The Human Odyssey

Life-Span Development

Third Edition

The Human Odyssey

Life-Span Development

Third Edition

Paul S. Kaplan
Suffolk County Community College and
The State University of New York at Stony Brook

Brooks/Cole Publishing Company
I(T)P™ An International Thomson Publishing Company

Pacific Grove • Albany • Belmont • Bonn • Boston • Cincinnati
Detroit • Johannesburg • London • Madrid • Melbourne • Mexico City
New York • Paris • Singapore • Tokyo • Toronto • Washington

Sponsoring Editors: *Peter Marshall and Jim Brace-Thompson*
Marketing Team: *Christine Davis, Lauren Harp, and Alicia Barelli*
Editorial Assistant: *Terry Thomas*
Production Coordinator: *Laurie Jackson*
Production Service: *The Clarinda Company*
Manuscript Editor: *Radhika Rao Gupta*
Permissions Editor: *May Clark*
Interior Design: *Lois Stanfield, LightSource Images*
Interior Illustration: *The Clarinda Company*
Cover Design: *Roy R. Neuhaus*
Cover Illustration: *Jane Wooster Scott*
Typesetting: *The Clarinda Company*
Cover Printing: *Phoenix Color Corporation*
Printing and Binding: *World Color*

For more information, contact:

BROOKS/COLE PUBLISHING COMPANY
511 Forest Lodge Road
Pacific Grove, CA 93950
USA

International Thomson Publishing Europe
Berkshire House 168-173
High Holborn
London WC1V 7AA
England

Thomas Nelson Australia
102 Dodds Street
South Melbourne, 3205
Victoria, Australia

Nelson Canada
1120 Birchmount Road
Scarborough, Ontario
Canada M1K 5G4

International Thomson Editores
Seneca 53
Col. Polanco
11560 México D. F., México

International Thomson Publishing GmbH
Kőnigswinterer Strasse 418
53227 Bonn
Germany

International Thomson Publishing Asia
221 Henderson Road
#05-10 Henderson Building
Singapore 0315

International Thomson Publishing Japan
Hirakawacho Kyowa Building, 3F
2-2-1 Hirakawacho
Chiyoda-ku, Tokyo 102
Japan

Printed in the United States of America
10 9

Library of Congress Cataloging-in-Publication Data
Kaplan, Paul S.
The human odyssey : life-span development / Paul S. Kaplan. —3rd ed.
p. cm.
Includes bibliographical references and indexes.
ISBN 0-534-34951-X
1. Developmental psychology. I. Title.
BF 713.K379 1998
155—dc21

97-19669
CIP

To My Wife

Leslie Rochelle Kaplan

My Companion on Our Odyssey

Brief Contents

Contents

Part 1 Foundations

Part 6 Early Adulthood

Chapter 14 Physical and Cognitive Development in Early Adulthood / 315

Chapter 15 Social and Personality Development in Early Adulthood / 337

Part 7 Middle Adulthood

Chapter 16 Physical and Cognitive Development in Middle Adulthood / 364

Preface

> "I wish I had taken a course like this years ago, when I had small children."
>
> "I now understand my parents better. Why didn't I see it all along?"

These sentiments are often expressed by students after they have taken their first course in human development. Sometimes the behavior of others, especially those who are much younger or older than we are, seems incomprehensible and unpredictable. Many people are baffled when children protest after their usual bedtime ritual is changed, or when older people treat their social activities as commitments. In addition, controversial issues involving day care, early intervention, bilingualism, multiculturalism, moral development, child abuse, and violence are of intense interest, and it is often difficult to separate myth from fact. Developmental psychology can often make the seemingly inexplicable understandable and can help us predict future challenges an individual may face. There is a certain excitement involved in understanding behavior and in being able to anticipate behavioral and motivational changes.

The excitement also arises from respect for an individual's subjective experience. As people face predictable challenges in life, many choices arise and many paths open. Modern developmental psychology sees relationships as reciprocal—the individual is both affected by and affects the environment. *The Human Odyssey* seeks to convey this combination of predictability and individual experience.

In this edition of *The Human Odyssey,* many new issues are covered, the material has been substantially updated, and new theoretical approaches are presented. However, three basic principles that guided the first two editions remain.

First, this book demonstrates a basic respect for the reader. *The Human Odyssey* speaks directly to the reader as the story of development unfolds. It is designed to present the material in a clear, interesting, readily understandable manner. It offers scientific support for statements it makes without becoming pedantic or condescending.

Second, the distinction between education and indoctrination is consistently maintained. A textbook author is responsible for offering both sides of an issue, describing a theory's strengths and weaknesses, and telling readers frankly if a particular problem doesn't have an answer at this time. It is easier to cite research showing that some popular viewpoint is correct—to take a trendy view and run with it. It is also easier to show readers a simplistic, one-sided point of view or to leave the impression that no loose threads or opposing views exist. However, most issues are not so clear-cut. Controversies and differences of opinion abound, which contribute to the vibrancy, dynamism, and excitement of developmental psychology. *The Human Odyssey* remains committed to telling both sides of a story; it seeks to clarify disputes, placing them into sharper focus for the reader.

In addition, controversial issues are not omitted from this book because they are "too hot to handle." In Chapter 3, one of the most controversial books of our time, *The Bell Curve,* is critiqued. Issues surrounding bilingual programs are discussed in Chapter 7, as are questions surrounding child support in Chapter 15.

Third, *The Human Odyssey* offers a balance among childhood, adolescence, and adulthood. One objection many professors have to life-span development texts is that they seem to be childhood and adolescence texts, with adulthood sections tacked on as an afterthought. This is not the case with *The Human Odyssey.* The entire text takes a life-span perspective, with balanced coverage of childhood and adulthood. Research on adulthood is much more plentiful now than it was 15 years ago, thus allowing more complete coverage of adulthood.

Developmental psychology is a dynamic field; a text on the subject must reflect this. At the same time, basic research and traditional interests remain relatively stable. The third edition of *The Human Odyssey* combines change with stability in the following manner.

New Perspectives

The growing awareness of the importance of experiences unique to people from different groups within our pluralistic society is reflected in this edition. Research continually shows variations in child rearing strategies, worldviews, attitudes, and experiences that have not yet been adequately explored. These perspectives are presented in a psychological, a social, and sometimes a historical context. The acknowledgment that people from various groups can have different experiences and interpretations, and that these have validity, is a great advance. At the same time, we must neither overemphasize group membership, thereby ignoring individual differences, nor emphasize the differences between groups while ignoring similarities. *The Human Odyssey* presents cultural and subcultural experiences, differences, and similarities without neglecting individual differences.

Another change in perspective is the conception of the individual as embedded in many contexts. This contextualism allows us to view the individual as involved not only with the immediate and extended family and friends, but as enmeshed in a variety of environments, including the community and political system. For example, such factors as the quality and the affordability of day care are often determined by entities (the community or the state legislature, for example) far removed from the family unit; however, these factors greatly affect all family members. Economic changes in a society strongly influence people's work experiences at different stages of life, and, in turn, indirectly affect the children in that society. Viewing the individual as developing in multiple contexts, some far removed from the traditional family, brings to light new understanding of how segments of a society interact and affect each other.

Pedagogical Features

A text is a learning tool. To be useful, it must contain pedagogical features that make the content more interesting and applicable. This edition continues the strong emphasis on pedagogical features that marked the previous editions. A new feature, *Questions Students Often Ask,* presents specific questions that students frequently voice as they work their way through the course. These questions, which have been phrased as they are often heard in the classroom, are answered briefly. Another new feature is a 20-item multiple-choice review at the end of each chapter.

Each chapter also contains one of four major features: *New Perspectives, Controversial Issues, Our Multicultural Society,* and *Forming Your Own Opinion.* These features focus on issues of current interest. For example, the *New Perspectives* feature in Chapter 2 presents chaos theory; in Chapter 5, the issue of childhood vaccinations is examined. The *Controversial Issues* feature in Chapter 9 considers the controversy surrounding spanking children, and, in Chapter 20, physician-assisted suicide is explored. *Our Pluralistic Society* features include discussions of whether bilingual programs work (Chapter 7) and of identity and minority status (Chapter 13). The *Forming Your Own Opinion* feature in Chapter 4 examines reproductive surrogacy; Chapter 11 contains a discussion about raising a moral child.

In addition, every chapter begins with 10 true-false statements that are repeated after the paragraph in the text in which they are answered. All key terms are set boldface in text and defined both at the bottom of the page and in the glossary at the end of the book. A point-by-point summary appears at the end of each chapter. Last, pictorial views of demographic changes are found in datagraphic features.

Content

The most challenging aspect of writing a revision is deciding what to change. The content of the previous edition has been updated to reflect current research, but some areas that have either been introduced or expanded significantly should be mentioned here. In Chapter 1 (and throughout the text), an extensive emphasis on the contexts of development is introduced, and new coverage of time-lag and sequential designs is offered. In Chapter 2, "Theories of Development," extensive coverage of ecological theory, the importance of theory, and new trends in developmental psychology are discussed. Chapter 3, on genetics, describes twin and adoption studies and models of genetic/environmental interaction. In Chapter 4, "Prenatal Development and Birth," new material on technology and reproductive alternatives and on the effects of cocaine is included.

In Chapters 5 and 6, covering infancy and toddlerhood, new material on vaccinations, culture and emotions, advances in attachment theory, the father-child relationship, and new research on day care has been added. In Chapter 7, on language and communication, culture and early language usage is introduced, and the discussion of bilingualism has been expanded.

Chapters 8 and 9, covering early childhood, offer more information on nutrition, children's health, preschool education, the only child, subculture and discipline, compliance, and child rearing in different subcultures. Chapters 10 and 11, which discuss middle childhood, contain new material on elementary school, multicultural education, gender differences in the school experience, homelessness, and aggression, including exposure to crime and violence.

New perspectives on risk taking, drug use, violence, values, acquaintance rape, sex education, and homosexuality are discussed in the chapters on adolescence, 12 and 13. In addition, expanded coverage of the junior high school and high school experience—including the varying experiences of males and females, and of adolescents from different minority groups—can be found.

The early adulthood chapters, 14 and 15, offer new material on Generation X, women and theories of adulthood, spousal violence, the transition to parenting, and gay and lesbian households. Chapters 16 and 17, the middle years of adulthood, contain new research on the health of people from minority groups, women's health issues, personality in mid-life, young adults living with their parents, and relationships with adult children. The later adulthood chapters, 18 and 19, offer new information on nutrition, alternatives to nursing homes, elder abuse, grandparents raising grandchildren, and volunteering. Finally, Chapter 20, "Death, Dying, and Coping With Loss," contains new material on physician-assisted suicide and on the death of a child. Although this list is far from exhaustive, it gives an idea of some of the new material included in this edition.

Examples and Practical Applications As in the previous editions, the text is filled with anecdotes and examples that enliven the discussions and improve comprehension. The practical applications come directly out of research that has been conducted, thus showing the relationship between research and practice.

Ancillaries

Ancillaries for this edition include the following:

1. *Study Guide:* The study guide contains chapter study questions with a review, important terms and concepts, multiple-choice and true-false practice tests, and chapter activities.
2. *Instructor's Manual:* The instructor's manual contains chapter learning objectives, lecture notes, discussion questions, action/reaction case studies, suggestions for teaching, student activities, and transparency masters.
3. *Test Bank:* The test bank contains approximately 1200 multiple-choice questions and 150 essay questions, with correct answers and page references to the main text. The test bank is available electronically in Macintosh and Windows platforms as well as in hard-copy format.
4. *Film and Video Library:* Instructors may choose from a variety of programs from Films for the Humanities and Sciences and the Annenberg/CPB Discovering Psychology series.
5. *Web Site:* For each chapter in the book, the web site provides several useful Internet links and additional study questions. Students and instructors can access the web resources through *http://psychstudy@brookscole.com*

A Word About References

Students often ask why a text must be heavily referenced; few readers will refer to the original sources. References are important because they give credit where credit is due and demonstrate that developmental psychology is based on the work of others. References do require a great deal of space, especially those that contain many names. After much deliberation, we decided to continue using the American Psychological Association citation style, with one change: Where there are more than three authors, the term *et al.* has been used the first time the citation appears. Technically, *et al.* should be used at first mention only when the citation refers to six or more authors; however this style is unwieldly and interferes with smooth reading of the material. The full reference is cited in the bibliography at the end of the text.

Acknowledgments

Writing and producing a text is a team effort. Developmental editors, production editors, professional reviewers, artists, and many other professionals are involved and often go unappreciated. I have had the good fortune to deal with excellent editors, Peter Marshall and Jim Brace-Thompson, at West and at Brooks/Cole. In addition, this book would not be a reality without the patience, encouragement, and help of Laurie Jackson and Emily Autumn during the production phase. I would also like to thank David Quinn and Joyce Gabrielle of Suffolk Community College's Western Campus library for their help in obtaining some difficult-to-find sources for this text. The professional reviews of the second and third editions were instrumental in helping me make decisions about what to keep, what to expand, and what to delete. I would like to acknowledge the following members of the academic community for their help: Daniel R. Bellack, Trident Technical College; Carole Carroll, Middle Tennessee State University; Vern Dorschner, Central Lakes College; Trisha Folds-Bennett, College of Charleston; Robert Poresky, Kansas State University; Robert Stowe, Central Connecticut State University; Vince Sullivan, Pensacola Junior College; and Thomas Thoms, Pearl River Community College.

Finally, no project of this size could be completed successfully without the encouragement and support of my family. I would like to thank my wife, Leslie, and my daughters Stacey, Amy, Jodi, and Laurie, for their patience, understanding, and encouragement which made the writing of this book easier and more pleasant.

Paul S. Kaplan

Chapter 1

The Challenge of Human Development

Chapter Outline

Are the Following Statements True or False?

1. No developmental changes of importance take place after age 40, with the exception of a decline in physical abilities.
2. Older adults are more likely than younger people to be cautious and to value accuracy over speed when presented with a problem to solve.
3. Developmental changes in thinking and emotional response are caused solely by learning but those involving physical abilities and growth are caused by genetic factors.
4. A person's diet during childhood can affect that person's adult health status.
5. A child's poor early experiences, before the age of three years, are so powerful that later improvements in the child's life will have little positive effect on the child's behavior and development.
6. About one child in four is growing up in a one-parent family.
7. By the year 2010, Latinos will comprise the largest minority group.
8. Children living in poverty in the United States have lower rates of vaccination for childhood diseases than middle-class children.
9. More than 20% of all American children live in poverty.
10. Observation is a valid tool for conducting research.

Answers to True-False Statements 1. False: see p. 2 2. True 3. False: see p. 4 4. True 5. False: see p. 6 6. True 7. True 8. True 9. True 10. True

Life-Span Development: Studying Change and Stability

Two children were busy playing when a disagreement broke out. It was quickly settled when one told the other that "my mother said so." Young children see their parents as authority figures whose commands are law and whose pronouncements are to be accepted as truth. However, within a few years children realize that parents aren't always right. Then in adolescence, the child may think that his or her parents are rarely correct or that they are out of touch. In late adolescence or early adulthood, this may change to an appreciation of the parents' point of view. Mark Twain once wrote, "When I was a boy of 14, my father was so ignorant I could hardly stand to have the old man around. But when I got to be 21, I was astonished at how much *he* had learned in 7 years" (in Rees, 1994, p. 337). Children's attitudes toward their parents continue to change in middle adulthood.

Think about the changes in your life. Some are so gradual that they are difficult to see; others are more obvious. Changes in the way young children think and feel and in what they can do are relatively easy to spot because these changes occur so quickly. However, development continues over the entire course of the life span. Developmental changes that occur in adulthood occur more gradually but are no less real. **Life-span developmental psychology** is concerned with the study of constancy and change throughout the course of a lifetime from conception to death (Baltes, 1987). During one's lifetime, changes occur in many areas. Physical changes are obvious over the life cycle, but people change intellectually (cognitively) as well. A 3-year-old child does not think in the same manner as a 9-year-old. Adolescents do not think in the same way as middle-aged people do. This does not mean that people change so much that there is no continuity; you may change a great deal between adolescence and middle adulthood, but you are still the same person.

True or False?
No developmental changes of importance take place after age 40, with the exception of a decline in physical abilities.

Questions Students Often Ask

I find it difficult to accept the idea that older people are still "developing." I don't see it.

You're not alone in this. There are two reasons for the problem people often have in accepting life-span development. First, we often equate growth with development. Since children and adolescents grow quickly and noticeably, we don't have any problem understanding this in terms of development. Physical growth cannot be used as a measure of adult development. However, middle-aged and older adults also develop. For example, adults think somewhat differently from younger people, being more practical in their approach. Their physical appearance changes, as does their view of the world. Another reason for the difficulty is that whatever changes take place in adulthood happen relatively slowly whereas those in childhood and adolescence occur at a quicker pace and in a shorter amount of time.

The changes that occur throughout life are usually predictable because they are systematic and successive (Fisher & Lerner, 1994). If you know that a child is now crawling, you can predict that typically the next step is standing. You would expect a 1-year-old child to stand

life-span developmental psychology The study of human development that is concerned with describing, explaining, and at times modifying the changes that occur over the entire life span.

Developmental psychology is the study of how people change over the life cycle.

or walk with some help, to require frequent changing of diapers, and to be unable to communicate verbally. You would expect a 5-year-old to talk, to be toilet-trained, to ask questions, and to wander easily around the house. You would also expect their interests and concerns to differ at different ages; for example, teenagers have different interests and concerns than their grandparents. However, individual differences are important. Although developmental psychologists can generally predict when the majority of children will walk or talk, some children will do so before others.

Quantitative and Qualitative Change

Developmental psychologists catalog changes into two categories: quantitative and qualitative (Appelbaum & McCall, 1983). Some changes, however, are both quantitative and qualitative.

Any changes that involve an increase or decrease in some characteristic are quantitative. If we charted the number of teeth in a person's mouth, we would see a gradual increase until all the baby teeth were in, then a decrease as the baby teeth are lost, and then a gain as the permanent teeth come in. The person keeps that permanent set of teeth until late adulthood when tooth loss may slowly begin. Height and weight also fit into the category of quantitative change. **Quantitative changes** involve changes in amount, frequency, or degree (Miller, 1993). Such changes are usually quantified easily, for example, in terms of inches or pounds.

Qualitative changes involve changes in process, function, structure or organization. For instance, older people may solve certain types of problems differently from younger people. In general, older people are more likely to be cautious, to value accuracy over speed, and to stay with a strategy longer once they adopt it than are younger adults (Botwinick, 1984). What is important here is not whether older adults solve more or fewer problems correctly, but that they approach problem solving differently. Because people approach problems or think differently does not mean that one way of problem solving is necessarily better than another; differences do not necessarily mean deficits.

To understand the difference between quantitative and qualitative change, try this experiment. Cut out 16 pictures from various magazines: 4 pictures of food, 4 of pieces of furniture, 4 of toys, and 4 of items of clothing. Ask children of various ages first to look at all the pictures and then to try to recall as many pictures as they can after a minute or two of study. As you would expect, the older children will remember more items than younger children will, thus indicating a *quantitative* change in ability to recall information. However, if you had observed the children studying the pictures, you would also have noticed a *qualitative* change in the strategies they used to help them remember the items (Kail & Hagen, 1982). For example, younger children usually do not make use of categories whereas older children do.

> ***True or False?***
> Older adults are more likely than younger people to be cautious and to value accuracy over speed when presented with a problem to solve.

Basic Themes in Life-Span Development

The study of life-span development is based on several themes that will be developed throughout this text. These themes define the concerns and basic premises of the field.

Developmental Changes Occur Over the Entire Life Cycle

Some people believe that development is synonymous with growth. This narrow definition ignores adult development altogether. Development is a lifelong process; the study of life-span development has gained momentum

quantitative changes Changes that can be considered solely in terms of increases or decreases, such as changes in height or weight.

qualitative changes Changes in process, function, structure, or organization.

and continues to thrive. The increase in interest may be tied to demographic changes, as people are living longer. Today, researchers are looking for early behavior or events that might predict functioning later in life (Baltes, 1987). Interest in life-span development has also been sparked by the many popular best-sellers that explain developmental changes in adulthood.

Developmental Changes Are Influenced by Genetic and Environmental Factors

What causes developmental changes? Psychologists argue that genetic and environmental factors contribute to developmental changes. You may have heard some changes result from genetics and others from environmental factors, but such thinking is antiquated. Some areas of development, such as physical growth, are indeed determined mostly—though not entirely—by one's genetic endowment. Other areas, such as computer programming skills, are affected mostly by one's environment. However, both genetic and environmental determinants are important in understanding behavior.

> ***True or False?***
> Developmental changes in thinking and emotional response are caused soley by learning but those involving physical abilities and growth are caused by genetic factors.

Psychologists use the term **maturation** to describe the unfolding of an individual's unique genetic plan. Maturation largely explains such things as the first appearance of baby teeth, the onset of menstruation in adolescent girls, and the physical aging process. Maturation depends primarily on the individual's genetic master plan, which functions as a timetable of sorts and largely (but not entirely) determines when certain events will occur. The plan may also limit the speed of progress. For example, before babies can walk they must have the necessary strength and balance, which is determined largely by maturation (Stewart, 1980). However, we must also consider such important environmental prerequisites as adequate nutrition and experience (Cratty, 1986). Infants need opportunities to practice their skills and it is usually easy to provide them with these basic experiences.

The importance of both the environment and genetics is also shown in the aging process. Aging itself is thought to be under genetic control, but people who take good care of themselves show fewer signs of aging (Plomin, DeFries, & McClearn, 1990). People who get little exercise, eat a diet rich in fat, smoke cigarettes, drink alcohol immoderately, and do not get enough rest are likely to show signs of aging much earlier than people who have better health habits.

The maturation process proceeds in much the same way for people in all cultures and is determined largely by internal signals. Learning, on the other hand, is determined largely by external events. Any relatively permanent changes in behavior caused by interaction with the environment result from **learning.** By definition, such changes cannot be the result of maturation. When a child recites the alphabet or imitates a brother's fear of spiders, or when an adult plays one way with a son and a different way with a daughter, learning has occurred.

A person's understanding of gender roles, morality, and problem solving is dependent on learning, but we cannot see learning. We can only infer from behavioral change that learning has taken place. A person who was unable to balance a checkbook a week ago but can do so now is said to have learned.

In contrast to maturation, learning is extremely dependent on the environment. Children learn what they see and experience. Children whose parents habitually fight, lose their tempers, and behave aggressively may well learn to be aggressive themselves.

To fully understand the nature of development, we must appreciate both genetic and environmental factors and how they interact. Let us say that it is helpful to have good hand-eye coordination and quick reflexes to hit a baseball well. Let us further hypothesize that genetic factors underlie these abilities. An individual who has better hand-eye coordination and faster reflexes may thus have an initial advantage while playing baseball. However, an individual who is given no practice in hitting would never reach his or her potential. At the same time, through constant practice, an individual with average hand-eye coordination and reflexes may become a very good baseball player. What complicates the issue, though, is that it only makes sense to talk about genetic contribution within a particular context. The genetic contribution to the ability to swing a bat well is probably more important at the major-league level, where the ball is thrown at 90 miles an hour with considerable skill, and less important at the neighborhood level, where practice is probably sufficient to hit the ball reasonably well.

The same analysis may be used for understanding a number of other characteristics, such as intelligence. As will be discussed in Chapter 3, to understand intelligence, both the genetic endowment of the individual and the environment must be taken into account. For example, two children with similar genetic potential who are raised in very different environments will have different intelligence scores. A child raised in an enriched and stimulating environment will have a higher IQ than a child raised in an unstimulating environment. However, we must also take into account the genetic factor. If five people from similar environments and backgrounds were exposed to an enriched and concentrated educational

maturation A term used to describe changes that result from the unfolding of an individual's genetic plan. These changes are relatively immune to environmental influence.

learning Relatively permanent changes in behavior resulting from interaction with the environment.

program, some of them would still do better than others partially because of differences in genetic endowment. The environment may encourage or discourage the development of a genetic potential in a certain area, and different aspects of our genetic potential may be developed depending upon the environment in which we find ourselves.

We should also beware of thinking that these abilities or characteristics are something that you either have or do not have. In reality, hand-eye coordination and intelligence can best be understood in terms of a continuum, with most people falling somewhere in the middle and relatively fewer people having very high or extremely low abilities. Chapter 3 deals extensively with genetic influences over the life span and the interaction of heredity and environment.

Factors That Determine Development Express Themselves Cumulatively

Whenever we seek the cause of a behavior, we often look to the person's early childhood. A child's early experience is certainly important. Children who do not receive enough emotional care may show abnormal behavior patterns that limit later social and emotional functioning (Rutter, 1995). Indeed, the psychological makeup of terrorists has been linked to childhood experiences involving hopelessness and rage and a lack of nonviolent role models; the only effective role models terrorists had belonged to terrorist groups. In addition, about half the terrorists studied described a life-threatening childhood illness that few in their culture survive. One possible explanation is that this led them to deny the risk of death in adulthood (Goleman, 1986a).

Such characteristics as aggression and altruism (doing something for others without expecting a reward) can be traced to childhood influences (Eisenberg & Mussen, 1989). Research also finds that early nutrition is important both in later obesity and heart disease (Whitney, Cataldo, & Rolfes, 1994). Plasma cholesterol is a major factor in heart disease. In countries where the incidence of heart disease is high, children have average-to-high levels of plasma cholesterol, whereas in countries where the heart disease rate is lower, children have low levels of the substance (deBruyne & Rolfes, 1989).

> ***True or False?***
> A person's diet during childhood can affect that person's adult health status.

It seems that we only need look at factors in childhood to explain adult behavior. But consider these two cases:

> Boy, senior year secondary school, has obtained certificate from physician stating that nervous breakdown makes it necessary for him to leave school for six months. Boy not a good all-around student; has no friends—teachers find him a problem—spoke late—father ashamed of son's lack of athletic ability—poor adjustment in school. Boy has odd mannerisms, makes up own religion, chants hymns to himself—parents regard him as "different."
>
> Girl, age sixteen, orphaned, willed to custody of grandmother, who was separated from alcoholic husband, now deceased. Mother rejected the homely child, who has been known to lie and steal sweets. Swallowed penny to attract attention at five. Father was fond of child. Child lived in fantasy as the mistress of father's household for years. Four young uncles and aunts in household cannot be managed by the grandmother, who is widowed. Young uncle drinks, has left home without telling the grandmother his destination. Aunt, emotional over love affairs, locks self in room. Grandmother resolves to be more strict with granddaughter since she fears she has failed with own children. Dresses granddaughter oddly. Refused to let her have playmates, put her in braces to keep back straight. Did not send her to grade school. Aunt on paternal side of family crippled; uncle asthmatic (Goertzel & Goertzel, 1962, p. xiii).

These descriptions of the early environments of two children would make it difficult for you to give a positive prognosis for their later adjustment or accomplishments in life. But the first case describes Albert Einstein, and the second describes the early life of Eleanor Roosevelt, wife of President Franklin D. Roosevelt and a powerful figure in her own right. So it is apparently not so

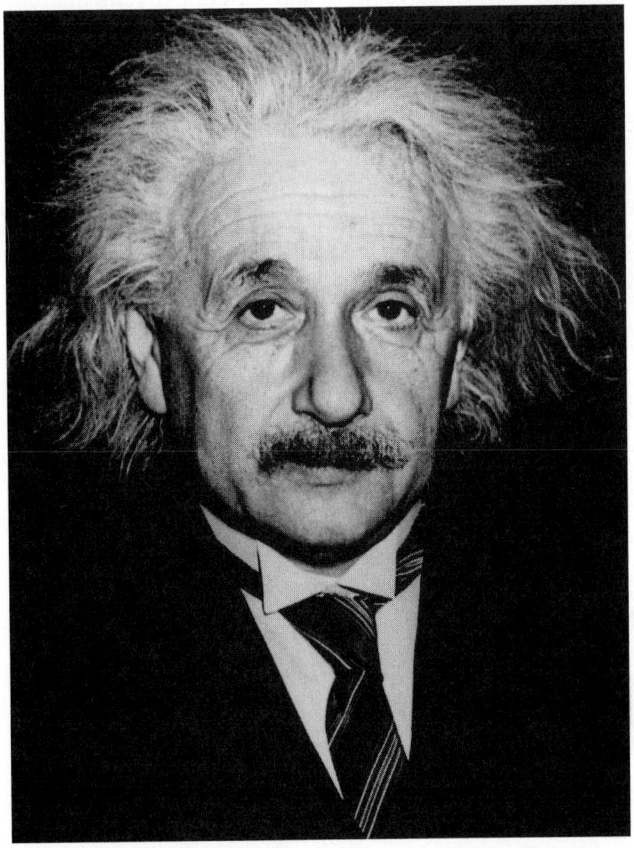

The case of Albert Einstein demonstrates how difficult it can be to make predictions for people based on early childhood experiences.

easy to make sweeping generalizations and predictions based on early childhood data.

Later experiences can compensate at least partially for poor early experiences. Children raised under very poor conditions are often delayed in many areas of development, but with extra care and attention, the effects of their environment can to some degree be compensated for (Bornstein, 1995; Clarke & Clarke, 1976).

True or False?
A child's poor early experiences, before the age of three years, are so powerful that later improvements in the child's life will have little positive effect on the child's behavior and development.

Psychologists often focus on early experience because most children who have a poor start continue to be victims of a poor environment throughout childhood and adolescence, thus developing poor interpersonal relationships in adulthood. If children enter school already behind in certain important skills and nothing is done to help them catch up and improve, they may fall further behind and never fulfill their potential. This can affect vocational opportunities, the nature of their social world, and their interests in adulthood. In other words, often early childhood experience seems so important because there is no change in the environment in later childhood. Where a positive change does occur, better outcomes are the rule. Prevention is easier and superior to remediation, and it is best to create a positive early environment for children instead of trying to reverse the problems caused by poor early experience.

Challenges People Face as They Develop Are Somewhat Predictable

People face particular challenges during certain periods of their lives. The 2-year-old begins the task of becoming toilet trained, the 6-year-old must cope with school, the 13-year-old with puberty, the young adult with occupational considerations and marital questions, the middle-aged person with the loss of parents, and the older adult with retirement and chronic illness. Such challenges are roughly related to age, but they need not be. A young adult can lose a parent and a child can suffer a chronic illness.

People Are Affected by the Historical Time in Which They Live

The generation of the 1960s and 1970s was greatly affected by the Vietnam War; the present generation views that war as history. The present generation is used to computers; older people are not. Many younger people do not remember a time when women were expected to be full-time homemakers and when a female lawyer or doctor was unusual. Today, more than one third of the medical degrees and a little less than half the law degrees are awarded to women (Statistical Abstract, 1996).

Questions Students Often Ask

How could early experience be so important if the child doesn't remember anything from that point in life?

I can see your point. I don't know how extensive your early memories are but mine are very fragmented. Yet you are assuming that you must have an active, present memory of something for it to affect your behavior and development. This may not be true. You may have forgotten a number of incidents that happened in first grade, yet you wouldn't say that you weren't affected by your first-grade teacher. In addition, early experience may set in motion a series of interactions that may continue throughout childhood. For example, suppose that one parent reacts to the care-giving of her infant with patience and joy, while another parent acts bothered and cold. The first infant may react with a smile, which may cause the parent to vocalize and begin a positive relationship. In the second case the infant may react differently, setting up a different pattern. Most psychologists believe that even at the earliest ages children are learning about relationships.

The effect of growing up in a particular time period is known as the **cohort effect.** Look at the differences between generations. Twenty-five years ago, one child in ten grew up in a single-parent household, but currently it is about one in four (U.S. Bureau of the Census, 1994). The present generation has received more education than any previous generation. Events that occur at a particular point in time—such as economic depressions, epidemics, and revolutions—affect people's lives greatly. People in the same generation share common experiences (see Figure 1.1). We talk about the baby boom generation born between 1946 and 1964 and the generation born in the 1970s called *generation X* (Meredith & Schewe, 1994). The differing experiences of the generations must be taken into consideration when evaluating their behavior and attitudes.

True or False?
About one child in four is growing up in a one-parent family.

Social and Demographic Changes Are Potent Influences on Behavior and Development

Think about how our society has changed. Not long ago, few women went to college or entered the professions and women were expected to have many children. Today, women attend college in large numbers, enter the professions, and most women with children are employed at least part time. Women are having fewer children as well. The roles of both men and women have

cohort effect The effect of belonging to a particular generation, of being raised in a certain historical time.

COHORT CARTOGRAPHY

Six cohorts define the U.S. consumer market

The Depression Cohort

Born: 1912 to 1921
Coming of age: 1930 to 1939
Age in 1994: 73 to 82
Current population: 13 million
Share of adult population: 7 percent

People who were starting out in the Depression era were scarred in ways that remain with them today—especially when it comes to financial matters, like spending, savings, and debt. The Depression Cohort was also the first to be truly influenced by the contemporary media: radio and especially motion pictures.

The World War II Cohort

Born: 1922 to 1927
Coming of age: 1940 to 1945
Age in 1994: 67 to 72
Current population: 11 million
Share of adult population: 6 percent

People who came of age in the early 1940s were unified by a common enemy and shared experiences. A sense of deferment was especially strong among the 16 million Americans in the military and their loved ones at home. Consequently, the World War II Cohort became intensely romantic. Although it was not a boom time, unemployment was no longer a problem.

The Post-War Cohort

Born: 1928 to 1945
Coming of age: 1946 to 1963
Age in 1994: 49 to 66
Current population: 41 million
Share of adult population: 21 percent

Members of the 18-year Post-War Cohort benefited from a long period of economic growth and relative social tranquility. The expectation of good times became ingrained in the society. But global unrest, the threat of nuclear power, and the Cold War generated a need to alleviate uncertainty in everyday life. Post-War adults enjoy feeling comfortable, secure, and familiar.

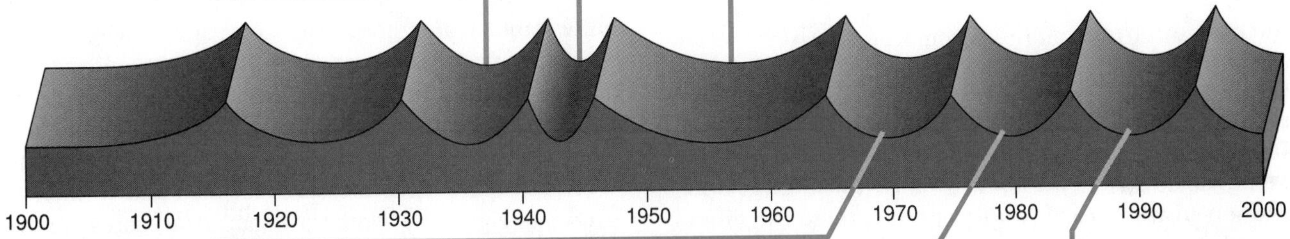

The Boomers I Cohort

Born: 1946 to 1954
Coming of age: 1963 to 1972
Age in 1994: 40 to 48
Current population: 33 million
Share of adult population: 17 percent

The two boomer cohorts are separated by the end of the Vietnam conflict. The Kennedy assassination, followed by those of Martin Luther King and Robert Kennedy, signaled an end to the status quo and galvanized the large boomer cohort. Still, the Boomer I Cohort continued to experience economic good times and wants a lifestyle at least as good as the one experienced as children in the 1950s.

The Boomers II Cohort

Born: 1955 to 1965
Coming of age: 1973 to 1983
Age in 1994: 29 to 39
Current population: 49 million
Share of adult population: 25 percent

After Watergate, something changed people coming of age in America. The idealistic fervor of youth disappeared. Instead, the Boomer II Cohort exhibited a narcissistic preoccupation with themselves, which manifested itself in everything from the self-help movement to self-deprecation in the media. Changes in the economy had a profound effect on this group. Debt as a means of maintaining a lifestyle made sense.

The Generation X Cohort

Born: 1966 to 1976
Coming of age: 1984 to 1994
Age in 1994: 18 to 28
Current population: 41 million
Share of adult population: 21 percent

Generation X has nothing to hang on to. These are children of divorce and day care, the latch-key kids of the 1980s. They are searching for anchors with their seemingly contradictory "retro" behavior: the resurgence of proms, coming-out parties, and fraternities. Their political conservatism is motivated by a "What's-in-it-for-me?" cynicism.*

Figure 1.1
*A more detailed and flattering description of generation X can be found in Chapter 15 and of the baby boomer generation in Chapter 17.
Source: Meredith & Schewe, December 1994.

changed much over the past two decades. Men participate more actively in child care, although certainly 50–50 splits are rare.

Another social change is the "greying of America." Predictions for populations in developed countries for the next 50 years show that the rate of childbearing will be low and the proportion of elderly people will rise markedly (Easterlin, 1996). In 1995 about 12.8% of all Americans were over 65 years of age, but by the year 2025 the percentage of elderly people is projected to rise to 28.4% of the total population (Statistical Abstract, 1996)! The elderly will become an even more important economic and political force in developed countries. They will also require social and medical services, and governments need to consider how they will meet the needs of an expanding elderly population in the future.

Another change is the increasing percentage of minority group members in many Western societies. Today, one in every four Americans is a member of a minority group (Bradley, 1991). African Americans form the largest minority group, accounting for about 12% of the population. However, the Latino population grew tremendously during the 1980s and in 1994 it comprised 10% of the nation. By the year 2010, Latinos will be the largest ethnic group (Statistical Abstract, 1996). In addition, the number of Asians and Pacific Islanders in the United States doubled in the 1980s ("New Face," 1991). African-American and Latino youth now constitute about 27% of the current child population, but this is estimated to grow to about 33% in the year 2010 (SRCD, 1991). The future welfare of society will depend upon the success of people in these groups, a greater percentage of whom are being raised in poverty and often experience prejudice and discrimination.

True or False?
By the year 2010, Latinos will comprise the largest minority group.

Individual Experiences Are Important

Even if you are the same age as your friend and therefore grew up in the same historical period, there are differences between the two of you. You have had different personal experiences. The death of a parent at an early age, divorce, winning the lottery, severe illness, and unemployment are examples of significant events that can occur in the lives of people and are relatively unpredictable. Developmental psychology takes these events as well as a person's subjective experience into consideration.

Intervention Can Affect the Course of Development

Since environmental factors influence development, we can intervene at certain points of development to enhance it or change its direction. Special programs are designed to stimulate premature infants to enable them to function better in life (Hack, Klein, & Taylor, 1995). Preschool programs are designed so that children can improve their skills and succeed later in their school years. Interventions can also be effective at later ages. Older workers can be taught new skills, and elderly people can learn new ways to solve problems (Denney, 1982).

Stability, as Well as Change, Is Seen in Human Development

So far we have been looking at change, but what of stability? Some characteristics, such as personality traits, are quite stable in adulthood. Paul Costa and colleagues measured the traits of extroversion, openness, and neuroticism (a measure of emotional instability, depression, and anxiety) in more than 10,000 people of different ages (Costa et al., 1986; Costa & McCrae, 1986). The average scores on these three measures for men and women are shown in Figure 1.2. Note how stable the scores are over the adult years. The researchers concluded that personality seems to be predominantly stable in adulthood. Children who showed temper tantrums at 8 to 10 years of age were later judged to be less controlled and more irritable and moody than their even-tempered peers (Caspi, Elder, & Bem, 1987).

Because specific behaviors change with time, stability is sometimes difficult to see, but the underlying personality structure may still be similar. For instance, if we examine the intensity of a child's reactions to a stimulus we find an interesting progression. An intense child may cry loudly at the sound of thunder at 6 months, laugh hard when a parent plays roughly at 1 year, rush to greet his father and get hiccups when laughing hard at 5 years, and tear up an entire page of homework if one mistake is made or slam the door of his room when teased by his younger brother at 10 years (Thomas, Chess, & Birch, 1970). We would hardly expect a 10-year-old to show the same behavior as a 1-year-old, even

Individual differences are also important in understanding development. How would your life change if suddenly you found yourself a lottery winner?

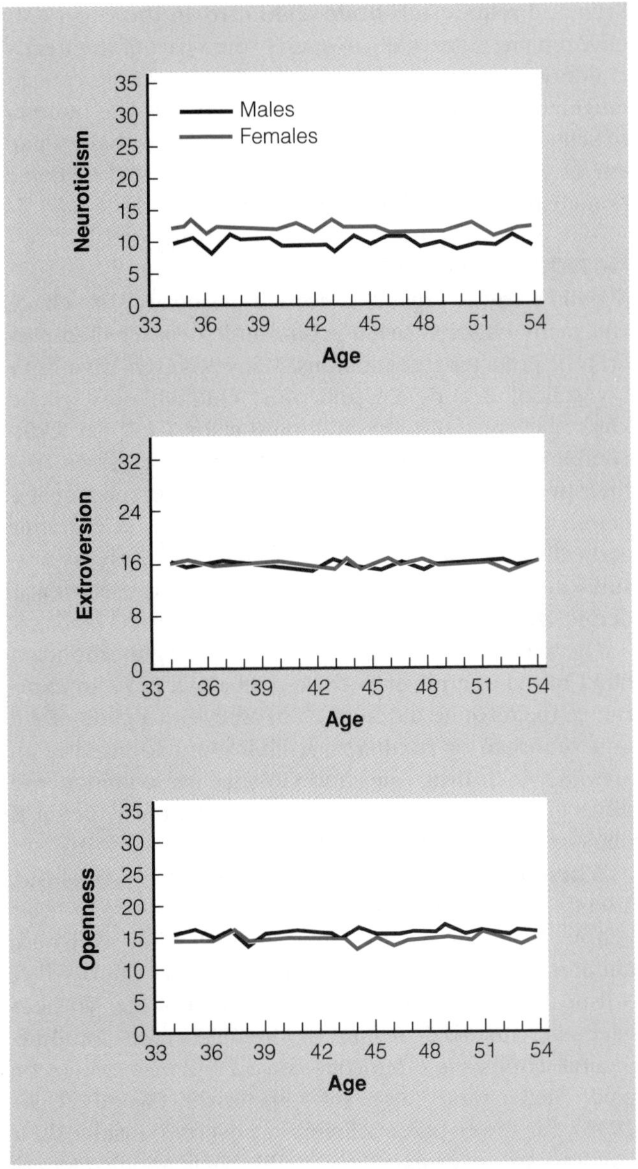

Figure 1.2
Stability of Personality in Adulthood This graph shows the mean levels of neuroticism, extroversion, and openness to experience for men and women aged 34 to 54 years. The findings from this study support the conclusion that personality is generally stable in adulthood.
Source: Costa et al., 1986.

though the same structure—in this case, intensity—underlies all these behaviors and is relatively stable.

Social Influences Are Reciprocal

It is far too easy to look at these themes and come to the conclusion that outside influences, parents, teachers, friends, and even psychologists act upon a passive organism, as a potter does on clay. This is not the case, for it ignores the effect the child has on these people. Do you remember a child in school who was always being discourteous to others, whose health habits were poor, who did not seem to have the social skills necessary to interact with others, and who was aggressive? This child was probably rejected. We could look at how the other students in the class treated the child. But more correctly, we should also look at how this child's behavior affected others. It is necessary to look at both how the child affects and is affected by others (Clarke & Clarke, 1986).

This perspective emphasizing how both parties in an interaction affect each other is called **reciprocal interaction** and is becoming more popular with developmental psychologists. We affect and are affected by the people around us. Spend some time observing the interactions between a parent and an infant. Perhaps the parent hugs the baby, who responds with a smile. The parent then says something to the baby, who reacts with a vocalization. The baby's vocalization brings a string of verbal praise from the parent. For years, psychologists have looked at the caregiver-child relationships in terms of what the mother or father did to the child, but the effect of the child on the parents was rarely considered. Today, developmental psychologists look at how each affects the other.

In the preceding example, the actions of both parties served as responses and stimuli, which prompted new actions. The baby's smile stimulated the parent to speak to the child, and this in turn stimulated the baby to vocalize. The interaction proceeded rapidly, with both parties affecting the behavior of the other. The system is bidirectional, with information flowing from one party to the other and back again (Bell, 1968, 1979).

Development Occurs Within Specific Contexts

Development does not occur in a vacuum. Each individual's life is embedded in a series of multilevel contexts (Kreppner & Lerner, 1989). The most immediate context is the family, but other contexts such as the school, peer group, neighborhood, and religious institution may be important. The different facets of the environment affect each other. Political changes, such as the availability of government- and private-sponsored day care services may affect interactions in the family, and changes in the family structure, such as more mothers seeking employment, may affect the economic and political system. The functioning of a individual then is the product of interactions between the person and the many facets of the environment that continually emerge and change over time (Fisher & Lerner, 1994). This interaction is mediated by the individual's genetic endowment. The contextualization of development is one of the most important changes in developmental psychology in the past decade and deserves special attention.

Contexts of Development

We all develop in multiple contexts, but are rarely aware of how some of them affect us. The most obvious context

reciprocal interaction The process by which an organism constantly affects and is affected by the environment.

is the family, and questions about family structure, relationships within the family, child-rearing techniques, sibling interactions, and grandparent involvement may be asked. People also develop in the context of their peer group, neighborhood, and school, and in their cultural, religious, and ethnic environment as well as developing within a particular historical period.

Focus on the Family

The family is the most important context for development. The family today in the United States (and in many other developed countries) is quite a different institution from what it was even 30 years ago. The traditional family consisting of a mother who is a homemaker, a father who is employed full time, and two children is far less common. Only about 5% of the families of children entering school today have an employed father and a full-time homemaker mother (Barney & Koford, 1987), largely because of the greater number of single-parent families and the rise in the percentage of mothers who are employed. In the United States about half of all white children live in nuclear families with both parents, as compared to about a quarter of all African-American children and a little more than a third of all Latino children (New York Times, August 30, 1994).

The number of single-parent families has increased substantially, and more than one million children each year are affected by divorce. Most divorced mothers and fathers remarry, and many children of divorce will go through a series of marital transitions from intact family to single-parent family to stepfamily relationships (Hetherington, Stanley-Hagan, & Anderson, 1989).

Other changes in family life have also occurred. Today, most mothers are employed at least part time (U.S. Department of Labor, 1994). Many of them have young children and require substitute child care. In the late 1990s children are more likely to spend some part of their early childhood in day care or some kind of substitute care arrangement. Supervision is a key concern as the number of self-care, or latchkey, children (who do not have a parent or older person waiting for them when they come home from school) has increased.

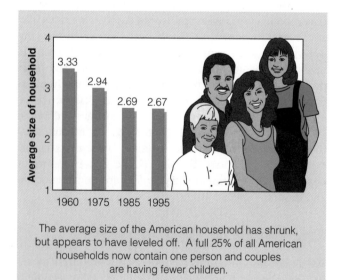

The average size of the American household has shrunk, but appears to have leveled off. A full 25% of all American households now contain one person and couples are having fewer children.

Datagraphic
The Shrinking American Household
Source: Data from Statistical Abstract, 1996.

School and Community

A child's day is organized around attendance at school, and many children begin school much earlier than children of preceding generations. Many children have nursery school experience, and most children now attend kindergarten, about half attending it for a full day. Unfavorable comparisons between American children and their peers in other countries on various measures of academic achievement have produced changes in curricula and calls for educational reforms (Kaplan, 1990). As a result, kindergartners today are likely to be exposed to academic work.

The child is also a product of the neighborhood. A child raised in a poverty-stricken area will have an experience that is quite different compared with a child raised in a suburban or rural area. A child who is raised in an area in which drug sales and violence are common will differ greatly from a child raised in an area in which it is unusual to even lock one's doors.

Where one lives and, to some extent, the school one attends is dependent upon socioeconomic status. People living in poverty tend to live in areas where children are exposed to more violence (McLoyd & Wilson, 1991). Poverty affects every area of life. Without adequate financial resources, medical care for low-income families is often substandard and bills cannot be paid. Vaccination rates are also lower (Wood et al., 1995). Far fewer parents living in poverty consider their children to be in excellent health than middle-income parents (Adams & Benson, 1990). Poverty is related to many problems, such as homelessness, prematurity, inadequate nutrition, and lack of intellectual stimulation in the home.

True or False?
Children living in poverty in the United States have lower rates of vaccination for childhood diseases than middle-class children.

About 14.5% of all people lived in poverty in 1994 (Wolf, 1995). About 22% of all American children live in poverty (Statistical Abstract, 1996). This is an increase from 15% in 1970, and children are much more likely to live in poverty than are adults (Larson, 1992; Huston, 1991). African Americans, Latinos, Native Americans, and some subgroups of Asian Americans are more likely than white Americans to live in poverty (Wolf, 1995). The gap between rich and poor is wider in the United States than in most other industrialized countries (Bradsher, 1995).

True or False?
More than 20% of all American children live in poverty.

Why has poverty increased over the last two decades? First, the number of single-parent families has risen, and poverty among female-headed families is much greater than poverty among married couples (Burns & Scott, 1994). Most are the product of divorce, but the number of single parents who are unmarried teenagers has increased dramatically. Presently more than 65% of all women giving birth between the ages of 15 and 19 are unmarried (Klerman, 1991a; Glazer, 1993). Other reasons for the increase in the number of children living in poverty are the loss of blue-collar, well-paying jobs and the inability of federal poverty programs to keep up with the need (Huston, McLoyd, & Coll, 1994).

The Media

The influence of the media must also be recognized. Children spend more time watching television than any other activity except sleeping (Dorr & Rabin, 1995). People are greatly influenced by what they see on the television or in the movies as well as by what they read and what they listen to on the radio. Many people are concerned about the effect that violent television programs or violent song lyrics may have on children. In the future all television sets will come with a v-chip, which allows parents to screen out programs containing violence, profanity, or nudity (Healey, 1995).

On the Job

In adulthood, one's day is organized around a job. The world of work has become more competitive, and the growth of service industries and the decline of manufacturing have changed the vocational landscape. More jobs require reading ability, and workers have more desire for some responsibility in decision making.

Culture

A child raised within the Japanese culture encounters a different set of values and attitudes and has a different life experience than a child raised in Egypt. Often what seems strange or unusual to one individual may be very commonplace and natural to another. Trading for profit is not very common among young children in the United Kingdom or the United States, but it is very common in Zimbabwe, Africa (Jahoda, 1983).

Specific ways of dealing with developmental challenges are influenced by one's culture. Misunderstandings can arise when two cultures interact. Medical and agricultural volunteers learned this lesson doing volunteer work in New Guinea among the Dani tribe. Each morning the volunteers would buy food from the Dani farmers. The Dani would hold up the fingers of one hand to indicate how much currency they would accept for their vegetables. One volunteer noticed that they would often walk away disappointed, and none of the advisers could understand why since they always paid the price indicated. The Dani would not talk about their disappointment. Finally, one of the Dani who worked in the hospital solved the mystery for the volunteers.

When you hold up two fingers you are indicating that you want two of whatever you are signaling. However, in the Dani culture, what you want is indicated by the number of fingers that are *not* raised (Riccardo, 1997). When a Dani farmer held up two fingers he was signaling his desire for three items, whereas he was only being given two items, hence his disappointment. Also, in Dani culture, it is considered inappropriate to complain.

One's general outlook on life and priorities are prescribed by one's culture. For example, these volunteers were able to fly in some candy canes and gave them out to those who were present during an assembly. This was a rare treat for the Dani, who are very poor. The volunteers became concerned when they finished giving out their supply and saw many people coming over the hills to join the assembly. Would there be a confrontation between those who had candy canes and those who did not? Sharing is a value much admired by the Dani, and those who had been given the treats shared them with the newcomers without any protest.

Cultures differ in many ways, including in child-rearing strategies, values, customs, and language. Although we often notice and emphasize the differences between other cultures and our own, we should be aware of similarities as well.

The Subcultural Context

It is easy to accept cultural differences, especially in cultures that are very different from our own. However, within complex societies such as our own, a number of groups exist each of which differ from the majority culture in attitudes, child-rearing strategies, beliefs, values, and communication patterns. If these minority groups differ significantly from the dominant culture and think of themselves as different, they are considered subcultures (Light, Keller, & Calhoun, 1994). The principle minority groups within the United States are African Americans, Latinos, Asian Americans, and Native Americans. Subcultures need not be ethnic or racial groups, for we may speak of a subculture of teenagers or older people living in retirement communities.

Subcultures exist within a larger, dominant culture and not completely apart from it. Understanding the values, child-rearing strategies, and attitudes of a particular group is vital to understanding the context in which people develop and will be explored in detail in Chapter 9. For instance, African-American children often take on family responsibilities quite early and are raised within extended kinship networks that offer support

Our Pluralistic Society: Cultural Cautions

A few years ago the concept of American society as the melting pot was popular, that is, the concept that minority groups melted into American society as they took on the values of the dominant culture. Today, because the melting pot seems not to explain our society anymore (if it ever did), many psychologists and educators increasingly look at American society as well as many other Western societies as being culturally pluralistic, in which a number of cultural groups exist side by side. This new perspective has the advantage of encouraging the appreciation of how an individual's culture affects behavior and development.

To what extent should a person's cultural, religious, and racial group membership be taken into consideration when trying to understand behavior? Is an 8-year-old Latino child's experience in the United States that much different from that of an 8-year-old white or African-American child? The answer is both yes and no. Certainly some of the developmental concerns of both children are similar, as they are both in the third grade and dealing with similar developmental problems. However, their experiences may be different in other contexts. The Latino child may live in a different neighborhood, speak a different language, and may be raised using different strategies. Although there are many similarities, a person's experience may be greatly affected by the cultural environment.

In addition, each group has a different history both in the United States and in the country of origin. The historic lack of opportunity available to some minority groups may influence their attitudes towards authority, education, and local and national politics (Ogbu, 1992).

An understanding of cultural differences is important for people who are working with families (Franklin, 1992; Harry, 1995). For example, psychologists working with African-American families may fail because they do not use the strengths of the family, which often include extended family members, and the religious and community institutions available (Martin, 1995).

The importance of understanding the diverse groups that comprise most Western societies today is reflected in many sections of this text. We will continually be looking at the experiences of children and adults from the many minority groups that live together in the United States and Canada. At first glance, taking into consideration the cultural influence in people's lives would seem both obvious and relatively easy. This is not the case, however, because looking at a culture often means making generalizations and the emphasis on culture has many pitfalls attached to it.

Mistake Number One: Defining a Person by His or Her Group Membership

If you were told that someone was African American, Latino, or Native American, how much would you really know about the person? One problem is the tendency to define people in terms of their culture and to forget about the individual. Although understanding culture is important to appreciating the behavior and values of the person, we ought not to forget the individual.

It would be truly unfortunate if the new appreciation of culture led to increased stereotyping. People usually think of stereotyping in terms of negative images, such as the way Native Americans are stereotyped in the older movies. Yet, today when we try to understand a culture, we may be in danger of stereotyping everyone belonging to a particular group and overemphasizing group affiliation. For instance, if certain minority group cultures emphasize sharing, this does not mean that every person in the group does so. People then stereotype the individual as someone who should share because they believe the culture values this behavior.

Mistake Number Two: Treating Minority Groups as Single, Unified Entities

People often view a minority group as a unified, monolithic whole rather than as a fragmented entity (Ryan, 1994). At

and comfort. Many Latino children are raised in an atmosphere that stresses cooperation and family pride rather than competition. Many Asian-American children are used to a child-rearing regimen that emphasizes family obligations and many Native American children are raised with a value system that emphasizes group activities and sharing. Perhaps these seem like overgeneralizations; indeed, not every Native American, African American, Latino, or Asian American will be raised under these circumstances. Although our new appreciation of culture and the experiences of people from minority groups is appropriate, the danger of overgeneralization and stereotyping is great, and can lead to other difficulties (see Our Pluralistic Society: Cultural Cautions on pp. 12–13).

Discovery: Research in Human Development

Discovering how and why a change occurs—and describing the nature of that change—is exciting. Researchers actively seek such information through well-defined methods of data collection and experimentation. These methods allow us not only to understand some of the mysteries of development but also to answer many practical questions. Developmental psychologists rely on methods that are systematic and objective. Researchers must clearly define the subjects in the study, the manner in which the study will be performed, and the statistical analyses used. This produces a study that allows others to replicate the study, checking its results and expanding

Our Pluralistic Society: Cultural Cautions (continued)

times, the differences between subgroups in the minority culture are misunderstood. For example, Latinos do not all belong to the same group. People from Cuba, Mexico, and Puerto Rico differ greatly. They often consider themselves Mexican, Puerto Rican, or Cuban rather than Latino.

Latinos may share some elements of culture and attitudes, but they are certainly not identical. Various Asian groups such as Japanese, Vietnamese, and Chinese also differ greatly in attitudes, language, and background, so it is important to understand the varied nature of different cultures.

Mistake Number Three: Ignoring Acculturation

There are no pure forms of minority culture. Whenever a minority group comes into contact with the majority culture, some change occurs. It may take a few generations, but change is inevitable. This is called **acculturation.** Acculturation occurs when contact between cultures affects the cultural patterns of one or both groups (Hernandez, 1989).

Mistake Number Four: All Minority Group Members Are Poor

It is inaccurate to assume that all members of minority groups are poverty stricken. About 40% of all Asians and Pacific Islanders have incomes over $50,000 per year. The African-American and Latino middle class is growing in number and many live in the suburbs and not in the inner city (O'Hare & Frey, 1992). Although people from certain minority groups are overrepresented in the ranks of the poor, it would be incorrect to ignore the substantial numbers of minority-group families who are *not* living in poverty. It is important to differentiate socioeconomic status from minority-group status.

acculturation The process by which contact between cultures affects the cultural patterns of one or both groups.

Mistake Number Five: Idealizing the Minority Group's Culture

It is important not to idealize one culture and denigrate another culture. One culture should not be portrayed as faultless and pure, in battle against the bad dominant culture. Saying that American culture values individuality more than some other cultures does not mean that American culture is superior. Cultural differences must be understood and appreciated. Although our new appreciation of the importance of culture is to be applauded, we ought not steep cultures in myths and half-truths and adopt simplistic notions about the merits or demerits of a particular culture.

Mistake Number Six: Emphasizing Nothing but Differences

Most often when people talk about culture they speak about cultural differences. Too often, the differences are emphasized and we do not take into consideration the similarities in people's hopes, attitudes, and values. Although cultural differences are illuminating, it would be wrong to leave the impression that members of one minority group differ in every, or even most, respects from members of other minority groups or the majority group.

When speaking about different cultures, some generalizations are inevitable. The purpose of an explanation of culture is not to stereotype families, but to become aware of attitudes, values, and beliefs that may come into play when interacting with people of a particular group (Salend & Taylor, 1993). It is also important to appreciate the situation in which they now find themselves and to understand their history. Yet, our appreciation of the importance of culture and minority-group experience must not be allowed to increase our stereotypes or to reduce our appreciation of individual differences. Cultural background is an important factor in determining an individual's developmental experiences, but it is only one of a number of factors that comprise the context of development.

upon its conclusions. Researchers can adopt a number of strategies or methods. Each strategy has its own strengths and weaknesses, but each can contribute to our knowledge of human development.

Naturalistic Observation: Describing Behavior

Sometimes researchers observe events as they occur in the native environment. This method is called **naturalistic observation.** For example, Bonnie Klimes-Dougan and Janet Kistner (1990) wanted to know whether abused preschoolers would react differently from nonabused children when faced with distressed peers. The researchers watched abused and nonabused preschoolers on a playground react to naturally occurring crying, screaming, or verbalizations such as "ouch," "stop," or "help." (Reports of the children's abuse had been documented by state officials. The last incident of abuse had occurred many months prior to the study.) They found that abused preschoolers showed more aggression towards, as well as withdrawal from, distressed peers than did nonabused preschoolers. Abused children were more likely to initiate actions that caused others distress. These results are especially interesting because these inappropriate responses persisted despite prolonged exposure to and interaction with nonabusive peers and care-givers at a day care center. Certainly new approaches to countering these early experiences are required.

naturalistic observation A method of research in which the researcher observes organisms in their natural habitat.

True or False?
Observation is a valid tool for conducting research.

Naturalistic observation has its limitations. First, observers may disagree about what they have seen. To counter this possibility, sometimes it helps to videotape the events being studied. Second, observers themselves may influence a subject. Would you act the same way if someone were watching you? The very presence of an adult sitting in a classroom or watching parents play with their children may cause subjects to act differently. Research shows that some subjects try to present themselves in their best light, while others may have the opposite reaction (Repp et al., 1988). For this reason, observations must be conducted such that the observer blends into the background as much as possible. Third, although naturalistic observation yields interesting information, it cannot tell us anything about cause and effect. When people are being observed in their natural environments, no effort is made to control the many factors than may influence behavior. From this study we can make no statement about why abused children act the way they do.

Case Studies

What if you wanted to know how a particularly effective teacher structures the classroom and lessons (Pierce, 1994), or understand the experience of a child who was abused but is still functioning well (Herrenkohl, Herrenkohl, & Egolf, 1994)? You would study this one individual, trying to obtain as much relevant information as possible. You might observe the child and interview the child's parents and teachers. A researcher following the progress of a subject over an extended period of time, painstakingly recording behavior and seeking to identify patterns, is conducting a **case study** (Harrison, 1979). Case studies can be especially useful when investigating an unusual situation, one in which relatively few people find themselves. For example, one case study investigated an 11-year-old boy who was verbally gifted, had a learning disability in mathematics, and had a serious health impairment. The child was receiving homebound instruction and had little contact with the school. The investigators looked at the child's learning characteristics and educational experiences to discover something about the unique experiences of this child (Moon & Dillon, 1995).

Case studies also can be useful in generating experimental questions that can then be looked at using other means (Wells, 1987). They also present a unique look at the individual, which is sometimes necessary because other methods of research rely on the group.

Although a valuable technique, the case-study approach is of limited use. One can never be quite certain that the person being studied is similar to other people who are the same age or who have the same particular condition. Therefore, it is necessary to do many case studies to demonstrate a common behavioral pattern. Case studies also cannot determine cause and effect. In addition, by their very nature, such observations are time-consuming and expensive.

The Survey Method

What if you wanted to find out how satisfied 5000 women were in their marriages, how children feel about eating vegetables, or how older people feel about being grandparents? In these cases, you would probably use a **survey** or interview method. In a survey, researchers ask a number of people questions about their own or others' behavior or attitudes. Answers are then tabulated, analyzed, and reported.

Psychologists frequently use surveys to collect data, sometimes with surprising results. For example, what if you wanted to find out how parents discipline their children? When 500 parents of children under age 12 were sampled and the findings compared with the results of a similar survey in 1962, the changes were significant (Figure 1.3). The most preferred method of discipline now is time-out, which involves removing children from a situation that is reinforcing to one that is less reinforcing, whereas spanking was the most widely used method in 1962 (Bruskin/Goldring Research, 1993).

Surveys present many challenges. For instance, before we can make any general statement about the change in preferred strategy, we must be certain that the parents answering the questionnaire were representative of other parents across the nation. To do so, we would have to know how the survey was conducted. For instance, if the survey was conducted by telephone in the afternoon, the study would have left out women who work during the day. Second, some people just refuse to fill out questionnaires. Those who refuse to participate in a survey may be different in some ways from those who do answer, making interpretation of the data more difficult. Third, you cannot be certain that respondents are telling the truth about how they feel or act. Finally, it is difficult to construct a fair and unbiased questionnaire. The researcher must be quite careful about how the questions are worded. For example, imagine being asked a number of questions concerning how you discipline or punish your child. If the question is "How often do you spank your child?" you might answer one way, but if the question is "How often do you beat your child?" you might answer that quite differently. Certainly, this did not occur in the study on discipline just described but the general warning about bias should be kept in mind.

Surveys can be very useful because they allow the researcher to gather a great deal of data in a fairly short amount of time. However, questionnaires must be constructed with care, the sample carefully chosen, and the interpretations cautiously made.

case study A method of research in which one person's progress is followed for an extended period of time.

survey A method of study in which data is collected through written questionnaires or oral interviews from a number of people.

Naturalistic observation is a valuable research technique, but the presence of an observer may influence the subjects' behavior, so this researcher is observing through a one-way mirror.

Correlations: Finding Relationships

Researchers involved in collecting and analyzing data sometimes want to find the relationships between two elements in the environment. For example, a relationship exists between poor behavior in class and grades. Researchers use the term **correlation** to describe such a relationship.

A correlation can be positive, negative, or zero. A positive correlation indicates that relatively large scores on one factor are associated with large scores on another and that relatively small scores on one factor are associated with small scores on another. As intelligence increases, so does academic achievement. A positive correlation exists between physical activity and longevity, that is, as vigorous activity increases so does length of life (Lee, Chung-Cheng, & Pafenbarger, 1995). A perfect positive correlation is written +1.00.

correlation A term denoting a relationship between two variables.

A negative or inverse correlation indicates that as one factor increases the other decreases. A perfect negative correlation is written −1.00. For example, we may find a negative correlation between misbehaving in class and grades on a child's report card: the greater the misbehavior, the lower the grades. A zero correlation indicates that there is no relationship between the two factors; for example, there is no relationship between shoe size and the child's intelligence.

Most correlations are far from perfect. The correlation between scores on an intelligence test and achievement in school as measured by grades hovers between .50 and .60, which is high but not anywhere near perfect (Kubiszyn & Borich, 1987). Other factors besides intelligence, such as motivation and perseverance, are involved in school success. In addition, correlations do not tell us about cause and effect. Certainly students who misbehave tend to receive poor grades, but it may not be correct to state that misbehavior *causes* poor grades. There are other possibilities. Students who misbehave tend not to pay attention in class, study hard, do their homework, or do well on exams. It may be these factors, rather than misbehavior, that causes the poor grades. Only more experimentation can determine whether this is the case. A correlation only tells us that a relationship exists, the direction of the relationship (whether it is positive or negative), and the magnitude of that relationship.

Type of Discipline	1962	1992
Timeout	20%	38%
Lecture them (in a nice way)	23%	24%
Spanking	59%	19%
Take away television privileges	38%	15%
Scold them (not in a nice way)	17%	15%
Ground them	5%	14%
Take away allowance	4%	2%

Note: Parents could cite more than one method.
Source: Data from Bruskin/Goldring Research.

Figure 1.3
Parental Discipline: Methods of Discipline Favored by Parents, 1962 and 1992

Experimentation: Finding Causes

Often, the only way to answer an important research question is to conduct an **experiment.** Experimental studies may allow us to find cause-and-effect relationships. To do this the researcher controls the situation as much as possible, manipulating one or two elements of the environment. To illustrate, let's look at how Boyatzis, Matillo, and Nesbitt (1995) approached the question of the effect watching a popular children's television show, *The Mighty Morphin Power Rangers,* has on aggressive behavior.

In 1995, *The Mighty Morphin Power Rangers* was the most popular children's program on television. The

experiment A research strategy using controls that allows the researcher to discover cause-and-effect relationships.

Power Rangers are a group of racially diverse superheroes who battle monsters trying to take control of the earth. The National Coalition on Television Violence, which has analyzed violence on television since 1980, claims that it is the most violent children's program ever studied, averaging more than 200 violent acts per hour.

An ethnically diverse sample of 26 boys and 26 girls ranging in age from 5 to 11 years was randomly assigned either to an experimental group, which watched an episode of the program, or to a **control group** which did not. On the first day of the study, each child in the control group was observed while in regular play and the number of aggressive acts were recorded. The next day the experimental group watched the television show and then were allowed to play in their regular fashion while their play was observed and the number of aggressive acts were recorded.

The results showed that children who watched the Power Rangers program committed seven times the number of aggressive acts as the children in the control group. Boys were much more likely to be affected than girls, perhaps because so many more Power Rangers are males. An interesting observation is that a number of the violent acts, such as flying karate kicks, were almost exact replicas of what was seen on the program.

This study demonstrated that viewing this program leads to more aggressive actions. The authors suggest that the study needs to be replicated and extended using larger samples. For example, it would be interesting to test children individually by allowing each to view the program alone and then allowing the subjects to play with other children who had not viewed the video. Since this show is televised five or more times a week in many areas, the cumulative effect of such viewing is an interesting question as well. Finally, the Power Rangers sometimes admonish each other to fight in self-defense or to express one's anger responsibly, but these positive statements are embedded in violent actions and do not seem to be very effective. It would be interesting to investigate the effect of this show on children's prosocial behavior and conflict resolution.

The factors of an experiment that are manipulated are called **independent variables** and those that are measured are called **dependent variables.** In this study, whether the children watched the program or not was the independent variable, the number of aggressive acts was the dependent variable.

Experimental studies are often difficult to perform because a researcher has to exercise great control over the environment. Experiments require a control group, a yardstick against which to measure change. However, experimental studies are worth the extra effort because they can demonstrate cause-and-effect relationships.

Questions Students Often Ask

I often find that what I read in textbooks does not match my experience or even what I read in the newspaper. Why?

Let's say that you send your 3-year-old to a nursery school where she has a terrible experience. The teacher is not very good and her peers do not relate well to her. Your personal experience may well affect your view of nursery schools. Although a personal experience should not be denied, it does not mean that it is the experience of most children. Indeed, your experience could be atypical. The newspapers may also be more interested in publishing an atypical report because it is interesting or controversial. This is why impartial, well-designed research studies, which look at the experience of many people, are so important.

Longitudinal and Cross-Sectional Research

Developmental research is often concerned with measuring change over time. We may be interested in discovering how people of various ages approach problems or how people perceive right and wrong differently as they develop. Developmental psychologists have formulated several research designs that measure change over time.

To find out how people view environmental issues you could find groups of people of various ages and administer instruments that would accurately measure their attitudes to and practice of certain behaviors, such as recycling. This is an example of a **cross-sectional study.** On the other hand you could begin with a group of 20 4-year-olds and measure their attitudes and behaviors, wait 4 years and measure their personalities again, and then wait another 4 years and do it a third time, and so on. This is an example of a **longitudinal study.**

Cross-sectional studies are easier to conduct. Groups of subjects of different ages are tested at the same time and the results are compared. For example, in one cross-sectional study, people in four age groups, 20–29, 35–45, 53–67, and 70–83, were asked to read a story that contained highly emotional material as well as nonemotional material. Later they were asked to repeat everything they remembered about the passage they read about an hour before (Carstensen & Turk-Charles, 1994). The younger subjects processed about the same amount of nonemotional and emotional information, whereas older subjects

control group The group that acts as a comparison against which the experimental treatment is evaluated.

independent variables The factors in a study that will be manipulated by the researcher.

dependent variables The factors in a study that will be measured by the researcher.

cross-sectional study A research design in which subjects of different ages are studied to obtain information about changes in some variable.

longitudinal study A research design in which the same subjects are followed over an extended period of time to note developmental changes in some variable.

remembered a higher proportion of emotional material. Older people devote a greater amount of their cognitive resources to feelings than younger people do. The investigators suggest that when testing older and younger people, researchers often use neutral information without emotional content that may place older people at a disadvantage.

Cross-sectional studies are useful, but they have limitations. It is difficult to understand the growth and decline of any attribute over an extended period of time, because the same people are not being followed (Nunnally, 1982). In addition, when comparing subjects who differ significantly in age, the effect of growing up in a different generation (the cohort effect) must be taken into account. This problem is evident here. It is possible that the current generation of older adults attends more to emotional information but this may not be true of the next generation.

Longitudinal studies are more difficult to execute than cross-sectional studies. Subjects must be followed over some period of time and retested at stated intervals. However, such studies allow us to see changes in subjects over time. Such questions as, *Do obese children become obese adults?* and *Do aggressive teens remain aggressive during adulthood?* can best be studied using longitudinal research designs. Longitudinal studies can determine the changes in parenting styles over time or how the nature of interactions between parent and child change over time. For example, when fathers' parenting behaviors were assessed when their children were 13 months old and again at 5 years of age, total paternal involvement was found to have increased. During infancy, mothers were the primary care-givers and both parents were equally involved in play activities. When the children were 5 years old, fathers were more involved in the care-giving; the amount of social interaction with the child was about the same as it was when the child was an infant (Bailey, 1994). Still, mothers performed the greater share of the care-giving at both ages. Paternal participation was related to maternal employment. If the mother was employed the father participated more in the care-giving. Perhaps the mother simply had less time and so the father felt more responsible. In the history of developmental psychology, many important long-term longitudinal studies have been performed, some of which will be discussed, especially in the adulthood chapters.

Longitudinal studies also have practical limitations. They are more time-consuming, and maintaining contact with subjects over a long period of time is difficult. Some subjects move away; others simply do not return for follow-up interviews or do not return their questionnaires, leaving the researcher with incomplete data. It is difficult to determine whether those who drop out differ from those who remain throughout the study. Another problem is the effect of practice and retesting in some longitudinal studies (Blank, 1982). Let's say you want to measure changes in intelligence over the years. If you use the same or a very similar test, people might become wise to the test and show an improvement simply as a result of practice. On the other hand, using different measures may create problems because one measure may not be directly comparable to another. As in the cross-sectional approach, the cohort effect should be taken into account (Birren et al., 1981). Longitudinal studies performed 30 years ago are interesting, but they may be confounded by specific generational differences and may have to be updated.

Time-Lag and Sequential Designs

Cross-sectional designs measure at least two different age groups at one time whereas longitudinal studies measure one group of people over a particular time period. Neither design really differentiates the effects of aging from the cohort effect. For example, if people at 10, 30, and 50 years were found to have different views about environmental issues, do age differences necessarily explain these changes? The changes may be the result of a change in our culture and in our basic way of thinking about the environment.

In order to deal with this problem, different designs are used. In a **time-lag study**, two or more data collections occur at different times and data that already exists before the study was even planned, such as college or voting records, are used for comparison. You may examine the same variable in 30-year-olds today and compare them with similar studies done in 1970. For example, you may find data on people's opinions of environmental issues in 1970 and then use a similar survey to obtain data about today's early adults. If they are similar, you might then argue that age may have something to do with particular attitudes. However, if they differ greatly you may be witnessing a change in culture. The fact that two different groups of people were involved in this study also makes interpretation somewhat difficult (Hayslip & Panek, 1993).

Sequential designs are more complicated and require the study of at least two cross-sections or two longitudinal analyses (Stevens-Long & Commons, 1992). The researcher studies at least two different cohorts at two or more different times of measurement. For example, to measure health practices, including eating and exercise patterns, we could begin the study in 1997 with a sample of 10-year-olds and measure these behaviors every 5 years—this is a longitudinal study. In order to find out if there are any cohort effects we might then start another such study in 2007 of a different group of 10-year-olds and follow them every 5 years as well. Two longitudinal studies cover the same age ranges but at different times. Another way of conducting a sequential study is to use a cross-sectional approach comparing children who were 5, 10, and 15 years of age on these variables and then following them every 5 years. Some studies of intellectual

time-lag study A study that compares data presently gathered to data gathered at an earlier time, before the study was contemplated.

sequential design The use of at least two cross-sectional or longitudinal studies in one research study.

changes, especially in adulthood, use sequential designs (Schaie, 1994).

Questions Students Often Ask

Research methods are complicated and I don't expect to become an expert in them. Why do I have to know them?

Although an introduction to research methods won't make you an expert, understanding some basic principles involved is worthwhile. Let's say you saw the results of a survey on television or read about it in the newspapers. After reading the brief analysis of surveys in the text, wouldn't you ask some questions about how it was conducted? For example, how did they choose their subjects? What exactly were the questions asked? If you read about a relationship (correlation) between two variables, such as looking one's best and getting a job, you might now question whether that really means that looking your best caused *you to get that job. You might look for other possibilities, such as that looking your best made you feel more confident, and it is confidence that aided your presentation, getting you that job. The point is that an understanding of research methods helps you better analyze the claims you hear everywhere.*

Cross-Cultural Research

No research method is perfect, and each has advantages and disadvantages. We have assumed that researchers conduct the research in their own cultural setting with no language difficulties, but this may not be true. More and more research is being performed in other cultures. Conducting research in different cultures presents new problems and opportunities. Even executing research studies in one's own nation on subgroups or minorities whose cultures may differ can be difficult.

Cross-cultural studies are important and valuable if we are to extend our understanding of human development past our own borders. Some researchers even argue that unless we look at other cultures it is not possible to make any serious systematic attempt to understand human behavior and development, perhaps because our own cultural biases get in the way (Heron & Kroeger, 1981).

Cross-cultural studies yield many benefits. They help us extend and test theoretical approaches. For instance, Jean Piaget, whose theory is described in Chapter 2, believes that the sequence of cognitive development is invariant; that is, that children progress from Stage I to Stage II to Stage III in order without regressing or skipping any stages. Most cross-cultural studies confirm this part of Piaget's theory (Dasen & Heron, 1981).

Cross-cultural research also allows researchers to discover how people from other cultures handle their problems and develop. For example, a study of how Japanese and American mothers handle certain daily problems showed an interesting difference (Hess et al., 1986). Japanese mothers were more likely to appeal to feelings, for example, asking children, "How do you think I will feel if you don't eat those vegetables?", whereas American mothers were more likely to use appeals to authority or power, such as "I told you to eat those vegetables."

Cross-cultural research also widens our perspective and may serve to increase understanding between people and to reduce prejudice. We sometimes think that the way things are in our own country is the way they are throughout the world, but research on competition and cooperation, aggression, fathering, education, and gender differences and stereotypes have shown that this is not true (Adler, 1982).

Last, there is a tendency to be so centered on our own culture that we do not recognize the fact that people in other cultures can be ahead or behind on some characteristic, depending upon their environment and culture. It is especially important to look into the context of development to understand why a person develops in a particular manner (Rogoff & Morelli, 1989). We can only truly appreciate the importance of environment and culture and reduce our cultural isolation by looking at development in other cultures.

Cross-cultural research presents unique problems, one of which is accurate translation. Devising measuring instruments that can be used across cultures is another. The most serious problem, however, is that a concept may have one meaning in one culture and another in a different culture. For example, achievement in Western developed nations like the United States and Canada is an individualistic concept, whereas in some South Pacific islands it has meaning in a group context, where achievements can be shared for the mutual benefit of everyone in the group (Gallimore, Weiss, & Finney, 1974).

Despite these problems, cross-cultural research studies make valuable contributions to developmental psychology. Although in the past these studies emphasized the differences among cultures, today we are just as interested in discovering similarities among cultures (Heron & Kroeger, 1981).

Ethical Considerations in Research

Ethical problems arise whenever research is performed. In most universities today, committees review the ethics of each research proposal involving animals or human beings, and many professional organizations as well as the federal government have published ethical standards for research (Cooke, 1982). Most psychological experiments cause no physical or mental pain. Studies that contain anything considered even remotely dangerous are rare. Although there are many ethical questions in psychological research, two of the main concerns have to do with the issues of informed consent and deception.

Informed Consent

Federal guidelines specify that subjects should be told the purpose of the research, the procedures involved, and the risks and benefits. Subjects should also be presented with a statement noting that they are free to withdraw from the study and should be invited to ask questions about their participation.

Some studies involve small children, who naturally cannot give their permission. In such cases the study is explained to the parents, who then consent to the child's participation. If the child is above the age of 7, the child's consent should definitely be obtained (Cooke, 1982). However, the researcher should try to get the permission of children even younger than 7 whenever possible. Often, however, young children have difficulty understanding the research process, and their limited cognitive abilities do not allow them to understand their rights fully, especially their right to withdraw from the study (Thompson, 1990).

Recently, a new question of consent has been raised. In the past few years Congress has cancelled proposed studies funded by the federal government on sensitive topics, such as the sexual behavior of teenagers, because many legislators felt the questions were too graphic or offensive. In the past parents were often but not always informed that a questionnaire would be given to their children, but only if the parents objected by phone or mail would their children be prevented from participating. Under the new rule parents will have to sign their written consent to have their children participate on anonymous surveys on such topics as sexual behavior, religious attitudes, or illegal or antisocial activities (Lane, 1995).

Some social scientists claim that such a law would lead to tremendously increased costs and would also lead to questions about the accuracy of their studies, since parents would have to take a positive action—signing their consent—rather than simply a passive one—not objecting. In one school in which a survey on drinking and drug use was being conducted only 17 of 100 parents returned the form (Lane, 1995). Many parents, even those who do not object, may just not sign the consent form because of lack of time or interest. Perhaps a compromise would be best; a federal regulation requiring parental notification and allowing withdrawal by telephone but not requiring active agreement might satisfy the concerns of both sides.

Deception

The most serious ethical problem confronting researchers today is deception. Some researchers argue that they cannot always inform subjects about the true objectives of their study. If they do, the subjects may alter their behavior to match the desires of the researcher. What if the researcher wants to determine whether the gender of the author of a composition would affect students' evaluations of the work? The researcher may tell the subjects that the study is concerned with the content of the story itself and not mention the author's name, which appears at the top of the page and clearly reflects the writer's gender. Is this deception warranted? Today, sexism and racism are not fashionable, and subtle deceptions may be necessary if psychologists are to study these areas. Other psychologists disagree, arguing that deception is morally wrong and harmful to the profession (Baumrind, 1985).

Questions Students Often Ask

If you need to find something out, and the only way to do it is deception, there seems to be no choice. I don't see the problem.

Although deception is not used in most studies, it is used sometimes. Committees in major universities must consider whether there is any other way the question can be researched and weigh the costs and benefits. The benefits of research seem obvious, but the cost of deception can be high. Consider what would happen if you were deceived by a researcher whom you trusted. You volunteered for one study but were involved in something quite different. You were deceived. How would you feel about psychologists or psychology after that? Deception exacts a price on the field in terms of mistrust and should not be used without considerable thought.

This difference of opinion among researchers will continue. Researchers who use deception take extra responsibilities upon themselves. After the study, subjects must be informed as to the study's true nature. It is necessary to look into the possible impact of the deception on the subjects' self-esteem, feelings toward authority figures, and alienation from society, especially for subjects who already perceive themselves to be rejected or alienated from society (Fisher & Tryon, 1988). In addition, during the study subjects may acquire knowledge that may trouble them, and researchers must provide help for subjects trying to work through what they have learned about themselves (Holmes, 1976a; Holmes, 1976b).

People of different ages are vulnerable to different types of problems (Thompson, 1990). For example, challenges to a child's self-concept are likely to become more stressful with age. If a study purports to find a person's intelligence, the discovery of the figure will affect a child of school age or an adult more than a younger child. On the other hand, a very young child is more likely to be stressed if separated from an adult. We must continue to be aware and sensitive to the way people experience the research process.

Ready to Begin

This chapter examined the basic principles behind the life-span perspective and some of the research methods scientists use to uncover new information. But to place these new findings into perspective and adequately interpret these research results, scientists need to adopt theoretical perspectives that will allow them to ask the relevant questions and relate earlier experiences and behavior to later behavior. It is to these theoretical approaches that we turn next.

Summary

1. Life-span developmental psychology is concerned with the study of constancy and change in behavior throughout the life cycle from conception to death. Quantitative change is a change in amount, frequency, or degree; qualitative change is a change in process, function, structure, or organization.
2. Developmental changes are caused by the interaction of genetic and environmental factors. Maturation is the unfolding of the genetic plan. Any relatively permanent change in behavior that can be attributed to interactions with the environment is the result of learning.
3. Early childhood experiences have a profound influence on later development and behavior. However, the effects of a poor early environment can be remedied, at least to some extent, by improving the environment.
4. The effect of belonging to a particular generation is known as the cohort effect. Epidemics, economic depression, technological change, and revolutions may have an important effect upon the development of a particular generation.
5. When investigating relationships, developmental psychologists emphasize reciprocal interaction by looking both at how people affect and are affected by their environment.
6. People develop in multiple contexts including the family, peers, community, media, vocational world, cultural and religious environment, and the dominant political system.
7. There are many types of research. In naturalistic observation, the researcher carefully observes and records what occurs in the natural environment. The case study method involves carefully observing a subject for a substantial period of time and collecting a great deal of information about one person. Researchers using the survey method question a number of people, then tabulate and analyze the data. Researchers may attempt to discover correlations or relationships between variables. These relationships show the extent to which one factor is related to another. Researchers using the experimental method control the environment, allowing only the desired variables to vary. Such experiments may demonstrate cause and effect.
8. In cross-sectional studies, people from various age groups are tested at a particular time. In a longitudinal study, a single group of people is tested at certain intervals. In a time-lag study two or more data collections occur at different times and data that already exists before the study was even planned may be used. Sequential designs require the study of at least two cross-sections or two longitudinal analyses.
9. Psychologists are more interested than ever in performing cross-cultural studies. Such studies help us appreciate the many and varied ways in which culture can affect development.
10. Most psychological experiments cause no physical or psychological harm to their subjects. Most universities have committees that examine the ethics of each experiment. Two of the most common ethical problems involve informed consent and deception.

Multiple-Choice Questions

1. Which of the following is an example of a quantitative change?
   a. A child can now solve a jigsaw puzzle that he couldn't last week.
   b. An elderly person now uses lists in order to make up for a failing memory.
   c. A middle-aged person gains three pounds in a year.
   d. All of these are quantitative changes.
2. A qualitative change is a change in:
   a. process.
   b. amount.
   c. frequency.
   d. degree.
3. What is the problem with saying that growth is caused by genetic factors and the ability to add is caused by environmental factors such as being taught?
   a. We have no evidence that genetics is involved in growth.
   b. We have no evidence that learning and environmental factors are involved in doing mathematical problems.
   c. Environmental factors and genetics interact and both must be taken into consideration.
   d. Genetic factors are always most important to understanding all types of change, but the environment deserves some minimal attention.
4. The unfolding of the genetic plan is called:
   a. canalization.
   b. maturation.
   c. institutionalization.
   d. symbolic interaction.
5. You read that early experience determines the personality, emotional reactions, and behavior of the adult. According to research, this is:
   a. correct, and later experience can do little to change behavior.
   b. incorrect, because the infant does not remember what happens so infancy is not very important.

c. incorrect, because early experience determines later behavior and personality, but not later emotional reactions.
d. incorrect, because although early experience may be important, later experience can partially modify what is learned early in life.

6. The fact that you may differ from your parents because you were brought up during a different historical period is called the:
a. Spock effect.
b. cohort effect.
c. judgmental effect.
d. psi effect.

7. A child whines and a parent reacts with an angry stare that causes the child to cry more, which causes the parent to yell at the child. The term _________ describes how each person affected the other.
a. indirect causation
b. retroactive inhibition
c. individualized affectation
d. reciprocal interaction

8. The fact that people grow up affected by their families, peer groups, neighborhood, schools, and even the political system in which they live can be understood using the concept of:
a. formulation.
b. institutionalization.
c. covenants.
d. context.

9. What percentage of American children grow up in poverty?
a. 3%
b. 8%
c. 16%
d. 22%

10. One limitation to naturalistic observation is that:
a. people may act differently if they know they are being observed.
b. naturalistic observation does not allow the use of statistics to analyze data once it is gathered.
c. it can only be performed out-of-doors and is not useful in the home or classroom.
d. it is only effective for children, not for adolescents or adults.

11. A child who has just witnessed a tornado ripping up a family's home is followed for a few years. He is observed, interviewed, and so are his parents and other people who know him. This method of research is called:
a. multiple context.
b. a case study.
c. cross-sectional.
d. experimental.

12. If you wanted to find out how 1000 people feel about their job, what research method would you probably use?
a. case study
b. experimental
c. observation
d. survey

13. The key to the experimental method is:
a. the size of the sample.
b. control of the experimental situation.
c. the relationship between the experimenter and the subject.
d. the attitude the experimenter brings to the study.

14. Dr. Zimmer is conducting an experiment on the effect of being given leadership roles on the self-concept. Fifty children are randomly divided into two groups: one in which children are given leadership roles in various school activities and another in which they are not. The independent variable in this study is:
a. a measure of self-concept.
b. which children end up in the experimental group.
c. whether or not children were given leadership roles.
d. whether Dr. Zimmer or a colleague does the observation.

15. Dr. Forago is conducting an experiment on the influence of different parenting practices on honesty. In this experiment, the dependent variable is:
a. parenting practices.
b. who has and does not have two biological parents living with them.
c. a measure of honesty.
d. the attitudes that Dr. Forago brings to the experiment.

16. If a positive correlation exists between physical activity and longevity, we might expect:
a. people who eat a good diet to live longer.
b. people who engage in physical activity to live longer.
c. physical activity to predict happiness and contentment.
d. physical activity to be the prime cause of longevity.

17. If you were told that the correlation between two factors is .70, you would know that:
a. a high negative correlation exists between the two factors.
b. a perfect correlation exists between the two factors.
c. there is almost no correlation between the two factors.
d. a high positive correlation exists, but it is not perfect.

18. Dr. Nichols is comparing groups of 5- , 8- , and 10-year-olds on how they perceive government. Dr. Nichols is conducting a:
a. cross-sectional study.
b. longitudinal study.
c. cross-sequential study.
d. mixed design study.

19. Dr. Washington wants to see how personality changes over the life span. She chooses 200 5-year-

olds and then tests them every 5 years for the next 50 years. This type of study is called a:
a. cross-sectional study.
b. longitudinal study.
c. cross-sequential study.
d. mixed design study.

20. Which of the following is an ethical problem involved in developmental research?
a. deception
b. informed consent
c. how information the subjects learn about themselves may affect them
d. all of the above

Answers to Multiple-Choice Questions

1. c 2. a 3. c 4. b 5. d 6. b 7. d 8. d 9. d
10. a 11. b 12. d 13. b 14. c 15. c 16. b 17. d
18. a 19. b 20. d

Chapter 2

Theories of Development

Chapter Outline

Are the Following Statements True or False?

1. Theories can both describe present behavior and predict future behavior.
2. Freud argued that early parent-child experiences cause particular personality characteristics to develop.
3. People usually first think about their identities in early adulthood.
4. Most studies show that children after the age of 5 years think and solve problems in the same way as most adults.
5. Preschool children generally believe that everyone sees and experiences the world the way they do.
6. For people to learn something, they do not have to be reinforced directly.
7. The relationship between children and their parents may be affected by such long-range factors as their parents' work environment and parents' network of friends.
8. A person may play many roles, some of which may be in conflict with each other.
9. Developmental psychologists unanimously agree that the best way to understand development is through the use of stages.
10. Using one theory to understand cognitive development and another theory to understand social development is an inappropriate use of theory.

Answers to True-False Statements 1. True 2. True 3. False: see p. 29 4. False: see p. 30 5. True 6. True 7. True 8. True 9. False: see p. 41 10. False: see p. 44

How Will the Children React?

On the morning of January 28, 1986, millions of people of all ages around the country watched the long-awaited *Challenger* space shuttle launch on television. More children than usual were watching because the shuttle carried a teacher, Christa McAuliffe, who was to give a science lesson in space. Less than a minute and a half into the mission, the space shuttle exploded. Shock and grief spread throughout the country, together with some concern about how the children who had witnessed this tragedy would respond.

Is it possible to predict how children from different age groups would respond to the incident? Many developmental psychologists could have (and, in fact, did), because they know how people at various developmental levels reason and deal with information. The day after the tragedy, Nanci Monaco and Eugene Gaier (1987) conducted a study of teachers and students that in part demonstrated just how well psychologists' theories can be used to understand how people at particular developmental levels will react to an event. After presenting a short factual review and some background information about the tragedy, teachers asked students of various ages for comments and questions. The children's questions and comments could have been predicted by a person familiar with Jean Piaget's theory of cognitive (intellectual) development.

Why Is Theory Important?

Theories are powerful tools for understanding human development. Without a theoretical perspective, data cannot be interpreted. Let's say that you had access to a computerized database of research findings in human development. You ask for data on intellectual (cognitive) development. The computer spews out thousands of pages of data from study after study. How do you know which studies are germane to your questions? How do you pull the information together to make it intelligible? To give cohesiveness to this voluminous data, you adopt a theory. Theories, then, help us organize our research.

A theory can also help us explain behaviors. For instance, young children do not believe that an 8-ounce cup and an 8-ounce glass hold the same amount. How can you explain this? Piaget's theory maintains that children between the approximate ages of 2 and 7 do not understand conservation, that quantities remain the same despite changes in their appearance. Theories are also useful in predicting what will come next. Knowing what a child is doing at this point allows us to predict what the child will accomplish next, although the exact time the child will progress is more difficult to predict. If a person is negotiating the teenage years, Erik Erikson's psychosocial theory would emphasize the importance of an adolescent's developing a personal identity. Last, theories help us ask the right questions. Proponents of various theoretical perspectives ask different questions about the same behavior. Each theory seeks to understand why people act the way they do, but each approaches the subject differently. A behaviorist, for example, who explains behavior using principles of learning would be interested in discovering the rewards and punishments in a particular person's environment. A social learning theorist might look for the models in the person's life. Theories, then, allow us to relate one fact to another, to describe and predict behavior, and to focus our attention on specific questions.

Questions Students Often Ask

How do you know that a theory is "good"?

A number of criteria exist that determine whether the theory is a "good" one. For example, a good theory enhances understanding and is especially useful in making predictions. Ideally, a good theory is testable. In other words, researchers should be able to perform experiments that test the theory's hypotheses. However, many theories, such as Freud's, have been useful even though their basic ideas are difficult to test empirically. A theory also should be useful in understanding and predicting future behavior.

Good theories are inclusive: they help answer as many questions related to their particular area as possible. In addition, good theories are economical in that they introduce as few new terms as possible; also, good theories are clear and concise. Last, good theories should spark a great deal of valuable research.

True or False?

Theories can both describe present behavior and predict future behavior.

Developmental psychology offers a number of different theoretical approaches, but no single theory explains or predicts all behavior. Even within a particular area, such as social or cognitive development, a number of theories vie for acceptance.

Freud's Psychoanalytic Theory

According to Sigmund Freud (1900, 1923, 1933), three levels of awareness exist. The **conscious** involves one's immediate awareness and makes up only a small portion of the total mind. The **preconscious** comprises memories that can easily become conscious. Finally, some memories as well as certain impulses and wishes that are unacceptable to a person because they run counter to society's standards are stored in the **unconscious**—the portion of the mind that is beyond normal awareness. The unconscious shows itself in many ways, such as through dreams and slips of the tongue.

Freud (1933) also argued that behavior could be caused and maintained by early experiences that had apparently been forgotten. These experiences, often called *repressed memories,* are stored in the unconscious and are beyond normal awareness. Despite the lack of awareness, these memories can still have a profound effect on behavior. For instance, a person may experience sexual difficulties in a marriage because of a traumatic childhood sexual experience that the individual no longer remembers (DiCaprio, 1983).

Freud insisted that we may not be aware of our true motives or wishes because they are unacceptable to us or because society forbids us to gratify them. A child who is angry at her mother may kick a younger sibling instead of her mother—a situation referred to as *displacement*—and may refuse to admit to feelings of hostility towards her mother. The child is not lying, but rather is unaware of those feelings.

Freud explained the workings of the mind using three constructs (Freud, 1923, 1940): the **id,** the **ego,** and the **superego.** The id is the source of all wishes and desires. It is unconscious and exists at birth. The id wants what it wants when it wants it and cannot tolerate delay. It functions through the **primary process,** which entails instant gratification for every wish and desire. In this sense an infant is totally motivated by the id.

Within the first year, the ego comes into being. Needs such as hunger can be satisfied only by interacting with the real world. The ego, which is partly conscious, operates through the **secondary process,** or **reality principle,** and is responsible for dealing with reality and satisfying the needs and desires of the id in a socially appropriate manner. Whereas the id knows only its subjective reality (I want), the ego must also understand the world outside the mind and the self. As the child grows and matures, the ego grows stronger and learns to delay gratification and balance the desires of the id with the restraints of the third construct, the superego.

The superego is analogous to the conscience. It contains a set of principles gathered from interacting with others in society and serves as an internal gyroscope. The superego compares your behavior to your **ego ideal,** which is what you think you should be like. The superego is perfectionistic, seeking to inhibit the id's antisocial desires and causing an individual to experience guilt when transgressing (or even when just considering a misdeed) or pride when the person reaches a particular standard. The ego must mediate between the strictures of the superego and the desires of the id. Tension may arise from the pull of the id, society's prohibitions, and the weight of superego restraint. Life is a compromise, and

conscious Freudian term for thoughts or memories of which a person is immediately aware.

preconscious Freudian term for thoughts or memories that, although not immediately conscious, can easily become conscious.

unconscious Freudian term for memories that lie beyond one's normal awareness.

id In Freudian theory, the portion of the mind that serves as the depository for wishes and desires.

ego In Freudian theory, the part of the mind that mediates between the real world and the desires of the id.

superego In Freudian theory, the part of the mind that includes a set of principles, violation of which leads to feelings of guilt.

primary process The process by which the id seeks to gratify its desires.

secondary process or reality principle The process by which the ego satisfies the organism's needs in a socially appropriate manner.

ego ideal The individual's positive and desirable standards of behavior.

proper adjustment is a matter of maintaining a delicate balance.

The ego has a difficult job. Sometimes it is overwhelmed, and the tension that results is experienced as anxiety. If the anxiety becomes too great, the ego may defend itself by using a large number of protective maneuvers, called **defense mechanisms** (Table 2.1). A defense mechanism is an automatic and unconscious process that serves to relieve or reduce feelings of anxiety or emotional conflict (Laughlin, 1970).

Psychosexual Stages

One of Freud's most challenging theories is that of infantile and childhood sexuality, which states that infants and children experience sexual feelings. Freud did not believe that young children experience adult sexual feelings, but feelings of sensuality and pleasure. He saw life as the unfolding of the sexual instinct, called *eros.* The energy emanating from eros is known as the *libido,* which attaches itself to different portions of the body as the child matures and is the basis for Freud's theory of the stages of psychosexual development.

defense mechanism A behavior that serves to relieve or reduce feelings of anxiety or emotional conflict.

Freud (1933) stressed the importance of early experience in the formation of personality, and he focused attention on early parent-child interactions as determinants of later personality traits. The issue of early experience was discussed in Chapter 1 and the influence of early parent-child relations on particular behaviors is discussed in Chapter 6, when the nature of the early parent-child relationship is explored.

True or False?
Freud argued that early parent-child experiences cause particular personality characteristics to develop.

The Oral Stage At birth, the infant gains pleasure through sucking and, later, biting, both of which are oral activities. If a child is either frustrated or overly stimulated, he or she may become fixated and partially remain in a previous stage of psychosexual development; the child's personality will show some characteristic of this fixation. According to Freud, fixation at this stage, if it involves sucking, may lead to gullibility (accepting anything that is presented), dependence, inactivity, and a belief that others will provide the comforts of life.

Table 2.1 **Defense Mechanisms**
Defense mechanisms are used to reduce or eliminate unpleasant feelings such as anxiety or emotional conflict. This table shows some of the more prominent mechanisms.

DEFENSE MECHANISM	DESCRIPTION	EXAMPLE
Rationalization	Making up plausible but inaccurate excuses to explain some behavior.	A student who is getting poor grades in school explains it away by telling you, "It's what you learn, not your grades, that is important" or "Schools teach nothing useful anyway."
Denial	A person refuses to believe something has occurred or is occurring.	A person refuses to believe that someone has died or that he or she has a problem with using alcohol or other drugs.
Compensation	Making up for a real or imaginary deficiency by putting effort into a similar area (direct compensation) or into a different area (indirect compensation).	An unathletic person who feels physically inferior may buy bodybuilding equipment and work out until he is a first-class weight lifter (direct compensation) or put his efforts into schoolwork to become the best student he can (indirect compensation).
Reaction Formation	An individual experiences feelings that are unacceptable to him or her and so acts in a manner that is contrary to those feelings.	A junior high school girl who likes a boy may act very rude or even hit him to "prove" to her friends that she doesn't really like him.
Projection	Feelings that are unacceptable to oneself are transferred to someone else.	A child who feels angry at her mother for not driving her to a friend's house asks her, "Why are you angry with me?" instead of telling her she is angry at her.
Regression	Returning to a time in life that was more comfortable.	A 3-year-old boy who is talking and toilet-trained begins to talk baby talk and wet his pants after a baby brother is brought home from the hospital.
Repression	Memories are barred from consciousness so they no longer bother a person.	A person who accidentally struck another with his bat during a baseball game cannot remember the incident.
Displacement	The transfer of feelings from one person or object to another.	A child is angry at her father but yells at her brother.
Rechannelization (Sublimation)	Unacceptable impulses are rechanneled into socially appropriate pursuits.	An aggressive person learns to express himself through sports or music.

The Anal Stage At about 18 months of age, the libido becomes attached to the anal cavity, and this coincides with attempts to toilet-train the child. A power struggle over bowel and bladder control may give rise to anal retentive character. In such a case, the child shows such character traits as miserliness, obstinacy, and extreme orderliness and neatness. If, on the other hand, the child relents and releases feces, especially at inappropriate times, anal expulsive traits such as cruelty and messiness result.

The Phallic Stage At about age 4 the child's libido becomes attached to the sexual organs. The child now experiences sexual feelings toward the opposite-sex parent but fears that these desires will earn the displeasure of the same-sex parent and lead to punishment. The child wishes to be rid of the same-sex parent and have the opposite-sex parent all to himself or herself. This is called the *Oedipus complex* in boys and the *Electra complex* in girls. Children resolve this conflict by learning to identify with the same-sex parent. Problems in the phallic stage lead to a variety of disturbances in personality. For example, when the resolution of the Oedipal conflict is not positive, a boy will resent his father and generalize this resentment to authority figures later in life (Nye, 1975). According to this theory a number of sexual problems also date from difficulties in the phallic stage.

The Latency Stage From about age 6 until puberty, the child's sexuality lies dormant. Since a boy has identified with his father, he tends to imitate him at every turn. Boys have also repressed their sexual feelings toward their mothers, but since they are so young, this repression generalizes to all females. Thus, 8-year-old boys are likely to stay apart from 8-year-old girls. In a similar way, girls identify with their mothers. However, the resolution of the Electra complex in females is less severe, and at this stage girls show somewhat less of an aversion to boys than boys do to girls.

The Genital Stage The onset of puberty, with its hormonal changes and sexual arousal, moves the child out of the latency stage and into the genital stage. The young adolescent boy turns his attention to a girlfriend and the young adolescent female seeks a boyfriend. This is the beginning of mature adult sexuality.

Evaluation

Freud's emphasis on the importance of the early interaction between parent and child has been largely accepted by psychologists. Freud felt that poor experiences during the early stages left indelible marks on children, but today we have a more flexible view that believes that subsequent positive experiences ease the negative effects of poor early experiences. In addition, Freud's theory presented the development of the child in a stage setting that has become very popular. Some of Freud's ideas concerning the unconscious have been of great interest as well (Emde, 1992), and Freud's description of defense mechanisms has allowed psychologists a new understanding of behaviors that were incomprehensible in the past. Finally, Freud's theory has served as a focal point for criticism and as a basis for the development of other theories.

THEORY	BASIC PREMISES	VALUES AND STRENGTHS	CRITICISMS AND WEAKNESSES
Freud's Psychoanalytic Theory	1. Behavior is motivated by unconscious thoughts, memories, and feelings. 2. Life is the unfolding of the sex instinct. 3. The child's early experience is critical to the child's later personality. The manner in which the parents satisfy the child's basic needs is important to later mental health. 4. Children develop through a sequence of stages called psychosexual stages. 5. People protect themselves from anxiety and other negative emotions through unconscious and automatic reactions called defense mechanisms.	1. Encourages developmental specialists to look beyond the obvious visible behavior and seek insights into the unconscious. 2. Emphasizes the importance of the child's early experience and relationships, which in turn focuses our attention on the caregiver-infant relationship. The idea that later problems may be due to disturbed early relationships is challenging. 3. The concept of stages in Freudian theory has become a popular way of viewing the development of children. 4. Emphasis on sexuality, while debatable, still alerts us to the existence of sexuality at all ages. 5. Serves as a focal point for other theorists.	1. Since theory is based upon clinical experiences with troubled people, it may have more to say about unhealthy than healthy development. 2. Hypotheses are very difficult to test. 3. Failure to appreciate the importance of culture.

Questions Students Often Ask

I don't understand why we even study Freud anymore since no one seems to believe in anything he says. Why cover his theory?

It is somewhat of an overstatement to say that no one seems to believe anything *he says. Although it is true that Freudian thought is no longer as influential as it was, it has influenced and continues to influence some areas of developmental psychology and many other areas of the social sciences. For example, Freud's emphasis on the importance of the early parent-child interaction and the stage of infancy itself influenced many psychologists to look at the effect of early maternal deprivation. In addition, Freud's idea that people do not always think in a logical, rational manner is still important today (Miller et al., 1993). Freud's concept of defense mechanisms is challenging and his emphasis on childhood emotions is noteworthy. We should not forget that he developed the stage approach as well. Although Freud's influence in developmental psychology may be on the wane, it is hardly nonexistent.*

Psychoanalytic theory was formulated on the basis of Freud's clinical experiences (Cairns, 1983). Freud's patients were troubled, and psychoanalytic theory may have more to say about abnormal development than typical development. It may be a mistake to base our ideas concerning normal development and child-rearing on clinical experiences with emotionally troubled people. In addition, Freud's formulations are difficult to test empirically (Miller, 1993). Some of his concepts, such as *instinct* and *psychic energy*, are vaguely or even poorly defined, and none is defined in a manner that would make scientific testing easy. Finally, Freud's emphasis on sexuality was a product of the society in which Freud lived. Sexuality was frowned on in Vienna at that time, and the belief that sexuality was sinful and unhealthy may have been the cause of many of the problems Freud treated. Freud's ideas may not be as universal as Freud had thought.

Erikson's Psychosocial Theory

Although accepting some of Freud's concepts, a number of Freud's followers have rejected others. Freud's emphasis on sexuality troubled many, as did his lack of consideration for the effect of cultural differences on a person's development. Of all Freud's followers, Erik Erikson has had the greatest influence on the study of human development.

Erikson (1963, 1968) argued that human beings develop according to a preset plan called the **epigenetic principle,** which consists of two main elements. First, personality develops according to predetermined steps that are maturationally set. Second, society is structured so as to invite and encourage the challenges that arise at each particular stage. Maturation brings about new skills that open new possibilities for the person, but also increases society's demands on the individual's functioning. Societies have developed ways to meet the person's new needs at each step in the maturation process, such as parental care, schools, and occupations (Miller, 1993).

epigenetic principle The preset developmental plan in Erikson's theory consisting of two elements: that personality develops according to maturationally determined steps and that each society is structured to encourage challenges that arise during these stages.

Psychosocial Stages

According to Erikson each individual proceeds through eight stages of development from cradle to grave. Each stage presents the individual with a crisis. If a particular crisis is handled well, a positive outcome ensues. If it is not handled well, the outcome is negative. Few people emerge from a particular stage with an entirely positive or negative outcome. In fact, Erikson argues that a healthy balance must be struck between the two extremes. However, the outcome should tend toward the positive side of the scale. Although people can re-experience these crises during a life change, by and large the crises take place only at particular times in life. The resolution of one stage lays the foundation for negotiating the challenges of the next stage.

Trust Versus Mistrust The positive outcome of the stage of infancy is a sense of trust. If children are cared for warmly and lovingly, they are likely to trust their environment and feel that they live among friends. If parents are anxious, angry, or incapable of meeting a child's needs, the child may become mistrustful. Trust is the cornerstone of the child's attitude towards life.

Autonomy Versus Shame or Doubt Children who are 2 and 3 years old are no longer completely dependent on adults. Toddlers practice their new physical skills and develop a positive sense of autonomy. They learn that they are persons in their own right. If these children are either not allowed to do the things they can do or if they are pushed into performing tasks for which they are not ready, they may develop a sense of shame or doubt about their own abilities and fail to develop self-confidence. Parents can help children acquire a sense of autonomy by encouraging them to do what they can do for themselves.

Initiative Versus Guilt By the time children are about 4 years old, they can begin to formulate a plan of action and carry it through. The positive outcome of this stage is a sense of initiative, a sense that one's desires and actions are basically sound. Four-year-olds who are encouraged to form their own ideas will develop a sense of initiative. These children will become self-starters and accept challenges (Hamachek, 1988). Children who are punished for expressing their desires and plans will develop a sense of guilt, which leads to fear and a lack of assertiveness.

During the middle years of childhood, children develop a sense of industry if their accomplishments are valued.

Industry Versus Inferiority During middle childhood children must learn the academic skills of reading, writing, and math, as well as social skills. Children who succeed in acquiring these new skills and whose accomplishments are valued by others develop a sense of industry. Children who are constantly compared with others unfavorably may develop a sense of inferiority.

Identity Versus Role Confusion During adolescence children must start making decisions regarding their vocational and personal future and develop a sense of who they are and where they belong. The adolescent who develops a solid sense of identity formulates a satisfying plan and gains a sense of security. Adolescents who do not develop this sense of identity may develop role confusion, a sense of aimlessness and of being adrift. Erikson's concept of identity, which has sparked much research, is covered in detail in Chapter 13.

> ***True or False?***
> People usually first think about their identities in early adulthood.

Intimacy Versus Isolation The young adult who has already acquired an identity is ready to share that identity with others. In other words, young adults are ready for intimacy—the capacity and willingness to make commitments and to keep those commitments despite the sacrifices and compromises that may be necessary (Erikson, 1963). Intimacy is found in healthy marriages as well as in deep friendships. The negative outcome of the psychosocial stage of young adulthood is isolation—the inability or unwillingness to commit oneself to others. An inability to share one's innermost feelings and thoughts can cause isolation, which leads to loneliness and despair (Salkind, 1981).

Generativity Versus Stagnation The positive outcome of the next stage—middle adulthood—is what Erikson calls generativity, which is primarily concerned with establishing and guiding the next generation (Crain, 1992). Although it is well known that children need adults, the opposite may also be true—that adults need the younger generation. Generativity involves investing something of oneself in the future, such as through one's children or grandchildren or through other means such as community involvement and helping others or creative activities. Stagnation—the negative outcome of this stage—involves absorption in one's own personal needs and an inability or unwillingness to give to others (Salkind, 1981).

Ego Integrity Versus Despair The psychosocial crisis of later adulthood is described in terms of ego integrity versus despair. People with ego integrity realize that their life has been worthwhile. After years of facing challenges and problems, they can look back on a productive and purposeful life. People who see only missed opportunities may become bitter and depressed and develop a sense of despair.

Socialization, Culture, and History

Erikson broadened Freud's theory of growth and development by stressing the importance of socialization, culture, and history. His theory has a cultural basis in two areas. First, the resolution of each crisis depends on the person's interaction with the culture. The search for identity is different for an American than for a South Seas Islander. In our society, industry—the positive outcome of middle childhood—is somewhat dependent on formal school achievement. This is not true in many other cultures. Although children in every culture go through the same stages, each culture has its own way of directing and improving the child's behavior at each age (Miller, 1993). Second, cultures may change over time as institutions respond to the needs of a changing population. The institutions of one generation may not be adequate for the next. For example, the increase in the number of children with both parents employed and of single-parent families has brought about a greater need for alternative child care and the development of day care facilities.

Erikson also noted the importance of the historical period in which people live (Erikson, 1975). Each generation is raised under different social, political, and technological circumstances. Erikson has applied his theories to many great historical personalities, including Martin Luther and Gandhi (Erikson, 1958, 1969). Erikson believed that certain historical changes, such as industrialization or the Great Depression of the 1930s, result in institutions changing to meet people's needs.

Evaluation

Erikson's theory, which is clear and easy to understand, serves as an excellent introduction to the general concerns of people at different ages. His emphasis on the importance of culture, socialization, and the historical moment extends our view of the factors that influence people. Erikson's view of identity has become a cornerstone for understanding adolescence. Erikson's emphasis on the life cycle influenced psychologists greatly and he is credited for our new appreciation of adulthood (Levinson, 1986). He established three periods of adulthood—young adulthood, middle age, and later maturity—and gave us our first psychological maps of the tasks faced at each age. Erikson's work demonstrates the changing nature of the challenges that occur during certain periods of adulthood and emphasizes the way human beings interact socially with their environment.

Criticisms of Erikson's theory are similar to those of Freud's theory. Erikson's theory is difficult to test experimentally (Miller, 1993). Some support for Erikson's theory of identity exists, but little research has been done on the other stages. In addition, Erikson's theory is rather general and global, and some authorities doubt the existence of all of his stages (Thomas, 1979). Despite these criticisms, Erikson's theory offers a convenient way of viewing development throughout the life span.

Piaget's Theory of Cognitive Development

Children are not little adults; children think of and deal with problems differently than adults. The differences between the thinking of children and that of adults are sometimes seen as mistakes or as signs of resistance to growing up. This is not so, as the monumental work of Jean Piaget, who devoted his adult life to studying the cognitive (intellectual) development of children has shown (Beilin, 1992).

True or False?
Most studies show that children after the age of 5 years think and solve problems in the same way as most adults.

According to Piaget, development involves the continuous alteration and reorganization of the ways in which people deal with the environment (Piaget, 1970). Development is defined by four principal factors: *maturation, experience, social transmission,* and the *process of equilibration.* Maturation is the gradual unfolding of our genetic plan for life. Experience involves the active interaction of the child with the environment. Social transmission refers to the information and customs that are transmitted from parents and other people in the environment to the child. We can consider this the educational function in the broad sense. Finally, the process of **equilibration** defines development. Children seek a balance between what they know and what they experience.

equilibration In Piagetian theory, the process by which children seek a balance between what they know and what they are experiencing.

THEORY	BASIC PREMISES	VALUES AND STRENGTHS	CRITICISMS AND WEAKNESSES
Erik Erikson's Psychosocial Theory	1. Explains development in terms of the epigenetic principle. Personality develops according to predetermined steps that are maturationally set. Society is structured to encourage the challenges that arise at these times in a person's life. 2. Describes development in terms of eight stages from cradle to grave. Each has positive and negative outcomes. 3. Emphasizes the importance of culture and the historical period in which the individual is living.	1. Sees development as continuing over the life span. 2. Importance of culture and historical period adds to our appreciation of factors that affect people's development. 3. Provides a good general overview of crises that occur at each stage of a child's life. Some of these crises, such as identity versus role confusion, have become important in understanding specific periods in a person's life.	1. Difficult to test experimentally. 2. Theory is rather general.

When faced with information that calls for a new and different analysis or activity, children enter a state of disequilibrium. When this occurs, they change their way of dealing with the event or experience, and a new, more stable and advanced stage of equilibrium is established. In this way children progress from a very limited ability to deal with new experiences to a more mature, sophisticated level of cognitive functioning. For example, a child who believes that heavy things are big and light things are small is introduced to a styrofoam beam that looks like wood but is not made of wood. The child is forced into disequilibrium and is motivated internally to find out more and to establish a new equilibrium. This he does by changing his ideas.

Piaget did not believe that children are simply passive receivers of stimulation. Children interact actively with the environment, and their active experiences impel them to new heights in cognitive functioning and action. The child's cognitive development is based not only on information directly and formally received from parents and teachers but also on the child's personal experiences.

Functional Invariants: Organization and Adaptation

Piaget used the term **functional invariants** to refer to processes that characterize all organisms and operate throughout the life span (Bjorklund, 1995). Two of the most important processes are *organization* and *adaptation.* First, people must organize their knowledge in a way that makes the knowledge useful. Second, every organism must adapt to its environment in order to survive. Adaptation can be understood in terms of adjustment. As the forces in the environment change, so must the individual's ability to deal with them.

Organization: Cognitive Structures and Schemata

As children develop they perceive and deal with the world in more sophisticated ways. Piaget uses the term **schema** to describe an organized system of actions and thoughts that are useful for dealing with the environment and that can be generalized to many situations (Piaget, 1952). For example, an infant may place a block in her mouth and suck on it. This is the sucking schema. She may do the same with other items. The infant is also master of other schemata, including looking, listening, grasping, hitting, and pushing. Schemata are tools for learning about the world; new schemata are developed as the child matures. In infancy, the schemata are basic and involve types of overt behavior, such as sucking and picking things up; later on, schemata become more symbolic and mental. The 8-year-old given a block can mentally operate on the block. He can imagine placing two blocks together and taking them apart even if he does not always do so physically.

The symbolic schemata that characterize older children are called **operations.** An operation is an internalized action that is part of the child's cognitive structure. Such actions include plans or rules for solving problems (Piaget, 1974). Piaget wrote extensively about the operation of reversibility, that is, being able to return to one's point of origin. If 3 plus 5 equals 8, then subtracting 5 from 8 will leave 3. You can add something to 3 and then take it away and think your way from one condition to another and then return to the starting point (Phillips, 1975). Schemata and operations form what Piaget calls the *cognitive structure* of the child.

As children develop, their cognitive structures or abilities to deal with the outside world change and they develop more sophisticated strategies for dealing with information. For instance, consider what happens when a magnet is given to children in different stages of development. The infant merely puts the magnet in his or her mouth or perhaps bangs it against the floor. A 3-year-old might realize that some objects stick to or want to stay with the magnet. A 9-year-old child realizes that certain objects with certain characteristics are attracted to the magnet and tests which ones do so and at what distances. The adolescent forms an abstract theory of magnetism that involves the size and shape of the magnet and distance from the object (Miller, 1989).

Adaptation

The second major concept in Piagetian theory is adaptation, which involves two complementary processes: assimilation and accommodation. **Assimilation** refers to the "taking-in process"—whether of sensation, nourishment, or experience—by which input is filtered or modified to fit already existing structures (Piaget & Inhelder, 1969). When we assimilate something, we alter the form of an incoming stimulus to adapt to existing actions or structures (Piaget, 1983). For example, a child may bang a rattle against the side of the crib, but when given a plastic block, the child will assimilate it by also banging it against the crib.

Accommodation involves modifying existing schemata to meet the requirements of a new experience (Piaget & Inhelder, 1969). When we accommodate, we create new schemata or modify old ones (Brainerd, 1978). For example, a child may be very good at using a one-handed pickup schema, that is, lifting an item with one

functional invariants Processes that characterize all organisms and operate throughout the life span.

schema A method of dealing with the environment that can be generalized to many situations.

operation An internalized action that is part of the child's cognitive structure.

assimilation The process by which information is altered to fit into one's already existing structures.

accommodation The process by which one's existing structures are altered to fit new information.

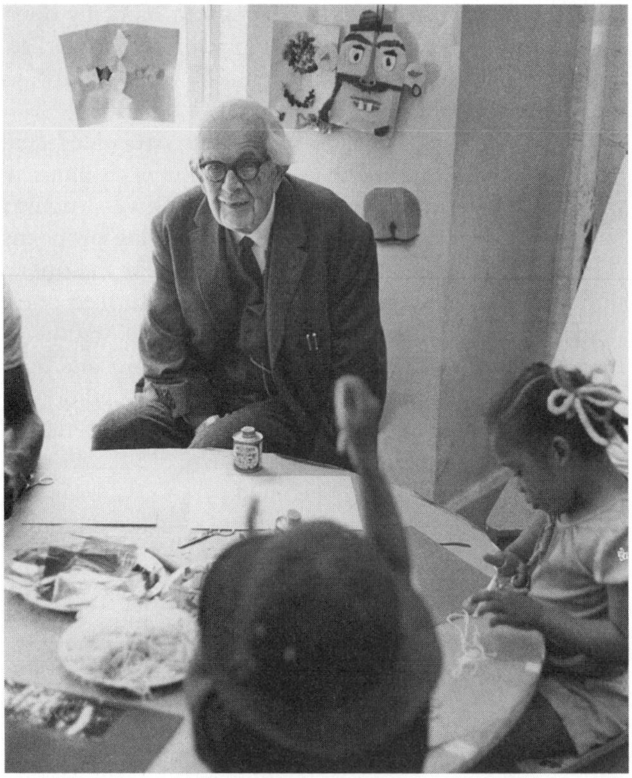

Jean Piaget conducted research by presenting children of varying ages with problems to solve, noting how they approached them and the nature of their reasoning.

hand, but when faced with a heavier item, the child has to accommodate, that is, use a two-handed pickup schema.

Assimilation and accommodation work together. A young child may point to a large Cadillac automobile and say, "Car." The child may then spot an old, rusty Volkswagen beetle and say, "Car." You are suitably impressed because even though the Cadillac and the Volkswagen are noticeably different, the child has understood that they were both cars—an example of assimilation. The child may later point to a large truck and say, "Car." You correct her, saying, "No, that is a truck." After a while the child points out a few more examples of trucks. She has accommodated. Now she has separated her conception of *car* from that of *truck*. The child then sees a van. She may put it in either category or even ask you what it is. Using assimilation and accommodation in this way the child begins to understand her world.

Stages of Cognitive Development

Piaget (1954) argued that children's cognitive development can be viewed as occurring in a sequence of four stages.

Sensorimotor Stage Between birth and about 2 years of age, children investigate their world using their senses (vision, hearing, etc.) and motor activity. They develop *object permanence,* the understanding that objects and people do not disappear merely because they are out of sight. The child's abilities in this stage are limited by an inability to use language or symbols (things that stand for other things). Children must experience everything directly through their senses and through feedback from motor activities.

Preoperational Stage Between the ages of 2 and 7 years, children negotiate the preoperational stage. Children can now use language and symbols, but their understanding of the world is limited. Children often believe inanimate objects are alive—that stuffed animals have a life of their own. The preschool child who described the *Challenger* tragedy with the words "the rocket died" was exhibiting such reasoning. Children in this stage are also egocentric, believing that everybody sees a situation the way they do. If a parent is tired or not feeling well, the child may bring the parent a favorite toy, not understanding that the parent would rather have some peace and quiet. Children in this stage are also *artificial,* which means that they interpret all natural phenomena as made by human beings. One child said, "Somebody shouldda moved the clouds" in response to the shuttle explosion. Children in the preoperational stage also tend to judge everything by appearance and do not understand *conservation*—the idea that the quantity of something may remain the same despite changes in its appearance. Preschoolers often do not understand, for example, that a short, wide glass and a tall, narrow glass can hold the same amount of liquid.

True or False?
Preschool children generally believe that everyone sees and experiences the world the way they do.

Concrete Operational Stage During this stage, which lasts from age 7 to about age 12, preoperational reasoning gradually is overcome. Children become less egocentric and can see things from other people's points of view. One child in the concrete operational stage noted, "It was sad that Mrs. McAuliffe's children lost their mother." Children in this stage also develop an understanding of conservation, understanding that an 8-ounce cup and an 8-ounce glass hold the same amount despite their different appearance. However, the child still has difficulty with abstract terms such as *freedom* and *liberty* and cannot reason in a scientific, deductive manner.

Formal Operational Stage During this stage adolescents develop the ability to test hypotheses in a mature, scientific manner and can understand and communicate their positions on complex ethical issues that demand the use of abstractions. They can consider hypotheses, deal with future orientations, and consider many aspects of a problem. When asked about the *Challenger* incident, many in this stage said that space exploration must continue because so much energy and time had already been committed to the endeavor, and they systematically looked at and evaluated positions regarding the future of manned space missions. Others looked at the possible lessons learned from the tragedy.

Evaluation

Piaget's ideas comprise the most influential theory in all of developmental psychology (Beilin, 1992). His explorations into the way children develop their concepts of time, space, and math, for example, show that young children see the world differently from adults. Parents and teachers must understand children's thought processes in order to serve the needs of youngsters better. Piaget's theory also recognizes previously unsuspected intelligence in infants and young children, and encourages us to determine what abilities infants possess at birth, what abilities children possess at later points in development, and what developmental processes allow children to make these transitions (Siegler, 1991).

Piaget's emphasis on the active, searching mind of the child has fascinated many. His theory implies that children should be encouraged to discover and to experience, that they are not mere passive receivers of stimulation. Children initiate action and react to stimuli in the environment and are shaped by and actively shape their own environment (Kagan, 1992).

Critics of Piaget's theory argue that Piaget underestimated the influence of learning on intellectual development and that there is evidence both for and against the idea that children progress through a series of stages in cognitive development (Flavell, Miller, & Miller, 1993; Siegler, 1991). Although there is little doubt that if you test Piagetian stage-related concepts such as conservation exactly the way Piaget did, you get the same results, different results are sometimes obtained if the test situation is altered. Some psychological studies show that children are more competent than Piaget thought. The nature of the task and of the past learning experiences of the child may be more important than Piaget realized (Flavell, 1992). In addition, some specific Piagetian concepts, especially egocentrism, have also come under fire. Finally, Piaget did not see any qualitative changes in thinking beyond formal operations. As we shall see in Chapter 14, other psychologists believe there are some important developments in reasoning that go beyond formal operations.

The Information-Processing Approach

Information-processing specialists investigate the way people take in, process, and act on information. Factors such as attention, perception, memory, the mediating processes by which people do something to the information in their mind, and their response system play an important role.

Information-processing specialists often use the computer as an analogy to the workings of the human mind, but they do not see human beings as computers or

information processing theory An approach to understanding cognition that delves deeply into the way information is taken in, processed, and then acted upon.

THEORY	BASIC PREMISES	VALUES AND STRENGTHS	CRITICISMS AND WEAKNESSES
Piaget's Theory of Cognitive Psychology	1. Children do not think or solve problems in the same manner as adults. 2. Emphasizes the importance of the child's active interaction with the environment. 3. Sees maturation and experience as more important than formal learning in the child's cognitive development. 4. Views cognitive development as occurring in four stages. Each stage shows a qualitative leap forward in the child's ability to solve problems and reason logically. 5. Most complete description of cognitive development from infancy through adolescence available.	1. Emphasizes the importance of active experience in a child's development. Leads to a view of young children as little scientists sifting through information and actively coping with the world. 2. Descriptions of the way in which children think and approach problems very helpful in understanding children's behavior. 3. Many of the sequences for understanding specific concepts are very challenging.	1. May underestimate the influence of learning on cognitive development and the nature of task on the child's performance. 2. Piaget's style of research has been criticized. Piaget presented children with a problem and sought to discover how the children reasoned and tried to solve the problem. His studies were not controlled.

robots. The computer analogy helps us understand how people of all ages solve problems and use information. What we type into the computer (input) is roughly analogous to information we gather from the environment through our senses. Some operations are performed on the information according to the program, and the information is encoded and stored in some way that is retrievable. Some processes must occur in our minds that enable us to attend to a particular stimulus, organize it, and remember it so it can be used in the future. The information that is retrieved and used if the proper command is given could be considered the output. In the human being the output could be some motor activity, such as moving the arm to catch a baseball, or may be verbal, such as the answer to a mathematical problem. Finally, an individual receives feedback—information about whether the movement or the answer was effective. Just as the title of a computer program gives some clue as to what the general results of the program will be, human beings may have an upper executive plan that coordinates these activities and guides purposeful behavior.

Information-processing theorists are interested in following the information through the system to learn how it is encoded, processed, and retrieved (Sternberg, 1985). Thus, they look at cognition on a very detailed level, investigating the processes of perception, attention, representation, memory, and retrieval.

The information-processing viewpoint is not always seen in a developmental framework, but it can be. Developmental changes in the ability to process information, control attention, and use memory strategies occur in a manner that allows developmental psychologists to take a developmental perspective. For example, elderly people process information more slowly than younger people. This partially explains why older adults take longer to learn and why they may have some difficulty understanding rapidly spoken speech.

Evaluation

The information-processing approach allows us to delve more deeply into the kinds of phenomena that interested Piaget. The Piagetian and information-processing viewpoints can complement each other, giving us new ways to analyze a person's cognitive growth.

The information-processing perspective is so new that it is difficult to evaluate at this point. It is hardly a unified field. Several models have been advanced to account for the numerous subprocesses such as encoding, memory, and retrieval involved in processing information. No one yet knows how far the computer analogy can be taken. More importantly, we also do not know whether the mind will yield to the step-by-step analysis of subprocesses vital to the success of the information-processing approach. Although the viewpoint is interesting, much work remains before we can truly judge its value for understanding how people develop and process information.

The Behavioral Approach

Behaviorists argue that the environment determines behavior and that if the environment is altered adequately, behavior change will follow. For example, suppose every time Kim is taken to the doctor he experiences some sort of pain—often an injection. After several visits, just seeing the doctor will cause Kim to cry. The sight of the doctor was probably neutral at first, but when paired a number of times with discomfort or pain, it eventually elicited crying. This is an example of a process of learning called **classical conditioning,** which involves the pairing of a neutral stimulus with a stimulus that elicits a particular response until the stimulus that was originally neutral elicits the response.

An **unconditioned stimulus** is one that elicits the response prior to the conditioning. In Kim's case, the shot is the unconditioned stimulus because it caused him to cry before the conditioning took place. An **unconditioned response** is a response to an unconditioned

behaviorist A psychologist who explains behavior in terms of the processes of learning such as classical and operant conditioning and emphasizes the importance of the environment in determining behavior.

classical conditioning A learning process in which a neutral stimulus is paired with a stimulus that elicits a response until the originally neutral stimulus elicits that response.

unconditioned stimulus The stimulus that elicits the response prior to conditioning.

unconditioned response The response to the unconditioned stimulus.

THEORY	BASIC PREMISES	VALUES AND STRENGTHS	CRITICISMS AND WEAKNESSES
Information-Processing	1. Emphasizes the importance of the manner in which people take in information, process it, and then act upon it. 2. Such processes as attention, perception memory, and processing strategies are studied.	1. Yields a detailed look at the processes involved in taking in and processing information. 2. May serve as a diagnostic aid in discovering where people have difficulties in solving problems.	1. It is not a unified approach. A number of models have been advanced. 2. It still awaits adequate testing.

stimulus. Kim's crying after receiving a shot is an unconditioned response. A **conditioned stimulus** is a previously neutral stimulus that elicits a response when it is associated with an unconditioned stimulus. Only when the doctor's presence was paired with the shot did it cause Kim to cry. Finally, a **conditioned response** is a learned response that is associated with the conditioned stimulus, that is, Kim crying when he sees the doctor.

Kim may also exhibit this response with a number of different people who look similar. This is called **stimulus generalization.** Experience will teach Kim to differentiate between the doctor and people who look similar. This occurs through the process of **discrimination.** He will cry when he sees the doctor, but not when he sees other people who look similar. Will Kim's fear ever end, or will he always cry in the doctor's office? Perhaps after many painfree visits to the doctor, Kim will no longer cry in response to the situation. This process is called **extinction.**

Classical conditioning is especially useful for understanding emotional response, such as a child's response to the voice of his parents or the experience of an adult at work when faced with a boss who always criticizes her. The boss at first did not cause great anxiety, but when paired with constant criticism, the boss may cause the worker to feel anxious every time she hears the boss's voice or sees the boss.

conditioned stimulus The stimulus that the organism has learned to associate with the unconditioned stimulus.

conditioned response The learned response to the conditioned stimulus.

stimulus generalization The tendency of an organism that has learned to associate a certain behavior with a particular stimulus to show this behavior when confronted with similar stimuli.

discrimination The process by which a person learns to differentiate among stimuli.

extinction The weakening and disappearance of a learned response.

In **operant conditioning** a person's behavior is followed by some event that increases or decreases the frequency of the behavior that preceded it. If the event increases the likelihood that the behavior will recur, the action is said to be *reinforced.* If it decreases the chances of its occurring, it is said to be *punished.* In operant conditioning behavior is governed by its consequences. If staying late at work results in an extra twenty dollars in your paycheck you have been reinforced for your behavior, and chances are you will do it again. The **reinforcer** is not always tangible; attention and praise can be and often are effective reinforcers.

As in classical conditioning, generalization and discrimination are important concepts and explain many behaviors. If Patrice is reinforced for being aggressive by getting what she wants, she will exhibit this behavior in many contexts. She begins by taking toys away from a younger brother and then generalizes this behavior with peers at school. But soon Patrice learns when this works and when it is counterproductive. She learns to discriminate. Children begin to learn that using profanity with friends may be acceptable, but it is not appropriate in front of Grandma. Aggression may help Scott get his way with some peers during childhood, but it is not effective in early adulthood when trying to talk his way out of a speeding ticket. Notice that the behavioral perspective emphasizes the past history of the organism and the stimuli in the present environment. No mention is made of what occurs in the mind, of thought process, or of memory. This perspective has been very useful for psychologists who look for reinforcers of behavior and will be used in the discussion on gender roles and aggressive and prosocial behaviors in Chapters 9 and 11.

operant conditioning The learning process in which behavior is governed by its consequences.

reinforcer An event that increases the likelihood that the behavior that preceded it will recur.

THEORY	BASIC PREMISES	VALUES AND STRENGTHS	CRITICISMS AND WEAKNESSES
Behavior Approach	1. Human behavior may be explained by the processes of learning including classical and operant conditioning. 2. The behavioral approach has been successful in modifying the behavior of people in many situations. 3. The behavioral approach does not deny consciousness and mental processes like thinking, but rather deals with behavior and development in a different manner. 4. Development is seen as continuous with no stages posited to explain progress.	1. Learning theories are clear, precise, and laboratory tested. 2. The emphasis on the environment is important.	1. Some consider it too mechanical. Its avoidance of mental processes such as consciousness and thinking may yield only a partial picture of behavior. 2. Sees little qualitative difference between humans and animals.

Evaluation

The behavioral view is valuable in pinpointing the importance of the environment. Even critics of behaviorism usually acknowledge that the environment has a tremendous effect on behavior (Rogers, 1980). Whether it has total control or whether internal, cognitive factors such as thinking and information-processing abilities must also be taken into account to understand the organism better is an issue between behaviorists and cognitively oriented psychologists. Another contribution of behaviorism is its emphasis on experimental methodology. Although it may seem stifling at times, experimental methodology produces high-quality work.

The most common criticism of the behavioral view of human development is that it is too mechanical. The approach makes human beings seem too predictable, and the avoidance of such concepts as consciousness, thinking, and subjective experience is a problem. It is doubtful that all human development can be understood on the basis of the principles of conditioning.

Social Learning Theory

People also learn by observing and imitating others. They do not always have to be reinforced or punished to change their behavior. They can learn by watching the consequences of others' behavior. If we see a person touch a hot stove and get burned, we do not have to repeat the action ourselves and get burned. **Social learning theory** investigates the process of imitation and observation learning (Bandura, 1986).

Imitation can be seen in many kinds of behaviors. Children learn to be aggressive or altruistic by observing respected models engaged in these behaviors (Mussen & Eisenberg-Berg, 1977). People also learn partly through observation how males and females are expected to act within a particular culture.

Sometimes children imitate exactly the gestures and words they see and hear, as when a 2-year-old girl pointed as if lecturing and called out to her sister, "Darn it, you better do that"—in an exact imitation of her mother. However, imitation is not always so exact. You may watch your favorite tennis players and try to imitate their play, yet you will be limited by your physical ability. We adapt what we see in a creative way that mirrors our own understanding of the situation and of our abilities.

Imitation can be seen as a four-step process (Bandura, 1977, 1986). A person must first pay attention to the model. Then the information must be retained in memory. The information must then be used in an attempt to reproduce the action. For example, a person watching a tennis player may try to use the player's stance. Last, some reinforcement must be available. According to Bandura, reinforcement provides people with information about what might happen in the future if they perform the particular behavior. Reinforcement can also motivate. People may remember the consequences of the behavior and then later use the information to attain their own ends. They do not have to experience the reinforcement personally.

social learning theory The theoretical view emphasizing the process by which people learn through observing others and imitating their behaviors.

> ***True Or False***
> For people to learn something, they do not have to be reinforced directly.

Social learning theorists believe that to understand how complex behaviors like helping and sharing are acquired, the relationship between behavior, environment, and personal and cognitive factors must be understood. Each factor can influence and, in turn, be influenced by the other two. For example, as a child tries to master reading, the teacher works with the child, whose reading improves greatly. This, in turn, produces changes in the environment in that the teacher may give the child a more positive evaluation and perhaps work harder with the child. At the same time, the child can now read different, more interesting books, allowing for additional choice. Here we see the behavior (learning to read and practicing reading) affecting the environment (the teacher's behavior and the physical composition of the room). At the same time, having more choice to read also affects the child's behavior. Having additional and more interesting books available, the child may want to read more. Notice that a change in the environment (having more books to read) can lead to a change in the behavior (reading). Similarly, success in reading influences the child's beliefs about reading. He may now choose to read more. His change in cognition (belief about himself) changed his behavior, while his behavior (learning to read) changed his beliefs about himself. His cognitive change, now believing that he can read, may alter his environment as well, because he may surround himself with more books in his room.

Social learning theorists divide behavior into two different processes: learning and performance. We learn—that is, acquire knowledge—through a number of processes, including observing others. However, whether or not a person will exhibit the behavior (performance) depends partly upon what Bandura calls **self-efficacy,** which is one's beliefs about what one can and cannot do in a particular situation (Schunk, 1996). Judgments of self-efficacy, whether accurate or not, affect one's choice of activities. People who believe a task is within their capabilities will attempt it whereas they will avoid activities that they believe exceed their capabilities (Bandura, 1982).

Evaluation

Social learning theory reminds us of the importance of imitation and observation in determining behavior and is useful in understanding the genesis of many kinds of be-

self-efficacy People's beliefs about what they can and cannot do.

Boys and girls who had watched an adult modeling violence were more likely to show violent behavior in that same situation than children who had not witnessed the model's violent behavior.

havior. It will be especially important when discussing the acquisition of social behaviors in Chapters 9 and 11.

Social learning theory is not without limitations, one of which is that it completely lacks a developmental framework (Cairns, 1979). The process of imitation is described in terms that give little consideration to maturation or to the differences between the imitative behavior of a toddler and that of an adolescent (Thomas, 1979). Thus, although social learning theory explains some behaviors very well, it is inadequate in explaining age-related developmental changes.

Ecological Theory

As discussed in Chapter 1 development occurs within a number of contexts: family, neighborhood, school, and culture, and within a particular historical time. This viewpoint is developed in a theoretical approach formulated by Urie Bronfenbrenner called **ecological theory** (Bronfenbrenner, 1979; 1986 Bronfenbrenner & Ceci, 1994).

Bronfenbrenner suggests that people live their lives enmeshed in many different environments at the same time. He uses the analogy of a set of Russian dolls each inside the other. People affect and are affected by the multiple layers of their environment. Ecological theory systematically links these environments to each other and notes how they operate and affect each other.

ecological theory A broad theory that attempts to describe the many environments in which people exist and the relationships between people and these environments.

THEORY	BASIC PREMISES	VALUES AND STRENGTHS	CRITICISMS AND WEAKNESSES
Social Learning Theory	1. Human behavior is partially explained through the process of imitation and observation learning. 2. The process of imitation may be explained using a four-step process involving attention, encoding and memory, behavioral reproduction, and, finally, reinforcement.	1. Is useful in understanding certain behaviors such as altruism and aggression. 2. Encourages us to look at the models in the person's environment.	1. Lacks a developmental framework. The process of imitation is viewed as the same no matter who is observing. 2. Does not explain age-related changes.

Four different environmental systems operate. The **microsystem** consists of the immediate interactions of the person and the environment. This face-to-face interaction may occur at home or in school (Bronfenbrenner & Crouter, 1983) and consists of what the individual is presently experiencing. The microsystem includes where a child lives, the people in the home, and the activities they do together. At first the child's microsystem is limited to the home and the family; as the child develops, additional settings become important and more people enter the child's microsystem.

The **mesosystem** involves the interrelationships among two or more settings in which the person actively participates. For example, the mesosystem includes the relationship between parents and the school, parents and the day care center, parents and the peer group. The entry of a child into a new setting causes changes in the other major settings. For example, the child's attendance in school may charge the pattern of activities and interactions occurring within the family (Bronfenbrenner & Crouter, 1983).

The **exosystem** involves settings in which the child is not actively involved, at least at the present time, but that affect the family and child, such as the parents' place of work, a class attended by other siblings, family network of friends, or the activity of the local school board. The exosystem may directly affect the child. For example, a school board voting to increase class size may impact on the child's education by affecting teacher-child interaction. Also, the insecurity that a parent may experience at work may impact negatively on parent-child interaction.

True or False?
The relationship between children and their parents may be affected by such long-range factors as their parents' work environment and parents' network of friends.

The **macrosystem** is composed of the ideology or belief system inherent in social institutions and includes ethnic, cultural, religious, economic, and political influences (Seligman, 1991). For example, people in the United States live under a economic and political system that differs from that of other countries. These differing social customs, ideologies, and economic systems affect the social institutions in the country and therefore the child. The availability of day care may depend on the political situation or the ideology of the system. Changes in social structure may also indirectly affect the child. For instance, the growth of single-parent families, increased family mobility, and changes in the status of women in the United States have an affect on all systems. Within each society a number of different micro-, meso-, and exosystems operate depending upon social class, ethnicity, and religious groupings.

Changes in one system cause adjustments in other systems. For example, the cultural norm of maternal employment affects the work place, the economy, community affairs, as well as the child's microsystem. Flexible hours, the need for more day care, and more sharing of household and child-rearing responsibilities may directly impact on the child's microsystem.

Ecological theory emphasizes the importance of looking beyond the current environment and of appreciating the relationships between them. A child's ability to learn to read in elementary school may depend not only on the way the child is taught in first grade but also on the relationship between the home and the school (Bronfenbrenner, 1979) and on decisions made by others about organization and staffing of schools. Changes in political, social, and economic factors also affect the child directly and indirectly. Because influence is reciprocal, the future of the environment or the person cannot be predicted reliably unless both are understood.

Ecological theory also looks at transitions such as going to school, becoming a parent, or entering the world of work because these result in significant changes in roles. Roles have the power to change how people are treated, how they behave, what they do, and even how they think and feel. These ecological transitions are the result of development and they also instigate developmental processes. A child's entrance into school changes the system from an exosystem into a mesosystem; immigrating to another country involves crossing macrosystem borders.

Evaluation

There is a growing appreciation of the various contexts that affect development (Parke et al., 1994). The fact that these systems affect each other and directly and indirectly affect children and adults expands our view of the factors affecting development. Transitions and changes in roles encourage us to ask questions about preparation for these transitions. Accepting the concept of reciprocal interaction means that the individual is not solely at the mercy of environmental factors but has the power to affect the environment as well. Last, ecological theory is broad enough to include social policy, cultural aspects of the environment, and other macro- and exosystems. Ecological theory will be consistently used in this text. Discussions of public policy and changes in society such as the growth of the one-parent family, economic changes, and other modifications in the exosystem and macrosystem will be linked to changes in parent-child interactions.

Although ecological theory is popular, it is very complex. Most psychologists would agree that looking at the entire context of development is desirable, but is it prac-

microsystem The immediate interactions between the individual and the environment.

mesosystem The interrelationships among two or more settings in which the person actively participates.

exosystem Settings in which the individual is not actively involved, at least at the present time, but yet affect the individual.

macrosystem The ideology or belief system inherent in social institutions including ethnic, cultural, and religious influences, as well as the economic and political systems that exist.

Bronfenbrenner urges psychologists to look at the many contexts and layers of the environment, each affecting the other. This includes the economic and political situation and the different ideologies and social institutions of the country called the macrosystem.

tical? A theory that views the individual as affected by so many social, political, and economic forces may simply be too complex to use as a basis for research. Although the conceptual view of ecological theory is valuable, it remains to be seen whether it can be practically used as a basis for research and interpretation.

Social Roles, Social Norms, Culture, and History

Each culture has its own **norms**—rules that regulate behavior in certain situations. For instance, parenthood brings with it new social roles and obligations. Some norms are based on a person's age. *Age norms* partially determine the types of behavior considered appropriate for people in different age groups. For instance, if we see a young person looking outrageously punk, we shrug it off. But if grandma tries to achieve the same look, we consider it an oddity. Age norms add constraints to behavior because people internalize them and realize how others may react to a given violation. Many societies also have age-status systems, in which people are given power and status based on their age; our society gives the elderly a fairly low status (George, 1990).

Each society also has its own **social clock**—an internalized sense of timing that tells people whether they are progressing too fast or too slowly in terms of social events in their lives (Neugarten, 1968). A 40-year-old who is still single or a 25-year-old who has not yet made an occupational commitment may experience internal as well as external pressure to do so. Social clocks depend partly on social class. People from lower income groups proceed through adult stages at a faster pace. They marry younger and tend to have their children earlier whereas people from higher socioeconomic groups can delay movement from one stage of adulthood to the next (Neugarten & Moore, 1968). A wealthy person can afford to lose a term in school or to postpone starting a

norms Rules that regulate behavior in particular situations.

social clock The internalized sense of timing that tells people whether they are progressing too fast or too slow in terms of social events.

THEORY	BASIC PREMISES	VALUES AND STRENGTHS	CRITICISMS AND WEAKNESSES
Ecological Theory	1. The person cannot be isolated from the context of development. 2. Human development is enmeshed in multiple environments at the same time. 3. Ecological theory links these environments to each other, noting how each operates and affects the others. 4. Transitions bring about changes in roles, which change how people think, act, and how they are treated.	1. Encourages a broader view of human development. 2. Shows how societal values and priorities that operate through public policy may affect the child. 3. Emphasizes the importance of specific transitions such as starting school or becoming a parent.	1. Theory is very complex, requiring an in-depth look at the many contexts of development. 2. Some question whether the theory can be practically used as a basis for understanding development.

career, but a poor person has less freedom to put off making educational and occupational choices.

Age norms and social clocks are affected by the historical period in which people live. Table 2.2 compares two identical surveys conducted 20 years apart. In the 1990s, retiring while still in good health and looking forward to years of leisure activity is not just a dream but a reality for millions whereas years ago, retirement simply meant illness and the inability to work. Couples used to have as many children as possible and spent most of their adulthood raising them. Today a good portion of adulthood is spent without children to raise. Social clocks change with historical periods. We are now more flexible in determining when people "ought" to take jobs, marry, or retire (Schlossberg, 1984).

People are also taking longer to proceed through each of these stages. In her recent book entitled *New Passages,* Gail Sheehy (1995) focuses on the effect living a longer, more productive life has on middle-aged people. It is difficult to call someone who is 60 "old" if life expectancy is close to 80 and the individual is active, alert, and leading a productive life. At the same time it takes longer for a young adult to become independent due to educational, financial, and housing difficulties.

Last, people's behavior can be understood partially by looking at the roles they play. A **role** is a set of behaviors, attitudes, obligations, and privileges expected of an individual who occupies a status (Light, Keller, & Calhoun, 1989). Children take on roles such as son, daughter, friend, and student, but roles become much more complex and numerous in adulthood. An adult may be a son or a daughter, still remain a student, be a parent, a worker, a supervisor, a volunteer in a community hospital, as well as take on a number of other roles.

role A set of behaviors, attitudes, obligations, and privileges expected of an individual who occupies a status.

Some of these roles may be in conflict with others, as a parent may want to be at a school play to see her son perform and also need to be at a business dinner to entertain clients. An adult who is friendly with a co-worker may find her roles in conflict if she becomes a supervisor (Schaefer & Lamm, 1995). Role overload may occur when people simply have too many roles to perform and find it difficult or impossible to perform each satisfactorily. A man with a family may find that he does not have enough time to carry out the obligations of a father, worker, and perhaps a son for a parent who needs care, in a way that measures up to his own standards. How well people view their performance of roles and how others view them may affect their satisfaction and happiness. To truly understand behavior, the changing nature of roles and how people cope with these changes must be investigated. People vary in how they see and carry out their obligations as parents and workers, and this variability adds to the richness and complexity of the life cycle.

True or False?
A person may play many roles, some of which may be in conflict with each other.

Developmental Theory: Yesterday, Today, and Tomorrow

Several of the important advances that have been made in theoretical approaches to human development deserve our attention. The theories of Freud, Erikson, and Piaget

Table 2.2 **What's the Right Time?**
Two surveys asking the same questions 20 years apart (late 1950s and late 1970s) have shown a dramatic decline in the consensus among middle-class, middle-aged people about what's the right age for various major events and achievements of adult life.

		LATE '50s STUDY		LATE '70s STUDY	
	APPROPRIATE AGE	MEN	WOMEN	MEN	WOMEN
ACTIVITY/EVENT	RANGE	% Who Agree		% Who Agree	
Best age for a man to marry	20–25	80	90	42	42
Best age for a woman to marry	19–24	85	90	44	36
When most people should become grandparents	45–50	84	79	64	57
Best age for most people to finish school and go to work	20–22	86	82	36	38
When most men should be settled on a career	24–26	74	64	24	26
When most men hold their top jobs	45–50	71	58	38	31
When most people should be ready to retire	60–65	83	86	66	41
When a man has the most responsibilities	35–50	79	75	49	50
When a man accomplishes most	40–50	82	71	46	41
The prime of life for a man	35–50	86	80	59	66
When a woman has the most responsibilities	25–40	93	91	59	53
When a woman accomplishes most	30–45	94	92	57	48

Source: Rosenfeld and Stark, 1987.

emphasized the importance of stages whereas other theories did not. Stage theories present development in terms of age-related periods in which people are faced with particular problems and have specific abilities. People in a particular stage should act or reason similarly. These theories see development as occurring in a steplike, discontinuous sequence. Progression from stage to stage occurs in an invariant order, and new skills develop from skills acquired in previous stages. Each person progresses through the same stages and cannot skip a stage, but people may enter or leave a particular stage at different times, so it is incorrect to simply equate ages with stages. The ages given throughout this text are only guidelines and should not be thought of as absolutes.

Other psychologists believe that development is a more continuous process and do not agree with the concept of stages. These psychologists see development in terms of smooth, small steps, explained by looking at past achievements. They see no stages, but rather gradual development. The question of whether people develop in a stagelike progression is still being debated. It may not be an either/or proposition. It is possible that some types of developmental change are discontinuous and can be understood in terms of stages while others are more continuous (Flavell, 1992).

True or False?

Developmental psychologists unanimously agree that the best way to understand development is through the use of stages.

Questions Students Often Ask

Many people use the idea of stages when they talk about children, such as about a 2-year-old only going through a stage. Piaget, Freud, and Erikson talk about stages while many others do not. Do people develop in stages?

There is evidence both for and against the stage concept, but the argument really comes down to whether the stage concept is really useful. For stage theories to hold, a child's behavior or thinking while in one stage should be constant. In other words, if a child is in stage Y, the child should relate to the world using behaviors that are stage Y behaviors. This does not seem to always be the case as people sometimes reason or act in agreement with their stage and sometimes do not (Flavell, Miller, & Miller, 1993). Even Piaget recognized this inconsistency. Some 2-year-olds react differently than stage theories predict. In addition, structuring the task differently sometimes shows children to be more competent than first thought.

But before you throw the stage concept out, remember that often children do act as stage theories predict. The concept of stages certainly has some utility and children of similar ages do act and reason in similar fashions.

Most psychologists who accept the concept of stage theories will admit that these stages are not as rigid as Piaget and others would have us believe (Flavell, 1992). They argue that stages, such as those Piaget advocated, explain a great many general properties of children's thinking. These psychologists look at specific changes within stages (Flavell, 1992). While accepting the fact that children are more competent that Piaget believed, they argue that there are limitations to their thinking as well.

There is no simple answer to the question, but it seems that stage theories are still useful. What we need to do is to realize that they are not as rigid as first proposed.

Second, the idea of reciprocal interaction is accepted by most psychologists, and we now understand the need to conceive of the organism as active in creating its own environment (Kagan, 1992). Rather than concentrating separately on the child or the parent we concentrate on how each affects the other.

Third, a new appreciation of the complexity of the environment is accepted. Theoretical approaches, such as ecological theory, suggest that the environment is not a simple conception. Changes in one environmental factor may influence changes in other factors, influencing the individual's development and behavior (see New Perspectives: Chaos Theory, pp. 42–43). Fourth, built into many relatively new theoretical approaches is an appreciation of the historical time in which the individual lives (Elder, Modell, & Parke, 1993). This appreciation emphasizes the changing nature of society and the fact that secular events and historical cycles are important to the understanding of development (Parke et al., 1994).

Fifth, a new appreciation of the importance of both cross-cultural work and cultural variation within a particular society now exists. We are now more aware of cultural and subcultural membership, and the need to do more research using samples of individuals whose experiences may not match those people from the majority group. We also need to discover to what extent our theories hold in other cultures. This cultural sensitivity is found in Erikson's theory and also is prominent in ecological theory.

Sixth, various areas of development interact with each other. Although it may be easier for conceptual purposes to look at the cognitive, physical, social, and biological aspects as separate realms, we know that these are integrated. The child's health may affect the child's cognitive abilities and the child's cognitive level may affect the child's health practices (Parke et al., 1994). This connection, although accepted, awaits further theoretical explanation. Finally, as we begin to appreciate how changes at very fundamental levels, such as brain chemicals, affect behavior we will need a theoretical bridge that links these changes with behavior (Flavell, 1992).

Which Theory Should Be Used?

Each theory in this chapter presents a different way of looking at development. The decision to use a particular

New Perspectives: Chaos Theory

"But we have soothed ourselves into imagining sudden changes as something that happen outside the normal order of things, an accident, like a car crash. Or beyond our control, like a fatal illness. We do not conceive of sudden, radical, irrational change as built into the very fabric of existence. Yet it is. And chaos theory teaches us," Malcolm said, "that straight linearity, which we have come to take for granted in everything from physics to fiction, simply does not exist. Linearity is an artificial way of viewing the world. Real life isn't a series of interconnected events occurring one after another like beads strung on a necklace. Life is actually a series of encounters in which one event may change those that follow in a wholly unpredictable, even devastating way (Crichton, 1990).

Dr. Ian Malcolm, famous fictional mathematician, explains chaos theory in Michael Crichton's *Jurassic Park.* Few people had ever heard of chaos theory before reading the book or seeing the movie. Yet chaos theory has had an impact on physics, mathematics, and biology, and now psychologists are beginning to take notice.

As an introduction to chaos theory, think of a child being raised in a carefully controlled environment. A psychologist checks every parental action to make certain it is in keeping with our best theories of how to optimize the child's development. Nutritionists carefully monitor the child's diet, and doctors make sure the child gets enough sleep. Specialists design the child's social interactions and determine the programs the child watches on television. The entire environment is controlled and nothing is left to chance.

This may sound like nonsense because it is not the usual way people live. It is not the way children are raised. In reality, chance occurrences affect everyone—children and adults. Theodor Geisel (Dr. Seuss) had just had his book *And To Think That I Saw It on Mulberry Street* rejected by more than 20 publishers when he ran into an old friend on Madison Avenue in Manhattan who just happened to be an editor of children's books for a major publisher. He was interested in seeing Geisel's work and gave him a contract 20 minutes later. The book was a huge success, beginning a spectacular career and the book has since had over 20 printings (Wallace et al., 1981). No one is claiming that Dr. Seuss would never have found a publisher, but the chance meeting that could not be predicted certainly changed Geisel's life and affected in some way the lives of many children. One of the theorists presented in this chapter, Albert Bandura (1982), discusses the notion that people's lives can be influenced by unusual and chance events. In the same way, people's environments are very complicated and real life does not allow for the type of control that would make prediction simple and neat.

Rather than considering these chance events as "error," chaos theory welcomes them and considers them a source of study (Duke, 1994). Chaos theory attempts to understand and explain events that seem spontaneous and seemingly unpredictable. Phenomena studied by chaos theory display three general characteristics. First, the behavior appears to be disordered and random, such as the branching of a lightning bolt or the path of a falling leaf. Second, these behaviors can change radically in response to very brief and seemingly insignificant events, as a child blowing on that falling leaf will change the pattern of its fall. Third, phenomena that appear chaotic may actually follow detectable patterns if one looks closely or knows how to look at them (Psychology Today, 1993).

Some people misunderstand chaos theory, arguing that behavior and development are unpredictable. Chaos theory proposes that, although a lack of predictability is to be expected when looking at specific patterns, definite patterns (which often include chance occurrences) are seen at a more global level of analysis (Duke, 1994). Chaos theory is actually a middleground between total regularity and total randomness (Duke, 1994).

To explain this, one needs to understand the concept of an attractor, which is a point or a pattern around which some phenomenon is drawn. Attractors allow a degree of predictability. For instance, if you place a hot coffee cup down in a room it may be somewhat difficult to predict its exact temperature 5 minutes from now, but you can predict that eventually the coffee will come to room temperature. The attractor concept allows us to understand how behavior can be seen as both stable and variable at the same time. The behavior of developing organisms is neither completely stereotyped nor random (Thelen, 1989). The behavior fluctuates, but only within limits, and within these boundaries we can see attractors. Traits such as morality, religiosity,

theory leads a researcher to ask specific questions. A researcher who uses a behavioral approach might concentrate on what reinforcers were present in a particular environment and on what behaviors the person had learned throughout childhood. A researcher using a Freudian perspective might ask questions about a person's unconscious motivations and early relationships with caregivers. A researcher using an information-processing approach would consider how people interpret their environment and decide what their alternatives are. Each theory adds something to our understanding of human development.

Questions Students Often Ask

O.K., which theory do you use?

I am asked this question more often than any other while teaching theories of development. The answer would depend upon what I am studying at the time. Some theories are plainly more useful for understanding some phenomena than others. For example, the

New Perspectives: Chaos Theory (continued)

competitiveness, or aggression around which much behavior seem to revolve may be considered attractors.

Looking at the nature of a long-term loving relationship may make the concept of attractors somewhat clearer. Anyone who has been in a long-term relationship knows that there are times in which, despite the constant love, more harmony or discord exists. If a researcher chooses a point at which the relationship shows more discord and then generalizes this to be the nature of the relationship, the researcher will be in error. If these patterns of harmony and discord are looked at over the long term both will be seen as part of the relationship. The fluctuations are real, and show a range of variation in the behavior within the relationship.

The pattern of behaviors around an attractor are recognizable but rarely identical. If asked to draw a number of circles, you would find that although all the drawings are easily recognizable as circles they differ somewhat in size and form. A memory of an event, for instance, may be seen as an attractor but the memory may vary somewhat with each telling of the event.

Why does this occur? Chaos theory uses the concept of sensitive dependence on initial conditions to explain this lack of exact recurrence (Barton, 1994; Mandel, 1995). If two sets of conditions differ by even a very small degree at the outset, the specific solutions will diverge dramatically in the long run (Barton, 1994). Consider a person going on a 20-mile hike with a compass that is off by only one degree (Duke, 1994). If the person discovers this problem after only 5 minutes or so, an easy correction can be made and the person will find that he is not far from where he should be. However, what if the person finds that a mistake has occurred after walking for many hours? Now that one-degree mistake means much more, and the person will be far from his goal and probably lost. Small differences in the initial conditions, many of which may not be known, can result in significant differences in the long term.

This is sometimes called the *butterfly effect,* originally credited to Edward Lorenz, a meteorologist and an important figure in the development of chaos theory. Could a butterfly flapping its wings in China affect the weather in Oklahoma (Mandel, 1995)? Theoretically, such a trivial event at a critical time may have an important effect on the way an emergent weather system develops. Minor local events may then serve to reduce predictability by altering the course of future events.

This same phenomenon may be important to understanding development. Psychologists look at major life events, especially traumatic ones, as causes of behavior. Chaos theory would have us look at small events that may occur at crucial times. A small discussion with a parent, a hug at the right time, or playing chess with a child may have as much or even a greater impact on a child's development than the major events that are often the focus of our research studies. Such minor events in the long run may be very important. Small changes in parenting practices or teaching strategies, especially when children are young, may not show immediate results but may be very significant over the long run (Duke, 1994).

How influential chaos theory will be is still a question. Many social scientists do not have the sophisticated mathematical knowledge necessary to fully appreciate the theory, which was originally meant for physicists and mathematicians (Mandel, 1995). The extent to which a theory borrowed from physics and mathematics can be applied to human development and behavior is also a question (Barton, 1994). In addition, chaos theory should not be seen as simply replacing earlier, more linear, deterministic models. Rather, it adds to the way we look at the world. Both our present models and chaos theory may eventually be brought together in some way.

In the book *Jurassic Park,* chaos theory predicted that the scientists and gamekeepers in the park filled with dinosaurs could not control everything, and the resultant adventures and tragedy of that situation follow. However, chaos theory has its positive side in that it leaves us with a deep sense of humility. It brings the mystery and adventure back into life. It emphasizes life's complexity and how small changes may reap large rewards over time, and how patterns of behavior may be similar yet not identical. However, it does not mean that predictability is impossible because over the long run events and behavior show patterns that can be identified. We may someday be able to understand how small changes at critical times fit into our lives, which may give us a better understanding of the entire course of human behavior and development.

maps Erikson designed for identity are quite useful for studying adolescence, and information-processing theory is especially useful when I look at memory. Often theories complement each other. Although Erikson's theory of adolescence is wonderful, Piaget's ideas about the formal operational stage and the development of the adolescent's ability to use abstractions certainly fit in nicely. Theories are usually not right or wrong; they are merely useful. I choose the theory that seems most useful at the time.

Many developmental psychologists are aware that there are numerous ways to look at a particular behavior. This is a strength, not a weakness, since each approach has something different to offer. Some developmental psychologists are eclectic; that is, they adopt the most useful theory to explore an area rather than work from only one perspective. Such eclecticism is healthy if it allows us to appreciate the many ways in which a particular behavior can be studied (Rychlak, 1985). Throughout this book we describe behavior from several different perspectives in order to gain a better understanding of the developing person.

> ***True or False?***
> Using one theory to understand cognitive development and another theory to understand social development is an inappropriate use of theory.

Summary

1. Theories give facts their meaning and help us interpret data. Theories allow us to relate one fact to another and predict behavior.
2. Freud's psychoanalytic theory emphasizes the importance of early parent-child relationships. Freud argued that children progress through five psychosexual stages that involve the unfolding of the sexual instinct. Some of Freud's concepts, such as unconscious motivation, defense mechanisms, stage development, and infantile and child sexuality, are of interest. Psychoanalytic theory has been criticized because it is difficult to test, considers sexuality the prime motivation, and emphasizes deviancy.
3. Erikson argued that people proceed through eight stages from cradle to grave and that each stage presents people with different tasks. If a task is successfully negotiated, there is a positive outcome. If not, there is a negative outcome. Erikson's theory provides a good framework for viewing human development and sees development as continuing throughout the life span. It has been criticized for being too broad and too general and difficult to explore experimentally.
4. Piaget investigated the cognitive, or intellectual, development of the child. He noted that children do not think like adults, and he described four stages through which children pass between birth and adolescence. Piaget also viewed the child as actively involved with the environment and stressed the importance of discovery. His theory has been criticized for underestimating the importance of formal learning.
5. Information-processing theory focuses on the way people take in, process, and act on information. Such factors as attention, perception, and memory are investigated. The approach is noteworthy because it can yield specific information about how a person solves a particular problem. However, it is not as well developed as other theoretical approaches, and only additional experimentation will determine how useful it will be.
6. Learning theorists, or behaviorists, do not emphasize the concept of stages but stress the importance of classical conditioning and operant conditioning. This approach is noteworthy because it emphasizes the importance of the person's environment in determining behavior. The behavioral perspective has been criticized for being too mechanical and for not adequately taking consciousness and thought processes into consideration.
7. Social learning theorists emphasize the importance of imitation and observation learning to the understanding of behavior. Social learning theorists argue that to understand how people acquire complex behaviors the relationship between behavior, the environment, and personal and cognitive factors must be apreciated. This perspective is valuable in that it reminds us of the importance of models and observation learning. It has been criticized as lacking a developmental framework.
8. Ecological theory takes a broader view of the environment. People are affected by multiple layers of context. The microsystem consists of the immediate interactions between the person and the environment. The mesosystem involves the interrelationships among two or more settings in which the person actively participates. The exosystem involves settings in which the person is not actively involved now, but that affect the family and child, such as the parents' place of work. The macrosystem is composed of the ideology or belief system inherent in social institutions. Changes in each system have an impact on other systems and eventually on the person's microsystem.
9. Culture, history, roles, and social norms are also important for understanding development. One's culture determines the rights and responsibilities of the individual. The historical period in which a person lives has a profound effect on his or her outlook. A social clock is an internalized sense of timing, telling us whether we are progressing too fast or too slowly in terms of social events. Each individual also plays many roles, which are sets of obligations that an individual possesses. Roles are more complex and complicated in adulthood and role conflict and overload may occur.
10. Theories in developmental psychology can be divided into two distinct types. Stage theories emphasize the idea that people develop in a particular sequence, or in stages. The sequence of stages is invariable, progress is always in the forward direction, and no regression occurs. However, people can enter and leave any particular stage at different ages, depending upon individual factors. Nonstage theorists do not agree with the concept of stages, seeing development as a more continuous process.
11. Developmental psychology lacks a unified theory that covers every aspect of development. A researcher will choose the theory that seems most useful in understanding the developmental phenomenon of interest.

Multiple-Choice Questions

1. Which activity is most important, according to Freud, during the first psychosexual stage?
   a. toileting
   b. sucking
   c. fighting
   d. reaching
2. Janette has a positive attitude towards others. She believes that people are basically good and she has an optimistic attitude. Janette has succeeded in attaining a sense of ________, according to Erikson.
   a. intimacy
   b. autonomy
   c. trust
   d. initiative
3. Ahmed is 15 years old and trying to understand who he is and where he belongs. The psychosocial crisis that Ahmed is going through is:
   a. initiative versus guilt.
   b. identity versus role confusion.
   c. intimacy versus isolation
   d. integrity versus despair.
4. Mrs. Jones is teaching her son how to spell words in English. Piaget would call this factor in development:
   a. accommodation.
   b. assimilation.
   c. social experience.
   d. social transmission.
5. A child is creating new schemata to account for new information. Piaget calls this process:
   a. assimilation.
   b. accommodation.
   c. operations.
   d. function autonomy.
6. A 4-year-old child sees that his father is tired and offers to read his father the child's favorite book. He feels that since it makes him feel better it will help his father. This is an example of Piaget's concept of:
   a. animism.
   b. artificialism.
   c. conservation.
   d. egocentrism.
7. Children begin to understand and use abstractions during which of Piaget's stages of cognitive development?
   a. oral stage
   b. preoperational stage
   c. stage of formal operations
   d. secondary stage
8. Critics of Piaget's theory claim that he:
   a. underestimated the importance of formal learning.
   b. underestimated the importance of personal experience.
   c. completely ignored maturation as a factor in development.
   d. did not offer a mechanism for change.
9. Dr. Simons is conducting research into how people take in information, represent it, and process and use it. His work is most in keeping with:
   a. Freudian theory.
   b. behavioral theory.
   c. psychosocial theory.
   d. information-processing theory.
10. Which theoretical viewpoint emphasizes the importance of learning for understanding development?
   a. Freudian theory
   b. information processing theory
   c. ecological theory
   d. behavioral theory
11. After numerous painful experiences at the doctor's office, little Steven cries when he sees the doctor. This is an example of:
   a. social learning theory.
   b. classical conditioning.
   c. operant conditioning.
   d. unconscious learning.
12. "Behavior is governed by its consequences," describes:
   a. operant conditioning.
   b. psychosocial crises.
   c. supply-demand theory.
   d. the Yerkes Dodson law.
13. One important criticism of the behavioral view is that it:
   a. does not give enough credit to the role the environment plays in determining human behavior.
   b. has not led to much research.
   c. ignores the importance of cognitive factors in development and behavior.
   d. overemphasizes the importance of the unconscious.
14. A child watches a friend help a fellow student who does not understand the work and helps another child at a later time. This is in keeping with:
   a. Erikson's concept of learned helpfulness.
   b. social learning theory.
   c. information theory's concept of required helpfulness.
   d. Piaget's concept of de-egocentrism.
15. Social learning theorists believe that to understand how people acquire complex behaviors such as helping others, psychologists must understand the relationship between the behavior, the environment, and:
   a. personal and cognitive factors.
   b. reinforcement structures.
   c. unconscious processes.
   d. terminal beliefs.
16. A 30-year-old who is still in school feels an internal pressure to graduate as soon as possible because he

feels that by this age he should be earning a living. This illustrates the:
a. social clock.
b. social perspectives.
c. cohort effect.
d. Dallas effect.

17. The theory that requires psychologists to take a very broad view of the environment and appreciate how events that occur far from the individual may still affect the person is called:
a. psychoanalytic theory.
b. information-processing theory.
c. ecological theory.
d. social learning theory.

18. The system in ecological theory that describes the basic political and economic ideologies of the society that may affect an individual is called the:
a. microsystem.
b. exosystem.
c. macrosystem.
d. mesosystem.

19. Which of the following statements about stage theories is correct?
a. People cannot regress from a higher stage to a lower stage.
b. People cannot skip a stage.
c. People may enter and leave a stage at different times.
d. All of the above are correct.

20. Which of the following theories would be a good example of a theory that emphasizes the continuity of development?
a. psychosexual theory
b. psychosocial theory
c. behavioral theory
d. Piaget's cognitive theory

Answers to Multiple-Choice Questions

1. b 2. c 3. b 4. d 5. b 6. d 7. c 8. a 9. d
10. d 11. b 12. a 13. c 14. b 15. a 16. a 17. c
18. c 19. d 20. c

Chapter 3

Genetic Influences Across the Life Span

Chapter Outline

Genetic Questions

Popular Misconceptions

Genetic Transmission

Determining Genetic Contribution

Genetic Influences on Physical Characteristics

Genetic Influences on Disease

Genetic Influences on Personality and Intelligence

Controversial Issues: *The Bell Curve*—The Most Controversial Book of Our Time

Not How Much, But How

Appreciating Complexity

Are the Following Statements True or False?

1. Traits influenced by genetic factors cannot be changed.
2. Genetic influence on development and personality is more important in childhood than in adolescence and adulthood.
3. Fraternal twins are no more genetically alike than any other pair of siblings.
4. If a family consists of five male children, the chances are quite small that the sixth child will be a boy.
5. If neither mother nor father shows a trait, the trait cannot be passed on to the children.
6. Children with the chromosomal disorder Down syndrome usually require institutionalization by the age of 5.
7. Because there is a genetic basis for alcoholism, the majority of the children of alcoholics become alcoholics.
8. Whether someone has an outgoing personality or a tendency to be shy is partially the result of genetic factors.
9. Identical twins reared apart are more similar in intelligence than fraternal twins reared together.
10. Intelligence scores can be modified through a program of intense training.

Answers to True-False Statements 1. False: see p. 48 2. False: see p. 49 3. True 4. False: see p. 50 5. False: see p. 51 6. False: see p. 56 7. False: see p. 57 8. True 9. True 10. True

Genetic Questions

You and your spouse decide to adopt a child. After a period of waiting you are told that an infant will be available for adoption very soon. Although you understand that you will not be told the parents' identities, would you have any questions about what the parents were like or their genetic background? Do you think you are entitled to some information about the parents?

You and your spouse have just been told that you are expecting twins. You have read about some amazing similarity among identical twins in temperament and behavior. Can you expect the personalities of your identical twins to be identical?

Mrs. M.'s mother had breast cancer and Mr. M's father has Alzheimer's disease. They are both in their 20s and, although they rarely speak about it, both Mr. and Mrs. M. are concerned about the possibility that they are at risk for developing these diseases. Do they have anything to worry about?

Popular Misconceptions

Interest in the genetic influence on development, personality, and physical and mental health is greater today than at any time in the past. New research showing that certain genes place people at risk for diseases or predispose people to act in a particular way constantly appears in newspapers. Yet, many people do not understand the true nature of genetic influence. For example, some people believe that having a gene for a particular trait means that the person is certain to show the trait. This is a gross overstatement. In most cases having a particular gene may predispose, that is make it more likely for an individual to show a trait, but the environment determines whether the individual actually shows it. If genetic endowment contributes to cancer or aggressiveness, someone who inherits these genes would have a greater chance of developing cancer or showing aggressiveness, but environmental factors would play a crucial role as well.

Some people incorrectly believe that if genetic factors underlie a trait, the trait cannot be altered. Genetic influence does *not* imply that the behavior cannot be changed. Although genetic endowment plays a part in determining intelligence, it is possible to raise the intelligence level of a child. Nothing is as damaging as the idea that genetic influence means that some behavior or characteristic is carved in stone.

> ***True or False?***
> Traits influenced by genetic factors cannot be changed.

Last, although some people accept the role that genes play in an infant's life, they do not understand that genetic influence continues throughout life. Genes turn off and on throughout the life span, causing changes in hormones and neurotransmitters and even structural alterations. As regards longevity, certain diseases, and even some aspects of personality, genetic influence is stronger in adulthood than in childhood. Evidence indicates that genetic factors involved in intelligence may be greater in adulthood than in childhood (McGue, Bacon, & Lykken, 1993). The process of aging (described in Chapter 18) is under genetic control, even though there are many theories of how and why we age (Hayslip & Panek, 1993). Some disorders, such as schizophrenia, involve inherited predispositions that usually show themselves in early adulthood. In the realm of personality, such traits as extroversion and neuroticism (emotional instability) have a genetic base. Genetic influence is expressed throughout the life span.

True or False?
Genetic influence on development and personality is more important in childhood than in adolescence and adulthood.

This chapter examines the nature of genetic influence in human development and personality and looks at some ways in which genetics and environment interact.

Genetic Transmission

The basic unit of heredity is the **gene,** which is composed of deoxyribonucleic acid (DNA). Human beings are believed to have between 50,000 and 100,000 genes (McKusick, 1989). A great international effort to locate each gene and determine its function, called the Genome Project, is now in progress, and this research has raised the possibility of new and exciting medical treatments.

Genes are carried on rod-shaped structures of various sizes called **chromosomes.** Each animal species has its own number of chromosomes. The normal human being has a complement of 46 chromosomes, or 23 pairs. The same 46 chromosomes are found in every cell of the body except in the **gametes,** or sex cells. In a process called **meiosis** the sex cells divide to form two cells containing 23 chromosomes each. This allows human beings to maintain the same complement of 46 chromosomes from generation to generation. The splitting of cells is random and which chromosome ends up in which of the split cells is a matter of chance. There are more than eight million different possibilities in this process alone.

During the process of meiosis, some genetic material on one chromosome may be exchanged with material from another (Cummings, 1995). This exchange is called **crossing over.** When crossing over is taken into consideration, the chances of any two individuals being genetically identical are practically zero. Although human beings share a common species inheritance, each person is also genetically unique, except for identical, or **monozygotic twins,** who result from a single egg and sperm and who share the same genetic composition. Fraternal, or **dizygotic twins,** result from two different eggs being fertilized by two different sperm and are no more similar than any other pair of siblings. The randomness of conception is quite impressive. About 300 million sperm are expelled in a single ejaculation (Greenberg et al., 1989), but only one sperm is necessary for conception.

gene The basic unit of heredity.

chromosomes Rod-shaped structures that carry the genes.

gametes The scientific term for the sex cells.

meiosis The process by which sex cells divide to form two cells, each containing 23 chromosomes.

crossing over The process occurring during meiosis in which genetic material on one chromosome is exchanged with material from the other.

monozygotic (identical) twins Twins who develop from one fertilized egg and have an identical genetic structure.

dizygotic (fraternal) twins Twins who develop from two fertilized eggs and are no more genetically similar than any other sibling pair.

Identical twins share precisely the same genetic makeup. Fraternal twins are no more genetically alike than any other pair of siblings.

True or False?
Fraternal twins are no more genetically alike than any other pair of siblings.

Whereas sperm are continually being produced in the testicles of the male, females are born with their full complement of egg cells. The average female infant comes into this world carrying approximately 800,000 eggs (Greenberg et al., 1989), although throughout her reproductive life she will probably use only about 350 (Smith & Neisworth, 1975).

Sex Chromosomes

Twenty-two of the 23 pairs of chromosomes look similar. However, the 23rd pair is different. These chromosomes, called the **sex chromosomes,** are responsible for determining the gender of the offspring. There are two types: X and Y. The genetic composition of a male is XY and females have two X chromosomes. When meiosis occurs, a male contributes an X chromosome and a Y chromosome; the female contributes two X chromosomes. If during conception the sperm carrying the X chromosome penetrates the egg's membrane, the offspring will be female. If the sperm carrying the Y chromosome penetrates the membrane, the child will be male. Figure 3.1 shows that the chances of the offspring being male are fifty-fifty. Environmental factors such as conditions within the vagina can also influence the "odds" of conceiving a male or female child.

sex chromosomes The 23rd pair of chromosomes, which determines the gender of the organism.

		Father	
		X	Y
Mother	X	XX	XY
	X	XX	XY

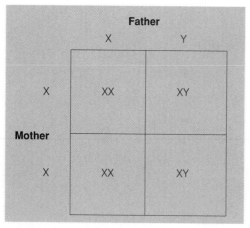

Figure 3.1
Determination of Sex The child's mother can contribute only an X chromosome, while the child's father can contribute an X or a Y. Statistically, 50% of the conceptions will produce males and 50% will produce females. However, other factors, such as conditions in the vagina, influence whether the X- or Y-carrying sperm will reach and penetrate the egg.

		Father	
		6	5
Mother	6	1 6 fingers 6 fingers	3 6 fingers 5 fingers
	5	2 6 fingers 5 fingers	4 5 fingers 5 fingers

Figure 3.2
Transmission of a Dominant Trait: Six Fingers When both parents have one gene for six fingers there is a 25% chance that a child will have two genes for six fingers and thus have six fingers. There is a 50% chance that child will have one gene for six fingers and, since this is a dominant trait, will have six fingers. There is only a 25% chance that a child will not have a gene for six fingers and so will have five fingers.

From a strictly genetic point of view, the chances are the same for each conception. Even if you have seven boys, the chances are still fifty-fifty that you will have a girl next; this is true for all inherited characteristics. Some people incorrectly believe that if their first child has a particular genetic problem, the chances of having a normal child are increased or decreased. Reproduction does not work that way. Every conception starts from square one, and the same odds exist for every pregnancy.

True or False?
If a family consists of five male children, the chances are quite small that the sixth child will be a boy.

Dominant and Recessive Traits

How do parents transmit traits to their offspring? With some select characteristics that are inherited because of one gene pair, the possibilities that an offspring will inherit a particular trait can easily be determined. Traits that follow this simple pattern are known as Mendelian traits, after Gregor Mendel who discovered and described this method of inheritance. A trait that is expressed when only one gene is present is considered a **dominant trait.** Traits that become visible only when two genes (one from mother and one from father) are present are called **recessive traits.**

Let's look at how dominant traits may show themselves by considering the example of a dominant trait, extra digits. Let us say that each parent has one gene for six fingers and one gene for five fingers. If the offspring inherits two genes for six fingers, the child will show six fingers (see Figure 3.2, frame 1). If the child inherits two genes for five fingers, the youngster will have five fingers (see frame 4). If one parent passes on a gene for six fingers and the gene from the other parent is for five fingers, the child will have one gene for six fingers and one for five fingers (see frames 2 and 3), and since six fingers is dominant, the child will have six fingers. Notice that as long as individuals have one gene for a dominant trait, they will show that trait. Several traits such as double-jointedness and some diseases such as Huntington's disease (discussed later) are dominant.

dominant traits Traits that require the presence of only one gene.
recessive traits Traits that require the presence of two genes.

Questions Students Often Ask

If six fingers is dominant over five and genetic diseases such as Huntington's disease are dominant, why are they so rare?

In order for a person to inherit these dominant characteristics they must be available in the individual's gene pool. A person can only inherit a characteristic if it is passed on by the parents. If the characteristic is not present in the parents' genes then the characteristic cannot be inherited. Although six fingers and Huntington's disease are dominant, they are very rarely found in the gene pool, so most people do not have the chance of inheriting them.

If neither parent shows a particular trait it can still be passed on to offspring so long as the trait is recessive. If both parents have one gene for a recessive trait such as the disease **cystic fibrosis,** a disease that causes respiratory problems, it is possible for a child to inherit the trait. If each parent has one recessive gene for the disease, neither parent will show signs of the recessive trait because

cystic fibrosis A severe genetic disease marked by digestive and respiratory problems.

two genes are needed for the trait to show. A person who has one gene for healthy functioning and one defective gene for a recessive trait is called a **carrier** because the individual will not show the trait but can pass the defective gene on to his or her offspring.

True or False?
If neither mother nor father shows a trait, the trait cannot be passed on to the children.

Suppose two carriers marry. What are the odds that any child would have the trait? To understand the possibility, two new terms must be introduced: **genotype** and **phenotype.** The genotype of a person refers to the specific composition of that person's genes. The phenotype refers to the observable characteristics of an individual. Phenotype and genotype may be the same or different. A person may have one hair color but choose to dye the hair, thereby changing the phenotype—that is, the color that is shown—but the genotype still remains. New hair that grows will show the original color.

Both the mother's and the father's genotypes in Figure 3.3 include one gene for cystic fibrosis and one gene for healthy functioning. Because the trait is recessive and requires two genes, neither the father nor the mother shows the trait and the phenotype is normal. However, either parent can pass the gene on to the offspring because both parents are carriers. If each parent contributes a gene for healthy functioning to the child, the child will not show the disorder; both the phenotype and genotype will be normal. There is a 25% chance that this will occur. If one parent contributes a gene for healthy functioning and one contributes a defective gene, the offspring will not show any trace of the disease. Because healthy functioning is dominant, it masks the defective gene. The phenotype is normal but the genotype is not, since the child is carrying the defective gene and can pass it on to the offspring. There is a 50% chance of this occurring. Finally, if both the mother and the father contribute their defective gene, the child will be both genotypically and phenotypically abnormal. The child will have cystic fibrosis and could pass the gene on to the next generation; there is a 25% chance of this occurring.

Polygenic Inheritance

Most human characteristics are influenced by many genes. The effects of the environment on the expression of one's genetic endowment also play an important role, which makes the relationship between phenotype and genotype more complicated.

carrier A person who possesses a particular gene or group of genes for a trait, who does not show the trait but can pass it on to his or her offspring.

genotype The genetic configuration of the individual.

phenotype The observable characteristics of the organism.

	Father: Normal Gene	Father: Cystic Fibrosis
Mother: Normal Gene	Normal Gene Normal Gene	Normal Gene Cystic Fibrosis
Mother: Cystic Fibrosis	Cystic Fibrosis Normal Gene	Cystic Fibrosis Cystic Fibrosis

Figure 3.3
Transmission of a Recessive Trait: Cystic Fibrosis When both the mother and the father carry the gene for cystic fibrosis, the chances are 25% that an offspring will have the disease (cystic fibrosis-cystic fibrosis), 50% that the child will be a carrier (cystic fibrosis-normal), and 25% that the child will not have the disorder or be a carrier.
Note: Some other genetic diseases such as Tay-Sachs disease and phenylketonuria are transmitted in the same way as cystic fibrosis.

When a characteristic is influenced by more than one pair of genes, the mechanism of inheritance is **polygenic.** The term **multifactorial inheritance** describes a trait that is influenced both by genes and by the environment. However, the terms *polygenic* and *multifactorial* are often used interchangeably. Skin color is a polygenic trait and four gene pairs may be involved with no evidence of dominance (Cummings, 1995). But the environment also influences the phenotype. If you have light skin and spend time in the sun, you will tan. Your genotype has not changed, but your outward appearance, or phenotype, has.

Sex-Linked Traits

Sex-linked traits are those that are transmitted on the 23rd chromosome pair (sex chromosomes). The X chromosome is three times as large as the Y and contains many more genes than the Y. Many of the genes found on the X chromosome do not exist at all on the Y, a fact that has profound consequences for males.

Consider what might happen if a female had one defective gene for a recessive trait and one gene for normal functioning that is found on the 23rd chromosome. Remember, females have two X chromosomes whereas males have an X and a Y. Assume that these genes are found only on the X, and not on the Y, the female would

polygenic inheritance Characteristics influenced by more than one pair of genes.

multifactorial inheritance Traits influenced both by genes and by the environment.

sex-linked traits Traits inherited through genes found on the sex chromosomes.

not show the effects of the recessive gene because she possesses a gene for normal functioning to counter it. But if she had children, she could pass on both the normal and the abnormal gene, but in this situation the child's gender becomes crucial.

As shown in Figure 3.4, if the mother contributes a normal X and the father contributes a normal X, as in frame 1, the child will be a female who will show no signs of the disorder and will not pass the disorder on to her offspring. If the mother contributes an abnormal gene on the X chromosome and the father contributes a normal gene for the same trait from the X, the child will be a female who will not show any signs of the disorder but will be a carrier like her mother (frame 2).

If the mother contributes a normal gene and the father contributes his Y, as shown in frame 3, the offspring will be a male who will not show any signs of the disorder or be able to pass the disorder on. In this case, because the X is normal, there is no need to be concerned. But if the mother transmits the defective X chromosome and the father a Y, the resulting male offspring will show signs of the disorder and may pass it on to the next generation (frame 4). The defective gene on the X has no corresponding normal gene to counter it, so the defective gene on the X is in a position to show itself.

Sex-linked traits usually involve female carriers, but it is the male who inherits the trait. Among the proven sex-linked traits are hemophilia and color blindness. Both hemophilia—a severe blood disorder involving a deficiency in the blood's ability to clot—and color blindness are determined by defective genes found on the X chromosome. Because a female has two X chromosomes, her chances of being color-blind or of having hemophilia are negligible. For example, red-green color blindness occurs in about 8% of all males but in less than 0.5% of females (Restak, 1988).

Could some differences between males and females be genetically determined? The fact that women usually outlive men may be partially explained by genetic endowment (Kermis, 1984). Psychologists differ sharply on such questions. Except for some genetic diseases and physical traits, the interaction of genes with environment is crucial to understanding the end product. However, it is tempting to explain some gender differences using the mechanism of sex-linked genetic transmission.

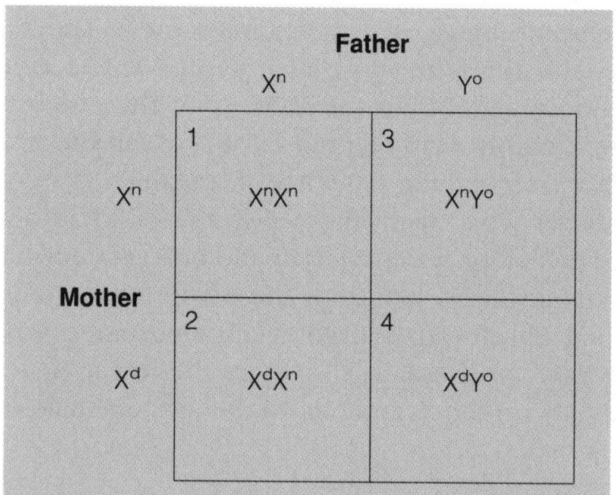

Figure 3.4
Sex-Linked Inheritance In sex-linked traits, females may carry the defective gene but do not develop the disorder.
n = normal
d = gene for a disorder—e.g., hemophilia or color blindness

Determining Genetic Contribution

If a particular characteristic, for example, intelligence or aggressiveness or alcoholism, is suspected to be influenced by genetic endowment, verifying our suspicions and estimating the extent of the contribution is necessary but often presents difficulties.

Consider the following. In a given family the father, mother, and two children are quite overweight. Going back a few generations you find that almost everyone in the family is overweight. Can you conclude that obesity is genetic? Although you might *suspect* genetic involvement, you cannot conclude that it is so from this information. It is possible that the children may have learned how to eat from their parents. Perhaps the parents were totally absorbed with eating and modeled eating everything on their plate and taking second and third helpings. The children may have learned that behavior.

Trying to separate the possible environmental (learned) aspects from the genetic involvement is difficult and requires specific methods. The term **heritability** is used to describe what proportion of the differences between people in a given population on a particular characteristic is caused by genetic factors (McClearn, 1993). Sometimes scientists use the term **environmentality** to describe the proportion of the variation between people in a given population on a particular characteristic that may result from environmental factors. Two methods useful for determining heritability are twin studies and adoption studies.

Twin Studies

Twin methods are based upon the fact that monozygotic (identical) twins have 100% of their genes in common and fraternal twins (dizygotic) as all other siblings have on the average of 50% of their genes in common (Kimble, 1993). A simple method for evaluating the heritability of a trait is to find the extent to which if one twin has the trait the other twin also will have it. This agreement between traits is called the **concordance rate.** If identical twins show a given trait much more often than fraternal twins do, some genetic influence can be assumed. If a trait is completely genetic, the concordance rate among

heritability The proportion of the measured differences between people in a given population on a particular characteristic due to genetic factors.

environmentality The proportion of the variation between people in a given population on a particular characteristic that is caused by environmental factors.

concordance rate A measure of the frequency with which both members of a pair of twins show the same particular trait.

identical twins is 1.00 and among fraternal twins is close to .50 (Cummings, 1995). When bipolar disorder, formerly called *manic depression,* occurs in one identical twin, it will also affect the other twin 70% of the time; if it affects one fraternal twin the other twin will develop this disorder in 15% of the cases (Milunsky, 1989). The difference suggests that genetic factors are involved but also that important environmental factors are present.

Sometimes it is possible to research twins reared apart and together, which yields additional data (McGue et al., 1993). When Albert Stunkard (1990) compared both identical and fraternal twins in their late 50s raised together and apart, the identical twins had almost the identical body mass, a measure of weight corrected for height, whether reared apart or together whereas fraternal twins varied much more than the identical twins even if they were reared together.

Questions Students Often Ask

I've read about identical twins reared apart being incredibly similar in attitudes and behaviors—for example, a set of twins in which each chose the same vocations and enjoyed the same leisure activities. How can you explain this?

Many of these similarities are not easy to explain. Of course, twins who share similarities are hounded by the news media while those who do not are left alone. It therefore seems as if this is somewhat more common than it is. Many identical twins reared apart show differences as well as similarities.

On the other hand, remember we now view all behavior as representing complex interactions between genetic and environmental factors. We would expect social behaviors such as liking sports or choosing a law enforcement career over office work to represent genetic as well as environmental forces. Identical twins with the same genes may have similar personalities and temperaments and this may cause them to choose similar activities. Some similarities are difficult to understand, for example, identical twins raised apart who married women with the same name and named their dogs the same name. However, with our new understanding of genetic/environmental interaction, many similarities can now be explained.

Twin studies have their detractors. Early twin studies sometimes depended solely on appearances and did not test for whether these twins were identical or fraternal. New measures that test for this characteristic have eliminated this problem, but interpreting older twin studies is still problematic (Cummings, 1995). The twin method also assumes that the environment of both twins is similar. It is possible that parents treat identical twins more similarly than fraternal twins. If this were so to any great extent it might explain the greater concordance rates between identical twins (Reiss, 1993). The greater concordance rate between identical twins would then be the result of a more similar environment than that experienced by fraternal twins. Some studies do show that the treatment of monozygotic twins is more similar than the treatment of dizygotic twins but this alone does not account for the results of studies on twins. Some even argue that identical twins know they are more similar and therefore may act in a particular manner. Studying twins and generalizing to the whole population has been questioned. Twins differ in many ways, for example, they are more likely to be premature, have lower birth weights, and perform worse on verbal tasks and language learning, although most of these differences disappear in the school years (Plomin, DeFries, & McClearn, 1990).

Adoption Studies

Studies of adopted children and their parents are also used to determine genetic influence. Consider a child of parents with a particular body mass adopted by parents with significantly different body mass. Will the child be more similar to the adoptive or the biological parents? Stunkard and colleagues (1986) compared adopted children's body mass to the body mass of their biological and adoptive parents. There was a clear relationship between adoptee weight class of *thin, medium, overweight,* and *obese* and the body mass index of the biological parents. There was no relationship between adoptee weight class and body mass of adoptive parents. Studies that compare adopted children's intelligence to that of their biological mothers and adoptive parents show a greater similarity to biological than adoptive parents (Horn, Loehlin, & Willerman, 1979; 1982).

Questions Students Often Ask

I now understand why I'm so overweight. Since it is in my genes, nothing can be done about it, right?

Wrong! Just because genetic factors may be involved does not mean that one cannot regulate one's weight. Studies certainly show that body mass is partially the result of genetic factors. However, this only means that people with a genetic propensity to be overweight must watch themselves and be more careful about what they eat.

Adoption studies have been roundly criticized because the placement of adopted children is certainly not random. It is possible that children may be adopted by people with similar backgrounds as the biological parents. Second, parents may treat an adopted child differently than a biological child. This could lead to greater differences between adopted siblings than between biological siblings for solely environmental reasons (Reiss, 1993). Third, it is frequently difficult to find information about the biological fathers of adopted children (Nigg & Goldsmith, 1994). Fourth, the timing of adoption is a major question. The longer the child stays with the biological parents the greater the influence of that environment. Last, it should be remembered that the womb itself is an environment (Lombroso, Paul, & Leckman, 1994).

Twin and adoption studies are often used to find and estimate any genetic contribution. However, these studies also show the importance of the environment. For instance, the Texas Adoption Project found that the intelligence scores of adopted children were more similar to their biological than to their adoptive parents. However, the relationships were all quite low and most of the variability was not the result of genetic influences but of socioeconomic factors, such as neighborhood, friends, and schools (Cummings, 1995).

In addition, heritability depends upon the population being measured and its environments. Many developmental psychologists have asked that professionals conducting such studies sample subjects from a wider range of environments and measure the environments more accurately (Rowe & Waldman, 1993). Last, these analyses of heritability consider groups and populations. Heritability differences are measured between groups of people not between individuals.

How does genetic endowment affect various aspects of development? Why is an understanding of genetics important to an appreciation of development and behavior?

Genetic Influences on Physical Characteristics

The most striking genetic influence involves physical appearance. Hair and skin color, the shape of the nose, body build, and a thousand other physical characteristics are directly influenced by genes. Evidence that body weight is affected by genetics is clear. One's adult weight is not entirely predestined, but some people may be more likely to become obese, and programs to prevent obesity should be targeted at children who are at risk for obesity.

Biologically speaking, most physical features are trivial. The color of a person's skin or whether one is slightly overweight makes very little difference from the point of view of biological functioning or intellectual ability (being grossly overweight increases one's susceptibility to certain illnesses). However, these and many other physical characteristics may or may not be valued by the society in which a person lives. Let's look at weight. Today, thin is "in," and overweight people suffer discrimination both in the workplace and in social interactions. The same is true of skin color, which is biologically trivial but may be socially important. Thus, any discussion of a physical characteristic must be investigated from both a biological viewpoint (does it lead to some advantage or disadvantage in functioning?) and a social perspective (how is that trait valued by the family and society?).

Genetic Influences on Disease

The March of Dimes Birth Defects Foundation (1987) has catalogued about 2000 confirmed or suspected dominant genetic disorders and over 1000 confirmed or suspected recessive disorders. There are some 250 confirmed or suspected genetic disorders transmitted through the X chromosome. Many of these diseases are rare, and some show great variability in the severity of their symptoms. About 3% of all newborns have some genetic birth defect, and about 1 in 200 have a chromosomal abnormality (Plomin et al., 1990).

Cystic Fibrosis Cystic fibrosis is a recessive genetic disease of the glands that produce mucus, saliva, and sweat. It affects many organs, including the lungs, liver, and pancreas. A person with cystic fibrosis has a low resistance to respiratory diseases and a tendency to become dehydrated because of excessive salt in the sweat. New antibiotics have increased the life expectancy of individuals with this disorder. Fifteen years ago the life expectancy of people with cystic fibrosis was 18 years, but today it is 28 years with many living into their 30s and 40s (Wolfson, 1996). Some women with cystic fibrosis are even having babies; in 1994 there were 60 births to women with cystic fibrosis but about one quarter of the babies were born prematurely. At this point, there is no cure for cystic fibrosis.

Recent research into this disorder shows great promise. Scientists have actually cured cystic fibrosis cells in the laboratory by inserting a healthy version of the gene that causes the disease (Angier, 1990a). A genetically engineered virus was used to place good copies of the gene into cells taken from the respiratory tract and pancreas of cystic fibrosis patients. As a result, the abnormal cells became healthier and functioned more normally. This is called *gene therapy*. Several genetic diseases may be conquered by gene therapy, which has already been used successfully on a very rare genetic disorder in which children do not have the ability to fight off any disease (Angier, 1990b; Ridker et al., 1995). However, progress in developing effective gene therapies against other conditions has been slow (Wheeler, 1995). Curing a few cells in the laboratory, although a significant achievement, is a long way from curing an actual individual so progress in using gene therapy is apt to be slow and fraught with difficulties (Knowles & Boucher, 1996; Alton, 1996).

Tay-Sachs Disease Some genetic diseases are more likely to be found in one group of people than another. For example, **Tay-Sachs disease** is most common among Jews whose ancestors came from Central and Eastern Europe, although members of any other group can inherit the disease. Infants born with the disease seem healthy at birth, but their progress slows after 6 months. The disease involves an inborn error in metabolism and is incurable. At the age of 2 or 3, the child dies. Many other diseases show a greater incidence in certain ethnic groups. For example, Italians are more likely to suffer from thalassemia (a blood disease), and phenylketonuria (an inability to digest a particular amino acid, which if left

Tay-Sachs disease A fatal genetic disease found most often in Jews who can trace their ancestry back to Eastern Europe.

Today genetic counseling can help people who believe they are at risk for a particular condition to discover the probability.

Today genetic counseling is available for people who believe they are at risk for a particular genetic disease. Genetic counselors help people by (a) diagnosing and describing particular disorders, (b) calculating the probabilities that a disorder will be transmitted to offspring, (c) helping people reach a decision based on genetic information as well as on ethical, religious, and cultural concerns, and (d) describing the treatment and resources available to those seeking such information. The ability to detect the presence of the gene for Huntington's disease and other genetic disorders gives affected individuals the information they need to plan their lives.

untreated may result in mental retardation) is more common among North Europeans. **Sickle cell anemia,** a blood disorder, is found much more commonly among African Americans and Latinos.

Huntington's Disease **Huntington's disease** is a rare dominant genetic disease that affects the central nervous system. It is caused by a defective gene on chromosome 4. The onset typically occurs after the prime childbearing years; the average age of onset is 35 years. The individual suffers from progressive mental deterioration and pronounced involuntary muscle movements. Woody Guthrie, the well-known folk singer, died from this disease. Today a test is available that can determine whether a person has the gene and therefore can help people plan their lives accordingly (Quarrel et al., 1987).

Questions Students Often Ask

My girlfriend just told me that her cousin has cystic fibrosis and since it also runs in my family we are both concerned about it. We've heard about genetic counseling but we're afraid the counselor will tell us not to have children.

You have the wrong idea about genetic counselors. They will give you the information and alternatives but they will not tell you what to do. Genetic counselors have very strict ethical guidelines to follow and will be able to answer your questions in a professional manner.

Phenylketonuria: A Success Story **Phenylketonuria (PKU)** is a rare recessive disorder that occurs in approximately one in 8000 births (March of Dimes, 1986b). It involves the inability to digest a particular amino acid called phenylalanine. If left untreated, brain damage leading to mental retardation results. Phenylalanine is found in all protein-rich foods, including fish, meats, poultry, eggs, milk, and bread products. It is also found in some soft drinks, many of which are now labeled. Most states require that a blood test be given, usually on the day the baby is scheduled to be discharged from the hospital (Plomin et al., 1990), to determine whether a newborn has PKU.

Phenylketonuria is treated with a special diet low in phenylalanine. During middle childhood the diet is relaxed or even abandoned. However, if the diet is abandoned too early, the child's intellectual abilities are negatively affected (Holtzman et al., 1986). Some people should remain on the diet for life, which is not easy because the amino acid is found in so many foods (DeAngelis, 1993). A woman who has PKU should consult a physician before she becomes pregnant because if she becomes pregnant while not on the diet, the baby is likely to be born with mental retardation because of the mother's abnormal body chemistry (March of Dimes, 1986b).

Down Syndrome Some inherited diseases are caused by chromosomal abnormalities rather than genetic defects. **Chromosomal abnormalities** are conditions in

sickle cell anemia An inherited defect in the structure of red blood cells found mostly in African Americans and Latinos.

Huntington's disease A dominant and fatal genetic disorder affecting the central nervous system.

phenylketonuria (PKU) A recessive genetic disorder marked by the inability to digest a particular amino acid and leading to mental retardation if not treated.

chromosomal abnormalities Conditions caused by too many, too few, or incomplete chromosomes.

which a person has too few, too many, or incomplete chromosomes. The most common of these abnormalities is **Down syndrome,** which occurs approximately once in every 1000 births and is caused by the appearance of an extra chromosome on the 21st pair (Plomin et al., 1990). The child has 47 chromosomes instead of the normal 46. The frequency of the disorder increases with the age of the mother as well as the age of the father. The risk for women under 30 is one in 1250 births, while for mothers between 35 and 40 it is 1 in 365 births; at age 40, the chances are 1 in 110 births (March of Dimes, 1987b). The disorder is also linked to the father. In 5% of the cases of Down syndrome the disorder is linked to the sperm (Antonarakis, 1991). In the United States, about 5000 children a year are born with Down syndrome (Dullea, 1989).

Most children with Down syndrome are identified either at birth or shortly after by their physical appearance. Unusual physical features include folded eyes, short digits, flat face, protruding tongue, and harsh voice (Sue, Sue, & Sue, 1990). Mental retardation is associated with the disorder, but the degree of mental retardation varies greatly. Today many children with Down syndrome are given special treatment, including special preschool programs that can improve cognitive functioning, and many score in the mildly retarded range on intelligence tests (Kaplan, 1996). Years ago most children with this disorder were institutionalized immediately after birth, but this is no longer the case. Many children with Down syndrome are now raised at home, which is usually beneficial.

True or False?
Children with the chromosomal disorder Down syndrome usually require institutionalization by the age of 5.

Not too long ago, the life expectancy for children with Down syndrome was 10 years or less. Congenital heart problems are common, and resistance to disease is low. However, medical advances have substantially increased the life expectancy of these children. Approximately 20% die during the first 2 years (Randal, 1988). However, the majority who survive infancy live well into adulthood (Baird & Sadovnick, 1987). After the age of about 40, people with Down syndrome appear to be more susceptible to diseases that are related to old age—many have brain lesions that look like the lesions of Alzheimer's disease, and many show symptoms of senility (Kolata, 1989). This may be because the genes associated with congenital heart defects and the brain changes associated with familial Alzheimer's disease are also found on the 21st chromosome. Much research is being conducted into the relationship between various genes on the 21st chromosome.

Down syndrome A disorder caused by the presence of an extra chromosome, leading to a distinct physical appearance and mental retardation of varying degree.

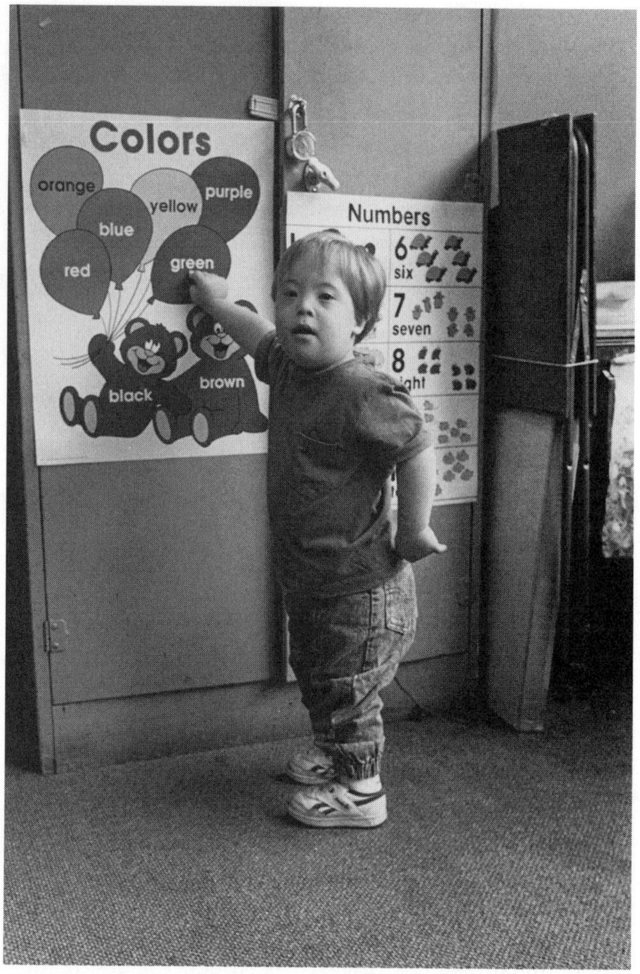

Down syndrome is the most common chromosomal disorder. It affects about 5000 children a year in the United States.

Some children with Down syndrome attend public schools (Schnaiberg, 1996). Although most are in special classes, some attend regular classes. They interact with nonretarded children and are tuned into the culture of childhood and adolescence. Some people with Down syndrome have been successful in the world of work with the help of job coaches and can live semi-independently, often in group homes (Kaplan, 1996).

Predispositions to Disorders

Not all genetically based disorders are transmitted directly. Sometimes a predisposition to a disorder, rather than the disease itself, is passed from parents to children. This is true of **schizophrenia,** alcoholism, and possibly bipolar disorder and Alzheimer's disease (Rose, 1995).

Schizophrenia Schizophrenia is a severe mental disorder characterized by hallucinations, delusions, emotional disturbances, apathy, and withdrawal. About 50% of the residents of mental hospitals at any one time suffer from the disorder. A number of twin and adoption studies have suggested that a genetic base for schizophrenia

schizophrenia A severe mental disorder marked by hallucinations, delusions, and emotional disturbances.

exists (Nigg & Goldsmith, 1994; McBroom, 1980). However, the evidence also indicates a strong environmental component. What appears to be transmitted is not the disease itself, but rather a tendency or predisposition to acquire the disorder. All environmental factors being equal, an individual with a family history of schizophrenia is at a greater risk for the disease than one with no family history of schizophrenia.

Prenatal, birth, and psychosocial factors also play a role. For example, some prenatal insults that cause brain abnormalities, lack of oxygen to the brain, and birth trauma; some cognitive deficits; and chaotic family situations with communication problems may be implicated (Mirsky & Duncan, 1986). Genetic factors may make an individual more vulnerable to schizophrenia but other factors can be important as well.

Bipolar Disorder and Alzheimer's Disease Studies indicate that other disturbances, including specific reading disorders, attention-deficit/hyperactivity disorder, and autism, may have a genetic base (Lombroso, Paul, & Leckman, 1994). Researchers at the University of London found that genetic factors may contribute to bipolar disorder, which is characterized by intense mood swings from euphoria to profound depression (Friend, 1994; Hodgkinson et al., 1987). In addition, some research indicates that a genetic factor may be implicated in Alzheimer's disease, a disease marked by mental deterioration in later life (Selkoe, 1991; St. George-Hyslip et al., 1987).

Alcoholism and Genetics Twin and adoption studies find a genetic basis for alcoholism (USDHHS, 1993). In a famous Swedish study Michael Bohman (1978) compared rates of alcohol abuse between adoptees and biological parents. Adopted sons whose biological fathers were alcoholic were three times more likely to become alcoholic than adopted sons of nonalcoholic fathers. If the mother was an alcoholic, the sons were twice as likely to become alcoholic. Studies also show a higher concordance rate for alcoholism among identical twins than fraternal twins (McGue, 1993; Sexias & Youcha, 1985). The conclusion of most studies is that there is a genetic predisposition to alcoholism (Gordis et al., 1990). However, there is also considerable evidence that environmental factors are important in alcoholism. Most children of alcoholics do *not* become alcoholic, and this phenomenon has not been adequately studied (Heller, Sher, & Benson, 1982).

Questions Students Often Ask

I don't understand how a group can be at risk for alcoholism or some other trait and still a majority do not get the disease or show the trait.

The concept of risk is a difficult one. If a group is at risk for a disease it only means that they have a better chance of getting it than the general population. The fact that the group is at risk tells us nothing about the percentage who will have the disease. For example, let us say that 5% of the population gets disease X. If we find that 15% of a certain group within the population develops this disease, this group is 3 times more likely to get the disease—this group is at a greater risk. Yet, if 15% get the disease, 85% do not (100 − 15 = 85). This explains how a group may be at risk and a majority still not develop the disease.

Children of alcoholics are certainly at an increased risk for becoming alcoholic. The majority do not because they have made a conscious decision not to follow in the path of their alcoholic relatives. Many realize that they are at risk and do not drink. I know that it seems unfair that someone with a biological predisposition cannot live the way other people do. This is the same with people with a biological predisposition to obesity or high blood cholesterol. Yet, this knowledge allows us to change our behavior to reduce our chances of becoming alcoholic or overweight.

True or False?

Because there is a genetic basis for alcoholism, the majority of the children of alcoholics become alcoholics.

Some studies find that the gene associated with alcoholism may be found on chromosome 11 because it is involved in alcohol metabolism (Rose, 1995). Studies have shown that alcoholics and nonalcoholics have enzyme differences in the ability to break down alcohol. Alcoholics metabolize alcohol differently than nonalcoholics and build up tolerance more easily (Schuckit, 1987). Marc Schuckit (1986) compared sons of alcoholic fathers to sons of nonalcoholic fathers. At the time of the study, none of the sons were alcoholics. Even with the same level of alcohol in their systems, the sons of alcoholic fathers reported that they were less intoxicated than the sons of nonalcoholic fathers did. Some metabolic difference may be responsible for this difference. In addition, several neurological and chemical differences have been found between the two groups (Cloninger, 1987; USDHHS, 1993).

Predispositions are inherited in a rather complex manner. Scientists are now trying to discover chemical or neurological markers that would allow us to discern which people are more at risk than others. These at-risk individuals could then seek information and counseling that would allow them to understand their situation and deal with it.

Genetic Influences on Personality and Intelligence

The importance of one's genetic endowment goes beyond specific physical characteristics and predisposition to particular disorders. One's temperament, behavioral traits, attitudes, rate of development, and intelligence are also affected by one's genes.

Table 3.1 **Measuring Children's Temperament**
Alexander Thomas, Stella Chess, and Herbert Birch found the majority of children could be classified as "easy," "slow to warm up," or "difficult," according to how they rate in key categories that are shown on a 9-point personality index.

TYPE OF CHILD	ACTIVITY LEVEL	RHYTHMICITY	DISTRACTIBILITY	APPROACH-WITHDRAWAL
	The Proportion of Active Periods to Inactive Ones	**Regularity of Hunger, Excretion, Sleep, and Wakefulness**	**The Degree to Which Extraneous Stimuli Alter Behavior**	**The Response to a New Object or Person**
Easy	Varies	Very regular	Varies	Positive approach
Slow to warm up	Low to moderate	Varies	Varies	Initial withdrawal
Difficult	Varies	Irregular	Varies	Withdrawal

Temperament

Each child is born with a **temperament**—an "individual style of responding to the environment" (Thomas, Chess, & Birch, 1970, p. 2). Alexander Thomas and his colleagues found nine characteristics that comprise temperament (see Table 3.1).

The majority of children fit into one of three general types. Children with "easy" temperaments are generally happy, flexible, and regular. These children get along well with almost everyone and present few problems to parents or teachers. "Difficult" children, on the other hand, are intense, demanding, inflexible, and cry a great deal. Children in the third category—"slow to warm up"—do not respond well to changes in their environment, but their reactions are not intense. They exhibit a low activity level and have a tendency to withdraw from new stimuli. Approximately 40% of the sample in the study by Thomas and his colleagues could be characterized as easy, about 10% as difficult, and another 15% as slow to warm up. The remaining 35% showed a mixture of behaviors and thus could not be categorized.

Some psychologists do not use these categories and propose a different constellation of behavior patterns that define temperament. For example, Buss and Plomin (1984) suggest that temperament comprises three characteristics: emotionality, activity, and sociability. *Emotionality* refers to the strength of arousal shown by infants in response to events. Emotional infants show strong fears, anger responses, or distress even to minimal negative stimuli and are less easily comforted. *Activity* is the extent to which the child requires movement and expends energy. *Sociability* is the child's desire for the rewards of being with other people, such as attention. There is no agreement on what factors temperament actually is made up of and different scientists have suggested different characteristics.

Early temperament is related to later behavior. For example, children considered undercontrolled at 3 years (a characteristic affected by temperament) scored high on measures of impulsivity, danger seeking, aggression, and interpersonal alienation at 18 years whereas inhibited children scored lower on many such measures (Caspi & Silva, 1995). However, the way people react to the child's temperament may explain this relationship, rather than consistency in temperament itself.

Whether temperament changes or remains stable is still at issue. Temperament seems to be relatively stable in infancy (Worobey & Blajda, 1989). After infancy, there is evidence both for moderate stability and for change. When children's temperament was measured at 2 months, 9 months, 6 years, and 15 years, substantial stability in activity level and a sociability factor were found. However, substantial change was found in a factor akin to emotionality (Torgersen, 1989). Perhaps some aspects of temperament change whereas others may remain stable. It is also possible that some traits may show stability for a time and then show change. One trait may remain stable for a time while another changes and vice versa (van den Bloom, 1994). If temperament is biological in origin, genes may turn on and off and different sets of genes may play a role at different stages of development (Buss & Plomin, 1984).

Children who exhibit different patterns of temperament show different physiological reactions. For instance, children who show withdrawal in novel social situations, are easily frightened, and show anxiety when challenged are often labeled behaviorally inhibited. Children who show the opposite behaviors and approach new situations with confidence are labeled behaviorally uninhibited. Genetic involvement is strong in these behavior patterns (Robinson, Kagan, Reznick, & Corley, 1992). Inhibited and uninhibited children differ on a number of physiological indicators, including heart rate and pupil dilation, suggesting greater reactivity on the part of the peripheral nervous system. Evidence that neurological differences are linked to increased vulnerability to negative emotions also exists (Rickman & Davidson, 1994). Yet, other factors are also important. Parental response and parental characteristics of extroversion, shyness, and avoidance also may affect the child's responses.

Could there be genetic differences in temperament among various cultural and geographically related groups? Four-month-old infants from Boston, Dublin, and

temperament A group of characteristics reflecting an individual's way of responding to the environment and thought to be genetic.

Table 3.1 **Measuring Children's Temperament (continued)**

ADAPTABILITY	**ATTENTION SPAN AND PERSISTENCE**	**INTENSITY OF REACTION**	**THRESHOLD OF RESPONSIVENESS**	**QUALITY OF MOOD**
The Ease With Which a Child Adapts to Changes in His or Her Environment	**The Amount of Time Devoted to an Activity and the Effect of Distraction on the Activity**	**The Energy of Response, Regardless of Its Quality or Direction**	**The Intensity of Stimulation Required To Evoke a Discernible Response**	**The Amount of Friendly, Pleasant, Joyful Behavior vs. Unpleasant, Unfriendly Behavior**
Very adaptable	High or low	Low or mild	High or low	Positive
Slowly adaptable	High or low	Mild	High or low	Slightly negative
Slowly adaptable	High or low	Intense	High or low	Negative

Source: Thomas et al., 1970.

Beijing were tested on differences in ease and intensity of behavioral arousal to visual, auditory, and olfactory stimuli. The Chinese infants were significantly less active, less irritable, and less vocal than the infants in the other two samples. These differences in reactivity are part of many measures of temperament and may be partly genetic in origin (Kagan et al., 1994). The fact of biological differences has been accepted for many years. For instance, the number of Rh-negative (a chemical found in the blood and discussed in Chapter 4) individuals in China is less than 1% but is greater than 15% in Europe (Cavalli-Sforza, 1991) and differences in response to medications have been noted (Lin, Poland, & Lesser, 1986).

Even though temperament appears to have a genetic basis, behavioral orientations may be affected by parenting practices and attitudes. In a study of infant temperament in three African societies, specific differences in temperament were attributed to each culture's child-rearing practices and parenting orientations (de Vries & Sameroff, 1994). For example, mothers of infants in the Digo culture are not very concerned with time and are more likely to respond to a child's immediate needs. There is little emphasis on how long a child should sleep or a specific feeding schedule. Perhaps as a result of this care-giving pattern, Digo infants were rated less regular than infants in the other two African cultures.

A child's temperament may affect the relationship between the parents and the child. Children respond differently to environmental events, and these responses affect their parents' reactions (Mohar, 1988). Mothers of nonirritable infants show a high level of visual and physical involvement from the first month, combined with a gradual increase in effective stimulation. They rapidly respond to positive signs from their infants. Irritable infants are confronted with less visual and physical involvement from birth, a very low level of effective stimulation, and a rapidly decreasing responsiveness. These behaviors became less acute by 6 months (van den Bloom & Hoeksma, 1994).

What does temperament mean to parents and children? Children are fortunate if their inborn temperament meshes with their parents' abilities and styles. The difficult child thrives in a structured, understanding environment, but not in an inconsistent, intolerant home. The child who is slow to warm up does best if the parents understand that the child needs time to adjust to new situations. If they do not, the parents may only intensify the child's natural tendency to withdraw. Thomas urges parents to work with their child's temperament rather than try to change it. Children who are slow to warm up should be allowed to proceed at their own pace. Gentle encouragement is best. Difficult children should be handled in a very consistent and objective way. Easy children may also face problems related to temperament because sometimes they are unable to resolve conflicts between their own desires and the demands of others.

It is generally agreed that temperament reflects behavioral tendencies, has biological underpinnings, is easiest to see directly in infancy, and becomes more complex as the child matures (Goldsmith et al., 1987). Psychologists disagree about just how much of an infant's behavior emanates from temperament, on the nature of the specific components that temperament comprises, and on whether the term *difficult child* should be used at all because of its negative connotation. Despite these differences, the concept of temperament is useful in understanding the factors that underlie a child's tendency to react to stimuli in characteristic ways early in life.

Rate of Development

Children develop at their own rate and their rate of maturation reflects their unique genetic master plan. Activities such as standing, crawling, walking, and talking depend largely, but not exclusively, on the child's genetic endowment. Statistics may show that the "average" child walks or talks at a particular age, but variations exist within the range of normal development. When children fall far behind these norms, the problem should be investigated.

It is important to recognize that within the broad "normal" range, some children develop faster than others. Serious consequences may follow from pushing a child to do something before that child is ready. **Readiness** implies that there is a point in development when a child has the skills necessary to master a particular task. When parents and teachers do not understand this, problems can result. For instance, if a child who does not understand the concept of "number" is forced by parents or teachers to try to add two numbers, the child is destined to fail. The child becomes frustrated because understanding numbers is essential to learning how to add. Bitter and unnecessary failure results. Repetition of such experiences may lead to a lack of self-confidence. The same argument is true for any challenge—mental or physical.

Behavioral Traits

If your parents are friendly and affectionate, will you be the same? Is extroversion (being outgoing) or introversion (being withdrawn) an inherited predisposition? Strong evidence exists that extroversion (being outgoing) and introversion (being withdrawn) are genetically based traits (Plomin et al., 1990). In an important twin study important genetic factors were shown to underlie behavioral inhibition and shyness (Plomin et al., 1990). Between 20% and 45% of the variability in extroversion, emotional stability, agreeableness, and being conscientious results from genetic factors (Loehlin, 1992; Rose, 1995). Traits such as mental agility, religiosity, traditionalism, conduct problems, job satisfaction, cheerfulness, depressiveness, danger seeking, self-acceptability, self-control, hostility, and pessimism are strongly related in identical twins reared apart and much less related in fraternal twins reared apart (Rosenhan & Seligman, 1995). The heritability is a bit below .5 on many of these characteristics, much lower than the 1.00 that would show complete genetic influence. Environment has a tremendous influence on personality, but a genetic basis for various personality traits exists (Holden, 1987; Tellegen et al., 1988).

Genes affect personality by exerting their influence on behavior at a more biological level of organization via enzymes and hormones. Genes influence physiological functioning, which in turn affects behavior.

> ***True or False?***
> Whether someone has an outgoing personality or a tendency to be shy is partially the result of genetic factors.

Attitudes and Social Behaviors

Perhaps the most challenging finding is that a genetic component underlies our attitudes and social behaviors. For example, about 30% of variability in job satisfaction results from genetic factors (Arvey, Bouchard, Segal, & Abraham, 1989). Vocational attitudes and work values such as achievement, comfort, status, safety, and autonomy are also influenced by genes (Keller et al., 1992). Genes may play a part in how people perceive the degree of parental warmth within the family (Rowe, 1983). Genetic influence is found for individual differences in sibling interactions involving competition and positive and negative behaviors (Rende et al., 1992) as well as perceptions of self-worth and competence (McGuire et al., 1994).

Behaviors once considered solely the product of the environment are now being reevaluated as being at least partially genetically based (Azar, 1997). This is not as strange as it seems. If *all* behavior is seen as being a phenotype influenced by environmental and genetic components, the change in outlook does not seem so radical (Rende et al., 1992). Because geneticists presently know of *no* genes for specific attitudes or behaviors, such as competition or warmth, genetics must affect behavior and attitudes through other systems, possibly through personality, which has a genetic basis (Chipuer et al., 1993). For example, in the case of self-report ratings of family environment, extroverted identical twins raised apart might perceive their rearing families as warm because of their own general extroverted outlook on life (Chipuer et al., 1993).

One personality factor that affects job satisfaction is labeled "positive affect," and reflects the individual's ability to experience enthusiasm and feelings of gratification and trust. Another factor, "negative affect," reflects a tendency to be fearful, suspicious, and dissatisfied. Both show high genetic influence (Tellegen et al, 1988). These personality dimensions may be the source of genetic influences. Genetic differences in sensory structures such as taste, hearing, and sensitivity to touch could affect attitudes towards food and loud music (Tessor, 1993). Differences in body chemistry such as hormones, which are genetically influenced, may predispose individuals to react in different ways. Differences in temperament may also affect other attitudes.

No one is denying the tremendous influence of environmental factors on attitudes and social behaviors. For example, as much as 70% of the variance in job satisfaction between people is due to environmental differences. However, looking at all behaviors as expressions of both genetic and environmental factors is a new and challenging way of viewing behavior and attitudes.

Intelligence

Is intelligence partly inherited? The issue of genetics and intelligence is fraught with controversy (see the Controversial Issues box on pp. 62–63), beginning with the problem that there is no single accepted definition of intelligence (see Chapter 10). The existence of a genetic component in intelligence is well accepted. Some authorities claim that it is impossible to estimate true heritability figures for human traits because we cannot control the environment (Feldman & Lewontin, 1975). Highly intelligent people create more stimulating environments than do less intelligent people. Heritability studies are based not on individuals but on populations, and one

readiness The point in development at which a child has the necessary skills to master a new challenge.

must know a great deal about the population and the trait being measured to understand the meaning of these figures. For example, the heritability figure for a group's ability to sing passably is probably low, because practice, persistence, training, and motivation—all of which are environmental—are most important. However, these factors do not account for the vocal qualities of some great singers. Almost any child might be able to learn how to sing, but not every child can become a great vocalist, no matter how much training is received. The heritability index would be different for the group of passable singers and for a group of great singers.

Questions Students Often Ask

If IQ is genetically based, my child's intelligence will be somewhere between my spouse's and my own, right?

Sorry, you're wrong. An individual's intelligence is not some average of the parents'. Although you certainly inherit half your genes from mother and half from father, intelligence is a multifactorial trait that cannot be understood just through averaging. Some children will have intelligence scores that are above those measured for their parents; others may have intelligence scores that are below. Heredity and environment interact in a very complex manner to produce intelligence. Your child's environment is not the same as yours or your spouse's, nor is it an average of both of your past environments. In addition, environmental factors involving friends, school, the media, and so many others also influence intelligence. Genetic factors interact with these enviromental factors, producing a unique individual with special abilities.

The data from adoption studies generally indicate that the intelligence levels of adopted children are more closely related to their biological parents than to their adoptive parents (Horn, 1983; Jencks, 1972). In the Texas Adoption Project, 300 adoptive families were studied when the adopted children were about 8 years old. Although the correlations were low, the intelligence scores of adopted children correlated better with their biological parents than with their adoptive parents (Loehlin, Horn, & Willerman, 1989).

The results of twin studies also show some genetic influence on intelligence. In the Louisville Twin Study (Wilson, 1977, 1983), identical twins, fraternal twins, and nontwin siblings were compared. The intelligence scores of the siblings were similar to those of fraternal twins, which would be expected because they each have about 50% of genes in common. Identical twins were more similar than other pairs. In a study of identical twins reared apart, Thomas Bouchard (1984) found that the average correlation of identical twins reared in different environments was .76, which is higher than for either fraternal twins or nontwin siblings reared in the same household and closer to the value found for identical twins in the same homes. When Thomas Bouchard and colleagues (1990) followed identical and fraternal twins separated in infancy and reared apart, they found that an astounding 70% of the variance in intelligence was associated with genetics. These results have been criticized, and many scientists believe that this figure is too high (Adler, 1991). Most studies yield values closer to 50% (Plomin & DeFries, 1980), which would ascribe approximately half to genetic factors and the other half to the environment.

True or False?

Identical twins reared apart are more similar in intelligence than fraternal twins reared together.

Modifying Intelligence

Some psychologists are afraid that studies such as these will be misinterpreted as meaning that the environment is unimportant. This is certainly not the case, and any heritability figure should be interpreted cautiously. Problems in defining intelligence and difficulties in research design combine to provide ammunition for both sides (Walker & Emory, 1985; Horn, 1985). Even the same set of data can be interpreted differently, especially if one researcher concentrates on one area of the study while another person favors data from a different area (McCall, 1981). Most psychologists accept the fact that an important environmental element underlies intelligence, since none of the correlations in the data noted previously are perfect. No matter which estimate of heritability one uses, both environmental and genetic factors are involved in intelligence.

Intelligence can certainly be modified environmentally. A number of studies testify to the modifiability of intelligence, but one by Skeels (1966) stands out. In the 1930s Skeels worked in a bleak orphanage, where the children received little attention and were subjected to a rigid schedule. The children had no toys, and the environment was depressing. Skeels took a special interest in two girls who rocked back and forth and spent most of their time in bed. These two girls were later transferred to a mental institution, where they came under the influence of an older, retarded woman who showered them with attention. Their behavior changed, and they became much more responsive.

Skeels decided to find out more about this phenomenon. A number of children were removed from the sterile setting of the orphanage and allowed to live with older mentally retarded people in a better environment. The children's intelligence test scores improved an average of 29 points, and one child's intelligence test score actually rose by more than 50 points. The group that stayed in the depressing environment of the orphanage was found to have even lower intelligence scores than when the study had begun.

The conclusion that a change in environment accounts for an improvement in intelligence has been accepted by most psychologists today, although the methodology has

Controversial Issues: The Bell Curve—*The Most Controversial Book of Our Time*

Rarely has a book generated as much fury and passion as *The Bell Curve* by Richard Herrnstein and Charles Murray. It was the subject for cover stories in various magazines and was even brought up during a presidential press conference (Finn, 1995). As soon as it was published, reviews and letters to the editor decried the book, often calling it racist. Unfortunately, much of the public reaction was not based on a careful reading of the book but on what people had heard about it. Although the book deserves much criticism, most reviewers focused on only one of its ideas, the most controversial portion of the book, and totally ignored other areas of the book.

What is it about the book that brings out such passions? In order to summarize the book's ideas, we will look at each of the book's four parts, presenting the authors' ideas and then noting some of the more thoughtful criticisms.

Part One

American society has become more and more stratified according to intelligence level. Those with the highest intelligence attend certain universities, serve in certain positions in society, and reap the rewards. They form a cognitive elite and interact with each other, often marrying each other. Intelligence scores become even more important as jobs become more dependent on intellectual skills. The authors argue that general intelligence underlies performance in every job and is a function of both genetics and the environment. As environmental influences become more equal, genes become more important. The authors emphasize the importance of genetics in the variability of intelligence between people, claiming that the heritability figure lies between .40 and .80 (Herrnstein & Murray, 1994).

Criticism

The idea that intellectual skills are becoming more important in our society and that America is becoming stratified by intelligence is intriguing, even if overstated. However, the relationship between skill level and intelligence is high but by no means perfect (Heckman, 1995). Factors other than ability, such as attitude and motivation, may also affect performance in school and on the job. Ability level and education are not the same, and people with less ability but with the motivation to study and attend school can succeed and reap the economic rewards of education (Heckman, 1995).

Some psychologists argue that there are many different kinds of intelligence, not just a general intelligence, an idea that will be discussed in Chapter 10 (Gardner, 1994). A person may be linguistically intelligent but not mathematically intelligent. Others have criticized the authors' use of a particular intelligence test in their assessment for technical reasons (Heckman, 1995). Last, the idea that some genetic factors affect intelligence is certainly accepted by most psychologists (Snyderman & Rothman, 1987), but the extent of the contribution is very much in doubt and depends upon the environment as well as the skill being measured.

Part Two

The book's primary thesis is that intellectual ability can be adequately measured by intelligence tests and high intelligence is related to many desirable behaviors and low intelligence to many undesirable behaviors (Finn, 1995). Most people score somewhere in the middle. According to the authors, people with low intelligence scores are more likely to drop out of school, be unemployed, give birth to out-of-wedlock children, use poorer parenting strategies, commit crime, and are less likely to be politically active. Low intelligence is a better predictor of these conditions than socioeconomic status. The authors' statistical evidence is based upon studies of whites, thereby circumventing any claim that racial variables confound their results. They emphasize that they are talking about groups, not individuals. They recognize that the intelligence of an individual is a poor predictor of other aspects of the individual.

Criticism

Much of the evidence presented in this section is based upon correlations and does not demonstrate cause and effect. Is it poverty that leads to many of these social problems? Is it lack of intelligence? Is it some interaction between the two, with perhaps other variables being involved? Although the authors argue that it is lack of intelligence many psychologists disagree. Environmental factors are often poorly described in many studies, making it difficult to determine what factors contribute to an outcome.

Part Three

In the third and most controversial part of the book, the authors argue that differences in measured intelligence occur among various racial groups. They argue that differences in intelligence between Asian Americans, African Americans and whites are found at every socioeconomic level and are not the result of any cultural bias among these tests. Although they believe that genetic factors play an important part in intelligence, they do not absolutely state that differences between racial groups are caused by genetics (Azar, 1994). Nor do they deny the possibility.

Criticism

Although the authors argue that intelligence tests do not discriminate on the basis of group membership, some psychologists believe that these tests do not take cul-

Controversial Issues: The Bell Curve—*The Most Controversial Book of Our Time* *(continued)*

tural differences into consideration (Kaplan, 1996). Cultural and environmental factors are not identical and therefore any discussion of causation is bound to be problematic. The fact that differences exist does not tell us anything about what *causes* the differences. Furthermore, heritability estimates are computed within the white population and their usefulness in comparing intelligence scores between races is dubious at best (Kaplan, 1996).

A larger problem is the misunderstanding of the term *heritability.* If the heritability of IQ is placed at .6, this means that 60% of the differences in IQ scores among individuals in a large group (not a race) is caused by genetic differences. Most people incorrectly believe that 60% of an individual's IQ is determined by genes (Wright, 1995). The authors state, that just because a trait is genetically transmitted in individuals does not mean that group differences in that trait are also genetic in origin. Heritability differs in different environments. These estimates apply only to the environment under study and say nothing about its modifiability.

Part Four

The authors argue that efforts to raise intelligence through social programs have basically failed. Resources have been taken from the intellectually able of all groups and directed toward those at the lower end of the scale, thereby reducing the educational experiences of gifted children.

The authors argue that we face a situation in which a caste system will arise as the differences between the cognitive elite and the affluent grow and an underclass of people of all groups with low intellectual ability is created. The authors have little hope that environmental improvements will be sufficient. The cognitive elite's fear of the underclass will create what the authors call the "custodial state" in which social programs may be expanded in order to reduce violence, child abuse, and disorganization. The government will take over more parenting responsibilities from those who are inadequate for the job; stricter policing and more segregation by class will result.

The authors argue that inequality of endowments is a reality that we must all accept. Trying to pretend that intelligence is unimportant or is easily modifiable leads to programs that do not work. The authors argue that any programs to improve the lot of people should be pegged at the correct level. For example, if many women who have babies out of wedlock have below-average intelligence scores, educational strategies that rely on abstract or future-oriented strategies will be of little use. If many adults who are chronically unemployed and without job skills have low intelligence scores, then job training should take this into account.

The authors state that the goal should be to create a society in which every person can find a valued place in the community. Since social problems are concentrated on the relatively few who have low intelligence scores, most people do succeed. In order to help these at-risk people, the authors say that society should make it easier to make a living, begin a business, and fill out one's tax form. Government bureaucracy and rules have become so complicated that many people cannot deal with them; simplification is a solution. The authors argue for swifter justice and encourage birth control, but are against government intrusion into the decision of whether or not to have a child. However, the authors argue that people who have children outside marriage should not receive support from the government.

Criticism

Few people would deny the importance of focusing educational and training programs on the ability level of the people being served or of the need to simplify rules to allow everyone to find their place. However, these ideas are rather simplistic. The book's critics fear that people may believe that intelligence is determined by genetic differences and that it is not malleable (Wright, 1995). Intervention can work and cognitive skills improved, especially through intensive educational experiences (Kaplan, 1996; Nisbett, 1994). Believing that people's cognitive abilities are set in stone and genetically determined allows politicians to withdraw their support from programs to improve the cognitive functioning of children (Gates, 1994).

Conclusion: The Wrong Stuff

Unfortunately, Herrnstein and Murray needlessly chose to complicate their ideas with a rather tired and dubious analysis of race and intelligence. As America approaches the 21st century advanced schooling and cognitive ability are certainly important and questions about people with less schooling and/or ability deserve discussion. Questions about what we must do to provide the opportunities for all people at all levels of ability to live reasonable lives and be valued should be raised without any discussion of the nature of general versus specific intelligence and the genetic basis for intelligence and without presenting intellectual differences in a racial context (Heckman, 1995).

The Bell Curve could have served as a source of debate on issues of individuality, stratification, and the cost-benefit ratio of governmental programs. Unfortunately, the one question everyone will remember relates to race and intelligence, a question that should have been put to rest 25 years ago.

been severely criticized (Longstreth, 1981). The genetic influence on intelligence does not limit the malleability of intelligence (Scarr-Salapatek, 1975); rather, the genetic factor affects the elasticity of intelligence. Few would argue that any enrichment program could turn a child of below-average intelligence into a genius, but a radical change for the better in the environment would probably have a significant effect on a child's intelligence score. Several programs have attempted to lift the intelligence scores of young children through a variety of educational programs aimed both at children and at their parents. Many of the programs have been successful in the short term. (These programs are discussed futher in Chapter 8.)

True or False?
Intelligence scores can be modifed through a program of intense training.

Not How Much, But How

Perhaps you are impressed with the sheer array of physical, cognitive, and personality traits and characteristics that are affected by one's genetic endowment. Developmental psychologists are not as interested in the degree of genetic involvement as in how genetics and environmental factors interact. It is relatively easy to say that we must appreciate the constant genetic interactions between environmental and genetic factors in order to understand personality and development. But what is the nature of this interaction and how does it occur?

The Additive Model

In some cases, an additive model seems to work. Some birth defects such as club foot (in which one or both feet are turned downward and inward toward the ankle) or cleft palate (a condition characterized by an opening in the roof of the mouth involving the hard or soft palate or both) are multifactorial (Vergason, 1990). People are either more or less genetically predisposed to the condition and their vulnerability is caused by a number of genes, each of which contribute in an additive fashion. Those with a vulnerability above a particular threshold will develop the condition *if exposed to certain environmental conditions.* Environmental conditions are most likely to have the greatest impact on genetically predisposed individuals. The problem with this model is that it explains relatively few characteristics and most complex behaviors, such as aggression or sociability, are expressed on a continuum. All persons are more or less sociable so the question is not whether the person shows a particular behavior but to what extent that behavior is manifested.

The Range of Reaction Model

Most human behaviors are the result of a highly complex reciprocal interaction between genetic and environmental factors. How our genes are expressed depends upon the environment in which we exist; how we respond to elements of our environment depends partially on our genetic endowment.

One of the most difficult developmental phenomena for people to understand is why two people exposed to the same environments can respond so differently. One explanation uses the concept of a range of reaction (Gottesman, 1974; Gottesman & Shields, 1982). According to this model, each genotype can produce a range of different phenotypes (its range of reaction) depending upon the environment. One's genotype allows an individualized range of possible responses to the environment. Genetics sets a limit and it is the environment that determines the path. People differ in their responses to similar environments because their genetic makeup differs. Two children exposed to an environment, perhaps one that is enriched or extremely unstimulating, will have different responses. Each child would be helped by the stimulating environment and hurt by the unstimulating environment but would be affected to different degrees because of innate genetic differences.

Genetic factors form the limits of individual reactions and the environment determines which path the individual follows. The child's genotype for intellectual ability allows for a number of phenotypical paths; the environment determines which path the child follows. Some psychologists view this model as too rigid. We cannot know the individual's genotype, and each new environment may have different influences on developmental outcomes, which cannot be stated in advance of actual research investigation (Gottlieb, 1991) so the limits cannot be known.

The Genotype/Environment Interaction Model

Perhaps the most interesting and controversial model describing how genes and environmental factors interact is advanced by Sandra Scarr and Kathleen McCartney (1983), based upon work by Plomin and colleagues (Plomin, DeFries, & Loehlin, 1977). This model suggests three different genotype and environment effects.

The first is a *passive effect* in which parents provide a rearing environment that is in itself affected by the parents' genes. Verbal ability is in some measure hereditary and parents pass on genes for this ability as well as create an environment in which this ability can be developed. The environment created by the parents is, in part, shaped by their genetic endowment.

The second type of genotype/environment effect is called *evocative* because it represents the various responses that people with different genotypes evoke from the environment. For example, smiling, active babies receive more social stimulation than passive infants. Quick, attentive preschoolers experience more pleasant, mutually satisfying interactions than uncooperative, distractible youngsters. A genetic basis exists for these behaviors. Some of the similarities in child-rearing strategies may result from the genetic similarities of these children

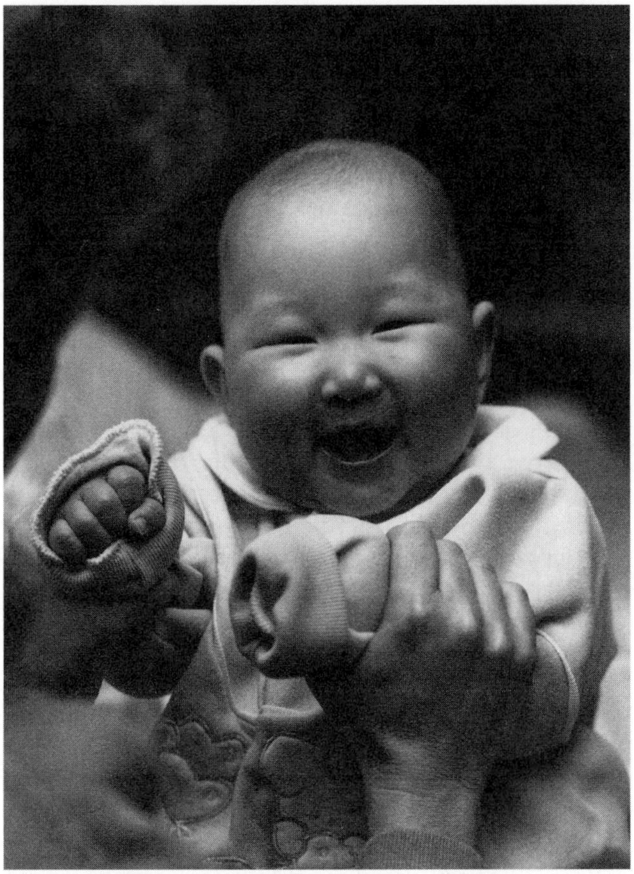

An active, smiling infant receives more social stimulation than a passive infant.

in that their behavior produces these parental reactions (Revelle, 1995). Some kinds of behavior evoke particular reactions from the environment.

The third kind of genotype/environment is the *active* kind and represents the child's selective attention to and learning from aspects of the environment that are influenced by the genotype. People seek out environments they find comfortable and stimulating. They actively select elements from the environment to pay attention to and learn about, sometimes called *niche picking* or *niche building.* These selections are related to the individual's motivation, personality, and intellectual ability, all of which are partially affected by genotype. This is the most powerful connection between people and environment. For example, someone who enjoys athletics pays attention to all kinds of athletic stimuli, selecting athletic activities and participating in them thus becoming a better athlete.

As children grow, the relative importance of the three kinds of effects changes. Although infants are active in structuring their experiences by selective attention, they do not have that much freedom or many opportunities. Their environments are created by parents and, according to this theory, reflect both genotype and environment. The effects of these passive genotype environments decline as the individual receives more opportunities to interact with the environment, replacing the passive effects with more active ones. The importance of evocative effects remains throughout life.

This model nicely explains the fact that fraternal twins, adopted children, and siblings seem to become more different as they grow older (McGue et al., 1993). The early home environment is similar but because of genetic differences their active/environment interactions differ. Identical twins, even when separated, remain more similar as they seek out similar experiences because they have the same genes. Scarr and McCartney (1983) argue that genes influence development by influencing the experiences children have, thereby becoming the quarterback of the nature/nurture team. Genes direct the course of human experience but experiential opportunities are required for development to occur. A restrictive environment does not allow children to develop their potential and abilities (Scarr, 1993).

This model offers a different way of explaining the dynamics behind a behavior. If we look at a child who is very warm and friendly and whose parents are the same, we might argue that the parents both model and reinforce such behaviors in their children. However, a genetic basis may underlie this and other traits in that parents create an environment consistent with their genes, the child evokes positive reinforcement by acting in a particular way partially because of genetic endowment, and lastly that the child seeks out these experiences partially because of genetic endowment.

One of the objections to the idea that genotypes drive phenotypes is that it relegates environmental influences such as child-rearing practices or intellectual stimulation to a lower level of interest (Baumrind, 1993). Parents may believe that if a genetic basis underlies behavior, they have no power to change things (Baumrind, 1993). Other critics are concerned that the overemphasis on genetic influences will discourage intervention efforts (Jackson, 1993). However, with the exception of some genetic diseases, heritability estimates can never be used to argue that the environment is unimportant. Often genetic factors do not even explain 50% of the variability. Genes do not fix behavior in concrete, although they may limit the possible outcome. People are not completely malleable. A shy individual cannot be converted into an extrovert, nor can an individual with mental retardation increase his or her intelligence score to 160 through some environmental interaction. There are limits, but environmental influences can be potent.

Appreciating Complexity

This new understanding of genetic/environmental interaction has implications for the three families described at the beginning of this chapter. Some information about possible genetic diseases might be helpful for adoptive parents; many professionals advocate that genetic family histories be made available to adoptive families (Bernhardt & Rauch, 1993). While accepting the fact of predisposition, parents must also appreciate the substantial effects that environment has on children. Parents can enhance the environment and allow children to maximize their abilities (Creedy, 1994).

Parents of twins should remember that although identical twins are certainly similar in many respects they differ in others. The stories of twins who show unusual similarities are trumpeted in the popular press but their differences are often not mentioned. Take the example of Raymond and Richard, identical twins separated shortly after birth. Raymond was adopted into a home of a rich doctor in the same town; Richard was adopted by a family that was always on the brink of financial disaster. Raymond had every advantage and never experienced poverty. Richard's father never had a job, and the family moved often. Though the boys were raised in different backgrounds, their intelligence scores were almost identical, and their character and emotional stability were as alike as if they had been raised together (McBroom, 1980). Raymond and Richard differed in many ways as well. Richard was more aggressive and self-reliant, probably because he had been protected less. Many identical twins differ greatly from each other (Ainslie, 1985). The parents of twins would be wise to recognize both the similarities and differences in their children.

The new evidence for genetic susceptibility to diseases holds much promise for developing tests that might identify those at high risk or offer very early detection of diseases, including some cancers such as breast cancer (Azar, 1995). Scientists may also discover what environmental elements trigger diseases. Yet, it is important to recognize that our knowledge is still in its infancy here and to understand the concept of a predisposition.

Some people yearn for the "good old days," when general statements about what was inherited and what wasn't could be made. Things were certainly easier then, even if they were almost always incorrect. The more modern view of the nature-nurture controversy is certainly more complicated and precludes making grandiose statements about heredity causing one thing and the environment causing another. It is clear that we cannot speak of nature without nurture or of nurture without nature (Creedy, 1994). Our present knowledge gives us the opportunity to marvel once again at the complicated process by which a tiny, one-cell fertilized egg develops into a person, who then, guided by both genetic endowment and environmental factors, can fulfill his or her great human promise.

Summary

1. The basic units of heredity are genes, which are carried on chromosomes. Human beings have 23 pairs of chromosomes. In the sex cells, however, the chromosome pair splits, so that each sex cell contains 23 chromosomes. The split is random, ensuring genetic individuality. The 23 chromosomes found in both the egg and the sperm cells combine during fertilization to maintain the same 46 chromosomes found in human beings.
2. The first 22 pairs of chromosomes appear to be alike, but the 23rd pair, the sex chromosomes, is different. A female has two X chromosomes, while the male has an X and a Y. The male determines the gender of the offspring, since he can contribute an X or a Y, while the female contributes only an X.
3. A trait that is expressed even if only one gene for it is present is called *dominant.* The trait that requires two genes to express itself is called *recessive.* The term *genotype* describes the genetic composition of the individual; the term *phenotype* refers to the person's observable characteristics. An individual's phenotype and genotype may be different.
4. When a particular characteristic is influenced by many genes, the mechanism of transmission is considered polygenic or multifactorial. The word *multifactorial* is sometimes used to denote characteristics influenced by a number of genes as well as by the environment.
5. Since the X chromosome is three times larger than the Y, a number of genes found on the X are not present on the Y. When there is some defect on the X, a male may not be able to counter its effects, since males possess only one X and the gene may not be found at all on the Y. Traits inherited in this manner are called *sex-linked traits.* Females normally do not show them, because they have two X chromosomes and only one normal gene is necessary to mask the effects of the defective gene. Hemophilia and color blindness are transmitted in this way.
6. The term *heritability* refers to that proportion of the measured variation between people in a given population on a particular characteristic that is the result of genetic factors. Scientists use twin and adoption studies to determine the extent to which a particular trait has a genetic basis. The agreement of twins on any particular characteristic is known as the *concordance rate.*
7. Genetic endowment affects one's physical characteristics. Since people react to one another on the basis of some of them, these characteristics can become socially important even if they are biologically trivial.
8. A number of genetic disorders have been discovered, including cystic fibrosis, Tay-Sachs disease, phenylketonuria, Huntington's disease, and sickle cell anemia. There is hope for helping people with such diseases through gene therapy.
9. Children with Down syndrome have 47 chromosomes rather than 46, the extra chromosome is found on the 21st chromosome. Such infants usually have mental retardation, although the degree of retardation varies.
10. There is a significant genetic component in schizophrenia and bipolar disorder, as well as in alcoholism. However, what is transmitted is not the

disorder itself, but rather a tendency or a predisposition to suffer from the disorder, given a particular environment.

11. Human beings are born with a temperament, an individual way of responding to the environment. Temperament shows considerable stability in infancy, and after infancy evidence for both stability and change exists. Different physiological responses may underlie temperament. Children's temperament may influence how others react to them. Genetic factors are also important in determining a child's rate of development.
12. Our genetic endowment influences our personality, probably by affecting our biological functioning. Several personality traits, such as introversion and extroversion, sociability, and activity level, appear to have a genetic basis.
13. All behaviors are the result of a complex interaction of genetics and the environment and these include characteristics such as attitudes and job satisfaction that are often thought to be completely environmental in origin. Genes may affect these behaviors through personality, genetic sensitivity to sensory structures, differences in body chemistry and temperament.
14. A genetic basis for intelligence exists, although there is much dispute over the heritability figures. An individual's environment greatly affects how these genes will be expressed. Education programs can raise the intelligence scores of children.
15. Some models seek to answer the question of how genes and environment interact to form a phenotype. The additive model notes that people are either more or less susceptible to showing a particular condition, which is manifested only if certain environmental factors are present. The model of range of reaction argues that for each genotype there are a number of possible outcomes and it is the environment that determines which is shown. Genetic factors restrict the number of outcomes. Three types of genetic/environmental interactions exist: *passive*, in which parents provide an environment for the child partly based upon their genotypes; *evocative*, in which the child's behaviors that are partially based upon the genotype influence how others react; and *active*, in which the individual, partially based upon the genotype, chooses which aspects of the environment to attend and to learn.

Multiple-Choice Questions

1. Which of the following statements is *incorrect?*
   a. Genetic influence affects children more than adults.
   b. Even if genetic factors underlie a particular behavior, it is subject to change.
   c. Traits such as extroversion and introversion are influenced by genes.
   d. Intelligence has a genetic basis.
2. You are looking at the chromosomes in the liver of a individual. You would expect to see ____________ chromosomes.
   a. 13
   b. 25
   c. 36
   d. 46
3. Twins that have exactly the same genes are called ____________ twins.
   a. monozygotic
   b. dizygotic
   c. heterozygotic
   d. immunozygotic
4. Mr. and Mrs. Jones have three boys. What is the chance of their next child being a girl?
   a. 75:25
   b. 60:40
   c. 50:50
   d. 75:25
5. If a characteristic requires only one gene to show itself the characteristic is considered:
   a. dominant.
   b. co-dominant.
   c. incompletely dominant.
   d. recessive.
6. Kerrie has brown eyes but uses blue contact lenses that make her eye color appear blue. She has changed her:
   a. genotype.
   b. phenotype.
   c. developmental quotient.
   d. secondary sex characteristic.
7. Studies of intelligence generally have shown that adopted children:
   a. are more similar to their adoptive parents than their biological parents.
   b. are more similar to their biological than adopted parents.
   c. do not resemble either their adoptive or biological parents in intellectual ability.
   d. resemble both their adoptive and biological parents to about the same degree.
8. A genetic disorder in which the production of mucus affects the respiratory system is:
   a. Huntington's disease.
   b. Down syndrome.
   c. cystic fibrosis.
   d. sickle cell anemia.
9. A genetic disease that is treated with a special diet is:
   a. cystic fibrosis.
   b. Huntington's disease.
   c. phenylketonuria.
   d. sickle cell anemia.

10. You are told that Jimmy has 47 chromosomes instead of 46, the extra chromosome being found on the 21st chromosome. Jimmy has:
    a. phenylketonuria.
    b. Down syndrome.
    c. fetal alcohol syndrome.
    d. Huntington's disease.
11. If a study shows that a genetic predisposition underlies a particular disease, the:
    a. environment can play no part in its development.
    b. environment may determine how severe the disorder is but not whether it will be shown.
    c. environment may still be important in determining whether the disorder is shown.
    d. disease must be potentially fatal.
12. Which of the following dimensions have been used to describe temperament?
    a. activity level
    b. emotionality
    c. sociability
    d. all of the above
13. Which of the following statements about temperament is false?
    a. Temperament appears to have a genetic basis.
    b. The use of the term "difficult" to describe temperament is controversial.
    c. Temperament is present at birth but its effects disappear by 1 year.
    d. A child's temperament may influence how other people treat him or her.
14. How can genetic factors operate to influence personality?
    a. Specific genes exist for extroversion and introversion.
    b. Genes may influence some hormones and other biological aspects of functioning.
    c. Personality can change one's genotype leading to changes in behaviors that underlie personality.
    d. All of the above are correct.
15. One problem in emphasizing the genetic influence on intelligence is that:
    a. people may believe that intelligence cannot be modified.
    b. the evidence does not indicate much, if any, genetic influence on intelligence.
    c. the genetic influence on intelligence is true only in childhood and not in adulthood.
    d. although genetic influence is shown by many studies, it is not accepted by most psychologists.
16. Perhaps the best way to look at the possibility that environmental improvement can change intelligence is to realize that:
    a. environmental improvement cannot alter intelligence.
    b. even modest improvements in environment can cause major, permanent increases in intelligence of about the same amount for everyone.
    c. environmental enrichment can alter intelligence, but always within limits.
    d. little or no research has been performed in this area and we do not know if any environmental enrichment can be successful.
17. Which of the following questions are developmental psychologists now most interested in?
    a. How much of a trait is influenced by genetics?
    b. Does genetic influence play any part in the development of the trait?
    c. How do genes and the environment interact to create a phenotype?
    d. If genetics underlies some trait, can the phenotype be changed?
18. A professor states that parents create the environment for their young child and the type of environment they create partially reflects the parents' genetic endowment. The professor is describing which genotype/environment interaction?
    a. active
    b. passive
    c. evocative
    d. primary
19. The fact that children who smile and are responsive get more social stimulation and attention than children who are withdrawn is an example of Scarr and McCartney's environmental/genetic effects called:
    a. evocative.
    b. passive.
    c. active.
    d. secondary.
20. One danger of our new appreciation of genetics is that people may:
    a. relegate the environment to a secondary status that it does not deserve.
    b. believe that most phenotypes have a genetic basis.
    c. believe that everyone suffers from a genetic disease of some type.
    d. seek to change the direction of medical research and emphasize genetic research.

Answers to Multiple-Choice Questions

1. a 2. d 3. a 4. c 5. a 6. b 7. b 8. c 9. c
10. b 11. c 12. d 13. c 14. b 15. a 16. c 17. c
18. b 19. a 20. a

Chapter 4

Prenatal Development and Birth

Chapter Outline

Are the Following Statements True or False?

1. The first organ to function prenatally is the liver, which detoxifies potentially dangerous chemicals.
2. The presence of people who smoke in the pregnant woman's environment can adversely affect the birth weight of the child.
3. The damage done by exposure to cocaine in the womb is permanent and environmental improvement does not seem to have any positive effect on the cocaine-exposed child.
4. The virus that causes AIDS can be transmitted through breast milk.
5. An Rh problem is caused by a virus that can be combatted by the use of antibiotics.
6. Older fathers, those who have their first child after age 35, spend more time with their children and are more nurturant than fathers in their 20s.
7. Once a woman has had one cesarean section to deliver a child, all later deliveries must also be by cesarean section.
8. The Lamaze method of birth emphasizes the importance of leaving the mother alone to meditate on her birth experience.
9. Premature infants are no more at risk for developmental problems than are infants born at term.
10. The United States has a lower infant mortality rate than every other industrialized country with the exception of Japan.

Answers to True-False Statements 1. False: see p. 71 2. True 3. False: see p. 75 4. True 5. False: see p. 77 6. True 7. False: see p. 83 8. False: see p. 84 9. False: see p. 85 10. False: see p. 86

The First Odyssey

Look through the window of a hospital nursery and watch the infants for a few moments. Some are sleeping, some fussing, and some crying. These infants all seem equally ready to begin their human odyssey. But is this so? In reality, some of these infants are already starting at a disadvantage because of adverse experiences in the womb and during the birth process. Every child deserves a fair chance to develop in a healthy manner but too often this is not the case because exposure to some agent before or during pregnancy may compromise development.

A number of environmental, physical, and viral agents can cause difficulties during pregnancy. Although the threats are real enough, the great majority of infants develop normally and emerge from the birth canal ready for life. About 7% of all the live births in the United states have low birth weight and 3%–7% percent have some recognizable birth defect (Wyrobek, 1993). Knowledge of the possible dangers allows prospective parents to alter their behavior to give their child the best start possible.

Prenatal Development

People often do not appreciate the importance of what transpires during the prenatal period and act as though it has no relationship to life outside the womb (Hofer, 1988). This is changing as scientific research is communicated to the public and people begin to appreciate the importance of the prenatal period.

The Beginning During ovulation, one egg is allowed to pass into the fallopian tube, where it is exposed to any sperm that are present. Although many sperm may surround the egg cell, only one will penetrate the cell's outer wall. At the moment of conception, the mother's egg cell is fertilized by the father's sperm. When this occurs, there is a rearrangement and an exchange of genetic material, and the genetic endowment of the new being is set for life. This fertilized egg, or **zygote,** continues to travel down the tube into the uterus, or womb.

In some cases, two eggs may pass into the fallopian tubes and be fertilized by two different sperm. The result is dizygotic, or fraternal, twins, two separately developing organisms that are no more genetically similar than any other pair of siblings. Identical twins develop from a single egg and a single sperm. Cell division takes place very early in development, and these twins have an identical genetic makeup.

The Germinal Stage It takes anywhere from a week to 10 days or so for the fertilized egg to embed itself in the lining of the uterus. During this period, called the **germinal stage,** the fertilized egg divides again and again and begins the process of specialization that results in the formation of its organs. On the second day, about 30 hours after fertilization, the cell divides into two new cells (Singer & Hilgard, 1978). At 60 hours, the two cells divide to become four cells. This division continues until, at the end of the first week, over 100 cells are present. On the fifth day after conception the cells rearrange to form a cavity. The hollow ball of cells is now called a **blastocyst.** The majority of cells are found in the outer

zygote A fertilized egg.

germinal stage The earliest stage of prenatal development, lasting from conception to about 2 weeks.

blastocyst The stage of development in which the organism consists of layers of cells around a central cavity forming a hollow sphere.

layer, called *trophoblast;* the smaller number are found in the inner layer, called the *inner cell mass* (Moore & Persaud, 1993). The outer layer will become structures that enable the embryo to survive, including the yolk sac, the allantois, the amnion, and the chorion. The yolk sac produces blood cells until the developing organism can do so on its own, at which point it disappears. The allantois forms the umbilical cord and the blood vessels in the placenta. The amnion eventually envelops the organism, holding the amniotic fluid, which protects the organism. The chorion becomes the lining of the placenta and the inner cell mass becomes the embryo.

The survival of the fertilized egg depends on the egg's ability to burrow into the lining of the mother's uterus and obtain nourishment from the mother's system. This process is called **implantation,** which begins at the end of the first week and is completed by the end of the second week (Moore & Persaud, 1993). Digestive enzymes are secreted that allow the blastocyst to embed itself in the maternal tissues; the blastocyst now develops the ability to feed off its host.

At about 7 or 8 days the inner cell mass has differentiated into two distinct layers: the *ectoderm* and the *endoderm.* The ectoderm will develop into the organism's external coverings, including the skin, hair, sense organs, and nervous system. The endoderm becomes the digestive system, the respiratory system, and the glands. At about the 16th day, another layer, the *mesoderm,* appears between the ectoderm and endoderm and develops into the muscles, connective tissues, and the circulatory and excretory systems.

As development continues, the amnion swells and covers the developing organism. The trophoblast develops projections, or villi, which penetrate the uterine wall, allowing the developing organism to get nutrients more efficiently. The villi on one side organize into the placenta, which is connected to the developing organism by the umbilical cord. The placenta delivers nutrients, removes wastes, and helps combat infection. The germ cell at the end of the first 2 weeks of life measures about 1/175 inch long (Annis, 1978).

The Embryonic Stage The **embryonic stage** begins at 2 weeks and ends at about 8 weeks after conception. At 2 weeks the tiny mass has just begun to depend on its mother for everything. It is hardly recognizable as a human being. Six weeks later, all the vital body organs will be present (Annis, 1978). During the embryonic period, changes occur at a breathtaking pace. Each system's development follows a particular sequence. On day 31, the shoulders, arms, and hands develop; on day 33, the fingers develop; and on day 34 through day 36, the thumb is completed. The organs form and begin to function in a primitive manner. The first organ to function is the heart, which circulates the blood to the placenta and throughout the developing body by the end of the third week (Moore & Persaud, 1993). The circulatory system of the embryo is completely separated from the mother's, and no exchange of blood occurs. All exchanges of nutrients and oxygen occur by diffusion. By the end of the first month, the ears, nose, and mouth begin to form, and arms and legs make their appearance as buds. Fingers and toes become defined. Internal organs are now rapidly developing. During this time of extremely rapid growth, the organism is most vulnerable to environmental insult. The embryo is capable of some primitive behavioral reactions. Reflex action occurs as early as the middle of the seventh week and the beginning of the eighth. If the mouth is stimulated, the embryo flexes its neck to the opposite side.

True or False?
The first organ to function prenatally is the liver, which detoxifies potentially dangerous chemicals.

The Fetal Stage During the last 7 months of development, the **fetal stage,** the fetus grows and develops at a tremendous rate. At the beginning of the third month the average fetus is 1¼ inches long and weighs less than ⅓ ounce. By the end of the third month, it is 3 inches long and weighs 1 ounce. Hormonal action during this third month causes the genitals to become defined. If the male hormone testosterone is secreted into the fetal system, it causes the development of male genitalia. In the absence of the male hormone, the fetus will develop female organs. During this third month the major organs are completed and bones begin to appear and muscles develop. The fetus now moves, kicks its legs, swallows and digests the amniotic fluid, and removes waste products through urination.

During the fourth month the fetus continues to grow at a fantastic pace. By the end of this month, it is 6 inches long and weighs 6 ounces. As it grows, it develops internally. By the fifth month the fetus sleeps and wakes at regular intervals, and some reflexes, such as hiccupping and swallowing, have developed. The fetus cries and may suck a thumb. At this point, the fetal movements are likely to be felt by the mother, although some mothers experience movement earlier. This is known as *quickening.* During the sixth month, the fetus attains a weight of about 2 pounds and a length of 14 inches. The facial features are clearly in evidence, and the fetus can make a fist.

During the last 3 prenatal months the fetus gains a layer of fat that will help keep the infant warm after birth. By the end of the 28th week, the fetus measures about 17 inches and weighs about 3 pounds. Traditionally, 7

implantation The process by which the fertilized egg burrows into the lining of the mother's uterus and obtains nourishment from her system.

embryonic stage The stage of prenatal development, from about 2 weeks to about 8 weeks, when bone cells begin to replace cartilage.

fetal stage The stage of prenatal development that begins at about 8 weeks and continues until birth.

months is considered the age of viability because the fetus has a reasonable chance of survival if born at this time. However, there is considerable individual variation in weight, health, and developmental readiness; some 7-month-old fetuses are more ready than others for an independent existence.

During the last 2 prenatal months, the fetus gains about half a pound a week. Its heretofore red, wrinkled appearance disappears somewhat as it puts on weight. The development of the lungs is especially important during these last months. At the end of its normal period of prenatal development (approximately 266 days), the infant is born. The entire process of fetal development proceeds without any need for conscious maternal intervention. It is directed by genetic forces that we are only just beginning to understand. However, the fetus is also affected by the environment.

Developmental Myths

People once believed that everything a woman did could have an effect on the fetus. Unusual occurrences in a pregnant woman's daily life were thought to influence the personality and physical well-being of the child. For instance, if a rabbit crossed the woman's path, some believed that the child would be born with a harelip (Annis, 1978). If the mother ate or squashed strawberries, the baby would have a strawberry-shaped birthmark. This belief in total environmental control was replaced by the idea that nothing the mother did really mattered. The placenta was viewed as a barrier that did not allow any dangerous elements into the infant's environment and rendered various poisons harmless.

In the 1960s this view was shattered when a medication called thalidomide taken by pregnant women between the fourth and sixth week of pregnancy for morning sickness was linked to the birth of thousands of infants in Europe with missing or deformed arms and sometimes legs (Cook, Petersen, & Moore, 1990). Far from being a total barrier, the placenta allows a number of substances to pass into the system of the fetus. Although we no longer believe the superstitions about rabbits and strawberries, we know that the environment greatly affects the health of the fetus.

The Developing Organism and the Environment

The embryo and fetus can be affected by many viruses, chemicals, and medications. Any agent that causes a birth defect is called a **teratogen.** The effects of these agents depend upon the type of agent, the dosage, and the genetic characteristics of the fetus. The time at which the fetus is exposed is also important, because some teratogens are more likely to produce birth defects if they are ingested at a certain time during the pregnancy. This is called the **critical period,** during which a developing organism is most susceptible to a particular teratogen (Moore & Persaud, 1993). The time at which the organ is developing most rapidly is the period of greatest vulnerability. Figure 4.1 shows the critical periods for the major organs; some organs such as the brain, teeth, and skeletal system have critical periods that extend into childhood.

Medication

A number of medications have been linked to birth defects, and the research findings on others are contradictory. Tetracycline, a commonly prescribed antibiotic, has been linked to permanent discoloration of the teeth and defective bone growth (March of Dimes, 1983). Some antibiotics seem safe, but our knowledge of most is limited (Knothe & Dette, 1985). Most teratogenic drugs cause defects that are noticeable at birth; one drug that does not fit this pattern is the synthetic estrogen called diethylstilbestrol (DES). From the 1940s through 1971 DES was widely administered to pregnant women who had a history of diabetes or who were apt to have miscarriages (N.Y.S. Department of Health, 1979). There seemed to be little cause for concern because the children born to these women were healthy as infants, but in 1971 a link was found between prenatal administration of DES and eight cases of a kind of cervical cancer usually found only in women over 50 years. The chances of a daughter born to a mother who took DES developing the cancerous condition are about 1 or 2 in every 1000 (Orenberg, 1981). However, many DES daughters suffer from genital tract abnormalities. All women whose mothers took the drug should be watched carefully by their doctors. DES sons are also affected by the drug, sometimes experiencing genital tract abnormalities and benign cysts that require attention from a urologist (N.Y.S. Department of Health, 1979). The DES story demonstrates that the effects of drugs taken during the prenatal stage may not show up for some time.

Questions Students Often Ask

Why is it so difficult to say for certain that a particular substance leads to this or that birth defect?

Researching teratogens is difficult. Even if a doctor finds that a parent took a particular medication or drug, it would still be difficult in most circumstances to ascribe the birth defect to this drug. People may have ingested a number of such drugs. In addition, people may not remember what they did during their pregnancy. Most people do not know much about their level of exposure to the drug. Many studies are correlational; that is, a relationship is found between a substance and some birth defect. This makes cause and effect difficult to establish. Because of these and other problems, scientists are often very careful about the statements they make.

teratogen Any agent that causes birth defects.

critical period The period during which a particular event has its greatest impact.

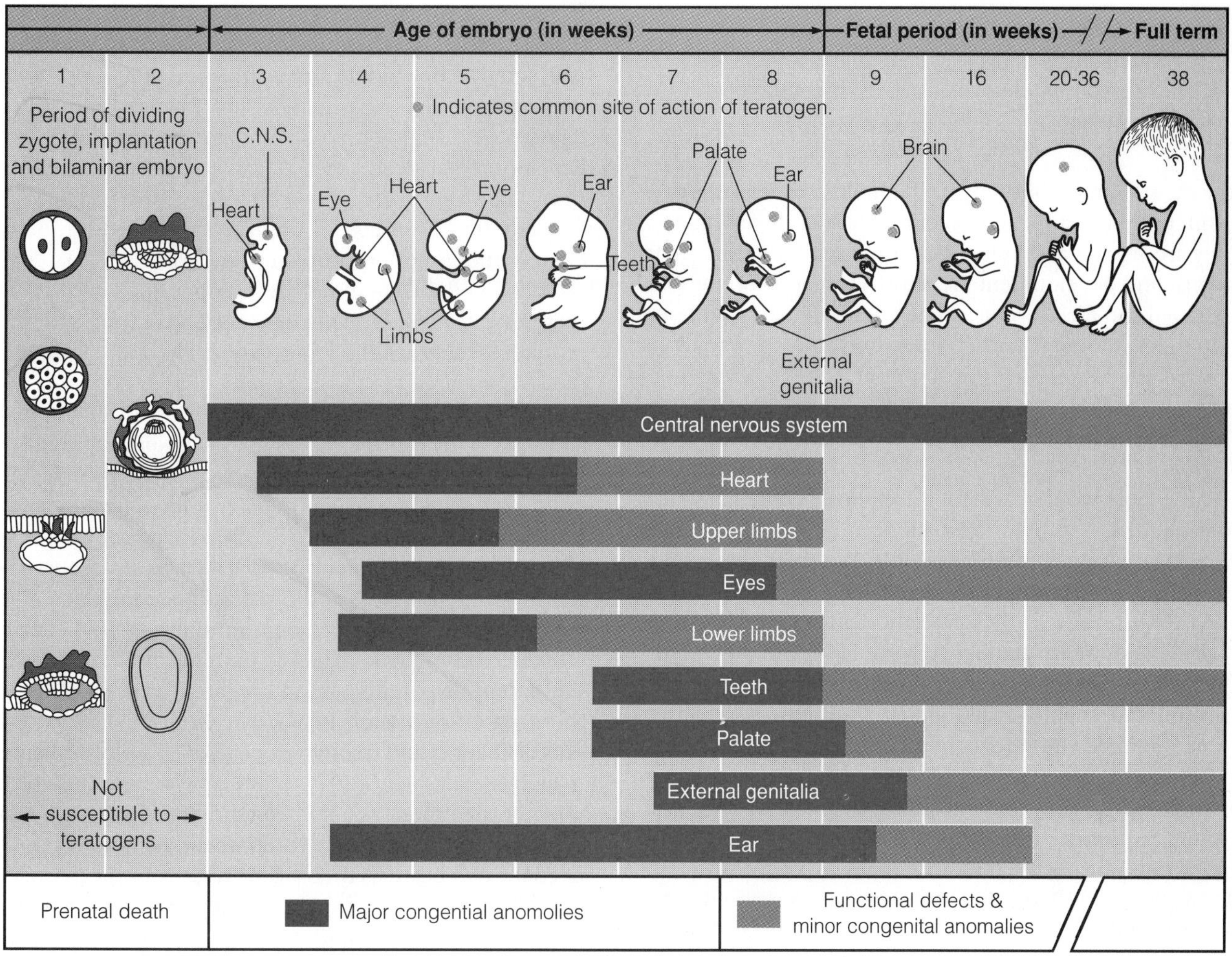

Figure 4.1
Critical Periods in Prenatal Development The darkest purple color shows the time during which that particular organ is at greatest risk.
Source: Moore & Persaud, 1993.

Drugs: Legal and Illegal

Most drugs taken during pregnancy are not prescribed by doctors. They are available either legally, such as nicotine and alcohol, or illegally, such as narcotics. The National Institute on Drug Abuse estimates that between 375,000 and 739,000 drug-exposed children are born each year—about 18% of all newborns in the United States (Sautter, 1992). Sometimes the damage is obvious whereas at other times it may not be noticed for a number of years.

Nicotine About 17% of all pregnant women smoke cigarettes during their pregnancy, although some estimates are a bit higher (Chomitz et al., 1995; Lancashire, 1995). Although the effects of nicotine are dose related, smokers are twice as likely as nonsmokers to have low-birth-weight babies (Lancashire, 1995). The infants of smokers weigh an average of 200 grams (about half a pound) less than infants of nonsmokers (Vorhees & Mollnow, 1987). In addition, infants of mothers who smoke are shorter; have smaller head, chest, arm, and thigh circumferences; and have lower neurological scores than the infants of nonsmokers (Metcoff et al., 1989). Maternal smoking is also linked to miscarriages and increased risk of sudden infant death syndrome. Women who stop smoking during pregnancy give birth to heavier infants (Floyd et al., 1993; Lieberman et al., 1995). Injurious long-term effects from maternal smoking include increased risk of academic difficulties, especially in reading; hyperactivity; and poor attention span (Naeye & Peters, 1984; Streissguth et al., 1984). Some evidence even exists that maternal smoking during pregnancy may sensitize the fetus' brain to the effects of nicotine and other chemicals in tobacco, making it more likely that the child will smoke when an adolescent. Various chemicals may alter the release of neurotransmitters in the brain and change the threshold of these systems (Kandel, Wu, & Davies, 1995).

Exposure to smoke in the environment, called *passive smoking,* is also related to lower birth weight (Martinez et al., 1994). Nonsmoking pregnant women exposed to cigarette smoke give birth to infants who weigh less than the infants of pregnant women who are not exposed to cigarette smoke in the environment (Eskenazi, Prehn, & Christianson, 1995).

> ***True or False?***
> The presence of people who smoke in the pregnant woman's environment can adversely affect the birth weight of the child.

Alcohol Some children of alcoholic mothers show a distinct physical appearance and pattern of development. They are shorter and lighter than other children, and their growth and development are slow. They show a number of cranial and facial abnormalities, heart defects, and poor motor development and coordination, and they tend to be mentally retarded (Sampson et al., 1995). Their mortality rate is also higher than average (Jones et al., 1974). These characteristics describe the **fetal alcohol syndrome.**

Since most women are not alcoholics, people generally consider the negative consequences of drinking something that happens to other people. However, even moderate drinking can affect the fetus. The term **fetal alcohol effect** is used to describe the less severe spectrum of damage done by alcohol (Casiro, 1994; Chomitz et al., 1995). Most common among these problems are severe learning and cognitive disabilities. The fetus is sensitive to alcohol, and the effects of alcohol on the fetus seem to be dose related, with lower doses resulting in some but not all of the characteristics of fetal alcohol syndrome. As little as one drink a day increases the risk of miscarriage during the middle months of pregnancy (Harlap & Shiono, 1980), and can lead to decreased fetal growth (Mills et al., 1984). Prenatal alcohol exposure to 1.5 ounces of alcohol per day is related to a decrease in psychomotor skills (Larroque et al., 1995).

Commonly Used Illegal Drugs Cocaine taken during pregnancy constricts the blood vessels in the placenta, decreasing blood flow to the fetus and increasing uterine contractions. The use of cocaine during pregnancy is related to infant mortality, low birth weight, prematurity, and a number of medical problems including neurological damage and malformed heart, lung, and digestive systems (Neuspiel & Hamel, 1991; Scherling, 1994). Head circumference is often smaller, and these infants are also shorter (Hadeed & Siegel, 1989). Infants exposed to cocaine in the womb are more irritable and tremulous than the average newborn and are often unable to respond to the human voice or face (Berger et al., 1990). They show more stress-related behavior (Eisen et al., 1991), and do not seem to be able to interact with others. They are emotionally labile and respond poorly to attempts to comfort them (Chasnoff, 1985, 1987).

fetal alcohol syndrome A number of characteristics—including retardation, facial abnormalities, growth defects, and poor coordination—caused by maternal alcohol consumption.

fetal alcohol effect An umbrella term used to describe damage to a child caused by the mother's imbibing alcohol during pregnancy that is somewhat less pronounced than fetal alcohol syndrome.

Many such infants are jittery and have an abnormally high-pitched cry. They are overwhelmed by sensations, and some stiffen while being touched. Some cry when they hear music or voices or are brought into bright lights; others simply tune out and go to sleep. They show developmental delays in walking and talking, and some throw tantrums. Later, these children show language delays, emotional difficulties, impulsivity, low frustration tolerance, and attention problems (Scherling, 1994).

These initial difficulties are compounded by the fact that these troubled infants may not receive the care they require. Sometimes the babies are abandoned in the hospital to be raised by a foster family or a grandparent who may or may not be capable of dealing with infants who show so many behavioral and physical difficulties. If the infant is taken away after birth by welfare agencies, the child's lot may be a string of foster homes. Children who remain with their mother or both parents are often subjected to an environment of poverty and inadequate parenting, which increases the risk of poor intellectual development. The parents often continue to use cocaine, which exposes the infants to extreme poverty because the parent or parents use all the family resources to buy the drug (Wrightman, 1991). The lifestyle of these parents is chaotic, and the rate of neglect and physical abuse is high (Besharov, 1989). Cocaine abusers are difficult to retain in treatment and it is common for these parents to relapse into cocaine use. Often, these parents claim the need for child care as their major reason for dropping out from drug treatment programs because many treatment facilities require separations for 18 months or longer. Some experimentation with allowing cocaine-abusing women in therapeutic communities to live with their children during treatment shows that these women remain significantly longer in treatment (Hughes et al., 1995).

The parenting techniques used by cocaine-addicted mothers are substandard. The mothers are rigid and show a lack of pleasure in relating to their infants, are not responsive to their infants, and show very little emotional involvement with them (Burns et al., 1991). The child's initial problems in relating to others are compounded by the parent's own difficulties, and the child often develops various cognitive and behavioral problems involving either withdrawal or aggressiveness (Rist, 1990). These infants experience congenital problems resulting from prenatal exposure and subsequent damage resulting from poor parenting and the deficient environments in which they spend their early years.

Some experts argue that the media has sensationalized the problem, often presenting the worst-case scenario. Daniel Griffith (1992), a prominent researcher in the field, notes that if we were to believe the media we would incorrectly think that all cocaine-exposed children were severely affected, that little can be done for them, and that all medical, behavioral, and learning problems shown by these children are caused directly by their exposure to cocaine. In reality, great individual differences exist in the behavior of children exposed to cocaine in utero. Many of the problems, especially oversensitivity to stimuli and problems in self-regulation, are caused by both the exposure to cocaine and other drugs in utero as well as the deficient environment in which so many of these infants are raised.

The most damaging belief is that nothing can be done for these children. This is simply not true, and society should not give up on these children (Mayes et al., 1992). Growing evidence exists that early treatment to eliminate drug use in pregnant mothers, along with prenatal care and follow-up examinations can improve the long-term behavioral competence of these cocaine-exposed infants (Chasnoff et al., 1992). When pregnant women who abused cocaine and other drugs received prenatal care, nutritional counseling, and drug treatment, the majority of their infants were carried to full term, with premature infants born less than a month early. These children showed many of the classical signs of drug exposure, but they were helped when their parents were taught effective child-rearing strategies. Since these infants showed a deficiency in the quiet-alert state, a state during which infants are best able to process information, care-givers were taught to use comforting techniques such as swaddling, offering pacifiers, and vertical rocking. The parents were taught how to maintain an appropriate environment as well as how to recognize when the child was approaching overstimulation. The majority of these children showed little difference at 3, 6, 12, 18, and 24 months from a group of nonexposed infants (Griffith, 1992). Only one third showed delays in language development and problems in attention and self-regulation. Early intervention to stop the drug use and to improve the environment can improve life for these children (Zuckerman & Frank, 1992). It is evident that cocaine-exposed infants and their families require immediate and intensive help if these infants are to have any chance of developing in a healthy manner.

> ***True or False?***
> The damage done by exposure to cocaine in the womb is permanent and environmental improvement does not seem to have any positive effect on the cocaine-exposed child.

The effects of marijuana smoking on the fetus are inconsistent, with some studies showing adverse effects. The use of marijuana has been linked to poor fetal growth and subtle neurological problems (Lester & Dreher, 1989; Zuckerman et al., 1989). Some studies have found behavioral differences for infants of mothers who are regular marijuana users, including lack of response to a light stimulus, tremors, and increased startling (Vorhees & Mollnow, 1987).

Babies of heroin addicts are born addicted to heroin and must go through withdrawal. They often show disturbances in activity level, attention span, and sleep patterns (Householder et al., 1982). Because these infants are frequently premature and very small, this is sometimes a life-or-death situation.

Over-the-Counter Drugs Some over-the-counter drugs can also be dangerous. If taken in the later months of pregnancy, aspirin may adversely affect blood clotting in both mother and baby (March of Dimes, 1983). Even normal doses of aspirin in the final months of pregnancy can prolong labor and pregnancy and cause maternal heavy bleeding both before and after birth (Mendelson & Mello, 1985).

Pollution and Radiation Pollution and radiation can also adversely affect the fetus and are therefore causes for concern. For example, PCB, a contaminant sometimes found in water and fish, can cause immature motor responses, behavioral abnormalities, and deficits in information-processing abilities such as visual discrimination (Jacobson et al., 1984; Jacobson et al., 1992). Exposure to relatively common compounds once used as insulating materials in electrical equipment is related to neurological and intellectual difficulties in infants and young children (Jacobson & Jacobson, 1996). These compounds have been banned but their residue remains and exposure can lead to developmental deficits.

Radiation has been linked to fetal deaths as well as to a number of structural defects in infants. There is no safe level of radiation. Because radiation accumulates in the body, repeated x-rays may be dangerous. Although there are times when an x-ray is medically required, pregnant women should avoid radiation as much as possible.

Disease and Pregnancy

Rubella (commonly called *German measles*) is generally a very mild disease, yet the effects of the rubella virus on a developing embryo can cause serious disorders, such as congenital cataracts and other eye disorders, ear damage, congenital heart disease, and central nervous system damage as well as fetal death (Rich, 1991). With the advent of a vaccine for rubella, epidemics should become a thing of the past. Unfortunately, not every child is being protected, and isolated cases of rubella-induced defects still occur.

Venereal Disease In recent years increased attention has been paid to the effects of **acquired immune deficiency syndrome (AIDS),** herpes, syphilis, gonorrhea, and chlamydia on the fetus. Evidence is great that such diseases, which are usually transmitted during sexual intercourse, pose significant dangers to the developing fetus.

Women who have herpes can transmit it to the baby during the birth process. If the herpes virus reaches the baby's organs or brain, the prognosis is not good, and

rubella A disease responsible for many cases of birth defects.

AIDS (acquired immune deficiency syndrome) A fatal disorder affecting the immunological system, leading to inability to fight off disease.

more than half may die (Corey & Spear, 1986). Antiviral treatment reduces the mortality rate, but impairment is still common (Stagno & Whitely, 1985). To prevent the spread of the disease, doctors often check for lesions in the birth canal and may recommend a cesarean section (discussed later in the chapter). Syphilis in the expectant mother can cause a number of defects in the infant, including bone and facial deformities and nerve deafness, as well as fetal death. A number of those children who survive birth will develop syphilis. If the mother-to-be receives prompt treatment, the fetus may not be infected. Many women who have gonorrhea may be totally unaware of it, since they often do not show any outward symptoms. Fetuses exposed to gonorrhea are often premature and blind. The standard practice of placing a protective solution in an infant's eyes at birth is to protect the baby against blindness in case the mother has gonorrhea. In many hospitals, erythromycin or tetracycline is used. Erythromycin combats chlamydia, an infection that can also cause blindness in newborns (Simkin, Whalley, & Keppler, 1984). Chlamydia is more common than gonorrhea and the infants of mothers with the disease may develop conjunctivitis and pneumonia and other lung disorders (Schachter, 1989). Chlamydia can also cause miscarriage, low birth weight, and infant death (March of Dimes, 1989). Unfortunately, women with chlamydia may not know that they are infected because they are often asymptomatic, but newer tests allow for better screening. Once the disease is diagnosed, it is relatively easy to cure.

Today, the gravest concern centers on AIDS, which is a fatal disease that affects the immunological system and leads to an inability to fight off disease (Rosenberg & Fauci, 1994). It is caused by a virus called the *human immunodeficiency virus (HIV).* It is estimated that 1 in 2200 infants born each year in the United States is infected with HIV (Onorato, Gwinn, & Dondero, 1994). AIDS is a worldwide concern; the World Health Organization projects that by the year 2000, 3 million women and children will have died from HIV-related disease and 10 million children will be born infected (Mofenson & Wolinsky, 1994; Wilfert, 1996).

Virtually all new cases of pediatric AIDS are caused by transmission of the virus prenatally or at birth (Anderson, Sedmak, & Lairmore, 1994; Rogers, Schochetman, & Roff, 1994). AIDS may also be transmitted through the breast milk of an HIV-positive mother (Landau-Stanton & Clements, 1993).

True or False?
The virus that causes AIDS can be transmitted through breast milk.

The rate of HIV transmission between mother and child and the factors that determine such transmission remain somewhat uncertain (Futterman & Hein, 1994). Studies in the United States and other Western countries describe rates of transmission between 15% and 40% (Dickover et al., 1996; Oxtoby, 1994). A number of factors have been suggested as predicting the likelihood of such transmission, including advanced HIV disease represented by altered immune status and a high level of the virus in the system (Anderson et al., 1994; Mofenson & Wolinsky, 1994). Other studies suggest that a high risk of transmission exists with women who become HIV positive during pregnancy itself (Oxtoby, 1994).

Infants infected with the virus are more likely than adults to develop symptoms of AIDS (Koup & Wilson, 1994; Sande, 1986). They show a more rapid progression from latent infection to symptoms to death for reasons that are unknown (Koup & Wilson, 1994). The pregnant woman is also more susceptible to various viral, bacterial, and fungal infections and is more likely to die from these infections (Minkoff & Duerr, 1994). Although AIDS is certainly found in every ethnic and socioeconomic level, low-income, urban women and children are disproportionately affected (Capell et al., 1992). Of all children who acquired the virus through transmission from mother to child, 59% are among African-American children and 26% are Latino children (Oxtoby, 1994). The reason is thought to be that many of these minority group women live in poor inner-city communities in which the prevalence of HIV infection among drug users is high.

The prognosis for these infants is very poor, and the probability of long-term survival is low at the present time (Peckham & Gibb, 1995). Two distinct patterns have emerged. Some infants have profound immune deficiency and opportunistic infections during the first months of life and most of these children die before the age of 5. AIDS is the seventh leading cause of death in the United States for children between the ages of 1 and 4 years. A larger group gradually develops the immune deficiency over a period of several years up to age 10 and show a pattern of disease development and mortality similar to that found in adults (Mayaux et al., 1996). These children with HIV live into the elementary school age and sometimes beyond.

The question of testing pregnant women for HIV is controversial. Some people argue that such information is vital and testing should be mandatory, which means without the permission or even the knowledge of the woman (Twomey & Fletcher, 1994). Opponents of mandatory testing argue that women at highest risk are most likely to receive poor, late, or no prenatal care, which would limit the benefits of the program. The program may also violate a person's civil rights. Today testing pregnant women for the HIV virus is highly recommended and is done voluntarily and in a routine manner (Cotton et al., 1994). One reason for the emphasis on early testing is the finding that giving AZT (zidovudine) to HIV-positive women during pregnancy prevents the transmission of AIDS in many cases (Dickover et al., 1996; Sperling et al., 1996). With this possible preventive treatment available, such screening is highly desirable (Twomey & Fletcher, 1994).

The Mother's Medical Condition

Maternal hypertension is related to poor fetal growth, increased perinatal death, and many neurological and developmental problems. Maternal diabetes is also related to many birth defects. These disorders are dangerous to the mother as well. In both cases, as with so many other maternal medical conditions, competent medical advice and prompt treatment may improve the chances of delivering a healthy child and safeguarding the mother's health.

With many more women planning their first pregnancy when they are over 30 years and so many teens giving birth, a relatively new concept called *preconception care* has been advanced that attempts to reduce a woman's reproductive risks before conception. These preconception programs include risk assessment, which involves identifying health risks such as inadequate nutrition, health promotion, and interventions to reduce risk (Jack & Culpepper, 1990).

The Rh Factor Perhaps the most famous maternal factor affecting the fetus is the **Rh factor,** which consists of a particular red blood cell antigen found in most human beings. Approximately 85% of all whites, 93% of African Americans, and nearly 100% of Asians, Native Americans, and Eskimos have the factor—that is, they are Rh positive (Stevenson, 1973).

In about 13% of white unions, the woman is Rh negative and the man is Rh positive. In such a situation, the baby may be Rh positive, which may be problematic. Because the mother's blood is Rh negative, her body reacts to the Rh positive antigen in the fetus as it would to an invading germ or virus—by creating antibodies. However, since the blood of the fetus does not mix with that of the mother during the pregnancy, the mother is not likely to manufacture antibodies that might injure the fetus. Few fetal blood cells cross the placenta. During the birth, especially if it is long and difficult, some cells *do* cross the placenta, and the mother will manufacture the antibodies.

Since the first child of these parents is not likely to be exposed to many of these antibodies, the infant's chances of survival are good. But once these antibodies are manufactured, they tend to remain in the mother's body. The mother also becomes more sensitive to this factor in later pregnancies. During the second pregnancy, the fetus will be exposed to the mother's antibodies, which will cross the placenta and destroy the red blood cells of the fetus (Ortho Diagnostic Systems, 1981). In each successive pregnancy the risk to the fetus becomes greater and greater, until the chances that a child will be born healthy are quite low.

Rh factor An antibody often but not always found in human beings.

Since 1968 a preventive vaccine for Rh problems has been available. Within 72 hours after each birth, miscarriage, or abortion, a shot of the vaccine RhoGAM is administered to block the production of these antibodies. Before this vaccine was available, about 10,000 babies died every year, and 20,000 more were born with severe birth defects from Rh disease (Apgar & Beck, 1974).

> ***True or False?***
> An Rh problem is caused by a virus that can be combatted by the use of antibiotics.

Current Issues

As people learn more about the prenatal period, new issues are proposed and old ones are perceived differently. Four such issues are especially current: (a) the relationship between the age of the mother and the health of the fetus, (b) maternal nutrition during pregnancy, (c) the father's responsibilities during pregnancy, and (d) the effect of new technology on mother and child.

Maternal Age

The number of women having their first child at age 30 or older has increased substantially. Many contemporary couples have postponed having children for economic and career reasons. Since the middle 1970s the birth rate for women above the age of 30 has grown steadily, increasing over 25%, although recently the birth rate for women over the age of 30 has stabilized (Lancashire, 1995).

First-time older mothers do very well. They are more likely than younger mothers to have good family support systems, economic stability, and to have planned the pregnancy. Certain age-related characteristics such as patience and judgment, which are important in parenting, are more likely to be present among older mothers, and some studies find that the age of the mother at birth shows a slight but consistent and positive association with the child's intelligence (Fonteyn & Isada, 1988). The years between 20 and 30 are the safest for childbearing. As a woman ages, the incidence of high blood pressure and delivery complications increases (Fonteyn & Isada, 1988). Older fathers (those having their first child above age 35) also do well. They spend more time in leisure activities with their children, have higher expectations for their children's behavior, and are more nurturing toward their children compared to fathers in their 20s (Heath, 1994).

> ***True or False?***
> Older fathers, those who have their first child after age 35, spend more time with their children and are more nurturant than fathers in their 20s.

While the physical risks of women in their 30s having children are somewhat greater, the availability of modern diagnostic procedures and better prenatal care reduces

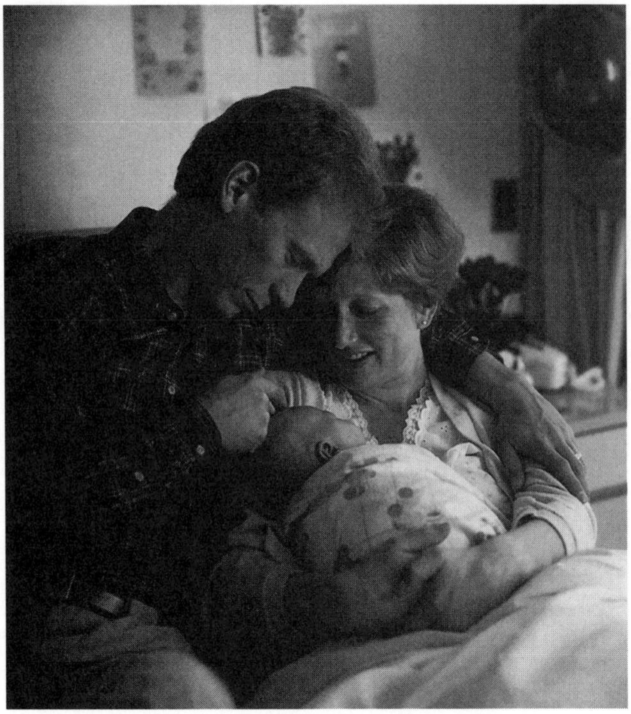

Many couples are deciding to wait to have their first child. Although the risks are somewhat greater, with good prenatal care, most women can give birth to healthy children.

these risks somewhat. If there is no evidence of chronic disease, the outlook for the intelligent mother entering the world of parenting in her 30s is quite good (Berkowitz et al., 1990).

Questions Students Often Ask

Are there increased risks for women over the age of 40 who want to have children?

The answer is a clear yes. The "older" mother is more likely to have high blood pressure and diabetes and to develop toxemia. Advanced age is also associated with Down syndrome; yet, with good prenatal care many older mothers can have healthy infants.

The number of births at the other age extreme is much more troublesome. The pregnant teenager belongs to the high-risk group for birth complications, birth defects, and prematurity (Croen & Shaw, 1995; Seitz & Apfel, 1994). This high rate of complications may be explained by the relationship between adolescent pregnancy and such factors as low socioeconomic status, poor education, and poor health care. Teenage mothers are likely to have repeat pregnancies and are less likely to receive high-quality prenatal care. Teenage pregnancy is part of a larger social and economic problem that must be approached educationally and medically and will be discussed in Chapter 12.

Maternal Nutrition

The mother's nutritional status before pregnancy is important too (Sizer & Whitney, 1988). The mother may have suffered from nutritional problems that affect her own physical development and health, reducing her ability to bear a healthy child. The pregnant woman's nutritional needs are far greater during this period. Malnourishment around conception may cause the placenta to fail to develop adequately, causing many different abnormalities. If this small infant is female, she runs an elevated risk of having a poor pregnancy outcome also. A woman's pregnancy then can adversely affect not only her children but her grandchildren as well (Whitney, Cataldo, & Rolfes, 1994).

The past two decades have seen renewed interest in maternal nutrition during pregnancy. The finding that chronic malnutrition during the prenatal stage leads to an irreversible condition in which the infant has fewer brain cells—as many as 20% fewer than the normal baby (Winick, 1976)—did much to spur the interest. Malnutrition is related to fetal deformities and impaired physical and intellectual development. Mental retardation, low birth weight, cerebral palsy, and increased susceptibility to disease have been traced to malnourishment during pregnancy (Annis, 1978). Infants who were malnourished during the prenatal stage also show abnormal behavioral patterns, such as withdrawal and irritability, and are often born prematurely (Ricciuti, 1980; Birch, 1971). Malnutrition is not restricted to indigent mothers, although it is most common in this group (Moore & Persaud, 1993); studies demonstrate that malnutrition can also lead to increased fetal deaths (DeBruyne & Rolfes, 1989).

Important research linking particular vitamins to fetal development and the possibility that supplements may prevent particular deformities has made nutrition before and during pregnancy an increasingly important issue. For example, giving folate supplements before and around the time of conception reduces the occurrence of neural tube defects, the most prominent of which is spina bifida in which the spine does not close properly (Rush, 1992). When a group of women with low levels of zinc were given dietary supplements that included zinc, their infants had significantly greater birth weight and head circumference than a group of women given multivitamin tablets that did not contain zinc (Goldenberg et al., 1995).

The Father's Role

Research demonstrates that the father's behavior can also affect the pregnancy and the subsequent health of the fetus. Paternal drug taking prior to pregnancy as well as exposure to radiation may affect the father's genes and in turn directly affect the child. The sperm are vulnerable to damage from drugs and other chemical substances. Paternal exposure to particular chemicals prior to pregnancy is implicated in such outcomes as spontaneous abortion, low birth weight, and birth defects (Olshan & Faustman, 1993). Some agents can lead to reduced sperm quantity and motility and abnormal sperm structure (Wyrobek, 1993). An increase in spontaneous abortion is found in the partners of men working in occupational settings in which they are exposed to vinyl chloride

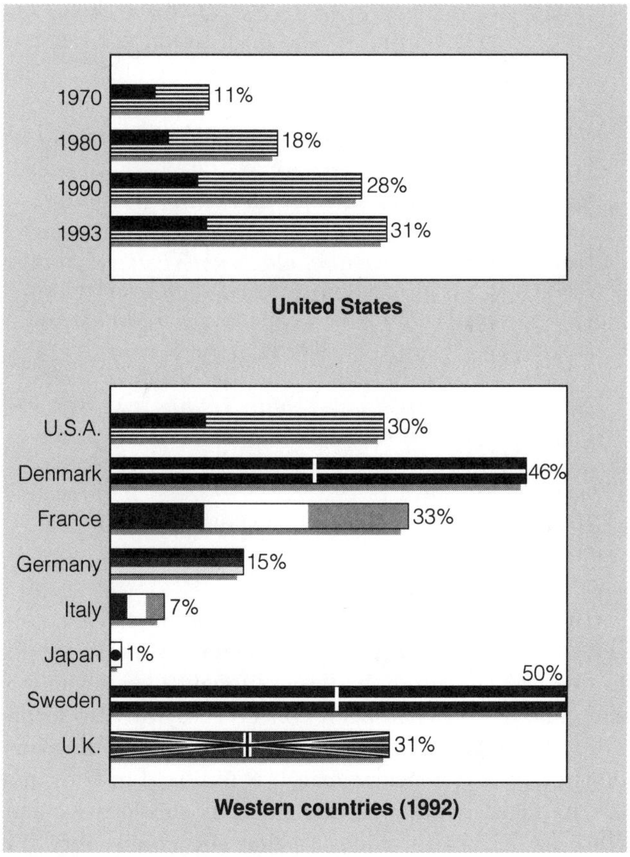

Datagraphic
Births to Unmarried Women (as percentage of all births)
Source: Data from Statistical Abstract, 1996.

or metals such as mercury (Aleser et al., 1989; Cohen et al., 1980; Cordier et al. 1991). Occupational exposure to chemicals used in the manufacture of rubber, plastics, and solvents is also related to an increased rate of spontaneous abortions (Lindbohm et al., 1991; Taskinen et al., 1989). Some studies report a relationship between exposure to particular chemicals or drugs and low birth weight, but the evidence is still contradictory (Olshan & Faustman, 1993).

Exposure to solvents and some pesticides have been linked to birth defects (Olshan, Teschke, & Baird, 1991). Although few studies have investigated the relationship between paternal smoking and use of alcohol and birth defects, one large study found paternal cigarette smoking associated with increases in cleft lip and cleft palate and various other birth defects (Savitz, Schwingle, & Keels, 1991). In another study fathers who had two or more drinks daily or at least five drinks on one occasion in the month before conception fathered infants who had lower birth weights than those who did not drink. The study controlled for such variables as maternal drinking, paternal smoking, paternal use of other drugs, and other factors (Little & Sing, 1987). Other evidence shows statistical links between exposure to particular chemical toxins and cancer in offspring (Wyrobek, 1993). Several childhood cancers primarily arise from mutations traced to sperm, mutations that may occur during cell division (Blakeslee, 1991).

How could these chemicals affect the outcomes of pregnancy? First, these chemicals may directly affect sperm, thus causing a birth defect (Cicero, 1994). Second, evidence indicates that some chemicals and drugs, including cocaine, may be found in seminal fluid and that transfer is possible (Olshan & Faustman, 1993).

The research on paternal exposure and adverse infant development is plagued by incomplete reports and by the very small number of people researched (Wyrobek, 1993). Often, in occupational and environmental studies, the amount of exposure is not well researched (Shore, 1995). In many cases, the Environmental Protection Agency admits that the listing of a chemical or drug as having adverse affects on sperm is based upon very few studies of each chemical and the results may be expected to change as more information is provided (Wyrobek, 1993; Wyrobek et al., 1994). In addition, the research is often inconclusive and a definitive statement is difficult to make. Despite the inadequacies in research, the literature to date suggests potential associations between exposure to drugs and chemicals and adverse pregnancy outcomes; certainly, more research is needed in this area.

The father's behavior also influences the expectant mother's actions. If women heed the warnings about drinking, smoking, and drug taking, they will increase their chances of giving birth to a healthy child, but if the father is indulging, the mother may find it more difficult to refrain from such behavior. The mother's need for emotional support places a responsibility on the father's shoulders. The father can help to reduce the stress and anxiety experienced by the mother by being willing to understand her special needs for support and assistance. Such willingness can help the mother through this unique time in the couple's life.

Technology and Reproductive Alternatives

About 1 in every 13 couples is infertile, which is defined as the inability to conceive after a year or more of intercourse without contraception (Higgins, 1990). In 40% of the cases of infertility the problem lies with the female; in 40% the problem lies with the male; and in 20% of the cases both spouses are responsible or the cause is unknown (Manning, 1982).

More couples are using high-tech reproductive treatment than ever before, and hope means everything to them. If you were told that a treatment had only a 10% chance of success, you wouldn't hold out much hope but the infertile couple concentrates on the 10% probability and accepts hormones, surgery, and other drug therapies that sometimes have annoying and painful side effects. Perhaps the most radical treatment is *in vitro fertilization* (IVF) in which the egg is taken from the woman's ovary through a process known as *laparoscopy,* which requires an incision. Next the egg is fertilized with the husband's sperm and allowed to develop for 2 days before being implanted in the womb. More than 10% of couples seeking infertility treatment advance to IVF (Halpern, 1989). This technique requires commitment and some suffering and is also expensive. Injections of hormones are required and much time is lost from work as the couple has to spend weeks near a fertility clinic. The chances that one cycle of in vitro fertilization will result in pregnancy is low, so a number of attempts may be required. In addition, there in an increased risk of prematurity in IVF pregnancies, and therefore some concern about the health of these infants (Rosenthal, 1992).

In vitro fertilization and other such techniques may go beyond helping couples who are infertile. What if a woman finds that she carries a gene that makes it quite likely that she will get breast cancer; she wants to have children but does not wish to pass this gene on to her children. Under such a scenario, would you choose or would you encourage your wife to choose in vitro fertilization in which the egg is fertilized outside the womb, have genetic tests conducted on these embryos, and have those without the gene reimplanted in the womb? Although a gene for breast cancer has been found, scientists are still probably some time away from being able to screen for it on a mass basis. However, with more genes for various diseases and medical conditions being discovered each year, the question is germane. Such a test is available for cystic fibrosis, and in one case eight embryos of a British woman with a gene for cystic fibrosis were screened for the gene, two were reimplanted, and one survived to term (Wright, 1994). This process, called *preimplantation diagnosis technique,* permits examination of embryos for genetic defects before they are transferred to the uterus.

Questions Students Often Ask

My friend said that in vitro fertilization is not natural and should not be used because it goes against nature. Does it?

A number of problems are associated with IVF, including its low success rate, its cost, and the controversial uses described in the text. Yet, the charge that it isn't natural or "goes against nature" is not one of these. Certainly becoming pregnant through IVF differs from the way it occurs in nature, but much of what we do improves upon nature. For example, people in the last century suffered from many diseases and many women died in childbirth. New and artificial medical procedures have saved many infants and vaccinations created by human research have been instrumental in increasing life expectancy. It is not necessarily logical to say that everything natural is good and that everything created by humans is not.

Given the present techniques, embryos can be conceived in vitro and preserved through cryopreservation. In one case a custody battle was fought over seven frozen embryos that had been conceived by in vitro fertilization (Angell, 1990). In another development, an ovum donated by a younger woman was fertilized in vitro, and the fertilized ovum was implanted in an older woman, who was given hormones so that she could carry the pregnancy to term (Sauer, Paulson, & Lobo, 1990). Menopause may no longer necessarily be the end of a woman's ability to bear children, which raises several ethical questions. Is it reasonable to help a woman become pregnant such that she will be 80 when her child is 18? On the other hand, men become fathers late in life, as did Charlie Chaplin at 73 and Anthony Quinn at 78, without stirring up any controversy (Phillips, 1994), although expensive technology was not required. Also, eggs used in IVF are often retrieved from young women and the process carries with it a small risk of infection that can lead to infertility. Is it fair to ask women, some of whom may be poor and require the money, to put their future fertility at risk? In response to these problems, the Canadian Royal Commission on Reproductive Technologies advocated that IVF be considered a proven treatment for only one type of infertility—blocked fallopian tubes—and that the procedure not be used for any other purpose (Phillips, 1994).

There has been a boom in multiple births due to the growing number of couples in fertility treatment. "I had panic attacks when I heard it was triplets, but I would rather have my hands full than empty," said one mother who gave birth to two boys and a girl after 11 years of infertility treatments.

Some advocates for people with disabilities are concerned

that routine genetic tests coupled with the new reproductive technology will lead to a subtle pressure on people to terminate pregnancies whenever a disability is detected. They also worry that insurance companies will refuse to cover children with disabilities by considering their disabilities as preexisting conditions that ought not to have occurred (The Progressive, 1994).

The new reproductive alternatives offer hope for infertile couples, but also raise many ethical questions (see Forming Your Own Opinion: Reproductive Surrogacy) that will have to be explored.

Technology: Pregnancy and Birth

Today a woman's experience of pregnancy and the birth process differs somewhat from that of her mother. Fetal monitors, which tell the doctor how the fetus is reacting to maternal contractions during labor and presents an early indication of any potential fetal distress, are commonly used. Many pregnant women have **sonograms** (also called *ultrasound*) in which sound waves are used to produce a picture of the fetus. Sonograms can be used to determine the gestational age of the child, to determine whether a woman is carrying twins, and to diagnose a number of rare but important fetal defects; it can be combined with other techniques to discover cardiac problems in the fetus (Chervenak, Isaacson, & Mahoney, 1986).

Some women undergo **amniocentesis,** in which a small amount of amniotic fluid is extracted from the womb. The fluid contains fetal cells that have been discarded as the fetus grows. These cells are cultured and examined for genetic and chromosomal abnormalities. In

sonogram A "picture" taken of the fetus through the use of ultrasonic soundwaves.

amniocentesis A procedure in which fluid is taken from a pregnant woman's uterus to check fetal cells for genetic and chromosomal abnormalities.

Forming Your Own Opinion: Reproductive Surrogacy

A 1991 trial in New Jersey startled the nation. Elizabeth and William Stern contracted with Mary Beth Whitehead that she act as a surrogate mother. Ms. Whitehead was impregnated with Mr. Stern's sperm through artificial insemination. Later, the surrogate mother did not want to give up the child and wanted custody.

The New Jersey court handled the case as a custody case, therefore declaring the contract unenforceable. The decision of the court awarded custody to the biological father and permitted Elizabeth Stern to adopt the child. However, this was overturned by the New Jersey Supreme Court, which awarded custody to William Stern but did not allow Elizabeth Stern to adopt the child, granting Mary Beth Whitehead visitation rights (Ragone, 1994).

The term *surrogate mother* is an inadequate one because it glosses over many important distinctions. For example, it is now possible to collect ova from almost any woman, fertilize the ova in the laboratory with sperm essentially from any man *(in vitro fertilization),* and implant a fertilized ovum into almost any woman with a uterus, either immediately or after a time during which the fertilized egg is frozen. None of the parties to this technological feat need know each other or the parties involved may be intimately related.

In the past 10 years or so many celebrated cases of surrogate motherhood have introduced questions that have never had to be answered before. Many cases involve a couple unable to have children and another woman who allows herself to be artificially inseminated with sperm. The second woman is called the *surrogate mother.* If the fertilized egg this woman nourishes is not her own but came from a different woman, would the woman still be called a surrogate mother?

Eugene Sandberg (1989) suggests the use of three different terms. The *genetic mother* is the producer or the donor of the egg, the *gestational mother* is the developer of the fetus, and the *nurturing mother* is the custodian of the child. Today the surrogate mother is usually a woman who carries her own fertilized egg for another couple, but this may not be so in the future. Most women who cannot have children can provide their own eggs but are unable to carry the infant adequately. The egg of such a woman can be artificially inseminated and implanted in another womb. This has already been done: A 48-year-old woman delivered triplets for her daughter in South Africa after fertilization of the daughter's egg outside the womb and embryo transfer. A lesser number of women will simply need a genetic surrogate—that is, a donor ovum—but will be able to carry the child themselves. In vitro fertilization and surrogacy may become more common in the future.

The objections that are frequently raised concerning surrogacy involve legal contracts and monetary issues as well as the potential exploitation of poor women to carry children for the wealthy. By the middle of 1992, England, Germany, and France had made such monetary contracts for surrogate parenting illegal and 18 U.S. states have passed laws sharply limiting surrogacy arrangements ("Making Money," 1992; Phillips, 1994). Unpaid surrogate parenting remains legal. There are eight established commercial surrogate mother programs in the United States, and a number of private individuals arrange surrogate contracts on a freelance basis (Ragone, 1994).

By the year 2000 some forms of surrogacy will probably become acceptable. However, many issues remain unresolved. For instance, should a contract between a woman who agrees to carry a fertilized egg to term be enforceable in a court of law? Should people who do so be paid? These and other legal and ethical questions are now being hotly debated.

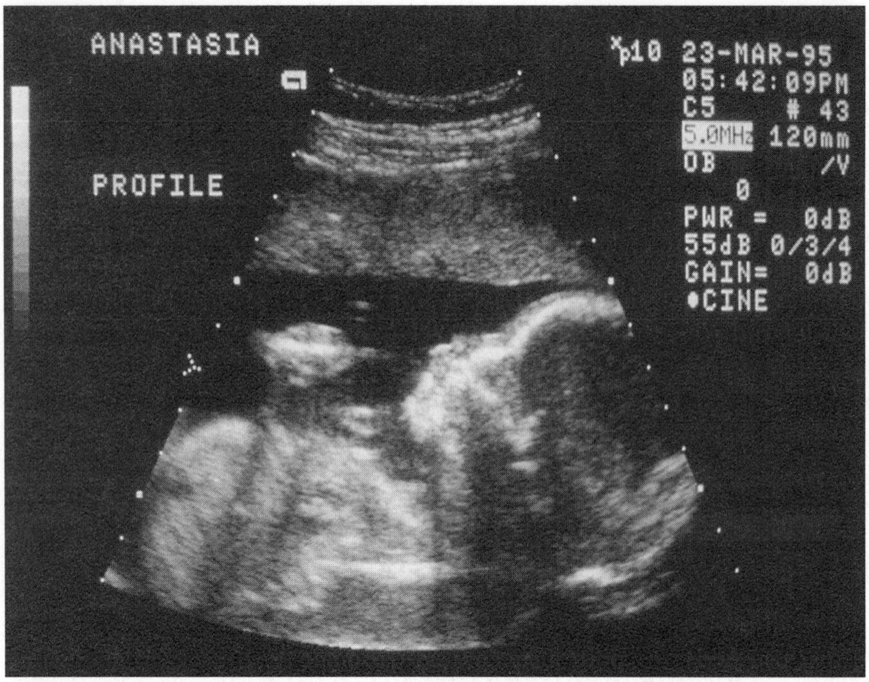

Sonograms, which are pictures of the fetus using sound waves, are helpful in diagnosing a number of problems as well as determining the exact gestational age of the child.

another procedure, called **chorionic villus sampling,** cells are obtained from the chorion during the 8th to 12th week of pregnancy and checked for genetic problems.

Both amniocentesis and chorionic villus sampling are not used for every pregnant woman because they require an intrusion into the area near the developing fetus. They are indicated when the mother is older or if there is some possibility of prenatal problems. The search for nonintrusive ways to screen for genetic problems is ongoing. One such screening test is a blood test called the *maternal serum alpha-fetoprotein (MSAFP)* test, which identifies fetuses that are at higher-than-average risks for certain serious birth defects and other problems. *Alpha-fetoprotein (AFP)* is a substance that all fetuses produce; some of it gets into the amniotic fluid, and a little actually enters the mother's bloodstream. Given between the 16th and 18th week of pregnancy, this test measures the amount of AFP in the pregnant woman's blood. If the amount of AFP is either high or low, other tests are usually performed (Clark & DeVore, 1989; March of Dimes, 1989). Work is ongoing to develop techniques based upon blood tests that will eliminate the need for invasive techniques such as amniocentesis and chorionic villus biopsy (Phillips, 1994).

Birth

Before birth the average infant spends about 266 days, counting from conception, or about 280 days, counting after the beginning of the last menstrual period, developing in the womb. A century ago most women gave birth at home, but today the overwhelming majority of births take place in hospitals. Information about birth is rarely taught in high school, and young parents may be ignorant of the basic facts surrounding the event.

The Three Stages of the Birth Process

The birth process is divided into three stages. During the first, or **dilation,** stage the uterus contracts and the cervix flattens and dilates to allow the fetus to pass through. The general term **labor** describes this process. This stage can last from about 2 to 16 hours, or even longer; it tends to be longer with the first child. When the contractions start, they usually come at approximately 15- to 20-minute intervals and are generally mild. Near the end of this first stage, the contractions change, becoming more difficult, longer, and more frequent. This period, lasting about an hour, is called **transition** and is the most difficult part of labor for many women (Tucker & Bing, 1975). By the end of this stage, the cervix is dilated to about 10 centimeters, and contractions occur every minute or so.

The second stage of birth involves the actual delivery of the baby. This **expulsion** stage is quite variable and can last anywhere from 2 to 60 minutes or more. In the average delivery, the baby's head appears first, an event referred to as **crowning.** The rest of the body soon follows.

The third stage of the birth process involves the **delivery of the placenta** (or afterbirth) and fetal membranes. During this stage mild contractions continue for some time. They help decrease the blood flow to the uterus and reduce the uterus to normal size.

Cesarean Birth

If it has been determined that there might be a problem in the birth process, the doctor may advise that the baby

chorionic villus sampling A diagnostic procedure in which cells are obtained from the chorion (an early structure that later becomes the lining of the placenta) during the 8th to 12th week of pregnancy and checked for genetic abnormalities.

dilation The first stage of labor, in which the uterus contracts and the cervix flattens and dilates to allow the fetus to pass.

labor A term used to describe the general process of expelling the fetus from the mother's womb.

transition A period late in labor in which the contractions become more difficult.

expulsion The second stage of birth, involving the actual delivery of the fetus.

crowning The point in labor at which the baby's head appears.

delivery of the placenta The third and last stage of birth, in which the placenta is delivered.

be removed surgically through the wall of the abdomen and uterus. This is major surgery that typically involves a longer hospital stay. **Cesarean sections,** as this type of birth is called, have become much more common in the past decades. Before 1965 cesarean sections were performed in about 2% to 5% of all births; today the rate stands at somewhat over 22% (Quilligan, 1995).

A number of explanations have been advanced for the dramatic increase in cesarean sections. The safety of the operation has improved markedly both for the mother and for the fetus. Other policies that have led to this increase include the practice of repeat cesarean sections on women who have already had one, the increased threat of malpractice suits, and an increase in the number of problems that now indicate the need for a section. Fetal monitors can alert a doctor to a possible problem early in labor, and the doctor may then opt to practice a conservative, defensive style of medicine rather than risk a possibly difficult vaginal delivery.

Questions Students Often Ask

Does a cesarean delivery affect the child's development?

The evidence is quite clear that there are no long-term problems from cesarean sections. Cesarean sections may be performed in emergencies when the infant is in distress and if fetal anoxia results, this may affect the child's development. However, evidence shows that the cesarean section itself does not lead to any long-term problems (Entwisle & Alexander, 1987).

The increase in cesarean sections has become a controversial issue in recent years. One way to reduce the number of such surgeries is to end the standard practice of automatically requiring a woman who has had one cesarean to deliver her other infants by the same method. Many women who have had a cesarean section are able to deliver vaginally in the future and the percentage of women doing so has increased substantially in the past decade (Goldman et al., 1993; Quilligan, 1995).

True or False?

Once a woman has had one cesarean section to deliver a child, all later deliveries must also be by cesarean section.

The Effects of Obstetrical Medication

In the United States obstetrical medication is almost routinely administered to women in labor. There is little question concerning the effects of such medication on infants in the first few days of life. Medicated infants are more sluggish than nonmedicated infants (Brackbill, 1979, 1982). In the second day of life heavily medicated infants sucked at a lower rate and for shorter periods of time and consumed less formula than infants whose mothers received no anesthesia or received local anesthesia (Sanders-Phillips, Strauss, & Gutberlet, 1988).

The real controversy concerns whether any long-term effects exist. Some studies find the effects of the medication on infant behavior strongest on the first day and reduced greatly by the fifth day, but some differences between the medicated and nonmedicated infants still existed (Murray et al., 1981). By 1 month there were few differences between the groups, but mothers of unmedicated babies handled their babies more affectionately whereas mothers of medicated babies spent more time stimulating their infants to suck. There were no differences in infant behavior, but the mothers perceived their babies differently. Mothers of medicated babies perceived their infants as less adaptable, more intense, and more bothersome. Of course, more difficult deliveries may account for some of these findings, but not all. Perhaps the major effects of medication, at least at 1 month, are found in the possible problems mothers have in interacting with infants who were heavily medicated during the first few days. Such problems may carry over and be more important in the long term than the medications themselves. Perhaps the early encounters set up expectations and problems that continue to influence the mother's responses.

Others argue that there are long-term behavioral differences (Lester, Heidelise, & Brazelton, 1982), especially when these children are faced with challenging tasks. At this point all we can say is that studies are mixed on the long-term effects of obstetrical medication on infants. The effects of such medication depend on the dosage, and a number of individual factors that are not well understood. Doctors are now more knowledgeable and aware of the possibility that medication may adversely affect the fetus (Finster, Pedersen, & Morishima, 1984).

Decisions About Birth

Not too many years ago parents were often robbed of the experience of birth. It was standard practice for mothers to be heavily medicated and separated from their infants for quite some time after birth and for fathers to be prevented from participating in the birth process and forced to wait outside the delivery room. Today the situation has changed and many parents are now able to choose to participate actively in alternative methods of birth. In addition, medical and hospital procedures are gradually changing. Birth centers are available for families who wish to give birth outside the high-technology atmosphere of a hospital. These centers may be useful for women who are at lower than average risk for problems in pregnancy (Rooks et al., 1989). It has even been suggested that birth centers be located inside hospitals so that if emergency treatment is necessary, it is easily accessible (Lieberman & Ryan, 1989). Midwife attended deliveries have also increased, but the overwhelming majority of deliveries still take place in the hospital under a doctor's supervision (Lancashire, 1995).

cesarean section The birth procedure by which the fetus is surgically delivered through the abdominal wall and uterus.

The Lamaze Method

The most popular alternative birthing method, called the **Lamaze method,** was developed by Fernand Lamaze. Lamaze advocated not only the father's presence but also the father's active participation in the birth process (Lamaze, 1970). Women are taught specific techniques to manage discomfort, reducing the need for painkillers. Relaxation techniques, breathing methods for the various stages of labor, and a number of other procedures help to reduce discomfort. Finally, the Lamaze method emphasizes the importance of experiencing the birth and of sharing an emotional event.

> ***True or False?***
> The Lamaze method of birth emphasizes the importance of leaving the mother alone to meditate on her birth experience.

Lamaze procedures accomplish their goals. They reduce the amount of medication required, and women giving birth using Lamaze techniques report less discomfort and a more positive attitude toward the process (Cogan, 1980; Charles et al., 1978). This does not mean that women feel no discomfort, although they do report experiencing less pain than women who do not undergo Lamaze training (Melzack, 1984).

The question of the effect the father's experience may have on the father-infant relationship is still in doubt. In a review of the research, Palkovitz (1985) found insufficient evidence to conclude that bonding is enhanced by the father's attendance at the birth. Studies that find positive results for father attendance slightly outnumber studies that find no differences, but these positive studies tend to be less rigorously performed. However, evidence does confirm that the father's attendance at birth and early contact with the infant enhance the marital relationship and the father's feelings of being included, which can have a positive effect on the family.

Complications of Birth

Most pregnancies and deliveries are normal, but sometimes problems such as anoxia and prematurity do occur that may have serious consequences later in childhood.

Anoxia

A deficiency of the oxygen supply reaching the baby, **anoxia,** is the most common cause of brain damage. Such damage may be inflicted either during the birth process or for some time during the prenatal period when the placenta is detached or infected. Anoxia can lead to a number of birth defects, including cognitive and behavioral problems (Wenar, 1994). Except in the more extreme cases, making predictions about the future development of anoxic children is difficult. Some anoxic children compare well with peers who did not suffer from anoxia. Anoxia increases the risk for developmental disability in cognitive and behavioral areas, but many anoxic children develop normally and show little difference from their peers when they enter school (Wenar, 1994). The quality of care may be most important in staving off possible problems (Sameroff & Chandler, 1975). The better the care, the less likely mildly and moderately anoxic children are to develop these disabilities.

Prematurity: Born at Risk

The greatest threat to an infant's survival is prematurity. A **premature infant** can be defined in terms of birth weight or the length of the gestation period. Currently a baby weighing less than 2500 grams (about 5½ pounds) or one who has been born less than 37 weeks after conception is considered premature. A birth weight below 1500 grams (about 3 pounds 5 ounces) is designated very low birth weight. Generally, low-birth-weight infants are categorized into two groups. In the first group are infants born below the weight expected for their gestational age. Some of these babies are born at their normal term, others are born earlier. These babies are called **small-for-date infants.** The other group involves what are called **preterm infants,** those whose birth weights are appropriate for their gestational age but who are born at or before 37 weeks from conception (Kopp & Parmelee, 1979).

Fifteen or twenty years ago the outlook for premature infants, especially the smaller ones, was very poor, but this is no longer the case. Even infants born very small—between 750 and 1000 grams—have about a 70% chance of surviving if they get good care. The smallest infants, weighing less than 750 grams, have about a two-thirds mortality, but even here there is more hope and increased survival compared to years ago. Unfortunately, some of the smaller infants show major disabilities when observed at 1 or 2 years of age (Ehrenhaft, Wagner, & Herdman, 1989).

> ***Questions Students Often Ask***
> I don't want to sound cold or hard, but should we be so aggressive in saving the lives of very, very small infants who often have major disabilities?
> *It is very expensive to treat children with very low birth weights (1500 grams or less). These costs include extended hospital stays with expensive technology, as well as additional medical, educational, and therapeutic costs because these infants often show extensive disabilities. Countries in Europe are far less aggres-*

Lamaze method A method of prepared childbirth that requires active participation by both parents.

anoxia A condition in which the infant does not receive a sufficient supply of oxygen.

premature infants Infants weighing less than 5½ pounds or born less than 37 weeks after conception.

small-for-date infants Infants born below the weight expected for their gestational age.

preterm infants Infants born before 37 weeks of gestation.

sive in such treatment, and allow parents to decide what treatment is appropriate (Tyson, 1995).

One point of view is that as a society we should make every effort to save every child that we are able to. The child born alive is a living being with rights to adequate medical treatment. Allowing too much discretion on which babies to treat could lead to infants with relatively minor or moderate disabilities being denied treatment. According to this view, it is best to treat every infant.

In the United States the Child Abuse and Treatment Act of 1984 (Public Law 98-457) sometimes referred to as the revised Baby Doe regulations *defines the withholding of medically indicated treatment as child abuse and neglect. The act notes that treatment may be withheld only when the infant is chronically and irreversibly comatose and treatment would be futile and merely prolong dying, or treatment would be both virtually futile in terms of survival of the infant and inhumane. Unfortunately, the terms "futile," "virtually futile," and "inhumane" are vaguely defined and make the act somewhat difficult to interpret (Tyson, 1995). It has been criticized for denying parents the rights to make medical decisions for their children.*

The rationing of resources is never easy to justify. If we have a finite amount of resources, where should they be placed? If an infant has a 10% chance of surviving and survival means extensive physical, mental, neurological, and emotional disability, should extensive efforts be made to save the child? These are difficult questions to answer, and full public discussion of the consequences of various policies is needed.

Premature infants are at risk for a number of physical and intellectual deficits during childhood (Horbar & Lucey, 1995). Children who are premature are more likely to have intellectual problems and learning difficulties than children who are not premature (Horbar & Lucey, 1995). In addition, premature infants are more likely to die during the first month of life, accounting for about half of all the deaths that occur during this time. There is no doubt that prematurity is a great cause of health and developmental problems.

True or False?
Premature infants are no more at risk for developmental problems than are infants born at term.

Not every premature infant suffers these setbacks. Some premature babies grow up to be superior children and to function well as adults. A variety of outcomes is possible, depending on the size and gestational age of the infant and on subsequent care and upbringing. The lower the birth weight and the shorter the gestation period, the more potentially serious the consequences. Premature infants are at risk not only because many diseased or genetically abnormal infants are born early but also because the premature infant is likely to be born into a disadvantaged environment. Although prematurity is found in every socioeconomic group, it is far more common in women who live in poverty or in those who are young. White women between 20 and 30 years of age have about a 3% low-birth-weight rate, whereas economically disadvantaged teenagers have a 9% rate (Kopp & Kaler, 1989). African Americans have about twice the risk of low birth weight as whites although some decline in the incidence of low birth weight has occurred for African Americans (Paneth, 1995; Lancashare, 1995). Socioeconomic factors alone cannot explain these statistics because the prematurity rate for Latinos is only slightly higher than for whites (Chomitz, Cheung, & Lieberman, 1995).

Although we do not know the reasons for most premature births, a number of factors have been implicated, including the maternal health and nutrition prior to pregnancy; maternal age, weight, and weight gain during pregnancy; maternal smoking and use of other drugs; uterine problems; and lack of prenatal care (Nathanielsz, 1995; Kopp & Parmelee, 1979). Cigarette smoking is the largest single modifiable risk factor and accounts for perhaps as much as 20% of the low-birth-weight cases (Shiono & Behrman, 1995). These factors correlate with social class

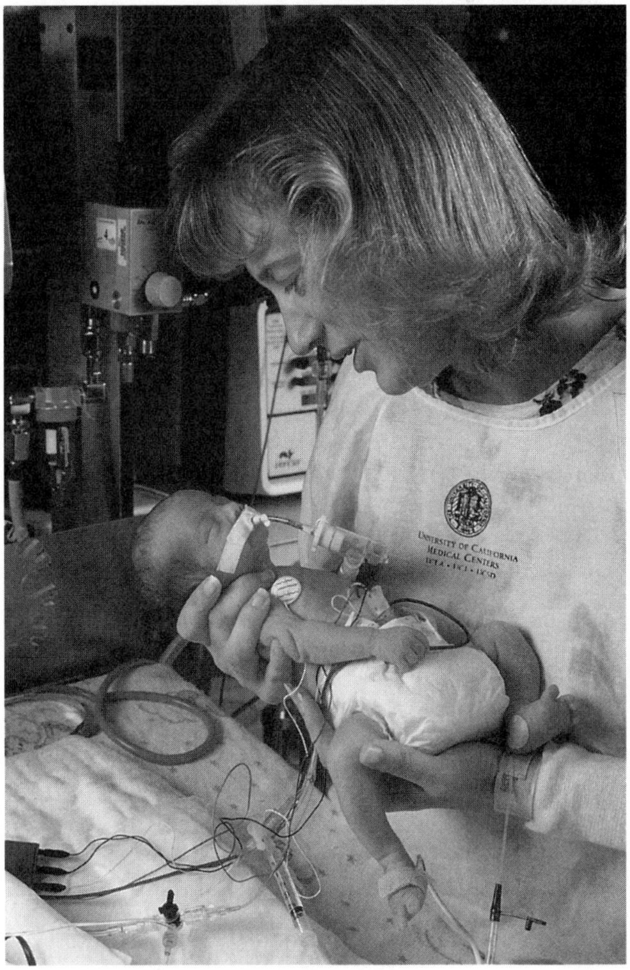

Advances in medical science have helped save many lives of premature infants.

(Hughes & Simpson, 1995) because women living in poverty are less likely to eat a nutritious diet during pregnancy and are much less likely to receive high-quality prenatal care. Their health prior to the pregnancy is also likely to be worse, and the crowded environments in which they live are not ideal as these women are exposed to more diseases. It is no wonder that children born to these mothers are at a double risk, being they are more vulnerable at birth and more likely to be exposed to poor living conditions afterward (Roberts, 1997).

Years ago severely premature infants were fed a very weak formula and placed in an oxygen-rich environment. However, too rich an oxygen supply led to a condition called **retinopathy of prematurity,** a disorder that causes blindness. Lack of proper nourishment resulting from being fed weak formula led to developmental problems. Today there are effective tube-feeding techniques, and sophisticated machinery is able to monitor the infant's vital signs. We are also aware that it is important that these children be stimulated. The effects of a deadening, nonstimulating hospital environment must be countered by giving the infants extra rocking and tactile stimulation as well as presenting them with things to look at and hear. Years ago the policy was to avoid touching premature infants, but today we know that this is counterproductive. Gentle massaging and a program of appropriate stimulation is very helpful in fostering growth, weight gain, and general development (Field, 1986). Various enrichment programs, some focusing on the child and others on the family, have been successful. In the Infant Health and Development Program premature infants were randomly assigned to an experimental group that received a training program based on child development principles, family support, and medical services, or to a control group that received only 3 years of medical care and a medical follow-up. The children who received the enrichment had significantly higher intelligence scores than the children in the control group and showed fewer behavioral problems (Hack, Klein, & Taylor, 1995). Such programs are highly effective in improving the neurological, motor, and psychological development of premature infants. Family support programs are also very successful in easing familial pressure and helping children to develop their cognitive abilities (Richmond, 1990).

Infant Mortality

Congenital birth defects, prematurity, and low birth weight are the leading causes of infant mortality. The rate of infant mortality in the United States has declined consistently since 1933 and as shown in Figure 4.2, continues to decline (MacDorman & Rosenberg, 1993). However, the United States ranks 22nd in the world in infant mortality and the decline in its mortality rate is not equal to that of other industrialized countries (Shiono &

retinopathy of prematurity A condition of blindness resulting from an oversupply of oxygen most often administered to premature infants.

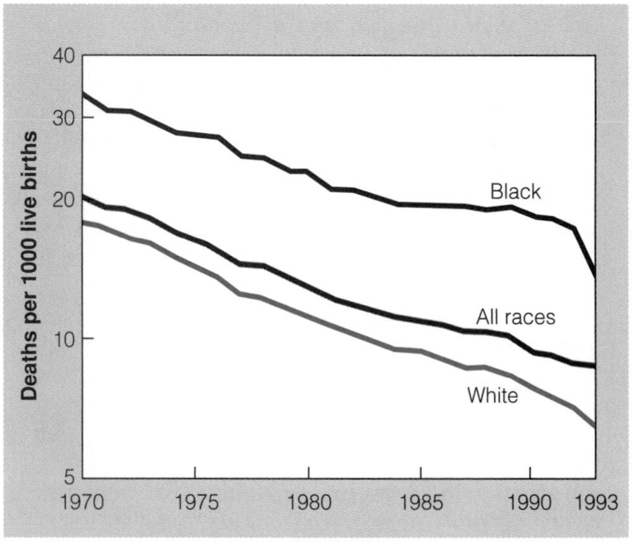

Figure 4.2
Infant Mortality Rates by Race: United States, 1970–93
Source: Centers for Disease Control and Prevention, National Center for Health Statistics, National Vital Statistics System and *Statistical Abstract*, 1996.

Behrman, 1993). Infant mortality is related to poverty and to a greater extent to poor education (Leviton, 1995). Many experts argue that the inability of poor pregnant women to get early and continuous prenatal care is one causative factor (Cooper, 1992).

True or False?
The United States has a lower infant mortality rate than every other industrialized country with the exception of Japan.

The lack of prenatal care, drug use, and other factors contribute to the infant mortality rate. Today more than three quarters of all pregnant women receive prenatal care during the critical first trimester, the highest level ever reported. The percentage of those who do not receive any medical attention until the third trimester or not at all has fallen to 5% (Lancashare, 1995). Fewer Latinos (except Cubans), Native Americans, and African Americans receive care in the first tremester (USDHHS, 1995). In order to improve the situation, access to health care before, during, and after pregnancy is required as are lifestyle changes such as reducing exposure to drugs.

After the Birth

By the end of the typical period of prenatal development, the average American male infant weighs approximately 7½ pounds and is approximately 20 inches long. The average female weighs slightly less, about 7 pounds, but is better equipped for life. She is about 4 weeks more mature, as measured by skeletal age (Annis, 1978), and is more neurologically advanced.

Hospitals have instituted specific procedures to measure the physical functioning of and the capacity for in-

Table 4.1 **The Apgar Scoring System**

The Apgar Scoring System is a relatively simple scale used to rate newborns on survivability. Each child is rated on each of the five behaviors listed below. Each behavior can have a score of 0, 1, or 2. (Highest possible total score is 10.) If the total score is greater than 7, no immediate threat to survival exists. Any score lower than 7 is cause for great concern. If the score is lower than 4, the infant is presently in critical condition.

AREA	SCORE		
	0	1	2
Heart rate	Absent	Slow (<100)	Rapid (>100)
Respiration	Absent	Irregular	Good, infant crying
Muscle tone	Flaccid	Weak	Strong, well flexed
Color	Blue, pale	Body pink, extremities blue	All pink
Reflex response			
Nasal tickle	No response	Grimace	Cough, sneeze
Heel prick	No response	Mild response	Foot withdrawal, cry

Source: Based on Apgar, 1953.

dependent survival of newborn infants. For example, infants may be evaluated using a rating system called the **Apgar Scoring System** (Apgar, 1953), which measures five physical characteristics: heart rate, respiration, reflex response, muscle tone, and color (see Table 4.1). The newborn is given a score of 0, 1, or 2 for each item according to a special criterion. For instance, if the newborn has a heart rate of 100 to 140 beats a minute, the infant receives a score of 2; for 100 beats a minute or below, the infant receives a score of 1; if there is no discernible heartbeat, a 0 is given (Apgar et al., 1958). Infants who receive a total score of less than 7 need additional supervision and care. The Apgar score can alert those responsible for the infant's care to a possible problem.

A more complex assessment for infants is the **Brazelton Neonatal Behavior Scale,** which provides information concerning reflexes and a variety of infant behaviors (Brazelton, 1990). Among the behavioral items are measures of responsiveness to visual stimuli, reactions to a bell and a pinprick, and the quality and duration of the infant's alertness and motor activity (Lester et al., 1982). The scale is a diagnostic tool but has also been used to research cross-cultural differences among infants.

Looking Ahead

The study of prenatal development and birth is both encouraging and frustrating. So much is known about preventing birth defects, yet some pregnant women continue to drink, smoke, and eat poorly, and do not always receive adequate prenatal care. Teenagers are giving birth at alarming rates, but little effort is expended to teach these young parents about the special needs of their infants. Improving programs to serve the needs of families at this important time of their lives is expensive. We pay for these failures in the years to come because problems that develop at this stage often lead to later psychological, social, and medical problems that force their attention on us. The new medical knowledge and advances mean that infants have a better chance of being born free of defects and of remaining healthy as they grow.

Apgar Scoring System A relatively simple system that gives a gross measure of infant survivability.

Brazelton Neonatal Behavior Scale An involved system for evaluating an infant's reflexes and sensory and behavioral abilities.

Summary

1. Fertilization occurs when a sperm cell penetrates an egg cell. The germinal stage begins at conception and lasts for about 2 weeks, during which time the fertilized egg travels down the fallopian tube and embeds itself in the womb. The embryonic stage lasts from 2 to 8 weeks; the heart starts to beat and other vital organs are formed. During the fetal stage, from 2 months until birth, the developing organism continues to develop internally and put on weight.
2. The critical period is the time during which a particular event has its greatest effect. Some teratogens are more dangerous at some times than at others. A number of environmental factors can adversely affect development in the womb, including drug use, pollution, radiation, and various diseases.
3. Smoking is linked to low-birth-weight infants and possibly to learning disabilities, prematurity, and cleft palate. Second-hand smoke can also injure the fetus. Children of alcoholics can suffer from fetal alcohol syndrome, a condition of retardation and physical defects. Even moderate drinking can cause some fetal abnormality, known as fetal alcohol effect.
4. The use of various narcotics during pregnancy is linked to many birth defects. The effects of cocaine are serious and the environment these children live in is often poor, which adds to the problems. Studies show that these children's development can be aided if they are given extra help.
5. Various diseases, such as rubella, AIDS, herpes, syphilis, gonorrhea, and chlamydia, cause fetal abnormalities or death.
6. The Rh factor is a particular red blood cell antigen. When the mother is Rh negative and the father is Rh positive, the offspring may be Rh positive, and prob-

lems may arise in the womb. Antibodies from the mother may pass through the placenta and kill red blood cells in the fetus. Today, women with such problems receive a shot of RhoGAM, which blocks the creation of the antibodies.

7. For financial and professional reasons, more women are having their first child when they are over 30. Although the risk is greater for both mother and baby, good prenatal care can reduce the risk somewhat. Older mothers and fathers are more stable and are very capable parents. Many pregnant teens do not get proper prenatal care, are exposed to many teratogens, and may be malnourished. The risk factor is very high for this group.
8. Serious malnutrition can lead to fewer fetal brain cells. Specific vitamin and mineral deficiencies may lead to fetal deformities. The effects of mild and moderate malnutrition are controversial, but malnutrition may serve to weaken the fetus. Giving specific nutritional supplements, such as folate and zinc, prevents some birth defects.
9. Paternal drug use prior to pregnancy may affect the father's sperm. If the father continues to drink and smoke, the pregnant woman may find it more difficult to refrain from such behavior herself.
10. Couples who have difficulty conceiving may seek treatment from fertility clinics. A number of new procedures are available, including in vitro fertilization in which an egg is fertilized by sperm in a laboratory and then implanted in the womb. The use of this and other fertility treatments raises many ethical and medical questions.
11. New technologies now give doctors and patients more information and choices. Sonography uses ultrasonic sound waves to create a picture of the embryo or fetus in the womb. Amniocentesis and chorionic villus sampling are used to discover genetic problems. A screening test for alpha-fetoprotein can alert the physician to a possible problem. Fetal monitoring during labor gives early warnings that something is wrong.
12. During the first stage of birth, the uterus contracts and the cervix dilates. The infant is delivered in the second stage, and the placenta during the third.
13. Cesarean births have increased greatly during the past 30 years as a result of improvements in the safety of such surgery, new technological aids that allow doctors to know sooner whether something is wrong, and the tendency for doctors to practice defensive medicine.
14. The Lamaze method of prepared childbirth emphasizes the importance of both parents' participation in the birth process. Relaxation is used to reduce discomfort, and the mother usually requires less medication.
15. Prematurity is the greatest threat to infant health because it is related to infant mortality and intellectual, neurological, and developmental disabilities. The cause of most cases of prematurity is unknown. Early intervention can help these infants develop more normally.
16. The average American male infant weighs about 7½ pounds and measures about 20 inches. Females weigh slightly less than males but are more mature as measured by skeletal age and are more neurologically advanced. After birth, the child may be rated on the Apgar Scoring System, which estimates the infant's physical condition and chances for survival.

Multiple-Choice Questions

1. The heart begins to function during which stage of prenatal development?
   a. germinal
   b. embryonic
   c. fetal
   d. organizational
2. You read that a particular drug affects the fetus much more at one particular time during prenatal development than at other times. This reflects the principle called the:
   a. time-line effect.
   b. linear effect.
   c. period of maximum retention.
   d. critical period.
3. Millie says that the effects of drugs taken during pregnancy or diseases experienced during the prenatal stage must show up either at birth or shortly after. To prove her wrong, you could use the example of:
   a. thalidomide.
   b. diethylstilbestrol.
   c. rubella.
   d. syphilis.
4. Dorothy is pregnant and does not smoke, but her husband and her mother with whom they live smoke heavily. Dorothy claims that this constant exposure to second-hand smoke affects the infant's birth weight. According to research, Dorothy is:
   a. incorrect, because it affects the infant's heart rate, not the birth weight.
   b. incorrect, because it affects the infant's coordination and physical functioning but not birth weight.
   c. incorrect, for there is no evidence that exposure to second-hand smoke affects birth outcome.
   d. correct.
5. A child whose mother used alcohol during pregnancy does not show physical signs of any disability but has learning and cognitive problems related to this alcohol use. This is called:
   a. fetal alcohol syndrome.
   b. fetal alcohol subclinical syndrome.

c. fetal alcohol effect.
d. alcohol toxic side effect.

6. Tina used cocaine when she was pregnant. You are observing her child-rearing practices. If Tina was similar to other mothers who use cocaine you would expect Tina to:
 a. smother the child with attention.
 b. show little emotional involvement with the infant.
 c. attend to the child's emotional needs but not to the child's cognitive needs.
 d. expect the child to understand her mother's problems at an early age.
7. The use of a vaccine for __________ has greatly reduced the incidence of birth-related problems caused by exposure to this disease.
 a. AIDS
 b. herpes
 c. rubella
 d. tuberculosis
8. Which of the following statements concerning AIDS is correct?
 a. Almost all cases of AIDS in children in the United States are caused by transmission during the prenatal stage or at birth.
 b. The virus that causes AIDS can be transmitted through breast milk.
 c. The prognosis for infants with AIDS is poor at the present time.
 d. All of these are correct.
9. Which of the following statements concerning having children in one's 30s is incorrect?
 a. People are delaying childbearing for economic reasons.
 b. Parents having their first child in their 30s are more stable than parents in their 20s.
 c. Older fathers spend more time with their infants than fathers in their 20s.
 d. Birth rates for people in their 30s continue to grow at a rapid rate.
10. Giving women nutritional supplements containing __________ around the time of conception may help to prevent neural tube defects.
 a. folate
 b. zinc
 c. iron
 d. vitamin E
11. Which of the following statements concerning paternal drug use and birth defects is correct?
 a. Some childhood cancers have been linked to defects in sperm.
 b. Exposure to certain pesticides and solvents is related to birth defects.
 c. Many of the studies relating paternal exposure to chemicals and later birth defects are based upon very small samples and incomplete information.
 d. All of the above are correct.
12. Mr. and Mrs. T. have had difficulty having a child. They consult a fertility clinic and decide to undergo a process whereby Mrs. T's egg is surgically removed and fertilized with Mr. T's sperm and then implanted into the womb. This procedure is called:
 a. embryo transplantation.
 b. in vitro fertilization.
 c. intensive preimplantation.
 d. preimplantation diagnosis.
13. Mrs. Peters is undergoing a test in which the doctor can take a picture of the fetus and determine the age of the fetus. This is called a:
 a. sonogram.
 b. visigram.
 c. perigram.
 d. audiogram.
14. Mr. and Mrs. Carr would like to know whether the fetus Mrs. Carr is carrying has Down syndrome. Mrs. Carr should have:
 a. a sonogram.
 b. an audiogram.
 c. a fetuscope.
 d. amniocentesis.
15. The number of cesarean sections:
 a. has continued to increase almost each year.
 b. has stabilized at a high level.
 c. cannot accurately be determined because doctors are reluctant to report them.
 d. has been dropping steadily as better methods of delivery are used.
16. Which of the following statements best describes the Lamaze method of childbirth?
 a. Both parents attend training sessions and the pregnant woman learns breathing and relaxation techniques.
 b. The lights are dimmed during birth and the birth is made as gentle as possible using a massage.
 c. The birth is accomplished in warm water with the father acting as an assistant midwife.
 d. The mother is given a medication that allows her to enter a twilight sleep and experience little discomfort.
17. An infant weighing less than __________ grams or having a gestation of less than __________ weeks is considered premature.
 a. 5500/28
 b. 2500/37
 c. 1800/39
 d. 1200/38
18. Which of the following statements concerning prematurity is correct?
 a. Prematurity is the greatest threat to newborns' health.
 b. Premature infants today are still at risk for intellectual and physical difficulties.

c. The cause of most cases of prematurity is unknown.
d. All of the above are correct.

19. America ranks ___________ in the world in infant mortality.
a. 5th
b. 10th
c. 18th
d. 22nd

20. Right after a baby is born, the doctor quickly assesses the child's heart rate, respiration, reflex response, muscle tone, and color to determine the child's capacity for independent functioning. The doctor is using the:
a. Denver II.
b. Bayley Scales of Infant Development.
c. Brazelton scale.
d. Apgar Scoring System.

Answers to Multiple-Choice Questions

1. b 2. d 3. b 4. d 5. c 6. b 7. c 8. d 9. d
10. a 11. d 12. b 13. a 14. d 15. b 16. a 17. b
18. d 19. d 20. d

Chapter 5

Physical and Cognitive Development in Infancy and Toddlerhood

Chapter Outline

Are the Following Statements True or False?

1. Infants are born farsighted but within a month or two develop normal vision.
2. Before 5 months of age, infants do not see color but, rather, shades of gray.
3. Infants are born deaf, but quickly develop their sense of hearing.
4. Infants at 8 months actually spend more time sleeping, crying, and feeding than newborn infants.
5. Most of the infant's reflexes become stronger during the first year.
6. Infants triple their weight within a year and increase their length by half.
7. The earlier toilet training begins, the longer it usually takes.
8. The 1-month-old infant believes that mother no longer exists when she leaves the room.
9. Intelligence tests given to normal infants at 6 months predict later school achievement quite well.
10. Parent-child interactions that are aimed at encouraging cognitive development should be fun for the child.

Answers to True-False Statements 1. False: see p. 93 2. False: see p. 94 3. False: see p. 94 4. False: see p. 96 5. False: see p. 99 6. True 7. True 8. True 9. False: see p. 115 10. True

Where's the Instruction Book?

"Babies should come with instruction books and their vocalizations with subtitles," a young mother of a 6-month-old admitted to me. "They cry, but can't tell you why. They stare—but you can't tell what they can really see. They seem to hear, but you can't tell what they are listening to. They may become cranky, but it is difficult to figure out what is wrong."

It isn't easy to care for infants or to understand their behavior. However, psychologists have made tremendous strides in understanding the sensory abilities and behavior patterns of infants and toddlers. Much of what we have learned is surprising, and as we tear away the curtain of mystery we become more impressed at the incredible abilities that even very young infants show.

The Newborn at a Glance

The newborn infant does not resemble the pictures we see on baby food jars, in soap advertisements, or in the movies. The newborn is covered with fine hair called **lanugo,** which is discarded within a few days. The baby's sensitive skin is protected in the womb by a thick secretion called **vernix caseosa,** which dries and disappears. The head is elongated and about one fourth of the baby's total length. The thin skin is pale and contains blotches caused by the trip through the birth canal. The head and nose may be out of shape, because their soft, pliable nature allows an extra bit of "give" during birth. They will soon return to normal, but it will be about a year and a half before the bones of the skull will cover the soft spots, called **fontanels.** The legs are tucked in under the baby in a fetal position and will remain that way for quite a while. The infant wheezes and sneezes and appears anything but ready for an independent existence.

lanugo The fine hair that covers a newborn infant.

vernix caseosa A thick liquid that protects the skin of the fetus.

fontanels The soft spots on the top of a baby's head.

How the Infant Experiences the World

As late as the 1960s some doctors and nurses believed that newborns were blind at birth, could not discriminate sounds, and could not feel pain. Many parents believed—and perhaps still believe—that newborns really can't taste and are not really sensitive to odors. The idea that young babies can learn from their experiences was not accepted (Lipsitt, 1990), and the notion that infants showed intelligence was also doubted. The newborn was considered a helpless being with few, if any, capabilities. After 30 years of research, however, we now know that infants are born well prepared for survival. The neonate is better adapted to the environment and more capable than most people think.

Before examining the physical and cognitive development of the child from birth through the second year of life, a few terms require definition. The term **neonate** refers to the baby's first month of life. The term *infant* refers to the entire first year of life. The *toddler* period begins at 1 year and continues until age 3 (Morrison, 1991).

One of the most important methods of testing an infant's sensory abilities is through **habituation,** the process by which an individual spends less and less time attending to a familiar stimulus (Brierly, 1976). If the same picture hung over your desk day after day, eventually you wouldn't even notice it. But if someone changed the picture would you notice the change? To respond to the new picture, you must notice that it is different.

Psychologists use the process of habituation to test a number of infant perceptual abilities (Streri & Pecheux, 1986). An infant is presented with one stimulus, and the baby's behavior is observed closely. At first the infant

neonate The scientific term for the baby in the first month of life.

habituation The process by which organisms spend less and less time attending to familiar stimuli.

shows some interest, but after a time the baby pays less attention to it, finally perhaps ignoring the stimulus altogether. If an increase in attention occurs when the infant is offered another stimulus, the infant has noticed the difference between the pair of stimuli.

The habituation design has been used on infants as early as the first few days after birth. Infants 1½ days old to 3 days old habituated to a checkerboard pattern placed on the side of the crib, and the 3-day-old infants habituated faster to visual stimuli than younger infants did (Friedman & Carpenter, 1971).

Another technique identifies infant preferences for one stimulus over another. Two stimuli are projected, one to the left and one to the right—if the infant gazes at the one on the left significantly more, infants of that age can be assumed to have a preference for that stimulus. To be certain that the infant's preference is for the stimulus rather than the fact that it is on the right or left, you would switch the positions of the stimuli.

Vision

Like adults, infants rely on the sense of vision for much of their information about the world. At birth, the visual apparatus of an infant is immature but functional (Aslin, 1987). What can an infant see?

Acuity and Accommodation Infants are very nearsighted. Neonates have a visual acuity of between 20/200 and 20/400 at birth, which means they can see at 20 feet what an older child with normal vision could see at 200 feet (Haith, 1990). The infant also has difficulty focusing; the best focal distance for the newborn is about 19 centimeters (7½ inches). This serves infants well; when a newborn is held by the mother, the baby's face is usually less than 6 inches away, so the infant is able to see the mother during feeding. Newborns do show some visual accommodation, about a third of the adult level (Bremner, 1988). Visual abilities improve quickly (Bronson, 1994). By the age of 2 months, the ability to focus approaches adult proportions (Aslin & Dumais, 1980). Within a year the infant's visual acuity approaches that of an adult (Haith, 1990).

> ***True or False?***
> Infants are born farsighted but within a month or two develop normal vision.

Form and Preference Newborns have visual preferences. They prefer curved lines to straight lines (Fantz & Miranda, 1975), patterned surfaces over plain ones (Fantz, 1963), and high-contrast edges and angles (Cohen, 1979). The infant's scanning is directed by rules (Haith, 1980) that cause the baby to concentrate on the outline of a figure rather than explore the figure's details (Milewski, 1976). By 8 weeks or so, infants develop more adult patterns of scanning and will investigate the interior as well as the contours of a figure (Bronson, 1994; Maurer & Salapatek, 1976). Research shows that infants are sensitive to patterned properties of stimuli from birth (Antell, Caron, & Myers, 1985).

A Preference for Faces? How can visual patterns and preferences help the newborn survive? Because the newborn depends on others for the basic necessities of life, a visual preference for human faces is adaptive. The discovery by Robert Fantz (1961) that this was true greatly excited the scientific world. Fantz showed infants two pictures—one on the infant's right, the other on the left—and measured the time the infant's eyes spent fixated on either one. Fantz found that infants preferred patterns to nonpatterned surfaces and that a picture of a face attracted the most attention (Figure 5.1). Perhaps the infant comes into this world programmed to recognize faces. Most studies have indeed shown that by 2 to 4 months of age infants prefer drawings of faces to any other drawings (Dannemiller & Stephens, 1988).

However, Fantz's argument that infants have a natural preference for faces may be premature. His conclusions have been reinterpreted in terms of the complexity of stimuli, and other researchers have not been able to replicate his work (Cohen, DeLoache, & Strauss, 1979). Others claim that in the absence of experience with faces, neonates do not show a preference for the face (Small, 1990). Perhaps both sides are correct; there is no final answer to this question. The infant has a preference for

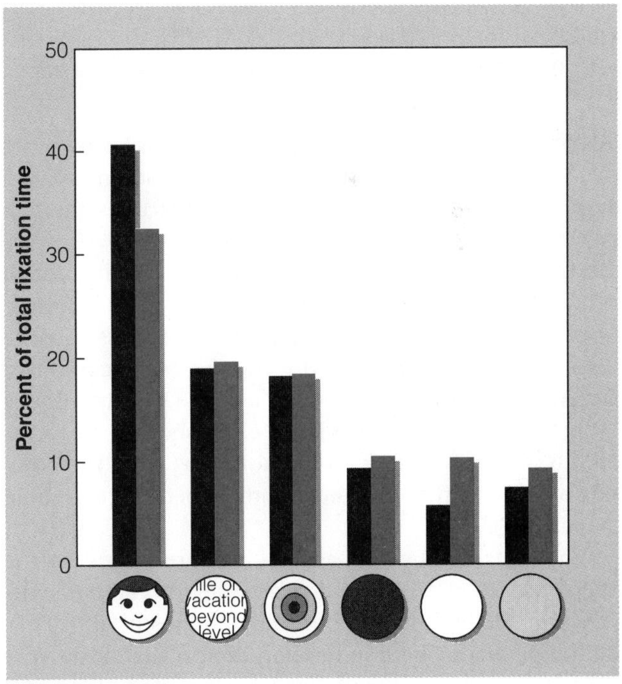

Figure 5.1
Visual Preferences in Infancy The importance of pattern rather than color or brightness was illustrated by the response of infants to a face, a piece of printed matter, a bull's-eye, and plain red, white, and yellow disks. Even the youngest infants preferred patterns. The darker bars show the results for infants from 2 to 3 months old; lighter bars, for infants older than 3 months.
Source: Adapted from Fantz, 1961.

complex stimuli; on a behavioral level this translates into an interest in faces, which are common complex stimuli in the infant's environment.

Can Infants Recognize Different Faces? There is some evidence that infants may recognize particular faces at very early ages. When presented with their own mother's and a female stranger's face, 2-day-old infants gaze longer at their mother's face (Bushnell et al., 1989). However, in other studies recognition of mothers was not confirmed until about 3 months (Kurzweil, 1988).

Color Vision The color vision of neonates is extremely limited. Neonates as young as 1 day old can tell the difference between a white stimulus and some shades of yellow-green (Adams, 1995); 4-day-old infants are able to discriminate red from green, and infants as young as 3 days of age prefer colored over noncolored stimuli (Adams, 1987; 1989). The size of the stimulus is important because in experimental situations neonates show some color discrimination to an 8-inch rectangle but not to a smaller one (Adams, 1995). Within some areas of the spectrum, neonates do not respond to color at all. At 1 month color vision improves only slightly and it is impossible to say whether neonates see color the same way as adults do. However, infants as young as 4 months do show the same color preferences as adults, gazing more at blue and red than at yellow (Banks & Salapatek, 1983).

True or False?
Before 5 months of age, infants do not see color but, rather, shades of gray.

Spatial and Depth Perception Do babies live in a two- or three-dimensional world? To test an infant's depth perception, Gibson and Walk (1960) designed an ingenious experiment. A stand was constructed above the floor, and an infant was placed on the stand, which contained two glass surfaces. The first was a checkerboard pattern, the other a clear sheet of glass. On the floor beneath the clear glass was another checkerboard pattern, giving the impression of a cliff. This experiment, using what is called the **visual cliff,** showed that children 6 months or older would not crawl from the "safe" side over the cliff even if their mothers beckoned to them (Figure 5.2).

When infants as young as 2 months are placed on the deep side of the cliff, the heart rate of these infants slows, indicating interest not fear (Campos et al., 1970). Although young children develop depth perception very early, it is only at 6 months or later that they develop a fear of the cliff. Dogs, goats, and cats show a much earlier avoidance of the cliff.

In sum, neonates do see and process information, albeit on a very limited basis. They see forms and can track slow moving targets, but their visual acuity and ability to focus are poor. Finally, they scan the field according to rules that may be innate, indicating that part of visual processing is inborn. However, visual abilities develop quickly, and these primitive prewired programs give way to more adult scanning and visual processing.

visual cliff A device used to measure depth perception in infants.

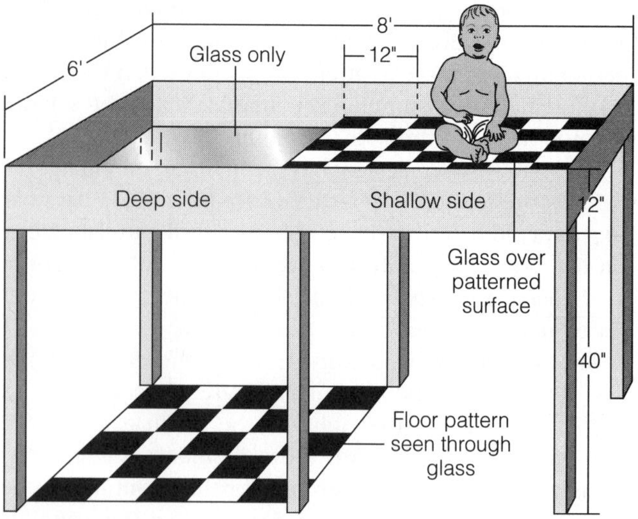

Figure 5.2
The Visual Cliff Apparatus
Source: Based on Gibson and Walk, 1960.

Hearing

Infants can hear from the moment of their birth (Wertheimer, 1961). Neonates as young as 3 days old turn their heads in the direction of a continuous sound (Muir & Field, 1979). The auditory threshold—the intensity at which the newborn is capable of hearing—is somewhat higher than in adults (about 10 to 20 decibels higher; Bremner, 1988). Some authorities believe that infants can hear in the womb, although this is debatable. Newborns only 3 days old will change their sucking behavior to listen to their own mother's voice rather than to another female's voice (DeCasper & Fifer, 1980). The newborn does not have extensive experience with the mother's voice so this effect may occur because the baby has heard its mother's voice while developing in the womb (Fifer & Moon, 1984). Neonates whose average age was about 2 days demonstrated a preference for a specific passage that their mother read out loud during the last 6 weeks before birth when compared with one they were not exposed to during the prenatal stage (DeCasper & Spence, 1986).

True or False?
Infants are born deaf but quickly develop their sense of hearing.

The neonate's auditory capability is better developed than the visual abilities. Studies have shown that newborns react to pitch, volume, and even rhythm (Eisenberg, 1970; Sansavini, Bertoncini, & Giovanelli, 1997), and coordinate their body movements to other people's speech rhythms (Condon & Sander, 1974). Human neonates

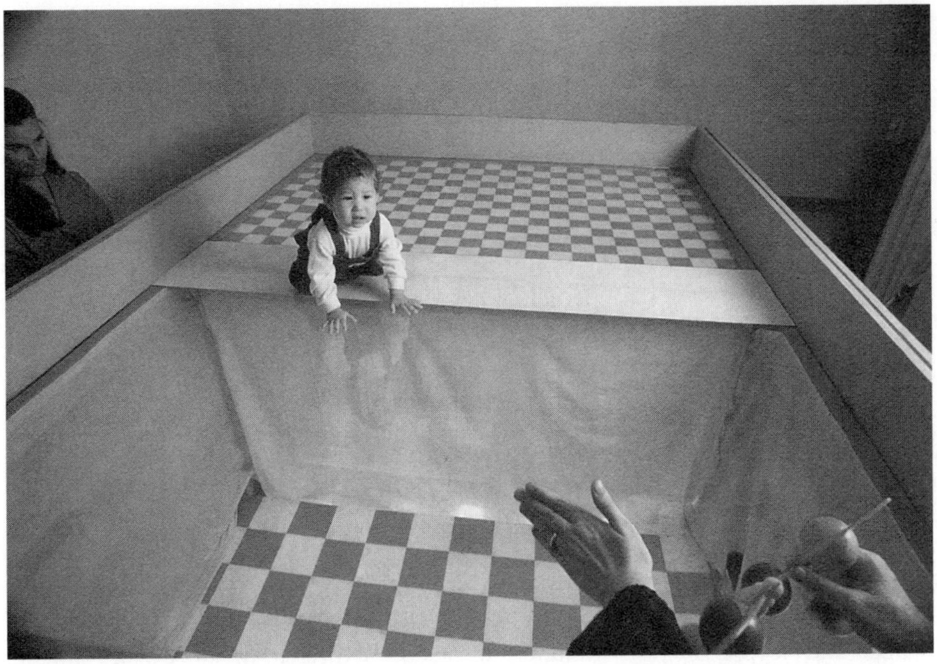

Babies develop depth perception at an early age. In this experiment, a 6-month-old infant would not crawl across what looks like a cliff even though the mother beckoned.

respond to most sounds within the human voice range (Webster, Steinhardt, & Senter, 1972) and are also more sensitive to higher-pitched sounds (Aslin, Pisoni, & Jusczyk, 1983). Infants are also tuned in to language from birth (Aslin, Pisoni, & Jusczyk, 1983), and as early as 1 month after birth, they can distinguish between the sound of a "p" and that of a "b" (Eimas et al., 1971).

Many stimuli provide information to more than one sense; they are multimodal in nature. The appearance of mother is also often accompanied by mother's voice. As people walk toward the infant, their voices become louder. Infants show evidence of understanding this in their first year (Lewkowicz, 1996). Five-month-old infants were placed where they could see two video screens, one with the motion picture of a train coming toward the infant and another with the train moving away; an audiotape corresponding to either event was played. Five-month-old-infants matched the auditory and visual information correctly, as measured by their visual fixation (Pickens, 1994).

Smell

Infants as young as 7 days old turn differentially to their mother's breast pad even if offered another woman's breast pad (MacFarlane, 1981), but this is not seen in 2-day-old neonates. Two-week-old breast-fed neonates can recognize the smell of their mother when presented with gauze pads that had been placed in the mother's armpits. However, these children cannot recognize their father's odors, and nonbreast-fed children cannot recognize either their mother's or their father's odors (Cernoch & Porter, 1985).

Even bottle-fed infants can identify the odor of lactating females. When presented with a pad that had been worn on the breast of a nursing mother and a pad that had been worn by a nonnursing mother, 2-week-old bottle-fed females turned preferentially toward the pad that had been worn on the breast by nursing mothers (Makin & Porter, 1989). This demonstrates that nursing mothers may produce a general odor that attracts infants as well as very specific odors that their own infants can recognize. Such discrimination on the basis of smell is impressive (Porter, Bologh, & Makin, 1988).

Taste

Newborns 1 to 3 days old prefer sucrose to glucose (Engen, Lipsitt, & Peck, 1973). When fed solutions that tasted bitter, sweet, sour, or salty, neonates only 2 hours old showed different facial responses to each taste except salty (Rosenstein & Oster, 1988). Some researchers note that the newborn is more sensitive to taste stimuli in early infancy than at any other time (Reese & Lipsitt, 1973). We can conclude that the sense of taste is functional in the neonate and well developed during infancy and toddlerhood.

Pressure and Pain

Neonates are responsive to tactile stimulation, especially around the mouth. They can feel pain from birth but are not as sensitive to pain for the first day or so. This may reduce some of the infant's perception of pain during the birth process. Within a few days this sense changes dramatically (Lipsitt & Levy, 1959), which contributes to the baby's ability to respond to painful stimuli that might be injurious. Some people conclude incorrectly that infants do not experience pain or interpret it as adults do. The infant does indeed experience pain from birth (Azar, 1996; Anand & Hickey, 1987). The human neonate's neural pathways as well as the brain centers necessary for pain perception are well developed.

The neonate is born with several sensory abilities that develop rapidly throughout infancy and toddlerhood. The infant actively seeks out new stimuli during attempts to experience and understand the world. This process is facilitated by changes in the sleeping-waking cycle. As infants mature, they spend more time awake and alert, which allows for even more exploration of their environment.

The Sleeping-Waking Cycle

The neonate's favorite activity is sleeping and the newborn infant has no day-night sleep cycle, as any parent

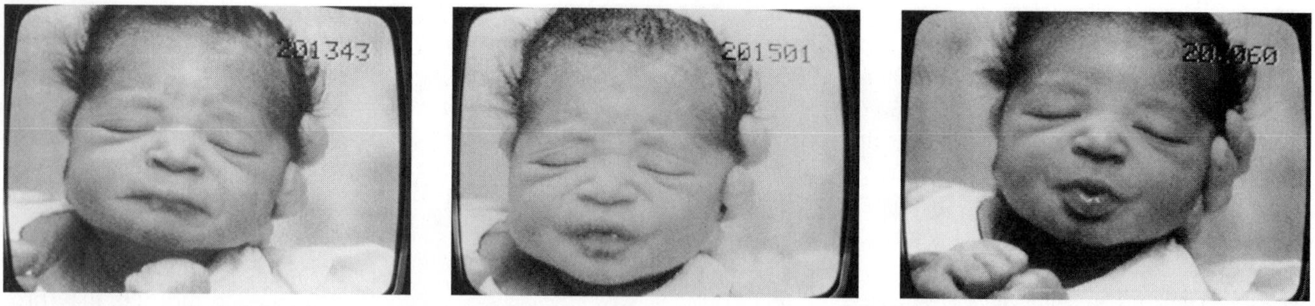

A sweet solution will elicit facial expressions in infants. Initial negative facial actions are followed by relaxation and sucking.

can attest (Harris, 1995). The neonate is as likely to sleep during the day as at night. The 24-hour sleep/wake cycle is usually established by between 12 to 16 weeks after birth, but individual differences exist and children continue to get up during the evening even after the pattern is established (Harris, 1995). The amount of time spent sleeping decreases during the first year. As infants proceed through their first year, they cry, feed, and sleep less (Michelsson et al., 1990).

> ***True or False?***
> Infants at 8 months actually spend more time sleeping, crying, and feeding than newborn infants.

Neonates, older children, and adults show some interesting differences in sleep habits. When both children and adults are awakened from sleep in which they show *rapid eye movements (REM),* they report vivid dreams. The typical adult spends about 20% of sleep time in REM sleep. Normally the adult begins in non-REM sleep and after about an hour switches to REM sleep. About 50% of infants' sleep—an astounding one third of their day—is spent in REM sleep (Harris, 1995; Roffwarg, Muzio, & Dement, 1966). Premature infants show even more REM sleep and REM periods are found in fetuses as early as at 18 to 20 weeks (Harris, 1995). In addition, infants typically begin their sleep patterns in REM sleep. By the age of 3 months the amount of REM sleep is reduced to about 40%, and infants no longer begin their sleep in that state (Harris, 1995; Minard et al., 1968).

The functions of sleep and REM are probably quite complex in the newborn. Perhaps newborns use the extra REM to provide a self-stimulatory experience because they sleep so much of the day. The fact that REM sleep decreases as waking time increases provides some evidence in that direction (Roffwarg et al., 1966). Other psychologists argue that the REM sleep fosters brain organization and development, which is particularly rapid at this stage of development (Berg & Berg, 1979).

Besides waking and sleeping, newborns experience a number of transitional sleep states that fit into neither category (Figure 5.3). As the infant grows, these transitional states decrease, and the infant's state can more easily be measured and classified. Peter Wolff (1969) argues that infants show seven sleeping or waking states:

1. Regular sleep: During this state, the infant lies quiet, subdued, with eyes closed and unmoving. The child looks pale, and breathing is regular.
2. Irregular sleep: In this state, the infant does not appear as still, showing sudden jerks, startles, and a number of facial expressions, including smiling, sneering, and frowning. The eyes, though closed, sometimes show bursts of movement, and breathing is irregular.
3. Periodic sleep: This is an intermediate state between regular and irregular sleep. The infant shows some periods of rapid breathing, with jerky movements followed by periods of perfect calm.
4. Drowsiness: In this state, the infant shows bursts of "writhing" activity. The eyes open and close and have a dull appearance.
5. Alert inactivity: The infant is now relaxed and has a bright, shining appearance but is inactive. The infant searches the environment, and breathing is irregular.
6. Waking activity: The infant in this state shows a number of spurts in activity involving the entire body. Respiration is irregular. The intensity and duration of these movements vary with the individual.
7. Crying: In this familiar state, the infant cries. Crying is often accompanied by a significant motor activity, and the baby's face may turn red.

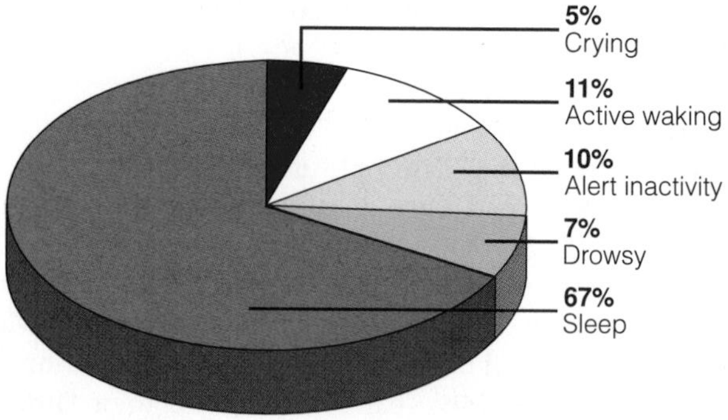

Infants spend more time sleeping than in any other activity.

Figure 5.3
Infant States
Source: Data from Berg, Adkinson, & Strock, 1973.

Knowledge of infant states is important because the response of an infant to a stimulus depends on the infant's state when tested (Parmelee & Sigman, 1983). Some reflexes are stronger and more reliable in one state than in another. The infant's sensory thresholds are also mediated by the baby's state. In the alert inactive state, infants may turn away from strong auditory stimuli toward more gentle voices. During the transition states, the infant can go either way. If the stimuli are pleasant, the infant is drawn out into an alert state and is more responsive. The amount of alertness an infant shows may affect the neonate's opportunities for early stimulation. Parents can interact for longer periods with an infant who shows more alert awake periods (Colombo & Horowitz, 1987). Infants learn about their environments most in periods of quiet alertness and attentiveness. An infant's state also influences adult behavior—when children cry, parents soothe them rather than play with them (Bornstein, 1995).

Infant Crying

Perhaps the most familiar infant state is crying. The cry of an infant has survival value. It informs others of the baby's condition and encourages parents to care for the infant. The infant's cry has a physical effect on parents. Mothers' heart rates increased as they watched videotaped recordings of infants, particularly their own, crying (Weisenfeld & Klorman, 1978). Parents' sensitivity and responsiveness to infants' cries have a powerful effect on infants. Infants whose mothers respond promptly to cries exhibited less crying in later months (Bell & Ainsworth, 1972). Babies who are held may become more secure and require less contact later.

Young parents are often concerned that they will not understand what the infant is communicating through its cry. However, there are qualitative differences in the cries (Wolff, 1969), and parents can usually understand the meaning of each cry from environmental cues.

The infant emits a number of different cries. The *hunger cry* is heard when the infant is hungry as well as when there is any environmental disturbance. It starts out arrhythmically and low in intensity but gradually becomes louder and more rhythmic. The *mad* or *anger cry* follows the same general pattern as the hunger cry, except it is more forceful because more air is pushed past the vocal cords. The *pain cry* is different. The first cry is much longer, as is the first rest period. It lasts as long as 7 seconds, during which time the infant lies still holding his or her breath. This is followed by the gasping intake of air and cries of shorter and varying duration. The pain cry begins suddenly, and no moaning precedes it. The initial segments of the pain cry are particularly potent stimuli for both adult males and adult females (Zeskind et al., 1985). Mothers with some experience are somewhat better than nonmothers at guessing the exact cause of the cries and spend more time in activities that might soothe the infant's distress (Gustafson & Harris, 1990).

The Infant's Ability to Learn

If newborns are to survive, they must learn about their new world. Even neonates can learn through the three processes of classical conditioning, operant conditioning, and imitation. Researchers report some success using classical conditioning with infants. The sucking reflex can be conditioned by sounding a tone that acts as the conditioned stimulus and following it by inserting a nipple, which acts as the unconditioned stimulus (Lipsitt & Kaye, 1964). After pairing the tone and insertion of the nipple, the infants sucked to the tone (conditioned response).

Operant conditioning is easier to demonstrate in neonates. Infants were allowed to suck on a nipple and were rewarded by being allowed to hear music (Butterfield & Siperstein, 1972). The longer they sucked, the more music they heard. Two-day-old infants sucked longer and longer to hear the music but would not do so if sucking led to the music's being turned off. Infants can be conditioned to turn their heads in a particular direction if rewarded with milk each time they turn in the desired direction (Sameroff & Cavanagh, 1979).

Many studies indicate that neonates are capable of imitative behavior. Newborn infants ages 0.7 to 71 hours imitated an adult's facial gestures of opening the mouth and sticking out the tongue (Meltzoff & Moore, 1983) and infants less than 3 days old can imitate head turning (Meltzoff & Moore, 1989). Infants 12 to 21 days old imitate facial and manual gestures (Meltzoff, 1977). Infants opened their mouths and stuck out their tongues when the same behaviors were modeled by an adult. There is also some evidence that neonates can match their own facial expression (happy face or sad face) to a model demonstrating these facial expressions (Reissland, 1988). Some studies, however, have not succeeded in replicating this imitation of facial gestures (Kaitz et al., 1988). Exactly when and what infants imitate is still debated, but the fact that they do is agreed upon (Anisfield, 1991).

Reflexes in the Newborn

Infants also enter the world programmed with a number of specific responses to the environment in the form of reflexes that enable them to deal efficiently with stimuli in their environment (Table 5.1). A **reflex** is a simple automatic reaction to a particular stimulus. Reflexes connected with feeding such as the **sucking reflex** are well established in the newborn. Place something in an infant's mouth, and the baby will suck vigorously. The infant also shows the **rooting reflex.** If you stroke the

reflex A relatively simple automatic reaction to a particular stimulus.

sucking reflex A reflex found in young infants in which an infant automatically sucks when something is placed in the mouth.

rooting reflex A reflex in young infants in which a stroke on a cheek causes the infant to turn in the direction of the stimulus.

Table 5.1 Some Neonatal Reflexes

REFLEX	ELICITING STIMULUS	RESPONSE	DEVELOPMENTAL DURATION
Babinski	Gentle stroke along sole of foot from heel to toe.	Toes fan out; big toe flexes.	Disappears by end of first year.
Babkin	Pressure applied to both palms while baby is lying on its back.	Eyes close and mouth opens; head returns to center position.	Disappears in 3 to 4 months.
Blink	Flash of light or puff of air delivered to eyes.	Both eyelids close.	Permanent.
Diving reflex	Sudden splash of cold water in the face.	Heart rate decelerates; blood shunted to brain and heart.	Becomes progressively weaker with age.
Knee jerk	Tap on patellar tendon.	Knee kicks.	Permanent.
Moro reflex	Sudden loss of support.	Arms extended, then brought toward each other; lower extremities are extended.	Disappears in about 6 months.
Palmar grasp	Rod or finger pressed against infant's palm.	The object is grasped.	Disappears in 3 to 4 months.
Rooting reflex	Object lightly brushes infant's cheek.	Baby turns toward object and attempts to suck.	Disappears in 3 to 4 months.
Sucking reflex	Finger or nipple inserted 2 inches into mouth.	Rhythmic sucking.	Disappears in 3 to 4 months.
Walking reflex	Baby is held upright and soles of feet are placed on hard surface; baby is tipped slightly forward.	Infant steps forward as if walking.	Disappears in 3 to 4 months.*

*The disappearance of the walking reflex has been questioned. Esther Thelen (Thelen, 1986; Thelen & Fisher, 1982) noted a similarity between the stepping reflex and infants' kicks when lying on their back. As infants mature, they show more kicking, and Thelen argues that these kicks are a forerunner of stepping. The walking reflex disappears because the increased mass of the legs alters the way infants can move. The infant's strength is sufficient when the body weight is supported as in the supine position (lying on the back) and the body's movement is aided by gravity. However, the strength is inadequate to lift the legs or support the weight when the infant is upright. The underlying mechanism, then, has not disappeared, but physical factors, such as muscle strength, make it impossible for the infant to show it.
Source: Dworetzky, 1984.

neonate's cheek, the baby turns toward that side to find the breast. The swallowing reflex is also well developed in the newborn. A number of digestive reflexes are also present, including hiccuping, burping, and regurgitation.

The functions of other reflexes either are unknown or can only be guessed at. If you slide your finger along a neonate's palm, the infant's fist will close. This **grasping reflex** is strongest at birth, weaker by 2 months, and usually disappears by about 3 months (Illingworth, 1974). In the evolutionary perspective, the grasping reflex might have some survival value. Most primates must hold on to their mothers for protection, and this reflex would facilitate that attachment. The reflex may have once had the same purpose for human infants. Persistence of this response well past the 3- to 4-month period may indicate brain damage.

If someone tickles the sole of an adult's foot, the toes curl in; when an infant's sole is stroked, the toes fan out. This reflex, known as the **Babinski reflex,** normally disappears by the end of the first year. One of the most interesting reflexes is the **walking (stepping) reflex.** If infants are held upright and slanted a little forward and the soles of their feet make contact with some hard surface, they will show stepping motions (Cratty, 1979).

Of all the reflexes, perhaps the strangest is the **Moro reflex,** which can be elicited in a number of ways. A sudden loud noise or a momentary change in position can cause infants to cry, extend their arms and legs while arching their backs, and then contract their limbs into a hugging position.

grasping reflex A reflex in which a stroke on the palm causes the infant to make a fist.

Babinski reflex A reflex in which stroking the soles of a baby's feet results in the baby's toes fanning out.

walking (stepping) reflex A reflex in which, if the baby is held upright and the soles of the feet are placed on a hard surface while the baby is tipped slightly forward, the infant makes a stepping movement.

Moro reflex A reflex elicited by a sudden loud noise or momentary change in position, causing arching of back, extension of the arms and legs, and finally their contraction into a hugging position.

Most of the strength of many infant reflexes declines and the reflex terminates with time, being replaced by behaviors that are voluntary. One popular theory argues that this occurs because the infant's cortex is not fully wired, so nature allows the infant to run on these programmed reflexes. With time, the cortex, which is responsible for more voluntary activities, takes control and actively inhibits these early reflexes. Slowly, voluntary behavior replaces many automatic responses.

True or False?
Most of the infant's reflexes become stronger during the first year.

Brain Development

The change from automatic, programmed, sensory, perceptual, and motor behavior to more voluntary activity is partly the result of the development of the infant's central nervous system. The newborn's brain, which weighs about 25% of that of a mature adult's, develops rapidly. By 6 months it is 50% of the adult brain's weight, and at 2 years of age, it weighs 75% of what an adult's brain may weigh (Brierly, 1976). Brain growth allows the infant to develop new skills and capabilities.

Most areas of the brain are not well developed at birth. The brain stem and spinal cord are most advanced (Hutt & Hutt, 1973) because they are involved in critical psychological functions and behavioral responses. Most areas of the upper region of the brain—the cortex—are relatively undeveloped. The sensory and motor areas are functional only at a primitive level. The neurons that carry instructions from the cortex to the motor nerves lack the insulating cover—called a *myelin sheath*—that is necessary to conduct impulses efficiently (Harris, 1995). The process of myelinization is faster in the sensory tract than in the motor cortex. This has survival value because the infant requires the information from the senses to safely negotiate the environment.

Between 3 and 6 months, a very important change occurs: the cortex develops. This switch from control by the lower, more automatic, section of the brain to control by the upper, more voluntary, centers affects behavior, allowing more voluntary behaviors to replace programmed behaviors.

The Brain and Experience

The brain does not develop in a vacuum. The brains of rats raised in an enriched environment differ from those raised in an impoverished environment (Rosenzweig et al., 1972). The brains of the rats from the enriched environment had more dendrites, which serve as receivers when neurons send messages to each other. Experience makes an imprint on the brain, and lack of basic experience may hinder the brain's development. Although brain development is partly programmed by genes, experience is important. Visual experience speeds up myelinization of nerves in the visual cortex (Morrell & Norton, 1980).

Wiesel and Hubel (1965) demonstrated the importance of the environment on brain development in a different way. They sewed one eye of a kitten closed for the first 4 to 6 weeks of life. After cutting the sutures and allowing the kitten the full use of its eyes, the cells that would normally process visual information for that eye were unable to do so. There is a critical period of 4 to 6 weeks in which the cortical cells develop an ability to process information from the eye. After that period, suturing the eye had little or no effect on the kitten.

To better understand how experience can influence the brain, William Greenough and colleagues (1987) argue that two different types of information and two different types of brain mechanisms should be taken into consideration. *Experience-expectant information* is environmental information that is common to all members of the species, such as being exposed to visual information. In many sensory areas the connections between nerve cells are overproduced, and which connections remain depends upon the individual's sensory experience. This explains the research showing that there is a critical period for the development of many sensory functions. Early sensory and motor experience is important for the healthy development of sensory abilities and motor skills (Bertenthal & Campos, 1987). If stimulation is absent during certain critical periods, important functions and abilities may never develop adequately.

The second type of information is called *experience-dependent information* and is unique to the individual. It involves learning about the environment and requires neurons to form new connections in response to the environment.

The development of the brain can help us understand cognitive development. Some authorities argue that there are spurts in the formation of the connections between neurons at particular ages, including 2 to 4 months, 7 to 8 months, 12 to 13 months, and 18 to 24 months in human infants. The first 4 months may also be one such period. These spurts are related to leaps in the infant's cognitive abilities (Fischer, 1987). This theory is controversial, and is rejected by some authorities (McCall, 1987).

Our new knowledge of the development of the brain links the brain's development with various sensory, motor, and cognitive abilities. It also demonstrates that the relationship between experience and brain growth is reciprocal: brain growth affects the child's abilities, and the child's experiences affect the growth and development of the brain.

Growth and Motor Development

Infants grow rapidly. They rarely wear their clothes out; they grow out of them first. Growth in the first year is remarkable. After losing some weight during the first week or two, most infants double their birth weight by 4 months and triple it by 1 year. Within 6 months the infant has grown more than 5 inches, and in the next 3 months, 3 more inches will be added to the baby's length. Length usually increases by 50% during the first year. After infancy, the growth rate slows perceptibly. If it continued at this rate, a 10-year-old child would be about 10 stories tall and weigh more than 220 tons (Brown, 1995). In the second year the child grows approximately 4 inches and gains less than 10 pounds (Lowrey, 1978; Whitney, Cataldo, & Rolfes, 1994).

True or False?
Infants triple their weight within a year and increase their length by half.

Most scientists believe that growth is basically a slow but regular process but some challenging research suggests a pattern of brief spurts and stops in which a child could grow as much as ½ inch in a day and then enter a considerable period of no growth (Lampl, 1994; 1995; Lampl, Veldhuis, & Johnson, 1992). This type of growth is called *saltatory growth,* after the Latin word *saltare,* which means to jump or leap. Growth is determined by the secretion of growth hormones. During these periods children are more irritable, sleepy, and hungry. These findings are still controversial at the present time, with some experts arguing that growth takes place in a more gradual manner (Heinrichs, 1995). Infants' growth and development are checked regularly by physicians. During these visits, children also receive their vaccinations. See New Perspectives on p. 102.

Principles of Growth and Development

Infants do not develop in a haphazard manner. Their development follows consistent patterns (Shirley, 1931) and is governed by principles that are now well understood. For instance, the head and brain of the infant are better developed at birth than the feet or hands. The **cephalocaudal principle** explains that development begins at the head and proceeds downward (*cephalocaudal* means from head to tail). Control of the arms develops before control of the feet. A second rule of development notes that organs nearest to the middle of the organism develop before those farthest away. The **proximodistal principle** explains why the internal organs develop faster than the extremities. It also correctly predicts that control of the arms occurs before control of the hands, which predates finger control (Whitehurst & Vasta, 1977).

Muscular development follows a path from control of the large to the fine muscles, the **mass to specific principle.** First, the individual develops control over the larger muscles responsible for major movements; then, slowly, control is extended to the fine muscles. This is why younger children use broad, sweeping strokes of the forearm or hand when coloring with a crayon. Only later does the child gain the dexterity to use finger muscles in a coordinated manner.

Development is also directional. It moves from a state of largely involuntary, incomplete control toward one of voluntary control, from undifferentiation toward subtle differentiation. Under normal circumstances new abilities arise from older ones.

cephalocaudal principle The growth principle stating that growth proceeds from the head downward to the trunk and feet.

proximodistal principle The growth principle stating that development occurs from the inside out—that the internal organs develop faster than the extremities.

mass to specific principle A principle of muscular development stating that control of the mass or large muscles precedes control of the fine muscles.

Motor Development

The first step a child takes is a milestone for the child and a joyous occasion for the parents. Motor advances open up new worlds of exploration (Whitall & Getchell, 1995), and lead to reciprocal changes in the parent-child relationship. The infant finds pleasure in the ability to explore. As children begin to walk, they show an increase in positive emotions and parents react more positively as well (Biringen et al., 1995; Campos et al, 1992).

Many smaller achievements lead up to walking. Mary Shirley (1933) made exhaustive observations of a group of children beginning on the day of their birth. All these infants progressed through the same sequence, leading up to walking. Shirley was interested only in when the baby would first perform any of the acts on her chart (Figure 5.4), such as sitting with support or standing with help, not in how well the baby performed the act. Each of these abilities is perfected with practice.

Although the sequence of motor development is standard, the ages noted are merely guidelines. Radical departures should be brought to the attention of a pediatrician, but there are no "average" babies. Each infant will negotiate each stage at his or her own rate. Some will stay longer at one stage than others. The age at which a child develops these abilities is a function of that child's maturation rate as long as the child is well-fed and healthy and has an opportunity to practice these skills.

The Effects of Practice and Stimulation

No one doubts that some opportunity to practice motor skills is necessary for development of those skills, but there are many roads to mastering them. Hopi children who were reared in the restrictive environment of the cradleboard still walked at about the same age as infants not reared on the cradleboard (Dennis & Dennis, 1940). These children received excellent stimulation and were allowed off the cradleboard more often as they matured. Some evidence for flexibility is also found in a study of children raised in a substandard orphanage in Lebanon who were well behind in their motor development at age 1 year because of environmental restriction. When they received more opportunity to practice these skills, they were much improved by age 4 to 6 years (Dennis & Najarian, 1957). The greater opportunities these children ex-

Figure 5.4
The Sequence of Motor Development Leading to Walking
Source: Shirley, 1933.

New Perspectives: Vaccinations—Is There a Problem Here?

I can remember my grandmother telling me about the death of her daughter at the age of 3 years from measles in New York City in the early part of this century. As she told the story, I could see her sadness and resignation. Deaths from childhood diseases were common in those days.

Table A **Conquering Childhood Diseases**
Major childhood diseases such as diphtheria, polio, and rubella have been virtually eliminated in the United States.

Reported Disease	Greatest Number of Cases, Year	Cases in 1994
Diphtheria	206,939 (1921)	2
Measles	894,134 (1941)	1,000
Mumps[a]	152,209 (1968)	1,500
Pertussis (whooping cough)	265,269 (1934)	4,600
Poliomyelitis (paralytic)	21,269 (1952)	0[b]
Rubella[c]	57,686 (1969)	200
Congenital rubella syndrome	20,000 (1964–1965)	9[d]
Tetanus	1,560[d] (1923)	51

[a]Mumps first became a reportable disease in 1968.
[b]Projected number of vaccine-associated cases, 5–10.
[c]Rubella first became a reportable disease in 1966.
[d]1992 data.
Source: Centers for Disease Control and Prevention, 1995.

How different the situation is today! The incidence of infectious childhood diseases has declined by 97% (see Table A) largely because of the development of effective vaccines, but cleaner water, public sanitation, and antiseptic hospitals also deserve some mention (Jost, 1993).

Many childhood diseases can be prevented by immunization—polio, measles, pertussis (whooping cough), mumps, rubella (German measles), tetanus, diphtheria, hepatitis B, and *Haemophilus* influenza B (Hib). A relatively new chickenpox vaccine and one for bacterial meningitis are also available. With the exception of tetanus, all these diseases are contagious (Robinson et al., 1994). The Public Health Services advisory committee on immunization recommends that by the age of 15 months children should have a basic series of vaccinations on a particular schedule, a sample of which is shown in Figure A. The progress made in reducing the prevalence of these diseases must stand as one of the greatest achievements of 20th-century science.

Children in the United States cannot enter school without proof of inoculation and so by age 6, almost all children are fully inoculated (Pollock, 1994). Yet, the record for younger children is disappointing and the Centers for Disease Control and Prevention (CDC) estimates that between about a third and a little more than half of all preschool children in the United States (up to 6.3 million) have not

Figure A
Recommended Childhood Immunization Schedule, United States, January–December, 1997

	DPT[1]	Hepatitis B[4]	Polio	H. Influenza B[5]	MMR[2]	Varicella[3]	TD
Birth		x					
1–2 months		x					
2 months	x		x	x			
4 months	x		x	x			
6 months	x			(x)			
6–18 months		x					
12 months							
12–15 months				(x)	x		
12–18 months			x			x[7]	
15 months							
15–18 months	x						
18 months							
4–6 years	x		x		(x)[6] or		
11–12 years					(x)		
14–16 years							x

[1]Diphtheria, pertussis, tetanus
[2]Measles, mumps, rubella
[3]Chickenpox
[4]Adolescents who have not previously received 3 doses of hepatitis B vaccine should initiate or complete the series at the 11- to 12-year-old visit. The second dose should be administered at least 1 month after the first dose, and the third dose should be administered at least 4 months after the first dose and at least 2 months after the second dose.
[5]Three H. influenza B (Hib) vaccines are licensed for infant use, and the schedule varies for doses after 4 months, depending upon the vaccine used.
[6]The second dose of MMR is routinely recommended at 4 to 6 years of age or at 11 to 12 years of age, but may be administered at any visit, provided at least 1 month has elapsed since receipt of the first dose.
[7]Varicella vaccine can be administered to susceptible children any time after 12 months of age. Unvaccinated children who lack a reliable history of chickenpox should be vaccinated at the 11- to 12-year-old visit.
Note: This information should not be used as a substitute for the medical care and advice of your pediatrician. There may be variations in treatment that your pediatrician may recommend based on individual facts and circumstances.
Source: American Academy of Pediatrics, 1997.

New Perspectives: Vaccinations—Is There a Problem Here? (continued)

received all 15 inoculations by their second birthday (Jost, 1993).

The percentage of American children vaccinated differs greatly by community. A significant difference exists between rates among poor and nonpoor children—significantly more poor children do not receive their inoculations (USDHHS, 1995). Some inner-city neighborhoods have only a 50% level of vaccination (Curry & Rosensteel, 1995) and the problem is particularly severe among homeless children. This disparity is alarming and, because poor children tend to live in clusters, the chances of an outbreak are greater.

The reasons for this lack of immunization are hotly debated. Some point to the cost of immunization (Children's Defense Fund, 1993), although poor children receive them free. Simply stated, immunizations are too expensive for some low- and middle-income parents. In 1982 the cost of a complete set of childhood vaccines was $23.29 whereas in 1992 it stood at $243.90 (Pollock, 1994). The pharmaceutical companies can be accused of profiteering and they are easy targets.

A more detailed investigation shows that the situation is just not this simple. First, if producing vaccines was so profitable, why has the number of companies making vaccines fallen from 12 to 5 between 1984 and 1994 (Pollock, 1994)? Fewer companies want to make vaccines because of the fear of liability for a child who has an allergic reaction, even to an approved vaccine (Pollock, 1994). Another component of the price that is rarely mentioned is the government tax on vaccines—$25 for a full set. Last, the cost of bringing vaccines to market is much higher today and approaches $200 million. Most of the research on new vaccines is privately conducted. New vaccines, such as those for hepatitis B and bacterial meningitis, which have recently been marketed, proved to be very expensive to develop and market.

The pricing policies of pharmaceutical companies should be scrutinized. Public officials have the responsibility to ensure that vaccine prices remain reasonable. However, the Public Health Services National Vaccine Advisory Committee did not identify cost as one of the most important barriers to immunization. The Committee argued that missed opportunities for administering vaccine, lack of access to health care, and lack of public awareness of the benefits of immunization were the most significant barriers.

The chief reasons for the lack of immunization of young children lies in the areas of health delivery and public awareness. Simply stated, it is too difficult to get children inoculated; too many barriers exist. Many public health clinics are not open at convenient hours and are understaffed. Some require the child to undergo a complete physical examination, to have a referral from a private physician, or to enrol in a comprehensive well-baby program before immunizations are given (Jost, 1993).

Public complacency is also a problem—most parents have never heard of the diseases their children need to be inoculated against. They do not know anyone who has ever contracted one and so do not see the urgency of protecting their children. Occasionally, we are reminded that many of these illnesses are not eradicated but rather just controlled. In 1989 major outbreaks of measles hit American cities with thousands of cases reported and more than 100 deaths recorded over a 3-year period (Jost, 1993). Language problems and cultural traditions that do not stress prevention hinder some parents from taking advantage of inoculation programs for their children (Curry & Rosensteel, 1995).

How can the percentage of infants and toddlers being inoculated be increased? Some advocate providing all immunizations free of charge, as is done in many other countries. In the United States, children on Medicaid and those who have no medical insurance are offered vaccinations free. However, since the federal government began funding immunizations in 1955 it has never required parents to prove financial need in order to get shots at public clinics. Most vaccinations are administered in private physicians' offices for a fee; some insurance policies do not cover the cost of vaccinations. There is a substantial debate on just how to distribute vaccines, where shots should be given, and who should receive them free of charge (Satcher, 1995; Thompson, 1995). Making inoculations free to everyone would be very costly, unnecessarily supporting upper- and upper–middle-class people who can pay for the shots themselves, and would not correct problems of service delivery and public apathy.

No matter how the inoculation problem is examined, the health care delivery system must be made easier to use. Longer clinic hours and the use of mobile vans to make vaccinations more accessible are needed. Computerization of records on a local basis would surely help. For example, some parents lose or do not bring their child's record of vaccinations, which can be a problem if they use different clinics. Computerization would permit timely reminders and keep track of each child's vaccinations. Physicians should routinely check a child's immunization status at every opportunity, including at hospitalizations and emergency room visits (CDC, 1993). Also, requiring proper inoculations for children entering day care is probably worth a try.

On the educational front, alerting parents and teachers of the importance of inoculations is necessary. Vaccination days are a possibility and community advertising, in languages that the people understand, is needed. Special campaigns improve vaccination rates somewhat, for example, volunteers going door-to-door to remind parents of opportunities to vaccinate their children. Nontraditional advertising, such as reminders on baby food jars and diaper boxes, is an interesting addition to public health programs (Robinson et al., 1995); computer-generated telephone reminders also help (Public Health Reports, 1993). *(continued)*

New Perspectives: Vaccinations—Is There a Problem Here? (continued)

State tracking can be especially helpful (The Economist, 1995). Georgia health officials carefully audit records of public clinics, providing feedback to clinic personnel about children who need additional inoculations. A child's immunization status is checked whenever the child enters any health clinic and the needed shots are administered. This program has raised the rate of immunizations for young children (Shalala, 1993).

The miracle of immunization has produced a worldwide reduction in childhood diseases. In 1967 the World Health Organization began a global program to wipe out smallpox. In 1977 the last case of smallpox occurred and 2 years later the WHO announced that for the first time a major disease had been completely eradicated from the globe. Vaccination rates are increasing markedly in developing nations (The Economist, 1994). The United Nations' active program is credited with saving 2 million lives a year (UNICEF, 1993). Even in politically unstable countries vaccination programs have gone forward. During the civil war in El Salvador U.N. agencies persuaded both warring parties to declare a cease-fire during national vaccination days!

The problems faced by health care workers in developing countries differ somewhat from those faced by developed nations. Some diseases, such as polio, that have been all but eliminated in the United States and Europe continue to cause concern especially in more isolated regions (Cooper, 1995). The limited health delivery systems of some developing countries cannot cope with multiple visits for vaccinations. The United Nations is now funding the development of a supervaccine that will allow all the vaccines to be given in one shot (CQ Researcher, 1993). Although it is doubtful that this can be accomplished, a more convenient vaccination schedule could help. The need for refrigeration is also a major problem in these countries. A major scientific breakthrough may be at hand that would involve drying vaccines such that they would not need refrigeration (The Economist, 1995). Also, if a vaccine costs more than $1 many countries simply will not be able to afford it, which is why many countries do not use the hepatitis B vaccine. New vaccines are needed around the world. Some are specific to certain geographic areas, such as the need for a vaccine for dengue fever and malaria in Africa and South Asia, and of course the entire world waits for the possibility of a vaccine for AIDS.

Progress from this point on will be more difficult to achieve. As more children receive their inoculations, only the more difficult cases or most remote geographic areas remain to be served. The challenge for public health officials is to deliver the inoculations conveniently, affordably, and effectively, convincing parents of the need to have their children inoculated. Many challenges lie ahead, but the real enemy is complacency, which robs people of the will to continue the age-old battle against infectious diseases, which for the first time in history, human beings finally are in a position to win.

perienced after age 1 were sufficient to counter their poor early environments. If corrected, some of the effects of a deprived environment can be reduced and children can catch up; if the environment doesn't improve, these children will not develop normal motor abilities.

In three studies of isolation and deprivation of infants, the results did not show a complete catchup (Razel, 1988). The idea that a small amount of practice later on is as good as a great deal of practice earlier is simply not true. These infants suffered severe and long-lasting difficulties. Although later training may help, the infant does suffer from early deprivation and such deprivation cannot be completely compensated for. The role of the environment in early motor development has been underestimated (Zelazo, Zelazo, Cohen, & Zelazo, 1993).

Most children receive at least minimal stimulation and some opportunity to explore their environment and do not suffer stimulus deprivation. To hasten motor development a number of programs have been advanced, and some research has shown the programs to be effective. Infants given training that capitalized on the stepping reflex enabled them to walk at an earlier age than expected (Zelazo et al., 1972). Six-week-old infants who were given two 3-minute daily sessions of exercise in stepping or sitting or both for 6 weeks showed these abilities well before infants in two control groups who did not receive the exercise program. The effects of the practice were specific, affecting only the skills trained. The improvement did not generalize to other skills (Zelazo et al., 1993). The group that received training in both stepping and sitting naturally showed improvements in both.

Some infant exercise programs are valuable (White, 1993) and help children to develop physical skills, but parents must take care not to put too much pressure on their children, seeking large gains and making such programs "work" rather than pleasure. Parents should be wary of stimulation programs that promise large gains in motor or cognitive development. Our efforts would better be spent on optimizing the environment, allowing each child to take advantage of opportunities to explore and learn when the child is ready, and helping the child practice these skills.

Focus on the Toddler

At 1 year of age the child enters the toddler stage. The defining skill that differentiates an infant from a toddler is the ability to walk (Bornstein, 1995). Toddlers are active, engaging beings with a mind of their own. There is

Toddlers have a great deal of energy and, because they don't always know what is dangerous, must be constantly monitored.

an exciting quality to their newfound capabilities, and they go from one activity to another with breathtaking speed. There is wonder in everything they do. As Alicia Lieberman notes, "Who else could show us so convincingly that a wet, muddy leaf lying on the ground is actually a hidden marvel, or that splashing in the bath can bring ultimate joy? Toddlers have the gift of living in the moment and finding wonder in the ordinary. They share those gifts by helping the adults they love to reconnect with the simple pleasures of life" (1993, p.1). Yet, accidents are common at this age. Obviously the health and safety of young children is a prime responsibility for parents. This is why it is important that the care-giver carefully evaluate the child's environment. It is a good idea to get down on your knees to look at the room as a toddler might see it. One parent who did this found nails sticking out of a piece of paneling, which could have injured the child.

Toddlers are no longer completely dependent on other people and they want to do things their own way. Most of all, toddlers are explorers who have to balance their need to be independent and competent with the need for protection, love, and care (Lieberman, 1993). The motivation to explore forms the foundation upon which learning occurs. Young children show a persistence and a drive to master skills. When learning to walk, the child may fall, get up, fall again, get up, and the pattern will continue (Hauser-Cram, 1996).

Toddlers can communicate verbally in an elementary manner. By age 2, a child may use up to 320 words, understands many more, and is beginning to put two or three words together. Two-year-olds use their verbal skills to show their independence, saying "no," "me do it," and "mine," often. Although they may understand some commands, they may still be unable or unwilling to carry them out. The increased motor behavior, desire for independence, and tendency to be negative explains why parents often call this age the "terrible twos."

During toddlerhood control issues take center stage. Resistance and angry behavior peak during the second year and then show a decline after and throughout the school years (Kopp, 1992). Mothers and fathers react more positively to 12-month-old than to 18-month-old children and self-reported enjoyment of child-rearing declines from 18 to 24 months (Fagot & Kavanaugh, 1993). Mild conflicts are common; conflicts between 2-year-olds and their mothers are twice as common as those between 4- or 5-year-olds (Lieberman, 1993). Temper tantrums peak at between 18 and 21 months but clearly drop by 3 years.

On the other hand, toddlers do comply with requests quite often and many parents manage to deal with their 2-year-olds, despite the increase in motor activity (Kaler & Kopp, 1990). Actually, the "terrible twos" label may help somewhat because parents may ascribe stubborn, negative behavior to the child's age and not to the child, telling themselves that the stage will pass (Lieberman, 1993).

Some families do have a very difficult time dealing with the typical behaviors shown by 2-year-olds and experience many management problems (Belsky, Woodworth, & Crnic, 1996). Families who have the most problems often use "negative control" strategies, which include statements and behavior that convey anger and irritation. Children in these poorly functioning families show more negativity and power struggles escalate constantly.

Much of the reason why parents believe that their toddlers are so difficult is that they compare them with older children as well as long for the days when the children took longer naps. Simply stated, many people have inappropriate expectations for toddlers and do not understand the way toddlers learn. Toddlers learn with their whole bodies (Gonzalez-Mena, 1986). They learn through action, learning far more through active manipulation than through listening. Toddlers are explorers who are absorbed in their world. When toddlers become interested in something, they can attend to it for a long time. As they approach the age of 3, they develop simple skills in the area of eye-hand coordination, and some of what seems like random exploration is reduced. The progression from movement that appears to occur just for the sake of movement to more controlled motor activity that seems increasingly oriented toward ends or consequences occurs during the toddlerhood stage (Bullock & Lutkenhaus, 1988).

Dealing with toddlers requires patience and skill. Toddlers hear many comments: protective ones such as "don't step in the road," admonishments to wash their hands and warnings to be careful or they will break something (Edwards, 1995). Children's compliance increases from the toddler through the preschool to the school years (Whiting & Edwards, 1988). Even children under the age of 2 comply when they understand a command and do not when they don't (Kaler & Kopp, 1990). When 18-, 24-, and 30-month-old toddlers were observed in situations in which their parents asked them not to interrupt, to stop playing, to clean up and so forth, children of different ages were compliant in some situations and not others. The group of 18- and 30-month-old toddlers was more compliant than the group of 24-month-old toddlers in a situation in which the parent stopped reading and told the child it was time to go on to a different activity, but 24-month-old toddlers were more compliant than 18- or 30-month-old toddlers when presented with two different problems, a sorting task and a puzzle that were too difficult, and told to work by themselves (Schneider-Roisen & Wenz-Gross, 1990)—to some extent compliance is situational.

One way to deal with toddlers is to give them choices (Gonzalez-Mena, 1986). For example, telling a child, "I don't want you walking around while you eat, but you can eat in either the blue chair or the red chair," can resolve a problem. Also, preventing dangerous behavior by physically intervening by gently holding an arm before it hits someone or knocks the pot of hot water off the stove may be necessary. Prevention is best, and some negative behavior, such as saying "no" or crying, are to be expected, especially when the child is tired.

Choices in Parenting

Most of the choices that affect children are made by their parents. These include feeding, the extent to which children will be treated differently because of their gender, and toilet training.

Infant Nutrition

Infants' nutritional needs differ from those of adults and nutritional decisions throughout infancy and childhood are important to the future health of the child. A majority of new mothers breast-feed their infants but a slow decline has been found in all groups (Ryan et al., 1991b). Recent evidence shows that full-time maternal employment is related to a reduced probability of breast feeding; a return to work on a full-time basis is related to the complete cessation of breast feeding. Women who work part-time are even more likely to breast-feed than women who are not employed at all (Lindberg, 1996). Women need some additional encouragement and education in how to return to work full-time and still breast-feed their infants.

The American Academy of Pediatrics recommends that infants receive breast milk for the first 6 to 12 months for good reason. Breast feeding has important advantages for both mother and baby (Lawrence, 1991). Mother's milk is the natural food for human infants and meets all the infant's nutritional requirements, with the possible exception of vitamin D (Whitney et al., 1994; Woodruff, 1978). Vitamin D deficiency is rarely seen in breast-fed infants because it is synthesized with the help of a normal amount of exposure to sunlight. Mother's milk contains a number of helpful substances not found in prepared formulas. Some antibodies protect the infant against intestinal disorders, and immunities are passed on in breast milk (Brown, 1995). Mother's milk also contains chemicals that promote the absorption of iron. In addition, the incidence of allergies is less in breast-fed infants than in infants raised on artificial formulas. Breast feeding also promotes better tooth and jaw alignment (Hamilton, Whitney, & Sizer, 1985). Some preliminary evidence relates breast feeding to the promotion of neurological development (Lucas et al., 1992). There are significant psychological benefits to the breast-fed infant; the close contact between mother and child encourages the growth and development of the mother-infant bond and satisfies the infant's need for warmth and physical contact.

Breast feeding is nutritionally sound and almost all women are biologically capable of it (Brown, 1995). But what about bottle feeding with prepared formulas? Certainly infants can be successfully raised on formula (Schmitt, 1979). Whereas the infant's natural nutritional and psychological needs are normally satisfied naturally during breast feeding, bottle feeding may require more thought and concern. The care-giver must be certain to hold the baby close to give him or her the physical contact that is so important to infants. Today, many infant formulas meet the nutritional standards set by the

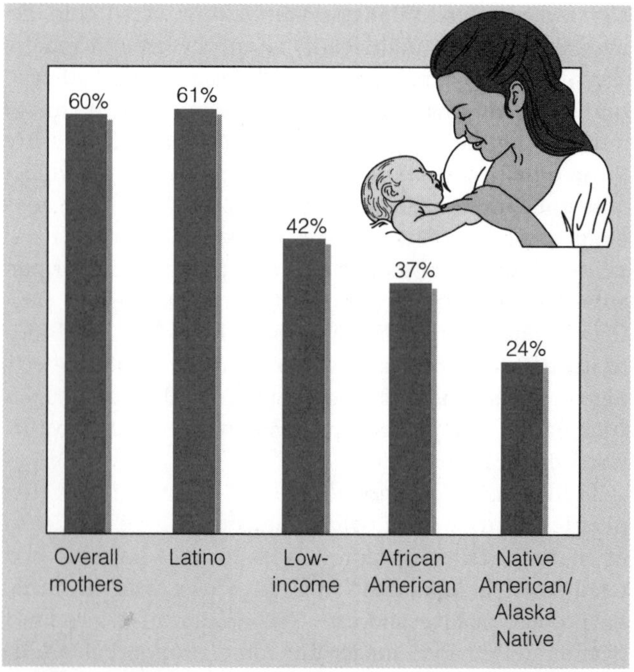

Datagraphic
Breast feeding in the United States
Source: Data from U.S. Department of Health and Human Services, 1996.

Committee on Nutrition of the American Academy of Pediatrics. Most formulas are based on fortified cow's milk, but the incidence of allergies to cow's milk is estimated to be less than 1% of infants (Woodruff, 1978). It may be necessary to bottle feed the child if the mother is taking certain medications. Breast-feeding mothers should watch their diet because caffeine, alcohol, and environmental contaminants may be transferred to breast milk (Brown, 1995).

Many women do not breast-feed very long; in fact most stop by 4 months. Mothers who receive early and repeated breast-feeding information are more likely to choose to breast-feed and to do so longer (Saunders & Carroll, 1988). Education may be an important key to increasing the percentage of women who breast-feed their infants.

Gender Differences—How Parents View Sons and Daughters

The first announcement made to the parents concerns the baby's gender. The first question people ask when told a new baby has arrived concerns gender (Intons-Peterson & Reddel, 1984). How important is gender to the way infants are treated? What physical differences exist at birth?

Gender Differences at Birth At birth the average male is about 2% longer and about 5% heavier than the average female (Doyle & Paludi, 1991). Females are more mature at birth and continue to develop at a faster rate. Girls are 4 weeks more advanced in skeletal development at birth (Tanner, 1970), and they reach motor milestones faster than males. The average female child sits up, walks, becomes toilet-trained, and talks earlier than the average male child (Kalat, 1980). Another difference is that the average female infant performs more rhythmic behaviors, such as sucking and smiling, than the average male infant (Feldman, Brody, & Miller, 1980). Males exceed females in large-muscle movements, such as kicking; they also show greater muscular strength and can lift their heads higher at birth (Korner, 1973). At the end of the first year males show higher activity levels, but because this is found through observation the question of bias is raised (Kohnstamm, 1989).

These early physical and developmental differences may affect parental behavior, magnifying the effects of the differences. The more developmentally superior females may be more responsive. By being capable of sitting up, walking, or talking at an early age they may be more reinforcing to their parents. Advanced development could then lead to more attention and different types of interaction with their care-givers. The differences in how parents treat their sons and daughters, however, are more often based upon their different expectations from each gender rather than on any real differences. For example, even when male and female infants are the same size, weight, and physical condition, parents see daughters as weaker and more sickly and males as sturdier and more athletic (Rubin, Provenzano, & Luria, 1974). When parents who merely had seen their newborns behind the nursery glass were asked to describe their children, both fathers and mothers described their sons as more alert and stronger and their daughters as more delicate (Rubin et al., 1974).

Some indirect evidence indicates that this labeling process continues throughout infancy and toddlerhood. When videotapes of 17-month-old children were shown to adults and the babies' genders were indentified, men described children labeled as male in such stereotyped terms as "independent," "aggressive," and "active" (Meyer & Sobieszek, 1972). These same babies were interpreted as delicate, passive, and dependent when they were told the children were female. In another study, 13-month-old infants were observed in a play group. Although no gender differences were found in assertive acts or attempts to communicate with adults, the adults attended more to boys' assertive behaviors and less to those of girls. Adults attended more to girls when the girls used less intense forms of communication. Eleven months later, gender differences were observed as boys were more assertive but girls talked to adults more (Fagot et al., 1985).

Questions Students Often Ask

I don't buy the idea that if a baby girl wears pink and a boy wears blue that this leads to some big differences later on, especially since we remember so little from that age period. What difference does it make?

Relating early treatment to later behavior is difficult in any area of interest, but in gender-related behaviors it is even more challenging. Differences exist in the way we treat sons and daughters and it is difficult to deny the behavioral differences that appear later on. Some people would have you believe that all we have to do is to look at the early parent-child interactions and we can predict later gender-related behaviors, especially those that differentiate between how girls and boys act. This is simply not true. Peers, teachers, the media, and a host of other agents of socialization have a complicated effect upon the individual.

Just because someone cannot remember what happens during infancy does not mean that it is not important. A pattern that begins in infancy may continue throughout childhood. It doesn't just end after the age of 2 years. In addition, the differences found in parent-child interaction, especially with toys, seems to indicate that different skills and potentials are unlocked by different toys and interactions and these may lead to greater interest in these skills. For example, if a little boy is given a baseball to play with and receives reinforcement for doing so, the boy may improve his skills, find it pleasurable, and do it more often thereby becoming better at it. A girl who is not given this type of feedback may not develop these skills.

The problem is that we are always looking for simple answers to what are complex questions. How parents treat their infants is important to their later gender-typed activities, but at the same time we do not find a direct input-output relationship between parental sex-typed treatment of infants and later behavior because other influences impact on the child.

As boys and girls develop, males are reinforced for attempts to develop gross motor skills involved in large-scale physical play more than females are (Smith & Lloyd, 1978). Boys are allowed to play alone more than girls (Fagot, 1978). Even the physical environment provided for boys and girls in infancy and toddlerhood differs. Boys are provided with more sports equipment, tools, and large and small toy vehicles. Girls are given more dolls and children's furniture. Girls are dressed in pink and multicolored clothes more often, and boys are dressed more in blue, red, and white (Pomerleau et al., 1990).

Gender-based differences in treatment continue as children develop. When mothers and fathers were videotaped playing with their 1- to 2-year-olds on two occasions, no differential reinforcement of boys and girls for masculine or neutral play was found, but the child's gender affected parents' choice of toys to use during the interactions (Eisenberg et al., 1985). Parents of boys chose more masculine toys, and parents of girls chose more neutral toys. Parental toy choice, but not parental reinforcement, was related to children's play choices. Parents did not actively discourage or encourage their young children to play with the toys the children chose themselves. However, merely by selecting play items parents encouraged their children toward some toys and away from others.

The fact that parents and children select the same sex-typed toys when they have a choice was amply demonstrated when parent-child pairs ranging in age from 18 to 23 months were observed during play (Caldera, Huston, & O'Brien, 1989). Each parent-child pair was asked to play with six different sets of toys. Toys were categorized as masculine (trains and wooden blocks), feminine (dolls and a kitchen set), and gender neutral (puzzles and shape sorters). Each set of toys was placed in its own covered box and parents and children engaged in play with these toys for 4 minutes after which they were told to put the toy away and go to the next.

Even when no alternatives were available and parents' involvement was controlled, toddlers showed less involvement with toys stereotyped for the other gender than with those stereotyped for their own gender and they more often rejected cross-gender toys than same-sex or neutral toys. Parents modeled more play with sex-stereotyped toys as well. Parents did not overtly promote play with same–sex-typed toys or discourage play with cross-sex toys. Some parents did have trouble complying with instructions when playing with cross-gender toys. One father playing with his daughter opened up a box with trucks and remarked, "Oh, they must have boys in this study," closed the box and returned to playing with dolls. Mothers and fathers both showed these tendencies.

The nature of the toys influenced parent-child interaction. When playing with masculine toys, especially trucks, few questions were asked and more distance existed between child and parent. A great many animated sounds were made rather than verbal statements. Feminine toys elicited closer proximity and more verbal interaction in the form of questions and comments. The neutral toys elicited the most positive verbal and informative verbal exchanges. These findings may have something to do with the nature of the neutral toys. Parents may associate puzzles and shape sorters with cognitive development. Generally fathers tend to be more concerned than mothers with gender-appropriate behavior and are more likely to give more negative feedback to boys who play with dolls and other soft toys.

Three main conclusions stand out quite clearly from the research in gender differences in early life. First, the initial differences between the genders are quite limited at birth. Second, the treatment of males and females tends to be more similar than different, although the differences may in the end turn out to be important. Parents give both sons and daughters affection and do not generally tolerate aggression from either. Third, although parents often do not vocalize their gender-stereotyped opinions, they may show them in their behavior with their children and certainly in their toy preferences. Fathers are stricter than mothers in reinforcing these stereotyped gender-appropriate behaviors, especially in their sons.

Toilet Training

One of the most common questions about toilet training is how early to start. Sometime in the course of the second year, toddlers begin to recognize the bodily sensations that allow them to control elimination. Besides the obvious maturational capability to control the muscles, there are individual and environmental factors involved in toilet training. Some children do not like being soiled. Others may be aware that their friends do not wear diapers and may train easily and quickly. Still others may require more time and have many accidents. Once a child is maturationally ready, toilet training should not take long. Children can be introduced to the potty, taught about the procedures involved, and given encouragement and social reinforcement. The pressure on the child should be minimized and parents should understand that some children will be ready for toilet training before others.

Some parents toilet-train before the child understands what is expected and can become a willing partner. The ability to do so is rarely shown before between 15 and 18 months and may not occur until 24 to 30 months or even later (Lieberman, 1993). Some toddlers initiate the process themselves by calling their parents attention to the fact that they are eliminating. Beginning the process too early can lead to frustration and negativism, and also makes the process slower. In one study McGraw (1940) started to train one twin from each of two pairs as early as 2 months of age; the siblings were allowed to wait. The early training did not help; the later-trained children trained much more quickly and soon caught up with others. Training started later is faster (Sears, Maccoby, & Levin, 1957). It is best to train a child when the child is ready.

True or False?
The earlier toilet training begins, the longer it usually takes.

Some parents place a great deal of importance on early toilet training. The expectation that a 1- or 2-year-old is going to be completely dry day and night not only is unreasonable but also may be harmful, for it leads to criticism from parents when the child has an accident. The age at which a child will be ready varies from child to child. Children's bowel control precedes bladder control, and the ability to control elimination in the day precedes the ability to do so at night; girls are also somewhat ahead of boys in this area (Oppel, Harper, & Rider, 1968).

The Wonder of Cognitive Development

During the first 2 years of life children develop a basic understanding of the world around them. They learn to recognize objects and people, to search for objects that are not in their field of vision, to understand cause and effect, and to appreciate the concept of space.

Piaget's Theory of Sensorimotor Development

The manner in which infants develop an understanding of their world was described in detail by Jean Piaget. The infant is negotiating the first stage of cognitive development, the **sensorimotor stage** (Piaget, 1962). This stage is called sensorimotor because infants learn about their environment through their senses (hearing, vision, touching) and their motor activity (reaching, grasping, kicking) (Piaget, 1967). Much of an adult's knowledge of the environment is not direct but rather symbolic, being based on words and language and requiring the ability to represent or create a mental picture of what is going on around the person. For instance, when your friend tells you not to sit on the chair that has spilled coffee on it, you don't have to see the coffee or get your pants soggy. You understand the idea behind the statement and can create a mental picture of what has happened. All this is far beyond the abilities of the infant. The infant learns much about objects through manipulation; in the second year the infant begins to show more symbolic understanding—for example, by talking on toy telephones (Bornstein, 1995).

Questions Students Often Ask

How can an infant's behavior be considered intelligence?

Piaget looks at intelligence in terms of changes in the way people deal with the environment. If infants change the way they deal with a toy or a natural phenomenon then they are showing intelligence. A young infant just places everything in the mouth; an older infant may use a utensil to stand for something else (symbolism).

The reason people have difficulty with the idea of infant intelligence is because we all take basic physical laws for granted. For instance, if we drop something we expect it to fall. We understand gravity very well. If I strike my hand against a wooden desk a particular sound is made. But infants do not know these things. They must learn about these simple ideas. The infant who kicks his foot against the crib post time and again is "learning" something about cause and effect; he is learning that when he does this . . . that will occur. One debt of gratitude we owe Piaget is for making us aware of this as well as proposing a sequence to explain how children begin to understand such physical laws as causality.

The Substages of Sensorimotor Development

It is easy to overlook the basic cognitive advances in infancy. The idea that objects exist even if they are out of sight or that by tugging a string with a toy on the end the toy will come toward you must be learned. Piaget described the development of such elementary concepts in terms of six substages. The sequence of substages is believed to be absolute but the ages that children enter or leave them may vary (Flavell, Miller, & Miller, 1993).

Reflexes (0–1 Month): Substage 1 In Substage 1 the infant is basically an organism reacting to changes in stimuli. The behavior of infants is rigid and reflexive. Infants are almost entirely dependent on these inborn patterns of behavior. These not only include sucking and grasping but more subtle behaviors such as eye movements, orientation to sound, and vocalization (Bjorklund, 1995). Behaviors are elicited by environmental stimuli over which they have little control and their range of behavior is limited. Infant reflexes are often modified in an infant's everyday experience. For instance, an infant may suck harder on a bottle containing milk than on a toy placed in the mouth (Siegler, 1991; Ault, 1977).

Primary Circular Reactions (1–4 Months) The most prominent feature of Substage 2 is the emergence of actions that are repeated again and again. These are called **primary circular reactions.** They are primary because they are focused on the infant's body rather than on any outside object (Phillips, 1975). They are circular because they are repeated. The infant is basically trying to re-create some interesting event. For example, an infant's thumb may drop into his or her mouth by accident. This is pleasurable, so after the thumb falls out, the infant attempts to find the mouth again (Bjorklund, 1995).

sensorimotor stage The first stage in Piaget's theory of cognitive development, in which the child discovers the world using the senses and motor activity.

primary circular reactions Actions that are repeated over and over again by infants and centered on the body.

Secondary Circular Reactions (4–8 Months) An important change occurs in Substage 3. **Secondary circular reactions** are observed. Infants now focus their interest not on their bodies but on the consequences of some action on their external environment. The infant does something that creates some environmental reaction. For instance, an infant shakes a rattle and is surprised to find that it produces a sound. The child may pause, then shake the rattle again, hear the sound, and continue the activity (Flavell, Miller, & Miller, 1993).

Coordination of Secondary Reactions (8–12 Months): Substage 4 In Substage 4 the child coordinates two or more strategies to reach a goal, thereby showing true intention. Means and ends are now separated. The child shows perseverance in spite of being blocked. For instance, if you place your hand in front of a toy, the child will brush it away. The child is using the brushing away behavior in order to use a reaching or grasping behavior (Piaget, 1952).

Tertiary Circular Reactions (12–18 Months): Substage 5 Infants in Substage 5 begin to use **tertiary circular reactions.** Although actions are still repeated and thus circular, they are no longer carbon copies of each other. Children now seek out novelty (Ault, 1977). They are little scientists, experimenting with the world to learn its characteristics and mysteries. The Substage 5 child picks up objects from the crib and throws them out, listening and watching intently to learn what they sound like and how they look on the floor (Willemsen, 1979). When you put them back in the crib, the child may throw them out again. Everything must be done physically. If a child wants to know whether a tricycle will fit under the table, he or she must physically do it; the child cannot tell just by looking at it (Bjorklund, 1995).

The difference between the child's using secondary circular reactions and tertiary circular reactions is variability (Ault, 1977). Suppose the child is placed in a playpen with lots of toys. The infant in the secondary circular reaction substage drops a block from a particular height again and again, without varying the action. The child in the substage of tertiary circular reactions may drop different items out of the playpen and vary their distances from the ground.

Invention of New Means Through Mental Combination (18–24 Months): Substage 6 Substage 6 marks the beginning of representation (Flavell et al., 1993). Toddlers can think about objects and the relations between objects without having to directly and physically act upon them. To some extent, trial and error can be performed in the mind (Bjorklund, 1995). The Substage 5 child uses trial-and-error experimentation but the Substage 6 child can try out alternatives internally by imagining them (Flavell et al., 1993). The child can now think of an object independent of its physical existence. Children can also use language now, putting words together meaningfully. This also reflects their ability to use symbols.

The character of play and imitation changes. Children are now capable of **deferred imitation;** that is, they can observe some act and later imitate it. Children also show some pretend play in this substage (Belsky & Most, 1982). Until now, spoons were something to suck on, eat with, or bang. Now a spoon may stand for or represent another, unrelated object, such as a person or a guitar. The infant has moved from the realm of coordinated actions to that of symbolic representation.

Object Permanence

"Out of sight, out of mind" the saying goes. Objects that are out of sight quite literally cease to exist for the infant. Most students are surprised to discover that infants must tortuously develop an understanding that objects exist outside their perception of them, an understanding known as **object permanence.** Researchers study the development of object permanence by hiding objects in a variety of ways and observing children's search patterns. Infants develop their ability to understand object permanence in a series of substages (Piaget, 1954).

In Substage 1 (0–1 month), infants look at whatever is in their visual field but will not search when an item or individual disappears. For instance, the infant looks at mother but doesn't search for her when she leaves the room (Ault, 1977). Instead, the infant looks at something else.

During Substage 2 (1–4 months), the infant will continue to look in the direction of an item after it disappears. A 2-month-old may follow mother but when she leaves the visual field, may continue to gaze at the point where mother was, not anticipating her reappearance at another place (Bjorklund, 1995). However, Piaget does not see this as true object permanence, because the search is basically passive (Piaget, 1954).

> ***True or False?***
> The 1-month-old infant believes that mother no longer exists when she leaves the room.

During Substage 3 (4–8 months), we begin to see some active search for items. Now if an object is partially covered by a handkerchief, the infant tries to lift the cloth to discover the rest of the object (Diamond, 1982). Children who drop something from a high chair look to the ground for it. It is as if they can now anticipate the movement of an item. The child at this stage does not show complete object permanence, however, for the search for the hid-

secondary circular reactions Repetitive actions that are intended to create some environmental reaction.

tertiary circular reactions Repetitive actions with some variations each time.

deferred imitation The ability to observe an act and imitate it at a later time.

object permanence The understanding that an object exists even when it is out of one's visual field.

den object consists only of a continuation of eye movement, some expectation that something in motion may continue its trajectory. The child will not search for an object if it is completely hidden from view.

In Substage 4 (8–12 months), the child will search for an item that is completely covered by a handkerchief. However, it is here that the child makes an error—called the *AB error*—that has fascinated psychologists for years. If the child is allowed to find the item in one place a few times and the item is then hidden elsewhere while the child watches, the child will search in the first location (Figure 5.5) (Wellman, Cross, & Bartsch, 1987). Once the infant finds the object at the new location, if the toy is again hidden at the original location, the infant will now make an error by reaching back to the location that was most recently correct (Diamond, Cruttenden, & Neiderman, 1994).

According to Piaget the child does not really have object permanence and has simply identified the object with a particular location (Diamond, 1982). Other psychologists disagree. For example, Baillargeon and Graber (1988) argue that infants may understand where the object is, but because they may not be able to integrate knowledge and action, they make the error. Still others suggest that the errors result from memory constraints and the child's inability to inhibit what was earlier a successful response (Diamond, Cruttenden, & Neiderman, 1994).

In Substage 5 (12–18 months), children can follow the object through the displacements. They no longer search for an item under the first pillow if it has been moved to a second one while they are watching (Piaget, 1954). The Substage 5 child's understanding of object permanence is far from perfect, however. Piaget designed a simple test to demonstrate the child's limitations. His daughter had been playing with a potato and placing it in a box that had no cover. Piaget (1954, p. 266) notes:

> I then take the potato and put it in the box while Jacqueline watches. Then I place the box under the rug and turn it upside down thus leaving the object hidden by the rug without letting the child see my maneuver, and I bring out the empty box. I say to Jacqueline, who has not stopped looking at the rug and who has realized that I was doing something under it: "Give Papa the potato." She searches for the object in the box, looks at me, again looks

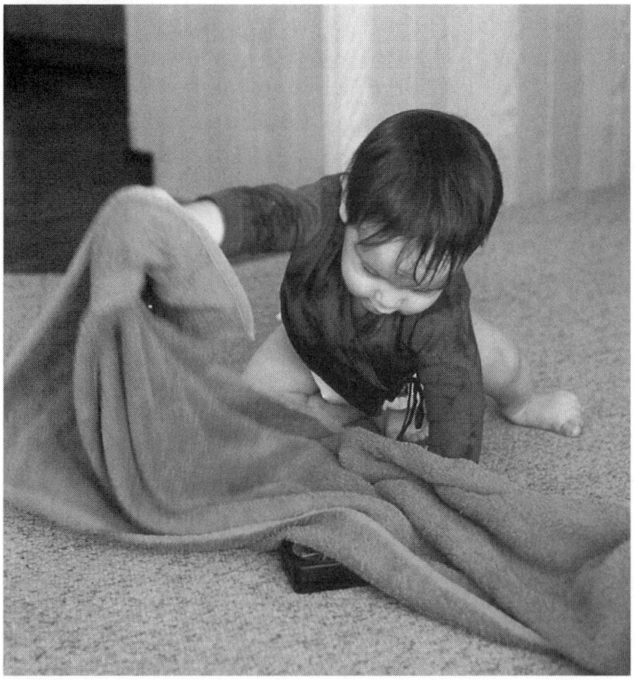

As infants develop, their search patterns become more sophisticated.

Figure 5.5
The Stage-4 Search Task The experimenter hides the object in the first location (1), whereupon the infant searches successfully (2). But when the experimenter hides the object at the second location (3), the infant searches again at the original location (4).
Source: Based on Bremner, 1988.

at the box minutely, looks at the rug, etc. but it does not occur to her to raise the rug in order to find the potato underneath.

Note that in this stage the movement from one hiding place to the other must be performed under the child's gaze. The child's search for a hidden object is still based on visual information. No logical inferences are formed, and there is no mental representation of the object.

During the last substage (18–24 months), children become free from the concrete information brought in through their senses. They can now construct a mental representation of the world and locate objects after a series of visible displacements. They can imagine where an item might be (Diamond, 1982).

Object Permanence and Infant Behavior

Piaget's description of the infant's cognitive development explains some common infant behavior. For instance, children in Substage 5 of the sensorimotor period who are dropping toys out of their playpens despite being asked to stop are not doing this out of any malicious intent. They are practicing tertiary circular reactions. In the old game of peekaboo, in which you cover your face with your hands then take your hands away, as a child gains more knowledge of object permanence, the child will pull down your hands, exposing your face. The child is validating the expectation that you are still there. Or perhaps a 4-month-old begins to cry hysterically after playing alone for a while. You notice that the baby has dropped a toy out of sight. Since children younger than 6 months do not actively search for hidden objects, you may find that merely picking it up and placing it in the baby's field of vision is enough to stop the crying.

The Sensorimotor Stage Under Scrutiny

Piaget's description of infant cognitive growth was a breakthrough. The basic sequences described by Piaget seem to hold (Harris, 1989) and studies conducted all over the world have generally supported Piaget's view of the sequence in which children develop these skills (Nyiti, 1982; Uzgiris, 1973). However, recent research has raised doubts about specific areas of Piaget's sensorimotor stage. The way Piaget presented the tasks to infants may have affected the infants' reactions. In addition, a fundamental error in logic may have crept into these studies: just because infants do not successfully complete a particular task does not mean they are unable to do it. Perhaps they have the ability to perform some task but either are not motivated to do so or cannot perform the motor activity required. Whenever an infant cannot perform a particular task, Piaget interprets the inability in terms of competency: the child does not have the cognitive sophistication necessary. But some psychologists are not so sure about that; if the physical composition of the task were modified, perhaps the results would be different.

There is much evidence to suggest that infants are more capable than Piaget believed (Johnson & Aslin, 1995; Flavell et al, 1993). Individual and situational factors influence the infant's performance. When examining object permanence studies, such factors as familiarity with the object and motivation must be taken into account. The infant's physical abilities may also be an important confounding factor in tests of object permanence.

The testing procedures themselves may lead investigators to make the logical error that performance always reflects competency. Even the type of cover used when hiding an object seems to make a difference. Nancy Rader and her colleagues (1979) studied object permanence in infants whose median age was 160 days. They hid plastic keys in a well and covered the keys with either a 12-by-12-inch washcloth or a 7-by-7-inch piece of manila paper covered with blue felt. Infants differed in their success with the task; some succeeded in uncovering the keys when the paper cover was used but not when the washcloth was hiding their toys. The awkwardness of the covers used in an object permanence test may affect the test's outcome.

Some psychologists argue that young infants show object permanence if tested somewhat differently from Piaget's standard procedures. When we separate knowledge from coordinated behavior, we find that infants may understand object permanence at a considerably earlier age than Piaget believed. A series of experiments by Baillargeon (Baillargeon et al., 1985; Baillargeon, 1987) with infants 3½, 4½, and 5 months old demonstrated that these infants understood object permanence. Infants were shown a screen moving through a 180-degree arc along a flat surface. The infants habituated to the moving screen (Figure 5.6). Then a box was placed behind the screen, and infants were shown either a possible or an impossible event. The possible event involved the screen's moving until it reached the box, stopping, and then returning to its initial position. In the impossible event the screen moved until it reached the box and then kept on going as though the box were not there (thanks to a hidden platform that dropped the box out of the way). It thus completed its full arc before reversing direction. The researchers argued that if the infants had object permanence and knew that the box continued to exist after it was hidden from view, they would pay more attention to the impossible event than to the possible event, since the impossible event should be novel and the possible event similar to the event to which they had been habituated. Infants beginning at 3½ months of age paid more attention to the impossible event, demonstrating that they knew the box did not disappear. Baillargeon argues that the results of these experiments show that Piaget's claim of object permanence being understood by infants at the age of 8 months or so needs to be reevaluated. Other studies using different formats find some knowledge of object permanence somewhere between the age of 2 and 4 months (Johnson & Nanez, 1995; Slater et al., 1994).

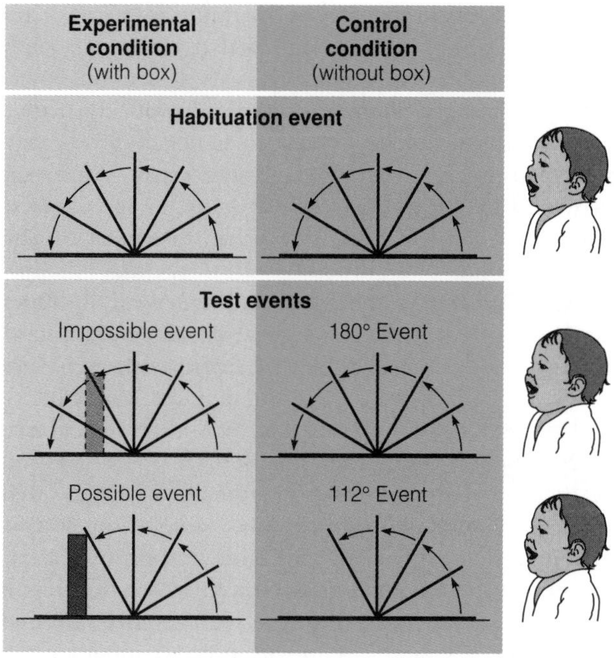

Figure 5.6
Schematic representation of the habituation and test events shown to the infants in the experimental and control conditions.
Source: Baillargeon, 1987.

Infants possess this notion long before they can perform the coordinated movements necessary to show their knowledge on the standard Piagetian task (Johnson & Aslin, 1995). Perhaps young infants do not show object permanence because most studies force children to engage in an active search, which involves eye-hand coordination and motor skills they do not yet possess. Most object permanence searches require the coordination of two distinct actions into a means-end sequence, for example, reaching for and removing a cover (the means) in order to grasp and play with a hidden toy (the end). The integration of separate schema into an intention means-end sequence does not occur prior to Substage 4 (about 8 months) according to Piaget, so Piaget may have been testing for object permanence using behaviors that he himself believed infants were not yet capable of producing (Flavell et al., 1993).

The same problem is found in representation. Piaget argues that it is not until 18 months (Substage 6) that representation is present, but studies of infants learning American Sign Language show that children as young as 6 to 7 months show clear symbolic signs (Meier & Newport, 1990). Piaget argued that in Substage 6 deferred imitation began, but again this is in doubt. When 9-month-old infants watched an adult model perform a series of actions such as pushing a button on a box to produce a sound, and were not permitted to do so right after the demonstration but were presented with the materials 24 hours later, they performed the action themselves at this later time (Meltzoff, 1988). Piaget's theory considers the substages as invariant, but it is now clear that these claims do not hold up well (Flavell et al., 1993).

Putting It All Together

Piaget's description of infant cognitive growth is an excellent starting point. He has focused our attention on infant cognitive growth and encouraged us to form more detailed questions with regard to such growth (Gratch, 1979). At the same time the evidence showing that other factors may affect performance should make us wary of generalizations about what an infant or toddler can or cannot do.

Infants follow Piaget's progression if tested in the standard Piagetian way. However, infants are very sensitive to the demands of the task. An analysis of what skills are necessary for success may yield information concerning why a child fails at a task. For example, when a child must retrieve a hidden object, eye-hand coordination skills, motor skills, three-dimensional perception, and memory abilities are required. Piaget did not detail these skills; that task remained for others. Children who fail a particular task may lack any one (or more) of the required skills or abilities. The simple fact is that if you test children the way Piaget did, you get his results. However, by looking more closely at the task, in this case realizing the importance of coordinating action with what the child knows, we begin to separate what the child knows from the specific ways in which Piaget tested these abilities. It seems likely that infants are more capable than even Piaget thought they were.

Information-Processing Skills

The idea that infants remember things is easy to demonstrate experimentally but difficult to comprehend. We rarely retrieve memories from infancy or toddlerhood, yet memory is basic to the learning process.

Memory

Research on early memory focuses on recognition and recall. The skill of **recognition** involves the ability to choose the correct response from a group of answers and is similar to the multiple-choice questions on a test. **Recall** involves producing the correct response on the basis of very limited cues and is similar to the task you face when taking an essay test.

Studies show that recognition is excellent even in young infants. When 3-month-old infants were presented with pictures of their mother, they were later able to tell the difference between their mother's face and that of a stranger (Barrera & Maurer, 1981). Some researchers are impressed not only with infants' recognition ability but also with their retentive abilities. Neonates can retain memory for specific sounds over a 24-hour period (Swain, Zelazo, & Clifton, 1993). Infants as young as 2 months were able to recognize a visual pattern and retain it for 24 hours (Martin, 1975); 5- to 6-month-old

recognition A way of testing retention in which the subject is required to choose the correct answer from a group of choices.

recall A way of testing retention in which the subject must produce the correct response given very limited cues.

infants familiarized with a face for only 2 minutes were able to recognize the face after a delay of 2 weeks (Fagan, 1973). This recognition memory is quite resistant to interference—it improves with age, with older infants showing superior retention on tests of recognition (Rose, 1981).

Infants are very sensitive to the conditions of the memory task. Three-month-old-infants can be conditioned to kick to move a mobile and respond at a high rate if they are tested after a 24-hour delay on the same mobile. However, they do not respond if they are tested with a different mobile. They remember the details of their training mobile and discriminate between the situations (Bhatt & Rovee-Collier, 1996; 1994). Infants are even sensitive to reminders. Infants between 2 and 6 months old were conditioned to kick their foot to activate a mobile suspended over their crib. They were then made to wait for varying periods of time. Two-month-old-infants showed retention for about 1 to 3 days, after just 2 days of training, 3-month-olds showed retention of about 6 to 8 days, and 6-month-old infants for 15 to 16 days (Hayne & Rovee-Collier, 1995). Even after these time periods, if infants are given a reminder by having the experimenter move the mobile around, infants show retention for longer intervals (Hayne, 1990). However, if the mobile is just placed over the child or the child sees the stand or ribbon (which had been attached to the foot and the stand), no memory improvement takes place. Reminders are only effective when infants encounter stimuli that are virtually identical to those present when the original learning occurred.

Questions Students Often Ask

Why can't I remember anything from when I was an infant?

The first answer is really another question. Why should you? Most of an infant's day is spent in activities that are hardly memorable, so the lack of memories would be expected. Infantile amnesia is an interesting phenomenon. Some psychologists explain it by referring to changes in encoding or retrieval that occur during the first few years. However, it is also possible that since memory retrieval occurs only when infants encounter stimuli that are virtually identical to those present during the original encoding situation, any changes in perception, attention, or the selection of which stimulus to look at, would make it less likely the individual would remember anything, especially after very long intervals. This need for specific cues to retrieve a memory makes it difficult, if not impossible, for useful memories to be retrieved by cues or in contexts that have not previously been encountered. Last, the acquisition of language may play a part. We do not know what happens to memories that were originally encoded without language, especially after an individual develops language. A retrieval failure might occur when linguistically capable individuals try to find memories that are primarily perceptually based (Hayne & Rovee-Collier, 1995).

Studies of recall are not as plentiful as research on recognition. Piaget (1968) argued that children do not show true recall before 1½ to 2 years of age, but today many psychologists believe that recall probably begins somewhere in the first year (Mandler, 1990). Eight-month-old infants show recall in certain situations. Brody (1981) first trained infants to touch a lighted face. When the infants did so, they were reinforced by the pleasant sounds of a music box, the sequential illumination of lights around the panel, and a view of a puppet rotating on a turntable for 3 seconds. After the infants had learned to touch the light for the reward, they were presented with a delay. After the face was lighted, the light was turned off and a screen covered the face for 250 milliseconds. Then the screen was lifted, and the infants were reinforced for touching the face that had been illuminated before the lowering of the screen. After the infants had learned this response, the researcher varied the amount of time in which the screen covered the face by 3, 6, and 9 seconds. Brody found that 8- and 12-month-old infants could remember the location of the stimulus during the 250-millisecond delay, but that only the 12-month-old infants could tolerate the longer delays.

The period between 8 and 12 months of age is one of rapid change in the infants' cognitive abilities. Neurological changes that improve memory occur (Kagan, 1979a, 1979). The infant develops the ability to retrieve older information spontaneously and apply it to current circumstances. This improvement in memory has behavioral implications. For instance, stranger anxiety is rare before 7 months, but it increases rapidly between this time and the end of the first year. Separation anxiety occurs when an infant shows anxiety at being left by the parent or care-giver. It emerges at about 8 or 9 months, rises to a peak at 13 to 15 months, and then declines. Kagan argues that these events are partly explained by the growth of the infant's memory abilities, which include the ability to retrieve past memories and anticipate future behavior based on past experiences. When the father of a 10-month-old leaves the room the child remembers the father's former presence and compares it with the current scene in which the father is not there. A child who cannot resolve the difference may be distressed by this event. In addition, the 10-month-old may cry when mother walks toward the exit without leaving. Kagan believes that this child can now generate hypotheses about what might happen in the future and anticipates the parent's exit.

Predicting Later Intelligence

We know that infants show intelligent behavior and are impressed by the development of their cognitive abilities. But do these infant abilities predict later cognitive abilities?

The most commonly used evaluation instrument for infants and toddlers is the **Bayley Scales of Infant Development,** which has recently been updated (Bayley, 1969; Psychological Corporation, 1993). The Bayley II contains three parts. The Mental Scale evaluates sensory/perceptual abilities, the ability to respond to various stimuli, memory, learning, and problem solving, and the beginning of verbal communication. The Motor Scale assesses the degree of control of the body, coordination of muscles, and movement. The Behavior Rating Scale provides information on attention, persistence, and emotional and social behavior. The Bayley Scales yield a valid description of the child's intellectual development at the time (Bayley, 1970) but do not have much predictive power with normal infants, until about 18 months (Francis, Self, & Horowitz, 1987; McCall, 1979). The Bayley Scales largely measure sensorimotor abilities whereas intelligence in older children depends largely on verbal abilities and learning.

True or False?
Intelligence tests given to normal infants at 6 months predict later school achievement quite well.

If this is true, psychologists would need to measure basic information processes that underlie future intelligence if they wish to predict IQ. Indeed, some information-processing skills predict later development (Dougherty & Haith, 1997; DiLalla et al., 1990). Infants who habituate more quickly develop better cognitive skills, as measured on such Piagetian tasks as object permanence during early toddlerhood (Miller et al., 1977) and speaking vocabularies at 12 months (Ruddy & Bornstein, 1982). Another skill is visual recognition memory at 6 months, which predicts scores on tests of cognitive skills from 2 to 6 years in preterm infants (Rose & Wallace, 1985a). Such information-processing abilities as the ability to encode visual stimuli efficiently and to remember visual or auditory stimuli are related to superior performance on traditional tests of verbal intelligence and language tests during childhood (Bornstein & Sigman, 1986). These represent basic information-processing abilities (Benson, Haith, & Fulker, 1993). Speed and efficiency of information processing, attention, and memory—all cognitive processes—may underlie intellectual functioning throughout life.

Other authorities believe that social variables are predictive of later intelligence. The socioeconomic status of the child in the first 12 to 18 months of life appears to be a good predictor of later intellectual development (McCall, Hogarty, & Hurlburt, 1972). Socioeconomic status is usually analyzed in terms of income, parental education level, and occupational rating (Rubin & Balow, 1979). Low-socioeconomic-status homes differ greatly from middle- and higher-socioeconomic-status homes, especially in the area of verbal behavior (Tulkin & Kagan, 1972). Mothers from low socioeconomic backgrounds talk much less to their infants. Perhaps because of lack of education or the stresses of poverty, they may not be able to provide the verbal stimulation or the environment necessary for their children to maximize their cognitive skills.

Yet the entire concept of socioeconomic status is far too broad and too general a consideration, and it ignores the wide variations that exist in intelligence within socioeconomic levels. General statements about the low-socioeconomic-status parent ignore these differences and stigmatize an entire group of people. Finally, socioeconomic status is not an easy variable to change. Poverty, lack of education, and a low-status job cannot be altered overnight by a child development specialist. It would be better to focus on the differences among families, variables such as parental responsiveness, the child's environment, and parenting skills, all of which can be improved (Ramey, Farran, & Campbell, 1979).

One instrument frequently used to measure various aspects of the home environment is called the Home Observation for Measurement of the Environment **(HOME) Scale.** This scale provides a measure of quality and quantity of the emotional and cognitive elements in the home setting (Elardo, Bradley, & Caldwell, 1977). Much convincing research demonstrates an important relationship between children's home environment and their health and development (Bradley et al., 1994).

The HOME inventory measures six factors, including the parent's emotional and verbal responsivity, the avoidance of restriction and punishment, the organization of the environment, provision of appropriate play materials, parental involvement with the child, and opportunities for variety in the daily routine. Information is collected through interviews and observation. The most widely used are the infancy and early childhood versions. Table 5.2 shows some selected items from the parental responsivity subscales of each of the HOME inventories. A substantial relationship exists between the home environment in the first year and intelligence at age 3 (Bradley & Caldwell, 1980), and between HOME scores at 2, 3, and 4 years and later intelligence (Bradley, 1989).

Evaluations of specific elements of the home are more efficient in predicting future intellectual growth than either infant tests or parental education (Elardo, Bradley, & Caldwell, 1975). For example, the intensity and variety of stimuli is related to intellectual development (Wachs, Uzgiris, & Hunt, 1971). Infant's positive experiences in verbal and symbolic learning; perceptual, spatial, and fine-motor experiences; color discriminations; and problem-solving activities are related to IQ scores at 3 years (Carew et al., 1975). The HOME inventory has been successfully used throughout the world (Bradley, 1993).

Bayley Scales of Infant Development A test of intelligence administered to infants between 2 months and 2½ years of age.

HOME Scale A scale that provides a measure of the quality and quantity of the emotional and cognitive elements in the home.

Table 5.2 Selected Items from Parental Responsivity Subscales of the HOME Inventory

Infant/toddler version	Parent responds to child's vocalization with a verbal response. Parent caresses or kisses child at least once during visit.
Early childhood version	Parent holds child close 10 to 15 minutes per day. Parent spontaneously praises child's qualities or behavior twice during visit.
Middle childhood version	Parent sometimes yields to child's fears and rituals (for example, allows night-light, accompanies child to new experiences). Parent responds to child's questions during interview.

Source: Bradley, 1989.

At this point, some tentative conclusions can be drawn. Such factors as the responsivity of the care-giver, parental involvement with the child, the variety of stimulation available, the organization of the environment, the caregiver's restrictiveness, and the play materials available at an early age predict later cognitive development. A healthy home environment in infancy usually stays that way throughout childhood; similarly, an unhealthy home environment in infancy rarely improves greatly as the child grows older. Some of the relationship between the environment during infancy and later intellectual ability is a reflection of the cumulative effects of the environment throughout childhood and does not solely demonstrate the importance of the earliest environment. In addition, some aspects of the home environment will probably be more important at different times.

Parents and Cognitive Development

Most factors that influence cognitive development are determined by the child's parents. Burton White (1971) studied the differences between mothers of competent infants and mothers of less competent infants and found three major differences. The mothers of competent children were designers—that is, they constructed an environment in which children were surrounded with interesting objects to see and explore. They were able to understand the meaning that an activity or experience might have for a child and build on it. Second, parents of competent children interacted frequently with their children in interplays that lasted for 20 to 30 seconds. The children were not smothered with attention, but the parents were always available and ready to help them experience events. They often labeled the environment and shared the child's excitement. Third, the parents of these children were not overly permissive or overly punishing. They had firm limits, but they were not unduly concerned about such minor things as mess and bother.

Most child specialists believe that parental activities that can optimize cognitive growth should be low-key and fun; the child should not feel pressured to achieve too early (Zinsser, 1981). Parental disappointment, anxieties, and expectations can be communicated to young children quite early and may hinder the very development that parents seek to improve. Infants and toddlers have limited attention spans and may go from activity to activity quickly. Equally important is understanding that enriched environments do not always lead to accelerated or enhanced cognitive or perceptual development. Enhanced environments help when there is a match between the encounter and the child's abilities (Hunt, 1961).

True or False?
Parent-child interactions that are aimed at encouraging cognitive development should be fun for the child.

The Question of Acceleration: The "American Question"

These suggestions aim at helping children develop their abilities at their own pace, not at accelerating infants cognitively to make them learn faster. This desire to accelerate is perhaps part of our culture. American educators and parents are often interested in the question of how fast or how early a child can accomplish some academic task. We are impressed with the child who reads at the age of 3 or solves algebraic equations at 8. Reflecting this fascination with speed, researchers have raised the question of whether infants can be accelerated through the period of sensorimotor experience. The entire idea really runs counter to Piaget's ideas.

Piaget was reluctant to make any recommendations to teachers or parents concerning how to maximize a child's potential, let alone how to accelerate the child (Vernon, 1976). Remember that Piaget's theory emphasizes the importance of giving children an opportunity to interact with their environment. It deemphasizes formal instruction. Parents may help their children by designing an environment that is appropriate for the children at their particular point in development and by elaborating on that environment, giving children plenty of opportunity to discover things on their own. Parents should be available to answer questions and interact with their child, but the emphasis is on discovery, not formal teaching and programming.

A number of programs emphasize adult directed activities that promise to teach infants to read early, identify famous artists, and so on. Most of these programs are not based on sound research. In these programs adults dictate how and when learning takes place. In Burton White's research on development, children during the first 18 months who were considered superior in development *chose* most of their activities, except of course for maintenance activities such as feeding and bathing (White, 1993). It is best to design stimulating environments for children and to interact with children so they gain appropriate skills. Rushing a child through these growth stages accomplishes little because accelerated development is not necessarily any better.

Conclusions

The infant begins life with certain programmed physical and cognitive behaviors. As the child matures and interacts with the environment, he or she develops new physical and cognitive skills that allow the infant or toddler both to explore the environment and to develop an understanding of the surrounding world. Labeling the environment, interacting in a positive manner with children, and encouraging children to investigate and explore their world are clearly helpful in promoting development. Parents can and should be active in these areas, but they must be careful not to overdo it, not to pressure their infants, not to believe that faster is always better, or to become schoolteachers instead of parents.

Summary

1. The neonate is born with characteristics and abilities that make survival possible. Newborns can see, hear, smell, taste, as well as experience pain. Their sensory abilities develop quickly.
2. Neonates spend most of the day sleeping and spend a great deal more time than adults do in REM sleep. The infant's state is related to behavior.
3. Classical conditioning, operant conditioning, and imitation have been demonstrated in the neonate. Young infants also habituate to stimuli, that is, they pay less and less attention to stimuli to which they are continually exposed.
4. The neonate is born with a number of reflexes, such as the sucking, rooting, grasping, and stepping reflexes. The functions of the Babinski reflex and the Moro reflex are not known.
5. The brain grows rapidly in the months following birth, and such factors as nutrition and experience are important in optimizing such growth.
6. Development occurs in a consistent pattern from the head downward (cephalocaudal) and from the inside out (proximodistal), and muscular development progresses from mass to specific.
7. Toddlers learn through doing, and they show a desire for independence. During toddlerhood the child begins toilet training. Children who are toilet trained later take less time to train. The toddler's physical abilities often outweigh the child's judgment, making home safety a first priority.
8. There are nutritional and health advantages to breast feeding, but children's nutritional needs can be satisfied through the use of approved formulas as well.
9. Girls are more mature at birth and develop at a faster rate than males. Females show more oral and facial movements. Males show more large musculature movements such as kicking and greater muscular strength. Parents tend to treat their infant sons and daughters differently. Activities requiring gross motor control are more likely to be reinforced in male infants. Fathers are more rigid in gender-stereotyping behavior than mothers. Parents choose sex-typed toys for their children.
10. According to Jean Piaget infants are in the sensorimotor stage, during which they use their senses and motor skills to learn about the world. They do not have the ability to create mental images or to use language or symbols to represent anything.
11. The development of object permanence—the understanding that an object or person exists even if it is out of sight—is an important achievement in infancy.
12. One should not equate competency (knowledge and ability) with performance. Performance depends on motivation, the type of task presented to the infant, and other environmental factors. Some recent experimentation demonstrates that infants are more capable than Piaget believed.
13. Infants have the ability to recognize faces very early. Infants between 8 and 12 months old have some recall abilities.
14. Scores on infant intelligence tests do not predict later intellectual ability very well for normal children. A relationship exists between later cognitive development and the responsiveness of the care-giver, parental involvement with the child, the variety of stimulation the child receives, the organization of the environment, and the play materials available.
15. Allowing children to explore their own world, labeling the environment, encouraging communication, reading to them, ensuring brief interactions in which parents share some experience with the child, and tailoring activities to the child's developmental level promote cognitive growth.
16. The so-called American question asks whether we can accelerate cognitive growth. Such acceleration was discouraged by Piaget, who believed that by designing an appropriate environment and giving children an opportunity to discover the mysteries of life, children can develop their cognitive abilities.

Multiple-Choice Questions

1. The term neonate describes a child between the ages of:
   a. 1 and 3 years.
   b. 1 month and 12 months.
   c. birth and 1 month.
   d. birth and 1 year.

2. Which statement concerning an infant's ability to see is *incorrect?*
   a. Neonates are born quite farsighted.
   b. The infant's ability to see improves rapidly from birth.
   c. Neonates prefer curved lines to straight lines.
   d. Neonates have some color vision but it is quite limited.
3. Psychologists often use an apparatus called the __________ to test young infants for depth perception.
   a. strange situation
   b. visual cliff
   c. valcap
   d. chromometer
4. Which statement concerning the auditory abilities of neonates is *correct?*
   a. Neonates can hear from the moment of birth.
   b. Neonates are most sensitive to sounds in the range of the human voice.
   c. Infants 1 month old can distinguish between some sounds in the environment.
   d. All of the above are correct.
5. Mrs. Campbell's 9-week-old daughter gets up often during the evening and she is concerned that it will continue. Based upon research, you could truthfully tell Mrs. Campbell that:
   a. she would be wise to take the child to the doctor and find out why the child cannot sleep through the night at that age.
   b. infants do not sleep through the night until about 1 year of age.
   c. her feeding patterns are probably keeping the child from sleeping through the night.
   d. this is normal and infants of that age do not sleep through the night.
6. Evidence indicates that infants 1 month old can learn through:
   a. classical conditioning and operant conditioning, but not through imitation.
   b. classical conditioning, but not operant conditioning or imitation.
   c. operant conditioning, but not through classical conditioning or imitation.
   d. classical conditioning, operant conditioning, and imitation.
7. An infant is given a picture on a screen to look at. After a while the infant pays less and less attention to the picture. Psychologists would say that ________ has occurred.
   a. generalization
   b. integration
   c. habituation
   d. substitution
8. As you stroke the cheek of an infant the infant turns towards you and opens his mouth. The infant is showing the ________ reflex.
   a. rooting
   b. Babinski
   c. Moro
   d. tonic-neck
9. The rate of growth after infancy:
   a. stays about the same until about 5 years of age.
   b. increases gradually until 6 years of age.
   c. decreases markedly.
   d. increases in toddlerhood but decreases after age 3 years.
10. Which principle explains why children first use their forearm to draw and then slowly use the small muscles in their fingers?
    a. cephalocaudal
    b. proximodistal
    c. mass to specific
    d. parallel development
11. Which statement about toddlers is correct?
    a. The major development that differentiates the infant from the toddler is talking.
    b. Toddlers are particularly adept at putting a particular thought into words in a variety of different ways.
    c. Enjoyment of parenting shows an increase from 12 months to 18 months and from 18 months to 24 months.
    d. Toddlers are action oriented and learn as they physically manipulate things.
12. Three women, Sally, Sarah, and Seena, all have 3-month-old infants and are breastfeeding them. Sally is returning to work full time, Sarah is returning to work part time, and Seena is staying home until the child is a year old. Based upon the research in the area, which of the following statements is *correct?*
    a. Sally is most likely to stop breast feeding.
    b. Sarah is most likely to stop breast feeding.
    c. Seena is most likely to stop breast feeding.
    d. There should be no difference in the probability that any of them will stop breast feeding.
13. Research consistently shows that parents of infants and toddlers:
    a. encourage sex-typed play activities.
    b. are more likely to be concerned about the health of their sons than daughters.
    c. actively discourage their sons to play with feminine toys and actively discourage their daughters to play with neutral or masculine toys.
    d. expect their infants and toddlers to understand their gestures and verbal statements beginning at 6 months of age.
14. Children in the sensorimotor stage at least until 18 months according to Piaget cannot use:
    a. their senses.
    b. their motor activities.
    c. a combination of senses and motor activities.
    d. symbols.
15. According to Piaget, a child will not search for an item that is completely covered until what age, at the earliest?
    a. 3 months
    b. 6 months

c. 8 months
d. 12 months

16. Modern studies of object permanence find that:
a. the concept itself is flawed.
b. children do not attain object permanence until well after the time Piaget suggested.
c. children may show an understanding of object permanence before Piaget thought possible.
d. object permanence cannot be measured accurately until a child can explain his motivations to the experimenter.

17. Concerning the memory of young infants, psychologists find that:
a. neither recognition or recall is found in infants below the age of 18 months.
b. neither recognition or recall is found in infants below the age of 12 months.
c. both recognition and recall is found in the first year.
d. infants as young as 6 months may remember something but forget it after a delay of less than 5 minutes.

18. The most popular way to measure infant abilities using a standardized test involves using the:
a. Infant Standard Form.
b. Bayley Scales of Infant Development.
c. Lemmington Scales of Infant Intelligence.
d. Bennington Behavioral Scales.

19. Chris argues that psychologists should look at the differences between families in their relationships and the structure of the child's environment in order to predict intelligence. To do this psychologists could use which of the following scales?
a. The HOME Scale
b. The Lexington Scale
c. Location Scales
d. Illinois Test of Psycholinguistic Abilities

20. Mrs. Davis asks a child development specialist how to accelerate her child through the substages of the sensorimotor stage. Piaget called the question of acceleration the:
a. hidden agenda.
b. American question.
c. precocious principle.
d. generation X question.

Answers to Multiple-Choice Questions

1. c 2. a 3. b 4. d 5. d 6. d 7. c 8. a 9. c
10. c 11. d 12. a 13. a 14. d 15. c 16. c 17. c
18. b 19. a 20. b

Chapter 6

Social and Personality Development in Infancy and Toddlerhood

Chapter Outline

Are the Following Statements True or False?

1. Fewer than one quarter of all mothers with infants are presently employed.
2. Adults usually agree on what emotions a young infant is showing.
3. Infants as young as 3 months can differentiate between a happy and a sad face.
4. The quality of infants' attachment to their mothers predicts children's future social maturity as well as their cognitive abilities during early childhood.
5. Fear of strangers is an abnormal response in older infants and toddlers and indicates a serious emotional disturbance.
6. Fathers in dual-earner families do more housework and participate more in child care than fathers in single-earner families.
7. In the United States mothers play with their infants and toddlers in a quieter and more verbal manner than fathers.
8. Infants become attached to their fathers as well as to their mothers.
9. Mothers who are employed are more likely to stress self-sufficiency in their children than mothers who are not employed.
10. Most children in day care attend large, institutionally run day care centers.

Answers to True-False Statements 1. False: see p. 121 2. True 3. True 4. True 5. False: see p. 132 6. True 7. True 8. True 9. True 10. False: see p. 136

Setting the Stage

Like so many American families, Lisa and Tim Walters needed every penny to keep their heads above water. With two children (Beth, 2 years, and Jon, 8 months) and a modest home, they were just breaking even each month. They had decided that Lisa would stay home and be a full-time homemaker until their youngest child entered elementary school. Then Lisa would return to work. This strategy combined Tim and Lisa's belief that the early relationship between mother and child was important with the reality of needing a dual income as the children grew.

But Tim was laid off from his job. Unable to afford a long layoff, he took a lower-paying position and returned to school for retraining. Trapped by car payments and a hefty mortgage, Lisa and Tim fell into debt. They finally decided that Lisa should go back to work.

Lisa and Tim are concerned. The 2-year-old will have to enter a day care program; the baby will be taken either to a day care center or to Lisa's mother's home. The parents have a host of questions. How will these constant but temporary separations affect their relationship with their children? How will Lisa's employment affect the family? Is day care harmful to children?

Many American families are asking the same questions. Over the past 30 years the proportion of employed mothers has increased dramatically, and today more than 60% of all women with preschoolers are employed (Statistical Abstract, 1996). More than half of all women with infants under 1 year of age also work outside the home.

True or False?
Fewer than one quarter of all mothers with infants are presently employed.

Many people equate the employed mother with the single parent—and indeed most single parents work—but more than half of all mothers in two-parent families are also employed. So the Walters's dilemma is not unusual, and the questions the Walters ask concern many parents today. This chapter investigates the emotional, social, and personality development of infants and toddlers and answers the Walters's questions.

Emotional Development in Infancy and Toddlerhood

The Functions of Infant Emotions

Infant emotions have two major functions or purposes. First, emotional expressions communicate the infant's state to others and encourage the care-giver to help the infant (Lamb, 1988). The smile of an infant reinforces the care-givers to continue the interaction; an infant's distress may cause the care-giver to search for the problem and do something about it. Second, emotions facilitate behavioral reactions to stimuli in the environment (Lamb, 1988). For example, interest is associated with many behaviors, including attention, learning, exploration, and play; sadness is associated with behaviors that may include avoidance and a reduction in motor activities (Termine & Izard, 1988).

Adults agree on the emotional expressions infants show (Emde et al., 1985). Both trained and untrained college students had no difficulty identifying infant emotional responses to a variety of events, ranging from happiness during playful interactions to pain from inoculations to the expressions of surprise and sadness (Izard et al., 1980).

True or False?
Adults usually agree on what emotions a young infant is showing.

What Emotions Do Infants Show?

Many parents argue that their very young infants show identifiable and definite emotions almost from birth. They are correct according to *differential emotions theory,* which states that young infants possess a limited number of emotions (Malatesta et al., 1989). These specific emotions are innate and include interest, disgust, physical distress, and a precursor of surprise, called a startle. Anger, surprise, and joy emerge in the next 4 months; sadness is seen at about the same time and fear emerges between 5 and 7 months (Izard & Malatesta, 1987). These emotions are referred to as *primary emotions,* because they appear early in life, can be easily recognized from facial expressions, and are found in infants all around the world. Such emotions result from biological programming (Izard, 1994), but learning exerts a strong influence as time passes and children learn what emotions are appropriate in particular situations.

Early infant emotions are related to specific infant behaviors. When newborns only 2 hours old were fed solutions that tasted bitter, sweet, sour, or salty, the infants showed different facial responses to each, except salt. When given a sour solution the infants compressed their cheeks against their gums, tightly squeezed their eyes, lowered their brows, and pursed their lips. The reaction to bitter included a mouth gaping, accompanied by elevation of the tongue in the back of the mouth and other actions that blocked swallowing. The authors note that some of the facial actions in response to the nonsweet stimuli are components of adult expressions of disgust, but they are not willing at this time to draw any conclusions about the subjective nature of these infant responses (Rosenstein & Oster, 1988). Other psychologists are willing to consider the responses in terms of emotional expression.

Young infants show definite emotional responses to particular stimuli. At 4 weeks babies show pleasure in response to a human voice or face. When researchers taught 2- to 4-month-old infants to pull a string tied to one arm to produce a pleasant visual and auditory stimulus, the babies displayed expressions of joy during the learning but anger when pulling no longer produced the pleasing sound or sight (Lewis et al, 1990; Sullivan et al., 1992).

Cognitive development also influences emotional expression. Consider the emotional expressions of 4- to 8-month-old infants who watched while someone wearing a scary mask approached them. The babies cried when the mask was worn by a stranger, but they laughed when their mothers wore the mask (Sroufe & Wunsch, 1972). This demonstrates that infants at this age can use cognitive appraisal to "decide" which emotion to show. Between 8 and 12 months infants develop the ability to plan and anticipate and can therefore show surprise when something unexpected happens.

Secondary Emotions

Other emotions such as shame, envy, guilt, contempt, and pride appear during the second year of life, and are called *secondary emotions* (Izard & Malatesta, 1987). These secondary emotions occur later in development and require more sophisticated cognitive abilities than primary emotions (Lewis, Alessandri, & Sullivan, 1992). For example, in order to feel envy the child must be aware of the difference between oneself and others, which typically develops at between 15 and 24 months (Lewis et al., 1989).

Some understanding of the nature of the self is necessary for toddlers to develop these more complex secondary emotions. The emergence of the distinction between the self and other is usually tested by placing some rouge on the nose of a child, allowing the child to see his or her reflection in a mirror and observing reactions that would show self-awareness, such as touching the nose. Between 15 and 18 months many infants begin to recognize themselves in a mirror, videotape, or picture, and by the end of the second year all children do this easily (Lewis & Brooks-Gunn, 1979; Asendorpf, Warkentin, & Baudonniere, 1996).

Some secondary emotions such as guilt, shame, and pride require not only a sense of self but an ability to evaluate one's actions against a standard. Beth understands that the bridge she just built with toy blocks is good because she evaluates it against some standard and therefore feels pride. This type of evaluation begins to emerge somewhere around 18 to 24 months, slightly after self-consciousness and becomes more sophisticated with time (Lewis et al., 1992). This increasing sophistication is nicely shown in a study in which children were given three tasks to perform, each of which had an easy and a difficult version. For example, in the easy puzzle-solving chore, children had to complete a 4-piece puzzle; in the difficult condition they had to complete a 25-piece puzzle that was missing some pieces. Children often showed pride when successful in the difficult but not in the easy task and shame when they failed at the easy rather than the difficult task. By the age of 3, children were not only capable of engaging in such self-evaluating behavior, but also of taking task difficulty into account. Both self-consciousness and a capacity for self-evaluation are necessary for children to regulate their own behavior and experience emotional reactions to doing something wrong (Asendorpf et al., 1996). Self-evaluative statements increase greatly between 19 and 29 months and are found in almost every child by 30 months (Stipek, Gralinski, & Kopp, 1990).

Culture and Emotion

Cultures have their own rules determining what emotions should and should not be shown in particular situations. Central nervous system development, learning, and cognitive advancements all enable children to expand their repertoire of emotions. Care-givers both model and reinforce their infants for showing certain emotions. Mothers show a rather narrow range of negative emotions and overwhelmingly positive emotions during the first 6 months (Malatesta & Haviland, 1982). As infants mature, mothers respond more to positive emotions and infants learn to present more pleasant expressions, which are more socially acceptable.

Cultures often demand that people control their emotions and sometimes mask their negative emotions. Children can do this in the last half of the second year. A 20-month-old child falls but cries only if Mom is present. (Why pass up an opportunity for a good hug?) Three-year-olds can hide their emotions quite well. Preschoolers were told not to peek at a toy when the experimenter left a room and observed them through a one-way mirror. Only 4 did not look, whereas 29 sneaked a peak. When asked, the overwhelming majority lied; insisting that they hadn't looked when they really had. The most important finding for our purposes is that observers could *not* tell who was lying and who was not by their facial and body movements (Lewis, Stanger, & Sullivan, 1989). It seems that 3-year-olds can mask their emotional expression and use verbal deception.

Questions Students Often Ask

I'm a little upset about children being able to lie with a straight face at that young age. Shouldn't parents teach their children to be honest about how they feel? *I understand how you feel. The finding that children can mask their feelings and lie by 3 years is somewhat troublesome. The fact that many cultures, not only our own, emphasize the importance of masking feelings and that there are social occasions on which this is desirable is small comfort.*

The key is to be aware of how one really feels. For example, if little Susie says that she doesn't like Aunt Ethel, a parent should not tell Susie that she has no "right" to feel that way or that she shouldn't feel that way. I've never understood why people need permission to feel one way or another. However, this does not give Susie the right to act any way she wants to. She still must treat Aunt Ethel with respect. The same is true of masking feelings. There may be times when you may not wish to tell others how you really feel for one reason or another; the real issue is whether you are aware of how you really feel. Then it becomes your decision as to when to show a particular emotion and when not to.

It may be unfortunate that a child's innocence is so short-lived, but we teach children to hide their real feelings sometimes for good reasons. The child who receives a shirt instead of that hoped-for toy from grandpa is told to show gratitude and say "Thank you" rather than show disappointment. Mother may say that she doesn't want to see anyone because she is tired, yet she may smile and say "Nice to see you" when a neighbor comes calling.

Can Infants Read the Emotional States of Others?

Even young infants are aware of their parents' facial expressions. Infants as young as 2 to 3 months—and possibly even newborns—can discriminate a variety of facial expressions (Nelson, 1987). Two-month-old infants can discriminate a happy face from a neutral face, and 3-month-olds can discriminate between happy, sad, and surprised faces (Nelson & Horowitz, 1983). Three-month-old infants recognize the difference between smiling and frowning expressions (Barrera & Maurer, 1981).

True or False?
Infants as young as 3 months can differentiate between a happy and a sad face.

It is only from about the age of 6 months that infants react to different expressions, reacting more negatively to a frowning, crying, or sad face than to a happy or neutral face (Kreutzer & Charlesworth, 1973). In the second half of the first year, infants not only can discriminate emotions but also are affected by them, therefore realizing that emotions have meaning (Bornstein, 1995).

Infants Seek Information from Others: Social Referencing

How are infants affected by the emotional expressions of others? The phenomenon in which a person uses information received from others to evaluate events and regulate behavior is called **social referencing** (Hornik & Gunnar, 1988). The approach that most studies take is to place an infant in an ambiguous or a novel situation while an adult displays a particular expression. The psychologist then observes how the adult's expression affects the infant's behavior (Rosen, Adamson, & Bakeman, 1992).

Social referencing is reliably found at about a year. Recall the example of the visual cliff described on p. 94. Consider what might happen if a 1-year-old is placed on the safe side of the cliff. The infant is uncertain about whether to cross. The mother stands at the other side of the cliff and either smiles, shows joy, interest, or fear. If her infant sees her showing a positive emotion, the infant in most cases will cross to the deep side. If the mother shows fear or anger, the infant is not likely to cross. If the visual cliff is adjusted so that it is obviously safe, very few infants reference their mother at all, and those who do and see mother showing fear, hesitate but cross anyway (Sorce et al., 1985).

Social referencing is most likely to take place in an ambiguous situation. Under such circumstances, infants actively search for information (Rosen et al., 1992; Walden & Ogan, 1988). Although the expressions that most influence infants' behavior are negative, such as fear and sadness, positive emotions also affect the

social referencing The phenomenon in which a person uses information received from others to appraise events and regulate behavior.

behavior of the infant. Although mothers are most often used in these studies, infants will show social referencing with their fathers and even to their day care providers (Camras & Sachs, 1991).

Attachment

What do children need in order to feel that the world is a positive place and that they are valued? What experiences in infancy will enable their children to feel confident enough to explore the world around them, develop satisfying peer relationships, and cope with adversity?

Many psychologists emphasize the importance of the early parent-child relationship. Erik Erikson (1963) argued that our basic attitude toward people develops from our early relationships with our care-givers. If our early needs are met in a warm environment, we develop a sense of **trust,** a feeling that we live among friends and that we can trust others. If, on the other hand, our needs are met with rejection or hostility, we develop a sense of **mistrust,** perceiving the world as a hostile, nonaccepting place, and become unable to relate warmly to others. Children's relationships and early experiences form the basis for how they will see the world later in life.

As children negotiate toddlerhood, it is important for them to gain a sense of **autonomy,** an understanding that they are individuals in their own right and have some control over their own behavior. However, if parents do not allow their children to do what they are able to do and are greatly overprotective or if they push their children into doing something for which they are not ready, children may develop a sense of **shame or doubt** concerning their ability to deal with the world around them. Encouraging children to do what they are able to do is the key to a child's developing a sense of autonomy. To better understand the nature of this early parent-child bond, an appreciation of attachment theory is necessary (Karen, 1990).

The Nature of Attachment

An **attachment** is a binding emotional tie that one person forms with another and that endures over time (Ainsworth, 1974). Infants become attached to the primary care-giver, in most instances the mother; but they also become attached to their fathers, their grandparents, and day care workers.

trust The positive outcome of Erik Erikson's first psychosocial stage, a feeling that one lives among friends.

mistrust The negative outcome of Erikson's first psychosocial stage, an attitude of suspiciousness.

autonomy The positive outcome of the second stage of Erikson's psychosocial stage, an understanding that the child is someone on his or her own.

shame or doubt The negative outcome of Erikson's second psychosocial stage, in which the child has a sense of shame or doubt about being a separate individual.

attachment An emotional tie binding people together over space and time.

Attachment is necessary for the survival and healthy development of the infant (Ainsworth, 1974; Bowlby, 1973). According to a famous attachment researcher, John Bowlby (1969), attachment is a product of evolution and ensures survival since it leads to the protection of the child by the care-giver and the enhancement of the child's development. Infants are not born with a natural affinity to their mothers; this affinity is learned (Waters & Deane, 1982). Attachment takes time to form, and it develops along with the child's cognitive abilities. Although attachment has biological roots, learning and cognition also play a part.

Attachment Behavior

Although infants begin to recognize the difference between strangers and familiar people in the first 4 months, it is only at about 6 months that proximity-maintaining behaviors, such as seeking out the care-giver when afraid or following the mother around, occur (Ainsworth, 1967). Attachment differs from **attachment behavior,** which involves actions that result in a child's getting closer to another person who is viewed as better able to cope with the world (Bowlby, 1982). Under certain circumstances, such as stress or anxiety, children are motivated to seek out the individual to whom they are attached. Such behaviors are shown only when a child's world is threatened in some manner (Colin, 1996). In safe circumstances the level of attachment behavior is low and the attachment figure is used as a secure base for exploration and play. The attachment system functions to balance proximity-seeking and exploratory behaviors. Under low-stress conditions the presence of the care-giver helps the child to explore the environment. As the situation becomes more stressful infants typically show more proximity-seeking behaviors.

The Consequences of Poor Attachment

Knowledge of the importance of attachment and attachment behavior has grown steadily over time. While working in a child guidance clinic, John Bowlby noticed how often the early histories of adolescents in trouble included severe disruptions in their relationships with their mothers. He came to believe that these disruptions had a negative influence on the children's development. Bowlby was also influenced by the work of Konrad Lorenz (1937) who found that geese will follow and attach themselves to the first object they see. When goslings opened their eyes and saw Lorenz, he became the object of attachment and they followed him everywhere. The geese were capable of forming such a relationship only in the first day and a half. This unlearned, rather rigid, irreversible behavior pattern is called **imprinting.**

attachment behavior Actions by a child that result in the child's gaining proximity to care-givers.

imprinting An irreversible, rigid behavior pattern of attachment.

Questions Students Often Ask

Aren't the first few days after birth crucial for the bonding between mother and child?

In many species, separation immediately after birth results in rejection. If a goat is separated right after delivery from her kid, she will reject it when reunited, but if the separation occurs 10 minutes after delivery, no rejection occurs. Years ago, Marshall Klaus and John Kennell stirred up controversy by arguing that such a sensitive period existed in human beings (Klaus & Kennell, 1976). In many hospitals, after birth the mother would go to the recovery room and the infant to the nursery. Even days later, contact was often limited. Klaus and Kennell suggested that this lack of early contact was responsible for some later problems in the parent-child relationship.

Most studies, though, have not found such a link, or they have found that any differences disappear in about 2 months (Lamb, 1982). Even when separations are long, as in the case of some premature infants, no significant differences in security of attachment were found between infants separated from their parents at birth and those who were not (Rode et al., 1981). Attachment is based on the cumulative effects of mother-child interactions, not on any single brief encounter. This does not mean that early contact is not desirable, only that it is not absolutely necessary. Newborn babies are not as isolated today, and fathers and siblings are often encouraged to visit them.

Other theorists and research studies showed that a breakdown in the early care-giver–child relationship can result in serious consequences (Rutter, 1979). Indeed, Freud (1935) argued that difficulties in this early relationship were the foundation for later emotional disturbance. Children who do not receive adequate care become anxious and are unable to relate to others. The tragic consequences of the lack of any care-giver–child bond was shown by Renee Spitz (1945, 1965) who compared children raised in an orphanage, where they received impersonal care from the staff, with children raised by their mothers in a prison nursery. The children raised in the prison nursery thrived, whereas those raised in the orphanage without much attention suffered greatly. Emotional disturbances, failure to gain weight, and retardation were common. The orphanage-raised children also suffered many more physical illnesses. Spitz coined the term **hospitalism** to describe these symptoms.

Children who have been deprived of a good early relationship with a care-giver can benefit greatly if the environment is improved. Wayne Dennis (1973) followed children raised in an orphanage in Lebanon; the children received little attention, and their life was one of uninterrupted boredom. When tested after the first year, they were extremely retarded, but they recovered quickly after being adopted. Those adopted before the age of 2 recovered well. At about 6 years of age, those who were not adopted were transferred to other institutions—one for males, the other for females. The institution serving the females was just as bad as the one from which they had come. When tested during middle childhood, the girls were quite retarded. The institution for males, however, was better run and provided a more stimulating environment, filled with toys, educational equipment, and films. The boys had a much higher IQ than the girls.

Dennis's observations lead to two conclusions. First, these children suffered from **stimulus deprivation,** that is, their environments were so unstimulating that it prevented them from developing normally. Second, the consequences of these unfavorable environments, although quite serious, could be remedied to some degree by placing them in better, more stimulating environments. The earlier this occurred, the better.

Years ago many psychologists believed that the care-giver–child bond was chiefly based upon feeding, that is, the satisfaction of the child's need for food, but a series of famous experiments by Harry Harlow brought this idea into grave doubt. Harlow raised rhesus monkeys with either a terrycloth mother or a wire mother. When frightened, the infant monkeys clung to the cloth mother even when the wire mother had fed them. They were greatly comforted by the softness of the cloth mother. But even though the monkeys raised with the cloth mother were more normal than those raised with the wire mother, they still exhibited abnormalities. They could not play normally, showed rocking movements, bit themselves, were withdrawn, and could not function sexually. Human infants also have this need for **contact comfort.** In other studies Harlow demonstrated that the injurious consequences of a lack of mothering could be, to some degree, reduced if the maternal deprivation is reversed early enough (Harlow & Harlow, 1962).

The Quality of Attachment

So far research had shown the importance of the care-giver–child bond, that it was not based upon feeding, and that the results of poor bonding could be partially repaired. However, most children do develop some attachment to a care-giver and the question remained as to whether the quality of that attachment would influence the child's development. This was one of the questions answered by Mary Ainsworth, a researcher who had originally worked with Bowlby (1967; Ainsworth et al., 1978). Her observations both in Uganda, Africa, and Baltimore, Maryland, pointed to the importance of the quality of attachment between parent and child. The infant's

hospitalism A condition found in children from substandard institutions, marked by emotional disturbances, failure to gain weight, and retardation.

stimulus deprivation The absence of adequate environmental stimulation.

contact comfort The need for physical touching and fondling.

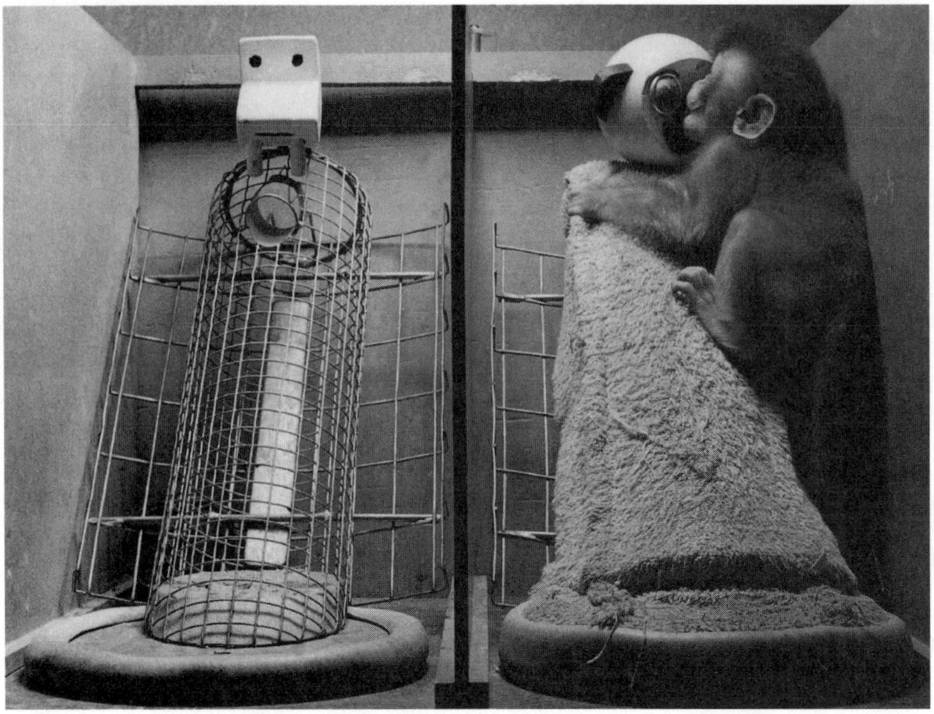

Regardless of whether the wire or cloth substitute mother fed the infant monkey, the infant ran to the cloth mother when frightened.

confident use of mothers as the secure base from which to explore was the primary evidence of **secure attachment** and a show of anxiety or anger was interpreted as **anxious attachment.** Ainsworth noticed that both in Uganda and Baltimore if the mother was present and the child's anxiety level was low, the child would roam all around the room and explore things. If the mother left the room, the infant in Baltimore became upset, but less so than the infant in Uganda. Ugandan children are kept very close and a mother's absense is unusual, whereas children in Baltimore were more used to the comings and goings of their mothers.

Such naturalistic observations are very time-consuming and difficult to control, so Ainsworth and her colleagues developed a structured way of measuring attachment behaviors using what is called the **strange situation** (Table 6.1), a procedure in which young children are observed as they experience a series of brief separations from and reunions with their care-givers (Ainsworth & Wittig, 1969; Waters & Deane, 1982). The strange situation is one way to determine the quality of attachment.

Using the strange situation, infants were originally classified into three major categories depending upon the pattern of behavior observed (Ainsworth, Blehar, Waters, & Wall, 1978). Later, a fourth category or major pattern of behavior was found, but is not used by every researcher (Main & Solomon, 1990; Waters, 1997). Infants are classified as having a secure attachment if, when reunited with their mothers, they greet them positively, actively attempt to reestablish proximity during the reunions, and show few if any negative behaviors toward them. Secure infants use their mothers as a base of operations to explore the environment when the mother is present (Ainsworth, 1979). When Mother leaves they may protest or cry but when she returns she is greeted with pleasure and the child wants to be picked up and held close. They are easily consoled. Infants who actively attempt to regain closeness, make contact, or interact with the parent following reunion are classified as secure (Main & Cassidy, 1988).

Infants classified as **anxious/avoidant** ignore their mother's entrance into the room during the reunion episodes and may actively avoid reestablishing contact (Main & Cassidy, 1988). They explore the new environment without using mother as a base of operations and don't care if their mothers are there. When Mother leaves, they are not affected and on return they avoid the mother. They do not try to gain contact when distressed and do not like to be held.

Infants classified as **anxious/ambivalent** show an angry resistance toward the mother upon reunion (Joffe & Vaughn, 1982). They may also show an inability to be settled by the parent on reunion. These babies show a great deal of anxiety upon entering the room even before the session begins and are quite distressed by the separation. In the reunion, they are ambivalent, both seeking and resisting close contact (Ainsworth, 1979). They are clingy from the beginning and afraid to explore the room on their own. They become terribly anxious and agitated upon separation, often crying profusely and refusing to be soothed.

secure attachment A type of attachment behavior in which the infant in the strange situation uses the mother as a secure base of operations.

anxious attachment A general classification of insecure attachment shown in the strange situation, consisting of avoidant behavior, ambivalent attachment behavior, or disorganized/disoriented attachment behavior.

strange situation An experimental procedure used to measure attachment behaviors.

anxious/avoidant attachment A type of attachment behavior shown in the strange situation in which the child avoids reestablishing contact with the mother as she reenters the room after a brief separation.

anxious/ambivalent attachment A type of attachment behavior shown during the strange situation in which the child both seeks close contact and yet resists it during the mother's reentrance after a brief separation.

Table 6.1 **The Strange Situation**

EPISODE	PEOPLE PRESENT	PROCEDURE
1	B, C, E	E shows C where to put B and where to sit, then leaves. If necessary, C gets B to start playing with toys.
2	B, C	C does not initiate interaction but may respond.
3	B, C, S	S enters, sits quietly for a minute, talks with C for a minute, and engages B in interaction or play for a minute.
4	B, S	C exits. S lets B play. If B needs comfort, S tries to provide it. If B cries hard, episode can be terminated early.
5	B, C	C calls to B from outside the door, enters, greets B, and pauses. If B needs comfort, C may provide it. When B is ready to play with toys, C sits in her chair. If B is very upset and needs extra time with C, episode can be prolonged.
6	B	C exits. B is left alone. If B cries hard, episode can be terminated early.
7	B, S	S enters, greets B, and pauses. If B is OK, S sits. If B needs comfort, S tries to provide it. If B cries hard, episode can be ended early.
8	B, C	C calls to B from outside the door, enters, pauses, picks B up, comforts B if necessary, and lets B return to play when ready.

Note: B = baby, C = care-giver, E = experimenter, and S = stranger.
Source: Colin, 1996.

Infants in the fourth group, **anxious/disorganized-disoriented,** shows many different behaviors. Sometimes the infant may first approach the care-giver and then show avoidance or suddenly cry out after having been quieted. The infant may also show contradictory behaviors at the same time, such as approaching the parent while taking great care not to look at him or her; some even show fear of their care-giver. They appear confused, apprehensive, and sometimes depressed (Hertsgaard et al., 1995). Many abused and neglected children act in this manner. Physiologically these infants show high levels of hormones indicative of stress (Hertsgaard et al., 1995; Grossman, 1993).

Generally, in most samples drawn from ordinary middle-class or working-class families in the United States, about 60% to 65% of infants are classified as securely attached, between 20% and 25% are avoidant, and about 10% are ambivalent. The percentage of infants who are considered disorganized-disoriented varies greatly with the sample used; about 5% to 8% in a typical nonclinical sample (Waters, 1997), although some estimates are a bit higher. In some clinical samples involving maltreated children or children whose caregivers suffer from some serious mental disorders the percentages can skyrocket to more than 50% (Colin, 1996; Lyons-Ruth et al., 1990).

Infant Attachment and Later Behavior

The difference in the way children react to a strange situation is interesting in itself. Its importance is increased by the many studies that find a relationship between type of attachment and later behavior and development. At 2 years of age, infants who were classified as securely attached at 18 months are more enthusiastic, more persistent, and less easily frustrated than the infants from the other two groups (Matas, Arend, & Sroufe, 1978). Securely attached infants are more socially and cognitively competent as toddlers (Waters, 1978). Securely attached infants also are better problem solvers during toddlerhood (Frankel & Bates, 1990). Securely attached children are more cooperative and comply more readily with mothers' instructions (Londerville & Main, 1981). Securely attached children at 18 months show a higher quality of play and more advanced verbal ability than anxiously attached preschoolers. The former are also more popular in middle childhood and show fewer negative and more positive emotions (Sroufe, Carlson, & Schulman, 1993). Anxiously attached youngsters are less effective in their interpersonal relations (Fagot, 1997), less successful in their efforts to master challenging tasks, and show a higher incidence of behavioral problems (van den Boom, 1994).

anxious/disorganized-disoriented A type of attachment behavior shown during the "strange situation" in which the child shows a variety of behaviors such as fear of the care-giver or contradictory behaviors such as approaching while not looking at the care-giver during the mother's reentrance after a brief separation.

> ***True or False?***
> The quality of infants' attachment to their mothers predicts children's future social maturity as well as their cognitive abilities during early childhood.

When children are rated on classification of attachment at 18 months and their behaviors observed at 4½ and 5 years, securely attached children are superior in social skills (Erickson, Sroufe, & Egeland, 1985). The quality of the attachment to Mother has implications for all close personal relationships and is related to increased competence in interpersonal relationships (Parke & Waters, 1989; Waters, Wippman, & Sroufe 1979).

Questions Students Often Ask

I'm impressed with the strange situation. Can I use it to test my child's security of attachment?

No, I strongly recommend against this. Please understand that the strange situation is simply and solely a research procedure and its power is based upon probabilities and percentages (Karen, 1990). It is not meant as a clinical assessment tool. In addition, some children can be mislabeled or, as will be discussed later, show patterns that may not result from parenting styles. It would be a mistake to misuse the strange situation.

Causes of Secure and Insecure Attachment

What causes some children to be securely attached while others are anxiously attached? The core construct explaining why children differ in attachment security is *maternal sensitivity,* which involves being aware of infant cues, interpreting them correctly, and responding promptly and appropriately (Smith & Pederson, 1988). One-year-old infants of mothers rated as highly sensitive are significantly more likely to be securely attached than those of mothers rated as less sensitive (Isabella, Belsky, & Von Eye, 1989). Mothers of secure infants are more involved with their infants, more responsive to their signals, more appropriate in their responses, and show more positive and less negative behaviors toward their infants than mothers of anxiously attached infants (Isabella, 1993).

Infants who show avoidant patterns of behavior in the strange situation have mothers who are significantly more rejecting than mothers of children placed in different categories. These mothers are angry, resentful, and irritable; consistently in opposition to baby's wishes; always scolding them; and physically interfering with what the infant is doing and often use verbal commands (Ainsworth et al., 1978). Because they are rejected, avoidant infants come to expect that interactions with the care-giver will be aversive or disappointing, which leads them to adopt a defensive strategy in which the child directs attention away from Mother and avoids her. These children may desire proximity but may experience rejection. Avoidant mothers are sometimes highly active in infant-mother interactions, even to the point of overstimulation, but are not sensitive to their infant's reactions.

Mothers of children classified as ambivalent are best characterized as inconsistent. They are less involved than parents of securely or avoidant children. While sometimes sensitive, they are more often insensitive. Their timing is poor, and they often interact when their babies are uninterested or otherwise engaged. They are underinvolved, unavailable, and unpredictable parents, which accounts for the angry, ambivalent behaviors shown by infants.

These patterns are relatively stable (Howes & Hamilton, 1992b; Sroufe, 1985), but they can change if there is a major improvement or a significant turn for the worse in the child's environment. A child may show a pattern of anxious attachment while the parents are going through a divorce and then later, if the parents solve their problems and become more sensitive to the needs of the child, show a more secure pattern (Waters, 1997).

If sensitivity is a key, then it should be possible to increase the probability of secure attachment through training aimed at promoting sensitivity. This has been successfully accomplished with parents of anxious/avoidant children. Parents were taught how to better read infant cues and to respond appropriately, and a change in attachment classification was sometimes accomplished (van den Boom, 1994).

Maternal Factors and Attachment

The care-giver–child relationship is influenced by the characteristics of the parent and the child. The care-giver's emotional problems may affect parent-infant relationships and lead to anxious attachments. Mothers who suffer from mental disturbance are not as responsive, resulting in children who are more likely to form insecure bonds. Mothers of anxiously attached children are prone to feelings of insecurity, which may result in maternal behaviors that affect the quality of the mother-child interaction. These mothers are less social and less empathic (Izard et al., 1991).

Another variable affecting attachment may be the care-giver's attachment status—how the child's parents remember their early relationship with their own parents. A relatively new method of assessing adult attachment, called the Adult Attachment Interview (AAI), is now available. The AAI is a structured 15-question interview that focuses on the early attachment experiences of adults and their current thoughts about them (Colin, 1996; Sagi et al., 1994). The adult is asked to choose five adjectives that describe the relationship with each parent in childhood and to give instances that illustrate each. Questions cover various aspects of the child's perception of their relationship with their parents. The interviewer assigns a classification to the subject's overall responses to these questions; four categories, *autonomous, dismissing, preoccupied,* and *unresolved,* are used.

Adults characterized as *autonomous* find it easy to recall and discuss attachment-related experiences. They are generally thoughtful, value their attachment experiences, and freely examine their past experiences (Benoit & Parker, 1994). The incidents they describe and their perceptions of how their parents affected them are coherent and they recognize the importance of their early experiences. They integrate both positive and negative experiences, tolerate flaws, and do not idealize their parents. They provide balanced and noncontradictory descriptions of their parents as loving or, if rejecting, understand why and show they have forgiven them.

Individuals classified as *dismissing* report few attachment memories of any value, do not value their memories, and show little concern for their early life. Sometimes the memories contradict each other as in saying that parents were perfect, an idealized view, yet describing rejection. Others simply cannot remember anything at all.

Those who are *preoccupied* are still enmeshed in their relationship with their parents, are extremely dependent on them, and still struggle to please them. They can tell many stories about childhood but cannot provide a coherent and organized description of early relationships. They often give tangential, irrelevant information and fail to use the past tense. Some may be intensely angry with their parents.

Subjects with an *unresolved* experience describe abuse, loss, or some other traumatic experiences and change quickly between positive and negative feelings, often giving irrational answers. They seem confused or disoriented when loss of a loved one or experiences of sexual or physical abuse are discussed.

Mothers' adult attachment scores predict subsequent mother-infant attachment for their own infants (Fonagy, Steele, & Steele, 1991; Ward & Carlson, 1995). For example, when the Adult Attachment Interview was administered before the birth of the child, it successfully predicted later attachment status (secure and anxious attachment) between mother and child (Benoit & Parker, 1994). Mothers who were autonomous generally formed secure relationships with their own children; those with dismissing models most often had infants who were classified as avoidant; mothers with preoccupied attachments usually had infants who were ambivalent, and mothers with unresolved models generally showed disorganized/disoriented attachments (Steele, Steele, & Fonagy, 1996).

Why does this intergenerational effect occur? Perhaps the parents' model of their early relationship influences their ability to perceive, interpret, and respond to their infants' signals (maternal sensitivity), which could influence attachment classification (Grossman & Grossman, 1990; Main et al., 1985).

Mothers with autonomous attachments are more sensitive to their infants and more likely to respond appropriately to signals (Haft & Slade, 1989). Preoccupied mothers respond almost at random to both positive and negative emotions and fail to read infant signals well during play. Dismissive mothers tune into children's behavior that expresses autonomy or separateness but fail to respond to or give poorer responses to infant's bids for comfort and reassurance.

The Care-Giver–Child Relationship

Perhaps the most important tenet of attachment theory is that individual differences in care-giver–infant attachment are based upon the type of relationship that the infant has with the care-giver (Bridges, Connell, & Belsky, 1988). Some care-givers are more competent than others, and we have some idea of the characteristics of competent care-giving. For example, parents who are attentive, meet the infant's needs, provide a relatively anxiety-free atmosphere, are skilled in the physical care of the infant, permit increasing freedom with development, show empathy for the infant, and are sensitive to infant cues are competent care-givers. These competent parents express positive emotions; provide a safe atmosphere in which the infant can explore; frequently interact with infants; touch, hold, and smile at their infants a great deal; and provide a stimulating atmosphere for their infants (Jacobson, 1978). The frequency of positive interactions in infancy is related to absence of problem behavior at 4 years (Pettit & Bates, 1989).

Attitudes and expectations also affect the parent-child relationship. Parents who have positive expectations about parenting adapt well to their new roles, whereas those who are overly anxious do not (Maccoby & Martin, 1983). Parents who know what to expect of a child at a particular age are less likely to lose their patience. For example, the parent who thinks that a newborn will sleep through the night or that a baby will be quiet during the parent's favorite television program is likely to be disappointed. Attitudes and expectations are somewhat related to age. Many young parents have unrealistic expectations for their infants, thinking of them as toys or dolls (Wise & Grossman, 1980). Reality may come as a shock and may affect the young parent's relationship with the child. Older mothers are more likely to have a positive attitude toward parenthood and to be more responsive to the needs of their children. They also report spending less time away from their children than do younger mothers (Ragozin et al., 1982). Perhaps older mothers are more secure and more likely to have realistic expectations of parenting.

The social support received from both family and friends is related to maternal sensitivity, which, as we've seen, is an important aspect of competence (Crockenberg & McCluskey, 1986). This is most true for parents of irritable infants and shows that mothers require the support of other people, especially when dealing with difficult infants or infants with special needs.

Bidirectionality

It is wrong to concentrate entirely on the characteristics of the care-giver. Parent-child interactions are based upon bidirectional influence (Cohn & Tronick, 1988) and are actually a chain of quick actions and reactions. An action on the part of the child prompts an action on the part of the parent, which may then elicit another action on the child's part, and so on. The beginning and the end of the interchange are difficult to define. Infants are small but powerful. Their power lies in the their "ability to compel action by their eye-to-eye gaze, smiling, crying, appearing helpless, or thrashing" (Bell, 1979, p. 824). Responsive care-givers lead to improved responsiveness on the part of the infant (Symons & Moran, 1987).

Synchrony Between Parent and Child Any understanding of the parent-child relationship must look at the second-by-second interactions between the two. This is often called **synchrony**—referring to the basic rhythms that underlie the interaction between parent and child (Schaffer, 1977). Watch a mother feeding her baby some mushy cereal, and the meaning of synchrony becomes obvious. The infant's head turns, the baby looks here and there, spits out a little, blows a bubble, and kicks both feet. At just the right second as the baby looks up, the mother has the spoon ready.

The timing is amazing. The infant also was an active participant, looking at mother at just the right moment, knowing what was coming. The timing was based on an accurate reading of cues for both. People who do not have regular contact with a particular infant often find it difficult to do things with the child. For instance, they may not be able to read the child's signals and may find themselves shoveling cereal into a closed mouth.

Mother and child must cooperate, and each must adapt to the other's behaviors (Osofsky & Connors, 1979). The development of the warm relationship hinges on the development of this synchrony, this understanding of what will happen next. The beginning of this mutual understanding, as well as the basic attachment sequence discussed earlier, starts at birth. In fact, synchrony has been related to attachment quality. Mother-infant pairs developing secure attachments are characterized by many well-timed, reciprocal, and mutually rewarding behaviors. Insecure relationships are characterized by interactions in which mothers are minimally involved, not responsive to infant signals, or in which mothers are intrusive (Isabella & Belsky, 1991).

Infant Temperament and Attachment

The nature of the care-giver–infant interactions depends not only on the characteristics of the parent but on the child as well. Certain characteristics of the child can help or hinder the formation of a viable care-giver–child relationship and influence the nature of their interactions. For example, the responsive, capable infant is more likely to elicit favorable responses than an infant who is unresponsive (Brazelton, Koslowski, & Main, 1974). Infants who are less sociable are less interactive with their mothers, and this may produce anxious attachment (Lewis & Feiring, 1989).

The most important infant characteristic affecting attachment is the child's temperament (see p. 58); (Seifer et al., 1996). Individual differences in how infants react may influence the way parents respond to the infant (Izard et al., 1991). Maternal behavior is much more positive when dealing with nonirritable behavior in infants than when dealing with infants who are constantly irritable (van den Boom & Hoeksma, 1994). Mothers of difficult children, who are characterized by negative emotionality, irritability, and fussy/crying behavior, often are less responsive to their child, which may lead to anxious attachment. Infants who are anxiously attached cry more, demand more attention, and show more negative emotions (Goldsmith & Alansky, 1987). Children with a less difficult temperament are more likely to show more secure attachment (Seifer et al., 1996).

A leading proponent of the importance of temperament, Jerome Kagan, uses the term *behavioral inhibition* to describe the tendency of some infants and young children to withdraw and show negative emotions in responses to new people, places, objects, and events (Garcia-Coll, Kagan, & Reznick, 1984). Such infants require a great deal of time to adjust to new situations and need to stay very close to their mothers. They show more negative emotions as well as elevated amounts of the hormone cortisol, which is implicated in stress reactions (Kagan, Reznick, & Snidman, 1987). A relationship exists between early irritability, anxious attachment, and behavioral inhibition (Calkins & Fox, 1992). The ambivalent attachment reflects high inhibition, the avoidant attachment reflects low inhibition.

Kagan (1984) argues that quality of attachment reflects temperamental responses to the strange situation and that anxious/ambivalent infants in the strange situation have the highest rates of fussy and difficult behavior as rated by mothers.

There is some disagreement about just how important temperament is to the establishment of a secure attachment (Vaughn et al., 1992; Seifer et al., 1996). The influence of temperament remains controversial, with some studies showing support and some not (Calkins & Fox, 1992; Nachmias et al., 1996).

Some Basic Concerns With Attachment Theory

Attachment theory, as it presently exists, provides us with a map for understanding the early care-giver–child relationship and its consequences. Problems and questions remain and criticisms of this approach deserve attention.

One question is the primacy of maternal sensitivity and care-giver variables generally. In our analysis we repeatedly looked at ways in which care-givers, most often mothers, who acted in particular ways "caused" various outcomes. Yet, some psychologists are not happy with what they see as a one-sided approach. One of the key assumptions of attachment theory is that security of attachment reflects variations in maternal behavior. Although some studies show good relationships between maternal sensitivity and other outcomes, some do not (Rosen & Rothbaum, 1993). The association between types of parenting and attachments yields mixed results and some research finds a low or even a nonsignificant relationship. The role of maternal sensitivity and outcome may not be as strong as originally proposed (Goldsmith & Alansky, 1987).

Although most attachment theorists will admit that children's characteristics may influence attachment, perhaps by influencing parents' behaviors, they do not accord them as much attention as some say is required (Rosen & Rothbaum, 1993). Other influences, including

synchrony The coordination between infant and care-giver in which each can respond to the subtle verbal and nonverbal cues of the other.

temperament, the family situation, family functioning, quality of marital relationship, cultural factors and very stressful events, may all be important (Rosen & Rothbaum, 1993).

Much criticism also centers around the use of the strange situation. It is an easy, quick way of measuring attachment but is artificial and would be better measured via a more naturalistic framework. When analyses of attachment status are conducted both in the strange situation and in naturalistic settings the relationships are very high, especially in determining securely and anxiously attached infants (Pederson & Moran, 1996). Even so, the limitations of the strange situation should be appreciated, especially in its use with atypical or culturally different populations (van Izendoorn et al., 1992). For example, when testing children with Down syndrome in the strange situation the percentage of those who cannot be classified increases substantially (Vaughn et al., 1994). Children who have Down syndrome do not become stressed as much as other children during separations (even when left alone) and so they do not seek or maintain contact in reunion episodes even if they seek proximity. Japanese children tend to react more strongly to separation, perhaps because in Japanese culture children are rarely separated from their mothers at an early age (Miyake, Chen, & Campos, 1985). To interpret research conducted in other cultures requires a better understanding of those cultures.

Kagan (1984) also questions the modern values that arise from the strange situation. Today we may value autonomy in children because so many mothers work, but this is not a quality that was that was admired by previous generations. If you are securely attached, you are motivated to adopt the values of your parents. If your parents value autonomy you will be autonomous, if they value dependency, you are more likely to be dependent. Because we value autonomy, other styles are considered less beneficial (Karen, 1990). Children who are classified as avoidant in the strange situation may have been conditioned to control their fearful responses. They learned control, not because they were poorly parented, but because control may be something their parents valued (Kagan, 1984).

Attachment theory is certainly useful and explains many of the needs and behaviors of young children. It is now a cornerstone of our understanding of the social and emotional development of infants. It is a dynamic theory that we hope will address these questions and criticisms in the future.

Fear of Strangers

Some time in the second half of the first year, parents are surprised by the way their infants react to kindly strangers. In the past the baby showed curiosity, but now the child may show fear, manifested by crying and agitation. Until about 4 months of age, infants smile even at strangers, but after that they do so less and less (Bronson, 1968). Most children go through a period in which they react with fear to strangers and even to relatives they do not see regularly. The stage usually begins between about 7 and 10 months of age and may last through a good portion of the child's second year (Lewis & Rosenblum, 1975).

Although some infants and toddlers show a fear of strangers, new research shows that others do not.

Some studies question whether this **fear of strangers** is inevitable. When an adult female was allowed to interact with infants and their mothers for 10 minutes before making any attempt to pick up the babies, and the mothers acted in a friendly manner toward the other woman, the infants were neither fearful nor upset and responded positively to the stranger (Rheingold & Eckerman, 1973). Infant response to strangers depends on the stranger and the context (Durkin, 1995). Infants show less or no fear of other children, perhaps because of the similarity in size (Lewis & Brooks-Gunn, 1972). Female strangers produce less fear than male strangers (Skarin, 1977). If the mother is present and the stranger appears in a familiar place, such as the child's home, the child is less anxious than when in an unfamiliar setting. In addition, when infants are allowed to investigate the situation on their own, they do not always show stranger anxiety. It is wrong, then, to conclude that stranger anxiety is inevitable or that the

fear of strangers A common phenomenon beginning in the second half of the first year, consisting of a fear response to new people.

appearance or lack of stranger anxiety indicates any problem (Goleman, 1989). Rather, we can say that stranger anxiety is reduced by a number of factors and depends upon the situation.

> ***True or False?***
> Fear of strangers is an abnormal response in older infants and toddlers and indicates a serious emotional disturbance.

Separation Anxiety

Separation anxiety begins at about 8 or 9 months and peaks at between 12 and 16 months (Metcalf, 1979). It can be found throughout the preschool period in some children, although it decreases with age. When the child can anticipate predictable separations, such as going to preschool, knows that Mother will return, is familiar with the environment, and is well acquainted with the substitute care-givers, the child's separation anxiety will decrease (Maccoby, 1980). Unpredictable separations, such as when a child must enter the hospital, are different because the child is now presented with a novel situation in an unfamiliar environment and with strange people.

How a child reacts to any separation depends on the child's age, how familiar the situation is, and previous experiences. In addition, if the child has familiar toys or a companion (such as a sibling) or is left with a substitute care-giver to whom he or she feels an attachment, separation anxiety will be reduced.

Even the possibility that the mother will leave can be enough to create some problems, especially in the unpredictable situation. For example, when Mother begins to pack for a trip, the child, anticipating the loss, may start to cry and cling to Mother. Any increase in the risk of a separation can trigger some anxiety (Bowlby, 1982).

Separation anxiety may also be a function of temperament. The brain-wave patterns of 10-month-old infants who cried both before and after separation from their mothers were different from the brain-wave patterns of infants who did not cry (Davidson & Fox, 1989). These differences may demonstrate that reactions to separation are at least partly based upon temperamental differences.

The Father-Child Relationship

Up to this point, it may have seemed as if children had only one parent—the mother. What about the father? We know a great deal about the mother-child bond, but what about the father-child relationship?

Where Is Father?

Fathers are not as involved with their infants and toddlers as they are with older children; they spend more time with older children (Gottfried et al., 1995). Most women have had more experience handling and caring for infants and toddlers than men have. This lack of experience, combined with the cultural prescriptions favoring mothers, causes fathers to be wary of interacting with their young children. In the United States mothers spend much more time with their children than fathers do.

You might say that this is understandable if Father works 40 hours and Mother is a full-time homemaker. But what happens if Mother is also employed full-time? Does Father participate more in child care or housework?

One clear trend is the greater participation of fathers both with housework and child care when Mother works (Gottfried et al., 1995). Men's average contributions to housework and child-rearing have about doubled since 1970, whereas women's contributions have decreased by a third. Child care by fathers has shown the most dramatic increases in the past decade. The level of paternal care has increased even since the mid-1980s and men contribute nearly one third to this activity in dual-earner couples (Parke, 1995). When mothers are employed, fathers spend significantly more time with their children on weekdays; changes in weekend time are not significant (Gottfried et al., 1995); this is especially true for time fathers spend with sons.

> ***True or False?***
> Fathers in dual-earner families do more housework and participate more in child care than fathers in single-earner families.

Despite the increase, men still participate much less in child care generally, and only minimally with their infants and toddlers (McBride & Mills, 1993; Hoffman, 1989). When couples with infants were asked to rate the average involvement of fathers on a 5-point scale (0 meant no participation, 5 performing the entire task), the mean score for all tasks was 1.7 for both child care (feeding, changing diapers, soothing baby when fussy, and getting up at night to care for the child) and housework. Interestingly, mothers' and fathers' ratings often did not match; fathers thought they were doing more than mothers' said they were (Deutch, Lussier, & Servic, 1993).

> ***Questions Students Often Ask***
> I can't stand it when I hear men say that they're "baby-sitting" for their own children or that they are "helping their wives." Why can't they realize that they are equal partners too?
> *These statements simply show that the burden of child-rearing still falls on the woman more than the man. Men's roles are not as well defined as far as child-rearing is concerned. Men are doing more today, but the completely equitable division of labor is very rare. Few men have had fathers who are the type of role model who shared equally in everything. The situation is improving but relatively slowly. The way we express ourselves is important, and such language is objectionable to women and some men who feel that parenting should be an equal partnership.*

separation anxiety Fear of being separated from care-givers, beginning at 8 or 9 months and peaking at between 12 and 16 months.

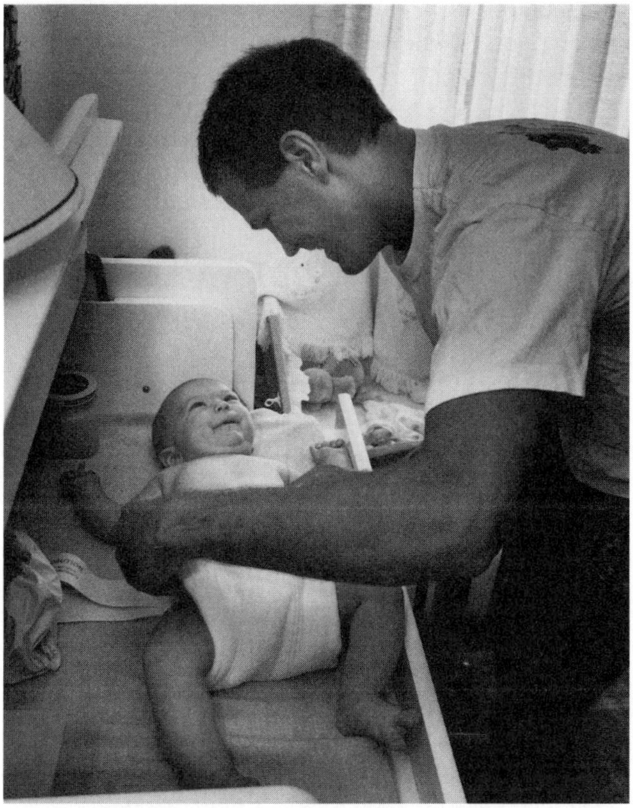

When both parents work, fathers help out somewhat more, although 50–50 splits are rare.

Although fathers are doing somewhat more, true equality in family life is not the case. Every study finds that even when both parents are employed, the disparity in time spent is very obvious (Coltrane, 1996). In her research for the book *The Second Shift,* which describes dual-earner families, Arlie Hochschild (1989) found that fathers do not do much housework or child care, despite media reports to the contrary. Hochschild argues that women in dual-earner families work an extra month each year of 24-hour days. Women work approximately 15 hours a week longer than men. Only 20% of the men in her study share housework equally. Even when couples share housework equitably, women do two-thirds of the daily jobs, such as cooking and cleaning up, and most of the daily chores with the children. Much of what men do involves home and car repairs. Men are likely to take their children on fun outings, while women spend more time on maintenance activities, such as bathing and feeding. Most studies find that there is little change in the division of labor and that employed women do twice as much housework as men (Benin & Agostinelli, 1988). Men tend to help out by shopping but don't do much ironing or washing of dirty diapers.

More paternal participation is needed to take some of the burden off the mother, and everyone benefits from the father's increased participation. Paternal involvement is related to children's having higher intelligence scores and better grades, greater social maturity, and better adjustment, including a greater internal locus of control (Gottfried et al., 1988; 1994; McBride & Daragh, 1995).

How Do Fathers Interact With Infants?

Mothers and fathers interact with their infants in different ways and for different reasons (Parke, 1995). Mothers are more likely to provide physical care for children, especially younger ones, and fathers tend more to play with children (Atkinson, 1987). In addition, fathers play in more physical and emotionally arousing ways, whereas mothers tend to play in a quieter, more verbal manner, using conventional games like peekaboo (Bridges et al., 1988; Hodapp & Mueller, 1982). Fathers also engage in more unconventional, unpredictable play, but mothers are more responsive to infant cues of interest and attention (Power, 1985); these differences remain fairly constant throughout infancy.

True or False?
In the United States, mothers play with their infants and toddlers in a quieter and more verbal manner than fathers.

These differences in interaction explain why children seek out each parent for different reasons (Biller, 1982). If a child seeks out Father for play and Mother for care, it is not a function of gender but a function of the child's differential experience with the two parents. The preference is based on the child's past experiences. This interactional difference is culturally determined. Swedish fathers and mothers do not play differently with their infants (Lamb et al., 1983), whereas American fathers and mothers show interactive differences. The qualitative differences between mother-child and father-child interactions decline somewhat in dual-earner families (Stuckey, McGhee, & Bell, 1982).

Why do fathers interact the way they do? The cultural expectation that women will do most of the day-to-day child care is one reason. Another is the idea that men may not know or understand what infants are capable of doing. Fathers who are less involved in child care attribute considerably less competence to their infants than mothers do. The more involved the man is, the less the difference between the man's ideas about what the infant can do and his wife's (Ninio & Rinott, 1988). Perhaps one reason why fathers tend to engage less often in verbal and toy play with infants is that they are unfamiliar with what their infants can do. Fathers also tend to see themselves as less skilled. Those who have more skills feel more competent dealing with their infants (McHale & Huston, 1984). This is why some research shows that parent education results in greater paternal involvement. Parent training can provide the knowledge and experience necessary to encourage fathers to take a more active interest in their child's development (McBride & McBride, 1993; Devlin et al., 1992).

Questions Students Often Ask

Why don't working women insist on a more equitable distribution of the work?

There are many reasons for this. First, some women believe that the housework and child care responsibilities are principally theirs whether or not they are employed. In addition, some may be afraid that insisting that the husband do more may adversely affect the marriage. Last, some do not believe that their husbands are capable of doing the work (Pleck, 1985).

Given the opportunity and enough encouragement, fathers can do a fine job with their children and are excellent managers, even though they are involved less in the day-to-day care-giving routines (Bhavnagri & Parke, 1991). They show many nurturant behaviors, and can be competent care-givers (Parke, 1979). Fathers can accurately recognize the meaning of infant cries and are responsive to the infant's signals and sounds (Parke, 1981).

Do Infants Become Attached to Their Fathers?

Despite limited interaction, infants do form an attachment to their fathers. The pattern of attachment behavior shown to fathers in the strange situation is about the same as that shown to mothers (Colin, 1996). In fact, infants become attached to many people, not just the mother. They show attachment behavior with grandparents with whom they have had frequent contact (Myers, Jarvis, & Creasey, 1987). The quality of this attachment depends on the history of the interactions the child has had with a person. It is not true that if love is portioned out to too many people, the amount available for Mother is less. "Love even in babies has no limits" (Schaffer, 1977, p. 104).

True or False?

Infants become attached to their fathers as well as to their mothers.

The attachment between Father and infant evolves in much the same manner as with mothers (Colin, 1995). Infants whose fathers were more affectionate and interacted more positively with them at 3 months showed secure attachments to their fathers at 1 year. Infants who are securely attached to their fathers spend more time looking at them and react emotionally when their fathers enter or leave the room. In addition, "well-fathered" infants are more curious and more likely to explore the environment, more secure, and more advanced in motor development (Biller, 1982). Infants tend to choose mothers over fathers when they are hungry, wet, or under stress, but in a stress-free environment, they show no preference and may even seek out fathers when they want to play.

Fathers and mothers mean different things to children, based on the roles they choose to fulfill (Parke, 1981). When Mother, Father, and a stranger are present, the child will stay closer to the mother than to the father, and closer to the father than to the stranger (Cohen & Campos, 1974).

Children attach themselves to many people, depending on the nature of the interactions. The quantity of the interactions is not as important as the quality. When one asks just what the role of the father is in the family, the answer given by Schaffer (1977, p. 104) is "just what he and his wife choose it to be."

The Employed Mother

One of the questions that bothers the Walters is what the effect of Lisa returning to full-time employment will be on the children. Mothers who are employed generally report being happy and satisfied. They emphasize the benefits of work, which include adult contacts, stimulation, and higher morale. When employed and nonemployed mothers are compared on measures of personal satisfaction, employed mothers often report being more satisfied. However, for mothers with children at home, happiness depends on whether the mother *wants* to be employed (Alvarez, Gove & Zeiss, 1987). The positive relationship between dual roles and happiness for women holds only for mothers who want to be employed.

Mothers who want to work but cannot for whatever reason show more depressive symptoms than mothers who are at home and want to be full-time mothers (Field, 1995; Hock & DeMeis, 1990), and depression in mothers is related to poorer child-rearing behaviors. Women who are employed but prefer to be home do not show increased depression, perhaps because they justify their

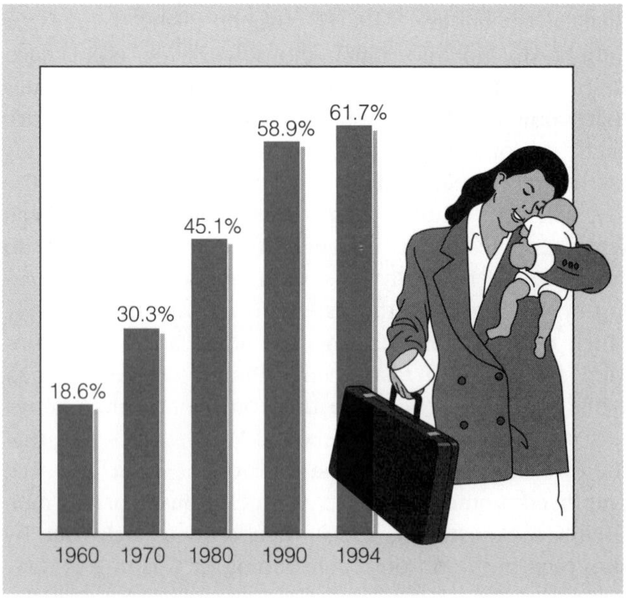

Datagraphic

Married With Young Children . . . And in the Labor Force The percentage of married women with children below the age of 6 who are employed has risen sharply over the years.

Source: Data from U.S. Bureau of Labor Statistics, 1996.

lifestyle on the basis of family need. They do, however, report greater anxiety about separation from their child (Hock et al, 1987). Employed mothers who want to work have much less anxiety about separation and far more positive attitudes toward leaving children with alternative care-givers.

Maternal satisfaction is related to better parenting and maternal health and better child-rearing outcomes (Gottfried et al., 1995). The more satisfied the woman is, the more likely she is to interact better with her family (Rutter, 1981). The woman who is satisfied being at home is just as happy as the employed woman.

Nonemployed mothers who are more concerned about their careers and employed mothers who are anxious about leaving their infants both have infants who exhibit more negative reunion behaviors than infants of mothers who express no role conflict (Hock, 1980). Highly anxious employed mothers are more intrusive than less anxious employed mothers, which may result in anxious avoidant attachment. These mothers may overcompensate and become very controlling rather than following their baby's cues.

How Employed Women Interact With Their Children

Mothers employed for more than 20 hours per week spend less time with their infants and preschool children but are as sensitive to meeting their children's needs as nonemployed mothers (Gottfried et al., 1995). Some studies show that employed and nonemployed mothers interact very similarly with their children (Hock, 1980) and that child-rearing practices do not differ (Yarrow et al., 1962). Any differences that do exist are reduced as the level of education of the mother increases (Hoffman, 1989; Lerner & Abrams, 1994). Often, educated mothers compensate for the lack of time spent with their children during the week by increasing the amount of time they spend with their children on weekends and during nonworking hours (Hoffman, 1989).

Some differences in treatment may be related to the child's gender. When mothers are employed, they interact more positively with daughters and less positively with sons whereas full-time homemakers interact more positively with sons (Stuckey et al., 1982). When interviewed, employed mothers of preschoolers described their daughters but not their sons in positive terms. Perhaps boys who may be somewhat more active and less compliant receive harsher words and generally less nurturant treatment.

Employed mothers emphasize independence training far more than nonemployed mothers (Hoffman, 1989) and stress being able to do things for oneself and being self-sufficient (Volling & Feagans, 1995). Girls appear to benefit from such training but boys may not. Stressing independence too early in sons has negative social consequences, in that it is related to less positive peer interactions.

True or False?
Mothers who are employed are more likely to stress self-sufficiency in their children than mothers who are not employed.

How Maternal Employment Affects Children

Maternal employment may be a positive influence on a girl's cognitive development. Daughters of working mothers tend to be higher achievers, possibly because the mother may function as a role model (Hoffman, 1979; 1989). Daughters of working mothers are usually very well adjusted, do well in school (although neither better nor worse than those of nonemployed women), and have higher career aspirations (Lerner & Abrams, 1994). Boys of employed mothers hold fewer gender-stereotyped ideas about what men and women can do (Lerner & Abrams, 1994).

Maternal employment does not adversely affect the cognitive development of lower-income males, and some studies find higher scores on measures of cognitive development among sons of working-class employed mothers. Studies of middle-class boys, however, sometimes show differences in cognitive development. Some studies find a slight trend for boys whose mothers are not employed full time to show higher intelligence scores compared to boys whose mothers work full time (Hoffman, 1979; Lerner & Abrams, 1994). A study of middle-class toddlers showed that sons of nonemployed mothers were more cognitively advanced than those of employed mothers. Not all studies have shown this superiority in cognitive development and one major study found no significant differences between middle-class children of employed and nonemployed mothers (Crouter et al., 1990). No differences in school competence were found between the children of employed and nonemployed mothers if they shared activities such as reading, playing, and talking (Moorehouse, 1991). Any disadvantage was found to occur only when mothers are employed full time, not when mothers are employed part time (Gottfried, Gottfried, & Bathurst, 1988).

Minor differences appear in social behavior between children of employed mothers and children of mothers who stay home full time. Preschool children of employed mothers are more peer oriented and self-sufficient (Schachter, 1981). Children of nonemployed mothers seek out more help and protection and show more jealousy. No differences in emotional adjustment are found. Some long-term studies find that children of employed mothers are less compliant and more peer oriented, but this depends on the nature of the nonmaternal care they receive (Hoffman, 1989). No relationship is found between maternal employment and juvenile delinquency or personality disorders (Crouter et al., 1990).

In summary, the effects of maternal employment can be either negative or positive, depending on many factors. Maternal employment neither hurts nor encourages children's development (Gottfried, Gottfried, & Bathurst, 1995). Children of mothers who are employed are not at risk for psychological maladjustment, poor self-esteem, immature social behavior, adjustment problems, or cognitive difficulties across the life span (Gottfried et al., 1995). Perhaps this is because other variables are much more important. For example, regardless of whether parents are employed, when children are less well monitored they receive lower grades than better monitored youngsters (Crouter et al., 1990).

Most women who work outside the home need to find substitute child care, the quality of which affects the child. Such factors as parental attitudes, level of education, the nature of the home environment, how the child is treated after parents come home from work, and the nature and quality of the substitute care are most important.

Day Care

Lisa and Tim Walters' concerns center on their children's experience in day care. Many people think of day care only in terms of large urban day care centers, but most day care does not take place in such centers (Figure 6.1). As you can see, children are much more likely to be cared for by a relative in their own home, or in someone else's home than in a day care center. There is a recent trend toward using more formal, organized day care facilities because they offer greater educational experiences, provide more reliable care, and are more likely to be regulated by some governmental agency (Hellmich & Peterson, 1996).

True or False?
Most children in day care attend large, institutionally run day care centers.

More children are cared for in family day care homes than in day care centers. Family day care homes, which generally serve six or fewer children, outnumber day care centers three to one. Such homes are conveniently found in many neighborhoods and every state has some regulations for these facilities, although only about 14% are licensed or registered with their individual states (Frankel, 1994). Parental satisfaction is high and well-trained providers do a better job than untrained ones.

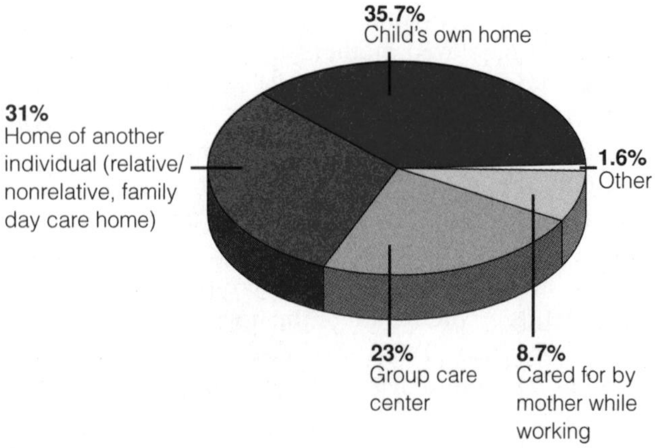

Figure 6.1
Child Care in the United States
Source: Data from Statistical Abstract, 1996

Infant Day Care

Children in day care form relationships with, and an attachment to, their substitute care-givers (Lewis, 1987). Children show less distress when left with a familiar care-giver than when left with a stranger, and they even show some distress when separated from the substitute care-giver (Ricciuti, 1974). The extent of this attachment depends on the quality of the day care worker's interaction with the child. Children show strong attachment behaviors to high-interaction care-givers, and low levels of attachment to low-interaction care-givers. In the presence of a high-interaction care-giver, the child feels secure enough to explore the environment. It is possible for a child to be securely attached to the day care worker and anxiously attached to the parents (Goossens & Ijzendoorn, 1990). Again, the quality, not the quantity, of the interaction is most important for the development of positive relationships.

Day Care and Attachment to Mother and Father

The effects of substitute care for infants on attachment quality is a matter of sharp debate among psychologists. Some research evidence demonstrates differences between home-reared and day care children on measures of attachment in a strange situation (Blehar, 1974). Negative effects are sometimes found for children who begin day care before their first birthday, but secure children who enter out-of-home care after their first birthday do not show any problems (Vaughn, Deane, & Waters, 1985). Barglow and colleagues (1987) measured attachment in infants whose mothers were employed and who were supervised in their own home by an unrelated person and found that these infants were more likely to show anxious-avoidant attachment patterns in the strange situation than infants whose mothers remained at home. However, more than half of those infants of working mothers showed secure attachment, and some as yet unidentified factors must moderate the effects of daily separations for these securely attached infants. In two studies of middle-class infants, children exposed to 20 or more hours of substitute care per week were more likely to be classified as anxiously attached than infants of nonworking mothers or mothers who worked less than 20 hours per week (Belsky & Rovine, 1987). Looking at this and other evidence, Belsky (1988) concluded that early substitute care may put a child at risk for anxious attachment and later social and emotional problems.

However, many studies have failed to find any heightened risk of anxious-avoidant patterns at all (Phillips, McCartney, & Scarr, 1987; Roggman et al., 1994). Much research around the world shows that such heightened risk is not inevitable. Bengt-Erik Andersson (1992, 1989) followed children in Sweden, some of whom had begun out-of-home day care at various ages and some of whom had no day care experiences. Andersson found that children who had entered day care in the second half of their first year were both better adjusted and academically superior at ages 8 and 13 years to children who had begun day care at a later age or who had no day care experience. Some authorities claim that the evidence is substantially weaker than Belsky suggests (Thompson, 1988). The percentage of those infants rated anxious-avoidant is higher but not dramatically so (Clarke-Stewart, 1988; 1989). Having a secure attachment to an alternative care-giver may even compensate for anxious attachment to a mother (Howes et al., 1988). Some evidence exists that for anxiously attached children, day care may serve a protective function in the areas of social involvement and self-esteem (Egeland & Heister, 1995). Anxiously attached children who received early day care showed more positive adaptations in many areas compared to anxiously attached children raised at home.

A recent, large, well-designed study of infant child care and its effects on attachment substantially clarified the situation (NICHD, 1996; Chira, 1996). First, the study concluded that the use of the strange situation was as valid for children who experience a great deal of child care as for children who do not. This is important because some authorities have doubted the meaning of infant behavior in the strange situation with children who have experienced many routine separations from their care-givers. This report seems to agree that at least in our culture, the strange situation is a valid measure of attachment quality and can be used with infants with differing experiences.

Second, the study found that mothers of secure infants were more sensitive and better adjusted psychologically than mothers of anxiously attached children. They were also better off economically. This is not surprising and matches much of the available research to date.

Third, and most important for this discussion, is the finding that child care features, in and of themselves, were *not* related to attachment security or anxiety avoidance specifically, as long as the home care situation was good. Rates of attachment security were not related to variations in the quality of day care, to the amount of care, to age of entry into care, the stability of care, or type of care used. However, low-quality child care, unstable care, or extensive care were each related to increased rates of insecurity when mothers were relatively insensitive. In other words, for vulnerable children, poor child care was related to poor outcomes. Children who experience dual risk, that is poor home care and poor day care, have the highest probability of showing insecure attachments to their mothers. Children receiving insensitive, poor care-giving at home and insensitive care from their mothers had anxious attachment rates ranging from 49% to 56%. Children in less risky conditions with better child care or better maternal care had an anxious attachment rate of 38%.

Fourth, the study found that extensive care for boys and limited care for girls were associated with somewhat elevated rates of anxious attachment. Perhaps boys are more vulnerable than girls to stress; more research is needed to fully explain these findings.

The report concluded that nonmaternal child care by itself does not constitute a threat to the security of the infant-mother attachment relationship. Nor does it foster secure attachment. Rather, poor, unstable, or more than minimal amounts of child care add to the risks already present when the child experiences poor parenting practices. As the results of this major study show, it is probably incorrect to simply blame infant day care; rather, the combination of family characteristics (especially lack of care-giver sensitivity) and poor day care may pose a danger. We can only wait for more on this important subject.

Other Aspects of Early Day Care

Attachment is not the only area of interest when investigating infant day care. The effect of early day care on the social and cognitive aspects of the child's life are also of interest. Preschoolers who entered day care before 6 months engaged in less inactive watching and solitary play and showed more cooperative play and positive emotions than those who entered after that age (Field et al., 1988). Attending high-quality day care is associated with more cooperative play and positive affect in preschool and with more leadership skills and enhanced popularity in elementary school (Field et al., 1991; 1988). However, there is no indication that similarly positive results would be found for a sample of children attending substandard day care centers.

Margaret Burchinal and colleagues (1989) compared groups of very poor children who were randomly assigned to receive extensive university-based intervention day care in a group setting, children placed in a regular community day care center, and children with little or no day care. The children in the day care groups began their experiences in early infancy—between 6 weeks and 3 months—and continued until kindergarten. The children in both day care settings showed better intellectual development, with the university program showing superior results. Infant day care and day care within the first 3 years are associated with higher reading and math scores for poor children (Caughy, DiPietro, & Strobino, 1994; Desai, Chase-Landsale, & Michael, 1989). Another study found no significant differences in language and intelligence between middle-class 3-year-olds of intact families who had attended high-quality day care since infancy and home-reared children (Ackerman-Ross & Khanna, 1989). The quality of day care, then, is important.

Others argue that children who experience early day care are at risk for heightened aggressiveness, noncompliance, and withdrawal in the preschool and early school years (Belksy & Eggebeen, 1991; Belsky, 1988; Volling & Feagans, 1995). A relatively small but statistically reliable relationship exists between extensive early day care and

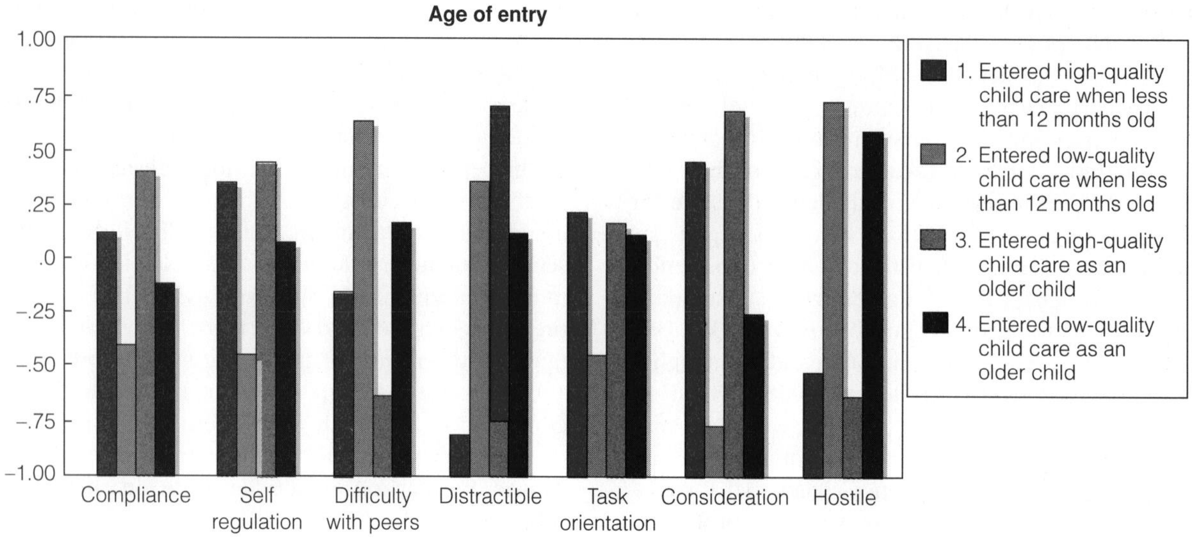

Figure 6.2
Social Adjustment of Children With Varying Child Care Histories
Source: Howes, 1990.

aggressiveness and social skills problems in kindergarten (Bates et al., 1994). Others suggest that early day care can have a negative effect on cognitive functioning in 3- and 4-year-old boys from higher-income families (Baydar & Brooks-Gunn, 1991). These families may provide better learning environments than those offered by nonmaternal environments.

Again, however, the quality of day care becomes paramount, as graphically shown in Figure 6.2. Carollee Howes (1990) followed a group of middle-class children who entered day care before their first birthday and children who entered between 1 and 4 years of age through their toddler, preschool, and kindergarten years. She found that early-entry children in low-quality care had the most difficulty with peers in preschool and were distractible and less considerate of others in kindergarten. Those who entered high-quality child care as infants were not much different from the children who entered high-quality care as older children.

When children enrolled in either high- or low-quality day care were examined, their social competence was related to many factors including family environment, temperament, and quality of day care. Smaller group size was related to more nurturance and less restrictiveness. The quality of the day care environment rather than the number of hours and age of entry had pronounced effects on social outcomes (Volling & Feagans, 1995).

Some children are more likely to be injured by poor day care. Children rated by their mothers as socially fearful are more likely to engage in nonsocial play and less likely to have friendly interactions with their peers if enrolled in low-quality day care. When in high-quality day care these children are actually more involved in friendly peer interactions and less in nonsocial play. Temperamental differences may make some children more vulnerable than others to the effects of a poor quality experience.

Day Care After Age 1

It is much easier to discuss day care after infancy because of the fairly consistent research that exists. Research supports the notions that if a child goes from a stimulating environment to a good day care center, little gain or loss will occur. But if a child goes from a nonstimulating environment to a stimulating environment, some gain will result. If a child goes from a stimulating environment to a poor day care center, negative effects would be seen. Indeed, the research supports these notions (Belsky & Steinberg, 1979). Children who attend day care are more self-confident, outgoing, assertive, verbally expressive, and self-sufficient and less distressed, timid, and fearful in new situations. They are also less polite, agreeable, and compliant with their mother's or care-giver's requests, somewhat louder and more boisterous, more irritable and rebellious, and have more temper tantrums than children who are not in day care. One reason for these findings is that few day care centers teach social skills or effective ways of settling disputes (Clarke-Stewart, Allhusen, & Clements, 1995).

Studies of intellectual performance show that these children do at least as well or better. An impressive longitudinal Swedish study that followed children who began day care during the toddler years found intellectual benefits for second-grade children who had spent considerable time in high-quality center-based day care early in life (Broberg, Wessels, Lamb & Hwang, 1997). Children from lower-income families are more likely than children from middle-income families to benefit and the quality of care is more important than the type of care.

Day care has no injurious effects on the cognitive development of low-risk children (Belsky & Steinberg, 1978). For disadvantaged children, an enriched day care program may encourage cognitive development. In some studies, the intelligence scores of disadvantaged children reared at home showed a decline over the first 3 years

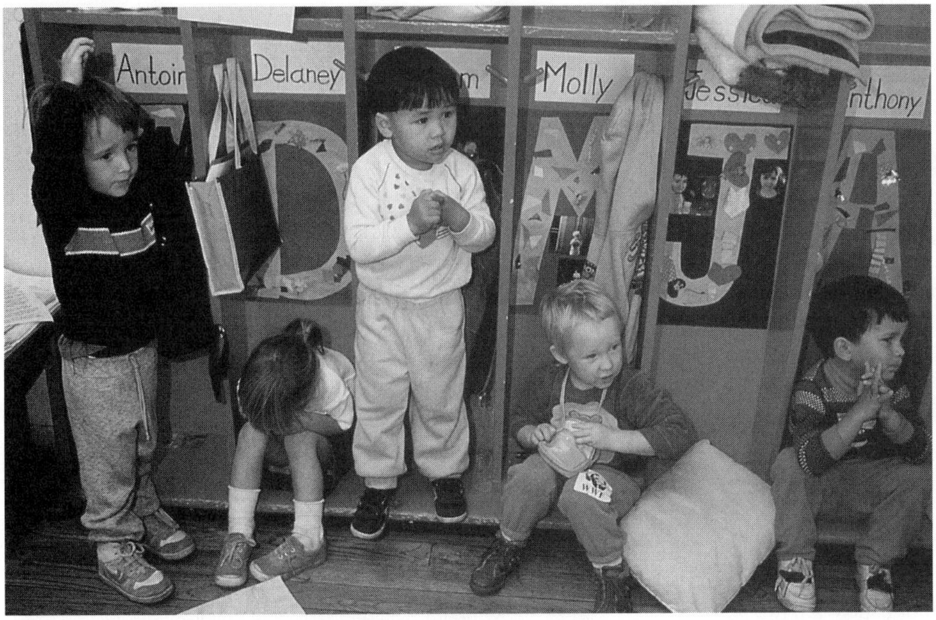

Studies show that generally the overall social-emotional adjustment of day care children is good and compares well with that of home raised children.

whereas the scores of those enrolled in day care did not. Studies show that the general overall social-emotional adjustment of day care children is good and compares well with that of children raised at home (Watkins & Bradbard, 1984; Etaugh, 1980). In summary, although there are differences in social-emotional adjustment, there is no evidence that day care causes serious emotional or social problems for children.

Questions Students Often Ask

I'm confused by all the research. I still don't think that day care is good for children.

Just as how maternal employment influences children is not a simple question, neither is the effects of day care on children. As ecological theory emphasizes, maternal employment and day care do not exist in a vacuum. They are influenced by many factors, such as the quality of day care and the quality of the parental relationships, which preclude simple answers. Day care in itself is neither positive nor negative. A good-quality day care combined with good parent-child relationships is best. The real danger seems to come from poor day care experiences when the home situation is also poor.

The answer is for families to do what they think is best for their own situation. Unfortunately, this is not always possible for many people who may find that despite their desire to stay at home they need to work or despite their desire to work they find that they must stay at home, perhaps because of the lack of of day care. People may often find themselves in positions they did not plan or seek. Having high-quality, affordable day care available gives people an option that is essential in today's world.

As regards the health consequences of day care there is definite evidence that children in day care facilities are sick more often, about 5 days more per year (Bell et al., 1989; Johansen et al., 1988). The strongest indicator for the amount of illness is the number of children in the room (Bell et al., 1989). There is also some fear that infants who require frequent changing of their diapers may be at risk for intestinal viruses because some illnesses may be spread through poor hygienic practices.

The Quality of Day Care

Much depends on the quality of the day care center, especially for vulnerable children in poor child-parent relationships. High-quality, stable child care is associated with positive later outcomes (Howes, Phillips, & Whitebook, 1992; Howes, 1988). Deborah Vandell and colleagues (1988) observed 4-year-olds during play at both good- and poor-quality day care centers and again 4 years later. Those from good day care centers had more friends, interacted better with peers, and were rated as more socially competent and happier at age 8 than those who attended poor-quality day care centers. Programs in more intimate settings with more care-givers lead to better linguistic development and more sophisticated play (Portner, 1995). Better day care is related to better cognitive development; children's cognitive activity is enhanced when child care facilities offer creative play activities and are staffed by teachers who engage the children in positive social interactions (Burchinal et al., 1995; Howes & Smith, 1995).

The day care center checklist (Figure 6.3) may be of some help in evaluating a day care center, including its structural qualities, child-adult ratio, group size, and teacher training. Process quality refers to the child's experience in day care, especially the provision of appropriate activities and social interactions with the teacher (Hagekull & Bohlin, 1995). Process quality is more strongly related to child outcomes than is structural quality, but both are important (Howes & Smith, 1995).

Although day care should not be thought of in terms of school, such activities as reading to children and playing social games can contribute to social and intellectual growth. Another factor is the ratio of care-giver to child. If attention and face-to-face interactions are vital to development in early childhood, the better this ratio, the more likely that day care will be a positive experience (Ruopp et al., 1983). Other structural factors such as

Space and Equipment (Yes ____ No ____)

____ ____ 1. There is adequate space to play.
____ ____ 2. Sufficient storage for material is available.
____ ____ 3. The furniture is child size and in good condition.
____ ____ 4. The temperature is comfortable (68 to 70 degrees).
____ ____ 5. The lighting is adequate.
____ ____ 6. Materials are available in sufficient numbers so children don't have to wait long to use them.
____ ____ 7. There is enough space outside or inside (a playground or a gym) for children to run or engage in other physical activities.
____ ____ 8. There is adequate space for resting.
____ ____ 9. The eating area is clean and bright.
____ ____ 10. Bathroom facilities are designed for small children.
____ ____ 11. Bathroom facilties are convenient.
____ ____ 12. Electrical outlets are covered when not in use.
____ ____ 13. First-aid supplies are available.
____ ____ 14. All equipment is in good repair (no broken toys or sharp edges).
____ ____ 15. Materials (e.g., pots or cages) are available for growing things or taking care of animals.
____ ____ 16. Books are visible.
____ ____ 17. Puzzles are available.
____ ____ 18. Adequate space is available for dramatic play (raised platforms, rows of wooden crates, etc.)
____ ____ 19. Emergency procedures are clear and the environment allows for safe exit in case of emergency.
____ ____ 20. Smoke detectors and fire extinguishers are evident.

The Program

____ ____ 1. There is an organized daily program.
____ ____ 2. There is variety within the program.
____ ____ 3. Students are encouraged to talk with each other.
____ ____ 4. Children participate in projects.
____ ____ 5. Activities are planned to encourage children to learn by using their senses.
____ ____ 6. Self-expressive activities such as painting and various forms of art are programmed.
____ ____ 7. Children are generally busy, not just sitting around.

The Program (Yes ____ No ____)

____ ____ 8. Children show evidence of learning through discovery and asking questions of the staff.
____ ____ 9. Small-group activities are encouraged.
____ ____ 10. Reading and storytelling are part of the program.
____ ____ 11. Activities that develop the large muscles are evident.
____ ____ 12. Activities that develop fine-muscle control are evident.
____ ____ 13. Boys and girls are encouraged to participate in all activities.

Teacher-Child/Teacher-Parent Relationships

____ ____ 1. Sufficient staff is available so that each child receives individual attention at some point in the day.
____ ____ 2. A warm relationship with the children is evident.
____ ____ 3. Staff circulates among all children and does not spend an inordinate amount of time with only one child.
____ ____ 4. Staff offers suggestions in a positive manner.
____ ____ 5. Staff trusts and respects children.
____ ____ 6. Staff encourages children to do things.
____ ____ 7. Staff does not use threats or punishment.
____ ____ 8. Staff does not smoke around the children.
____ ____ 9. Children understand their responsibilities.
____ ____ 10. Staff has sufficient training in the field.
____ ____ 11. Children seem happy.
____ ____ 12. Children seem to get along with one another.
____ ____ 13. Staff appears vigilant, knows what is going on at all times.
____ ____ 14. Staff and administrator encourage parents to visit and become involved.
____ ____ 15. Communication with parents, such as written notices of special events or changes in program, is adequate.
____ ____ 16. Checks on who can take child home (dismissal procedures) are adequate.
____ ____ 17. Staff/teacher conferences are held regularly.

Minimum Staff/Child Ratio for Centers

Age	Maximum group size	Staff/child ratio
Birth to 2 years	6 chldren	1 adult: 3 children
2 to 3 years	12 children	1 adult: 4 children
3 to 6 years	16 children	1 adult: 8 children

Figure 6.3
A Day Care Checklist It's not easy to choose a day care facility. The following checklist can be used as a basis for comparing day care centers.
Source: Adapted from Stines, 1983, and Clarke-Stewart, 1982.

safety, ventilation, security, cleanliness, staff turnover, and cost should also be considered.

The quality of day care is highly variable (Scarr, Eisenberg, & Deater-Deckard, 1994). Turnover rates of 40% are not unusual and harsh and detached care-givers are not uncommon (Phillips et al., 1994). Centers that serve high-income families provide the highest quality of care, probably because the staff is better trained and more sensitive to the needs of the children. The most uniformly poor care (measured in a variety of ways including teacher training and appropriateness of activities) is found in centers that serve middle-class children. Centers serving lower-income children often receive government support and some degree of standards are maintained. Those that serve middle-income children do not receive government support and do not have the financial resources to purchase high-quality care.

Most day care children receive mediocre care. Some care is so poor that it may be detrimental to children's emotional and intellectual development. Infants and toddlers are in the most danger of receiving poor care as four in ten are in centers that fail to meet basic health and safety needs (Miller, 1995a). During the spring of 1993, researchers rated only one in seven centers as developmentally appropriate, and one in eight centers was found to neglect children's basic needs. States with more

Controversial Issues: The Future of Child Care

Trends in child care that began as early as the 1970s will continue. For example, women will continue to enter the labor force, and there will be more pressure to increase the availability of day care.

Poor and divorced mothers of modest means obviously need day care. How can these women make a life for their children and themselves without affordable child care services? However, the need for day care services has increased among middle-class women, even in two-parent families, for whom finding adequate child care is difficult. It is estimated that on an annual basis it costs $7507 for a babysitter, $4680 for a day care center, and $3900 for family day care (Deely, 1996).

As demands for day care increase, the government as well as the private sector will have to make a greater commitment to it. One possible future trend is the direct involvement of school districts in day care. Consider the possibility of elementary schools having a separate wing for day care with the principal having overall responsibility for the school and day care center, while the center is physically separate and run by a director.

It is doubtful, however, that the schools or even employers will be capable of dealing with infant day care. Here, there may be a need for some radical rethinking. It may be that work schedules will have to be changed to allow mothers and fathers to care for their infants. Flexible work hours are already permitted in many companies. Mothers and fathers may also be allowed leave for some months after the birth of the child; in Sweden, such leave is provided with 90% pay. In the United States, recent legislation allowing parental leave rights without pay became law. Part-time jobs, job-sharing, and working from home may be the answer for others.

The extent to which government has a responsibility for managing day care or prescribing its availability by private industry raises many interesting questions. How much does the public want and is it willing to pay for such services? What is the government's responsibility in this area? We don't expect people to educate their children entirely by themselves, which is why public schools exist. The community as a whole has certain responsibilities and day care may be one of such responsibilities.

In the end, though, many of these arguments center around the balance between the individual's responsibility and community involvement. As the need for these services increases and their costs rise, the debate over how to provide such services and what part government should play will become more urgent. It is a debate that bears watching into the next century.

demanding licensing standards had fewer poor-quality programs (Miller, 1995b).

States need to create higher standards that take into account children's needs, eliminate exceptions from licensing standards, encourage professional accreditation, and increase financial investment. Many states still don't require child care workers be trained in first aid or that children attending have basic immunizations. Many states do not ban smoking around children nor do they even require child care facilities to be equipped with smoke detectors (Miller, 1995b). Nearly half the states do not limit the number of children in a group. The question of what the government's responsibility may be in this area is an important one (see Controversial Issues box on this page) and will have an important influence on the future of day care in this country.

Many Roads to Travel

Much has been said about meeting the needs of the child, and warm, responsive, understanding adults are required if children are to become socially and emotionally healthy. Yet the research shows there is no single way these needs must be met. As Chess and Thomas (1981, p. 221) note, "Just as the child's nutritional requirements can be met successfully with a wide range of individual variation, so can his psychological requirements." Many roads can lead to the same destination; parents can provide for their children's needs in many ways, taking into account the personality of the child, the child's own needs and requirements, and the family's circumstances.

Summary

1. According to differential emotions theory, infants' early emotions are innate. These are called primary emotions. Secondary emotions, such as embarrassment, require some understanding of the self as different from others. Others such as pride require the child to evaluate his state against others. Children begin to recognize themselves between 15 and 18 months and begin to evaluate themselves later.
2. Infants can recognize the difference between some facial expressions early in infancy, whereas recognition of other expressions takes more time to develop. It is only after about 6 months that infants understand the meaning of others' emotional expressions. By 1 year, children use social referencing and are affected by and guided by the facial expressions of their care-givers; by the last half of the second year they can mask their emotions.
3. Erik Erikson argues that the psychosocial crisis during infancy is trust versus mistrust. If the child's needs are met, the child develops a sense of trust. If not, a sense of mistrust develops. During toddlerhood, the psychosocial crisis is one of autonomy

versus doubt. Infants must develop a sense that they are people on their own.

4. Infants must attach themselves to a care-giver if they are to develop in a healthy manner. Children who have not had the opportunity to do so often experience significant developmental problems. The tragic consequences of maternal deprivation may be reduced if the child receives excellent care later on.
5. Attachment behaviors can be measured using a standardized procedure of brief separations and reunions known as the strange situation. There are four classifications of attachment behavior: secure attachment, anxious/avoidant attachment, anxious/ambivalent attachment, and anxious/disorganized-disoriented attachment. Children classified as securely attached are superior to the other classifications on a variety of measures. Children's attachment status is related to later behavior. Maternal sensitivity is related to attachment quality.
6. Parents' mental illness as well as their own attachment status may influence the attachment status of their infants. Children's temperament may also influence attachment status.
7. Many factors affect the parent-child relationship, including the age of the parent, attitudes and expectations of their parental role, the parents' background, and sensitivity to the infant's needs. The infant's abilities, temperament, and gender also affect the relationship. The parent affects the child, and the child in turn also affects the parent.
8. A child's fear of strangers begins sometime in the second half of the first year and lasts through most of the second year. Beginning at about 8 months of age and peaking somewhere between 12 and 16 months, children experience separation anxiety.
9. Infants form attachments to their fathers as well as to their mothers. Mothers and fathers interact differently with their infants: mothers often perform more of the daily care-giving chores and fathers play more physically with their children. Infants often seek out their fathers when they want to play and their mothers when they are in distress.
10. Men's contribution to child care and household chores has increased substantially, especially when their wives are also employed. Even so, mothers still do much more of the housework and child care than fathers do. Increased paternal involvement is related to better cognitive development and adjustment in their children.
11. Maternal employment is related to greater satisfaction as long as the mother *wants* to work. Employed mothers emphasize independence training more than nonemployed mothers. Maternal employment may positively influence daughters, and working mothers may serve as an achieving role model for their daughters. The differences in social behavior between children of employed and nonemployed mothers are minor.
12. Most children in day care are cared for by relatives. Family day care homes are also popular. Studies of children who enter day care before their first birthday show that these children are somewhat more likely to develop anxious attachment patterns, although the majority of such infants show secure attachment patterns. New research shows that poor-quality infant day care combined with poor-quality care at home may lead to anxious attachment patterns.
13. Children who enter day care after their first birthday show few differences compared to children raised at home. Day care children tend to be more peer oriented and more boisterous.
14. The day care experience may be positive, neutral, or negative, depending on the quality of the day care, the attitudes of the parents, and the parent-child interactions after work.

Multiple-Choice Questions

1. Which statement about employed mothers is *correct?*
   a. More than half the mothers of infants are employed.
   b. Most women with preschoolers are employed.
   c. More than half of all mothers in two-parent families are employed.
   d. All of the above are correct.
2. According to differential emotions theory, primary emotions are characterized by all of the above *except:*
   a. they appear early.
   b. they are culturally determined.
   c. facial expressions underlie each.
   d. they are biologically programmed.
3. Such emotions as shame, pride, and guilt are shown late in toddlerhood because:
   a. they require self-evaluation as well as self-consciousness.
   b. younger children do not have the physical ability to show their emotions on their faces.
   c. parents teach them not to show such emotions.
   d. children do not experience events before then that would require these emotional expressions.
4. Fifteen-month old Joseph looks at his mother for guidance as to whether to touch a new toy or not for he is not certain that it is safe. His mother smiles and he goes after the toy. This is an example of:
   a. positive reactivity.
   b. ambiguous sensitivity.
   c. social referencing.
   d. expressive targeting.
5. One-year-old Kara used to like to be held by just about any adult, but now she refuses and jumps back to her mother or father. Her parents are worried about this behavior. According to psychologists, this behavior is:
   a. unfortunate, and shows that some negative experience has occurred to this child.

b. unfortunate, for such an anxiety reaction predicts a very timid, socially underdeveloped preschooler.
c. excellent, for it means that the child will now develop a strong sense of self and self-confidence.
d. typical of the age, and some children show it more than others.

6. A child is frightened by a loud noise and runs to his mother. This type of behavior is called:
a. attachment behavior.
b. enduring behavior.
c. neurotic behavior.
d. primary behavior.

7. Mr. Somers argues that an absence of early mother love is the cause of many problems that we see when children are not given sufficient care. You are impressed by Wayne Dennis's work and so argue that:
a. Mr. Somers is completely correct.
b. stimulus deprivation is the problem and children can be raised by substitute care-givers.
c. there is insufficient research at the present time to determine whether early problems in infant-care-giver relationships have negative effects on children.
d. the negative effects are based upon the lack of such maintenance behaviors as feeding, changing, and bathing.

8. Parent-child relationships are based upon the extent to which parents can satisfy the physical needs of their children, says a friend. However, research conducted by ____________ disputes this effectively.
a. Skinner
b. Tanner
c. Harlow
d. Page

9. An infant in the strange situation ignores Mother's leaving and her returning. She does not seem to care if Mother is present. This pattern of behavior describes infants in the classification category of:
a. secure attachment.
b. anxious/ambivalent attachment.
c. anxious/avoidant attachment.
d. anxious/disorganized-disoriented attachment.

10. In a nonclinical well-parented group, the most common classification will be:
a. secure attachment.
b. anxious/ambivalent attachment.
c. anxious/avoidant attachment.
d. anxious/disorganized-disoriented attachment.

11. The most rejecting mothers are found to be those whose children are classified in the strange situation as:
a. avoidant.
b. ambivalent.
c. secure.
d. secondary.

12. The one common care-giver behavior that seems to differentiate children who are securely attached from those who are anxiously attached is:
a. love.
b. compassion.
c. involvedness.
d. sensitivity.

13. The most important child-related factor that influences quality of attachment is:
a. Apgar score.
b. the presence or absence of a physical disability.
c. temperament.
d. ability to verbalize.

14. As baby looks at her father, the father vocalizes, causing the child to smile and the father to laugh softly. Each affects the other. This is an example of:
a. bidirectionality.
b. learned helpfulness.
c. maximum coordination.
d. required helpfulness.

15. Mr. Seymour argues that when mothers are employed full time, modern fathers help out more than fathers did even 20 years ago. According to studies, Mr. Seymour is:
a. incorrect, because there have been no changes in what fathers do around the house.
b. incorrect, because research studies in this area have yielded mixed results with some showing husbands do more and some showing they do less.
c. incorrect, because fathers actually help out more when mothers do not work than when they do.
d. correct.

16. The results of most studies on the effects of maternal employment on children's development have found:
a. major emotional problems.
b. poor attachment behaviors indicative of later problems.
c. massive feelings of guilt on the part of children leading to defensiveness.
d. no major but some minor and inconsistent differences.

17. When comparing mothers who are employed with those who are not, one consistent finding is that mothers who are employed:
a. are less sensitive to the signals from their infants.
b. express more love and happiness when interacting with them.
c. engage in more early independence training with their children.
d. use harsher child-rearing techniques.

18. The greatest percentage of children in alternative child care are cared for:
a. at home.
b. in neighborhood day care houses.
c. at centers run by governmental or other nonprofit agencies.
d. at work.

19. Children who spend considerable time in day care compared to those who are at home with their mothers:
    a. show more aggressive behavior.
    b. are more peer oriented.
    c. are more comfortable in social situations.
    d. are characterized by all of the above.
20. The most important factor in determining whether the day care experience will benefit or detract from the child's development is the:
    a. child's verbal abilities.
    b. extent of father participation.
    c. quality of the day care experience.
    d. amount of time a child spends in day care.

Answers to Multiple-Choice Questions

1. d 2. b 3. a 4. c 5. d 6. a 7. b 8. c 9. c
10. a 11. a 12. d 13. c 14. a 15. d 16. d 17. c
18. a 19. d 20. c

Chapter 7

The Development of Language and Communication Skills

Chapter Outline

Are the Following Statements True or False?

1. American Sign Language, which is used by people with hearing impairments, is recognized as a true language.
2. Psychologists can now understand the general meaning of a young child's babbles.
3. In the second half of the second year, there is a rapid increase in the number of words the child can use.
4. For the average child, no grammatical improvements take place after the age of 6.
5. Children who use incorrect forms of words, such as "goed" and "drinked" instead of "went" and "drank," need formal language training.
6. At present, scientists have not been able to find any part of the brain responsible for language.
7. Parents use well-formed sentences, generally using the present tense, when speaking to toddlers.
8. Middle-class children use more complex sentences and fewer commands than children of working-class parents.
9. Psychologists argue that to have maximum benefit parents should read to their children at least four times per week.
10. Bilingualism leads to cognitive difficulties and academic problems in school.

Answers to True-False Statements 1. True 2. False: see p. 148 3. True 4. False: see p. 150 5. False: see p. 151 6. False: see p. 153 7. True 8. True 9. True 10. False: see p. 159

The Mysteries of Language

If you have ever lost your voice for a day or had such a bad cold that you could not hear well, you probably found it difficult to get through the day. Language and communication are such an enormous part of our lives, and yet we take them for granted. Infants who come into this world with no prior knowledge of any language learn their own language within a few years on the basis of very little formal teaching.

A related mystery involves children's ability to generate sentences they have never heard before. Spend an hour or so listening to preschoolers converse. The creativity involved in generating a new thought will amaze you. When children don't have a word for something they simply make one up! But the simplicity of a child's communication should not blind us to the wonder of how a child creatively uses language.

The Nature of Communication

Language and communication are not the same. Language is only one part of **communication,** which is the process of sharing information, including facts, desires, and feelings. Communication entails a sender, a receiver, and a message. **Language** involves arbitrary symbols with agreed-upon meanings (Shatz, 1983) and it is usually but not always verbal. American Sign Language is a manual language used by people with severe hearing impairments in the United States. It is a recognized language with a grammar of its own, even though it is not verbal (Kaplan, 1996).

communication The process of sharing information.

language The use of symbols to represent meaning in some medium.

True or False?
American Sign Language, which is used by people with hearing impairments, is recognized as a true language.

Young children can communicate without language and without speech. A toddler who wants a cracker but can't reach the cracker box may be capable of saying "cracker," but she does not have to do so to get her message across—she can cry or gesture instead. As receiver of the communication, the parent must interpret the message—not always an easy task because children mispronounce words or express their thoughts in individualistic ways.

The Nature of Language

Just what do children learn when they acquire language? Language has a number of subsystems, including **phonology, morphology, syntax,** and **semantics,** as well as the rules for social language use, sometimes called **pragmatics** (Figure 7.1). *Phonology* includes the sounds of a language, the rules for combining them to make words, and the stress and intonation patterns (Gleason, 1985). For example, the sound "kl" occurs in English, but "kx" does not. Children must learn how these sounds combine to become words. The

phonology The study of the sounds of language, the rules for combining the sounds to make words, and the stress and intonation patterns of the language.

morphology The study of the patterns of word formation in a particular language.

syntax The rules for combining words to make sentences.

semantics The study of the meaning of words.

pragmatics The study of how people use language in various contexts.

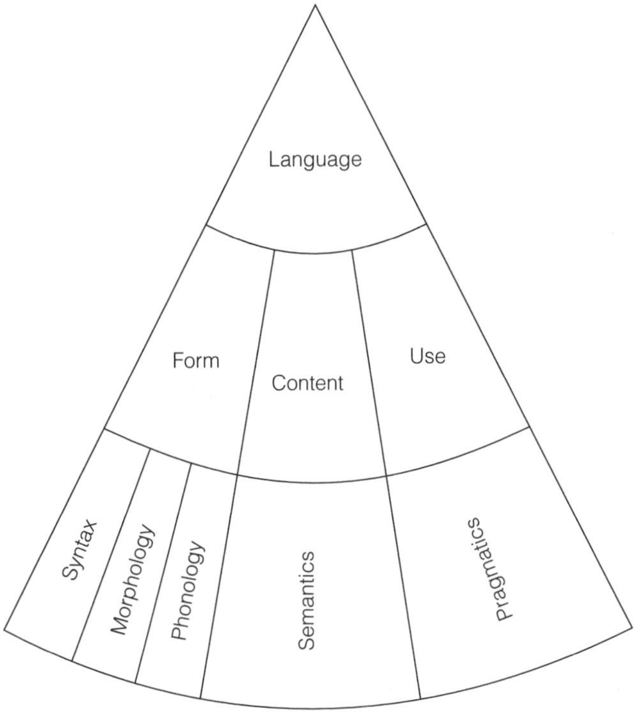

Figure 7.1
Subsystems of Language
Source: Owens, 1992.

morpheme is the smallest unit of meaning in a language. Some morphemes, such as "dog" and "little," can stand by themselves whereas others, such as "ed" and "ing," must be added to another word. The rules of morphology make certain that some sequences (such as "walked") will occur and that others (such as "walkness") will not. Every language has its own rules—called its *syntax*—for how to combine words to make sentences. For instance, "John hit Mary" conveys a meaning quite different from "Mary hit John."

Children must also acquire a vocabulary and understand what the words mean. This area is called *semantics* (Carroll, 1994). Children must also be able to use language appropriately to express their ideas efficiently, which is called *pragmatics.* For example, children must learn how to ask for something, how to greet others, how to apologize, as well as how to use language in social situations (Becker, 1988). Each language has its own rules, and each culture has its own idea of how language should be used. The general term **grammar** is used to refer to the total system of rules or principles that describe the phonology, morphology, syntax, pragmatics, and semantics of a particular language (Owens, 1992).

To communicate with one another, people must understand what others are communicating (called *comprehension*) as well as produce meaning themselves through language or gestures. People can comprehend many more words than they themselves produce. We recognize many more words in print and in someone else's speech than we ourselves use, and this imbalance remains throughout life.

morpheme The smallest unit of meaning in a language.

grammar A general term that refers to the total linguistic knowledge of phonology, morphology, syntax, and semantics.

The Development of Language

Few events bring parents as much joy as their child's first word. It is easy to forget that much has already taken place before the child says "Dada" or "car." Under normal circumstances, every human child in every culture proceeds through similar steps in reaching linguistic competence. The ability to use formal language and communication capabilities develops gradually over time (Elsen, 1995).

Prelanguage Communication

Communication between infants and their care-givers does not require language. Smiles, cries, gestures, and eye contact all form a basis for communication. The nonlanguage interaction between parent and infant approximates a conversation. Although very young infants cannot understand words, they do respond when their caregivers speak to them (Fernald & Simon, 1984), and some linguistic abilities are present almost from birth. One-day-old infants respond to speech sounds by moving their bodies in rhythm to the sounds (Condon & Sander, 1974). One-month-old infants are able to discriminate between certain vowels, such as "i-u" from "i-a," and "pa" from "pi" (Trehub, 1973). Neonates show some ability to discriminate vocalizations in their mothers' native language from those in another language (Mehler et al., 1988).

The infant's ability to respond to language and to other nonverbal cues leads to a kind of turn taking called *proto-conversations.* A parent speaks, and the baby responds by smiling or cooing. The parent then says something else, and the pattern continues. These interactions are spontaneous. Let's say a mother is playing with her baby. When the infant lets go of a toy, the mother says, "No, I don't want that any more. I want the ball." These interactions are the beginning of a conversation mode and are the basis for later communication. Such conversations are not as random as they seem. Mothers use a rising pitch when their infants are not paying attention and mothers want them to make eye contact (Stern, Spieker, & MacKain, 1982). In addition, yes-no questions are spoken with a rising pitch, whereas questions having to do with what and where as well as various commands are accompanied by a falling pitch.

The infant is also the master of another ability—**cooing.** Cooing involves the production of single-syllable sounds, such as "oo." Vowel sounds are often preceded by a consonant, resulting in a sound such as "moo." Infants enjoy listening to themselves vocalize, but these

cooing Verbal production of single-syllable sounds, such as "oo."

early vocalizations are not meant to be formal communication.

The next step in language development is **babbling,** which involves vowel and consonant sounds strung together and often repeated. Babbling may begin as early as 3 months and gradually increases until about 9 to 12 months of age, after which it decreases as the child begins to use words (deVilliers & deVilliers, 1978). Most infants are babbling by the age of 6 months (Silverman, 1995).

No one has been able to decipher the meaning of any of the babbles of infants. Although babbling begins as a relatively uncoordinated activity, social stimulation affects the amount of babbling children produce (Hegde, 1995). Although the variety and range of speech sounds produced is impressive, it does not approximate all the sounds that humans are able to produce (deVilliers & deVilliers, 1978).

> ***True or False?***
> Psychologists can now understand the general meaning of a young child's babbles.

Many of the important prerequisites for understanding language are shown at this point. Infants begin to pay attention to more frequently used words; 4½-month-old infants show a preference for listening to their own names over other names whether matched or not matched for sound stress patterns (Mandel, Juscyk, & Pisoni, 1995). For example, if the child's name is Joshua, the child shows a preference for the name over Agatha (same stress) or Maria (different stress). No one claims that children this young understand their own names, but they have the ability to recognize and respond to frequently occurring sound patterns, which is a prerequisite for later relating sounds to meanings.

By 7½ months infants show some capacity for detecting the sound patterns of words in fluent speech (Jusczyk, 1995) and begin to appreciate the nature of their own language. For example, in English most words have a stress on the first syllable. Nine-month-old American infants listen significantly longer to words with a strong/weak stress than with a weak/strong stress (Jusczyk, Cutler, & Redanz, 1993). This preference is not found in 6-month-old infants. Being able to pick out words from rapidly spoken sentences or to pay attention to the stress patterns of words shows the beginning of an understanding of the nature of words, which is a prerequisite for the later understanding of language.

The First Word

Children's earliest recognizable language is in the form of single words. Children usually utter their first word anytime between 10 and 15 months, but there is considerable individual variation. The development of the first 10 or so words is relatively slow, taking place from the later part of the first year gradually through the next few months (Durkin, 1995). Children's first words are related to those that they have heard frequently used by their parents (Hart, 1991). After they begin using language, the relationship between the frequency of parental use of particular words and children's utterances is much less (Barrett, Harris, & Chasin, 1991). According to one study, the most common words were *mom, dad, baby, kitty, duck, sock, good, see,* and *stop* (Hart, 1991).

Katherine Nelson (1973) studied early word acquisition in a number of children and was able to divide the children into two categories. **Expressive children** used words that were involved primarily in social interactions, such as "bye-bye" and "stop." The early language of **referential children** involved the naming of objects with such words as "dog" and "penny." These differing styles followed the linguistic style used by the children's caregivers. The parents of referential children named objects very frequently whereas those of expressive children directed their children's activities and emphasized social interactions. The early language of both groups differed. Referential children used many more words. Expressive children began to use language in a social context and referential children used it in a cognitive context, such as labeling items when looking at a book (Nelson, 1981). At 20 months referential children were more likely than expressive children to point out objects to their mothers (Goldfield, 1990).

These findings demonstrate that children's language is influenced by the language their parents use and that children may take different paths to arrive at linguistic competence.

Words at first are used in isolation and then gradually are generalized to similar situations. Babbling continues during this one-word stage. For years psychologists have argued about the meaning of one-word utterances. What does a child really mean when uttering the single word "jam" (Francis, 1975)? Does he or she mean that some jam is on the table or that the child wants jam on a piece of bread? Psychologists call this one-word utterance a **holophrase,** a single word that stands for a complete thought (Carroll, 1994). For instance, a child says, "up," and means "pick me up," or says, "wet," and wants to be changed. Parents must go beyond the word and use the context to interpret the child's ideas. But the child saying, "wet" may be labeling the condition and not want to be changed at all, which casts doubt on whether the child is really using one-word expressions to indicate entire thoughts.

Toddlers' Language

By around 18 to 20 months, most infants have a productive vocabulary of around 50 words. Words such as "no,"

babbling Verbal production of vowel and consonant sounds strung together and often repeated.

expressive children Children who use words involved in social interactions, such as "stop" and "bye."

referential children Children whose early language is used to name objects, such as "dog" or "bed."

holophrase One word used to stand for an entire thought.

"mine," and "hot" are common, although word usage is inconsistent. In the second half of the child's second year a rapid acceleration in vocabulary occurs (Woodward, Markman, & Fitzsimmons, 1994). It could be called a naming explosion, because about three-quarters of these new words are nouns. By 24 months, the child is using 320 words and by 30 months 570 words (Mervis & Bertrand, 1994).

True or False?
In the second half of the second year, there is a rapid increase in the number of words the child can use.

This vocabulary explosion is difficult to explain. It may be caused by some improvement in memory or some change in processing capacity (Woodward et al., 1994). Perhaps it is caused by some major cognitive advance, such as the child beginning to understand that everything can and ought to be placed in a category (Gopnick & Meltzoff, 1987). Between 20 and 22 months children show a spurt in comprehension as well (Reznick & Goldfield, 1992).

Children seem to employ a fast mapping strategy that enables them to connect a word and an object after only one or two exposures (Mervis & Bertrand, 1994). Between 2 and 5 years children seem to pick up words at an astounding pace (Rice, Buhr, & Nemeth, 1990). This is true both in production and comprehension. Between the ages of about 1½ and 6 years, children learn to comprehend over 14,000 words, which averages to about 9 new words a day (Rice et al., 1990). Young children learn words in a variety of contexts and situations, including from television programs, where the words are spoken quickly (Akhtar, Carpenter, & Tomasello, 1996; Rice & Woodsmall, 1988). Children can hold a verb or a noun in their minds while something is being done or said and await the label at a later time (Tomasello & Barton, 1994).

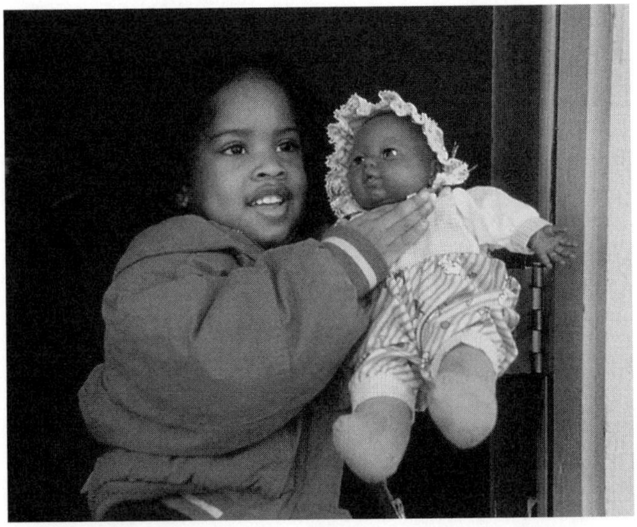

Toddlers use particular rules of word order. For example, to show possession, children use the possessor and then the item such as "baby, doll."

Some children, however, learn words more gradually and maintain a balance of nouns and other kinds of words, especially verbs (Goldfield & Reznick, 1989). This may mean that there is no single "correct" strategy and there may be more roads to linguistic competence than first thought.

It is easy to understand how children link a noun such as a chair with the label. Parents point out objects for young children, and this is how most children learn these nouns. But only in some Western middle-class homes is a conscious attempt made to point and label. In many other settings little immediate labeling takes place but children still learn their nouns; labeling is certainly beneficial but may not be necessary (Tomasello & Barton, 1994).

What about learning verbs? Parents label what they are doing, request the child's participation, or comment on their own or the child's pending action. The last of these is most important and seems to lead to the most rapid learning of verbs (Tomasello & Kruger, 1992).

During the toddler stage the child's vocabulary increases greatly, two- to three-word sentences are spoken, and the first pronouns, such as "I," appear. Some simple adjectives and adverbs are present, and the child often demands repetition from others. The child begins to announce intentions before acting and asks questions (Weiss & Lillywhite, 1976).

The two-word stage is well organized. The child's use of words is governed by rules, which make the communication easier to understand (Armon-Lotem, 1995). The meaning depends upon specific word orders (Owens, 1994). For example, when expressing ownership, toddlers use one word to stand for the possessor and another for the item, as in "mommy ball" or "baby doll." When the toddler wants something that has happened to happen again, the child will use a recurrence word, such as *more* or *nuther,* and then the object, such as "nuther cookie" (Owens, 1994). Young children use an agent-action form such as "Adam hit" or an attribution form such as "big ball" that are expanded on later (Durkin, 1995). Toddler language contains a number of these rules. When about half the child's utterances contain two words, the child begins to use three words and these sentences are still governed by specific rules.

The child's early speech leaves out small words like *a, to,* or *from* and concentrates on the more important words. This is called **telegraphic speech** because it is similar to the language found in telegrams, where the sender includes only the words absolutely necessary for communication. Examples are "mommy go store" and "baby take toy." These important phrases are commonly stressed by other speakers in the environment, which makes them easier to imitate and learn (Brown, 1973). Parents still must interpret the child's meaning according to the context of the remark, but the thoughts are communicated more precisely at this stage.

telegraphic speech Sentences in which only the basic words necessary to communicate meaning are used, with helping words such as "a" or "to" left out.

Language Development in Early Childhood

From ages 3 through 6 years, the child's vocabulary and sentence length increases. The child's style of speech also improves. By the end of the second and into the third year, young children use words to coordinate their actions with others, tell them what to do, protest others' actions, to make suggestions, and to negotiate a play activity and respond to others (Eckerman & Didow, 1996). Their use of language becomes more social and pragmatic. These advancements are shown in Table 7.1. At 3 years of age the child's sentences are well formed but very simple. By age 6 the child is using all parts of speech and can use language much more efficiently and effectively. By the end of the preschool stage, the child is making fewer grammatical errors, can sustain a conversation longer, has more focused conversations, and can attend longer to one topic of conversation.

Language Development in Middle Childhood

During middle childhood the child improves in every subsystem of language. The child uses more elaborate phrasing and uses the passive voice, as in "was sad," "got lost," or "was chased." After the age of 7 years, the child understands the *-ly* adverb form, and verb agreement with irregular nouns, such as "The sheep is eating," improves greatly. The child begins to use past participles, such as "eaten," and perfect tenses, such as "has been." These tenses develop slowly, and even though some forms are produced early in this stage, their use may be uneven until later in the period. This gradual language development is common in this period. For example, the conjunctions *if, so,* and *because* are used much earlier, but their full development does not occur until later in the period. Some forms, such as *although* and *therefore,* may not be used until late elementary school or early adolescence.

> ***True or False?***
> For the average child, no grammatical improvements take place after the age of 6.

The vocabulary of these children also increases. As most parents well know, school-age children become able to use language more subtly. Children's ability to get what they want now improves because they can see things from other people's point of view. This gives the child the ability to ask for things indirectly, as in "Gee, that cowboy hat looks great." Most parents understand that this is an indirect request. The school-age child can gain attention in a more socially acceptable manner, ask for things giving a rationalization, and more easily direct the actions of others. The child can now introduce a topic into the conversation, keep the conversation going for a while, and close the conversation less abruptly than can a younger child.

Adolescence and Beyond

Adolescents use language in more advanced ways; their ability to use and understand satire, metaphors, and similes is associated with cognitive advancements such as the ability to use abstractions. Adolescents have the cognitive sophistication to understand political cartoons, abstract poetry, and proverbs. Adolescents also show vocabulary gains, especially in some technical areas. In addition, their communication patterns change. Teenagers are better able to understand the communicative requirements of the situation and appreciate how people's moods and expectations influence their acceptance of communication. The adolescent can more easily bend language to meet the needs of the situation. The ability

Table 7.1 **Linguistic Advancements During the Preschool Stage**
During the preschool stage, the child shows great progress in language acquisition.

AGE	NUMBER OF WORDS USED	NUMBER OF WORDS PER SENTENCE	NEW DEVELOPMENTS
3	900	3–4	Sentences show subject and verb but are simple; uses present tense; use of words such as *when, time, today;* begins to use plurals and some prepositions; uses commands.
3½	1200	4–5	Rate of speech increases; asks permission *(may I?);* uses *couldn't* and *if* as conjunctions.
4	1500	5–5½	Demands reasons why and how; rhymes; questions a great deal; uses words such as *even, almost, like,* and *but;* understands most questions; has difficulty with *how* and *why.*
4½	1800	5½–6	Does not command or use demands as often; completes most sentences.
5	2200	6	Asks meanings of a particular word; asks function of items, and how they work; uses many types of clauses; discusses feelings; understands *before* and *after.*
5½	2300	6½	Makes fewer grammatical errors; sentences become more sophisticated.
6	2500	7	Uses all parts of speech to some extent; can define by function.

Source: Adapted from Weiss & Lillywhite, 1976; Owens, 1988; Kaplan, 1991.

to hint and make indirect requests, which began in middle childhood, improves greatly as well.

Adults are frequently judged on their linguistic abilities, including their vocabulary and the ability to express themselves. Adults who have limited linguistic abilities may find themselves limited in the job market and in certain interpersonal interactions, such as dealing with supervisors or making a positive impression at job interviews. Language abilities take on an importance for the entire life span; adults can improve their linguistic skills, and some further development can occur, which in adulthood depends largely upon the individual's lifestyle.

How Words Are Used

Striking differences exist between how children and adults use language. Young children overextend and underextend their use of words and follow grammatical rules with what seems to be blind devotion.

Overextensions and Underextensions

As they learn language, children make certain kinds of mistakes (Griffiths, 1986). For instance, a young child looking at a magazine might label every picture of a man "daddy" and every four-legged animal "dog." Such a child knows the identity of his or her father and is probably aware of the difference between a cat and a dog. The type of error in which children apply a term in a broader manner than is correct, called **overextension,** is probably more a problem of production than a problem of comprehension (Whitehurst, 1982). That is, children understand the differences, but they have difficulty producing the correct labels. This was demonstrated well in a study by Nelson and colleagues (1978), who found that children who would call all sorts of vehicles—airplanes, trucks, or even helicopters—"cars" could pick out the correct object when asked to do so. Children also show signs of **underextension**—that is, they use a term to cover a smaller universe than it should (Anglin, 1977). Young children often use "animal" to define only mammals and may deny that people, insects, or birds are also animals.

Why do children overextend and underextend? Perhaps children learn words and concepts in terms of basic features (Clark, 1974, 1978). This is called **semantic feature theory.** According to this theory, since dogs have four legs and hair, a child would call all four-legged animals with hair "dogs." Children learn that birds have feathers and fly so all animals fitting that description are placed into the category of "bird." However, the categories must be constantly updated: an ostrich has feathers and does not fly but is still a bird. Others argue that rather than learning specific features, the child actually develops a **prototype**—or the most typical instance of a category—and compares other instances to the category. When asked to state whether a new item fits into a category, people compare the new stimulus to the prototype; some examples are better prototypes than others. For instance, robins are better prototypes of birds than turkeys or penguins. How well a particular example fits a prototype affects how fast we process information—people will more quickly classify a robin than a penguin as a bird.

Categorization problems may also arise from the speech that is directed at children by adults (Anglin, 1977). When a child is young, parents are apt to use such terms as "car" and "dog" rather than "Chevrolet" and "German shepherd." This is functional because children need to recognize the difference between a car and a truck, but not between a Chevy and a Dodge, but it restricts the child's experience with labels. Overextension and underextension may also simply reflect the child's prevailing mental abilities and difficulty in categorizing items.

Overregularization of Rules

Once children begin to acquire some of the basic rules of English, they overuse—or, as psychologists say, overgeneralize or **overregularize**—them (Goodluck, 1986). Children will often overuse the rules of language, saying "seed" and "goed" for the past tense of "see" and "go." There is often an early period when the child correctly uses these irregular verbs before overegulization appears (Johnson, 1995). With experience, most children gradually learn the exceptions with little or no formal training.

> ***True or False?***
> Children who use incorrect forms of words, such as "goed" and "drinked" instead of "went" and "drank," need formal language training.

How We Learn Language

Psychologists struggle with the question of how a child develops from understanding but producing no language to using language with great ease. Four major factors contribute to our regrettably incomplete understanding of this process—the principles of learning, innate factors, cognitive factors, and social factors.

Reinforcement and Imitation

The first scientific attempts to explain language acquisition are credited to B.F. Skinner (1957) who believed that

overextension A type of error in which children apply a term more broadly than it should be.

underextension The use of a word in a more narrow context than is proper.

semantic feature theory A theory of semantic and concept acquisition arguing that people develop concepts in terms of a concept's basic features.

prototype The most typical instance of a category.

overregularization (overgeneralization) A type of error in which children overuse the basic rules of the language. For instance, once they learn to use plural nouns, they may say "mans" instead of "men."

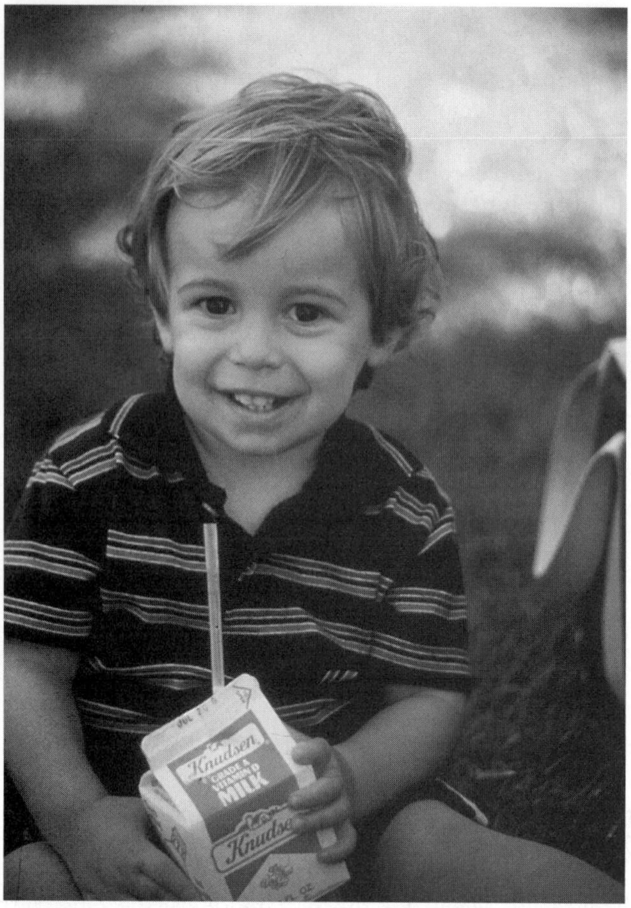

"I drinked the milks," Once children begin to master the rules of grammar, they often overgeneralize them.

language was learned in a similar way as everything else—through reinforcement and modeling. Language learning could be explained solely by environmental factors. According to Skinner (1957), operant conditioning—including the processes of reinforcement, generalization, and discrimination—is responsible for language development. Children are reinforced for labeling the environment and for asking for things. Through the processes of generalization and discrimination, children come to reduce their errors and use the appropriate forms. Children also imitate parental speech. Skinner looked at the acquisition of grammar as a matter of generalizing and making inferences. For example, a child may learn the meaning for the phrase "my teddy bear" and then infer that "my" can be used as in "my apple," "my television," "my" everything. As we shall see, this explanation of language development is sharply contested by others.

Reinforcement and imitation are involved in word learning. Words are symbols that stand for things or ideas. Children's early imitation depends upon a number of factors, including the nature of the sounds (some sounds are easier to produce than others), the stress pattern of the words, as well as how difficult the word is to imitate (Hura & Echols, 1996). The influence of imitation on word acquisition is evident. A parent who labels common, everyday items is likely to have a child who has a superior early vocabulary (Nelson, 1973). Children also learn words from older siblings and peers.

Other evidence exists that the processes of learning can affect both the number and the complexity of verbalizations. English- and Spanish-speaking 2- and 3-year-olds were exposed to a foreign language. Some children were reinforced if they used the language; others were not. For example, in the experimental group, if the child used the foreign word for a toy, the toy was immediately handed to the child. Those who were reinforced in this way used many more foreign words (Whitehurst & Valdez Menchaca, 1988). The reinforcement motivated the children to use the words from this new language. Other studies show that care-givers who reinforce their children for using complex language generally have children who indeed use such language.

Although imitation and reinforcement are helpful in understanding certain areas of language acquisition, they are inadequate to explain language acquisition itself. The overall amount of imitation decreases with age, especially after age 2 (Owens, 1992). In other words, the usefulness of imitation as a language-learning strategy decreases as language becomes more complex; imitation then becomes most important at the single-word level.

It is also very difficult to explain how children create original sentences using reinforcement and imitation. All children create original sentences they have not heard before. Strong evidence against imitation is the finding that children invent new words and new forms they have not heard around them (Marcus et al., 1992).

In addition, a child of limited cognitive abilities can master the complicated rules of grammar that even adults cannot explain—and do it all without formal training (Bloom, 1975; Durkin, 1995). The rules of whether to use "a" or "the" thing are very complicated and abstract. No one teaches children these rules and yet children use them correctly. They learn them despite the fact that adult speech is anything but fluent, containing errors, false starts, interruptions, fragments, and is spoken very quickly (Durkin, 1995); learning theory has a great deal of difficulty explaining how this occurs. Also, why do children make the same mistakes as they develop their language abilities, and why do they produce such childish speech patterns as telegraphic speech, which they do not hear around them? These problems have led some authorities to argue that some innate biological mechanism must be responsible for language acquisition.

Is Language Acquisition Innate?

Noam Chomsky (1959, 1965, 1972), the leading advocate for the biological, or **nativist explanation,** argued that human beings are programmed to learn language. Children only require exposure to language. Human beings are born with an innate, biological ability to learn

nativist explanation An explanation of language development based on biological or innate factors.

language—called a **language-acquisition device.** Children can acquire the grammar of the particular culture's language because their brain is biologically patterned to understand the structure of language. Children acquire and use the basic rules of language and form hypotheses about them, which they then test out.

It is difficult to explain grammatical constructions. Chomsky argues that since children learn abstract grammatical rules despite poor input means that they must have some basic understanding or capacity to understand language. Chomsky's position was excitedly received by many psychologists and psycholinguists (scientists who study the nature of languages), and it explains the interesting similarities we find in language acquisition around the world. Children in all cultures proceed through similar steps when learning language (Slobin, 1972) and make the same mistakes, similarities that can be accounted for if language acquisition rests on some shared neurological foundation.

In the nativist view, language acquisition is a maturational activity that coincides with brain development. Some authorities claim that there is a critical period between birth and adolescence for developing language (Lenneberg, 1967) and that if not developed during that time, the individual's language will be permanently disordered. There is evidence for and against this idea. What would happen if children were not exposed to any language? In a few cases of severe environmental deprivation and isolation this has occurred. When these isolated children are later exposed to language they are able to learn some early language but it is far from complete (Harris, 1995). The most interesting case is that of Genie, who was kept socially isolated from the age of 18 months until adolescence without any exposure to language (Curtis, 1977). After intensive speech and language therapy she reached a 2-year-old stage or so of language but did not really move past that. Her language usage consisted of two or three words loosely linked by meaning and without any grammatical construction (Harris, 1995). If the nativist theory is correct, why did she learn any language? If the behavioral theory is correct, why was her language so poor? This remains a mystery. Perhaps the mechanisms for learning simple language and more complex forms are different.

Although Chomsky's theory is controversial, everyone accepts the fact that human beings are born with an impressive vocal apparatus that allows them to develop speech and that specific areas of the brain are devoted to language. The cerebral cortex in human beings is divided into two hemispheres: the right and the left. Most people are right-handed, and almost all have their language functions centralized in the left hemisphere. Half the left-handed people also have their language areas localized in the left hemisphere (Gleason, 1985). This specialization is present by the age of 20 months, and other neurological changes related to language learning also occur early in life (Harris, 1995).

When specific areas of the brain are injured, certain language-related problems occur. The area responsible for producing speech is called **Broca's area,** and damage here causes difficulties in producing language, but not in language comprehension. Damage to another area, called **Wernicke's area,** causes a person to have poor comprehension and to use speech filled with nonsense words, even though the speech is fluent (Harris, 1995). The brain also has specific areas that are associated with written language (Gleason, 1985).

True or False?
At present, scientists have not been able to find any part of the brain responsible for language.

Some biological basis for language acquisition may exist. Human infants can make impressive phonetic distinctions and are attentive to speech quite early in life (Marean, Werner, & Kuhl, 1992). Some strategies for processing language may be innate (Slobin, 1973; McNeill, 1970). Infants show different brain wave electrical patterns to familiar and unfamiliar words (Harris, 1995).

One recent, but still controversial, area of research which may support the nativist position involves the question of how parents react to their children's ungrammatical statements? Parents correct their children's syntactical errors of word order, tense, or grammar about a third of the time. For example, if a child says "That are a monkey," the parent may say "That is a monkey." Parents also respond with expansions or recasts, reproducing major parts of the child's utterance while adding to it. For example, if a child said, "lady dress on," the parent might say, "The lady has a dress on." Although some authorities question whether the relatively small percentage of corrections and expansions really influences children's acquisition of language (Gordon, 1990), others argue that they may play an important role (Bohannon & Stanowicz, 1988; Bohannon, MacWhinney, & Snow, 1990).

Both the function and consequences of such corrective feedback, sometimes called *negative evidence* because it hypothetically shows children that something in their speech pattern is incorrect, is important to the Skinner-Chomsky debate. The nativist position is that since children are rarely informed about the grammatical correctness of their statements and learn language on the basis of relatively poor and limited linguistic input, the explanation of how language acquisition occurs must lie in the child's innate ability to learn language. On the other hand, parental corrections and expansions being important in shaping children's language would provide evi-

language-acquisition device An assumed biological device used in the acquisition of language.

Broca's area An area in the brain responsible for producing speech.

Wernicke's area An area in the brain responsible for comprehension of language.

dence for the more environmental explanations (Bohannon, Padgett, Nelson, & Mark, 1996).

A recent study found no relationship between recasts and children's subsequent grammar or self-corrections (Morgan, 1996; Morgan, Bonamo, & Travis, 1995). Recasts did not serve as corrections and did not repress grammatical mistakes, but they did encourage children to express themselves in a variety of ways. The results of this study may be seen as evidence for the nativist position. However, the study has been questioned on technical grounds, with some authorities arguing that the jury is still out (Bohannon et al., 1996), but its conclusions also have been defended (Morgan, 1996).

Weaknesses of the Nativist Position

The nativist position has also been criticized. Despite findings showing a neurological basis for language, the existence of a language-acquisition device has not yet been demonstrated (Moerk, 1989). In addition, even if we agree that a neurological basis for language exists, it does not explain the process involved in language learning. Finally, although the similarities between how children learn language around the world are impressive, evidence shows that there are some differences that reflect the nature of the language being learned (Akiyama, 1985), and the idea that children are programmed with a number of possible linguistic variations, although interesting, has not yet been adequately demonstrated. Others claim that the existence of a language acquisition device is not necessary to understand language acquisition and that cognitive and general learning principles are sufficient to explain language acquisition (Moerk, 1989). Although some biological foundation for learning language is probable, the nativist position does not fully explain language acquisition.

Cognitive Theory and Language Development

Language learning requires a number of cognitive processes, such as attention, information processing, and retention. For instance, paying attention to stimuli that are loud or connected to some vital activity (such as feeding), remembering them, making discriminations and judgments about them (such as whether they are the same or different), and classifying according to these judgments are all cognitive processes related to language learning (Peters, 1986). Cognitive psychologists argue that cognitive factors either precede or place a limit on language learning (Durkin, 1995). Children notice things in their environment and learn words best when parents focus on what children are paying attention to rather than forcing children to redirect their attention to something else (Dunham, Dunham, & Curwin, 1993). In order to create sentences children also need the cognitive ability to remember words. In addition, children must understand something about an object or an idea before using words in a meaningful manner. Linguistic growth necessarily parallels cognitive growth. The child first uses simple words to label things, then proceeds to define classes of things in terms of their more abstract qualities, such as color.

Piaget (1962) argued that language emerges from nonlinguistic sensorimotor intelligence and represents the ability to create and understand symbols. Studies have generally not supported the idea that sensorimotor intelligence is a prerequisite for *all* aspects of language learning, but children's performance on some Piagetian tasks does predict specific language achievements (Tomasello & Ferrar, 1984). It is difficult to understand how a child could express a thought such as "all gone" or understand the concept of disappearance unless the child understood some measure of object permanence (Rice, 1989). Toddlers all around the world use locational terms, such as "out," "down," and "on" (Bowerman, De Leon, & Choi, 1995), which they could not do without some spatial understanding.

Children first talk about what they know—favorite things, people, and activities (Rice, 1989); they name their bottles and other things that have meaning to them. In understanding semantic development, we now go beyond the idea that children merely hold a picture of an item in their heads and then attach the word symbol to this item. This simple association may be useful for simple words, but the child's understanding of the word and its meaning goes beyond this. As noted previously, semantic feature theory and cognitive theories based on the notion of prototypes have been advanced to account for how children develop their word knowledge. Modern cognitive approaches to linguistic development are searching for identifiable sequences in which the relationships between cognitive advancement and linguistic expression are related. Although cognitive advancements are not a total explanation for language development, cognitive processes cannot be ignored.

Social Interaction and Language Development

Children do not acquire language in a vacuum. They are affected by their total linguistic environment. Although there are many similarities in the way children develop their linguistic skills around the world, some individual differences are also found (Elsen, 1995). These differences are not merely in pace of learning, but in the path children take to learn language. Some individual differences in language development can be explained by the variations in the linguistic environments that surround different children.

At first glance, the linguistic environment appears to be confusing, and its level seems to be much too advanced for infants. However, early verbal interchanges are not confusing or too difficult for young children (Moerk, 1989). When people talk to infants, they modify their speech; parents talk to their older infants in shorter, well-formed sentences (Bowerman, 1981). The language that parents use when talking to toddlers is simple and repetitious. It contains many questions and commands and few hesitations, focuses on the present tense, and is high pitched and spoken with an exaggerated intonation (Garnica, 1977). The use of simplified speech and exaggerated intonation are found almost universally (Fernald & Morikawa, 1993). Mothers in different cultures modify their speech to match the cognitive abilities of their children. In short, parents' speech to their linguistically limited children is restricted; it uses common nouns and comments on what their children are doing (Molfese et al., 1982).

True or False?
Parents use well-formed sentences, generally using the present tense, when speaking to toddlers.

The use of simplistic, redundant sentences is normally referred to as **motherese** or **parentese.** All adults and many older children tailor their language to the age and comprehension level of younger children. Even young children use these strategies but are not as proficient in their use (Tomasello & Mannle, 1985). Four-month-old infants prefer to listen to motherese speech over speech directed at adults (Fernald, 1985). Infants are especially sensitive to pitch. The higher pitch used when talking to an infant elicits the infant's attention (Fernald & Kuhl, 1987). The child's reaction to parental speech determines the speaker's choice of words (Bohannon & Marquis, 1977). If a 2-year-old does not seem to understand, the adult immediately reduces the number of words in the next sentence. Children are not merely passive receivers of information—their comprehension or noncomprehension serves to control their linguistic environment.

Verbal exchanges between adults and young children do not constitute formal language lessons. However, there is no doubt about the influence that parental speech and reaction have on the child. A strong relationship exists between parental language and children's vocabulary, especially in early language development (Barrett et al., 1991; Hart, 1991). Language acquisition involves learning a social skill that is useful in the interpersonal context and is purely functional. The purpose of speech and language is to communicate one's thoughts, ideas, and desires to others.

The intense communication between parents and children begins before verbal language is developed. Even before they learn language, children actively communicate with their parents through gestures and vocalizations (Bruner, 1978a, 1978b), prelinguistic modes that are replaced later by standard linguistic modes. Between the transition from the prelinguistic mode to the first words, children use more and more gestures to make themselves understood and parents are particularly sensitive to these early attempts to coordinate gesture and vocalization (Harris, 1995). The interactions between parent and child are structured in the form of a dialogue and show a progression from the simple to the complex. Even though parents may not be aware of their role as teachers, they do teach their children their native tongue. The infant begins to communicate, and the parent responds; the interaction between the two is intense and functional.

Questions Students Often Ask
Why is the question of how children learn language so complicated?
I sympathize with students who want a clear concise answer to how a child learns language. Unfortunately we don't have one right now and may not have a complete model for the foreseeable future. One of the greatest problems is the increasing realization that children can take multiple paths to linguistic competence. Research in various cultures clearly shows that use of language differs in parent-child interactions and produces different types of early language. Yet, all children learn to speak and such flexibility makes it difficult to find one theoretical position that will fit all children.

Language is used to direct the actions of others. The child learns that communication involves signaling meaning, sharing experiences, and taking turns. The eminent psychologist, Jerome Bruner (1978a), sees language development in terms of problem solving. Children must solve the problem of how to communicate their wishes and thoughts to others. They learn language through this interaction with others and by using language actively. The opportunity to engage actively in communication is necessary. Children acquire grammar and vocabulary because they are useful to them in accomplishing their aim of getting across to others what they want and what they are thinking. Notice that in this conception of language development, parents tune their linguistic input to the ability level of the child. This theory is sometimes called the **fine tuning theory.** Fine-tuned speech is not just motherese; it is not just simpler sentences, but communication that is matched to the developmental level of the child and adapts as the child develops (Sokolov, 1993). It explains the finding that children encounter language in a very structured and progressively more difficult and complex manner. Language is learned as an extension of nonlinguistic communication. Bruner's theory is a kind of compromise between Skinner's and Chomsky's. Bruner believes that language develops from the interaction between the language and social environment created by the care-givers and whatever innate language potential children have (Levine & Mueller, 1988).

Culture and Early Language Usage

Cultural variation may help explain differences in language usage and development. For example, similarities and differences exist in the ways in which Japanese and

motherese (parentese) The use of simple repetitive sentences with young children.

fine tuning theory A theory noting that parents tune their language to a child's linguistic ability.

American mothers use language. When observed playing with their children both Japanese and American mothers accommodated to the special needs of their children by simplifying their speech, repeating themselves frequently, and using interesting sounds to engage their infant's attention. At the same time, Japanese and Americans differed in how they interacted with their infants, differences that were shaped by their cultural beliefs.

American mothers focused more on target objects and provided labels consistently. Japanese mothers were less likely to label toys, but used language more often in rituals of social exchange, such as giving and taking, and verbal politeness (Fernald & Morikawa, 1993). Japanese mothers were more likely to engage their infants in empathy routines encouraging the infant to show positive feelings towards a toy because cultural norms for polite speech are very important in Japan. Japanese mothers also used more baby talk and for longer. When asked, Japanese mothers typically explained their goals were to talk gently using sounds that they thought were easy to imitate. American mothers were more likely to report that their goals were to attract the infant's attention and to teach the infant words. They were more interested in fostering linguistic competence, whereas Japanese mothers used language to establish emotional bonds (Fernald & Morikawa, 1993). As a result, American children had larger noun vocabularies than did Japanese infants at 19 months.

These linguistic differences are now beginning to be investigated as a clue to the many paths children can take to become language proficient. Mothers from Argentina, France, Japan, and the United States were audiotaped as they spoke with their 5- and 13-month-old children, and their communications were analyzed. All mothers showed a change in their communication. Affect-salient statements, such as greetings, recitations of nursery rhymes, and endearments, comprised much more of the speech at 5 months than at 13 months. Information-oriented speech consisting of statements, questions, and reports about the environment ("You like the blocks"), increased greatly between 5 and 13 months (see Figure 7.2). But differences between cultures were significant. Argentine mothers showed much higher frequencies of direct statements than mothers in the three other cultures. Bornstein and colleagues (1992) note that traditional Argentine child-rearing is somewhat more authoritarian and directs the child's behavior while expressing care and love. American mothers asked many more questions, probably as a way to engage children. French mothers seemed to place less emphasis on stimulation and more on using language to establish closeness. French mothers address their infants much less frequently in a modified speech register than do American parents and use more typical adult-adult conversational tones than American mothers (Bornstein et al., 1992). Japanese mothers were highest in their use of affect-salient speech, using the most grammatically incomplete utterances and playing with sounds more than mothers in other cultures. Their goal was to empathize with their infants' needs (Bornstein et al., 1992). Mother-infant communication serves a socialization function and becomes part of culture.

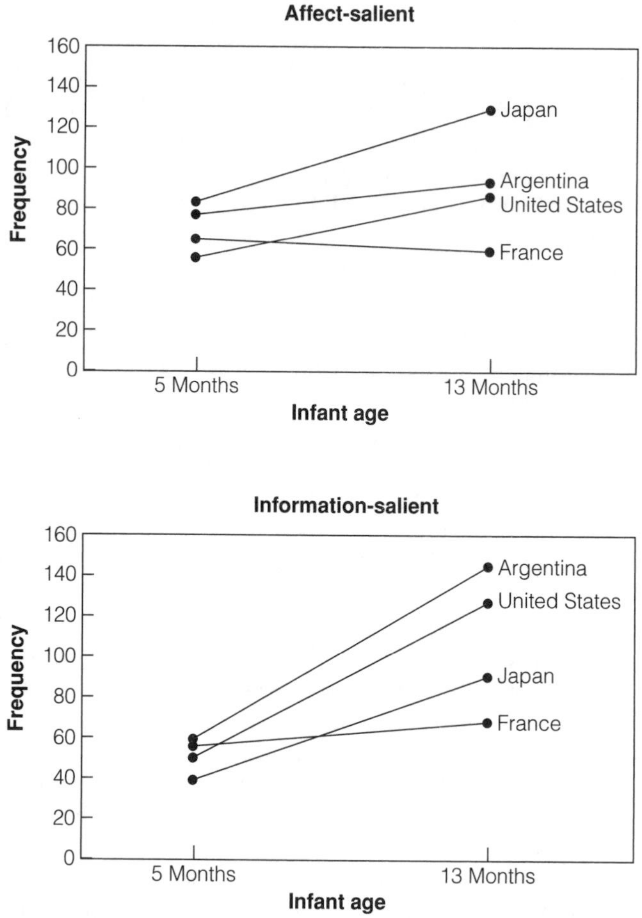

Figure 7.2
Maternal affect-salient speech (top) and maternal information-salient speech (bottom) to infants of two ages in four cultures.
Source: Data from Bornstein et al., 1992.

In looking at how parents communicate with their children we have taken a middle-class, mostly Western point of view. In many non-Western societies, young children are not spoken to very much. They are expected to learn language from what they overhear. Yet, despite this lack of linguistic interaction they do learn language. Although no one doubts that parental, care-giver or even sibling speech directly aimed at the child has an effect on children's language development, recent evidence demonstrates that overheard speech may also have an effect (Oshima-Takane, Goodz, & Derevensky, 1996). Younger children listen to what is said to others and sometimes show that they understand it (Dunn & Shatz, 1989). Although first-born children tend to reach the 50-word mark before later children, no differences exist at the 100-word mark (Pine, 1995). There is no indication that younger children learn early language at any slower rate. They do use it somewhat differently—they hear and therefore use more personal pronouns. Again, we conclude that there are many paths, some culturally prescribed, to linguistic competence (Oshima-Takane et al., 1996).

Although the influence of social forces on language acquisition seems obvious, the actual mechanisms are still not well understood (Durkin, 1995). Exactly how language may emerge out of the complex social interactions is difficult to explain.

Encouraging Linguistic Competence

Children learn language through an active process that involves exposure to a particular linguistic environment. The finding that the nature of this early linguistic interaction determines the child's later language abilities comes as no surprise. Children who are encouraged to verbalize and expand on their language skills develop superior language abilities (Hoff-Ginsberg, 1986).

In the United States the language environment of poor and nonpoor children differs (Walker et al., 1994). Economically impoverished families play fewer language games that are conducive to early language learning and ask their children less often for language (Hart & Risley, 1992; Walker et al., 1994). Middle-class children use more expansive language and do better in language activities in school. Children of working-class parents use simpler sentences and more commands (Olim, Hess, & Shipman, 1967). Children reared in poverty have fewer early language experiences associated with optimal language later on, and this leads to differences between middle- and lower-income children in later reading and academic achievement. Early language ability predicts success in school (Walker et al., 1994).

> ***True or False?***
> Middle-class children use more complex sentences and fewer commands than children of working-class parents.

However, language is functional and these children are not deficient in their own native environment. What they somewhat lack are the specific language abilities required in school. When we consider how well a child knows his or her own dialect, there is no deficiency in rate and amount of linguistic knowledge (Hart & Risley, 1992; Walker et al., 1994; Menyuk, 1977).

Helping Children Learn Language

Most suggestions for improving linguistic competence are based on the premise that children learn language both by listening and by participating. Parents and other adults, such as day care workers, can help children to develop their linguistic abilities in the following ways:

Giving the Child an Opportunity to Talk Acquisition of language is an active process. Children should have an opportunity to talk and to communicate their thoughts (Cazden, 1981). When children are young, ask questions that require more than just a "yes" or "no" answer.

Talking to Infants, Even at the Earliest Age Infants are sensitive to language and learn much about verbalizations and turn taking from early conversations. There are many opportunities to talk to a baby (Honig, 1988), such as when feeding, changing, or playing with the child. It is important to greet a toddler's verbalizations with approval, even though it is not always easy to understand what the child means. A child's gestures or emotional reactions can also bring a verbal interpretation from the care-giver. For example, if the child seems impatient, the care-giver can say, "I know you're hungry. I'm warming up your dinner." There is some evidence that the use of the pronoun "we" in statements with 2-year-olds relates positively to later cognitive abilities (Laks, Beckwith, & Cohen, 1990).

Expanding on the Child's Statements Middle-class parents often expand on their children's statements. For example, if the child says, "Throw ball," a parent might say, "Throw the ball to Daddy." Such expansions have a positive effect in broadening the child's language usage in some areas (Hovell, Schumaker, & Sherman, 1978).

Labeling Things in the Environment Children benefit from listening to speech that labels the environment.

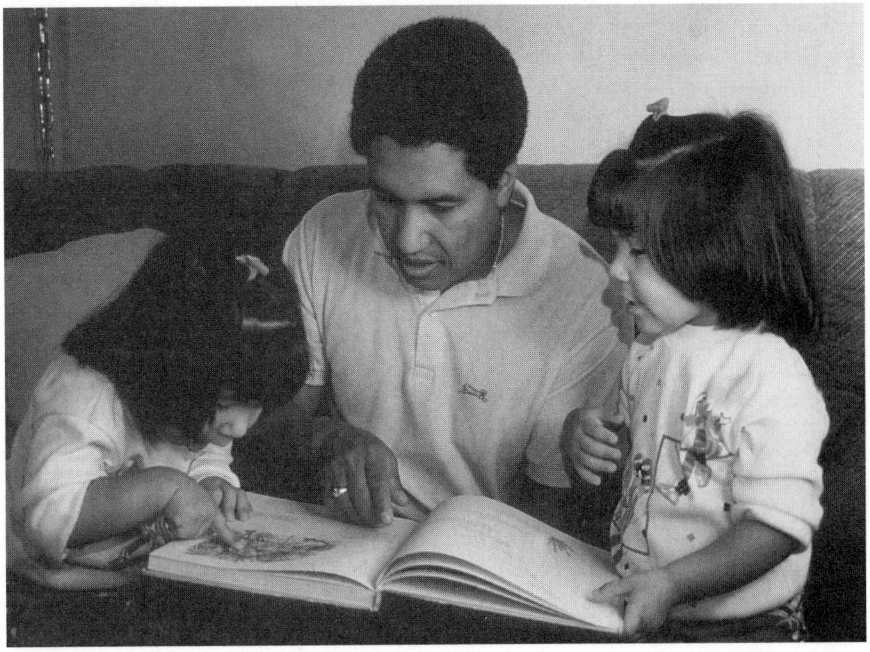

Reading to children is certainly beneficial. However, there are many ways to do this. Asking age-appropriate questions is one important way of improving a child's language abilities.

When a baby points at the bottle, it is worthwhile to say, "You want your bottle?" It is also beneficial to label one's action before one does something.

Asking Questions Children who are asked "wh-" questions often show better linguistic competence, especially superior syntax (Hoff-Ginsberg, 1986, 1990). Such questions involve sincere requests for information and questions that incorporate part of the child's previous utterances into the mother's speech. In addition, asking questions encourages a child to respond.

Modeling Correct Speech Because children tend to copy their parents, reasonably good linguistic models are important. Such techniques as finishing sentences, answering questions in an expanded way, and using adjectives contribute to a rich linguistic environment.

Questions Students Often Ask

It seems as if children have less manners than years ago; they don't say "thank you" as often or seem to be able to communicate in a rational manner. What can be done about it?

A little while ago, I drove one of my daughter's friends home, and she got out of the car, closed the door, and went into her house. My daughter cringed because she knows how I feel about the importance of a simple "thank you," especially since I had gone out of my way to drive her home. A few days later the girl asked my daughter if I would do it again. When my daughter informed her friend that she hadn't acknowledged the favor and that this was a problem, the girl could not believe it. She just didn't think a "thank you" was in order or meant anything.

Teaching children manners is part of a parent's job and enhances interpersonal competence. Popular children have better pragmatic skills than isolated and rejected children and are seen as more likable (Becker, 1988). Reinforcement and modeling can be used to teach manners. Role playing can also help. Perhaps one child can help another practice how to ask the teacher to regrade a paper or a store owner for a refund. Parents have the greatest responsibility in this area, but the school also shares in the responsibility.

Encouraging Verbal Interaction Using praise and engaging the child in meaningful verbal interactions is preferable to forcing a child to speak (Hess & Shipman, 1967).

Dialogic Reading

Perhaps the most popular way to help children develop their linguistic skills is by reading to them. The typical middle-class child enters first grade with many more hours of one-to-one picture book reading than the child from a low-income family (Adams, 1990). One-third of the children in the United States enter kindergarten unprepared to learn, most of them lacking in vocabulary and sentence structure crucial to school success (Carnegie Foundation, 1991).

A British study found significant differences between lower- and middle-class preschool children in number of books owned by children and frequency of visits to libraries, measures that predicted phonological awareness (awareness of specific sound clusters), which serves as a basis for learning to read, even after intelligence is equalized (Raz & Bryant, 1990). A significant relationship exists between the frequency of reading to children during the early childhood stage and later reading, spelling, and intelligence at 13 years of age (Stevenson & Fredman, 1990). Parents who reported having read to their children more regularly during the preschool years had children with higher reading scores than parents who had rarely read to their children. For maximum benefit, children should be read to at least four times a week. Those who were read to less than this amount achieved less well.

True or False?
Psychologists argue that to have maximum benefit parents should read to their children at least four times per week.

There are many ways to read to children. I have witnessed parents whizzing through books at breathtaking speed, not giving children any opportunity to process the material. I have also seen parents stop and ask questions, allowing the child to take over the story and expanding on the child's abilities. As the child matures, the child may participate more and more in the reading process. Active participation is most helpful, for example, asking age-appropriate questions when the child is old enough to respond. When reading a story, you might ask the preverbal youngster to point to a character or object on the page. Verbal children can be encouraged to label objects in the story and answer questions about them. Older children can be encouraged to discuss the story.

The importance of such an interactive reading climate was demonstrated in a study by Grover Whitehurst and colleagues (1988). Parents of toddlers were divided into two groups. Parents in the experimental group were instructed to (1) ask open-ended questions that require more than a yes/no response, (2) ask function/attribute questions (e.g., "What is the farmer doing?") to encourage the children to tell more, and (3) use expansions (repeating statements with some additions, such as saying "big dog" if a child said "dog"). Parents were also told to respond positively to the child's attempts to answer questions and to reduce the number of questions that could be answered by pointing. These techniques required the child to talk about the pictured materials. The control group parents were instructed to read in their normal manner. After 1 month children in the experimental group scored significantly higher on measures of expressive language ability and showed a higher mean length of utterance, a greater use of phrases, and a lower frequency of single words. Nine months later, the differences were somewhat less but still present.

Should bilingual children be taught subjects other than English in their native language or in English?

One type of reading, called *dialogic reading,* in which children take on the role of storyteller while the adult is the active listener, asking questions, adding information, and prompting the child to enhance descriptions of the story is related to linguistic growth (Arnold, et al., 1992). As the child becomes more skillful at telling stories, the adult asks more open-ended questions and avoids yes-no questions. This type of reading improves the linguistic skills of young learners as well as the language skills of those who are already advanced in language (Arnold et al., 1994; Whitehurst et al., 1994). This active form of reading can be included into day care programs with excellent results (Whitehurst et al., 1994).

The Bilingual Puzzle

Many children live in homes in which more than one language is used. English is used very sparingly in some of these homes. What is the effect of the bilingual experience on children? English is often their second language, and their success in the United States depends partly on learning standard English.

Knowing more than one language can be a great advantage. However, research in the 1950s indicated that bilingual children did poorly in school and showed difficulties in both languages (Segalowitz, 1981). These studies have been criticized for their poor methodology and the questionable testing devices used. Today, an about-face has occurred on the issue of bilingualism. We now know that bilingualism itself does not lead to intellectual or cognitive problems in school (McLaughlin, 1977; 1978). Some of the difficulties encountered by bilingual students stem from poverty, poor housing conditions, lack of intellectual stimulation, and other socioeconomic variables (Diaz, 1985). There is evidence that bilingual children are high in verbal and nonverbal intelligence scores and show more cognitive flexibility (Segalowitz, 1981). These children also enjoy advantages in concept formation and creativity (Padilla et al., 1991). Some authorities argue that this is true only in a balanced bilingual situation in which both languages are encouraged and if the child is allowed to develop full competence in both languages (Padilla et al., 1991). However, bilingual students often are not given an opportunity to continue their native language, which means that some are relatively poor in their primary language (Crawford, 1987).

True or False?
Bilingualism leads to cognitive difficulties and academic problems in school.

Questions Students Often Ask

Doesn't being bilingual lead to problems because children go back and forth between two languages and don't learn either well?

In the 1950s when socioeconomic status was unfortunately linked with bilingualism, people had all sorts of ideas as to why bilingual children did not do better in school. When socioeconomic status is controlled, we find that bilingual children have advantages. The problem is that many bilingual children have a poor knowledge of both English and their native language.

We often make the mistake of believing that children who can speak two languages have an excellent knowledge of their first language and often a somewhat poorer knowledge of their second. Many children, especially if they come from poverty backgrounds, have a poor grammatical knowledge of their native language as well. In fact, children with a good knowledge of their first language have an easier time learning English. This is one reason why some people advocate continuing instruction in the child's native language along with instruction in English.

Bilingualism itself does not cause any difficulties and there is some evidence that bilingual children have certain advantages over their monolingual peers. Second, poverty and bilingualism are often confused. Many minority groups in the United States who speak a language other than English suffer from the degradations of poverty, including poor self-concept, disillusion-

Our Pluralistic Society: Do Bilingual Programs Work?

The number of children in the United States whose first language is not English is expected to continue growing into the next century. No one knows the precise number of children who have limited English proficiency (LEP), but it is estimated at 1.9 million (U.S. Department of Education, 1993). Nine of ten LEP elementary school students come from impoverished backgrounds (U.S. Department of Education, 1993). Their success in climbing out of poverty depends on academic achievement and partly on learning standard English, but what is the best way to teach children English whose native language is something else?

Today, most jobs that provide a reasonable standard of living require education. Our goal is not just to teach immigrants basic English but to help them gain the necessary academic skills to succeed in high school and perhaps beyond. Every child who spends a great deal of time in the United States will eventually learn enough English to function in the community. However, the type of English used in advanced schooling differs. It is more abstract, technically more exacting, and uses a higher-level vocabulary. A child learns the type of social English necessary for conversation within 3 years, but learning academically appropriate English takes much longer: between 5 and 7 years (U.S. Department of Education, 1993).

A number of new approaches are being tried out in communities across the country. Generally, these programs can be viewed as a continuum between the active encouragement and use of the primary language on the one hand, sometimes called *native language emphasis,* and the increased focus on English called *sheltered English* or *structured immersion,* on the other (Gerstein & Woodward, 1994).

Some educators propose that a bilingual program be introduced in the school, and that subjects such as math and social studies be taught to Spanish-speaking students in Spanish until the children are sufficiently fluent in English. At the same time these children would receive instruction in standard English. Advocates of such an approach, such as Jim Cummins (1989), argue that the use of the native language empowers these students and reinforces their cultural identity. He argues that once children have learned to read in Spanish they do not have to learn to read all over again; they transfer what they have learned.

The structured immersion or sheltered English approach assumes that proficiency in English can be best attained through well-designed content instruction where English is used, but at a level that is constantly modified and expanded as the child's abilities increase. Teachers control their classroom vocabulary, using concrete objects, gestures, and many instructional strategies so students understand the academic material. In some cases students receive native language instruction for 30 to 90 minutes a day at school, but English is used the majority of the teaching day.

Students in such programs learn English while they develop basic academic skills. This is the approach used successfully in Quebec, Canada with English-speaking students, with Southeast Asian immigrants in elementary school, and with Latino-American youth at the secondary level (Gerstein & Woodward, 1994). In the two-way program both Spanish and English are used to teach both Spanish- and English-speaking students. During the Spanish part of the day Spanish-speaking students explain lessons to their English-speaking peers; the roles are reversed during the English part of the day. Unlike traditional bilingual programs, two-way programs don't segregate students (Donegan, 1996).

In a longitudinal study of low-income immigrants, mainly from Mexico, no significant differences in achievement or academic engagement were found among students taught using any of three different bilingual approaches, two of

ment, discrimination, and lack of opportunity. The effects of poverty rather than bilingualism may actually cause many of the problems cited by teachers in the public schools.

Although we have reevaluated our ideas on the psychological consequences of bilingualism, it is most important that children learn English. Children who leave school knowing mathematics, science, and social studies but functioning poorly in such language-related areas as reading, writing, and speaking, have poorer prospects for educational advancement and jobs. Many programs have been instituted to teach English to nonnative speakers, children whose primary language is something other than English (the controversy is discussed in the Our Pluralistic Society box on this page.). These programs need to be continually evaluated to ensure that these children are learning and using English.

Questions Students Often Ask

I've read about a movement to make English the national language of the United States. This seems reasonable— why is it controversial?

Most people would agree with you, at least initially. Indeed, polls show that 86% of American voters and 81% of all immigrants support legislation to make English the official language of the United States (Mujica, 1996 a & b). Other polls find somewhat lower percentages, with 73% in agreement, but all show it to be a very popular stance (Headden, 1996). The United States would not be alone, as 69 other countries have official language policies (Mujica, 1996b). Yet problems abound.

Some people argue that making English the official language shows disrespect for the customs of minority group members or implicitly asks people to stop speaking their first language. Others point to this

Our Pluralistic Society: Do Bilingual Programs Work? (continued)

which were structured immersion and native-language emphasis (Ramirez, 1992). Admittedly, research is difficult in this area because of discrepancies in program emphasis and differences between how the program is designed to operate and the reality of the services provided. A supposedly native-language program may feature more English than planned, and a structured immersion program may use more of the primary language.

Evaluations of bilingual programs generally are mixed; some evidence shows that the programs have helped students achieve scholastically (Crawford, 1987; Willig, 1985). Other researchers disagree, noting that these programs have not been as successful as hoped (Porter, 1990; Baker & de Kanter, 1981).

Bilingual education has become a political issue—what started out as an educational program to give new immigrants a better chance at success about 25 years ago has turned into a ten-billion-dollar political football. Bilingual education has been made a rallying point for safeguarding one's own culture; those on the other side see it as a dangerous attempt to divide society by emphasizing cultural divisions and deemphasizing the learning of English.

No matter where one stands on the issue of bilingual education, its serious practical shortcomings are all too clear. Programs have often been inflexible and unresponsive to parents' and children's needs. For example, in one case a child born in Brooklyn, New York whose mother came from Puerto Rico, lived in a household in which only English was spoken. The boy was placed in a regular classroom until the third grade when he was moved to a program that taught him in Spanish for all but 45 minutes a day. Seeing his lack of progress, his mother begged to have her son returned to an English-only class. Her request was met with the question, "Why, don't you feel proud to be Hispanic?" (Headden, 1996). Some students also stay much too long in programs that were supposed to be transitional, some for as long as 9 years. Bilingual education programs were meant to allow children to remain current in all other subjects while they learn English. After 3 or 4 years children should switch over to classes taught exclusively in English. Children would then theoretically be fluent in two languages. Unfortunately, some students hear English for as little as 30 minutes a day. Although art, music, and physical education are supposed to be taught in English, often they are not. A serious charge is that some Latino children are placed in bilingual programs not because they show deficiencies in English but because they simply don't read well; such children require remedial not bilingual help. Another practical problem involves what should be done when parents do not want their children in such classes (Donegan, 1996).

These and other practical problems do not necessarily mean that bilingual education is a failure. Many worthy programs have practical flaws that can and must be addressed. It is obvious that we need to define our goals for bilingual education more clearly and solve the practical problems that plague inflexible pro grams.

The debate continues and Americans are split on the need for bilingual education. It is not just a matter of teaching children enough English so they can get along in the society. There is more pressure now to teach bilingual children sufficient English so they can succeed in advanced schooling. What is obviously needed is a relatively quick way of accomplishing this. Any successful strategy requires a complex balance between the use of native languages and English (Gerstein & Woodward, 1994). It is hoped that new experimentation in the next decade will provide educators with an answer to this challenge.

as just another example of intolerance and anti-immigrant feelings. Although some people who favor such legislation may indeed be intolerant, support of such legislation does not make someone intolerant. Other languages could be used at home, in the street, or in other settings.

People who are against making English the national language are sometimes labeled as wanting to see the United States fragmented and disunited. This is not true; people can be against the proposal and still understand the need for unity in governmental institutions and law.

Proponents of making English the national language often argue that such a policy would encourage immigrants to learn English faster because all official proceedings would be in English (Mujica, 1996b). They claim that accommodating the more than 300 languages spoken in the United States reduces the incentive to learn English. If people do not learn English quickly, they risk continuing poverty, which may lead to a permanent underclass (De La Pena, 1993). If ballots, government communications, and other official documents are in other languages, there is less need to learn English, and such linguistic problems would lead to a dependence on government and a lack of understanding of a large amount of information not found in native languages (Buckley, 1996). Last, there is the question of national unity. If English is not made the law, Americans may find themselves divided.

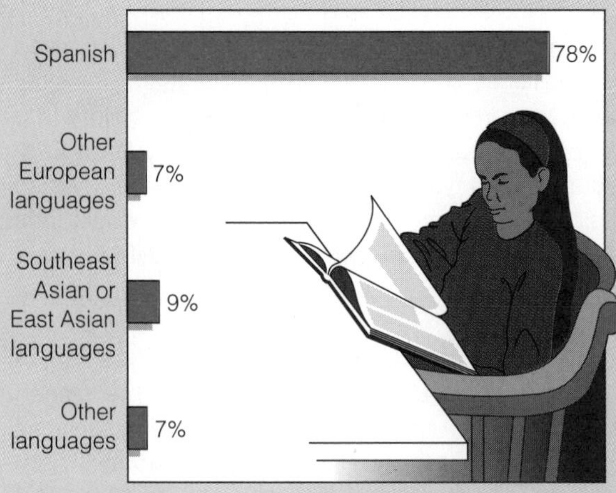

The majority of children with limited English proficiency speak Spanish as their primary language.

Datagraphic
Children with Limited English Proficiency
Note: The figures add up to 101% due to rounding.
Source: Data from U.S. Department of Education, 1993.

Those opposed argue that the legislation is unnecessary and counterproductive (Underwood, 1996). There is no evidence that the use of English is threatened or that the use of languages other than English fragments American society (Madrid, 1993). Some argue that it communicates a message that Americans who do not speak English are somehow less a part of the country. Others argue that an English-only approach would limit the ability of some Americans to function well in society. Some benefits of citizenship would be denied, since people would not be able to understand the written part of the driving test or court papers. This raises constitutional issues (Baxter, 1995). A strict English-only law would make it difficult or impossible to use translators in court or even in some hospital settings. How could people who do not understand English follow court proceedings or pay their taxes accurately?

Some proposed English-only laws are very strict, requiring all governmental forms to be in English, while others are largely symbolic, for example, declaring English the official language but providing exceptions for health, safety, and civil and criminal justice (Headden, 1996). This issue will remain very controversial into the next century.

A Wonder Rediscovered

The modern approach to language acquisition takes both the laws of learning and the biological basis for language learning into consideration, but it also looks at the nature of the interactions between the child and the parents. This position views language development as a carefully orchestrated progression of interchanges between active learners and active teachers, who may not be aware of the role they are playing in a child's language development.

As we begin to tear down the curtain of mystery that surrounds language development, we can appreciate the wonder of it all. The simple sentence of a child is not just an imitation of what the child has heard, nor is it something preprogrammed. It is a creative expression of an inherently human ability. Looking at it from this standpoint, we can see that learning our native tongue is perhaps the greatest intellectual feat any one of us ever performs.

Summary

1. Communication is the process of sharing information and can be verbal or nonverbal. Language is a set of agreed-upon, arbitrary symbols used in communication and consists of a number of subsystems, including phonology, morphology, syntax, semantics, and pragmatics.
2. Infants communicate with the people around them by smiling, crying, and gesturing. They are sensitive to speech sounds from the moment they are born.
3. Babbling, which involves verbalization of vowel and consonant sounds, begins as early as 3 months. Children utter their first word anytime between 10 and 15 months of age. Some psychologists argue that children use one word, called a ***holophrase,*** to stand for an entire thought. The toddler uses specific and simple grammar. Beginning at about 18 months, children's vocabulary expands very quickly. The child's early sentences are called telegraphic because they contain only the words that are absolutely necessary to communicate meaning.
4. The length of a child's sentences gradually increases, vocabulary increases, and more adult grammar is found as the child develops. Although the most dramatic improvements are seen in the first 5 or 6 years of life, language development continues throughout middle childhood and adolescence.
5. Young children make predictable errors. They overextend, using words in a wider manner than is proper, and underextend, using words more restrictively than is appropriate. Children also overregularize or overgeneralize rules; when children begin to learn the rules of a language, they use the rules indiscriminately and have difficulty with exceptions to the rules.
6. Behaviorists, such as Skinner, use the processes of reinforcement and imitation to explain language acquisition. Chomsky argues that a human being is programmed to learn language and merely requires exposure to a language in order to master it. The nativist position sees language acquisition as having a

biological basis and stresses the importance of maturation.

7. Cognitive psychologists argue that such factors as attention and memory are involved in language acquisition. In addition, they believe that to use a word correctly, a child must know something about the object.
8. Adult speech to young children is well-constructed and consists of short, simple sentences with many repetitions. Parents from different cultures use language in different ways. Parents fine tune the level of their speech to the individual abilities of their children.
9. The linguistic environment that surrounds a child is important in the acquisition of language. Middle-class parents tend to use expansive language whereas working-class parents tend to use more restricted speech patterns. Parents can help to optimize their children's language learning by asking questions, expanding on their children's statements, reading to their children, modeling good grammar, and giving their children an opportunity to speak.
10. Early reading is especially important, but to be most effective, children should be read to at least four times a week and should actively participate in the reading.
11. Recent studies stress the advantages of bilingualism. Bilingual programs are controversial, and much research concerning the best way to teach English to bilingual students remains to be performed. Every child should learn standard English.

Multiple-Choice Questions

1. American Sign Language is:
   a. a recognized language with a grammar of its own.
   b. manual signs used in English word order.
   c. a language with no official grammar or word order.
   d. not considered a language at all.
2. Jon understands that "ch" is a sound in English. This is an achievement in the area of:
   a. morphology.
   b. pragmatics.
   c. semantics.
   d. phonology.
3. How many morphemes does the word "unreliable" have?
   a. one.
   b. two.
   c. three.
   d. four.
4. "Please, let go me right now," is not proper English. The sentence contains an error in:
   a. semantics.
   b. morphology.
   c. syntax.
   d. phonology.
5. A child learns that the word "cow" refers to a different animal than the word "dog." This is an achievement in the area of:
   a. semantics.
   b. morphology.
   c. phonology.
   d. syntax.
6. A child learns to say "thank you" after being given a new toy. This is an improvement in the area of:
   a. semantics.
   b. phonology.
   c. syntax.
   d. pragmatics.
7. Which statement concerning babbling is *correct?*
   a. Most infants are babbling by 6 months.
   b. Scientists have not been able to understand any meaning behind babbling.
   c. Reinforcing babbling with attention can increase the amount a child babbles.
   d. All of the above are correct.
8. In their early language some children use words that regulate social interaction such as "hi" and "bye-bye." Katherine Nelson would label such children:
   a. referential.
   b. candid.
   c. expressive.
   d. determinate.
9. Lisa says "food" when she wants some bread and butter. This single word is called a:
   a. buffer.
   b. holophrase.
   c. button.
   d. fragment.
10. Jason is about 18 months old and knows about 50 words. If Jason is like most other children we might expect him to:
    a. gradually learn words at a rate of about one per week.
    b. show a tremendous increase in vocabulary usage, especially in the area of nouns.
    c. use more verbs than nouns.
    d. begin to use complete sentences of four and five words.
11. Gayle seems to be able to learn a new word after only one or two exposures. This ability is called:
    a. detailed engrossment.
    b. emergent semantics.
    c. fast mapping.
    d. warp learning.
12. "Mommy, go gym," is an example of:
    a. telegraphic speech.
    b. formal operational language.
    c. evident speech.
    d. fine tuning speech.
13. Taneequa calls every animal with four legs a dog. This is an example of:
    a. overenthusiasm.
    b. underprocessing.

c. overextension.
d. personalism.

14. Which statement would be most likely made by B.F. Skinner concerning language development?
a. Cognitive growth explains a great deal of language development.
b. A child's language learning is based upon an innate understanding of the structure of language.
c. Children learn language as they do most every behavior through reinforcement, imitation, generalization, and discrimination.
d. Children learn language when they receive active and formal lessons in how to pronounce and use particular words and phrases.

15. "Children are preprogrammed to learn language and only require some exposure to their native language," is a statement that would be made by a person who is arguing which of the following approaches?
a. cognitive theory.
b. learning theory.
c. the fine tuning approach.
d. the nativist approach.

16. Which statement concerning the neurological basis for learning language is correct?
a. Most people's language abilities are located on the left side of the cerebral cortex.
b. The area responsible for speech is called Broca's area.
c. Damage to Wernicke's area of the brain impairs a person's comprehension.
d. All of the above are correct.

17. The communication by parents to young children that often consists of simplified speech emphasizing the present tense is known as:
a. motherese.
b. dimentionality.
c. consequential speech.
d. metacognitive speech.

18. Dr. Ellinger argues that parents adapt the level of their speech to their children's abilities, changing their language to meet the abilities and needs of their children. She is basically arguing for the:
a. seven cycle system.
b. word level theory.
c. process-product system.
d. fine tuning theory.

19. Which statement about reading to children is correct?
a. Generally, middle-class children are read to more often than children who live in poverty.
b. Children who are read to by their parents are more likely to show superior linguistic skills.
c. For the best results, children should be read to at least four times a week.
d. All of the above are correct.

20. Which conclusion about being bilingual matches the latest research?
a. Bilingualism is a hindrance to academic achievement.
b. Bilingualism is an advantage in learning English but a disadvantage in learning math and science.
c. Bilingualism is no disadvantage, and bilingual children may have certain advantages over their monolingual peers.
d. Bilingual children do better in school but show more conduct-related problems.

Answers to Multiple-Choice Questions

1. a 2. d 3. b 4. c 5. a 6. d 7. d 8. c 9. b
10. b 11. c 12. a 13. c 14. c 15. d 16. d 17. a
18. d 19. d 20. c

Chapter 8

The Physical and Cognitive Development of Preschoolers

Chapter Outline

The Time-Life Remover
Physical Development in the Preschool Years
Children's Health: A World View
Cognitive Development in the Preschool Years
Information-Processing Abilities
Home, Television, and Nursery School
Controversial Issues: How Early Should a Child Start School?
Two Dangers

Are the Following Statements True or False?

1. If preschoolers are allowed to choose foods for themselves, they will choose a nutritious diet based upon the specific tastes of various kinds of food.
2. The mortality rate of young children around the world has stayed about constant since 1960.
3. During the preschool years the child begins to reason in a manner that is very similar to that of an average adult.
4. Most preschoolers do not believe that dolls and cartoon characters are real.
5. The child's attention span at 4 years is about the same as an adult's.
6. Three-year-old children can only remember an event that happened to them for about 6 months, after which it disappears from their memory.
7. Preschoolers are more rigid than elementary schoolchildren in their understanding of what should take place and the order in which events should occur.
8. Preschoolers spend more time watching television than engaging in any other activity except sleep.
9. Children attending Project Head Start classes are less likely than their peers who did not attend the program to be held back in school or placed in special education classes during their school career.
10. The curriculum of today's kindergarten is more likely to include training in basic academic skills than it was a generation ago.

Answers to True-False Statements 1. False: see p. 168 2. False: see p. 170 3. False: see p. 172 4. True. 5. False: see p. 177 6. False: see p. 178 7. True. 8. True. 9. True. 10. True.

The Time-Life Remover

"She (turned) almost full blue. My mother was screaming at me to get away from her. I ignored her. I knew what to do. I said to my mother,"I saw this on *Benson* (a television situation comedy). I lifted her up and banged her on her feet. She bended over and she coughed and it plopped out." This is how 5-year-old Brent Meldrum saved the life of 6-year-old Tanya Branden, who had something stuck in her throat. Brent is the youngest person ever known to have used the Heimlich maneuver, which he calls "the time-life remover" (Hero, 5 can do it but can't say it, *Los Angeles Times,* 1986, August 7, p. 2). In another incident, a 5-year-old child whose mother collapsed in front of him called 911 and waited for the ambulance outside the house as he had been told to do by the police. He had learned how to call 911 in kindergarten (Burke, 1990).

These incidents demonstrate how great the physical and cognitive capacities of preschoolers are. Yet we are often surprised when preschoolers sometimes attribute living qualities to inanimate objects, can't understand that squat 8-ounce cups and tall 8-ounce glasses hold the same amount, and have difficulty solving what seem like simple problems.

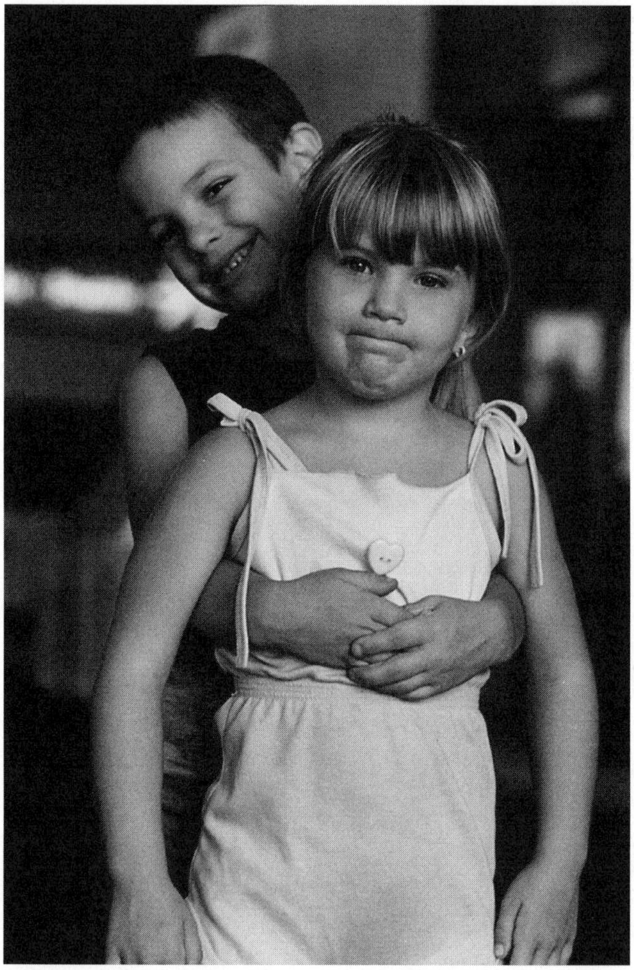

Five-year-old Brent Meldrum saved the life of six-year-old Tanya Branden by using the Heimlich Maneuver. Brent had seen it on television.

Physical Development in the Preschool Years

The expanding motor abilities of preschoolers allow them to attend to what is going on around them instead of having to concentrate just on how they walk and hold things. Preschoolers can participate in many physical activities, satisfying some of their curiosity about the world and learning from their experiences. Their physical skills give them more independence. They interact more frequently with other children and learn from these social interactions. Many youngsters attend a preschool in which their new physical and sensory abilities are used as tools to encourage social and cognitive growth.

Growth and Development

The rate of growth slows during the early childhood years. About twice as much growth occurs between the first and third years as between the third and fifth years (Cratty, 1986), but growth is still readily apparent during this period. Boys are a bit taller and heavier throughout this stage and remain so until about the age of 11 (Hamill, 1977). The preschool child grows approximately 3 inches a year, although variations from the statistical average are to be expected. Scientists usually speak of a range of heights and weights (between the 25th and 75th percentiles) that are usual for a child of a certain age in a particular culture. Deviations from this range may not indicate a problem, but they may alert doctors to a possible difficulty and encourage them to look into the situation.

During the preschool period, body proportions change. At age 2, the head is about one-fourth the total body size; by age 5½, it is one-sixth the body size; and at adulthood, it is about one-tenth (Cratty, 1970). The preschooler gradually loses that babylike appearance because the amount of fat decreases, the added weight resulting from growth and development of muscle tissue. Boys generally have more muscle tissue whereas girls have a bit more fat, but many individual differences can be found. At the beginning of this preschool period, children usually have a full set of baby teeth, which they begin to shed at the end of this period.

Motor Skills

By the beginning of the early childhood period children can walk with ease. They are as likely to run as to walk, their movements are smoother, and they turn corners better. Large muscles are still much better developed than fine muscles, but by the age of 4 the child can hold a pencil somewhat like an adult and can fold a paper diagonally (Heinicke, 1979).

Children at this stage master many motor skills, including running, jumping, hopping, skipping, and climbing (Table 8.1). The advances in fine motor control are also impressive, although fine motor control lags behind gross muscle development and control. The more subtle development of fine motor control shows itself in the way a child controls a crayon or pencil. Babies use their entire fists. Toddlers progress to holding the crayon fairly well but use their wrist for drawing, while preschoolers by about age 5 have improved to the point where they are now holding the crayon better and using the small muscles in the fingers for control. Still, they must concentrate, and the effort lacks the smoothness it will have later. Both maturation and practice are responsible for this improvement in control and coordination (Kellogg, 1970).

Table 8.1 **Development of Locomotor Skill**

LOCOMOTOR SKILL
Running
3-year-old
Runs with lack of control in stops and starts
4-year-old
Runs with control over starts, stops and turns
Speed is increasing
5-year-old
Running well established and used in play activities
Speed is increasing
Jumping
3-year-old
42% are proficient
Jumping pattern lacks differentiation
4-year-old
72% are proficient
Jumping pattern characterized by more preliminary crouch
5-year-old
81% are skillful
Overall jumping pattern more smooth and rhythmical
Hopping
3-year-old
Can hop ten times consecutively on both feet
Great difficulty experienced with hop pattern
4-year-old
33% are proficient at hopping
5-year-old
79% become proficient during this year
Climbing
3-year-old
Ascends stairs using mark time foot pattern
During this year ascending stairs is achieved with alternate foot
Descending stairs mostly with mark time foot pattern
4-year-old
Ascends and descends stairs with alternative foot pattern
5-year-old
Climbing skill increases
70% can climb a rope ladder with bottom free
Skipping
3-year-old
Skip is characterized by a shuffle step
4-year-old
14% can skip
One-footed skip still prevalent
Overall movement stiff and undifferentiated
5-year-old
Skips mostly on balls of feet
72% are skillful
Can skip with alternate foot pattern

Growing Independence and the Need for Supervision

Children use their motor skills to explore the environment and do things on their own. They can dress themselves with some degree of care, eat independently, and play by themselves for significant periods of time. Advances in both gross and fine motor control open new opportunities for play. Preschoolers no longer need to be watched every second, and active, independent preschoolers are engaging beings. Yet their motor skills and desire for independence are greater than their mental ability to understand what is good for them, which can lead to problems in the areas of safety and nutrition.

Safety

Accidents are the leading cause of death during the preschool years (Statistical Abstracts, 1996). The most common causes of accidental death are motor vehicle accidents, drowning, fires, and poisoning. Although not all accidents can be avoided, precautions—such as using restraints in cars, fencing and locking pools, and placing poisons in locked storage cabinets—can prevent many of them.

Nutrition: Why Preschoolers Eat What They Eat

Infants eat—or don't eat—what is given to them. However, preschoolers know what foods are in the house and can tell you what they want. They may want a particular cereal and cry until they get it, refusing anything else; 3- and 4-year-old children can rank their food preferences, and these preferences are related to eating habits (Birch & Fisher, 1996; Birch, 1979).

Conflicts between parents and their young children over nutrition revolve around two areas: what preschoolers' eat and how much. Research into both these areas show that parents often have a poor understanding of their children's nutritional needs and make serious mistakes in the way they feed them.

Children's food preferences are the major determinant of their food intake, and children do not eat what they do not like (Birch & Fisher, 1996). A preference for sweet and a rejection of sour or bitter foods is present in newborn infants (see Chapter 5). Although neonates are neutral in their response to salt, some preference is shown by 4 months of age. This preference is modifiable, and infants who are fed lower-salt diets show less of a preference for salt than infants who are fed a higher-salt diet (Harris, Thomas, & Booth, 1990). The preference for salt shown by young children is largely based upon their experience with salt. In fact, children show a preference for foods to which they are exposed over a long period of time. If they are used to heavily sugared or salted food, they prefer them (Sullivan & Birch, 1990).

Why do children seem to prefer foods high in sugar, fat, carbohydrates, and salt, which are not very nutritious? First, children have an innate preference for sugar, making these foods more palatable. Second, rich foods are often served on holidays and special occasions, providing an association between these foods and pleasant memories. Cake and ice cream are more likely to be served at birthday parties than are fruits and vegetables. Third, substances that impart flavor to food are often fat soluble (they are absorbed by the fat in the food) so that high fat foods are often very flavorful (Birch and Fisher, 1996). Fourth, foods that are nutritious, such as vegetables, are also more likely to be the ones associated with parents' coercion. Parents are more likely to demand that children eat their vegetables than their ice cream sundae. Nutritious foods are often linked to tension and pressure. Fifth, many sugary foods are advertised on television, which makes them even more appealing to children. Spend a Saturday morning watching children's television, and you'll find that the commercials are often more colorful and impressive than the programs themselves! Most commercials glorify processed and sweet foods, thereby encouraging poor eating habits. It is not surprising that the diet of many preschoolers is filled with high-calorie, low-nutrition foods—especially snacks, since preschoolers receive much of their information about food from watching television. Finally, many parents use sweets as rewards, which is another mistake. Learning to eat right is an important skill learned in childhood; apples or carrots are better snacks than cookies or candy.

Preschooler's food preferences are shaped by many factors, some of which are social. Preschoolers will prefer foods that their peers select, and nursery school teachers also have some influence on food selection (Birch, 1986; 1987). Parents can also act as models. Parents who do not eat vegetables but are always snacking on potato chips may find their children doing the same. Preschoolers who have the greatest amount of fat in their diet by choice are those whose parents consume such foods (Fisher & Birch, 1995). Parents may offer their children sugary, high-fat foods that they themselves prefer. Cultural factors also enter the picture. For example, in the traditional Mexican village, children are regularly exposed to older siblings and parents eating and enjoying hot peppers, often in hot sauces. This encourages the young child to like the burn of these peppers, which is not innately preferred (Rozin, 1996).

Since children have a natural preference for sweets, and learning and experience are so important in food preference, parents must actively choose the foods they wish to offer their preschoolers. Most children will not select a nutritionally balanced diet on the basis of taste alone. Parents must act as gatekeepers, offering their children a variety of healthy foods and limiting their exposure to sweets. When children are allowed to create meals freely from a variety of foods, they often choose more highly sugared foods than when they know their parents are watching them (Klesges et al., 1991). Sweets should not be banned altogether because doing so makes them even more alluring to children; parents should limit and control the availability of and children's access to junk food.

> ***True or False?***
> If preschoolers are allowed to choose foods for themselves, they will choose a nutritious diet based upon the specific tastes of various kinds of food.

Many people incorrectly believe that children will innately choose the most healthy foods and will seek out the necessary nutrients. Except for a few substances such as salt, the evidence for "natural wisdom" is quite weak, even in animals (Galef, 1991). This mistake is often based on a misunderstanding of a classic study conducted by Clara Davis (1939; 1928) in which youngsters were allowed to eat what they wanted from a variety of foods they, themselves, chose and, indeed, they thrived. This has been incorrectly summarized as meaning that people will eat a healthy diet prompted by some internal mechanism. What is rarely stated is that Davis only offered the children healthy foods.

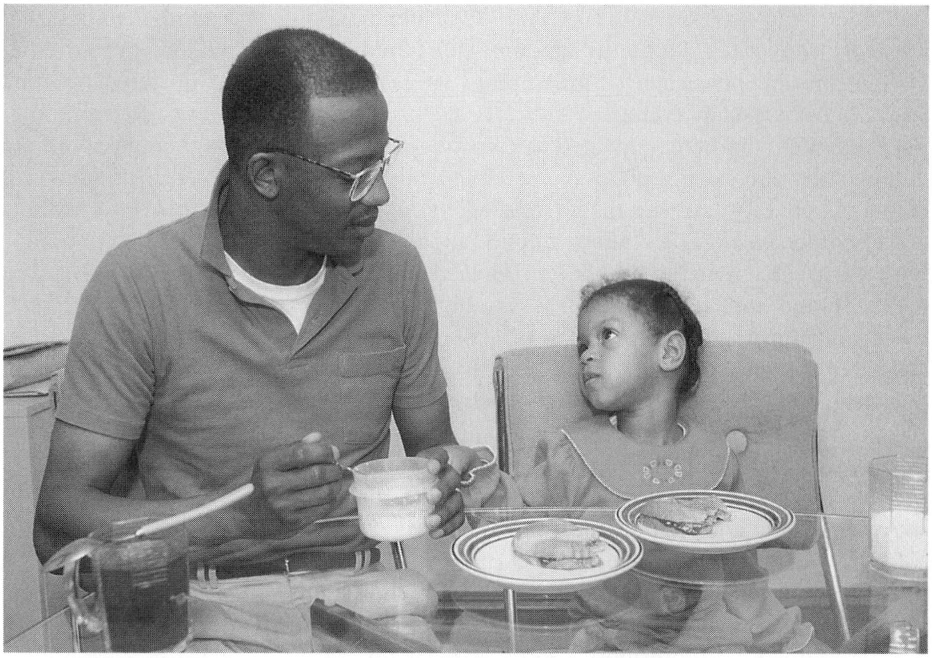

Conflicts over how much a child should eat are usually unnecessary.

Parents often complain that their young children reject new foods, especially those that are healthy and low in fat and refined sugars. This is typical behavior for preschoolers, and with repeated opportunities to eat the food, this aversion is sometimes reduced. It may take a number of exposures and tastings. Many parents believe that a child's initial rejection represents some unchangeable dislike. The child is then viewed as finicky, and the food is never offered again. Since children's food preferences and selection are linked to familiarity of foods, offering these foods again at a later date increases their familiarity and makes them more palatable. It is best to offer one new food at a time, in small amounts, and at the beginning of the meal when children are most likely to be hungry. The child makes the decision to accept or reject the food; no power struggles should ensue. Children who are coerced or forced to try new foods are less likely to try them again than if they are given the choice themselves (Birch, 1987).

The second area of parental concern is how much the child should eat. Many parents overestimate the amount of food that young children need to eat. When their children prefer to eat less than parents consider healthy, parents become anxious and reason that their children cannot control their portion size, but this is incorrect.

Children's appetites are variable, usually decreasing at about 12 months, probably in accord with the decrease in the rate of growth (Hamilton & Whitney, 1982). Children need and demand more food during periods of rapid growth than during slower periods (Whitney, Cataldo, & Rolfes, 1994). Parents need not control their children's portion size to make them eat more. Preschoolers have a natural internal mechanism that modulates the amount of food they eat.

Young children are sensitive to the energy density of their foods, which is the extent to which a particular food provides carbohydrates, proteins, and fats—all energy nutrients (Birch & Fisher, 1996). Young children adjust their meal size on the basis of energy density, eating larger quantities of less-energy-dense foods and smaller quantities of energy-rich foods; even infants do this. Healthy infants compensated for energy differences in their formula consuming more dilute (54 kcal.) formula than the richer (100 kcal.) formula so that total energy intake was similar to that of infants fed the standard formula of 67 kcal energy density (Fomon, 1993). This same effect is found in preschoolers (Birch et al., 1991; Kern et al., 1993). When 2- to 5-year-old children were offered the same menus on 6 days with no limitations, their total energy intake was relatively constant for each child over a 24-hour period. A high energy intake at one meal was often followed by a low energy intake at the next and vice versa (Birch et al., 1993). When the energy density of some foods was changed by replacing fat with a fat substitute with no energy value but the same taste, the children adjusted to the change so that the total energy intake across 2 day blocks was almost the same. Children, then, have an internal sense of how much to eat and can regulate their meal sizes quite successfully.

However, some parents actually teach their children to ignore their inner feelings of satiety and pay attention to external cues. For example, parents may reward their children for finishing everything on their plates or restrict them from doing some activity until they have eaten what parents feel is a reasonable amount. Other parents act in an authoritarian manner during feeding ("Eat what I give you right now!"), which teaches preschoolers to pay attention to external cues and makes them less sensitive to their internal cues (Johnson & Birch, 1994). When children pay attention to their internal cues of being satisfied they tend to eat less; when they are focused on external cues they do not respond to the energy density of their foods and eat more (Birch et al., 1987). Parents who are truly concerned about the amount their child eats should consult a physician, but pressuring young children to eat more is usually counterproductive.

Children should be encouraged to eat slowly, to enjoy companions and conversation at the table, and to stop eating when they are internally satisfied. It is best to serve smaller portions and allow second helpings if they wish. Physical activity should be encouraged. Children's meals should include a variety of healthy foods that meet nutritional needs and are matched to individual appetites. In addition, foods should be warm but not hot because children's mouths are very sensitive, and flavors should be mild because children have more taste buds than adults do. Young children can also help to plan and prepare meals. Parents should also be constantly alert to the dangers of choking. Round foods, such as grapes, nuts, hard candies, tough meat, popcorn, chips, and hot dog pieces are difficult for young children with few teeth and can easily become stuck. Last, breakfast is often children's best and most important meal, for they are usually hungry in the morning and therefore more likely to be cooperative. Since many families unfortunately place little emphasis on breakfast, a plan to improve children's diets should begin with providing a nutritious breakfast.

Children's Health: A World View

Children's death from disease is very rare in Western countries. However, this is not the case in most of the world. One death in every three in the world is a child under the age of 5 (Grant, 1988). Each week, more than 250,000 children die in developing countries from infection and malnutrition.

The leading cause of death in young children is diarrhea. Most of these children can be saved if they receive a therapy known as oral rehydration therapy, a system of actions that begins with parents giving children a special solution that parents can make from sugar, salt, and water in the correct proportions. Other steps are taken to prevent dehydration. If the diarrhea persists, the child is given a specially formulated mixture called ORS, or oral rehydration salts. ORS is produced around the world, and each dose costs about 10 cents. About half of all diarrhea cases in the world's poorest countries are now treated with oral rehydration but in some remote areas it is still not available (Bellamy, 1996).

Other diseases such as measles, tetanus, and whooping cough kill millions each year. Polio is rare in the United States, but outbreaks are not uncommon in underdeveloped nations. These diseases can all be eliminated through vaccinations costing about five dollars per child and, as we saw in Chapter 5, significant progress is being made throughout the world in this area.

Acute respiratory infections also kill many children and can sometimes be prevented or treated using antibiotics administered by community health workers. Still, many parents do not know how to distinguish between a bad cough and a more serious lung infection.

Last, malnutrition contributes to perhaps as many as one-third of childhood deaths. Nutritional problems are related to economic status. Although there is still a lack of food in many places, in some areas the problem is the lack of information about how to feed and when to seek professional help. This information must cover breast feeding, inoculations, illness prevention, special feeding during and after illness, and when to consult a doctor. Safe water is also necessary, as is information about sanitary waste disposal.

True or False?
The mortality rate of young children around the world has stayed about constant since 1960.

The fact that children are dying of maladies that can be easily prevented or cured is tragic. Yet, tremendous progress has been and is still being made, often under the direction or prodding of the United Nations through such international organizations as UNICEF. In almost all areas of the world, the mortality rate for infants, toddlers, and preschoolers has been reduced (Figure 8.1). In the Middle East and in northern Africa the rate of childhood deaths is now a quarter of what it was in 1960 (Bellamy, 1996). Disease prevention and treatment, as well as access to clean water, is responsible for this improvement. One area

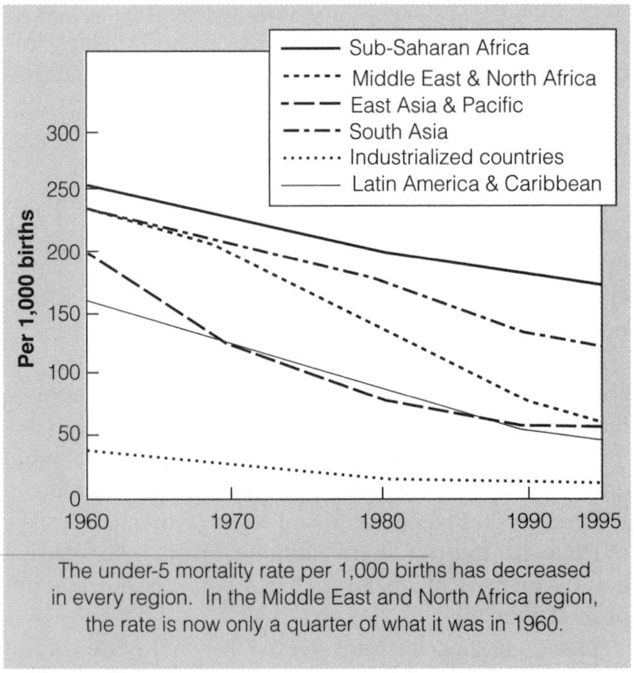

Figure 8.1
Under-5 Mortality Rate Dropping
Source: UNICEF, 1996.

that is increasingly affecting the health and mortality rate of the world's children is the destruction of their communities from violence and war.

Improving the health of people around the world is also a social movement, for parental behavior and attitudes need to be changed as well (Grant, 1988). If parents do not ensure that their children receive inoculations, know how to deal with diarrhea, or make use of available medical and nutritional programs, any program is bound to fail.

Although a good deal of progress has been made, a great deal more remains to be done, and the United Nations has proposed targets for controlling certain diseases and improving the environment. (The goals for the year 2000 are shown in Table 8.2). The emergence of low-cost ways of dealing with major health problems opens up new and exciting opportunities for improving the health of the world's children, and progress will continue to be made well into the future.

The health of children within the United States is also a great concern. Most children are covered by medical plans but about 13.7% are not (Statistical Abstract, 1996). More children are covered by Medicaid than ever before but this is offset by the decline in poor children covered by private plans (Lewit & Baker, 1995). Access to medical care is related to economic status. Poor children are much less likely to see the doctor for preventive medicine or when they are ill. Providing access to adequate medical care for all is an important concern within the United States.

The second health challenge—that of changing people's attitudes and behaviors—is probably as great here as it is in other countries. A number of health-related changes in attitude and behavior, including changes in the way we feed our children (such as a reduction in junk food) and helping young pregnant women to abstain from drugs and lead healthy lives, are required.

The challenges of protecting and improving children's health differ between developed and developing countries. Industrialized countries offer better access to information and spend more on healthcare. Getting the needed medications and vaccines to rural areas in developing countries whose transportation systems are poor is difficult. But changing attitudes and parental behaviors is a challenge in every country, and any improvement in this area must be based upon a knowledge of the local cultural attitudes and practices.

Table 8.2 **Social Goals: 2000**

The end-of-century goals, agreed to by almost all the world's governments following the 1990 World Summit for Children, may be summarized under 10 priority points.

GOALS FOR THE YEAR 2000

1. A one-third reduction in 1990 under-5 death rates (or to 70 per 1000 live births, whichever is less).
2. A halving of 1990 maternal mortality rates.
3. A halving of 1990 rates of malnutrition among the world's under-5s (to include the elimination of micronutrient deficiencies, support for breastfeeding by all maternity units, and a reduction in the incidence of low birth weight to less than 10%).
4. The achievement of 90% immunization among under-1s, the eradication of polio, the elimination of neonatal tetanus, a 90% reduction in measles cases, and a 95% reduction in measles deaths (compared with preimmunization levels).
5. A halving of child deaths caused by diarrheal diseases.
6. A one-third reduction in child deaths from acute respiratory infections.
7. Basic education for all children and completion of primary education by at least 80%—girls as well as boys.
8. Safe water and sanitation for all communities.
9. Acceptance by all countries of the Convention on the Rights of the Child, including improved protection for children in especially difficult circumstances.
10. Universal access to high-quality family planning information and services in order to prevent pregnancies that are too early, too closely spaced, too late, or too many.

Source: UNICEF, 1996.

Cognitive Development in the Preschool Years

The advances in motor control and coordination in early childhood enable preschoolers to master their physical environment and learn about their world. Preschoolers actively encounter the physical world and try to comprehend the phenomena they see around them. Their expanding physical abilities allow them to experiment with all sorts of activities and bring them into contact with many new social situations. Their physical development therefore has an impact on their cognitive development.

Preoperational Thought

The distinct manner in which preschoolers think was described by Piaget, who argued that children from age 2 to age 7 years progress through what he called the **preoperational stages.** It is a stage marked by many advances but also by many limitations (Table 8.3).

By the time children enter the preoperational stage they can use symbols, that is, they can use one thing to represent another (Siegler, 1991). Children may use a spoon to represent a hammer, or a toy person to represent the mail carrier. Children can also use language. Words represent particular concepts and objects. Another example of representation first seen at the end of the sensorimotor stage is **deferred imitation.** The child watches something, stores the information, and performs

preoperational stage Piaget's second stage of cognitive development, marked by the appearance of language and symbolic function and the child's inability to understand logical concepts such as conservation.

deferred imitation The ability to observe an act and imitate it at a later time.

Table 8.3 **The Preoperational Stage**

In this stage, children can use symbols and can judge on the basis of appearance. However, they cannot perform mental operations such as reversibility. This stage is a long one, lasting from about 2 to 7 years of age. Children in the later part of the stage are much more advanced than those in the earlier part. Remember, it is incorrect to simply use age to judge cognitive abilities, because children enter and leave a stage at their own individual rate.

CHARACTERISTIC	EXPLANATION	EXAMPLE
Symbolic function	The ability to use one thing to represent another.	A child can use a spoon to represent a hammer. The ability to use words also requires the use of symbols.
Deferred imitation	The ability to observe an act and imitate it at a later time.	A preschooler can see the teacher exercising and can imitate similar actions at a later time without the teacher's presence.
Inability to seriate	The process of placing objects in size order.	Preschoolers cannot place ten blocks of wood in size order.
Inability to classify	The process of placing objects in different groupings.	Younger preschoolers cannot group plastic objects of varying shapes and colors by shape or color.
Appearance and reality	The tendency to judge on the basis of appearance.	A child shown a red car will correctly identify the color. If a filter that makes the car look black covers the car, the child will say the car is black. When the filter is removed, the child will again identify the car as red.
Inability to conserve	The inability to understand that quantities remain the same despite changes in their appearance.	If shown two equal-sized lumps of clay, the preschooler will know they are equal. If one is flattened out, the child will believe that one lump has more clay than the other.
Centering	The tendency to attend to only one dimension at a time.	When comparing the contents of a small thin beaker and a short fat beaker, the preschooler will do so by comparing only one dimension of each, probably height, and will ignore the differences in width.
Irreversible thinking	The inability to begin at the end of an operation and work back to the start.	Preschoolers do not understand that if you add 4 to 2 to make 6, then you can take 2 away from 6 to make 4 again.
Egocentrism	The inability to understand someone else's point of view.	If shown a display and asked how someone standing opposite them is seeing it, preschoolers will not be able to visualize the other person's perspective. Preschoolers believe that the world revolves around them.
Animism	The tendency to ascribe the attributes of living things to inanimate objects. The belief that inanimate objects have a consciousness or are alive.	A preschooler believes that the balloon soared to the ceiling because it did not want to be held.
Artificialism	The belief that natural phenomena are caused by human beings.	A preschooler will see a lake and say it was made by a group of people digging and then filling it up with water from hoses.

the action at a later date. To do this, the child must preserve a symbolic representation of the behavior during the intervening time. For example, hours after a child sees a sibling doing exercises, the child may do a version of the same exercises.

How Preschoolers Reason

Preschoolers often reason differently from adults. Adults reason either inductively or deductively. **Inductive reasoning** proceeds from the specific to the general. After examining a number of specific cases, the conclusion may be reached that children who do not do their homework do not receive good grades. Adults also use **deductive reasoning,** beginning with a general rule and proceeding to specifics. They may form a rule concerning homework and grades and then apply it to specific cases.

inductive reasoning Reasoning that proceeds from specific cases to the formation of a general rule.

deductive reasoning Reasoning that begins with a general rule and is then applied to specific cases.

Preschool children reason from particular to particular, called **transductive reasoning.** The simplest example of such reasoning is that if A causes B, then, according to the preschooler, B causes A. The child's understanding of causality is based on how close one event is to another. As Pulaski notes, "The road makes the bicycle go; by creating a shadow one can cause the night to come. The thunder makes it rain, and honking the horn makes the car go" (1980, p. 49).

> ***True or False?***
> During the preschool years the child begins to reason in a manner that is very similar to that of an average adult.

Seriation and Classification

Parents are often surprised when preschoolers use different logic or have difficulty with problems that seem so

transductive reasoning Preoperational reasoning in which young children reason from particular to particular.

simple to adults. For instance, preschoolers simply cannot seem to put a series of sticks in order from biggest to smallest, an operation called **seriation.** Later in the preoperational stage children can do this task but, are unable to insert a new stick into an existing display (Piaget, 1952; Siegler 1991).

Preschoolers cannot classify items, at least at the beginning of the preoperational stage. When young children are given a number of squares, triangles, and rings of different colors and asked to put those that are alike into a pile, most children younger than 5 do not organize their choices on any particular logical basis. They may put a red triangle and a blue triangle together but then throw in a red square. No central organizing principle is evident. Some young children do not understand the task at all. Later in the preoperational stage some progress in **classification** is made. The child can sort items on the basis of one overriding principle—most often form—but fails to see that multiple classifications are possible.

Preschool children also have difficulty understanding subordinate and superordinate classes. For example, a child may be shown seven green beads and three white beads, all made of wood, and asked whether there are more green beads or more wooden beads. The child will usually say more green beads (Thomas, 1995). Preschoolers have difficulty with these problems, called *class inclusion problems,* since they seem unable to make comparisons across levels.

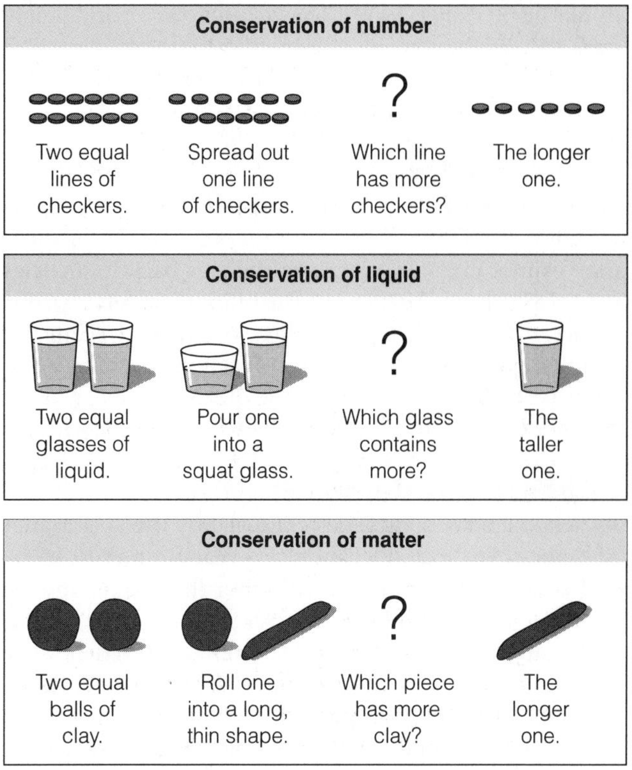

Figure 8.2
Conservation When presented with the problems seen above, preschoolers give answers (indicated in the right column) that differ from those of older children. Preschoolers have difficulty with conservation problems.

Transitive Inferences

Preschoolers also cannot seem to understand **transitive inferences,** such as who is quickest if Susan is quicker than Donna and Shirley is quicker than Susan (Artman & Cahan, 1993). The preoperational child views comparisons as absolute (Piaget & Inhelder, 1974) and does not understand that an object can be larger than one thing and at the same time smaller than another.

Conservation Problems

Nowhere are the preschooler's difficulties so obvious as in the inability to solve conservation problems (Figure 8.2) (Howes, 1990). **Conservation** involves the ability to comprehend that quantities remain the same regardless of changes in their appearance. You can test this out yourself in a number of ways. For example, show a preschooler displays of seven pennies in which the coins are either grouped close together or spread apart. The 4-year-old is certain that the spread-out display has more pennies than the display that is packed closer together. Or show the child two equal lumps of clay and roll each lump into a ball. Then, while the child is watching, roll one ball into a worm and ask the child which clay form has more clay. The preschooler fails to understand that the forms are still equal in size and believes that one has more clay than the other. Or show a preschooler two identical half-filled beakers of water. The child will tell you the amounts of water are equal. Now transfer the water from one beaker to a squat cup and ask the child which container has more water. The child will usually say that the taller beaker contains more liquid.

Why can't preschoolers solve these simple tasks? The answer lies in certain characteristics of preschoolers' thinking.

Characteristics of Preschoolers' Thinking

Most preschool children can concentrate on only one dimension at a time (Piaget & Inhelder, 1969). This is known as **centering.** Because containers are *shaped* differently, preschoolers believe that one container is larger than the other. Preschoolers rely on a visual comparison and believe that a tall, narrow glass contains more liquid than a short, fat cup. They can attend to only one measure at a time (i.e., length *or* width), and appearances confuse them. Centering is not confined to laboratory tasks. Properational children often use height as a means of estimating age. The taller the person the older the child

seriation The process of placing objects in size order.

classification The process of placing objects into different classes.

transitive inferences Statements of comparison, such as, "If X is taller than Y and Y is taller than Z, then X is taller than Z."

conservation The principle that quantities remain the same despite changes in their appearance.

centering The tendency to attend to only one dimension at a time.

thinks he is (Piaget, 1969). They center on size and height cues. When they are not distracted by these cues they can use others, such as facial characteristics, which are likely to lead to a better guess (Bjorklund, 1995).

Irreversibility

Preschoolers also cannot reverse operations **(reversibility).** If a clay ball is rolled into a worm in front of them, they cannot mentally rearrange the clay back to its original form (Piaget, 1929). This inability to reverse an operation affects preschoolers' answers to what seem like simple questions. When a preschooler was asked whether he had a sister, he said he did and gave her name. When asked whether his sister had a brother, he said no.

Appearance Versus Reality

Preschoolers are sometimes confused by the appearance of objects. For example, show a 3-year-old a red toy car and cover the car with a green filter that makes the car look black. Now hand the car (without the filter) to the child and put the car behind the filter again. When asked what color the car is, the child says "black" (Flavell, 1986). Preschoolers are perception-bound, basing their judgments on how things look to them at the present time, and they have difficulty going beyond visual information. The ability to separate reality from appearance increases markedly between 3 and 5 years of age (Gopnik & Astington, 1988).

Care should be taken not to overestimate children's difficulties in this area (Deak & Bauer, 1996). Children have the most trouble when deception is used, such as the example just described using the filter (Woolley & Wellman, 1990). Preschoolers can easily distinguish toys, pictures, and pretend actions from reality. They know that people who are playing at something are just playing and that a picture is a picture and not real. Young children understand very well that a cactus cannot be made into a porcupine, no matter how much the cactus looks like a porcupine (Keil, 1989). The appearance-reality difficulty depends on the type of situation presented to the child.

Egocentrism

Underlying all the child's reasoning is a basic **egocentrism.** Piaget (1954) argues that children see everything from their own point of view and are not capable of taking someone else's view into account. Young children believe that everything has a purpose that is understandable in their own terms and relevant to their own needs. Preschoolers see the entire world as revolving around them. The sun and moon exist to give them light; mothers and fathers exist to give them warmth and to take care of them.

This egocentrism is seen in children's interpretations of their physical world and their social world. Children who know their left hand from their right may not be able to identify correctly the left and right hands of a person standing opposite them. Nursery school teachers are aware of this, and when facing preschoolers, they raise the left hand when requesting that the children raise their right (Davis, 1983). Piaget showed a model of three mountains to young children and asked them to consider how the display might look to a doll sitting in different positions around the model. Preschool children could not do this accurately, because they reason that everyone sees the world as they do. For example, after I had had a particularly hard day my 4-year-old came over and asked if I wanted her to read to me. Since stories make her feel better, she supposed they would do the same for me.

Animism and Artificialism

One of the charming aspects of early childhood is the child's tendency to ascribe attributes of living organisms to inanimate objects, which is called **animism.** A preschooler may bump into a desk, smack it, and say, "Bad desk!" A book that falls from a shelf does not want to be with the other books. A balloon that has soared to the ceiling does not want to be held. Animism is most characteristic of the early part of this stage. It becomes less evident as children reach the age of 4 or 5 (Bullock, 1985).

The child's reasoning also reflects **artificialism,** the belief that natural phenomena are caused by human beings. This is a natural outgrowth of what children see around them. Everything is viewed as intentional and organized for human use, so children explain the world in terms of human causation (Piaget, 1928), such as believing that Lake Geneva was not created by natural forces but dug by a group of men (Pulaski, 1980). My daughter once noticed a half moon and innocently asked, "Who cut the moon in half?" Since she was familiar with her sandwiches being cut in half, she believed that someone had to have cut the moon in half as well.

Children also believe in magical thinking to some extent (Piaget, 1930). Children may believe that it is raining because they wished it. Indeed, half of all 4-year-olds in one study believed that a fairy does magic in the real world and three-quarters believed that a magician does real magic, while many fewer 6- or 8-year-olds believed so (Phelps & Woolley, 1994). Children may be simply evoking magic to explain events that violate their expectations or for which they simply have no adequate physical explanations.

Recent Challenges to Piaget's Views

After all this, it must seem that preschoolers are described more by what they cannot do than by what they can

reversibility Beginning at the end of an operation and working one's way back to the start.

egocentrism A thought process in which young children believe everyone is experiencing the environment in the same way they are. Children who are egocentric have difficulty understanding someone else's point of view.

animism The preschooler's tendency to ascribe the attributes of living things to inanimate objects.

artificialism The belief that natural phenomena are caused by human beings.

(Beilen, 1992; Flavell, 1985), and their charm results from their ignorance. Preschoolers' reasoning appears reasonable to them; it only seems illogical from an adult perspective.

Many of Piaget's ideas concerning the limitations of preschool thought have recently been challenged. Psychologists now realize that preschoolers may not be as limited as first thought. Perhaps preschoolers can classify, are not so egocentric, and can perform transitive inferences—if the situation is structured correctly.

The observations Piaget made of preschoolers using his standard testing procedures are well founded, and no one seriously doubts their reliability (Gelman & Baillargeon, 1983). If you test a preschooler the same way Piaget did, you will get the same results. However, the assumption that because preschoolers fail these tests they cannot seriate, classify, or decenter is questionable. Perhaps if we tested the children differently they might succeed. Indeed, this is exactly what researchers have found. Preschoolers can arrange things in size order, classify items, and understand inferences if we tailor the tasks to the preschooler's interests and abilities. First, we have to strip away anything that might distract the child, leaving only the elements most essential to the task. Second, the task situation must be familiar because preschoolers are easily distracted and do poorly in strange situations (Brown, et al., 1983). Their abilities are also easily taxed, so that memory and lack of comprehension can affect performance.

Simple modifications in Piaget's method can change the results of the experiment. For example, Inhelder and Piaget (1964) argued that children can seriate if they can place the items in correct order, put additional items into the series, and correct any errors. However, Piaget used a total of 10 sticks in his observations to conclude that true seriation did not occur at this stage. When a similar approach is taken with 4 sticks instead of 10, three-quarters of the 3- and 4-year-olds could put the sticks in size order, about four-fifths could insert new sticks into the order, and all the children could correct the incorrect insertions (Koslowski, 1980). These children possess the ability to seriate, but 10 sticks are simply too many for the preschooler to deal with at one time.

Piaget noted that children had difficulty with class inclusion problems. Yet, studies show that children do understand superordinate and subordinate classes. Even 2- and 3-year-olds understand that a hammer is a type of tool and a cabinet is a piece of furniture (Blewitt, 1994). Some of Piaget's ideas have been greatly expanded. At the end of the sensorimotor stage children develop the ability to represent, that is to use one object to stand for another. An 18-month-old may pretend that a paper plate is a hat and put it on his head. Representation goes far beyond this simple idea, as shown by a series of intriguing studies performed by Judy DeLoache and her colleagues (1987; 1991a & 1991b; DeLoache, Kolstad, & Anderson, 1991). A young child watches as a miniature toy dog is hidden somewhere in the scale model of a room. The scale model exactly corresponds to the actual room. The child is then asked to find a larger miniature toy dog hidden in the same place in the real room. The 2½- and 3-year-old children are told that the scale model of the room is identical to the real room. Will the children be able to use the scale model as a guide to discover where the item in the larger room is hidden? When these and other similar studies are conducted, most of the 3-year-olds but very few 2½-year-olds are able to use the models and succeed at the task.

Memory problems can be ruled out as an explanation for the failure of the 2½-year-old children since they understood the directions and later are generally able to find the toy in the scale model. Younger children seemed to understand everything except the relationship of the model to the room. De Loache argues that the failure of the younger children is caused by the dual nature of the model. The scale model is both a symbol of the larger room but also is a real thing in itself. To succeed in the task, children have to be able to think about the model as both representing the larger room and as a thing in itself. The younger children could not think about the model in two different ways at the same time, but the 3-year-olds could (DeLoache, 1987). The younger children looked at the scale model as an interesting object in itself and not as a symbol.

In fact, when 2½-year-old children are shown where an object is hidden in a picture of the room rather than a model they do much better at this task. They do use the picture as a guide. De Loache theorizes that even very young children understand that a two-dimensional picture is a symbol and not the thing itself. They know that a picture of a dog is a representation of a dog. The picture does not require a dual orientation and so even the 2½-year-old children can succeed at the task (DeLoache, 1991). These studies show that although a child may be in the preoperational stage and therefore capable of using symbols in some fashion, this does not mean that they do so in the same way as older children and adults do.

Piaget's conception of egocentrism has also been the focus of much criticism (Ford, 1979). Under specific circumstances preschoolers are not egocentric—that is, they can understand the viewpoint of others. John Flavell and his colleagues (1981) found that preschoolers understood that objects with different sides, like a house, look different from various perspectives, but that objects with identical sides, like a ball, look the same. In another experiment, 1- to 3-year-old children were given a hollow cube with a picture pasted to the bottom of the inside. The children were asked to show the picture to an observer sitting across from them. Almost all the children who were 2 years or older turned the cube away from them and toward the observer, demonstrating some understanding of the other person's perspective. (Flavell et al., 1993; Lempers, Flavell, & Flavell, 1977). Young children, then, can take someone else's perspective at certain times but not others, perhaps because two levels of perspective taking exist. Young children understand that another person does not always see the object in exactly the same way as the child does, but this is basically an all or none concept; the child simply understands that others may see it differently (Flavell et al., 1993). The older child at about age 4, begins to develop a more mature understanding of the conflicting ways that objects can be represented.

Other important cognitive changes occur at about age 4 as well, for example, the ability to understand the distinction between appearance and reality. In the standard test, children are shown an object that looks like one thing but is really something else, such as a sponge that looks like a rock, and are asked an appearance question (What does it look like?) and a reality question (What is it really?). Children under the age of 4 believe that it is not only a sponge but also looks like a sponge (Flavell, Flavell, & Green, 1983). Four-year-olds understand that it looks like a rock but is a sponge. The older child understands that an object can be represented in more than one way, depending upon how one looks at it. Some new evidence indicates that young children fail to understand this because of limitations in their information-processing ability, that is, they cannot hold in mind two conflicting object identities at the same time (Rice et al., 1997). When these information-processing requirements are reduced, children who fail the standard test succeed. When 3-year-olds who failed the standard task were presented with an eraser that looked like a peanut along with a real eraser and a real peanut that were identical in appearance and asked the reality and appearance questions, they answered correctly (Brenneman & Gelman, 1993). The presence of both objects helped the young children hold both identities in mind.

These changes in thinking at about age 4 are also shown in children's understanding of the nature of beliefs. In one standard task, a child watches as something, perhaps candy, is hidden in a box. The child is then asked to leave the room and the box is filled with pencils while the candy is moved to another box. When the child returns and is asked where the candy is hidden, the child obviously guesses that it is in the original box. An older child or adult would understand that they had held a false belief and simply change their mind about where it was hidden. They would understand that another person would make the same mistake in the absence of any other information. However, 3-year-olds believed that another child would actually believe there were pencils in the box and stated that they themselves always believed that (Gopnik & Astington, 1988). Four-year-olds after realizing they had been tricked, laughed and understood that another child would still think that the candy was in the original box. They understood the nature of their false belief and that their representation of the items' location could be wrong and changed their beliefs.

Children begin to understand the nature of these false beliefs at age 4 but locational beliefs are not the only ones that emerge at this age. Three-year-olds who were told that other children thought it acceptable to bite another child or wear pajamas to school refused to believe that others could believe this (Flavell, Mumme, Green & Flavell, 1994). Older children have the ability to understand the nature of these false beliefs. This finding holds despite situations in which younger children are given great help to understand the nature of these beliefs (Sullivan & Winner, 1993), and has been found not only in Europe and North America but around the world, for example, in Baika pygmies of Cameroon, Africa (Avis & Harris, 1991). Children fail to falsely believe partially because they do not remember what they originally believed (Gopnik & Astington, 1988). They may also fail because 3-year-olds lack the conceptual ability necessary to solve problems by switching beliefs (Perner, 1991).

The understanding of false beliefs is part of psychologists' interest in how children understand mental processes such as dreams, memories, and beliefs. As young children mature, they gain a more sophisticated understanding of representation and beliefs, and 4-year-olds seem to have a great advantage over younger children in this area (Schaffer, 1996). Beginning at this age, children's thinking changes as they come to to understand that the same world can be experienced in many different ways by different people, that each person may have a different belief about reality. They begin to infer mental states in others and see them as an explanation for behavior. They understand that people's beliefs are important and some of them are false.

These changes, which begin to appear at age 4, show a new awareness of the nature of the world and demonstrate that even very young children are not as egocentric as Piaget had believed. Children's understanding of the world is a great deal more sophisticated than Piaget believed, although it is admittedly incomplete.

Even the concept of animism is under fire. Only a third of all the 3-year-olds tested in one study attributed emotional states to dolls (Gelman, Spelke, & Meck, 1983). Although some preschoolers think cartoons and dolls are real, most do not (Prawat, Anderson, & Hapokeiwicz, 1989). Children are animistic in some ways, but we must be careful not to overgeneralize. The point is not that Piaget was wrong but rather that Piaget underestimated young children's abilities because some of the tasks he had them perform were too demanding.

True or False?
Most preschoolers do not believe that dolls and cartoon characters are real.

Questions Students Often Ask

Was Piaget right or wrong? Why can't we get a definite answer to this?

Not everything can be answered by a simple "yes" or "no." The situation is more complicated. If you use Piaget's definitions, his criteria for achieving skills such as seriation or class inclusion, and test children exactly the way he did, you will get the same results.

His studies have been replicated many times. However, if you change the way you test the children by varying the task demands, studies show that you can get different results.

This is not really surprising. The easiest example is Piaget's criteria for success in seriation (placing things in size order). He used 10 sticks and few preschoolers were able to do it. But what makes 10 sticks the standard? If fewer sticks are used (4) many young children can seriate. The new research does not contradict Piaget as much as add a dimension to his work and cause us to look at the task demands. Most importantly, it should keep us from generalizing that a child cannot do something and perhaps look at the demands of the task.

Other Piagetian skills have been taught to children at younger ages than thought possible. Gelman (1969) trained children to conserve by teaching them to respond to relevant cues and to ignore apparent visual ones. Children have been taught to solve class inclusion problems as well (McCabe & Siegel, 1987). Although there are some doubts about the degree to which children transfer their learning to other situations, the studies demonstrate that young children are more flexible in the development of their reasoning processes than first thought.

Harmonizing the Views

Putting this new information into perspective is difficult. Can preschoolers seriate and understand causality in a more or less mature manner? At first glance, the research seems contradictory, but it is not. Under certain circumstances, preschoolers can do things Piaget did not think possible. However, if the situation is complicated or requires more memory and verbal skills than they have, preschoolers fail at these tasks.

These findings have practical implications. People working with preschoolers must design an environment in which tasks are simplified and memory requirements are minimized, and they must be certain that preschoolers understand what is required of them if they are to bring out these newly developing skills. Under these circumstances, preschoolers can do some surprising things. This is not to say that a child at any age can learn anything; limitations exist. However, too often people have reached conclusions about what young children can and cannot do, only to find that preschoolers can do more than they thought possible.

Information-Processing Abilities

The importance of the demands of the task are also shown in the preschool child's information-processing abilities. Developmental changes in attention and memory affect the child's behavior and capabilities.

Attention

Two aspects of attention are most commonly studied; **attention span,** which is the time period a child can spend on a given task, and **selective attention,** the ability to concentrate on one stimulus and ignore extraneous stimuli. Adults who work with preschoolers and designers of television shows aimed at young children do not expect them to maintain their attention for long periods of time. Compared to older children and adults, preschoolers have shorter attention spans, although a significant increase is seen during early childhood (Ruff & Lawson, 1990). A fourfold increase in attention span is found between the ages of 1 and 4 (Anderson & Levin, 1976).

True or False?
The child's attention span at 4 years is about the same as an adult's.

The ability of young children to consciously attend to a particular stimulus when faced with competing stimuli is limited, but improves through the preschool period. Preschoolers do not spontaneously restrict their attention to important stimuli unless the stimuli stand out or unless the children receive training (Woody-Ramsey & Miller, 1988). Preschoolers are easily confused when the situation becomes too complex (Miller & Harris, 1988). In fact, preschoolers' attention is more affected by such stimulus characteristics as color, movement, and novelty than older children and adults' attention. Older children and adults have a greater ability to tune out a physically attractive stimulus and pay attention to another less attractive but more important stimulus. As children mature, their ability to control their attention, to discriminate between what is and is not most important, and to adapt their attention to the demands of a situation improves (Bjorklund, 1995; Flavell et al, 1993). One reason for the improvement in attention span is the increase in the ability to tune out extraneous information (Ruff & Lawson, 1990)

Questions Students Often Ask

Why do young children have such short attention spans?

They don't. I hear this quite a bit but it is not true. Young children have an attention span that is reasonable for them. The reason it seems so short is that you are comparing them to older children and adults, which is not fair.

The fact that the preschooler's attention can be gained and to some degree held by using elements of sound, color, novelty, and movement is well-known, but the

attention span The time period during which an individual can focus psychological resources on a particular stimulus or task.

selective attention The ability to concentrate on one stimulus and ignore extraneous stimuli.

preschooler's ability to comprehend the material should not be ignored. Preschoolers pay attention to messages that they understand. The preschooler's shorter attention span requires that material be presented in small segments. Tasks and their directions must be simple and given in a way that young children can understand. Specific instructions as to where to place their attention may be of some help (Hochman, 1996). Because preschoolers are more easily distracted, competing environmental stimuli should be reduced or eliminated.

Memory Skills

Children need to remember material for it to be useful. Preschoolers' memory skills are far superior to those of toddlers. Between 2 and 4 years of age, their already good recognition skills improve (Perlmutter & Myers, 1979). Their ability to use language allows them to store memories using words. Even young children can show impressive memory for events. When children who were 3 or 4 years old when they went to Disneyworld were interviewed 18 months later, all of them remembered a great deal about their trip. Older children remembered more details and did not require as many prompts (Bjorklund, 1995).

> ***True or False?***
> Three-year-old children can only remember an event that happened to them for about 6 months, after which it disappears from their memory.

Any parent will tell you that children are rather selective in what they remember. Children always seem to remember the toy that you said you would buy them, probably because interest is an important factor in what preschoolers as well as toddlers as young as 2 remember (Somerville, Wellman, & Cultice, 1983).

Preschoolers show some interesting limitations in the memory strategies they use. Adults shown a group of pictures and asked to remember them might first group them into categories (foods, buildings, people), then rehearse them. Preschoolers do not use these strategies on their own (Kail & Hagen, 1982; Schneider & Pressley, 1989). If they are instructed to do so, their memory for the list improves (Flavell & Wellman, 1977).

As in the case of Piagetian tasks, we must be careful not to overgeneralize because the characteristics of the task and the test conditions are most important. When 18- to 24-month-old children watched an experimenter hide a toy, were told to remember its location so that they could find the item later, and then were distracted for 4 minutes, the children actively tried to remember where it was. They frequently interrupted their play to talk about the hidden toy and its location, which suggests that the idea that preschoolers are nonstrategic needs rethinking (DeLoache, Cassidy, & Brown, 1985). Preschoolers *do* use some strategies for remembering, such as pointing and looking, but their use of verbal strategies is limited (Kail & Hagen, 1982).

Young children also may not understand the demands of the task. Lynn Appel and colleagues (1972) presented pictures to 4-, 7-, and 11-year-old children using one of two different instructions: "Look at the pictures" or "Remember the pictures." Children did not seem to know that the problem requires some voluntary, purposeful cognitive activity. Indeed, the 4-year-olds did not act any differently when presented with either instruction, but the older children did. Perhaps preschoolers show such poor use of memory strategies because they do not understand what memory tasks entail (Flavell & Wellman, 1977). Four-year-olds, but not three-year-olds, understand that chances of forgetting increase with age (Lyon & Flavell, 1993).

Unfortunately, many studies of memory in young children have used artificial situations that require recalling new information for its own sake (Paris & Lindauer, 1982). Children 3 to 7 years of age were asked to remember a list of five words under two different conditions. Under one condition, the children played a game of grocery store and had to recall the items so they could buy them. Under the second condition, children were simply told to remember the items. Children recalled significantly more items under the first condition than under the second (Isotomina, 1975). Children tested on the task of remembering a list did quite well when the words fell into familiar categories, such as names of their teachers and television shows (Lindberg, 1980).

Developmental differences in forgetting also exist. Young children forget more quickly and forget more material than older children (Howe, 1991). They show the same interference effects, that is, something they learn presently can interfere and cause forgetting of something they learned earlier and vice versa (Howe, 1995). Forgetting can be reduced by reminding the preschoolers of some part of the memory at a later time, a process known as *reinstatement* (Howe, Courage, & Bryant-Brown, 1993). Such reinstated memories are more durable and less likely to be forgotten than the original memories. For instance, 2-year-old children were shown 12 common objects that were then hidden around the room. The children learned the locations of the objects. Some children were later shown the objects but no mention was made of the hiding place, while others were not shown anything. Those children receiving cues (reinstatement) made far fewer errors (Howe et al., 1993).

We find that children can remember more and do begin to use strategies. But young children are easily confounded, and artificial tasks are likely to reveal their limitations. Taken as a group, the studies in cognition and memory should keep us from generalizing about what abilities children do or do not have. Children who may not show these abilities when tested in a certain way do not necessarily lack them. Instead, it is important to note the situations in which children can and cannot successfully perform particular tasks.

The Importance of Prior Knowledge

When we lay down memories, we do not do so in a vacuum; we often have a framework on which to hang our memories. For instance, before hearing about Columbus, we may have seen a film about explorers or know what an explorer does. This makes learning about Columbus easier. Psychologists focus on the importance of what people know—their knowledge base—to what people are trying to know or remember (Chi & Glaser, 1985). Their findings show that the more people know, the easier it is for them to lay down new memories, possibly people who have some prior knowledge have already formed what cognitive psychologists call schemata.

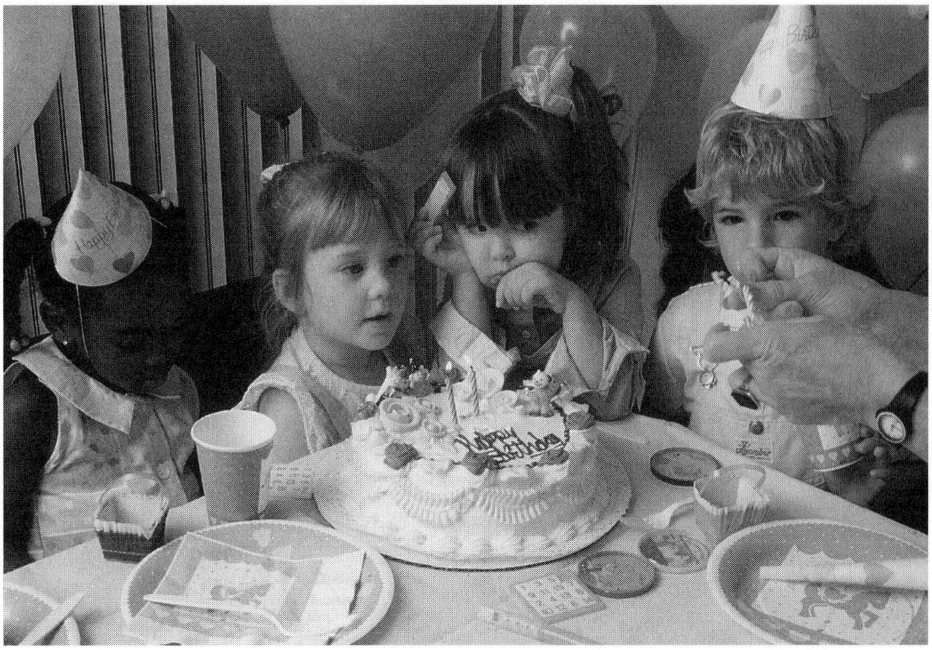

Children develop scripts—that is an understanding of what is supposed to happen in a certain situation, such as a birthday party, and in what order.

A **schema** is an organized body of knowledge that functions as a framework for describing objects and relationships that generally occur (Leahey & Harris, 1997). Schemata (the plural of *schema*) can contain both knowledge about and rules for using knowledge. A schema for a dog may contain information about the dog's physical features and activities and different aspects of a dog's behavior as well as how to treat dogs. If a situation resembles previous situations represented in a schema, the schema is activated, encouraging better organization and interpretation of information (Schneider & Pressley, 1989).

Consider a preschool teacher talking about hospital procedures and telling students about a nurse taking a patient's blood pressure. Students with some prior knowledge of hospitals would understand or visualize this scenario better than students without this knowledge. Such prior knowledge might involve the roles of various people at the hospital, various hospital procedures, and the types of instruments used in hospitals. These schemata underlie our understanding of events and allow us to interpret and clarify what we experience or learn (Chi & Glaser, 1985). The more we know about hospitals and their procedures, the easier it is to understand what goes on in a hospital.

Schemata allow us to encode additional information more meaningfully because new information can be linked to already encoded information. It also allows us to fill in gaps and to infer. As children mature, their schemata become more complicated, richer, and more flexible. A child's background may contain a great deal of information in one area and not very much in another. Since preschoolers generally do not have very rich experiential knowledge, it is not unusual for them to have difficulty remembering some things while easily remembering others. Some of the differences between preschoolers and children in middle childhood result from the richer memory of the latter.

A similar concept to schema is **script,** a type of schema that involves knowledge of the events that make up an episode as well as the sequence of the events (Eiser, Eiser, & Jones, 1990). Numerous scripts exist, including those for birthday parties, job interviews, and a school day. Adults show a great deal of agreement on these scripts, as do young children on familiar scripts. Four-year-olds and even younger children describe daily events at home, in a day care center, or at a McDonald's restaurant in much the same way as an adult would (Nelson, 1978). Scripts give order to the child's life (Fivush, Kuebli, & Clubb, 1992). Young children find it easier to remember memories that fit into their regular scripts. Preschoolers have a limited ability to plan for the future and scripts seem to help them to anticipate future events (Hudson, Shapiro, & Sosa, 1995).

Scripts form the basis for remembering familiar stories and events. If you are given information and are familiar with the script, you can fill in missing information. Prior knowledge represented by the script makes the story easier to follow. When young children are presented with a script that contains an event that is out of order and are asked to recall the event, they either omit the misordered event or put it in the place that is in keeping with their knowledge of how it usually is (Bauer & Thal, 1990; Nelson & Gruendel, 1981). Children recognize deviations from the proper script and correct them (Wimmer, 1979). Preschoolers remember stories incorrectly if the stories differ from their familiar scripts. For instance, children

schema (information processing) An organized body of knowledge that functions as a framework describing objects and relationships that generally occur.

script A structure that describes an appropriate sequence of events in a particular context.

invent and put appropriate material in stories when they cannot recall what they were told (Mandler & Johnson, 1977).

Knowledge of scripts also affects how children make inferences. Children who are told that Renaldo went to a restaurant and is drinking milk do not need to be told that Renaldo probably looked at a menu or drank his milk from a glass. They infer it because they are familiar with the script. Script knowledge also affects behavior. Preschoolers who are familiar with scripts interact more easily; script knowledge facilitates turn-taking, play, and conversation (Furman & Walden, 1990).

The scripts of older and younger children differ. Preschoolers are more rigid in their ideas of what should take place and when (Wimmer, 1980). Older children also produce more alternative paths in their scripts. For instance, when describing how to make a campfire, they offer more possible paths to accomplishing the task than younger children do.

Preschoolers, being rather rigid in their scripts, will often rebel if people do things that are not in keeping with their idea of the script. Changes in scripts can trouble younger children more than older children. A 2-year-old who was usually given a bath after dinner became very upset when bathed before dinner because she thought she would not be fed (Hudson, 1990). Preschoolers may become confused or annoyed if baby-sitters or substitute preschool teachers do things differently than their parents or regular teachers. Scripts become more flexible and more complex as children develop. Both scripts and schemata are culturally dependent. When people move to another country or even to a different part of the same country, scripts and schema may change.

True or False?
Preschoolers are more rigid than elementary schoolchildren in their understanding of what should take place and the order in which events should occur.

Home, Television, and Nursery School

The child's cognitive abilities are affected by his or her environment. A preschooler's environment is more complex than a toddler's environment. Expanding physical and communicative abilities enable the child to explore and learn more. Three areas of influence on preschoolers' cognitive development are their home, what they watch on television, and what they experience in preschool.

The Home

The characteristics of the home environment can develop or retard the child's cognitive abilities. Children who are more cognitively advanced come from homes in which language is used expansively. Such children are encouraged to express themselves, to label the environment, and to describe their world. Parents who give information, explain events, read to their children, and encourage curiosity and exploration help to develop their children's minds so that when the children enter elementary school, they are ready for new challenges (Katz, 1980).

Even when not directly involved in a parent-child interaction, children observe those around them. If preschoolers see their parents and older siblings enjoying reading, they are more likely to develop a positive attitude toward reading.

Parents can help their children develop their cognitive abilities in a number of ways. Almost every activity can be a learning experience and can be made enjoyable. Children can learn to recognize similarities, shapes, and colors and to explore their environments safely.

There are two models here. The first views parents as environmental engineers who at the appropriate times provide materials and opportunities that help their children explore and learn about the world. Such parents construct an environment rich in opportunities, allowing their children to discover the world at their own pace and stimulating them to think. Although Piaget never listed recommendations on child-rearing (Vernon, 1976), such a strategy is in line with his thinking. The child learns through discovery, and the child's readiness is taken into consideration. Formal instruction is deemphasized, and the everyday experiences of the child are educational. A simple walk around the neighborhood becomes a learning experience. There are traffic signs, people working, and a hundred different things to discuss. The other approach emphasizes formal instruction; parents actively teaching their preschooler skills, with less emphasis on self-discovery and more on planned activities that impart knowledge.

Both these extreme positions should be questioned. The parent who merely produces an environment but does not actively interact with the youngster is not maximizing the child's experiences. On the other hand, too formal or unnatural a structure may cause a child to resent the parents and reject the instruction as a joyless and "grim business" (Zinsser, 1981). Not all preschoolers can be early readers; many do not have the physical abilities, such as the ability to focus on printed words, necessary for success in reading. Such children may feel inadequate for not living up to their parents' expectations, and the resulting tension could interfere with their development.

Television

Some 98% of all American households have television sets, and many have an extra set for the children. Children begin watching television before their first birthday and have favorite programs by their second or third birthday. They spend more time viewing television than doing anything else except sleeping (Dorr & Rabin, 1995). The television is on for 7 hours a day in the average American home and preschoolers and kindergartners watch about 3 hours of television a day (West, Hausken, & Chandler, 1992); other estimates are somewhat higher (Condry, 1989). Many parents use the television set as a baby-sitter, and the children of such parents may not watch appropriate programming. However, there are television shows that are produced just for young children.

True or False?
Preschoolers spend more time watching television than engaging in any other activity except sleep.

Many toddlers absolutely love Barney, the purple dinosaur that appears on a television show called *Barney and Friends,* which has been a tremendous financial success (Kroninger, 1995). Barney is constantly upbeat, singing songs and reminding children to do such things as brush their teeth and be nice to each other. The show takes place in a suburban setting and features happy children singing happy songs and learning simple lessons.

Parents and other adults don't always feel very positive about Barney (Ferguson, 1993), probably because the show is so unabashedly sweet, but the show is not produced for them. The more serious criticisms of the show are that it does not recognize the existence of unpleasant realities. Giggles and unconditional love, happiness and prompt conflict resolution are appealing, but are they honest reflections of reality (Levy, 1994)? Pain, sorrow and frustration—natural feelings that young children experience—simply are not addressed on the show. Barney changes sadness to happiness instantly. For example, when Barney trips on a toy and falls, he is bruised and in pain, but he giggles. Barney convinces a child who is afraid to get a shot that there is nothing to be afraid of at all. Would it be better in the first instance if he had shown the pain and in the second if the child were told that the shot would hurt only for a second? These criticisms are debatable, but they should be discussed.

Sesame Street is a television program directed toward teaching youngsters basic numerical, language, and problem-solving skills. Its goal is to promote intellectual and cultural growth, especially in disadvantaged preschoolers (Comstock & Paik, 1991). It emphasizes cognitive concerns, although over the years it has covered cooperation, tolerance for others, and developing healthy attitudes. The show stresses literacy and interpersonal communication, and counters stereotypes by showing nontraditional role models (Walsh, 1996; Van Evra, 1990).

Sesame Street is fun to watch, and children from all ethnic and socioeconomic backgrounds do so (Rice et al., 1990). It is broadcast in 130 countries, and 14 countries have co-productions of the program tailored to their own cultures, including a mixed-race South African *Sesame Street* and a peaceful Israeli-Palestinian version. A Russian *Sesame Street* production called *Ulitsa Sczam* introduces Zeliboba, a lovable free spirit from a Russian fairy tale, as Bert and Ernie's friend. It takes place in a courtyard next to a cottage. Its values include racial harmony, peaceful dispute resolution, respect for the environment, and equal rights for women (Cooperman, 1996).

Barney is a favorite character of very young children.

Children who watch *Sesame Street* regularly learn its central concepts and have an advantage over those who do not watch. These advantages seem to hold regardless of the socioeconomic level, sex, or ethnicity of the viewer (Ball & Bogatz, 1970; Bogatz & Ball, 1971). Children gain more from the program if they watch it with a parent who can interpret the material and act as a guide (Peters, 1977). Children also imitate the cooperation they see if they are placed in a situation like the one on television, but no generalized effects have been found (Watkins et al., 1980). Watching *Sesame Street* also has a positive effect on children's vocabulary development (Rice et al., 1990).

The show has been criticized for having a very fast, perhaps frenetic, pace, which some have linked to attention span problems in children (Cooperman, 1996; Tower et al., 1979). *Sesame Street* also shows negative behaviors, such as violence and trickery. Finally, some have criticized its approach to literacy, saying that although learning letters is important, emphasizing the meaning of written passages would be better (Mates & Strommen, 1995). There are no signs or posters to read, and few vignettes involve written material, such as reading menus, letters from others, or written directions. Little is said or shown about the usefulness of reading or of reading for pleasure (Mates & Strommen, 1995).

Mister Rogers' Neighborhood is a slower-paced, adult-led show that emphasizes interpersonal skills, imagination, and understanding of one's emotions (Tower et al., 1979; Singer & Singer, 1976). Research on *Mister Rogers' Neighborhood* shows that the program is successful in promoting prosocial behaviors, although its effects are not lasting (Friedrich & Stein, 1973). When preschoolers watched *Mister Rogers' Neighborhood*, aggressive cartoons, or neutral programs daily for 9 weeks the children who saw *Mister Rogers' Neighborhood* improved in task persistence and prosocial behavior, such as cooperation. Watching the show also led to an increase in fantasy play and imagination (Tower et al., 1979; Singer & Singer, 1976)—a noteworthy increase, since fantasy and pretend play are considered important aspects of a child's development (Rubin, Fein, & Vandenberg, 1983). Children who show more imaginative play have better social skills, show greater concentration and more positive affect, are less impulsive, and show more internal control (Tower et al., 1979). The success of *Mister Rogers' Neighborhood* demonstrates that a deliberately slow-paced, repetitive show can successfully aid cognitive and affective development (Singer & Singer, 1983).

The slow pace of *Mister Rogers' Neighborhood* has also been criticized for sometimes making young children restless (Singer & Singer, 1976). But there is a tradeoff in pacing: In one study kindergarten and first-grade children attended more to fast-paced programs but showed greater recall for the material in slow-paced shows (Wright et al., 1984). Television has a great potential for helping preschoolers develop cognitively and socially. Commercial television has learned something from the success of these shows, and its offerings have improved. However, television has a long way to go to reach its potential in this area.

Questions Students Often Ask

Do you agree that there's nothing on television? I won't let my kids watch it.

That's your choice. Some parents agree with you and a few do not even own a television set. I respect the choice. I have had students who grew up in rural areas without television and they did not see themselves as deprived. On the other hand, some programs are valuable and some are entertaining. I generally believe that self-control can be taught by having a television but limiting its use.

Preschool Education

The third environmental factor influencing cognitive development is preschool education. Nursery school attendance has shown consistent growth in the United States over the past 30 years. The need for many mothers to enter the labor market and the growth of one-parent families account for part of this increase (Hernandez, 1995). Some parents also worry that unless their children receive a preschool education, they will enter elementary school at a disadvantage. The importance of preschool education for young children is now widely accepted, especially as a means of helping children from disadvantaged groups who have traditionally not achieved well in school, but middle-class families are also sending their children to nursery schools in increasing numbers. Many children living in poverty will attend government-funded preschools, and private nursery schools are available to those with the resources to pay (Mare, 1995).

Preschool programs differ greatly from each other and today are collectively grouped under the heading of early childhood care and education (ECCE) (Gomby et al., 1995). **Compensatory education** involves an attempt to compensate for some difference between one group and another. Many preschool programs, such as Project Head Start (discussed later), try to help children from economically disadvantaged families develop the attitudes and skills necessary for later success in school.

There are many approaches to preschool education. Some emphasize the importance of social skills and emotional development and include stories, listening to music, art, and trips in their programs and encourage cooperation and sharing (Morrison, 1991). Others are more cognitively oriented. Many are sponsored by religious groups and emphasize moral education and personal and family-related activities. It is not easy to compare different types of early childhood programs because their goals may differ somewhat, but some comparisons are available. One study compared child-centered early childhood and kindergarten programs that emphasized children's choice of activities, a playlike rather than worklike atmosphere, warm, supporting teachers, and the encouragement of social interaction with more structured programs emphasizing teaching basic skills in structured, heavily performance-oriented programs. Children in the more structured, teacher-directed instructional programs showed better performance on a test of letters/reading achievement. However, children in the child-centered programs were superior in measures of motivation; they had higher expectations for school success, showed less dependency on adults, showed more pride in their accomplishments, seemed to enjoy their work more, and claimed to be less anxious than the children in the work- or teacher-oriented programs. The researchers argue that young children's perceptions of their own competence can be injured by being asked to perform in a negative social context. It is important to make certain that all early childhood programs have warm, responsive, supportive teachers that create an optimistic atmosphere in the classroom and support social interaction. The researchers did find some academically based classrooms that had these qualities, which demonstrates that it is not

compensatory education The use of educational strategies in an attempt to reduce or eliminate some perceived difference between groups of children.

a simple either-or situation (Stipek, Feiler, Daniels, & Milburn, 1995).

Generally speaking, nursery schools accomplish their purposes. Children who attend nursery schools are generally more advanced than those who do not. This is especially true for children in lower-income groups (Minuchin & Shapiro, 1983). Children who attend preschool programs are more socially competent, outgoing, self-assured, curious, independent, and persistent on a task than those who do not attend, and are better adjusted, more task oriented, goal directed, persistent, cooperative, and friendly in elementary school (Clarke-Stewart & Fein, 1983).

There is no question that nursery school has a positive effect on children from low-income areas and for children at risk for developing later problems in school. The question of the benefits of nursery school for middle-class children and those not in the at-risk category is still controversial. Some evidence now is emerging on this issue. A study of middle-class elementary school children found advantages in reading and language skills for boys who had attended a preschool; no effect was found for girls (Larsen & Robinson, 1989).

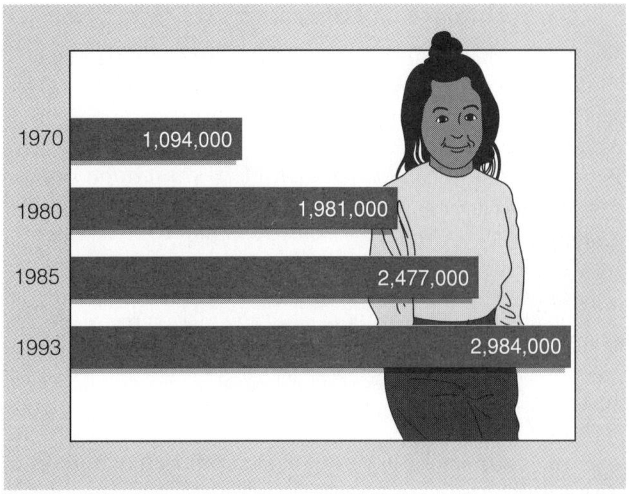

Datagraphic
Nursery School Enrollment The number of preschool children enrolled in nursery school has increased greatly.
Source: Data from U.S. Bureau of the Census, 1994.

Project Head Start

Children from impoverished backgrounds who enter school behind their middle-class counterparts are likely to fall further behind as they progress through school. Perhaps if these children could attend a preschool that would help compensate for their different experiences, this cycle could be stopped and such children would have a reasonable chance for academic success. This was partly the thinking behind one of the greatest educational social experiments of the past 50 years: **Project Head Start.**

Since its inception in 1964 about 14½ million American children have taken part in Head Start, and the program continues to expand (Head Start, 1995). The hope is that a program instituted early enough could give children living in poverty a head start in school and reduce or eliminate the social-class differences in educational achievement (Zigler & Berman, 1983).

Head Start programs have broader goals than most other preschool programs. All Head Start programs must provide services in four areas: education, health, social (and psychological) services, and parent involvement (Barnett, 1995; Head Start, 1995). Children learn to work and play independently, become able to accept help and direction from adults, gain competence and worth, sharpen and widen their language skills, be curious, and grow in ability to channel their inner, destructive impulses.

Students who participate in Head Start as well as other preschool programs are significantly less likely to be retained in grade or to be found in special education classes; they are also much more likely to graduate from high school (Barnett, 1995). The results of studies on reading and mathematics achievement for children who attended a Head Start program are mixed, with some showing Head Start children achieving more in mathematics and reading than children from other preschool programs (Lazar & Darlington, 1982; Darlington et al., 1980). Head Start is also given some of the credit for the improvement in SAT scores among minority youth (Carmody, 1988). Other advantages have been found, especially for Head Start programs in which parental participation is stressed. The children of parents who were very active in Head Start as board members and volunteers, for example, performed better on achievement tests (Washington, 1985). Involvement in the program is often the first community involvement for many parents, and most authorities believe even more emphasis should be placed on involving parents (Sprigle & Schaefer, 1985; Oyemade, 1985).

Project Head Start A federally funded compensatory education program aimed at reducing or eliminating the differences in educational achievement between poor and middle-class youngsters.

True or False?
Children attending Project Head Start classes are less likely than their peers who did not attend the program to be held back in school or placed in special education classes during their school career.

Children who attend Head Start programs show gains in cognitive ability as measured by intelligence scores, but those gains do not continue as children progress through second and third grade (Westinghouse Learning Corporation, 1969). This is often called the *fadeout phenomenon;* that is, the gains in intelligence are temporary, and by the second grade or so, Head Start children do not differ in intelligence from peers who do not attend the program. Perhaps one reason these cognitive gains may fade out is that many children who graduate from Head Start attend substandard schools (Viadero, 1994).

Questions Students Often Ask

Has Head Start been a success or not? If it doesn't result in lasting improvements in IQ, why bother with it?

There is nothing magical about IQ. Head Start is a success in many other areas, such as graduation rates and lower rates of retention. The evidence on academic achievement is positive, although not as overwhelmingly so. These accomplishments are impressive. Research shows that if we want more we must start somewhat earlier, provide more intensive services, and emphasize parent services.

How can preschool programs lead to better outcomes despite their temporary influence on IQ? First, even temporary enhancement in intelligence may ease the transition to elementary school, reducing the likelihood of tracking and increasing the probability of immediate success that may carry over into later grades. Second, it may influence parents as well as teachers to have more positive expectations for these children (Entwisle, 1995). Head Start may also lead to better self-esteem, academic motivation, and social competence (the ability of young children to select and carry out their interpersonal goals), which influence school performance (Barnett, 1995; Zigler & Berman, 1983).

The Perry Preschool

Head Start is the largest and most famous early childhood program but other more intensive programs can make a powerful difference in the lives of young people. The Perry Preschool Program demonstrated the effectiveness of preschool programs with children at risk for failure (Schweinhart & Weikert, 1981). Children aged 3 and 4 from Ypsilanti, Michigan, who lived in poverty and whose families showed many characteristics predictive of later school failure, were randomly assigned either to an experimental or a control group. The intervention consisted of extensive preschool experiences over a two-year period. The curriculum was based upon the idea that children are active learners who gain from having direct experience with objects and talking about their experiences. Children were given some choice of activities, carried them out, and were asked to recall and represent their experiences verbally or through pictures. Emphasis was placed on problem solving, independent thinking, and social development, and sometimes on small group activities in cooking, art, music, and games (Weikart, 1988). Teachers also visited each mother and child at home for 90 minutes once a week during the school year.

The differences between the two groups were impressive. The children attending the Perry Preschool began kindergarten with an intelligence score of 95 compared to 84 for the control group. Those who attended the preschool showed greater motivation in elementary school, had greater aspirations for college at age 15, and devoted more time to homework. They also achieved much more than the control group. Many fewer required special education and those who did needed it for fewer years. Parents were more pleased with their child's performance and, as rated by elementary school teachers, these children were better behaved. Many more also graduated from high school and entered postsecondary education. The program participants also committed fewer delinquent or criminal acts and those they committed were less severe (Barreuta-Clement et al., 1987). They were also much less likely to be arrested for drug use or drug dealing (Yoshikawa, 1995).

The reduction in juvenile delinquency and arrests is a finding of studies of other preschool programs as well (Zigler, Taussig, & Black, 1992). Although the exact reason for the decrease in juvenile arrests is not completely understood, perhaps the early success these children experienced carried over throughout their school years, reducing frustration and producing a more positive attitude toward school and life in general. Others suggest that since factors leading to delinquency include a history of antisocial behavior, low verbal ability, and inconsistent and harsh parenting practices, perhaps early childhood programs that include parental involvement directly reduce these problems (Yoshikawa, 1995). Long-term gains are also found as these children mature. By age 27 those who were in the experimental group were better educated, had higher earnings, were less likely to be on welfare, and showed lower crime rates (Barnett, 1993). The most successful preschool programs usually combine early education and family support services and involve parents.

The Future of Head Start and Early Childhood Programs

It isn't really fair to compare a national program with thousands of centers with a special program that was run as an experiment, although the Perry Project has served as a model for other preschool programs (Harper, 1987). The Perry Project spent more money per child, had a better child-teacher ratio and was able to make more home visits than Head Start programs. The benefits of any early childhood program are affected by structure (class size, ratio of children to teachers), intensity of services provided, and curricula (Frede, 1995). As noted, those that serve both the child and the family have the best track record. Better programs are also closely monitored for quality control and tend to start earlier.

The investment in Head Start and other preschool programs has increased greatly and most Americans support them. Some recent changes and additions to the Head Start menu include demonstration projects to help low-income students maintain and enhance the benefits they received in their earlier years in Head Start, and new programs for infants and toddlers and their families, which were started in 1994 (Head Start, 1995). Head Start faces a number of challenges. The quality of Head Start's program seems to vary considerably among centers (Barnett, 1995). In addition, at present it serves only about a third of eligible preschoolers. Some even argue that it should be expanded to include those children who are slightly above the poverty level (Zigler & Muenchow, 1992). It must also strengthen its parent programs and its health and nutrition segments, which are so important to its success.

The need for such comprehensive early childhood programs is growing and Head Start, as well as other preschool programs, have much to offer. However, Head Start is not an antidote to poverty, but it offers the hope that children who traditionally have not been successful in school will have a better chance to succeed.

Kindergarten

Do you remember your kindergarten experience? Chances are you attended for a half-day, were never tested, (except perhaps for vision), and spent the day in playlike activities designed to stimulate your curiosity and social competence. Visit most kindergartens today, and you will be very surprised at the changes.

The most obvious change is that today's kindergartners are much more likely to attend a full school day (Olsen & Zigler, 1989). The change to a full day was made for many reasons. Some claim that we now expect kindergartners to accomplish more in that year and that a full-time program meets these goals. Others argue for a more practical reason: Parents who are employed want their children to attend a school full time as soon as possible (Honig, 1995). In addition, many children have had some preschool experience and are used to time away from the home, making day-long kindergartens more practical. However, some authorities question whether the full-day kindergarten is developmentally appropriate.

Another significant change is the increasing use of screening and readiness tests at these young ages. Screening to identify children at risk has become more common both in preschool and in kindergarten. Some tests are used to screen students for problems that would prevent them from school success. Such students may then be referred for a more rigorous examination or be placed in some special program (Kaplan, 1990; Walsh, 1989). Other tests, called *readiness tests,* seek to determine which skills the children have or have not already acquired; these tests are used to make instructional decisions. If a teacher receives information that a student does not have a particular skill, some program might be instituted to help the child develop that skill.

The most profound and controversial change in kindergarten is in curriculum. Over the past two decades, academic skills have been increasingly emphasized. In the past, play was the basis of kindergarten, but this is changing. Programs now are more likely to stress academic skills and group instruction and use commercially prepared materials more (Nall, 1982). Kindergarten reading programs are now pencil and paper oriented, with dittos, texts, and workbooks (Willert & Kamii, 1985). Some believe that "kindergarten is what first grade used to be" (Walsh, 1989, p. 385). The pressures for this change come from state-mandated standards that require skill mastery, first-grade teachers who want their students to have certain skills prior to entering the grade, and parents who want kindergarten to place more emphasis on academics than the preschools their children attended (Walsh, 1989).

True or False?

The curriculum of today's kindergarten is more likely to include training in basic academic skills than it was a generation ago.

Questions Students Often Ask

My child learned more in the last year of nursery school than in kindergarten. Why?

This is the dilemma many kindergarten teachers confront. Consider the kindergarten teacher who faces a class with some children who have never been out of their mother's presence and have not attended preschool and others with 2 or 3 years of preschool. Although the movement in the United States is towards more academics, not everyone thinks it is correct and some teachers would rather emphasize social skills and developing a positive attitude towards learning. Many parents have academic goals for their children, some of which are appropriate, some not. Kindergarten teachers often face parents who are disappointed that their children are not reading, even though most children are probably not ready to do so at this point. Still, kindergarten must do a better job of serving students who have had extensive preschool experience.

Not many studies have evaluated these new changes in the modern kindergarten. Most studies that have been performed find that the longer school day and more extended periods of time spent on academics, including language, reading, and mathematics, do increase standardized test scores, especially on some readiness tests (Olsen & Zigler, 1989). This is especially true for children from at-risk populations. The findings on middle-class children are more mixed but again positive. Whether these children do better in the long run is still questionable. There is much less evidence to support changes in motivation or general intellectual ability that might lead to significant long-term change (Olsen & Zigler, 1989).

There has been a reaction against this increased emphasis on the academic. Some ask whether we are making inappropriate demands on young children, overemphasizing fine motor skills and desk work (see Controversial Issues: How Early Should a Child Start School? on p. 186). Are we rushing children into reading and academic enterprises that they are not ready for? This is a difficult question to answer. Others argue that problem solving, motivation, interest in learning, and social competence are not emphasized enough.

Controversial Issues: How Early Should a Child Start School?

Will children in the future attend a preschool completely paid for by the government? Will the child in the year 2000 be compelled to begin school at an early age? These questions are now being asked by many who see the extension of the public school system to the preschool years.

If research shows that preschool experiences may enrich a child's cognitive and social growth, why not require all preschoolers to attend school? The movement to open public schools to 4-year-olds is gaining strength (Hymes, 1987) for many reasons. The increased number of children whose parents are employed and who must attend day care, the increased popularity of nursery schools, and the fact that special groups of children attending preschool programs gain from such programs have all lent weight to the arguments for beginning public education at a younger age than children do today.

There are problems, though. The data on middle-class, preschool-age children are mixed, with some studies showing preschool benefits for middle-class children and other studies showing no differences. The greater benefits are found for lower income children (Kagan, 1985). In addition, funding a universal public school program for 4-year-olds will be very expensive. Most important, there are possible dangers, especially of pushing children to read and write before they are ready and overselling the public on what 4-year-olds can be taught. These dangers are well brought out in David Elkind's 1987 book *Miseducation.* No educator or psychologist is opposed to teaching children to read or write when the children are ready. However, "only between one percent and three percent of the children are reading with comprehension before entering kindergarten and the majority of children do not show interest in how to read until ages 5 or 6" (Elkind, 1987, p. 185). We are miseducating our children if we push youngsters into academic situations for which they are not ready. Too often, educational programs designed for school-age children are being written down to the level of 4-year-olds. Elkind believes that we place these young children at a risk for short-term stress and long-term personality damage and that these programs do not serve any useful purpose or have any lasting benefits. Some of these programs pay little attention to individual differences in development and learning styles. Similar questions are being asked about the kindergarten curricula as well (Egertson, 1987).

The question of universal education for preschool children is controversial. Elkind reminds us that any such program must be developmentally related to the child's needs and abilities, and he encourages us to question the appropriateness of academic training for young children. Others argue that appropriate education can be offered to preschoolers and that the public schools ought to get involved. The controversy is an ongoing one, with no clear answer in sight.

Overall, we can conclude that high-quality, developmentally appropriate preschool experiences do not injure the child or cause later academic problems. The evidence shows that such experiences may even help children, especially those from lower socioeconomic backgrounds. Yet the public should not be oversold on what such programs can accomplish. Such programs may also constitute a danger if too much pressure is placed on young children to develop academic skills before they are ready. As the push for earlier schooling gains ground, we will be forced to make decisions. Should these programs focus on academic or on social skills? Should participation be voluntary or required? These questions need to be debated and answered using research results from relevant studies and a thorough analysis of what is in the best interests of young children.

This issue haunts every kindergarten program as well as many nursery school programs. Should we emphasize academic skills or more social-motivational ones? One expert, Bettye Caldwell (1989), argues that it is not an either-or situation. Preschools and kindergarten must provide a blend of education and care, which Caldwell labels "educare." They must offer a "developmentally appropriate mixture of education and care, of stimulation and nurture, of work and play" (Caldwell, 1989, p. 266).

Two Dangers

Cognitive development during the preschool period is certainly impressive. Piaget described the preschooler's abilities and limitations, and new research shows just how sensitive young children are to task type and the environment in which the task is performed. We now also have a better understanding of how important it is for children to be ready for the formal school experience and of the part the home, television, and preschool programs can play in fostering a child's cognitive development.

Yet in the midst of the tremendous interest in preschool education and cognitive development, two cautions are necessary. First, there is a real danger of overemphasizing early cognitive education, making parents quasi-teachers who grimly and joylessly drum facts and skills into children's heads (Zinsser, 1981). Second, there is a danger that social and personality development will be submerged in the rush to "school" our children. Social and personality development are just as important, and people sometimes forget that children learn much through interacting with other people and during play. It is to the preschooler's development in these areas that we turn next.

Summary

1. During the preschool years, the rate of growth declines. Preschoolers develop a number of motor skills, including jumping, running, and hopping. The development of the large muscles precedes that of the fine muscles.
2. The leading cause of death among preschoolers is accidents, many of which can be prevented.
3. Although death from disease is rare in Western countries, many preventable diseases as well as malnutrition claim many lives in the developing countries. There has been great progress in reducing the death rate, improving inoculation rates and water quality, and providing medical care. New, inexpensive treatments are now available. The challenge is not only to provide medical treatment and food but also to provide information and to change attitudes.
4. According to Piagetian theory children between about ages 2 and 7 are in the preoperational stage. These children can now use symbols and have the capacity to view an action, remember it, and repeat it later.
5. Children in the preoperational stage tend to be egocentric (see everything from their own point of view), sometimes believe inanimate objects possess animate qualities, and reason transductively (from specific event to specific event). Preschoolers have difficulty placing things in size order (seriation) and, at least at the beginning of this stage, have problems sorting items into different classes (classification).
6. Preschoolers cannot solve conservation problems (challenges that involve the understanding that quantities remain the same even if their appearance changes). Their tendency to center on one dimension and their inability to reverse operations are responsible for their problems in this area.
7. New evidence shows that many of these abilities are present if preschoolers are tested on tasks that are meaningful to them, and clearly defined. However, these abilities are fragile, and preschoolers will not show these skills all the time.
8. The attention span of preschoolers is superior to that of toddlers, but it is still not as long as it will be in middle childhood. Children are attracted by many aspects of the situation, such as movement, color, and loud noise. As children grow up, their ability to voluntarily focus their attention in a planned, organized manner increases. This ability is not well developed in the preschooler.
9. Preschoolers do not spontaneously use verbal strategies, such as rehearsal, but they do show such strategies as looking and pointing. Children do better in familiar situations and with tasks that are meaningful to them.
10. The child's knowledge base affects memory and performance on a number of tasks. Both children and adults possess a number of scripts or structures describing the sequence of events in a particular situation. These form the basis for understanding events.
11. Parents who label the environment, encourage their children's curiosity, and read to them tend to maximize their children's cognitive development.
12. *Barney and Friends, Sesame Street,* and *Mister Rogers' Neighborhood* are successful children's television shows that combine entertainment with instruction.
13. More and more preschoolers are attending early childhood education programs. These programs differ from one another in philosophy and methods of teaching. The evidence generally shows that children who attend preschools gain from the experience.
14. Project Head Start is an attempt to help close the gap between children from lower socioeconomic backgrounds and their peers from middle-class backgrounds. While the immediate gains in intelligence are not sustained throughout elementary school, children who attend these programs are less likely to be held back or be found in special education classes, and more likely to graduate. Some studies show that they also do better in mathematics and reading.
15. The Perry Preschool Project is an experimental program that successfully improved achievement and led to a reduction in delinquency.
16. A number of changes have been made in the kindergarten curriculum. Full-day kindergartens have become more popular, more screening and readiness tests are being used, and the curriculum has become more academically oriented. All these changes are very controversial, with some authorities claiming that the emphasis on academics at this age is inappropriate.

Multiple-Choice Questions

1. Which statement about the growth and physical abilities of preschoolers is *correct?*
   a. The rate of growth declines during the preschool years.
   b. Boys generally have more muscle during the preschool years.
   c. Large muscles are better developed than fine muscles.
   d. All of these are correct.
2. The leading cause of death during the preschool years in the United States is:
   a. cancer.
   b. AIDS.
   c. accidents.
   d. malnutrition and undernutrition.

3. The most important factor determining what a preschooler eats is:
   a. parental reinforcement.
   b. the child's food preference.
   c. the specific need for a particular vitamin that a certain food may contain.
   d. peer influence.
4. Three-year-old Cindy rejects new foods and her parents do not know what to do. Which of the following is the best course of action?
   a. Cindy has a problem with self-starvation and requires immediate medical attention.
   b. Cindy's behavior is unusual but parents should accept it and not try to offer any new foods.
   c. Cindy's behavior is common and parents should offer the food again on another occasion.
   d. Cindy's behavior shows a defiance of the parents' and if allowed to continue will lead to defiance in other areas as well.
5. The most common cause of death for young children in the entire world is:
   a. diarrhea.
   b. respiratory disease.
   c. cancer.
   d. AIDS.
6. Which of the following statements about the abilities of young children as they enter the preoperational stage is correct?
   a. children show deferred imitation and the ability to understand symbols.
   b. children can conserve and seriate.
   c. children can use deductive logic and solve class inclusion problems.
   d. children can classify and seriate.
7. A child reasons that since it is still light outside it isn't bedtime yet, but once it becomes dark he should go to bed. This is an example of:
   a. inductive reasoning.
   b. deductive reasoning.
   c. incidental reasoning.
   d. transductive reasoning.
8. A 4-year-old is shown a bouquet containing five roses and three tulips and asked whether there are more roses or more flowers. The child will probably say:
   a. more flowers.
   b. more roses.
   c. more tulips, even though it wasn't mentioned.
   d. he or she can't count that high.
9. Two 5-year-olds are arguing over who has the most juice. They actually have the same amount but because one is drinking from a 6-ounce cup and the other from a 6-ounce glass, the amounts look different to them. They are arguing because they do not yet understand:
   a. transitivity.
   b. class inclusion problems.
   c. conservation.
   d. seriation.
10. Young children can concentrate on only one dimension at a time when comparing things. This is called:
    a. egocentrism.
    b. transitivity.
    c. transferability.
    d. centering.
11. A preschooler believes that all children have brothers because he has a brother. This is an example of:
    a. irreversibility.
    b. centering.
    c. egocentrism.
    d. artificialism.
12. A child asks his mother whether her sewing up the seams of his favorite stuffed animal will hurt it. This is an example of:
    a. animism.
    b. egocentrism.
    c. artificialism.
    d. classification.
13. Studies showing that young children sometimes seriate, solve class inclusion problems, and conserve show that:
    a. Piaget was essentially incorrect about the nature of preschoolers' thought.
    b. children can solve any problem at any level of development if they understand the problem.
    c. children are very sensitive to the nature of the task demands.
    d. these skills can be easily taught to children who then can transfer them to other similar problems.
14. Which statement about information processing is *correct?*
    a. Preschoolers don't use such verbal memory strategies as rehearsal on their own.
    b. Young children forget things faster than older children.
    c. Interest is an important factor in the memory of young children.
    d. All of the above are correct.
15. Three-year-old Tanisha can tell you what happens and the order of activities in her nursery school class. Psychologists call this a:
    a. script.
    b. formality.
    c. belief.
    d. void.
16. Preschoolers spend more time in which activity than any other except sleep?
    a. playing with parents.
    b. eating.
    c. watching television.
    d. drawing.
17. A criticism of *Sesame Street* is that it:
    a. does not emphasize the meaning of reading in daily life.
    b. it is too slow and children become restless watching it.

c. does not emphasize cognitive concerns.
d. is designed for older children but watched by younger children.

18. Long-term studies of Head Start show all of the following *except:*
a. improvements in graduation rate.
b. Head Start graduates are less likely to need special education services.
c. Head Start graduates are less likely to be left back.
d. lasting improvements in intelligence scores.

19. An experimental preschool program that led to impressive long-term gains is called the:
a. Perry Project.
b. McDonald's Program.
c. Northern Program.
d. Indiana Project.

20. The most controversial change in kindergarten is the:
a. increased involvement of parents in the educational process.
b. emphasis on academic work.
c. emphasis on social skills.
d. change from female to male teachers.

Answers to Multiple-Choice Questions

1. d 2. c 3. b 4. c 5. a 6. a 7. d 8. b 9. c
10. d 11. c 12. a 13. c 14. d 15. a 16. c 17. a
18. d 19. a 20. b

Chapter 9

The Social and Personality Development of Preschoolers

Chapter Outline

The Land of Make-Believe
I Like Me: Self-Concept in the Preschool Years
The Mysteries of Play
The Rise of the Peer Group
The Sibling Experience
Parents and Preschoolers
Child Abuse
Controversial Issues: To Spank or Not to Spank?
Gender-Role Acquisition
Ready for New Challenges

Are the Following Statements True or False?

1. Five-year-olds do not understand the difference between play and work.
2. Psychologists do not believe there are any consistent gender differences in play.
3. Rough-and-tumble play is actually a form of aggression.
4. The qualification for being a friend in early childhood is being a playmate.
5. The most common conflicts among preschoolers are over possessions.
6. Siblings are more likely to fight than to play with each other.
7. Children whose parents allow them maximum freedom with few, if any, restrictions are usually self-reliant and show excellent self-control.
8. Reports of child abuse have increased substantially over the past 10 years.
9. The overwhelming majority of abused children grow up to abuse their own children.
10. Research has failed to establish any consistent gender differences in behavior or cognitive abilities.

Answers to True-False Statements 1. False: see p. 192 2. False: see p. 193 3. False: see p. 193 4. True 5. True 6. False: see p. 197 7. False: see p. 199 8. True 9. False: see p. 207 10. False: see p. 208

The Land of Make-Believe

"Let's play Barbie dolls," Annie said to her reluctant babysitter as she dumped her dolls onto the carpet. She proceeded to set the scene, telling her sitter exactly what she expected her to do. This time Barbie was captured by a witch who put her in jail. The time before, she was the mommy and the sitter played the part of the children. During that domestic scene, the children were told that their parents were going out, and although they wanted to come along, they couldn't because it would be too late. After telling them a story, Annie put the children to bed.

Preschoolers are very different from toddlers. Preschoolers interact with a wider variety of people, and have a good idea of what they want and what they don't want. Their interactions with their parents are more verbal because they can both express themselves better and understand others with greater ease. Their expanding world offers new challenges in getting along with others as they seek satisfying interpersonal relationships outside the family. At the same time, they become more aware of their environment and begin to develop some idea of how boys and girls act in their society, which forms the basis for their later understanding of gender roles.

A Sense of Initiative

Preschoolers are able to plan, and they enjoy being on the move and taking the initiative (Erikson, 1963). Erikson considers **initiative** the positive outcome of this preschool stage and the negative outcome is **guilt.** If parents appreciate the importance of encouraging a preschooler's plans and curiosity, the child will leave the stage with a sense of initiative. The preschooler is an active experimenter, who tends more to begin than to finish things. Preschoolers have many ideas: let's bake a cake, go to the movies, eat at McDonalds. If a child's curiosity bothers the parents and the parents react with verbal scorn and restrictions, the child is likely to become timid and fearful.

I Like Me: Self-Concept in the Preschool Years

One morning, Annie was playing outside in her yard by herself. An adult neighbor watched the preschooler for a while as the girl played a pretend game. After a while, the adult opened the window and asked Annie where her parents were. "Oh, they are inside having breakfast." "Where is your brother?" asked the neighbor. "He is reading in his room," Annie replied. "But aren't you lonely?" asked the neighbor. The little girl looked up, smiled, and said, "No, I like me."

Psychologists have for many years been interested in the child's emerging self- concept. The *self-concept* is the picture people have of themselves. Children are not born with a self-concept; it develops as children mature. By the time children are 3 years old, they have differentiated themselves from the outside world and understand that they are distinct, unique individuals.

In early childhood, the self-concept is based on external factors, such as physical characteristics (Burns, 1979); possessions (Damon & Hart, 1982); and activities, such as baseball. When preschoolers were asked to respond to such statements as, "I am a boy/girl who . . .," more than half of all the responses referred to a particular action (Keller, Ford, & Meacham, 1978). Self-descriptions focus on what is visible and tangible (Damon & Hart, 1988). The preschooler describes concrete observable behaviors and specific examples but tends not to generalize. A girl who

initiative The positive outcome of the psychosocial crisis of the preschool period, involving development of a respect for one's own wishes and desires.

guilt The negative outcome of the psychosocial crisis of the preschool period, resulting in a sense that the child's acts and desires are bad.

likes basketball and baseball will not say she likes sports; a boy who likes cats and dogs will not say he likes animals. It is not until middle childhood that personality characteristics take center stage and personal comparisons with others, such as "I am taller," become common.

Preschoolers do show the beginnings of a psychological sense of who they are (Eder, 1989). Preschoolers can describe inner states and emotions. They sometimes make statements such as "I don't feel good with grownups," or "I usually play with friends." The self-concept is cumulative; what is formed in early childhood can be modified if there is some major change in the child's life. The child's experiences form the basis for later generalizations. Other people help to define the nature of this self-concept both by the way they treat the child, for example, not letting a little girl get dirty but allowing a little boy to do so, or by evaluating some behavior or desire, such as by telling children that they are good (or bad) at drawing (Durkin, 1995). Preschoolers who are told that their socially acceptable initiatives are good are likely to evaluate themselves in such terms. Such early experiences can directly affect behavior. There is a significant correlation between self-concept and cooperative behavior; that is, preschoolers who have a positive sense of themselves are more likely to show cooperation and other helping behaviors (Cauley & Tyler, 1978).

The Mysteries of Play

Play is such a natural part of childhood that we tend not to think very much about it. **Play** is an activity that is performed for sheer enjoyment with no ulterior motive. The focus of play is on the child rather than on what the child is holding, bouncing, or coloring. Play activities are performed for their own sake (Vandenberg, 1978), with no payoff or reward involved (Fogel, Nwokah, & Karns, 1993).

Even young children are certain about the differences between play and work. Kindergarteners believe that work is what they *have* to do and play is what they *want* to do (Wing, 1995). Play is freely chosen and self-directed whereas work is obligatory and controlled by others. Work is about what some adult, such as a teacher, wants and play is about what the child wants. If they have to finish an activity it is work; if they are allowed to switch to others it is play. Children see "work" as fun to some extent but play is *always* fun. Later, children become even more sophisticated, labeling some activities as a "little work" or a "little play." Work, then, to young children does not always mean drudgery.

> ***True or False?***
> Five-year-olds do not understand the difference between play and work.

play An activity dominated by the child and performed with a positive feeling.

The Development of Play

Children of different ages play in characteristically different ways. A baby is uninvolved with other children, and anything that occurs may hold an infant's interest for only a few seconds. Such **unoccupied behavior** is the first stage of play. Later in the first year children play with simple toys, banging them against something or dropping them. They are basically exploring the properties of the toy and are still uninvolved with any other children around them. They may play simple peekaboo games with a parent, but the other individual is essentially a toy, and no mutuality is evidenced.

Solitary play or independent play can be seen in young children and remains important in the second and third years of life. However, the transition to a more social type of play can be seen in **onlooker play** (Parten, 1932). During this stage children watch others with considerable interest and frequently ask questions about what others are doing. However, they are not yet able to join in and remain on the outside. This leads to a type of play in which children may seek out the company of others but still do not interact with them.

After the second year children are often brought together with their peers. These 2-year-olds engage in **parallel play.** They play in the presence of other children, but not with them. They do not really interact or cooperate with one another. We get the feeling that if one child were to leave, the other child could go on alone without any problem. The quality of the sand castles built by either child does not depend on the participation of the other. Parallel play is found throughout the preschool period, but it decreases with age. It is the primary play behavior of 2-year-olds and of some 3-year-olds (Smith, 1978).

Active interaction with others emerges during early childhood. Annie can both play by herself, with her parents and sitter, and with children her own age. Preschoolers actively associate with other children (this is called **associative play**) and may share, cooperate, argue, and play together, but few of these periods are sustained. There is a flightiness to preschoolers' play and interactions with others. Much of their play involves physical practice of skills that have been or are being mastered. Preschoolers' play is often physically exhausting.

Beginning in the later part of the preschool period and continuing into middle childhood, children actively in-

unoccupied behavior A type of play in which children sit and look at others or perform simple movements that are not goal related.

solitary play Independent play in which the child plays by himself or herself.

onlooker play A type of play in which the child watches others play and shows some interest but is unable to join in.

parallel play A type of play common in 2-year-olds in which children play in the presence of other children but not with them.

associative play A type of play seen in preschoolers in which they are actively involved with one another but cannot sustain these interactions.

dulge in **cooperative play** with one another. This involves a more or less unified group of children playing a particular game, often in which one or two children lead. Children are able to take specific parts in a game and have a more mature understanding of what their role is in the group. There are often distinct rules to the game. Some children act as leaders and allot roles to others. Sometimes rebellions break out in the ranks, but children's need for one another is obvious. As children develop, the amount of their social play increases, as does their ability to sustain their attention during play, which allows for longer interactions (Huff & Lawson, 1990). Even though children play more with others as they age, they still play by themselves quite a bit.

Questions Students Often Ask

I pass playgrounds with no one playing in them. My own children seem to be hypnotized by the television. Are children playing less than years ago?

There are some authorities who believe that children are playing less than they did years ago and in a less social manner. When Parten's earlier work on the types of play was replicated, Barnes (1971) found that children were playing in a less social manner than they did 30 years earlier. Perhaps the amount of television viewing, parents' understandable fears about children's safety, an increased emphasis on schooling, and video and computer games may partially explain this. There is also more emphasis on adult-led, adult-supervised play than in years past.

Pretend Play

Pretend or **dramatic play** involves taking on the roles of others, and requires the ability to imitate and to put oneself in another's place. The latter ability is primitive in young preschoolers and develops slowly as children find themselves in different social situations. Most dramatic play centers on common home situations and everyday challenges. However, some involves participation in fantasy, including children's protecting others from monsters and putting themselves in fairy tales as specific characters. This was seen in Annie's play with her sitter. In imaginary play, objects can take on new functions and identities, and new roles are spontaneously adopted as a scenario unfolds (de Lorimier, Doyle, & Tessier, 1995). This dramatic play is spontaneous and flexible, and its sophistication increases with age. Children who engage in a great deal of such play are better at perspective taking, role taking, and are more socially competent. Some evidence indicates that training children in pretend play skills leads to improvements in these skills (Lillard, 1993).

Pretend play can start as early as toddlerhood, when a child begins to use symbols (Piaget, 1962). Dramatic play declines as children enter middle childhood but does not disappear (Johnson & Yawkey, 1988). Gender differences are common. Boys more often refer to buildings and repair vehicles and girls prepare meals or care for babies (Wall, Pickert, & Bigson, 1989). Children sometimes try to work through their concerns and problems in their play (de Lorimier et al., 1995). Since children sometimes use pretend play to cope with their problems, to master situations, or to explore the roles of those around them, it is a very developmentally important phenomenon.

True or False?

Psychologists do not believe there are any consistent gender differences in play.

Rough-and-Tumble Play

One type of play that adults observe often with some displeasure is **rough-and-tumble play.** Such behaviors as play fighting, chasing, wrestling, sneaking up on someone, carrying another child, holding, and pushing can fall into this category (Humphreys & Smith, 1987). Adults often discourage rough-and-tumble play because they are afraid someone will get hurt, that it will escalate into real fighting, or because they believe that it will teach antisocial or aggressive behavior (Pellegrini & Perlmutter, 1989).

The chances of someone being injured by accident are greater in rough-and-tumble play than if children are busy drawing pictures, but rough-and-tumble play should not be confused with aggression (Pellegrini, 1995). Rough-and-tumble play takes place when no dispute is occurring, whereas aggressive behavior often occurs in the course of disputes, especially those involving property. In rough-and-tumble play, children take turns playing roles, whereas in aggression this is not the case. When rough-and-tumble play ends, children do not separate, nor do they have angry feelings towards one another; the opposite pattern is found in aggressive behavior (Humphreys & Smith, 1987).

True or False?

Rough-and-tumble play is actually a form of aggression.

Recently psychologists have asked for greater tolerance of rough-and-tumble play. Besides providing the obvious practice of physical skills, such play, some claim, can lead to cooperative games. If you ever played tag, you might remember that the game was governed by rules and involved changing roles from being chased to being the chaser. Rough-and-tumble play is also related to children's social problem-solving and negotiation skills, and popularity with peers (Humphreys & Smith, 1987). Rough-and-tumble play is related to social competence, whereas

cooperative play A type of play seen in the later part of the preschool period and continuing into middle childhood, marked by group play, specific roles, and active cooperation for sustained periods of time.

pretend play (dramatic play) A type of play in which children take on the roles of others.

rough-and-tumble play Physical play such as play fighting, chasing, and wrestling.

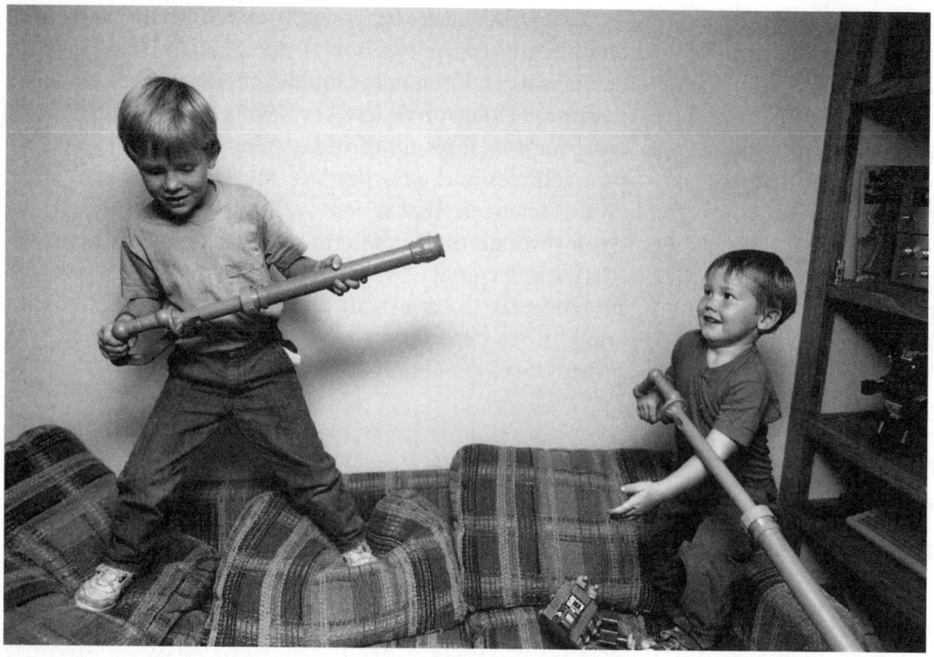

Parents discourage rough-and-tumble play because it is noisy and can escalate to real fighting, but rough-and-tumble play has some developmental benefits.

aggression is not (Pellegrini, 1995; 1987). Children (mostly boys) who engage in rough-and-tumble play are liked and are good problem solvers, whereas the opposite is true of children who engage in aggressive behavior.

Does rough-and-tumble play with friends usually turn into the real thing, requiring adult intervention? Studies show that both popular and unpopular children engage in a similar amount of rough-and-tumble play (Coie & Kupersmidt, 1983). However, when popular children engage in this sort of play, it does not escalate into aggression, whereas such play by unpopular or rejected children often does (Pellegrini, 1988). Unpopular children may not have the social skills to understand the limits of rough-and-tumble play. Also, unpopular, aggressive children may interpret rough-and-tumble play as a provocation, thereby eliciting aggressive responses from them (Dodge & Frame, 1982).

Gender Differences in Play

Gender differences in play, as shown in pretend play, start early. Boys are more aggressive and engage in more rough-and-tumble play. These differences appear in cultures around the world, whether the culture is essentially tribal or technologically advanced (Whiting & Whiting, 1975).

When same-gender groups of 4½-year-old children were brought three at a time into a mobile home from which the furnishings had been removed and some toys provided, boys and girls played differently. The girls organized themselves and made rules (DiPietro, 1981). They argued, but they did not resort to physical means of persuasion. The boys played more roughly, often wrestling. They did not seem angry, nor did they attempt to injure one another; they simply played differently from the girls.

Although some may argue that males are biologically predisposed to such behavior, other explanations are possible. Since various societies expect males to act more aggressively, males may simply be complying with society's expectations. The possible presence of some biological predisposition does not negate the importance of learning.

The Benefits of Play

People tend to overlook the contributions play makes to a child's development. The physical benefits of play are the most obvious. Children tossing a ball around are exercising their muscles and improving their eye-hand coordination. As they play, children refine their skills and become more self-secure and assured (Isenberg & Quisenberry, 1988).

In the psychosocial realm, play provides practice in social skills. It allows children to handle social situations involving dominance, conflict, and cooperation and teaches them to share power, space, and ideas (Hamburg, 1994; Rubin & Howe, 1986). Children can explore new ways of handling conflicts as they suspend reality, switch roles, and control a situation (Johnson & Yawkey, 1988). Role playing encourages children to become less egocentric and provides children with practice in role taking (Saltz & Johnson, 1974). Play also allows children to express their feelings and work through conflicts, regulating their aggressive behavior (Hamburg, 1994; Kramer, 1996). Pretend play helps children develop a variety of social and group skills. The frequency with which children engage in social pretend play is positively related to teacher ratings of social competence, peer popularity, and social role-taking ability (Connolly & Doyle, 1984).

In the cognitive realm, play encourages children to improve their planning and problem-solving abilities. During pretend play children figure out the scripts of various situations. Play promotes creativity and flexibility because it allows children to experiment without fear of the consequences (Johnson & Yawkey, 1988).

Play is an important developmental activity. Many of the preschooler's interpersonal interactions occur in the context of play and during the preschool years the child's interpersonal relationships with peers, siblings, and parents change dramatically.

The Rise of the Peer Group

As children negotiate the preschool stage, the number of children they play with at one time increases. Preschoolers are no longer limited to one-on-one situations. Groups of three or four children are not uncommon, with boys' playgroups being larger than girls' (Benenson, 1993; Fabes et al., 1996).

Children's social interactions are affected and limited by their cognitive abilities. The preschooler's world is more complicated than the toddler's world, and preschoolers must acquire knowledge that allows them to behave appropriately in different situations. For example, a preschooler may not be required to share toys much at home, but sharing may be necessary in the day care or nursery school setting (Small, 1990). Children can be only as social as their cognitive functioning will allow (Bjorklund, 1995). A child who cannot take the perspective of another may not voluntarily choose to help another child who needs help, whereas a child who can see things from someone else's perspective may choose to share or simply help the child with a problem. As their cognitive skills improve, so does their ability to interact in more complex ways with others and to better resolve their conflicts. Psychologists are very interested in the relationship between cognitive development and social behavior, termed **social cognition.** Some of the areas of prime interest right now are interpersonal relationships, aggression, prosocial behavior, turn taking, and moral development.

Most preschoolers' interactions with others, especially with their peers, are positive (Hartup, 1970). Preschoolers clearly prefer some children over others. They play with certain children quite often, with others once in a while, and completely ignore others (Hartup, 1989). The child's individual behaviors determine whether they are accepted or rejected (Ramsey, 1995). Children who are aggressive and unfriendly are rejected, whereas children who share, reward other children, and have good communication skills are more accepted. You can see the beginnings of friendship as preschoolers react more positively and are more responsive to friends than to other children. Preschoolers do play with children whom they do not consider friends, and they often use a temporary friendship status as a way to obtain entry into a group. While some friendships are maintained over the year, most children make new friends and separate from old friends (Howes, 1988).

The qualification for friendship among preschoolers is simply being physically present and willing to play (Rubin, 1980). For the preschooler, a friend is a playmate, and friendships are not based upon any real intimacy. The goal of young children's friendship and peer interaction generally is play (Gottman & Mettetal, 1986), and the great concern of friendship is maximizing the level of enjoyment (Parker & Gottman, 1989). Young children describe a friend as someone who is rewarding to be with, whereas older children describe friends in terms of empathy and understanding (Bigelow & LaGaipa, 1975). Preschoolers with superior social skills form friendships more easily than preschoolers with fewer skills (Hazen & Black, 1989). As children interact with others, they become more selective in their playmates (Ladd & Price, 1993; Ramsey, 1995). Preschoolers take on different roles with different playmates, being more dominant in one relationship than another (Ross & Lollis, 1989). When playing with the same child over a long period of time, for instance a year, they show moderate stability in their behavior—that is, the level of sharing and imitation stays relatively stable within that relationship (Park, Lay, & Ramsay, 1993).

True or False?
The qualification for being a friend in early childhood is being a playmate.

One tendency that begins in early childhood and that will become commonplace in middle childhood is having mostly same-sex friends (Powlishta, 1995; Diamond, LeFeurgy, & Blass, 1993). Such findings are found across many cultures (Whiting & Edwards, 1988). About a third of all best friendships cut across gender among 3- and 4-year-olds, but that drops to less than a quarter among 5- and 6-year-olds and becomes practically nonexistent for 7- and 8-year-olds (Rickelman, 1986).

There are many possible reasons for this change. Perhaps children see children of their own gender as more compatible in their play style. That is, boys may be aware that other boys will permit rough-and-tumble play (Alexander & Hines, 1994). Perhaps adults reinforce children for playing with other children of the same gender. The development of gender role stereotypes, such as the belief that girls don't play with certain kinds of toys, may also be a factor (Gottman, 1986). For whatever reason, as children get older they play more with children of their own gender and less with children of the other gender.

Prosocial Behavior

If you observe preschoolers at play, you will notice that sometimes they share and help, while at other times they flatly refuse to do so. Behaviors such as sharing, helping others in need, and comforting others are called **prosocial behaviors** (Eisenberg et al., 1996). A specific type of prosocial behavior, called **altruism,** involves actions that help others, that are internally motivated, and for which no reward is expected. Generally, older children show more prosocial behavior than younger children.

Preschoolers infrequently share with, help, and comfort others (Eisenberg-Berg & Hand, 1979). They are much more likely to agree to help when asked to do so by adults than when their peers make the request (Eisenberg et al., 1985). When they carry out a request from adults,

social cognition The relationship between cognition and knowledge about and behavior regarding social situations and relationships.

prosocial behaviors Actions that are intended to help or benefit another individual or group.

altruism A type of prosocial behavior that involves actions that help people, that are internally motivated, and for which no reward is expected.

they usually are doing so in obedience to an authority figure. Although peers make more requests for help, compliance with adults is much more common. Altruistic behavior is rare, and relatively few helping behaviors are self-initiated. Yet, most preschoolers perform such self-initiated behavior at some time or another; thus, preschoolers are indeed capable of self-initiated helping behavior but do not offer it very often (Stockdale, Hegland, & Chiaromonte, 1989).

Some preschoolers respond with comforting to their peers' distress much more than others. Children with easy temperaments, those who have a great deal of peer contact, and those who are friendly with the child in distress are more likely to help (Farver & Branstetter, 1994). Children who attend a preschool in which prosocial behaviors are taught or actively promoted develop more cooperative skills. Children who show the most prosocial behavior have excellent social skills, are popular, and are able to delay gratification (Eisenberg et al., 1996; Fabes et al., 1994).

Prosocial behavior increases with age, perhaps because older children are more adept at taking the perspective of other children and can empathize more. This explains why even among preschoolers the ability to empathize and to take on others' roles is related to prosocial behavior (Roberts & Strayer, 1996). Older children are much more likely have these skills, being somewhat less egocentric, and to share when there is no reward or adult pressure to do so. When they do, they justify their behavior on altruistic grounds.

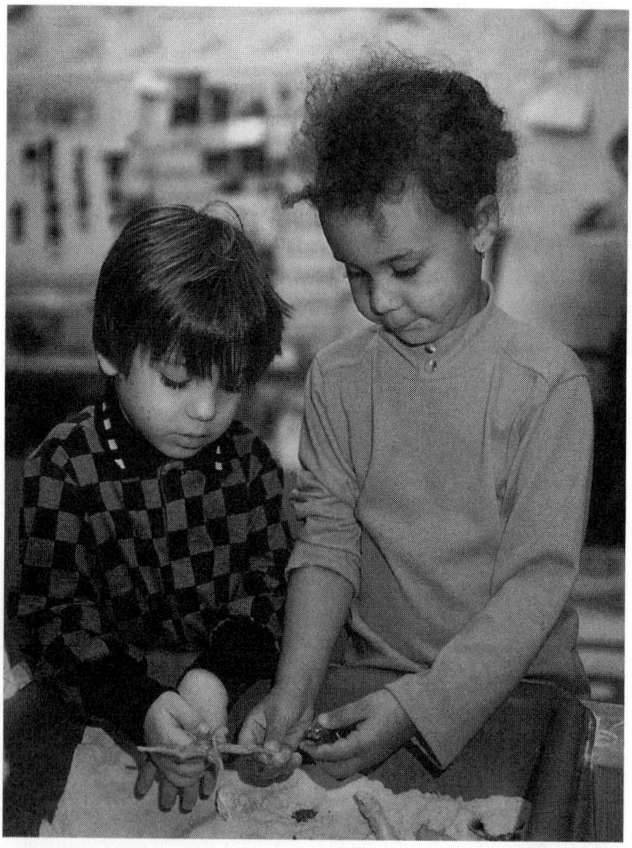

Although toddlers may share sometimes, preschoolers are frequently in situations that require sharing, such as being with a friend or in a nursery school setting. They are much more likely to share if directed to by an authority figure.

Conflict

Preschoolers engage in fewer arguments than one might think, and those that occur are relatively brief and end without parental interference. Conflicts are quickly resolved in mostly nonaggressive ways. The most common involve conflicts over possessions (Ross, 1996; Lauresen & Hartup, 1989). One child wants a toy that the other is playing with at the time. The second most common are conflicts over another child's actions or lack of action, as when a child refuses to take on a role assigned to him or her. The third category involves factual disputes, which are far less common than the other two types of conflict. By about 4½ or 5 years of age disputes in the first two categories occur at about equal rates (Shantz, 1987).

True or False?
The most common conflicts among preschoolers are over possessions.

The most common way of solving conflicts in this period is insistence (Eisenberg & Garvey, 1981). Conflicts are most likely to end when one child surrenders the toy to the other or keeps it by defending it. The second most common strategy is simply to explain why the child should give up the toy to someone else. Preschoolers communicate verbally in the course of the conflict, often explaining their actions and feelings (Vespo, Pedersen, & Hay, 1995). They also have some idea of property rights (Ross, 1996). Other strategies, such as suggesting alternatives and compromise, are not used very often, even though they are more likely to end the conflict. Most conflicts have one definite winner and one definite loser.

In about a quarter of the conflicts, verbal and/or physical aggression is used (Hay & Ross, 1982), but this percentage decreases with age. Aggression itself decreases with age. Aggression can be divided into two categories (Hartup, 1974). *Instrumental aggression* involves struggles over possessions. It is not personal, and its aim is to secure an item. *Hostile aggression,* on the other hand, is person oriented and is aimed at injuring the other party. Most young children act aggressively to wrench a toy from someone else or to gain space. The finding that aggression decreases with age probably stems from the striking decrease in instrumental aggression. As children mature, verbal alternatives replace physical means (Parke & Slaby, 1983).

However, aggression itself is a fairly stable individual characteristic, even in early childhood (Cummings, Iannotti, & Zahn-Waxler, 1989; Olweus, 1979). In other words, aggressive children in early childhood tend to become aggressive children in middle childhood even though the overall amount of aggression they show declines.

The Sibling Experience

By their first birthday, children spend almost as much time with their siblings as with their mothers and far more than with their fathers (Dunn, 1983). Discussions about siblings usually revolve around sibling rivalry, but siblings encourage prosocial actions and fill definite psychological needs. Not only do siblings play together and experience firsthand each other's joys and pains, but they also often help one another. Sometimes they provide each other with support and affection that may not be forthcoming from their parents (Dunn & Kendrick, 1982). Siblings often perform a teaching function, as younger children imitate their older siblings.

Sibling interaction is fairly predictable. Older children initiate more prosocial as well as combative behaviors, and younger children imitate more (Abramovitch et al., 1986; Vandell & Bailey, 1992). Brother-brother relationships involve the most conflict (Vespo et al., 1995; Stoneman & Brody, 1993). Older siblings clearly dominate younger ones. The distinctions lessen over time, but birth order rather than age is the cause of the domination. Although combative behaviors occur, prosocial and play-oriented behaviors constitute a majority of the interactions. People are wrong to think that sibling relationships are primarily combative or negative. Sibling relations often grow warmer with time; and in adulthood, siblings give each other great support in family crises. Sibling relationships are more likely to be pleasant when parents discuss with their older children how the younger child feels (Howe & Ross, 1990). In addition, more conflict and fewer friendly relationships are reported in families in which mothers are more responsive or affectionate to one child (Brody, Stoneman, & Burke, 1987). Therefore, the way parents act toward their children can influence sibling relations.

True or False?
Siblings are more likely to fight than to play with each other.

Questions Students Often Ask

Does birth order make a difference?

So much has been written about birth order that a simple answer to this question is really very difficult. There is no doubt that the experience of being the first born or last born is different. Many psychologists have tried to describe behaviors or characteristics that are more likely to be found in a first-born than in a second-born child. Birth order is only one of many factors that are important. For example, first born children tend to get more attention and are brought up strictest while later-born children, especially the youngest, are allowed to do things at an earlier age. The problem with birth order studies is that their findings are sometimes contradictory, and other factors such as ethnicity, gender, and socioeconomic status enter the picture. In some cultures being the oldest brings with it tremendous responsibility while in others it does not. In some cultures gender is more of a defining characteristic than birth order. Although birth order within a particular family may have some effect on the child's experiences and therefore the individual's development, it is difficult to make predictions based upon just this factor alone.

We all know families in which the children seem so different in personality, social skills, and physical abilities and wonder how this could be so. The answer is relatively simple. From an environmental viewpoint no two children really experience the same environment. They are born at different times, their parents may be more or less at ease with their roles, and may be in a different financial position. Male and female siblings may be treated differently.

From a genetic viewpoint, siblings (except for identical twins) have about half their genes in common. Half of their genes are not the same and this type of inheritance is called ***nonshared inheritance*** (Plomin & Daniels, 1987). Siblings are more similar to each other genetically than cousins or nonrelated people, but they also differ greatly from each other. When environmental and genetic factors interact, great differences in outcomes may be expected. People sometimes overestimate sibling similarity in both environment and genetics and underestimate the nonshared qualities of both.

The Only Child

Not all children have siblings. About 10% of all marriages result in the birth of one child. The so-called "only" child has been the victim of many generalizations, few of them flattering. Some people pity the only child because of a lack of siblings and others consider these children spoiled or selfish or even believe that the only child might be more likely have problems interacting with others (Falbo & Poston, 1993). Modern studies do not find the only child to be disadvantaged and find some definite advantages. A review of many studies found that only children have very positive relationships with their parents and that mothers of only children spend more time with them, engage in more conversation, and give them more information (Falbo & Polit, 1986; Polit & Falbo, 1987). The size of these differences is not large when only children are compared to those with one or two siblings but the differences become more distinct when only children are compared to children from larger families (Furman, 1996).

A great deal of research on the only child is conducted in China, where an ongoing national policy to encourage families to have only one child seeks to reduce the population growth. Young people are encouraged to marry later, the public is educated on methods of birth control, and economic incentives are used to encourage parents to have only one child (Yang et al., 1995). When this program was begun, there was some question as to how this emphasis on one child per family would affect the academic ability and personality of the children. The research evidence has been surprising. The results are clear that only children are more advanced in cognitive development (Yang et al., 1995) and show superior school achievement when compared to those with siblings (Wan, Fan, Lin, & Jing, 1994); this is found in Western studies as well.

Only children are somewhat less anxious, less fearful, and less likely to be depressed (Yang et al., 1995). Some authorities feared that these children would be little emperors, overindulged and spoiled. Although some studies show they are a bit more likely to be self-centered (Falbo & Poston, 1993), they are not spoiled. They are well adjusted and their social skills are similar to firstborns who have siblings (Falbo & Polit, 1986). The evidence shows that only children show superior cognitive and academic skills and that the differences in personality are neither great nor negative. Children do not seem to suffer from being the only child in the family.

Parents and Preschoolers

Although preschoolers interact more with peers and siblings than they did in toddlerhood, parents continue to be the major influence. This relationship changes during the preschool stage. Preschoolers have a greater sense of independence and can do things on their own. Parents also expect their preschoolers to have some control of their basic actions, especially aggressive responses (Mills & Rubin, 1990). Parents use stricter discipline when they are convinced the child can understand the rules and act appropriately (Dix, Ruble, & Zambarano, 1989). For example, what if a 2-year-old breaks a figurine that was sitting on the coffee table? A parent who does not believe that the child understood or is responsible for the behavior will react with disappointment, perhaps even annoyance, yet with understanding. The parent who believes the child does understand is more likely to yell or punish. Most parents believe that preschoolers can control their actions, at least to some degree, so a sterner type of discipline is seen in these years than in the toddler years.

Parenting Styles

Parents differ in the ways they control their children's behavior. Parenting styles have been perceived in terms of two factors: responsiveness and demandingness (Baumrind, 1989). Responsiveness refers to parental warmth, consideration of the needs of the child, and using a reasoning approach to discipline. Demandingness refers to the extent to which parents set firm rules and expect good behavior from their children. Some parents exercise a great deal of direct control whereas others believe that fewer rules are better. Some parents are much more responsive than others. The effect of differing parenting styles was investigated by Diana Baumrind (1967, 1971, 1978, 1980) and further developed by other psychologists (Maccoby & Martin, 1983).

Authoritarian parents try to control their children's conduct by establishing rules and regulations. Obedience is greatly valued, and the threat of force is used to correct behavior. A parent's decisions cannot be questioned—the authoritarian parent's word is law. Authoritarian parents are very controlling but are less warm and responsive to their children.

Permissive parents make few demands on their children. They are nonpunishing, are open to communication, and do not attempt to shape the children's behavior. The children regulate their own activities. When necessary, permissive parents use reason rather than power to control their children. They emphasize self-regulation over conformity to rules (Fagot, 1995). Permissive parents are noncontrolling and nondemanding but can be relatively warm.

Authoritative parents encourage verbal give-and-take and explain the reasons behind family policies. Both autonomy and discipline are valued. Limits are set, but the child's individuality is taken into consideration. The parents are warm and do not see themselves as infallible (Baumrind, 1971).

Rejecting-neglecting parents are essentially not engaged with their children. They are neither responsive nor demanding. They do not monitor their children's activities and provide little or no structure. Some may actively reject their own children whereas others simply neglect their responsibilities.

As a group, the children of authoritative parents are the most self-reliant, self-controlled, explorative, and contented. They have higher levels of self-esteem and better impulse control (Paikoff & Brooks-Gunn, 1995). The children of permissive parents are not self-reliant or self-controlled nor do they explore the environment. The children of authoritarian parents are discontented, withdrawn, and distrustful. Children of neglectful and rejecting parents are perhaps the worst off of any of the other groups (Schaffer, 1996). Adolescents from such homes score the poorest on measures of adjustment and psychosocial competence and show psychological and behavioral dysfunction. They are consistently at risk for drug abuse and delinquency (Lamborn et al., 1991).

The children of authoritative parents seem to thrive. Authoritative parents combine firm control, encourage-

authoritarian parenting A style of parenting in which parents rigidly control their children's behavior by establishing rules while discouraging questioning.

permissive parenting A style of parenting marked by open communication and a lack of parental demand for good behavior.

authoritative parenting A style of parenting in which parents establish limits but allow open communication and some freedom for children to make their own decisions in certain areas.

rejecting-neglecting parenting A style of parenting in which parents are not involved in their children's lives, being neither demanding nor responsive.

Authoritarian parents tell their children what to do and allow no questioning.

ment of individuality, and open communication, producing children who are independent and competent. They are also warmer and more nurturant than authoritarian parents. Some permissive parents are warm; others are cool and detached with their children. Authoritative parents are certainly demanding, but they are also warm, rational, and receptive to the child. This combination of high demandingness and positive encouragement of the child's independent striving is best. Parental control does not interfere with independence as long as children are given an opportunity to develop their own abilities and make their own decisions, within limits. Yet the total parental control that authoritarian parents exercise produces children who are less competent, less contented, and suspicious. Warmth and discipline are the keys to producing independent, competent children.

True or False?
Children whose parents allow them maximum freedom with few, if any, restrictions are usually self-reliant and show excellent self-control.

Relating parenting style to outcome is not as easy as it seems. First, parents do not use a single style when dealing with their children's misbehavior. They often vary their discipline practices according to the nature of the particular misdeed. A combination of power assertion and reasoning is used in response to antisocial acts, such as lying and stealing, whereas reasoning alone is used in response to failures in showing concern for others (Grusec, Dix, & Mills, 1982). Second, as we shall shortly see, cultural differences complicate the relationship.

Discipline Style

A parent's attempts to control a child's behavior can be placed in one of two categories. **Power-assertive discipline** involves physical punishment, yelling, shouting, and forceful commands; **love-oriented discipline** involves praise, affection, reasoning, showing disappointment, and withdrawing love (Maccoby & Martin, 1983). Each parenting style uses discipline in a different way, resulting in different outcomes. Authoritarian parents rely on punishment, which gets them obedience in the short term and rebellion in the long term. Permissive parents rarely use any type of discipline, and this can result in a child who lacks direction and self-control. Authoritative parents use both approaches, depending on the situation, but they encourage independence by allowing children freedom within limits. Authoritative parents notice the change in a child's verbal and physical abilities and tailor the discipline to the child's emerging abilities. Authoritarian parents use power-assertive discipline; authoritative parents use both power-assertive and love-oriented discipline. Permissive parents use very little discipline, but when discipline is necessary, they use reasoning, a love-oriented approach.

These discipline styles interact with the emotional tone of the parent-child relationship. When restrictiveness occurs within a context of warmth and acceptance, it can lead to such positive outcomes as obedience and nonaggressiveness as well as less positive outcomes such as lack of assertiveness and lack of creativity. When it occurs in the presence of hostility, it leads to withdrawal and anxiety (Becker, 1964). In investigating techniques of discipline, both the type of approach (power-assertive or love-oriented) and the emotional tone of the relationship (warm or hostile) must be considered.

Disciplinary style may have a direct influence on a child's approach to resolving conflicts with peers. Mothers who rely on power-assertive discipline have children who are less accepted by peers. These children believe that aggression and intimidation, such as threatening to hit another child, are likely to lead to successful outcomes (Hart, Ladd, & Burleson, 1990).

Because their physical abilities are greater, preschoolers can get into more trouble than infants or toddlers.

power-assertive discipline A type of discipline relying on the use of power, such as physical punishment or forceful commands.

love-oriented discipline A type of discipline relying on the use of reasoning or love.

However, their ability to use language gives parents more options in dealing with their misbehavior. As children mature, they respond to a more rational approach. Preschoolers respond better to suggestions, while toddlers respond better to simple commands (McLaughlin, 1983). Parents who realize that their preschoolers' verbal abilities give them more options are likely to change their discipline strategy and use more complicated verbal techniques instead of mere commands.

When "Do It or Else" Doesn't Do It

It is not difficult to get young children to do what you want; parents are bigger, stronger, and have more power. A more important consideration is whether they internalize the lessons that parents want to teach and conduct themselves well when no authority figure is present. When children internalize parental teachings, they begin to accept their parents' values, such as "don't hit someone" and "share your toys," as their own belief and behavior system. Recently, two forms of compliance have been identified. In *situational compliance* the child will accede to parental demands but feels no internal obligation. In *committed compliance,* children embrace and endorse the lessons and internalize them (Kochanska, Aksan, & Koenig, 1995; Kochanska & Aksan, 1995).

A pattern of parental discipline based upon explanation and negotiation rather than the pure use of power increases committed compliance. Parental warmth, sensitivity, responsiveness, authoritative child-rearing, and more child-centered family management are variables that are related to the ability to regulate one's own behavior (Gralinski & Kopp, 1993). Toddlers who have warm relationships with their parents are more likely to become preschoolers who internalize parental teachings (Kochanska, Aksan, & Koenig, 1995). Authoritarian child-rearing emphasizing the unbridled use of power is linked to deficits in internalization (Kochanska & Aksan, 1995).

Some early internalization may be linked to imitation of parental behavior and parental reinforcement of good behavior, but after age 3 cognitive factors play an important role (Kochanska, 1994). At this age, internalization requires both the child's accurate perception of the parent's viewpoint and acceptance of it (Kochanska, 1994). The clarity of a parent's position and the child's ability to understand it are important factors. Acceptance or rejection depends upon the emotional climate of the home; warmth is related to more acceptance if the correction seems well intentioned, if it is seen as appropriate, and if the child is motivated to comply with it (Perry, 1994). Even preschoolers are aware of appropriate interventions (Killen, 1991). Internalization is fostered by teaching, by setting example, by social reinforcement of the correct behavior, and by arranging the environment so that the desirable behavior occurs naturally (inviting friends who usually share over to the house), along with child-centered discipline techniques.

The child's emotional reactions may encourage or discourage internalization. Children may react to a correction with fear or anger, which might hinder internalization, or empathy, which may promote it (Hoffman, 1994). Others argue that some power assertion and love withdrawal may be needed to get the child to pay attention to the message. Too little arousal and the child may ignore the parent; too much and the resultant fear and anxiety prevent acceptance (Grusec & Goodnow, 1994b). Appropriate arousal directs the child's attention to the consequences of the actions.

Subculture and Discipline

Child-rearing methods are directed towards producing people who can survive and thrive within a particular culture. In American and many other Western societies, autonomy and independence are valued; other countries place more emphasis on interdependence and being a part of a larger group. This can lead to different child-rearing strategies. For example, Mayan mothers strongly disapprove of the Western middle-class custom of allowing infants to sleep alone and they reacted to an explanation of such Western customs with shock, disapproval, and pity for the child, regarding it as something close to child neglect (Morelli et al., 1992). Mayan child-rearing methods are targeted towards establishing an enduring closeness with their children. North American mothers place a great deal of emphasis on stimulation compared to both Dutch and Japanese mothers (Corter & Fleming, 1995). Societies differ in the types of relationships parents wish to form with their children, the child-rearing strategies they use, as well as their attitudes toward parenting in general. The range of parenting strategies used around the world is impressive (Corter & Fleming, 1995; Holden, 1995).

Linking parenting style to outcome, as in Baumrind's work, makes intuitive sense. However, it may be more applicable to North American people of European ancestry than to other groups. Authoritative parenting that leads to academic achievement among European-American adolescents does not do so among Asian-American youths (Darling & Steinberg, 1993).

Chinese and other East Asian parents often rate very high on scales measuring authoritarianism and restrictiveness and low on authoritativeness (Chao, 1994). Among American middle-class children this is related to a lack of achievement, but Asian children do very well in school under this type of parenting (Dornbusch et al., 1987). Authoritarian parenting has a different meaning in these cultures. Our society equates strictness with parental hostility, mistrust, and aggression, but many Asian societies interpret a desire for obedience and strictness in terms of caring and involvement.

The Chinese term "chiao shun" means training or educating, and Asian parents often see their child-rearing strategies as educating or training children in the self-discipline necessary for academic and vocational success. This type of training requires a tremendous amount of devotion and sacrifice, especially on the part of the mother who provides a very nurturing environment in the early years, being consistently available and responsive. The elementary school child receives support as well as demands for achievement in school so as to meet societal and family expectations for success. The training takes place in the context of a supportive, highly involved, and physically close mother-child relationship. Parental care, concern, and involvement are synonymous with firm control of the child. This control and governance called "guan" has positive connotations. Table 9.1 shows some statements that Chinese parents are more likely to agree with than are American parents of European descent. What we might label authoritarianism is what traditional Chinese parents might label training, which goes well beyond the authoritarian concept.

Another problem in interpreting differences is that looking at a particular ethnic group does not take into consideration differences within the culture and the effects of acculturation (see p. 13). Not all Latinos or Asian Americans raise their children one way, and when people from different cultures settle in another country some changes take place. Chinese mothers from Taiwan are more restrictive than Chinese American mothers, and white American mothers are the least restrictive (Chiu, 1987). The experience of living in America resulted in some changes in traditional child-rearing practices.

Other factors besides culture may influence child-rearing strategies, the most important being education.

Table 9.1 **Chinese and European-American Statements**

IDEOLOGIES OF CHILD DEVELOPMENT AND LEARNING
Children are by nature born good.
*Parents must begin training child as soon as ready.
Children can improve in almost anything if they work hard.
*Mothers must train child to work very hard and be disciplined.
*Mothers teach child by pointing out good behavior in others.
The best way child learns how to behave is to be around adults.
*When child continues to disobey you, he or she deserves a spanking.
IDEOLOGIES OF THE MOTHER-CHILD RELATIONSHIP
*Mothers primarily express love by helping child succeed, especially in school.
A mother's sole interest is in taking care of her child.
*Children should be in the constant care of their mothers or family.
Mothers should do everything for child's education and make many sacrifices.
*Child should be allowed to sleep in mother's bed.
*Child should be able to be with mother and taken on errands and gatherings.

Note: *Starred statements indicate a significant difference between Chinese and European-American parents.
Source: Chao, 1994.

Educated parents are more likely to use reasoning and talking while less educated parents use more power-assertive strategies (Kamii & Radin, 1971).

What all this boils down to is the need to take an ecological viewpoint regarding parenting. To best understand parenting we must look at parental goals, the methods used to reach these goals, and the style of parenting adopted (Darling & Steinberg, 1993). As we look at some of the differences in child rearing among the four most prominent minority groups in American society, we will emphasize the characteristics that they value, the family structure, and the child-rearing practices used.

Child-Rearing in African American Homes

No minority group family has been subjected to more analysis as the African American family. African American families are characterized as having one of three structures. A large number of basically middle-class or working-class families that do not differ greatly in structure from majority families make up one group. Another group is poor African Americans with a stable family structure and a potential for economic and social mobility. The third is a group for families with unstable structures, composed of people with poor job skills and insufficient education.

Multigenerational family structures are somewhat more common in African American families than in the general public, with grandparents being more involved in child-rearing. Older children often help take care of their younger siblings and have after-school child care responsibilities. A strong work ethic can be found in these families. Adolescents often enter the work force before their white cohorts and help their family with their income.

Child-rearing practices also differ. Often, the emphasis is placed on people orientation, rather than on object orientation. For example, when African American children reach for an object or surface, their attention is often redirected to the person holding them. The interaction between mother and child tends to be a rhythmic volley of speak and respond. Many African American children are accustomed to a higher-energy, faster-paced home with a great deal of concurrent stimulation. Extended kinship networks involving cousins and other relatives are a source of strength. Traditional values stress interdependence, security, establishing a positive self-image, persevering in the face of adversity, and establishing a positive racial identity (McAdoo, 1991). Socializing children to deal with prejudice and racism is also common (McAdoo, 1991). Organized religion and spirituality are important community resources and sources of inspiration.

Child-rearing stresses obedience and respect for elders. African American parental disciplinary practices are somewhat stricter and parent focused (Baumrind, 1972), but such practices may be seen as necessary, especially in poor families from areas that are racked by violence (Kelley, Power, & Wimbush, 1992); such attitudes may be related to safety (Kelley, Sanchez-Huckles, & Walker, 1993).

The ecological view is especially important here. African Americans growing up in a ghetto use functional child-rearing strategies, even though they differ from middle-class techniques, and teach self-reliance, resourcefulness, the ability to manipulate situations, mistrust of people in authority, and the ability to ward off attack (Ogbu, 1981).

Child-Rearing in Latino Homes

Latinos come from many different countries but are united by a common language. Certain attitudes and family features are common to all Latino families but differences also occur. For example, mothers originally from the Dominican Republic are stricter than mothers from Puerto Rico (Wasserman et al., 1990).

Families emphasize sharing and cooperation rather than competition. Often the individualism and competition of American schools is in conflict with what the child is taught at home (Delgado-Gaitan & Trueba, 1985). A sense of family pride and loyalty is also nurtured. The orientation is usually to the present and a belief in destiny is instilled. A sense of individual dignity not based upon economic status is emphasized, which differs somewhat as the general society tends to value people based upon their economic or social positions (Garcia Coll et al., 1995).

The traditional role expectations demand that men be virile, somewhat aggressive, and protective of women, the well-known machismo attitude (Bigner, 1994). Machismo has often been criticized but it actually refers more to the man's responsibility to his family. Family loyalty often supercedes individual interests, and older children often have child care responsibilities. Multigenerational family structure used to be typical, but is somewhat less common today. The roles of mothers and fathers are often clearly defined, with fathers being more authoritarian and mothers being more involved in child-rearing. Traditional male and female role expectations have been somewhat relaxed with more joint parental decision making today (Garcia Coll et al., 1995).

Frequently, Latino mothers differentiate between the roles of mothers and teachers, emphasizing the maternal role. Latino families are warm and nurturant, showing some indulgence towards young children (Vega, 1990). The emphasis is placed on close mother-child relationships, interpersonal competence, the proper demeanor, and a sense of pride (Harwood, 1992). A child is expected to be calm, obedient, courteous, and respectful toward adults (Garcia Coll et al, 1995). Latino parents endorse stricter disciplinary standards than other parents as well. They place less emphasis on achievement and on reaching developmental milestones early. Many children do not get as much cognitive stimulation in their early years as white children do. Latino parents are more concerned with the child's physical well-being and behavior than with the development of cognitive skills.

Child-Rearing in Asian American Homes

Many Asian American children experience a very different child-rearing regimen compared to most other Americans. American parents foster self-reliance, assertiveness, and speaking one's own mind but Asian American children, especially those from the Pacific Rim countries, are taught to view their role within the society and the family in terms of obligations. Asian American children are taught to think of family first and to subjugate their own desires and concerns to the larger good of the family. For many Asian Americans individual behavior reflects either shame or pride on the family (Morrow, 1987).

Asian American families place the individual as secondary to the family. Many Asian American children are taught that displays of anger and displeasure are to be avoided. Social customs demand strict adherence. Communication is often indirect and outward displays of emotion are not encouraged, except with infants (Slonim, 1991). Child-rearing practices in infancy and early childhood are indulgent but become more demanding after 5 years. These lenient, nurturant, and permissive ways stem from the belief that young children are not capable of understanding what they do (Kelley & Tseng, 1992). The later emphasis on strictness occurs because older children are thought to be capable of understanding what they do so demands for emotional self-control and self-discipline increase (Garcia Coll et al., 1995). Asian American children are accustomed to a fairly structured and formal setting. Parental control, obedience, discipline, an emphasis on education, filial piety, respect for elders, a desire to minimize conflict, and a respect for obligations and tradition are common features of Asian American child-rearing (Lin & Fu, 1990).

Asian American parents view their primary role as one of teacher (Kelley & Tseng, 1992). Children are taught that through hard work, moral living, and diligence they will fulfill their potential and make the family proud.

Child-Rearing Among Native Americans

More than 500 Native American tribal units are recognized by the federal government, and 200 distinct tribal languages are actively spoken (Brown, 1993) so a general Native American child-rearing strategy or culture is difficult to discern. The traditional Native American community is collective, cooperative, and has extensive noncompetitive social networks (Harrison et al., 1990). In Native American families responsibilities for child-rearing are typically shared among many caring adults including parents, extended family members, and other adults. A great value is placed on age and life experience, and parents often seek advice from older family members or elders in the community. Children are treated somewhat permissively and there is less interference in the affairs of others and regulation of activities (Williams, 1979). For instance, Navajo children do not need permission to eat or sleep; they eat when they are hungry and sleep when tired (Phillips & Lobar, 1990). Children master self-care skills and participate in household responsibilities, which fosters self-sufficiency (Garcia Coll et al., 1995). Being part of a group and blending in are important virtues and asserting one's individuality is not encouraged (Nazarro, 1981).

Sharing is an important value that is learned very early; however, people in authority are supposed to share what they have (Lewis & Ho, 1979). Saving for the future, an ideal among the dominant culture (though not always practiced), is relatively unimportant. One's worth is measured by one's willingness and ability to share, therefore the accumulation of wealth is not as respected (Slonim, 1991). Strong extended-family structures are common although not as prevalent as years ago.

Patience is a virtue taught by many Native American tribes. Native American children may not seem competitive by the standards of the dominant society since they have been taught to wait patiently for their turn without having to be assertive. Native American children are also frequently given choices and are allowed to participate in adult activities (Pepper, 1976).

Punishment: Uses and Abuses

During our discussion of discipline and child-rearing, we sidestepped the issue of punishment. For many families, punishment is synonymous with discipline, but there are important differences. *Discipline* involves control of others for the purpose of holding undesirable impulses or habits in check and encouraging self-control. It may include reasoning and positive reinforcement for the correct behavior. Discipline also occurs before the infringement. **Punishment** is a process by which an undesirable behavior is followed by a negative consequence. It is administered after the damage is done and is always negative. Its purpose is to decrease or completely eliminate a behavior in a particular circumstance. Most behaviors are correct in one instance but not in another. Hitting a child to get a toy is unacceptable, but defending oneself when being hit by another child may be acceptable. Punishment may teach a child what *not* to do, but it does not provide any instruction in what the child *should* do under certain circumstances.

Psychologists recognize that punishment may sometimes be necessary but they are concerned about the type of punishment used and the way it is administered. Punishment can be administered in two ways (Sarafino, 1996). First, a positive reinforcer may be removed; for example, a parent may take away a toy or turn off the television set to punish misbehavior. The second procedure involves a parent's following the child's undesirable action with an unpleasant action—a child who whines may be yelled at or spanked.

punishment The process by which some aversive consequence is administered to reduce the probability that misbehavior will recur.

Although punishment can decrease the frequency of an undesirable behavior, it often fails because it is administered incorrectly. It may be overused by some parents who never compliment their children but are always quick to criticize and even threaten physical punishment. To be effective, punishment should be strong enough to deal with the offending behavior yet not so strong that it interferes with the parent-child relationship. It should be swift, certain, and combined with rewards for the correct behavior (Altrocchi, 1980). Unfortunately, parents often delay punishment, use it inconsistently, are overly severe, and constantly threaten their children—practices that are ineffective in the long term.

Some parents are proud to be severe disciplinarians and do not spare the rod. They claim that spanking works and find it difficult to understand why other parents do not use as much punishment (see Controversial Issues: To Spank or Not to Spank? on pp. 204–205). To the casual observer the harshly disciplined child may seem well behaved, but a deeper look reveals a different picture. Harsh punishment is effective in temporarily decreasing the undesirable behavior, but over the long term it is less successful and can even be damaging (Sarafino, 1996). Children may correct their behavior temporarily, especially in the presence of the feared parent, but their frustration and anger builds up and eventually explodes; such children may become sullen and suspicious of authority.

Child Abuse

Sometimes punishment goes beyond the point of reason and leads to abuse. About two thirds of the incidents of child abuse can be related to parental attempts to discipline or control their children's behavior (Gil, 1970). **Child abuse** occurs when parents intentionally injure their children. **Child neglect** refers to a situation in which the physical care and supervision of the child is inadequate or inappropriate, for example, a child who comes to school each day dressed inadequately for the bitterly cold weather. Reports of child abuse have increased substantially over the past decade. All states now require such professionals as doctors, nurses, and teachers to report suspected cases of child abuse or neglect. There are twice the number of reports for neglect as for abuse. Despite the widespread publicity surrounding some celebrated cases of abuse in day care centers and foster care settings, only 2% of the confirmed cases occur in these settings, and that figure has been consistent over the past 9 years (NCPCA, 1996). In 1995, 1215 children died from abuse or neglect and about half (46%) had had either current or past contact with child protective agencies.

child abuse A general term used to denote an injury intentionally perpetrated on a child.

child neglect A term used to describe a situation in which the care and supervision of a child is insufficient or improper.

Controversial Issues: To Spank or Not To Spank?

In the area of discipline, no topic is as controversial as spanking or corporal (physical) punishment. Some parents believe strongly in corporal punishment, whereas others rarely or never resort to it; the emotional debate on spanking has been going on for years.

In Sweden and several other countries it is against the law for parents or teachers to use corporal punishment. The legislation is not part of the criminal code, but is a statement of national policy. It is also used to identify parents who need help disciplining their children (Straus, 1991a). A 1979 Swedish law states that "a child may not be subjected to physical punishment or other injurious or humiliating treatment" (Haeuser, 1990, p. 53). Other forms of discipline, including time-out, the judicious use of rewards, denial of privileges, and talking out conflicts, are advocated.

Spanking remains a more accepted disciplinary technique in the United States, although there is a growing movement to make it less acceptable. In February 1989 The University of Wisconsin and the American Academy of Pediatrics Provisional Committee on Child Abuse convened the Wingspread Conference whose participants included experts in such areas as pediatric medicine, psychology, social work, and law enforcement. No call for legislation was made, but participants urged a national campaign to educate parents to the possible injurious effects of corporal punishment as well as the use of preferable alternatives. Several other major organizations joined the chorus against corporal punishment.

Spanking is the most common form of physical punishment. Somewhere between 70% and 90% of American parents spank their children at least once in a while (Wauchope & Straus, 1990). Spanking is most commonly used when children are between 3 and 5 years of age and then declines (Lytton, Watts & Dunn, 1988). Older children are also physically punished, and one out of three 15-year-olds is spanked (Straus, 1991a) and the threat of physical punishment is even more common (Davis, 1996).

When a sample of college-educated mothers of 3-year-olds was interviewed, three quarters said they used corporal punishment. Mothers reported spanking an average of two and a half times a week, totalling about 130 spankings a year. Of a total of 537 serious child misbehaviors reported, 16% ended in spanking. Most spankings occurred at home between 5 p.m. and bedtime and were witnessed by others (Holden, Coleman, & Schmidt, 1995). Aggression was the behavior most likely to be followed by a spanking, although violating the rights of others such as taking someone else's toys also resulted in spanking. In one third of the cases mothers spanked only after warnings were ignored. In 65% of the spankings mothers reported they actually felt happy or neutral before the child's misbehavior, but in 35% they claimed to already have been in a bad mood.

Many factors influence the amount of corporal punishment used in a given home. One obvious factor is the attitude parents have towards physical punishment: Those who believe it is effective and acceptable are much more likely to use it extensively. In addition, some groups are more likely to use punishment, including those who are less educated and are younger. Their use of such punishment may be related to many factors including having experienced such punishment when they were growing up and considering it appropriate, lack of understanding of the alternatives, experiencing more stress, or the seeming need for a quick strategy to reduce the misbehavior.

True or False?
Reports of child abuse have increased substantially over the past 10 years.

Questions Students Often Ask

Is there really more child abuse today, or are we simply more aware of it and more willing to report it?
Child abuse is certainly not a new problem; it has existed for centuries. Social scientists also understand that when people become aware of a particular problem it is more likely to be reported. In addition, today there is somewhat less tolerance for the attitude that anything a parent does is his or her own business. You can certainly make a case that the increase in reporting is partly the result of an increase in awareness and a change in societal attitudes. Yet, we also know that child abuse reports have increased substantially even since 1986, a time when people were certainly aware of the problem. So it seems that awareness may be one reason for the increase in reports but an actual increase in child abuse may also have taken place.

The results of child abuse are serious and extensive (Trickett & McBride-Chang, 1995). They include language delays, poor self-concept, aggression, social and emotional withdrawal, and poor social relationships with peers (Hennessy et al., 1994; Mason, 1993; Salzinger et al., 1993). Abused children show poor interpersonal problem-solving skills and interpret the social behavior of others more negatively (Dodge, Bates, & Pettit, 1990). Children who are abused have lower intelligence scores and are at an increased risk for depression, suicide, and drug abuse (Wisdom, 1989).

Controversial Issues: To Spank or Not To Spank? (continued)

Difficult children are more severely disciplined than children with easy temperaments (Eisenberg & Fabes, 1994) and certain offenses are more likely to lead to spankings than others. An aggressive misbehavior is three times more likely to elicit a spanking than a conventional misdeed, such as failure to pick up clothing (Catron & Masters, 1993). Both parental attitudes toward spanking and child behavior are significant predictors of the frequency of physical punishment. A positive attitude sets the stage for using physical punishment after a punishable offense has taken place.

Boys and girls are just about as likely to be physically punished during early childhood (Holden et al., 1995; Lytton & Romney, 1991). However, as they grow older boys are much more likely to receive physical punishment (Gelles, 1978), which may reflect their greater defiance, disobedience, or aggressive behavior (Anderson, Lytton, & Romny, 1986).

Those in favor of spanking argue that it is merely a discipline technique that is effective and essentailly harmless, although more and more advocates are seeing it as a technique of "last resort" (Davis, 1994). Advocates of spanking argue that it is a clear, short-lived, and immediate way to discipline. They cry foul when critics of physical punishment claim it leads to child abuse or serious physical harm because they do not see a swat on the behind as abuse. Linking spanking with child abuse is denounced as false logic that only serves to muddy the debate.

Critics of spanking argue that it is demeaning and ineffective punishment that can lead to very serious consequences. Spanking may work in the immediate situation but is ineffective in the long term because it causes resentment, and it does not lead to internalization and better self-control. Children may stop their behavior out of fear but have not learned how to behave when the authority figure is not present. Meaningful discipline, they argue, involves teaching children self-control; spanking only teaches them that might is right. Spanking also teaches children that aggression and violence are acceptable, and parents serve as aggressive models for their children. Too often, critics argue, spanking is not a reasoned response but rather an emotional one as a parent strikes out at the child when angry (Dix, Reinhold & Zambarano, 1990). Critics claim that spanking is the lazy parents' way to discipline, because other, sounder methods require more time and effort. Critics also claim that parents can become addicted to spanking; if it stops the behavior in the short term, parents will use it more and more until it becomes the discipline technique they use most often.

Finally, some critics argue that physical punishment is related to a whole range of negative developmental outcomes including delayed impulse control, impaired psychological adjustment, delinquency, later child abuse, and aggression (Holden et al., 1995; McCord, 1991; Straus, 1991).

The spanking debate demonstrates how child-rearing strategies can become emotional topics with symbolic meanings. Whenever I discuss spanking and physical punishment in class, each side tends to discount what the other side is saying; those in favor of corporal punishment casting their critics as "permissive," while those against corporal punishment consider the others "abusive" or at least "inadequate" parents. Those in favor of corporal punishment would like to see acceptance of spanking as a discipline technique. Those opposed to corporal punishment do not necessarily want legislation outlawing it as much as they would like to educate people on better ways to discipline children. Both sides in this debate want to capture the hearts and minds of American parents.

Sexual Abuse

Sexual abuse has been the subject of much discussion in the media. **Sexual abuse** may be defined as forced, tricked, or coerced sexual behavior between a younger person and an older person (Gelles & Conte, 1990). Sexual abuse is the least reported type of abuse and is generally considered to be grossly underreported, partly because it is often not recognized as abuse (Clark, 1993).

According to reported incidents, sexual abusers are mostly men and girls constitute the majority of victims (Finkelhor & Baron, 1986; Gelles & Conte, 1990). Sexual abuse is most likely to occur between people who are related, but a child may also be victimized by a stranger. The consequences of sexual abuse can be both physical—such as venereal disease and pregnancy—and emotional. Long-term effects include depression, self-destructive behavior, anxiety, feelings of isolation and stigmatization, social withdrawal and isolation, poor self-esteem, difficulty trusting others, substance abuse, and sexual maladjustment (Trickett & McBride-Chang, 1995; Clarke, 1993). One fifth of all victims of sexual abuse develop serious long-term psychological problems (AMA, 1992). Recently, maturational and biological consequences have been reported. Some sexually abused girls mature earlier, have different hormonal reactions to stress, and may even develop impaired immune functioning. Abuse could thus alter the biological processes of development by changing the timing of hormone release (DeAngelis, 1995).

Parents should remind their children not to accept money, favors, or rides from strangers. Children should be told that if they think they are in danger, it's okay to make a scene by running away and screaming for help. Because

sexual abuse Forced, tricked, or coerced sexual behavior between a younger person and an older person.

the sexual abuser may be someone they know and trust, children should be told that they do not have to agree to demands for physical closeness—even from relatives. Finally, children should be encouraged to report any instances of people touching them in intimate places or of asking them to do the same.

Many schools have programs that teach young children about sexual abuse. At this point it is not possible to demonstrate whether these educational efforts are successful in reducing sexual abuse, but studies do show that children learn these lessons and their knowledge improves (MacMillan et al., 1994a). One concern of sexual abuse prevention programs is that they might have a negative effect on children by making children frightened of strangers or uncomfortable about physical affection. Studies generally show that this does not occur (Wurtele & Miller-Perin, 1987a and b). These programs should be included in the school's regular health curriculum.

Emotional Abuse

Not all child abuse is physical. Consider the parent who constantly yells at and berates his or her children. Imagine a 4-year-old who has just spilled some juice hearing a parent shout, "You're a stupid, rotten kid. If I had any sense I'd give you away!"

Defining **emotional** or **psychological abuse,** is difficult (Baumrind, 1994; Rosenberg, 1987). Certain parental actions can lead to a loss of self-esteem in the child and interfere with the child's emotional development, but defining these actions and describing remedial steps can be difficult. Conceptually, such parental behaviors as rejecting, isolating, terrorizing, ignoring, and corrupting constitute psychological maltreatment (Garbarino, Guttman, & Seeley, 1986). The most frequent form of emotional abuse is verbal aggression or threatening (Davis, 1996). These forms of abuse frequently produce emotional and behavioral problems in children (Hart & Brassard, 1987). Unfortunately, an objective definition of emotional maltreatment is not yet available that would allow mandatory intervention to reduce such abuse (Kelton & Davison, 1987). In the absence of such specific guidelines, the courts have taken a hands-off attitude toward all but the most extreme forms. Perhaps in the future the more obvious cases will be identified and some help for both parents and children will be forthcoming.

Why Are Children Abused?

To understand the causes of child abuse, the characteristics of the parents, the child, and the situation must be taken into account.

Abusive Parents As a group, parents who physically abuse their children are impulsive, have unmet dependency needs, have a poor self-concept and a poor sense of identity, are defensive, and project their problems onto their children (Green, Gaines, & Sandgrund, 1974). They believe in the value of physical punishment, are afraid of spoiling their children, and have difficulty empathizing with them (Kelley, Grace, & Elliott, 1990). Abusive parents seem to derive little enjoyment from parenting or from life in general, and show little satisfaction with the child, nor do they express affection to the child. They are isolated from the community and do not encourage autonomy or independence, yet they still have high expectations for their children (Trickett et al., 1991).

These characteristics are general ones; many parents who are impulsive and isolated, for example, do not physically abuse their children, and this has led many professionals to deny that there is any definite "abusive" personality (Green, Gaine, & Sandgrund, 1974). A personality profile of a parent is not an accurate predictor of abuse.

Questions Students Often Ask

I think all parents who abuse their kids are mentally ill. Their children should be taken away from them so they won't hurt them any more. Why doesn't the child protective department just do this so the children won't be further hurt?

Most parents who abuse their children are not *mentally ill and are not in need of hospitalization or sedation. Only about 5% to 10% of abusive parents require this type of care. Parents who abuse their children do need help and have personal and interpersonal problems, but studies do not find that they are generally mentally ill.*

Some studies compare abusive and nonabusive parents' child-rearing practices. Abusive parents have lower rates of interaction, more negative interactions with their children, use more verbal and nonverbal aggression and fewer positive responses when managing behavior, and provide less instruction (Chilamkurti & Milner, 1993).

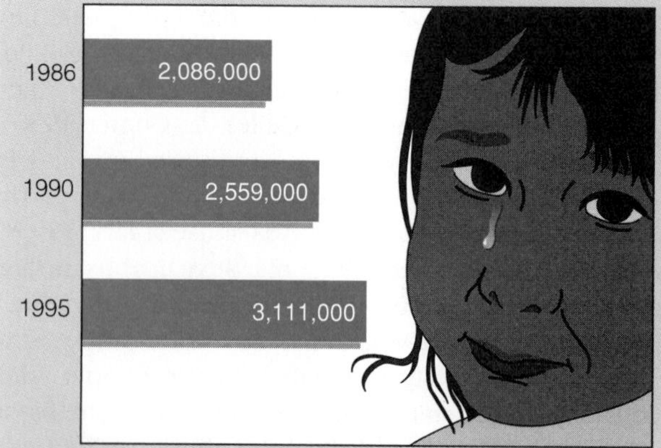

The number of reports of child abuse continues to rise.

Datagraphic
Reports of Abused Children
Source: Data from the National Committee to Prevent Child Abuse, 1996.

emotional or psychological abuse Psychological damage perpetrated on the child by parental actions that often involve rejecting, isolating, terrorizing, ignoring, or corrupting.

Physically abusive parents also use more severe forms of punishment, such as striking the child's face, hitting the child with an object, or pulling the child's hair (Trickett & Kuczynski, 1986). They evaluate their children's behavior more negatively and have more unrealistic child-related expectations (Milner & Chilamkurti, 1991). They judge their children very harshly and use fewer reasoning techniques (Trickett & Kuczynski, 1986).

Between 25% and 35% of individuals who were physically abused as children grow up to abuse their own children (Kaufman & Zigler, 1987), so the generalization that abused children grow up to abuse their own children is greatly overstated (Wisdom, 1989). Although certainly children who are abused are more likely than the general population to abuse, most people who were abused do not abuse their own children.

True or False?
The overwhelming majority of abused children grow up to abuse their own children.

Why would some children who have suffered abuse or neglect perpetuate similar patterns of behavior in adulthood? Perhaps repeated exposure to aggressive parents provides children with a model of what a parent is, and such children use this model in their own parenting, with little thought of the alternatives or concern with why they are doing it (Simons et al., 1991). How then do we explain the majority of abused and neglected children who do *not* abuse their own children? People who break the cycle of abuse tend to have received emotional support from a nonabusive adult during childhood, participated in therapy during some time in their life, or had a nonabusive, more emotionally stable mate with whom they shared a satisfying relationship. Those who continue the cycle of abuse experience significantly more life stress and anxiety and are more dependent, immature, and depressed (Egeland, Jacobovitz, & Sroufe, 1988). Therefore, the presence and influence of other supportive and nonabusive adults and/or a helpful counseling relationship are two factors that may reduce the possibility of abuse.

The Abused Child Certain characteristics may predispose a child to being a victim of abuse. Some people feel uneasy at any suggestion that the child contributes to the problem. It is easier to see a child as a helpless victim of a vicious adult than to look at a child's characteristics that may bring out the worst in a parent. No one is excusing abusive behavior or blaming an innocent victim. However, a child's personality or physical and intellectual characteristics, in combination with an inadequate parent, may cause problems (Parke & Collmer, 1975). For instance, prematurely born, physically challenged, or mentally retarded children are abused more often (Friedrich & Boriskin, 1976). All such children need special care, and children whose needs are greater are at greater risk for abuse.

Abusive parents often hold unreasonable expectations for their children and distorted perceptions of what their children are capable of doing (Chilamkurti & Milner, 1993; Martin, 1978). Children with physical, emotional, or mental disabilities often cannot meet their parents' expectations and are more likely to be abused. A premature baby who requires a great deal of care may be more than an impulsive, unrealistic parent can handle, so the parent may resort to violence to quiet the child. As the child grows, the pattern is reinforced; physical violence keeps the child in line until it becomes well established and continues throughout childhood. These abused children often justify the parent's actions on the basis of their own behavior, believing themselves to be generally bad (Dean et al., 1986). The child whose needs are greater, who engenders anger in a parent, or who is difficult to care for is more likely to set in motion abusive parental responses that may become the standard parent-child interaction.

The Situation Any situation that raises the level of tension and stress can promote abuse. For instance, neglect and abuse increase when economic problems within the community increase (Steinberg, Catalano, & Dooley, 1981). Unemployment and underemployment are stressful situations, and parents may displace—that is, transfer their feelings from one person or object to another. Thus, the child may become the object of a parent's anger toward the boss or the life situation in general. Although child abuse and maltreatment can be found in all social groups and neighborhoods, they are more prevalent where people are poor and isolated and live in areas of high unemployment (Coulton, Korbin, Su, & Chow, 1995).

Preventing Child Abuse

Programs to deal with child abuse have focused on both prevention and treatment. Programs aimed at preventing abuse may enroll parents in educational programs and offer child development courses in high schools. Such courses teach students child care techniques, provide them with information concerning children's nutritional and emotional needs, and tell parents where they can go for help. Other programs include giving information at health fairs and promoting drop-in centers at which parents can talk with other parents, social workers, or counselors (McCauley, 1992). The most effective prevention programs against physical child abuse and neglect involve home visits from trained professionals who help parents to develop better parenting skills and to cope with the many challenges of parenting (MacMillan et al., 1994b).

Many approaches have been used to treat child abusers. Social work, individual and family therapy, self-help groups such as Parents Anonymous that provide emotional support, and group treatment can all claim some success. The victims of abuse need help. Abused children show many behavioral disturbances that affect learning and development but improve even when only a mild to moderate improvement occurs in the home situation. Early identification is one factor in successful treatment.

Gender-Role Acquisition

Gender is one of the first and most obvious distinctions that children make in classifying others. Children as young as 2 years of age have some understanding of the differences, and by 3 or 4 years most children can accurately apply sex-stereotyped labels to toys, activities, household tasks, and even adult occupations (Turner & Gervai, 1995). From about 3 years of age, consistent gender differences in preferred toys and play activities are evident, with boys playing more with toy vehicles, balls, and blocks and girls engaging more in artistic activities and playing with dolls and dressing up (Huston, 1983). Gender differences in personality and social interaction are less pronounced in the preschool stage and appear somewhat later (Turner & Gervai, 1995).

Gender Differences

Is the average male more aggressive than the average female? Is the average female better at verbal tasks than the average male? The term **gender difference** describes the differences between the genders that have been established by scientific research. For example, the average female matures more rapidly than the average male. Eleanor Maccoby and Carol Jacklin (1974) reviewed more than 1600 studies on gender differences and concluded that only four differences appeared consistently. Most studies indicate that (a) males are generally more aggressive than females, a finding that is common across many cultures, (b) girls have better verbal ability, (c) boys excel in visual-spatial ability, and (d) boys excel in mathematical ability. A number of other supposed differences were not supported by scientific studies. The hypotheses that girls were more suggestible, had lower self-esteem, were less motivated, were more sociable, were better at rote learning, were less analytical, were affected more by heredity, and learned better using their auditory sense than boys were dismissed as not supported by the research. A number of other hypotheses were still in question, including the questions of male dominance, female compliance, female nurturance, male activity level, female passivity, and male competitiveness.

> ***True or False?***
> Research has failed to establish any consistent gender differences in behavior or cognitive abilities.

As valuable as it is, the work of Maccoby and Jacklin is not the last word on the subject and has been criticized for several reasons. For example, Block (1976) noted a number of technical objections to the way the review of the literature had been performed. Others reviewed much of the same literature and came to different conclusions, suggesting that women are more suggestible and more fearful and that men are more active (Eaton & Ennis, 1986; Eagly, 1978). Some studies find that girls are more empathic, more compliant, and seek more approval from adults than boys (Turner & Gervai, 1995).

Three considerations should be kept in mind when assessing any positive findings on gender differences. First, even though a difference between the genders on some characteristic, such as verbal ability, is found, it tells us nothing about its cause. Are males generally more aggressive than females because of some environmental factor, such as reinforcement, some genetic or hormonal factor, or some interaction between the two? Even the finding that a genetic or hormonal element may underlie the behavior does not mean that the behavior itself cannot be modified; a genetic contribution does not imply immutability. Rather, the individual's genotype may influence the range of possible behaviors, but the behavior is determined by the environment.

Second, most gender differences should not be seen as absolute because the overlap between the sexes is tremendous. The average difference between the sexes on any particular trait is normally very small, even if it does exist. The differences between individuals within the same gender are far greater than the average differences between males and females. Thus, although males generally seem to perform better at advanced mathematics, you will find excellent female math students and males who are terrible at math. The genders are more similar than they are different.

A gender difference might be found in one circumstance but not another, which makes global statements about one trait or another questionable. For example, consider a study of the social interactions of preschoolers: Some of the children have same-gender partners whereas others have opposite-gender partners. What if when paired with boys, girls behaved more passively, allowing the boys to play with the toys while the girls watched. However, when paired with other girls, the girls showed no evidence of passivity and intense social interaction was the rule. Would it be fair to conclude that girls are more passive than boys? Gender differences are often situational, and it is incorrect to generalize (Maccoby, 1990).

Gender Identity, Gender Stability, and Gender Consistency

Children develop their understanding of gender in a particular developmental progression (Slaby & Frey, 1975). First, they establish a **gender identity,** which is an awareness of being male or female. Evidence indicates that at about age 2, children become aware of the labels "boy" and "girl" (Schaffer, 1981) although they do not use them correctly all the time. After establishing gender identity,

gender differences The differences between males and females that have been established through scientific investigation.

gender identity One's awareness of being a male or a female.

These children are showing sex-typed behavior in their choice of toys.

children learn that their gender is stable **(gender stability).** In other words, children know that they were boys or girls when they were younger and will become men and women when they grow up. Finally, children develop **gender consistency** (also called **gender constancy**), the understanding that boys remain boys whether or not they have long hair or play female-oriented games. Gender identity is more easily understood by children than gender consistency, with gender stability lying somewhere between. The average age of attaining these understandings differs widely. For example, although the average age for attaining gender consistency was 55 months in one study, some attained it as early as 41 months, while others did not understand the concept until 67 months of age.

This developmental progression explains some of the unusual behavior we find in young children. If children have not gained an understanding of gender stability or consistency, they may believe that if Daddy grows his hair long, he will become a woman like Mommy. A little girl might believe that if her brother wears a dress, he will become a girl like her.

Sex Typing and Gender Roles

Consider the following statement: "Women cook, take care of the children, ask for help, are rescued from trying circumstances (by men), and play with dolls. Men work full-time jobs, don't ask for help, are action oriented, and are strong." Such generalizations still exist in our society. **Sex typing** is the process by which an individual acquires values and behaves in a manner more appropriate to one gender or another. Sex-typed behavior can be seen in many areas of development—for example, boys playing with trucks and girls playing with dolls. Such behavior patterns as methods of aggression, behavior while dissecting a frog, and emotional expressiveness are examples of sex-typed behavior. Girls learn that crying is acceptable when they are sad; boys learn to hold their sadness in. Boys avoid showing an interest in babies; females pay more attention to infants (Blakemore, 1981).

gender stability Children's knowledge that they were of a particular gender when younger and will remain so throughout life.

gender consistency (constancy) Children's knowledge that they will remain boys or girls regardless of how they act, dress, or groom.

sex typing The process by which an individual acquires the attitudes, values, and behaviors viewed as appropriate for one gender or another in a particular culture.

When we add up all the behavior patterns and psychological characteristics that seem appropriate for each gender, we are describing the concept of **gender roles,** which permeate many other roles. Not only are gender roles involved in the choice of occupation (truck drivers are men, nurses are women), but they also are related to a number of social expectations. For example, consider some social conventions in the areas of dating and family life—the male picks up the female at her house for the date and drives the car, and the male is the primary breadwinner. Some of these conceptions are changing, but many are still with us today.

Just how children acquire the behaviors that are considered appropriate for their gender is a matter of great interest and controversy. No single approach adequately explains it, but each has something to offer.

The Biological Approach

No biological factor successfully explains why males may act one way and females another. Instead, a number of biological factors are suggested that may be taken into account when studying gender roles.

Hormones Males produce more testosterone; females produce more estrogen. In laboratory studies the hormone testosterone is linked to aggressive behavior (Rogers, 1976). However, variations in human behavior cannot be explained merely by citing hormonal factors because learned behavior is also important. Money and Ehrhardt (1972) studied children who were born with ambiguous genitals. Some were surgically altered very early in childhood, and these children made successful

gender roles Behaviors expected of people in a given society on the basis of whether an individual is male or female.

adjustments to their gender if the surgery took place before the age of 2. Those who became female, however, were tomboyish, showing more rough-and-tumble play. This tendency might be caused by the greater concentrations of testosterone in their systems. Perhaps males are more inclined to be aggressive than are females. Despite this inclination, however, every psychologist notes the overwhelming importance of learning in this area.

Hormone levels during sensitive periods in early life may have an organizing effect on the brain, encouraging the development of certain neurons. The brains of animals given doses of hormones show changes, and these may relate to behavioral changes in aggression, parenting, and rough-and-tumble play (Ruble, 1988).

Differences in Maturation The average female is born more ready for life than the average male is. Females are more advanced in central nervous system development and bone formation (Doyle & Paludi, 1991). Some gender differences may be caused by the interaction of rates of maturation and the environment surrounding the child. For example, while gross muscle development in males is superior, females develop fine muscle control more quickly (McGuinness, 1976, 1979). Because children are apt to do both what is easiest and what yields the most positive reinforcement, males may turn their attention to activities in which gross muscle ability and reaction time are vital. Having better fine motor control, females are more likely to concentrate on tasks that require such control. This would mean that society merely reinforces an existing difference in abilities. The interaction of maturation and the environment may also help explain why boys have so many more reading problems than girls. Females have a greater attention span, and their eyes are better developed by the time they enter school, which suggests that the average male may find language skills more difficult and may require additional instruction.

Genetic Differences Genetic differences on the 23rd chromosome may also affect behavior. The male Y chromosome contains many fewer genes than the female X chromosome, and some characteristics—such as color blindness—are sex-linked. There is evidence that this may also be true of spatial ability, although some studies cast some doubt on this (Vandenberg & Kuse, 1979).

Even if you are impressed by the biological approach, assignment of unequal roles on the basis of biological argument cannot be justified; in the case of gender roles and behavior, biology is not destiny.

Behavior Theories

The most obvious reason why males and females act differently is that they learn to do so. Children's learning experiences can be roughly divided into two categories: (a) boys and girls are treated differently and reinforced for different actions; and (b) the role models for boys and girls differ, and children learn at least some of their gender role by observing others.

Different Treatment for Sons and Daughters Parents do expect different behaviors from sons and daughters, expecting sons to be stronger and tougher (Richmond-Abbott, 1983). Parents provide sons with different toys and decorate their rooms in a "gender-appropriate manner" (Rheingold & Cook, 1975). Although parents may not consciously reinforce young children for playing with gender-stereotyped toys (e.g., boys with trucks, girls with dolls), they actively channel their children into such standard play (Eisenberg et al., 1985). The same parents who may say it would not bother them if their son played with dolls are likely to provide him with only balls, gloves, and trucks to play with.

Girls are viewed as more fragile, and parents play with sons more roughly than they do with daughters (Bee, 1978). Parents also supervise daughters more, allowing sons more freedom (Block, 1979). Boys are also more likely to be discouraged by adults and peers from engaging in gender-inappropriate behavior (Langlois & Downs, 1980). Fathers are more likely than mothers to treat sons and daughters differently (Lytton & Romney, 1991). A father is more likely to criticize his son when he sees him playing with dolls than he is to criticize a daughter who is observed beating up a Bobo doll.

Males are more likely than females to hold rigidly to sex-typed behaviors. Even though preschool boys and girls both prefer gender-stereotyped toys, boys avoid cross-gender toys more often than girls do (Lobel & Menashri, 1993). Indeed, preschool boys choose sex-typed toys and cling to their choices even if told that the toys not chosen are appropriate for both boys and girls; it is also easier to get girls to switch toy preferences than boys. Females show more flexibility in behavior than males. Preschoolers judge female gender-role violations less harshly than male gender-role violations (Smetana, 1986). As children enter middle childhood they become somewhat more lenient in this regard (Katz & Ksansnak, 1994). One consistent finding is that parents reinforce gender-typed play activities and toy choices, but more so for boys than girls (Fagot & Hagan, 1991; Lytton & Romney, 1991).

In an analysis of many studies on parental treatment of children, the only areas in which parents treated sons and daughters very differently were in encouraging sex-typed activities (such as in play) and certain sex-stereotyped characteristics, and even here the findings are modest (Lytton & Romney, 1991). In the United States and Canada there were no significant differences in such variables as parental warmth, encouraging dependence, restrictiveness, interaction, encouragement of achievement, or verbal interaction. Boys are not necessarily reinforced more than girls for aggressiveness (Maccoby & Jacklin, 1974). Studies from other Western countries show a significant gender difference for physical punishment with more being meted out to boys, but this tendency is slight and not significant in North America.

The fact that parents emphasize sex stereotypes in play and household chores may have far-reaching effects. For example, boys' toys provide more opportunity for manipulation and visual-spatial skills, which may lead to better skills in these areas (Block, 1983). Some authorities, however, are more impressed by the similarities than the differences (Lytton & Romney, 1991; Maccoby and Jacklin, 1974). The evidence in most areas is very weak for differential treatment. The question is not whether boys and girls are treated differently, but whether these differences are enough to explain later sex-typed behavior patterns. Although some differences in treatment do exist, it is difficult to see how they could be the sole determinants of later personality and behavioral differences between the sexes; they are only one part of the puzzle and another part may be found in the understanding of the role models that surround a child.

Role Models and Imitation The use of modeling and imitation to explain the acquisition of gender role is appealing. A boy who sees his father cooking dinner and enjoying it gets the idea that it is manly to cook dinner for the family. Because parents are the most important people in the life of preschoolers, the children may model themselves after them (Mischel, 1970). For example, daughters of mothers employed outside the home hold less traditional role concepts and have higher aspirations than girls whose mothers are not employed. They benefit from observing that Mother as well as Father is valued in the labor market and performs useful functions outside the home. Mothers who participate more in nontraditional male-typical household chores and child care tasks have children who are less typical in their gender-activity preferences (Serbin et al., 1993).

Children are also exposed to models in the outside world—for example, peers, teachers, and characters in children's books and on television. Even though it is difficult to analyze the effect these models have on a child's understanding of gender roles, their role should not be minimized.

Psychoanalytic Theory: Identifying With Parents

No theory is more controversial than Freud's ideas about the development of sex-typed behavior. According to Freud (1925), the development of gender roles arises from events that occur during the **phallic stage.** Until early childhood both boys and girls have similar psychosexual experiences, but during the phallic stage the little boy experiences sexual feelings toward his mother, views his father as a rival for his mother's affection, and resents his father. The child fears that his father will find out how he feels and will retaliate by castrating him; this is called the **Oedipus complex.** At the same time, the father is respected as a model of masculinity who is superior to the child. As he matures, the little boy represses his feelings toward his mother and identifies with the father. In this way, he becomes like his father and takes on the "appropriate" gender role.

The process with females, called the **Electra complex,** is more convoluted. The little girl is also originally sexually attached to the mother but slowly turns her attention to her father when she realizes that she does not have a penis (Mullahy, 1948). Blaming her mother for her lack of a penis, she competes with her mother for the father's attention. She does not have to resolve this situation fully because she doesn't have to worry about castration. Freud believed that because girls may never fully accept the "appropriate" gender role, women were more likely to have personality difficulties than men (Freud, 1933; Schaffer, 1981).

An important idea underlying the psychoanalytic concept of gender roles is **identification.** Children identify with the same-gender parent and thereby acquire the appropriate gender role. Perhaps the most controversial portion of this theory involves Freud's argument that the girl's discovery that she lacks the male organ is a turning point in her life. Freud sees every imaginable character trait of females beginning with this "penis envy," including feelings of inferiority, physical modesty, envy, and psychosexual difficulties. Freud's ideas in this realm have been largely rejected by developmental psychologists because of inadequate evidence (Sears, Roe, & Alpert, 1965). The clinical problems Freud noted can be interpreted in terms of the social roles traditionally thrust on women by society (Horney, 1939, 1967). In addition, even though the Oedipus complex has been found in a number of societies (Kline, 1972), it is not universal (Mead, 1974).

Gender Schema Theory

The cognitive component is missing from all these theories. According to **gender schema theory,** once a child develops gender identity at about the age of 2 (Carter & Levy, 1988), children develop a gender schema, or a body of knowledge about what boys and girls do. This body of knowledge helps them organize and interpret information and influences their preferences and activities (Bem, 1981; Martin & Halverson, 1981). As children learn society's gender schema, they learn which characteristics are related to their own gender—and therefore to themselves—and which are not. Sandra Bem (1981) notes that part of the gender schema for boys is strength; nurturance is part of the schema for girls. The strong-weak dimension appears to

phallic stage Freud's third psychosexual stage, occurring during early childhood, in which the sexual energy is located in the genital area.

Oedipus complex The conflict in Freudian theory in which the boy experiences sexual feelings toward his mother and wishes to rid himself of his father.

Electra complex The female equivalent to the Oedipus complex; the female experiences sexual feelings toward her father and wishes to do away with her mother.

identification The process by which children take on the characteristics of another person, often a parent.

gender schema theory A theory of gender role acquisition in which after developing gender identity the child acquires a body of knowledge about the behaviors of each gender, which helps the child organize and interpret information and guide behavior.

be absent from the female gender schema; the nurturant dimension is almost absent from the male gender schema. Children apply this same schema to themselves and choose to attend only to the possible dimensions of personality and behavior that are applicable to their own gender.

One of the advantages of gender schema theory is that it explains why children maintain their gender stereotypes even when confronted with contrary information. Once a child learns his or her schema, such knowledge biases the way information is processed. Most research shows that gender-consistent information is remembered better than gender-inconsistent information (Liben & Signorella, 1993; Signorella & Liben, 1984). Children remember best information that fits their gender schema and may even change information that is inconsistent so that it becomes consistent with their beliefs (Welch-Ross & Schmidt, 1996). For example, a child who thinks that only boys can be soldiers and hears of a female soldier, may change the gender of the soldier to suit his or her own beliefs. Gender schema theory thus argues that children are internally motivated to conform to their gender-based cultural standards (Levy & Carter, 1989).

Gender-Role Theories Reconsidered

No single theory can adequately explain how a child acquires a gender role, but each theory adds greatly to our knowledge (Turner & Gervai, 1995). Behavior theory makes us aware of how important the differential treatment of boys and girls by adults can be. Social learning theory stresses the importance of imitation and the models that surround the child. While few scientists today believe that biological explanations by themselves are sufficient to explain gender roles, maturational, hormonal, and genetic differences add pieces to the puzzle. Despite the problems inherent in the Freudian approach, the importance of identification and the part that both parents may play in the socialization of the child are important to remember. Gender schema theory emphasizes the importance of a child's intrinsic motivation to find out about gender roles and adds to our understanding of why it is so difficult to get people to alter rigid ideas about gender roles.

A number of relatively new findings have changed the way we look at sex typing and gender role formation. For example, at first people thought that gender role acquisition was basically completed before children enter school. Today we know that a great deal of change occurs in middle childhood and indeed across the life span. It was also once assumed that parents were the primary socializers, but today the focus expands to other influences including siblings, peers, teachers, and the media. Also, it was once thought that it was important and even necessary for children to adopt traditional sex-typed behaviors, but today we know that it may not be adaptive and that individual differences in the gender schema are to be expected (Katz & Ksansnak, 1994).

The Limitations of Traditional Stereotypes

It definitely matters whether or not you have a narrow or a broad definition of what is appropriate for your gender. Let's say that little Joey feels like crying but refuses to do so because he's been told it is not manly. He decides that it's best not to express his emotions because emotional expression remains inconsistent with his definition of gender role. Later in life, Joey may have difficulty expressing his feelings and his definition of being male will limit his flexibility. Little Katie, who believes that girls don't get dirty or take leadership positions, has also limited her future activities unnecessarily. Even children raised in nonsexist homes can astonish us with their stereotyped notions about male and female roles. Simply exposing a child to nontraditional models is not sufficient, direct instruction on the irrelevance of gender for occupations and particular behaviors is necessary and more effective in reducing stereotypes (Bigler & Liben, 1990).

Ready for New Challenges

The preschooler's social world expands rapidly and parents, peers, nursery school teachers, and siblings all have an effect on the child in many areas including the self-concept, development of a sense of initiative, interpersonal competence, and the development of an understanding of gender role. Preschoolers are active, curious, and playful. If parents and teachers encourage healthful activities, preschoolers gain the sense of initiative that Erikson believes is so important. If parents set limits in a loving atmosphere and allow preschoolers some freedom to choose, the children become competent and independent and develop a positive view of themselves. They are, then, ready for the challenges of middle childhood.

Summary

1. The psychosocial crisis of the preschool years can be understood in terms of initiative versus guilt. Preschoolers can express their desires and act upon them. Their self-concept is described in terms of their physical characteristics and possessions; a child's self-concept can affect behavior.
2. Play is an activity performed for sheer enjoyment with no ulterior motive. Young children understand the differences between work and play. Play helps develop a child's mental, physical, and social abilities and allows the child to experiment with new roles. The complexity of play increases with age. Both pretend play and rough-and-tumble play have important developmental benefits. Boys play more roughly than girls.
3. Preschoolers have more contact with peers than when they were toddlers. Although some preschool

friendships last throughout the year, most are temporary and lack intimacy.

4. Preschoolers do show some prosocial behavior but little altruistic behavior. Prosocial behavior increases with age. Most children's conflicts are settled without the aid of adults, most often when one child gives in to another.
5. Siblings may offer support and help as well as serve as sources of discord. Although antagonistic behavior among siblings is not uncommon, most interactions are positive and play oriented. Evidence indicates that being an only child does not have any negative effects on the child.
6. Baumrind identified three types of parenting styles. Authoritarian parents seek to control a child's every action, causing the child to become suspicious and withdrawn. Permissive parents allow almost total freedom and rarely use discipline. Their children do not show much self-control or self-reliance. Neglectful parents are neither demanding nor responsive to their children. Authoritative parents give their children freedom within limits. Their children are competent and self-controlled.
7. Child-rearing strategies depend upon parental goals, repertoire of strategies, and parenting style. Culture and subcultural affiliation influences the goals and parenting strategies used.
8. Discipline involves training in self-control; punishment involves inflicting physical and/or psychological pain for violating a rule. Punishment is most effective when it is just sufficient to reduce or eliminate the offending behavior, swift, certain, and combined with positive reinforcement for the correct behavior.
9. Abuse and neglect are major societal problems. To understand abuse, the characteristics of the parents, child, and situation must be taken into account. Sexual abuse is the least reported type of abuse. Psychological or emotional abuse involves such actions as rejecting, isolating, terrorizing, ignoring, and corrupting. Many parents who physically abuse their children can be helped to stop abusing them.
10. Research has generally found that males are more aggressive than females, that girls have greater verbal abilities, and that boys excel in visual-spatial tasks and ability in mathematics. Gender differences tell us nothing about the cause of the differences; the differences between individuals within the same gender are greater than the average differences between males and females.
11. Gender roles involve the behavioral patterns and psychological characteristics appropriate for each sex. Biological factors—including hormonal, genetic, and maturational differences—have been advanced as explanations for these differences between the genders, but a completely biological explanation is untenable. Children learn their gender roles through operant conditioning and imitation of role models in the environment. Freud saw gender roles in terms of the resolution of the Oedipal complex in the phallic stage, when children identify with the parent of the same gender. Gender schema theory argues that once a child knows his or her gender, the child develops a body of knowledge about what boys and girls do. This helps children organize and interpret information and influences their preferences and activities.

Multiple-Choice Questions

1. Four-year-old Larry tells his parents what he wants to do and how he feels. His parents encourage him and Larry feels that what he wants is good. Erikson would say that Larry will develop an appropriate sense of:
   a. happiness.
   b. generativity.
   c. initiative.
   d. perseverance.
2. Which of the following descriptions is *least* likely to be made by a preschooler?
   a. I like spaghetti.
   b. I am a boy.
   c. I play with games.
   d. I am loyal.
3. Two children are playing but they do not seem to interact much. If one left, the other could go on playing the same way. This describes ____________ play.
   a. industry-type
   b. cooperative
   c. parallel
   d. individualized
4. Hassan and his friends choose sides and play a game of baseball with each person assigned a position in the field and in the batting order. This describes ____________ play.
   a. cooperative
   b. indigenous
   c. tangential
   d. rough-and-tumble
5. Which of the following statements about pretend play is *correct?*
   a. Pretend play declines in middle childhood.
   b. Children who engage in a great deal of pretend play have better role-taking skills.
   c. The pretend play of girls and boys shows differences.
   d. All of the above are correct.
6. A psychologist is studying the influence of cognitive development on social behavior in such areas as moral development, sharing, and conflict management. The psychologist is studying:
   a. parapsychology.
   b. social cognition.

c. personality development.
d. script analysis.

7. The major qualification for friendship in the preschool stage is that a person:
a. must be reliable and honest.
b. be present and ready to play.
c. be happy and loyal.
d. be dominant yet willing to listen.

8. Which of the following statements about prosocial behavior and altruism is *false?*
a. Altruism involves doing something for someone without any hope of a reward.
b. Preschoolers do not engage in as much prosocial behavior as children in middle childhood.
c. Preschoolers do not engage in any altruistic behavior because they cannot take the perspective of other people.
d. Preschoolers are more likely to engage in prosocial behavior when they are asked to by an adult than if they are asked by a child.

9. Two preschoolers are having a conflict. It is most probably over:
a. who should be first to do something.
b. whether a preschooler really did what he or she claimed to do.
c. one child's refusal to play a particular part in dramatic play.
d. possessions.

10. Aggression declines as children progress from the preschool to the middle childhood period probably because ____________ aggression declines.
a. hostile
b. instrumental
c. forceful
d. interpersonal

11. You are watching siblings interact as part of an observational study. Which of the following observations would *not* be in keeping with the conclusions of most previous studies?
a. Older siblings start more conflicts.
b. Younger siblings imitate more.
c. The greatest amount of conflict is between brothers.
d. Most interactions are combative rather than playful.

12. Mr. and Mrs. Temple do not set many rules, are always available for consultation, but depend upon their children to regulate their own behavior. They fall into Baumrind's parental style called:
a. authoritarian.
b. permissive.
c. authoritative.
d. personable.

13. If you were studying children's internalization of parental ideas you would probably find that preschoolers:
a. cannot internalize parental instructions because they do not have the cognitive sophistication to do so.
b. are more likely to internalize if their parents use power assertive discipline in which the consequences for misbehavior are formidable.
c. will internalize parental lessons if they are told to verbally repeat rules to themselves until they know them by rote.
d. are more likely to internalize their parents' lessons if they understand them and accept them.

14. One problem of linking specific parenting styles to the later behavior of children is that:
a. parenting style cannot be measured.
b. culture and subcultural differences must be taken into account.
c. parenting styles are learned.
d. children may or may not understand the style that a parent is using.

15. Which of the following statements concerning child-rearing practices in minority groups is *correct?*
a. African American parents emphasize a people-centered rather than an object-centered orientation.
b. Latino American homes emphasize sharing and cooperation rather than early cognitive development and competition.
c. In Asian American homes parents are very lenient with young children but become much stricter in middle childhood.
d. All of the above are correct.

16. Which of the following does *not* apply to parents who abuse their children?
a. impulsive
b. believe in physical punishment
c. socially isolated
d. high rates of interaction with their children

17. The most effective programs to prevent child abuse involve:
a. psychotherapy.
b. teaching children to reason with their parents.
c. home visitations by professionals.
d. providing reading material on parenting to those at risk for abusing their children.

18. Which of the following is not a gender difference that has been reliably found in the research?
a. Males are more aggressive than females.
b. Females have greater verbal ability.
c. Girls have lower self-esteem.
d. Boys have superior visual-spatial ability.

19. The research on how parents differentially reinforce their sons and daughters shows the greatest support for the idea that parents reinforce their:
a. sons' and daughters' play and toy preferences.
b. sons to be more aggressive.
c. daughters to be more dependent.
d. sons to achieve more.

20. Dr. Davis states, "Once children understand their gen-

der, children then develop a body of information about their gender's attitudes and behaviors, which influences information processing and guides behavior." She is talking about which of the following theories?

a. involvement theory
b. behavioral theory
c. psychoanalytic theory
d. gender schema theory

Answers to Multiple-Choice Questions

1. c 2. d 3. c 4. a 5. d 6. b 7. b 8. c 9. d
10. b 11. d 12. b 13. d 14. b 15. d 16. d 17. c
18. c 19. a 20. d

Chapter 10

Physical and Cognitive Development in Middle Childhood

Chapter Outline

Are the Following Statements True or False?

1. The rate of growth actually increases during middle childhood.
2. Elementary school children today are more active than they were a generation ago.
3. Elementary school children often overestimate their physical abilities.
4. School-age children can solve abstract, hypothetical problems if they are given the time.
5. When elementary school children claim they understand something, a parent or teacher can be reasonably certain that they do.
6. Both parents and children rate elementary schools more positively than secondary schools.
7. Today there are no differences in achievement between children who come from middle-class and poverty backgrounds.
8. American children enter elementary school with a greater knowledge base than Japanese children.
9. Children whose time spent watching television is restricted read more.
10. Most children who are academically gifted are socially backward.

Answers to True-False Statements 1. False: see p. 217 2. False: see p. 218 3. True 4. False: see p. 220 5. False: see p. 224 6. True 7. False: see p. 227 8. True 9. True 10. False: see p. 236

Letting Go

About 10 years ago a television commercial showed a parent bringing her young child to the bus to go to school for the first time. As sentimental music played, the mother's hand let go of her child, symbolically representing independence for the child as he entered the bus, the school, and a new world. The school experience dominates the middle years of childhood. Many things change, and more demands are made on the child.

Physical Development in Middle Childhood

Middle childhood is a time of horizontal growth, of gradual changes in height and weight. Slowly, the child's forehead and abdomen become flatter, the arms and legs more slender, the nose larger, the shoulders squarer, and the waistline more pronounced. Although the changes may be less spectacular than those that occur in earlier years, they are no less important.

Height and Weight

The rate of growth continues to decline during middle childhood until about the age of 12. Girls are a bit shorter than boys until adolescence, but because girls experience their adolescent growth spurt about 2 years earlier, they are taller for a couple of years. By age 14 or so, boys regain their height advantage (Tanner, 1990).

True or False?
The rate of growth actually increases during middle childhood.

Boys and girls weigh about the same amount at 8 years of age (Black & Puckett, 1996). Then girls become heavier at about 9 or 10 and stay heavier until they are about 14½ years old, when boys equal or surpass girls (Tanner, 1990).

Nutrition

No one doubts the importance of nutrition. Children who are chronically hungry and malnourished often suffer growth retardation and severe cognitive impairment. When hunger is temporary and nutritional deficiencies mild, children experience more subtle problems such as poor academic performance (Whitney & Rolfes, 1996). Poor eating habits, such as missing breakfast, are related to lower performance on tests of arithmetic (Kruesi & Rapoport, 1986).

The middle childhood years are the parents' best and perhaps last chance to influence food choices, but nutritional supervision wanes during this period. Most children in the fourth through eighth grades choose their own breakfasts, lunches, and snacks (National Center for Nutrition and Dietetics, 1991), and they are deeply affected by what they see on television, which encourages them to eat poorly. The most common TV commercials aimed at children are for toys and games, cereals and candy, soda, and other snacks (Condry, Bence, & Scheibe, 1987), and children ask their parents for these foods (Taras et al., 1989).

Questions Students Often Ask

When my children watch television, all I see are commercials for candy, cereal, toys that they don't need. I think food ads should be banned on children's TV programs.

Many people are upset at the ads that are directed to young children. Although young children understand the difference between the program and the commercial, they fail to comprehend that someone is trying to get them to buy a certain product. The problem with banning these types of commercials is that it would interfere with free-speech rights. People have the right to communicate over the airwaves within the legal limits of the law. Cigarette ads are banned because of their proven relationship to disease. Although the candies and cereals advertised may not be very nu-

tritious it is difficult to say that they are as harmful as cigarettes. If we continue to ban anything that is objectionable, we may interfere with the free and open exchange of information.

Relatively few studies have been conducted on the eating habits of children during their middle childhood years. One major study, the Bogalusa Heart Study, found a consistent pattern of overconsumption of foods high in saturated fat, sugar, and salt, with snack or junk foods high in these elements accounting for about one third of the children's total caloric intake (Berenson et al., 1982). This is unfortunate, since a recent government report noted that children and adolescents with a high cholesterol level are much more likely to have a high cholesterol level in adulthood and advocated that children eat a low-fat, low-cholesterol diet (Lane, 1991). Recent studies show that the effects of poor diet begin early. At least 40% of elementary school children show at least one risk factor related to later heart disease such as high blood pressure, high cholesterol, or obesity (Black & Pucket, 1996). Nutritional education is certainly an important concern.

Childhood Obesity

There is no relationship between birth weight or weight in infancy and later obesity. Overweight infants most often grow into children who are normal in weight. However, beginning in the toddler years and preschool period and continuing throughout the middle years of childhood, being overweight is associated with continued obesity.

Children are heavier today than they were 20 years ago, having gained about 5 pounds over the past two decades (Whitney & Rolfes, 1996). The main problem appears to be a lack of exercise (Schlicker, Borra, & Regan, 1994). Children are more sedentary than ever before. In a 1992 survey of 6- to 9-year-olds, fewer than half of all children surveyed said they played outside after school or on weekends whereas 80% watched television (International Food Information Council, 1992). Obesity is also more common today, and there is a relationship between the number of hours children spend watching television and obesity and blood cholesterol (Klesges, Shelton, & Klesges, 1993; Obarzanek et al., 1994). Many children in school do not get enough exercise nor do they engage in any strenuous physical activity (Parcel et al., 1987); many students do not receive any daily physical fitness training at all in school (Brody, 1990).

True or False?
Elementary school children today are more active than they were a generation ago.

Obese children are more likely to be shunned, to have fewer friends, and to have a poor body image (Mendelson & White, 1985). They may suffer discrimination and be teased. They often begin puberty earlier but stop growing at a shorter height (DeBruyne & Rolfes, 1989).

Although obesity has a genetic component, most obese people overeat and are not sufficiently active. Some children learn to eat the wrong foods and consume empty calories from junk food each day. Obesity in children is difficult to correct. Because very heavy dieting can injure children as they develop, it is usually not recommended. One promising approach is to feed children in a nutritious way that will help them maintain a constant weight while they grow. This promotes normal development while restricting the accumulation of body fat (Cataldo & Whitney, 1986). Other approaches involve providing psychological support and increasing the amount of exercise the child gets. One successful program involved placing parents and children on a diet and exercise routine, requiring attendance at weekly meetings and reinforcement. Under this regimen, parents and children lost weight. After 10 years the parents had gained the weight back, but the children were less likely to have done so. Other suggestions include eating healthier snacks and portion control.

Health Education

Nutritional education is only one part of a larger effort, called *health education,* which deals with physical and

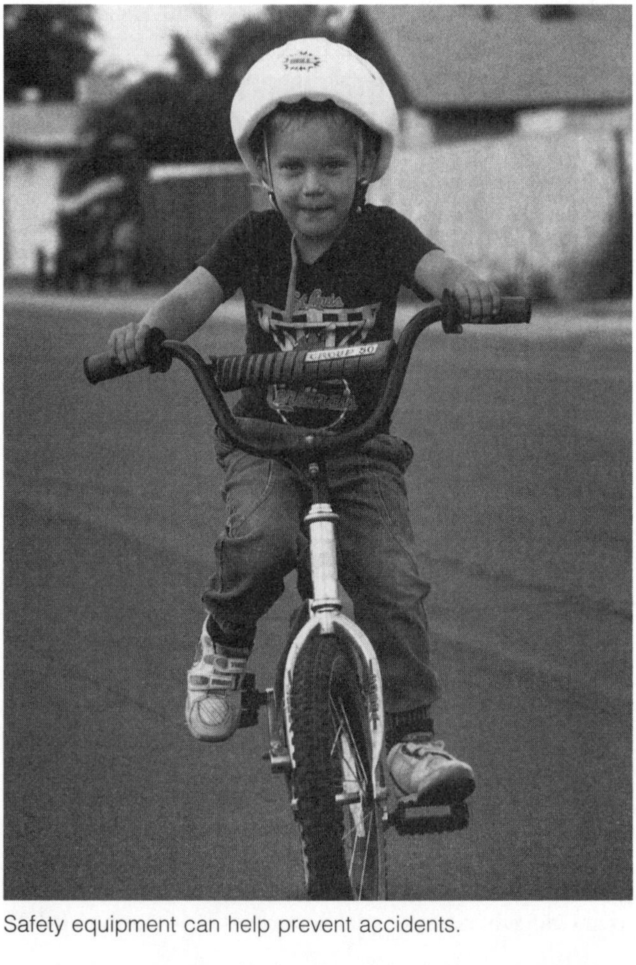

Safety equipment can help prevent accidents.

emotional health. Health education programs focus on how certain practices, such as drinking and smoking, affect the body. These programs can be beneficial if they are comprehensive. A survey conducted by the Metropolitan Life Foundation found that children in grades three through twelve who had taken at least 3 years of health education were less likely to drink alcohol, smoke, use other drugs, or ride with a driver who had been drinking than children of the same age who had 1 year or less of health education (Brody, 1989). These children were also more likely to exercise regularly, wear seat belts, eat breakfast every day, and brush their teeth.

Another area of health education is safety and accident avoidance. The most common cause of death in middle childhood is accidents, and deaths from bicycle accidents are a major concern. The use of safety helmets could reduce the risk of head trauma and injury. Appropriate safety equipment for skateboarding and rollerblading would help as well. The most common hazards and safety problems for school-age children are found in Table 10.1, along with suggested topics to discuss with children (Pillitteri, 1992).

Children in middle childhood often overestimate their ability to perform tasks both just beyond and well beyond their ability (Plumert, 1993). Elementary school children believe themselves to be more capable than they really are and take physical risks such as riding bicycles too fast or climbing too high (Black & Pucket, 1996). Some accidents are caused by errors in judgment when children overestimate their abilities and perhaps run through traffic believing they are faster than they really are; this is especially true of younger elementary school children (McKenzie & Forbes, 1992). Other accidents may result from failure to follow simple rules like looking both ways when crossing the street.

True or False?
Elementary school children often overestimate their physical abilities.

Dentition

The shedding of **deciduous teeth** is perhaps the most obvious physical occurrence during early middle childhood. For children, losing their teeth is a sign that they are growing up, but the gaps left in the mouth can cause temporary cosmetic problems as well as difficulty in pronunciation.

Human beings have a complement of 20 baby teeth and 32 permanent teeth. The first permanent tooth is usually the "6-year molar," which does not replace any baby tooth (Smart & Smart, 1978). This tooth may erupt

deciduous teeth The scientific term for baby teeth.

Table 10.1 **Preventing Accidents in the School-Age Child**

ACCIDENT	PREVENTIVE MEASURE
Motor Vehicle Accidents	Encourage children to use seat belts in a car; role model their use. Teach street-crossing safety; stress that streets are no place for roughhousing, pushing, or shoving. Teach bicycle safety, including advice not to take "passengers" on a bicycle and to use a helmet. Teach parking lot and school bus safety (do not walk behind parked cars, wait for crossing guard, etc.).
Community	Teach to avoid areas specifically unsafe, such as train yards, grain silos, back alleys. Teach not to go with strangers (parents can establish a code word with child; child does not leave school with anyone who does not know the word). Teach to say "no" to anyone who touches them whom they do not wish to do so, including family members (most sexual abuse is by a family member, not a stranger).
Burns	Teach safety with candles, matches, campfires—fire is not fun. Teach safety with beginning cooking skills (remember to include microwave oven safety such as closing door firmly before turning on oven; not using metal containers). Teach not to climb electric poles.
Falls	Teach that roughhousing on fences, climbing on roofs, etc., is hazardous. Teach skateboard safety.
Sports Injuries	Wearing appropriate equipment for sports (face masks for hockey, knee braces for football, batting helmets for baseball) is not babyish but smart. Teach not to play to a point of exhaustion or in a sport beyond physical capability (pitching baseball or toe ballet for a grade-school child). Teach to use trampolines only with adult supervision to avoid serious neck injury.
Drowning	Children should learn how to swim and that dares and roughhousing when diving or swimming are not appropriate. Teach not to swim beyond limits of capabilities.
Drugs	Teach to avoid all recreational drugs and to take prescription medicine only as directed.
Firearms	Teach safe firearm use. Parents should keep firearms in locked cabinets with bullets separate from gun.
General	Teach school-agers to keep adults informed as to where they are and what they are doing. Be aware that the frequency of accidents increases when parents are under stress and therefore less attentive, special precautions must be taken at these times. Some children are more active, curious, and impulsive and therefore more vulnerable to accidents than others.

Source: Pillitteri, 1992.

at any time between 4½ and 8 years of age (Krogman, 1980). It is not easily recognizable, and it may become decayed and lost if not properly cared for. Some parents do not put much effort into dental care for their young children, thinking they have "only baby teeth" anyway. This is unfortunate, because premature loss can lead to dental problems, including difficulties with the bite. As a rule, girls lose their baby teeth before boys do.

Motor Skill Development

By the time children enter elementary school, they have developed many motor skills. They can run, climb, gallop, and hop. Skipping is just being mastered, as are throwing, catching, and kicking; balancing is reasonably good. During the next 6 years, motor skills are refined and modified (DeOreo & Keogh, 1980).

During middle childhood running speed and the ability to jump for distance increase. The ability to throw both for accuracy and for distance also improves (Cratty, 1986), as does balance. These improvements are the result both of maturation and of practice. Boys are superior in running speed and throwing whereas girls excel in tasks that require agility, rhythm, and the ability to hop (Cratty, 1986). Boys are also stronger than girls during this period, but girls show more muscular flexibility. As with almost all gender differences, the overlap between the genders is great (Lockhart, 1980), and training and motivation are important factors. Frequently, boys are more motivated to perform on tests of physical ability and are more likely to practice certain skills, such as throwing, that involve the large muscles. In addition, the differences between the average boy and girl on many of these tasks are not very great; if girls are encouraged to develop their skills, they can improve them greatly.

As boys and girls get older, however, differences in their physical abilities become more noticeable. Differences in performance before the age of about 11 or 12 are small (Corbin, 1980b), but during adolescence males continue to improve while females tend to level off or may even decrease in physical ability. The decreased performance may result from a lack of motivation, fear of physical injury to female internal organs, or fear of appearing too masculine (Corbin, 1980b); it may also be related to society's expectations. For example, males are expected to participate in rugged sports that require strength, and females are more likely to be encouraged to engage in physical activities that demand agility. Females may not be taught the same physical skills as males. Society's different expectations for the physical abilities and training of males and females are somewhat reduced today from what they were even 20 years ago, but they are still present.

Motor skill development has an effect on the self-concept. Children who think of themselves as clumsy often do not have a positive self-concept. This may also lead to social problems because physical activities are part of the social scene of middle childhood. Children may not want to take part in games because they are afraid to be embarrassed and this may lead to a vicious circle in which less practice leads to lower ability, which leads to a further fear of embarrassment and the tendency to practice motor skills even less.

Cognitive Development in Middle Childhood

Children start elementary school at the beginning of middle childhood and their cognitive development is naturally a great concern. Children's abilities to pay attention, remember what they learn, and use information and skills to solve problems are crucial to school success. As children enter first grade the long preoperational stage is drawing to a close, and children are entering the **concrete operational stage.**

The Stage of Concrete Operations

The shift from the preoperational stage to the concrete operational stage is gradual. The child does not go to sleep egocentric and unable to fully understand classification and conservation and wake up with fully developed abilities in these areas; these skills develop gradually over the years (see Table 10.2).

During the concrete operational stage, children can deal with concrete objects rather than with abstractions when they consider change (Siegler, 1991). They must either see or be able to imagine objects. In this stage children who are presented with a purely verbal problem that involves hypotheses cannot solve the problem but have no difficulty if it is explained in real, concrete terms. This is one reason why children have difficulty understanding the long-term, probable effects of such behaviors as poor nutrition and find it easier to understand direct, concrete, and immediate cause-and-effect relations involved in certain safety-related concerns (Olvera-Ezzell et al., 1994).

> ***True or False***
> School-age children can solve abstract, hypothetical problems if they are given the time.

The Decline in Egocentrism

Children in the stage of concrete operations become less egocentric. They understand that other people see the world differently, and they seek to validate their own view of the world. This is accomplished through social interaction, during which they can share their thoughts and verify their view of the world (Piaget, 1928). In addition, they can now take the perspective of the other person and imagine what others are thinking of them in a relatively simple way (Harter, 1983). They are capable of being more sensitive to the feelings of

concrete operational stage Piaget's third stage of cognitive development, lasting roughly from 7 through 11 years of age, in which children develop the ability to perform logical operations, such as conservation.

Table 10.2 **The Concrete Operational Stage**
In the stage of concrete operations, children can deal with information that is based upon something they can see or imagine. They can mentally operate on objects but cannot deal with abstractions.

CHARACTERISTIC	EXPLANATION	EXAMPLE
Conservation	Children in this stage understand that things remain the same despite changes in appearance.	A child develops the ability to understand that a ball of clay can change shape and still contain the same amount of clay.
Ability to Classify	Students can place objects into various categories.	Elementary school students can now group different animals as mammals.
Ability to Seriate	Students can place things in size order.	Children can arrange a series of sticks in terms of length or weight.
Ability to Reverse Operations	Students can follow a process from beginning to end and then back again.	If a teacher rolls a ball of clay into a long, wormlike structure, a child in this stage can mentally recreate the ball of clay.
Inability to use Abstractions	Students cannot deal with abstract material, such as ideas and statements not tied to something observable or imaginable.	Children may find political cartoons and proverbs puzzling because they cannot understand their abstract meaning.

others and imagining how others would feel in various situations. Their language becomes less egocentric. Preschoolers often use such pronouns as "he" and "she" without offering enough information for the listener to know to whom they are referring because they assume that since they know who they are talking about, others do so too (Pulaski, 1980); as the child matures, this tendency is greatly reduced.

Reversibility and the Ability to Decenter

During middle childhood the limitations of preoperational thought begin to fade slowly. Children develop the ability to reverse operations—to realize that if you roll a clay ball into a long worm, you can reverse your operation and recreate the ball of clay. One 6-year-old proudly told his mother that he learned that 3 plus 2 equals 5. After praising him, his mother asked him how much 2 plus 3 was, to which the child said that he didn't know because he he hadn't learned that one yet (Bjorklund, 1995). The child in the concrete stage of operations understands reversibility and has no difficulty with this. Children also develop the ability to decenter—to take into consideration more than one dimension. Children now realize that the increase in the length of the clay worm compensates for the decrease in its width.

Conservation

The crowning achievement of the concrete operational stage is the ability to conserve (Bisanz, Morrison, & Dunn, 1995). The simplest example is the famous beaker experiment described in Chapter 8, in which a researcher pours equal amounts of a liquid into two identical beakers that are long and thin. Then, in front of the child, the contents of one tall beaker are poured into a squat beaker. The preschool child cannot take both height and width into consideration and cannot reverse the operation of pouring, attending only to the end state, which makes conservation impossible (Piaget & Inhelder, 1969). However, school-age children find such a problem relatively easy and may even show surprise when younger children cannot get it right.

Conservation of number, substance, weight, and volume occur at different ages but in a specific order. Piaget (1952) noted this uneven performance within a developmental stage and used the term **horizontal decalage** to describe the phenomenon whereby the child has acquired the underlying principle for solving a problem such as conservation but is not able to apply it across contexts.

Conservation of Number When children are shown seven pennies either grouped close together or spread out, a 4-year-old is certain that the spread-out display has more coins than the other display. A 6- or 7-year-old develops a sense of conservation of number and knows that the spacing does not matter.

Conservation of Weight A 7-year-old may understand that no clay is lost during the transformation from a ball to a long worm, but this child probably will not understand that both pieces of clay still weigh the same. Conservation of weight comes later, at about age 9 or 10 (Piaget & Inhelder, 1969).

Conservation of Volume When two balls of clay are shown to a child the child should understand that the clay balls are equally large and weigh the same. Then put the clay balls in two identical beakers containing equal amounts of water and show that the balls displace the same volume of liquid because they cause the level of water to rise to the same height. Now change the shape of one of the balls and ask whether it would make the

horizontal decalage The unevenness of development in which a child may be able to solve one type of problem but not others, even though a common principle underlies them all.

water level rise to the previous height (Diamond, 1982). Typically, the ability to solve conservation problems concerning volume comes last, appearing at about age 11 or 12 (Piaget & Inhelder, 1969).

Seriation and Classification

School-age children also further develop the ability to seriate and to classify. They can easily arrange a series of sticks first by mass, later by weight, and finally by volume (Bjorklund, 1995). Their ability to classify also improves greatly. In fact, school-age children are known for their propensity to collect things (Kegan, 1982), thereby practicing their skills of classification. They begin to understand that an item can be classified in many ways and can belong to a great many classes at one time.

How the School-Age Child Thinks

The school-age child's thought processes are a great improvement over those of preschoolers. The logic of preschoolers often defies analysis for a parent who is unfamiliar with Piaget's theories. The more logical, less egocentric ways of elementary school children are easier to undestand.

Although every individual achieves concrete operational thought (Howes, 1990), Piaget was well aware that children in other cultures show variability in the age at which they develop concrete operational skills (Bringuier, 1980). Children in rural Iran showed 2-year, 3-year, and even 4-year delays in passing through the same stages as compared with their urban peers. Environmental influences become more important as a child becomes older. Many studies show that poor rural children with no schooling who have little contact with the developed world do more poorly on Piagetian tasks than urban schoolchildren (Laboratory of Comparative Human Cognition, 1983). Such factors as schooling, urbanization, and the relevance of a particular skill for a society affect the onset of concrete operational abilities (Dasen & Heron, 1981).

Limitations of Concrete Operational Thought

The cognitive abilities of school-age children show a number of limitations. For instance, ask a 7-year-old to interpret a proverb such as "You can lead a horse to water, but you can't make him drink," and you will be very surprised at the answer. The child may say something about not being able to force an animal to drink, may appear puzzled, or may attempt a literal interpretation of the saying. These children do not understand the more general, abstract meaning of the saying. Political cartoons also require the ability to think in the abstract so children do not understand them very well. Teachers who are aware of this may attempt to explain difficult concepts, such as democracy, in more concrete terms that children can understand, perhaps through elections in class, instead of trying to define concepts in abstract, dictionary terms.

Children also have difficulty with hypothetical situations. When asked, "If all dogs were pink and I had a dog, would my dog be pink?" children often rebel (Ault, 1977), insisting that dogs are not pink, and that's that. Children in the concrete stage of operations have difficulty accepting hypothetical situations. For example, children in the concrete operational stage believe that all illness is caused by germs and that to be healthy all you need do is follow some rigid rules. Children are able to understand the immediate consequences of a particular act, for example, running while holding a pair of scissors, but have much more difficulty understanding delayed consequences. They have problems associating two events that are separated by a considerable period of time (Olvera-Ezzell et al., 1994).

Information-Processing Skills

The elementary school child's information-processing skills are superior to those of the preschool child, and attention and memory improve greatly during middle childhood.

Attention

Preschoolers' ability to voluntarily pay attention to a relevant stimulus is limited, and they are easily distracted. The ability to pay attention despite interference improves with age (Dempster, 1992). As children mature, their ability to control their attention, to discriminate between what is and is not most important, and to adapt their attention to the demands of the situation improves (Wittrock, 1986). Their ability to choose what to attend to also improves (Flavell, 1985). These abilities are primitive in preschoolers and develop over the elementary school years. During middle childhood children can also switch attention from one task to another more quickly (Bjorklund, 1995; Pearson & Lane, 1991).

Recall, Recognition, and Memory Strategies

No matter how it is measured, memory improves as children negotiate middle childhood; short-term memory improves with age from 5 to 10 years. The typical 5-year-old can recall four or five numbers after a single presentation; a 10-year-old can recall six or seven numbers (Williams & Stith, 1980). Recognition memory is generally good at all ages, but it too improves with age as does recall (Dirks & Neisser, 1977). Retention is also superior in both recall and recognition.

Children in middle childhood also begin to use verbal memory strategies on their own. During first and second grade young children can often use an organizational strategy when prompted, but fail to apply the strategies spontaneously when given a memory task (Alexander & Schwanenflugel, 1994). When 5-, 7-, and 10-year-olds were asked to remember pictures while researchers measured the rehearsal strategies used, very few 5-year-olds showed any rehearsal whereas most 7-year-olds did once, but only relatively few used the strategy regularly (Flavell et al., 1966). Almost all the 10-year-olds verbalized, and most did so consistently. Spontaneous rehearsal is seen more often as children negotiate middle childhood (Flavell et al., 1993).

Rates of forgetting decline significantly during middle childhood (Brainerd & Reyna, 1995) and children process material much faster (Eaton & Ritchot, 1995). As children progress through middle childhood, they also become aware that some strategies are superior to others. Second-graders show no preference for categorization over rehearsal, and while sixth-graders demonstrate a clear preference for more sophisticated strategies such as categorization (Justice, 1985). Progress in understanding the relative effectiveness of different strategies continues through the elementary school years.

Metamemory

Consider this problem: 8-year-old Rachel comes home from school and tells her mother that she has to learn the state capitals. Up to her room she goes to learn them but comes down a few minutes later, telling her mother that she is finished studying. Her mother tests Rachel, but to the chagrin of both, Rachel doesn't know many of them. Her mother is angry, believing that Rachel just wanted to go outside to play, and Rachel is confused because she thought she knew them.

This scene is relatively common in many homes. Although it is possible that Rachel was pulling a fast one on her mother, it is just as probable that she really thought she knew them. Rachel may have a problem with **metamemory,** which is an individual's knowledge of his or her own memory process. The process of remembering something requires deciding what must be done, doing some operation (such as rehearsal), and finally checking or monitoring how one is doing (Kail, 1990); both diagnosis and monitoring are in the realm of metamemory.

John Flavell (1985), a pioneer in metamemory research, suggests that metamemory should be understood in terms of two major categories. The first is sensitivity. Children must understand—that is, be sensitive to—the meaning of instructions, which often involve words like "remember." Although this may be a problem for very young children, most school-age children have no trouble with such instructions.

The second category involves three variables that interact to determine how well an individual performs on a memory problem. The first is knowledge of one's own memory abilities: young children tend to overestimate the number of items they can remember (Flavell, Friedrichs, & Hoyt, 1970). The second involves the nature of the task. Young children often have difficulty separating the important material from the not-so-important material (Brown & Smiley, 1977). In addition, children must learn what is required of them. When 6-, 8-, and 10-year-olds were tested on their recognition of pictures after a few minutes, a day, or a week only the older children studied longer when told they would have to remember the material for a longer period of time (Rogoff, Newcombe, & Kagan, 1974). The third variable is knowledge of strategies. As children mature, they gain the ability to use more strategies and to understand when one strategy is more useful than another.

metamemory A person's knowledge of his or her own memory process.

Older children are also more likely to use reminders when they need to remember something. Many young children don't even understand that reminders should be placed where they can be seen. When children were asked to remember the location of a penny hidden inside one of four identical opaque cups with lids, almost half the 4- and 5-year-olds thought that hiding a paper clip inside the cup with the penny would be a useful reminder (Beal, 1985). Older subjects think of many more different strategies than younger children, and are better at planning their approaches to solving real-world problems.

Metamemory is a promising area of research. Just because a child says he or she understands the material does not mean that the child does understand. In addition, academic progress may be related to a child's ability to comprehend his or her own level of understanding. In his influential book *How Children Fail* (1964), John Holt noted that part of being a good student is understanding one's level of comprehension. Good students may be those who often say they do not understand and are aware of their level of knowledge. Poor students may not really know whether they understand the material. Holt notes, "The problem is not to get students to ask us what they don't know; the problem is to make them aware of the difference between what they know and what they don't" (1964, p. 29). Older children have a more realistic and accurate picture of their own memory abilities and limitations than younger children (Flavell, Miller, & Miller, 1993); metamemory improves with age.

This child does not know his work after studying. Perhaps he does not know what he knows and what areas he does not understand.

> ***True or False?***
> When elementary school children claim they understand something, a parent or teacher can be reasonably certain that they do.

Some evidence indicates that children can be taught to improve their understanding of memory and their use of strategies (Flavell et al., 1993). One way to do this is to ask the children right before material is taught or read what they think they should know, what they need to know, and what they would like to know and then help them to focus their attention on these areas (Gray & Coolsen, 1987). This is important because children who understand what they know and don't know are better readers and capable of using a variety of strategies, such as rereading and changing speed, to enhance comprehension.

Elementary School

It is crucial that children in elementary school master reading, writing, and arithmetic because they form the basis for later success in school and influence how they see themselves. Erik Erikson viewed the psychosocial crisis of this stage in terms of *industry versus inferiority.* Children who do not measure up to other children in these skills may feel inferior, while children who do well develop a positive sense of achievement and a sense of industry.

Reading is fundamental to school achievement, and learning to read at the appropriate time is crucial to academic success. Failure to learn to read by the end of first grade is associated with later academic failure. This does not mean that a poor reader in the second grade cannot be helped, but without special help, children who are behind tend to stay behind.

Unfortunately, students spend relatively little time reading in or out of school (Rothman, 1990). About half the students in grades four, eight, and twelve report reading 10 or fewer pages each day for schoolwork. This is unfortunate because the more children read, the better their tested skills. Exposure to print and reading time is related to better reading (Echols et al., 1996). Parental involvement is also a key to boosting children's reading; parents who read and show that they value the activity influence their children (Madden, 1996). If parents read for enjoyment, children may do the same. In addition, parents can encourage reading by listening to the child read and providing a wide choice of materials (Carbo & Cole, 1995).

Mathematics is also an important core subject. American students spend less time on and do more poorly in mathematics than do children in many other countries. One study of first-grade and fifth-grade students from Japan, Taiwan, and the United States found that students from Japan and Taiwan were superior to U.S. students on basic mathematical skills (Stigler, Lee, & Stevenson, 1987). The differences can be explained by the time devoted to these skills as well as by the practice demanded of students.

Rating the Schools

Elementary schools have largely escaped the criticisms of the school system; almost all of the discontent seems directed at the secondary school. The famous report, *A Nation at Risk* (National Center on Excellence in Education, 1981), that led to much educational reform was aimed almost entirely at high schools. Polls consistently find more parental and community support and approval for elementary schools than secondary schools. Half of all elementary school students give their school an "A" or "A−" overall rating, but only one third of the secondary school students do so. The parental totals show a similar trend, with more parents rating their neighborhood elementary school higher than their local high school. Many more children rate their elementary school teacher "A" or "A−" than secondary school students and again, this trend is found for parents as well (Education Poll, 1995).

> ***True or False?***
> Both parents and children rate elementary schools more positively than secondary schools.

A number of factors may be at work here. Elementary school children stay in one class with one teacher for most of the day whereas secondary school students have

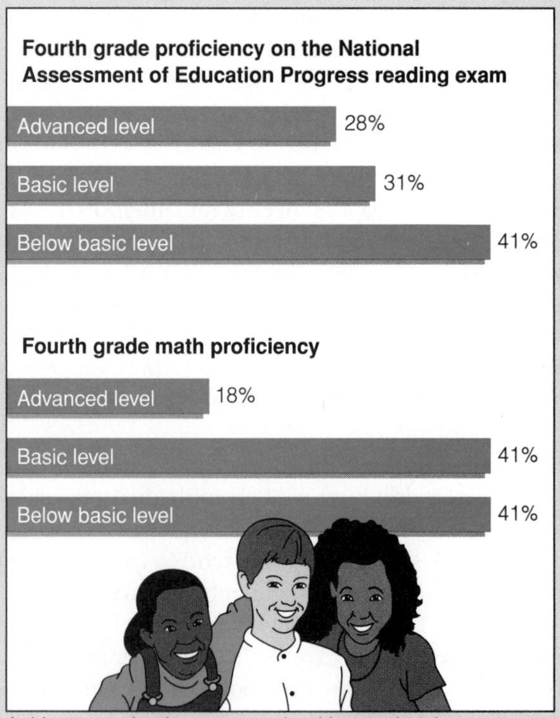

Achievement in elementary school is a national concern.

Datagraphic
Student Achievement
Source: Data from Education Week: January 22, 1997.

many teachers so it is likely that students and their parents have closer relationships with elementary school teachers. Parents take somewhat more of an interest in elementary school work because it is much easier for them to understand. In addition, the mandate of the elementary school to teach the basics is understandable and clear to the general public; the mandate of the secondary school is somewhat more ambiguous (Bracey, 1996). When elementary schools are criticized it is most often for failing to address the difficulties of children from minority groups.

Many African American and Latino children do not achieve as well as would be desirable. Between one third and one half of the gap in achievement between African Americans and whites was closed in the 1970s and 1980s, but the progress has recently slowed (U.S. Department of Education, 1993b). Unfortunately, the emphasis placed on the underachievement of African American children has led to them being stereotyped as underachievers (Slaughter-Defoe et al., 1990). This is unfair because many minority children succeed academically.

Much of the problem is directly related to poverty and all the factors that go with poverty including poor housing, greater exposure to violence, lower parental education, poor access to health care, and lack of family stability (Ford & Harris, 1996). Academically successful African American 6-year-olds come from supportive homes, have smaller families, are above the poverty line, and have mothers with higher IQs and are relatively better educated. Having a large family reduces the amount of attention each child receives and may also lead to more authoritarian parenting. Children who are less successful have mothers with lower levels of intelligence and less education, come from larger families, and experience less support in the home (Luster & McAdoo, 1994). The greater the number of risk factors present the more likely it is that the child will fail.

When sixth-grade gifted African American students were compared to African American students in regular classes and in classes for potentially gifted students, those in regular classes perceived lower parental achievement orientations and expressed greater concerns about peer relations and pressure. Gifted African American students reported higher achievement orientations, higher perceived parental achievement orientations, and had more positive perceptions of academically successful students. Students in all classes strongly supported achievement and valued school success but only those in the gifted class were working up to their potential. Children in regular classes were more likely than other students to experience negative peer pressure to achieve. Counseling that centers on self-awareness may help to close the gap between values and achievement, as would exposure to more positive role models. For instance, the lack of role models in math and science may discourage achievement in these areas (Rech & Stevens, 1996).

A similar situation exists among some Latino children. Their proficiency in reading, math, and science has improved but a significant gap remains (U.S. Department of Education, 1995b). Much of the gap is attributable to poverty as well, but the most important barrier is language (Duran, 1989; see Chapter 7). Latino immigrants, especially those from Mexico, arrive in the United States with fewer educational and economic advantages than other immigrants or people born in the United States (Schnaiberg, 1996).

Americans don't seem to want significant changes in their elementary schools, although formal rote learning has been de-emphasized and discipline is not as strict. Newer methods of learning include cooperative learning in which students work as a team, experiential learning, and the use of projects and exhibitions (Darling-Hammond, 1994). Another area of change is in preparing children for school and in easing the transition from preschool to elementary school (Fleck, 1995). As noted in Chapter 8, a new Head Start initiative emphasizes the continuation of services into the early elementary school years. In addition, building a parent-teacher partnership in which parents work with teachers to encourage their children's mastery of basic skills is now being emphasized. Studies show that such cooperation can be effective (Whitehurst et al., 1994).

Computer technology has also entered the elementary school classroom and one of the greatest concerns of both elementary and secondary school students is their inability to obtain sufficient time on the computers (USA Today, 1996). More time and effort must be spent investigating the best use of such technology (Woronov, 1994). All too often computers are found only in isolated labs and teachers often have difficulty scheduling classes or finding the right software (Whitehead, Cain, & Graves, 1994).

Cultural Pluralism: Multicultural Education

Another major change in the curriculum is based on our increasing awareness that we live in a diverse society. At one time, the concept of the melting pot was popular, that is, the notion that minority groups melted into American society and they took on the values of the dominant culture. Today, the melting pot does not explain our society anymore, and America is instead a culturally pluralistic society, one in which a number of cultural groups exist side by side. This change requires that educational practice be modified to serve the new demographic and cultural realities in the United States and other Western countries (Hilliard, 1980).

One of these modifications is the provision of what is called **multicultural education** to students. Multicultural education means different things to different people

multicultural education A multidisciplinary approach to education aimed at teaching students about the cultural heritage of various groups and the many contributions each group makes to society.

Many schools are proud of their computer equipment but more work needs to be done on using this technology to aid learning in an organized and meaningful manner.

(Ryan, 1994). Some see it as a way of providing more information about the contributions of minority groups whereas others emphasize the importance of reinterpreting history and the American or Canadian experience in terms of how it affects different groups or in terms of encouraging a wider, global view of society. Finally, the multicultural perspective is a political movement that seeks to empower minorities.

Five possible approaches to multicultural education are suggested (Sleeter, 1993). The first approach called teaching the exceptional and culturally different, aims at helping students in minority groups to "make it" in society as it currently exists. Culturally relevant materials are used, and programs are instituted to bring students up to grade level. The emphasis is on changing the educational opportunities of minority students by focusing less on the majority student.

The human relations approach fosters positive interpersonal relationships among members of diverse groups in the classroom and strengthens children's self-concept and self-esteem. Advocates of this approach are concerned with how children feel about one another and how they relate to each other (Winter, 1994/1995). Teaching about cultural differences and similarities, avoiding stereotypes, and emphasizing every group's contributions to American society are incorporated into the curriculum. Often, ethnic fairs and special celebrations are held to introduce certain cultures to students.

Single-group studies focus on a particular group, such as women or people with disabilities, raising consciousness about how each group experiences history, its culture, its contributions, and how it relates to the dominant society.

The approach Sleeter actually calls multicultural reconstructs the entire educational process to promote cultural pluralism. Curriculum content is reorganized around knowledge of various cultures, often starting with the cultures within the school (Marshall, 1995). Students are actively encouraged to analyze life situations and to use their native language; all students are encouraged to learn a foreign language. Students debate issues from the point of view of different groups. The academic emphasis is on achievement, and the entire curriculum is rewritten to emphasize multicultural understanding, often using content developed through the single group and human relations perspectives.

The last approach, the multicultural/ social reconstructionist approach, combines the multicultural approach with an activist component. It includes everything in the multicultural approach, but also focuses on social action.

Educators have voiced some concerns about multicultural education, some claiming that multicultural perspectives seem to dwell solely on the negative experiences of minority groups and especially on their school experiences (Garcia & Pugh, 1992); others fear that it will fragment American society (Krauthammer, 1990; Schlesinger, 1994). Even those who are in favor of multiculturalism fear that indignation and anger rather than rigorous academic criticism will be taught (Winkler, 1990); some tempering of the rhetoric on both sides would be welcome (Price, 1992).

The emphasis on cultural pluralism has led to changes in curriculum. A greater emphasis has been placed on showing how history has affected each group. For instance, a person of European ancestry may see Columbus as the explorer who opened up the New World to settlement by Europeans, eventually leading to the establishment of the United States and other countries. However, Native Americans may see Columbus as the explorer whose voyages ushered in the era of European encroachment on Native American lands and of the wars that would bring many tribes to the brink of extinction.

A greater appreciation of different cultural practices and beliefs can lead to better understanding between groups, but many cultures must be studied, not just the culture within the school. Students in heavily populated Latino areas who study their culture learn to appreciate it and be proud of their heritage. To be truly multicultural, though, these students should be exposed to other cultures as well. If one of the goals is to teach students to communicate and interact with people of different cultural backgrounds, then education must be truly multicultural and emphasize the similarities as well as the differences between cultures (Hernandez, 1989).

Success in School

In a technological society, success in school opens the door to better jobs and a better future. The general achievement of a child in school depends on school, home, and individual variables.

The School

Factors such as a safe and orderly environment, clear goals, administrative leadership, high expectations, instruction in the basic skills, and frequent monitoring of student progress have been suggested as differentiating successful schools from less successful ones (Lezotte, 1982; Cohen, 1982). A good relationship between home and school is also important. Especially in the early grades and in schools where students require remedial work, smaller classes are an advantage (Rutter, 1983).

The Home

Children who live in poverty do not do as well as those who do not. Poverty is negatively related to academic achievement across all racial and ethnic groups (Duncan, Brooks-Gunn, & Klebanov, 1994). Children from poor families live in crowded conditions, receive poorer health care, have fewer books, go on fewer field trips, have lower career aspirations, and may not know how to succeed in public school (Kaplan, 1990). Poorer children generally come to school less advanced cognitively. These conditions may lead to failure, and a vicious circle can ensue: Failure leads to lack of interest and motivation, which leads to more failure. These children's expectations for success are also lower, although they increase with age (Fulkerson, Furr, & Brown, 1983).

> ***True or False?***
> Today there are no differences in achievement between children who come from middle-class and poverty backgrounds.

The correlations between socioeconomic status and academic achievement range anywhere from a low of +.1 to a high of +.8 (White, 1982), with a correlation of +1.00 being perfect. Although socioeconomic status is correlated with achievement, it can explain only about 5% of the final results in academic achievement. The traditional indicators of socioeconomic status are occupational level, education, and income, but many studies also include such factors as family size, educational aspirations, ethnicity, and the presence of reading materials in the home.

Measures of home atmosphere, such as the availability of books and educational aspirations correlate more highly with academic achievement than measures of socioeconomic status. Because of this, we would do better to concentrate on which home factors affect academic achievement.

Parents who are involved without being overcontrolling can help to improve their children's achievement, and moderate levels of supervision rather than very high or low levels are positively related to achievement (Ginsburg & Bronstein, 1993; Kurdek et al., 1995). Praising children for their successes, stating expectations in a nonchallenging manner, acknowledging children's feelings and needs, and providing choices and alternatives are positively related to achievement (Ginsburg & Bronstein, 1993; Levitt, Guacci-Franco, & Levitt, 1994). Parents who read to their children, help them with homework, take them to the library, and expand their language skills give their children a boost. Parents can further help children to improve their school performance by checking their homework, reinforcing reading for pleasure, restricting time spent watching television, and generally encouraging learning. By concentrating on home environment instead of socioeconomic status, we turn our attention away from a particular group and toward particular parent-child relationships, home variables, and child-rearing strategies. Socioeconomic status may mask truly important home variables that are good predictors of academic achievement.

Unfortunately, many parents become less involved with their children's cognitive development when they enter elementary school. Harold Stevenson, a noted researcher whose work includes comparisons of American children to Asian children, found that American children often enter school with more knowledge and motivation than Asian children in Japan and China, but that Japanese and Chinese students are soon doing better. Stevenson argues that many American families provide a stimulating atmosphere for their preschoolers by reading to them and taking them to museums and on outings. When American children enter elementary school, however, parents often seem to believe that it is solely the school's job to educate the child (Rothman, 1991), an attitude that hinders the achievement of American children.

> ***True or False?***
> American children enter elementary school with a greater knowledge base than Japanese children.

Television and Reading

One home factor often blamed for children's lack of basic skills is excessive television viewing. Some argue that watching television substitutes for reading as a leisure activity, thereby reducing the time children spend reading which, in turn, reduces reading ability. When fifth-graders were asked to rate leisure activities, reading ranked seventh out of nine categories, with television ranking first (Greaney, 1980). Indeed, a negative relationship exists between television viewing and reading, and between television viewing and academic achievement (Johnson, Cooper, & Chance, 1982). Television has an especially adverse effect on reading when the skill is being acquired, during the early years of elementary school (Van Evra, 1990). The relationship between television and poor reading skills is greatest for children who are heavy viewers (Comstock & Paik, 1991).

Television viewing may not always be the cause but the symptom of a problem. It may well be that children who find it difficult to read are frustrated and turn to television as an outlet. Also television viewing displaces more than just reading; it displaces physical activity and any activity that is valued less than television viewing.

It would be a mistake to blame poor reading skills on television viewing. The cognitive abilities of the child, the values of the home and school, and the child's attitude toward reading are also important factors that enter the equation. Some excellent readers watch quite a bit of television (Neuman, 1982). Thus, television may be one factor that inhibits reading, but it cannot shoulder the entire blame, which must be shared by the home and the school (Comstock & Paik, 1991).

Restricting television viewing can improve reading, at least in the short term. Consider what happened when 6-year-olds were matched and randomly assigned to a restricted television viewing group or an unrestricted group. In the restricted group, the children watched half as much television as they had previously watched. The results showed that restricting television did improve performance on intelligence tests and that the children did spend more time reading (Gadberry, 1980).

True or False?
Children whose time spent watching television is restricted read more.

Individual Factors

Individual variables, such as work habits and intelligence, also influence a child's success in school.

Attitudes, Motivation, and Work Habits

Highly motivated students with positive attitudes toward school do better than children who dislike learning and school and don't care how they do. One reason put forward for male superiority in mathematics in the later grades is that males expect to do better. These higher expectations are found as early as the first grade, even though the grades and abilities of boys are not superior to those of girls (Entwisle & Baker, 1983). Differences in performance are not inevitable, especially when females have positive attitudes toward math (Paulsen & Johnson, 1983). Also, children who know how to study and how to take tests are likely to do better than those who don't; work habits and study skills can be taught. Students who use their time effectively, involve themselves in classroom activities, show interest in the subject matter, and pay attention in class do better (Alexander, Entwisle, & Dauber, 1993).

Intelligence

Of all the factors that contribute to academic achievement, none is more controversial than intelligence. **Intelligence** has been defined as the ability to profit from one's experiences, a cluster of cognitive abilities, the ability to do well in school, and whatever an intelligence test measures (Kaplan, 1990). Howard Gardner, a respected expert in the field, defines intelligence as "an ability to solve problems or to fashion a product which is valued in one or more cultural settings" (1987, p. 25). Piaget viewed intelligence as an ongoing process by which children use qualitatively different ways to adapt to their environment.

Most people see intelligence in terms of academic achievement. One of the more popular and newer conceptions of intelligence is advanced by Howard Gardner (1987a; 1983) and called the **Theory of Multiple Intelligences.** Gardner argues that seven different types of intelligence exist: linguistic, logical-mathematical, musical, spatial, bodily kinesthetic, interpersonal (social skills), and intrapersonal (the understanding of one's own feelings; Figure 10.1). Other approaches look at the nature of how children take in and process information.

Clearly, the definition one uses affects the way intelligence tests will be constructed. Most intelligence tests are targeted at school-age populations, and there is a high correlation (about .6) between school achievement and performance on intelligence tests (Kubiszyn & Borich, 1987); that is, children who score very high are likely to do better in school. The correlation between scores on IQ tests and standardized tests of achievement is even higher, falling within the range of .7 to .9. Intelligence tests can predict future school success, and children who score very low may have difficulty in school. However, notice that the correlation is not perfect, meaning that other factors, including motivation, background, and work habits, affect how a child performs in school. Some psychologists believe that such factors as motivation and adjustment must be assessed if we are to measure the intellectual competence of children (Scarr, 1981).

The Stanford-Binet and Wechsler Tests

In the early 1900s Alfred Binet created a test to identify students who would not benefit from traditional education. Binet used a series of tests that measured a sample of children's abilities at different age levels. At each level, some children performed better than others and Binet simply compared children's performances on these tests to those of others in the age group. If a child had less knowledge than the average child of the same age, that

intelligence The ability to profit from experience; a cluster of abilities, such as reasoning and memory; the ability to solve problems or fashion a product valued in one's society.

Theory of Multiple Intelligences A conception of intelligence advanced by Howard Gardner, who argues that there are seven different types of intelligence.

Linguistic

Language skills include a sensitivity to the subtle shades of the meanings of words

Logical-Mathematical

Both critics and supporters acknowledge that IQ tests measure this ability well

Musical

Like language, music is an expressive medium—and this talent flourishes in prodigies

Spatial

Sculptors and painters are able accurately to perceive, manipulate and re-create forms

Bodily-Kinesthetic

At the core of this kind of intelligence are body control and skilled handling of objects

Interpersonal

Skill in reading the moods and intentions of others is displayed by politicians, among others

Intrapersonal

The key is understanding one's own feelings—and using that insight to guide behavior

Figure 10.1
Gardner's Conception of Intelligence
Source: U.S. News and World Report, November 23, 1987.

child was said to be less intelligent; if the child knew more, the child's intelligence was said to be higher. Binet used the term **mental age** to describe the age at which the child was functioning.

Later, another psychologist, William Stern, proposed the term **intelligence quotient,** or **IQ,** which is arrived at by taking the mental age of the child and dividing it by the child's chronological age (age since birth) and then multiplying by 100 to remove the decimal. The problem with the IQ is that it assumes a straight-line (linear) relationship between age and intelligence. This is not the case, especially after the age of 16. The original Binet test has gone through a number of revisions and today is called the Stanford-Binet Intelligence Test.

Beginning in the late 1930s, David Wechsler began to develop another set of individualized intelligence tests.

mental age The age at which an individual is functioning.

intelligence quotient (IQ) A method of computing intelligence by dividing the mental age by the chronological age and multiplying by 100.

The third edition of Wechsler Intelligence Scale for Children (WISC) contains a number of subtests that can be divided into two categories: verbal and performance. The verbal subtests measure verbal skills such as information and similarities and the performance subtests measure nonverbal skills such as completing pictures and putting together puzzle pieces (Wechsler, 1991). A composite, or total, intelligence score may also be obtained.

Today a statistically sophisticated way of calculating the intelligence scores, called a *deviation IQ,* is used. This involves a comparison of a child's performance with the average performance of a large group of children of the same age. The average is still 100. If every 8-year-old child in the United States were to receive an intelligence test, most scores would probably cluster around the middle, the 100 mark, with fewer scores being found on each extreme. Scores closer to the average are much more common than those further away. More than two thirds of all children have intelligence scores between 85 and 115 and very few, less than 3% have scores above 130 or below 70.

How Intelligence Tests Can Be Misused

In recent years, much controversy has arisen over the use of intelligence tests. Some criticism has been directed at the possible cultural bias against minorities (Hickson, Blackson, & Reis, 1995). Are intelligence tests fair to children from minority groups? In 1971, a group of parents of African American children who were placed in classes for children with mental retardation sued in federal court, claiming that the placements were discriminatory because they were based on intelligence tests that were culturally biased. Eight years later, the court ruled that IQ tests *were* culturally biased. This famous decision, *Larry P. v. Riles,* meant that intelligence tests could no longer be used as the sole basis for placing children in special classes (Rothstein, 1995).

Opponents of intelligence tests often emphasize the negative social outcomes of testing, such as the overrepresentation of students from minority groups in special education. Children from minority groups may be unfairly stigmatized as less intelligent. Others point to the different experiences of minority group children. For example, on an older version of a standardized intelligence test, a child is asked: What would you do if you were sent to buy a loaf of bread and the grocer said he did not have any more?

Professionals constructing the test thought the answer go to another store was reasonable and it certainly is. Yet, more than a quarter of all children from minority groups said that they would go home if such a situation arose. When asked why they answered this way the children simply told investigators there were no other stores in the neighborhood (Hardy et al., 1976). Many such examples show that the differential experiences of children from various minority groups affect the ways in which they answer questions on intelligence tests, which leads some groups to argue that IQ tests discriminate against test takers who don't fit into the white middle-class profile. (On some individual intelligence tests, a child may be asked to explain the answer and will be given credit if the answer is logical).

Vocabulary, too, can cause difficulties because they may be inappropriate for children whose primary language is not English (Kaplan, 1996). Children from the majority culture may be very comfortable with the setting, the format of the test, and the types of questions asked whereas children from various minority groups may not be as comfortable (Duran, 1989).

Others argue that these tests are based on the reasoning style of the dominant group and do not take into consideration that possibility that children from various minority groups may reason differently and may have different cognitive styles (Helms, 1992). For example, tests are constructed so that each question has only one right answer that is determined by the normative majority group response because it is assumed that intelligent people will think in that particular manner. But people who grow up with different cultural beliefs may view the world differently and possess different cognitive styles and therefore see alternative answers to a question; these answers are considered incorrect by the test constructors (Helms, 1992). For example, a person who is raised to believe that emotions and logic are equally important may have difficulty understanding a problem in which a person is reasoning about the best solution without any emotional input (Helms, 1992). Another problem is the interpretation of intelligence, as if it were a fixed quality etched in stone. As we have noted many times, it is not. Intelligence can change with one's experience.

Finally, although scores on an intelligence test correlate with academic achievement, there is a tendency to overrate the test's predictive abilities and to categorize children rigidly (Kaplan, 1977). For example, one of my acquaintances was shocked when her child's fifth-grade teacher told her that her son was doing fine considering he had an IQ of "only" 105. Children can really suffer if intelligence test scores are used in such a manner.

Proponents of testing argue that the problem with intelligence tests is the way they are used, not their construction or what they indicate. They do predict, albeit not perfectly, academic success across ethnic groups (U.S. Department of Education, 1993a). Intelligence tests scores do not indicate the cause of the difference in intelligence between groups of children; recent studies report that poverty and home environment explain the overwhelming majority of this difference. When poverty and home environmental variables are controlled, differences between the scores of African American and white children are narrowed considerably and all but eliminated (Brooks-Gunn, Klebanov, & Duncan, 1996).

One major problem is that the type of intelligence measured by intelligence tests relates to academic skills, not to "common sense" or the ability to solve real problems; intelligence tests do not really measure adaptation to life. This is readily admitted even by those who prepare intelligence tests (Wechsler, 1991). In fact, some argue that intelligence tests may be related to success in school but emotional intelligence, which includes delaying gratification, persistence, and other personal and emotional qualities, better predicts success in life after school (see New Perspectives on p. 231).

If people would look at these tests as demonstrating past learning and understand that they are not global measures of functioning, just narrow measures related to school achievement, the tests would be understood for what they are. These tests do not measure overall learning potential in every area, but do predict how well the child will do in the schools as they are now constructed (U.S. Department of Education, 1993a). The tests could be improved by removing questions with obvious cultural bias and making the test-taking procedures more culture-friendly by giving children unfamiliar with such tests an opportunity to become familiar with the test format. In this way low test scores would not be ascribed to some deficiency in ability but rather to a lack of particular skills necessary to negotiate schools the way they are now structured; low scores indicate a need for action, rather than an indictment of the child.

Questions Students Often Ask

I think IQ tests don't really mean anything and should be banned from use in the schools. Why do we still use them?

There are many psychologists who agree with you, at least up to a point. Besides the question of cultural bias, there is the problem with the misunderstanding of what intelligence tests measure and about how they are used. I once did some work for a school district that routinely gave teachers access to the intelligence scores of all children; it was printed on their records. (The district used group intelligence tests or tests of cognitive ability). When I asked why a teacher would need the scores and how they would be used, it was difficult to get an answer, but eventually I was able to get the process changed.

At times, the results of a good individual intelligence test can be useful. For example, performance on each of the subtests of the WISC can offer important information that may help professionals understand the child's strengths and weaknesses (Petti, 1988; 1987). For example, if a student scores low on the WISC subtest of information, a teacher may realize that the student lacks a knowledge base. A student who is weak in finding missing details in pictures may overlook arithmetic signs and punctuation marks. Intelligence tests can offer important information and they do correlate with achievement, but they should be used only to help rather than hurt students.

Properly used, the tests would become sources of diagnostic help for the teacher. Low scores would indicate

New Perspectives: Emotional Intelligence—How's Your EQ?

When you think about genius or brilliance you probably think of someone who has a very high IQ and who does very well in school. IQ is related to educational achievement, which may determine the college you attend, the type of degree you get and, ultimately, your job. But the fact that two people with very similar IQs and similar backgrounds who enter the same field do not achieve equally means that other factors besides IQ must be at work. Other skills may determine how well a person does on the job. For example, an individual who cannot get along with others, who comes in late, or who cannot handle anger or frustration is not likely to rise to the top.

If you were asked to list those skills necessary to create a successful marriage or to lead a satisfying life, it is unlikely that intelligence, as defined by standardized tests, would be high on your list. Other factors such as social skills, persistence, being able to express oneself and manage conflict, and the ability to delay gratification would probably be higher on your list.

Some argue that psychologists have overemphasized IQ and underestimated the importance of these personal and interpersonal abilities (Epperson et al., 1995). Daniel Goleman (1995), in his best-selling book *Emotional Intelligence,* extends and redefines our idea of what it is to be smart. Goleman believes that emotional intelligence is a more accurate predictor of success than IQ is. Emotional intelligence determines how well a person does in life. Goleman argues that IQ contributes only 20% to the factors that relate to success in life, leaving 80% to other factors, primary among them being emotional intelligence. Emotional intelligence involves self-awareness, impulse control (delaying gratification), persistence, self-motivation, empathy, being able to handle one's emotions, and having social skills. Goleman groups these qualities under a single term—*character.*

Goleman believes that people have both a rational and emotional mind, which usually act in harmony and in balance. Children who can understand and handle their emotions get along better with others and have a better chance of succeeding in school. Despite average or above-average IQs, children who are impulsive, disruptive, and unable to control their emotions are at high risk for academic failure, alcoholism, and crime.

Consider the following study. A researcher invites young children individually into a room and tells them that they can have a marshmallow right now but if they wait they can have two; the researcher then goes away for about 20 minutes. Some children grab the treat immediately and some wait. When these children reach high school, parents and teachers find that those who at the age of 4 were able to delay gratification and wait grow up to be better adjusted, more popular, more confident, and more dependable teenagers. They are more socially competent, personally effective, and better able to cope with frustration. Those who grabbed the treat are more likely to be lonely, easily frustrated, stubborn, and to have difficulty dealing with stress. Those who could delay gratification have an intelligence score on the average of 21 points higher (Shoda, Mischel, & Peake, 1990). Goleman argues that the ability to delay gratification and control one's impulses is a master skill, a triumph of reasoning over impulse, and is a powerful predictor of success and achievement.

Goleman relates the lack of emotional intelligence to such problems as violence, depression, crime, and even eating disorders because all these problems show our inability to deal with our feelings. These problems cry out for remedial emotional education, which holds the promise of reducing the core problems in our society.

Goleman points to curricula that can be presented to children to teach these skills. These qualities of character can be taught and nurtured if we become aware of them and understand their relationship to learning and to life. People can learn to become more aware of their own feelings and to manage anger and depression. They can learn people-oriented skills such as showing empathy, being gracious, and reading social situations effectively.

Goleman's book has been sharply criticized. One criticism is that the book makes it too easy to believe that people with a high IQ have very low emotional intelligence and vice versa; this is not true (Adelson, 1996). Years ago, Lewis Terman (1925) conducted studies demonstrating that people with high IQs also can be sociable and sensitive; in fact, there may be a relationship between high IQ and high emotional intelligence.

The lack of any real definition for emotional intelligence is also bothersome, and Goleman does not suggest any way to measure emotional intelligence (Seligman & Sullum, 1995). His claim that improving emotional literacy will improve academic success and performance requires evaluation. Much more hard evidence is necessary. In addition, it is difficult to understand how school teachers who have limited time in which to teach core subjects will be able to find the time to teach skills that represent emotional intelligence. Finally, emotional literacy education has been criticized because it may lead to conformity, to the notion that there is a "right" and a "wrong" way to feel.

Goleman's work is valuable in that it shows us that IQ is a rather narrow construct that has its uses and its limitations. He demonstrates that the skills measured by an IQ test are not the only skills necessary for success in life. Yet, we should be careful not to dismiss cognitive intelligence as unimportant or to believe that IQ and emotional intelligence do not or cannot coexist in the same person. The concept of emotional intelligence reminds us that personal and emotional skills can be nurtured and then used in a way that can make our lives richer and more satisfying.

a need for different types of instruction. Test scores would only be part of an assessment, and other sources of information would be used to obtain a more complete picture of the child's functioning. No standardized test can provide such a picture.

In an attempt to free standardized tests of any bias, culture-fair tests have been formulated that depend less on language abilities and speed of responding and eliminate items that reflect differential cultural or social experiences. Such tests use matching, picture completion, copying, block designs, analogies, spatial relations, and ability to see relations between patterns (Brown, 1983). But a perfect culture-fair test has yet to be invented, and some argue that culture-fair tests are impossible (Cahan & Cohen, 1989). Even if such a test is formulated, it is questionable whether it will predict school performance as well as our present standardized tests.

Boys, Girls, and the School Experience

Even though no gender differences exist in intelligence, girls perform better than boys on measures of reading, verbal fluency, spelling, and mathematical computation while boys are superior in mathematical reasoning and problems involving spatial analysis (Halpern, 1986; Marshall & Smith, 1987). A great deal of overlap occurs, with some girls performing better than boys in mathematics and some boys reading better than girls. Boys believe they are more competent in math and science whereas girls believe that they are more competent in reading, even in first grade before they have had much experience in school (Eccles et al., 1993). Females are less likely to repeat grades and also show higher writing proficiency in fourth grade (U.S. Department of Education, 1995c).

Girls may have an advantage over boys in elementary school. The atmosphere of elementary school is feminine, with its great percentage of female teachers and its emphasis on obedience and activities that require fine motor coordination. Boys and girls experience school in different ways, and both male and female teachers value the stereotyped feminine traits of obedience and passivity rather than those of aggressiveness and independence (Etaugh & Hughes, 1975).

Teachers interact with boys and girls differently, interacting more with high-achieving boys than with high-achieving girls (Good, Sikes, & Brophy, 1973). When teachers attend to task-oriented activities in class, boys receive more attention than girls (Fagot, 1977). In addition, when children demand attention, teachers respond to boys with instructions and to girls with nurturance (Beal, 1994). Girls are also given more attention when physically close to teachers whereas boys are given more attention when they are far away. Perhaps teachers expect good behavior from girls but believe that boys need to be encouraged to behave well. Male and female teachers are not very different in their views of student behavior; it is possible that these interactions reinforce physical proximity and conformity in girls and more task-oriented behavior in boys.

A study by the American Association of University Women (1992) found widespread discrimination in teachers, texts, and tests. Teachers pay less attention to girls, and some tests remain biased against girls or stereotype or ignore women; even though girls get better grades, they are still shortchanged.

Teachers observed over a 3-year period called on boys more often than girls, offered boys more detailed and constructive criticisms, and allowed boys to shout out answers but reprimanded girls for doing so (Sadker & Sadker, 1985). Teachers consistently underestimate their female students' abilities in math (Kimball, 1989) and females have less confidence in their math abilities, and with less confidence comes lower performance. Boys get more detailed instruction on the correct approach. Girls are frequently told they are right or wrong and given the right answers. These differences are not deliberate, and even female teachers show these patterns (Kerr, 1991).

Not everyone agrees that girls are shortchanged. Some authorities argue that the some of the research reviewed is questionable, that some research findings run contrary to their assertions, and that the strides in educational achievement made by women are often disregarded (Schmidt, 1994).

The media often depicts males as experts in technology and teachers often direct questions about technical material to boys. In the home, the computer is more likely to be in the boy's room than the girls' or in a common area, so fewer girls are familiar with the computer (Koch, 1994). In school, girls do not go to the computer room during lunch as often as boys do. No one actively stops them, but some girls believe that computers and math are not their domain; they must be encouraged to go to the computer room if they are to become familiar with computers (Sadker & Sadker, 1994).

Children With Exceptional Needs

About 9.5% of all children between the ages of 6 and 18 years receive special education services (U.S. Department of Education, 1994). They include children with **learning disabilities,** communication disorders, or **mental retardation,** those who show behavior disorders, have visual or auditory impairments, or are physically challenged. The overwhelming majority have mild disabilities (Kaplan, 1996). Another 3% of the population is categorized as gifted and also require special services.

learning disabilities A group of disorders marked by significant difficulties in acquiring and using listening, speaking, reading, writing, reasoning, or math skills.

mental retardation A condition marked by subnormal intellectual functioning and adjustment difficulties that occurs before a person is 18 years of age.

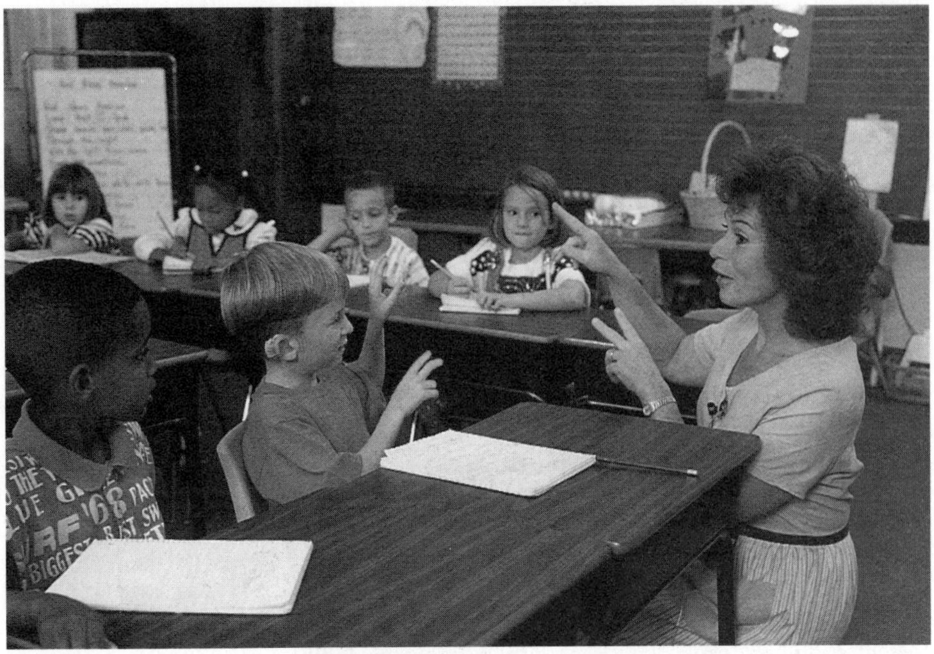

Proponents of the inclusion movement believe that all services to children with disabilities ought to be delivered within the regular classroom.

The most important law mandating educational services for children with disabilities is the Individuals with Disabilities Education Act, originally called the Education for All Handicapped Children Act, Public Law 94-142 (Kaplan, 1996). This law does not cover gifted children, although many districts have special programs for gifted children. The law requires all children with disabilities to receive a free, appropriate education, and it provides procedures to safeguard the rights of children with disabilities. The law also requires accountability, because educators must develop an individualized education program (IEP), which states the goals of the child's schooling and the methods for attaining them. Parents have the right to participate in all phases of their children's placement and education. The law also mandates that the child be placed in the least restricted environment; this means that each student with a disability must be educated in an environment that is no more restrictive than absolutely necessary.

Today, a relatively new movement called **full inclusion** maintains that all children with disabilities should be served in the regular classroom with the aid of various professionals and aides. The classroom teacher would have the primary responsibility for educating all children, and would have the help of a support team. The entire educational system, the school, and the classroom would be adapted so that students with disabilities receive virtually all their education with their peers who do not have disabilities (Stainback & Stainback, 1984; 1991).

Recently there has been a call to identify and educate disabled infants, toddlers, and preschoolers. The Education of the Handicapped Act Amendments of 1986, PL99-457 requires services to be offered to young children who have disabilities, usually defined in terms of developmental problems (Bernstein & Morrison, 1992; Howard et al., 1997). These children do not require a definite diagnosis; eligibility depends upon developmental and behavioral criteria (Bagnato, Neisworth, & Munson, 1993). Today, about half a million children below the age of 5 receive special services.

Learning Disabilities

Despite attending class and having the same teachers as their peers, some children do not learn well. More children with disabilities are diagnosed as having a learning disability than any other disability. Children with learning disabilities show significant difficulties acquiring and using listening, speaking, reading, writing, or reasoning skills or mathematics. They do not achieve up to their age and ability in some basic skill. The problem is not the result of sensory handicaps such as blindness, mental retardation, emotional disturbance, or any environmental, cultural, or economic disability (Federal Register, 1977). To diagnose a learning disability, three factors must exist: (1) academic problems, (2) a discrepancy between ability and performance, and (3) problems that are not the result of exclusions noted previously (Kaplan, 1996).

full inclusion A movement that would provide all special services for children with disabilities in the regular classroom.

Questions Students Often Ask

It seems that every child who has problems with school is considered to have a learning disability. Why is it so common now?

Children with learning disabilities have always been with us, but years ago they were not diagnosed correctly. Children with learning disabilities would quit school and go to work because schooling wasn't required. The recognition of learning disabilities as a cognitive problem and the emphasis on providing disabled students with a better education explains some of the increase in the diagnosis. Other factors may also be involved, such as the possibility that some children who have difficulty learning to read are placed in the category because no other services are available and that the classification is more socially acceptable than mental retardation or emotional disturbance.

Children with learning disabilities may show problems in perception, motor skills, communication, and memory strategies. For example, they may have difficulty discriminating "p" from "b," or they may not perceive the position of the stimuli correctly, reversing letters or words and reading "saw" for "was." These problems are common in young children, but they persist in children with learning disabilities. Such children often do not use memory or learning strategies, such as rehearsal, appropriately and show poor organization skills and short-term memory problems (Swanson, 1994).

Psychologists now believe that a primary feature of learning disability is a deficit in phonological awareness (McBride-Chang, 1995; Wagner, Torgesen, & Rashotte, 1994). Phonological awareness involves a number of skills, for example, understanding that words can be divided into sounds such as "c," "a," "t" in "cat." Others involve being able to blend sounds such as "fl" in "flower" and simply being able to recognize the beginning sound of a word. The inability to blend, segment, rhyme, and manipulate sounds can cause children to have problems recognizing words (Hansen & Bowey, 1994; O'Connor, Jenkins, & Slocum, 1995). These phonological problems cause children with learning disabilities to have trouble abstracting and transferring. For example, when taught to read "pine" and "shark" children with learning disabilities are not better able to identify "fine" and "dark" (Lovett et al., 1994). Studies show that when these phonological skills are integrated into reading instruction, children with learning disabilities make significant progress (Hatcher, Hulme, & Ellis, 1994).

Children with learning disabilities also experience social problems. They may be rejected because of the way they interact with others (Tur-Kaspa & Bryan, 1995; Vaughn, 1985). Learning-disabled children may not interpret verbal communications properly and often respond in inappropriate or insensitive ways (Haager & Vaughn, 1995). As the child grows up, such problems as slow information processing, distractibility, poor self-concept, reading problems, and lack of organization continue but many people with learning disabilities find ways to compensate (Gerber, Ginsberg, & Reiff, 1992; Gerber et al., 1992; 1990). A large study found that 81% of all learning-disabled students are involved in some productive activity such as working, continuing their studies, or rearing children 1 year after leaving high school (Viadero, 1989).

Learning-disabled children are often diagnosed in elementary school as problems appear. They receive help in the cognitive and the social areas through special techniques developed for working with learning-disabled students. Direct-instruction methods directly pinpoint academic problems and teach children the necessary skills. Because children with learning disabilities have difficulty choosing the correct strategy (Butler, 1995), another approach is to teach these children learning strategies, such as how to approach a task or how to monitor their progress, as well as organizational skills (Lovett et al., 1994).

Attention Deficit/ Hyperactivity Disorder

If you spend a few minutes with a child who is easily distracted, hyperactive, and impulsive, you begin to appreciate the patience and skill required for dealing with such children. Children who show these symptoms are classified as having an **attention deficit/hyperactivity disorder (ADHD).** These children have difficulty in school, and their relationships with their teachers are often strained. A connection exists between attention and hyperactivity problems and learning disabilities, but figures vary widely on the percentage of children with learning disabilities who also show attentional problems (Stanford & Hynd, 1994). The best estimate is that between 15% and 20% of children and adolescents with learning disabilities show ADHD (Silver, 1990). Between 3% and 5% of all children are estimated to have ADHD (Burcham & Carlson, 1995; Fowler, 1991), but others find a lower incidence (Viadero, 1993). Many children with ADHD show conduct difficulties, including fighting, disobedience, and rule breaking (Weiss, 1990).

Children with ADHD are inattentive, impulsive, and, in many cases, show hyperactivity (Fowler, 1991). Originally, psychologists focused on the hyperactivity, but today the attentional problems and impulsivity as well as the hyperactivity are emphasized and three specific types of ADHD are recognized: one in which inattention predominates, another in which hyperactivity and impulsivity are the primary symptoms, and a third in which all three major symptoms exist (American Psychiatric Association, 1994). Children with ADHD have social problems; they often are seen as bothersome, socially awkward, disruptive, talkative, loud, and aggressive (Wicks-Nelson & Israel, 1997).

Between 30% and 50% of these children carry some of the symptoms of ADHD into adulthood. They do not fidget as much, but they are likely to be impulsive and to have difficulty forming relationships.

Children with ADHD are often treated with stimulant medications, most commonly Ritalin, that make them calmer and more attentive (DuPaul & Barkley, 1993). About 70% show increased attention and reduced impulsivity and activity levels (Swanson, et al., 1991). They become somewhat more compliant as well (Forness & Kavale, 1988). Evidence indicates that mothers and teachers interact more positively when children are less disruptive and impulsive (Barkley et al., 1984). Some evidence indicates that the social status of these children improves as their disruptive behavior decreases, but peer appraisals of these children still are not as positive as for nonhyperactive children (Whalen et al., 1989).

attention deficit/hyperactivity disorder (ADHD) A condition used to describe children who are impulsive, overly active, easily distracted, and inattentive.

Questions Students Often Ask

Is it true that changing the diet of children who are hyperactive works?

Sorry, but it doesn't, at least not for most children. Some years ago, a physician, Dr. Benjamin Feingold, noted that hyperactivity was related to the consumption of food additives, such as preservatives and artificial colors and flavors. He claimed that if hyperactive children were put on a diet free of these compounds, a significant number would improve (Feingold, 1975). Although some clinical support for the Feingold diet has been found (Burlton-Bennet & Robinson, 1987), controlled experimental studies have not supported its effectiveness (Barkley, 1990; Silver, 1987). A few young children may show hyperactive responses to artificial food additives, but generally the negative effects do not seem as widespread as formerly claimed (Smith, 1991). The success rate of the diet is also lower than has been asserted by its supporters (Johnson, 1981). The diet may be effective for some but not the majority of children affected with ADHD.

The medications used to treat ADHD have been widely criticized because they treat only the symptoms, not the underlying cause, and may produce unpleasant side effects such as insomnia, which often diminish after a dosage reduction (Barkley, 1990). There is also evidence that although effective in reducing the symptoms in the short run, medication is not effective in the long run unless given with other treatments, probably because the aggressive and antisocial behavior is not being treated (Weiss, 1990). The overall benefits may disappear when the medication is halted (Hinshaw & Erhardt, 1993). Other critics say that these drugs are being overprescribed. No one claims that the drugs will improve intelligence or even schoolwork, only that they reduce the symptoms. Drug therapy is not always the treatment of choice; the very idea of a child having to take medication for years should make us cautious. Some authorities claim that such treatment should be used only as a last resort, and then always in combination with another type of treatment.

Another approach to treating ADHD (which may be used in combination with medication) involves manipulating the environment and its reinforcement. For example, providing structure and solid routines and using positive reinforcements can be helpful (Abromowitz & O'Leary, 1991; Walden & Thompson, 1981). Some teachers complete a brief checklist that indicates whether the child has met specific behavioral goals for the day. The checklist is sent home, signed by the parent, and returned to the school. The parents provide appropriate reinforcers at home that have been carefully designed for the child. If the child has not met the criteria for success, some privilege is forfeited. Some claim that behavioral intervention is superior to medication (Gadow, 1983). Sometimes, programs to improve academic performance are offered as well and academic success may also help children in the areas of attention and behavior (Wicks-Nelson & Israel, 1997).

Mental Retardation

The public holds many stereotypes of people with mental retardation and is often surprised to learn that most people with mental retardation cannot be identified by their physical appearance and that many work in competitive employment. Today the future of children with mental retardation is somewhat brighter than in the past, with many being able to live productive and meaningful lives.

Mental retardation is characterized by significant subaverage intellectual functioning, which exists along with limitations in at least two areas of personal functioning such as communication, self-care, home living, social skills, community use, health, and safety. It must be shown before the age of 18 years (AAMR, 1992). General intellectual functioning is usually measured by some score on an individualized intelligence test (e.g., below 70 on the Wechsler Intelligence Scale for Children), and adaptation is often measured by behavioral scales.

Children with mental retardation are often classified according to their intelligence level; mild (50–70), moderate (35–55), severe (20–35), and profound (under 20). Most children with mental retardation are classified as mildly retarded and do not look any different from the general population, although both their gross motor skills, such as jumping ability, and their fine motor skills, such as those involved in finger dexterity, often lag behind other children (Kaplan, 1996). Children with mild mental retardation often have difficulty with schoolwork and show many cognitive difficulties, among which are slow information processing, short-term memory problems, and the inability to generalize from one situation to another similar one (Kaplan, 1996). Children with mild mental retardation are diagnosed in elementary school when it becomes apparent that they are performing on a lower academic level. If they receive proper vocational education many can lead independent lives (Hickson, Blackson, & Reis, 1995; Kaplan, 1990). They require not only job skills but training in social and behavioral skills as well. They can work successfully in unskilled or semiskilled jobs, and studies show them to be effective workers (Levy et al., 1992; Gaylord-Ross et al., 1987), who frequently show a lower turnover than nonretarded workers (Brickey & Campbell, 1981).

People with moderate mental retardation will probably not be able to live independently because they are very slow, especially in language development. Their educational program stresses self-help skills, proper behavior, and limited simple verbal communication. The vast majority of moderately retarded people need some care throughout their lives, and special instruction in self-contained classrooms is the norm. Moderately retarded individuals are often employed in sheltered workshops or through supported employment where the environment is noncompetitive and friendly, in jobs that may involve sorting and packaging. These individuals may live in group homes with other people who have mental retardation or other disabilities.

Most severely or profoundly retarded children have multiple disabilities, including sensory and motor problems. Special programs help these children to develop basic survival and self-help skills.

A major change is now taking place in the classification of children with mental retardation. Instead of using *mild, moderate, severe,* and *profound,* which emphasize the intelligence scores, a new system advanced by the American Association on Mental Retardation (AAMR) classifies children according to the intensity of the support services required once a child is determined to have mental retardation (Table 10.3). This classification system emphasizes the child's strengths and weaknesses in the psychological, health, and environmental areas.

Attempts to help people with mental retardation center on education and on developing the social and personal skills necessary for success in the outside world. There is also a movement toward community-based group homes, where people with mental retardation can live in dignity and with a degree of independence. The watchword is *normalization,* which is the trend toward trying to integrate the individual into normal society as much as possible. The degree to which this can be accomplished depends on the level of support available, the education and social training the person receives, and public acceptance that people with mental retardation are individuals with full rights in the community.

Table 10.3 **Definition and Examples of Intensities of Supports**

INTERMITTENT
Supports on an "as needed basis." Characterized by episodic nature, person not always needing the support(s), or short-term supports needed during life-span transitions (e.g., job loss or an acute medical crisis). Intermittent supports may be high or low intensity when provided.
LIMITED
An intensity of supports characterized by consistency over time, time-limited but not of an intermittent nature, may require fewer staff members and cost less than more intense levels of support (e.g., time-limited employment training or transitional supports during the school to adult period).
EXTENSIVE
Supports characterized by regular involvement (e.g., daily) in at least some environments (such as work or home) and not time-limited (e.g., long-term support and long-term home living support).
PERVASIVE
Supports characterized by their constancy, high intensity; provided across environments; potential life-sustaining nature. Pervasive supports typically involve more staff members and intrusiveness than do extensive or time-limited supports.

Source: AAMR, 1992.

Gifted and Talented Children

When the word *gifted* is mentioned, people usually think in terms of people with a high intelligence. Children who score considerably above average on intelligence tests are indeed gifted, but is that all there is to it? What about the child who is artistically gifted or very creative? The federal government defines a gifted child as any child who either has demonstrated or seems to have the potential for high capabilities in general intellectual ability, specific academic aptitude, creative or productive thinking, leadership ability, or the visual and performing arts (Gifted and Talented Children's Act of 1978). The underlying educational assumption is that the unique skills and abilities of these children require special curricular alterations (Hershey, 1988).

Stereotypes of the gifted sometimes prevent society from meeting the special needs of such children (Treffinger, 1982). For example, many people believe that the gifted are socially backward, have little or no common sense, and look down on other people (Rickert, 1981). These stereotypes should be laid to rest; gifted elementary school children tend to be well accepted by nongifted children and are rather popular (Cohen, Duncan, & Cohen, 1994). Gifted children are not generally isolated, and their interpersonal relationships are good (Austin & Draper, 1981). Besides being fast learners and interested in school, gifted children tend to be well-adjusted, energetic, physically healthy, intuitive, perceptive, a bit rebellious and original, and show superior concentration skills (Scott, 1988; MacKinnon, 1978). They see relationships among diverse ideas and are curious (Tuttle et al., 1988). However, the gifted are not a homogeneous population (Juntune, 1982), and although most are well adjusted, some are not.

True or False?
Most children who are academically gifted are socially backward.

Two general approaches are taken to the education of the gifted. *Acceleration* involves the child's skipping a particular grade or particular unit and being placed in a more challenging situation. When children are accelerated, they complete courses of study in less time or at a younger age than usual (Reynolds & Birch, 1988). Early admission to school, skipping courses, or special accelerated courses that allow a child, for instance, to do 2 years of math in 1 year are typical of accelerated programs.

Sometimes students take college courses in high school (Pendarvis, Howley & Howley, 1990). Some people object to acceleration because of possible social problems or gaps in the child's knowledge base, but no evidence exists to support these fears (Feldhusen, Proctor, & Black, 1986; Swiatek & Benbow, 1991; Sayler & Brookshire, 1993).

In *enrichment* programs gifted children stay in their grade but do work that goes much beyond the usual work of students their age. Their educational experience is deeper and varied and requires curriculum modifications (Schiever & Maker, 1991). It may include Saturday classes, after-school seminars, or working on projects (Feldhusen, 1991). Children may either be kept in their usual classroom, be placed in a special room for a few hours a day, or even be placed in separate classrooms. The problem with enrichment is that sometimes it translates into more work, rather than work that is qualitatively different. Assigning 20 math problems instead of 10 is not enrichment; in some ways it can be seen as a punishment! Gifted children require a program that is *qualitatively* different from their age mates if they are to fulfill their potential. Many schools are looking at giftedness in a more global sense and trying to serve children who may be gifted in the arts, music, or in the leadership area (Davis & Rimm, 1994).

Questions Students Often Ask

Gifted children make it in society anyway, so why allocate scarce resources to their special education?

As a group, gifted children do succeed, but some do not, and many do not work up to their special abilities. I hear this claim at many school board meetings by parents of children not in the gifted program. The fact is that academically gifted children deserve some services, just as children who have artistic, musical, or athletic abilities deserve some special attention. The amount of money spent on programs for the gifted is usually very small, and when they are canceled, the saving for the district is minimal. Some acceleration strategies can even save a district money because children may graduate early, and many enrichment strategies don't cost anything at all because they can be done in the regular classroom.

The Total Child in School

The middle years of childhood are dominated by a child's school experiences. School-age children are expected to learn to read, write, and do mathematics proficiently. When children succeed in school, they develop a positive sense of achievement about their work, which Erik Erikson calls *industry*. School is more than a place of academic learning; it is also a place to meet friends, to learn to deal with social situations, and to begin to develop more personal autonomy. Children during the middle years of childhood are deeply affected by an ever-widening variety of social experiences, and it is to these experiences that we turn next.

Summary

1. During middle childhood, the rate of growth slows. Children's motor skills improve and are refined with maturation and experience. Physical changes during this stage are gradual.
2. Elementary school children today actually weigh more than their peers did a generation ago, probably because they are less active. Although obesity has a genetic component, most overweight children eat too much and do not exercise. Treatment for obesity may involve following a nutritious diet, providing psychological support, and beginning an exercise routine; any such plan should be executed under a doctor's care.
3. Teaching good health habits in the areas of nutrition, safety, and exercise is an important part of the parents' and schools' responsibility. Many children overestimate their physical abilities.
4. According to Piaget, the school-age child is negotiating the stage of concrete operations. Egocentrism declines, and improvements occur in the ability to solve problems that entail reversibility, the ability to decenter, seriation, and classification. The crowning achievement is the development of the ability to conserve. The child develops the ability to conserve number, substance, weight, and volume.
5. Children in the stage of concrete operations are unable to understand abstractions and hypothetical problems.
6. During middle childhood, children's ability to voluntarily use their attentional strategies improves greatly, as do their memory abilities. Children begin to spontaneously use verbal memory strategies, such as rehearsal and categorization.
7. The term *metamemory* describes an individual's knowledge of the memory process. Metamemory abilities increase during the school years.
8. Children in elementary school are expected to learn how to read, write, and successfully solve mathematical problems. Mastering these basic skills influences a child's self-concept and self-esteem. Elementary schools are rated more positively by parents and students than secondary schools.
9. A child's academic achievement is affected by the school and teachers, the pupil's socioeconomic status, the home environment, gender, attitudes, motivation, work habits, and intelligence.
10. There are many different approaches to defining intelligence. Performance on intelligence tests is related to school achievement, but other factors—such as motivation and adjustment—are important. Intelligence tests have been criticized for a variety of rea-

sons, most important of which is that they may be biased against children from some minority groups, and their value is still being debated.

11. Public Law 94-142 requires school districts to provide an appropriate free education for every child. It also mandates educational accountability through an individualized education program. Finally, it requires that children be placed in the least restrictive educational environment. The full-inclusion movement advocates providing special educational services in the regular classroom. Infants, toddlers, and preschoolers with disabilities are legally entitled to special services today as well.
12. Children who achieve much below what their intelligence and educational experiences indicate they should be achieving are considered to have a learning disability. This disability may not be the result of cultural differences, socioeconomic level, or sensory disability. Children with attention deficit/hyperactivity disorder are impulsive and distractible; they often have difficulty in school and with interpersonal relationships.
13. Most children with mental retardation are mildly retarded and many can be educated to lead productive, independent lives. Children with moderate retardation are taught self-care and some skills, but only rarely can they live independently. The severely and profoundly retarded often require institutional care. A new classification system based upon the type of support services required rather than the intelligence level of the child is now being used.
14. Gifted children have superior intellectual, creative, or academic capabilities or manifest talent in leadership or in the performing or visual arts. Gifted children are generally well-adjusted.

Multiple-Choice Questions

1. Which of the following statements about the physical development of elementary school children is *correct?*
   a. The rate of growth increases substantially during this stage of childhood.
   b. Children really do not grow in middle childhood, but rather gain weight and muscle making them look more like adults.
   c. Girls are actually significantly taller than boys until adolescence.
   d. The rate of growth declines during middle childhood.
2. Mr. and Mrs. L's child weighed 13½ pounds at birth while Mr. and Mrs. W's child weighed 4¼ pounds at birth. According to research:
   a. Mr. and Mrs. L's child is more likely to become obese.
   b. Mr. and Mrs. W's child is more likely to become obese.
   c. Both children will most probably become obese because children who weigh above and below average are more likely to become obese.
   d. Scientists can make no prediction about obesity from birth weight.
3. The main reason children weigh more than they did a generation ago is because of:
   a. ingestion of more fatty foods.
   b. lower metabolism rates.
   c. greater levels of anxiety.
   d. lack of exercise.
4. A first-grader is estimating whether she can jump a certain distance. If she is similar to other children her age, she will:
   a. overestimate how far she can jump.
   b. underestimate how far she can jump.
   c. accurately estimate how far she can jump.
   d. refuse to estimate how far she can jump.
5. If you were measuring the physical abilities of a large group of elementary school boys and girls, you would expect *all* of the following except:
   a. the boys to run faster.
   b. the girls to be more agile.
   c. the girls to show better rhythm.
   d. the girls to be stronger.
6. You would expect which of the following during the stage of concrete operations?
   a. an increase in egocentrism
   b. an ability to understand conservation of weight
   c. an inability to reverse operations
   d. an increase in the tendency to center on one dimension at a time
7. The fact that conservation of number, weight, and volume occur at different times even though the principle of conservation underlies all is referred to as:
   a. primary masking.
   b. sequential masking.
   c. horizontal decalage.
   d. reciprocal inhibition.
8. Children in the concrete stage of operations have difficulty understanding political cartoons because they:
   a. cannot seriate.
   b. have difficulty with classification.
   c. have difficulty with abstractions.
   d. cannot reverse operations.
9. Which of the following statements about memory in middle childhood is *correct?*
   a. Children forget less than when they were preschoolers.
   b. After about age 7, children use memory strategies such as rehearsal on their own.
   c. Children process information more quickly than when they were preschoolers.
   d. All of the above are correct.
10. Your teacher tells you that some students "don't know what they know and don't know what they

don't know." Your teacher is talking about the psychological concept of:
a. reciprocity.
b. metamemory.
c. involvement.
d. episodic discontinuation.

11. Which of the following statements concerning children's reading is *correct?*
a. Most students in elementary and secondary school read on the average of 40 pages per day.
b. There is no relationship between the amount of reading children do and their reading skills.
c. One key to improving children's reading ability is for parents to read more and show they value this activity.
d. All of the above are correct.

12. Jeff notes that children's television viewing has a negative influence on children's reading achievement. According to studies, Jeff is:
a. wrong, because good readers watch as much television as poor readers.
b. wrong, because children who watch a good deal of television actually read more because they see so many signs and so much print material on television.
c. wrong, because it may affect teenagers who use television programming as a means of escape but does not adversely affect the reading skills of elementary school students.
d. correct.

13. The differences in mathematical achievement between children in the United States and those in Japan and Taiwan are mainly the result of the:
a. lack of interest in math that American students show.
b. feeling on the part of American children that math is simply not useful.
c. difference in school time allotted for math.
d. superior abilities that students from Japan and Taiwan have for math.

14. You are taking a poll of how parents and children view their local schools. If your results agree with the research in the field:
a. parents and students will view their high schools as better than their middle school and elementary schools.
b. parents and students will view their middle schools as superior to their elementary and high schools.
c. parents and students view their elementary schools more positively than their middle and high schools.
d. parents view their high schools as better and students view their elementary schools as better.

15. Which of the following is *not* one of the different types of intelligence discussed by Howard Gardner in his theory of multiple intelligences?
a. bodily-kinesthetic
b. logical-mathematical
c. common-relevant
d. musical

16. The key question concerning the use of intelligence tests on children of minority groups is whether:
a. the test results predict academic achievement.
b. the tests are culturally biased.
c. teachers should be given the students' scores.
d. intelligence tests take too long to administer.

17. Which of the following statements concerning how teachers treat male and female students is *correct?*
a. Boys are allowed to shout out answers, while girls are criticized for it.
b. Boys receive more detailed instruction on their errors.
c. Teachers interact more with high achieving males than with high achieving females.
d. All of the above are correct.

18. According to federal law:
a. children with disabilities must receive a free, appropriate education.
b. children who are gifted must receive special education.
c. only children with moderate to severe rather than mild disabilities must receive special educational services.
d. every student with a disability must be given private tutoring.

19. Children with attention deficit/hyperactivity disorder are often treated with:
a. diet.
b. cooperative learning strategies.
c. medications such as Ritalin.
d. electroconvulsive shock.

20. Which statement about mental retardation is correct?
a. Most children with mental retardation do not look any different from their peers who do not have mental retardation.
b. Most children with mental retardation score below 50 on a standardized intelligence test.
c. Most children with mental retardation process information too fast, making them impulsive.
d. All of the above are correct.

Answers to Multiple-Choice Questions
1. d 2. d 3. d 4. a 5. d 6. b 7. c 8. c 9. d
10. b 11. c 12. d 13. c 14. c 15. c 16. b 17. d
18. a 19. c 20. a

Chapter 11

Social and Personality Development in Middle Childhood

Chapter Outline

Are the Following Statements True or False?

1. Parents show more physical affection and spend more time with their children during middle childhood than they did during the preschool stage.
2. During middle childhood, children raised in authoritarian settings are better adjusted than those raised in authoritative households.
3. After a divorce the custodial parent becomes stricter and the other parent becomes more permissive.
4. Daughters have more difficulty accepting the remarriage of their mothers than sons.
5. Homeless children are more likely than poor but housed children to attend a Head Start program, receive their full set of vaccinations, and attend elementary school regularly because they are watched more closely by social service agencies.
6. Aggressive children in middle childhood do not have any friends.
7. Boys and girls tend to form same-gender playgroups during middle childhood.
8. Elementary school children are more flexible in their gender stereotypes than preschoolers.
9. As children progress through the elementary school years, they are more likely to judge right and wrong on the basis of the consequences of an action rather than intent.
10. As children mature, they tend to share with other children more often.

Answers to True-False Statements 1. False: see p. 243 2. False: see p. 243 3. True 4. True 5. False: see p. 248 6. False: see p. 249 7. True 8. True 9. False: see p. 251 10. True

Through a Child's Eyes

Karen quickly looked around and put the wallet in her pocket. No one had noticed. The wallet contained a lot of money, and she wanted to buy so many things. She could return it, since she knew the man who had lost it. Karen's parents would want her to return the wallet, but they were so busy with their own problems, and Karen was considered the "bad one" anyway. Karen's parents were always saying how dumb Karen was, and Karen's father usually lost his patience when trying to explain something to Karen. In fact, the only adult Karen had any respect for was her aunt, who frequently listened to her, tried to help her, and would give her a kind word.

Then Karen saw her best and almost only friend, Linda, and got an idea. Karen could take Linda on a shopping spree. To Karen's surprise, Linda thought Karen should return the wallet, because the person who lost it might really need the money. Karen valued Linda's opinion and realized that if she returned the wallet, there might be a nice reward. Yet she still couldn't decide what to do. Now that Linda knew about the wallet, Karen had to make up her mind quickly.

Looking at Middle Childhood

Children's social networks expand significantly during middle childhood and the number and importance of their friendships increase (Ladd & Le Sieur, 1995). Children of this age receive feedback from many more sources and develop a sense of their own abilities, strengths, and weaknesses. At the same time, elementary school children's relationship with their parents undergoes a subtle but definite shift toward greater independence. All over the world the first years of middle childhood mark a major change in children's relationships with adults (Collins, Harris, & Susman, 1995). They are expected to be more responsible for their own actions and develop a sense of right and wrong. They are likely to be faced with moral and ethical dilemmas concerning cheating, lying, and stealing, as well as to face situations calling for prosocial qualities, including helping and cooperating with others. These changes take place slowly over a number of years, and the theme of more gradual change is found throughout the research on this period of development.

Industry and Inferiority

School-age children are faced with many academic challenges. If they succeed, they gain a sense of **industry**—the sense that their work and efforts are valued. Children with a sense of industry enjoy learning about new things and experimenting with new ideas. They show more perseverance and can accept criticism (Hamachek, 1988). If they do not succeed, they develop a sense of **inferiority**—a belief that they are incompetent and do not measure up to their peers (Erikson, 1963). Children whose parents compare them unfavorably with their siblings may stop trying to succeed. One difficult parenting task is valuing the individual competencies of each child in the family. Even if parents avoid direct comparisons, implicit comparisons exist.

Comparisons can cause a special problem for minority-group children, who during middle childhood become

industry The positive outcome of the psychosocial crisis in the middle years of childhood, involving a feeling of self-confidence and pride in one's achievements.

inferiority The negative outcome of the psychosocial crisis in the middle years of childhood, involving the child's belief that his or her work and achievements are below par.

aware of how their group compares with the majority. These children often learn that their group is not as valued (Spurlock & Lawrence, 1979), and they may develop a sense of inferiority.

The Misunderstood Latency Stage

According to Freudian theory the child has now negotiated the Oedipal situation and enters the **latency stage.** A boy resolves his Oedipal problem by identifying with his father ("me and you, Dad") and repressing his feelings toward his mother, and indeed all females. Girls experience less pressure to resolve their conflicts in this stage, and many do not fully do so. Sexuality in the latency stage is hidden or latent, and a segregation of children by gender appears. Boys play with boys, and girls play with girls. Freudians claim that children have repressed their feelings toward the opposite sex in order to resolve their Oedipal conflicts and contact may reawaken these disturbing emotions. Sexuality, however, is not absent in this stage, it is only hidden from view.

The Developing Self-Concept

The **self-concept** begins to develop in infancy, when children differentiate themselves from the outside world. In early childhood the self-concept is based on external factors, such as physical characteristics, possessions, and such abilities as playing a sport well. Especially after age 8, a shift from physical to psychological conceptions of the self takes place (Damon & Hart, 1982). Personality characteristics take center stage. Children in this stage often refer to their personal attributes, interests, beliefs, attitudes, values, and relationships with the opposite sex, and talk less about possessions and appearance. As self-concept develops, there is a change from an external frame of reference to an internal frame of reference. Children's descriptions of themselves become more stable and more comprehensive in middle childhood.

The self-concept evolves from a combination of feedback children receive from peers, parents, and teachers and their evaluation of their own subjective experiences. Children whose parents continually tell them that they have "no brains" and are "stupid" may believe it. However, children are not just passive recipients of feedback. Children evaluate their own experiences and see themselves as being good, bad, aggressive, calm, or honest and compare their experience against a standard set by society, parents, peers, and finally, by themselves. Even in the absence of direct feedback, they evaluate their experiences. If a child's experience is not in keeping with his or her sense of self, the child may reject the subjective experience. For instance, children may believe they are honest and have difficulty coming to grips with the fact that they cheated during an exam or, as in Karen's case, kept something that didn't belong to them. The experience of dishonesty may not match their conception of themselves as honest.

In middle childhood children receive feedback from many more sources. They encounter more children and adults, not all of whom will like them. Some feedback is likely to be negative or conflicting, which is especially troublesome for children who already have low **self-esteem** (Smith & Smoll, 1990). In addition, children's newly developing cognitive skills affect their self-concept and self-esteem. Children in the concrete operational stage can reason more logically, thereby verifying the attributes of self. Children become especially good at developing a self-theory from inductive (specific) experience. They may conclude that they are smart because they are good at reading and mathematics (Harter, 1983) or honest because they returned something they found. Children now develop the ability to take another person's point of view, as Linda did when she reasoned that the person who lost the wallet might need the money (Froming, Allen, & Jensen, 1985). They test their self-concepts by comparing themselves with others, and because they are no longer as egocentric, they develop the ability to imagine what others think of them. This allows them to anticipate evaluations and to correct their behavior or to evaluate an action and react to it emotionally with pride or disappointment.

A child's self-concept colors how the child interprets certain situations as well as his or her behaviors and attitudes. For example, if Karen is faced with a difficult arithmetic problem and believes she is a poor student, she will probably give up easily. If she has a positive view of her math skills she will approach the problem with the expectation that she will succeed. Children with a positive view of their physical self will join in and play baseball with the other children, but those who don't think they are good enough will refuse to join in. A vicious circle ensues, for children who do not play will not develop their abilities to their fullest. They fall further behind their peers, which makes them refuse to play at all and leads to a further lack of development.

The child's self-concept and self-esteem also affect his or her ability to learn. Children who possess strong self-esteem volunteer their ideas more often in class whereas those with low self-esteem are often overwhelmed by school tasks. Positive self-esteem is related to better adjustment in school, more independence, less defensive behavior, greater acceptance of others, and better school achievement (Gurney, 1987).

The self-concept also affects how information is processed. If children think that they are bad, they will believe such feedback from other people. In this way, the self-concept can set a self-fulfilling prophecy in motion. Believing that someone will say something negative causes children to anticipate poor evaluations, reject positive feedback, and even to interpret neutral feedback as negative.

latency stage The psychosexual phase, occurring during middle childhood, in which sexuality is hidden.

self-concept The picture people have of themselves.

self-esteem The value people place on various aspects of their self.

The Family

The parent-child relationship changes in middle childhood. Parents show less physical affection for their children, are not as protective, and generally spend less time with them (Maccoby, 1980). As in previous years, mothers have more frequent interactions with their children involving care-giving and household tasks, while fathers engage in more physical and outdoor play.

> ***True or False?***
> Parents show more physical affection and spend more time with their children during middle childhood than they did during the preschool stage.

Parents expect children to regulate their own behavior and show greater autonomy and independence at home, in school, and in peer group interactions. Children are encouraged to take on more responsibility (Collins et al., 1995). Temper tantrums are fewer, and the frequency of disciplinary encounters decrease between the ages of 3 and 9 years. When disciplinary exchanges do take place, parents less frequently engage in physical punishment and are more likely to use other techniques, such as forfeiting a child's privileges, reminding children of their responsibility, and appealing to the child. Parents' appeals are based less on power and more on fairness, a return of favors, and reminders that parents have more knowledge and experience. Despite these changes, which result from the child's increasing age and abilities, general parenting values remain stable; a parent who is very strict remains so, and a parent who is responsive remains responsive (McNally, Eisenberg, & Harris, 1991).

During the early years of middle childhood, children strive to please their parents and teachers and derive great pleasure from reaching the goals these adults set for them and from acting in a way that meets their standards. Later in this stage the child's peers become more important, and fitting in and being accepted in the group take center stage. Children begin to identify less with adults and more with peers. They become more argumentative, discourteous, and rebellious and complain about what they perceive as unfairness. These children now see their parents' authority as having limits, although they agree more with their parents than they will later (Smetana, 1989). Ten-year-olds believe that decisions that affect only them, such as choosing friends, are outside their parents' authority (Tisak, 1986). Parents are now seen as fallible human beings who can be, and often are, arbitrary and wrong.

Child-Rearing Strategies Reconsidered

The original studies by Diana Baumrind (see Chapter 9) on child-rearing strategies were based on observations of nursery-school children. She continued her studies of these children when they were 8 or 9 years old. Children, especially boys, raised by authoritarian parents continued to have problems; these boys showed less interest in achievement and withdrew from social contact. Children who were raised permissively lacked self-confidence and were not achievement oriented. Children raised by authoritative parents were again superior. The combination of firm rule enforcement, demands for more mature behavior, better communication, and warmth led to a desirable outcome, which also leads to greater self-esteem (Coopersmith, 1967).

> ***True or False?***
> During middle childhood, children raised in authoritarian settings are better adjusted than those raised in authoritative households.

Neither the unbridled use of power nor the permissive style benefits most children. Demanding either total, unquestioning obedience or nothing at all does not lead to independence or social maturity. Children of authoritarian parents (like Karen's parents) lack social competence with peers, do not take the initiative, lack spontaneity, and have external rather than internal moral orientations to right and wrong. Children from permissive families are impulsive and aggressive and lack independence and a sense of responsibility. Children of authoritative parents are independent, take the initiative in the cognitive and social areas of life, are responsible, control their aggressive urges, and have self-confidence and high self-esteem (Maccoby & Martin, 1983). Baumrind (1989) concludes that parents who are both demanding and responsive usually produce children who are most socially responsible.

Taken as a whole, the research on parenting in middle childhood yields no surprises. Children benefit when their parents show warmth and acceptance, set and enforce appropriate rules, listen and respond to their children, and give them some room for personal choice, responsibility, and freedom. In middle childhood parental behavior has to strike a delicate balance between assistance and respect for the autonomy of the child (Krappman, 1989).

The Changing Family

The American family today is a far cry from what it was even 30 years ago. The number of single-parent families has increased substantially and about one million children each year are affected by divorce. Many children live with stepparents, the overwhelming majority with stepfathers and biological mothers. If trends continue, 61% of all American children will spend some part of their childhood in a single-parent household before their 18th birthday. Most divorced parents remarry so many children go through a series of marital transitions, from intact-family to single-parent family to stepfamily relationships (Hetherington, Stanley-Hagan, & Anderson, 1989).

The Experience of Divorce

The most common reason why children live in single-parent families is divorce, an experience that affects the entire family forever. Even 5 and 10 years later, a parental

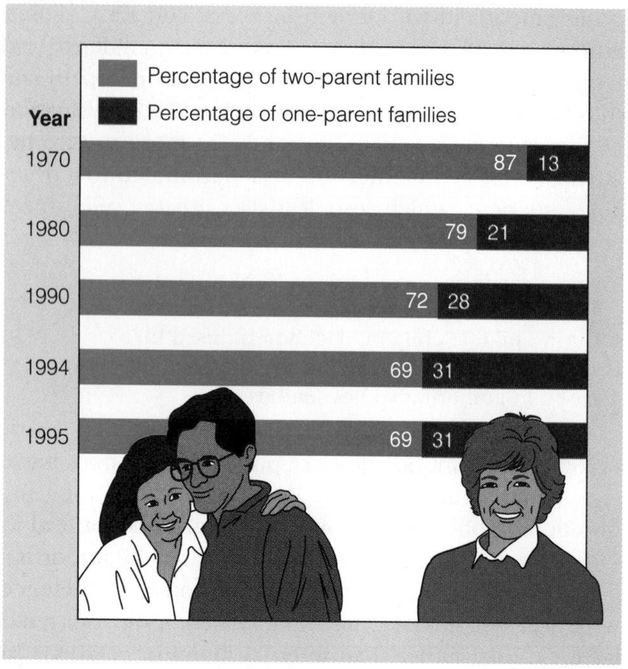

Datagraphic
The Growth of One-Parent Families
Source: Data from U.S. Bureau of the Census, 1996.

divorce remains the central event of childhood and casts a "long shadow" over those years (Wallerstein, 1983, p. 233). Divorce itself brings many changes; the child's world is torn asunder, and the child's lifestyle is disrupted. Financial problems may force the family to move to a new neighborhood, altering the child's daily routine. Most children do not see such changes in a positive light, even years after the divorce (Wallerstein, Corbin, & Lewis, 1988).

Immediate Reactions to Divorce Almost all children find divorce a painful experience, and their early reactions may include anger, depression, and guilt (Weinraub & Gringlas, 1995). Children often show behavioral changes such as regression, sleep disturbances, and fear. Children may grieve for the absent parent and may respond with aggression or noncompliance (Hetherington et al., 1989). Parent-child relationships also change. The custodial parent, usually the mother, becomes stricter and more controlling, while the other parent becomes permissive and more understanding, although less accessible. Both parents make fewer demands on children to mature, become less consistent in their discipline, and have more difficulty communicating with the children (Hetherington, Cox, & Cox, 1978). Parents' discipline practices become poorer (Forgatch, Patterson, & Skinner, 1988), and conduct problems are not uncommon (Brody & Forehand, 1988).

True or False?
After a divorce the custodial parent becomes stricter and the other parent becomes more permissive.

After the initial period, some children show a remarkable ability to recover, while others do not. Some adapt well in the early stages, and some show delayed effects. How quickly children recover from the initial shock depends on whether a stable environment is created after the divorce and on the social supports available to the child (Kurdek, 1981). Often, however, such supports are not available. Parents are confused and must rearrange their own lives. Relatives are often judgmental, and their relationships with both the parents and the children may change. Peer relationships may suffer because some children feel guilty about what is happening. Family friends may be forced to take sides and maintain contact with only one parent. The main social supports are weakened at a time when increased support is vital.

Questions Students Often Ask
I keep reading that children of divorce "suffer." I'm divorced, and I don't think all kids suffer. What can be done to help those children who do suffer?
There is quite a bit that can be done. Divorce is a very personal experience for parents and the children. Just as parents don't see the marriage in the same way, children don't always view their home situation in the same manner. If the home before the divorce was racked with a tremendous amount of open conflict, divorce can lead to a reduction in such open hostilities, which is beneficial for the children. Yet most children do not see divorce as positive. The keys to helping children "recover" involve getting along civilly with one's ex-spouse (not always easy), trying to regain a stable home environment after the divorce, offering children the social and emotional support they require including answering their questions, and monitoring changes in children's behavior.

Long-Term Effects of Divorce Many of the initial reactions either become less severe or disappear by the end of the first year to 18 months (Hetherington, 1979; Portes et al., 1992). The long-term effects of divorce on children can be severe. In one study of children whose parents divorced during their middle childhood years, half had improved functioning, and about one-fourth of the subjects had become significantly worse (Kelly & Wallerstein, 1976).

Children from one-parent families do not differ in academic ability or intelligence, but they are absent from school more often, are more disruptive, have lower grades, and are viewed by teachers as less motivated (Minuchin & Shapiro, 1983). They evaluate their families more negatively than children from intact families (Parish, 1990). They are more likely to have emotional problems, although the majority do not show these difficulties (Chase-Lansdale, Cherlin & Kiernan, 1995). When children whose parents were divorced when they were in middle childhood were followed, Wallerstein (1987) found feelings of sadness, neediness, and an increased sense of vulnerability expressed by a majority of these older children. Even though it had been 10 years since the divorce, the children spoke sadly of their loss of the intact family, and especially of the lack of contact with their noncustodial parent. They expressed a great concern about being betrayed in relationships, and were very anxious about personal commitments. Half the boys and one-fourth of the girls were considered poorly adjusted and at high risk at this 10-year follow-up.

The long-term effects of divorce depend on a number of postdivorce factors. In fact, postdivorce stressors have a greater influence on children's mental health than the divorce itself (Sandler, Tein, & West, 1994). Post-divorce adjustment is much better if parents can cooperate after divorcing (Bronstein et al., 1994). If parents continue to quarrel after the divorce, the children suffer (Berger, 1995; Wallerstein, 1983). Children have a much more difficult time coping with stress when there is a great deal of conflict between parents (Portes, Haas, & Brown, 1991). Unfortunately, according to one study about 50% of parents continue to argue after the divorce is final (Stark, 1986).

More people today are using mediation services rather than entering an adversarial court procedure to settle disputes; mediation reduces tension and stress for everyone (Dillon & Emery, 1996). Parents seem more satisfied with mediation, and compliance rates with decisions are impressive. Parents are more likely to cooperate with each other and the noncustodial parent is more likely to remain involved (Dillon & Emery, 1996; Emery, Matthews, & Kitzmann, 1994).

Children of all ages do better when their parents maintain a warm relationship with them (Hess & Camara, 1979). When adolescents were divided into three groups—divorced/good relationships with parents, divorced/poor relationships with parents, and intact/good relationships with parents—those who were from families with divorced parents and that had a good relationship with both parents showed no more cognitive or behavioral problems than those in the intact/good relationship group. These good relationships buffered the child against the problems of divorce (Wierson et al., 1989). Last, adjustment problems are less severe if financial problems and parental conflict are minimized and if social supports exist (Kurdek, 1981). Unfortunately, parents' difficulties involving finances, loneliness, fear, anxiety about the future, and the loss of social supports reduce their ability to give the children what they need to soften the blow of divorce (Weinraub & Gringlas, 1995).

Divorce and the Age of the Child Children of various ages experience divorce somewhat differently. Preschoolers react quite negatively, often showing regressive behavior and separation anxiety, although most do recover from the initial shock after a year or so (Allison & Furstenberg, 1989). Continued deterioration after one year is linked to continuing family disorder. Preschoolers do not understand what is going on, and parents do not explain very much to preschoolers. They may blame themselves and fear being abandoned by their parents (Wallerstein et al., 1988). School-age children experience loyalty problems, including feelings that they have to choose between their parents. Elementary-school children feel powerless and frightened and frequently are angry at one or both parents; they may support one parent against the other. About one-half of these children show severe drops in achievement during the first year (Wallerstein et al., 1988). Adolescents have a difficult time coping with anger, often showing acute depression, acting-out behaviors, emotional and social withdrawal, and anxiety about their future. They are often disturbed by the fact that the family's financial problems no longer allow them to purchase things they formerly could buy.

Does Divorce Affect Boys and Girls Differently? One research finding that is generally but not unanimously accepted is that the long-term effects of divorce are greater for boys than for girls (Doherty & Needle, 1991). Boys are much more likely to suffer psychologically, socially, and academically and to show acting-out behaviors than are girls (Hetherington et al., 1989). The reasons for this are not definitely known. In the majority of cases, mothers gain custody, and perhaps the absence of the male authority figure may have an especially injurious effect on boys (Huston, 1983). However, psychologists now appreciate the influence fathers have on their daughters' development. Girls raised by their mother have more difficulty relating to men later on. Girls from divorced families are more flirtatious, sexually precocious, and seductive, and girls raised in widowed families are more withdrawn (Hetherington, 1972). Paternal absence clearly affects daughters as well as sons.

Family Discord and Behavior Problems

Studies comparing children from intact families with children from divorced families often conclude that the latter have many more problems and attribute the problems to the divorce or the behavior of the parents after the divorce. A different approach attributes some of the problems to conditions in the home that existed long before the divorce took place. Family turmoil—whether it ends in divorce or not—creates problems for children (Emery, 1982). The more open and intense the hostility, the more serious the children's problems.

Marital turmoil is also related to underachievement in school. One interesting longitudinal study assessed the personalities of children from intact families, families that later experienced divorce. The behavior of the boys prior to divorce was affected negatively by the stress in the family, and such problems as uncontrolled impulsiveness and aggressiveness were common. The behavior of girls was found to be less affected than that of boys. The researchers conclude that some of the problems considered to be consequences of divorce may be present prior to divorce (Block, Block, & Gjerde, 1986).

Stepfamilies

Many divorced people remarry, forming families that consist of one biological parent and one stepparent. Children have to adjust to living with a new parent, and each individual comes to the new family after having experienced a loss. Children have to obey a new set of rules, and the stepparent and biological parent must learn to share the children with the other biological parent who lives elsewhere. In addition, children may need to learn to live with stepbrothers and stepsisters. On the positive side, the remarried mother's financial situation improves and she gains some additional emotional support (Hetherington & Stanley-Hagan, 1995). Stepparents may not instantly fall in love with their stepchildren, and stepchildren may resent or merely tolerate the presence of the stepparents and their children.

Stepfamilies present unique problems. In the period following a remarriage, children must accept the remarriage and resign themselves to the fact that their biological parents will not get back together again. Children may resent their new stepparent's attempts to discipline them and may feel that the new parent is a threat to their relationship with their biological parents (Hetherington et al., 1989).

Directly following the remarriage, the children may show more problem behaviors. Most younger children eventually form a reasonably good relationship with a competent stepparent, but adolescents may have more difficulty and may challenge the new family more actively. There is some evidence that girls have more difficulty adjusting to remarriage than boys (Brand, Clingempeel, & Bowen-Woodward, 1988). Remarried mothers are apt to experience more parent-child conflict, especially mother-daughter conflict (Hetherington & Stanley-Hagan, 1995). Over time, preadolescent boys in families with stepfathers are more likely than girls to show improvements in their adjustment. Perhaps girls develop very strong relationships with their mothers during the time when their mothers are unmarried and see the stepfather as a threat to this relationship. Perhaps the presence of a male increases the tension in the family more for a daughter than for a son.

> ***True or False?***
> Daughters have more difficulty accepting the remarriage of their mothers than sons.

Readjusting to a new family takes time (Bray, 1988). Successful stepfathers initially spend more time establishing good relationships with their stepchildren and are warm and involved, but do not initially assert too much parental authority (Hetherington & Stanley-Hagan, 1995; Hetherington et al., 1989). While acceptance of the stepfather by stepsons is related to the behavior of the stepfather toward the stepson, this is not the case with stepfather-stepdaughter relationships, where there is no correlation between the two and acceptance is much more difficult to achieve (Hetherington et al., 1989). Stepmothers are more active and involved in discipline than stepfathers. When positive relationships exist between stepparents and stepchildren, the children are less aggressive and show higher levels of self-esteem (Clingempeel & Segal, 1986).

It is commonly believed that children do not thrive in stepfamilies because the adjustments are so difficult. However, the most common finding of studies comparing stepfamilies with nuclear families on adjustment or cognitive functioning is that there is little or no difference (Clingempeel & Segal, 1986). When stepfamilies are compared with single-parent families, the presence of a stepfather is found to reduce some of the negative effects of divorce for boys, and males score higher both on measures of cognitive development and measures of adjustment (Oshman & Manosevitz, 1976; Santrock, 1972).

Although stepfamilies are faced with many adjustments, research shows that living in a stepfamily can be a positive experience, depending upon the quality of the relationship between parents and children.

Latchkey or Self-Care Children

When Karen comes home from school, neither of her parents is home. Both her parents are employed, and Karen spends about 2½ hours after school alone. Karen is one of the growing number of **latchkey** or **self-care children.** More than 1.6 million children between the ages of 5 and 14 years, some 7.6% of all children, are alone after school (Fields, 1994). The public is greatly concerned about the safety and development of latchkey children (Campbell & Flake, 1985). A nationwide poll found

latchkey or self-care children Elementary school children who must care for themselves after school hours. (Junior high school students are sometimes included in the definition.)

Many elementary school children return home from school to an empty house. New research emphasizes the importance of parents knowing where their children are and communicating with them on a regular basis when the children are home alone.

that teachers think that the lack of supervision at home after school is a major reason for lack of achievement (Flax, 1987); many parents agree.

Are these opinions substantiated by research? Some studies find a patten of few if any differences in social development between latchkey children and children who have a parent waiting for them (Vandell & Corasaniti, 1988). Hyman Rodman and colleagues (1985) compared self-care children with children who come home to adult care on such variables as self-esteem, locus of control, social adjustment, and interpersonal relationships and found no significant differences.

Laurence Steinberg (1986) criticized this research because Rodman used children who usually went directly home after school. Steinberg also argued that the public was more concerned about the possibility that these unsupervised children might get into trouble, especially since other studies have shown that lack of parental monitoring is related to substance abuse, delinquency, and poor school achievement (Bradley, 1995). Instead, Steinberg measured susceptibility to peer pressure in children grades five through nine and found that children and adolescents who report home after school were not significantly different from other children but that children who were removed from adult supervision were more susceptible to peer pressure to engage in antisocial activity. Adolescents whose parents knew their children's whereabouts were less susceptible, even if the supervision was somewhat lax. Unfortunately, nearly half of the self-care youngsters do not go directly home (Steinberg, 1988). Steinberg concludes that parental monitoring is most important and that even long-distance monitoring, such as when children call their parents at work to tell them that they're home, can be useful; negative effects are most likely when children are not monitored regularly (Golambos & Maggs, 1991).

Still another important factor may be the reason that children find themselves in the self-care situation. When fifth- and sixth-graders who were alone or with younger siblings were compared with non–self-care children, few differences were found, but those that were found may be important (Diamond et al., 1989). Latchkey boys had more behavior problems, as described by both parents and the children themselves, and tended towards lower academic achievement. However, since the status of being a latchkey child may be dependent upon poverty and living in a one-parent family, the authors suggest that behavior problems may result from the stresses of a one-parent family living in poverty rather than the latchkey situation. Children who come from lower-income families or those who experience a great deal of anxiety may have more difficulties in the self-care situation, which is why it may be important to find out why a child is in self-care.

With the number of self-care children increasing, some organizations offer courses for children and their parents. The courses encourage parents to evaluate their children's maturity level and ability to be alone. They also teach children safety and survival skills, such as how to talk to strangers on the phone, discriminate between emergencies and nonemergencies, and care for younger siblings. Children who take these courses feel more confident about handling both emergencies and everyday situations. However, the children strongly wish that a parent were home with them or would call them. They experience a sense of independence and accomplishment, but they also feel frightened, lonely, and bored (Freiberg, 1996; Gray & Coolsen, 1987). Children who are home often see television as their only companion. Other help comes from telephone helplines, which children can call for help with minor domestic emergencies, conversation, information, or advice concerning problems with friends (Peterson, 1990).

It is difficult to interpret all the work on latchkey children because there are so many important variables. The definitions used sometimes differ, and the nature of the family situation that forces the child into the self-care situation may be important. However, there is an important difference between those children who come directly home and whose parents use some sort of supervision and those who do not, and parents should be encouraged to provide long-range supervision for their children.

Homeless Families

Homelessness is very much in the news today. Although most homeless people are single adults, the fastest growing segment of the homeless population today is families with children (Anderson & Koblinsky, 1995). It is difficult to estimate the number of homeless people because many are hidden as they sleep in automobiles, on the roof of a tenement, in campgrounds, or double up with others. A 1994 survey found that 3.6% of the population had been homeless sometime in the past 5 years (Link et al., 1995); about a quarter of all homeless people are children (National Alliance, 1991: Spaide, 1995).

The homeless family is most likely to be headed by the mother, and most families have histories of moving often (Bassuk, Rubin, & Lauriat, 1986). About half of the mothers have completed high school, but only a third have worked for longer than 1 month (Bassuk & Rosenberg, 1988).

Becoming homeless is a process that often begins with a family's being forced to leave an apartment because of nonpayment of rent or fire (Gewirtzman & Fodor, 1987). The next step is often to double or triple up with other families (Foscarinis, 1991). This sharing continues until the family is asked to leave, possibly because of the constant tension of overcrowding. Having little or no income and nowhere to go, these families then become homeless.

Research generally shows that homeless families are more similar to than different from other poor families but that homeless parents have experienced more disruptions in their early life than other poor people (Milburn & D'Ercole, 1991). One-third of the mothers heading homeless families report having been abused during childhood, and two-thirds have experienced major

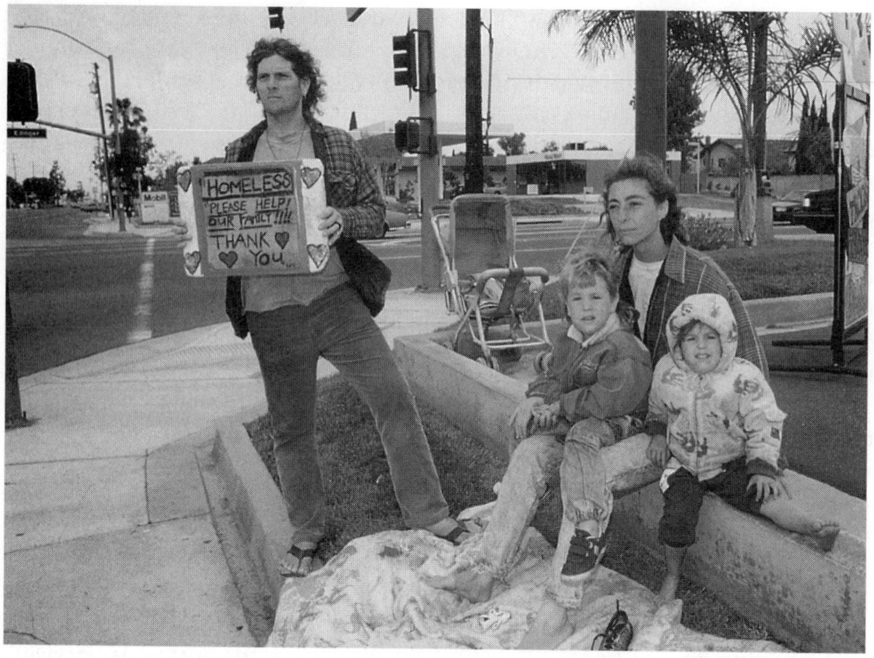

Homeless children show many deficits, especially in language. Their families need permanent housing and extensive social services.

family disruptions, such as divorce in their early life. Homeless mothers are more likely than poor single mothers who have housing to report an early experience that includes being in a foster home, running away for a week or more, living on the street for a time, or being physically or sexually abused (Bassuk & Rosenberg, 1988). The frequency of alcohol and drug abuse and serious psychiatric problems is also greater among the homeless mothers than among poor, housed mothers (Bassuk & Rosenberg, 1988; Robertson, 1991). Many homeless mothers are survivors who have endured disrupted childhoods including violence and life in shelters or on the streets (Rog et al., 1995b).

Homeless mothers are believed to lack all family contact and to have been abandoned by family and friends, but this view is actually only half true. Although these families presently have no one to turn to and are isolated, this is often because they have already used up their social supports. Homeless mothers actually have more contact with parents and friends than poor but housed mothers (Shinn et al., 1991). However, homeless women are unable to receive any support from these people because they are likely to have used their help in the past.

Homeless families may live in hotels or in temporary shelters. In shelters families sleep on cots in an open room that lacks privacy and cooking facilities. Young children may run through the facility or simply lie on cots; there are few toys and no play area (Gewirtzman & Fodor, 1987).

Studies comparing homeless children raised by single mothers to housed children who are very poor and also raised by single mothers demonstrate that homeless children are at a greater risk for medical, developmental, and educational problems (Hausman & Hammen, 1993). For example, homeless children experience a greater number of acute and chronic health problems than other poor children (Rafferty & Shinn, 1991). They are more likely to have delayed immunization schedules and elevated blood lead levels and to show higher rates of abuse and neglect (Alperstein et al., 1988). Fewer homeless mothers receive adequate prenatal care and the rate of prematurity is higher (Chavkin et al., 1987). Evidence also indicates that more homeless children have iron deficiencies and are at risk for delayed or stunted growth (Molnar, Rath, & Klein, 1990). Homeless children are also more likely to show developmental problems than poor but housed children (Molnar et al., 1990). The most common problem is a delay in language development (Whitman et al., 1990; Rafferty & Shinn, 1991), and visual motor development problems are also found (Rescorla, Parker, & Stolley, 1991). For such children at risk, Head Start programs could help. Yet, significantly fewer homeless children are enrolled in preschool programs than poor housed children (Rescorla et al., 1991). Homeless children are also more likely to show such psychological problems as depression and anxiety (Bassuk et al., 1986). Sleep problems, withdrawal, and aggression are also relatively common (Bassuk & Rubin, 1987).

Most homeless children are enrolled in public school, but their attendance is spotty and they are more likely to drop out of school (Gewirtzman & Fodor, 1987; Molnar et al., 1990). Homeless children are more likely to read and do mathematics below grade level and to be retained in grade (Rafferty & Shinn, 1991).

True or False?
Homeless children are more likely than poor but housed children to attend a Head Start program, receive their full set of vaccinations, and attend elementary school regularly because they are watched more closely by social service agencies.

Although the long-term effects of homelessness on children are not yet known, it is clear that this is a population not only at risk but currently suffering physical, emotional, and psychological damage. What can be done? Temporary shelters must provide children with day care, Head Start Programs, medical care, and space for physical activity. Shelters must provide case management services that allow referrals to other programs and movement to transitional housing (Rog et al., 1995a).

Obviously, affordable, permanent housing is required. Many families can go directly from shelters to service-enriched permanent housing in which they pay only a reasonable amount of rent and receive special services. These services can include child care, social support, self-help programs, job services, health care, mental health care, substance abuse counseling and treatment, transportation assistance, and programs like Head Start, but service-enriched permanent housing is often unavailable (Rog et al., 1995a). Both affordable housing and extensive social services are necessary if these at-risk children are to develop in a healthy manner.

Best Friends

During middle childhood, the influence of peers and friends grows substantially. Elementary school children form their own groups and interact extensively with them. Children learn social skills from their peers and obtain information by comparing themselves with others. Such interactions foster a sense of group belonging (Rubin, 1980) and help children learn self-control. Children in middle childhood see the peer group as most influential in the areas of activities and social behavior (O'Brien & Bierman, 1988). As children grow they see parents less often as the most important providers of companionship, and children of the same gender become more important in this area (Buhrmester & Furman, 1987). Much social interaction takes place in the school yard and on the school bus.

During the school years, children's ideas about friendship change, and they now see support, helping, sharing, and affection as more important and physical characteristics as less important (Berndt & Hoyle, 1985; Furman & Bierman, 1983). As children mature, they start to care about psychological compatibility (Rubin, 1980). Friends tend to be similar to each other in prosocial as well as antisocial behavior (Hartup, 1996). Friendships are based on such deeper values as intimacy, trust, loyalty, and faithfulness (Berndt, 1981). As children develop, their definition of friendship depends less on concrete behaviors and is more abstract (Shantz, 1983). It changes from the self-centered orientation of perceiving friendships as self-satisfying to perceiving friendships as mutually satisfying, and from an emphasis on momentary or transient positive interactions between individuals to a relationship that endures over time and through conflict. For these changes to occur, advances in cognitive functioning are necessary. Children cannot develop mutuality unless they can take a friend's point of view into consideration, an ability that develops in middle childhood. Although friendships are somewhat more stable than during the preschool period, only moderate stability in friendships and social group membership is found during elementary school (Cairns et al., 1995).

Elementary school children are often found in small groups (Berndt, 1989). Children are aware of the standards of the group, and much of the communication in these friendship groups is in the form of gossip (Parker & Gottman, 1989). This gossip concentrates on an exploration of the similarities among group members, reveals attitudes and beliefs that members share, and often involves criticizing other children. As children gossip, they affirm their norms and the values of the group. For example, they may criticize another child because he is bossy and aggressive, tells lies, or is a tattletale.

Rejection

Not all children make friends easily. Some children are more popular and make friends easier than others. Children who are popular and have many friends are physically attractive; share interests with other children; are friendly, outgoing and enthusiastic; know how to give positive reinforcement; and have interpersonal skills (Hartup, 1970; Dion, 1973). Popular children are helpful, friendly, considerate, and follow the rules of peer interaction (Dunn & McGuire, 1992). Late in middle childhood, traits like loyalty and empathy become important. Deviant and negative reactions to others are related to rejection (Hartup, 1983).

There seem to be two types of unpopular and rejected children. First, there are children who can be described as anxious, lonely, and depressed and who have low self-concepts (Patterson, Kupersmidt, & Griesler, 1990). Rejected boys who are not aggressive are often rated by their teachers as being shy, passive, and socially insensitive (Dunn & McGuire, 1992). Second, there are unpopular children who are aggressive (Dodge et al., 1990). Many aggressive children are rejected, and those who show both aggression and little prosocial behavior are rejected most often (Dunn & McGuire, 1992). These patterns are relatively stable. Children who are aggressive in second grade show acting-out behavior in fifth grade, and children who are socially incompetent and isolated in second grade show emotional problems such as anxiety and depression in fifth grade (Hymel et al., 1990).

Aggressive, unpopular children sometimes do have friends, usually other aggressive or unpopular children (Cairns et al., 1988). Aggressive children are often members of very solid peer clusters throughout elementary school.

> ***True or False?***
> Aggressive children in middle childhood do not have any friends.

One way to help unpopular children is to teach them the social skills they lack. However, children who learn social skills need to be included in programs that allow them to show and practice their new skills (Bierman & Furman, 1984). These social abilities predict school achievement. Beginning as early as kindergarten, children who keep their old friends and can make new ones are better adjusted and develop more positive attitudes toward school.

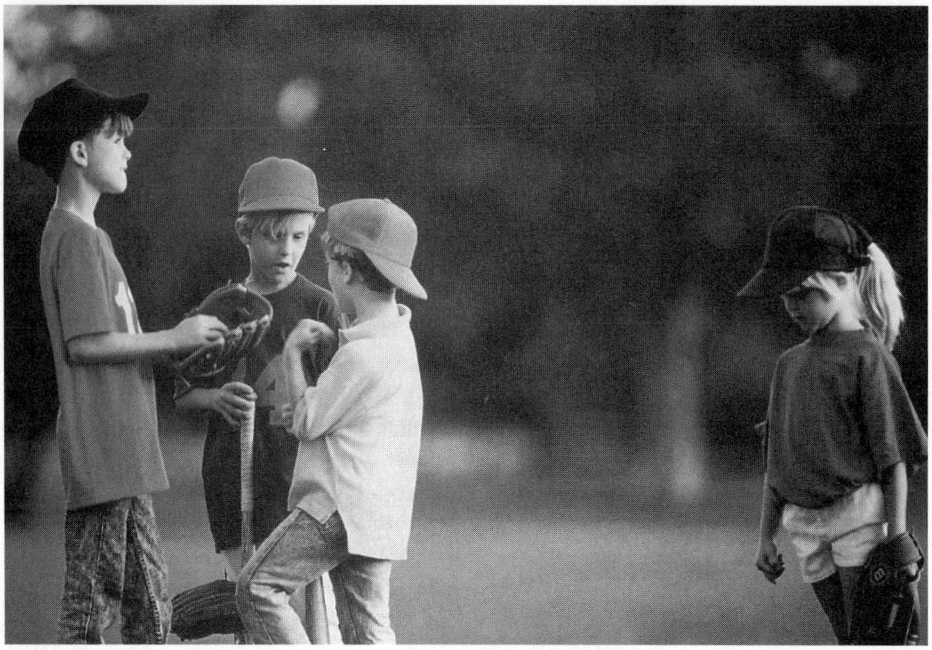
Segregation by gender is one of the hallmarks of middle childhood.

Friendship Patterns and Gender

Same-sex friendships are the rule during middle childhood. Boys and girls do talk with each other, but their relationships lack intimacy and involvement. Active rejection of the opposite sex is rare; avoidance is the usual course of action (Hartup, 1983). Whatever cross-sex friendships do develop are less stable than same-sex relationships. This segregation reaches its peak during the late elementary school or early junior high school years (Schofield, 1981). Of course, individual differences do exist, and some fast-developing seventh graders may be ready to develop cross-sex friendships.

> ***True or False?***
> Boys and girls tend to form same-gender playgroups during middle childhood.

Freud explained this segregation in terms of the resolution of the Oedipal situation, as described earlier in this chapter. Other interpretations for gender segregation have been advanced, including lack of compatibility in play, encouragement from parents to form friendships with children of the same sex, and the formation of gender-role stereotypes (Hartup, 1983). For example, boys do not expect girls to want to join in their games (Schofield, 1981), perceiving girls as having different interests and participating in different activities. They may also be aware of the relationships between the genders that await them during adolescence, including dating, romance, and sex. Peer pressure may also be a factor. A sixth-grade boy interested in forming a relationship with a girl may find himself under peer pressure not to do so. The young girl may be the butt of rumors and jokes and may find it easier to avoid a boy than to risk her friends' criticism. Whatever the reason, the growth of same-sex friendships during this period helps the child develop the ideals of friendship and intimacy that prove so important when the child begins to form cross-gender relationships in adolescence.

Gender Stereotypes: Alive and Well in the 1990s

As children proceed through middle childhood, they become more flexible in their understanding of gender relations and show more tolerance for others (Katz & Ksansnak, 1994). They become somewhat less rigid in their stereotypes (Huston, 1983). After about age 7 children no longer accept such stereotypes as absolute and are willing to make exceptions (Carter & Patterson, 1982). This tendency should not be overemphasized, for children have limits to what they will accept, and boys are more likely to resist change than girls are (Katz & Walsh, 1991). Boys show an increased preference for male-stereotyped activities, but girls do not show the same growing preference for stereotypical female activities (Carter & Patterson, 1982).

> ***True or False?***
> Elementary school children are more flexible in their gender stereotypes than preschoolers.

Moral Development

The second Karen picked up the wallet, she was faced with a moral question. Moral questions arise whenever a person is in a position to do something that can help or harm someone else (Carroll & Rest, 1982). Moral issues are very much in the news, and concern about instilling values in youth is growing (see Forming Your Own Opinion: Raising a Moral Child on pp. 252–253).

Piaget's Theory of Morality

Piaget looked at morality in terms of how a child develops a sense of justice and a respect for the social order. He argued that children's understanding of rules follows a general sequence. Preschoolers and children in the early school years consider rules sacred and untouchable and created by an all-powerful authority figure. In this stage, called **moral realism,** rules are viewed as inflexible, and justice is whatever the author-

moral realism The Piagetian stage of moral reasoning, during which rules are viewed as sacred and justice is whatever the authority figure says.

It is acceptable for girls to take on some of the stereotyped competencies of males. Do you think boys are as free to adopt such "female-sterotyped competencies" as being gentle or playing with dolls?

ity or law commands. The letter, not the spirit, of the law is important, and children become upset if people try to change the rules. Children believe in the absoluteness of values, and during these years they evaluate acts on the basis of their consequences and not on an individual's intent or motivation.

At about age 7 or 8, children reach the intermediate stage. Children now interact with peers and develop some type of reciprocal understanding. What is fair is more important than the position of authority. Punishments may or may not be fair, depending on the crime committed.

The stage called **moral relativism** emerges at about age 11 or 12. Children become more flexible and allow rules to be changed. They take extenuating circumstances into account and weigh them when making moral judgments. For example, ask a young child, "Who was naughtier—the child who broke one dish trying to sneak into the refrigerator to get some jam or the child who broke three dishes trying to help her mother?" Children in the stage of moral realism claim that the second child was naughtier, but children in the stage of moral relativism argue that the first child committed the worse act. Children younger than 7 years old rely primarily on consequences when evaluating another person's actions; children older than age 10 or so rely on intentions. Between about age 7 and age 10, children rely on either one of these (Ferguson & Rule, 1982).

moral relativism The Piagetian stage of moral reasoning in which children weigh the intentions of others before judging their actions as right or wrong.

> ***True or False?***
> As children progress through the elementary school years, they are more likely to judge right and wrong on the basis of the consequences of an action rather than intent.

Piaget's ideas in this area have been criticized. First, making judgments about who is naughtier is a very special type of moral judgment. Piaget does not deal with questions about what a child should do (Rest, 1983). Second, a number of studies have varied such factors as the amount of damage and the degree of intentionality and found that under certain circumstances, even small children understand that deliberate damage is naughtier. Piaget's findings are valuable, despite the narrow area of moral development they cover; however, the most complete theory of moral reasoning was developed by Lawrence Kohlberg.

Kohlberg's Theory of Moral Reasoning

Heinz's wife has cancer. There is a drug that might cure her, but the only dose is owned by a pharmacist who wants a great deal of money for it. Heinz doesn't have the money. Should he steal the drug? Lawrence Kohlberg (1969, 1976) presented dilemmas like this to many subjects, and after careful study, he proposed a model that describes the development of **moral reasoning.** Kohlberg saw moral reasoning as developing in a three-level, six-stage sequence. These stages are sequential and universal, that is, they are applicable to every culture, and no stage is ever skipped. Each stage requires more sophisticated skills than the one that precedes it.

How would you have answered Heinz's dilemma described above? Most students state immediately that Heinz should steal the medication. But Kohlberg was not interested in the answer itself. It is the reasoning behind the choice that is of interest and that determines what stage of moral reasoning a person is in. As Kohlberg's three levels and six stages are reviewed below, keep in mind that it is the moral reasoning, not the answer itself, that determines one's stage of moral development.

Level I: Preconventional Morality At the **preconventional morality** level, people make decisions on the

moral reasoning An approach to the study of moral development, stressing the importance of the child's ideas and reasoning about justice and right and wrong.

preconventional morality Kohlberg's first level of moral reasoning, in which satisfaction of one's own needs, and rewards and punishment, serve as the basis for moral decision making.

Forming Your Own Opinion: Raising a Moral Child

Parents, schools, and communities are wrestling with the problem of raising children who are decent and moral. At a time when supervision of children is more tenuous and life is infinitely more complicated, the question of how to raise virtuous children becomes more urgent. Serious evidence of social disintegration involving arrests and criminality is splashed all over the news; we seem to be a society in crisis. We also see the problems of intolerance and bigotry and wonder if anything can be done to improve the situation. People are now asking what parents, schools, and the community itself can do to improve children's moral development. One survey found that 71% of all Americans believe it is more important to teach values than academic subjects, and respect for others topped the list (Wagner, 1996).

Years ago, special programs called *values clarification courses* were advocated. These emphasized the importance of children experiencing the process of valuing rather than attempting to transmit certain values to children (Raths, Harmin, & Simon, 1966). Students were challenged to discover their own values. The teacher offered a number of anecdotes, simulations, and other activities that aimed at getting students to freely adopt and clarify their own values.

These courses were severely criticized because so much stress was placed on process and so little on the end result (Ryan, 1981). There is no right or wrong (Bauer, 1987). Some authorities claim that fostering values cannot be left to self-discovery, and students cannot be allowed to find their own values without input from adults (Ryan & Greer, 1990). Such a hands-off approach runs the risk of children developing antisocial or prejudiced values, so an open-ended format is rarely practiced today (Herbert & Daniel, 1996).

A similar approach uses Kohlberg's dilemmas, such as the case of Heinz, in an attempt to improve moral reasoning. Students are encouraged to play the role of different characters within the dilemmas. A dilemma is presented to the class in the form of a story, and the students determine how the situation should be resolved, giving reasons for their solutions, which are shared in group discussion. Kohlberg also argued that schools should be transformed into just communities, which involves establishing democratic structures and student participation in making and enforcing rules and policies (Oser, 1990). Some schools that have adopted some participatory democratic practices have given students a real voice and have decided to mandate restitution for victims of theft and to let students voluntarily switch classes to achieve greater racial integration.

On the surface, agreement on the type of values to be transmitted would seem easy to obtain. However, problems abound, especially in the area of priorities (Wagner, 1996). If you were a school administrator responsible for a new program for instilling values in your students, how would you rank order the following values in order of their importance to your program?

_____ a. self-discipline
_____ b. altruism
_____ c. respect for the environment
_____ d. respect for authority
_____ e. tolerance for others who may be different
_____ f. patriotism
_____ g. compassion
_____ h. obedience
_____ i. self-sacrifice
_____ j. courage

Two sets of values, espoused by two different philosophical approaches, vie for public support. One might be called *character education* and emphasizes such values as self-discipline, patriotism, respect for authority, obedience, perseverance, and courage. These are often perceived as

basis of reward or punishment and the satisfaction of their own needs. If Karen reasoned at this level, she might keep the wallet because it satisfies her immediate desires. On the other hand, she might not, because she is afraid of getting caught and being punished. Morality is defined strictly by the physical consequences of the act.

Stage 1: Punishment and Obedience Orientation An individual in Stage 1 avoids breaking rules because doing so might lead to punishment. This person shows complete deference to rules and does not consider the interests of others.

Stage 2: Instrumental-Relativist Orientation In Stage 2, the right actions are those that satisfy one's own needs and only sometimes the needs of others. However, the only reason for helping others is that they will then owe you something, to be collected at a later time. There is a sense of fairness in this stage, and a deal is acceptable.

Level II: Conventional Morality At the **conventional morality** level, conformity is the most important factor. The individual conforms to the expectations of others, including the general social order. Karen might keep the wallet if she reasons that anyone would keep it—and it's just too bad for the owner. On the other hand, she might not keep it if she reasons that it is against the rules and she would not be doing the "right" thing or being a good girl.

conventional morality Kohlberg's second level of moral reasoning, in which conformity to the expectations of others and society in general serves as the basis for moral decision making.

Forming Your Own Opinion: Raising a Moral Child (continued)

conservative virtues, sometimes religious in nature even though they are not associated with any particular religion. On the other side are the citizenship values, which include altruism, democracy, civility, tolerance, respect for the environment, compassion, and self-esteem. The argument today rages over which values our children should be taught. Those who emphasize more traditional values often claim the breakdown of society is due in some measure to the loss of these values, to indulgent parenting, and they advocate a return to respect and deference to authority, firmness, and character training. Those who favor citizenship values are concerned that traditional values are often "preachy" and moralistic, and they consider them more divisive than citizenship values (Wagner, 1996).

Parents can use both verbal and action-oriented methods to foster moral development in their children. Parents who encourage their children to participate in discussions of moral issues, especially those that occur in real life, and listen to their children's ideas and present other points of view promote moral reasoning in their children (Walker & Taylor, 1991b). An action component is also important and children must be encouraged to put their values into action.

Unless a concerted effort is made to build opportunities to put their values into practice, children may verbalize these values without really internalizing them. The most important ingredient may be to provide actual experiences that allow children to place their values into action. These activities may involve community- and school-based volunteer programs that emphasize helping others and improving the environment. No matter what values are decided upon, an emphasis on actually "living" the values needs to be included in the program.

Some schools have initiated programs in which older children help other children through peer tutoring. Visiting and helping in soup kitchens, shelters, hospitals, and day care centers is also beneficial (Spaide, 1995).

The same emphasis on action is needed to reduce prejudice. We now know that just placing children together does not seem to encourage tolerance and respect for others. When many schools were integrated, it was assumed that physical proximity would encourage interaction, dispel prejudice, and reduce intergroup problems. However, the results have not been particularly promising (Weyant, 1986). We have not seen the expected precipitous drop in racial prejudice or the increases in interaction between African Americans and white Americans. The findings are similar for the research on integrating children with disabilities into the regular classroom (Kaplan, 1996).

The lack of progress should have been predicted. Gordon Allport (1954) argued that to succeed in reducing prejudice, contact needs to fulfill three characteristics: (a) the groups must have equal status, (b) they should share a common goal, and (c) they must engage in activities supported by authority figures. Unfortunately, status differences often exist, and many classrooms do not encourage cooperation. Active cooperation can be increased, however, by using cooperative learning strategies in which two or more students work together to reach some common goal. By sharing the same goal, students can overcome their prejudices.

In the future, children will face the same social and economic problems we deal with today. The need for tolerance and understanding between groups, self-discipline, and the ability to delay gratification will be as great as it is today. In the future, activity-based programs will supplement programs aimed at attitude change so that students will be encouraged to live their ideals and practice what they preach. The school and community will have to actively confront the social and moral problems that so plague our society if we are to prosper in the next century.

Stage 3: Interpersonal Concordance, or "Good-Boy/Nice-Girl" Orientation Living up to the expectations of others and being good are important considerations for a person in Stage 3; the emphasis is on gaining approval from others by being nice.

Stage 4: "Law-and-Order" Orientation A person in Stage 4 is oriented toward authority and maintaining the social order. The emphasis is on doing one's duty and showing respect for authority. Sometimes people in this stage reason, "If everyone did it, then . . .".

Level III: Postconventional Morality People in the **postconventional morality** level have evolved moral values that have been internalized. These values are individualized and do not depend on membership in any particular group. Usually such moral reasoning does not occur until adolescence at the earliest, so we would not expect Karen to show such reasoning. However, if this dilemma occurred at a later age, she might return the wallet because she herself values honesty and integrity, even if it means she has to do without something. In Karen's case, the reasoning for keeping the wallet is admittedly strained. However, she might reason that the person who lost it does not need the money as much as she and Linda need it and that even if she were caught, she would be helping another human being in need—her friend. Karen's values of friendship, loyalty, and giving to others would become most important here.

postconventional morality Kohlberg's third level of moral reasoning, in which moral decisions are made on the basis of individual values that have been internalized.

Stage 5: Social Contract, Legalistic Orientation

In Stage 5, correct behavior is defined in terms of individual rights and the consensus of society. Right is a matter of personal values and opinions, but the emphasis is on the legal point of view.

Stage 6: Universal Ethical Principle Orientation

In this highest stage, Stage 6, correct behavior is defined as a decision of conscience in accordance with self-chosen ethical principles that are logical, universal, and consistent. This involves being able to weigh the ethics of various viewpoints and reasoning, and creating abstract guidelines to direct one's behavior (Kohlberg & Kramer, 1969).

People rarely reason solely in one stage. More often, they are predominantly in one stage while partly in the stages that come before and after. Change involves a gradual shift in the percentage of reasoning from one stage to the next higher stage (Walker & Taylor; Walker, 1988).

Moral Reasoning and Gender

In Kohlberg's stages the emphasis in the higher stages of moral reasoning is on justice, individual rights, and the rights of others. Higher moral reasoning seems to have little to do with interpersonal relationships. According to Carol Gilligan (1982), women have a different orientation to moral questions. They see moral questions more in terms of how these issues affect interpersonal relationships rather than in strictly individualistic terms, whereas men emphasize individual rights and self-fulfillment.

The differences in moral reasoning are rooted in the varying experiences boys and girls have in childhood. For example, boys learn to be independent, assertive, achievement oriented, and individualistic and to attach great importance to the rule of law; this is similar to Kohlberg's Stage 4 perspective. Women are raised to be more concerned with the rights and needs of others and to be interested in interpersonal relationships (Hotelling & Forrest, 1985). They are more oriented toward interpersonal connectedness, care, sensitivity, and responsibility to other people rather than toward abstract principles of justice (Muuss, 1988). They tend to see moral difficulties as conflicts between what they themselves want and the needs and wants of others, and they may base their decisions on how relationships with others will be affected. Harmony rather than justice may be the guiding principle. Sensitivity to the needs of others instead of strict individual rights becomes the criterion to apply in such dilemmas. This seems more like the Stage 3 perspective. Gilligan notes, however, that neither reasoning is superior—the stages are just different, and the differences should be understood and respected.

Karen may look at how her actions might affect her relationships with others rather than simply looking at some abstract rules of justice. Some interesting evidence in favor of this point of view comes from studies showing that 5- and 7-year-old boys and girls settle their disputes differently. Boys are more likely to use threats and physical force and to pursue their own goals whereas girls try to reduce conflict and improve harmony (Miller, Danaher, & Forbes, 1986). Boys also experience more conflict with peers than girls do.

Gilligan's ideas are controversial, with some studies failing to find consistent gender differences (Galotti, 1989; Walker, 1984, 1989). People often display both forms of moral judgment. When asked to report real-life dilemmas, females offer more personal and relationship-oriented dilemmas than males, and these may evoke more care-based moral judgments than other dilemmas (Wark & Krebs, 1996). One reason why females seem to make more care-based moral judgments than males is because females choose to discuss more care oriented moral dilemmas. Even here, the differences are small and gender differences in moral reasoning are found on only a few moral dilemmas. In fact, both genders used more justice-based than care-based moral arguments (Wark & Krebs, 1996). People don't view all the dilemmas in predominantly care- or justice-oriented ways; people invoke different forms of moral judgment in response to different types of dilemmas.

Perhaps there are two types of moral reasoning, and males and females use both types of reasoning in about the same degree (Yatsko & Larsen, 1990). Even if consistent gender differences are subsequently not supported by research, Gilligan's contribution lies in broadening our view of moral reasoning to include the idea that the moral person may integrate concepts of abstract justice and concern for others (Muuss, 1988).

Is Moral Reasoning Related to Moral Behavior?

Would a person reasoning at Kohlberg's Stage 5 act differently from a person reasoning at Stage 1? As the individual progresses toward Stage 6, we would think that moral behavior such as honesty and resisting temptation would increase. Indeed, most studies find a relationship between moral reasoning and moral action (Blasi, 1980; Kohlberg, 1987a), but the strength of the relationship varies from area to area. Some support is found for the idea that people at higher moral stages are more honest, but there is little support for the idea that people at the post-conventional level resist social pressure to conform in their actual moral actions. Only relatively weak associations are found between progressing to higher levels of moral reasoning and whether a child will cheat, yield to temptation, or behave altruistically if there is a personal cost attached to it (Maccoby, 1980). For example, college students were found to cheat less as the level of their moral reasoning increased. However, although subjects low in moral judgment cheated more, those high in moral judgment also cheated when the temptation became strong (Malinowski & Smith, 1985). Therefore, although there is a relationship between moral reasoning and moral behavior, other factors help to determine whether a person will perform a particular act.

Evaluating Kohlberg's Theory Kohlberg offers a valuable framework for understanding moral development, but his theory has been seriously criticized, partly because of its emphasis on moral reasoning rather than behavior. It is often thought that Kohlberg was not interested in behavior, only in reasoning but this is really not the case. Kohlberg just believed that the best way to understand behavior was to understand moral reasoning (Turiel, 1990). However, the discrepancy between reasoning and action is a problem. For whatever reason, people sometimes proceed in ways they think are theoretically best, and sometimes they do not (Chandler & Boyes, 1982). Also, because it is possible to reason at any level and still find a reason to cheat, lie, or steal, more predictability is needed. Kohlberg's theory also assumes that a person should reason fairly consistently in different situations. That is, a person predominantly reasoning at Stage 4 would reason mostly at this stage and a little at the two surrounding stages. Although there is not much research in this area, the few studies that do look at this issue do not support this consistency (Wark & Krebs, 1996; Hoffman, 1988). When people begin to reason at higher stages they seem to retain the ability and the willingness to reason at the lower stages as well (Carpendale & Krebs, 1995).

Questions Students Often Ask

Why study moral reasoning at all?

It is tempting to look at particular types of behavior and avoid the complexities of examining reasoning. However, when people are faced with moral choices and have the time to consider them, their reasoning becomes an important factor in their choice of which course of action to follow. I do agree that moral reasoning is only one aspect of the process, but it is an important one.

Kohlberg's use of hypothetical dilemmas is also problematic. We know a great deal about hypothetical dilemmas like the case of Heinz but very little about real-life moral judgments (Wark & Krebs, 1996). Kohlberg's theory would be better if he had depended more on actual life experiences and less on verbal responses about hypothetical situations (Vitz, 1990). Kohlberg argued that the earliest stages of moral reasoning were not based upon universal ideals but were restricted to particular situations, whereas the later stages were more universal and not situational. However, research shows that children as young as 3 and 4 years understand that some actions like hurting others and stealing are universally wrong, and that other behaviors such as dress codes are based upon societal conventions and are more changeable (Wainryb, 1993).

Perhaps moral reasoning may be only a part of the overall process people use to convert environmental information into an action sequence. According to Rest (1983), there are four stages to this sequence. First, a person must be sensitive enough to notice and evaluate a situation in terms of moral questions. Then the person attempts to reason the problem out. (This is where Kohlberg's moral reasoning theory fits in.) In the third stage, environmental influences are taken into consideration. (How much will the decision personally cost the person? How important is getting a good grade when cheating may be easy?) Finally, there may be practical difficulties in implementing the plan of action. (You may want to help someone who has just suffered a heart attack but not know how to perform cardiopulmonary resuscitation).

The Psychoanalytic Conception of Morality

When children are considering an action, do they hear a "small, critical voice" exhorting them to improve their behavior? Do they experience guilt if they do something forbidden? Psychologists who follow Freud believe so. They view morality as involving the development of the **superego**. Children between the ages of about 4 and 6 resolve their sexual fantasies toward their parents by identifying with the parent of the same sex and the superego arises out of this identification.

The superego consists of two parts: The **ego ideal** and the **conscience**. The ego ideal consists of the individual's standards of perfect conduct, formed when the child identifies and internalizes the ideals and values of the adults around him or her. The conscience causes the child to experience guilt when misbehaving (Eidelberg, 1968; Freud, 1933). Before the superego is formed, all resistance to temptation exists outside the individual (Solnit, Call, & Feinstein, 1979). Children are afraid that they will lose their parents' love or that their parents will punish them. After the formation of the superego, the regulation is internalized. Even if the parents are not present, the child acts in ways that would make the parents proud and experiences guilt when acting badly.

Research on the psychoanalytic conception of morality is mixed. Children do identify with older people, including their parents (Kline, 1972), but their moral values are hardly carbon copies of their parents' values. Although some similarity exists, children do not totally copy their parents (Damon, 1983).

The Learning Theory Approach to Morality: Studying the Behavior Itself

Some psychologists approach moral development by studying the behavior itself—sharing, helping, giving, lying, stealing, and being aggressive—instead of looking at the moral reasoning of the individual. They explain moral behavior in terms of the situation, the child's background,

superego In Freudian theory the part of the mind that includes a set of principles, violation of which leads to feelings of guilt.

ego ideal The individual's positive and desirable standards of behavior.

conscience Part of the superego that causes the individual to experience guilt when transgressing.

the models available to the child, and the reinforcers present in the environment.

Learning theorists argue that moral behavior, like any other behavior, is learned. Operant conditioning explains some of it. Children who are reinforced for giving and sharing are more likely to give and share. Social learning theorists add imitation to the picture. Much of behavior is influenced by watching how others—both adults and peers—deal with life's challenges (Bandura, 1986). This may not always be the case, since we do not imitate everything we see, and such factors as the character of the model, the consequences of the behavior, and our own characteristics affect whether or not we imitate (Bandura, 1977).

Cognitive factors, such as how we perceive the situation and process the information, are also important. For instance, aggressive children are more likely than nonaggressive children to believe that aggression will get them what they want and find it easier to be aggressive (Perry, Perry, & Rasmussen, 1986). Another factor is the child's competence to deal with a particular situation (Mussen & Eisenberg-Berg, 1977). Children who feel that they are competent may act one way; if not, they may act in a totally different manner.

Prosocial and Antisocial Behavior in Middle Childhood

It is tempting to divide people into those who are honest and helpful and those who are not, into those who give and share and those who are selfish. In their landmark studies, Hugh Hartshorne and Mark May (1928) tested thousands of children on a number of different tasks and concluded that children's behavior varied with the situation. A child could be honest in one situation and not in another. One who cheated on an athletics test might or might not cheat on an arithmetic test (Cairns, 1979). This situational view of honesty prevailed for some time, but later research using statistical techniques not available to Hartshorne and May discovered a carryover of honesty from one situation to the next, although it was not very strong (Burton, 1963). It seems that some people are more honest than others, but we cannot say that a person will be honest in every situation.

Helping Others

Social scientists have identified a number of factors that affect prosocial behavior. One of them is culture. Americans pride themselves on being prosocial and they donate a good deal of money to charity, yet American children are not as willing to share or to give as much as children in other societies. Children from India, Kenya, Okinawa, Mexico, the Philippines, and the United States were observed in a variety of social interactions. All the Kenyans and most of the Mexican children showed prosocial behavior in amounts that exceeded the median of all children in the study; only a small percentage of the American children exceeded this median. Prosocial behaviors were encouraged in cultures in which children lived in extended families and had greater responsibilities and where the social structure was simpler (Eisenberg & Mussen, 1989). Cultures that emphasize obligation to the community, trust, and cooperation rather than individualism and self-reliance are more likely to produce people who are prosocial and more conforming (Stevenson, 1991). A study of children in Japan, Taiwan, and Minnesota found that Asian children were raised in a more community-oriented manner and engaged in more friendly behavior and prosocial interactions than children raised in Minnesota. Those who grow up in small villages and rural areas are more cooperative than those who grow up in urban environments (Eisenberg & Mussen, 1989).

Another variable is child-rearing, which is related to culture. Parents who use reasoning techniques combined with affection raise children who practice prosocial behavior (Hoffman, 1979). This is especially true if parents make an effort to point out to children the effect of such behavior on others. Explaining rules clearly and linking rules to their consequences is also important. In addition, children who see their parents helping and sharing are more likely to do so also.

Even within particular cultures, there are wide individual differences in prosocial acts. One variable is age. Although young children show some prosocial behavior, cooperation and sharing increase somewhat with age (Durkin, 1995; Peterson, 1983). This may result from cognitive growth; the ability to take someone else's viewpoint increases because there is a decline in egocentrism (Eisenberg et al., 1987). Improvements in moral reasoning occur and may lead to an increased ability to experience empathy. **Empathy** is an emotional response resulting from understanding another person's state or condition (Eisenberg et al., 1996). A positive relationship exists between the ability to feel empathy and cooperation, socially competent behavior, and the inhibition of aggression (Eisenberg, 1989). The ability to empathize is a strong predictor of just about all types of prosocial behavior, especially in males (Roberts & Strayer, 1996). The reason empathy is somewhat more important for males than females is that social norms require women to show prosocial and nurturant behavior but men are under less pressure to do so.

True or False?
As children mature, they tend to share with other children more often.

Prosocial moral reasoning is also linked to prosocial behaviors (Carlo et al., 1996). People who are focused on themselves and what they can get are less likely to be helpful and generous than those who are concerned with the experiences and problems of others.

empathy An emotional response resulting from understanding another person's state or condition.

Aggression and Antisocial Behavior

Almost all parents have to handle aggression in their young children at one time or another, and aggression is a growing problem at home, in the schools, and in the community (Henry, 1994). Concern about being the victim of aggression is widespread in young children. When children between the ages of 7 and 12 years were asked about their worries, the three most common areas were school, health, and personal harm (Silverman, La Greca, & Waserstein, 1995). Worries about being physically harmed or attacked were the most frequent response reported by children, and this survey was not conducted in a high-crime area! The risk of exposure to violence during middle childhood is increasing (Lorion & Saltzman, 1993). Children's perception of violence in their communities is related to their reports of fear, distress, and depression both at home and in school (Osofsky, Wewers, Hann, & Fick, 1993).

Very aggressive children show deficits in social skills; they don't interact well with other children and often criticize them (Patterson et al., 1990). Aggressive children often aggress against each other, and are more aggressive when interacting with other aggressive children than when interacting with nonaggressive children (Coie, Dodge, & Christopoulus, 1989). When aggressive children are placed in small groups with children who are not aggressive, rates of problem behavior decrease (Dishion et al., 1991). Aggressive children often do poorly in school and are therefore tracked together in a class, which gives them even fewer chances to interact with better-adjusted children.

Aggressive children are likely to be male. Between three and six times as many boys as girls are referred to mental health agencies for aggressive behavior (Cullinan & Epstein, 1982), and boys are also more likely to be the targets of aggression (Cairns, 1979). Gender differences are rather constant across age and culture. Some argue that hormones predispose males toward aggression (Maccoby & Jacklin, 1980), and the evidence for this hormonal theory in animals is strong. In humans the evidence is far from conclusive, with some arguing that it is an important factor and others denying it (Schaffer, 1996). The debate will continue for many years, but both sides readily acknowledge that social factors are involved in aggressive behavior.

It is wishful thinking to believe that the aggressive child will grow out of it (Cullinan & Epstein, 1982). Aggression is rather stable over long periods of time for both boys and girls (Olweus, 1977, 1979, 1982). When children were followed from middle childhood through early adulthood, the more aggressive 8-year-olds became the more aggressive 30-year-olds (Huesman, Lagerspetz, & Eron, 1984).

Ingredients for Aggression

The same factors that we noted were responsible for prosocial behavior—culture, personality and cognitive factors, and family relationships—operate to influence aggressive children as well. Certain cultures encourage or at least tolerate aggressiveness. If aggressiveness is modeled in society, it is thought to be the proper way to deal with problems. Our own society seems to have a love/hate relationship with violence. Violence is condemned and punished (albeit violently), but our heroes use violence freely, sometimes without regard for the law, and children see violence—some of which is rewarded—all around them.

Family variables are also important. Many aggressive children come from very stressful family backgrounds that are marked by poor parental monitoring and the overuse of power by parents (Dishion, 1990). Children who watch their parents argue violently, are hit hard and often, and find that they get what they want by being aggressive toward others grow up to be aggressive (Parke & Slaby, 1983). Children who witness violence in the home or an acceptance of violence on the part of the parents as a way to settle disputes may learn that it is acceptable (Comer, 1995). In a series of studies, children were exposed to live or filmed models acting aggressively against a Bobo doll. When given the opportunity to play with the doll, the children usually imitated whatever they saw. If exposed to aggressive actions, they acted aggressively; if shown constructive actions, they imitated those actions (Bandura, 1986; Bandura, Ross, & Ross, 1961).

A child may also be rewarded for aggression which leads to more aggression (Becker et al., 1994). If a child takes things away from other children and is allowed to keep them, the child learns that the consequences of aggression are positive and will continue to behave aggressively; aggression becomes the characteristic method of dealing with desires and frustration.

Certain child-rearing strategies, such as permissiveness and punitiveness, are related to aggression in children (Sears et al., 1957). Very permissive parents tend to raise aggressive children, and the more punishing the parents, the more aggressive the children. The combination of permissiveness and punitiveness leads to the most aggressive children. If parents allow their children to vent their aggressive impulses, children think it is acceptable. Then they are harshly punished for it, which causes frustration and anger, which in turn leads to further aggression. The aggressive behavior does not remain confined to the home—parental use of physical punishment is related to children's aggressiveness at school (Eron, Walder, & Lefkowitz, 1971). Aggressive children are often not monitored properly and are plagued by inconsistent discipline (Kazdin, 1994). Their parents often use aggressive punishment in response to almost any transgression and expect aggressive behavior from their children (Strassberg, 1995). Other patterns associated with aggression include a very controlling parent combined with a resistant child or a very passive child with a domineering parent (Barth & Parke, 1993); children raised in these situations do not learn the proper social skills.

The parent-child interactions that lead to some very aggressive behavior patterns have been identified by

Patterson (1986; Patterson, DeBaryshe, & Ramsey, 1989). Any criticism from the parent causes the child to respond aggressively, which causes the parent to withdraw from the interaction. The child, then, is reinforced for the aggressive response.

Peer groups also influence aggressive behavior (Parke & Slaby, 1983). This may occur in three ways. First, children may model themselves after a violent individual, especially if the model gains something of value through violence. Second, the peer group may reinforce the violent deeds. Although aggressive individuals are often rejected by the majority of children, they may find a group in which this behavior is acceptable. Third, the social norms of the peer group may also influence aggressive behavior—some groups reject violence more than others.

In addition, cognitive factors must be taken into consideration. Children who are aggressive attribute more aggressiveness to others, seeing peer behavior as more provocative than it really is and then retaliating (Crick & Dodge, 1996). If children are asked to imagine that someone spills water on them during lunchtime and are given no additional information, aggressive children are much more likely to believe that it was done on purpose than nonaggressive children (Hudley & Graham, 1993). Aggressive children can be taught to perceive these behaviors differently and to give other children the benefit of the doubt, to more correctly identify social situations, and to better distinguish between intent and accident (Hudley & Graham, 1993). Aggressive children also expect positive outcomes from their own aggressiveness and often do not understand that other alternatives are available. Aggression becomes simply a way for them to get what they want.

Exposure to Crime and Violence

Although culture, child-rearing variables, and cognitive functioning contribute to aggression, the influence of the child's neighborhood on aggressive behavior may be underestimated (Osofsky et al., 1993). Children who live in poor neighborhoods are exposed to more antisocial behaviors by other children and do not have as many nonaggressive models. Young children living in high-crime areas deal with death more frequently and at a much younger age. When elementary school children living in a very high-crime area were surveyed, almost all had witnessed a violent act and over half had been victims of some form of violence. Weapons were a common sight, and some of the violence occurred in the home. Fears of violence were intense, and many children showed stress reactions, including a pervasive sense of fear and vulnerability, problems concentrating, had thoughts of violence intruding on their consciousness, and sometimes became inured to the violence. Some admitted becoming violent themselves and adopting an uncaring attitude. Such reactions as hypervigilance, withdrawal, suspicion, reduced impulse control, and increased risk taking were common (Martinez & Richters, 1993). Many of these children were taught "avoidance" skills, including to dive or run when they heard shots or not to sit near windows.

These reactions are commonly found among children in war zones around the world (Lorion & Saltzman, 1993), and there are similarities between people who live in such communities and those who live in combat areas (Cairnes & Dawes, 1996). Aggression may be the response to living in unsafe and stressful environments; children may learn to anticipate aggression and respond to it with violence (Kupersmidt et al., 1995). Young children who live in very violent areas are often traumatized by recurring violence, worry about their safety, and show a desire for revenge (Osofsky et al., 1993).

Not all children living in these areas are so affected, just as not all children living in war zones suffer from major behavioral problems—about 20% actually do (Garbarino & Kostelny, 1996). Some children cope better with these oppressive circumstances (Punamiaki, 1996), perhaps because their families provide a buffer against the violence (Zahr, 1996). Youth exposed to crime and violence are at significant risk for developing a number of psychological problems including anxiety, depression, phobias, and aggressive disorders (Berman et al., 1996), and parents often underestimate the amount of violence to which their children are exposed. Exposure to violence is an important ingredient in societal aggression and must be dealt with effectively if we are to reduce the overall amount of aggression in society.

Prosocial and Antisocial Behavior and Television

Children spend a great deal of time watching TV, and its effect on behavior has been thoroughly researched. It is one factor implicated both in prosocial and antisocial behavior.

When groups of preschoolers were exposed to aggressive cartoons, *Mr. Rogers' Neighborhood,* or neutral films, the children exposed to the prosocial programs displayed more positive behavior than children in the other groups (Friedrich & Stein, 1975). Elementary school children were shown a *Lassie* program in which a boy risked his life to save the dog; other children were shown either a *Lassie* program without such prosocial behavior or a situation comedy. Later, each child had an opportunity to help puppies in distress, but to do so they would have had to forfeit an opportunity to win a valuable prize. The children who had witnessed the prosocial program were more likely to help the puppies (Sprafkin, Liebert, & Poulos, 1975). Thus, watching prosocial programs can have a positive effect on children's behavior (Van Evra, 1990).

Viewing violence has been linked to aggression. By the time children graduate from high school, they have seen 13,000 violent deaths on television (Gerbner & Gross, 1980), and two-thirds of all television programming aimed at children is violent. The evidence indicates that viewing violence on television increases the probability of violent action (Liebert & Sprafkin, 1988). Short-term effects are easy to document (Wood, Wong, & Chackere, 1991). If two groups of children who are similar in aggressiveness are compared after one group sees a violent program and the other does not, the first group will react more aggressively. The same short-term effects are found for studies of children who play violent videogames—such play is related to increased aggressiveness (Williamson, 1987; Griffiths, 1991).

Television viewing also increases risk-taking behavior in children. When 6- to 9-year-old boys and girls watched the same programs edited for risk-taking behavior, the children who viewed the risk-taking version of the program, which included running while holding dangerous items, moving at very fast speeds, handling explosives, or hanging or jumping from dangerous heights, were more willing to take risks (Potts, Doppler & Hernandez, 1994). Long-term exposure may desensitize children to physically dangerous behaviors and also provide fearless role models. Indeed, an analysis of injuries to television characters found that almost no injuries have serious consequences for the victims nor do they last beyond the immediate scene (Potts & Henderson, 1991). Most injuries are minor despite the seriousness of the violence that causes them. According to social learning theory, seeing the consequences of an act presents observers with important information that can determine the likelihood that the person will imitate the action, so the lack of consequences is a concern.

Although some people seem to be more susceptible to violent suggestion than others, children of both genders and of all ages, social classes, ethnic groups, and personality characteristics may be affected (Huesmann et al., 1984). Both males and females may be equally influenced, with people who are more aggressive within each gender being more affected than others. Although children at every age are susceptible, they are particularly sensitive during late middle childhood—around 8 or 9 years of age (Eron et al., 1983). Exposure to violence peaks at about the third grade, but the correlation between aggressiveness and viewing violence increases until ages 10 to 11, suggesting a cumulative effect beyond this sensitive period.

Questions Students Often Ask

I've watched a great deal of violent television and I haven't been affected. How can the research linking aggression and violent programming be correct?

Violent programming increases the likelihood that people will aggress; it does not ensure it. Background, cultural, and cognitive factors are all involved in the result. In addition, what makes you think you haven't been influenced? You may not be aware of the influence but it is still there. Perhaps you are more accepting of violence as a way to solve problems or have become more desensitized to violence as a result of viewing such programs. You might not attribute your attitudes to watching violence on TV, but it still may be a factor in the development of your attitudes.

Seeing violence that appears justified and realistic has a greater effect on children than seeing violence that appears unjustified or brings negative consequences to the aggressor. These realistic and violent shows are very popular with children (Gable, 1994). Even fictional programs show violence as being pervasive and violence is sometimes used as a type of humor. The effect of television violence is greater if the viewer is already angry or frustrated.

Television may influence children's aggressiveness in a number of ways (Liebert & Sprafkin, 1988). First, some children may directly imitate what they see on television. Second, televised violence disinhibits aggression. People have certain inhibitions against violence, and witnessing aggression may reduce these inhibitions. Third, television violence may lead to antisocial attitudes and encourage children to accept violence as a way of dealing with problems. We get used to violence on television and come to accept it as a normal part of life (Drabman & Thomas, 1975), a process called ***desensitization***.

Questions Students Often Ask

Why doesn't watching television reduce aggression since viewers get their aggressions out in this way?

The catharsis theory states that people get their negative impulses out by watching such programs, but it just doesn't work that way (Brehm & Kassin, 1996). Many studies have found that people who watch these programs are actually more likely to be violent, not less. Watching violence does not reduce the urge to be violent, it acts as a model for aggression.

However, the relationship between aggression and television violence does not demonstrate cause and effect. For example, television may lead to aggressiveness in children, but aggressive children may also simply watch more aggressive television (Eron, 1987). In an analysis of two very large, long-term studies, Leonard Eron (1982) concluded that aggressive children prefer to watch more violent behavior, establishing a circular pattern. Eron reasons that aggressive children are unpopular and spend more time watching television. The violence that they see reassures them that their behavior is appropriate and teaches them new ways to act aggressively. This makes them even more unpopular and sends them back to the television for another dose of violence. Children who are aggressive are often heavy viewers of crime dramas, adventure shows, and cartoons, especially very violent ones (Sprafkin, Watkins, & Gadow, 1990). They are also more likely to identify with the violent characters than nonaggressive children are (Sprafkin et al., 1992).

Whatever the reasons, the link between aggression and viewing violence on television is well established (Comstock & Paik, 1994). Exposure to violent programming increases the probability of aggressive behavior and reduces prosocial behavior as well (Donnerstein, Slaby, & Eron, 1994). According to some authorities between 5% and 15% of all antisocial or illegal acts can be linked to exposure to violent television programming (Comstock & Paik, 1994; Graham, 1994; Silver, 1995).

Recent surveys show some reduction in television violence (Newsday, 1996), but parents have the ultimate responsibility for monitoring the programs their children watch. The V-chip, which allows parents to program out objectionable television shows, may make this somewhat easier but nothing will take the place of parental monitoring and guidance.

A Time of Gradual Change

Middle childhood is often seen as a time of horizontal growth, as the calm before the many changes that occur in adolescence. Unfortunately, this has led to the mistaken notion that middle childhood is a stagnant period. Unlike the earlier years of childhood and the coming years of adolescence—when cognitive, physical, and social growth are more obvious—changes during the middle years are more gradual, and we must look harder to find them. The child's social world is expanding as friends and teachers become more important, and children are given more freedom and responsibility at home. Because parents will not be with their children all the time, children must develop their own sense of right and wrong and decide how they will handle their interpersonal relationships.

These trends are seen in Karen's dilemma. No parents or even adult figures are present to tell her what to do. She must reason and act on her own and decide whether to give the wallet back or keep it. Her background, her relationship with her parents, her self-concept, and numerous other factors will influence her reasoning and final behavior.

It comes as no surprise that psychologists have found that children who emerge from middle childhood with a positive self-concept, good working relationships with their parents, healthy relationships with friends, and a good feeling about their own academic and social capabilities are ready to tackle the challenges that await them during adolescence.

Summary

1. Children's social network expands significantly in middle childhood. According to Erikson, the positive outcome of middle childhood is the development of a sense of industry and the negative outcome is a feeling of inferiority.
2. Freud noted that after resolving the Oedipal situation children enter a latency stage, during which sexuality is hidden. Boys' and girls' groups are segregated.
3. During middle childhood, the self-concept shifts from physical to psychological characteristics. Children receive feedback from many different people. Their self-concept develops from a combination of this feedback and their own evaluation of their subjective experiences.
4. Children's relationships with their parents change during middle childhood. Children become more independent and later in the stage are greatly influenced by peers. They also become more argumentative and question parental judgment more often.
5. Children's immediate reaction to divorce involves anger, depression, and guilt. Normally children recover from the initial shock after a year or so, but the long-term effects of divorce can be serious if parents continue to argue, if serious financial problems exist, and if social supports are unavailable. The use of divorce mediation can reduce some of the stress.
6. The stepfamily situation requires adjustment on everyone's part. Stepfathers who attempt to build a good relationship with the children before trying to discipline them do better than if they do not first attend to the personal relationships.
7. Children who must take care of themselves after school are called latchkey or self-care children. Evidence indicates that if the child comes right home after school and is monitored even from a distance by the parents, negative results do not ensue. However, many children do not go straight home after school and are not monitored. Some schools and social agencies offer training for self-care children.
8. Most homeless families are headed by mothers, many of whom have suffered serious disruptions. They have generally used up the support of family and friends and find themselves with nowhere to go. Homeless children suffer many more health problems, developmental problems such as lags in language development, and psychological problems such as depression and anxiety compared with children who are poor but housed. Homeless families need permanent, affordable housing and intensive psychological and social services.
9. Friendships in middle childhood are based upon psychological compatibility. Children's conceptions of friendship change over time as they become more cognitively sophisticated. Children who are popular tend to be friendly, have good social skills, share interests with their peers, and be physically appealing. Rejected children are anxious, depressed, or aggressive.
10. In middle childhood boys show an increased preference for stereotypical male activities but girls do not show such a preference for stereotypical female activities.
11. Piaget and Kohlberg both advanced theories of moral reasoning. Piaget noted that young children do not take intention into consideration when judging actions and that they see rules as unchangeable. Older children are more flexible and consider intent when judging actions. Kohlberg explained the development of moral reasoning in terms of three levels, each of which contains two stages. The reasoning underlying the moral decision, not the decision itself, determines the level of moral reasoning.
12. Carol Gilligan argues that while males are oriented

toward individual rights and legal issues, women are more concerned with how their decision will affect their social and interpersonal relationships. Although there is evidence that two different styles of moral reasoning exist, the idea that they are gender related is very controversial.

13. Freud viewed morality in terms of the development of the superego. The child identifies with the parent of the same sex and internalizes ideals and values.
14. Behaviorists are more interested in studying moral behaviors—such as cheating and altruism—than in the reasoning behind the behavior. The environment as well as the situation itself affects moral behavior.
15. Some cultures encourage more prosocial behavior than others. Children are more likely to show prosocial behavior when parents use rational methods of discipline and point out how the child's behavior helps others. The models children observe around them, as well as the reinforcers they experience or witness, are also important. Children's prosocial behavior increases with age because they become less egocentric.
16. Children who observe a great deal of aggressive behavior at home, who are harshly disciplined, or who are taught that aggression is an acceptable method of getting what they want tend to be aggressive. Aggressive children interpret the actions of others as provocative and are more likely to use violence as a response. Living in a violent neighborhood may affect children's development and behavior.
17. Most studies indicate that observing violent behavior on television makes it more likely that a child will act aggressively; it also desensitizes children to violence.

Multiple-Choice Questions

1. Victor is proud of his achievements and abilities. According to Erikson, Victor has achieved a sense of:
   a. intimacy.
   b. candidness.
   c. industry.
   d. satisfaction.
2. You are listening to a lecture on Freudian theory and the speaker says that sexual feelings are hidden because of the resolution of the Oedipal conflict. The speaker is talking about the __________ stage.
   a. genital
   b. latency
   c. anal
   d. pretense
3. When investigating the child's self-concept, you would expect a 9-year-old compared with a 4-year-old to make fewer statements concerning:
   a. possessions.
   b. attitudes.
   c. values.
   d. personal attributes.
4. The number of disciplinary encounters with parents __________ for children aged 3 through 9 years.
   a. increases
   b. decreases
   c. stays about the same
   d. increases until age 7 and declines after that
5. An 8-year-old child is described as impulsive, aggressive, and lacking in independence and a sense of responsibility. The child's parents are most likely to have used a(n) __________ style of parenting.
   a. authoritarian
   b. authoritative
   c. combinational
   d. permissive
6. The most common reason children live in single-parent families is:
   a. the mother never married.
   b. divorce.
   c. death of a parent.
   d. desertion of a parent.
7. Which of the following statements about children's adjustment to divorce is *correct*?
   a. The immediate reaction of children to divorce is negative.
   b. Many children show improvement between a year and 18 months after the divorce.
   c. Children find recovery more difficult if parents still argue after the divorce.
   d. All of these are correct.
8. Your child must spend some time alone at home before you come home from work. You decide to call the child or have him call you a few times between 3 and 5 p.m. and make certain that he knows he must come home directly from school. According to studies in the field:
   a. your child will still be adversely affected and will be more likely to show behavior problems, especially aggression.
   b. your child will actually do better in school since he will have more time to finish his homework.
   c. your practices should significantly reduce the probability of problem behavior developing.
   d. these practices make the parent feel better but have little or no effect on the possibility of the child developing behavioral problems.
9. Which statement concerning homeless children is *correct*?
   a. Homeless children are more likely to show language problems than poor but housed children.
   b. Homeless children are more likely to be immunized than poor but housed children.
   c. Homeless children do not attend school.
   d. All of the above are correct.

10. Much of the communication in groups of elementary school children is in the form of:
    a. directions.
    b. gossip.
    c. commands.
    d. emotional expressions.
11. Children who are most rejected combine which of the following characteristics:
    a. shyness and anxiety.
    b. aggression and little prosocial behavior.
    c. depression and apathy.
    d. fearfulness and little sharing.
12. Elementary school children 8 and 9 years old:
    a. are less likely to agree with gender stereotypes than when they were preschoolers.
    b. are more likely to agree with gender stereotypes than when they were preschoolers.
    c. completely reject the idea of gender stereotypes.
    d. are just as likely as preschoolers to believe in gender stereotypes.
13. In Piaget's stage of moral development called ____________, children believe that rules are absolute and justice is whatever the authority figure says it is.
    a. moral singularity
    b. moral relativism
    c. moral realism
    d. stage 1: amoral
14. A child says that you should not steal because you will get caught and punished. This is the reasoning in Kohlberg's level called:
    a. postconventional.
    b. conventional.
    c. preconventional.
    d. semiconventional.
15. A child says you should help others because it is what you are supposed to do. The child's reasoning is representative of Kohlberg's level of moral reasoning known as:
    a. postconventional.
    b. conventional.
    c. preconventional.
    d. semiconventional.
16. A friend states that Carol Gilligan's argument concerning moral reasoning is that women reason at a higher level than men. Your friend is:
    a. correct.
    b. incorrect, because Gilligan argues that they reason in the same manner.
    c. incorrect, because Gilligan argues that men and women reason differently; neither is superior to the other.
    d. incorrect, because Gilligan argues that only middle-aged women reason at a higher level than men.
17. Which of the following statements concerning prosocial behavior is correct?
    a. The relationship between empathy and prosocial behavior is greater for females than for males.
    b. Cultures that emphasize individuality produce more prosocial behavior than those that emphasize community.
    c. The decline in egocentrism in middle childhood is related to an increase in prosocial behavior.
    d. All of the above are correct.
18. Lois claims that children in elementary school are not really that concerned about violence because they do not witness much. According to studies, Lois is:
    a. correct.
    b. incorrect, in that elementary school children are more likely to be the victims of violent crimes than teenagers.
    c. incorrect, in that elementary school children are very concerned that they will be the victims of violence.
    d. incorrect, because children of this age group may witness violence but it does not seem to bother them very much.
19. Which statement concerning aggressive children is *correct?*
    a. Aggressive children often come from homes in which harsh punishment is used.
    b. Aggressive children may learn to aggress by watching others aggress.
    c. Aggressive children have parents who show more approval of the use of aggression as a way to solve problems.
    d. All of the above are correct.
20. A discussion is being held on the influence of television on elementary-school children. Doris claims that short-term studies show that watching violence increases the probability of violence. Dennis claims that aggressive children actually watch less aggressive television programs than nonaggressive children. Harry claims that seeing realistic violence influences children more than cartoon like violence, and Heidi argues that television is responsible for between 5% and 15% of the violence in society. The statement made by ____________ is incorrect.
    a. Doris
    b. Dennis
    c. Harry
    d. Heidi

Answers to Multiple-Choice Questions

1. c 2. b 3. a 4. b 5. d 6. b 7. d 8. c 9. a
10. b 11. b 12. a 13. c 14. c 15. b 16. c 17. c
18. c 19. d 20. b.

Chapter 12

Physical and Cognitive Development During Adolescence

Chapter Outline

Are the Following Statements True or False?

1. The sequence of developmental changes in adolescence is still largely a mystery.
2. As a group, 12-year-old girls are actually taller than 12-year-old boys.
3. Accidents are the greatest cause of teenage mortality.
4. Even if their weight is within the normal range, most teenage girls still want to lose weight.
5. Most people with anorexia nervosa, a condition marked by self-starvation, come from poor, uneducated, lower-income families.
6. The ability to interpret proverbs and political cartoons develops during adolescence.
7. As a group, adolescents show a higher desire for sensation and variety than do adults.
8. More college freshmen believe that it is important to be well off financially than it is essential to develop a meaningful philosophy of life.
9. Most adolescents believe in God.
10. The United States has the highest teenage pregnancy rate of all developed countries.

Answers to True-False Statements 1. False: see p. 265 2. True 3. True 4. True 5. False: see p. 270
6. True 7. True 8. True 9. True 10. True

It Will Pass

Many people consider adolescence a period of life marked by emotional swings, unrealistic ideas, and egocentrism. Teenagers are viewed as physically mature children who are not quite normal, negotiating a period in which they show some deviant, confused, but understandable behavior that will magically disappear by the end of adolescence. Some of this confusion is caused by rapid physical changes and the more subtle cognitive development that take place during this period. Adults really don't take adolescents' opinions and ideas very seriously, since they believe teens will cast these ideas aside as they negotiate early adulthood. At the same time, adolescents are required to make choices, for example, in the area of sexual activities, which have far-reaching consequences, and the public shows its anxiety over these decisions. Adolescent risk taking is an important concern (Carnegie Council, 1990).

Adolescence can be viewed more positively as a series of "firsts" (Siegel & Shaughnessy, 1995). It is the time of one's first kiss, first dance, first job, first date, first crush, and first love. It is a time of looking at the world in a new and different manner, of considering the future. It is the first time one experiences the intense feelings that come with deeper relationships. Many adolescents may not be prepared for these firsts, but viewing adolescence in this way makes it something more than just a bothersome period.

Questions Students Often Ask

Why don't people take adolescents, especially early adolescents, seriously? Why don't people like adolescents?

It isn't that people don't like early adolescents; they just don't take them very seriously. Adolescence is a period of transition in every area of development. Think back to your early and middle adolescent days. Do you remember any behavior that today would embarrass you? Looking back, how would you rate your behavior with the opposite sex? Adolescence is a time of "firsts." It is a time to try out new roles and behaviors and of being placed into new social situations. You are probably more at ease now with the opposite sex than you were then.

I know a number of people who cringe when they interact with their younger adolescent brothers and sisters because they do not remember that period. These are difficult years in which teens must get used to physical and social changes, and that takes time, understanding, and social experience.

Early adolescence is really a transition within a transition. It serves as a transition between childhood and the later phases of adolescence. It is an awkward period that people do not always look back to with fondness, as they sometimes do the periods of late adolescence. For these reasons early adolescents are not really given as much respect as they should be.

Puberty and Adolescence

Some people use the terms **puberty** and **adolescence** synonymously. Puberty refers to the physiological changes involved in the sexual maturation of the individual as well as to other body changes that occur during this period (Sommer, 1978). Body changes directly related to sexual reproduction, including maturation of the testes in males and of the ovaries in females, are called **primary sex characteristics.** Changes that are not directly related to reproduction but that distinguish boys

puberty Physiological changes involved in sexual maturation, as well as other body changes that occur during the teen years.

adolescence The psychological experience of the child from puberty to adulthood.

primary sex characteristics Body changes directly associated with sexual reproduction.

from girls are called **secondary sex characteristics.** These changes include beard growth in males and breast development in females. Adolescence refers to the stage from puberty to adulthood and covers all the psychological experiences of the person during that period. Puberty is a biological ripening and adolescence is a behavioral and cultural ripening (Krogman, 1980).

The sequence of changes that takes place in early adolescence is predictable. However, the timing of the changes varies considerably from person to person. For example, the average age of the first menstrual flow among American teens is approximately 12.8 years (Tanner, 1990), but a girl may begin menstruating any time between ages 10 and 16½ years and still be within the normal range.

True or False?
The sequence of developmental changes in adolescence is still largely a mystery.

Development of the Female Adolescent

The growth spurt is one of the earliest and most recognizable body changes. Because this spurt begins about 2 years earlier in girls than in boys, 12-year-old girls are generally taller and heavier and have larger muscles than 12-year-old boys (Tanner, 1970). Shortly after the growth spurt begins, girls develop breast buds and their hips increase in breadth. Then, when the growth spurt is at its maximum, changes occur in the genital organs; these include maturation of the uterus, vagina, labia, and clitoris as well as the breasts.

True or False?
As a group, 12-year-old girls are actually taller than 12-year-old boys.

When physical growth slows considerably, menarche (the onset of menstruation) takes place. At this point, a number of other changes in fat and muscle composition also occur. Menarche, then, is one of the later changes. Following menarche, most of the changes are nonsexual, including further changes in body shape and voice (Krogman, 1980).

Menstruation

Of all the body changes that occur in adolescence, menstruation is the most dramatic. Today, most female adolescents have at least been given some biological information about what is happening (or about to happen) to them. They are subjected to fewer restrictions, and discussion today is likely to be more honest. When a group of ninth-grade girls was asked about their preparation for their first menstrual experience, almost all said they were either well prepared or "somewhat" prepared (Koff & Rierdan, 1995). Most girls had discussed menstruation with their mothers, but discussions with sisters, nurses, and doctors were also relatively frequent. Information also came from classroom discussions and the media. Many emphasized the importance of a calm, supportive, reassuring environment as well as being given information as to what to expect and do.

secondary sex characteristics Physical changes that distinguish males from females but are not associated with sexual reproduction.

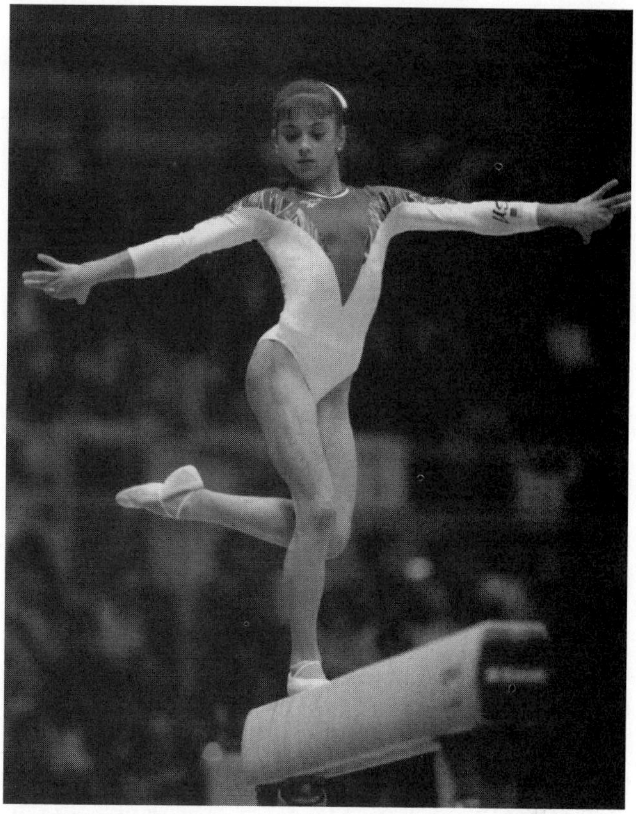

Women champions in the Olympics are often younger than their male counterparts, partly because of their earlier maturation.

Despite being somewhat prepared for it, most girls consider menarche mildly stressful and it is greeted with mixed feelings (Koff & Rierdan, 1995). Most report some physical distress and an immediate desire for privacy. Girls who are less prepared or who begin menstruating very early are most likely to evaluate the experience negatively. Although the experience produces some confusion and ambivalence, especially in those who are very young or who are not well prepared, it is not as traumatic as once thought (Ruble & Brooks-Gunn, 1982; Brooks-Gunn & Ruble, 1982).

Development of the Male Adolescent

The first signs of puberty in males are the growth of the testes and scrotum along with the appearance of pubic hair. This is followed about a year later by a spurt in height and the growth of the penis. The prepubertal growth spurt in males occurs approximately 2 years after the average female has experienced her growth spurt and takes the boy well beyond the height of the average female.

As is often the case, we can predict the sequence of events, but the time at which they occur varies from person to person. The trunk and legs elongate and leg length reaches its adult proportions before body breadth. The last growth change to occur is a widening of the shoulders. The voice deepens and facial hair appears. Muscles develop, in part because of the secretion of testosterone, and the heart and lungs increase in size dramatically, as does the number of red blood cells.

The Secular Trend: Taller, Earlier, and Heavier

In the past 100 years or so each new generation has been taller and heavier than the preceding one. In addition, each new generation has entered puberty at a slightly earlier age. These as well as other developmental tendencies—known collectively as the **secular trend**—have been the focus of much research. Since 1900, children each decade have been growing taller at the rate of approximately 1 centimeter and heavier by ½ a kilogram (1.1 pounds) (Katchadourian, 1977). Menstruation is also occurring at an earlier age (Tanner, 1990). The peak adolescent growth spurt is occurring earlier as well.

The secular trend is thought to result from improvements in health and nutrition, to a decline in growth-retarding illnesses during the first 5 years of life, and better medical care. The trend is definitely leveling off, or may even have stopped, in the United States and Western Europe (Tanner, 1990), possibly indicating that there are limits to how much these factors can affect the onset of puberty and influence the course of the physical changes that occur during this stage of life.

What Causes Puberty?

Three structures are thought to be primarily responsible for puberty: the hypothalamus (a part of the brain); the pituitary gland; and the gonads, or sex organs—the testes in males and the ovaries in females (Chiras, 1993). The hypothalamus produces chemicals known as releasing factors that are carried in the bloodstream to the pituitary gland, stimulating it to produce substances called gonadotropins, which stimulate the gonads. The gonads then produce the sex hormones that cause pubertal changes in the body (Sommer, 1978).

The level of hormones in the body is kept in balance. During childhood, the gonadotropin level is quite low, but secretion of these hormones increases in later childhood. The gonads grow and produce more sex hormones. The hypothalamus is sensitive to sex hormones circulating in the body. As the amount of sex hormones increases, the output of the releasing factors from the hypothalamus decreases, thereby reducing the pituitary's output of gonadotropins and regulating the amount of sex hormones in the body. As the individual matures, the hypothalamus becomes less sensitive to these hormones, increasing the amount of gonadotropin-releasing hormones in the system, and the pituitary output of gonadotropins climbs. This rise increases the production of sex hormones, thereby inducing puberty (Chiras, 1993).

The changes that take place during adolescence are largely determined by hormones, one group of which is the sex hormones. Scientists use the term **androgens** to refer to the group of male hormones, including testosterone, and the term **estrogens** to denote a group of female hormones, including estradiol (Kalat, 1981). Although both males and females produce both sets of hormones, males produce more androgens and females produce more estrogens. During adolescence the sex hormones are secreted into the bloodstream in great quantities. The androgens cause secondary sex characteristics—such as lower voice, beard growth, the growth of hair on the chest and in the underarm and pubic areas; estrogens encourage breast development and broadening of the hips (Kalat, 1981).

Timing of Puberty

As any observer of adolescence can attest, the timing of growth and development varies widely. Adolescents of similar ages can be more or less developed. For many years, the question of puberty's timing was simply explained in terms of genetic and dietary factors (Moffitt, Caspi, Belsky, & Silva, 1992). In societies in which medical care and nutrition are of good quality, developmental differences between people were ascribed to genetic factors. Although everyone agrees that genetic factors are important they do not account for all the variations (Steinberg, 1989).

Some authorities point to environmental factors as possible co-determinants of pubertal timing (Belsky, Steinberg, & Draper, 1991). In some specific cases, environmental factors can even override genetic factors in this area. Very intensive physical training can delay puberty and menstruation (Warren et al., 1991; Warren et al., 1986). Teen dancers have later ages of menarche than other girls. Usually, mothers and daughters are quite similar in age of menarcheal timing (Garn, 1980). When girls enrolled in dance company schools were compared to girls who did not attend such schools, a relationship between mother and daughter's age of menarche was found only for the nondancers, not for the dancers (Brooks-Gunn & Warren, 1988).

Other psychosocial factors also play a role. Family conflict and paternal absence in childhood predict a moderately earlier age of menarche (Moffitt et al., 1992). Better family relations, including lack of conflict, the presence of the father, and lower amounts of stress are associated with later onset of menarche (Graber, Brooks-Gunn, & Warren, 1995). The mechanisms linking family relationships and status to pubertal development have not yet

secular trend The trend toward earlier maturation today, compared with past generations.

androgens A group of male hormones, including testosterone.

estrogens A group of female hormones, including estradiol.

been identified, although hormonal pathways are probably involved (Graber et al., 1995).

Early and Late Maturers

Most people are neither very early in maturing nor very late but fall somewhere in between. There is some evidence that teens who mature either very early or very late may be affected by this experience. Early-maturing males have a substantial social advantage over late maturers. Adults rate early maturers more positively than late maturers. Early-maturing boys are considered more masculine, more attractive, and better groomed; they also have advantages in athletic competition, which may lead to popularity and increased self-esteem (Dusek, 1996).

Early-maturing males are also more likely to show behavioral problems at school, to be truants and delinquent, and are more likely to use drugs than their later-maturing peers (Andersson & Magnusson, 1990; Duncan et al., 1985). Early-maturing boys may form friendships with older boys and may be drawn into such behaviors.

Late maturers are considered tense and childish and are seen as always seeking attention. Peers see them as bossy, restless, less attractive, and having less leadership ability (Jones & Bayley, 1950). Late maturers are also viewed as more rebellious and dependent (Mussen & Jones, 1957), demonstrating a basic conflict in their personalities. Late maturers of college age have not yet resolved their basic conflicts from childhood, tend to seek both attention and affection, and do not gain positions of dominance or leadership (Weatherley, 1964). The late maturer separates himself psychologically from his parents and his peers. Early and average maturing boys are very similar in personality, so early maturation itself may not be the benefit it has been thought to be. It may be that what has actually been measured in previous studies is the lack of late maturation.

Late maturers continue to have problems into their 30s (Jones, 1957). The late maturers are still less settled, less self-controlled, more rebellious, and they have lower self-esteem. Not all the findings are negative, however, because late maturers also are more assertive and insightful. In addition, early-maturing boys become less active, more submissive, and less curious as they mature (Peskin, 1967, 1973). Although the early-maturing boy may have a social advantage, the later maturer is superior in some intellectual areas. Early maturers have more personal and social success but are not as happy in their marriages as later maturers (Ames, 1957). In their 40s the differences diminish greatly, and some personality advantages are found in favor of later maturers; early maturers become more conforming and rigid whereas the late maturers become more flexible and more insightful (Jones, 1965). The problems that seem to arise in early maturers in middle age—namely, inflexibility and being very conforming—are present even in adolescence (Peskin, 1973).

The results of studies of early maturation in females are inconsistent (Aro & Taipale, 1987). In a longitudinal study of sixth- and seventh-graders, early-maturing girls felt better about their futures, were more popular with boys, and dated more often and earlier than later-maturing girls (Simmons & Blyth, 1987). They were more likely to engage in early sexual activity (Gargiulo et al., 1987). They were more independent but less likely to get good grades and more likely to get into trouble in school. Early-maturing girls are more socially accepted by boys, but have less time to prepare for the social world. Later-maturing girls are more likely to be anxious and show higher levels of self-doubt, but are under far less social pressure. Because girls mature about 2 years earlier than boys, later-maturing girls may develop along with their male peers. Late-maturing girls are more gregarious, poised, and assertive (Atwater, 1996).

Early-maturing girls seem especially vulnerable to being pressured into engaging in risky behaviors. They are also more likely to be delinquent, use drugs, have eating disorders, and to have problems in school (Aro & Taipale, 1987; Koff & Rierdan, 1993). Early-maturing girls may be more popular with boys (an advantage), but more upset and anxious because of the social pressure to date and have sex. Perhaps this explains why early-maturing girls in schools with older peers are not as well adjusted as those who are in the highest grade in school (Blyth, Simmons, & Zakin, 1985). One important study argues that early maturation simply increases problems that are already present. When girls who matured early, on-time, and late were compared, an increase was found in problem behaviors for the early-maturing girls (ages 13 and 15 years). When early-maturing girls with a history of problem behavior were compared with those who did not have such a history, only girls with a history of problems showed the increase in behavioral problems (Caspi & Moffitt, 1991). Early maturers without a history of behavioral problems were no different from girls who were on-time maturers. Early maturation is a stressful time that magnifies the differences among individuals that exist even before adolescence.

Early-maturing girls are less satisfied with their physical characteristics and have a more negative body image than later maturers (Duncan et al., 1985; Brooks-Gunn & Warren, 1985). Later-maturing girls tend to be somewhat taller and thinner, more nearly approximating the cultural ideal of beauty in Western society, whereas early-maturing girls are shorter and have more body fat. By tenth grade most of these differences are significantly reduced or even, in some cases, nonexistent.

The timing of puberty may affect how parents deal with their teenage children. Parents perceive they have less conflict with early-maturing sons than with moderate- or late-maturing sons. On the other hand, early-maturing daughters are perceived to be a source of more stress and anxiety for their parents than late- and on-time maturing daughters (Savin-Williams & Small, 1986).

It is more difficult to draw conclusions about the effects of pubertal timing on girls. The situation is more complicated and less clear, and whatever effects are found are much less and more transient than they are for boys. Perhaps the best conclusion is that there are both advantages and disadvantages to early and late maturation for girls, but that the basis for the difficulties experienced by some early maturing girls may be present before puberty and not necessarily the result of puberty.

The Health of Teenagers Today

Adolescence is considered a period of life during which health is excellent. To some extent, this is true, especially if one considers the adolescent mortality rate, which is lower than any other group, with the exception of young children (Millstein, 1989). Relatively few adolescents now die from disease, which is in sharp contrast to the early part of this century when death from disease was common for this group. The most common causes of death in this age group are (a) accidents (most of which are motor-vehicle related), (b) homicide and violent crimes, and (c) suicide. The adolescent mortality rate has declined over the past 20 years, mostly because of a reduction in motor vehicle accidents; safer cars, reduced speed limits, an increase in the legal age of drinking, and the use of seat belts. Despite this decline, the accident death rate for youth 19 years and younger is higher than for any other age group (Sells & Blum, 1996).

True or False?
Accidents are the greatest cause of teenage mortality.

The second most common cause of death is homicide. Deaths from violence have increased greatly, especially among young people, and homicide is the number one cause of death among African-American males (USDHHS, 1996). The general level of violence throughout society is a national crisis; violence and delinquency will be further discussed in Chapter 13.

Suicide

Suicide is the third leading cause of death among people between 15 and 24 years of age (Worsnop, 1991). Each year, more than half a million young people attempt suicide and, unfortunately, about 5000 succeed (Neiger & Hopkins, 1988; Statistical Abstract, 1996). Males complete suicide much more often than females, but females attempt suicide more often than males; the difference is probably because males use more lethal methods to commit suicide (often firearms). Whites have higher suicide rates than African Americans, but the highest suicide rates are among Native Americans.

The most common cause of suicide is depression (Comer, 1995). A sense of hopelessness seems to overwhelm the victim (Farberow, 1985). When psychological autopsies (analyses of why suicides occur after they have already taken place) are performed, certain factors appear, which include drug and alcohol use; prior suicide attempts; depression; antisocial or aggressive behavior; and family histories of suicide (Garland & Zigler, 1993). Most adolescents who attempt suicide have experienced many stressful events in childhood, with a marked increase in stress in the year preceding the attempt. Having someone in the family who talks about, has attempted, or has actually committed suicide also increases the risk (Lawton, 1991).

Whenever a suicide occurs in a community, people start looking for reasons and clues, and indeed in a majority of cases, clues are found. About 80% of the adolescents communicate their feelings and intentions to other people before attempting suicide (Shafii et al., 1985). Research provides some clues to predict the possibility of suicide, but, unfortunately, people do not always pay attention to them. For instance, many people believe that people who talk about suicide never actually do it, but this is not so. People who talk about suicide are actually *more* likely to attempt it. Other warning signs include giving things away and talking about "ending it." A previous attempt at suicide is also a warning that a future attempt might be made if the predisposing factors are not controlled or adequately dealt with (Colt, 1983). When a child experiences extreme anxiety, depression, and hopelessness, people around the child should be aware that suicide may be contemplated.

Some schools offer classes in which students are taught how to recognize the warning signs and help their troubled friends. Such classes also introduce students to the community resources available. Some report positive results, including gains in understanding suicide prevention techniques (Nelson, 1987). One interesting outcome is that most of the teens questioned after the program reported that they were more likely to use a hotline to help themselves (Viadero, 1987).

Some authorities doubt the effectiveness of such programs and are concerned by their possible negative effects on already troubled students. A review of prevention programs found that the most effective programs were based upon sound empirical knowledge, including a clear understanding of risk, and collected evaluative data (Price et al., 1989). Most suicide prevention programs fail on both accounts. In an attempt to destigmatize suicide, the programs often deny that suicide victims experience mental disturbance. Additionally, suicide is sometimes incorrectly portrayed as a reaction to common stress and its incidence is often exaggerated. Deemphasizing the link between emotional disturbances and suicide serves no one, and many students only remember the link between stress and suicide.

Many prevention programs also do not reach the populations at greatest risk, which include dropouts, runaways, and youths who are arrested and incarcerated (Garland & Zigler, 1993). When students are asked what schools should do about suicide, they ask for special programs for troubled teenagers, programs for parents on how to be better parents, and information about hotlines and drop-in groups (Lawton, 1991).

One promising preventive approach is to help students improve their problem-solving skills and their confidence that they can influence the situation (Cole, 1991). Finally, reducing the availability of firearms and targeting education of at-risk populations, such as friends of people who have committed suicide and runaway youths, may also be effective in preventing suicide (Garland & Zigler, 1993).

Body Image

Just about every television situation comedy has a scene in which the entire family is waiting for the teenager to leave the bathroom after having just broken the "total time spent in the bathroom" record. Teenagers' bodies change quickly and these bodily changes require adjustments both in thoughts and in feelings (Richards et al., 1990). Although some teens cope very well with these changes, many are not always comfortable with their new bodies. Many want to change aspects of their physical selves—mostly their height, weight, and complexion (Burns, 1979). The combination of peer pressure and media advertising encourages teens to try to conform to a stereotyped socially approved body image. As teens proceed through adolescence, their wish for physical changes that they cannot have, such as being taller, declines (Bybee, Glock, & Zigler, 1990).

A good part of one's self-esteem in adolescence is determined by body image. There is a link between physical attractiveness and high self-esteem and between dissatisfaction with one's body and low self-esteem (Grant & Fodor, 1986). Girls are much more likely to suffer from poor body image than boys and are generally less satisfied with their bodies (Galambos, Almeida, & Petersen, 1990; Paxton et al., 1990). For example, although 81% of the subjects in one sample of teenage girls were assessed to be within the ideal weight range or even underweight, 78% wanted to weigh less, and only 14% were satisfied with their current weight (Eisele, Hertsgaard, & Light, 1986). Girls tend to overestimate and boys tend to underestimate how fat they really are (White, Schiecker, & Dayan, 1991). Many girls who try to lose weight really do not need to and some adolescent boys who should lose some weight do not think that they need to do so. Girls are much more likely than boys to base their self-esteem on their body image; which may be one reason why teenage girls are more likely than boys to suffer from depression and to have low self-esteem (Allgood-Merten & Lewinsohn, 1990). Poor body image and the behaviors instituted to control weight are related to disordered eating in female adolescents (Paxton et al., 1991). The problems with body image continue in adulthood, although most adult women do have a positive view of their body (Backley, Warren, & Bird, 1988).

True or False?
Even if their weight is within the normal range, most teenage girls still want to lose weight.

Nutrition and Eating Disorders in Adolescence

It stands to reason that adolescents' preoccupation with body image would affect their eating habits. The recommended daily allowances increase for most vitamins and minerals during the teenage years (Rolfes & DeBruyne, 1990). Nutritional needs are greater during adolescence than during any other time of life, with the exception of pregnancy or lactation (Whitney, Cataldo, & Rolfes, 1994). Some teenagers eat a balanced diet whereas the diets of others are deficient (Whitney & Hamilton, 1984). The most common problems are skipping breakfast and snacking excessively (Hertzler & Frary, 1989). Some become overly preoccupied with their body image and may attempt self-starvation or roller-coaster dieting (Newell et al., 1990).

About half of all female adolescents are trying to lose weight at any one time (Serdula et al., 1993). Most of this dieting involves adopting a low-fat or low-calorie diet, eating less, and perhaps increasing physical activity, behaviors that are usually considered healthy (French et al., 1995). However, a substantial number of adolescents try to lose weight in dangerous and unhealthy ways. These unhealthy weight loss practices have been reported by girls as young as 9 years of age (Berg, 1992).

Obesity Obesity is a major concern (Dusek, 1996) because being overweight increases risks for hypertension and coronary disease and leads to negative body images and poor self-concepts. Obesity creates a social problem for the teen because our society equates beauty and attractiveness with being thin; the obese person is out of step with current fashion. The obese person also faces discrimination by peers (Fowler, 1989). Obese children generally become obese teens, and obese teens are very likely to become obese adults (Epstein, 1987). Parental supervision of eating habits wanes during the teen years as the adolescent gains personal freedom. Social and academic pressure may lead to increased caloric intake. Many students use food to quiet their anxiety, and the less physically active life many older teens lead runs counter to the active life of childhood. Many teenagers eat diets that are high in fat and sugar and they do not really cut back on their consumption of these foods (Carruth & Goldberg, 1990).

Obesity has no easy cure. Teens need nutritional information because they eat an enormous amount of junk food, and their diet is often rich in starch but deficient in basic nutrients (Miller, 1980). In addition, many teens use crash diets, semi-starvation, or fad diets in a desperate attempt to lose or maintain weight, which can cause physical damage, especially to the kidneys, and are not effective in the long run. Perhaps a combination of increased physical activity under a doctor's supervision, nutritional information, a reduction in the consumption of junk food, and psychological support provided by peer group and family members can help obese teens lose weight and keep it off. However, long-term weight loss is difficult, and the battle against fat is a lifelong process.

Anorexia Nervosa **Anorexia nervosa** is a disorder marked by self-imposed starvation and involves an abnormal fear of becoming obese, a disturbance of body image, significant weight loss, and a refusal to maintain even a minimal normal body weight (American Psychiatric Association, 1994). It can be fatal in some cases. Anorexics have an appetite, but they are proud of being able to control their hunger. About 96% of all anorexics are female. This gender imbalance may be caused by the difference between how females and males are socialized to perceive their bodies. Females tend to see their bodies as effective only if they are attractive, which means thin, while males prize dominance, which translates into large proportions and physical strength (Grant & Fodor, 1986).

Anorexics usually show little overt rebellion toward their parents, but they suffer deep conflict on the dependent-independent dimension. They are often raised in educated, success-oriented, middle-class families that are quite weight conscious. They are also perfectionistic and are described by their parents as model children (Smart, Beaumont, & George, 1976).

True or False?
Most people with anorexia nervosa, a condition marked by self-starvation, come from poor, uneducated, lower-income families.

Anorexics are obsessed with food, weight loss, and compulsive dieting and are quite active physically, participating in socially accepted activities such as sports or in unusual ones such as running up and down the driveway until exhausted (Wenar, 1994). Even after they lose a significant amount of weight anorexics do not stop, but continue until they are too thin to be physically healthy. Losing weight becomes an obsession, and they fear they will lose control if they eat normally. Controlling their weight becomes their obsession. Changes in their physiology, thinking, and personality occur. They misperceive their weight, believing they are fat or about to become so; they often complain about feeling bloated after eating very small amounts of food (Wenar, 1994). Their condition becomes serious as their body begins to waste away. Menstruation ceases, they become ill and anemic, they cannot sleep, they suffer from low blood pressure, and their metabolism rate decreases (Bruch, 1978). In most cases depression is also found (Herzog et al., 1992).

The cause of anorexia is still a mystery. There is evidence for a genetic predisposition, as studies find a much higher concordance rate in identical than fraternal twins (Kendler et al., 1991). One theory emphasizes the effects on teens of our society's view of very thin being glamorous and the popularity of books on dieting (Nagel & Jones, 1992). Yet females receive mixed messages, because the same women's magazines are likely to give advice on how to make rich desserts, and at social functions women find themselves surrounded by calorie-rich foods. Unable to integrate these messages, the anorexic develops a fear of losing control and of eating too much and gaining weight. Freudian theory asserts that anorexia is a defense against sexuality and an attempt to regress to a preteen stage, especially since the anorexic stops menstruating. Those emphasizing a family approach note that anorexics come from rigid, overprotective families in which conflicts are avoided and people are overinvolved with each other, which interferes with formation of a personal identity. Still others believe that there is some basis in biology or that the dysfunction is neurological (Muuss, 1985).

Bulimia Imagine eating a gallon of ice cream and dozens of brownies and doughnuts and then purging your system of the food by forcing yourself to vomit. Such a dangerous pattern of behavior is characteristic of another eating disorder known as **bulimia.** Bulimia involves recurrent episodes of overeating followed by different behaviors intended to control weight and body shape, including vomiting and the overuse of laxatives. Bulimics maintain relative normal weight and the fluctuations in body weight are rarely extreme enough to be life-threatening, but the behaviors are abnormal and purging can cause serious physical problems. A characteristic set of disturbed attitudes to shape and weight, sometimes referred to as the *morbid fear of fatness,* exists (Fairburn et al., 1991). The overwhelming majority of bulimics are women.

Bulimics are aware that their behavior is abnormal but are afraid of losing control. Depression and extreme self-criticism are common after the binge. Often the food is sweet, easy to chew, high in calories, and is eaten very quickly. The binge-eating may be brought on by some emotional difficulty, such as stress, loneliness, depression, rejection, or rage (Muuss, 1986). Bulimia is often preceded by dieting (APA, 1994).

Bulimics believe that if they eat a small portion of a forbidden food they will completely lose control and they often jump from one eating fad to another. They make lists of forbidden foods and begin by denying themselves these foods only to break down later and binge. They have unreasonably high goals and may believe that if they gain any weight at all they will become fat or that if they cannot stick to a diet they are failures (Muuss, 1986).

Bulimics are perfectionistic, high achievers, and fearful of losing control. They often believe that others are watching them, and they constantly worry about how others perceive them. Bulimics are likely to have histories of mood swings, are more extroverted than anorexics, become easily frustrated and bored, and may abuse drugs (Fahy & Eisler, 1993).

anorexia nervosa A condition of self-imposed starvation found most often among adolescent females.

bulimia An eating disorder marked by episodic binge eating and purging.

The treatment for anorexia and bulimia is varied. The first priority is to restore anorexics to a reasonable weight, which sometimes requires hospitalization. In severe cases intravenous feeding is necessary. Family therapy that focuses on the relationships among family members and behavior modification to reinforce the anorexic to eat properly may be required (Muuss, 1985). Cognitive behavioral therapy is sometimes used for both anorexics and bulimics in an attempt to challenge their misconceptions and attitudes about eating and weight control (Wilson & Fairburn, 1993). It is important to change the way these adolescents think, for example, their belief that weight determines one's value as a person, and the bulimic's low self-esteem and perfectionism (Garner, Fairburn, & Davis, 1987). Longer-term therapy focuses on body image and interpersonal problems, making anorexics more aware of their underlying difficulties with autonomy and helping them to find other ways to assert their independence (Bruch, 1986); separate treatment for depression may be needed. Therapy can be very effective, but relapses are not uncommon (Sarafino, 1994).

Cognitive Advances in Adolescence

Adolescents are capable of perceiving the world as other people do and evaluating themselves, for example, their physical selves, as they think others will. Their self-consciousness seems to stem from their ability to consider how other people might be evaluating them and then to act to influence this assessment.

The idea that "people will think I am . . ," is especially powerful in early and middle adolescence. Other cognitive changes that relate directly to behavior are taking place, although they are less obvious. These changes allow teens to think differently from elementary school children and to begin to develop their own values. During the elementary school years, children can perform operations involving classification and reversibility. During the stage of formal operations, adolescents develop the ability to generate and explore hypotheses, to make logical deductions, and to use abstractions (Rutter & Rutter, 1993); their thinking can be described as formal, scientific, and logical (Miller, 1993).

The Stage of Formal Operations

Between the ages of about 11 or 12 and 15 years, many adolescents enter the **formal operations stage** (Table 12.1) and develop some interesting capabilities (Piaget, 1972; Inhelder & Piaget, 1958). These abilities develop gradually and an adolescent may show one skill but not another at a particular point in their development.

Combinational Logic When elementary school children are given a problem and are asked to find all the possible alternatives, they usually will not approach the

formal operations stage The last Piagetian stage of cognitive development, in which a person develops the ability to deal with abstractions in a scientific manner.

Table 12.1 **The Formal Operations Stage**
In the stage of formal operations, adolescents develop the ability to deal with abstract information and theoretical propositions. They can formulate and test hypotheses in a scientific manner.

CHARACTERISTIC	EXPLANATION	EXAMPLE
Combinational logic	The ability to find all the possible alternatives.	When asked what the president could have done in a certain situation, a teenager will produce a great many alternatives, some real, some impractical. If given five jars of colorless liquid and told that some combination will yield a yellow liquid, an adolescent will use an efficient and effective strategy that will produce all possible alternatives.
Separating the real from the possible	The ability to accept propositions that are contrary to reality and to separate oneself from the real world.	A teenager can discuss propositions such as, "What if all human beings were green?"
Using abstractions	The ability to deal with material that is not observable.	An adolescent understands higher level concepts such as democracy and liberty as well as the abstract meaning in proverbs.
Hypothetical-deductive reasoning	The ability to form hypotheses and use scientific logic.	A teenager uses deductive logic in science to test a hypothesis.

task in a scientific manner. For example, Inhelder and Piaget (1958) presented subjects of varying ages with five jars of a colorless liquid and told them that some combination of these chemicals would yield a yellow liquid. Preschoolers, who are in the preoperational stage, simply poured one into another, making a mess. Children in the concrete stage of operations combined the liquids but did not approach the task systematically. Adolescents formed a strategy for making all possible combinations of liquids and finally solved the problem. By the age of 13, between 80% and 90% of all children show this ability (Byrnes, 1988).

Adolescents can give all the possible solutions to a particular problem. If asked why something might happen, they understand that there are many different motives behind behavior. If asked the question "Why didn't Justin do his homework?" adolescents will provide a number of answers—some possible and many improbable. This demonstrates another similar skill—being able to divorce oneself from what is real.

Separating the Real and the Possible "What if human beings were green?" Ask a child this question, and the youngster may insist that human beings are not green. But adolescents can accept a proposition and separate themselves from the real world (Ault, 1977). They can form hypotheses and test them, which entails separating oneself from the real and considering what might be possible. Adolescents can reflect on a verbal hypothesis even though its elements do not exist in real life.

Some parents may have difficulty with adolescents who can and do suggest alternatives that may not be feasible or that parents simply do not like. The separation of what *is* from what *can* or *could be* allows adolescents to begin to think about a better world. Their "why" questions are based on possibilities divorced from reality, and they are capable of suggesting alternatives. But their lack of experience in the real world limits their ability to consider these possibilities in practical terms.

Using Abstractions The ability adolescents have to separate themselves from the trappings of what is real stems partly from their newfound ability to create and use abstractions. Children in the stage of concrete operations have difficulty understanding political cartoons and such sayings as "You can lead a horse to water, but you can't make him drink." They are still reality bound and therefore have difficulty with abstract thought and may actually picture a horse being led to water. But adolescents develop an ability to interpret abstractions, which allows them to develop internal systems of overriding principles. They can now talk in terms of ideals and values. Freedom, liberty, justice, and other such concepts take on added significance when they are separated from their specific situational meaning and adolescents are able to form their own values based on these overriding principles.

> ***True or False?***
> The ability to interpret proverbs and political cartoons develops during adolescence.

Hypothetical-Deductive Reasoning These emerging abilities allow the adolescent to engage in hypothetical-deductive reasoning—basically, the ability to form a hypothesis, which then leads to certain logical deductions. Some of the hypotheses may be untestable—such as "What if all humans were green?"—whereas others can be investigated scientifically. This type of reasoning is necessary for scientific progress. No one has ever seen an atom, but the developments in atomic theory have greatly affected our lives (Pulaski, 1980).

Thinking About Thinking Adolescents also develop the ability to think about thinking (Ault, 1977). Teens can look back on their own thought processes and see one thought as the object of another. This ability allows them to consider the development of their own concepts and ideas as well as to consider how others think. For

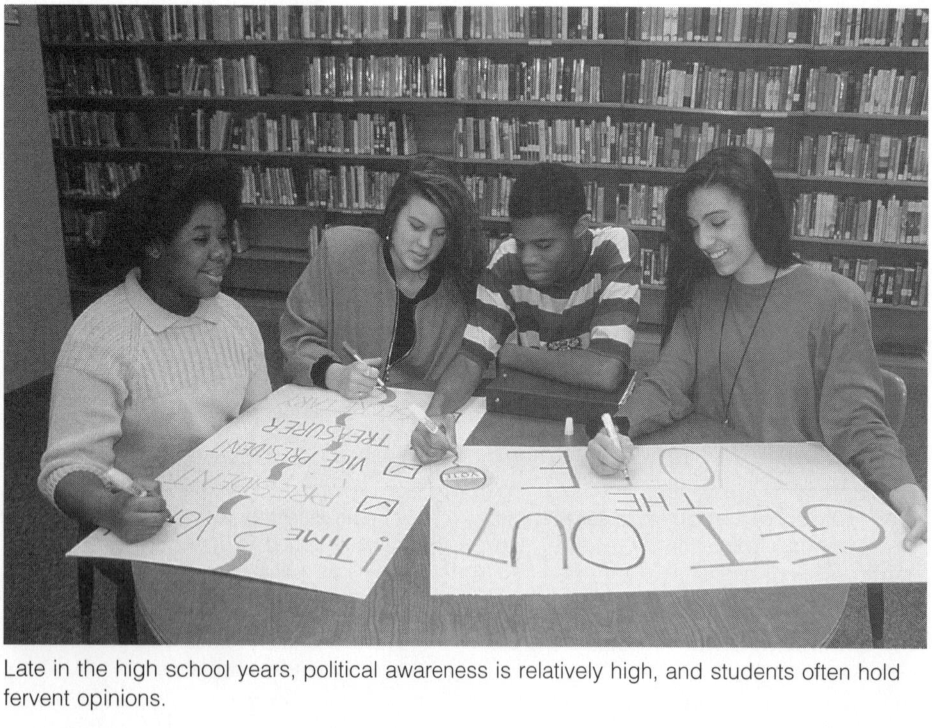

Late in the high school years, political awareness is relatively high, and students often hold fervent opinions.

example, in social situations a teen may follow this line of thought: he's thinking that I'm thinking that he's thinking about her (Miller, 1993, p. 63).

The ability to use combinational logic, interpret abstractions, and engage in hypothetical-deductive logic combine to allow adolescents to reason about problems on a higher level than they could during childhood. Adolescents are capable of accepting assumptions in the absence of physical evidence, developing hypotheses involving "if-then" thinking, testing these hypotheses, and reevaluating them (Salkind, 1981). Piaget saw the attainment of formal operations as the crowning cognitive achievement. He viewed formal operational reasoners as scientists who devise experiments on the basis of theoretical considerations and interpret their results within a logical framework. This mode of thinking is quite powerful (Siegler, 1991); it is also more flexible, because adolescents can consider a number of alternatives, weigh them, and then discard those that do not fit the situation. This ability to attack problems logically has great value in mathematics, science, and in life generally.

This type of reasoning develops gradually over the years and is dependent on the task and context (Rutter & Rutter, 1993); that is, adolescents may use the ability in one situation in which such reasoning is appropriate and not in another.

Evaluating Piaget's Ideas Not all adolescents—or even all adults—reason on this level (Neimark, 1975). Although older adolescents tend to be further along in using formal operational thinking, they do not use it on every problem where it would be appropriate (Roberge & Flexer, 1979). Only about half the adult population attains the final stage of formal operations (Muuss, 1982).

Why doesn't everyone show formal operational reasoning? Some claim that people may be competent enough to succeed at a task but for one reason or another do not perform it successfully (Flavell & Wohlwill, 1969). People fail because of fatigue, the way the problem is structured, or lack of experience with problems requiring such abilities. There is some evidence that people can be taught to use formal operational reasoning when appropriate (Kuhn, et al., 1979; Danner & Day, 1977).

Others suggest that not all people require the use of formal operations in their daily life. Consider the cross-cultural differences that have been discovered. Studies of formal operations show that people in non-Western cultures generally perform more poorly when presented with Piagetian tasks that require formal operational reasoning (Dasen & Heron, 1981). Piaget's stage of formal operations may be applicable only to adolescents in Western technological societies who are exposed to a great deal of formal education. Indeed, schooling does seem to be an important variable in determining whether people reach the formal operational stage. Schooled non-Western adolescents do better on these tests than unschooled non-Western adolescents (Rogoff, 1981).

Such evidence led Piaget (1972) to reevaluate this area of his theory. He recognized that education, vocational interests, and society and culture determine performance on tests of formal operations. Perhaps the environments necessary to progress to concrete operational thinking are basic and exist in the overwhelming majority of societies, but formal operational reasoning may require a more technological, structured environment and a particular type of stimulation found most often at the upper levels of schooling. At these levels, the nature of the environment may have a greater effect on performance than at earlier levels. What Piaget viewed as the ultimate achievement may only be so in Western cultures. We have little idea what may constitute the ideal last stage of cognitive growth in some other societies.

Finally, even within the same age groups in Western societies, some people perform better than others on tasks requiring formal operations. People mature at different rates and are exposed to different challenges. Individual differences in attaining formal operations skills should be expected, and indeed are found.

Adolescent Thought Processes

Adolescents often show a self-consciousness (especially early adolescents) that is legendary. In fact, early adolescent eighth-graders in one study were found to be significantly more self-conscious than younger children and older adolescents (Elkind & Bowen, 1979). Adolescents often look at themselves in the mirror and imagine what others will think about them. Adolescents can now think about thoughts—both their own and those of others. However, although teenagers can understand the thoughts of others, they fail to differentiate between the objects toward which these thoughts are directed and those that are the focus of their own thoughts (Buis & Thompson, 1989). Because teens are concerned primarily with themselves, they believe everyone else is focusing on them, too, and that others are as obsessed with their behavior and appearance as they are. The inability to differentiate between what one is thinking and what others are thinking constitutes what David Elkind (1967) called **adolescent egocentrism.** This leads to two interesting concepts: the imaginary audience and the personal fable.

The Imaginary Audience Adolescents often believe that when they walk into a room everyone focuses their attention on them. Then they anticipate the reactions. Adolescents are always on stage when in front of others (Elkind, 1985). Teenagers create an imaginary audience, believing that everyone is looking at and evaluating them. The people in this "audience" are real, but the audience is imaginary because most of the time the adolescent is not the focus of attention.

adolescent egocentrism The adolescent failure to differentiate between what one is thinking and what others are considering.

Adolescents are quite self-conscious. They believe others see and evaluate them in the same way as they see themselves.

The **imaginary audience** phenomenon leads to self-consciousness and the adolescent's mania for privacy (Peterson & Roscoe, 1991). Self-consciousness stems from the conviction that others see and evaluate them in the same way that they see themselves. The mania for privacy may come either from what Elkind calls a reluctance to reveal oneself or from a reaction to being constantly scrutinized by others; privacy becomes a vacation from evaluation.

As adolescents dress, act, and groom, they imagine how others will see them. Elkind notes that when the boy who combed his hair for hours and the girl who carefully applied makeup meet, both are more concerned with being observed than with being the observer. The imaginary audience disappears to a considerable extent during later adolescence. Self-consciousness seems to decline as people proceed from mid-adolescence to late adolescence (Hudson & Gray, 1986), but self-awareness increases. Teens begin to realize that people may not react to them the way they think they will. They also realize that people are not as interested in them as they thought.

The Personal Fable "You can't know how it feels to be in love with someone who doesn't know you exist," said one adolescent to his parents. He was convinced that only he could suffer such feelings of unrequited love, of loneliness, of despair. As adolescents reflect on their own thoughts and experiences, they come to believe that what they think and experience is absolutely unique and special. This is known as the **personal fable.** Teenagers may also believe they are invulnerable to harm, resulting in one of the most controversial behaviors found in adolescence—risk taking.

imaginary audience A term used to describe adolescents' belief that they are the focus of attention and being evaluated by everyone.

personal fable Adolescents' belief that their experiences are unique and original.

Risk Taking

We are often confused by the seemingly illogical behavior of teenagers as they take incredible risks involving drug overdoses, drunk and dangerous driving, and unprotected sex. Since risk taking seems to be a pattern in that adolescents who engage in one risk are much more likely to engage in others, a common cause may underlie them all. (Arnett & Balle-Jensen, 1993).

Some risk taking is explained by the personal fable. Teenagers are told that they are at the height of their physical and mental powers, that their future is bright and unlimited, and that they are unique. They tend to believe that they are invincible and that nothing bad can happen to them. They take risks, believing that the laws of physics and biology somehow do not apply to them. "It won't happen to me" is the philosophy that makes risk taking easy. Some support for the personal fable explanation of adolescent sexual risk taking exists. Many sexually active adolescents justify not using contraception with some variation of "I thought I (or my partner) couldn't get pregnant" (Quadrel et al., 1993). Belief in the personal fable declines at a much slower rate than belief in the imaginary audience (Lapsley, Milstead, & Quintana, 1986).

However, the personal fable cannot be the total explanation for adolescent risk taking. Adolescents are able to discriminate risky behaviors from safer ones (Alexander et al., 1990) and some studies find little or no difference in adolescents' and adults' understanding of the consequences of a particular risky action, such as driving while drunk (Beyth-Marom et al., 1993). A variation of the personal fable is found in adults as well; adolescents and adults both see themselves at less risk than others (Quadrel, Fischoff, & Davis, 1993). Even adolescents who are high risk takers understand the negative consequences of their behaviors (Dolcini et al., 1989). Perhaps adolescents' sense of indestructibility and their lack of awareness of the possible negative consequences of an action are simply shows of bravado or courage (Yando et al., 1994).

Another explanation for risk taking involves teenagers' desire for sensation seeking, which is related to risk-taking behavior (Arnett, 1992). Sensation seeking provides adolescents with novelty and an intense experience. The need for variety and sensation is highest in adolescence and declines thereafter. Both individual and cultural differences can be found in sensation seeking. In cultures characterized by individualism and independence, such as the United States, there is less parental monitoring and fewer restrictions on self-expression. These individualistic cultures are more likely to spawn sensation seeking than cultures that emphasize obedience and conformity (Arnett & Balle-Jensen, 1993).

True or False?
As a group, adolescents show a higher desire for sensation and variety than do adults.

Adolescents also have the need to assert their independence by not conforming to the standards of older people. Adolescents may take risks to deal with feelings of inadequacy or to gain inclusion into a group (Gonzalez et al., 1994). Adolescents may also understand the risks but choose to ignore them because the immediate benefits are far more attractive than the fear of possible consequences.

Morals and Values in Adolescence

The newfound abilities to understand abstract and overriding principles and values—such as freedom, liberty, and justice—and to separate the real from what is possible allow adolescents to formulate their own personal principles and ideas about right and wrong. They begin to think about how the world can be changed and to question the nature of various systems as well as the meaning of justice and morality (Siegler, 1991). As their thinking becomes more abstract, their idealism grows but so does their sense of uncertainty as older, established beliefs are modified (Rutter & Rutter, 1993).

Cognitive Development and Moral Reasoning

Lawrence Kohlberg, whose theory of moral reasoning was discussed in Chapter 11, argued that moral reasoning is related to cognitive growth and that higher stages of moral reasoning require more sophisticated cognitive abilities. As adolescents develop their formal operational skills, they begin to show higher levels of moral reasoning (Kohlberg, 1987a). Teens become concerned about the world of ideas, and willingly debate various moral and political perspectives (Miller, 1993).

The Higher Stages of Moral Reasoning Stage 4 of moral reasoning is oriented toward doing one's duty and maintaining the social order for its own sake. Stage 5 has a contractual legalistic orientation that emphasizes not violating the rights of others and respecting the welfare and majority will of others. Stage 6 is a more individualistic orientation, in which decisions are made involving one's own conscience and principles. Adolescents who are developing formal operational skills are better able to reason at these higher levels of moral reasoning, but many adolescents do not function at this level. In fact, even most adults do not develop beyond Stage 4 (Shaver & Strong, 1976).

The individual's stage of moral reasoning affects behavior in that the higher the stage of moral reasoning the less likely an individual is to engage in risky sexual behavior (Hubbs-Tait & Garmon, 1995). For example, the relationship between knowledge about AIDS and changes in sexual behavior depends upon the individual's level of moral reasoning. AIDS knowledge and risky sexual behavior are inversely correlated; that is as knowledge increases, risky sexual behavior decreases for higher-level reasoners but not for lower-level reasoners. This is also true for behaviors that reflect honesty and altruism. In other words, people who are at higher stages of moral reasoning tend to use the knowledge they obtain in a different manner, allowing that knowledge to influence their behavior.

A number of reasons explain why some people use Stage 6 reasoning while others do not. One of them is the competency-performance argument. Cognitive advancement makes more sophisticated moral reasoning possible but does not ensure it; other factors may also enter the picture. One variable is the content of the problem (Fischer, 1980); another is the consequences of the moral decision. When people are faced with a dilemma in which the personal consequences are great, they are likely to demonstrate lower-level moral thinking (Sobesky, 1983). Generally, when people are confronted with a problem, their cognitive skills form the upper limits of their abilities to reason, but the situation itself affects their actual behavior.

The adolescent's moral reasoning cannot be neatly placed in a single stage (Kohlberg, 1969) because they sometimes operate on a higher level, but at other times they operate on a lower one (Holstein, 1976). Thus, moral reasoning may be inconsistently applied to various problems and parents may have difficulty understanding their child's highly moral stand on one issue and lower-level reasoning on another.

The development of formal operations gives the adolescent the tools with which to solve a problem at the higher levels of moral reasoning, but it does not mean that these tools will be used. Formal operations are necessary but not sufficient for the development of higher moral reasoning processes. Many other factors, including personal qualities, family background, and the characteristics of the situation, determine whether these abilities will be used.

Values, Attitudes, and Religious Beliefs

An individual's values and beliefs are forged during adolescence. Each year since 1966 the attitudes and values of college freshmen have been surveyed. In the late 1960s students were more interested in social interpersonal morality. By 1975, however, the climate had changed, and students were more interested in personal achievement and this trend, although moderating, has continued. Many more adolescents in the 1960s believed that it was essential to develop a meaningful philosophy of life than in 1995, and many more adolescents in 1995 believed it was important to be well off financially (Sax et al., 1995). The changes in freshmen's views of social roles are startling. In the late 1960s more than half the freshmen believed that married women should stay home and look after their families, whereas less than one quarter believed the same in 1995; Table 12.2 depicts some of these changes.

***Table 12.2* Changes in Freshmen's Attitudes**
Alexander Astin and his colleagues surveyed nearly 6 million first-year college students. Some of their results are described below.

PERCENTAGE WHO	1970	1995
Identify themselves as politically liberal	34	21.1
Identify themselves as middle of the road politically	45	54.3
Identify themselves as politically conservative	17	20.3
	1966	**1991**
Plan to major in business	14	15.3
	1968	**1995**
Plan to pursue elementary or secondary teaching careers	21.7	9.3
	1986	**1995**
Are involved in programs to clean up the environment	15.9	22.5
	1967	**1995**
Believe it is essential or very important to be very well-off financially	44	74.1
Believe the activities of married women are best confined to the home and family	57	24.3
Believe it is essential or very important to develop meaningful philosophy of life	83	41.9

Source: Data from Sax et al., 1995.

True or False?
More college freshmen believe that it is important to be well off financially than it is essential to develop a meaningful philosophy of life.

Adolescents see law and politics differently from the way younger children see them. Preadolescents look at law and government in concrete, absolute, and authoritarian terms and evaluate them on the basis of how they affect particular individuals—for example, that seat belts are necessary because they protect the driver and passengers. Older subjects are less authoritarian and more sensitive to individual rights and personal freedom. Adolescents may see the conflict between requiring seat belts for the good of everyone and the loss of personal freedom that comes with regulation, a conflict that younger children do not see.

The political attitudes of today's freshmen are different from what they were just two decades ago (Sax et al., 1995). They are somewhat more likely to be middle of the road than years ago. Freshmen are more liberal on issues of personal freedom. For example, the belief that homosexual relationships should be prohibited continues to decline even since the 1980s.

Adolescents are affected by their environment, including the style of parenting used by their mothers and fathers. Authoritative parents are more likely to have children whose values are somewhat similar to their own and permissive or authoritarian parents tend to have children whose values differ more substantially from their own (Clark, Worthington, & Danser, 1988).

Adolescence is a time of questioning and examining belief systems, and religious beliefs and affiliations are areas that are reevaluated. Cross-sectional studies of religiousness by age show an overall decline in religiousness during adolescence (Donahue & Benson, 1995). By the end of adolescence teenagers are less involved in religious activities than they were as young teenagers (Benson, Donahue, & Erickson, 1989). This is often seen as a natural stage in religious development when all forms of authority are questioned and thinking becomes more critical.

About three quarters of all adolescents believe in God and most pray at least occasionally (Donohue & Benson, 1995). Adolescents have a more abstract notion of God than young children and do not see a Supreme Being as a physical entity. About half of all adolescents consider religion "important" or "very important" (Benson, 1993; Bachman, Johnston, & O'Malley, 1993). Women are more religious than men and African Americans are more religious than whites (non-Latinos) (Donahue & Benson, 1995; USDHHS, 1996).

True or False?
Most adolescents believe in God.

Religious belief and practice have a significant but relatively modest negative correlation with drug and alcohol use (Donahue & Benson, 1995), and with premarital sexual intercourse in that religious people are less likely to engage in premarital sex or use drugs. Religious youth are more likely to be involved in service projects and lower rates of violence are also related to religiousness.

Sexual Expression

The physical changes that occur in adolescence bring sexuality into stronger focus. The cognitive changes that occur allow adolescents to develop their own values and guide their choices in this area.

The Revolution in Sexual Attitudes

Traditional attitudes toward sexuality reflect the double standard. Males were permitted sexual freedom; females were denied it. Males were encouraged to experiment, yet sanctions against female sexuality were great. The sexual

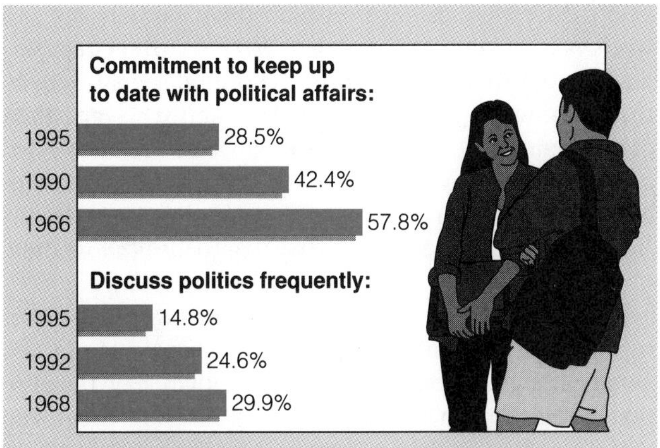

In recent years, college freshmen show less interest in political affairs, a worrisome trend.

Datagraphic
Interest in Politics
Source: Data from Institute for Higher Education Research, UCLA, 1996.

needs of males were recognized, but females' desires were denied, even within marriage. At least to some degree, however, the double standard has been reduced and attitudinal differences between males and females have narrowed.

The attitude change is in the direction of greater acceptance and a live-and-let-live orientation to sex. Sexual behavior is considered more a matter of personal choice than the business of society (Chilman, 1983). Adolescents' attitudes are likely to be much more permissive than those of their parents.

The revolution in attitudes appears to have been greater for females than for males, probably because women had more conservative attitudes to start with. Yet the idea that sex itself is viewed as a casual act or that the attitudes of males and females are identical is false. Males have more liberal attitudes toward sexuality than females and females are more likely to see sex as part of a loving relationship (De Gaston, Weed, & Jensen, 1996; Wilson & Medora, 1990). Females are also more likely to believe that birth control must be used and that no one should be pressured into sex; they are more likely to frown on premarital sex than males. Males are more likely to believe that it is right to demand sex from a girlfriend and that a woman is more responsible for birth control than the man (Carver et al., 1990). More women are committed to abstinence, are somewhat less permissive in their views, and are more likely to see adolescent sexual activity as a barrier to future goal attainment and to report less pressure from friends to have sex (Harvey & Spigner, 1995).

Both male and female teenagers become more permissive as the relationship they are in gets more serious; both believe that more sexual intimacy is proper when one is in love or engaged than when one is dating without affection or even with affection but without love (Roche, 1986; Roche & Ramsey, 1993). However, males are more permissive than females in what they believe is appropriate at the beginning stages of dating. In the later stages—which include dating only one person, being in love, and engagement—the differences for the most part disappear. In general, males expect sexual intimacy earlier in the relationship and females tie sexual intimacy to love and commitment (Roche, 1986).

Questions Students Often Ask

Why is sex considered a "problem"? It seems to me the problem is society's lack of acceptance of sexuality in young people.

"Sex" is not the problem; immature and irresponsible sexuality creates problems. Venereal disease and teenage pregnancy cannot be seen as anything but problems. STDs are medical problems and teenage pregnancy is a social problem. Very early initiation into sex is more likely to be linked to drinking, lack of achievement in school, and risky sexual behavior. It is difficult to think of a 13-year-old as mature enough to make sexual decisions. I agree that sexuality should not be viewed as "unnatural" or a "problem," but the consequences of certain types of sexual behavior can lead to unfortunate consequences.

Adolescent attitudes toward sexuality are affected by their relationships with their parents, their cognitive abilities, peer relationships, and the media. Many television programs and rock videos encourage liberal sexual attitudes and these have an effect on some teens (Howard, 1985; Strouse, Buerkel-Rothfuss, & Long, 1995). When satisfaction with the family is high, media influences are not as great as when familial satisfaction is low.

Dating

The age at which teens begin to date has declined. In 1924 girls started to date at the age of 16, while today it is about 13 years (Thornton, 1990). Adolescents from nonintact families begin to date earlier than those from intact families (Coleman, Ganong, & Ellis, 1985). Formal dating seems to have declined somewhat, and more informal meetings have become more common. Girls complain more about their parents' rules concerning dating than do boys, probably because parents are stricter with girls. Because girls date somewhat older boys, they experience increased pressure for sexual activity, which often causes parents to become stricter and more protective (De Gaston, Weed, & Jensen, 1996).

Dating affords an opportunity to interact and learn about others and to try out different relationships (Cox, 1990). Later in adolescence and continuing into early adulthood, dating becomes somewhat more serious because the possibility of mate selection enters the picture. Dating is fraught with anxiety, and disappointment and rejection are quite common (Greenberg et al., 1989).

Acquaintance Rape

One serious problem during dating that has recently received attention is acquaintance rape (also called date rape) and dating violence. It is not rare, but reliable figures are very difficult to obtain. One study of college students found that 40% of the women and 30% of the men either received or inflicted violence on their date and between 15% to 25% of all women experience date rape (Lane & Gwartney-Gibbs, 1985; Finkelson & Oswalt, 1995; Ward et al., 1991).

Questions Students Often Ask

Why is date rape suddenly such a problem today?

Date rape has always been a problem, but it is only recently that people have become aware of it. It still is not taken as seriously as it should be. In the past, women were blamed for being in a man's room or wearing certain types of clothing. This "blame-the-victim" attitude is somewhat less prevalent today but still is relatively common. Even when these rapes are reported, proof is difficult because acquaintance rape is a crime that occurs in private between two people who know each other and may have been dating.

Most women do not report date rapes to the authorities because they believe that their own behavior will be judged negatively, they feel embarrassed, or they feel some responsibility because they were under the influence of alcohol at the time (Finkelson & Oswalt, 1995).

Sometimes women who are raped may not identify their experiences as rape (Koss et al., 1987). Acquaintance rape does not meet the stereotyped image of rape (Strong & DeVault, 1995). About half the rapes are perpetrated on first or casual dates, by romantic acquaintances. It is important for rape victims to receive counseling and support as soon as possible.

Some date rape is the result of men who see their date as a source of sexual pleasure or who do not believe their date's refusal to allow certain sexual activities. Men expect sex earlier in relationships than women do, and women often face the problem of how to encourage a relationship without engaging in more sexual activity than they want (Komarovsky, 1985). Men who rape their dates are likely to have coercive fantasies, are aggressive, and accept the myth that women want to be coerced or believe that women really don't mean "no" when they say "no" (Greendlinger & Byrne, 1987). False ideas allow them to blame the victim (Blumberg & Lester, 1991).

Attitudes toward rape need to be changed as studies repeatedly reveal misconceptions and ignorance. In one study of high school students, more than half believed that some women provoke men into raping them, and that some girls encourage rape just by the way they dress (Kershner, 1996). Forced intercourse in some situations is not always seen as wrong by some adolescent males and females, an incredible belief (Feltey, Ainslie, & Geib, 1991). High school seniors were asked to read a vignette describing an obvious date rape. Some students were shown a picture of the victim dressed provocatively, others the victim conservatively dressed, and the rest were not shown any photograph. The findings are shown in Table 12.3. About one third of the students shown the provocative picture believed that the girl was partially responsible and that the boy was justified, or denied that the girl in the vignette was even raped (Cassidy & Hurrell, 1995). That no gender differences were found means that both males and females need rape education.

Women can take steps to reduce the possibility of date rape. The American College Health Association (1986) suggests, among other things, that women communicate limits, be assertive, not place themselves in vulnerable situations, not give in to pressure, and avoid excessive use of alcohol and other drugs. For men, communication, understanding that being turned down for sex is not a personal rejection, accepting the woman's decision, and avoiding alcohol and other drugs are advised. There is also a movement to begin antirape education in high school (Rich, 1991), and many colleges have initiated programs aimed at reducing acquaintance rape.

Table 12.3 **Percentage of Responses by Photograph Condition**

ITEM	PERCENTAGE PROVOCATIVE	PERCENTAGE CONSERVATIVE	PERCENTAGE NO PHOTO
Jennifer was responsible for John's behavior.			
Agree	37	4.3	5.5
Disagree	63	95.7	94.5
John was justified in having sex with Jennifer.			
Agree	31.5	6.9	7.3
Disagree	68.5	93.1	92.7
John raped Jennifer.			
Agree	63	89.7	84.4
Disagree	37	10.3	15.6

Source: Cassidy & Hurrell, 1995.

Sexual Behavior

Most people believe that a sexual revolution, a tremendous increase in the rate of sexual intercourse, has taken place. Has there been a revolution in sexual behavior?

Different studies show somewhat different statistics, but the trend toward earlier sexual experiences is clear. American men and women are more likely than ever to have intercourse by the age of 18 years. Among those born between 1963 to 1973, 61% of the men and 58% of the women had had intercourse by age 18. For those born 30 years earlier, the percentages were 43% for males and 32% for females (Hollander, 1996).

Adolescents generally overestimate the percentage of their peers engaging in sex and this may exert some pressure on teens to sexually experiment at a younger age (Leland & Barth, 1992). Indeed, one great concern is that teens are beginning their sexual experiences earlier; a third of the boys and more than a quarter of the girls have their first sexual experience by their 15th birthday (Carnegie Council, 1995).

The strongest predictor of sexual activity for teenagers of both sexes is alcohol consumption. Many teens engage in sexual intercourse after drinking (Harvey & Spigner, 1995). Alcohol use is associated with the early onset of sexual activity and more frequent sexual activity; this is especially true of high-risk sexual behavior, such as having unprotected sex.

Certain personality and social variables differentiate those teens who become sexually active at very early ages (in their early teens) from those who become active at the age of 17 or 18. Early onset and persistence is related to delinquency, emotional depression, and lower grades. It is associated with more childhood behavioral problems, antisocial behavior, and early use of alcohol and other drugs (Tubman, Windle, & Windle, 1996). Perhaps the antisocial behavior is indicative of poor impulse control and is related to sensation seeking and risk taking. Little parental monitoring exists (Capaldi, Crosby, & Stoolmiller, 1996), and teens who engage in sexual intercourse at an early age have comparatively poorer communication with parents (Casper, 1990). The poor family relationships and rebellion cause the adolescent to seek acceptance from peers through sexual activity. Whatever the combination of reasons for very early sexual behavior, such sexual behavior is related to personal and familial difficulties and the profiles of these teenagers may differ from the profiles of those who begin having sex later in adolescence.

The increase in premarital sex is now accepted by most researchers. However, whether one wants to call this a revolution or an evolution depends on one's personal point of view. The change in attitudes has been more radical than the change in behavior. The explanations for the increase are many and varied. Some explain it in terms of more open coverage by the media, the reduction of sanctions against premarital sex, the movement toward women's equality, the increased availability of contraceptives and abortion, earlier maturation, and the faster pace of our society.

Contraceptive Use

If rates of premarital sex have increased substantially and attitudes are more liberal, what about contraceptive use? Only 45% to 59% of all women used contraception at their first intercourse (Mauldon & Luker, 1996); studies conducted in Mexico and Germany find similar percentages (Huerta-Franco et al., 1996).

Most sexually active teens have had intercourse at least once without using any form of birth control. Often these teens report being either drunk or high at the time (Leland & Barth, 1992). Girls are more likely to depend upon male contraceptive methods when they first begin to be sexually active. Early use of contraception begins a pattern of safer sexual practices (Mauldon & Luker, 1996). Although there is some evidence that contraceptive use is increasing, many teens still run the risk of an unwanted pregnancy.

We often think that the sexually active teen is a well-informed person and knowledgeable about the facts of conception, but the research shows otherwise (Morrison, 1985). Many teens do not believe that a pregnancy can result the first time they have intercourse and do not know the time during the menstrual cycle when the greatest risk of pregnancy exists. On various tests of sexual knowledge, teens answer only about half of the questions correctly (Carver et al., 1990; Leland & Barth, 1992).

Contraceptive use has increased somewhat lately, but is still at a low level. Adolescents know something about the different methods of contraception, with older teens knowing more than younger teens. However, mistakes and misunderstandings are quite common (Scott et al., 1988). Research shows that sexually active teens do not necessarily know more about contraception than teens who are not sexually active (Padilla & Baird, 1991).

Teen attitudes toward contraception are negative or neutral at best. Many do not believe that even the reliable forms of contraception really work. Many teens simply do not consider the possibility that they will get pregnant, and if they do think about it, they do so fleetingly. The need for sex education would seem obvious, but what to teach and the effects of sex education are areas of controversy (see Controversial Issues: Sex Education on pp. 280–281).

Adolescents do not use contraception regularly because of erroneous beliefs about fertility, indifference to becoming pregnant, ignorance about where to get contraceptives, and negative attitudes toward contraceptive devices themselves (Morrison, 1985; White & DeBlassie, 1992). Some are uncomfortable about obtaining birth control. Some teenagers do not visit a family planning clinic because they think that they need their parents' consent (Brooks-Gunn & Furstenberg, 1989). Some teens are afraid to use oral contraceptives or say that they are not in a continuous sexual relationship. The fact that contraception must be planned and that planned sex is unromantic and lacks spontaneity may be another reason for the sporadic use of contraceptives. Many teens also deny being sexually active and may not be mature enough to admit that they are engaging in intercourse (Dreyer, 1982). The first sexual encounter is rationalized as an accident—a moment of passion or a chance event. Most methods of birth control demand that the person acknowledge that he or she is sexually active (Pestrak & Martin, 1985), but many adolescents are not cognitively

Controversial Issues: Sex Education—Just the Facts?

Everyone agrees that reducing the prevalence of adolescent pregnancy and combating the spread of AIDS and other STDs are worthy goals (Leland & Barth, 1992). The question that divides the public is how to attain these goals (Frost & Forrest, 1995).

People generally argue that the family should be the basic transmitter of education about sexuality. However, the statistics show that parents are not talking to their children about sex in an honest and open manner. A poll conducted by Planned Parenthood found that although teens cite their parents as the most important source of information on sex, pregnancy, and contraception, only a third had discussed contraception with their parents. Those who had discussed it were much more likely than those who had not to use contraceptives if they were sexually active (Wattleton, 1987). When a great deal of communication occurs, teens are also more likely to share the sexual values of their parents. Parents find it difficult to talk with their children about sex and such communication is often inadequate or even nonexistent.

The schools have a responsibility in the area of sex education as well and state education departments either strongly recommend or mandate the teaching of sex education and AIDS education (Haffner, 1992; Kirby et al., 1994). As many as 80% of all parents favor sex education in schools, although those opposed are often a very vocal minority (Miller, 1995; Barron, 1987). When sex education is offered in school, less than 3% of all parents refuse to let their children participate (Scales, 1978).

Most parents want contraception taught and about 65% of all American adults support condom availability in the schools (Roper Organization, 1991), although some are concerned that this will encourage sexual activity. However, the most comprehensive sex education programs that may include on-site availability of condoms do not lead to greater sexual experimentation (Kirby et al., 1994). Studies of HIV prevention programs that included promotion and distribution of condoms do not find an increase in sexual activity among adolescents (Sellers, McGraw, & McKinlay, 1994).

Do these programs do any good? Do they help students postpone becoming sexually active? Do they encourage the use of contraceptives among those that are sexually active? The results are mixed. Many sex education programs have failed to achieve their goals or have only had a small positive effect (Firestone, 1994; U.S. Office of Technology Assessment, 1992). However, other programs have been successful. For example, a large national representative survey of women found that the likelihood of a teenage woman using some contraceptive method at first intercourse increases by about one third following instruction about birth control. If contraceptive education occurs in the same year that the teen becomes sexually active, the odds that any method is used increase markedly (Mauldon & Luker, 1996). Students who receive school-based contraceptive education are more likely to talk to their parents (Mauldon & Luker, 1996).

Recent research offers some clues as to why some programs fail while others succeed. One major reason for failure is that many programs spend so much time on safe, noncontroversial topics such as basic biological information and so little time on contraception and disease prevention issues. Discussions of risk taking are far too general. Sex education frequently comes too late, after students have already begun having intercourse (Rodriguez & Moore, 1995).

Ineffective programs generally are less focused and cover too many areas. These programs also do not take a clear stand against unprotected sex. They may try to adopt a nonbiased, nonjudgmental model, encouraging students to simply make their own decisions (Kirby et al., 1994). Studies show that this is not effective, probably because spontaneous, unprotected sex is often considered romantic and produces short-term immediate pleasure whereas waiting or using contraception involves long-term planning. Ineffective programs are also often lecture centered, with an adult providing biological information or warnings without dealing with the pressures to have sex that are so common in teenage life.

able to cope with these facts. For example, the personal fable enables adolescents to believe that they won't get pregnant. Some teens show here-and-now thinking and some younger teens find the entire subject of conception difficult to understand.

Questions Students Often Ask

I think that to be effective schools must give out contraceptives. My girlfriend says this would be promoting sex and taking away parental rights. Who is right?

Giving out contraceptives in school is certainly controversial. Although studies definitely show that it does not lead to greater amounts of premarital sex, some people argue that it is just not a function of the school. I agree that sex education is the province of the home but too many studies show that parents just aren't communicating with their children. That leaves the schools with a mission of educating children. The question is really how to effectively teach sex education in a way that will lead to sexual responsibility.

Sexually Transmitted Diseases

Concern about sexually transmitted diseases (STDs) has increased with the spread of AIDS. Other sexually trans-

Controversial Issues: Sex Education—Just the Facts? (continued)

An evaluation of four effective programs found that the rate of teenage sexual initiation fell by as much as 15% during the year or two following participation in such a program. Programs that emphasize delay are more effective with younger adolescents and among older adolescents these programs significantly increase the percentage of sexually active older adolescents who consistently use contraceptives (Frost & Forrest, 1995).

In one interesting program conducted in Baltimore, junior and senior high school students received sex education as well as information presented by social workers on the services offered at a clinic. For several hours each day, staff members assigned to each school made themselves available for individual counseling. After school, a special clinic across the street or a few blocks away offered open group discussion and individual and group counseling that emphasized personal responsibility, goal setting, parental communication, and health care, including contraception. The results showed better knowledge about contraception and sex (something other studies have shown), as well as a delay in the age of first intercourse. Students attended the clinic sooner after initiating sexual activity, and there was an increased use of contraception among those who were sexually active. This behavior was especially noticeable among the younger teens, who usually show less responsible sexual behavior. The program altered behavior partially because access to high-quality free services, including professional counseling, was assured (Zabin, Kantner, & Zelnik, 1979).

Successful school-based programs share a number of elements. Effective programs focus on reducing sexual risk-taking behaviors that lead to HIV and other STDs or pregnancy. Some emphasize abstinence as the best way to avoid unintended pregnancy and STDs, or urge adolescents to delay intercourse. Others emphasize specific methods of contraception and how to obtain them (see Table 12.4). They all emphasize life skills, which involves helping students to set goals for their lives, to learn to say no to sex, and, most importantly, to negotiate and communicate within relationships. It is also important to dispel the myth that almost everyone has sex by the age of 15 or so, a prominent belief that leads to pressure to have early sex (Mahler, 1996). Many successful programs specifically teach resistance skills (how to say no), which are associated with a later age at first intercourse if presented with biological information and AIDS education (Ku, Sonenstein, & Pleck, 1993).

The most effective programs are also based upon solid theoretical considerations, most often using a social learning theory approach. Social learning theory, as applied to sex education, posits that a behavior such as delaying intercourse or using contraception is affected by an understanding of what must be done to avoid intercourse or use protection (knowledge), a belief in the benefit of delaying sex or using protection (motivation), the belief that particular skills or methods of protection will be effective (outcome expectancy), and the belief that one can use these skills or methods of protection (self-efficacy).

Effective programs provide basic information about the risks of unprotected intercourse but use active, engaging methods such as small group discussions, role playing, and brainstorming; and address the social or media influences on sexual behavior, including the social pressure to have sex. They sometimes use peer leaders or respected peers to model and practice communication and negotiation skills. Every successful program devotes time to communication, negotiation, and refusal skills.

These programs are not value-free, they have a definite value orientation. They reinforce group values and norms against unprotected sex and are tailored to the experience and needs of the students (Kirby et al., 1994; Mahler, 1996). Unfortunately, many communities still use programs that are ineffective. Now that we have learned a great deal about what works and what doesn't communities should insist that their sex education programs be based upon the research on effectiveness rather than on habit or wishful thinking.

mitted diseases such as syphilis, gonorrhea, herpes, and chlamydia, whose incidence is increasing, also can lead to serious health consequences. Although the prevalence of STDs in other industrialized nations remains low, the rate in the United States shows a rapid rise (Ericksen & Trocki, 1994); one in six sexually experienced teens has had a sexually transmitted disease (Sellers, McGraw, & McKinlay, 1994).

Women with untreated chylamydia or gonorrhea can develop an infection that can lead to infertility and other problems, as well as infections in their infants. Syphilis increases the risk of miscarriage and can cause infection in infants. Teens may be HIV positive and not know it because the long incubation period for the disease, averaging 11 years, means that many people infected as teens will get AIDS when in their 20s or 30s (Sellers et al., 1994). AIDS education and prevention is vital in adolescence because the behaviors of some adolescents put them at risk for acquiring the virus.

A history of drinking and drug taking, having a number of sexual partners, and the inconsistent use of condoms increases the risk of contracting STDs (Ericksen & Trocki, 1994; Centers for Disease Control, 1992b). Generally, boys engage in more high-risk sexual activities than girls (Leland & Barth, 1992). Girls report having fewer sexual partners and question their partners about high-

Table 12.4 **Teenage Pregnancy Prevention Programs**

POSTPONING SEXUAL INVOLVEMENT

A school-based educational curriculum that was initially implemented in Atlanta, Georgia, among eighth graders, Postponing Sexual Involvement is based on social influence and social inoculation theories and takes the position that youth this young should abstain from sex. The classes, which are taught by older teenagers (11th and 12th graders), include activities to help youth identify the source of and motivation behind pressures to engage in risky behavior (including sex) and to assist them in developing skills that will help them resist such pressures. These classes are accompanied by a series of sessions on human sexuality (including discussions of contraceptives) that are taught by hospital staff. A total of 10 classes are presented over a three-month period.

REDUCING THE RISK

A second school-based educational curriculum, Reducing the Risk, was initially implemented in several schools in California. Targeted to high school students (primarily 10th graders), it is based on several social learning theories and includes activities that teach adolescents the skills they need to resist pressures to engage in risky behavior. The classes attempt to instill students with the norm that unprotected intercourse is to be avoided, either by not having sex or by using contraceptives. The curriculum, which consists of 15 sessions presented over a three-week period, is presented by specially trained high school teachers.

SCHOOL/COMMUNITY PROGRAM

This program, which used a multifaceted approach to reduce teenage pregnancy in a rural community in South Carolina, included several components that generated active community participation. First, district teachers, administrators, and special service personnel attended graduate-level courses covering issues related to sexuality education and adolescent decision-making, self-esteem, communication, and influences on sexual behavior. Program staff helped teachers integrate sex education into ongoing courses at all grade levels (kindergarten through 12th grade). The project recruited clergy, church leaders, and parents to attend minicourses and used newspaper and radio to spread its messages. Concurrently, a school nurse who was active on the program's task force provided contraceptives to students, and a comprehensive school-linked clinic in an adjacent building provided students with contraceptive services and supplies.

SELF CENTER

The Self Center program linked school-based sexuality and reproductive health education and counseling with the provision of medical services at a nearby clinic. These services were implemented in both a senior and a junior high school located in Baltimore, Maryland, in the community surrounding Johns Hopkins University. Commitment for the program was first obtained from the schools superintendent, principals, health committee, and health department. A team consisting of a social worker and nurse practitioner staffed each school's Self Center every morning, conducting homeroom and classroom lectures, informal individual counseling, small-group rap sessions, and educational encounters. These health care workers also made appointments for students to obtain contraceptive and reproductive health care services at a nearby clinic where they were employed in the afternoons.

TEEN TALK

Teen Talk, an educational curriculum based on the health belief model and social learning theory, was designed for use in both educational and community-based settings and consists of six two- to two-and-a-half-hour sessions. The goal of these sessions is to alter adolescent behavior by raising teenagers' awareness about the probability that they might personally become pregnant or cause a partner to become pregnant; the serious negative consequence of teenage maternity and paternity; the personal and interpersonal benefits of delayed sexual activity and consistent, effective contraceptive use; and the psychological, interpersonal, and logistical barriers to abstinence and consistent contraceptive use. The curriculum includes both presentation of factual information and small-group discussions in which adolescents are confronted with the risks and consequences of adolescent pregnancy and are then presented with information and techniques for avoiding these risks and consequences, including role-playing exercises that give adolescents a chance to practice communicating in sexual situations. The curriculum was designed to be implemented either by family planning or health agency staff or by school staff trained in a two-day workshop.

Source: Frost & Forrest, 1995.

risk sexual behaviors more often, although evidence shows that lying about one's sexual history is very common (Leland & Barth, 1992). Failure to disclose having previous sexual partners, not using condoms, and failure to disclose testing positive for HIV or other STDs is common both among men and women (Desiderato & Crawford, 1995). Condom use is especially inconsistent when the adolescents are drinking.

Teenage Pregnancy

One in five 14-year-old girls today will become pregnant before reaching the age of 18, and more than 1 million teenagers become pregnant each year (Henshaw, 1994). The United States has the highest teenage pregnancy rate of any developed nation (Harvey & Spigner, 1995; Zabin, Sedivy, & Emerson, 1994). This is a serious problem among all groups, but it is most serious among minority-group youth who are even more likely to become pregnant in adolescence (Ladner, 1987).

True or False?

The United States has the highest teenage pregnancy rate of all developed countries.

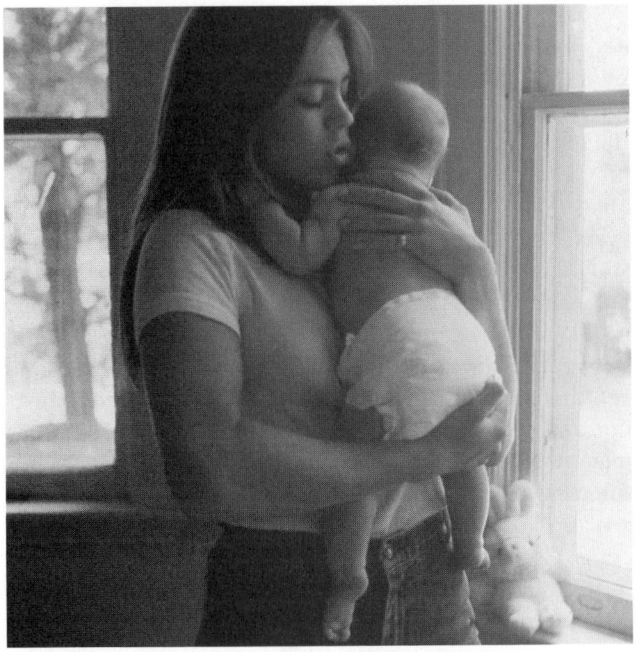

Studies find that teenage mothers are likely to live in poverty and have difficulties raising their children.

The odds are quite high that a second pregnancy will occur within the next 3 years as more than half the teenage mothers say that they had not used any form of contraception at last intercourse, despite stating that they wanted no more children at this time (Maynard & Rangarajan, 1994). Women who are poor or very young are most likely to become pregnant again. Teenage pregnancy and parenthood are greater problems today than they were in the past. Although the teenage birthrate was higher in the 1950s than it is today, the majority of teenage births today, unlike then, occur out of wedlock (Davis, 1989; Statistical Abstract, 1996).

Consequences of Teenage Pregnancies The vast majority of teen childbearing is unintended. The consequences of adolescent pregnancies are serious for the entire family. Whether there is a marriage or not, an adolescent pregnancy affects the future of everyone concerned.

The Infant Infants born to teenage mothers have more health problems than the average infant. Babies born to teenagers have lower birth weights, are more often premature, and have a greater chance of having a birth defect (Carver, Kittleson, & Lacey, 1990). The younger the woman the more likely it is that the child will have birth difficulties, including low birth weight and premature birth (Leland et al., 1995). Some of these problems appear to be caused by maternal age. Two studies following white, middle-class American teenagers found that they were more likely to deliver premature or small-for-date infants and that these infants were more likely to have birth defects than women with similar habits in their 20s (Fraser, Brockert, & Ward, 1995; Croen & Shaw, 1995). Age was a risk factor whether or not the mother had smoked. Within each group other factors, such as marital status, educational level, drug usage, and prenatal care, affected the pregnancy outcome; those who were poorly educated, used drugs, and did not receive adequate prenatal care had poorer outcomes. Those who had inadequate care were twice as likely to give birth to premature infants and these children were also more likely to live in poverty and to be abused.

The Mother Pregnancy is the most common reason why female students drop out of school (Ladner, 1987). Having a child before age 20 significantly reduces schooling among females in all ethnic and racial groups (Klepinger, Lundberg, & Plotnick, 1995). Perhaps as a direct consequence to this lack of educational attainment, mothers who have babies in their teens have lower incomes and hold lower-prestige jobs than their classmates. They also express less satisfaction with their jobs in their 20s and one half of teen mothers go on welfare within a year (Face up to sex education, 1993).

Family support is vital to these young mothers and their babies. Those who receive family support adapt better than those who do not receive social, psychological, and financial help (Furstenberg, 1981). Teens who live in one-parent families, have sex before age 14, and either do not use contraception or do so inconsistently are most at risk (Rodriguez & Moore, 1995). In many cases, their parents had talked with them about sex too late (Rodriguez & Moore, 1995). They were not close to their families and they did not think that they had bright futures; teenagers who see a future for themselves are less likely to become pregnant.

The Young Mother as Parent The young mother does not seem to be ready for her role. Most of the children of teenage mothers will live in homes in which the father is not present and are very likely to live in poverty. Adolescent mothers tend to be impatient, insensitive, and prone to punish their children; they show less empathy toward their children (Baranowski, Schilmoeller, & Higgins, 1990). Their behavior is characterized as highly physical and less verbal than that of more adult mothers (Garcia-Coll, Hoffman, & Oh, 1987). They are also less responsive and involved, show less positive emotion toward their children, and have lower HOME scores. When adolescent mothers were compared to older mothers while feeding their babies, the adolescent mothers were less expressive, showed less positive attitudes, and vocalized less to their infants than the older mothers. During play, adolescent mothers showed less patience and less inventiveness (Culp et al., 1991).

Children born to adolescent mothers lag behind their peers in cognitive, social, and academic performance and are at greater risk for maladjustment than their peers (Dubow & Luster, 1990). Teenage parents require help to raise their children successfully. If support is received from the mother's family, the general outlook on life as well as psychological adjustment improves (Schilmoeller, Baranowski, & Higgins, 1991).

Programs to improve the interactions between teenage parents and their children are quite successful and significantly lower the child abuse rate (Murray, 1995). One program sends child development specialists to homes on a weekly basis for about 2 years. It offers child care services that allow mothers to prepare for a better life, as well as instruction on child-rearing. Young parents are taught the difference between harsh and firm parenting. Parents who participate have more realistic expectations of children and development; some programs involve fathers as well. These programs are cost effective because they reduce the costs of later delinquency, abuse, and unemployment.

The Father Only a minority of children born to teenage mothers are fathered by teenagers (Weinstein & Rosen, 1994); most are 20 years old or older. When the father is an adolescent, he may not admit paternity perhaps out of ignorance, disbelief, or refusal to accept the obligations of fatherhood (Furstenberg, Brooks-Gunn, & Chase-Lansdale, 1989). Profiles of the unwed teen father show that he is frightened, withdrawn, and confused, and often feels guilty about his girlfriend (Barret & Robinson, 1981). He may not admit paternity out of fear, and many young fathers cannot deal with the pregnancy at all (Freedman, 1986). Teenage fathers are often poorly educated, are less likely to graduate from high school, and often have economic difficulties (Hardy & Duggan, 1988; Ladner, 1987). They often have dead-end jobs and, faced with the difficulty of supporting a family, many "slide into unemployment" (Freedman, 1986, p. 5).

Many teenage fathers are concerned about supporting a new family, finishing school, and about the welfare of the child and mother and their relationship with their in-laws. Their feelings of alienation are great (Elster & Panzarine, 1983). Many have some contact with the baby but often it is not extensive and does not continue; the degree of contact depends upon the continuing nature of their relationship with the mother. These fathers often do not provide much if any financial support (Toledo-Dreves, Zabin, & Emerson, 1995).

The Extended Family Most parents are shocked to learn that their unwed daughter is pregnant (Furstenberg, 1976). Teens who seek abortions do not usually consult their parents, but teens who carry their pregnancies to term almost always do. When the decision is made to bear the child, there is a definite progression from anger and disappointment to gradual acceptance and a growing closeness between mother and daughter. The quality of the relationship between the pregnant teen and her parents during the pregnancy determines what happens after the birth. If the bond is close, the young mother is much less likely to marry and is apt to stay with her parents (Furstenberg, 1981).

Most young mothers will stay at home if their mother says she will help them. Young mothers who are helped by their parents, especially until the child goes to school, are in a better economic position than those who leave home to live on their own. Grandmothers provide much of the child care in these situations (see Chapter 19). Many young mothers who return to school are better off years later, although problems do exist and the benefits should not be overstated. As the child matures, family relationships may deteriorate; the child's mother remains in a subordinate position to her parents because she is dependent on them.

Other siblings may be affected. They may need to help out and sometimes their share of the family's resources may be reduced if the mother returns to the home with the child. The younger sisters of childbearing adolescents are also at risk of bearing children themselves as adolescents. Compared with those whose older sisters did not bear children, these young teens have a more accepting attitude toward nonmarital adolescent childbearing, perceive younger ages for typical life events such as the best age to get married or have children, are more pessimistic about school and careers, are more likely to smoke and skip school, and are more likely to be involved in sexual relationships (East, 1996). These differences are present even when such variables as age, family size, educational level of the family, income and welfare status, mother-daughter communication, and other family experiences are taken into consideration; older sisters seem to serve as role models.

It is clear that young parents need help. Whether they marry, and whether they live at home or try to make it on their own, teenage parents need counseling and support from the time the pregnancy begins through the prenatal period and delivery and into the early years of parenthood. Because subsequent pregnancies are common, sex education is also necessary.

Sexual Orientation: Homosexual Behavior

Some adolescents express their sexuality in relationships with people of the same sex; such experiences are labeled *homosexual.* Between 3% and 10% of all men define themselves as gay and between 1% and 3% of all women define themselves as lesbian (Fay, Turner, Klassen, & Gagnon, 1989; Strong & DeVault, 1995). The number of people who have engaged in homosexual behaviors, often as teenagers, is much larger but when such behavior occurs only once or twice it does not necessarily mean that the person is gay (Rice, 1989). Despite this contact, most become exclusively heterosexual.

The term *gay* is now used to describe both males and females whose primary sexual orientation is toward members of the same sex. The term *lesbian* is used only to describe women whose sexual orientation is to other women. The term *bisexual* describes sexual behavior directed toward members of both the same and the opposite sex. Homosexuality does not define one's sex role, personality, attitudes toward life or physical appearance, only one's sexual orientation.

The origins of homosexuality are controversial. Recent work shows that homosexuality may have a genetic component (Savin-Williams, 1988). This finding reopened the debate on causation in the public press (Gelman et al., 1992). Indeed, twin studies offer evidence of genetic involvement. When one identical twin is homosexual more than 50% of the time the other twin is also homosexual. The percentage is reduced to less than 20% for fraternal twins or other siblings (Bailey & Pillard, 1991; Whitman, Diamond, & Martin, 1993). Since the concordance rate for twins is nowhere near perfect, there is much evidence for environmental effects as well.

Physiological differences have also been found, especially in the hypothalamus (LeVay, 1991). Even if we accept these differences as important, their interpretation is controversial because cause and effect are often difficult to separate. Some early experience may cause changes in the brain; some chemical or hormonal event during the prenatal stage may change the very structure and organization of the brain (Meyer-Bahlberg et al., 1995; Gelman, 1992). There is evidence that some gay and lesbian adults have been exposed prenatally to certain hormones that could affect sexual orientation through their effects on brain organization and structure (Berenbaum & Snyder, 1995; Meyer-Bahlburg et al., 1995).

These biological findings may be combined with environmental factors and it is fair to say that sexual orientation is probably shaped by a complex interaction of social and biological influences (Money, 1987; Paul, 1993). Perhaps some biological predisposition may affect social behaviors, such as causing youngsters to gravitate to a certain type of play or social relationship, which lead to homosexual identities. Some sex hormones may influence preferences for aggressive or stereotypical masculine or feminine behaviors. These early behavioral preferences may affect the parent-child relationship and how others see and relate to them. These behaviors may alienate a son from his father and cause him later to seek from males the affection he did not receive as a child (Green, 1987).

Although no single child-rearing pattern is found among people who have homosexual identities, domineering, overprotective mothers and uninvolved fathers are seen with some frequency (Bell, Weinberg, & Hammersmith, 1981). A similar argument is made for lesbians, who as a group perceive their mothers as cold and distant (Bell et al., 1981). These patterns are not applicable for all and may be important only in the presence of certain genetic or biological predispositions. Obviously, many pieces are missing in our attempt to explain the origins of homosexuality.

For adolescents whose primary orientation is toward members of the same sex, the teenage years may be difficult. Most are confused about it, half try to deny it (Newman & Muzzonigro, 1993). These teenagers may reject their sexual orientation, hide it from their family, and find it very difficult to cope with their feelings. Our society is not supportive of such sexual orientations; and discrimination, taunting, and violence are common. Society shows its fear of homosexuality, called ***homophobia***.

Even people who do not show homophobia may believe myths about homosexuality. For instance, some people believe that gays are readily recognized and that they show a particular behavior pattern. The truth is that most gays cannot be identified simply by their looks or behavior (Greenberg et al., 1989). Some also believe that all gay men are effeminate but only about 15% of gay men are effeminate (Voeller, 1980). Those who do show "effeminate" behavior tend to stand out, but the great majority who do not show this behavior go unnoticed. In addition, people sometimes confuse sexual orientation with gender identity. Contrary to many people's opinions, gays are comfortable with their gender and do not want to change (Comer, 1995). There is also no identifiable "homosexual personality" nor are people who engage in homosexuality more prone to psychopathology. Last, some people consider homosexuality to be a mental illness rather than a sexual orientation; however, the American Psychiatric Association does not consider homosexuality a mental disorder (American Psychiatric Association, 1994).

Questions Students Often Ask

I thought you could tell that someone is gay from their looks. I saw a gay rights parade, and I think I could tell. How can you say you can't tell by appearance?

Some gay men look or act effeminate, although not everyone who is effeminate is gay. These are the gay men that are visible, but the overwhelming majority of gay men do not look or act any different from heterosexuals. In the regular course of a day, you would never know their sexual orientation. Those gay people who are visible tend to be those who stand out because of their physical appearance. You might then believe that these are the only people who are gay. The large majority who do not look or act any differently do not stand out and you do not realize they are gay.

Usually the adolescent experiences homosexual feelings for years before he identifies himself as gay. The average gay male does not identify himself as gay until the age of 19 or 21 years (Strong & DeVault, 1995). Often the first phase in acquiring such an identity involves awareness of one's own feelings and recognition of one's emotional and physical desires. This phase is marked by fears of discovery and confusion. In the second phase, the individual actually acknowledges these feelings. The third phase involves a self-definition of being gay, which is difficult because society still considers it deviant. Families must deal with this acknowledgment. Some gays may go through two additional phases. One involves entrance into a gay subculture, including acquiring gay friends and frequenting gay bars and clubs. The final phase involves entrance into a gay or lesbian love affair, and most gay individuals have experienced at least one long-term relationship (Strong & DeVault, 1995).

Not all gays "come out," that is, publicly acknowledge their homosexuality. Some may acknowledge their own feelings but may not wish to publicly identify with the gay subculture. Coming out is often difficult and creates a crisis in the family, but gradually families accept the situation and adjust to it (Holtzen & Agresti, 1990).

Prejudice, discrimination, and even violence against homosexuals is common. The extent of the prejudice is shown by a national survey of white, African American, and Latino adolescents concerning their attitudes toward homosexuality and homosexuals; ethnicity was not a factor. The majority (59%) disagreed either "a lot" or "a little" with the idea that "I could be friends with a gay person" (Marsiglio, 1993). As in so many areas we have looked at, there is need for education.

Adapting to Change

It is easy to recite the list of physical changes that occur in adolescence, but more important is an understanding of the subjective experience of each adolescent in coping with these changes. Although it is more difficult to cite the cognitive changes that take place during adolescence, their contribution to adolescent behavior should be appreciated.

Teenagers need help in adapting to changes and new opportunities and decisions they face. Parents and teachers can actively assist by helping teens to develop their decision-making abilities, understand the possible consequences to their decisions, evolve their own moral and ethical ideals, and feel positively about themselves and what they want in life. This is not an easy task and it cannot be accomplished through lectures but can be successfully promoted through a combination of understanding, guidance, and dialogue.

Summary

1. Puberty refers to the physiological changes that lead to sexual maturity; adolescence refers to the individual's psychological experiences from puberty until adulthood. The sequence of physical development during adolescence is predictable, although the age at which each change occurs varies from person to person.
2. Females normally experience their growth spurt before males do, after which the genital organs and breasts develop, and then menstruation occurs. In males, pubic, body, and facial hair appear after the growth spurt. At about the same time, the sexual organs mature. Deepening of the voice and enlargement of the shoulders occur later.
3. The fact that each new generation for the past 100 years or so has been taller and heavier and has menstruated earlier than the previous one is known as the *secular trend.* It is leveling off or even stopping in the United States.
4. Early maturation in males is a social advantage during adolescence and early adulthood. In middle adulthood, however, early maturers tend to be less flexible and less insightful. The effects of early and late maturation in females is less important and the differences often disappear in later adolescence. Early-maturing girls are more likely to date early and get into trouble; later-maturing girls are more likely to have a positive body image.
5. Suicide is the third leading cause of death among adolescents, with accidents leading the list. Most suicide victims are depressed and have a pervading sense of hopelessness. Many give clues, such as talking about suicide or giving treasured items away, or have a history of a previous suicide attempt or a suicide in their family. Suicide prevention centers are effective in giving help in emergency circumstances.
6. The health of teenagers is usually considered excellent. However, teenagers tend to engage in behaviors that have negative health consequences both for the near and the long term.
7. Nutrition and eating disorders are not uncommon in adolescents. Obesity is a major medical and social problem. Anorexia nervosa, a disorder involving self-imposed starvation, can be fatal. Bulimia involves binge eating and purging of the system.
8. During the stage of formal operations adolescents develop the ability to find possible alternatives to problems, to separate the real from the possible, to form and test hypotheses, to interpret abstractions, and to think about their own thoughts.
9. Adolescents often have difficulty differentiating between their own thoughts and those of others, which leads to egocentric thinking. Out of this egocentrism comes the imaginary audience, in which adolescents often believe everyone else is looking at them, and the personal fable, in which they believe their experiences and thoughts are absolutely unique.
10. Adolescent risk-taking behavior may be related to the personal fable, but is also influenced by the adolescent's desire for new experiences, sensation seeking, and variety. Some adolescent risk takers do so to flaunt their courage or to show their nonconformity or opposition to authority.
11. According to Kohlberg, adolescents' more sophisticated cognitive abilities allow them to function at higher levels of moral reasoning. Most people, however, do not develop past Kohlberg's Stage 4. In adolescence, there is a positive relationship between the level of moral reasoning and prosocial behavior.
12. During the past 20 years values relating to personal achievement have become more prominent than

those having to do with one's relationships with society. Most adolescents believe in God and religious beliefs can have an effect on the behavior of adolescents.

13. Adolescent attitudes toward sexuality are more liberal than in the past. Females are still more conservative than males, although the gap is narrowing. Males expect intimacy sooner in a relationship than females do. Teenagers are beginning to have sex at earlier ages than years ago. Sexually transmitted diseases are a major problem.
14. Many sexually active teens do not use contraception regularly. Use increases with age, and there has been some increase in the use of condoms, but use is still inconsistent. Many teens do not use any contraception at all because they deny their sexuality, do not believe they can become pregnant, believe that contraception diminishes the romantic nature of the experience, or are ignorant of the biological facts of life.
15. Teen pregnancy is a widespread problem for everyone concerned. Infants born to teenage mothers have more health problems, and teen mothers are more likely to drop out of school. Teenage mothers do not tend to engage in behaviors that would optimize the child's development. Teenage fathers are often found in dead-end jobs.
16. The term *gay* is used to describe males and females whose primary sexual orientation is toward members of the same sex. The teenage years are frequently difficult for teenagers whose primary orientation is homosexual, and these teens may have difficulty coping with feelings. People hold a number of myths about homosexuality. Most gay males are not effeminate and are comfortable with their own gender identity. Homosexuality is not a mental disturbance. Acquiring an identity as gay occurs in a number of distinct phases.

Multiple-Choice Questions

1. The physiological changes that are involved in sexual maturation are referred to as:
   a. climacteric.
   b. puberty.
   c. initiative.
   d. pulsation.
2. Twelve-year-old Holly is taller than most of the boys in her class. This is:
   a. unusual, for boys are usually taller at this age.
   b. common, for girls are generally taller at this age.
   c. neither usual nor unusual, for as a group there is generally no difference in height between boys and girls at this age.
   d. almost impossible, as the average boy goes through his growth spurt quite a bit before the average girl does so.
3. Today's generation of women are taller and begin menstruating at a earlier age than women of generations ago. This is called the:
   a. primacy effect.
   b. species corrective trend.
   c. primary evolutionary effect.
   d. secular trend.
4. Which of the following bodily structure is *not* thought to play a great role in the significant physical changes that occur in early adolescence?
   a. the gonads
   b. pituitary gland
   c. hypothalamus
   d. reticular activating system
5. The timing of puberty can be affected by:
   a. nutrition.
   b. genetics.
   c. conflict in the home
   d. all of the above.
6. As compared to those maturing later early maturing boys:
   a. have a social advantage.
   b. are less likely to be truant.
   c. are considered more tense and are always seeking attention.
   d. are described by all of the above.
7. Early maturing girls are:
   a. less satisfied with their bodies.
   b. more likely to be delinquent.
   c. initially more popular with boys.
   d. described by all of the above.
8. The three most common causes of death among adolescents are:
   a. accidents, suicide, and AIDS.
   b. suicide, cancer, and homicide.
   c. accidents, homicide, and suicide.
   d. accidents, respiratory illness, and suicide.
9. Lee is a 16-year-old girl. If she is typical of other girls her age, she will:
   a. be satisfied with her body weight.
   b. want to lose weight.
   c. want to gain weight.
   d. not be concerned with her body weight.
10. Which of the following statements concerning nutrition in adolescence is *correct?*
    a. The recommended daily allowances for vitamins and minerals are somewhat lower than they are for younger children.
    b. The diets of adolescents are variable, with some eating a good diet and some not eating a healthy diet.
    c. The most common nutritional problem in adolescents is self-starvation.
    d. All of the above are correct.
11. Adolescents suffering from anorexia nervosa can be expected to show all of the following behaviors *except:*
    a. fasting.

b. great amounts of physical activity.
c. overt rebellion to their parents.
d. depression.

12. An adolescent can understand political cartoons and proverbs because the individual develops the ability to understand and use:
a. abstractions.
b. combinational logic.
c. seriation.
d. integration.

13. An adolescent thinks that everyone is looking at him and evaluating his appearance and behavior. This is known as the:
a. personal fable.
b. primary process.
c. imaginary audience.
d. mirror image.

14. The higher the level of moral reasoning, the more likely the person is to:
a. use information about risk to guide behavior.
b. believe that independence is an important concern in life.
c. argue with parents about political and social issues.
d. form close interpersonal relationships.

15. Adolescents are likely to show values that are relatively close to those held by their parents if their parents used a/an ____________ style of child-rearing.
a. authoritarian
b. authoritative
c. permissive
d. unidirectional

16. Which of the following statements concerning religion and religious involvement is correct?
a. As adolescents proceed through the period they tend to be somewhat less religious.
b. Women tend to be more religious than men.
c. Most teenagers believe in God.
d. All of the above are correct.

17. Adolescent males and females are likely to have different ideas on:
a. acceptability of coercion in sexual relationships.
b. responsibility for birth control.
c. when in the course of a relationship sexual intercourse is appropriate.
d. all of the above.

18. Which of the following statements about date rape is *incorrect?*
a. Most date rapes are reported to the authorities, but most often after 1 week.
b. It is common for people to blame the victim, for example, to feel that if she dressed provocatively she is also at fault.
c. Men who are guilty of date rape often do not believe that the woman really means "no" when she says it.
d. Alcohol is often a factor in date rape.

19. Ryan claims that more teens are sexually active at earlier ages than in the recent past. Doris argues that three quarters of all teens today use some form of contraception during their first sexual experience. Nita claims that the use of contraceptives has increased somewhat over the past 20 years. Jerry claims that most teens are not well informed about sex and do not have a good knowledge of the biology of sex. All of these people are correct *except:*
a. Ryan.
b. Doris.
c. Nita.
d. Jerry.

20. Which of the following statements concerning homosexuality is *correct?*
a. Homosexuality is not considered an emotional disorder.
b. There is some evidence for genetic involvement in homosexuality.
c. Most gay people *cannot* be identified as such from their physical appearance.
d. All of the above are correct.

Answers to Multiple-Choice Questions

1. b 2. b 3. d 4. d 5. d 6. a 7. d 8. c 9. b
10. b 11. c 12. a 13. c 14. a 15. b 16. d 17. d
18. a 19. b 20. d

Chapter 13

Personality and Social Development During Adolescence

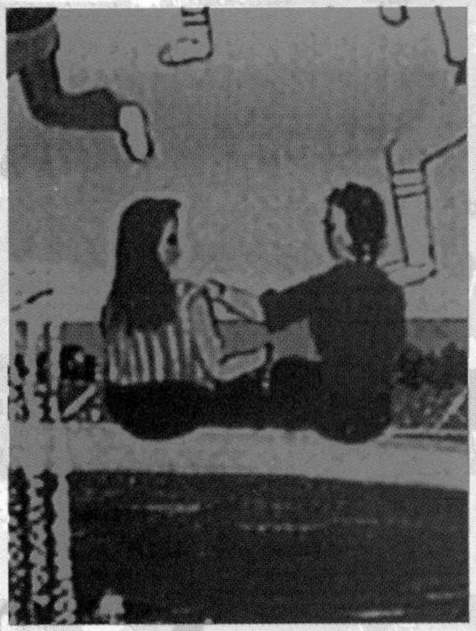

Chapter Outline

Rites of Passage

Personality and Self-Esteem in Adolescence

In Search of an Identity

Our Pluralistic Society: Identity and Minority Status

Relationships With Parents and Peers

School Days

Career Choice

Drug Use and Violence

Exploding the Myths

Are the Following Statements True or False?

1. Psychologists today view adolescence as a time of inevitable and continuous storm, stress, and conflict with authority figures.
2. Adolescent girls are more likely to show depressive symptoms than adolescent boys.
3. Periods of confusion in adolescence usually signal the probability of mental illness.
4. When parents communicate with their adolescent children, they tend to explain their own views rather than try to understand their teens' opinions and attitudes.
5. Friends try to control the adolescent's behavior more than parents do.
6. Within the past two decades high school course work has become more rigorous.
7. Most high school dropouts actually like school and read on grade level but find themselves bored and unchallenged.
8. The percentage of women doctors and lawyers has stayed about the same for the last 15 years.
9. Drug use by adolescents has increased markedly since the early 1990s.
10. Children who witness domestic violence are actually less likely to engage in violent behavior because they are aware of its consequences.

Answers to True-False Statements 1. False: see p. 291 2. True 3. False: see p. 293 4. True 5. False: see p. 299 6. True 7. False: see p. 304 8. False: see p. 304 9. True 10. False: see p. 310

Rites of Passage

In some Native American tribes, each 14- or 15-year-old male is taken to a sweat lodge, where his body and spirit are purified by the heat. A medicine man advises and assists him with prayers. The adolescent is then brought to an isolated spot where he fasts for 4 days. He prays, reflects on the medicine man's words, and awaits a vision that reveals to him his path of life as a man in society (Heinrich, Corbine, & Thomas, 1990).

A **rite of passage** is a ritual that marks the movement of people from one social status to another (Schultz & Levenda, 1987). These ceremonies are almost universal and most often involve a separation from society, some preparation or instruction from an elder, a transition (usually a special ceremony of some kind), and a welcoming back into the society with some acknowledgement of the person's changed status (Delaney, 1995). Some faiths have rites of passage, for example, the Bar or Bat Mitzvah in Judaism, a ceremony that Jewish boys and girls take part in during early adolescence that marks their spiritual arrival at adulthood.

High school graduation is a rite of passage in a technologic society. Adolescents are isolated in schools from the rest of society for a good part of the day. They are taught by teachers who are older and specially chosen by society. The graduation ceremony, with its special dress and formal setting, may be thought of as a transition (Delaney, 1995). But not all adolescents graduate or attend their graduation and more importantly, the teachers' relationship to students lacks the moral and spiritual function so prominent in rites of passage. The bond with society is also not necessarily strengthened. This rite of passage is very weak compared to those in more traditional societies. Sometimes young people create their own rites of passage: attempts to imitate adult behavior through cigarette smoking, drinking, and early sex. The change in status is acknowledged by peers and some social solidarity exists, but the lack of adult leadership and continuity with society make such transitions incomplete.

rite of passage A ceremony or ritual that marks an individual's transition from one status to another.

Some communities are moving towards providing such transitions. In an attempt to combat the social problems in their communities, some African American communities have initiated programs to restore traditional African values such as interdependence, spirituality, and respect for elders (Warfield-Copock, 1992). Adolescents are instructed in many areas, some philosophical and some practical, and an overnight retreat planned by elders and modeled on African tradition is experienced.

In our society, during the long transition between adolescence and adulthood teenagers are expected to gain their independence from their parents, yet stay in touch with their family. They are expected to achieve a separate personal identity, yet stay within a range of acceptable alternatives. Their relationships with their parents and peers are expected to change in a fundamental way. At the same time, they take on increased responsibility for their own work and begin to make vocational decisions. This reformulation of relationships and increased responsibility occurs in the context of a large, impersonal society that offers a bewildering number of choices, so it is no wonder that adolescence is a time of stress. The average adolescent experiences more negative stressful events than the average preadolescent and these stressful events result in more negative emotions than were experienced during childhood (Larson & Ham, 1993). Rejection, school problems, the challenge of more intimate relationships, the temptations of drugs, as well as taking on greater responsibilities lead to a more stressful existence. This chapter looks at how adolescents deal with these difficult tasks and examines some of the major challenges confronting adolescents today.

Storm and Stress?

G. Stanley Hall was responsible for the first modern look at adolescence in 1904. In his two detailed volumes he brought together much of what was known about adolescence. He wrote about growth, the development of motor skills, the intellect, psychological and sexual development, and the emotional problems of adolescents (White, 1994). But Hall is most famous for his conception of adolescence as a period of "storm and stress," as a time of crisis and psychological upheaval. Adolescence is marked by intense conflict between adolescents and parents as teens make the break from dependence on family to a more independent existence. The individual exiting adolescence is a fundamentally different person from the person who entered it.

Developmental psychologists accepted this view of adolescence for decades. However, beginning about 20 years ago psychologists began taking a different perspective (Coleman, 1978). Many adolescents do not experience tremendous conflict with their families and report good relationships with them as the renegotiation of power and autonomy occurs within the family context. Although no one denies that some conflict occurs, the more modern view does not see intense and continuous conflict as inevitable (Larson & Ham, 1993). The individual exiting adolescence is fairly similar to the one who entered it and there is no general upheaval in personality or self-concept.

True or False?
Psychologists today view adolescence as a time of inevitable and continuous storm, stress, and conflict with authority figures.

Personality and Self-Esteem in Adolescence

Self-esteem is moderately consistent throughout adolescence (Alsaker & Olweus, 1992) in that adolescents with high self-esteem or low self-esteem tend to stay that way. Since only moderate consistency is found, there is some room for movement.

Generally, males show greater self-esteem than females. A longitudinal examination of adolescents found moderate levels of stability when a large group was followed. However, many individuals showed substantial but not radical changes in self-esteem. The self-esteem of males tended to increase from early adolescence to early adulthood and many, but not all, females showed declines (Block & Robins, 1993). More girls than boys have low self-esteem in adolescence and this difference may become even greater in later adolescence. Between the sixth and ninth grades the percentage of males with high self-esteem increases slightly (still less than half), while the proportion of females with high self-esteem decreases from one-third to a bit more than one-quarter (Abernathy et al., 1995).

Depressive symptoms are also more common among adolescent girls than boys. This is a switch from childhood, where depressive symptoms were more prevalent among boys (Nolen-Hoeksema, Girgus, & Seligman, 1991). The reversal occurs at around age 13 or 14 years (Ge et al., 1994). Girls' symptoms increase while boys' symptoms remain relatively stable after this age. Boys react more negatively to stressors in childhood, but the pattern seems to be reversed in adolescence. Although stressful events affect both boys and girls, they seem to affect adolescent girls somewhat more.

True or False?
Adolescent girls are more likely to show depressive symptoms than adolescent boys.

Puberty marks a change in vulnerability to stress for girls, and they are more disrupted by changes in peer relations. Girls are more concerned with body image and may be more troubled by the physical changes of adolescence than boys (Gavin & Furman, 1989). Perhaps the emphasis on physical appearance and the higher standards for females may be one reason. It may be that fundamental conflicts in society's view of females make it more difficult for girls to form an identity and to mesh their personal desires with the interpersonal orientation that is a basic part of their socialization. Boys and girls may differ in their search for an identity, but this search is difficult for both.

In Search of an Identity

Who am I?
Where do I belong?
Where am I going?

These three questions typify the adolescent's search for a personal identity (Ruittenbeck, 1964). Erik Erikson (1959) saw the positive outcome of adolescence as the formation of a solid **identity,** while the negative outcome of adolescence is an aimlessness known as **role confusion**—the state of not knowing who one really is. Adolescents are walking a tightrope. Their task is to surrender the old, dependent ties and childhood identifications with their parents and develop a separate identity while continuing a healthy relationship with their elders (Siegel, 1982). To function as adults they must be able to make their own decisions, but the attitudes and values gained from their parents during childhood serve as anchors, providing security in a sea of change. Adolescents

identity The sense of knowing who you are.

role confusion In psychosocial theory the negative outcome of adolescence, which involves a failure to develop a personal identity and feelings of aimlessness.

who totally abandon these values may become bewildered and utterly confused. In addition, surrendering older ideals assumes them all to be worthless—a conclusion that is difficult to support.

Questions Students Often Ask

Is finding an identity more difficult today than years ago?

Although there is no way to research this, I would have to say that it is. Years ago adolescents had fewer alternatives open to them. News travelled slowly and parental values weren't challenged as quickly as they are today. Conventional thought gave women and people from some minority groups few choices as well. Today, the situation is different. Television, the print media, and the movies bring instant information to the community from all over the world. Along with this information explosion, teenagers are exposed to different values and many new choices. Although no one seriously believes that racism or sexism have been eliminated from society, certainly women and members of minority groups have greater opportunities now.

Young people today have many more choices and a greater degree of freedom to choose their own course. These factors combine to make forming an identity more difficult today than it was a hundred years ago. Society is changing at a faster rate than ever before, thereby making it more difficult to form some aspects of one's identity. The skills needed for young people to prosper in the years ahead are likely to change as society changes. Not long ago a high school education was considered relatively unnecessary, computers were the toys of science fiction writers, and manufacturing jobs were considered secure. The lack of stability in society means that teens must predict what vocations and skills will be needed in a changing world if they are to prepare adequately for the future.

Although there is a global identity, identity has many aspects, including the personal, religious, occupational, interpersonal, and racial/ethnic identity (see "Our Pluralistic Society: Identity and Minority Status," pp. 294–295). An individual may have developed one of these identities and not another (Meeus & Dekovic, 1995). Achieving an identity requires exploration, which one researcher called the "work" of adolescence (Grotevant, 1987). Adolescents have a difficult course to chart, one that may be marked by confusion, mood swings, self-doubt, impulsivity, and some conflict with others (Kidwell et al., 1995).

The Four Identity Statuses

Achieving an identity depends on two variables: crisis and commitment (Marcia, 1967). In a **crisis,** one actively faces and questions aspects of one's personal identity. For instance, a college student may have to choose a major and be faced with this decision when approaching the junior year. In the personal sphere, the student may be dating someone for a while and may have to decide whether to get more deeply involved. Today, many use the term *exploration* instead of *crisis* (Meeus & Dekovic, 1995). **Commitment** relates to the presence or absence of a decision (Flum, 1994). An individual making a commitment follows a plan of action that reflects the decision. A person who investigates many vocational choices and decides on a particular career will follow the appropriate course of study. The decision to end a relationship or to become engaged leads to different behavioral paths.

Adolescents differ in the extent to which they have experienced crises or made commitments. A prominent researcher in this field, James Marcia (1967, 1980), grouped adolescents into four categories, according to their experiences with crises and commitments (Table 13.1). One group of adolescents, termed **identity diffused,** consists of adolescents who may or may not have experienced a crisis but have not made any commitments. They show a lack of concern about identity issues. The **identity foreclosed** group consists of teens who have not experienced a crisis but have made commitments anyway. The **identity moratorium** group contains adolescents who are presently experiencing a crisis but have not yet made any commitments. The **identity achievers** group consists of adolescents who have already experienced crises and made their commitments.

Identity status is not engraved in stone. People can move from one group to another as they experience a crisis or make a new commitment. An unusual experience might lead one back to a moratorium. For example, after spending a number of years preparing to become a newspaper reporter, one young woman could not find a job and had to search for an occupational identity all over again. A divorced person may have to search anew for a personal or social identity because the original one is no longer viable. Because identity status is related to specific attitudes and behaviors, each status deserves more detailed study.

Identity Diffusion An individual who shows identity diffusion has not made any commitments and is not presently in the process of forming any. The adolescent may or may not have experienced a crisis. Even if there has been a crisis, it has not resulted in any decision (Waterman, 1982). Identity-diffused people may actively seek noncommitment, actually avoiding demanding situations. They may also appear aimless, aloof, drifting, and

crisis In psychosocial theory a time in which a person actively faces and questions aspects of his or her own identity.

commitment In psychosocial theory making a decision concerning some question involved in identity formation and following a plan of action reflecting this decision.

identity diffusion An identity status resulting in confusion, aimlessness, and a sense of emptiness.

identity foreclosure An identity status marked by a premature identity decision.

identity moratorium An identity status in which a person actively searches for an identity.

identity achievement An identity status in which a person has developed a solid personal identity.

Table 13.1 **James Marcia's Four Identity Statuses**

IDENTITY STATUS	DEFINITION
Identity Diffusion	An identity diffuser may or may not have experienced doubt over goals and values; he or she does not evidence a serious or realistic inclination to examine concerns about goals and values; he or she expresses no commitments to an ideology or to career plans.
Identity Foreclosure	A foreclosure displays a commitment similar to that of the identity achiever but has not appraised alternatives to personal goals and values; choices often express parental preferences.
Identity Moratorium	A moratorium has questioned goals and values and considered alternatives but is still doubtful and uncommitted; an active effort to become informed and to make suitable choices is predominant.
Identity Achievement	An identity achiever has experienced doubt (crisis) in personal goals and values, has considered alternatives, and is committed at least tentatively to some expressed value positions and career plans.

Source: Hummel and Roselli, 1983.

empty (Orlofsky, Marcia, & Lessor, 1973), but they are not mentally ill. Their psychological profiles appear normal (Oshman & Manosevitz, 1974), although their self-esteem is not very high. They may show excessive dependence on peers and often give in to the wishes of their peers. They do not believe they are in control and find it difficult to plan ahead or make firm decisions (Flum, 1994); they also tend to distrust others. The excessive conformity to group expectations means that very little individual growth takes place.

Some students become alarmed at this description because they have experienced periods in which the description closely fits them or someone they know well. But identity diffusion is a problem only when a person leaves adolescence without making tentative steps toward commitments. A period of confusion often precedes establishment of a firm identity (Erikson, 1959). There may be two types of diffusion: one that is permanent and one that is temporary (Flum, 1994).

True or False?
Periods of confusion in adolescence usually signal the probability of mental illness.

Identity Foreclosure Do you know people who seem to be in control, have known what they wanted from a very early age, and appear confident and secure? These seemingly lucky people have made a commitment, but it may not be their own but one handed down to them by their parents. They identify very well—perhaps too well—with their parents. For example, some people may go into their parents' business because they were always expected to. They were not permitted—or did not permit themselves—to search for alternatives. A young woman may have married very early in life and not explored any alternatives to early marriage. Identity-foreclosed people are very certain about their future plans and spend little time on self-examination (Flum, 1994).

Identity foreclosure can be a secure status, and these individuals are frequently envied by their peers because they have a definite direction. However, this security is purchased at a price. The path is not one they might have chosen, and foreclosed individuals sometimes find themselves mired in an unhappy lifestyle later in life (Petitpas, 1978).

Some adolescents may be foreclosed because they do not have the opportunity to explore or to know what is available. Many poor and minority youths do not believe they have many choices. Some must enter the labor force as soon as possible to support themselves and their families; others may not have the basic academic skills necessary for more advanced study, which would allow them to explore alternative vocational opportunities. Such teens are foreclosed by circumstances, by lack of knowledge about their choices, or by their belief that they do not have any control over their own destinies.

Identity Moratorium Adolescents who are presently experiencing a crisis but whose commitments are vague are considered to be in the moratorium status—a period of delay in which a person is not yet ready to make a definite commitment (Erikson, 1968). They explore many possibilities, some of them radical, but their final commitments tend to be more conservative.

The moratorium status is not a happy one and adolescents engaged in identity exploration show more self-doubt, confusion, and conflict with parents and other authority figures (Kidwell et al., 1995). Those in this state experience apprehension and fear as they search for meaningful commitments (Flum, 1994); they are often found alone, thinking about and considering their options.

Identity moratorium is the least stable of all the stages (Waterman, 1982), but it may be necessary for a person to experience it so that once a person does make a commitment, it is his or her own, made after a period of searching for answers.

Identity Achievement Identity achievers have made it. They have experienced their crises, solved them, and made their commitments. Their goals are realistic, and they can cope with shifts in the environment (Orlofsky et al., 1973). These independent personal identities are

Our Pluralistic Society: Identity and Minority Status

Identity development is a complex task for all youth, but it is particularly complicated for adolescents who belong to ethnic and racial minority groups (Spencer & Markstrom-Adams, 1990). These youths find themselves in two cultures: one dominant that sometimes does not fully recognize their group's contributions, and one shaped by their ethnicity or race. Developing a positive ethnic identity is related to a positive sense of selfesteem and self-efficacy (Bagley & Copeland, 1994; Smith, 1991).

When dealing with the majority culture and society, people from ethnic and racial minorities have four different choices. They can separate from the dominant group and emphasize their unique values and culture, having little or no interaction with the dominant culture. Another choice is assimilation, in which minority group members choose identification with the dominant society and cut all ties to their own minority group. Integration is a third option, which involves identification and involvement in both the dominant culture and the minority culture; marginality is a lack of involvement in either the minority or the majority culture. Minority group members who can be classified as integrated show better psychological adjustment and have higher self-esteem than those who choose the other options (Phinney, Chavira, & Williamson, 1992).

Developing an ethnic or racial identity is a complicated process and occurs in many different ways. One basic process, first advanced to explain African American identity formation, suggests a stagelike approach (Cross, 1989; 1978; 1971). In the *preencounter stage,* individuals see the world from the point of view of the majority group and devaluation of one's own group may also occur. During the second or *encounter* stage, the individual has some experience that forces him or her to reconsider this view. This reexamination may cause the individual to become antagonistic toward the majority group and identify strongly with the minority group. During the next stage, called *immersion-emersion,* the individual adopts a posture that is exactly the opposite of the one held in the preencounter stage—he or she totally adopts a new frame of reference and looks at everything from the point of view of the minority group. The individual uses many outward expressions and symbols of the minority culture and total immersion in the culture occurs; the dominant culture is now completely rejected. In the next stage, *internalization,* a more balanced, bicultural, pluralistic, and less ethnocentric view is adopted (Cross, 1978). The individual is secure in attachment to the group and committed to the culture but accepts the mainstream culture as well, showing more tolerance for diversity. In the final stage, *internalization-commitment,* the individual becomes politically involved in order to improve the minority group.

This theory has been criticized as too simplistic (Parham, 1989). There may be many paths to developing an ethnic identity and not everyone proceeds through every stage; people differ greatly on just how strongly they identify with their own ethnic and racial group. However, it can serve as one approach for understanding the process.

A minority group member who opts for full assimilation, which often means rejecting one's own minority group culture, may be rejected by both the majority and the minority culture. Separation and embeddedness in one's own cul-

not carbon copies of their parents' identities, nor are they totally the opposite. The identity includes some parental values and attitudes and omits others; such young people are well adjusted (Bernard, 1981) and have good relationships with peers and authority figures (Donovan, 1975). Identity achievers have the best grades (Cross & Allen, 1970) and have better study habits than people at any other status (Waterman & Waterman, 1971); they also perform better under stress (Muuss, 1982).

Becoming an identity achiever is not something that is commonly accomplished in early or middle adolescence. The number of identity achievers increases with age and the number of adolescents in the foreclosure and especially in the diffusion stages declines. The period between 18 and 21 years seem especially crucial to the development of an identity. Before this time, the overwhelming number of adolescents are either foreclosed or diffused (Archer, 1982; Meilman, 1979), and only very limited changes occur before or during the high school years (Waterman, 1982). The experience of schooling, especially college, seems to encourage young people to question and then make commitments.

Probably the most important finding is that identity achievement has been linked to the depth of intimacy developed in early adulthood. The ego crisis of young adulthood can be expressed as intimacy versus isolation, and much more will be said about this in Chapter 15 (Erikson, 1968). Intimacy involves the development of very close personal relationships whereas isolation involves a lack of commitment. Intimacy requires that two people share their identities without a complete merging of selves. Problems may occur for people who choose marriage or parenthood as a way out of an identity dilemma. These people really have not resolved the identity issue—it is still on the back burner, waiting for an opportunity to show itself. Resolution of identity issues can be delayed but not always shelved forever.

People in the moratorium and achievement statuses experience deeper levels of intimacy than people in the other two stages (Fitch & Adams, 1983; Orlofsky, Marcia, & Lessor, 1973). Although the basic relationship be-

Our Pluralistic Society: Identity and Minority Status (continued)

ture poses problems as well because it devalues the majority group. The rejection of the dominant culture makes participation in it difficult. The bicultural alternative in which people see themselves as existing both in the dominant culture as well as their own culture is a possible solution.

Another approach to understanding the development of ethnic identity is based on Erikson's and Marcia's work (Phinney, 1989). Many minority youth begin by internalizing the views held by the majority group of their own group. This is similar to identity foreclosure in that people may take on the values to which they have been exposed. This does not always have to be negative. It is often stated that minority group youth simply accept negative self-images that are projected onto them by society. Indeed, Erikson (1968) theorized that minority youth were prone to develop a negative identity as a result of accepting these images. However, studies do not show this to be so: positive self-attitudes are commonly found (Spencer & Markstrom-Adams, 1990). Other processes must be at work in the community or at home that counter these messages. It is also possible that some minority youth have not been faced with issues of ethnicity and therefore give little thought to them. These young people may not consider ethnicity very important and do not think about it. This might be considered diffusion, but little research has been conducted in this area. Phinney sees these two states as constituting a general first stage in identity formation.

A period of exploration or moratorium then ensues, which involves experimentation, inquiry, and an attempt to clarify personal implications of ethnicity (Phinney & Tarver, 1988); this is the second stage of the process.

Last, there is identity achievement, during which questions are resolved and commitments are made; people feel better about who they are and gain confidence as they grow to accept themselves as members of a minority group. When high school juniors from a number of minority groups were studied, half the subjects were diffused or foreclosed, with one-quarter in the moratorium and one-quarter in the identity achievement stage (Phinney, 1989). The percentages were very similar across minority groups.

The process of ethnic identity development has implications for overall adjustment. Minority group membership alone is not related to adjustment. Minority adolescents who have explored and are clear about the meaning of their ethnicity show higher scores on self-evaluation, sense of mastery, social and peer interactions, and family relations than diffused and foreclosed adolescents. Ethnic identity, not membership, is the key to understanding self-esteem and adjustment.

A number of different approaches explain the process of forming an ethnic identity. Adolescents from minority groups must come to grips with the extent of their identification with both the minority and majority cultures. There is no one way to do this and no single solution is best for everyone. Different people will identify more or less with various aspects of the dominant culture and their particular subculture. What is clear, however, is that people must personally explore what it means to belong to a minority group and come to a personally satisfying ethnic identity, one that allows them to feel comfortable with their relationships with the majority and the minority communities.

tween identity and intimacy is valid, some authorities now claim that the relationship may be slightly different for males and females. Some women can deal successfully with intimacy issues prior to achieving identity but very few men can (Schiedel & Marcia, 1985). This surprising finding may have to do with the difference between the search for identity that males and females conduct.

Do Males and Females Take Different Paths to Identity Formation?

Males and females may approach identity formation from different perspectives. Their searches and their abilities to explore alternatives may differ. Males tend to focus on intrapersonal factors, such as vocational identity and personal identity whereas women are more likely to tie their identities to interpersonal relationships (Schiedel & Marcia, 1985). Compared to men, women's relational identities are stronger, more important, and are developed at a higher level than their occupational identities (Meeus & Dekovic, 1995). Girls are more actively involved in exploring relationships than boys, and derive more self-confidence from them.

Carol Gilligan (Gilligan, 1988; Gilligan, Rogers, & Brown, 1990) argues that in adolescence women are faced with a dilemma: they have been raised to value human relationships and to define themselves in terms of their relationships with others. If they begin to think and act such that their own desires and goals show and they become self-sufficient, they label themselves, and risk being labeled by others, as selfish. Yet the selfless giving to others may not allow their own strivings to be realized. Gilligan and colleagues (1990) argue that this conflict is based upon concerns of inclusion and exclusion. Inclusion involves connecting with and giving to others, and is a central value for women. Exclusion involves being centered on oneself and one's own desires and needs. Gilligan (1988) notes that selfishness connotes the exclusion of others and selflessness the exclusion of self. The conflict is between concerns about being generous and the emerging individualism of many females (Lyons, 1990). Often, women solve this problem by silencing their special and distinctive voices, by not offering opinions, and by losing self-confidence in a pattern that may continue through adulthood. Young women must find an answer to the dilemma of inclusion and exclusion.

Relationships With Parents and Peers

Relationships with peers and parents change substantially in adolescence. Family relationships are renegotiated and a new relationship with peers is established. These modifications in relationships can be stressful. The most common calls for help to a National Telephone Hotline for teens involve problems with peer or parent relationships (Teare et al., 1995). Beginning in early adolescence, the amount of time spent with peers is often greater than that spent with parents and other family members (Fuligni & Eccles, 1993); much of this time is casually supervised or unsupervised.

Parental and Peer Influence

Adolescents become more emotionally autonomous and idealize their parents less. They depend somewhat less on their parents and more on their peers, which is accompanied by increased susceptibility to peer influences (Steinberg & Silverberg, 1986). The peer group serves a number of functions in adolescence: it provides support for adolescents who are striving for independence, because peers are facing similar challenges. Adolescents often turn to their friends for advice and comfort (Fuligni & Eccles, 1993) and peers help adolescents to develop social skills and an identity (Coleman, 1981). The peer group serves as a reference group through which teens can evaluate their own actions. Adolescents' self-esteem and emotional well-being are linked to having positive friendships; adolescents who describe their friendships more positively have higher self-esteem and fewer emotional disorders (Barrera, Chassin, & Rogosch, 1993). Peers can also influence school adjustment and behavior, both positively or negatively (Berndt & Keefe, 1995).

It is difficult to determine exactly how peer influence operates. Do friends influence a teen to change attitudes and behavior, or do teens simply choose friends who think and act the same way they do? Peers with particular needs, personalities, and interests select others who are similar for friendships. People who drink, smoke, or show high levels of aggression seek each other out as do people who show high or low levels of school achievement (Cairns et al., 1988; Hogue & Steinberg, 1995). Adolescents who are antisocial relate to each other (Dishion, Andrews, & Crosby, 1995). Teenagers who internalize and experience a great deal of depression and anxiety choose friends who show similar levels of internalized distress (Hogue & Steinberg, 1995).

Friends also shape or reinforce others who show these attributes (Hogue & Steinberg, 1995) and this is a type of socialization. It is very difficult to distinguish between the influence of selection and socialization. Research shows that both are important; for example, adolescents who are aggressive form relationships with other aggressive children and then they influence each other through modeling and reinforcement. This is a pattern suggested for drug use, in which drug users both select other users as friends and then influence each other to continue using drugs (Fletcher et al., 1995).

Peer influence is usually considered negative but it shouldn't be. Peers may influence each other for or against a particular behavior (Brown, Classen, & Eicher, 1986). For example, peers may influence adolescents to use or not to use drugs and alcohol, to achieve or not to achieve in school (Mounts & Steinberg, 1995). In addition, peers and parents may exert influence in the same way, connecting parent and peer support (Meeus & Dekovic, 1995; Meeus, 1993).

Adolescents in late junior high and early high school (eighth- and ninth-graders) seem to be most influenced by peers. Conformity to peers for antisocial acts peaks during the ninth grade and declines thereafter (Berndt, 1979). It is also the time of the greatest number of arguments between parents and children as the push for independence is particularly strong at this point. The heightened susceptibilty to peer influence during early adolescence decreases as adolescents age (Steinberg & Silverberg, 1986); there is some disagreement, however, as to when this takes place.

Parents do not suddenly find themselves without influence in adolescence. They continue to be important sources of support, guidance, and love during this stage. The parenting style in adolescence continues to be a major factor that influences the behavior of teenagers. Adolescents whose parents use an authoritative parenting style show superior academic achievement and psychological development (Dornbusch et al., 1987; Steinberg, Elmen, & Mounts, 1989).

Communication with Parents and Peers

Communication with peers differs greatly from communication with parents during adolescence. Parents are more directive, sharing their wisdom whereas communication with peers often shows greater mutuality and sharing of similar experiences (Hunter, 1984). This communication difference may spring from the nature of the parent-child relationship, which is dominated by parents, whereas peer relationships tend to be more mutual (Fuligni & Eccles, 1993). Parents may not like to listen to adolescents who are in the process of formulating their own values and opinions, especially if their children take positions that are different from theirs. On the other hand, parents may counter these unwanted views with a long lecture, which is usually an ineffective method of communication. Parents tend to concentrate more on explaining their own viewpoints than on trying to understand their child's views (Hunter, 1985). In short, parents are more directive with their adolescents, while peers tend to share more and appear to be more open with each other. In addition, much parental communication comes as criticism. This is unfortunate, because positive and supportive communication enables children to explore their identity in greater depth. Parents who support their children by creating an atmosphere that fosters respect for the opinions of others, mutuality, and tolerance make it possible for children to explore identity alternatives (Grotevant & Cooper, 1986). Adolescents who have the support of their families actually feel freer to explore these issues (Cooper, Grotevant, & Condon, 1982).

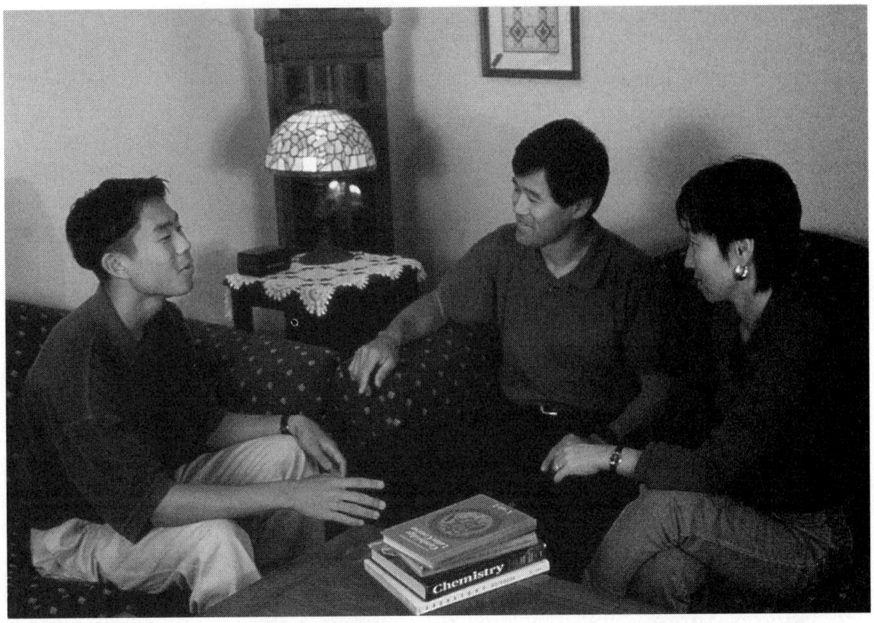

It is important for parents and teenagers to talk with each other. Unfortunately, adults are frequently more interested in explaining their point of view to teens than in listening to them.

Adolescents perceive the communication differences between parents and peers more clearly than parents do. They see significantly less openness and more problems in intergenerational communication (Barnes & Olson, 1985). However, communication problems exist on both sides.

True or False?
When parents communicate with their adolescent children, they tend to explain their own views rather than try to understand their teens' opinions and attitudes.

Questions Students Often Ask

I've heard a great deal about the generation gap. Parents and adolescents exist in different worlds; I think the generation gap is what causes problems.

The term generation gap *is often used to denote what is seen as the ever-widening gap between the standards, values, and opinions of generations. Most studies find that the generation gap is more apparent than real (Lerner et al., 1975). Adolescents and their parents possess very similar beliefs about the value of hard work, education, and desirable personal characteristics (Gecas & Seff, 1990). Religious beliefs, work, and educational issues show more variability within the adolescent population than between parents and children. The differences that do exist are often more a matter of degree or intensity than anything else. Adolescents overestimate the gap between their parents and themselves whereas parents consistently underestimate it. Each group views the other as more conservative than it actually is. Perhaps parents want to see themselves as closer to their children, while adolescents are motivated to separate themselves from their parents. All this could also reflect poor communication between the generations.*

Renegotiating Relationships With Parents

Communication problems make it difficult for adolescents to renegotiate their relationships with their parents. Adolescents must redefine their relationships with their parents and their roles within the family in preparation for leaving the family and leading independent lives (Feldman & Gehring, 1988). This redefinition is explained by two popular models (Grotevant & Cooper, 1985). The first sees the adolescents severing their ties with parents, often leading to a new dependency on peers. The other sees parent-child relationships as basically stable throughout adolescence and downplays the idea that meaningful conflict arises.

In the newer perspective the relationship between adolescents and their parents is seen as moving toward a new symmetry and equality as the years of adolescence roll by. This view sees autonomy and remaining connected with one's family as complementary, not opposite, processes. Adolescents who consider themselves most autonomous rate their relationships with their parents as close, perceive their parents as role models, and often turn to their parents for advice (Kandel & Lesser, 1969).

Adolescence is not a time of complete break or total stability. Instead, a gradual renegotiation between parents and adolescents takes place as the relationship changes from an authoritarian, superior-subordinate relationship to one of greater mutuality (Grotevant & Cooper, 1986). The growth of independence and autonomy does not require severing ties with parents and refusing to use them as pillars of emotional support. Parents continue to be called upon to support the adolescent's growth and development in many areas, including identity formation and independence (Ryan & Lynch, 1989). Earlier evidence tended to overemphasize the separateness of adolescents from their families and underestimated the family connectedness that continues to exist (Feldman & Gehring, 1988). Most adolescents report closeness and positive feelings between themselves and family members (Barnes & Olson, 1985).

Conflict Between Parents and Adolescents

Although psychologists no longer view adolescence as a time of constant and intense conflict, any parent of an adolescent will tell you that it is not free of conflict either. Sometimes the conflict is over the timing of being allowed to do something. Adolescents believe that they should be able to do things at a younger age than their parents do. They hold a different timetable for independence, which causes some conflict. It is not that parents refuse to accept their children's growing independence and competencies, they just see specific privileges and behaviors as appropriate at a later time. When sixth-graders were asked to decide the age at which they expected to engage in certain behaviors, their estimations were almost always earlier than those of their parents (Table 13.2). The researchers surveyed only the parents of boys but suggest that since the parents of girls are usually even more conservative, they would expect the differential to be somewhat greater. When these behaviors are ranked in terms of the ages at which both parents and peers think something should be allowed, the order is very similar (Feldman & Quatman, 1988).

Parents yield power more often and more easily in some areas than others. For example, both parents and children see personal issues, such as what programs to watch on television and what clothes to wear, as determined by the child to a great extent. There are also some moral issues that both see as legitimate concerns for parents, but as adolescents proceed through this period, more issues are deemed personal and their own business. Large discrepancies are found between adolescent and parental judgment of the limits of parental rights in areas of personal safety and friendship issues, and most battles involving autonomy are fought over these issues.

It is not conflict itself that weakens parent-child relationships, but the inability to settle conflict satisfactorily. For example, parents and adolescents might get along better if they tried to understand issues from each other's viewpoint and ceased to make each issue a battle of wills. If more time was spent defining the issue rather than testing each other's will, parents and adolescents could arrive at a solution that both could live with more often. For example, an argument over a messy room can be resolved by a cleaning schedule that both can live with (Steinberg & Levine, 1991).

A warm and supportive family atmosphere promotes successful negotiation of disagreements and keeps conflict to low or moderate levels. When the conditions are hostile or coercive, no one truly listens and conflict can escalate to unhealthy levels. Unfortunately, conflict between teens and parents increases during early and middle adolescence in family environments that are hostile and coercive, and parent-adolescent relationships tend to improve gradually in warm supportive environments (Rueter & Conger, 1995). Families that do not resolve disputes successfully find that these become long-running, festering problems that weaken the par-

Table 13.2 **When Should Children Be Allowed to Participate in Specific Activities?**
Average age at which teenagers and parents believe activities should begin or when children should be allowed to:

	GENERATION	
	Child	Parent
Overall Timetable	15.6	16.6
Composite Scores		
Oppositional Autonomy	15.0	15.6
Autonomy	15.7	16.6
Social	15.3	16.2
Leisure	14.7	16.4
Items		
1. Choose hairstyle even if your parents don't like it.	14.8	14.1
2. Choose what books, magazines to read.	13.2	14.3
3. Go to boy-girl parties at night with friends.	14.8	13.9
4. Not have to tell parents where you are gonig.	17.2	18.9
5. Decide how much time to spend on homework.	13.0	15.0
6. Drink coffee.	16.0	17.5
7. Choose alone what clothes to buy.	13.7	14.7
8. Watch as much TV as you want.	14.3	14.7
9. Go out on dates.	15.4	16.1
10. Smoke cigarettes.	20.3	20.5
11. Take a regular part-time job.	16.2	16.6
12. Make own doctor and dentist appointments.	17.4	17.9
13. Go away with friends without any adults.	15.8	18.5
14. Be able to come home at night as late as you want.	17.7	19.4
15. Decide what clothes to wear even if your parents disapprove.	15.8	16.0
16. Go to rock concerts with friends.	16.1	17.3
17. Stay home alone rather than go out with your family.	14.5	15.0
18. Drink beer.	18.9	19.3
19. Be able to watch any TV, movie, or video show you want.	15.3	17.4
20. Spend money (wages or allowance) however you want.	13.4	14.1
21. Stay home alone if you are sick.	13.4	14.2

Source: Feldman and Quatman, 1988.

ent-adolescent relationship. Adolescent reports of severe and unresolved disagreements are associated with many adjustment and conduct problems as well as alcohol and drug abuse (Brook, Whiteman, & Finch, 1993; Rueter & Conger, 1995).

Successful Parenting of Adolescents

Successful parenting of adolescents requires some change in parenting practices. Parents must expect children at age 17 to make some decisions on their own; parents also must realize that some renegotiation of power is necessary. This is reflected in parental behavior, as parents are more autocratic and interact in a more rule-based manner with their 11-year-olds than with their 17-year-olds. Although parents enforce fewer rules as their children progress through adolescence, they become more uncomfortable with their role as parents (Newman, 1989). This change towards greater mutuality and sharing power is not an easy one for parents.

Parents try to control the behavior of adolescents much more than do friends (Hunter & Youniss, 1982), but these attempts decrease as the adolescent enters college. Parents need to relax some of the earlier restrictions and give their adolescents more opportunities to make decisions independently. Some parents simply believe that high levels of restrictiveness are best; others believe their children are not yet ready for any increase in autonomy. Yet, if this is not done, adolescents may become more alienated and turn away from their parents. Adolescents who see no change in parental restrictiveness and no increase in self-determination report higher level of peer advice-seeking and a greater orientation towards peers compared to those who perceive a decline in parental restrictiveness and more decision-making opportunities.

> ***True or False?***
> Friends try to control the adolescent's behavior more than parents do.

On the other hand, some parents take a hands-off attitude. Parental permissiveness is related to susceptibility to antisocial peer influence (Steinberg, 1987). The idea that parents of young adolescents should back off and let children "grow up" is simply wrong; supervision and monitoring are required, especially in early adolescence when children are so vulnerable (Carnegie Council, 1994). Adolescents who are not monitored or supervised get into more trouble, and a rapid reduction in parental monitoring may be seen as a loss of parental interest.

These two views are not in conflict. If we look at control in terms of monitoring and supervision, such as making certain homework is done and knowing what the adolescent is doing and where, such control is related to competence and is positive. However, trying to control every facet of adolescent life; being confrontational, and not allowing adolescents any freedom to make decisions is not related to positive outcomes (Kurdek & Fine, 1994).

The Good News

The restructuring of relationships during early and middle adolescence may be difficult, but the parent-child relationship improves by late adolescence and conflict decreases (Furman & Buhrmester, 1992). The increase in autonomy does not mean complete emotional disengagement from parents. The autonomy occurs in the atmosphere of connectedness within the family (Hill, 1987). This increase in autonomy occurs gradually and usually without tremendous storm and stress. It involves increasing self-management as rules are changed and develops within the context of the family (Alessandri & Wozniak, 1989).

School Days

Most adolescents meet their friends in school where they must deal with the more complex interpersonal relationships of adolescence. It is in the school that the more advanced academic skills necessary for the world of work are partially developed and that information about jobs, college, and future careers is most available to students. The secondary school is a different place today than it was even 20 years ago.

The Junior High/Middle School Experience

The junior high school and middle school were originally designed to bridge the gap between the relatively easy curriculum of the elementary school and the more demanding work of high school (Smith, 1987). They were also advocated on a developmental basis: early adolescence is a period of rapid physical, cognitive, and social changes, a transitional period in which children have different needs that may be best met in a school environment fundamentally different from that of elementary school (Walker, Kozma, & Green, 1989). Adolescence is a critical period; and the potential for increased risk-taking in many areas—delinquency, sex, and drugs—calls for a special environment dedicated to the needs of adolescent students (Manning & Allen, 1987).

Most children adapt well to the change from elementary to a middle/junior high environment. A minority of students will experience problems, and girls are somewhat more likely to do so than boys because of the multiple stresses that girls experience at this time. For many girls the transition to junior high school coincides with many other developmental changes, especially physical ones, whereas this is not the case for the boys (Simmons et al., 1979). Girls are much more likely to be in the midst of significant physical changes between sixth and seventh grade than are boys.

The transition to junior high brings some complaints even from students who adjust well. Many adolescents feel a sense of anonymity in junior high school, which impacts negatively on their self-concept (Thornburg & Glider, 1984). Students do not believe their teachers are

The change from the more personal elementary school experience to the more impersonal secondary school experience is usually accomplished with few problems, but students do have their complaints, one of which is that their teachers don't know their names.

as warm and caring, and they perceive the school as more impersonal.

The most troublesome finding is a reduction in school-related motivation and an increase in behavioral problems. A number of differences between junior high school and elementary school classrooms may contribute to this decline in academic motivation and confidence in one's abilities. Junior high classrooms are characterized by more emphasis on teacher control and discipline, and fewer opportunities for student decision making. Teacher-student relationships are less positive and less personal, with very little individual attention and more public evaluation. Junior high school teachers see themselves as less effective, especially with low-ability students. Some authorities even argue that junior high school work actually requires lower-level cognitive skills than in later grades of elementary school. Finally, junior high school teachers grade lower and are stricter in their grading system (Eccles et al., 1993).

Some of these changes emanate from structural differences. The lack of personal attention is built into the system if a junior high school teacher teaches five classes of 30 students each instead of one class of 30 students all day.

Two detailed reports by the Carnegie Corporation (1995, 1989) emphasized the importance of the early adolescent period, young adolescents' tendency towards experimentation, and the "unprecedented choices and pressures" that adolescents experience. The reports argued that middle schools do not meet the needs of young people in a changing world. A number of changes were suggested, including dividing large middle grade schools into smaller communities for learning, teaching a core academic program, eliminating tracking by achievement level, more teacher involvement in decision making, fostering health and fitness, connecting the school with the community through service opportunities, and establishing partnerships with community organizations. They also advocated the use of cooperative learning strategies, social and life skills training, and a curriculum that strengthens problem-solving abilities and higher-order thinking; some rethinking of the junior high school experience is in order.

High School

The overwhelming majority of adolescents now attend high school, a change from earlier in the century when the high school graduate was a rarity. However, achievement is a great concern. The congressionally mandated National Assessment of Educational Progress (NAEP) tests fourth, eighth, and twelfth graders (high school seniors) in a number of areas. The results of the nationwide test in U.S. history and geography were disappointing, with most high school seniors unable to reach even the basic level of achievement (Lawton, 1995b, c). Reading scores declined slightly for seniors between 1992 and 1994, and stayed the same for fourth and eighth graders. Writing and math skills are also major concernts. Only half of all seniors do an adequate job solving problems that require decimals, fractions, and percentages (Carnegie Council, 1995).

There is also some good news on the high school front: enrollments in advanced science and math courses have increased (West, 1994). Graduation rates are up, and the percentage of high school students taking core academic subjects increased significantly in the past decade (Toch, Bennefield, & Bernstein, 1996). High school work has become more rigorous over the past two decades.

The school reform movement flowered in the 1970s and 1980s, and, despite disappointments in the present achievement of students, high school students are performing somewhat better today than years ago. Much of the reform was initiated by the National Commission on Excellence in Education's study entitled *A Nation at Risk* (1981). The commission documented many problems in the educational system and recommended, among other things, stricter requirements for graduation, especially in English, mathematics, science, foreign language, and social studies; a longer school year; and curricula reform. The trend towards greater rigor in the secondary school, especially high school, will continue into the near future.

True or False?
Within the past two decades high school course work has become more rigorous.

Some of the calls for higher standards are based upon studies showing that American students in high school do more poorly than high school students in other countries, such as China and Japan. These students spend more time in school, more time studying at home, and are exposed to a more rigorous curriculum (Fuligni & Stevenson, 1995; Stevenson, Chen, & Lee, 1993). After agreeing that higher standards are necessary, it is difficult to proceed (Applebome, 1996); many states have moved toward developing new standards but they are often general and imprecise. Very few states have developed standards that are clear enough to be used as part of a formal curriculum. National standards are difficult because the United States has a long history of local control.

Questions Students Often Ask

I always hear that Japanese high school students do better than American students do. But aren't they more anxious and don't they have fewer social relationships because they study so much?

Sorry, you're wrong. It is true that Japanese and Chinese students spend more time engaged in school work, and Americans spend more time socializing, watching television, and especially at part-time work (Fuligni & Stevenson, 1995). The lives of Chinese and Japanese students are no less balanced, although they date less and part-time work during the high school years is very uncommon in Japan and Taiwan. In addition, there is no evidence that the pressure to succeed causes psychological problems. Although the emphasis on academics leads to somewhat more academic pressure, American students report much more pressure in jobs and sports. The overall level of anxiety and adjustment is similar among high school students in all three countries. Cross-cultural differences in frequency of complaints among cultures are relatively small. High academic achievement does not have to come at the cost of psychological maladjustment. (Crystal et al., 1994).

Another major change is the movement toward minimum competency testing in high school, intended to ensure that each graduate has certain basic skills. The testing is an outgrowth of the movement to improve educational accountability and be certain that a high school diploma certifies some basic knowledge. The great majority of states now require some form of minimum competency test, although tests vary in what they measure and in the cutoff for success.

There has also been a call for high schools to focus on health, moral, and family issues. For example, there is a clamor for more drug and sex education programs and for courses covering family living that include basic information on child development, relationships, and similar topics.

A report on the restructuring of high schools called *Breaking Ranks* advocated some far-reaching structural changes. Many high school students feel that few people really know them and anonymity is a major problem, as it is in junior high (Maeroff, 1996). Limiting high school enrollment to 600 students would help to solve this problem. In addition, each student should have a personal adult advocate who can serve as a liaison between the student and others in the school environment. Practical learning is also emphasized and a guarantee that students can meet performance standards in entry-level jobs issued. It would also permit employers to return students lacking basic skills to high schools for additional training (Henry, 1996a). A full-time teacher should be asked to teach no more than 90 students per day to ensure individualized attention. Schools should be required to develop a long-term plan for using computers and other technologies. The report also advocates teaching a core set of values stressing that possession of weapons, drugs, and violence will not be tolerated as well as providing students with some role in decision making within the school. The practicality of these structural changes is questionable in the present economic environment (Henry, 1996a).

Making the curriculum more rigorous, including more science and math, emphasizing reasoning skills, and increasing the number of hours or days that students attend school are suggested. However, a startling analysis of high school education looks at the problems from a completely different point of view, claiming that a teen culture that does not value academic achievement is the key problem. After group discussions with many students and parents, Steinberg and colleagues (1996) argue that all the improvement in curriculum and standards will not work unless a change takes place in students' attitudes. Students must come to school interested in and committed to learning. They found that roughly 40% of the students admitted they were just going through the motions in school; disengagement was pervasive. The problem stems from a teen culture that does not reward or encourage achievement. Some students surveyed reported deliberately hiding their capabilities due to concerns about what friends might think. Few students believe their friends think it is important to get good grades. Most said that they could bring home grades of C or worse without their parents getting upset and many students said they do not do the homework they are assigned.

Parents are also disengaged from the educational process and do not attend school functions such as open school week and teacher conferences; a quarter of all parents do not know how their children are doing. American students are much busier with television, socializing, and working part time than students in other countries, with academics not being given the same attention.

Steinberg argues in favor of providing more parenting education to draw parents into their children's schools, adopting a system of national academic standards and examinations, cutting back student work hours, and making it harder for them to go through the motions. This analysis is sure to cause controversy (Viadero, 1996a). Some authorities do not believe that adolescents are any more disengaged than years ago, or that their conclusions are overgeneralized. Others argue that curriculum and school reforms are more practical than trying to change home or peer group reactions.

Whatever stand people take on high schools, there is no doubt that changes are needed on many levels. Curricular modifications, structural changes and higher standards are necessary, but as Steinberg reminds us, the need to find ways to change the climate of lack of support for achievement may be important as well.

Gender and Achievement in High School

Adolescent girls and boys do not achieve identically in secondary schools, even though they have no significant differences in intelligence. In elementary school girls do at least as well as boys, and perhaps better. Elementary school teachers value female competencies, and females may find that their teachers greatly value and praise their noncompetitive, highly social, more obedient behavior. Boys have a more difficult time and are punished more often. However, in secondary school males begin to value school achievement more, and teachers value the gender-role competencies of males more highly (Bernard, 1981). The gap between males and females closes rapidly in high school (Kaplan, 1990).

The fact that males catch up and females lag in high school does not tell us anything about the reasons it happens. Theories abound, but few real facts have been offered. Women are as achievement oriented and as persistent as men. The areas of greatest underachievement are science and math, and it is in these areas that much work remains to be done.

Two recent studies found that many teachers of math and science ignore girls in favor of boys and the gap on science standardized tests may actually be widening, while the gap in math is narrowing. Those girls who do well do not continue. Teachers consistently underestimate their female students' abilities in math (Kimball, 1989). Female students have less confidence in their math abilities, and with loss of confidence comes loss of performance (Junge & Dretzke, 1995). Boys get more detailed instruction on the correct answers. These differences are not deliberate, and even female teachers show these patterns (Kerr, 1991). Differential teacher attitudes and behaviors may discourage female students from taking advanced science and math courses. Simple training can improve teacher behaviors in this area.

In some cases, school personnel including teachers, administrators, and guidance counselors discourage girls from taking particular courses. A bright girl may be advised not to take an advanced math course. This type of blatant sexism has been held up to public scrutiny and criticized as it should be. However, such examples are probably less common than the subtle communication of expectations: females are not actively restricted from these areas—they are simply not encouraged to take such courses (Sadker & Sadker, 1994). Lack of encouragement produces similar results.

Studies show that girls do not take as many science and math courses in high school (Terwilliger & Titus, 1995). This reduced interest in science and math may begin when students are in middle school. By the time advanced courses in high school are chosen, a considerable gender difference is found. Girls take advanced biology, and boys choose physics and advanced chemistry. As girls proceed through high school, they see science and math as less and less relevant to their futures. Once girls avoid high school math, they close out some career options or at least make them more difficult (Murray, 1995a).

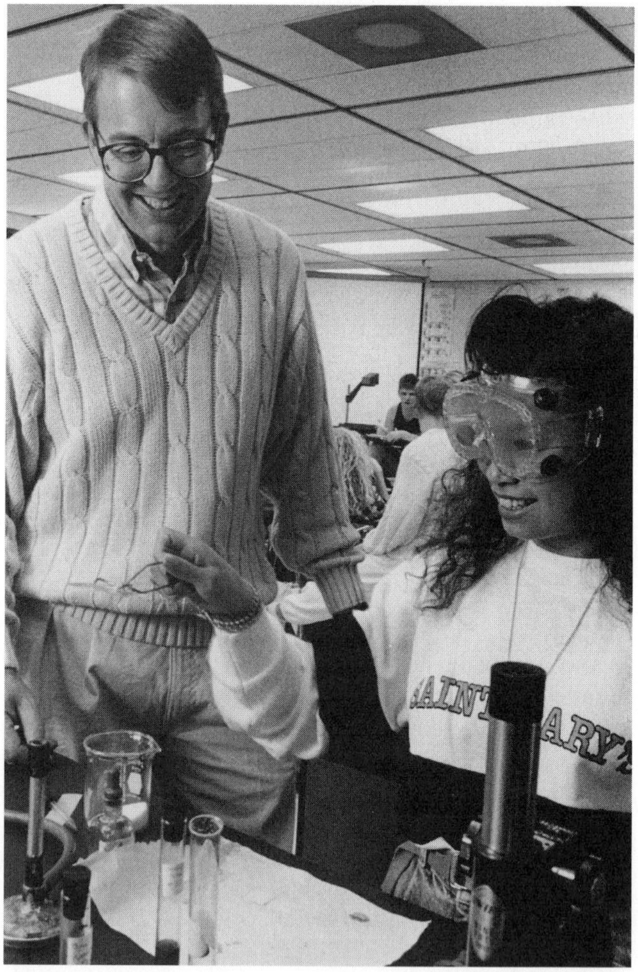

Fewer girls than boys take physics and chemistry or consider the physical sciences as possible future careers. This is changing very slowly.

Minorities in High School

Over the past years measures of academic achievement in reading, writing, and mathematics for both African-American and Latino youth have improved but remain below comparable white students (Toch et al., 1996). Historically, minority youth—especially those from lower-income backgrounds—have not achieved well in school (Reed, 1988), and college attendance is lower for minority group youth (DeBlassie & DeBlassie, 1996).

Grouping these youths from different cultural groups together under the heading of minority youth is a major problem. These young people come from different cultural, environmental, and social backgrounds and may have different difficulties. For example, Latinos as well as other minority youth may have poor English language skills and require specific help in this area. In addition, many Latinos come from a background that emphasizes cooperation more than individual achievement, which does not mesh with the more individualized achievement orientation of American schools. Native American children are also raised to value individual achievement less and group-oriented achievement more, which may lead to difficulties in school (LaFromboise & Low, 1989). The family values of interdependence with others and sharing may not be reflected in school. In addition, these youngsters may be reluctant to talk in school, and communication patterns may be different.

African American youth face a combination of social and environmental problems. A disproportionate number of African American children live in poverty, poor housing, and crime-ridden areas, and many are born into single-parent families (Edelman, 1985). Children born into single-parent families are especially vulnerable to school failure, since they are more likely to live in poverty, have poorer health, and their mothers are less likely to promote optimal development and are under more stress (Comer, 1985). Programs that aim at overcoming these problems can help, especially if they emphasize parental involvement (Comer, 1985). Many schools in primarily African American neighborhoods lack adequate funds and are not safe and orderly.

Asian Americans have always been thought to do well, and indeed they have succeeded. However, the stereotype of the bright, conscientious, quiet Chinese or Japanese student is very limiting and may give teachers unreasonable expectations based only upon ethnic identity. These students frequently have limited English skills (Huang, 1989) and may also have difficulties negotiating a culture whose values differ greatly from those they learn at home (Nogata, 1989).

One common thread that unites many minority youth is poverty. Often, students from poor backgrounds are labeled unintelligent and channeled into less challenging programs. Their attitudes toward school and their motivation may be poor, and they often see little relationship between what they learn in school and the real world. They may have no safe and quiet place to study, and the level of family support may be low. They suffer higher suspension and dropout rates (Reed, 1988). Poor academic achievement is more often a consequence of cultural, social, and environmental factors than of lack of ability (Gibbs & Huang, 1989).

There is no single answer to the problem of underachievement among adolescents. We must rid ourselves of the idea that all students learn or can be taught in the same way. Students from different cultural and experiential backgrounds may respond to different teaching styles and methods. Teachers who teach minority youth can become more knowledgeable about their students' cultural and family backgrounds and can observe other teachers who are effective with these children (Kaplan, 1990).

Dropping Out of School

One of the most serious academic problems is the high school dropout rate. High school dropouts are more likely to live at or near the poverty level, to experience unemployment, and to depend on government for support (Schmidt, 1993; Steinberg, 1989).

Although the majority of students finish high school, many do not. Students from minority groups have a higher dropout rate than middle-class youths. In the past, African Americans dropped out of school at a much higher rate than whites, but today the gap is narrowing substantially (Henry, 1994). Latinos still lag behind in high school completion; their problems include poverty, poor language skills, and poor educational attainment by parents (DeBlassie & DeBlassie, 1996). Moreover, many more Latinos drop out before or in the early years of high school (Education Week, November 3, 1993).

The most common signs of possible early school withdrawal are consistent failure, grade level placement be-

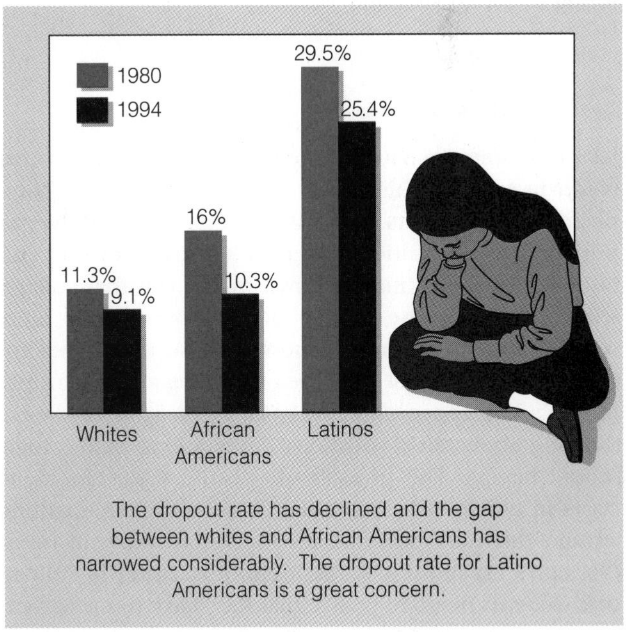

1980
1994
29.5%
25.4%
16%
10.3%
11.3%
9.1%
Whites
African Americans
Latinos
The dropout rate has declined and the gap between whites and African Americans has narrowed considerably. The dropout rate for Latino Americans is a great concern.

Datagraphic
Dropping Out: 1980 and 1994
Source: Data from U.S. Bureau of the Census.

low average, poor attendance, active antagonism to teachers, disinterest in school, low reading ability, unhappy family situations, and conduct problems in school (Brooks-Gunn, Guo, & Furstenberg, 1993; Horowitz, 1992). School holds little promise for dropouts, who as a group are poor readers. They also show a history of school-related problems, including high rates of delinquency and school suspension (Sprintall & Collins, 1984). Dropouts have poor grades, experience failure, and show little or no interest in school; many of these students have been left back a grade. They often come from large families or have backgrounds of poverty, discord, and divorce (Zmiles & Lee, 1991).

True or False?
Most high school dropouts actually like school and read on grade level but find themselves bored and unchallenged.

Most factors that differentiate graduates from dropouts are present before these teens drop out. Low self-esteem, higher rates of delinquency, and higher rates of drug abuse are found before the students stop attending school, so these factors are not consequences of dropping out. Dropping out is not an event as much as it is the result of a long process of failure, poor adjustment, low aspirations, low intellectual stimulation, and poverty; it can be predicted.

Many school districts recognize that the dropout problem is serious and requires bold new approaches. Because the problem is such a complicated one, the solution may require a variety of programs and approaches. Some school districts have instituted promising programs in which potential dropouts attend alternative schools or work-study programs and receive more attention and tutoring in basic academic skills.

Career Choice

"If I only knew what I wanted to be, I'd be able to do better in school." This is one of the more common complaints of adolescents. Erik Erikson acknowledged the importance of a vocational identity (Erikson, 1968). The interrelationship is nicely shown by the fact that college students who choose occupations that mirror their measured abilities and interests show more successful resolutions of Erikson's first six stages, including identity formation in adolescence (Munley, 1975; 1977). Students begin thinking about their vocational futures long before high school begins. The process of vocational development starts in childhood as children observe the occupations around them and imagine themselves working in them (Super, 1953). But it is in high school and later in college that students begin to realize that they have to make a career decision. Ideally, people take their abilities, interests, and future goals into consideration when they choose a vocation; but chance factors also enter into the equation.

Vocational choice is a conscious choice only when people can consider what they want to do and then follow some program of study or training to achieve it. Conscious career choice is viable only for people who believe they have the opportunity and the resources to succeed and who live in an environment that makes it possible for them to carry out their plans (Drummond & Ryan, 1995). For some women and members of many ethnic and racial minority groups, this is not always the case.

Women and Careers

The overwhelming majority of women are in the work force, and most teen girls believe their future involves employment. Findings from studies investigating the vocational choices of women are contradictory. Some studies show little difference in vocational choice between male and female students in high school (Kramer, 1986); others show that females have lower aspirations (Delisle, 1992). Women experience both internal and external barriers in making vocational decisions to enter fields in math and the physical sciences. The external barriers include sexism, discrimination, and lack of role models. Some internal barriers include fear of being considered too bright and falling back onto very traditional societal roles (Delisle, 1992).

Although women are still overrepresented in clerical and service positions and some professional fields such as elementary school teachers and librarians, more women are entering nontraditional fields. A nontraditional field is one in which more than two-thirds of the workers are of the other gender (Hayes, 1986). Women are making substantial but uneven progress, as shown in Figure 13.1. The percentage of women doctors, lawyers, computer scientists, and architects has increased significantly.

True or False?
The percentage of women doctors and lawyers has stayed about the same for the last 15 years.

Many women face problems in career planning that males do not. For example, men are socialized into the role of breadwinner but women have developed dual roles as mothers and workers, which often limits their career choices. Women are sometimes reluctant to enter careers in the sciences because they see problems combining family life and a career in this area. Although women are now entering nontraditional careers such as law and medicine, women who enter chemistry, physics, and engineering are still rare.

Why? Teachers, professionals, and even peers have been known to discourage women from pursuing a particular career because they think it is inappropriate. Television and movies rarely show women in scientific fields, and when they do, the women seem incapable of having a normal family life along with a career. Parents sometimes propagate sexist attitudes by discouraging daughters from pursuing certain fields.

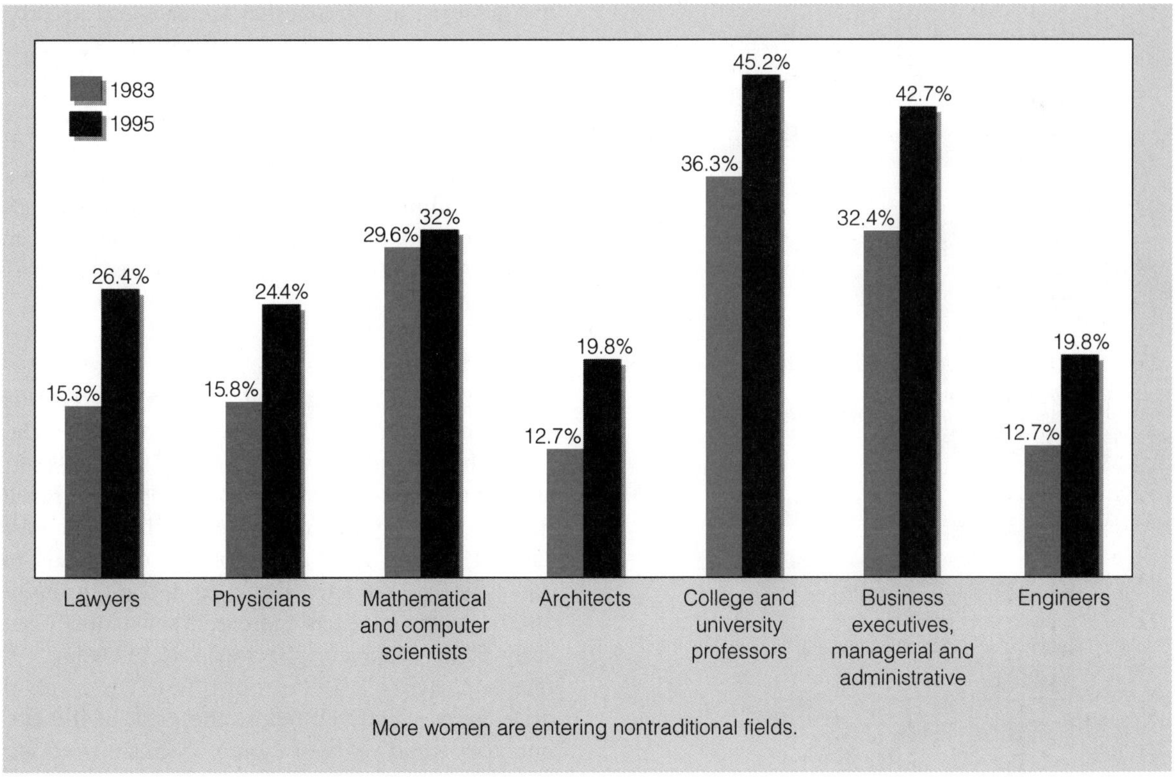

Figure 13.1
Percentage of Women Entering Nontraditional Professions
Source: Data from Department of Commerce, 1996.

We can conclude that more females will see employment outside the home as part of their future and many more will enter male-dominated occupations. Although concern about vocational choice is reasonable and the elimination of the barriers that negatively affect the achievement and career plans of women is important, some politically correct view of how a woman should live should not be foisted on students. Too often, older stereotypes have been replaced by newer ones. For instance, one female student felt rather guilty because she wanted to pursue a career in elementary school teaching. Her decision was not greeted with approval by her counselor, teacher, and friends, who believed she could "do better." Women should be encouraged to enter the field of their choice unencumbered by artificial barriers.

Socioeconomic Status

Career choice is a misnomer for the poor, many of whom belong to minority groups. Many poor adolescents do not have any choices, or at least do not see any. Many poor African American males have no real period of career exploration. They may have a succession of unrelated jobs for 50 years, with no discernible career pattern.

Occupational choice may also be limited by lack of academic skills and economic resources or by racial discrimination, complicated by the lack of high-achieving role models. Adolescents from middle-class families believe they can influence their own futures—that is, they have an internal locus of control. But this is not true of poorer youngsters, who often have an external locus of control and see themselves as at the mercy of the system, the outside world, or luck. They are more fatalistic in their outlook (Farmer, 1978); why plan if you don't have the power to change things?

There is both good and bad news concerning career choices for minorities. The proportion of African Americans in white-collar, professional jobs and technical specialties has increased (Figure 13.2). While some progress has been made, the progress has been slow. In addition, the unemployment rate is greater for minority youth than for white youths. This higher unemployment rate probably reflects both the lack of skills and the high percentage of school dropouts found among minority youths.

Studies show that minority group youth know less about different types of occupations than majority youth, and since occupational knowledge influences choice, this is one place to start (Drummond & Ryan, 1995). A successful work experience program for minority students may involve providing better occupational information, relating academic skills to future career requirements, providing job-related experience, and teaching job-finding and interviewing skills. This can be accomplished through informational seminars, career luncheons with role models, business representatives speaking to students, job fairs, career tours, and counseling (Miller & Cunningham, 1992).

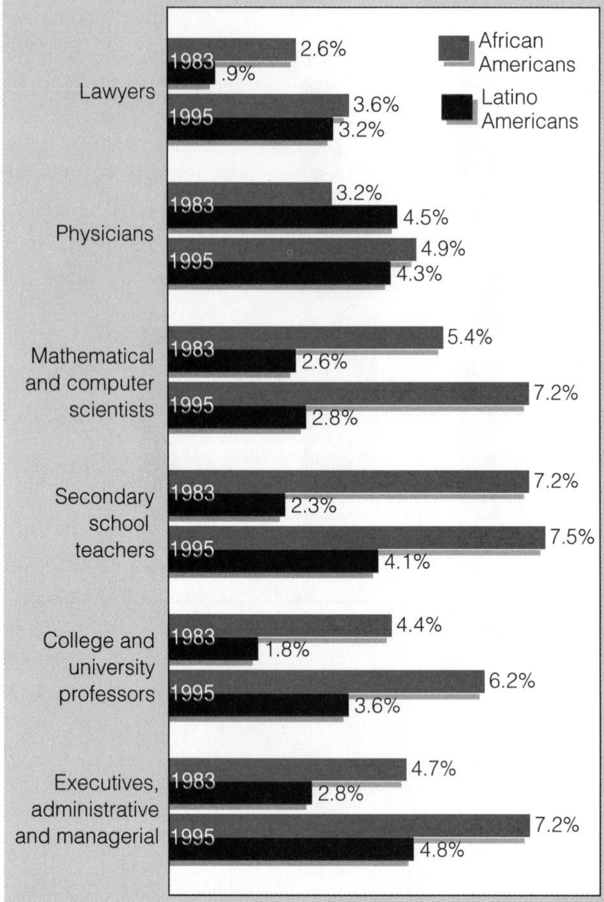

African Americans and Latino Americans have made some progress towards entering the professions.

Figure 13.2
Professional African Americans and Latinos
Source: Data from Department of Commerce, 1996.

African Americans and some members of other minority groups have a long history of discrimination and lack of opportunity. Difficulties in achievement may be caused by prior negative experiences and a history of discrimination that now pervades the culture. African American and Latino youth often believe that they will face a labor market that will not offer them rewards equal to the effort they put in and the educational credentials they may attain. Their lack of motivation may be a response to the belief that their educational efforts may not pay off (Ogbu, 1992, 1981, 1978). To change perceptions, job opportunities must be opened up to minorities so they can see for themselves the value of schooling; role models must exist to show that it can be done. Unfortunately, in many poverty-stricken communities those who succeed move out to other communities and the role models of successful business and professional people may not be at hand. Schools in poverty neighborhoods must be adequately funded, and students must be given an opportunity to learn in schools that are safe and secure, and in an environment conducive to learning.

Drug Use and Violence

Adolescents between the ages of 12 and 17 years say that the most important problems facing people their age are drugs and violent crime (Center on Addiction and Substance Abuse, 1995) so these problems deserve special attention.

Drug Use

Since 1975 the *Monitoring the Future Study* has measured the extent of drug use among high school students by sampling thousands of students from all around the United States (NIDA, 1995). The results from the 1995 survey are compared with earlier surveys in Table 13.3 and an analysis of the data leads to three conclusions. First, after a marked decline throughout the 1980s, drug usage has increased substantially since the early 1990s (Johnston, Bachman, & O'Malley, 1995; Stephenson, Henry & Robinson, 1996). The levels of illicit drug use are still well below the peak of the late 1970s but the trend is worrisome (Johnston et al., 1995; USDHHS, 1995).

Second, a trend also exists for youngsters to become involved in drugs at an earlier age (Leshner, 1995). Substance use has increased substantially for adolescents in the sixth through ninth grades (Stephenson et al., 1996). Third, the percentage of adolescents who appreciate the dangers of drugs has declined greatly. Since the early 1990s fewer students understand how harmful drugs are (Johnston et al., 1995; Leshner, 1995). This leads to an increase in peer tolerance for drug taking and eventually to increased drug use.

True or False?
Drug use by adolescents has increased markedly since the early 1990s.

Alcohol Alcohol is the most frequently used drug (Johnston et al., 1995). Alcohol use has remained fairly stable over the past few years, but it remains at a very high level. Although people tend not to take alcohol use seriously, the facts prove otherwise. More than half of all inmates convicted of violent crimes were drinking before they committed the offense (New York State Council on Alcoholism, 1986). A little less than half of all people killed in motor vehicle accidents are adolescents under the influence of alcohol (Wodarski, 1990). The carnage on our highways has caused an outcry, and many states have raised the legal age for drinking to 21 years. Higher minimum drinking ages, stricter laws, and increased educational efforts have been effective: there has recently been a decline in the number of alcohol-related automobile accidents involving young people.

Table 13.3 **Monitoring the Future Study: Trends in Prevalence of Various Drugs for Eighth-Graders, Tenth-Graders, and High School Seniors**

	Eighth-Graders		Tenth-Graders		Twelfth-Graders	
	1991	1995	1991	1995	1991	1995
Marijuana/Hashish						
Lifetime	10.2%	19.9%	23.4%	34.1%	36.7%	41.7%
Annual	6.2	15.8	16.5	28.7	23.9	34.7
30-day	3.2	9.1	8.7	17.2	13.8	21.2
Daily	0.2	0.8	0.8	2.8	2.0	4.6
Cocaine						
Lifetime	2.3	4.2	4.1	5.0	7.8	6.0
Annual	1.1	2.6	2.2	3.5	3.5	4.0
30-day	0.5	1.2	0.7	1.7	1.4	1.8
Daily	0.1	0.1	0.1	0.1	0.1	0.2
Crack Cocaine						
Lifetime	1.3	2.7	1.7	2.8	3.1	3.0
Annual	0.7	1.6	0.9	1.8	1.5	2.1
30-day	0.3	0.7	0.3	0.9	0.7	1.0
Daily	*	*	*	*	0.1	0.1
Heroin						
Lifetime	1.2	2.3	1.2	1.7	0.9	1.6
Annual	0.7	1.4	0.5	1.1	0.4	1.1
30-day	0.3	0.6	0.2	0.6	0.2	0.6
Daily	*	*	*	*	*	0.1
Stimulants						
Lifetime	10.5	13.1	13.2	17.4	15.4	15.3
Annual	6.2	8.7	8.2	11.9	8.2	9.3
30-day	2.6	4.2	3.3	5.3	3.2	4.0
Daily	0.1	0.2	0.1	0.2	0.2	0.3
*Alcohol***						
Lifetime	70.1	54.5	83.8	70.5	88.0	80.7
Annual	54.0	45.3	72.3	63.5	77.7	73.7
30-day	25.1	24.6	42.8	38.3	54.0	51.3
Daily	0.5	0.7	1.3	1.7	3.6	3.5
Cigarettes (any use)						
Lifetime	44.0	46.4	55.1	57.6	63.1	64.2
Annual	NA	NA	NA	NA	NA	NA
30-day	14.3	19.1	20.8	27.9	28.3	33.5
½ pack + per day	3.1	3.4	6.5	8.3	10.7	12.4

*Less than 0.5%.

**The wording of the questionnaire was changed in 1993; the new questionnaire requires heavier use to elicit a positive response.

Source: Data from National Institute on Drug Abuse, Monitoring the Future Study, 1995.

Nicotine Despite all the studies linking smoking to cancer, heart disease, and so many other health-related problems, smoking remains a national problem (Johnston et al., 1995; NIDA, 1995; Nelson et al., 1995). A greater percentage of high school seniors smoke than adults. Most adolescent smokers say they will quit in a few years, but this does not happen. White teenage girls are most likely to smoke, but smoking among African American boys has doubled since 1991 (Friend, 1996). Smoking is not just an American problem, but one that is growing worldwide (Abernathy, Massad, & Romano-Dweyer, 1995).

Illicit Drugs Teenage use of marijuana has increased significantly since 1991 at every grade level (Pina, 1995; USDHHS, 1995). Some marijuana users believe that no lasting effects occur after the high wears off. This is not true, as shown by a study of college students who were marijuana users but had not smoked for most of a month before testing: heavy users still performed worse on measures of attention and general learning (Painter, 1996).

Cocaine and Crack Of all the illicit drugs, cocaine has recently received more media attention than any other substance. Cocaine is a stimulant that affects the central nervous system and produces feelings of euphoria. Physiological effects include extreme changes in blood pressure, increases in heart and respiration rates, insomnia, nausea, tremors, and convulsions. Cocaine use can lead to paranoid behavior, and potent forms like crack are especially addictive.

The use of cocaine and crack has increased for eighth- and tenth-graders, and use by twelfth-graders has stayed relatively stable (Johnston et al., 1995). The percentage of students in each grade who felt that people are at great risk of harming themselves by trying crack cocaine has decreased markedly since 1991.

Can Drug Abuse Be Predicted?

If we could predict who is most likely to become a drug abuser, we could commit our resources more effectively. The factors predictive of drug abuse can be broadly placed in three categories; individual characteristics, family (parent-child) factors, and peer group influence.

Individual Characteristics Although there is no single personality pattern that is predictive of drug abuse, some characteristics do stand out. A pattern of undercontrolled and antisocial behavior at young ages predicts drug abuse (Shedler & Block, 1990). Children who are described as undercontrolled at ages 3 and 4 are more likely to use drugs in adolescence (Block, Block, & Keyes, 1988). Disruptiveness in kindergarten, and aggression and disruptiveness in elementary school is related to early drug use (before the age of 14 years) (Dobkin et al., 1995).

Drug users are more likely to have low self-esteem, to equate drug use with entertainment, and to have weaker family ties, whereas nonusers equate drugs and alcohol with negative consequences and show higher self-esteem and stronger family ties. Light to moderate users fall somewhere between these two extremes (DeAngelis, 1994). This pattern in which heavy users differ from light users and nonusers is commonly found with other drugs, such as marijuana, as well. For example, regular heavy users are much more rebellious and angry, show a lack of responsibility, and score high on measures of sensation seeking (Brook et al., 1981). They see themselves as inadequate, have friends who smoke marijuana heavily, often come from turbulent homes filled with discord, and show an inability to conform to rules. The differences between light users and nonusers are more subtle: nonusers have more affectionate relationships with their fathers (Brook, et al., 1981), and users are more defensive and rebellious (Mayer & Ligman, 1989).

Family Relations

Adolescents who describe their family lives as troubled and who are alienated from family at the age of 7 years are more frequent users and abusers of drugs in adolescence (Shedler & Block, 1990). Marital discord is related to substance abuse (Mayes, 1995), as is physical and sexual abuse (Mayes, 1995). In addition, teenagers are more likely to use drugs if their parents do so as well (Mayes, 1995).

Certain types of parenting seem to predispose adolescents to abuse drugs. Parents who are cold, forbidding, or neglectful tend to produce children who act out and are aggressive, and who are more likely to take drugs (Stein, Newcomb, & Bentler, 1993). Problem drinkers and illicit drug users often describe having experienced inconsistent parenting, a lack of family cohesiveness, and conflict. Less conflict and a warm parent-child bond is associated with less adolescent drug abuse (Brook, Nomura, & Cohen, 1989). Parents who abuse drugs may show poorer parenting strategies, which may predispose their children to the use of drugs. When these children grow up and have their own children they may continue this type of parenting (Stein, Newcomb, & Bentler, 1993). Adolescents who believe that their families manage stress well by working together are at a reduced risk for using drugs. Warm family relations provide a buffer against drug use perhaps by reducing the need for escape and providing models and lessons in how to deal with stress (Stephenson et al., 1996). Lack of adult supervision is also related to drug use.

A child's personality characteristics may influence the parenting practices used. For example, a child's aggressiveness may cause parents to resort to inconsistent and inappropriate discipline, which may then lead to poor family relationships that encourage drug use (Stice & Barrera, 1995). Poor and inconsistent parenting may cause children to react in a way that isolates them from others and results in a tense family situation.

Peers

Most parents believe that peer pressure is the primary reason teens use drugs; two-thirds of adolescents cite peer pressure as one reason. However, the overwhelming majority of teenagers say they use alcohol and other drugs for the high or to forget their problems (Boeck & Lynn, 1995). Peer pressure is certainly a factor but despite the availability of marijuana, cigarettes, and alcohol many teenagers do not smoke or drink. Having friends who smoke or drink has an influence on the adolescent, but peer pressure does not operate in a vacuum (Graham, Marks, & Hansen, 1991). Peer influence is mediated by the quality of the parent-child relationship (Chassin et al., 1993). The better the relationship, the less likely it is that peer pressure to use drugs will be effective. Adolescents who take drugs or are at risk for taking drugs may select as friends other adolescents with similar interests and outlooks on life who then expose them to drugs and both model and reinforce their use (Swain et al., 1989).

Not all adolescents, even those at risk, will become drug abusers. A number of protective factors mediate between risk and outcome. For example, a positive attitude towards school and health, valuing academic achievement, and understanding the health consequences of drug use predict less drug-taking behavior. Warm relationships with parents who show interest and discuss problems as well as parental supervision and family rules about dating, curfews, and chores deter drug abuse by improving family relationships, regulating time, and clearly showing what behaviors are and are not valued (Jessor et al., 1995). One way to combat drug abuse is to reduce factors that lead to at-risk status and increase factors that seem to buffer the child against drug abuse.

Drug Education

To prevent and combat illegal drug use Americans favor a broad-based strategy consisting of education, treatment, and law enforcement (Brown, 1995; Office of National Drug Control Policy, 1996). Drug prevention should start early, since studies show that children are starting to use drugs at an earlier age (Jones et al., 1990). Students whose parents communicate with them about drugs and are involved in community and school activities are half as likely to use illegal drugs (Manning, 1994).

A decade ago teenagers knew more about drugs than do today's teenagers. Drugs were always in the news years ago and parents of that generation were more likely to talk to their children about the dangers of drug abuse. The phenomenon of one generation knowing so much more about a particular subject than the newer generation is called **generational forgetting** (Johnston et al., 1995). Teens hear less now about the consequences of taking drugs but they receive more encouragement for using drugs. The lyrics of many popular songs display pro-drug sentiments and have drug-related themes. Ado-

generational forgetting The phenomenon in which the older generation knows more about a particular area than the newer generation.

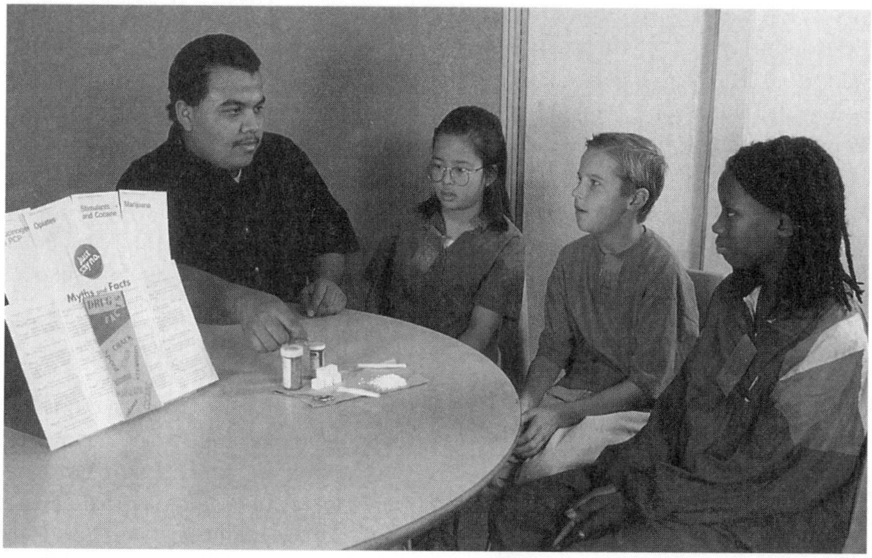

Everyone is in favor of drug education programs, but how to make them effective is the real question.

lescents today hear fewer cautions and more reassurance and encouragement for drug use.

Many drug prevention programs have not been as successful as educators would like (Goodstadt, 1987; Tobler, 1986), partly because these programs cannot eliminate the social problems that may lead to drug abuse. A student may abuse drugs for immediate pleasure, as a means of experimentation, to show rebelliousness, and because of peer pressure. Drugs may also be used as an escape from the harsh realities of life, such as failure, rejection, and family problems, and these conditions are much more difficult to remedy (Forbes, 1987; Tower, 1987). To be effective, drug education programs must deal with the issue of how to help students find alternative ways of dealing with their problems.

Students certainly need factual information about the dangers of drug use, but accurate information is only one aspect of drug education. Correcting misconceptions about the percentage of users can also reduce drug use. For example, as is true for students of all ages, college students often overestimate the number of peers who drink heavily on campus. When students are informed of the real figures, their perceptions change and this actually reduces alcohol consumption on campus (DeAngelis, 1994).

Most modern drug education programs go beyond just saying no or telling students why they should say "no" and teach adolescents *how* to say no (Murray, 1995b). Modern programs attempt to build drug resistance skills and improve the adolescent's involvement in community and school since so many drug abusers are alienated from family, community, and society in general (Murray, 1995b). For example, Project Star attempts to steer children away from gateway drugs. It is a 5-year program that teaches drug resistance skills, encourages parents to talk to their children about drugs, looks for ways to increase a nondrug use ethic in the community such as alcohol-free sporting events, and encourages community involvement in antidrug programs. Life Skills Training is a program that seeks to increase adolescents' ability to deal with life stress rather than escaping through drug use. Teachers are trained to focus on specific skills; students are shown how to cope with anxiety and tension. Assertiveness skills are also taught, such as how to resist pressure and evaluate advertising. Sessions focus on social skills, such as how to improve rapport, compliment others, and increase one's social network.

No single drug prevention program will work for everyone. Some adolescents, such as those who are homeless or runaway teens who have used drugs, need more help (Edmonds, 1995). Drug treatment is required and reduces crime in the community; for every dollar spent on treatment, the public saves seven dollars in criminal justice and health costs (Office of National Drug Control Policy, 1996).

Violence and Delinquency

There is no denying the rising tide of violence in our schools and parks and on our streets (Allen-Hagen et al., 1994). Violence is far too commonly seen by children and adolescents. Violence is a problem in urban and suburban schools and reports of violence have increased 75% since 1980, with more adolescents and children being both perpetrators and victims (Hall, 1994).

According to a Harris poll, one-third of junior and senior high school students have been involved in fights involving weapons and many avoid particular parks and playgrounds (Henry, 1996b). Even young 7- to 10-year-olds are anxious about violence, and have a fear of violence and death. There is a link between violence and drug use; students who carry guns are almost 15 times as likely to use cocaine, and much more likely to drink and smoke marijuana (Manning, 1994).

The most modern view of violence and delinquency sees it as a developmental problem that may begin very early in life. A number of risk factors exist that can be categorized as family, individual/peer, school, and community. These factors often interact, making it difficult to separate one from the other.

Family Processes and Relationships

Children who are rejected by their parents, who grow up in conflict-ridden homes, or who are not properly supervised are at a great risk of becoming delinquents (Wright & Wright, 1995). Cold, unloving parents who are overcritical often produce aggressive children. Delinquent adolescents usually have poor relationships with their parents. Many homes that yield delinquents lack a family routine and consistent discipline and are headed by parents who yell, threaten, and nag but do not follow through and are unable to deal with family problems (Wilson & Herrnstein, 1985). Family relations are characterized by rigidity, lack of cohesion, little positive communication, rejection, and indifference. Indeed, many delinquents come from neglectful homes and these children are often alienated from their parents and do not internalize their moral rules.

Very often, the parents of delinquents either use discipline that is either very severe and punitive or very lax (Fox, 1985). A link between child abuse and witnessing violence in the home and later aggression is often found (Mason, 1993). Children raised in homes where domestic violence or child abuse occurs are more likely to show aggression (Holden & Ritchie, 1991). Witnessing or experiencing abuse teaches children to solve their problems using violence, and prevents them from experiencing empathy for others and reduces their ability to deal with stress (Siegel & Senna, 1991).

True or False?
Children who witness domestic violence are actually less likely to engage in violent behavior because they are aware of its consequences.

Delinquency is somewhat more prevalent in single-parent families, perhaps because of the history of family conflict and the lack of supervision (Wells & Rankin, 1991). Mothers of single-parent families often have more difficulty controlling their teenagers (Dornbusch et al., 1985). However, marital discord is a better predictor of delinquency than family structure (Loeber & Stouthamer-Loeber, 1986). That is, a discordant family situation, whether or not the family remains intact, is related to more teen behavior problems. Teenagers who believe that their parents know what they are doing and whom they are with are less likely to engage in criminal acts than unsupervised youths.

Individual/Peer Factors

The personality profiles of delinquents differ from their nondelinquent peers. Children with background factors related to delinquency were identified when they were in fourth grade and when these children reached 12 or 13 years, those who were delinquent were compared to those who were not. As a group the delinquents were more unempathetic, egocentric, and manipulative and had poorer impulse control (John et al., 1994). Remember that this is a comparison to others from similar backgrounds and with similar risk factors who did not become delinquent. Delinquents are impulsive, resentful, socially assertive, defiant, suspicious, and lacking in self-control; they often feel inadequate and see themselves as lazy or bad (Conger & Petersen, 1984).

Peers also model and reinforce aggressive behavior. Aggressive children and adolescents seek out peers with the same characteristics and then reinforce each other for their aggressive behavior. Gang violence is increasing and is becoming more violent (Howell, 1994).

School

Academic failure and a lack of commitment to school are also related to delinquency (Catalano & Hawkins, 1995). Delinquents show a history of school-related problems, including high rates of misbehavior and school suspension (Sprintall & Collins, 1984).

Community Factors

People can be affected by the violence they see around them. As noted earlier, many adolescents witness violence in their homes and communities, which contributes to their own violent behavior. Adolescents who become frustrated by witnessing crimes might act out their frustration by committing a violent act themselves. Angry statements, belligerent gestures, television violence, and interpersonal violence stimulate violent behaviors (Shakoor & Chalmers, 1991).

Questions Students Often Ask

I'm sick of always seeing teenagers blamed for the increase in crime. Pictures of juveniles committing crimes make all teenagers look guilty. Are adolescents responsible for the recent increase in crime?

It does seem that an entire generation is blamed for the crimes of a relative few, but some of the increase in violent crime is the result of an increase in youth crime. According to Department of Justice figures, 19% of the increase in violent crime in the United States between 1983 and 1992 was due to an increase in juvenile crime (Snyder, 1994), which means that most of the increase was caused by adults committing more crime. In addition, most arrests of teenagers are not for violent crimes. Only 6% of all juvenile arrests are for violent offenses (Allen-Hagen, Sickmund, & Snyder, 1994). However, youth crime, gang crime, and general aggression has increased.

Delinquency is not necessarily a permanent condition. Although adult criminals have a history of juvenile delinquency, most adolescents who have delinquency problems do not go on to lead lives of crime (Moffitt, 1993; 1990). The earlier the criminal behavior begins the more long lasting it is likely to be.

Protective Factors

These factors are cumulative and the greater the number that exist the more likely the child will show aggressive behavior and delinquency (Catalano & Hawkins, 1995). Yet, not all children who grow up in violent homes become violent adults (Wright & Wright, 1995). Along with risk factors, protective factors also come into play; these protective factors either reduce the impact of the risk factors, or change the manner in which the adolescent reacts to them. Many delinquency prevention programs try to enhance the protective factors.

These protective factors fall into the same four categories. Such personal characteristics as warmth, flexibility, and being socially oriented are related to less delinquency (Hawkins & Catalano, 1992). Families that are marked by greater amounts of support, affection, and supervision serve as buffers against violence. Non-aggressive peers also serve as checks, as do community programs that emphasize inclusion and school programs that enhance social and academic competence.

Can Violence Be Curbed?

Psychologists know enough about what makes a child violent to fashion effective prevention programs. Since there are many paths to violence, there are many different programs that can be successful. Some successful prevention programs attempt to improve family relationships and begin in the first 5 years (Bilchik, 1995). Programs that prevent abuse, improve parenting skills, and reduce violence in the family are very successful.

Programs that prevent academic failure and promote social competence also prevent delinquency. As we saw in Chapter 8, programs such as the Perry Preschool program are very successful in reducing later delinquency. When the social and intellectual development of children as young as 3 or 4 years old is fostered, children grow up with a greater sense of social competence. The arrest record for participants in the Perry Preschool program (see p. 184) was 7% compared to 35% for control subjects (High/Scope Educational Research Foundation, 1993).

Programs that emphasize conflict resolution and social skills training look promising (Lawton, 1994). However, they should not be seen as a one-time fix but must be a long-term and consistent part of education because students today need such skills desperately. In 1993 a Louis Harris poll found that more than half the teenagers surveyed said it was almost impossible to back off from a confrontation (Rubin, 1995). With the increasingly violent reactions of some students, yesterday's punches are more likely to take the form of a shootout today. Conflict resolution programs can help. For example, in New York City the Resolving Conflict Creatively program aims at reducing violence and promoting cooperation by offering students a special curriculum that deals with how to resolve conflicts and peer mediation. Evaluations have been positive, with teachers and administrators reporting less physical violence in the classroom (Bilchik, 1995). Other programs seek to bring the alienated teen some community attachment through community work, and combine this with parent education programs. Community programs can help by offering mentoring and coaching relationships, and structured programs focusing on social skills and alternatives to gang membership, as well as providing a safe haven in the community for youngsters. They teach social and communication skills, goal setting, nurture interests, and give recognition for good work (Carnegie Council, 1994). Evidence shows that community youth programs promote constructive behavior, reduce high-risk behavior, and help reduce feelings of isolation and alienation; unfortunately, few American communities have such programs

Questions Students Often Ask

Psychologists seem to want to coddle criminals. I think we need tougher enforcement of laws to make people, including adolescents, pay for their crimes with jail time. Why are psychologists so soft on crime?

You'll get no argument from me on the need to catch and punish criminals. But that is only one part of crime prevention. Unfortunately, whenever people talk about prevention, they are seen as being "soft on crime." Violent offenders should be caught and punished. People should understand that there are consequences to their behavior. However, the overwhelming majority of teen arrests are not for violent crimes and even for some teens who are arrested for such crimes, violence may not be a way of life. We must find ways to reduce aggression and property crimes without sending everyone to expensive prisons. Once the offender completes serving his sentence, programs to reduce recidivism should be enforced. These may include job training. Prevention of crime through programs such as those described in this book is good policy. If interventions can help turn a child who is aggressive into an upright member of the community, the investment is worth it, especially since the cost of prevention is so much lower than the cost of punishment.

Other programs emphasize family intervention for improving behavior management and promoting family cohesion. Delinquents usually have negative interpersonal relationships with others, including family members. Some programs hope to reduce these negative interactions by teaching the parties better ways to interact (Henggeler et al., 1986). Others have tried to alter the cognitive and social skills of these troubled youth by teaching them to interpret social situations differently (Guerra & Slaby, 1990).

The National Atmosphere

It is common to hear public officials blame the film and the music industry for glorifying violence. Whether or not the media causes the problem, it certainly reinforces the theme of violence. However, some professionals are now seeking to use Hollywood in order to show a different way to approach teen problems. For example, the Center for Health Communications of Harvard University works with entertainment professionals on such shows as *Beverly Hills 90210, Family Matters,* and others to use scripts on responsible ways to deal with violence, eating disorders, and smoking without preaching. Antiviolence themes are created and alternatives to violence are shown (Rubin, 1995).

Public awareness combined with attempts to prevent and deal with violence are beginning to have an effect; evidence shows that some progress is being made, but more needs to be done (Portner, 1996).

Exploding the Myths

The popular belief that adolescents give up their dependence on their parents and form a total dependence on their peers is incorrect. The commonly held belief that parents' relationships with their adolescents are uniformly poor must also be reevaluated in view of recent research.

During adolescence young people are faced with important decisions in every area of life. A great deal has recently been written about moral education and the nature of personal choices. As we have seen, parents need not abdicate their special relationship with their children during this stage. Supervision and guidance are part of a parent's responsibilities, but so is preparation for independent adulthood. Constant criticism, harsh punishment, and strict warnings are often ineffective, especially if they occur in a cold, hostile environment. Adolescents are affected most by what they see and experience—and communication is extremely important.

As Haim Ginott said, "Character traits cannot be taught directly: no one can teach loyalty by lectures, courage by correspondence, or manhood by mail. Character education requires presence that demonstrates and contact that communicates. A teenager learns what he lives, and becomes what he experiences. To him, our mood is the message, the style is the substance, the process is the product" (1969, p. 243).

Summary

1. Erik Erikson viewed the formation of a personal identity as the positive outcome of adolescence. Role confusion—failure to answer the fundamental questions of identity—is the negative outcome of the stage.
2. James Marcia extended Erikson's conception of identity to include four identity statuses. Identity diffusion is a status in which a person has not begun to make any commitments. This status is considered negative only when an individual leaves adolescence without making reasonable progress toward finding an identity. Identity foreclosure is a status in which a person has made commitments prematurely. Identity moratorium is a temporary status in which an individual is not ready to make commitments but may be exploring possibilities. Identity achievers have gone through their crises and made their commitments. People who are identity achievers are generally more ready to form intimate relationships.
3. Males and females may take different paths to identity formation. Males focus on intrapersonal factors, while women tend to tie their identities to interpersonal relationships. This is changing, however, as many women now seek to balance a career with family responsibilities.
4. Peer influence increases in adolescence but does not replace that of parents. Most adolescents have good relationships with their parents. The period of adolescence is best seen as a time when children renegotiate their relationship with parents.
5. Parents are more likely to be directive, to want to share their wisdom, and to explain their views than to listen to the opinions of their teens. Peer communication shows more give-and-take.
6. Junior high school was established to ease the transition to high school and to provide for the rapidly changing social needs of young adolescents. Most children adapt well to the transition. Junior high has been criticized for not providing students with an adequate educational experience.
7. High school academic work is becoming more rigorous, and students are now taking minimum competency tests.
8. Most high school dropouts have average intelligence scores, but lack academic skills, have little interest in school, and show a history of school-related problems. They are more likely to come from poor, large families or families in which there is discord and divorce.
9. The choice of a vocation affects one's entire lifestyle. For many women and minority group youths, vocational choice is limited. However, women have made progress entering male-dominated occupations and more minorities are entering the professions. Many minority adolescents do not have high vocational aspirations, lack adequate role models, and find their choices limited by lack of academic skills and economic resources or by discrimination. These youths are less likely to believe that they have the power to influence their own futures.
10. Drug use among teenagers has increased significantly since the early 1990s and adolescents are using drugs at an earlier age. Teens also have less knowledge of the consequences of drug use than years ago. Some individual characteristics, such as undercontrolled and antisocial behavior, troubled family relationships and peers who reinforce and model drug taking can increase the risk of drug abuse. Drug education must give the facts but also build drug resistance skills.
11. Violence is a national concern. Factors that influence violence include personality characteristics such as poor impulse control, parental behaviors such as parental rejection, and peer reinforcement and models. Some violence prevention programs appear to be successful. Children who are rejected by parents or grow up in conflict-ridden homes and are unsupervised are more likely to become delinquents.

Multiple-Choice Questions

1. G. Stanley Hall perceived adolescence as a time of:
   a. compromise.
   b. increased belief in spirituality.
   c. storm and stress.
   d. all of the above.
2. Which statement about depressive symptoms in adolescence is *correct?*
   a. Girls show more depressive symptoms than boys.
   b. Adolescent girls seem to react to stress more negatively than adolescent boys.
   c. Boys show more depressive symptoms in childhood than girls.
   d. All of these statements are correct.
3. After considering many alternatives, Taneesha decided to become an engineer and is now enrolled in an electrical engineering program. This is an example of a:
   a. crisis.
   b. career expansion.
   c. commitment.
   d. compensation.
4. Tina does not believe she controls her life, distrusts others, and finds it difficult to plan ahead. She actively avoids commitment of any kind. She would probably be placed in Marcia's identity status of:
   a. moratorium.
   b. secured.
   c. foreclosed.
   d. diffused.
5. Wyatt is now actively evaluating his religious beliefs but has come to no conclusion yet. He feels uncomfortable and often finds himself thinking about the meaning of life. He would most probably be placed in which of Marcia's identity statuses?
   a. achiever.
   b. moratorium.
   c. foreclosed.
   d. disposed.
6. Joseph claims that people who are aggressive seek out others who are aggressive and are reinforced for being aggressive by their friends. According to research, Joseph is:
   a. correct.
   b. correct that they seek out aggressive friends, but they do not really reinforce each other for aggression.
   c. correct that they reinforce each other for aggression, but they do not especially seek out aggressive adolescents.
   d. incorrect in everything he said.
7. Children from homes in which parents use which of the following child-rearing strategies show the best achievement and psychological development?
   a. authoritative.
   b. indulgent.
   c. authoritarian.
   d. industrious.
8. Which statement about parent and peer relationships is *incorrect?*
   a. Parents try to control their adolescents' behavior more than peers do.
   b. Parent communication is more directive and shows less mutuality than communication between peers.
   c. Parents have more rules for their younger adolescents than for their older adolescents.
   d. Parents are more uncomfortable with their roles when their adolescents are in early adolescence than when they are in late adolescence.
9. Many students in junior high school complain:
   a. that the work is so much harder than in elementary school.
   b. about the lack of discipline in the classroom.
   c. that they have too many decisions to make.
   d. that their teachers don't know who they are.
10. Steinberg and colleagues' recent analysis of American high school students emphasized:
    a. the importance of curriculum changes.
    b. a peer culture that does not reinforce achievement.
    c. the fact that parents are more involved in school-related issues than ever before.
    d. the importance of vocational information given earlier in the student's high school career.
11. Which of the following statements about dropping out of high school is *correct?*
    a. Latinos have a higher dropout rate than African Americans or whites.
    b. Most high school dropouts have long histories of school-related difficulties.
    c. The African American dropout rate has been substantially reduced.
    d. All of the above are correct.
12. Which of the following statements about women and careers is correct?
    a. Women are still overrepresented in clerical and service positions.
    b. Women comprise the large majority in some professional fields, such as elementary school teachers and librarians.
    c. The percentage of women entering what were once male-dominated fields like law and medicine has increased significantly.
    d. All of the above are correct.
13. Your friend says that adolescents from poor backgrounds go through the same process of vocational choice as middle-class adolescents. According to research, your friend is:
    a. correct.
    b. incorrect, because adolescents living in poverty have less knowledge of occupations.
    c. incorrect, because adolescents living in poverty

have little or no motivation to enter the world of work.

d. incorrect, because adolescents living in poverty actually have a greater belief in their ability to influence their future work lives than middle class adolescents.

14. The prevalence of drug use between 1991 and 1995 shows:
   a. an increase.
   b. a decrease.
   c. about the same amount of use.
   d. an increase for most drugs but a decrease for heroin and alcohol.
15. When the smoking patterns of seniors in high school are compared with those of adults:
   a. seniors are more likely to smoke.
   b. seniors are a little less likely to smoke.
   c. seniors are much less likely to smoke.
   d. about the same percentage of seniors smoke as adults.
16. You are studying the perception of adolescents as to how many of their peers take drugs. If your study is similar to others in the field, you will find teenagers:
   a. very accurate in their estimates.
   b. tend to underestimate the levels of peer drug use.
   c. overestimate the levels of peer drug use.
   d. underestimate the amount of marijuana use but overestimate the amount of alcohol use.
17. The fact that teens of a generation ago know more about drugs than teens today is known as:
   a. the generative response.
   b. generational experience.
   c. motivated forgetting.
   d. generational forgetting.
18. The fact that delinquent behavior is more likely to occur in single-parent families than intact families is probably due to:
   a. lack of supervision.
   b. lack of love.
   c. inability to communicate.
   d. parental feelings of inadequacy.
19. Which of the following characteristics would you *not* expect to find in the personality of delinquents?
   a. a tendency to be manipulative.
   b. egocentrism.
   c. lack of empathy.
   d. high impulse control.
20. Which statement does *not* seem to fit a description of the homes that produce delinquents?
   a. The parents of delinquents are often cold and unloving.
   b. The homes that produce delinquents often have a strict family routine.
   c. The parents of delinquents are often very critical.
   d. The parents of delinquents often are inconsistent in their attempts to discipline.

Answers to Multiple-Choice Questions

1. c 2. d 3. c 4. d 5. b 6. a 7. a 8. d 9. d
10. b 11. d 12. d 13. b 14. a 15. a 16. c 17. d
18. a 19. d 20. b

Chapter 14

Physical and Cognitive Development in Early Adulthood

Chapter Outline

Adulthood: Paths, Choices, and Developmental Periods
Generation X
Physical Development in Early Adulthood
Stress in Early Adulthood
Cognitive Functioning in Early Adulthood
Morals and Ethics in Early Adulthood
Our Pluralistic Society: Americans With Disabilities—Quiet No More
Choices and Pathways

Are the Following Statements True or False?

1. Today's young adults are more dissatisfied with their lives than their elders.
2. Women are less likely to rate their health as "excellent" in early adulthood than are men.
3. Early adult men are more likely to perceive themselves as overweight than early adult women.
4. The present generation of young adults is eating a healthier diet than the last generation of young adults.
5. Brisk, regular walking can reduce the chances of an individual developing heart disease.
6. Most of the people who quit smoking cigarettes are early adults.
7. The majority of all the people with AIDS are between the ages of 20 and 40 years.
8. Young adulthood is the least stressful stage of adult life.
9. Early adults tend to look at problems in a more abstract, theoretical manner than adolescents do.
10. Most adults say that they believe in God.

Answers to True-False Statements 1. False: see p. 317 2. True 3. False: see p. 319 4. True 5. True 6. False: see p. 321 7. True 8. False: see p. 325 9. False: see p. 327 10. True

Adulthood: Paths, Choices, and Developmental Periods

In what ways do the developmental changes and tasks of adulthood differ from those of childhood? Just as children and adolescents face tasks that are identifiable and predictable, so do adults. Adults face challenges in areas such as marriage, raising a family, work, and creating an independent life structure that are fundamentally different from those faced by children.

Developmental changes in adulthood also tend to be more gradual than changes in childhood. As you look at photographs of yourself as a child, you can easily guess your age. During childhood, changes in physical appearance and abilities happen at a quicker pace and are much more noticeable. Changes in adulthood are more gradual and hardly noticed from day to day, from month to month, and often from year to year.

In addition, the developmental periods that precede adulthood—infancy, toddlerhood, early childhood, middle childhood, and adolescence—have fairly well defined points of entry and, for each except adolescence, exit. Infancy ends at 1 year when the child can walk; middle childhood begins when the child enters elementary school. The boundaries in adulthood are less clear. It is difficult to determine just when someone enters or leaves early adulthood.

Perhaps the most important difference is that adults have many more paths and choices they can take. An adult can choose whether to marry, to have children, where to live, which job to take, when to leave one job for another, and whether to remain in a marriage. Children are told to go to school, when to go to bed, and are allowed to make relatively few decisions on their own.

Generation X

Today's early adults are members of a cohort, often referred to as *Generation X,* which includes people born approximately between 1965 and 1977 (Zill & Robinson, 1995). They are, by far, the most maligned cohort of the last century.

This group of young adults was seen as disillusioned, alienated, apathetic, and aimless (Meredith & Schewe, 1994; Sommerfeld, 1995). Baby boomers, the generation now entering and negotiating middle age, often perceived them as a generation of whiners, always complaining and unhappy (McCarthy, 1994; Zill & Robinson, 1995). Many young adults disapprove of and refuse to identify themselves as members of Generation X (Russell & Mitchell, 1995). Lately, this unflattering portrait has given way to a more thoughtful and research-based analysis. The picture that emerges is of a generation with some differences from their parents, the baby-boom generation born between 1946 and 1964, but not as different as early analysts believed.

Questions Students Often Ask

I dislike the whole concept of Generation X. Even its name is demeaning. Why can't we get rid of the label?

I agree with you. It is a poor name for a generation, but until someone with clout comes along to change it, we are stuck with it. Some baby boomers don't like their generation's label either. The label isn't as important as the negative attitudes it implies. These attitudes are clearly changing, and research shows that they are either untrue or overly simplistic. Despite the challenges, especially the economic challenges, that young adults must meet, people of this generation have better relationships with their parents and achieve a more reasonable balance between work, family, and leisure than the previous generation.

Some of the adjectives used to describe Generation X are just plain wrong. For example, younger workers are not overly dissatisfied with their jobs. Although some polls find them a bit more dissatisfied with their jobs than other groups (American Enterprise Institute, 1994), one recent poll of employees of major corporations found that workers under the age of 30 were more satisfied with their jobs than any other age group, and showed more confidence in their companies than their baby-boomer parents (Carson, 1995).

These young people are definitely not apathetic or uninvolved. Reports from nonprofit organizations across the nation show early adults volunteering for meaningful community service in increasing numbers (Sommerfeld, 1995). Many college freshmen, about 60%, perform some community work and many continue to do so throughout their college years (McCarthy, 1994). This may indicate a return to idealism, although it is not the political activism of the 1960s (Sommerfeld, 1995).

A series of polls find that the attitudes of Generation X on many subjects are very similar to those held by other generations (American Enterprise Institute, 1994). They are no more dissatisfied with their lives than their elders. They are actually less dissatisfied with the way things are going in the United States at this time, and do not differ significantly from their elders in their confidence in government. They do not differ appreciably from the older generations on most questions about government spending, except that they favor more spending on environmental issues. They are somewhat more likely than their elders to believe that people get ahead based on hard work, and are as committed to working hard as their elders.

True or False?
Today's young adults are more dissatisfied with their lives than their elders.

People in *all* age groups see the economy as shaky; 80% of Americans between 18 and 29 years see it that way, the same percentage as those over age 60, while 83% of their parents believe that the economy is not very strong. This generation has embraced social change, for example, the changes in women's roles, and very few believe that a woman's place is in the home. This generation is more sensitive to the way others feel and more accepting of other points of view (Ritchie, 1995). They appreciate diversity, whether it is defined by ethnicity or sexual preference (Ritchie, 1995). This generation has grown up with technology and is very comfortable with it. They see cellular phones, computers, fax machines, and e-mail as essential parts of their lives (Ritchie, 1995).

The generation is more conservative than early adults in the previous generation. This is especially true for the men (American Enterprise Institute, 1994). Despite this conservatism, they are less likely than other age groups to believe that there is too much government regulation of business. They are also more likely to argue that government should be active in solving problems, and are in favor of a wide variety of government services.

Early adults of Generation X are more likely to have experienced the divorce of their parents than previous generations. Even those who were raised in intact families probably know others in the family or friends whose parents divorced. More than 40% of all young adults spent some time in a single-parent family by the age of 16 (Zill & Robinson, 1995). They are more likely than previous generations to have extended families, including stepparents and stepsiblings; they are also more fearful and cynical of intimacy and marriage.

Their economic situation is also different from what their parents faced as early adults. Generation Xers witnessed the success of their own parents in an expanding economy, but now face more financial problems than their parents did. Economic trends such as global competition and the loss of high-paying manufacturing jobs has caused this generation's earnings to drop relative to those of the previous generation. Every generation in the past believed that it would do better than its parents; early adults in this generation will have difficulty doing so, and they know it (Zill & Robinson, 1995).

Today's young adults are less confident of their jobs, incomes, and relationships (Zill & Robinson, 1995). This insecurity may be caused by the rapid changes they experienced in family structure as well as the present economic uncertainties and is an understandable reaction to their experience.

Early commentators argued that Generation X blamed the older generation for its problems. If that is so, it hasn't affected the relationship between Generation X early adults and their baby-boomer parents, which is somewhat better than the relationship was for the baby boomers. This is especially true for those whose parents have remained married (Zill & Robinson, 1995). In one survey 51% of all early adults said that they admire their parents more than anyone else, and 29% described their mother or father as "my best friend" (Ritchie, 1995). They like the same classic rock and roll music as their parents and feel some obligation to their parents for all they have done for them; there is no evidence of general resentment among Generation X.

It is good that they get along fairly well with their parents for they are staying much longer with their parents before going out on their own. The proportion of women in their 20s living in their parents' home rose from 17% in 1977 to 24% in 1993, and for young men from 30% to 35%. Late marriage and the high cost of housing are the major reasons for their inability to move out of their parents' homes (Zill & Robinson, 1995).

Despite the fact that Generation Xers are less likely to read literature for enjoyment or even newspapers for information, they strongly believe in the importance of education (Zill & Robinson, 1995; National Enterprise Institute, 1994). They recognize the importance of continuing their education. They are much more likely to visit art museums and to appreciate the visual arts (Zill & Robinson, 1995).

Finally, early adults are more open in their desire to balance job, family life, and leisure than baby boomers (Ritchie, 1995). Women in Generation X want to continue working, but place more importance on home and family life than their baby boomer parents did. The older generation of women who made sacrifices, broke stereotypes, and conquered barriers in the workplace may see Generation X women as unappreciative of their role as pathfinders.

What is the future of Generation X? They have real reason for optimism, despite the belt-tightening in industry and their experiences in relationships. Since they are getting married later and having children when they are older, their marriages may be somewhat more stable than those of their parents (Ritchie, 1995) and they may be pleasantly surprised when they succeed in the workplace. Despite their present economic problems they do not seem unhappy with their jobs. This is the first generation to be smaller than the preceding one and they are likely to have more opportunities for advancement as they age (Carson, 1995).

Physical Development in Early Adulthood

Most young adults are healthy (Table 14.1). When asked to rate their own health, the overwhelming majority say they are either in "excellent" or "very good" health. Early adult women are somewhat less likely to rate their health as "excellent," but are just as likely to say they are in very good health (Statistical Bulletin, 1993).

True or False?
Women are less likely to rate their health as "excellent" in early adulthood than are men.

Young adults don't get sick very often, and when they do, they bounce back quickly. In the United States fewer than 10% of adults between ages 18 and 44 have a chronic disease, such as diabetes, heart disease, or cancer, compared with 85% of those over 65 years (George, 1996; Troll, 1985).

The death rate is also much lower for early adults than for older groups. Accidents and AIDS are the leading causes of death (USDHEW, 1995). Some recent figures show that AIDS has just overtaken accidents as the leading cause of death in all Americans ages 25 to 44 (MMWR, 1995). The death rate throughout young adulthood is higher for males than for females.

Height and Weight

According to one viewpoint the average male reaches his adult height at 21.2 years and the average female reaches her adult height at 17.3 years (Roche & Davila, 1972), another argues that people continue to grow in their 20s, reaching their adult height somewhere in their mid-20s (Troll, 1985). Although these increases in height are trivial, the average person's increase in weight in young adulthood can become a problem.

Adults continue to gain weight until about age 55, after which progressive weight loss seems to be the rule (Troll, 1985). The weight gains in adulthood are greatest between the ages of 25 and 35, and those who are already somewhat overweight gain the most weight. Many adults have sedentary jobs, which contributes to a reduction in physical activity. Unless caloric intake is reduced, a gain in weight may occur (Newman, 1982). In addition, as people age and become less active, the amount of muscle tissue decreases, and bone tissue becomes less dense. People who were lean and muscular in their 20s may weigh the same at the age of 40 and yet appear much fatter (Whitney, Cataldo, & Rolfes, 1994). Fat may be distributed differently as people age, causing people to appear heavier.

This gradual weight gain in early adulthood is unfortunate because being overweight is related to many diseases including heart disease, hypertension, and diabetes. As soon as young adults see their weight edging up it is time to battle it (Hellmich, 1994). Many adults are concerned about their weight gain and the most popular method of weight loss is consuming fewer calories (Serdula et al., 1994). In every age group women are much more likely than men to consider themselves overweight.

Table 14.1 **Self-Reported Health Evaluations by Age and Sex, U.S. Adults, 1990**

	TOTAL			18–24		25–44		45–64		65 & over	
Characteristic	Both Sexes	Men	Women	Men	Women	Men	Women	Men	Women	Men	Women
Health Status	100.0	100.0	100.0	100.0	100.0	100.0	100.0	100.0	100.0	100.0	100.0
Excellent	34.8	38.6	31.4	50.2	38.6	44.9	38.4	32.0	26.5	18.9	16.2
Very Good	29.2	28.7	29.6	28.7	34.4	31.3	32.2	26.8	26.7	23.8	24.1
Good	24.8	22.7	26.8	18.8	22.1	18.6	22.8	26.6	30.8	32.3	34.1
Fair	8.2	7.1	9.2	1.9	4.3	4.0	5.4	9.8	11.3	17.4	18.6
Poor	3.0	2.9	3.0	0.4	0.6	1.2	1.2	4.8	4.7	7.6	7.0

Source: NCHS, 1990 Health Promotion and Disease Prevention supplemental survey to National Health Interview Survey. Reported estimates, analyses and computations by the Health and Safety Education Division, MetLife.

True or False?
Early adult men are more likely to perceive themselves as overweight than early adult women.

Health Concerns

Adults today are more concerned about what they eat, how they exercise, and what they weigh than in the recent past (Niknian, Lefebvre, & Carleton, 1991). More people believe that it is possible to prevent cardiovascular disease and know their own blood pressure, have their cholesterol measured, and exercise more regularly than in the past (Garrity et al., 1990). Many life changes occur during early adulthood, including becoming a spouse, a full-time worker, and a parent; these changes may cause changes in sleeping, eating, and exercise patterns. The active adolescent may find that he or she is now sitting at a desk all day. A person who used to sleep very well at night may find that he or she must wake up during the night to care for a baby. Habits formed in early adulthood can cause problems later on. For instance, the most consistent predictors of cardiovascular problems in middle age are blood pressure, serum cholesterol, and smoking, all of which are the result of habits that appear in young adulthood and perhaps even earlier (Garrity et al., 1990).

Diet

The diets of young adults have changed and generally for the better (Popkin, Siega-Riz, & Haines, 1996). Adults pay more attention to their diet than in the past and consume less saturated fats, salt, and sugar. High intake of fat and low intake of fruits and vegetables is associated with the development of a number of chronic conditions, including obesity, cardiovascular diseases, and even some cancers (Hunt et al., 1995). Doctors commonly advocate that their patients decrease their calorie intake, consume less fat, red meat, cholesterol, eggs, and dairy products and increase their consumption of vegetables, fruits, fiber, and fish. However, despite the improvement in diet, many adults do not consume enough of these healthy foods. About half the adult population consumes no fruit or fruit juice daily, and about one in five does not eat vegetables on a daily basis. Less than 30% of the adult population consumes the recommended daily intake for fruits and vegetables (Patterson et al., 1990).

True or False?
The present generation of young adults is eating a healthier diet than the last generation of young adults.

Many factors influence diet, including culture and upbringing. For example, low-income Mexican American women's dietary practices may partially protect them against lung and breast cancer. However, with acculturation into American society, their food habits change and their rates of these diseases begin to approach those of the general population. Alcohol and tobacco use increases and corn tortillas are replaced by bread. The diet of second-generation Mexican American women of childbearing age is much worse than that of their mothers. When data on consumption of eight nutrients was surveyed, first-generation women consumed more vitamins A and C, folic acid, calcium, and protein than second-generation poor Mexican American women or a group of white women (Guendelman & Abrams, 1995).

Questions Students Often Ask

One doctor says this, another says that. One "expert" on nutrition recommends this, another recommends that. I don't know what to believe.

You're right that all these announcements are confusing. Many amateurs make overly general or overly optimistic statements. But you are wrong if you think that scientists don't agree on some general aspects of health. For example, the need to exercise, to reduce fat in the diet, and to stop smoking cigarettes are found in most of the studies. This is not to say that people who smoke, don't exercise, and eat a high-fat diet have no chance of living long lives, just that they lower the chances through their health habits. Those who eat a healthy diet, exercise, and don't smoke have a better chance of living a longer life. There are no guarantees, only probabilities.

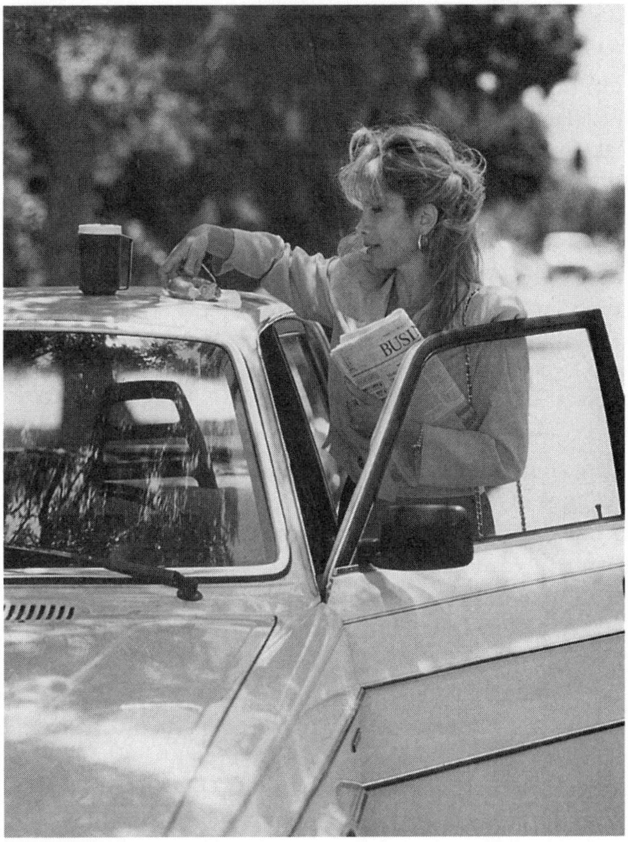

Young adulthood is a time of stress and some young adults do not take the time to eat properly.

The American public is faced with having to make sense of the many findings that bombard them daily. Just look at the supermarket tabloids and listen to some of the pronouncements made on television. Some celebrity is always telling people of the amazing diet that allowed him or her to lose 15 pounds in 2 days and enabled the person to live a truly meaningful, more spiritual life and almost win the Boston Marathon (Marshall, 1995). Together with premature announcements from experts, many people are confused. Most of the changes advised by experts in the field, involve an increase in the consumption of vegetables and fruit, a shift from animal- to a plant-based diet to decrease obesity and high blood pressure, and reduce the incidence of diabetes, heart disease, and some cancers. However, more controlled research is necessary to establish the effects of changing diet on health.

Exercise and Health

Every health-related study of adults emphasizes the importance of exercise. Exercise that requires increased oxygen consumption, called *aerobic exercise*—including brisk walking, jogging, bicycling, and swimming—is the best. For maximum advantage exercise should be performed regularly (at least four times a week), be sustained, and exercise the heart (Diekelmann, 1977); a Sunday-morning jogger or a Wednesday-evening bowler will not receive the greatest benefits.

The regular exerciser can achieve the same cardiac output with a lower heart rate (Strand, 1983), and the heart and circulatory systems do not have to work as hard during more vigorous activity. Research shows that regular exercise plays a part in preventing cardiovascular disease (Curfman, Gregory, & Paffenbarger, 1985), and physical inactivity is linked to increased mortality and a variety of diseases, including cardiovascular disease, diabetes, and even certain forms of cancer (Schechtman et al., 1991). Physically active people live longer than those who are not (Paffenbarger et al., 1993). Even adjusting for obesity and hypertension, a sedentary lifestyle is related to cardiac disease and mortality (Yaeger et al., 1995).

Exercise also burns up calories and can improve one's appearance. Regular exercise can lead to an increase in feelings of well-being, and exercises such as running and weight lifting have been found to improve the self-concept of depressed people (Ossip-Klein et al., 1989). Exercise reduces anxiety and tension (DeVaney & Hughey, & Osborne, 1994) and most people who exercise cite health as their main motivation (Leepson, 1992).

The idea that one has to actually suffer to gain from exercise is false, and may have discouraged many sedentary people from exercising (Siegel, Brackbill, & Heath, 1995). Although aerobic exercises are beneficial, only between 10% and 22% of all adults exercise at that level (Leepson, 1992; USDHHS, 1991). However, even a moderate amount of exercise can help to ward off heart disease and other chronic diseases (Blair et al., 1989; Manson & Lee, 1996). The benefits of moderate exercise, including walking for pleasure, gardening, yard work, housework, and dancing, are considerable (Leepson, 1992).

Exercise should be considered in terms of movement and strength improvement. According to medical evidence, to prevent heart problems later in life most people need to incorporate exercise into their leisure activities. One study of college alumni found that leisure activities that burn up at least 2000 calories a week were effective in reducing one's chances of having a heart attack (Paffenbarger et. al, 1978). This is equal to 1 hour of fast walking at 4 miles an hour each day or 30 minutes of jogging a day. However, other combinations—which include stair climbing, cycling, and swimming—are also effective. Even low-level activities, such as regular walking and gardening, offer some protection, but only if they are done regularly (Curfman et al., 1985; Manson & Lee, 1996). More vigorous activities probably confer additional protection, and activities using up 7.5 calories a minute—such as cycling, swimming, and running—are ideal (Morris et al., 1980). Building muscles is also important because people often lose some muscle strength as they age.

True or False?

Brisk, regular walking can reduce the chances of an individual developing heart disease.

Walking and slow jogging are the most popular forms of exercise for adults. They are the easiest, safest, and least expensive kinds of exercise and put little stress on the body, certainly much less than running. For example, the legs of a runner or high-impact aerobicizer absorb the impact of more than four times the body's weight as compared with just two and a half times the body weight for walkers (Leepson, 1992). Generally, the higher the individual's income and education level the more likely he or she is to exercise. The exception is walking, which is practiced almost equally by people with low and high incomes. Even adults who are sedentary, obese, or have health problems and are usually less likely to exercise are willing to walk (Siegel, Brackbill, & Heath, 1995). Of all the adults who claimed to be involved in some physical exercise during the past month, about half were walkers.

The evidence showing that increased activity equaling 2000 calories a week can help prevent later heart attacks is important. Simple changes in lifestyle can be a start. For instance, since walking uses about 3 to 7 calories a minute, a person walking briskly might consume an average of 5 calories a minute for 30 minutes, expending 150 calories, compared with only 45 calories used up while sitting in an auto. Climbing stairs consumes about 11 calories a minute, and a person who climbs twenty flights of stairs a day can burn about 50 calories. This

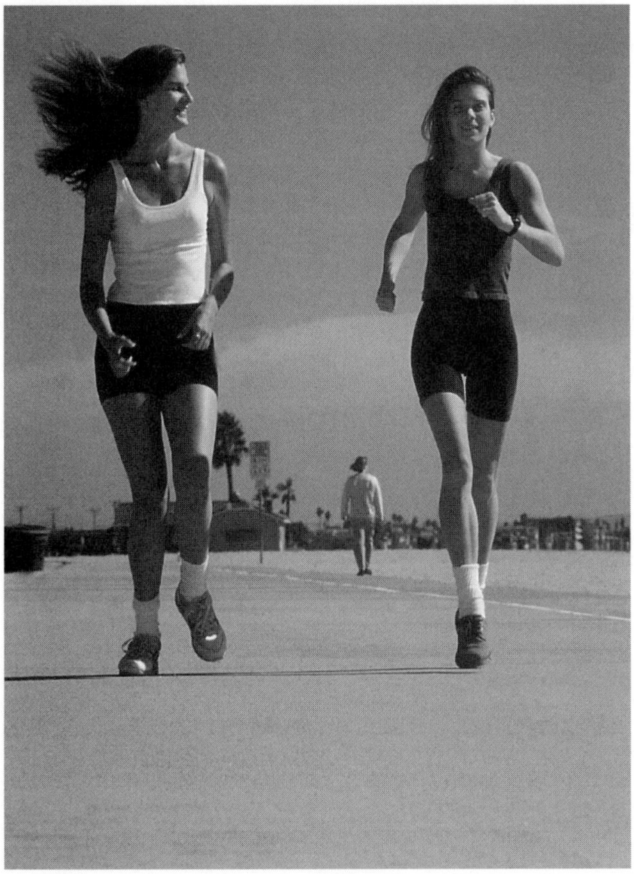
Young adults must build physical exercise into their busy schedules.

may contribute to the amount needed to reduce heart problems. Before beginning an exercise program, adults should consult their doctor and have a physical examination.

One definite concern is the percentage of people who start a program and then discontinue it. Many exercise programs have a dropout rate more than 50% during the first few months. Higher rates of continuous participation are possible with encouragement (Lombard, Lombard, & Winett, 1995). Some companies form exercise groups as a way to encourage physical activity. Simple strategies such as prompting with a telephone call once in a while can be effective.

Healthy behaviors such as exercise and good nutrition often are found together and behaviors such as smoking, lack of exercise, and poor nutrition that lead to poor health often coexist. There is a strong and inverse relationship between physical activity and fat consumption: those who are not very physically active tend to eat the most fat and those who are more active eat the least (Simoes et al., 1995). Physical inactivity is more common among smokers.

Drug Use

A sharp decrease in drug use occurs in early adulthood (Chen & Kandel, 1995; Frank, Jacobson, & Tuer, 1990), but this is not true for cigarette smoking. People who smoked in adolescence on a daily basis tend to continue the habit into early adulthood. The proportion of daily users of alcohol and marijuana declines greatly in early adulthood. Almost no initiation into drinking alcohol, or smoking cigarettes, or using illegal drugs occurs after age 29, probably because of the added responsibility of marriage and family life, an increased awareness of the dangers of drinking and driving, and the trend toward a healthier lifestyle. A cohort-related reduction in alcohol consumption occurred among young adults between 1981 and 1991 (Johnson et al., 1995)—that is, in 1991 early adults were drinking less than early adults did in 1981.

Although cigarette smoking has decreased during the past 30 years, about a third of all young adults still smoke (Statistical Abstract, 1996). The decline in men's smoking has been much greater than the decline in women's smoking; if this trend continues, smoking prevalence among adult women will be greater than among men. Smoking prevalence is lower among people with a high school or greater education, regardless of ethnicity (Escobedo & Peddicord, 1996). Most of the general decline in cigarette smoking is achieved by the greater number of people quitting, although some decline in the initiation rate has occurred (Breslau & Peterson, 1996; Pierce et al., 1989). Some young adults quit when they get married or become parents or are employed in companies that do not allow smoking, but quitting is greater among middle-aged adults than young adults. Those over 40 years of age are more likely to quit than younger smokers, probably because they are more aware of smoking-related illnesses with advancing age (Cohen et al., 1989). Light smokers and those who began after age 17 are more likely to quit than heavy smokers or those who began early in adolescence (Escobedo & Peddicord, 1996; Hajek, West, & Wilson, 1995). The strongest predictor of smoking cessation is level of education. Those who complete college are much more likely to quit than those with no college education, perhaps because they are more likely to find themselves in environments in which smoking is frowned upon. College-bound students are much less likely to smoke as well (Johnston, O'Malley, & Bachman, 1993). These same trends are reported in Canada, the United Kingdom, Norway and Sweden (Pierce, 1989).

True or False?
Most of the people who quit smoking cigarettes are early adults.

There are also dangers from breathing in smoke from cigarettes, called *passive* or *secondary smoking.* When healthy subjects between the ages of 15 and 30 who had never smoked but had been exposed to smoke on a regular basis were compared to a similar group who had not smoked and to a group of smokers, changes in the arteries considered early predictors of cardiac problems were found in both the passive and the active smokers (Celermajer et al., 1996).

The decrease in the prevalence in smoking over the last few decades is the result of the public's growing belief that smoking is a health risk; to the modern emphasis on a healthier lifestyle; and even perhaps to the increasing militancy of the nonsmoking population, which discourages smoking in its presence. Many workplaces now ban smoking, and where smoking is banned, smokers report a reduction in consumption of over 25% (Borland et al., 1990). People are trying to stop on their own and community encouragement may be helpful (Lando et al., 1995).

AIDS

No disease in the past 100 years has had the shocking effect that acquired immune deficiency syndrome (AIDS) has had on the American public in the past several years. AIDS is caused by the human immunodeficiency virus (HIV) that cripples the body's natural defenses, leaving the body vulnerable to opportunistic diseases that healthy bodies fight easily. The fear of AIDS is prevalent in our society (Mariner, 1995). The most common age group affected are early adults; males between 20 and 40 years comprise 80% of those diagnosed with AIDS (Statistical Abstract, 1996). More than a million and a half people in the United States carry the AIDS virus but do not meet the definition for AIDS. The World Health Organization estimates that by the end of 1994 there were about 5 million AIDS cases worldwide and the number is expected to increase (Stine, 1996).

> ***True or False?***
> The majority of all the people with AIDS are between the ages of 20 and 40 years.

Symptoms of AIDS include unexplained weight loss, oral thrush (an infection of the tongue and mouth), persistent diarrhea, coughing or shortness of breath, skin rashes and spots, bruising and bleeding, and severe fatigue (Gong, 1985a). Even if an individual is not showing the symptoms, he or she may be carrying the virus and may transmit it to others.

AIDS is transmitted through contact with infected blood and other body fluids (Fisher, Fisher & Rye, 1995), and is often transmitted through sexual intercourse. Although sexual transmission of the disease during homosexual intercourse is most common, the proportion of HIV acquired through heterosexual contact has increased greatly in the United States from 2.3% of all cases in 1983 to 9% in 1993 (Stine, 1996). The well-publicized case of Earvin "Magic" Johnson, who tested positive for HIV, brought this point very suddenly to the attention of the public (Woodard, 1992). The case of Tommy Morrison, a prizefighter whose HIV-positive status was discovered just hours before a fight in Las Vegas, led to many states requiring that all fighters be tested for HIV. Heterosexual transmission continues to increase in the United States and risky behaviors are common. Almost as many adults report engaging in high-risk sexual activity as report taking risk reduction measures (Catania et al., 1995). Many individuals, particularly men and singles, report multiple partners. Condom use, which offers some protection against AIDS, has increased somewhat but is still inconsistent. Heterosexuals with a history of risky behaviors rarely obtain testing prior to cohabitation or marriage and do not use condoms consistently with their primary sex partner (Catania et al., 1995). Only between 8% and 19% of married people having extramarital affairs use condoms (Choi, Catania, & Dolcini, 1994).

Although AIDS is found in every strata of society, some groups, such as gay men, are at greater risk than others (Fisher et al., 1995). In 1981 all reported cases of AIDS were in gay men; in 1993 46% of all cases were in this group. An increase in the percentage of intravenous drug users and heterosexuals as well as educational programs targeted towards the gay community explains the change in figures. Unfortunately, some evidence shows that younger gay men are not adopting safer sexual behaviors to the same extent as older gay men, and some relapse into unsafe behavior is occurring (Hays, 1992; Lemp et al, 1994). AIDS education programs and vigilance must continue.

Intravenous drug users are obviously another group at risk, and as many as one-third of all the intravenous drug users may be HIV positive. The AIDS virus is spread as intravenous drug users share needles, making it possible for infected blood to pass from one person to another. It is the second largest group and in some large cities the largest HIV-positive group (Muir, 1991). The majority of intravenous drug users are males and, if heterosexual, their partners are women. These female sex partners are one bridge across which the AIDS virus enters the general population. Another is through prostitution, since about a third of the female intravenous drug users admit to engaging in prostitution to pay for their drug habit or rent (Stine, 1996). As discussed in Chapter 4, AIDS is also transmitted from mother to child prenatally or during birth.

Casual contact does not seem to spread the disease. Studies of families living with people who have AIDS find that they generally do not catch the virus from casual contact. However, the general public is frightened of even casual contact with a person with AIDS and stigmatizes people belonging to groups at risk for HIV (Altman, 1986).

At the present time there is no cure for AIDS, although some medications—such as *zidovudine* (formerly called *azidothymidine,* or *AZT*), which stops the virus from reproducing—show promise for treatment of the disease (Rabkin, Remien, & Wilson, 1994). Other drugs, such as ddI (Videx) and ddC (Hivid), are used as well and also stop HIV reproduction and produce fewer side effects than AZT. ddC is used in combination with zidovudine

(Stine, 1996). ddI and ddC are not considered the first line of antiviral treatment at the present time; other antiviral treatments are in the testing stage and some will be available quite soon.

People can reduce their chances of contracting AIDS by taking some simple precautions. Since AIDS is spread most often through sexual contact, it is recommended that people refrain from engaging in sexual practices that might cut or tear the skin, avoid sex with people who engage in activities that place them at greater risk for contracting the virus (such as intravenous drug use), always use condoms, and take whatever other precautions are necessary to avoid transmission of the virus. Intravenous drug users are urged not to share needles. The correct use of condoms is highly recommended as a way to reduce the chances of infection (Stein, 1995; Vermund, 1995).

Some argue that abstinence, monogamy, and drug education should be emphasized to fight the spread of AIDS. Others, although agreeing that delaying the onset of sexual activity is desirable and viewing drug education as necessary, argue that other methods are required, especially for sexually active adolescents. They advocate education about condom use, partner selection, and reducing the number of partners (Hein, 1993).

Some advocate giving out condoms free in high school; others advocate needle exchange programs that would give intravenous drug users clean needles. Needle exchange programs show promise of reducing the transmission of AIDS (Coutinho, 1995). Some countries, such as the Netherlands and the United Kingdom, have such programs but they are strongly opposed in the United States for fear that giving out condoms shows a tacit approval of such sexual activity and would lead to more sexual behavior and that offering needles would lead to an increase in drug use. After carefully looking at the studies in the area, The Centers for Disease Control strongly recommended the implementation of such programs (Nadel, 1993). It is unfortunate that the battle between people interested in stopping the spread of AIDS is occurring at a time when unity in the fight against AIDS seems to be essential (Vermund, 1995)

Younger adults know a great deal more about AIDS than older adults. Knowledge of AIDS in the general population is relatively high in many areas, especially concerning modes of transmission (Adams & Hardy, 1991). Studies show that although high school and college students know that AIDS is spreading through the heterosexual community, a majority continue to practice unsafe sex. Despite widespread awareness of risks such behaviors as unprotected sex remain common, and preventive behavior is inconsistent among all segments of the community (Fisher et al., 1995). We know that gay men who successfully reduce their risks report greater peer support for behavioral changes and believe that their friends have already made such changes (Kelly et al., 1991). Counseling programs that aim at educating intravenous drug users also show some success (Stephens, Feucht, & Roman, 1991). Unfortunately, although many people are changing their behavior to safer practices in response to the AIDS epidemic, some fail to maintain these practices and lapse back into high-risk behavior (Joseph et al., 1990).

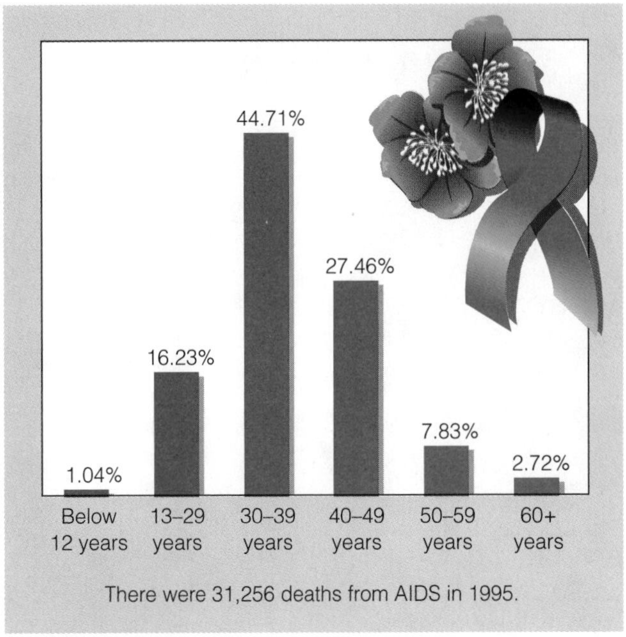

Datagraphic
Distribution of AIDS Cases in 1995 by Age
Source: Data from U.S. Centers for Disease Control and Prevention, 1996.

Education does not necessarily lead to reductions in risky behavior. Perhaps Gerald Stine puts it best; "in general people, especially young adults, do not do what they know. They sometimes do what they see, but most often do what they feel" (Stine, 1993, p. 401). In short, knowledge is necessary but it is insufficient for behavioral change. For example, although people may know something about AIDS, do they really believe that they are at risk if they perform a behavior? Do they believe that using a condom can protect them? People must be aware of the facts, such as that one unprotected episode can lead to AIDS, as well as believe that they have the power to prevent AIDS. People who use condoms are more likely to believe that they are acting responsibly and that they will help prevent AIDS (Fisher et al., 1995).

AIDS must be fought on three levels. First, new treatments and ways to combat the disease must be found through research. Second, people must be educated about how to reduce the risk of contracting the disease. Third, there must be an educational program aimed at separating myth from fact and at eliminating the stigma of AIDS. The suffering of the AIDS patient is often forgotten. Since many patients are young adults, their care is often left to aging parents, forcing a new and unwanted dependency on both patient and family. The AIDS sufferer must not only come to accept the diagnosis but also deal with the rejection and stigma attached to the disease.

The picture most of us hold of the professional athlete is a young adult in the mid 20s. Indeed, people are at their peak at this time.

The Physical Abilities of Young Adults

One tragedy of AIDS is that it strikes mostly young adults in the prime of life and at the height of their physical abilities. Indeed, physically speaking, young adulthood marks the peak of physical prowess. Most Olympic athletes in rigorous competition such as running and jumping tend to be in their early to middle 20s (Tanner, 1964); people hit their peak in physical strength, speed, and agility around this age (Newman, 1982). Some adults have disabilities that may interfere with some ability or function. Disabled adults today have a better chance of succeeding because new laws give them particular rights; society's attitudes have also changed (see Our Pluralistic Society: Americans with Disabilities—Quiet No More pp. 332–333).

The capacity to perform physical labor at extreme temperatures begins to decline before the age of 30 (Stevens-Long, 1984). Cardiac output—the volume of blood pumped by the heart each minute—decreases about 1% a year beginning at age 20 (Kohn, 1977). There is a slow decline in strength after age 30 and a gradual decrease in muscular endurance after age 25 (Rosentsweig, 1980). Between the ages of 30 and 40 there is some loss of speed and agility (Newman, 1982) and a gradual decrease in the secretion of gastric juices after age 30, which may explain the increase in digestive problems later in young adulthood (Timiras, 1972). Reaction time increases too—it takes longer to respond to a stimulus; a 17% increase in reaction time occurs between the ages of 20 and 40 (Stevens-Long & Commons, 1992; Bromley, 1974).

Any decline in these abilities is gradual and slight in early adulthood and probably goes unnoticed by most people (Troll, 1985). Most of the gradual physical decline is probably as much the result of disuse of muscles as of degeneration of muscles. Individuals who exercise can remain in excellent physical shape. Indeed, cross-cultural research demonstrates that older people in other cultures in which activity is the rule do not show some of the signs we attribute to aging, including reduction in strength and agility (Rosentsweig, 1980).

Sensory Functioning

During young adulthood sensory functioning remains excellent, although some gradual changes do occur. Visual acuity is perhaps best at the age of 20 and remains relatively constant until age 40 (Timiras, 1972). The changes that do occur are minor and inconsequential (Botwinick, 1984). There is a small decline in the ability to see details after age 25 or 30 years (Stevens-Long, 1984). It also takes longer for the eyes to adapt to the dark (Corso, 1981). Hearing declines a little from about age 20, especially for high-pitched sounds (Birren, 1964). There is little indication that smell, touch, or taste declines at all during the young adult years.

Physical Functioning and Cognitive Processes

Physical fitness and illness affect cognitive processes, and cognitive processes affect the body. For example, people who are overweight often have poor self-esteem, and people who are in good physical shape are likely to have a more positive self-concept (Burns, 1979). This interaction is quite apparent in the area of stress.

Stress in Early Adulthood

Stress is not always easy to define. For our purposes *stress* is an unpleasant state in which people perceive the demands of an event as taxing or exceeding their ability to satisfy or alter those demands (Brehm & Kassin, 1996). It is a good thing that the young adult is at his or her physical peak during this time because early adulthood is an especially stressful time of life (Milsum, 1984), and the average young adult must negotiate many major and minor life changes. Men and women, ages 25 to 44, re-

stress An unpleasant state in which people perceive the demands of an event as taxing or exceeding their ability to satisfy or alter those demands.

port experiencing more stress than any other age group (Statistical Bulletin, 1993). The most common stressor is money. Other causes of stress involve placing pressure on oneself, work load, children's needs and demands, and living up to the expectations of others including spouses, co-workers, and bosses (Clark, 1992).

True or False?
Young adulthood is the least stressful stage of adult life.

Stress is constantly discussed in the media and reducing stress seems to be one of our national obsessions, probably because stress can and often does affect health. Stress is linked to a number of illnesses and to mortality rates (Adler & Matthews, 1994; Krantz et al., 1985). Stress can lead to physiological changes such as increases in heart rate and blood pressure. If prolonged, these changes can be dangerous, sometimes leading to **psychosomatic** or **psychophysiological disorders,** which are real physical disorders in which stress and emotional reactions play a part. Disorders like ulcers, colitis, and high blood pressure are related to the body's reaction to stress.

Stress can affect health in any of three ways. First, stress has a direct negative impact on physiological functioning by raising blood pressure and pulse rates and increasing gastric secretions, which places a heavier burden on the internal organs. Second, chronic stress causes quantitative and functional changes in the immune system that are related to reduced efficiency (Kiecolt-Glaser & Glaser, 1992; Kiecolt-Glaser et al., 1987; O'Leary, 1990). Researchers find that the immune systems of unemployed, separated, or divorced individuals weaken (Kiecolt-Glaser et al., 1988; Arnetz et al., 1987). A relationship between stress, weakening of the immune system, and increased susceptibility to disease exists (Jemmott & Locke, 1984; Jemmott & Magloire, 1988). In one interesting study, nasal drops containing one of five different minor viruses were administered to healthy subjects (Cohen, Tyrell, & Smith, 1991). Subjects reporting higher stress showed greater rates of infections for all five viruses. Stress causes the increased production of certain hormones such as epinephrine, norepinephrine, and cortisol; and increases in the levels of these hormones often precede suppressed immune system functioning and the development of disease (Jemmott & Locke, 1984). Third, people under stress often show poorer health habits; they may become inattentive, increasing the likelihood of a traffic accident, or use drugs such as alcohol or tobacco to reduce their tension. They may not sleep or eat well. In these ways, stress may affect health directly and indirectly (Cohen & Williamson, 1991).

Psychosomatic or **psychophysiological disorders** Physical disorders, such as ulcers and colitis, that are contributed to or caused by emotional factors, including reactions to stress.

The Stressors of Young Adults

Stressors can be divided into three different categories. The first involves changes in one's life, the second daily hassles, and the third the stress that may arise from catastrophes such as wars or natural disasters.

Life Events Changes in life can cause stress. Holmes and Rahe (1967) formulated a scale that rated 43 life events according to the amount of stress each imposed upon a person (Table 14.2). The more changes in life events and the higher ranking of the events, the greater the chance of mental or physical illness. Note how many of the events are tied to young adulthood: marriage, pregnancy, gaining new family members, and work-related events. Older adults experience stress, too; the greatest stressor—loss of a spouse—is most likely to occur in old age. However, the number of life changes in young adulthood that take place in a relatively short amount of time is impressive. Even positive changes—such as marriage, the birth of a child, or buying a house with a substantial mortgage—are stressful. Studies generally find that people who experience more negative changes are more likely to experience physical illness, mental disorder, or some other problem (Monroe, Thase, & Simons, 1992). Some stressors, such as unemployment may lead to other stressors as well, for example, more marital tension; stressors are interconnected with each other.

One weakness of this scale is that it does not measure how people perceive the change. One person may perceive a particular event as more stressful than someone else. To rectify this problem, other scales measure not only the stressful events themselves but also the individual's perception of these events (Sarason, Johnson, & Siegel, 1978). An individual is also asked to mention any stressor not listed and to rate each stressor. Gender- and culture-based differences may then become apparent; for example, some people may find prejudice and discrimination a greater stressor than others.

Young adults seem to take stressful events harder than middle-aged adults. When asked to describe how disruptive certain life events were, older people consistently provided lower ratings; they worry less than younger people and report less job stress (Chiriboga & Cutler, 1980).

Acculturative Stress If you were to immigrate with your family to another country, you would bring with you the attitudes and values of your country of origin and have to adjust to those of your new country. Immigrants face acculturative stress, which is stress that comes from having to acclimate to a new culture (Rogler, Cortes, & Malgady, et al., 1991). The immigrant must often learn a new language, and adapt to different customs and traditions. Immigrants may face prejudice, and find their social status reduced from what it was in their country of origin. A doctor who immigrated to the United States from Eastern Europe found he had to take new courses

Table 14.2 **The Social Readjustment Rating Scale**
Life changes bring about stress, and too many changes within a relatively short amount of time increase the chances that a person will suffer mental illness, physical illness, or both.

RANK	LIFE EVENT	MEAN VALUE	RANK	LIVE EVENT	MEAN VALUE
1	Death of spouse	100	24	Trouble with in-laws	29
2	Divorce	73	25	Outstanding personal achievement	28
3	Marital separation from mate	65	26	Spouse beginning or ceasing work outside the home	26
4	Detention in jail or other institution	63	27	Beginning or ceasing formal schooling	26
5	Death of a close family member	63	28	Major change in living conditions (e.g., building a new home, remodeling, deterioration of home or neighborhood)	25
6	Major personal injury or illness	53	29	Revision of personal habits (dress, manners, associations, etc.)	24
7	Marriage	50	30	Trouble with the boss	23
8	Being fired at work	47	31	Major change in working hours or conditions	20
9	Marital reconcilliation with mate	45	32	Change in residence	20
10	Retirement from work	45	33	Changing to a new school	20
11	Major change in the health or behavior of a family member	44	34	Major change in usual type and/or amount of recreation	19
12	Pregnancy	40	35	Major change in church activities (e.g., a lot more or a lot less than usual)	19
13	Sexual difficulties	39	36	Major change in social activities (e.g., clubs, dancing, movies, visiting, etc.)	18
14	Gaining a new family member (e.g., through birth, adoption, older person moving in, etc.)	39	37	Taking out a mortgage or loan for a lesser purchase (e.g., car, TV, freezer, etc.)	17
15	Major business readjustment (e.g., merger, reorganization, bankruptcy, etc.)	39	38	Major change in sleeping habits (a lot more or a lot less sleep, or change in part of day when asleep)	16
16	Major change in financial state (e.g., a lot worse off or a lot better off than usual)	38	39	Major change in number of family get-togethers (e.g., a lot more or a lot less than usual)	15
17	Death of a close friend	37	40	Major change in eating habits (a lot more or a lot less food intake, or very different meal hours or surroundings)	15
18	Changing to a different line of work	36	41	Vacation	13
19	Major change in the number of arguments with spouse (e.g., either a lot more or a lot less than usual regarding child-rearing, personal habits, etc.)	35	42	Christmas	12
20	Taking out a mortgage or loan for a major purchase (e.g., for a home, business, etc.)	31	43	Minor violations of the law (e.g., traffic tickets, jay-walking, disturbing the peace, etc.)	11
21	Foreclosure on a mortgage or loan	30			
22	Major change in responsibilities at work (e.g., promotion, demotion, lateral transfer)	29			
23	Son or daughter leaving home (e.g., marriage, attending college, etc.)	29			

Source: Holmes and Rahe, 1967.

in the United States, learn a new language, and pass a test. He had to work as a part-time taxi driver and found it very difficult. In addition, immigrants must decide the extent to which they wish to preserve their native culture.

The Link Between Life Events and Illness Although there is evidence that people exposed to a great number of stressful events are more likely to develop some sort of physical or mental illness, the relationship between stressful events and illness is not strong (Flowers & Eisen, 1994; Rowlison & Felner, 1988). When exposure to stress-related events is used to predict future illness, the correlation is about .30, too low to make predictions about whether any individual will become ill (DePue & Monroe, 1986). Many people with high scores on these scales simply do not become ill (Krantz, Grunberg, & Baum, 1985), perhaps because of their high ability to cope or because they interpret these stressors as challenges.

Daily Hassles While Holmes and Rahe concentrated on specific stressful events, other researchers emphasized the importance of daily problems and stressors. We all are exposed to daily hassles, those little stressors that mount up. The traffic jam that causes us to be late for a meeting, a cranky child, the television that breaks 2 days after the warranty runs out, and the inability to lose that extra 5 pounds—all contribute to the stress in our lives.

Environmental insults—such as crowding, noise, and pollution—are stressful, too (Oskamp, 1984). Daily hassles have a substantial affect on one's health and well-being (Affleck et al., 1994), and their effects are serious and long-lasting (Bolger et al., 1989). Scales that measure daily hassles find that the most common ones involve weight, health of a family member, rising prices, home maintenance (indoor), too many things to do, misplacing things, home maintenance (outdoor), property taxes, crime, and physical appearance (Delongis, Folkman, & Lazarus, 1988; Kanner et al., 1981).

Catastrophes By their very nature, catastrophic events are unpredictable and devastating. Fires or floods, destruction from war, and hurricanes or tornadoes that rip through houses destroying everything in their paths are both overwhelming and uncontrollable. Because these events are largely unpredictable, they are not easy to study. One exception was the mammoth 1980 eruption of Mount St. Helens in Washington state, which was widely predicted by geologists and gave scientists one of the few opportunities they have ever had to study people's functioning before and after a major natural calamity (Adams & Adams, 1984). Significant increases in emergency room visits, an increase in calls to hot lines, and many more demands on mental health services were found even months after the eruption. An increase in the death rate and in stress-related illness also occurred. Anxiety disorders, use of alcohol, and phobic reactions all showed increases (Rubonis & Bickman, 1991).

Stress: The Individual Factor

There is certainly a relationship between stress and illness, but much of the evidence is based on correlations (Cohen & Williamson, 1991). Although we have good evidence that stress results in poorer immune functioning, the relationship between these changes and illness is not always present (O'Leary, 1990). For example, a number of adverse changes were found in the immune systems of medical students taking exams but no association between immune measures and illness was seen (Glaser et al., 1987).

Why some people are adversely affected by stress while others are not is an important question. In all measures of stress and disease the relationship may be positive but far from perfect. Stress itself is a transaction between the individual and the environment (Lazarus, 1993). The experience of stress is dependent upon the nature of the stressor and the individual's internal abilities to cope with it. Not all negative events cause psychological distress; distress arises only when the stressor makes demands on the individual that exceed the individual's ability to cope (Lazarus & Folkman, 1984). Some people simply cope with stress better. For instance, people whose coping styles include a great deal of self-blame when under stress show greater immune system impairment than those who are not as hard on themselves (Peterson, Seligman, & Vaillant, 1988). People who have other people to talk to and receive support from show less immune system involvement during stress (House, Landis, & Umberson, 1988). How we perceive stress, our ability to cope with it, and our personality may mediate the relationship between stress and the immune system and stress and illness.

The influence of stress on the individual shows the interconnections between physiological and psychological events. It also shows the importance of cognitive functioning because the individual's thinking patterns greatly affect how stress impacts on the individual's health.

Cognitive Functioning in Early Adulthood

Piaget had little to say about adult cognitive development, considering the stage of formal operations to be the final qualitative level of cognitive functioning (Piaget, 1970). However, some psychologists argue that adults use styles of reasoning called **postformal operational reasoning** that go beyond formal operations or are qualitatively different from formal operational reasoning. Any appreciation of postformal reasoning must begin with an understanding that adults face problems that are more practical and have many more constraints than those faced by children and adolescents (Labouvie-Vief, 1980, 1984). The abstract, principle-based logic of formal operations may not be as useful in dealing with practical problems. For example, adolescents using formal operational reasoning may look at all the alternative solutions to a problem as if the problem existed in a vacuum, but adults cannot and do not do this. Adults face many ethical and practical constraints, including money, time, and political concerns, which limit the solutions they will investigate. Gisela Labouvie-Vief (1990) notes that while the theme of youth is flexibility, the hallmarks of adulthood are commitment and responsibility. Adults need to adopt one course of action and disregard others. Adults faced with an issue or a problem may need to strike a balance between what is most logical and what is the most practical solution. This more pragmatic viewpoint differs greatly from the theoretical, abstract concept of cognitive functioning that characterizes formal operations (Labouvie-Vief, 1984). Last, adults often see problems within a particular context whereas adolescents are more theoretical. Adults always view a given problem in the context of their life and interpersonal relationships (Rybash et al., 1995).

> ***True or False?***
> Early adults tend to look at problems in a more abstract, theoretical manner than adolescents do.

postformal operational reasoning An expression used to describe any qualitatively different reasoning style that goes beyond formal operational reasoning and develops during adulthood.

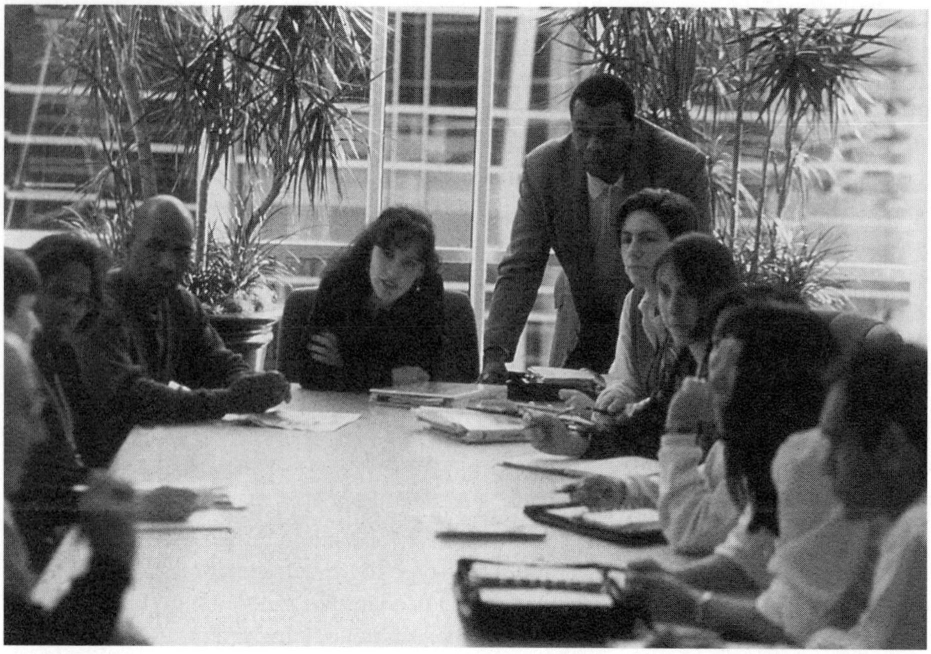

Does the reasoning of adults and teenagers differ? Some research finds that adults are more practical and that adults often find they must balance what is most logical with what is possible.

Relativistic Thinking

Jan Sinnott (1981, 1984) argues that adult thinking is often characterized by **relativistic thinking,** which involves the understanding that knowledge depends upon the subjective experiences and perspective of the individual. Such thinking is especially important for interpersonal relationships because different frames of reference may cause people to view situations differently. Adults are more likely to show this understanding of relativity when dealing with real-life problems than when dealing with abstract problems. All knowledge is seen as influenced by its context, which continually changes. Absolute prediction is therefore viewed as impossible because people are unique and events are continually changing (Kramer, Kahlbaugh, & Goldston, 1992).

An important study showing postformal relativistic thinking was conducted by William Perry (1968), who interviewed a group of students over their 4 years at Harvard. Freshmen approached intellectual and ethical problems believing that there was only one correct response and that the professors would teach it to them. Later, students came to believe that everything was relative, and they experienced difficulties, since if all knowledge and values are relative, the values seem equally right and wrong. Finally, Perry found that these students reached a level where they became committed to a viewpoint in addition to accepting the relative nature of truth. They came to believe that some viewpoints were better researched and had more evidence supporting them than others. Perry (1981) argued that there was a progression from a belief in absolute truth to a belief in full relativism and finally to a new equilibrium of commitment in the face of relativism.

Dialectical Thinking

Another prominent theorist, Michael Basseches (1980, 1984a, 1984b), suggests that postformal adult thinking is governed by what he calls **dialectical thinking,** in which people accept the idea of constant change and try to create order in the midst of this change. Basseches (1984a) gives an interesting example of this type of thinking in the decision to divorce. A formal operational approach to divorce would be that divorce was the result of one of three interpretations: I was inadequate as a partner, my partner was inadequate, or our initial choice was flawed. A dialectical approach would look at how experiences and internal and external changes led people to grow in different directions such that they could no longer stay together.

Besides seeing the world as constantly changing and evolving and taking the context into consideration, dialectical thinking also involves appreciating and accepting contradiction in the real world. The dialectical thinker knows that many viewpoints can coexist and that each may contain worthy elements. Contradictions are resolved by defining the thesis, defining its antithesis, and finally reaching a synthesis. Basseches (1984a) noted that a freshman in an interview stated that college is a place where ideas are exchanged (thesis), but then argued that such an exchange could occur in a coffeehouse in Paris or anywhere that people talk to each other (antithesis). Finally, the student came to the conclusion that people in a college are more qualified to give an opinion on their own subject and that some opinions are supported by more and better research than others (synthesis). An antithesis need not be the exact opposite of the thesis. It can be something that is simply left out. When Basseches (1980) administered an instrument measuring dialectical thinking to faculty members, college seniors, and college freshmen, he found that the faculty showed more such thinking than seniors, who showed more such thinking than freshmen.

relativistic thinking Thinking that involves the appreciation that knowledge depends upon the subjective experiences and perspective of the individual.

dialectical thinking Thinking that shows the appreciation of constant change in life and shows the capability of accepting contradiction in the real world.

Dialectical thinking may be a further development of relativistic thinking, which is the first postformal type of thought (Kramer, Kahlbaugh, & Goldston, 1992). Statements about social, interpersonal, and intrapersonal issues were written in absolute, relativistic, and dialectical terms and shown to people between the ages of 16 and 83 years. When subjects were asked to choose the statement that approximated their own thinking, a positive relationship was found between dialectical beliefs and age. Relativistic thought was relatively common in college students and early adults. As subjects negotiated early adulthood, more dialectical thinking began to appear because people come into greater contact with contradiction.

What Is Postformal Thought?

Table 14.3 shows a comparison of formal and postformal thought. Deirdre Kramer (1983) noted that postformal thought has three shared features: (1) knowledge is relative and not absolute; (2) contradiction is a basic aspect of the real world (an individual can both like and dislike another person at the same time); and (3) contradictions can be integrated (i.e., synthesized in fact, thought, and emotion) into some coherent entity. Rybash and colleagues (1995) add that postformal thinkers view reality as changing and realize that the context is important rather than believing that absolute, hypothetical principles operate in every context.

Intelligence in Early Adulthood

Although style of reasoning is certainly important, the area of cognitive functioning that is most popularly researched is intelligence. The meaning of intelligence for adults is in question. Intelligence is correlated with academic achievement (Horn & Donaldson, 1980), and this may have some meaning for children, but what meaning does it have for a 30-year-old adult who is out of school? Because intelligence tests are geared toward younger people, testing adults is questionable (Willis & Baltes, 1980). Children spend a great deal of their time acquiring knowledge, but adults spend a great deal more time applying that knowledge (Schaie & Willis, 1996). Adults are more concerned about the consequences of their actions and often actually face in real life the issues that many adolescents discuss as academic exercises.

Questions Students Often Ask

Does the fact that adults think differently from teens explain some of the problems in communication between them?

That is certainly one possibility that has not been examined by researchers much. Parents are faced with different problems, tend to see practical limitations on solutions, and must resign themselves to imperfection. Teenagers who are developing formal operations often see things as being divorced from reality, as either right or wrong, and as illogical. Older people may not take teens as seriously as they should because they do not see the teen as "worldly wise." A teen may see a parent's understanding of practical issues as reflecting a lack of values and concern. This may be one reason for lack of communication, but it is certainly not the only one.

Another problem involves individual differences. Some researchers argue that individual differences become even more important in adulthood (Fischer & Silvern, 1985), which makes generalizing from studies of groups

Table 14.3 **A Comparison of Formal and Postformal World Views**

WORLD VIEW OF THE FORMAL THINKER	WORLD VIEW OF THE POSTFORMAL THINKER
Logical analysis will reveal the permanent and absolute laws and principles that regulate the behavior of the elements and entities that reality comprises. Knowledge, because it can be logically deduced, is viewed as absolute and noncontextual.	Logical analysis has limits because logic is a construction of the mind, rather than a given or reality. Knowledge, because it is a construction of the mind, must be nonabsolute and contextually relative.
Reality is best described as a collection of closed, static, unchanging systems at rest.	Reality is best described as a whole that consists of multiple, integrated, self-transforming systems in movement.
Reality consists of systems as well as variables within systems that are independent of one another and can be separated from one another "one at a time."	Reality consists of systems and variables within systems that are totally interdependent of one another and thus cannot be separated from one another "one at a time."
Unidirectionality of variables (linear causality).	Reciprocal influence of variables (nonlinear causality, interactiveness).
Parts of a whole exist independent of the whole.	Parts of a whole are constituted by their relationship to the whole.
Avoidance and separation of contradiction.	Acceptance of contradiction and synthesis into more inclusive wholes.
Emphasis on the hypothetical and abstract.	Emphasis on real events that characterize real life.

Source: Rybash, Hoyer, & Roodin, 1986.

of adults to individuals difficult. Adults differ very widely in their cognitive experiences after graduation. Some never read a book and do not use advanced logic in their jobs; others are constantly learning and using complex problem-solving skills. Intelligence defined in terms of adaptability is very difficult to measure in adults. We have not had much success in determining what cognitive abilities are part of an adult's everyday experience (Kuhn, Pennington, & Leadbeater, 1983). It is not known what role formal logic or deductive reasoning plays in an adult's everyday world (Labouvie-Vief, 1980, 1982). Also, because there are many different kinds of intelligence (Gardner, 1983), emphasizing verbal intelligence may be unfair to artists, musicians, or mechanics, who have excellent problem-solving skills within their own discipline, but who may or may not have superior verbal intelligence.

Last, many intelligence tests rely on speed, which may have some general relationship with memory or other abilities. As we age, speed of response is reduced; speeded items may estimate intelligence in children, but such items may place older people at a disadvantage (Salthouse, 1994).

Most young adults do very well on intelligence tests (Schaie, 1994). When subjects were tested over six major testing periods for 35 years, almost all abilities were seen to peak in young adulthood; some skills peaked in very early middle age (Schaie, 1994).

Fluid and Crystallized Intelligence

Raymond Cattell (1963) argued that although intelligence may consist of a number of abilities, two factors are most important: fluid intelligence and crystallized intelligence. **Fluid intelligence** is essentially the basic capacity for learning and problem solving and is independent of education and experience (Sattler, 1974). It refers to such abilities as memory, reasoning, and the speed at which the mind works (Brim & Kagan, 1980). **Crystallized intelligence** is basically learned knowledge (such as information and skills) and what we might call wisdom. The abilities that comprise crystallized intelligence increase over most of the life span and certainly throughout early and middle adulthood (Figure 14.1), but the curves for fluid abilities look very different (Figure 14.2), showing a decline beginning sometime in early adulthood. Notice that although each ability has a different curve, the general pattern of decline over the course of adulthood is obvious; the reason for this decline is thought to be small changes in the central nervous system (Horn & Donaldson, 1980).

This analysis is not accepted by everyone (Schaie & Hertzog, 1982); however, despite the controversies in the field of intelligence, some tentative conclusions are possible. First, any decreases in fluid intelligence in young adulthood are quite minor and hardly noticeable in daily life. Second, crystallized intelligence increases throughout this period. Third, although scientists may argue over whether groups of people show predictable changes in intelligence, they agree that individual differences are important to any understanding of intelligence. Fourth, the entire concept of intelligence may require some revision; its usefulness for describing adult intellectual functioning is questionable, since adults are doing or have already done the things the tests were designed to predict.

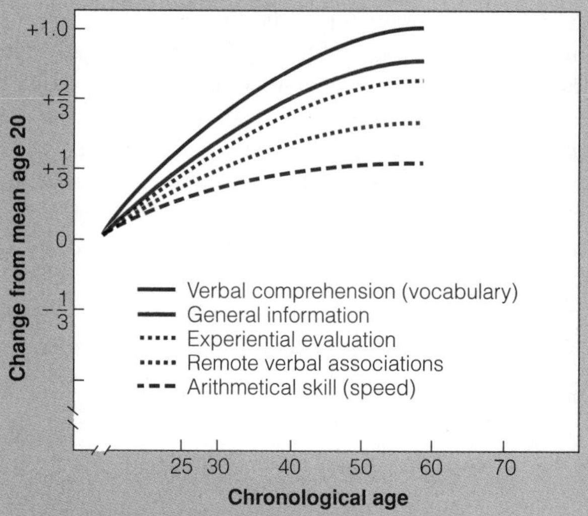

Most abilities that represent crystallized intelligence increase throughout early and middle adulthood and into late adulthood.

Figure 14.1
Changes in Crystallized Intelligence Over the Live Span
Source: Horn and Donaldson, 1980.

Morals and Ethics in Early Adulthood

Ideals

Idealism is identified with adolescence. The development of formal operational reasoning and college experiences often result in the formation of fervent beliefs. The ideals of adolescence change gradually in early adulthood, but they are not abandoned. Adolescent values tend to be abstract and absolute; they are polar, largely philosophical and symbolic, and are based on very partial experience and an impatience for change that may not be reasonable or practical. Things are either right or wrong, but the desire to end the wrongs is not realistically based on possibilities or practicalities.

This all changes in early adulthood, when ideals become more pragmatic and more emphasis is placed on applying them in the real world. Conformity peaks in the early high school years and the decline continues into

fluid intelligence The basic capacity for learning and problem-solving, independent of education and experience.

crystallized intelligence Learned knowledge and skills.

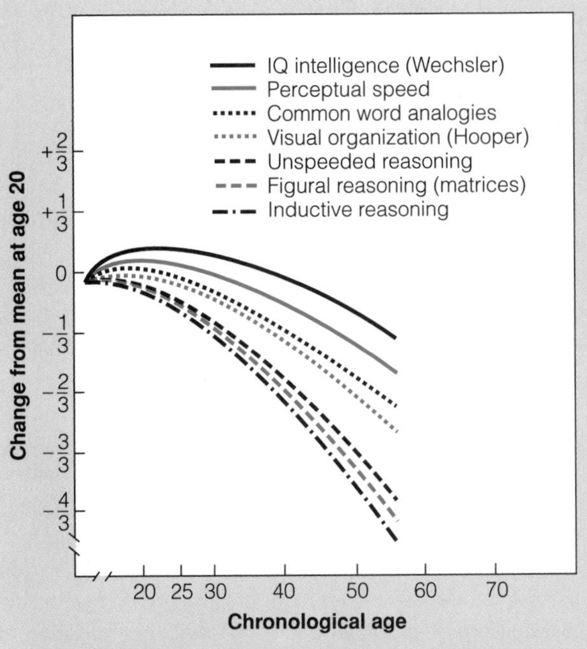

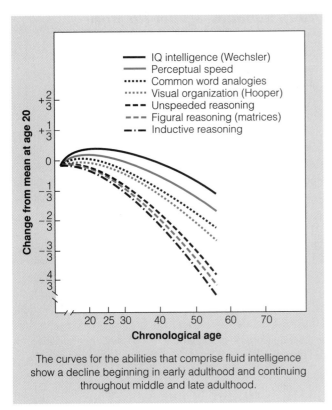

The curves for the abilities that comprise fluid intelligence show a decline beginning in early adulthood and continuing throughout middle and late adulthood.

Figure 14.2
Changes in Fluid Intelligence Over the Life Span
Source: Horn and Donaldson, 1980.

early adulthood, allowing adults to make more independent decisions (Brehm & Kassin, 1996).

Attitudes

Do people become more conservative and less likely to change with age? The rapid changes that occur in young adulthood involving marriage, children, and career require a certain amount of flexibility. Once these choices have been made, an increasingly conservative stance can be seen, and there is less flexibility in attitude. The area of strongest rigidity is vocational interests (Glenn, 1980). Changes are quite common from the age of 15 to 20, and then they decrease until there are few changes in vocational interest after age 40. More changes in attitudes and values are seen in early adulthood than in middle or late adulthood; attitudinal changes appear to be greater among young adults than among older adults (Hoge & Bender, 1974).

Religion

Children's religious beliefs and behaviors are greatly influenced by their parents, whom they tend to imitate. A decline in traditional religious beliefs occurs as adolescents experience college life. This liberalization on views concerning traditional religion continues during early adulthood, but the changes are not very dramatic. However, during early adulthood there is no decline and may even be an increase in spirituality (Baird, 1990). Many of the important decisions faced by young adults—including marriage, children, abortion, divorce, and personal ethics—have to do directly with religious beliefs and teachings.

About 95% of the American population believes in God, and many are active in religious organizations (Gallup & Castelli, 1989). Beginning at age 25, more than half say their religious beliefs are very important to them. Church attendance also increases with age, as does confidence in organized religion (Princeton Religion Research Center, 1980). A sizable minority of young adults attend religious services and believe in an organized religion.

True or False?
Most adults say that they believe in God.

Questions Students Often Ask

Why isn't religion given a more significant place in psychology?

Religion and spirituality certainly do influence people's development and behavior. People vary greatly in their beliefs, their religious practices, and the extent to which religion affects their behavior. It is not easy to study religion; religion consists of belief and practice, and someone may believe but not attend formal worship. In addition, some people may claim to be very religious but may talk and utter statements or behave in a manner that runs counter to the principles of their own faith. In short, religion is difficult to study.

Religious beliefs can have a far-reaching influence on personal and social life (Paloutzian & Kirkpatrick, 1995). Religion has a restraining effect on divorce, perhaps because religious people often agree on gender roles and life goals (Spilka, Hood, & Gorsuch, 1985). Having firm religious beliefs is associated with marital happiness, being able to maintain loving relationships, and higher levels of life satisfaction (Ellison, 1991). Religious people are less likely to engage in extramarital sexual activity, more likely to avoid illicit drugs, and less likely to abuse alcohol (Gorsuch, 1995; 1988); in short, religious beliefs have a significant effect on certain areas of decision making.

Moral Development

Ideals, attitudes, and religious values influence an individual's beliefs about right and wrong. Lawrence Kohlberg's theory of moral reasoning, as described in Chapters 11 and 12, is important here. Most adults reason at the conventional level (Kohlberg's Stages 3 and 4) and believe in upholding laws and conventions. When Kohlberg's original 1956 sample was followed for 20 years, reasoning at Stages 1 and 2 (the preconventional level) declined and reasoning at Stage 4 (doing one's duty) increased. Moral reasoning at Stage 5 (postconventional reasoning) was not found until ages 20 to 22, and it never

Our Pluralistic Society: Americans with Disabilities—Quiet No More

Almost one in four American adults has a disability (U.S. Bureau of the Census, 1995). The incidence of disability increases greatly with age, and many more elderly adults than younger ones have hearing, visual, or orthopedic impairments. A significant percentage of younger adults have disabilities too. For example, 6% of all Americans between the ages of 18 and 24 years, some 250,000, have disabilities (Hogan & Lichter, 1995). Disabilities are more common among African Americans, Native Americans, and Latinos. Since minority group status is often associated with poverty, such factors as poor access to medical care, poor preventive care, violence, and accidents may partially explain these figures.

The unemployment rate for adults with disabilities is very high (Allen, 1993). The many reasons for this, include educational and training difficulties, societal attitudes, difficulties adjusting abilities to particular jobs, and prejudice and discrimination.

Improvements in education, new training approaches, and the use of technology can help, but too often lack of opportunity and sometimes prejudice are the culprits. For example, consider these three situations:

> Lauren has a severe visual impairment but is qualified to do a job as long as she is given a talking calculator and some additional services. She is told that the company does not want to provide such services and she is not given the job.
>
> Dean has a learning disability that does not allow him to easily fill out applications or take a written test. The job he applied for does not require these skills but he is told that the company requires that he take a written test to get the job. He could pass the test if it were given orally.
>
> Kesia has an orthopedic disability. She is qualified for the job she has applied for, but is told that it is company policy that everyone have a driver's license. Even though a license is not needed to perform the duties of the job, she is not hired.

Each of these companies is violating the law and is liable to legal sanctions. On July 20, 1990, President George Bush signed into law the Americans with Disabilities Act (ADA), which ushers in a new era of opportunity for disabled people. This law will require some changes in the physical aspects of work, but will also require some major changes in attitude.

The ADA extends basic civil rights protection already given to members of minority groups and women to people with disabilities. In addition, it requires businesses with more than 25 employees to make changes so that people with disabilities can have an equal opportunity in the workplace.

The ADA guarantees equal opportunity for individuals with disabilities in employment, public accommodation, transportation, state and local government, and telecommunications (NARIC, 1993). The law prohibits firms from discrimination in the hiring or promotion of workers with physical or mental impairments. It requires employers to provide "reasonable accommodations" in both the application process and employment. The ADA outlaws tests that screen out applicants who have disabilities (O'Keeffe, 1995; Klimoski & Palmer, 1995).

It also requires restaurants, stores, and other public accommodations to widen doorways, provide ramps for people in wheelchairs, and make inner-city buses accessible to individuals with disabilities. Businesses must make new buildings and grounds conform to strict codes for access. Renovated or new hotels, retail stores, and restaurants will have to become accessible and barriers now existing must be removed if "readily achievable" (Berko, 1992). The law covers a full range of public accommoda-

rose to above 10% of the subjects (Colby et al., 1980). The stage of moral reasoning attained is also related to educational attainment (Speicher, 1994) in that education seems to stimulate thinking about various issues, which promotes moral development during early adulthood. Going to college may challenge previously held beliefs and values and stimulate young adults to examine and challenge their parents' beliefs.

Some argue that moral reasoning peaks in late adolescence and then regresses during early adulthood. However, when moral reasoning is measured differently, using a standard of commitment in relativism (believing that views besides one's own are possible) and of tolerance rather than in terms of absolute hypothetical principles of justice, progress in moral reasoning is seen. Such progress depends upon having experienced moral conflict when making behavioral choices (Murphy & Gilligan, 1980). During early adulthood behavior may become more ethical and principled as people act in a way that is more congruent with their own judgments of right and wrong (Stevens-Long, 1990).

In Chapter 11, we discussed the thesis that women see moral questions differently. Gilligan (1982) argued that women see them in terms of how they affect interpersonal relationships and needs of others whereas men see them in a strictly legalistic, individualistic manner. Evidence shows that people use both approaches in looking at moral questions. Carol Gilligan and colleagues (1990) argue that Kohlberg's highest stages overemphasize logic and cognitive control and do not give enough credit to caring, sensitivity, and emotion. To truly understand adult morality, the two perspectives need to be integrated, which requires postformal reasoning. Making a final decision involves appreciating and accepting

Our Pluralistic Society: Americans with Disabilities—Quiet No More (continued)

tions including lodging, restaurants, theaters, stores, rail depots, museums, parks, private schools, and health spas. The ADA requires car rental agencies to equip autos with hand controls for drivers who need them and telephone companies to provide operators who can pass on messages from people who must use special phones with keyboards. Private clubs and religious institutions are exempt from the law pertaining to accommodations.

The most controversial provision of the act requires companies to make "reasonable accommodations" for employees with disabilities. An accommodation is any change in the work environment or the way that things are usually done to create an equal employment opportunity for people with disabilities (Allen, 1993). A wide variety of these accommodations are required both in the application process and on the job.

Some accommodations involve accessibility, such as providing wider isles. Other accommodations must be made in the hiring process. For example, an individual with a learning disability may not be able to pass a written test for a job, and may require a verbal presentation. This change would be expected as long as the job did not require a great deal of reading. The rule that every employee must have a driver's license must be amended to allow an individual who cannot drive because of a disability a chance at the job, as long as driving is not an integral part of the job. Other possible accommodations involve providing raised letters on elevator control panels or a computer interface for verbalizing what is written on the screen so that an individual with a visual disability can work (Kaplan, 1996). They may involve changes in the use of technology, for example, providing a telecommunications device that would allow a person with an auditory impairment to use the telephone (Marczely, 1993; McCrone, 1994).

Reasonable accommodations in the job itself may require restructuring jobs, modifying work schedules, purchasing equipment, or changing training procedures. For example, an employer may be required to allow the worker with cancer who must spend 1 day each week receiving chemotherapy to work four 10-hour days (Allen, 1993). A disabled worker may require different tools to work on the job, which are crafted in a way that takes the disability into account.

The law also notes that these accommodations should not place an "undue burden" upon the employer. Although many large firms have been adapting their workplace over the years, smaller firms fear the cost. However, the costs of most of these accommodations can be kept down. For example, wooden ramps are less expensive than concrete ramps, and attaching a buzzer on the front door, which would allow the owner to open the door, is probably legal. The cost of providing reasonable accommodations may not be great for many companies. Only about 22% of all employees with disabilities require any accommodations at the worksite at all. Of those who do require accommodations, in 31% of the cases these modifications will cost nothing; in another 19% of the cases the changes will cost less than $50 (Eastern Paralyzed Veterans Association, 1992). Unfortunately, the language of the law is vague, and phrases such as "reasonable accommodations" and "undue burden" will require interpretation by the courts.

Many people with disabilities would like to work, and the ADA will open up new opportunities by requiring changes in the workplace. Disabled people themselves require better education and job training, including job-finding skills. The nondisabled population must change its attitudes towards people with disabilities and better understand the nature of the various disabilities. With legal advances, attitudinal changes, and better job training and education, more Americans with disabilities will take their place as equals in the workplace.

the contradiction between justice and compassion; our approach to understanding moral reasoning must be broadened if we are truly to understand the phenomenon.

Choices and Pathways

This chapter emphasized the importance of understanding the gradual nature of the changes that occur in early adulthood that are influenced by the choices we make. We can eat a healthy diet, exercise, continue developing our intellectual abilities, or not.

Different choices eventually lead to different experiences. Personal background, learning, and socialization are factors influencing our choices, but so are our subjective experiences and personal goals. According to the modern conception, adulthood is not a passive state during which the aging process takes its toll, cognition steadily declines, and social interaction becomes limited; rather, adulthood is a period that demands adapting to new circumstances and making various choices. It is a time of both challenge and choice, and it provides us with opportunities for growth and personal fulfillment.

Summary

1. The challenges of adulthood are identifiable and predictable. Adults have more choices than children.
2. Today's young adults are members of Generation X. They value balancing work and leisure, do volunteer work, and tend to feel insecure about relationships, and work. They are more comfortable with technol-

ogy and are no more dissatisfied than their elders with the state of the nation and government in general. They recognize the need for lifelong learning.

3. Most young adults are in excellent or good health. Both men and women gain weight throughout the early adulthood stage, probably because with age they become less active but have not yet begun to restrict their intake of calories.
4. Adults are now more health conscious than they have been in the past. Although their diets have improved somewhat in the past decade or so, adults still do not consume enough fruits and vegetables.
5. Regular exercise is advantageous to health. It improves cardiovascular functioning, burns up calories, and increases feelings of well-being. Low-impact exercise such as regular walking is beneficial. People should see a doctor before beginning an exercise program.
6. Most drug use declines in young adulthood, with the exception of cigarette smoking. AIDS is an important concern of young adults. AIDS is spread through shared needles among intravenous drug users, sexual contact with an HIV-positive partner (heterosexual or homosexual), or prenatally or at birth if the mother is HIV positive. Although many people are changing their behaviors in response to the AIDS crisis, some lapse into high-risk practices.
7. Although early adulthood represents the peak of physical conditioning, some abilities begin to decline during the late 20s and throughout the 30s. These reductions are hardly noticeable. The same pattern of slight decline is found in sensory functioning as well.
8. Young adulthood is a very stressful period. Stress may result from life events, such as getting married, as well as from the hassles of everyday life. Catastrophes may also cause stress. Some studies suggest that chronic stress is related to poorer immune system functioning as well as behavioral changes that may lead to illness. Young adults must learn to deal with these stresses.
9. Piaget considered formal operations to be the highest level of cognitive functioning. However, some psychologists argue that adults show reasoning that goes beyond formal operations. Formal operational reasoning is abstract, scientifically logical, and often useful for solving problems that do not have to be seen in an overall context. Adults must solve practical problems that are embedded in a particular context and whose solutions are limited by practical factors. Adults develop the understanding that knowledge is relative, that is, that knowledge depends upon one's perspective. Adults engage in dialectical thinking in which they understand the dynamic nature of life, can understand and accept contradictions, see problems in context, and synthesize opposing positions into a well-thought-out conclusion. Some evidence shows a progression from absolute to relativistic to dialectical thinking.
10. Most young adults perform well on intelligence tests, but the idea of using formal intelligence tests to measure adult intelligence has been criticized by some psychologists.
11. Fluid intelligence is the basic capacity for learning and problem solving, including memory, reasoning, and speed of mental work. Crystallized intelligence is learned knowledge, such as information and skills. Fluid intelligence begins to decline in young adulthood, whereas crystallized intelligence continues to increase during early and middle adulthood and into old age.
12. In early adulthood emphasis is placed on what can be realistically accomplished. Although young adults change their attitudes less than they did in adolescence, their attitudes are more flexible than they will be in middle and old age. Most young adults believe in God. Religious beliefs have an effect on certain areas of life, such as divorce, nonmarital sexual activity, and drug use.
13. The majority of early adults reason at Kohlberg's conventional level of moral reasoning. Young adults are more likely to believe that other views besides their own are possible and to be more tolerant than adolescents.

Multiple-Choice Questions

1. Which of the following statements about Generation X is *correct?*
   a. Its members are proud of the generation's label and identify with it willingly.
   b. Members of Generation X show a great deal more job dissatisfaction than their baby-boomer parents.
   c. Today's generation of young adults have much less confidence in government than their elders.
   d. Today's generation of young adults are more insecure in their relationships and their jobs.
2. Which statement about the health of young adults is *incorrect?*
   a. Most young adults rate their health good, very good, or excellent.
   b. Young adult females are more likely to rate their health as excellent than young adult males.
   c. Most young adults do not suffer from chronic diseases.
   d. Young adults are not ill very often and when they are ill tend to bounce back quickly.
3. Susan claims that the way young adults eat is worse than ever. Tanisha argues that most adults consume the recommended amount of fruits and vegetables but eat too much snack food. According to research:
   a. Susan, but not Tanisha, is correct.
   b. Tanisha, but not Susan, is correct.

c. Susan is correct only for males and Tanisha only for females.
d. Neither is correct.

4. Most people say they exercise:
a. to lose weight.
b. to look better.
c. for health purposes.
d. because they find it the most enjoyable activity in their day.

5. The most popular exercise for adults is:
a. weight training.
b. running.
c. walking.
d. stair climbing.

6. Herminia claims that as people proceed through the early adult years, drug use is greatly reduced. The only exception is:
a. alcohol.
b. marijuana.
c. hallucinogens.
d. tobacco.

7. The strongest predictor of whether someone will try to stop smoking is:
a. educational level.
b. age when they started smoking.
c. a sign of breathing problems.
d. having a parent who stopped smoking.

8. Which statement about the spread of AIDS in America is correct?
a. The percentage of cases involving heterosexuals has increased markedly.
b. Intravenous drug users and gay men are still populations that are most at risk for AIDS.
c. Most of the adults with AIDS are young adults.
d. All of the above are correct.

9. The two terms that best describe the changes in physical abilities that occur during the early adulthood period are:
a. significant and sudden.
b. gradual and slight.
c. continuous and disturbing.
d. inconsistent and significant.

10. Dr. Simons is testing four groups of subjects as to the amount of stress they are under. Group 1 consists of young adults between the ages of 25 and 44; Group 2 consists of middle-aged people between the ages of 45 and 54; Group 3 contains people between the ages of 55 and 64; Group 4 contains people between the ages of 64 and 80. If his research agrees with other studies in the area, which group will report the most stress?
a. Group 1.
b. Group 2.
c. Group 3.
d. Group 4.

11. One distinctive problem with scales that measure the effects of negative life changes on health is that they do not:
a. use adequate statistical models.
b. take into account the individual's interpretation of the changes.
c. positively correlate with actual illness, only with people's feelings about being ill.
d. take into account the fact that more than one negative event may occur in a short time period.

12. The type of stress immigrants face when they have to deal with differences in tradition and political systems between their native and adopted country is called ______ stress.
a. immigrant
b. emigrant
c. naturalized
d. acculturative

13. One difference between the thinking of adults and adolescents is based upon the idea that the problems adults face are:
a. more narrow in scope.
b. more practical.
c. more logical.
d. more interpersonal and less materialistic.

14. Each individual has a different frame of reference that must be taken into consideration. This is a basic idea in ______ thinking.
a. formal operational
b. relativistic
c. problem finding
d. secondary

15. Two types of postformal reasoning found only in adults are:
a. initial and secondary.
b. problem-finding and problem-solving.
c. relativistic and dialectical.
d. formal and concrete.

16. One problem in measuring intelligence in adulthood is that:
a. no modern intelligence tests measure intelligence in people between the ages of 18 to 21 years.
b. adults often refuse to take intelligence tests.
c. adult intelligence is more affected by genetic factors than children's intelligence.
d. intelligence tests for adults should measure application, whereas those for children should measure acquisition.

17. The type of intelligence that is concerned with flexibility and speed in problem solving is called .
a. crystallized.
b. fluid.
c. continuous.
d. secondary.

18. You are looking at a measure of fluid intelligence on groups of people who are in their 20s, 30s, 40s, and 50s. If your data looks like research that has been conducted in the past, you should find:
a. very little difference between the groups.
b. progressive reductions in fluid intelligence with age.

c. progressive but small increases in fluid intelligence with age.
d. no discernible pattern at all.

19. Concerning attitudes and morality in early adulthood:
a. vocational interests become more fixed with age.
b. ideals become more practical and realistic with age.
c. educational experiences seem to promote thinking about moral issues.
d. all of the above are correct.

20. According to Kohlberg:
a. most young adults can be found in Stages 5 and 6.
b. few young adults reach Kohlberg's most advanced stages of moral reasoning.
c. young children actually show more advanced moral reasoning than adults.
d. no young adults, but most adolescents reason at Kohlberg's most advanced stages.

Answers to Multiple-Choice Questions

1. d 2. b 3. d 4. c 5. c 6. d 7. a 8. d 9. b
10. a 11. b 12. d 13. b 14. b 15. c 16. d 17. b
18. b 19. d 20. b

Chapter 15

Social and Personality Development in Early Adulthood

Chapter Outline

Are the Following Statements True or False?

1. The median age of first marriage for both males and females has increased over the past four decades.
2. Wives are generally more sensitive and responsive to messages from their husbands than husbands are to their wives.
3. Women are more likely to demand a divorce than are men.
4. People look for different qualities in their second spouse than they did in their first.
5. People who are single by choice believe they are happier than people who are married.
6. Young adults who cohabit express strong attitudes against marriage.
7. When a couple has a child, the division of labor in the marriage becomes more traditional.
8. The overwhelming majority of children raised by gay or lesbian parents consider themselves heterosexual.
9. Today's employees are more loyal to their companies than workers in the past.
10. The majority of workers say they are satisfied with their jobs.

Answers to True-False Statements 1. True 2. True 3. True 4. True 5. True 6. False: see p. 350 7. True 8. True 9. False: see p. 358 10. True

Good-bye to Ozzie and Harriet

In the 1950s the typical family portrayed on most television situation comedies consisted of a breadwinner husband, a homemaker wife, and two or more children. This "ideal" American family shown in such early shows as *Father Knows Best* and *The Adventures of Ozzie and Harriet* reflected what was commonly thought of as the average American family's composition, attitudes, values, and behaviors.

Today's families are different. People delay marriage, divorce rates have climbed, cohabitation has increased, the number of single mothers has risen, and both single and married women have entered the work force in tremendous numbers (McLanahan & Casper, 1995). The family with a full-time homemaker mother and an employed father is a rarity today. Some predict the "death of marriage and families," but this does not seem to be the case. People still get married and remarried, but families have taken on a different structure and new types of living arrangements have become more common.

The lives of adults center about two dimensions: close interpersonal relationships and work. The importance of relationships is noted in Erikson's view that the psychosocial crisis of young adulthood can be seen in terms of **intimacy** versus **isolation.** The young adult makes commitments to other people, most often reflected in marriage. The negative outcome of the young adult years is isolation—the unwillingness or inability to commit oneself to others.

The second area of tremendous importance is work. George Vaillant (1977) analyzed the results from a longitudinal study called the Grant Study, which followed Harvard University students throughout their adult years. He emphasized the importance of vocational pursuits during early adulthood, finding a period in development for men in their 30s that he called *career consolidation,* during which men concentrate on their careers. Their focus is likely to become quite narrow, and they tend to be conforming and materialistic. Most people eventually grow out of the crassness of this stage. At age 40, men become less compulsive about their vocational pursuits and become "explorers of the world within." This change arises chiefly from a reexamination of talents and values.

The world of work as we approach the 21st century is a different place than it was 50 years ago. In the 1950s the United States accounted for about half of the world's total output in goods and services, was the acknowledged leader in almost every area, and international trade offered little competitive pressure (Levy, 1995). How different the situation is today, with increasing global economic competition, pressure towards greater worker productivity, and a greater emphasis on education and skill in the workplace. Real wages (adjusted for inflation) have declined, especially for young workers, and the two-earner family is a necessity (Mare, 1995). Today, with corporate downsizing and the uncertain nature of employment, people are changing jobs more often and find lifelong learning necessary for job advancement (Kasarda, 1995).

Some people find these changes very disturbing. Any significant change causes discomfort, an idealization of the "good old days," and a desire to return to the comfort of the past. But these changes also bring about opportunities and challenges that can lead to growth and development. More than anything else these changes lead to an increased number of choices for young adults.

intimacy The positive outcome of Erikson's psychosocial crisis of young adulthood involving development of close interpersonal relations, most often typified by marriage.

isolation The negative outcome of Erikson's psychosocial crisis of young adulthood, resulting in a lack of commitment to others.

Personality in Early Adulthood

When investigated in terms of traits such as extroversion, neuroticism, openness to experience, agreeableness, and conscientiousness, personality appears to be stable over the adult years (McCrae & Costa, 1990). This is especially true after the age of 30 (Whitbourne et al., 1992).

Changes do take place in other areas, though, such as attitudes, self-confidence and personal commitment. Over the early adult years, scores on measures of trust versus mistrust, identity versus role confusion, and intimacy versus isolation show increasingly favorable resolutions. Between ages 31 and 42 years increasing scores on autonomy versus shame and doubt, and initiative versus guilt are found. An increasing sense of personal control also occurs in the 30s (Whitbourne et al., 1992). Other changes, including a more realistic, practical world view and a greater willingness to commit oneself to others, reflect cognitive changes discussed in Chapter 14. As early adults proceed through their 20s and 30s they take on new responsibilities, make important lifestyle choices, and make new commitments.

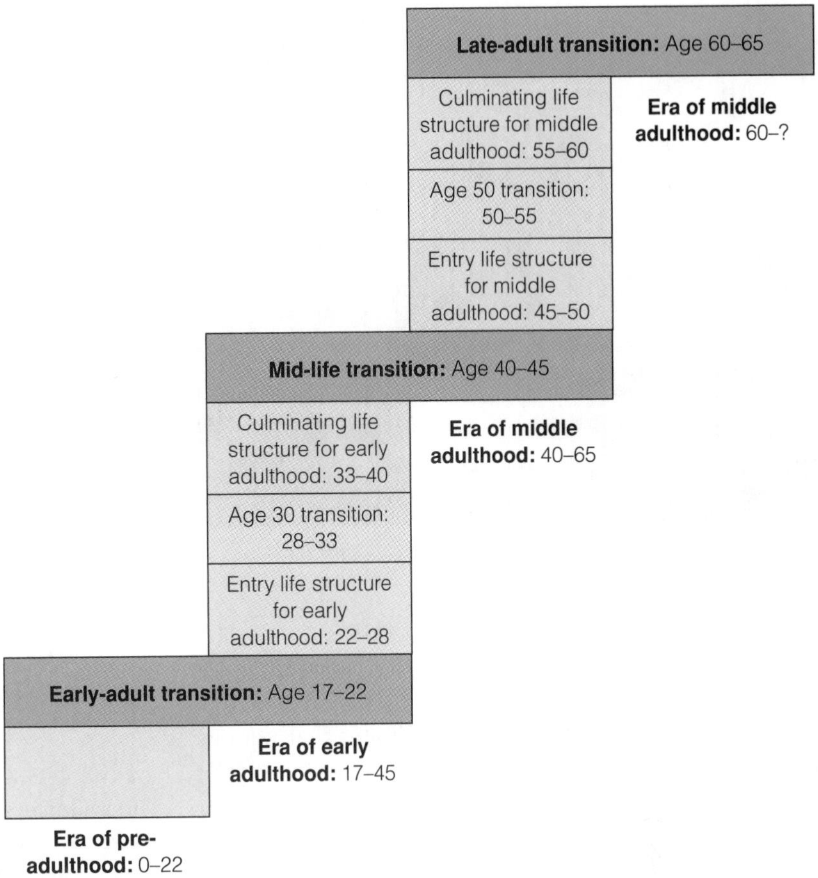

Figure 15.1
Developmental Periods in Early and Middle Adulthood
Source: Adapted from Levinson, 1978.

Levinson's *Seasons of a Man's Life*

Some psychologists emphasize the dynamic changes that occur as adults are challenged to adapt to new but predictable challenges in adulthood. Most notable among these psychologists is Daniel Levinson (1978, 1980, 1986, 1996), whose book *The Seasons of a Man's Life* had a tremendous impact on our thinking about adulthood. Beginning in 1969, Levinson conducted a longitudinal study of a group of 40 men age 35 to 45, who were asked to tell the stories of their lives. Levinson then analyzed the hundreds of pages of transcripts, looking for differences and commonalities in the men's experiences. Although Levinson has since died, he also conducted in-depth interviews with women, which were published in 1996 (Levinson, 1996).

The Four Eras of Life Levinson divided a person's life into four eras (Figure 15.1). The *preadulthood era* extends from birth to age 22 and is a time of rapid growth in every area of life. The second era, called *early adulthood,* lasts from age 17 to age 45, during which time a man establishes himself professionally and raises a family. The era ends with his reaching a senior position in his occupation. It is a period of rich satisfaction in terms of love, sexuality, family, and occupational advancement. However, it is also marked by marital, parenting, and vocational problems as well as by many personal choices. *Middle adulthood,* from about age 40 to 65 years or so, is a time of great transition, reappraisal, and coping with diminished physical abilities. It is also a time of achieving a dominant position and seeking more meaning in one's own life as well as giving to others. In *late adulthood,* about age 60 and older, the man has to confront the problems of aging. In addition, he must cope with the changing relationship between himself and society, finding a new balance and becoming more interested in realizing and using his inner resources. Levinson suggests that another era, *late-late adulthood,* exists beyond, but he does not describe it in detail.

Levinson's Periods of Adult Life Within these eras Levinson identified a number of periods that do not flow into each other but are connected by transitional periods (Levinson, 1978; 1986). Each transition involves termination of an existing life structure and initiation of a new one. During these transitions, each of which contains its own developmental tasks, a person must reappraise and modify his plans. Levinson notes that each period begins and ends at a particular age, with a range of about 2 years above or below the average. This chapter focuses on the early adulthood years; the transitions and plateaus of the middle adult years will be discussed in Chapter 17.

The Early-Adult Transition (ages 17–22) The early-adult transition forms the bridge between adolescence and adulthood. One task of this transition is to change one's life structure by altering one's relationship with parents and institutions. This involves separating oneself from one's family. A person may leave his home and par-

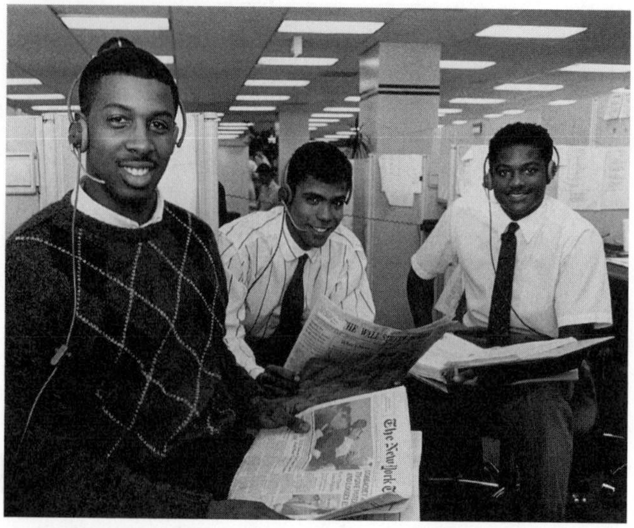

Early adulthood is a time of creating a life structure and making commitments in both relationships and work.

ents and become more self-sufficient; internally, he must explore the new possibilities offered by the adult world and make tentative choices. Levinson notes that people can live with their parents and still become more self-sufficient.

Entry Life Structure for Early Adulthood (ages 22–28) The first transition is followed by a rather stable period in which a new life structure is created. Many men create a **dream**, which is a vision of the life they would like to have; the dream both directs and motivates people. Although not everyone has a dream, those who do are deeply affected by it. The key elements of this period are exploration and creating a new and stable structure so that "the dream" can be fulfilled. This involves exploring the self and the world of work, making choices, and searching for alternatives. It also means making a new home and family life and increasing commitments. Decisions about occupation, love relationships, lifestyle, and values, which are not always lasting, are made. In the vocational realm at about this time, some people find *mentors,* people who help them at work, teaching them how to navigate around obstacles in their vocational path. The mentor relationship is very important because mentors guide their younger colleagues, helping them to succeed and to avoid the pitfalls that sometimes arise at work.

The Age-30 Transition (ages 28–33) Now that the exploratory period is over and the person's lifestyle is more or less established, questions about vocational and familial choices abound. *Did I make the right choices? Although I care about my spouse, do I really love him or her?* This is a time of great introspection. Levinson sees this period as an opportunity to correct one's mistakes and create the basis for a more satisfactory life. People who do not make commitments when in their twenties may be bothered by their lack of roots and feel that it is time to make a change. This transitional stage ends either with major changes or with a recommitment to family and occupation.

dream A vision of what a person would like his or her life to be like in the future.

Culminating Life Structure for Early Adulthood (ages 33–40) The next major task is to build a second life structure and work toward the dream within this framework. The dream consists of one's future goals and aspirations, and of the lifestyle one would like to have. This consists of two subtasks. The first is to establish one's own place in society, to anchor oneself to career and family, and to deepen one's roots. The second is to work toward advancement. Stability and progression are the key words here. During this period, family and vocational demands are especially high. Between the ages of 36 and 40 is a distinct phase that Levinson calls "becoming one's own man." Ambition peaks and the person may take on more responsibility on the job. The person is eager to accomplish goals, becomes more independent, and is more likely to speak with confidence and authority.

The Seasons of a Woman's Life

In a similar study of women, Levinson (1996) found a parallel underlying order in the lives of women as well, with the same transitions and plateaus. Although the basic structure of the theory seems applicable to both men and women, Levinson emphasized the importance of *gender splitting,* the creation of a division between men and women. Every society has some such divisions, and, according to Levinson, the more rigid structures of our society are being modified. In what Levinson calls the *traditional marriage enterprise,* the split between female homemaker and male provider was definite. The domestic sphere was reserved for women and the public or occupational sphere for men. Work was split between women's work and men's work. When Levinson interviewed homemakers, college faculty members, and businesswomen, he found that gender splitting was a problem. Traditional homemakers had difficulty sustaining the gender splitting in the face of societal changes and paid a price in terms of limiting their self-development. Career women had difficulty breaking down barriers in male-dominated occupations and in pushing for a more equitable division of household duties within marriage.

Men's and Women's Experiences: Similar Yet Different

Men and women face different challenges and deal with them differently. Male "dreams" rest primarily on careers and are individualistic and independent. Female "dreams" more often involve combining work and family life and are defined in terms of relationships with others. Women's dreams are often *split dreams;* that is, they are divided between career and marriage goals (Roberts & Newton, 1987). Even among professional women, only a small percentage have work-related goals as the sole component of their "dream."

This gender-related difference in dream content is also found in other areas of adult experience. Carol Gilligan (1982) notes that whereas separation and autonomy are basic to the male, attachment and empathy are of central importance to females. By the time children reach adolescence, males and females have different orientations toward social experiences and relationships. Appreciating the importance of relationships for women is the key to understanding female development. Autonomy and personal identity are important clues to male development.

Women's occupational choices often take their split dream into account, as they look for vocations that will allow them to care for a family and maintain employment. Women may take somewhat longer to commit to an occupation than men (Roberts & Newton, 1987).

The age-30 transition marks a major change in women's lives. Homemakers go through a time of intense questioning and feel the need for something outside the home. Work becomes an important component in their lives. Jobs are a source of satisfaction, making them feel more equal in marriage. Becoming more involved in the job world is somewhat difficult because women often continue to be responsible for the home as well. Career women also experience a transition at the age of 30 that is painful. They find the world of work not as fulfilling, caring, or logical as they expected. The struggles within the company are often viewed as painful. They reappraise their own career path and family aspirations. Married women may experience marital crises, and divorce is not uncommon. This period is one of exceptional questioning and turmoil.

Women who stressed marriage and motherhood in their 20s may develop more individualized goals in their 30s, and women who had focused on their career may become more concerned with marriage and family. Women's development is more deeply affected by their desire for or rejection of marriage and children than men's. The age-30 transition may place pressure on women to establish an intimate relationship if they have not already done so. This was found to be true even for a group of female attorneys whose image of womanhood included self-sufficiency and self-support. Every one of these women still envisioned a long-term intimate relationship and found the age-30 transition a point of reappraisal and concern (Roberts & Roberts, 1987).

Levinson found that women received much less mentoring than men. In addition, whereas at the ages of 33 and 40 men are settling down, women's lives do not seem as settled as they take on work and interpersonal commitments. Levinson noted a period in the late 30s called "becoming one's own man", in which men show more self-confidence and leadership abilities. Women go through this stage as well, appropriately called "becoming one's own woman" (Levinson, 1996; Roberts & Newton, 1987).

Levinson's Work in Perspective

One criticism of Levinson's theory concerns his biographical approach to research. These interviews are not empirical and his conclusions are based upon common threads that are woven through each person's life story, which may be subject to memory distortions. Levinson argues that the biographical method is an effective and flexible tool for reconstructing a person's life course and allows us to understand the complexities of adult life (Levinson, 1986). Levinson proposes that, despite much variability in the timing of specific life events, the basic structure of his theory is age specific (Lemme, 1995); not everyone agrees. Others raise the question of whether Levinson's theory is applicable to minorities and people living in poverty.

Marriage

Most people marry some time in early adulthood, but the age of first marriage has risen substantially. The median age at which people marry rose from a low in 1956 of 22.5 years for males and 20.1 years for females to 26.5 years for men and 24.5 years for women in 1993 (Footlick, 1990; Wolf, 1996). This trend may continue. Young people today are under less pressure to marry young, and the need for extensive education beyond the high school level means that many people cannot afford to marry at an early age.

> ***True or False?***
> The median age of first marriage for both males and females has increased over the past four decades.

Choosing a Spouse

Few decisions in life are as important as the choice of a spouse, and yet most theories about the reasons that people choose one person over another have not successfully explained the dynamics of the choice. Adults generally agree that people should not get married unless they are in love (Furstenberg, 1987). Other reasons may complement love—for example, the desire for companionship, children, or financial security. Most people have been taught that love is the foundation of marriage, but this tells us nothing about why people fall in love with some people and not with others, and why some people who fall in love get married and others do not.

Marriage choice is mediated by a number of factors. Although we think of ourselves as completely free to marry anyone we want to, most people are limited by their economic and social positions in life. For instance, if you come from a poor family, what are your chances of meeting and dating a millionaire's son or daughter? Also, your family's wishes that you marry a person with similar characteristics and upbringing may affect your choice. Perhaps the most common finding is that people date and marry others who are similar in age, race, education, social class, and intelligence level (Knox &

Schacht, 1991). People who marry usually share similar backgrounds, religious beliefs, interests, and personality characteristics.

Questions Students Often Ask

Don't opposites attract in selecting a mate? I have a friend who is very talkative, and he just found a partner who loves to listen.

At one time it was theorized that people who are complementary opposites marry (Winch, 1958). For example, a person who is dominant seeks out a person who is not. We now know, however, that except in fairly rare cases, this does not occur. It may seem more common than it is because such a marital relationship stands out when we spot it.

Similarity has been related to better chances for marital happiness (Schoen & Woolridge, 1989); this is called the **similarity theory of mate selection.** We are more comfortable with people who are of similar educational and experiential backgrounds. There is pressure toward marrying people from one's own race, religion, and ethnic group, although this is decreasing somewhat. Approximately 15% to 20% of all marriages are interfaith; the percentage of interracial marriages is less than 2% of all the marriages in the United States, but this is a substantial increase, even since 1970 (Strong & DeVault, 1995). Such patterns probably will continue and perhaps even increase in the late 1990s and beyond (Burnette, 1995; Berardo, 1990). People also tend to choose partners who are psychologically similar to themselves, that is, who share certain personality characteristics such as being extroverted (Strong & DeVault, 1995).

Although similarity is certainly a factor, its importance seems to be declining somewhat. In addition, it does not tell us anything about the process by which a commitment for marriage is made. The most popular way of looking at this process is to see the commitment as occurring in a gradual manner as illustrated in Murstein's (1976, 1982, 1987) **stimulus-value-role theory.** According to this theory, selection of a marital partner is viewed as a three-stage progression, with each stage involving more intimacy than the last. In the stimulus stage, people are attracted to each other on the basis of such external features as physical attractiveness, poise, dress, personality, and reputation. In the second stage, the value stage, values are compared. Communication proceeds to a deeper, more personal level. The couple begins to talk about their dreams, fears, hopes, and concerns. They explore their political and religious attitudes and reflect on how comfortable they are with each other; self-disclosure increases. Sometimes marriage occurs after this stage, but couples must often go beyond to the third stage.

In the third or role stage, people ask themselves whether the roles they see themselves playing in the future are compatible with those of their partner. People consider how they function together and compare their relationship with their concept of the ideal relationship.

People take in stimulus, value, and role information throughout the relationship and the steps are somewhat less qualitatively distinct from one another with smoother transitions (Murstein, 1987). Others disagree with the idea of stages, believing that there are many pathways to commitment, which may develop differently for various couples (Surra, 1990). Mate selection is a complicated phenomenon, one that is not well understood.

Love and Marriage

Americans are raised on the concept of **romantic love.** Movies and television programs show a great deal of romantic love, most of it out of wedlock, and much poetry is written about it. Love is an important part of the marital relationship, but defining it is difficult, if not impossible.

Many social scientists argue that two types of love exist: romantic love and realistic love. Romantic love is basically erotic in nature; there is a strong need for the presence of the loved one and for physical contact. It is characterized by the belief that a person has only one true love and by idealization of the loved one.

Realistic or companionate love is more characteristic of people who have been involved in a relationship for an extended period of time. It is less intense, but it involves steady concern and caring. People in a realistic love relationship do not expect their partner to be perfect and do not believe that love will solve all their problems. Romantic and passionate moments do occur, but they are not as intense as before (Schultz, 1984). When high school seniors, people married for about 5 years, and people married for 20 years were compared on love attitudes, the high school seniors and the older group were found to be quite romantic—much more so than those who had been married 5 years. The older group tended to believe that the person they married was the only one for them, probably because people are likely to feel this way when so much time has been invested in a relationship. The lack of romantic feeling in the group married for 5 years is understandable, because some of the initial fantasy had turned to realism. These couples were still very much in love, but their love had probably become more reality-based because of having to make a living and care for children.

similarity theory of mate selection The theory of mate selection emphasizing that people attract and marry on the basis of underlying similarities in a variety of areas.

stimulus-value-role theory The theory of mate selection that sees the selection of a marital partner as a three-stage progression involving initial attraction, value comparisons, and analyses of role compatibility.

romantic love Love that is basically erotic in nature and involves a strong need for the physical presence of the other and for physical contact.

realistic or companionate love Love that is characteristic of people in a long-term relationship involving steady concern and caring.

Robert Sternberg (1986) views love as a dynamic quality of relationships composed of three elements: intimacy, passion, and commitment. Intimacy is the emotional attachment that two people experience, requiring open communication and self-disclosure. Intimacy involves wanting to promote your partner's welfare, feeling happy with your partner, holding your partner in high regard, being able to count on and understand your partner, sharing, receiving and giving emotional support, and self-disclosure (Sternberg & Grajek, 1984). Passion refers to romantic and physical aspects of the relationship. Commitment is the desire to maintain the relationship, a willingness to stay with the relationship, to work things out, and to devote oneself to it. The strongest predictor of satisfaction and endurance within a relationship is commitment (Whitley, 1993).

Marital Satisfaction

It might surprise you to learn that most married Americans are satisfied with their marriages. In a nationwide study, 61% said they had excellent or very good marriages (27% excellent marriages and 34% very good marriages). In the overwhelming majority of excellent marriages, the spouses spent more than three-quarters of their nonworking time together. They had a close friendship, showed a great deal of affection in public, and showed respect for each other and each other's needs. They report fairness, cooperation, and sharing of jobs. Most women who report having excellent marriages say that they share decision making equally with their husbands (Schwartz & Jackson, 1989).

Marital Sex

Most adult sexuality takes place within marriage (McCammon, Knox & Schacht, 1993), but the importance of sex varies from couple to couple. Sexual satisfaction is vital for some; for others, sex is less important, and tenderness and loving concern are more important. Most married partners are satisfied with their sexual relationship. Most Americans who respond to surveys say that sex with their partner makes them feel wanted, and that they are generally pleased with their sexual relations. The overwhelming majority say that they receive great physical pleasure and great emotional satisfaction from their sex lives (Michael et al., 1994; Laumann et al., 1994).

The frequency of sexual relations decreases with age and years in the relationship (Ard, 1990). Most people attribute the decline to lack of time or energy, or to being used to each other (Michael et al., 1994; Blumstein & Schwartz, 1983). Various daily worries, including vocational and child-rearing concerns, are also involved. The presence of young children may inhibit parents, and child-rearing responsibilities may make parents too tired to consider their own intimate relationship. The focus of sexuality changes with age from an emphasis on passion and sexual intimacy to one in which tender feelings of affection and loyalty are more important (Reedy, Birren, & Schaie, 1982).

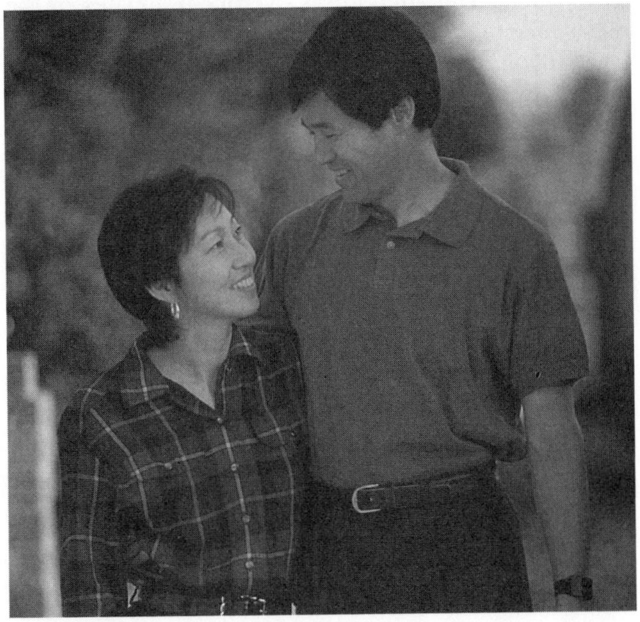

Despite what is trumpeted in the media, most married people are satisfied with their marriages.

Communication: Is Anybody Listening?

The strongest predictor of marital success is the quality of communication (Cate & Lloyd, 1992; Goleman, 1985). Satisfaction is higher when people can discuss their experiences and solve problems without completely sacrificing their own interests. People who feel that their partner understands their needs express greater satisfaction with the marriage. Measures of communication predict marital adjustment and satisfaction, especially after the first year.

Communication patterns show some gender differences. Wives are generally more sensitive and responsive to messages from their husbands than husbands are to their wives, both in regular conversations and during times of conflict (Noller & Fitzpatrick, 1991). Husbands offer more neutral messages such as "it doesn't matter to me," while wives give both more positive and negative messages and fewer neutral messages.

> ***True or False?***
> Wives are generally more sensitive and responsive to messages from their husbands than husbands are to their wives.

Studies of communication emphasize the importance of giving support, sharing emotions, and being sensitive to and understanding the spouse's needs and feelings. Communication patterns often differentiate happy couples from unhappy couples. Distressed and nondistressed couples report conflict on the same topics, but distressed couples have more frequent conflicts and spend more time in conflict (Noller & Fitzpatrick, 1991).

Distressed couples often report that one spouse communicates his or her feelings while the other does not. Distressed couples often communicate negatively and are more likely to command, disagree, criticize, and put each other down whereas happy couples are more likely to agree, approve, and use humor and laughter. Distressed couples express fewer positive feelings and more negative feelings, and these negative feelings are reciprocated by the spouse while the positive ones are not (Noller & Fitzpatrick, 1991).

Happily married spouses are very good at understanding what their partners mean when they express themselves, but in troubled marriages this is not so (Goleman, 1985). Spouses in unhappy marriages often misunderstand each other but are unaware that they do. Happy couples show a high degree of responsiveness and share everyday events with each other. Without such sharing, tension and perhaps even estrangement can result. Some specific examples of positive and negative communication are found in Table 15.1.

Self-disclosure—communicating personal information to another individual—is also a factor in marital satisfaction (Surra, Arizzi, & Asmussen, 1988). Self-disclosure is related to commitment and helps build bonds of trust between people (Boland & Follingstead, 1987). Studies of satisfied couples show the importance of trusting and confiding in one another, trying new ways of dealing with problems, and expressing caring and affection daily (McCubbin et al., 1988).

Distressed couples show more negative communication patterns than nondistressed, satisfied couples. In satisfying relationships, positive interchanges are the rule whereas distressed couples are caught up in what Wilson and Gottman (1995) call "cycles of negativity," which are very difficult to break.

Table 15.1 **Characteristics of Productive and Nonproductive Communication**
Some patterns of communication add to understanding, while others are potentially harmful to a relationship.

PRODUCTIVE COMMUNICATION	NONPRODUCTIVE COMMUNICATION
1. Avoidance of behaviors in column 2.	1. Blaming—"You're lying around the house while I do the work."
2. Neutral statement rather than accusation—"I thought we agreed . . ."	2. Name calling—"lousy lover," "tramp."
3. Acknowledgment of responsibility for partner's discomfort—"Well, I guess we did discuss sharing the work."	3. Threatening—"I'm going to leave."
4. Expression of willingness to alleviate problem—"What do you want me to do?"	4. Using sarcasm—"What would you know about sensitivity?" "Right again, Sherlock."
5. Positive labeling of suggestion—"It would be nice if . . ."	5. Being judgmental—"You're being hateful and mean."
6. Reciprocity—"I'll handle it Mon./Wed./Fri."	6. Changing issues—"No sex again tonight."
7. Positive expression at end of conflict—"Okay. I guess I'm on for Thursday night, eh?"	7. No attempt to stop escalation of conflict.
8. Brief—Each person takes two turns speaking.	8. Lengthy—Each person takes six turns speaking.

Source: Knox, 1985.

Conflict in Marriage

Conflict itself does not necessarily lead to marital distress or divorce. Almost half of the divorced people in one study said that they seldom quarreled, and only two in ten said they argued constantly (Hayes, Stinnett, & DeFrain, 1981). Gender differences during conflict are not that great, but wives generally set the tone of the argument and husbands are more likely to try to avoid and withdraw from the conflict rather than solve it. As the wife criticizes, the husband withdraws and does not communicate at all, which leads to more hostility on the part of the wives (Roberts & Krokoff, 1990).

Whether conflict will lead to marital distress depends upon how it is handled. Some rules for handling conflict successfully involve not belittling the other person, not dismissing the other person's ideas as unimportant, trying to understand the other person's viewpoint, not talking down to the other party, not getting angry or raising one's voice, and not being sarcastic (Jones & Gallois, 1989).

Violence Between Partners

Sometimes marital disagreements can lead to violence. High-profile cases, such as the O.J. Simpson murder trial, bring spouse abuse onto the front page of the nation's newspapers. The attention is overdue. Estimates of the prevalence of spousal abuse differ, but between two and four million women in the United States are severely assaulted by their partners each year (Sommers, 1994). About half of all women murdered in the United States are killed by current or former partners, and between one-quarter and one-half of all homeless families headed by women left home to escape domestic violence (Mason, 1993).

Almost all abused adults in shelters are women, and most cases of abuse that are publicized involve the aggression of men against women (Johnson, 1995). However, physical violence is also perpetrated by women; one large study found that in about two-thirds of the families in which the husband had been violent, the wife had also been violent, and that women initiate the violence about as often as men (Flynn, 1990; Stets & Straus, 1990). Most of the severe injuries are suffered by women, probably because men are physically bigger and stronger. However, women are much more likely to use violence as a form of defense or in retaliation against husbands or dates (Flynn, 1990).

Two different types of spousal abuse may exist (Johnson, 1995). The first, called *patriarchal terrorism,* is abuse that arises from men's desire to control their wives, either by the threat of violence or its actual use. Violence becomes a control tactic, along with the use of children, economic sanctions, and threat of isolation. These men believe that their role is one of domination and do not allow their wives any autonomy. Such abuse escalates; it increases in frequency and intensity over the years. The escalation is prompted by either the partner's resistance to the control or the man's need to flaunt his power and control, even if the woman has yielded. These wives often show a resignation, blaming themselves, and may continue to return to their battering husbands. This type of abuse often results in major injury.

The second type of abuse called *common couple violence* involves occasional outbursts of violence from either husbands or wives or both. Conflicts get out of hand and result in violence when the perpetrator cannot handle the anger or lacks conflict resolution skills. This type of violence results from tension within the home and an inability to cope with differences of opinion and frustration. It does not tend to escalate. In a 1-year follow-up study, 5.8% of all people who had used minor violence had escalated to more severe forms the following year, about 94% had not. This would explain why a widespread battered husband syndrome does not exist despite the studies showing that both husbands and wives can be violent. Most cases of extremely battered wives are the result of patriarchal terrorism, which differs greatly from this more common type of violence. The destructive nature of "common couple violence" should not be minimized. It damages the relationship, and the children who witness it come to believe that this is what relationships are all about, and physical and psychological injury occurs.

The causes of family violence are multiple and complex. Abuse is a learned behavior that has deep psychological and sociological roots. It often occurs in the context of an argument most commonly over housekeeping, sexual or social activities, money, and children (Straus, Gelles, & Steinmetz, 1980).

Perhaps the most famous factor in the transmission of violence from one generation to the next, known as the *cycle of violence,* involves children either being abused or watching their parents use violence and then using violence themselves when they are adults. Both men and women who received very harsh punishment as children are at increased risk for assaulting their spouses as well as abusing their own children (Simons, Johnson, Beaman, & Conger, 1993). Being abused increases the chances that women will engage in domestic violence and also raises their chances of being victims of domestic assault (Downs, Miller, Testa, & Panek, 1992). As in the case of child abuse discussed in Chapter 9, increased risk does not mean that most adults who were mistreated will do the same to their spouses (Lackey & Williams, 1995); in fact, over half the women who experience violence were not harshly punished as children (Simons et al., 1993).

Why are people with a childhood history of abuse or of witnessing abuse more likely to be violent? First, early in life these people learn that physical force is a way to settle conflict. Family aggression provides a role model, including one for being a victim. Second, women who are abused tend to meet and marry violent men. Children exposed to harsh punishment may become noncompliant, and have difficulties with their social skills and school life. As was noted earlier, rejected children become friends with other rejected children. These adolescents and young adults are often attracted to events and activities that bring them into contact with men who have hostile and aggressive attitudes, who they then date and marry (Simons et al., 1993). Experiencing violence in one's family or viewing it can predispose an individual toward abuse, but it is not the sole determining factor (Gelles & Conte, 1990).

Another factor in spouse abuse involves the inability to express oneself. When abusive males cannot explain their point of view, they become frustrated and resort to violence. In addition, many abusive males are emotionally dependent on their partners and feel very jealous and possessive. They often use violence as a way to keep a spouse from leaving. Finally, abusive males are less assertive than nonabusive males and may use violence to "prove" that they are men.

Conditions within the individual's life can heighten the risk of domestic abuse. Women with certain conditions are more likely to be abused. Women who are pregnant or HIV-positive are more likely to be victims of domestic violence (O'Campo et al, 1995; Rothenberg & Paskey, 1995). One consistent finding is that violence is related to stress (Gelles, 1987). Disappointments and family problems that cause stress may set the stage for spousal abuse (Gelles, 1989). Other factors may then come into play and determine how the individual will react to the stress. These reactions to stress may be mediated by the person's coping abilities, income level, the quality of the marriage, the social support available, and alcohol use (Gelles, 1994). Some people have the ability to cope with stress better than others and can deal with disappointment and anger without resorting to violence. Although abuse is found in all income levels, people from lower-income backgrounds are more vulnerable. People in poverty are faced with more stress and often have fewer resources available to mediate the stress. The worse the quality of the marital relationship, the greater the possibility of abuse. Conflict often precedes aggression and may interact with alcohol and other drug use to produce domestic violence (McKenry et al., 1995).

Couples who are violent display more negative communication and have difficulty resolving conflict because their problem-solving skills are compromised. Social support in the form of friends and family may enable frustrated individuals to talk their problems out.

People who are isolated are more likely to be violent. Two factors that seem to inhibit violence among those who have experienced it in their own childhood are social attachment to others, most principally to one's spouse but also to friends and family, and the belief that there are negative sanctions from others for engaging in spousal abuse (Lackey & Williams, 1995). When men believe that their wives would leave or friends and family would disapprove and lose respect for them or that they would be arrested, they are less likely to engage in violence.

The results of such violence are varied but highly negative. Besides the obvious physical injury and sometimes death, wives who are abused report a great deal of depression and anxiety (Christopoulus et al., 1987), and high rates of psychological distress (Gelles & Harrop, 1989).

It may be easier to understand the sad pattern of violence on the part of the husband than to understand why the wife does not leave. Even many professional workers sometimes view the woman as partially responsible for her victimization, which is the ultimate in blaming the victim (Andrews & Brewin, 1990). Some cases of wife beating and child abuse go on for years and many women do not leave at all. Sometimes the wife leaves for a short period of time and then returns, only to be abused again. Battered wives may return because they hope their husband will change, have nowhere to go, fear that their husbands will find and punish them for leaving, are concerned about their children's need for a father, or cannot support themselves financially (Hyde, 1985). The longer someone has been married, the more she has committed herself to the marriage and the less willing she will be to leave (Strube & Barbour, 1983). Women who are employed are less likely to stay (Gelles, 1980), probably because they are not totally dependent on their husbands for financial support.

Women who remain with abusive partners see their relationship in a more positive light. (This is true only for physical and not for verbal abuse.) Many women in abusive relationships are not abused every minute of the day, and their husbands may be "nice guys" on the outside and repeatedly regret their abusive behavior. They can at times be loving and kind. Many women believe that their relationship with their husband is not as bad as other people's relationships. However, when verbal abuse occurs all the time, women find themselves unable to see the positive.

Verbal abuse and physical abuse often go together, but not always (Stets, 1990). As one battered wife put it, "Bruises, cuts, etc. heal within a short time. When you listen to someone tell you how rotten you are and how nobody wants you day after day, you begin to believe it. Verbal abuse takes years to heal but before that happens, it can ruin every part of your life" (Herbert, Silver, & Elard, 1991 p. 322). Many of these wives are not naive, and 80% of battered wives who stay believe that they will be battered again.

Victims of abuse need shelters, hotlines to call for immediate help, and police protection as well as counseling. The effectiveness of shelters seems to depend upon whether the woman is ready and willing to take some control of her life. If she is, shelters can reduce the likelihood of violence. If she is not, shelters have little impact (Gelles & Conte, 1990). Between one-third and two-thirds of battered women in shelters return to their partners (see Gelles & Conte, 1990). The abuser needs to be restrained but also requires counseling. If two different types of spousal violence exist, different interventions may be effective with one type of abuser and not the other. More research is needed. Group counseling programs for violent men can be effective, but only if the individual finishes the program (Gelles & Conte, 1990).

Who's Doing the Dishes? Division of Labor

Most married women are employed outside the home. As was discussed in Chapter 6, husbands do help out more when wives are employed, but not much more (Demo & Acock, 1993; Rexcoat & Shehan, 1987). The division of labor remains lopsided even in households in which the husband is presently unemployed (Brayfield, 1992). On the average, men only do one-third of the domestic work (Greenstein, 1995). This situation becomes worse when the couple has children, as fathers do not participate very much in the day-to-day care of the children, leaving most of it to mothers.

Consider the wife who works all day at a job outside the home and then comes home to find that she is expected to do almost everything in the home as well. We might expect her to become somewhat disenchanted, and the evidence shows this happens in some cases.

Sharing housework and child care means more than freeing the wife to do other things that she might want to do. Wives interpret their husband's participation as signs of love, support, and concern (Pina & Bengtson, 1993). Their husbands lack of help might lead to a reduction in marital satisfaction. Satisfaction with the division of labor in both household and child care is related to satisfaction for both men and women (Heinicke, 1995). There are definite advantages when husbands participate more equally in these duties (Pina & Bengtson, 1993). Such sharing decreases depression in wives, and increases marital satisfaction, and leads to an increased sense of personal well-being (Perry-Jenkins & Folk 1994).

However, not all women are equally distressed by lack of help from their husbands. Research shows that the consequences of this unequal division of labor depend upon how wives perceive and interpret it, and these perceptions are filtered by her concept of gender roles (Greenstein, 1995). Although most women are aware of their unequal responsibilities, not all women see this division of labor as unfair (Thompson & Walker, 1989). Women who have very traditional views of the husband/wife relationship consider housework to be their responsibility even if it is not fairly distributed. They are aware of the inequality, but it does not affect their marital satisfaction because they believe that this additional work is part of their role (Greenstein, 1995). That is not the case with women who have more nontraditional ideas about the division of labor and among many women who work full time. These wives expect their husbands to help out more and when husbands don't, their marital satisfaction is greatly reduced. They don't see the unequal sharing of duties as appropriate or legitimate (Pina & Bengtson, 1993). Especially for these wives, husband participation is connected to feelings of support, which in turn are associated with higher marital quality and positive well-being (Pina & Bengtson, 1993).

Both spouses are vulnerable to marital dissatisfaction when they perform more of the domestic duties than their perception of gender roles allows. Wives with nontraditional attitudes but traditional roles are less satisfied. Men will also express dissatisfaction if the domestic duties are more equally divided and they believe that male and female roles should be more traditionally defined (McHale & Crouter, 1992). Before entering into marriage or parenthood today, some understanding of each partner's roles is necessary. With gender attitudes changing, the division of labor is more important than ever (Suitor, 1991).

Marital Satisfaction and the Life Cycle

Which stages of life are the most and which the least satisfying? Marital challenges and growth opportunities change with the presence or absence of children and their ages. The challenges of caring for the constant physical and emotional needs of infants differs from the responsibilities of helping adolescents develop. Family life can be divided into eight stages (Figure 15.2). Some authorities combine a few of these stages, for example, of becoming a parent, parenting preschool children, and parenting elementary school children into one stage (Carter & McGoldrick, 1989). The family's place in the family life cycle is determined by the age of the oldest child; this approach emphasizes the specific challenges that arise at each stage.

Marital satisfaction is high at the beginning of marriage, and then decreases as children are born and are raised. When children are grown, marital satisfaction increases (Glenn, 1990). Generally, the early and later stages are the most satisfying.

The life cycle approach has been criticized for focusing only on the traditional two-parent, intact family. Cohabiting couples, families affected by divorce, families of people who have remarried, single parents, and gay and lesbian families are variations in family structures not covered adequately by this model. Second, the relationship between the presence of children and marital satisfaction is not as strong as once believed and is more complicated than the life cycle model proposes. Children may cause stress but also feelings of pride and accomplishment.

Divorce

Divorce is a reality for about 1,200,000 couples each year (Edwards, 1995). As shown in Figure 15.3, the divorce rate has declined since hitting its peak in 1979, but remains high (Singh et al., 1995). Divorce is a permanent part of American life (White, 1990). About half of all divorces occur during the first 7 years of marriage, one-third occur within the first 4 years (Kurdek, 1991a). It is estimated that between 40% to 60% of all new marriages

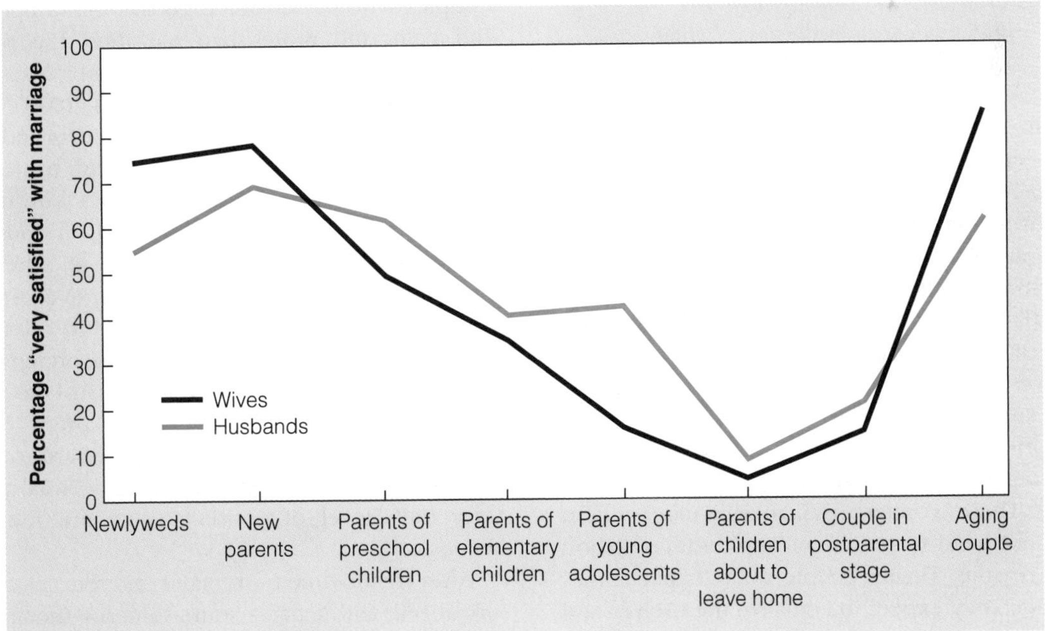

Figure 15.2
Marital Satisfaction Across the Life Span
Source: Adapted from Rollins and Feldman, 1970.

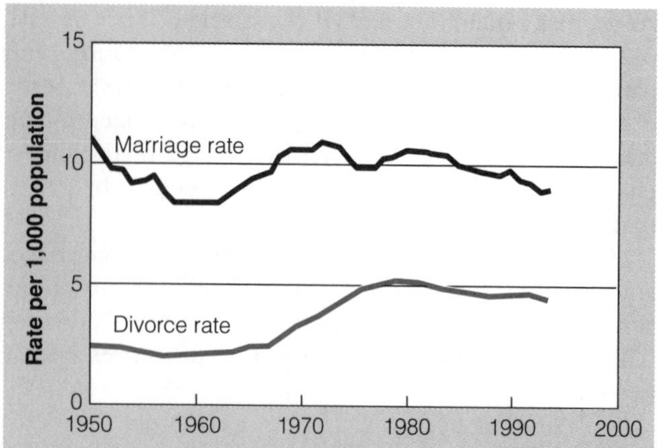

Figure 15.3
Marriage and divorce rates: United States, 1950–1994
Source: Singh et al., 1995.

will end in divorce; the exact figure depends upon the study (Edwards, 1995; Wineberg, 1994).

Questions Students Often Ask

It is hard to be optimistic about marriage with all these problems. Were marriages much happier in the past? *Although on the surface this may seem to be the case, I'm never sure if it really is. Certainly roles were better defined in the past, but I don't know if all those marriages that lasted were necessarily happy. If someone is very unhappy in a marriage today, divorce is a definite option. This was not available years ago. Years ago, few women had the ability to support themselves and their children. Different historical periods bring different challenges for marriage, but I would hesitate to say the they were necessarily happier.*

The increase in divorce is caused by many factors. The advent of no-fault divorce laws, which allow either spouse to gain a divorce without having to prove the other guilty of adultery or mental cruelty has increased the divorce rate (Nakonezny, Shull, & Rodgers, 1995). The stigma attached to being divorced is not nearly as great as it was in the past. Historically, many women stayed with their husbands because they had no other means of supporting themselves. Today, because more women are employed they are less likely to feel the need to stay married. Career-oriented women with college educations are more likely to get divorced than other groups of women (Glick, 1984). These women are financially independent and thus do not need to stay in an unpleasant situation for financial reasons. Finally, people today expect more out of marriage; they expect to actualize themselves and grow within the marriage. Older studies of reasons for divorce usually note that drinking or nonsupport were important factors. Newer studies emphasize breakdowns in affection and communication. People seeking divorce give many reasons for their decision; communication problems, unhappiness, incompatibility, emotional abuse, financial problems, infidelity, disagreement about gender roles, sexual problems, and alcohol problems are among the most prominent (White, 1990).

Why People Divorce

Divorce is not simply the result of a decline in marital satisfaction. Although marital satisfaction declines with time, marital stability increases (Karney & Bradbury, 1995). In other words, despite a decline in marital satisfaction with time, marriages are more stable with age and couples are less likely to divorce. The continuation of a marriage or its demise depends upon weighing the attractions of all aspects of the relationship, the barriers to leaving the relationship (financial or religious), and the presence of attractive alternatives outside the marriage. Marriages end when the attractions of the relationship are few, the barriers relatively weak, and the alternatives are inviting (Karney & Bradbury, 1995).

Women are more likely than men to initiate divorce. In about three-quarters of divorces, the woman initiates the proceedings (Wallerstein & Kelly, 1980). It is not uncommon for the other spouse to be surprised at the decision, although he or she will readily admit to problems in the marriage. Mutual agreement on divorce is relatively rare. The person who is most surprised is likely to experience the greatest stress, but both spouses suffer.

True or False?
Women are more likely to demand a divorce than are men.

The Consequences of Divorce

Couples who get divorced go through a period of crisis and pain, and more than half find the process very distressing. Divorced people report personal disorganization, anxiety, and loneliness (Myers, 1989). One's daily routine is disrupted, and social supports and friendships change. Divorced people are likely to find it more difficult to continue their friendships with couples they knew before the divorce. Remaining friends with both parties after a divorce is difficult; at other times the single person may not fit in with an evening of couples getting together. However, friends and relatives are important sources of support for divorcing individuals. After the divorce, it is not unusual to experience negative emotions, but these are often balanced by positive feelings, such as looking forward to a better life (Raschke, 1987). When the marriage was marked by a very high level of conflict, there are fewer negative feelings.

After the divorce both males and females are more disorganized, and it takes some time for them to put their new lives in order. Divorce may even lead to physical problems; studies show that divorced people have poorer health, a higher mortality rate, and more accidents than married people. The physical and psychological health of married people is superior to that of separated and divorced people (Kurdek, 1991a; White, 1990).

The experiences of divorced people with and without children differ. The divorced person without children need not have any contact with the former spouse, and studious avoidance is quite common. Each person is free to establish a completely independent life. There is less quarreling after the divorce; contact, although less frequent, is more friendly (Masheter, 1991). When children are involved, financial support is usually an issue, as are child-rearing practices.

Four different patterns of contact with former spouses have been identified (Stark, 1986). In 12% of the cases studied, ex-spouses could be placed into the *Perfect Pals* group. These ex-spouses remained friends and continued to be actively involved in each other's lives. In 38% of the cases, the ex-spouses could be described as *Cooperative Colleagues.* They had a moderate amount of interaction, were mutually supportive, and minimized potential conflicts, but were not as involved with each other as the Perfect Pals group. Twenty-five percent of the couples fell into the category of *Angry Associates.* They, too, had a moderate amount of interaction, but the interactions were marked by conflict. They had difficulty separating the spouse and parent roles. The most troubling quarter of the sample were called *Fiery Foes.* They had very little interaction with each other and argued whenever they did interact. They did not cooperate at all in parenting and were unable to be civil to each other.

How do people see divorce years later? One study found that while half the men opposed separation and divorce at the beginning, two-thirds expressed a positive view of divorce 5 years later. Only 30% of all males responding in the study were content, though. The number of women viewing divorce as positive decreased, although still more than half considered it a positive step (Kelly, 1982). Within 2 years of the divorce, divorced women perceive themselves as less depressed, less anxious, drink less, and have fewer health problems (Hetherington, 1993). Many are proud of their independence and their ability to cope, even though the postdivorce situation can be stressful. Most are happier in their new situation than in the last year of marriage before the divorce (Hetherington, 1993).

Most people eventually do start a new life and build new relationships. The healthier and better adjusted a person is before the divorce, the more quickly that person is likely to adjust to divorce (Wallerstein & Kelly, 1980). Often only one of the divorced spouses shows an improvement (Wallerstein, 1986). Even 10 years after the divorce, feelings of anger are common. However, the majority do recover and rebuild their lives, and we find increases in general happiness and self-esteem 2 years following the divorce (Hetherington, Cox, & Cox, 1976).

Remarriage

About three-quarters of all people who divorce will remarry (Bumpass, Sweet, & Martin, 1990). The younger the divorced person, the more likely he or she is to remarry. Divorced men are more likely to remarry than divorced women. Women with children are much less likely to remarry than those without, especially those with three children or more. The average interval between divorce and remarriage is about three years (Giles-Sims & Crosbie-Burnett, 1989). About half of these remarriages result in children being born, most often within the first or second year of the remarriage (Wineberg, 1990).

One obvious difference between first and second marriages is that people are older in their second marriage (Ganong & Coleman, 1994). Courtships tend to be shorter, sometimes because the parties knew each other before the divorce and they feel that they are marrying someone who allows them to be themselves (Furstenberg & Spanier, 1984). Most people blame their divorces on marrying the wrong person, and they look for different things in their second spouse than they did in the first. They are more pragmatic than romantic. The first time, they emphasized appearance, ambition, and occupational status; the second time they place importance on stability and respect. Expectations for the marriage are lower (Furstenberg, 1982). In addition, they are more informal when dating, and rather than project an ideal image, they present themselves honestly. The unhappy experience of the first marriage makes an indelible impression on the choice for the second.

True or False?
People look for different qualities in their second spouse than they did in their first.

Remarried people are satisfied and happy, and just as in first marriages, satisfaction declines somewhat over time (Coleman & Ganong, 1991). However, people who remarry are more likely to get divorced (Karney & Bradbury, 1995). The divorce rate is about 25% higher for second than for first marriages (Ihinger-Tallman & Pasley, 1987; Martin & Bumpass, 1989), possibly because people are not as ready to allow an unhappy remarriage to go on for as long as they did the first. The presence of stepchildren may also increase the chances of a divorce. Although children do not select the new spouses, they do have the power to "de-select" the spouse by creating conflict in the house (Ihinger-Tallman & Pasley, 1987). The challenges of the stepfamily are many, and remarried people have less tolerance for problems. Monetary difficulties and child-rearing problems are the most prominently mentioned reasons for remarriage failures (Berman, 1987).

The Single Alternative

Most people intend to get married, but not every young adult will marry (Bureau of the Census, 1995). Some will remain single by choice or circumstances and others may choose to cohabit. The last 25 years has witnessed a dramatic increase in the percentage of men and women in their twenties who are single due to the trend to delay marriage, expanded employment options for women, and a reduction in societal pressure for women to marry (Strong & DeVault, 1995). The longer people wait to get married, the less likely they are to marry, probably because they become more used to their lifestyle.

Singles who do not wish to marry emphasize the advantages of their status, including freedom to have a variety of relationships, to travel, and to move with spontaneity (Knox & Schacht, 1991). Singles are also likely to go out more than are married people, but they do admit to being more lonely (Strong & DeVault, 1995). The individual who is single by choice gives priority to career and autonomy. Singles have more control over their own lives and destiny, and more time for personal development and self-fulfillment. Single men and women focus on their independence and believe in egalitarian roles. Single women are accustomed to living on their own without being supported.

Single adults base their social lives on friendships and are very involved with siblings and other family members (Cavanaugh, 1993). Singles may be involved in community service projects as well. Although there is less pressure to marry today, single people have to deal with others' expectations that they will marry. America is a couple-oriented society and fitting in as a single adult is sometimes difficult. Still, most singles have a social network of their own and report being satisfied and happy with their careers and friendships (Alwin, Converse, & Martin, 1985). Singles believe they are happier than people who are married, and people who are married believe they are happier than singles.

True or False?
People who are single by choice believe they are happier than people who are married.

Cohabitation

Cohabitation, living together without being married, is becoming increasingly common in the United States and Canada, and indeed throughout the entire western world (Hall & Zhao, 1995; Loomis & Landale, 1994). About 5% of all women between the ages of 14 and 44 are cohabiting at any one time (London, 1991), but about half have cohabited at some time by the age of 35 (Bumpass & Sweet, 1989). About a third of all cohabiting households contain children, because in many cases at least one of the partners was previously married (Bumpass & Sweet, 1989). Rates of cohabitation have increased because people are getting married at a later age, allowing more time for cohabitation before marriage, an increased tolerance towards premarital sex, and women's decreased dependence on marriage.

cohabitation The state of living together without being married.

People may decide to cohabit for a variety of reasons: as a temporary convenience or simply as a continuation of an affectionate relationship in which two people enjoy each other but do not want to marry. They may also view cohabitation as a trial marriage or a temporary alternative to marriage until they feel ready for the commitment of marriage. Some consider it a permanent relationship, another form of singlehood (Rindfuss & Vanden Heuvel, 1990). Formerly married men and women may be more cautious about marrying again, and may use cohabitation as a way to test compatibility. Although some people who cohabit may do so for economic reasons, most have a strong emotional relationship.

People who cohabit do not differ from those who do not in social adjustment or socioeconomic status, but do differ on measures of religiosity. People who identify closely with their religious group are less likely to cohabit (Thornton, Axinn, & Hill, 1992). Cohabitation is not a threat to the institution of marriage, for those who favor cohabitation also express favorable opinions of marriage (Hobart, 1993).

True or False?
Young adults who cohabit express strong attitudes against marriage.

Cohabitation is far from a permanent relationship for most (Teachman & Polonko, 1990). About half the relationships end within a year (Lauman et al., 1994) and less than a quarter go on to marriage (Browder, 1988).

Cohabiting relationships differ in some ways from marital relationships. There is somewhat less commitment, especially among men, than in marital relationships. In addition, whereas married people pool their money, cohabiting couples maintain their financial independence. Also, in cohabiting relationships the woman is expected to work and support herself even if she is going to school (Strong & DeVault, 1995).

Although married couples who live together before marrying each other regard the experience as positive, the research shows that for many, cohabitation is no real advantage (Watson & DeMeo, 1987). There is more physical violence in cohabiting relationships than in married relationships (Stets & Straus, 1990). When people who are dating, married couples, and cohabiting couples are compared, violence is most common among the cohabiting couples (Lane & Gwartney-Gibbs, 1985; Stets & Straus, 1989). In addition, studies do not find that marriages preceded by cohabitation are any better or more satisfying than the marriages of couples who do not cohabit (De Maris & Rao, 1992). Cohabitation before marriage is associated with a lower perceived quality of communication for wives, and lower marital satisfaction as well as less satisfactory marital adjustment for both spouses (Booth & Johnson, 1988; DeMaris & Leslie, 1984).

Although people assume that living together as a couple before marrying or remarrying is an effective way to reduce the risk of divorce, studies show that this is not so (Hall & Zhao, 1995). The divorce rate for couples who lived together before marriage is actually higher than for the general population (Glenn, 1990); about a third higher than married couples who did not cohabit (Bumpass & Sweet, 1989). Perhaps living together undermines the idea of formal marriage and reduces commitment (Axinn & Thornton, 1992).

One standard argument in favor of premarital cohabitation is that it is a trial marriage to test the couple's compatibility. Although the evidence clearly shows that cohabitation does not lead to an improved marital relationship, it does not clarify the oft-stated point that it may have prevented many potentially bad marriages. It does show that the benefits may not be as great as some would like to believe.

Parenting

"Making the decision to have a child—it's momentous. It is to decide forever to have your heart go walking around outside your body" (Stone, 1989, p. 34). The decision to become a parent has major consequences for both spouses and for the marriage. Although most couples want to have children, some do not have this desire.

To Have or Have Not

Parenting is now considered a choice for people, mainly because of the availability of birth control and a change in societal attitudes. Although still a relatively small minority, more couples are electing not to have children (Somers, 1993). Some women declare their desire not to have children early in life—well before they get married—and seek out a mate who agrees with that plan. Some couples delay having children, often for career reasons, until they make the decision not to have children at all (Wolf, 1996). They tend to be well educated, to live in urban areas, and to have more nontraditional views of sex roles than their parents do (Somers, 1993). These women are more committed to their careers and are often professionals (Ambry, 1992). Couples who are asked why they want to remain child-free often cite freedom from child-care responsibilities, opportunity for self-fulfillment, more satisfactory marital relationships, female career considerations, monetary advantages, concern about population growth and the general state of world affairs, general dislike of children, doubts about parenting ability, concern about physical aspects of childbirth, and freedom to work or to travel (Houseknecht, 1987; Richmond-Abbott, 1983).

Most studies find that child-free marriages are satisfying to both partners (Somers, 1993). Studies find a higher degree of marital satisfaction among child-free couples than among couples with children (Strong & DeVault, 1995). Voluntarily child-free adults believe that they are viewed negatively, especially by other parents. Child-free women especially believe that they are the victims of stereotyping. Voluntary child-free marriages are happy and both husband and wife are satisfied. It is an option that is taken by a comparatively small minority of couples. Couples who decide on child-free marriages must be strong because they are going against the current of societal expectations.

The Transition to Parenting

The arrival of the first child is a major transition in life (Levy-Shiff, 1994). This is especially true for the mother, who is more involved in the daily care of the child. The family interaction will now change as the focus is placed on meeting the needs of the child. Although problems will arise, such as a need for family reorganization, most young parents report feelings of self-fulfillment, finding a new meaning in life and increased family cohesiveness (Miller & Sollie, 1980). After the birth, positive as well as negative changes are bound to accur.

One important change is what social scientists have called the *traditionalization of the marriage.* Role division becomes more traditional no matter what the employment status, educational status, preexisting division of labor before the child, and sex-role ideology (Levy-Shiff, 1994). After a month or so, the extra help given by the father decreases somewhat, and, as we noted in Chapter 6, mothers tend to do more at home than fathers whatever the age of the children.

True or False?
When a couple has a child, the division of labor in the marriage becomes more traditional.

How does becoming a parent affect a marriage? Carolyn and Philip Cowan (1992) followed couples for 5 years beginning in the prenatal period. In many cases, both husbands and wives showed a modest but significant decrease in marital satisfaction during this time. Not all couples showed such a decline in marital satisfaction, and about 18% actually showed an improvement in marital satisfaction. That figure increased significantly for those who participated in a support group program. No one reason was found for this decline in satisfaction, but the physical strain of child care, increased financial responsibilities, restrictions on parents, and redefinition of roles may all play a role. Discrepancies in expectations were important, and when there was a large discrepancy between wives' expectations and husbands' involvement in child care, a greater decline was found in marital satisfaction. Poor communication was also an important factor.

The problems in some families of new parents may exist long before the first infant arrives. Couples who report the most marital difficulty after having an infant tend to be those who had experienced the most strain even before they became parents. Couples with a history of being able to work out differences continue to do this and report the least dissatisfaction. Couples with more satisfying marriages work together effectively with their children. Succeeding as a couple after becoming parents requires striking a delicate balance between dreams and reality, between one's own needs and the demands of the other members of the family. The study showed that professionally led groups could significantly reduce the stress and the risk of divorce for expectant couples. The most consistent factor predicting satisfaction was paternal involvement with baby, especially in care-giving.

Motherhood

Even when a woman welcomes a pregnancy, her initial reaction might be one of both doubt and joy. Her doubt may come from some concern about her ability to parent. The mother-to-be might also feel more vulnerable, distressed about the physical changes in her body, and anxious about her infant's physical condition (Field, 1980). At the same time, positive feelings about the pregnancy are common. Bearing a child changes a woman's status and life. The woman may see herself as more responsible and mature, but also as more restricted. Some women expect to be tied down by the demands of young children but feel that there will be time for personal freedom later, when the children have grown up.

After the birth, a period of postpartum blues is not uncommon (Hopkins, Marcus, & Campbell, 1984). Between 50% to 70% of all new mothers experience the maternal blues, while about 10% experience postpartum depression, a more severe reaction (Kraus & Redman, 1986). Hormonal and psychological factors are considered probable causes, and stress has been implicated as well (Pfost, Stevens, & Matejcak, 1990).

The presence of a child in the family brings about changes in routine. Because the mother is likely to take on the greater share of the child-rearing responsibility, she feels additional stress (Barnard & Martell, 1995). She is expected to know how to do everything, even though child care is not instinctual. Mothering can be challenging because of loss of personal time, the need to gain role skills, nighttime care, and sleep deprivation (Barnard & Martell, 1995).

Despite the stress, parents report feelings of creativity, accomplishment, and competence from having and rearing children (Williams, 1977). When asked how much satisfaction they obtained from each of several areas of life—including jobs, marriage, leisure activities, housework, and being parents—parents reported that all areas provided some satisfaction, but none as much as parenthood. When parents were asked how having a child changes a person's life, the answers were primarily positive. Despite the many problems and self-doubts, parenting is a significant source of satisfaction in adulthood (Hoffman, 1982).

Fatherhood

New fathers experience fewer lifestyle changes than new mothers. Fathers are usually not as ambivalent about a wanted pregnancy, because they do not anticipate as many changes in their lives. The overwhelming majority find fatherhood very satisfying (Findlay, 1985). However, fathers may find themselves under a good deal of pressure when it comes to financial considerations, which is often their primary concern.

Society's view of fathering has changed over time from father as provider to father as nurturer as well. There is a significant trend toward looking at parenting in terms of non-gender-specific behavior (Atkinson & Blackwelder, 1993). That is, parenting is seen as a set of behaviors and skills that can be performed by both mothers and fathers. The traditional father was aloof and distant. He may have provided some emotional support for the mother, but his primary job was to support the family and had little or no involvement with the children (Fein, 1978). In the 1960s this began to change to what is called the modern view. Fathers came to be regarded as important to the successful development of the children and vital in certain areas—including the proper development of masculinity and femininity, academic performance, and moral development. Paternal guidance and presence were deemed important, which is significantly different from the traditional view.

Men may model their fathering practices after those of their own father. Fathers who are nurturant and involved tend to have children who grow up and treat their children the same way. Some men, though, may compensate for the lack of relationship they had with their own father and try to become more involved with their own children.

The emergent perspective on fathering is that men are psychologically able to participate in all parenting behaviors and that children's lives are improved by the opportunity to develop a personal relationship with both parents. Fathers are no longer seen as deficient in child-rearing skills just because they are males. This new view is reflected in the sections on fathering throughout this text.

Much is written about participation of the father in child care, but mothers are still much more involved than fathers. The situation is changing, but too slowly for some women. We still hear fathers talking about having to "baby-sit" their children or "helping out once in a while with a bottle," as if they were doing their wives a favor. The father's role as parent is secondary to the mother's, even if she is employed full time (Cowan & Cowan, 1992).

Fathers who are more involved often but not always have had nurturant and involved fathers who served as models (Parke, 1995). On the other hand, some involved fathers are compensating for the deficiencies in their childhood relationships with their own fathers (Baruch & Bennett, 1986).

Other factors that differentiate involved from noninvolved fathers include positive attitudes towards fatherhood and parenting skills. Fathers who reject the idea of a biological basis for sex differences in parenting and believe they have care-giving skills are more likely to be involved. In addition, maternal support is important. Mothers who actively encourage their husbands to become involved are more likely to have husbands who participate in child care responsibilities (Parke, 1995). Finally, the better the quality of the marital relationship, the more likely the father is to be involved with the children. In fact, the father-child relationship is more sensitive to changes in the marital relationship than the mother-child relationship (Belsky, 1984).

Single Parenting

The United States has a higher proportion of single-parent households than any other developed country. In 1995, of the estimated 67 million children under the age of 18, about 16.5 million were living with their mother only and about 2.5 million with only their father (U.S. Bureau of the Census, 1996). More than half of all children living in single-parent families have experienced a divorce. The second largest group of children have mothers who have never married. Although births to unmarried teens makes up a large percentage of these births, many single unmarried mothers are found in older groups (U.S. Bureau of the Census, 1996). Single motherhood has been increasing among women in their 20s (Weinraub & Gringlas, 1995). A small minority are widows. Most singles giving birth have limited job skills and inadequate support networks. About half of all single mothers live in poverty; one of every two single mothers lives below the poverty level whereas only one in ten two-parent families is poor (McLanahan & Booth, 1991).

Single parents claim that financial difficulties are their number one postdivorce problem (Amato & Partridge, 1987). Financial problems are greatest for poor women, women with no education or little employment experience, and women who have custody of small children. Since these women are primarily responsible for child-rearing and providing economic support they are at a greater risk of poverty than when they were married (Maccoby et al., 1993). Disparities in income between white and African American women are significant during marriage, but following divorce white women experience a greater decline in standard of living; the income of divorced white and African American women is about the same (Morgan, 1991). Even if the wife and children have not fallen into poverty, their standard of living drops greatly (Garrison, 1994). One significant reason for low income is lack of child support (see New Perspectives on p. 354). Many divorced people overcome these economic and social problems, although it takes a significant amount of time and effort to do so.

If single parents are to provide for themselves and their families, they often need to find jobs. Yet, the employment opportunities for single parents are often limited because of their need to care for young children and the lack of available day care services (Maccoby et al., 1993). Single mothers often must increase the number of hours they work in order to improve their lot financially. Employed single mothers are often constantly on the verge of financial disaster and earn on the average of only about a third of what employed working men make, partly because women make less than men, work fewer hours, and often have poorer job skills and need to arrange for child care.

The everyday problems of being a single parent are many. For example, a woman may have to give up a good job because child care is unavailable before and after school. Children may also have to give up opportunities such as after-school tutoring or soccer club if their parent cannot find someone to drive them to and from school. Even though divorced households eventually restabilize, they are less organized and mothers report feeling overloaded by all that they have to accomplish (Hetherington & Stanley-Hagen, 1995). They perceive themselves as more able parents, but do report more child-rearing stresses, especially in the area of monitoring and control of children (Hetherington, 1993).

Often the noncustodial parent—especially right after a divorce—will indulge the child and give him or her everything possible, as well as agree with the child's complaints against the custodial parent. This may undercut the custodial parent's authority, making discipline difficult. Sometimes the custodial parent tries to turn the child against the other parent; at other times, the child may play one parent against another.

Fathers who have custody have their own problems. Many must learn a child-rearing routine that is foreign to them, and they suffer the same problems of loneliness and lack of child care that single mothers do. Despite

New Perspectives: Child Support—Not as Simple as People Think

We call them "dead beat dads." Some states take away their driving licenses until they make arrangements to pay their child support. The stories of men who do not pay child support, and of the wives and children who live in unnecessary poverty make us angry. Politicians speak out against these delinquent fathers and the public is told that all we need to do is find some way to force them to pay up.

It is common knowledge that many men do not pay the child support and alimony awarded to their ex-wives. About 51% of all women awarded child support payments receive their full payment whereas 24% receive partial payment. One in four, 25%, receive no payment at all (U.S. Bureau of the Census, 1996). Fewer women with children who live below the poverty level receive full child support. African American and Latino women with young children are less likely to be awarded child support payments and are less likely to receive them (Franklin, Smith, & McMiller, 1995; U.S. Bureau of the Census, 1996).

What happens when fathers have custody and mothers are required to pay child support? The number of father-headed families has substantially increased since the 1960s, although there are still many more families headed by single mothers. Father-only families with children have substantially higher incomes than mother-only families, but even so, almost 20% live in poverty. Relatively few fathers are awarded child support, but only about half of these receive any payment at all (Meyer & Garasky, 1993); dead-beat moms exist as well.

Why don't fathers pay? It is easy to mention irresponsibility or feelings that the award was not fair as a reason for nonpayment. However, there are other factors that contribute to the problem. Some men simply cannot pay because they are unemployed or underemployed or because they are alcoholics or drug abusers. Others may get remarried and have other child care responsibilities and may be unable to support two families. Even wives who do receive support regularly are likely to find that the support is not sufficient. Women with young children often seek employment only to find that affordable child care is not available.

It has become popular to suggest that after divorce the woman's standard of living decreases greatly and the ex-husband's increases (Weitzman, 1985). Such studies have been presented to Congress and have become part of the conventional wisdom. However, other studies suggest that there are reductions in income for both spouses (Corcoran, Duncan, & Hill, 1984; McLanahan & Booth, 1989). In addition, some argue that many studies purporting to show that the ex-wife's income drops substantially do not take into consideration the fact that divorced women often increase their hours at work (Kitson & Morgan, 1990). However, most women find that their incomes decrease after divorce and many cannot maintain a decent standard of living; divorced women with young children comprise a large proportion of the poor.

Delinquent payments by men who can pay but do not make a large difference only in the upper middle and upper classes (Salt, 1991). Although there is no doubt that improved child support collection policies are important, and should be instituted, they will have only limited success for poor fathers and those from the lower middle class. A person earning very little cannot pay enough, no matter what percentage is ordered, to sustain two households (Salt, 1991). There is no way that one poor or lower middle-class income can support two households.

This has led to a number of suggestions. Some advocate cost-sharing mechanisms in which the actual cost of raising the child is shared on a percentage basis. Others argue that additional payments, if necessary, should be made through tax money or Social Security. Perhaps the actual amount awarded should be given by government programs and the government should then collect what it can from the ex-husbands. Others note that often the ex-husband feels alienated from the family, and having some agreed-upon amount, frequent visitation rights, and mediation can increase payments (Peterson & Nord, 1990). Paternal involvement seems to be one key. We know that fathers who are involved with their children are more likely to pay child support. In addition, fathers who have some input in the child-rearing decisions are more likely to pay. Paying child support, visitation, and participating in child-rearing decisions seem to go together (Seltzer, 1991). When fathers participate in any one of these, they participate in the other two. However, there are circumstances in which father involvement may be inappropriate.

Fathers who can pay and do not certainly should be found and the money collected. However, this will not in itself lead to a reasonable standard of living for poor and lower middle-class women and children. Some additional programs may be required. Since we know that visitation, participation in child-rearing decisions, and paying support seem to be linked, we need to encourage paternal input and reduce the ex-husband's alienation from his family.

The child support issue is clearly more complicated than just finding ways to collect the support that is ordered by the courts. We need to debate additional methods for supplementing income and look at both sides; we also need to find ways to encourage ex-husbands to stay involved in their children's lives and pay their fair share toward supporting them.

these problems, single parenting does have rewards. If the home was filled with violence, it is less violent now. If it was fraught with emotional conflict, the conflict is reduced.

Stepparenting

Imagine marrying into a one-parent, two-child family in which certain patterns have been established. As the new parent you must learn how to discipline the children, what changes are feasible, and what areas must be left alone. It is a difficult job, and one for which little training is available.

Stepparents often feel very confused about their role (Ihinger-Tallman & Pasley, 1987), and indeed the rights and responsibilities of stepparents are unclear. In general, stepparents have many of the responsibilities of parents but virtually none of the rights, such as the right to sign for routine medical care or visitation rights or custody in a divorce (Giles-Sims & Crosbie-Burnett, 1989; Fine, 1989). However, despite the lack of rights, stepparents are expected to take on financial, educational, and social responsibilities. Stepmothers are expected to perform a nurturant role in the family, but some power continues to rest with the biological parent, who is likely to be overcritical of the stepmother's efforts.

As noted in Chapter 11 when we discussed the stepfamily from the children's perspective, stepparents do have an effect on their children (Parish, 1982; Duberman, 1973). Just as the experience of the child in a stepfamily can be positive or negative, so can it be for the stepparent. Some stepparents are proud of their stepchildren while others consider them a bother and a source of constant conflict. Still others are not very involved with their stepchildren. Stepparenting is a delicate and sometimes difficult role but one that can bring satisfaction.

Gay and Lesbian Households

As more gay men and lesbians live openly according to their sexual preference, more households are established. Four types of relationships have been noted in the gay community. Some gay men have no special lover and are involved with a variety of partners. Some have a regular lover but do not live together. Others openly live with a special partner but sometimes have sexual experiences outside, while many couples have closed relationships and limit their sexual experiences to each other, resembling heterosexual couples in their exclusivity. Closed couples are becoming more numerous, and gay men are increasingly limiting their sexual partners and reducing their risk of AIDS (Berger, 1990). Closed relationships are characterized by greater levels of social support and interdependence. Lesbians tend to develop sexual relationships more slowly and many of these relationships develop out of friendship (Wolf, 1996).

Gay men and lesbians enter longer-term relationships for the same reasons that straight people do—for love, life satisfaction, and security (Peplau, 1981). Most often, both partners continue to be self-supporting (Peplau & Gordon, 1982). In gay and lesbian relationships household chores are shared somewhat differently than in heterosexual relationships. Compared to both married and gay couples, lesbian couples tend to share tasks, while gay couples and married couples are most likely to have one partner perform most tasks. With married couples, this is almost always the wife (Kurdek, 1993b). In the first year of a relationship, gay couples share tasks but after that they are allocated on the basis of skill and work schedule; the division of labor is more equal than in heterosexual relationships.

Gay, lesbian, and heterosexual couples show more similarities than differences in the areas of conflict. No differences are found in disagreements over power, personal vices such as drinking or smoking, intimacy, or in job or school commitments. In general, heterosexual couples argue more over social issues, such as politics and dealing with in-laws than gay men or lesbians, and gay men and lesbians argue more over distrust and jealousy (Kurdek, 1994). As members of a minority group that is often harassed (D'Augelli, 1992), perhaps lesbians and gay men have more similar views on many controversial issues, such as gay rights. The problem of jealousy and distrust is a bigger one for gay men and lesbians probably because a former lover may remain in the same social network. As with heterosexual couples, frequency of conflict is related to dissatisfaction in the relationship.

Gay Men and Lesbians as Parents

About 20% of all gay men have been married and about half have at least one child (Allen & Demo, 1995). About a third of all lesbians have been married, and half have children (Falk, 1989). Between 5000 and 10,000 lesbians have borne children through artificial insemination (Seligmann, 1990).

In the past gay men and lesbians have been prevented from adopting children and have lost child custody cases just because of their sexual preference. This is caused by prejudice and incorrect assumptions. For example, some people believe that children raised by gay men or lesbians will have more difficulties with their gender roles or will be more likely to be abused. Others fear that this will lead to the children having homosexual preferences, too. These assumptions are all false (Falk, 1989). Studies of children living with gay or lesbian parents show that the overwhelming majority become heterosexual (Green, 1982; 1978). Studies of the sexual orientation of the adult children of gay fathers show that more than 90% are heterosexual (Bailey et al., 1995).

> ***True of False?***
> The overwhelming majority of children raised by gay or lesbian parents consider themselves heterosexual.

This does not mean that being raised in a gay or lesbian environment has no effect on children's conception of relationships. One would expect any child raised in a loving and warm environment with gay or lesbian parents to be more accepting of such relationships and, indeed, this is the case. When the children of lesbian and heterosexual single mothers were followed from childhood into early adulthood, children from lesbian family backgrounds were a little more likely to admit to some same-gender sexual attraction but no significant differences in sexual orientation were found. People raised in such circumstances are more willing to admit such attraction than those raised in heterosexual homes. When asked about sexual identity, almost all the young adults with lesbian mothers identified themselves as heterosexual, but significantly more stated that they had considered or thought it was possible that they would experience same-gender attraction or have a same-gender relationship (Golombok & Tasker, 1996). This was especially true for daughters and the young adults raised by lesbian mothers were more likely to have had such a relationship. People raised by lesbian mothers are more open to these relationships than those raised in heterosexual homes, but the overwhelming majority become heterosexual.

Evidence shows that children reared in gay or lesbian homes do not differ significantly in intellectual functioning from children raised in heterosexual households. When the children raised by lesbian couples who had the child through artificial insemination were compared with matched heterosexual families, no significant differences in the children's cognitive functioning or behavioral adjustment were found. The quality of the couple's relationships were similar, but lesbian parents did show more parenting awareness skills (Flaks et al., 1995). This last finding is not surprising because women, both heterosexual and lesbian, show more awareness of parenting skills. Child-rearing practices were also similar. No current research shows significant differences in parenting or outcomes between lesbian and heterosexual mothers (Strong & DeVault, 1995; Falk, 1989).

Although the housework and decision making are shared in lesbian households, biological mothers are more involved in child care, and nonbiological mothers spend more time in paid employment (Patterson, 1995). Just as in heterosexual married households, when lesbian couples share the child care more evenly mothers are more satisfied and children are better adjusted. Even within the context of these more egalitarian arrangements, more equal sharing of child care is related to better outcomes for biological mothers and their children, although the differences are somewhat smaller than in heterosexual homes.

Gay fathers can be effective parents, and those living in stable relationships provide good parenting. Most gay fathers have positive relationships with their children, and gay fathers want their children to have stable environments. No significant differences in parenting are found between gay, lesbian, and heterosexual parents, with the exception that heterosexual parents try harder to provide opposite-sex role models (Harris & Turner, 1986/1985).

It remains to be seen what status society will give these relationships in the future and which rights will be accorded and which rights will be withheld. It is clear that gay men and lesbians would like the right to get married. At present, no state allows homosexual marriages, although Hawaii is considering it. Some cities allow a commitment ceremony and permit the couple to register in a city clerk's office as domestic partners (Adams, 1996). Whatever the stand on marriage, the old arguments against gay and lesbian parenting should be put to rest. No evidence shows that being raised by gay or lesbian parents injures children in any way (Patterson, 1992).

Questions Students Often Ask

If lesbian and gay parents can be good parents, shouldn't they have the right to get married and take on the responsibilities and receive the benefits of marriage?

At the present, no state recognizes gay marriages, but that may change in the future. Gay men and lesbians have won some rights. In 1989 the New York State Court of Appeals made an historic ruling involving a gay couple who had lived together for 10 years. When one of the men died, the other man wanted to take over the rent-controlled apartment, which, according to law, could be done only by a family member ("Homosexual Families and the Law," 1989). The court ruled in the man's favor. We used to think of a family in terms of blood relationships, but now we look at the amount of time people live together, whether they are economically interdependent, and whether they think of themselves as a couple. Other important issues involve medical coverage and other family benefits.

Friendships in Early Adulthood

Friends form the basis for social life, and their support and help can be vital in times of crisis. Most friendships in young adulthood are based on proximity and similarity. We tend to become friendly with people who live close to us and who are in similar economic circumstances (Kahn, 1984). Women especially are likely to be friendly with neighbors, and often their children are friends too (Athanasion & Yushioka, 1973). Shared interests and attitudes are also important. All these factors work together because people who live near each other are likely to have similar incomes, social status, and attitudes.

Same-sex friendships formed by men and women differ. Women's friendships are likely to be deeper and more intimate than friendships between men (Caldwell & Peplau, 1982). Across all age groups, men are less expressive and are more likely to talk about sports, politics, and business, whereas women are more likely to share their feelings and problems (Fox et al., 1985).

Questions Students Often Ask

My best friend is a girl my age whom I have known for years. There is no sexual relationship, yet my fiancée seems to object to it. Why is it so difficult to have opposite-sex friends?

After marriage, most friendships are same-gender friendships. Cross-gender friendships are rare because people's expectations for marriage include both sexual and emotional exclusivity. Yet, there is some evidence for some tolerance. More than 80% of one sample of college women thought it acceptable for a spouse to go to the movies with a female friend, but less than 33% thought it acceptable for a spouse to dance to the stereo with such a friend (Weis & Felton, 1987).

Friendships formed in early adulthood tend to endure, probably because families follow the same developmental course and share the same problems (Lowenthal, Thurnher, & Chiriboga, 1975). Young adults tend to have more friendships than they had in late adolescence or will have in middle or late adulthood (Weiss & Lowenthal, 1975).

On the Job

People tend to associate money with the words "career" or "job." But pay is just one aspect of the world of work. Work keeps a person busy: about 80,000 hours—or 30% of one's lifetime—is taken up by work (Miller, 1964). Work yields personal satisfaction and is a significant source of social interaction as people often form friendships at work. Work also affects one's self-concept. Satisfaction with one's job is related to general happiness, and vocational success is related to self-esteem (Marshall, 1983).

Young adults typically are interested in advancement, but in middle adulthood, job security becomes more important (Krausz, 1982). This is mirrored in job mobility statistics, which show that workers in their 20s tend to change jobs more often than workers in their 30s (Bockino, 1997). Middle-age workers change jobs even less often.

The Changing Workplace

At one time a worker may have thought that he or she would work for one company for a lifetime and that hard work would equal success and security on the job. The firm would offer security and the employee would respond with loyalty. This is no longer true, as the workplace of the 1990s differs from the workplace of 30 years ago.

First, the basic industrial pattern in the United States and other Western nations has changed, as service-related industries have increased greatly while manufacturing has declined (Barringer, 1990). Older manufacturing industries, which have traditionally paid fairly well, have been closed as overseas competition has increased. The decline will continue, but at a somewhat slower rate; by the year 2000 manufacturing in the United States will employ slightly fewer people than today (Personick, 1990).

Second, jobs today require more education and skills. The workplace is changing faster than ever, with new industries, such as biotech and computer-related industries, growing. These industries require more technical skills. Third, there is more insecurity in the workplace. Only 55% of all workers in a recent study believed that their companies provided job security, a decline from earlier studies (Reinemer, 1995). Some of this insecurity is caused by the downsizing of firms (Adler, 1993a). In an attempt to become more competitive, companies have laid off workers, requiring the remaining workers to become more productive. If this continues, the workplace may become an even more insecure place than it is today.

Fourth, the growth of temporary workers, part-time workers, and contract workers has changed the vocational landscape. By the year 2000 half of all jobs will be held by these temporary workers (Sixel, 1995). The "temping of America" has a number of alarming implications: temporary jobs usually do not offer health insurance or retirement benefits. The ability to save on these fringe benefits is one of the reasons why temps are so popular with employers. This may not go on forever,

Workplaces are becoming more technical, requiring greater education and skills.

as these workers may begin to demand medical insurance in the future.

Are Today's Workers Different?

Today's workers are also changing. The modern worker is better educated than ever before (Mare, 1995). Most manual workers have completed high school, and one-fourth have had some college experience. The number of college-educated workers has increased substantially. On the other hand, many more jobs require basic academic skills, such as reading, or more advanced skills, such as computer literacy, than ever before. Educated workers are more likely to want to exercise some control over decision making on the job and to show their competence. Perhaps the supervisor-worker relationship needs to be reevaluated.

Another major change is in the area of the work ethic—the idea that work is valuable for its own sake. As noted in the discussion of Generation X, (see Chapter 14), this generation of workers values a balance between work and leisure more than their baby boomer parents did. For many, working conditions and time off have become more important than more traditional factors (Featherman, 1980). However, there is much evidence that work remains an important part of the life experience (Yankelovich, 1982).

Workers are also showing less company loyalty (Albany & Van Fleet, 1983). People who are unhappy at work are more likely to leave for a more interesting job, and workers today are less likely to feel that they owe the company anything, even if they were trained at company expense. This lack of company loyalty may simply reflect the lack of job security and feelings of dissatisfaction some people experience in their jobs. Many workers now understand that they will probably change jobs more frequently than their parents did. The higher the person's education level, the more jobs he or she holds over a lifetime (U.S. Department of Labor, 1993).

True or False?
Today's employees are more loyal to their companies than workers in the past.

These new attitudes are reflected in the career desires of many young adults. When asked what they want from their jobs, many young adults cite not only money and advancement but also interest and a feeling of accomplishment. People expect more from their careers today. It remains to be seen whether the world of work can satisfy these demands. Also, many more women and minorities are in the workforce and will comprise an even greater percentage in the future.

There has been a great increase in split-shift marriages, in which one parent works in the day and another in the evening (McEnroe, 1991). About one out of every six employed mothers with children under 14 holds an evening or night job or works a rotating shift. The same is true for one of every five working fathers. Dad watches the children when Mom is at her job, and vice versa. For some, this split shift is the answer to the problem of day care. In addition, many service industries require weekend and evening work. The globalization of industry is another cause of night work, since some industries doing business overseas must work when it is daytime in Europe or Asia.

These changes also create employee demands, such as those for leaves of absence, part-time schedules, flexible time, and job sharing. Studies show that men want these as much as women do (McEnroe, 1991).

Job Satisfaction

A relationship exists between life and job satisfaction (Tait, Padgett & Baldwin, 1988). Although the relationship between job satisfaction and performance on the job is complex, evidence exists that worker satisfaction has an impact on how workers perform their job (Iaffaldano & Muchinsky, 1985; Ostroff, 1992). Job dissatisfaction is related to absenteeism and high turnover rates, as well as to the physical and mental health problems of workers (Youngblood, Mobley, & Meglino, 1983).

Studies show that people are generally satisfied with their jobs. The opinion surveys of workers over many decades show that between 80% and 85% consistently state that they are satisfied in their jobs (Glenn & Weaver, 1985; Smither, 1994). Some recent surveys show a smaller percentage, about 65% as satisfied or very satisfied but the idea that most people are dissatisfied with their jobs is simply not true (Reinemer, 1995).

True or False?
The majority of workers say they are satisfied with their jobs.

Job satisfaction can be investigated using a developmental framework but the results depend on whether a longitudinal or cross-sectional method is used. When people are followed longitudinally through their work lives, satisfaction is high at the beginning, probably because they are newly self-sufficient, and the whole world of work is new. Then there is a steep decline in worker satisfaction, followed later by an increase (Rhodes, 1983). If workers are grouped by age (cross-sectionally), a tendency towards increasing satisfaction with age is found. Younger workers express less satisfaction with their jobs than older workers (Hall, 1986; Reinemer, 1995). Part of the dissatisfaction younger workers feel (after the first flush of pride of having a job) may arise because they tend to be given the least creative and fulfilling work, whereas older, more experienced workers may be able to choose the most interesting jobs. In addition, satisfaction with pay increases with age.

Spillover From Home to Work and From Work to Home

Does what happens at work affect what happens in the home? One concern is that unhappiness on the job may spill over to the family (Barnett, 1994; Bergermaier, Borg, & Champoux, 1984). When employed mothers and fathers with young children were studied, those who felt that their work was challenging, complex, and stimulating were more likely to engage in better parenting behaviors, which included less harsh discipline, more warmth, and greater responsiveness (Greenberger, O'Neil, & Nagel, 1994). Adults whose jobs were more challenging and stimulating were generally more satisfied, which may contribute to their better mood at home and to more positive interactions with their children.

Excessive stress on the job is related to poorer interactions at home. When the job and home lives of male air traffic controllers were studied, measures of workload and stress were related to less favorable interactions at home. Work stress decreased the quality of the father-child interaction (Repetti, 1993;1989).

Spillover also is found in the other direction. Satisfaction with family roles is as important, or even more consequential, for men's and women's well-being than satisfaction with work role (Greenberger & O'Neil, 1993). The notion that men are obsessed by work and are less affected by what happens at home is just untrue. Some research shows a greater spillover from home problems to work for men than for women, perhaps because they are less experienced at handling family stressors than women (Barnett, 1994). In addition, a good home situation can buffer both men and women against the pressures of the workplace.

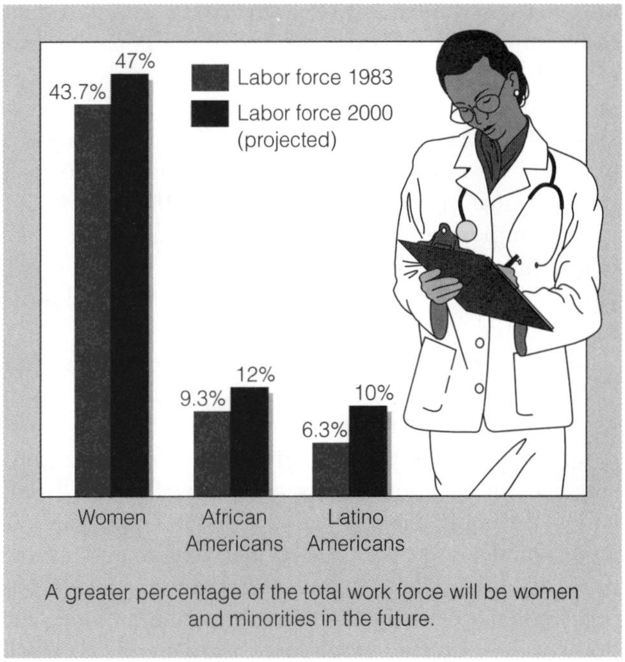

Datagraphic
Women and Minority Participation in the Labor Force
Source: Data from Fullerton, 1990; U. S. Bureau of Labor Statistics, 1996.

Women and Employment

More than 70% of all young adult women are in the labor force (U.S. Bureau of the Census, 1996) and the percentage of all women in the labor force has been increasing greatly. The weekly earnings of women has been growing faster than those of men but are still below their male counterparts. Women are narrowing the wage gap, but the median weekly earnings of women is still approximately 76.6% of men's earnings. This is an increase of more than 11 percentage points between 1985 and 1994 (U.S. Bureau of the Census, 1996).

The increase in women's employment is the result of changes in values, needs, and family structure (Crispell, 1995). With the present reduction in real wages and the higher cost of living (especially for housing), many more women have to work in order to maintain a reasonable standard of living. Values have also changed and many women desire to work or return to work after having a child because they may value both work and family roles. There is a great deal more support for women to work and it is now the norm. Changes in the family structure also have affected the workplace as the number of single and divorced women have increased.

Women are returning to work after having a child somewhat faster than in years past (Yoon & Waite, 1994). In 1993 Congress passed the Family and Medical Leave Act, which guarantees the same or a comparable position upon return from leave and requires the employer to continue the health care benefits during this period. This may increase the time some women stay at home after childbirth, but it is doubtful that this will outweigh the income considerations.

Women's complaints about the workplace have become more strident over the years. Although women express satisfaction with their jobs, they believe that the old-boy network holds them back. Women also recognize their progress in the job market and that benefits have improved. As noted in Chapter 13, they have made solid progress entering middle management (Kilborn, 1995). Although women hold few positions in very senior management, this will change in the future. It takes between 20 and 25 years for any aspiring manager, regardless of gender or race, to move to the peak and because this is the first generation of college-educated and career-oriented women, it is not surprising that women are not yet adequately represented at this level (Russell, 1995). Although no one doubts that discrimination exists, the situation is bound to improve.

Women believe that equity is needed in the areas of salaries, job opportunities, and benefits. However, more women today than in 1970 believe that sex discrimination holds them back in the workplace. About a third of all workplace discrimination cases filed in 1994 were for gender discrimination (a little more than a third were for racial discrimination) (Hansen, 1995). The two most common complaints are violations of the Equal Pay Act of 1963, which prohibits payment of different wages to men and women doing the same work, and violation of Title VII of the Civil Rights Act of 1964, which bars employment discrimination on the basis of race, color, religion, national origin, or gender, and prohibits retaliation against employees. In about half the cases, adequate proof of discrimination is found, while in the other half it is not. There is a large difference between claims filed and those substantiated.

Women are demanding more child care options, leadership opportunities, and an end to wage discrimination. As women progress up the career ladder, they encounter more obstacles, and the gap between expectation and reality becomes greater (Townsend & O'Neil, 1990). Family issues, including flexible work schedules and parental leave, will need to be addressed. Men will be under more pressure to help out at home; seven of ten women in one poll wanted more help from their husbands at home, and this was a source of resentment (Townsend & O'Neil, 1990).

The Two-Career Marriage

In most marriages today both spouses are employed (Crispell, 1995). The advantages of this include greater financial independence, intellectual growth, and a more equal distribution of power in the marriage. The problems involve a possible decline in interaction between husband and wife and the possibility of role strain. Success in dual-career marriages is possible when there is flexibility, mobility, a balance of independence and interdependence, and communication (Maples, 1981).

Many two-career couples delay having children until they are older. Because women are expected to care for the children, even in families in which both spouses are professionals, women are more likely than their husbands to cut down on their work hours (Grant et al., 1990). The mother remains the primary care-giver for the overwhelming majority of preschool children (Brayfield, 1995).

Partners in two-career marriages often have to cope with role overload and role conflict. **Role overload** occurs when the responsibilities of a particular role are more than the energy and time available to perform the duties (Wolf, 1996). Parents may not feel they have enough time to do everything that they need to do. **Role conflict** occurs when the performance of one role makes it difficult to meet the requirements of another role. For example, should one stay late to finish that important project for work or go to the child's dance recital? Both husbands and wives experience role conflict and role overload. Role conflict is especially common for people with young children who often try to juggle many roles at one time (Hughes et al., 1992). High levels of role conflict and role overload make it difficult to concentrate on the marriage and may negatively affect the emotional tone of communication (Paden & Buehler, 1995).

Role reduction, in which parents spend fewer hours at work, is one way to reduce role conflict and role overload. Wives especially tend to reduce their time commitments at work when they experience role conflict or overload. Another method is to reduce one's standards for performing one or more roles. For example, if one is trying to juggle the roles of parent, worker, and housekeeper, reducing one's expectations about how clean the house should be may reduce the strain. Others may be able to help take over some obligations in the home, which might mean that one's standards may have to be compromised.

Some jobs offer flexible schedules, which may allow the parents to better balance all their responsibilities. Those who have such options show less marital and parental stress (Guelzow al., 1991). Telecommuting from home, that is working from home via computer, may be another option as is job sharing. In addition, sometimes cognitive restructuring, that is attempting to redefine stress or negative situations in more neutral or positive terms may help (Paden & Buehler, 1995). There is no single strategy that works, and each individual has to find strategies to cope with the demands of multiple roles.

Leisure

Most Americans believe that the amount of time they have for leisure has decreased dramatically. However, studies of available leisure time show that the average amount of leisure time of most Americans has not decreased at all and for many has even increased (Cutler, 1990). There is, however, a perception of a time famine in America. Women with no children at home have more free time than women with children, but as children age these differences become less (Robinson, 1990).

Why this seeming contradiction between perception and reality? Some people certainly do have less leisure time, especially when you compare their situation now to what it was perhaps when they were younger. For example, a two-career couple with two children is likely to have less time for leisure now than before they had children. By comparing two different periods of life, they begin to believe they have less leisure time, when in reality studies usually compare young adults now with young adults 30 years ago.

Many Americans feel rushed (Robinson, 1990). This is especially true for women in two-income families (Gibbs, 1989). Those who report always feeling rushed are those with the least amount of free time, such as employed

role overload A state in which the responsibilities required in a particular role are more than the energy and time available to perform the duties.

role conflict A state in which the performance of one role makes it difficult to meet the requirements of another role.

mothers with young children. Those who feel rushed work more hours per week than the average person and spend more time caring for children. They do less housework and engage in **time-buying behavior;** that is, buying time-saving goods and shopping more efficiently.

Perhaps it is what people are doing with their leisure that causes them to believe they have less of it. Passive forms of leisure, such as watching television, have increased—along with talking and relaxing—since 1965. How does this compare with the emphasis on active participation in sports? Many leisure products compete for the 4 to 5 hours a week Americans devote to sports and hobbies (Cutler, 1990); weekend vacations have also shown a small rise.

Choices and Pathways

Life in the late 1990s for young adults offers many more options. There is a greater tolerance for different lifestyles now and a greater freedom to choose. With these choices comes the need to assess one's own personal desires and to understand what one wants from a relationship and a career. Each path offers specific challenges and limitations. If young adults know what they want and how they want to live, the late 1990s can offer many opportunities for personal satisfaction and growth.

Summary

1. Many changes are taking place in family and work structure. These changes enhance the choices available to young adults.
2. The basic concerns of early adulthood lie in the areas of love and work. Personality traits are stable, especially after age 30. Changes occur in one's sense of commitment and feelings of personal control. Erikson emphasizes the importance of developing close relationships with others. Levinson sees adult development in terms of eras and periods, each with its own problems and challenges. Periods of transition alternate with periods of stability. The experiences of men and women are similar, but women's dreams are likely to be split between work and family while men's dreams concentrate on individual accomplishment. Women are also more concerned about the roles that society expects men and women to play.
3. Most young adults marry, but the age of first marriage is increasing. Some authorities believe that similarity is the key to understanding mate selection. The stimulus-value-role theory suggests that the decision to marry entails a three-stage progression toward a deeper sense of intimacy. Two types of love, *romantic* and *realistic,* exist. Sternberg argues that love consists of intimacy, passion, and commitment.
4. Most people report satisfaction with their marriage and with their sex life within marriage. Although the frequency of sexual intercourse declines with age, it is not seen as a major problem as long as the couple's relationship is good.
5. Marital satisfaction is related to communication and the ability to handle conflict constructively. Both women and men can be abusive, but since men are generally stronger, women are more at risk for serious injury. Women are more likely to use violence in retaliation or self-defense. Witnessing violence or being the victim of violence in childhood increases the risk of violence in a later relationship. Abusive males often have a history of using physical force to settle disputes, may be drug dependent, and may have difficulty expressing their emotions.
6. Marital satisfaction is also related to a more equal division of labor in household and child-rearing duties. An unequal distribution with the mother doing so much more than the father is more likely to destabilize marriages when the mother holds nontraditional attitudes and expects more help. Communication and companionship are keys to marital satisfaction and adjustment.
7. The divorce rate has stabilized at a high level. Reasons for the high rate are that divorce is easier to obtain, there is less stigma attached to being divorced, women are increasingly able to support themselves, and people expect more from marriage. Breakdowns in affection and communication are commonly cited as reasons for divorce. Divorce is a wrenching experience, but most divorced people manage to rebuild their lives. Divorced women with young children often have serious economic difficulties. Remarriage is common. Stepparenting is a challenging role that may be a satisfying experience or fraught with anxiety and conflict.
8. Early adulthood offers many different lifestyle choices. Single people enjoy their freedom, autonomy, and self-fulfillment, and they have a social network of friends and family. Others choose to cohabit. Most cohabiting couples break up within a year. There is no evidence that those who eventually marry have marriages that are any more satisfying than those who did not cohabit. The divorce rate for these marriages is actually higher.
9. Most couples want to have children, those who can have children but choose not to tend to have happy marriages. The transition to parenthood can be stressful and parenting groups can be helpful. Motherhood brings with it joys, strains, and self-doubt. Our conception of fathering has changed, and the emergent viewpoint is that fathers are able to participate in all aspects of parenting.
10. Single-parent families are common today, primarily because of the high divorce rate. The number of unmarried women giving birth has also increased.

time-buying behavior Buying time-saving goods and shopping more efficiently.

11. Evidence indicates that gay men and lesbians can be excellent parents and that most children raised by gay men or lesbians are heterosexual.
12. The workplace has changed a great deal in the past 30 years. Manufacturing employment has decreased and service industry jobs have increased. Companies have become more efficient and laid off workers, causing an increase in insecurity. The growth of temporary workers is also changing the landscape of the workplace. In addition, many jobs require more education. Today's workers are different from those of previous generations in that they are better educated, value their leisure time more, have less company loyalty, and want more autonomy and input in the decision-making process. There are more women and members of minority groups in the labor force, and many people are working evenings, weekends, or split shifts.
13. Most young adults are generally satisfied with their jobs. There is evidence for spillover from home to work and from work to home.
14. Women continue to enter the workforce in increasing numbers. They have succeeded in entering middle management and will hold senior positions as they "age" into them. Many members of minority groups as well as women complain about inequities in the workplace.
15. Two-career marriages are also becoming more common as both marital partners establish and maintain their careers. Role overload and role stress are major challenges.
16. Americans believe that they have less leisure time today than years ago, although studies do not show this. Americans feel rushed. Most Americans spend their leisure time in passive pursuits, such as watching television.

Multiple-Choice Questions

1. According to Levinson, one major gender difference is that:
   a. women's dreams are split dreams, emphasizing both family and work, whereas men's dreams are primarily vocational in scope.
   b. women receive more mentoring than men.
   c. men show a period in their late 30s in which they are more confident whereas women become somewhat more confused and anxious at that age.
   d. men's lives show periods of plateau and transitions whereas women's lives do not.
2. The negative outcome of the psychosocial crisis of early adulthood is a sense of:
   a. guilt.
   b. stagnation.
   c. isolation.
   d. depression.
3. The age of first marriage has:
   a. increased for both men and women since the 1950s.
   b. increased substantially for men but not for women since the 1950s.
   c. increased for women but not for men since the 1950s.
   d. stayed about constant since the 1950s.
4. Which of the following statements about the similarity theory of mate selection does *not* reflect recent research?
   a. People are more comfortable when they share the same interests.
   b. There is often pressure to marry within one's racial, ethnic, and religious group.
   c. The importance of similarity in mate selection has increased.
   d. Most people marry someone in a similar socioeconomic group.
5. Sternberg believes that there are three components of love, which include:
   a. caring, sharing, and working together.
   b. intimacy, passion, and commitment.
   c. romantic, helpful, and simplistic.
   d. erotic, exotic, and companionate.
6. Concerning sexuality within marriage:
   a. the frequency of sex increases during the first 5 years, then decreases slowly after.
   b. most married people say they are satisfied with their sex lives.
   c. about half of all married people consider themselves dissatisfied with their sex lives and consider divorce.
   d. although most men are pleased with their sex lives, most married women are not.
7. Whether the unequal division of labor within the family will deeply affect the wife's satisfaction with the marriage depends upon:
   a. whether she has traditional or nontraditional ideas about gender roles.
   b. her ability to complete all tasks without feeling tired or depressed.
   c. whether she understands that husbands are willing to help out more if asked.
   d. the number and intimacy level of friends.
8. Dr. Masters would like to predict marital satisfaction in couples married for 5 years. She would be served best if she chose an instrument that measures:
   a. physical attraction.
   b. communication.
   c. personality.
   d. personal feelings of adequacy and well-being.
9. Which statement concerning communication between spouses is *correct?*
   a. Husbands communicate more neutral messages than wives.
   b. Husbands are generally not as emotionally responsive as wives.

c. One pattern of communication leading to dissatisfaction is when the wife communicates criticism and her husband withdraws.
d. All of the above are correct.

10. Mr. Waverly is investigating a case of spousal abuse. The man committing the abuse witnessed his father abusing his mother during childhood. He is not possessive or jealous, cannot communicate his feelings, and is not very assertive. The only characteristic that does not fit the research is:
a. the fact that the man witnessed violence in the family when he was a child.
b. that he is not possessive or jealous.
c. that he is not very assertive.
d. the fact that he cannot communicate his feelings adequately.

11. Which of the following statements about divorce is *correct?*
a. The longer people are married the greater the divorce rate.
b. Women are more likely than men to initiate divorce.
c. Divorced people are actually healthier than married people.
d. All of the above are correct.

12. Which of the following statements about remarriage is *correct?*
a. The courtship is usually shorter than in the first marriage.
b. Couples in unhappy second marriages do not wait as long to divorce.
c. Financial and child-rearing problems are the most common reasons for divorce in second marriages.
d. All of the above are correct.

13. People who are single by choice:
a. emphasize the benefits of being able to do what they want when they want.
b. admit to being more lonely.
c. believe they are happier than married people.
d. are described by all of the above.

14. Cohabiting couples usually:
a. divide the household duties more equitably than married couples.
b. do more housework than married couples.
c. show more financial independence from each other than married couples.
d. are much less violent towards each other than married couples.

15. Sharon and Leslie just had their first children. Sharon is a full-time homemaker; Leslie works full time in a library. Both their husbands are also employed full-time. If their marriages are similar to what is described in the literature:
a. Sharon, but not Leslie, should see a move towards more traditional gender roles.
b. Leslie, but not Sharon, should see a move towards more traditional gender roles.
c. Both Sharon and Leslie should see a move towards more traditional gender roles.
d. Neither Sharon or Leslie should see a move towards more traditional gender roles.

16. The most significant concern of single parents is:
a. social integration into the community.
b. the attitude of others towards their status.
c. financial difficulties.
d. their ability to deal with stress.

17. Josh claims that almost all children raised by gay or lesbian parents identify themselves as heterosexual in adulthood. According to research, Josh is:
a. correct.
b. correct for children raised by gay men but not for those raised by lesbians.
c. correct for children raised by lesbians but not for those raised by gay men.
d. incorrect for both children raised by gay men or lesbians.

18. Which of the following statements about the current world of work is *incorrect?*
a. Manufacturing jobs have increased in the United States but require more skills than in the recent past.
b. Workers show less company loyalty than in the past.
c. The number of temporary and part-time workers is increasing at a rapid rate.
d. The modern worker is better educated today than in the past.

19. Which statement concerning women and employment is *correct?*
a. Women have made good progress getting jobs at the top level of management.
b. Women are not returning to work after giving birth as quickly as they did years ago.
c. More than 70% of all early adult women are presently in the workforce.
d. All of the above are correct.

20. Taneesha finds that it is difficult to juggle the roles of worker, parent, and homemaker. She finds that she has to be in two places at one time, which of course is impossible. Taneesha is experiencing:
a. role overload.
b. role conflict.
c. role confusion.
d. inadequate role conversion.

Answers to Multiple-Choice Questions

1. a 2. c 3. a 4. c 5. b 6. b 7. a 8. b 9. d
10. b 11. b 12. d 13. d 14. c 15. c 16. c 17. a
18. a 19. c 20. b

Chapter 16

Physical and Cognitive Development in Middle Adulthood

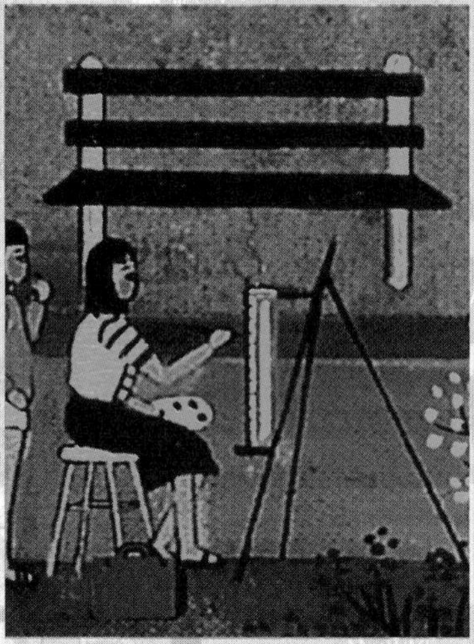

Chapter Outline

Are the Following Statements True or False?

1. The present generation of middle-aged people, called the baby boomers, are more individualistic than past generations.
2. Women going through menopause report a similar degree of bothersome symptoms across cultures.
3. The time it takes to react to a stimulus increases with age.
4. Hypertension is called "the silent killer" because it has no noticeable symptoms.
5. As people age, they show a more casual and careless attitude towards their health practices.
6. By its very nature, a vegetarian diet cannot be healthy.
7. About two-thirds of all middle-aged people exercise three times a week.
8. If you follow a group of people through middle age, their general intelligence will show a significant decline.
9. Middle-aged people show major decline in recognition memory.
10. In middle adulthood, a decline occurs in the ability to solve abstract problems, but the ability to solve practical problems improves.

Answers to True-False Statements 1. True 2. False: see p. 370 3. True 4. True 5. False: see p. 374 6. False: see p. 377 7. False: see p. 377 8. False: see p. 386 9. False: see p. 387 10. True

What Does 40 Mean to You?

Some ages have particular meanings in our culture; 21 is often thought of as the age of adulthood, and 18 is the age for gaining some rights and responsibilities, such as the right to vote. Teenage girls often have sweet-16 parties, and 65 is the age at which one enters later maturity. For most people, 40 means the start of middle age.

Most people have an ambivalent attitude toward middle age. The comedian Jack Benny joked for decades that he was 39. Our culture does not view aging in a positive light and the physical and cognitive signs of aging are unmistakable in middle-aged people.

However, as Gail Sheehy (1995) in her best-selling book *New Passages* notes, middle age is not what it used to be; it's much better. People are now taking longer to proceed through each stage of adulthood, since life expectancy is so much greater, and the stages of adulthood are shifting upwards by as much as 10 years. At age 40, people can still look forward to about half of their life or even more. Sheehy claims that instead of emphasizing decline, today's men and women are embracing a healthier, more active lifestyle, and creating what she calls a "second adulthood" in which they live more meaningful and creative lives.

The specifics of Sheehy's ideas are less important than her general positive outlook, which rejects the notion of middle age as one of decline and stagnation, and substitutes the idea of a healthy, creative middle age. Middle-aged people have the ability to customize their lives and live them to the fullest.

Middle-aged people enjoy life on a much grander scale than young adults. Their incomes are higher, their perspective on life is somewhat different, and they experience less anxiety than young adults and cope with it better. This positive view of middle age is not often echoed in a youth-oriented culture in which the media emphasizes the negative aspects of aging rather than its opportunities.

The Baby Boom Generation Hits Middle Adulthood

Seventy-seven million adults (4 in 10 adults) belong to what is called the **baby boom generation,** born between 1946 and 1964 (Gibson, 1993). When World War II ended, millions of men who had been in the armed forces were discharged and many had waited to have families. The peak years of the baby boom were from the late 1940s through the early 1960s (Figure 16.1). The boom continued for a number of years while these couples completed their families. The first baby boomers hit age 50 in 1996, when the youngest baby boomers turned 30 (Russell, 1995). This generation of middle-aged people is the largest in history.

The very size of this generation caused problems as it matured. When the baby boomers entered school, many districts were forced to build new facilities. Child-related industries, such as those producing toys and baby food, boomed along with them. So many applied to colleges and universities that those educational institutions had to expand to accommodate them. Now many of these people are approaching or negotiating middle adulthood. They are approaching the years of peak earnings and they have enormous economic power (Figure 16.2). People in their late 40s and 50s are the most affluent group (Russell, 1995). In the early 21st century, when they begin to retire and reach later maturity, they will demand the Social Security and social services they deserve, thereby placing a tremendous burden on these services.

baby boom generation The generation born between 1946 and 1964 now entering or negotiating middle age. It is the largest generation in the history of the United States.

One's 40th birthday seems to have a special meaning as a passage to middle age.

People of the baby boom generation differ greatly from the previous generation. They are a bit taller, the women are a bit lighter than their mothers, and the men weigh about the same as their fathers. They eat differently, consuming more chicken, fish, and low-fat milk and less beef. They smoke a bit less and exercise more. They enjoy better health than their parents did at this age, and they are more likely to believe that they can influence their health status than older generations (Waldrop, 1991).

They are a well-educated generation, averaging 12.9 years of schooling. More than 84% have completed high school, and 25% have had 4 or more years of higher education. They have experienced the openness of the sexual revolution of the late 1960s and early 1970s and are much more likely to be divorced than their parents at the same age and to remarry. A 40-year-old woman today is more likely than her mother was to be employed outside the home. Baby boomers tend to own their own homes and often have to balance family life with a career (Hall & Richter, 1985).

The one word that seems to define this generation is individualism (Russell, 1995). This generation was raised to think for themselves and be independent. When parents in the 1950s and 1960s were asked about their child-rearing practices, they believed that learning to think for oneself was the most important quality to nurture (Russell, 1993). The children of these baby boomers will probably be even more independent and self-sufficient because independence is an even higher priority for baby-boomer parents.

True or False?
The present generation of middle-aged people, called the baby boomers, are more individualistic than past generations.

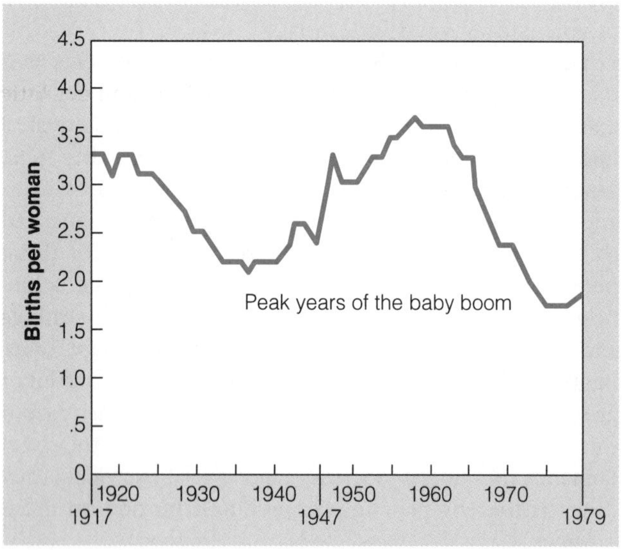

Figure 16.1
Fertility Rates for Women, 1917–1979
Source: Based on Bouvier, 1980.

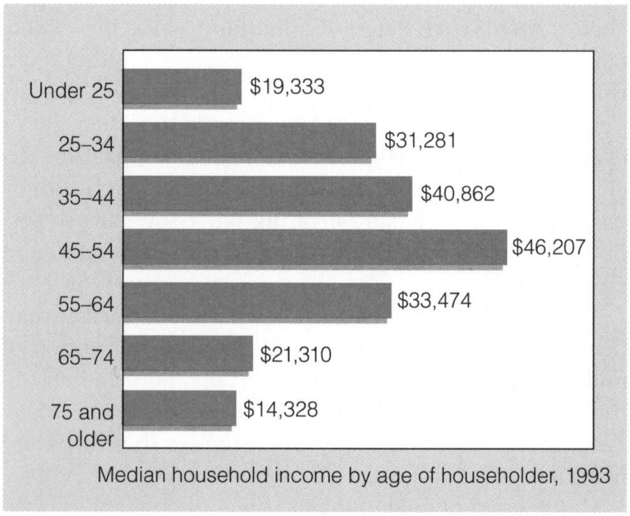

Figure 16.2
Mid-life Milestone: Affluence Hits Its Peak Householders age 45 to 54 have the highest incomes.
Source: Russell, 1995; data from Census Bureau, 1994 Current Populations Survey.

This generation has experienced radical changes in technology and economics, and it has been relatively difficult to predict its desires and behavior. Now as this generation enters middle adulthood, it should be more predictable and more stable. After age 45 people are less likely to divorce or marry and about half of workers aged 45 to 54 have been with their current employer for 10 years or more (Waldrop, 1991). As baby boomers age and their children grow, many will have somewhat more discretionary income to spend than did previous middle-aged generations. However, the dreams of this generation are somewhat grander, perhaps because of their education and opportunities, and many will never reach their goals. In the 1980s the baby boomers' real income declined, housing ownership fell, and promotion prospects were lower. This is a generation that may have to deal with the failure to live up to its own expectations (Light, 1988). Most baby boomers admit that they sometimes or always feel burned out by their jobs (Russell, 1995). The children of baby boomers tend to stay longer at home. One in four middle-age families has an adult child living at home (Russell, 1995).

It is wrong to paint a one-dimensional picture of this generation. Those born at the beginning of the boom in 1946 differ greatly from those born in the 1960s. The older baby boomers are entering middle adulthood whereas the younger ones are still raising young children. As an older baby boomer, I remember shelter drills in school in which we prepared for an enemy attack; I also remember the civil rights movement of the 1960s and I have a flashbulb memory of where I was when John Kennedy was assassinated. I remember the cost of my first house, and I was somewhat taken aback the first time I realized that some cars today sell for what I paid for that house. I can also remember raising my young children during the incredible inflation that hit in the early 1980s. Younger baby boomers are more likely to remember Earth Day and to find home ownership is more difficult to achieve. This generation may be divided into those born between 1946 and 1954 and those born between 1955 and 1964, since they experienced different things (Light, 1988). Younger baby boomers differ in their habits; for example, they are less likely to watch the news and feel less able to influence government. They are also more likely to delay marriage (Gibson, 1993).

The arrival of the baby boom generation at middle adulthood has a number of implications for society and the social sciences. This generation is more affluent and is now entering the period of life when many will reach the top of their earning power so their preferences for food, leisure activities, and material comforts may dominate the marketplace. Because they are better educated, they may expect more self-direction and autonomy in their jobs. The large number of baby boomers means that as they move through middle adulthood into later maturity and begin to suffer from long-term debilitating illnesses, they may tax our existing health care resources and require an increasing amount of social services. Their fertility rate is low and they have fewer biological children to take care of them when they age (Dorch, 1995; Longino, 1994). This generation has a much healthier lifestyle, smoking less and eating healthier so perhaps they will not be as dependent or experience the same rates of disability as their parents' generation (Longino, 1994). This new generation is ready to tackle the developmental tasks and concerns of middle adulthood.

Aging in Middle Adulthood

Some of the physical changes of middle adulthood are quite visible. They include graying hair, wrinkles, and weight gain. By age 50 half the population has gray hair. Middle-aged women may see their hair thinning and baldness is a concern for many middle-aged men (Felton, 1991).

The tendency of middle-aged people to gain weight is a definite problem. Fat often replaces muscle along the midsection, which makes the middle-aged person look fatter. Muscles decrease in mass. The metabolic rate declines in middle age, and if people do not reduce their caloric intake, a slow but steady weight gain is the result. Even if middle-aged people maintain a consistent weight, they may actually be putting on fat. A decline in muscle tone, strength, and stamina also is found around age 40 (Felton, 1991).

Environmental factors, such as exposure to the sun can increase wrinkles, since the ultraviolet rays make skin less elastic. Cigarette smoking reduces the blood supply to the skin, affecting the skin adversely (Katchadourian, 1987). Physical fitness, coordination, and flexibility often decline in middle age; it takes longer to get in shape, and it is harder to maintain that shape (Newman, 1982).

These changes usually take place gradually so people hardly notice them day to day. You don't put on 30 pounds overnight, or go in one month from a well-conditioned adult to one who has difficulty walking half a mile. People who are overweight, smoke, and get little exercise are likely to show the effects of these physical changes more than people who watch their diets, refrain from smoking, and exercise.

Awareness of Aging

Young people often want to look older, but what of middle-aged people? Joan Montepare and Margie Lachman (1989) investigated self-perception of age, fears of aging, and life satisfaction from adolescence to old age by asking people between the ages of 14 and 83 how they felt, how they thought they looked and acted, and how old they wanted to be. A changing pattern with age was found. Adolescents held older age identities, feeling that they were older than they looked and acted, whereas young adults were fairly consistent with their true age. However, both middle-aged and older adults most often reported younger age identities—that is, they felt younger and wanted to be younger than they were.

It is possible that middle-aged people see themselves as being in better health than previous generations, and do not accept the negative stereotypes of middle age. They see themselves as younger because they do not *feel* old. This is in keeping with Sheehy's ideas that the present generation of middle-aged people sees new opportunities and believes that they are more in control. It is also possible that some middle-aged people deny the fact that they are aging because they are more disturbed by it. People who define themselves in terms of their youthful appearance may fear aging.

Some theorists of adulthood stress the importance of turning from defining oneself physically to valuing wisdom and experience (Peck, 1968), as well as the importance of coping with the diminished physical abilities of middle age (Levinson, 1978). In middle adulthood people may have to care less about youthful appearance and physical performance and more about judgment and experience (Shanan, 1983).

The greater the discrepancy between subjective and actual age, the greater the fears of aging and the less life satisfaction expressed among middle-aged people. Women show more subjective discrepancies than men. In fact, men and women experience the physical aging process somewhat differently, and society perceives aging men differently from aging women. We have a double standard of aging in our society (Sontag, 1972, 1977). Although both men and women negotiate the inevitable aging process, aging affects women more than men. A man may find that he has to give up football and basketball and go on to other sports or that he can no longer beat his 18-year-old son at tennis, but his aging is seen as graceful. His graying is said to show maturity, and his features are now considered handsome in a mature way (Schaffer, 1981). A woman is often advised to try to keep her youth as long as possible and to fight the aging process. Even with this double standard of aging, there is evidence that women at mid-life see their bodies positively (Backley, Warren, & Bird, 1988). Most people are realistic about the aging process and take pride in the way they look and take care of themselves. Accepting that one is 40 years old may be important, but what 40 means to the individual may be the key.

Sexuality in Middle Adulthood

When many people think about sexuality, they imagine teenagers or young adults in the throes of passion. The idea that parents, and especially grandparents, are sexually active is rejected, if the idea even occurs at all. I was once lecturing on the increase in interest in sexuality shown by this generation's middle-aged and older people, when one 18-year-old blurted out, "My father maybe, but my mother—never!" When college students were asked to estimate the extent of their parents' sexual activity, half these students believed that their parents had sexual intercourse about once a month or less (Pocs & Godow, 1976). The researchers had no real data on how often these students' parents engaged in intercourse, but compared with Kinsey's data of about seven times a month for people in their 40s, these students were drastically underestimating their parents' sexual activity. Younger people refuse to see older people as having any interest in sex.

Sex in Marriage: The Middle-Aged Couple

Some physical changes in middle adulthood can affect sexual interest and activity but do not really interfere with—and may even enhance—the enjoyment of sex. The well-known research team, Masters and Johnson (1966) studied married couples, unmarried males, and unmarried females throughout late adolescence and adulthood and found that sexual response could be conceptualized as occurring in four stages. In the arousal stage, the penis becomes erect and the woman's vaginal secretions increase. Muscle tension increases, the body becomes flushed, and the heart rate increases. During the plateau stage, the penis is fully erect and the vagina is well lubricated. The uterus becomes elevated, and the testicles become enlarged and also somewhat elevated. In the orgasm stage, a pulsating release of sexual tension occurs, followed by the resolution stage, in which the body returns to its normal state. In males, the resolution stage is followed by a period of inactivity, called the refractory period, in which genital activity is not possible.

The most common effect of aging on male sexuality is that each stage of the cycle lasts longer. Thus, the older male takes longer to obtain an erection but is capable of maintaining one for a longer period of time before ejaculating. This can actually lead to an improvement in a couple's sex life, because the man can prolong the experience, allowing his partner more time to reach a climax. Other physical changes in males include a reduction in testosterone levels between the ages of 40 and 60 (after which it levels off), an increase in the refractory period, and a qualitative change from an intense genital focus to a more diffused generalized pleasure (Knox, 1985).

Some of the changes in middle-aged women that relate to sex have a similar effect. It takes longer for a middle-aged woman to become aroused. Vaginal lubrication takes longer and is less intense (McCammon, Knox, & Schacht, 1993). Middle-aged women also have fewer contractions during the orgasm stage (Rosen & Rosen, 1981). Sexual interest remains high, and there is evidence that postmenopausal women have an increased interest in sex (Knox, 1985).

When sexual problems occur in aging couples, they are much more likely to be caused by situational or psychological problems than by physical difficulties. Married people are generally pleased with their sex lives (Hunt, 1974). Men peak in their sexual activity in their mid-20s and women peak somewhat later. However, two-thirds of the people in their 50s report having either a moderate or a strong interest in sex (Pfeiffer, Verwoerdt, & Davis, 1974). Sexuality is affected by many things other than age, including illness, the use of medications, and personal problems (Weg, 1989).

The frequency of sexual intercourse varies widely, but declines with age, as shown in Figure 16.3 (Call, Sprecher, & Schwartz, 1995). A different longitudinal study of marital partners from their mid-20s to their mid-40s found somewhat different frequencies of sexual intercourse but the same decline in frequency with age (Ard, 1990). Husbands who reported that they experienced "great enjoyment" declined with age a little but the percentage of wives who reported "great enjoyment" actually increased a little. Most women reported experiencing orgasm either "always," "almost always," or "usually," and relatively few men experienced erectile problems.

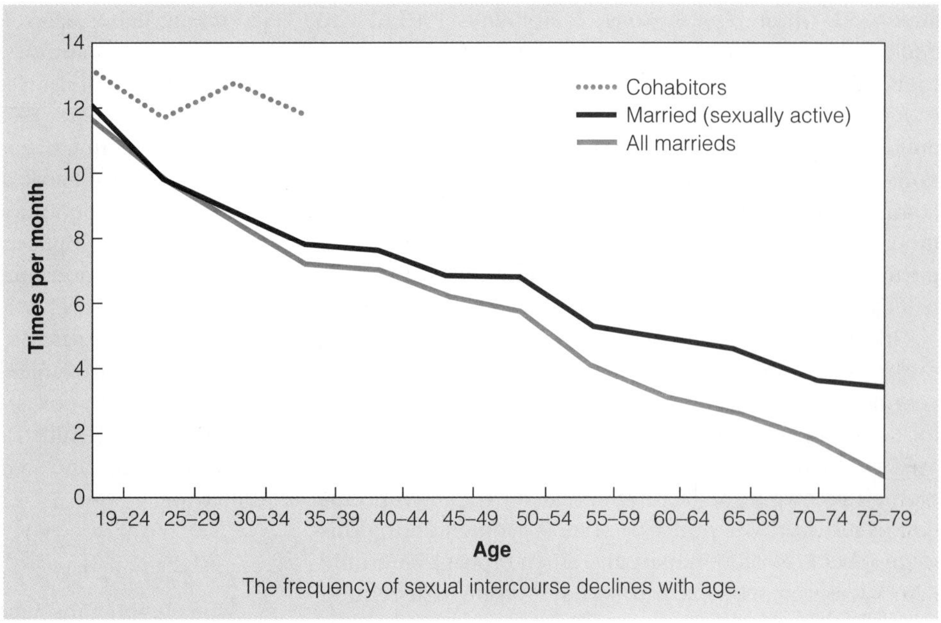

Figure 16.3
Frequency of Sex Last Month by Age and Marital Status
Source: Call, Sprecher, and Schwartz, 1995.

Most couples report marital satisfaction after 20 years of marriage, despite their reports of having sex less frequently. Marital happiness obviously does not depend upon frequency of sex, nor is it essential that sex be tremendously satisfying. The quality of feelings and other emotional aspects appear more important. When sexuality is considered only in terms of genital activity, we do a disservice to people of all ages, because hugging, touching, and stroking are also part of sexuality. People remain sexual beings all their lives; what may change is the way they express their sexuality (Weg, 1989).

The degree of sexual activity middle-aged adults engage in depends on their sexual practices in early adulthood (Pfeiffer & Davis, 1972). People who had a high interest in sex and were sexually active in their younger days continue to remain interested in sex as they grow older. Although age is the most important factor associated with marital sexual frequency, marital happiness is the second most important (Call et al., 1995). Other factors associated with life changes, such as having young children, health difficulties, and attitudes towards sex may reduce or increase the frequency of sex as well.

Menopause

Few events in an individual's life have been as misunderstood as **menopause**—the cessation of a woman's menstrual cycle. Another term often confused with menopause is **climacteric,** which encompasses all the physical changes that bring someone from a state of fertility to a state of infertility. The climacteric is the counterpart to puberty, whereas menopause is the counterpart to menstruation (Timiras & Meisami, 1972). Traditionally, women going through menopause have been characterized as unreliable, emotional, and difficult (Sheehy, 1992). Today we know that this is a false assessment, one that is potentially harmful to middle-aged women.

Physical and Psychological Signs of Menopause

Menopause is the result of changes in the follicle cells in the ovaries that make them unable to respond to various hormones from the pituitary gland. This causes a reduction in estrogen secretions. The estrogen levels in the blood remain relatively constant until about age 40, when they decline until about age 60, after which they tend to stabilize (Spence, 1989). Estrogen and progesterone secretion declines as the functioning of the ovaries decreases. The pituitary still tries to stimulate the ovaries to produce sex hormones, but the ovaries do not respond. Ovulation ceases, the menstrual cycle disappears, and the woman becomes infertile (Strand, 1983). Some estrogen is produced even after menopause by the adrenal glands, and the ovaries continue to produce some as well. Most of the estrogen is produced by fat tissue, which converts androgens to estrogens (Dan & Bernhard, 1989).

Most women experience menopause somewhere between the ages of 42 and 52 years; the average age is

menopause The cessation of a woman's menstrual cycle.

climacteric A term used to describe all the physical changes bringing someone from a state of fertility to one of infertility.

about 50 (Masters, Johnson, & Kolodny, 1991). The decline of estrogen precipitates the physiological symptoms associated with menopause (Doering, 1980). Although a number of physical symptoms may be reported, including depression, irritability, dizziness, heart palpitations, headaches, and insomnia (Spence, 1989), the most common is hot flashes (Dan & Bernhard, 1989). In a much-quoted British study, 30% to 50% of all women reported experiencing some of these symptoms, with about half experiencing hot flashes (McKinlay & Jeffreys, 1974).

Although many women experience some discomfort, the majority do not find the symptoms of menopause very bothersome and most do not seek medical treatment for them (McKinlay, Brambilla, & Posner, 1992; Neugarten, 1970a). Many studies concentrating on menopausal women receiving medical treatment for their symptoms do not reflect the experience of most women during this stage. Over 80% of menopausal women report either mild or no symptoms, but 20% report symptoms that require them to seek medical care (National Institute of Aging, 1986).

Although depression is often identified with menopause, menopause does not cause depression. Any depression may be caused by the attitudes some women may have towards menopause. Women who experience depression during menopause often are women who have experienced depression earlier in adulthood and any depression that occurs is brief (McKinlay et al., 1991). When women in menopause were studied for over 2 years, menopause led to few changes in psychological functioning, and none in anger, anxiety, or total depression scores (Matthews et al., 1990). However, women who expected to have major symptoms during menopause did show an increase in depression and other symptoms, showing the importance of attitude (Matthews, 1992).

Women's Attitudes About Menopause

Most women report feeling neutral or relieved by their menopause (Adler, 1991). When women were asked to select causes of stress that bothered them, very few cited menopause as a major source of worry. When asked what they disliked about middle age, only 1 out of the 100 questioned mentioned menopause. There were very few women who could not mention anything good about menopause; about a third of the sample could not think of anything bad about it (Neugarten, 1970b).

Women may be negatively affected by their attitudes toward menopause (Matthews, 1992), many of which are caused by our cultural emphasis on youth and fears of aging. For example, in Chinese society, where old age is venerated, they do not even have a word for "hot flashes" (Banner, 1992) and menopause is not even an issue. A study of symptoms of menopause in Japan, Canada, and the United States found a much lower frequency of hot flashes and feelings of depression in Japanese women (Avis et al., 1993). Women in these societies also differed in eating habits, exercise, number of children, and other factors, so the authors could make no direct statement about causation. In a survey of various cultures around the world, Griffen (1977) found a number of different reactions to menopause. In eight cultures, postmenopausal women did not show any behavioral changes. Women in India greeted menopause with relief. In a small minority of cultures, menopause is considered a disorder. In other cultures restrictions imposed on women during the childbearing years, such as against eating certain meats, are lifted at menopause. In many cultures, the end of fertility marks an improvement in the lives of women, freeing them from both cultural restriction and the risks of childbirth (Public Health Reports, 1994). Cultural beliefs are likely to affect one's view of menopause as well as one's behavior.

True or False?
Women going through menopause report a similar degree of bothersome symptoms across cultures.

Other life stresses such as loss of one's social network, divorce, and death of a parent are associated with higher rates of menopausal symptoms (McKinlay, McKinlay & Brambilla, 1987). In addition, the degree of anxiety women experience partially depends on how they feel about no longer being able to have children, what they know about the symptoms of menopause, and their anxiety about aging (Newman, 1982). Young women often dread menopause, perhaps because they confuse physiological changes with the negative connotations of growing older. The attitudes of women who have already negotiated menopause are quite positive (Neugarten et al., 1963). The women were aware that it brought freedom from the worry of pregnancy and an upsurge in sexual interest and activity occurred.

Treatment of Symptoms

A medical treatment available for women who experience serious physiological symptoms at menopause is hormone replacement therapy (HRT), which involves supplying additional estrogen to the system. Because estrogen replacement is associated with an increase in endometrial cancer (cancer of the lining of the uterus), another hormone—progestin—is also administered because it reduces the danger of this type of cancer (Dan & Bernhard, 1989). Unfortunately, progestin can also cause cyclical bleeding, and its long-term consequences are not yet known (Schmitt et al., 1991). Since women take this therapy for relatively long periods of time, it may place some elderly women at risk for other health disorders, such as gallstones and perhaps even hypertension (Dan & Bernhard, 1989; Strickland, 1988). Long-term hormone therapy (for 10 years or more) is also linked to increased risk of breast cancer (Public Health Reports, 1994). Nonmedical treatments involve getting sufficient physical exercise, eating a diet rich in calcium, and refraining from smoking or drinking alcohol (Greenberg et al., 1989).

The Male Climacteric

We are slowly accumulating research data showing that males also experience a climacteric, although it is slower and more gradual (Bischof, 1976). Between the ages of about 40 and 60, testosterone levels decline, causing a decrease in the size of the testes. Fewer sperm are produced, ejaculatory force is diminished, and the size of the prostate gland increases. Although sperm production continues well into old age and men as old as 90 have been reported to father children, there is a decline both in number and motility of sperm after about age 50 (Spence, 1989).

Enlargement of the prostate may lead to urinary tract problems, and cancer of the prostate during middle age is not uncommon. Mood swings and changes in self-concept also occur, but these problems are more likely to stem from difficulties in coping with aging than from the biological changes themselves (Williams, 1977).

Sensory Changes in Middle Adulthood

The sensory changes that occur in middle age follow the same pattern as the physical changes just described. They are relatively minor, noticeable, take place gradually over the course of many years, and have little effect on the average lifestyle of middle-aged persons.

Vision

A decline in visual acuity occurs after the age of 45 or so (Fozard, 1990). By their mid 40s, half the population needs glasses and almost everyone needs some sort of correction for visual acuity by their late 50s (Schaie & Willis, 1996). Middle-aged people may have difficulty seeing things very far away; reading may also become a problem, because the aging eye may also have more difficulty focusing on close objects. The middle-aged person holding a newspaper at arm's length is a common sight. Because middle-aged people have difficulty with both near and far vision, they often wear bifocals to compensate for these visual problems. Most serious visual problems do not occur until older ages.

Other effects include a thickening and clouding of the lens of the eye, which may increase sensitivity to glare (Kline & Scialfa, 1996). Dark adaptation is less efficient and together with glare problems may make it less comfortable to drive at night. Middle-aged people may need more light in order to see, probably because of a reduction in pupil size (Saxon & Etten, 1978).

Hearing

The ability to hear also declines in middle age, especially for high-pitched sounds (Schaie & Geiwitz, 1982). This condition, called **presbycusis,** is probably caused by a general degeneration of the auditory system. Men show this decrease before women, possibly because more men than women are exposed to noise pollution in their occupations, such as assembly-line work (Marsh & Thompson, 1977). They do not lose their ability to hear these frequencies, but they find it difficult to hear them unless the volume is increased (Corso, 1971).

About 1 in 5 middle-aged people experience difficulties in hearing, compared with 3 in 4 elderly people (Schaie & Willis, 1996). Middle-aged people also find it more difficult to discriminate certain sounds from others and to distinguish the sounds they want to hear from background noise (Slawinski, Hartel, & Kline, 1993). Speech perception becomes more a problem after age 50, and the problems are greatest when some distortion or interruption is present or when the speech is rapid (Fozard, 1990). For most people the practical significance of these hearing losses is not great. Middle-aged people may only need a bit more volume and to concentrate more, and they may not even be aware of the decline in their ability to hear.

The Other Senses

Whatever decline occurs in the other senses is quite small. A gradual loss of sensitivity to sweetness and saltiness takes place (Moore, Nielsen, & Mistretta, 1982). Early adults show more sensitivity to taste than middle-aged adults (Weiffenbach, Cowart, & Baum, 1986). The decrease in the number of taste buds and the higher threshold of sensitivity begins to show itself in the 40s but is of little importance in middle adulthood (Saxon & Etten, 1978).

The changes in the ability to smell are more controversial, and although some decrement may take place, it does not appear to be important (Walk, 1981). Sensitivity to touch begins to decline at age 45 and to pain at about 50. However, since the tolerance for pain decreases as well, pain becomes a significant problem, especially in old age, as we shall see in Chapter 18 (Katchadourian, 1987).

Reaction Time

Perhaps the most consistent finding is that some slowing of most processes occurs in middle adulthood (Salthouse, 1993; Schaie, 1989). The time it takes to respond to a stimulus—called *reaction time*—increases with age (Newman, 1982). Reaction time is measured in two different ways. **Simple reaction time** involves pressing some key or making some response after detecting a

presbycusis The decline in the ability to hear high-pitched sounds.

simple reaction time The time required to make a response after detecting a stimulus.

stimulus—for example, when a buzzer rings, the subject must push a button as soon as possible. **Choice reaction time** involves making one of a number of choices, depending on the stimulus presented—for instance, subjects may be asked to push one button when a red light comes on and another when a blue light is flashed. No matter which sense organ is stimulated, an increase in reaction time is found as a person ages.

True or False?
The time it takes to react to a stimulus increases with age.

Both simple reaction time and choice reaction time are adversely affected by age. To succeed on a test of choice reaction time, a subject must first identify which signal has been presented, then make the choice, then initiate the action. All these processes slow to some extent, causing an increase in reaction time. The fact that so many processes slow with age has led authorities to use the term "speed of behavior" rather than "reaction time." Reaction time connotes the act of responding itself whereas speed of behavior is more neutral and takes into consideration other components, such as perception and decision making, which also slow with age (Birren & Fisher, 1992).

If every older person performed worse than every younger person in every study of reaction time and mental processing, it would be easy to explain the slowdown. But this is not the case. In one experiment, the reaction times of men above age 70 and of young men of about 20 were tested (Botwinick & Thompson, 1968). Younger subjects were divided into two groups: athletes and nonathletes. As a group the elderly subjects showed slower reaction times than the young athletes did, but they were not much slower than the nonathletes. In fact, 30% of the younger subjects were slower in reaction time than the fastest 30% of the older sample. The speed of the young nonathletes varied considerably, with some performing better than the older people and some not doing as well. This appears to be true as well when comparing middle-aged adults with younger adults. Age is one factor explaining the slowdown, but other individual factors are also important. When age is correlated with speed on a number of different behaviors, the time it takes to react to stimuli generally increases with age. Yet the relationship is relatively low, showing that more is involved than simple age (Salthouse, 1985). Other variables include the subject's health, motivation, and training.

A number of theories attempt to explain this increase in the time necessary to respond to a stimulus with age. Some argue that there is a general slowing in the central nervous system, that one consequence of aging is a reduction in the speed at which impulses are conducted in the central nervous system (Botwinick, 1984). Another theory argues that neural noise is responsible. As people age, cells begin to fire more at random, creating neural noise and making it difficult for older people to differentiate one stimulus from the other. Still others argue that it may result partly from a change in strategy, as older people show more cautious behavior (Welford, 1977). It is possible that some combination of these theories is correct.

Nothing to Fret About

None of these changes is really very disturbing for a number of reasons. First, a person's general physical health should be taken into consideration. In healthy middle-aged people who take care of themselves by exercising and practicing good health habits, any declines are not nearly so great as in adults who do not follow these health practices. Second, the declines that do take place may have no effect at all on a person's day-to-day life. The increase in reaction time of a fraction of a second makes no difference in one's daily life. Whether one responds to a telephone signal a tenth of a second later makes little difference. Third, middle-aged people can compensate for some of the decline with eyeglasses, hearing aids, and, above all, experience. Finally, most of the changes reflect more the need of each sense for a higher level of stimulation to function than any traumatic reduction in the sensory functioning itself (Newman, 1982). For example, middle-aged people may find that they need more light to read or that they need to turn up the volume slightly to hear the voices on the television set.

Health in Middle Adulthood

Physical functioning is affected by health considerations and research shows that middle-aged people are quite concerned about their health. After the age of 30, the number of deaths from accidents declines, and deaths from disease increase. Between the ages of 45 and 64, cancer is now the most common cause of death; heart disease is second (U.S. Department of Health and Human Services, 1995).

Yet, there is good news. The death rate for heart disease has declined (Prager, Turczyn, & Smith, 1993). Although the overall death rate from cancer has not shown the same decline, progress has been made in treating many cancers and survival rates for some cancers are on the rise.

Heart Disease and Hypertension

Coronary heart disease (CHD) is a term used to describe a number of cardiac disorders resulting from inadequate circulation of blood to local areas of the heart muscle. A **heart attack (myocardial infarction)** involves the death of a part of the heart muscle caused by an interruption of the blood supply (Anderson, 1987). A heart

choice reaction time The time required to make one of a number of choices depending on the stimulus presented.

heart attack (myocardial infarction) The death of a part of the heart muscle because of interruption of the blood supply.

In some sports, older champions such as Arnold Palmer continue to play on a tour in which they compete with other older aged champions.

attack is caused by a thrombosis, a clot blocking one or more of the coronary arteries, small vessels that supply blood to the heart. A blood clot lodges in a coronary artery, restricts the flow of blood to the heart muscles, and cuts off the supply of oxygen and nutrients thereby depriving the heart muscle of oxygen and damaging and killing cells (Chiras, 1993).

The problem is in the arterial walls. As people age, their arteries lose their elasticity and begin to thicken. This hardening of the arteries is called **arteriosclerosis.** Although we do not know the exact cause of this phenomenon, we do know that it is associated with genetic factors, hormones, diet, and certain diseases, such as diabetes (Napoli, 1982). Although most people have some form of the condition, they experience no bothersome symptoms.

One form of arteriosclerosis is called **atherosclerosis,** in which the inner walls of the artery are made thick and irregular by a fatty substance called plaque. This plaque consists of a fat called cholesterol as well as other materials. The blood clots on top of this plaque. Because the elevated levels of cholesterol react with clotting factors in the blood, the blood clot does not disintegrate but actually grows. When these plaques block the blood flow or break off and lodge somewhere else in the coronary artery, a portion of the heart is starved for lack of oxygen and nutrients and dies. The person has now suffered a heart attack (Gasner & McCleary, 1982). The formation of atherosclerotic plaque results from a combination of stress, poor diet, lack of exercise, smoking, and heredity factors among others. The narrowing of a coronary artery by plaque does not necessarily result in a heart attack unless the narrowing is quite severe. Less severe narrowing does make the vessel more susceptible to blood clots. When a clot forms in the vessel at the site of narrowing or when a clot that originated elsewhere in the body lodges in the narrowed vessel, trouble begins (Chiras, 1993). If an artery that serves the brain is obstructed, brain cells will be starved, and some loss of function may occur. We call this a *stroke.* The outcomes of heart attacks vary. The size of the area as well as whether it interferes with the electrical activity of the heart are key factors in determining initial survival (Chiras, 1993).

Although a stroke or heart attack may occur suddenly, it is actually the result of many years of arterial narrowing. Atherosclerosis often begins in childhood. At first, lesions arise in the lining of the arteries, often by age 10 or 15. These later progress to fatty or fibrous plaques and eventually to large complicated lesions. They can result in *angina pectoris* (pain in the chest), heart attack, or sudden death (U.S. Department of Health and Human Services, 1989).

Many factors can contribute to atherosclerosis, including high blood pressure, high blood cholesterol levels, and cigarette smoking. The higher the blood cholesterol level, the greater the severity of atherosclerosis (Grundy, 1986). As the heart pumps, arteries expand to accommodate the blood flow. Because arteries that are hardened and narrowed by plaque cannot expand, blood pressure rises. The increased blood pressure puts a strain on the heart and damages the walls of the arteries even more. Atherosclerosis, then, is a self-accelerating process (Rolfes & DeBruyne, 1990). As pressure builds up in the artery, the wall may become weakened and balloon out, forming an aneurysm. (Aneurysms can also be caused by other factors.) An aneurysm can burst, and if this happens in a major artery, it can lead to massive bleeding and death.

Hypertension, or high blood pressure, contributes to many heart problems. High blood pressure damages and weakens the lining of the coronary and cerebral (brain) arteries and causes vascular problems in the brain. It can also damage the eyes and kidneys and injure the heart muscle, and it contributes to arteriosclerosis (Gasner & McCleary, 1982). About 38% of all American adults have hypertension (USDDHS, 1991), but only in about 10% of the cases is the actual cause known (Anderson, 1987). Hypertension is called "the silent killer" because in the early stages it does not have any noticeable symptoms. Only

arteriosclerosis A condition in which the arteries lose their elasticity as they harden.

atherosclerosis A condition in which the inner walls of the artery become thick and irregular because of a buildup of plaque.

hypertension High blood pressure.

by having their blood pressure checked can people be certain that it is within normal limits.

True or False?
Hypertension is called "the silent killer" because it has no noticeable symptoms.

The higher the blood pressure, the greater the risk of heart attack. Obesity makes hypertension worse by adding extra capillaries through which blood must be pumped. Although the role of salt is still controversial, salt is also implicated in high blood pressure, and studies on animals have linked salt intake with blood pressure (Schmeck, 1995). Some people may be more sensitive to salt intake than others. Most of the salt consumed in Western countries comes from commercially processed food. The three major risk factors for coronary heart disease include elevated blood pressure, high blood cholesterol levels, and cigarette smoking, all of which can be modified (Muscat et al., 1994). These factors have a cumulative effect: the more factors present in a person's life, the greater the likelihood of developing heart disease (Siegel et al., 1993).

Prevention and Treatment of Heart Disease and Hypertension One reason for the decline in deaths from heart disease is medical breakthroughs, including better medication to control hypertension and improved surgical procedures. Credit must also go to preventive steps taken by people who are now better educated about the risks of heart disease. Most people today are aware of the risk factors involving blood pressure, cholesterol, and smoking (Lenfant, 1987; Schucker et al., 1987). More people than ever are taking steps to control the risk factors associated with heart disease. People are lowering serum cholesterol, smoking less or not at all, and generally managing hypertension better (Sytkowski, Kannel, & D'Agostino, 1990).

Questions Students Often Ask

I've seen on television that some people control their heart conditions just with radical changes in behavior. Does this really work?

Yes, it can. Dean Ornish (1990) compared a sample of 41 patients aged 35 to 75 who had blocked arteries. Twenty-two of his patients were assigned to an experimental group that made radical changes in lifestyle. Those in the experimental group ate no animal products, with the exception of egg whites and up to a cup of nonfat milk or yogurt a day. The diet had no more than 10% fat and consisted primarily of vegetables, grains, and fruits. Dietary boredom, a problem with many programs, was reduced or eliminated by having the dishes designed by well-known chefs. The patients walked for 30 minutes a day and met as a group twice a week for 4 hours to walk, talk, eat, meditate, and practice stretching and breathing exercises. Nineteen others were assigned to a control group who made some moderate changes in diet. Most went on a 30% fat diet, and most exercised but did not practice stress reduction techniques.

One year later, 18 of the 22 patients in the experimental group showed significant unblocking of the arteries; 3 showed some slight progress, and 1 patient who did not comply showed a progression of coronary artery disease. The patients also reported a 91% reduction in chest pain. In the control group, 10 of the 19 showed progression of blocked arteries. Those who exercised more and ate fewer calories showed some unblocking. On the whole, this group actually reported a significant rise in the frequency of chest pains. This study shows the possible advantages of changing lifestyle in a fairly radical manner. However, despite the positive results of this study, some have questioned whether people can really make the radical changes necessary and sustain them for long periods of time; this remains to be seen.

The older a person is, the more likely he or she is to change his or her lifestyle to a healthier one. When young, middle-aged, and older adults were asked about such factors as sleep habits, avoidance of salt, diet, and how they coped with stress, the results clearly showed that as people age, they begin living healthier lives. The middle-aged group was more likely than younger adults to eat a balanced diet, obtain good medical information, avoid smoking, use salt sparingly, and eat high-fiber foods. The elderly were even more likely than the middle-aged subjects to take these steps. The same pattern held for stress reduction, with middle-aged people reporting avoidance of stress, having a good family life, avoiding anger, and thinking more positively than younger adults, but less so than the elderly. The only health practice that declined with age was exercise (Prohaska et al., 1985). However, this may change somewhat in the future, as young adults—who exercise at a higher rate than young adults did a generation ago—reach middle age and, it is hoped, continue the practice.

True or False?
As people age, they show a more casual and careless attitude towards their health practices.

We have often noted that genetics can have a predisposing influence in many areas and can increase or decrease risk. The risk factors of obesity and hypertension occur in families and have a genetic basis. However, appreciating the genetic possibilities should not cause us to forget about environmental factors. Even in the absence of genetic factors, there is a significant association between obesity and many cardiovascular disease risk factors, including high blood pressure and the consumption of fat (Newman et al., 1990). Lifestyle, then, remains important regardless of risk factors.

Cancer

About one out of every three persons alive today will have some form of cancer (McCarthy, 1993). No other disease has a greater emotional impact. It is the second leading cause of death in the United States (first in middle age), responsible for 22% of all deaths in this country (Williams, 1991). By the year 2000 cancer will probably overtake heart disease as the leading cause of death in the United States (Rubin, 1996).

Although many pieces of the puzzle are still missing, scientists have a general idea of how cancer develops. During the initiation phase, substances, called *carcinogens,* which change normal cells into cancerous ones, enter the cells. They cause mutations or genetic mistakes that alter cell functioning that are then passed on when cells reproduce. Every minute millions of cells in the body divide, doing so in a controlled manner regulated by genes (Brown, 1995). Each of us possesses a group of genes that when mutated can lead to cancerous growth. These genes are called proto-oncogenes and play a key role in cellular growth. When mutated by radiation, ultraviolet light, and chemical carcinogens, these genes produce cancer. Viruses may also cause cancer when they affect proto-oncogenes (Chiras, 1993).

After this initial change in the cells occurs, a key role is played by other substances called tumor promoters, which are not carcinogens but hasten the development of cancer after the damage is caused by carcinogens (Whitney, Cataldo, & Rolfes, 1994). During this promotion phase of cancer, the cells with altered DNA divide, producing a large number of abnormal cells; this may take anywhere from 10 to 30 years. These tumor promoters change benign slow-developing tumors into malignant ones. Just as some chemicals encourage cancer development, others may retard it. Finally, unless they are hindered by the body's defenses or corrected by outside treatment, these abnormal cells continue to divide, leading to the progression phase during which the body loses control over the abnormal cells, the normal functions of the tissues erode, and the cancer cells metastasize, that is, migrate to other tissues (Brown, 1995; Rolfes, & DeBruyne, 1990).

As with heart disease, personal habits and environmental factors can affect the likelihood of developing one or another form of cancer. The American Health Foundation submits that approximately three-fourths of cancers in the United States can be attributed to lifestyle and environmental factors. Others argue that the figure is as high as 90% as diet, smoking, alcohol intake, and exposure to toxins in the environment such as asbestos, chemical pollutants, and radiation take their toll (Committee on Diet and Health, 1989). The environment plays a very important role. For instance, immigrants to Australia and Canada from countries in which the prevalence of breast cancer is low eventually show a higher incidence of breast cancer, one that is similar to that of native-born Australian and Canadian women (Newsday, August 3, 1995). Some people appear genetically susceptible to some forms of cancer, in that when exposed to certain environments they have a greater chance of developing cancer. Again, genetic factors do not imply immutability because lifestyle is very important.

The most common causes of cancer deaths in middle age are lung cancer and breast cancer. An estimated 80% of all lung cancers occur in cigarette smokers (USDHHS, 1995; Williams, 1991). Deaths from lung cancer in men have escalated in the past 30 years as we see the results of all the past smoking. An increase in lung cancer among women is occurring as a result of women's increased use of tobacco since the middle of this century. The surgeon general states that cigarette smoking is the single most preventable cause of premature death in the United States (U.S. Department of Health and Human Services, 1988; Thun et al., 1995).

Breast cancer is a prominent cause of cancer deaths in women. Breast cancer affects about 1 woman in 10, which makes it a very serious problem. Many people who receive treatment early survive (Newsday, May 17, 1995).

Not all cancers have increased in incidence. There has been a major reduction in cancer of the stomach since the 1930s as Americans have reduced their consumption of smoked foods. In the United States, refrigeration and canning are common ways of preserving food. In Japan, however, the rate of stomach cancer is much higher because the Japanese eat much more smoked foods. Deaths from Hodgkin's disease and testicular cancer have declined dramatically while those for colon and rectal cancer have declined moderately over the past 25 years (Rubin, 1996); the death rate for breast cancer has leveled off.

Many cancers can be treated successfully if they are discovered early. New procedures, possibly using DNA testing, may allow doctors to detect cancer at a very early stage, allowing for a better chance of recovery (Friend, 1994). For women, self-examination and periodic medical exams that often include mammography can help to detect breast cancer early, and lead to more successful treatment. For men, self-examination can lead to early detection of testicular cancer. Other forms of cancer, such as cancer of the colon, can be detected early through other medical tests.

Treatment for cancer often includes radiation and chemotherapy, which are aimed at killing the cancer cells. Today, experimentation is taking another track as some drugs under development are trying to get the cancer cells to behave the way normal cells do (Cooke, 1991).

Diet

The nutritional concerns evident during the early adulthood stage—namely, ingestion of too many calories for the amount of physical activity engaged in—become even more pronounced during the middle adult years. People are likely to be even less active, and the basal metabolism rate (the rate at which food is burned) decreases so that even if caloric intake remains the same, a person will gain weight (Long & Shannon, 1983), perhaps a couple of pounds a year. During this stage of life, fat intake—which increases risk of heart disease and cancer—as well as calorie intake should be reduced. In addition, certain minerals are especially important. Women's need for iron remains high, at least until menopause. For postmenopausal women, receiving their daily calcium is vital, but few women meet the suggested daily requirement (Whitney, Cataldo, & Rolfes, 1994). Long-standing inadequate calcium intake is one factor implicated in osteoporosis, a disorder in which the bones become brittle and lose their mass (see Chapter 18).

Obesity in middle age is a problem that is not taken as seriously as it should be. In a study over an 8-year period of middle-aged American women, a full 40% of the coronary heart disease cases were attributed to excess weight. In the heaviest cases, a full 70% were attributed to excess weight (Manson et al., 1990). This has stimulated more efforts to understand and treat obesity (Van Itallie, 1990). Obesity is a causative factor for heart disease, hypertension, and diabetes (Phillips, 1995). Losing weight in middle age is linked with a reduced risk of heart disease (Hazzard, 1995; Katzel et al., 1995).

Today many authorities argue that the risk of coronary heart disease is increased by consuming foods high in cholesterol and saturated fat, and reduced by decreasing the amount of fats consumed. If cholesterol and high fat have the effect of accelerating the process of atherosclerosis, avoiding substances high in cholesterol might reduce one's risk. Clinical studies have shown that changes in diet can reduce blood cholesterol and therefore reduce the risk of heart disease (Hully et al., 1991; USDHHS, 1989). However, it is not clear whether cholesterol levels in the blood are exclusively influenced by diet; cholesterol levels may be affected by certain chemicals in processed food and by other complicated processes not well understood. Most investigators and the American Heart Association see such a link, at least in most people. Other dietary changes for reducing heart disease risk include eating a high-fiber, high-complex-carbohydrate, adequately balanced diet without too much caffeine, alcohol, or salt (Rimm et al., 1996; Rolfes & DeBruyne, 1989).

Diet is related to an estimated 60% of all cancers in women and 40% of all cancers in men (Committee on Diet and Health, 1989). Some diets seem to promote cancer. Cancer-promoting diets are high in fat (especially among those who are obese); low in fruits, vegetables, and fiber; and contain excessive alcohol and smoked foods cured with salt or nitrites. Specific cancers are related to certain dietary influences. Breast cancer rates are higher among populations with high-fat diets because fat affects the levels of hormones that act on the breast. The most common cancer of the digestive tract is cancer of the colon. There is a link between high-fat, low-fiber diets and increases in cancer of the colon. It is thought that dietary fat increases the secretion of bile acid into the intestine and that these acids enhance cancer development. Fiber seems to dilute bile acids and counters their adverse effects on the colon (Williams, 1991). Diets that are protective against cancer are high in fruits, vegetables, and fiber (Brown, 1995).

People who regularly consume fruits and vegetables have a lower risk of developing cancer than those who eat few of these foods (Brown, 1995). Inadequate intake of vitamin A has been linked with cancer of the lung, bladder, and larynx; vitamin C may help to prevent the formation of cancer-causing agents, especially in the esophagus and stomach (Hamilton, Whitney, & Sizer, 1991). Perhaps the most important discovery is the possibility that consumption of cruciferous vegetables (named for their cross-shaped blossoms), such as cauliflower, cabbage, Brussels sprouts, and broccoli, may offer some protection against cancer (Whitney, Cataldo, & Rolfes, 1994). Only about one-third of all American adults consume the recommended amount of fruit and vegetables (Krebs-Smith et al., 1995).

"Anti-cancer" dietary regimens require a reduction of total fat and caloric intake to reduce obesity; ingestion of more fiber and of green, orange, and yellow fruits and vegetables (especially from the cabbage family) (Boyle & Whitney, 1989). Since immoderate alcohol consumption increases the risk of cancer of the mouth, larynx, and esophagus, reducing alcohol consumption is recommended (U.S. Department of Health and Human Services, 1988).

Diet may have an effect at each step of cancer development, and it should not be forgotten that the immune system plays a role in cancer prevention and healthy nutrition makes the immune system stronger (Poirier, 1987). However, other factors, such as environmental exposure to cancer-causing substances and genetics, may be involved in cancer and no one knows the extent to which such dietary corrections will help reduce the risk. In addition, much of the research linking diet and disease is based upon correlational data, that is, the finding of a relationship between two variables. We should not confuse correlation with causation (Perl, 1991). Many studies do not have the controls necessary to make statements about causation.

Every 5 years, dietary recommendations known as Dietary Guidelines for Americans are developed by a joint committee of experts from the Department of Agriculture and the Department of Health and Human Services (Burros, 1996). The most recent guidelines contain some strong language and some surprises. The guidelines advocate eating more fruits and vegetables, reducing intake of processed meats such as sausage and salami, as well as limiting salt. They specifically warn adults about the dangers of creeping overweight, that is gaining a few pounds a year in adulthood, and they emphasize the importance of exercise as a way to control weight.

For the first time, these guidelines include a positive statement about the healthfulness of vegetarian diets.

What is most controversial in the guidelines is the acknowledgement that moderate alcohol consumption may promote health, including lowering the risk of heart disease, and is not in itself a health hazard. The dietary guidelines do not encourage people to drink and specifically mention that excessive alcohol consumption leads to many problems such as liver damage, hypertension, and weakened hearts (Public Health Reports, 1994a).

> ***True or False?***
> By its very nature, a vegetarian diet cannot be healthy.

Exercise

The psychological and physiological benefits of regular exercise for middle-aged people are very well documented and are similar to those for young adults as described in Chapter 14 (Blumenthal & McCubbin, 1987). Exercise enables the body to better deal with stressors (Blumenthal et al., 1988). It is also important in both prevention and treatment of obesity. Maintaining a physically active life is one way to reduce heart disease risk at all ages (Brink, 1995). In the Honolulu Heart Program, middle-aged men and elderly men 65 to 69 years were followed for more than a decade. The rate of coronary heart disease in active men was 30% lower than the rate of less active men. The rate of heart disease in active elderly men was less than half the rate of sedentary elderly men (Donohue et al., 1988). The risk of developing coronary heart disease in the sedentary population is almost twice as high as in the active population. A healthy lifestyle, including exercise, reduces a number of cardiac risk factors, including high blood pressure and high cholesterol (Gebhardt & Crump, 1990). The Centers for Disease Control found that the percentage of the U.S. population at risk for heart disease from lack of activity was 59%, which exceeded the percentage at risk from high blood pressure, cholesterol, or even smoking (Powell et al., 1987).

The importance of exercise is shown in a massive study of healthy men and women who were followed for 8 years (Blair et al, 1989). For both men and women the risk of death was three to five times higher for those least fit compared to those who were most fit. This was true across age groups and remained applicable even when risk factors such as smoking, blood pressure, weight, and family history of heart disease were taken into account. Some recent evidence suggests that regular exercise during middle and late adulthood may protect against some forms of cancer, including colon cancer. When men who were moderately or highly active were compared to those who were sedentary, the active individuals had about half the risk of colon cancer of those who were inactive. The protection lessens or disappears when people stop exercising (Lee et al., 1991).

Lack of exercise is a factor in cognitive decline as well (Bunce, War & Cochrane, 1993). The reasons are difficult to understand, but may involve blood flow and oxygen supply to the brain. Moderate levels of fitness that can be attained by most adults are related to less decline in memory and reaction time (Brink, 1995). There is even some evidence that exercise improves cognitive processes (Tomporowski & Ellis, 1986). In one study, aerobic exercise led to an improvement in measures of fluid intelligence but had no effect on crystallized intelligence (Elsayed, Ismael, & Young, 1980). Exercise improves simple response time, and individuals who exercise show a greater resistance to distractions (Dustman et al., 1984). Physical fitness also contributes to improvements in mood and self-concept. For example, regular swimming has been associated with feeling better and a more positive mood (Berger & Owen, 1983).

Although physical activity is clearly beneficial to health, most American adults do not exercise regularly. Although up to half of all American adults say they exercise regularly, more exacting investigations by public health experts reveal that the figure is lower; between 10% to 20% exercise regularly three times a week and about 30% exercise sporadically; at least 50% are sedentary (Leepson, 1992).

> ***True or False?***
> About two-thirds of all middle-aged people exercise three times a week.

Smoking

Smokers have a greater chance of suffering from cardiovascular disease, lung cancer, and emphysema. More than 400,000 Americans die each year from smoking as the habits of the 1950s and 1960s take their toll ("Death Toll," 1991). Smoking prevalence is decreasing across all races and both genders but at a slower rate for women than for men (Prager et al., 1993).

Passive smoking —that is, the inhaling of others' smoke by nonsmokers—is linked to various illnesses. When a group of rural, married women who were nonsmokers and disease free were followed over a 20-year period, cardiovascular mortality among women whose husbands smoked was significantly greater than among women whose husbands did not smoke (Humble et al., 1990). It is estimated that exposure to 25 or more years of smoking throughout childhood and adolescence doubles the risk of lung cancer (Janerich et al., 1990).

Does quitting smoking during middle age improve one's health? The answer is an emphatic yes. The benefits of smoking cessation rapidly accrue, and the longer the period of abstinence, the more ex-smokers reduce their chances of cancer and heart disease, although whether they ever reach the level for nonsmokers is still a controversy (Ockene et al., 1990; Tosteson et al., 1990).

Improving People's Health

In 1990 the Public Health Service in partnership with the National Academy of Science's Institute of Medicine announced health-related objectives in a program called Healthy People–2000. The program established 300 measurable objectives in the areas of health promotion, health protection, and provision of medical services. Federal, state, and local authorities and private organizations are involved in activities designed to meet these goals.

Table 16.1 shows some objectives that are especially relevant to the middle aged. The conclusion that people are living somewhat healthier lives is inescapable. Significant progress has been made in reducing cholesterol levels and controlling hypertension, and a steady decline in coronary artery disease and in stroke has been attained. Today, one in five Americans has a high cholesterol level as compared to one in four Americans a decade or so ago. The number of people being treated for high blood pressure who have that condition under control has increased significantly. Survival rates from heart disease and stroke are much improved as well (McGinnis & Lee, 1995). More people are using cancer detection services, particularly mammograms. The number of people who exercise regularly has increased slightly and more people are eating low-fat diets. Fewer people are smoking and using alcohol and other drugs and many more workplaces have health promotion programs.

Public awareness and interest in health issues has increased in recent years and middle-aged people think more about their health than younger people (Hooker & Kaus, 1994). Some middle-aged people are motivated to engage in healthy behaviors because they want to look better and feel better. However, they are more likely to be motivated to live healthier lives because they fear getting cancer, not being able to maintain their independence, or losing their mental faculties (Hooker & Kaus, 1994).

Questions Students Often Ask

The suggestions for a healthier life seem so obvious: exercise, eat right, and give up smoking. Why don't people follow through?

It is always easy for someone who exercises, eats a healthy diet, and has never smoked to tell others who don't engage in these healthful activities to change. Although it isn't easy, some have changed but many others find it very difficult. People don't change, feel they cannot change, or, in some cases, simply do not want to change for many reasons. One is habit. People often criticize middle-age people for not exercising or eating right but early adults and adolescents don't either. The cumulative effects simply show themselves in middle age. It is difficult to begin an exercise regimen if you haven't exercised in years, or to eat a healthy diet if you haven't for many years. It is not easy to give up cigarette smoking as it is an addiction. Still, many people have been able to exercise more, eat a healthy diet, and give up smoking.

Some people may choose not to change, either because they do not believe the health warnings, feel they don't apply, or simply rationalize them away with the "Tomorrow I could get hit by a truck" mentality. The odds are that you won't be hit by a truck, but it is hard to change attitudes.

Another problem is maintaining good health habits. Some people find it difficult to exercise given their very busy schedule. When they come home from work they are tired. Some people are embarrassed or bored by exercise. Not only is individual motivation important, but social reinforcement and environmental change is useful. For example, exercise can be a social activity and since people reinforce each other it is more effective to exercise in a small group. Not buying processed foods and refined sugars helps as well.

Company Policy

People require information and encouragement to change their health habits. People who understand the

Table 16.1 **Mid-Decade Status for Objectives: Healthy People 2000**

	BASELINE	(YEAR)	UPDATE*	RIGHT DIRECTION
More people exercising regularly	22%	(1985)	24%	Yes
Fewer people overweight	26%	(1974–1980)	34%	No
Fewer people smoking cigarettes	29%	(1987)	25%	Yes
More workplaces with health promotion programs	65%	(1985)	81%	Yes
Fewer work-related deaths per 100,000 population	7.7	(1983–1987)	7.9	No
More people with clean air in their communities	49.7%	(1988)	76.5%	Yes
Fewer coronary heart disease deaths, per 100,000 population	135	(1987)	114	Yes
Fewer deaths from strokes, per 100,000 populations	30.4	(1987)	26.4	Yes
Better control of high blood pressure	11%	(1976–1980)	21%	Yes
Decrease in cancer deaths, per 100,000 population	134	(1987)	133	Yes
Increase in screening for breast cancer	25%	(1987)	55%	Yes

*Updates are from 1992 to 1995.
Source: Adapted from McGinnis & Lee, 1995.

link between disease and such factors as controlling one's weight, restricting fat in the diet, giving up smoking, and exercising are more likely to do so (Jepson et al., 1991). Health promotion information can be delivered through community resources, including newspapers, local radio and television stations, and school-based programs. Indeed, the media seem to have an effect on people's health practices (Niknian, Lefebvre, & Carleton, 1991).

Educational campaigns can be somewhat effective. A study of a communitywide effort in five cities where educational campaigns were aimed at improving health practices such as reducing cholesterol levels through diet and improving physical activity found significant improvements (Farquhar et al., 1990). Knowledge may not always be sufficient to cause the changes in behavior, but it is a good starting point.

Many employers realize the importance to their company of health maintenance, and health promotion programs in industry have increased. There is increasing recognition that companies gain when workers are healthy and fit and that health programs have motivational and attitudinal benefits (Pritchard & Potter, 1990).

Health education programs in the workplace vary greatly. They may involve newsletters, health fairs, health screenings, and educational programs to generate interest. They may emphasize the modification of sedentary lifestyles and may even include strength training. In some programs, the company actually provides equipment and may remove unhealthy temptations such as candy from the vending machines and replace it with fruit.

Studies of company-sponsored fitness programs demonstrate that they can lead to improved employee health, especially if they are accompanied by counseling (Baum, & Tsai, 1986). Programs consisting of consultations on weight loss, smoking, and stress management improve fitness and engender increased feelings of well-being while reducing coronary risk factors (Blair et al., 1986). Such programs are cost effective, leading to lower accident, turnover, and absentee rates (Pelletier, 1988; Bartera, 1990; Warner et al., 1988). Absenteeism has been shown to drop anywhere from 20% to 55% for programs between 1 and 5 years long (Gebhardt & Crump, 1990).

A health promotion program must also deal with stress. There are two important differences between stress in early adulthood and stress in middle age. First, it takes longer for middle-aged people to cope with and bounce back from stress (Chew, 1976). Second, the effects of stress are cumulative and take time to show up. In middle age they may finally take their toll with heart attacks and other illnesses.

Many companies recognize the relationship between stress and illness and other work-related problems such as absenteeism and have established programs to help employees deal with stress. Such programs may involve physical activity, relaxation training, and alcohol and drug counseling. Such programs can reduce absenteeism and visits to the medical office significantly.

Minorities and Health Status

The average American adult is healthier today than a generation ago. Americans are living longer and data from such programs as Healthy Americans 2000 show that health practices seem to be improving somewhat. However, averages can be deceptive. When considering death rates and other health statistics, general trends in the population can be deduced but the state of health in minority communities may be obscured. At the same time, progress in a particular health problem in a minority group, such as the reduction in high blood pressure among African Americans, may not be noticed unless we focus on the health concerns of minority groups.

The health of minority group adults is a mixed picture, but one which leads to some concern. Generally, Latinos, Native Americans, and African Americans have higher death rates than whites in middle age. Minority group members are also less likely to have any health insurance (USDHHS, 1995).

African Americans have a high death rate compared to other groups in our society (Plepys & Klein, 1995). Their death rate from cancer is much higher (USDHHS, 1995). The most important reasons for this excessive mortality is the greater prevalence of high blood pressure and diabetes among them, which makes heart disease more difficult to treat (Newsday, 1996). In addition, more African Americans than whites are not covered by any type of health insurance. Their health status also lags behind that of whites; about twice as many African Americans report their health as fair to poor (USDHHS, 1995).

Latinos have health problems such as diabetes, obesity, and alcoholism and also are much less likely to have health insurance coverage (Kaplan, 1996). There is great variability, however, with many more Mexican Americans than people from Cuba or Puerto Rico not being covered.

The death rate for Asian Americans is 40% lower than for any other major group at every age (USDHHS, 1995). However, in some Asian American communities, the incidence of tuberculosis is much higher than in the general population (Public Health Reports, 1993a).

The death rate for Native Americans is higher than for the general population (USDHHS, 1995). Native Americans have a low life expectancy and many die before the age of 50. Alcoholism is probably their greatest health problem and an estimated one out of three Native American deaths is caused by alcohol (CQ Researcher, 1992). Cirrhosis of the liver caused by excessive alcohol consumption is much more prevalent among this group than in the rest of the U.S. population. Native Americans are also more likely to smoke (Public Health Reports, 1993b).

Some minority groups have higher death rates probably because of social and behavioral factors (Williams, Lavizzo-Mourey, & Warren, 1995). One reason for the disparity is that access to health care is unequal (see Controversial Issues feature on pp. 380–382) (Blenden et al., 1989). Minority group members are less likely to be covered by insurance plans. In addition, minority group members are more likely to be treated in hospital clinics,

Controversial Issues: The Crisis in Medical Care

Americans spent $949.4 billion on health care in 1994, an increase of 6.4% from the previous year (U.S. Department of Commerce, 1996). Health care costs continue to escalate and health care in the United States costs 40% more than in any other country (Bingaman, Frank, & Billy, 1993). The rate of increase has moderated somewhat, but the increases are still well above the annual rate of inflation.

Costs have increased because of higher provider fees, expensive medical technology, consumers' lack of knowledge, consumers not caring about payment, (since insurance companies often pick up the tab), fee-for-service systems that reward doctors for doing more services, services provided in hospitals rather than in less expensive settings, and the increasing number of older clients (Frank, 1993; Kerrey & Hofschire, 1993). Another reason for increased costs is the tremendous increase in malpractice suits in the 1980s (Frank, 1993). Some doctors, such as orthopedic surgeons and obstetricians/gynecologists may pay very high annual insurance premiums. Defensive medicine—extensive and perhaps unnecessary medical tests—is sometimes the result. Another reason for the increase, one that is not widely publicized, is administrative costs. As many as one in four health care dollars is spent on the massive paper work required to run the unwieldy health care system (Daschle, Cohen, & Rice, 1993). Many of you may remember becoming frustrated over the number of forms to fill out, the problem of dealing with insurance companies, and the sheer unfriendliness of the system, sometimes called the hassle factor.

A second problem is that about 35 million Americans do not have any health coverage at all (Kerrey & Hofschire, 1993). The percentage of Americans with no health insurance varies with age, ethnicity, and income (see Figure A). Because Medicaid has been expanded, more children are covered, but the percentage of those with no coverage is still more than 14%. People with low income, often members of minority groups, are much more likely to be uninsured (USDHHS, 1995).

Although most Americans now obtain health insurance coverage through their employers, the overwhelming majority of all Americans without health insurance are either working or live in a home that is headed by a worker (Frank, 1993); the low-income working family is most affected. Despite government programs that cover the elderly and some people who live in poverty, the problem of lack of insurance and of underinsurance continues to grow. Some Americans have access to the best, most modern health care, a number are inadequately covered, and some that are simply not covered at all.

The twin problems in American medical care, cost and access, defy a quick and painless solution (Kerrey & Hofschire, 1993). Health care in the United States is in crisis. If it were just a matter of covering the uninsured with health insurance, we could acknowledge the need, debate the costs, and find some way to provide the coverage. But the problem is much deeper and lies in the tremendously high costs of health care that have forced health insurance premiums through the ceiling and show no signs of abating (Frank & VandenBos, 1994). Simply stated, health care in the United States is becoming more expensive and less affordable for millions.

There is a widescale call for changes. Pressure to reform medical costs—including those under government programs—is growing and Americans believe that fundamental changes are necessary. The health care debate of the 1990s has resulted in hundreds of bills to reform the system. Most would guarantee universal access, many would reform liability, but they differ widely on what services would be covered, who would run the system, and how it would be paid for (Daschle et al., 1993). Many states have also entered the health care reform debate in an effort

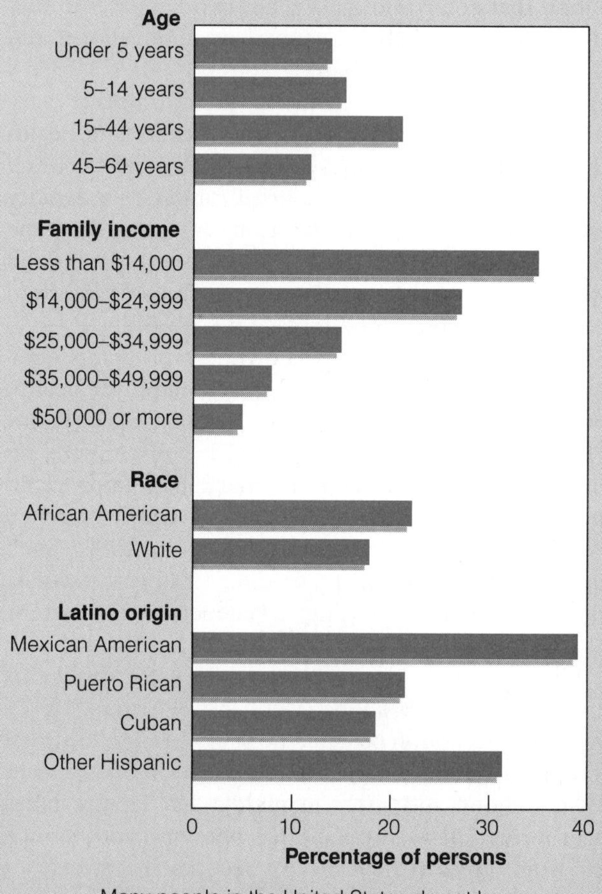

Many people in the United States do not have any health insurance.

Figure A
Percentage of persons under 65 years of age who are uninsured by age, family income, race, and ethnicity: United States, 1980–1993

Note: Percents include persons not covered by private insurance, Medicaid, Medicare, and military plans.
Source: Centers for Disease Control and Prevention, National Center for Health Statistics, National Health Interview Survey.

Controversial Issues: The Crisis in Medical Care (continued)

to cover their population and reduce costs. Hawaii is sometimes held up as a national model in which employers are required to provide health coverage and pay at least 50% of the premiums. Other programs pay for the very poor or people who otherwise would not be covered. Many are placed in a managed care plan that reduces costs (Frank, Sullivan, & DeLeon, 1994). However, Hawaii is an isolated state and not really in competition with its neighbors. Other states have neighbors who are economic competitors; raising costs by covering everyone and forcing employers to pick up the bill could force employers to move to neighboring states where it is cheaper to operate.

Whatever system is adopted, some very difficult questions will have to be answered. For example, people do not use health care services equally. The most ill 10% of the population accounts for twice the benefits of the other 90%. In addition, some procedures such as organ transplants are extremely expensive. The health problems of the most ill individuals drive up the overall health care costs for everyone. Should there be limits to medical coverage? Should a 75-year-old be allowed to have very expensive transplant surgery?

How can costs be controlled? One possibility is individual case management, in which attempts are made to reduce costs on a case-by-case basis. For example, by providing a ramp at the home of an elderly person, the hospital stay for hip replacement can be reduced. Some hospitals could specialize in certain unusual treatments like transplants, and health plans could negotiate fixed fees for such procedures. Large firms could provide medical coverage or pay into a supplemental plan and negotiate standard fees. A more radical approach is a bill that would require all major health care needs to be paid for by the government. However, extending medical coverage to all would not control costs, and controlling costs is certainly a priority.

One solution may lie in competition, which is currently very limited in the field of medicine (Bingaman, Frank, & Billy, 1993). A middle-aged man with a prostate problem that requires an operation will be sent to a specialist. The patient may be very concerned about his condition and may not even ask about the charges, knowing that most of the cost is covered by insurance. Under a plan called managed competition, people would not shop for insurance but would join a large private group at work or be assigned to a public group. The sponsor would arrange insurance for everyone in the group and solicit bids from private insurers and providers. Enrollees would insist on low costs because they will want more coverage for the money, and only basic coverage would be tax deductible. The problem with this system is that this would effectively eliminate choice, and people who want different doctors would be forced to pay for them privately. However, what if one is not pleased with the care from the group's doctor but cannot afford a private physician?

The Jackson Hole Model proposes creating Health Insurance Purchasing Cooperatives (HIPCs) sometimes called *alliances,* which are organizations that would act as purchasing agents for consumers. These would offer consumers standardized benefit packages from a number of providers, together with information on costs and quality (Bingaman, Frank, & Billy, 1993). Because so many consumers would be involved they would have some leverage. Consumers could purchase any one of a number of plans but the individual consumer would have to pay the difference between the least expensive plan offering the required services and other more expensive plans. During certain periods each year, consumers would be allowed to change providers. The plan would also create accountable health partnerships that would monitor the programs, looking for places to economize and to expand. The HIPC would actually buy the health care program from these Accountable Health Partnerships (AHPs), which offer benefit packages that meet their standards.

Other experts look to Canada as a model. Canadians choose their own doctors, and the government picks up the bill. Costs are controlled by provincial governments, which negotiate physician fees and hospital reimbursement. Canada spends 30% less per person than the United States, but some Canadians complain of long waits for treatment. Another problem is that the government model may stifle innovation because providers would have no incentive to improve the quality of their care. Canada benefits greatly from improvements in U.S. medical technology. Under some kind of managed competition, providers might find an incentive for innovation that would make their group more desirable.

Another highly controversial approach is to limit the introduction and use of new and expensive medical technology. Much life-saving technology is very expensive, and curbing its use is one way to reduce costs. Americans seem to want these high-technology discoveries but do not want to pay for them.

Some advocate a single-payer or single-collector system, either the government or a government agency, that would raise all the funds necessary, perhaps through a single tax (Daschle et al., 1993). This would actually reduce administrative costs. Despite what many people believe, Medicaid and Medicare administrative costs are only about 2% of the total. The single-payer system would also allow for better studies of utilization and reduce duplication (Daschle et al., 1993). Although other countries find that this reduces cost, it would be a radical change for the United States and it is doubtful that it will be adopted (Frank & VandenBos, 1994).

Managed care through a **health maintenance organization (HMO)** provides all health care services within a par-

health maintenance organization (HMO) Medical organizations that have a system for providing health care to members within a geographic area and that offer an agreed-upon set of basic and supplemental health and treatment services.

(continued)

Controversial Issues: The Crisis in Medical Care (continued)

ticular network of physicians. The fee per month is higher than some medical insurance, but it is constant and can be budgeted for (Sizer & Whitney, 1988). Overall, it is a less expensive system. By the year 2000 as much as 65% of the U.S. population will receive care through HMOs (Weiner, 1994). Although HMOs are more cost effective, they offer the consumer little or no choice.

The problem of providing health care to all Americans is a daunting one. It is clear that extending health insurance to those not covered, although necessary, will be expensive and will not curb expenses. Some change is required, but just what change will Americans allow? It would be unfortunate if a medical plan for America did away with the incentive to develop sophisticated life-saving technology, even though this is inherently expensive. It would be unfortunate if people were forced into a group care situation in which they would have no choice.

The American public agrees that health care reform is necessary. Americans also demonstrate a constant support for the expansion of medical and health expenditures (Navarro, 1987). The contradictions in the reforms Americans want in health care are staggering. In one study, 75% of those interviewed stated that competition would be the most effective way to reduce costs, and 75% also agreed that the government should become more involved and regulate rates (Blendon et al., 1994).

People use medical care more as they age. Chronic diseases such as cancer, heart disease, and arthritis require much care. The real issues are how to provide medical care at a reasonable cost, continue to evolve better ways of treatment, and still deliver services that will satisfy the consumer. The debate will continue into the future, and it is clear that everyone involved, including health care providers, the government, insurance companies, and the general public, will have to participate in this debate. Any system that is installed will be costly.

emergency rooms, and other health care settings where they receive care from a different health care provider each time (Blenden et al., 1989). It is not known why members of some minority groups are less likely to receive life-saving procedures, such as bypass surgery, than people from majority groups with similar conditions. The possibility of unequal treatment by the medical establishment must be seriously considered.

Another reason for the disparities may be that many people from minority groups were raised in poverty and may be the first generation to achieve middle-income status. Adult health is affected by health and risk factors that were present in childhood. Studies show that childhood socioeconomic conditions and medical problems may increase vulnerability to medical problems in adulthood (Williams, 1990). For instance, poor nutrition in childhood may be a factor in problems in adulthood. Parental disadvantage is related to low birth weight, which is also associated with other risk factors in middle age (Blane, 1995). It may take a few generations before this vulnerability is negated.

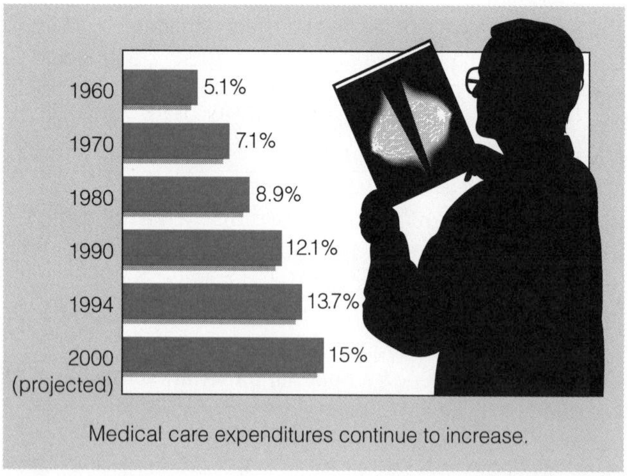

Datagraphic
Medical Care Expenditures as Percentage of Gross National Product

Source: Data from U.S. General Accounting Office, 1991; U.S. Health Care Financing Administration, 1996.

A major reason for differences in survival between groups is probably the greater participation by certain groups, for example whites, in risk reduction and early warning programs (Davis et al., 1994). For example, cholesterol screening programs often attract older, well-educated, nonsmoking white women (Muscat et al., 1994).

This does not mean that there are no biological differences that might increase one group's susceptibility to particular disorders. Sickle cell anemia is found mostly in African Americans and Tay-Sachs disease in Jews. However, geographical origin, not race, may be a key factor. The sickle cell trait provides some protection against malaria and developed as a response to environmental conditions. In this way, biological differences may reflect the adaptation of human groups to environmental conditions.

Socioeconomic Status, Education, and Occupational Status

Too many people equate race/ethnicity and socioeconomic status. The differences associated with race or ethnicity are much smaller than those associated with socioeconomic status (House et al., 1990). When racial disparities in health status are adjusted for socioeconomic level, the differences are either completely eliminated or at least greatly reduced (Keil et al., 1992). The problem is that a disproportionate number of people in minority groups are poor.

People from every ethnic group who are educated and have high-status jobs live longer and are healthier (Blane, 1995). People with higher levels of income, education, and occupational status have lower rates of disease in both the industrialized and developing countries. Among middle-aged people who did not finish high school the death rate is about twice as high as among college-educated people (Prager et al., 1993). There is an inverse relationship between education and risk factors such as blood pressure, cholesterol, and smoking, and this helps to explain the survival data (Adler et al., 1994; Bucher & Ragland, 1995). People who are educated live in more favorable environments, have better access to health care, and are more likely to follow health and medical advice (Prager et al., 1993; Prager et al., 1994). As educational status improves, health practices improve as well. The relationship between these socioeconomic factors and health is a graded association with health and socioeconomic status related at every level (Adler et al., 1994). People with high levels of education and occupational status may also be high in self-efficacy; believing that they can influence their health. In turn, people who believe they can influence their own health are more likely to engage in healthy behaviors. Many more people in minority groups are poor and as people from minority groups gain entrance into occupations that are better paying, the disparity should be reduced.

All three variables are usually correlated. People who are educated usually fill the higher-status jobs. The material resources of parental homes are strong predictors of educational attainment, which in turn is a strong predictor of occupation and labor market success.

Improving Health in Minority Group Members

Since many more members of minority groups lack health insurance, this is an important place to start. Many people, especially those who are poor, do not see the same doctor twice, relying on emergency rooms. The doctor is not familiar with the family's history and needs. Community-based programs can help. In one Los Angeles program, trained lay people were selected to serve as messengers, recruiters, and organizers to improve early cancer detection programs in their communities. They were asked to identify barriers to people's participation in these programs, spread information about program availability, and provide support services such as child care and transportation when needed. Churches enthusiastically supported the program and increases in the number of African American and especially Latino women screened for cancer were significant (Davis et al., 1994). No single method of communication is universally effective and many community-oriented programs use multiple sources such as local television spots, leaflets, and direct contact through mail and telephone reminders (Dignan et al., 1994).

Progress has been made in many areas, but more needs to be done. In 1993 a number of special research centers around the country were funded in an attempt to further research efforts to prevent, diagnose, and treat illnesses among minority populations (Public Health Reports, 1993). Because health impacts so many aspects of life it is important to begin now to target at-risk populations and attempt to reduce the disparities even more.

Women's Health

Would it surprise you to discover that few women take part in studies on heart disease even though coronary disease is the leading cause of death among women (though not in middle age) (Glazer, 1994)? Would it surprise you that women might react differently to medications than men?

Many studies on aging have excluded women, especially those dealing with cardiovascular disease. In 1990 the General Accounting Office reported that women were generally underrepresented in drug trials funded by the National Institutes of Health (Glazer, 1994). Medications may affect women differently because of hormonal and metabolic differences, and this needs to be researched.

Congress now requires the National Institutes of Health to include women in all studies of diseases and conditions that

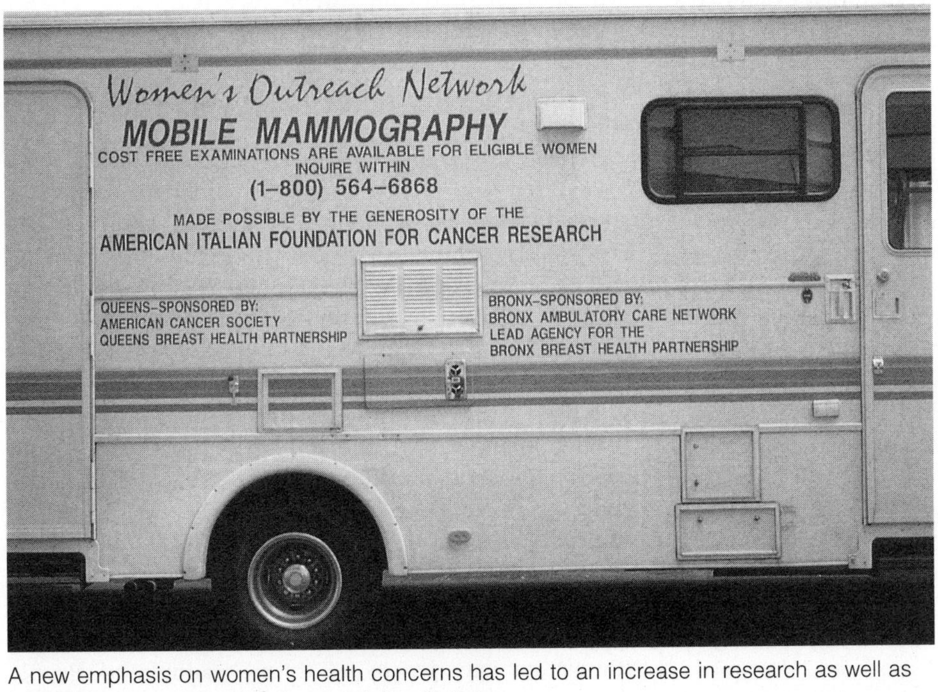

A new emphasis on women's health concerns has led to an increase in research as well as an increase in awareness of women's health issues.

may affect them. It requires drug companies to do the same and to report research on gender differences. These new rules are opposed by some. Women were excluded from clinical trials for a number of reasons, one of which was pregnancy. The rule against using women in many drug trials was to protect the fetus from possible damage. Not only would any harm to the fetus from a medication be tragic, it would also lead to law suits and liability. In addition, women's heart problems usually begin about 10 years after men's and longitudinal studies would thus take much longer.

Many researchers argue that the new requirements will make studies much more expensive. One important cardiovascular study of thousands of men in the 1970s cost 115 million dollars. If a sufficient number of women were included to analyze differences between the gender's risk factors in a valid way the study would cost 3 billion dollars. In addition, the new requirements assume that clinically important differences between men and women are the rule, not the exception, a theory that many doctors reject (Angell, 1993). Even, the premise that women have been excluded from most clinical trials is doubted as many more projects that focus exclusively on one gender do so on women, not men. Women's health has not been harmed by the orientation of past studies and women's death rates from heart disease have fallen at the same rate as men's death rates. Many researchers agree that women should be included in more studies but only where there is reason to believe that some differences will emerge.

Another area of concern is the desire for more research funding to be placed into areas of women's health. Due to intense lobbying, the funding for breast cancer research quadrupled in the early 1990s (Glazer, 1994). In 1990 the National Institutes of Health created a new office of research on women's health. In 1991 a massive study of 160,000 postmenopausal women that examined issues involving heart disease, breast cancer, and osteoporosis began (Schneider, 1993). Although the increase in research is welcomed some argue that the study is not designed as well as it should be, is too large, and overly expensive (CQ Researcher, 1994).

The medical establishment has been accused of being insensitive to the concerns of women. Women may show some differences in risk factors and disease progression and this needs to be researched and acted upon. Some desire a new medical specialty devoted to the entire spectrum of women's health, not just reproductive disorders (Johnson, 1994). Often the only training in women's health that doctors have is in obstetrics and gynecology. This is insufficient, and many doctors do not understand that women may have other concerns. Doctors frequently fail to allow women to share in decision making. Having a medical specialty devoted to women's health would stop the periodic increases and decreases in interest in women's health that seem to occur. A specialty would allow doctors to be trained not only in reproductive biology but in the different effects diseases and therapies have on women, as well as in such social issues as domestic violence and sexual abuse.

Others argue that at a time when everyone is concerned with the need to create more generalists, it is difficult to convince people of the need for a new specialty (Glazer, 1994). In addition, what goes on in the doctor's consulting office does not have much to do with what occurs in research centers, so the argument that the creation of a specialty would generate funding is doubtful (Harrison, 1994). The need is really to make all specialties of medicine more user friendly to women and that requires increased awareness.

Whether a new specialty is created, the need for more research into women's health issues is compelling, as is the need for greater understanding of the possible differences in risk factors and reactions to medications between men and women. This new interest must be translated into research studies that are well designed and based upon scientifically validated hypotheses. Most of all, what is needed is increased sensitivity to women's issues and better medical training so that more doctors are aware of women's concerns and can be more effective in dealing with women's health problems.

Cognitive Development in Middle Adulthood

The idea that health inevitably declines in middle age has been refuted. Health habits, which are under the person's control, are the keys to good health. But what happens to intelligence and problem solving as we age? Does lifestyle have an effect on cognitive functioning as well?

Intellectual Abilities

Which of the following statements is true?

* Intellectual abilities increase in midlife.
* Intellectual abilities decrease in midlife.
* Intellectual abilities remain stable throughout middle adulthood.

Actually, research supports all three statements. One reason for this is that individual differences—for example, health, education, and mental and physical fitness—are factors that are especially important in midlife and beyond. People who are healthy and do not abuse drugs score higher on intelligence tests than those who are not well or use drugs. Educated people tend to have an edge in intelligence testing because they are apt to remain intellectually active throughout life.

When people are followed throughout late adolescence and middle adulthood, we find that the intelligence of some people increases while that of others decreases; still others stay relatively stable in intelligence. One study found that people whose intelligence increased had traveled extensively overseas, had spouses whose adult intelligence was high, and had enjoyed stimulating experiences all through adulthood. People whose intelligence had decreased had drinking problems and experienced little mental stimulation (Honzik, 1984). Until about age 70 the differences between people of the same chronological age are greater than the differences between age groups (Schaie & Parham, 1977). Individual differences in reaction time, memory, and fluid intelligence become more important with age. Data collected on adults ranging from 16 to 74 showed that differences in performance on general intelligence, verbal aptitude, numerical aptitude, spatial aptitude, form perception, and other abilities not dependent upon speed are quite small until at least age 65 (Avolio & Waldman, 1994).

K. Warner Schaie and his colleagues (1990) followed certain basic abilities—such as verbal meaning, the ability to comprehend words (a measure of recognition vocabulary), spatial orientation (the ability to mentally rotate objects in two-dimensional space), inductive reasoning, number concepts, and word fluency—over 7-year periods in a group of individuals ranging from age 25 to 81. This study called the Seattle Longitudinal Study continues and some of its findings are found in Figures 16.4 and 16.5 (Schaie, 1994). Longitudinal data show that before age 60, average age declines in abilities cannot be reliably confirmed, except for word fluency, which has a significant speed component (Schaie, 1994). Most abilities peak in early midlife, plateau until the late 50s early 60s and then show decline, initially at a slow pace but accelerating as the late 70s reached (Schaie & Willis, 1993). The ages at which certain abilities peak and declines begin, though, are controversial and depend upon whether one uses cross-sectional or longitudinal studies.

Cross-Sectional and Longitudinal Studies of Intelligence

Whether a research study shows a decline in intelligence depends somewhat on the type of study being conducted. If a cross-sectional study—comparing groups of people in their 20s, 30s, 40s, and 50s—is performed, some decreases in intelligence are found. If a longitudinal format—comparing the same people over a long period of time—is used, significant declines are not found in middle age, at least not until age 60 (Whitbourne & Weinstock, 1979). The Seattle Longitudinal Study noted previously provides us with cross-sectional and longitudinal data. The difference in pattern is impressive. According to the cross-sectional data, three of the abilities peak in young adulthood and show age declines, steepest for spatial orientation and inductive reasoning and less pronounced for word fluency (see Figure 16.5). Verbal meaning and number concept peak in middle age. Verbal meaning shows some decline in old age (Schaie, 1994). As we noted in previous chapters, cross-sectional studies confound age and the different experiences of various generations. The longitudinal data tell a somewhat different story, showing modest gains for all abilities from young adulthood to early middle age. The age of peak performance differs depending upon the ability measured (see Figure 16.4). Again, declines (except in word fluency, which appears at age 53) are not significant in middle age.

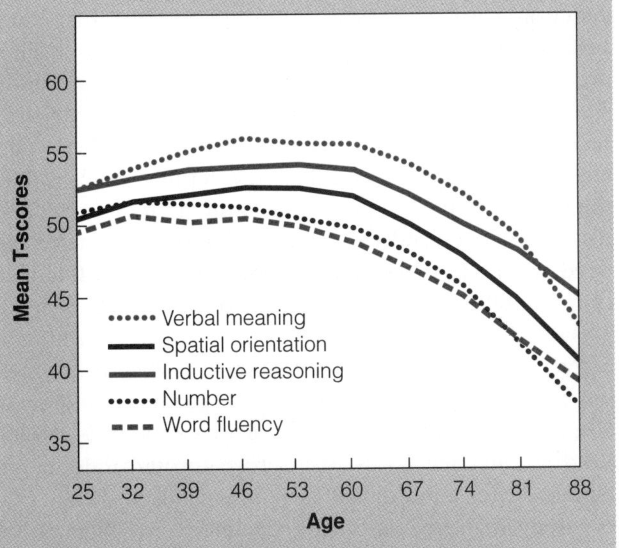

Using a longitudinal design, reliable declines are not found until age 60 or older for most abilities.

Figure 16.4
Longitudinal Estimates of Mean T-Scores for Single Markers of the Primary Mental Abilities
Note: From 7-year within-subject data.
Source: Schaie, 1994.

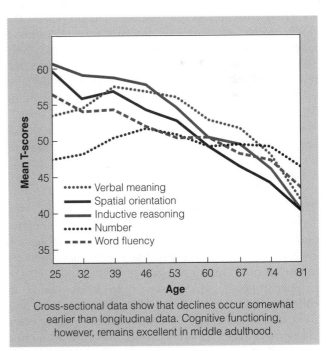

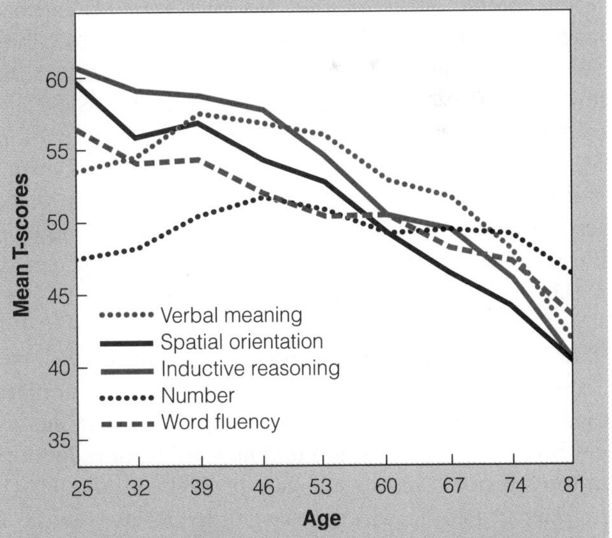

Cross-sectional data show that declines occur somewhat earlier than longitudinal data. Cognitive functioning, however, remains excellent in middle adulthood.

Figure 16.5
Cross-Sectional Mean T-Scores for Single Markers of the Primary Mental Abilities
Note: 1991 data.
Source: Schaie, 1994.

True or False?
If you follow a group of people through middle age, their general intelligence will show a significant decline.

Most cross-sectional studies that compare older adults to younger adults show that younger adults do somewhat better than middle-aged adults and that middle-aged adults do somewhat better than older adults (Willis, 1989). For example, declines in verbal ability in cross-sectional studies may be found in early middle age whereas in longitudinal studies they occur much later, sometimes very late in middle age or early in late adulthood, and the decline is much more gradual (Willis, 1989). Another interesting point is that the age at which there is a decline in general intelligence in cross-sectional studies has been increasing as educational opportunities and living standards have improved (Storfer, 1990). The difference in results between cross-sectional and longitudinal designs occurs for many reasons, including the cohort effect and the problem of averaging intelligence scores.

The Cohort Effect Suppose you perform a cross-sectional study comparing people in their 20s, 30s, 40s, and 50s on some intelligence test and find that scores get lower over the years. How do you interpret your results? The results may be real, or they may be caused by the generational differences between the groups, called the **cohort effect**, which is the effect of living in a particular historical period. The cohort effect is considered a major issue when comparing 60-olds with 20-year-olds, but society is changing so fast that comparing a person entering middle age with one entering young adulthood may not be fair today. Perhaps the most important cohort effect regarding intelligence is the result of differential levels of schooling between the generations. It is difficult to compare groups of people from different generations using intelligence tests because educational background is so important to performance on these largely verbal tests. Other generational differences involve changes in lifestyle and favorable technological change (Schaie et al., 1992).

The Problem With Averaging Intelligence Scores

To solve this problem, you decide to perform a longitudinal study. You test the same group of 20-year-olds every 5 years for 30 years and find no significant reductions in intelligence. This approach is problematic too. First, a number of people will probably drop out as your study continues and will tend to be the least educated and those who are physically ill. Thus, your study may be comparing an ordinary group of 20-year-olds with a superior group of 50-year-olds. Also, the stability of intelligence noted in longitudinal studies may reflect the averaging of different abilities measured under the heading "intelligence." In other words, some aspects of intelligence may increase whereas others may decrease, thereby averaging out.

Fluid and Crystallized Intelligence

The relationship of age to different abilities varies, depending on what is being tested and how it is measured (Salthouse, 1989; Denney, 1982). For instance, **fluid intelligence** (the basic capacity for learning and problem solving, including such abilities as memory and the speed of mental work) tends to decrease beginning in early adulthood (Botwinick, 1977; Horn & Cattell, 1966); nonverbal and abstract abilities also decline with age (Bayley, 1970). Studies on the nonverbal performance subtests of the Wechsler Adult Intelligence Scales, such as making a design out of blocks and completing a picture in which something is left out, show a decline in nonverbal abilities with age (Albert & Heaton, 1988; Honzik, 1984). On the other hand, **crystallized intelligence** (which involves learned knowledge and skills) tends to increase throughout middle adulthood (Horn & Donaldson, 1980). Information, comprehension, and vocabulary show increases in middle age (Sands, Terry, & Meredith, 1989).

One reason for the decline in fluid intelligence is the slowing of performance with age. When measuring fluid intelligence in middle-aged people, reducing the speed requirements for the test produces better results and the decline, although still present, is much flatter (Hertzog, 1989). This may result from a slowing in the rate of thinking itself.

Another possible reason for a decline in fluid intelligence and not in crystallized intelligence is that many people use their verbal skills throughout life but allow nonverbal skills—which may not be as useful in middle age—to decline. When abilities are exercised, they remain relatively constant throughout most of adulthood, but abilities that are not used decline (Denney, 1982). Adults might find nonverbal tasks more difficult merely because they have not used those particular skills for years. Indeed, studies have found that as people age they find tests of fluid ability more difficult than verbal tests (Cornelius, 1984).

Even those who claim that there is a decline throughout adulthood find that the decline in fluid intelligence is moderate until after age 50 or older whereas crystallized intelligence tends to improve through middle age and into later adulthood (Horn & Donaldson, 1980). Others deny that any significant decline in intelligence occurs during middle age at all (Schaie & Hertzog, 1983).

There is little disagreement that intellectual abilities decline sometime in adulthood—the question is when and

cohort effect The effect of living in a particular generation or historical period, particularly important to consider when comparing generations.

fluid intelligence The basic capacity for learning and problem solving. It is independent of education and experience.

crystallized intelligence Learned knowledge and skills.

why. It is obvious that using intelligence itself is a problem because it is composed of so many different skills. The evidence shows that intellectual abilities do not show reliable decreases in middle adulthood, with the exception of those that heavily involve speed.

What causes the decline is of vital interest and remains controversial. No one really knows why fluid intelligence decreases, and the theories attempting to explain this phenomenon are mainly repetitions of theories seeking to explain the increase in reaction time with age. If the decrease is caused by central nervous system decline resulting from the normal aging process (Horn & Donaldson, 1980), we will all be affected to some extent as we age. On the other hand, the evidence that people who are mentally active and physically fit and who watch their eating and health habits show few if any of these declines indicates that experience is probably as important as, if not more important than, physiological factors.

Memory

Memory shows some very modest changes in middle age. Visual memory declines only minimally until age 60, after which is declines significantly (Giambra et al., 1995). Auditory memory shows a decline between the ages of 20 and 40, and does not decline after that. Tactile memory shows a gradual decline with age. There is no evidence that sensory memory—memory that lasts for only a second before it must be attended to—changes much over the life span (Craik & Jennings, 1992). The number of items held in short-term memory—memory that lasts for about 30 seconds—increases during childhood, peaks in early adulthood, and declines thereafter (Baltes et al., 1980). The differences in short-term memory ability throughout middle age are relatively small (Galinsky & Judd, 1994). Working memory involves the preservation of information while processing the same or other information (Salthouse & Babcock, 1991). Again, these differences are relatively small (Cambell & Charness, 1990), with significant declines in working memory appearing after age 60 (Dobbs & Rule, 1989). Whatever differences occur are probably the result of a reduction in speed (Salthouse, 1994; 1993).

Long-term memory declines somewhat during middle adulthood, but again the changes are not great. There is an age-related decline in recall, with young adults performing better than middle-aged adults, who in turn do better than the elderly. However, recognition remains excellent (Craik & Jennings, 1992). In one study young adults right out of high school and adults of about 50 years of age were tested on both recall and recognition of high school acquaintances. In terms of recognition, the older adults did just about as well as the 18-year-olds even though they had been out of high school for so many years (Bahrick, Bahrick, & Wittlinger, 1975). Whatever reductions in memory abilities do occur are probably the result of an increase in the time people take to process information as they grow older (Salthouse & Kail, 1983). In addition, when the memory task is similar to one faced by the individual in the course of the day, middle adults do quite well. For instance, when people 18 to 59 years old were asked to learn and remember the names of four individuals, no age-related differences were found. However, when asked to recall the names of 15 individuals, not a situation that occurs in real life very much, performance differences were found (Crook & West, 1990).

True or False?
Middle-aged people show major decline in recognition memory.

Middle-aged people can easily improve their memory by using better organization and imagery. When young, middle-aged, and older adults were tested on free recall of words from a list, middle-aged people benefited from instructions on how to use visual imagery while the others did not (Mason & Smith, 1977). When middle-aged people are taught how to organize material, their memory ability improves.

Finally, people who use their memory do well on tests of memory. When adults of various ages were compared on memory ability and strategies used, those attending school, regardless of age, were more similar to each other than they were to their age mates who were not attending school perhaps because the educational experience requires people to practice their memory skills. Declines in memory and memory strategies may not be caused by aging alone. The researchers note that "adults of the same age may differ in memory performance, and adults differing in age may perform similarly" (Zivian & Darjes, 1983, p. 519).

The results of these studies are heartening. Some age-related declines may occur in recall, but not in recognition memory. As people age, it may take them longer to recall certain events, but these changes are not serious and do not appear to affect daily functioning; activity and practice appear to be important. In addition, the slight loss in recall can be compensated for by better organization and the use of imagery.

Learning and Problem Solving in Adulthood

Some people are surprised to discover that little or no differences in adult learning occur until about age 60. This is especially true if the material is meaningful for the adult. A decrease in performance on abstract problems begins in early adulthood, but performance on realistic and practical problems peaks in middle age (Denney & Palmer, 1981). Again, speed may have something to do with this. Slower processing may impair abstraction because less relevant information is simultaneously available when needed (Salthouse, 1994). In an extensive study—known as the Baltimore Longitudinal Study—learning and memory tasks were analyzed cross-sectionally across the age span and very small age differences were found prior to age 60 (Arenberg & Robertson-Tchabo, 1977).

True or False?
In middle adulthood, a decline occurs in the ability to solve abstract problems, but the ability to solve practical problems improves.

Steven Cornelius and Avshalom Caspi (1987) constructed an everyday problem-solving inventory that measures six domains, including experience as an economic consumer, dealing with complex or technical information, managing a home, resolving family conflicts, resolving conflicts with friends, and resolving conflicts with co-workers (examples are found in Table 16.2). When a group of people between age 20 and 78 were studied, everyday problem-solving performance displayed a linear increase with age, with older adults performing better than younger adults. This study agrees with others that show increases in practical problem solving for middle-aged people. However, it is necessary to point out that this material was not very complex, and more research is needed on the effects of complexity on problem-solving ability.

Experience is another factor in problem solving. Many people aged 40 to 65 have had a great deal of experience solving problems in their areas of expertise. Their expertise may equalize their performance on tasks associated with problem solving in these areas (Morrow et al., 1994).

There are some differences between middle-aged and younger learners in the learning process. The retrieval and response time of older learners tends to be greater (Salthouse, 1993). Allowing additional time for study and learning will lead to better performance. Everyone performs better under these conditions, but the middle-aged and the elderly are likely to benefit more from these changes. Sometimes middle-aged people need help in organizing new material, especially if it is unfamiliar.

Questions Students Often Ask

Despite all the encouraging sentiments about middle age, I still see it as a time of decline. I am a bit embarrassed, but I still don't see it as a very desirable time of life.

This is a common feeling, especially in younger people. We live in a very youth-oriented culture that fears aging. In addition, we place emphasis on outward appearance and compare ourselves to young adults. We also live in a fast-changing world, one that does not value experience and wisdom. In such a culture it becomes difficult to appreciate the advantages that middle-age people have in their view of the world, their income, and, as we will see in the next chapter, their acceptance of who they are. The news on middle adulthood shows that, with the exception of speed of response, very few negative changes need take place as we age; much of course depends on one's lifestyle.

Back to School

Even a casual look around a college campus will tell us that more middle-aged adults are taking courses and graduating from colleges and universities than ever before. For some, a career change necessitates further training. A man who found he could not get anywhere in the mailroom returns to school for accounting courses. A homemaker returns to school to prepare for a job selling insurance. Others return to school to broaden their horizons. A middle-aged man once told me he was taking courses in psychology, philosophy, and mythology and loving it because doing so gave him the chance to use his mind, something he could not do on his boring job. Some have no specific goals in mind but return to school because they crave more stimulation. Others might return to school to fulfill the dream of receiving the college education they either could not or did not pursue when they were younger.

Middle-aged learners have a number of assets when it comes to learning (Haponski & McCabe, 1982). The life experiences of adults often help them to contribute more to the class. Adults also show a greater eagerness to learn and more commitment, and they spend more time studying and are willing to

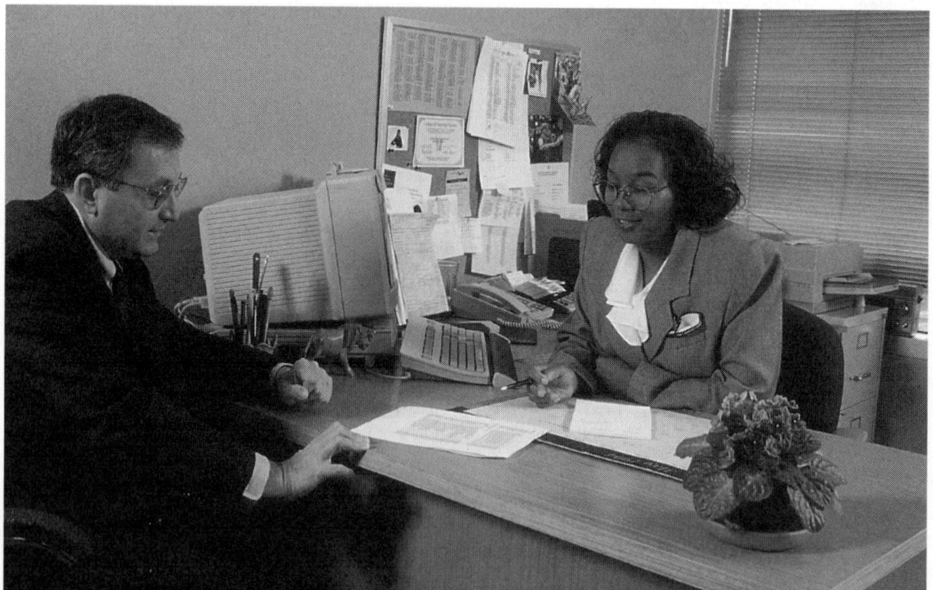
Middle-aged people sometimes return to school to prepare for a different career. If you were hiring people, would their age make a difference?

ask questions. They often have a better idea of their goals. The limitations of older learners are that they show a greater susceptibility to fear of failure and experience greater external pressures, which make it difficult to study.

The ability to learn is based upon many factors other than memory; it also depends upon motivation. Any stagnation that occurs in middle age results more from a loss of motivation than to any changes in mental abilities. It may take an older individual somewhat more time to learn difficult material, but this disadvantage can be compensated for by greater experience and a more mature approach to learning (Katchadourian, 1987); this may be an advantage in a world that is burdened by an oversupply of raw data. The problem may be how to select what is most important, and in this area middle-aged people may just show an advantage.

Learning Throughout Adulthood: A Model

No one knows the extent to which the relatively small age-related changes in learning and memory affect middle-aged people trying to learn something new. As we have seen, the changes do not seem very great. Some difficulties probably arise because the abilities required in academic areas have not been used extensively for years. Nancy Denney (1982) argues that there is a definite decline after early adulthood in abilities that are not exercised but that practice and experience clearly have an influence on cognitive abilities; Figure 16.6 demonstrates

Table 16.2 **Everyday Problem-Solving Inventory: Sample Situations and Responses From Each Problem Domain**

DOMAIN	SITUATION AND MODES OF RESPONSE
Consumer	You have a landlord who refuses to make some expensive repairs you want done because he or she thinks they are too costly. a. Try to make the repairs yourself. b. Try to understand your landlord's view and decide whether they are necessary repairs. c. Try to get someone to settle the dispute between you and your landlord. d. Accept the situation and don't dwell on it.
Information	A complicated form you completed was returned because you misinterpreted the instructions on how to fill it out. a. Obtain more information on how to complete the form correctly. b. Try to figure out on your own what was wrong. c. Ask someone to fill out the form for you. d. Blame the company for not making the instructions more clear.
Home	You would like to leave your home at night to attend a meeting or concert but are unsure whether it is safe for you to be out alone. a. Take precautions to ensure your safety. b. Reevaluate how important it is to attend. c. Ask someone to accompany you. d. Avoid worrying about it.
Family	Your parent or child criticizes you for some habit you have that annoys him or her. a. Try to change your behavior. b. Try to evaluate realistically whether the criticism is valid. c. Do not change your habit but avoid it when the person is around you. d. Ignore the criticism.
Friend	You would like to get some friends to come visit you more often. a. Invite them to your home. b. Try to figure out why they do not seem to make an effort to visit you. c. Accept the situation and do nothing. d. Do not be overly concerned about it and turn your attention to other things.
Work	You find out that you have been passed over for a better job or job promotion that you wanted. a. Try to find out why you did not get the job. b. Try to see the positive side of the situation. c. Accept the decision and do not pursue it. d. Complain to a friend or the other person about the unfairness of the decision.

Note: Following each problem situation, the four modes of response are problem-focused action (a), cognitive problem analysis (b), passive-dependent behavior (c), and avoidant thinking and denial (d).
Source: Cornelius and Caspi, 1987.

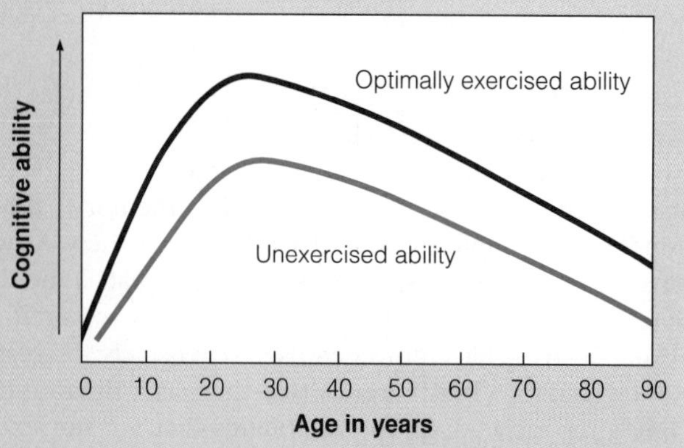

The curve for unexercised abilities reflects biological potential and normal experience. The curve of optimally exercised ability reflects the ability learned through optimal training and exercise. The space between the curves shows how practice and training affect performance. Notice how much better people do when their abilities are exercised.

Figure 16.6
Developmental Functions of Unexercised and Optimally Exercised Cognitive Abilities
Source: Denney, 1982.

this concept. Unexercised abilities are a function of biological potential as well as normal environmental experience. Optimally exercised abilities reflect the maximum ability attained by a normal, healthy person under optimal training and exercise. The space between the curves in Figure 16.6 is the amount by which both practice and training affect performance. Denney uses the example of running to illustrate how this model operates. The curve for unexercised ability indicates how well an individual could run at any age with no training, and the optimal exercise curve shows how well that person could perform with the best training. Notice that with enough training, an individual could run better at age 50 than he or she could at age 20 with no training. However, a 70-year-old with training would not do as well as a 20-year-old without training.

If this curve was used to analyze cognitive abilities, it would show a decline starting in early adulthood for unexercised abilities—for instance, abstract problem solving. However, people can improve their abilities throughout life with training and practice, and the decrease in exercised abilities is not as much as for unexercised abilities. The curve for optimally exercised abilities also is shown to decline, although the decline may not occur until later in life. Individual variation is great and depends on native ability, training, and experience. Different abilities follow different curves over the life span. For instance, the curve for nonverbal abilities, such as picture completion and block design, shows a curve similar to that for unexercised abilities because these abilities are not used very much in adulthood. Verbal abilities are exercised and remain stable throughout middle adulthood. Since traditional laboratory tests of problem-solving skills often use problems that are abstract, one would expect a decline, and indeed one is found. However, when middle-aged people are asked to solve practical problems, they show an improvement through their 40s and 50s and some decline after that.

A Positive Look at Middle Adulthood

What do the physical, sensory, and cognitive changes of middle adulthood mean? For most middle-aged people they mean very little. Many sensory deficits can be compenstated for, and although a middle-aged person may no longer be able to defeat a well-trained younger person in a strenuous game of tennis or in a laboratory reaction-time exercise, does it really matter? The important factor is one's attitude and the recognition that these changes do not restrict the enjoyment of life or participation in most activities. The finding that trained middle-aged people actually perform better than untrained early adults (Denney, 1982) shows that practice and activity can change the curve of decline greatly. Finally, the findings that individual differences in health, interest, motivation, experience, and training are more important than any biological factors in solving real problems demonstrate that how one lives makes all the difference.

A person who views no longer being able to have children, defeat youngsters in tennis, or read a newspaper without glasses as catastrophes is likely to go through a crisis of personal confidence. If, on the other hand, a more realistic and optimistic attitude is taken, middle-aged people can adjust to these changes and enjoy the financial and experiential rewards of middle adulthood.

Summary

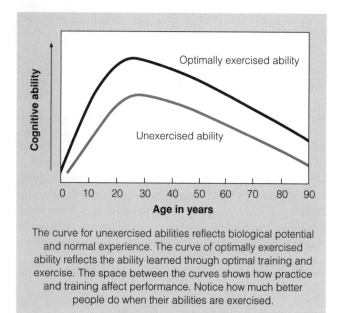

1. The baby boom generation consists of people born between 1946 and 1964. The oldest baby boomers are turning 50 and the youngest are in their 30s. The baby boom generation differs greatly from their parents in eating habits, attitudes, and education; this group is very individualistic.
2. The new look at middle age does not deny the effects of aging such as gray hair, wrinkles, redistribution of weight, and a general slowing. Rather, it emphasizes the middle-aged individual's ability to create a meaningful life and make lifestyle decisions.
3. Evidence indicates that middle-aged people today engage more frequently in sexual intercourse than middle-aged people did a generation ago. Physical changes in the sexual organs during middle age lead to an increase in response time in all phases of sexual response. Although frequency of sexual intercourse is reduced, sexual satisfaction is high.
4. *Menopause* is cessation of a woman's menstrual cycle; *climacteric* refers to all physical changes that bring someone from fertility to infertility. During menopause, women may experience physical symptoms, especially hot flashes, but most cope well with

the discomfort. Cultural, attitudinal, and personal factors may affect the physical symptoms experienced. Postmenopausal women have positive attitudes toward menopause because it brings freedom from pregnancy. Males may also proceed through a climacteric, although it is much more gradual than that experienced by women.

5. During middle age sensory declines occur, although they do not affect daily life much. Visual acuity worsens, and glare becomes a problem; hearing also declines somewhat. Declines in taste, smell, and touch sensitivity are small. Reaction time increases, probably because the impulse conduction in the nervous system becomes slower.
6. Heart attacks are more frequent in middle age, and hypertension is a major problem. However, over the past 30 years better medical care and changes in lifestyle have reduced the death rate from heart disease. Older people tend to be more careful about their health habits than young adults, with the exception that they get less exercise. Cancer is the most common cause of death in middle adulthood. Cigarette smoking and diet have been linked to cancer. There is a relationship between heart disease and cancer and diet. Watching one's weight and eating more fiber, fruits, and vegetables are now widely advocated.
7. Stress is a factor in heart disease, and many companies are instituting stress-reduction programs and more actively encouraging good health habits in their workers. Besides providing educational programs, these companies offer counseling, fitness programs, nutritional guidance, and help in overcoming smoking and drinking problems.
8. The health of minority groups is a special concern as unequal access to health care, poverty, and lack of use of prevention and early detection techniques may place people at risk. Women's health issues include the lack of women subjects in many studies, the treatment of women with medical needs, diseases of special concern to women, and the need for greater research funding.
9. Studies show that fluid intelligence continues to decline with age, but crystallized intelligence may increase. The decline is probably caused by an increase in the time it takes to process material. Individual differences in cognitive functioning are great and increase in importance with age.
10. Memory declines little if at all in middle adulthood. There is some decline in recall, but recognition remains excellent.
11. Middle-aged people benefit when they are given additional time to study and learn, and when they receive help in organizing new material. Abilities that are exercised show less decline than those that are not exercised, and different abilities show different curves of decline throughout middle adulthood.
12. The ability to solve realistic problems improves throughout middle adulthood; there is some decline in the ability to solve abstract problems.

Multiple-Choice Questions

1. Which of the following statements concerning middle age is *incorrect?*
   a. The physical changes that occur in middle age are noticeable.
   b. Most physical changes in middle age occur gradually.
   c. Metabolic rate increases somewhat in middle age.
   d. Physical fitness declines in middle age.
2. A word that best defines the baby boom generation is:
   a. conformist.
   b. scientific.
   c. individualistic.
   d. pessimistic.
3. Sexual problems in middle age are most likely caused by:
   a. physical changes in the body.
   b. psychological factors.
   c. lack of sexual motivation.
   d. mental illness.
4. Which statement concerning marital sexual satisfaction is correct?
   a. Most people in middle age are satisfied with their marital sex.
   b. In happy marriages between middle-aged partners, the frequency of sex increases with age.
   c. Men's enjoyment of sex increases with age but women's enjoyment declines somewhat in middle age.
   d. Marital satisfaction depends mostly on sexual satisfaction.
5. Keith says that menopausal symptoms are universal and the same percentage of women in each society experiences these symptoms. According to research, Keith is:
   a. correct.
   b. incorrect, because research shows there are no physical symptoms in menopause.
   c. incorrect, because women in some societies do not even go through menopause.
   d. incorrect, because different percentages of women in various societies report symptoms.
6. The changes in sensory functioning in middle age require:
   a. a change in attitude on the part of middle-aged people because they cannot read for as long or listen to music for the same amount of time.
   b. a greater intensity of the stimulus.
   c. medical treatment for moderate to major medical problems.
   d. all of the above.
7. A group of middle-aged people and young adults are asked to throw a switch if a red pattern is shown on a screen and to push a button if a yellow pattern is shown. You would expect:
   a. both groups to show the same reaction time because both groups will have some fast and some slow individuals.

b. the group of middle-aged people to show a faster reaction time because this is a test of choice, not of simple reaction time.
c. the group of younger adults to show a faster reaction time because younger adults are generally faster than middle-aged people.
d. the middle-aged people to show a faster reaction time on throwing the switch and the early adults to show a faster reaction time on pushing a button because the former requires experience and the latter does not.

8. The death rate from cardiovascular disease in the last 20 years has:
a. increased greatly.
b. declined substantially.
c. stayed about the same.
d. increased in men but declined in women.

9. One healthy practice that seems to decline with age is:
a. getting sufficient rest.
b. eating a healthy diet.
c. coping effectively with stress.
d. exercise.

10. The most common cause of death in middle age is from:
a. heart disease.
b. cancer.
c. diabetes.
d. accidents.

11. One new recommendation in the most recent dietary guidelines for Americans is the statement that:
a. a vegetarian diet is healthy.
b. eating meat is inherently unhealthy.
c. eating fruit is more important than eating vegetables.
d. eating vegetables is more important than eating fruit.

12. Which statement about exercise is *incorrect?*
a. Regular exercise reduces one's risk of heart disease.
b. Regular exercise may decrease the risk of colon cancer.
c. Lack of exercise is a factor in cognitive decline.
d. Most middle age Americans exercise on the average of three times a week.

13. Dorothy would like to quit smoking but does not think that a 46-year-old person who does so will improve her health. According to studies she is:
a. unfortunately correct.
b. incorrect, because she will actually be more healthy than those who never smoked.
c. incorrect, but the benefits may take 15 years or more to show themselves.
d. incorrect, and the benefits are immediate and lasting.

14. The group with the lowest death rate in middle age is:
a. Latinos.
b. African Americans.
c. Native Americans.
d. Asian Americans.

15. Which of the following statements about women and the medical community is *true?*
a. Women have been excluded from some major studies on cardiovascular disease.
b. Funding for research into breast cancer has increased dramatically over the past few years.
c. Women may react differently to some medications than men because of hormonal differences.
d. All of these are true.

16. Concerning cognitive abilities as people negotiate middle age, individual differences become:
a. more important.
b. less important.
c. do not change in importance.
d. almost disappear.

17. Which type of study is most likely to show differences in intelligence?
a. a cross-sectional study.
b. a longitudinal study.
c. a questionnaire.
d. a crystallized study.

18. Ahmed compares 50-year-old women to 20-year-old women on a number of abilities that comprise intelligence, finding that the 20-year-olds score higher. When interpreting his data, he takes into consideration the fact that they are from different generations. This is called the ____________ effect.
a. validity
b. Piagetian
c. cohort
d. domino

19. Which term best describes the change in short-term and working memory in middle age?
a. significant
b. moderate
c. small
d. nonexistent

20. The model of cognitive abilities advanced by Nancy Denney emphasizes that:
a. healthy eating and physical exercise are the keys to intellectual functioning.
b. an attitude that a person can alter the present and the future is required for positive social adjustment to occur.
c. people who practice skills tend to function better than those who do not practice such skills.
d. meditation and relaxation exercises can aid in keeping intellectual ability high.

Answers to Multiple-Choice Questions

1. c 2. c 3. b 4. a 5. d 6. b 7. c 8. b 9. d
10. b 11. a 12. d 13. d 14. d 15. d 16. a 17. a
18. c 19. c 20. c

Chapter 17

Social and Personality Development in Middle Adulthood

Chapter Outline

Are the Following Statements True or False?

1. People in middle age are at the top of their earning power.
2. Middle-aged people tend to look at the time they have left rather than time since birth.
3. A woman's dream, or the lifestyle she wants, changes from an emphasis on marriage in early adulthood to an emphasis on work alone in middle adulthood.
4. Most middle-aged men experience a significant crisis during early middle adulthood.
5. People in their 50s see life as more exciting than people in their 40s do.
6. Personality characteristics remain stable throughout middle adulthood.
7. More couples divorce during middle adulthood than during early adulthood.
8. Most parents see the period of raising adolescent children as the most satisfying of their parenting careers.
9. The empty-nest stage, the time at which all the children have left home, is experienced positively by most adults.
10. The relationship between middle-aged people and their parents is marked by strain and obligation.

Answers to True-False Statements 1. True 2. True 3. False: see p. 397 4. False: see p. 398 5. True 6. True 7. False: see p. 402 8. False: see p. 404 9. True 10. False: see p. 406

Middle Adulthood: Challenge Amid Stability

Jeremy and Tasha, both in their 40s, live with their two children Ronnie, age 17, and Shana, age 15, in the suburbs of a major city. Jeremy wakes up each morning at 6 for his commute to the city where he owns a small business. Tasha works as an accountant for a mid-sized firm in the area. Both Jeremy's and Tasha's parents live about an hour away and they see them fairly often. Despite their busy schedules, Jeremy and Tasha have some outside interests. Jeremy loves golf and is involved in a local youth group. Tasha is involved with the community theater group and volunteers at a shelter.

Jeremy has owned his business for 15 years, and Tasha has been working for the same firm for 10 years. In his early adulthood, Jeremy was employed at a number of large retail stores in managerial positions but decided to leave and start a business. Tasha worked at a few large accounting firms before deciding to make a career at the moderately sized firm that presently employs her. They bought their house 5 years ago after moving three times during their 20s and 30s. Neither has any plans to find a new job and they have no plans to move.

How calm and stable their lives seem. But appearances can be deceiving. Although their daily lives are stable, they face a number of challenges. Jeremy's father has Alzheimer's disease and his mother is having more difficulty dealing with it. Ronnie is argumentative and seems unappreciative of everything Tasha does. Jeremy and Tasha also find that they don't see each other much and when they do they are tired. They aren't communicating well and find that some of their arguments occur because they spend so little time together. In addition, they aren't sure that they are happy with their work. Jeremy's business has not expanded as much as he thought it would and he is somewhat disappointed, and Tasha admits to being bored. Yet, they know that they are lucky they have such good jobs; their best friend, Seth, just lost his middle-management job after his company merged with another.

In the Middle of Everything

Middle-aged people are in the middle of everything. In fact, they are sometimes called the *sandwich generation.* At the midpoint of their lives, they find themselves sandwiched between younger and older people both at home and at work. At home, they often must deal with teenage children as well as elderly parents. At the same time, they are in the middle of their work careers and must deal with younger workers as well as those who have been working even longer than they have. They are considered neither young nor old by society; they have arrived at that in-between period.

Middle adulthood brings with it special challenges. As parents and sometimes friends die, middle-aged people are forced to face their own mortality. They begin to recognize the limits of their own physical and psychological abilities and to understand that they may not achieve all they had hoped to. They assess their careers and the meaning of success or failure (McIlroy, 1984). They are likely to be raising adolescent children, and constantly reminded that a newer, fresher generation is coming into maturity. Their parents are also growing older and may need additional help.

However, many middle-aged people are at the top of their earning power and can influence the decisions of others. This is the generation that is very much in command. Their maturity and experience enable them to help both the older and the younger generation with social support, advice, and sometimes financial resources. The mentor role is a very satisfying one.

People in middle adulthood are in the middle of everything. They are often sandwiched between the needs of the older and younger generations.

> ***True or False?***
> People in middle age are at the top of their earning power.

Middle adulthood is a time of very gradual change amid stability. It is easy to see the stability in the daily lives of people like Jeremy and Tasha, but it is somewhat more difficult to see the changes that take place slowly over the course of the period. This chapter examines the challenges of middle adulthood and investigates how the generation in the middle copes with those challenges.

The Tasks of Middle Adulthood

Every age brings with it problems and challenges, and middle adulthood is no exception. It is the diversity of these challenges that is impressive.

Dealing With One's Own Mortality

During middle age, people are most likely to experience a personal trauma, such as the death of a parent or their own serious illness or that of a friend (Russell, 1995). Such occurrences are not uncommon in middle adulthood, and they cause people to confront their own mortality.

A New Time Perspective

At middle adulthood a change in time perspective occurs (Neugarten, 1968a). Middle-aged people tend to look at the time they still have left rather than at the past. They often speak of time running out, and there is an increased emphasis on using time wisely.

> ***True or False?***
> Middle-aged people tend to look at the time they have left rather than time since birth.

Recognizing Biological Limitations and Health Risks

Although today's middle-aged people are likely to be in better shape than their parents, they are scarcely able to compete with well-conditioned young adults. Middle-aged people must come to grips with the cumulative effects of their diet, smoking, drinking, and lifestyle in general. Young adults often believe they will live healthier lives when they get older, but middle-aged people do not have that luxury and may find it difficult to change health habits that are deeply ingrained.

Reorientation to Work and Achievement

In the American dream the worker who once polished door handles works his way up to become president of the company. Some people make it, but many do not; there is simply less room at the top. This realization forces some reevaluation.

Reassessment of Important Relationships

In mid-life parents deal with adolescent children who eventually leave home, at which time they are left with an **empty nest**—a home without children. These parents have more money, more time to spend together, and fewer responsibilities. After years of child-rearing, married couples must get to know each other again. Couples in middle adulthood tend to reexamine their aims and goals (Steinberg & Silverberg, 1987). At the same time, their own parents are growing older and may require help. Middle-aged adults are often caught between the needs of their children and the needs of their parents.

empty nest The state of the family after the last child leaves home.

Restructuring Identity and Self-Concept

The challenges in the area of family, career, and physical development may make it necessary to reassess and restructure one's identity and self-concept. Consider the individual for whom success on the job is most important. Then imagine that person being laid off or finding out that the big promotion is not coming through. Consider the woman who has spent so many years giving to her children finding that she now has time for herself but does not know what to do with it. Questioning values, achievements, and the meaning of life is also a part of middle adulthood (McIlroy, 1984). Sometimes people discover aspects of themselves that have been neglected—for example, a woman may rediscover her ambition, or a man may take up a new interest, such as music, art, or carpentry.

Do these tasks reflect only the experience of the white middle class? Although white middle-class people are more likely to face these problems and challenges, interviews with blue-collar workers show similar themes (Danielson & Cytrynbaum, 1980).

Middle Adulthood in Perspective

Mid-life is a fertile area for theorizing, but the basic tenets of reevaluation, change, and recommitment are common themes. The theories outlined here are based primarily on observations of the experiences of males.

Erikson: Giving to Others

Erik Erikson (1963) sees the psychosocial crisis of middle age as the attainment of **generativity,** or a sense of giving to others, versus **stagnation** and self-absorption. Generativity means giving not only to one's own children but also to one's grandchildren and the community. It involves seeing some part of one's legacy transferred to a new generation. It may involve creative work and the ability to open oneself up to new experiences. Generativity is primarily concerned with guiding, nurturing, and teaching the younger generation, as well as generating products that benefit others (McAdams & de St. Aubin, 1992). Middle-aged people accomplish this through their children, but generativity goes far beyond this rather narrow idea and may include work settings, professional activities, volunteer work, and participation in religious and political organizations (Petersen & Klohnen, 1995). Stagnation involves self-centeredness.

Generativity is seen as arising from both a cultural prescription and an internal need (McAdams & de St. Aubin, 1992). Society expects middle-aged people to use their resources to help the next generation. Middle-aged people show a desire to create or influence something that will live on after them, a sort of symbolic immortality.

In his elaboration on Erikson's theory, Robert Peck (1968) notes the importance of changing one's social emphasis from stressing sexuality to dealing with people on a more social level as companions. As their physical powers wane, middle-aged people must come to value wisdom over physical powers and maintain their mental flexibility.

If Erikson is correct, you would expect middle-aged people to practice generativity more and to engage in more activities that involve giving to others. When young, middle-aged, and older adults were compared, middle-aged people scored higher than young and older subjects on concern for the next generation and actions that reflected this concern (McAdams, de St. Aubin, & Logan, 1993).

Levinson's Theory: The Dream at Mid-Life

Levinson (1978) noted that in early adulthood, people often form a picture of what they want in life in terms of their goals and lifestyle. This vision of the future or dream may direct early choices and serve as a motivator. Not everyone has or even should have a dream but the existence and nature of the dream may affect later development.

Men's dreams are usually individualistic, pertaining to work and occupational attainment. Women's dreams are more likely to be split between career and marriage goals (Roberts & Newton, 1987). Even among professional women, only a small percentage of women show work-related goals as their primary component. Men's dreams feature an image of the independent achiever in an occupational role, whereas women's dreams are more relational, showing women within relationships with others.

The basic choices are made by middle age. Most people are married by then, many are divorced and remarried, and basic career choices have been made. Some will have succeeded in creating a lifestyle consistent with their dream, some will have failed, and some may be still forging that lifestyle. The dream plays an important role in adaptation to middle age. Men at mid-life who have a dream, are striving toward their dream, or have succeeded in fashioning a lifestyle consonant with their dream perform better on a number of indicators of mental health compared with those who have failed at their dream or given their dream up (Drebing & Gooden, 1991).

Women often find that a change occurs in their dream. When well-educated, upper-middle-class, employed women were questioned about the content of their dream, a decline in content for marriage/intimacy and family was found and a major increase was found in the personal areas of life, which appear to take center stage in women's dreams in mid-life (Drebing et al., 1995). Women in mid-life emphasize being themselves and fulfilling themselves as people. Most, but not all, studies find the importance of the work role increases as well, but this occurs along with an increasing emphasis on de-

generativity The positive outcome of Erikson's psychosocial crisis of middle age, which involves giving oneself and one's talents to others.

stagnation The negative outcome of Erikson's psychosocial crisis of middle age, in which one becomes completely absorbed in oneself.

veloping their abilitites and self-fulfillment. More personal elements come into focus during middle age.

> ***True or False?***
> A woman's dream, or the lifestyle she wants, changes from an emphasis on marriage in early adulthood to an emphasis on work alone in middle adulthood.

How does the dream affect women at mid-life? Although the presence of a dream is not related to overall mental health, women who never form a dream are more likely to experience anxiety. Many more women in midlife are still working towards their dreams than men, perhaps because their dreams are split or because they delay focusing on work or personal elements until middle adulthood. Success in achieving at the dream is related to lower amounts of depression, but not to other aspects of mental health.

Fulfilling a dream requires the support of one's spouse, parents, and perhaps children. Men and women both formulate dreams that contain the wife as supporting the husband's goals but not the other way around. Wives show many accommodations to their husband's goals in order to keep the marriage vital, but much less is shown in the other direction. Although many women find support for their strivings from their husbands and parents, others find resistance and opposition.

The most important finding, however, is that dream support is clearly related to particular aspects of mental health. No matter what the content of the dream or the woman's success in fulfilling it, having people support one's striving is related to mental health. This confirms the importance of relationships and social support in maintaining emotional functioning in women. Women's mental health is related more to receiving social support for the dream than in succeeding at the dream! Although having a dream and succeeding at the dream is important, receiving the social support to strive towards it is even more important for women.

Levinson's View of Mid-Life Crisis

Levinson argues that entrance into middle age brings about a personal struggle and a period of time for reevaluating one's entire life structure. Levinson (1978) believes that in middle age, three specific areas must be addressed. First, there is the inevitable need to deal with the transition to middle age just as there is a need to deal with other life transitions.

The second task in mid-life transition is to integrate what Levinson calls the *great polarities,* which involve four conflicts that arise during this transition. The first polarity is *young/old.* The person entering middle age is neither young nor old. If one clings to youth, however, one does not adjust to the challenges of middle age. If being young is surrendered completely, the risk of rigidity increases. The second polarity is the *destructive/constructive* problem. Middle-aged people are aware of the transient nature of many achievements, their own mortality, and the extent to which others have hurt them and they have hurt others. The desire to be more creative and to leave some sort of positive legacy is experienced. The *masculine/feminine* issue is a third polarity. Gender lines become less important, and men must come to terms with the feminine as well as the masculine side of their nature. Finally, the fourth polarity, the *attachment/separation* polarity, must be resolved. The need for attachment to others must be integrated with the need for separateness.

The third task in mid-life transition is to build a new structure for successful negotiation of middle adulthood. Some people make significant changes in external commitments, such as changing careers or getting a divorce. For others, recommitment is in order. However, even if there is a recommitment, marital relationships do change. Levinson found that 80% of his subjects found this period a time of great struggle. These men described crises that were either moderate or severe, and they questioned every aspect of their selves and their lives. During this period people sometimes become mentors to others. At times, it is the wife who reassesses the marriage. She may want changes, and the husband may be the one who opposes them. Other theorists, such as Roger Gould (1975), also see the need for a basic reevaluation of life during these years.

Mid-Life Crisis: Fact or Fiction?

The idea that middle adulthood is a period of crisis has recently become popular. Magazine articles announce that people in middle age face a crisis of reevaluation and of confidence. The term **mid-life crisis** has actually become part of our language. We read in the print media about people married 20 years who suddenly have affairs and split up, men suddenly changing careers, and women discovering that what they have is not what they want and making some radical shift. Although most people believe that this is a time of reevaluation, is it a time of crisis?

To understand this, we must first define the term. A *mid-life crisis* is a perceived state of physical and psychological distress that results when a person's internal resources and external social support systems threaten to be overwhelmed by developmental tasks that require new adaptive resources (Cytrynbaum et al., 1980). People at mid-life are faced with tremendous tasks—for example, dealing with their own mortality, recognizing their biological limitations, and reorienting themselves to work—which cause distress that threatens to overwhelm their ability to cope. Vaillant says, "The term *mid-life crisis* brings to mind some variation of the renegade minister who leaves behind four children and the congregation that loved him in order to

mid-life crisis A perceived state of physical and psychological distress that results when a person's internal resources and external social support systems are overwhelmed by developmental tasks that require new adaptive resources. (*Note:* Both *mid-life crisis* and *mid-life transition* are used interchangeably to refer to the period of questioning that may occur at the beginning of middle age. There is a general agreement that questioning does occur, but whether the term *crisis* should be applied is controversial.)

drive off in a magenta Porsche with a 25-year-old striptease artist" (1977, p. 222).

Levinson (1996) believes that his concept has been misunderstood, in that the popular press uses the phrase to denote an inappropriate or maladaptive response to a stressful event. The developmental crisis that he believes occurs at middle age arises when a person has great difficulty meeting the tasks of the period. Such a crisis is not solely negative; it may be painful both to the individual and others, but can also lead to greater fulfillment if one forms a more satisfying life structure.

Levinson argued that people in middle age negotiate a period of self-recrimination, asking such questions as "Where did I fail?" Questions like "Who am I?" and "What do I want to do with the rest of my life?" become important too, just as they were in adolescence. Levinson noted five possible outcomes for the mid-life crisis:

1. Advancement within a stable life structure. The men in this group made up a majority of Levinson's sample and had achieved a moderate degree of success and stability; however, they wanted more. For example, some novelists wanted not only to write another successful novel but also to win the Pulitzer prize and receive acclaim. There is a recommitment in this group—one last push to make it.

2. Serious failure or decline within a stable life structure. The men in this group were unable to advance in their occupation, and their marriages were lifeless and failing. They had to face their failures. "What do I do now that I can't make foreman or president of the board of directors?" is a typical question for this group. Some never recover from recognizing their failure; others may begin to define success more broadly and may recover.

3. Breaking out or trying for a new life structure. Some men broke out of old patterns. The breaking-out included some significant change, such as quitting a job, moving to another region, or leaving a wife. The next years were spent building a new structure, which is difficult at this age, so the new life is often a compromise. The outcome for the men who broke out was quite variable. Some were disappointed with the results; others were pleased.

4. Advancement that itself produces a change in life structure. A few men received promotions that produced qualitative changes in their lifestyles. For example, one worker received an extraordinary promotion, becoming a full manager of the purchasing department at age 37 and becoming head of manufacturing at 40. These promotions allowed him to move to a different neighborhood and adopt a different lifestyle but did not always yield positive results.

5. Unstable life structure. Men in this group were not able to stabilize their lives and were unfulfilled. They changed jobs, lovers, and spouses frequently and were unable to cope with life's tasks. One man was not able to hold a stable job, even though he was 37 years old. Another changed jobs frequently, was involved with drugs, did not marry, and formed no stable interpersonal relationships.

The mid-life crisis can provide opportunities for growth. Gould (1978) also noted the occurrence of a mid-life crisis between the ages of 35 and 43, which he called the *crisis of urgency.* He saw mid-life as a kind of second adolescence and every bit as turbulent. People become aware that they are mortal, that time is running out, and make one last attempt to achieve their goals. Life becomes unstable and uncomfortable. Gould believed that the age at which the conflict occurs depends on the person's personality, lifestyle, and subculture. Others point to the fact that family instability, marital infidelity, and physical problems from stress, such as ulcers, hypertension, and heart disease, increase significantly during this period (Rosenberg & Farrell, 1976).

However, most psychologists do not believe that the mid-life transition is a crisis, (Kruger, 1994). Psychologists often find little evidence of any dramatic change, but see it as a period of continuous rediscovery (Vaillant, 1977). When a scale measuring distress was administered to men between the ages of 33 and 70, no age differences in the amount of turmoil were found (Costa & McCrae, 1990). People who did experience a crisis during middle age were prone to having crises at other points in their lives and had long-standing adjustment problems. Hedlund and Ebersole (1983) interviewed men between the ages of 35 and 39, 41 and 46, and 48 and 53 regarding mid-life, including the meaning and usefulness of their lives, their fulfillment of "the dream," and their productivity. No age differences were found in these areas, leading the investigators to argue that reevaluation may be a continuous process rather than occurring only during mid-life. Support for the existence of a crisis in both mid-life and during the empty-nest years is slight and exists mostly when clinical populations or nonrandomly selected samples are used (Chiriboga, 1989).

The mid-life crisis is a reality for some but not for the majority. Some place the number of people who consider mid-life a crisis at 12% (Rosenberg & Farrell, 1981), and others place it even lower, at between 2% and 5% (Guttman, 1987).

True or False?

Most middle-aged men experience a significant crisis during early middle adulthood.

Questions Students Often Ask

I see middle-aged people having mid-life crises, and people I speak to claim they've had them. How can researchers say that this is the exception rather than the rule?

People who are having real crises in their lives tend to stick out in the crowd. This is one reason why the mid-life crisis seems more common than it really is. Some people who go through what they consider a mid-life crisis may believe everyone else must have had the same experience and communicate this to others. Research shows us the overall general trend but, an individual's experience may differ from this trend.

Most psychologists today do not consider the mid-life period to be a time of crisis. It is, however, a time of transition, marked by self-doubt and some confusion. Although they are not immobilized, many people find the mid-life self-examination difficult (Tamir, 1989). However, radical changes are the exception, not the rule. As Janet Belsky notes (1988, p. 63), "Few of us move to Tahiti or violently reject everything we have done in the past forty years. Nor do we suddenly leap to maturity when our hair grows gray." Yet reevaluations triggered by life events do occur and increased reflection is common. Still, this reevaluation is rarely a crisis, and most people handle it well.

A Word About the Fifties

Gail Sheehy (1995) in her best selling book, *New Passages,* refers to the "Flaming Fifties" because the fifth decade is a time of optimism, freedom, and adventure.

Although relatively little research has been done on this decade of life, the research that does exist is quite positive (Karp, 1988). People at this age see life as exciting versus the boredom of the 40s (Russell, 1995). When women who varied in age from 26 to 80 years were asked to rate the present period of life as *first-rate, good, fair,* or *not so good,* many more women in their 50s rated their life as "first rate" than younger or older women (Figure 17.1) (Mitchell & Helson, 1990). They take great satisfaction in their accomplishments and become somewhat more spiritual (Edmondson, 1993). Fewer complaints are noted and many people achieve top posts in business and government when in their 50s (Russell, 1995). The 50s are the time of preserving one's health, the environment, and establishing one's financial stability (Fracese, 1993).

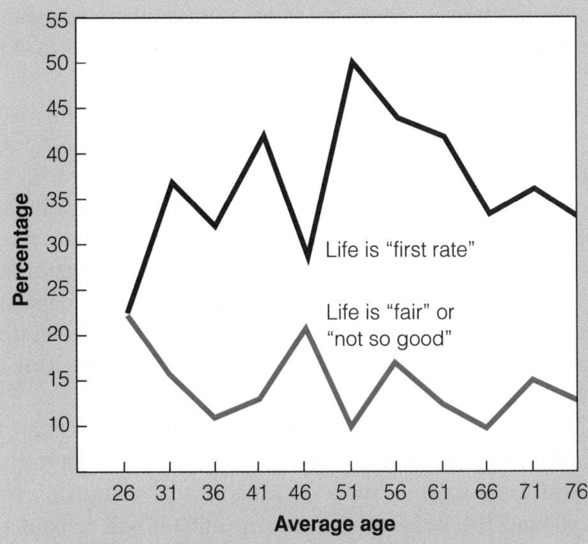

The percentage of women who say life is "first rate" peaks in the 50s.

Figure 17.1
Percentage of Women Who Say Their Life is "First Rate" or "Fair/Not So Good"
Source: Mitchell & Helson, 1990.

True or False?
People in their 50s see life as more exciting than people in their 40s do.

As people progress through their 50s, the idea of aging comes into much sharper focus (Katchadourian, 1987); such a person may be the oldest person at work. Experiencing the deaths of friends and parents and becoming a grandparent makes it hard to escape the reality of aging. The 50s is a decade of reminders (Karp, 1988). It is in this decade more than in the 40s that gender differences break down. Men in late middle age are not afraid to be nurturing and compassionate, and women are not afraid to be assertive and to take on leadership roles (Guttman, 1987). When professionals in their late 50s were interviewed, men tended to reduce their involvement in work and become much more selective about what they were doing (Karp, 1988). Women who had begun their careers later in life showed more occupational vitality and growth. Men felt freer from their occupational lives whereas many females felt an urgency to accomplish something vocationally because they had not been free to do so earlier.

Many 50-year-olds know they are no longer young but cannot believe it. One person in an interview told of his surprise when he first heard an insurance salesman on television inquire, "Do you know someone between the ages of 50 and 80?" The man's response was, "My God, he's talking about me!" People feel that they are still youthful but experience their physical selves differently. Some experience major life-threatening illnesses, such as heart attacks or major surgery; physical decline is more apparent, and is a precursor of old age. At about age 50 men fear a loss of sexual capacity but not of attractiveness, whereas women fear a loss of attractiveness but not of sexual capacity (Strong & DeVault, 1995). Thoughts about retirement increase, and the grandparent role reminds them of where they are on the life cycle. People in their fifties begin to feel they have wisdom; they feel self-confident and able to cope. They see the larger perspective, claiming now they know what is important and what is not.

The 50s is a decade of reminders, of excitement, and of freedom. People are reminded of their mortality and aging, but it is a time of growing self-confidence and opportunity, of feeling free, and feeling psychologically youthful.

Personality in Middle Adulthood

Two different trends can be found in the research on personality. As noted in Chapter 15, studies measuring traits demonstrate a pattern of impressive stability. In a study of middle-class adults aged 45 to 70, long-term stability for social extroversion and agreeableness was found (Conley, 1984). Impressive evidence on stability for such traits as flexibility, introversion/extroversion, and neuroticism occurs in the literature (Costa & McCrae, 1988). During times of severe stress, these characteristics actually show themselves in more extreme ways (Caspi & Bem, 1990). For example, irritable and explosive men became more irritable and more explosive during the Great Depression of the 1930s (Elder & Caspi, 1988).

When does this stability first begin to show itself? In a study that compared personality over 50 years, the lowest level of personality stability occurred between late adolescence and early adulthood, which means that the role changes so common in early adulthood, including assuming new roles as spouse, parent, and worker, may create some personality instability (Haan et al., 1986). When the California Psychological Inventory was administered to female college seniors at age 21, then at 27, and finally at 43, the evidence for stability was considerable, and the relationship between 27 and 43 was stronger than between 21 and 27 (Helson & Moane, 1987). The evidence for stability is overwhelming, especially once we go beyond the early years of early adulthood (Kogan, 1990).

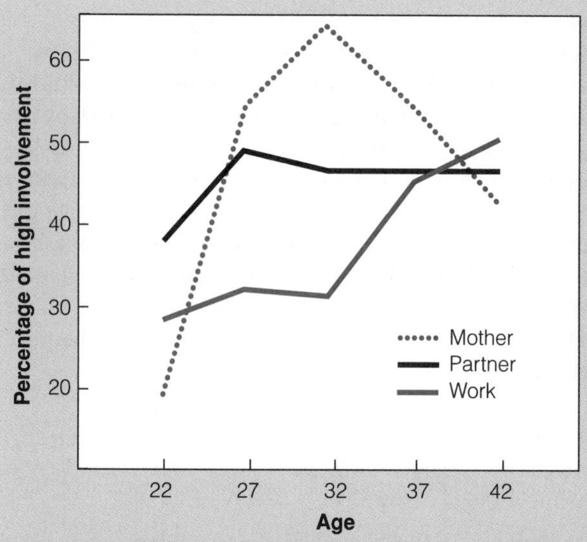

In the beginning of middle age, involvement in work increases.

Figure 17.2
Percentage of Sample (N = 105) Women Reporting a High Level of Involvement in Designated Roles at 5-Year Intervals From College to Mid-Life.
Source: Helson & Moane, 1987.

True or False?
Personality characteristics remain stable throughout middle adulthood.

An equally impressive viewpoint is that age-related changes in personality do occur but these cannot be found using traits. By their very nature, traits are stable and relatively insensitive to the changes that occur with age. The attempt to make the measurement of traits reliable and valid across adolescence and adulthood makes them insensitive measures of change (Helson & Moane, 1987).

When other indices besides traits are used, some change is found (Whitbourne et al., 1992). Evidence shows that middle age is a time for more giving to others, reflecting Erikson's consideration of generativity. According to Levinson's theory, by the time middle age rolls around the adult has created a first life structure in the 20s, gone through the age-30 transition, settled down in the 30s, and in the late 30s striven to become one's own person and to achieve a recognized place in the world. Mid-life transition, the aging of children, and having to deal with older and younger members of the family may cause changes in the way people act and feel.

People in middle age show more confidence in their abilities and coping strategies, impulse control becomes more internalized, and people tend to become more self-disciplined and independent. As people proceed through middle age they become more passive in the way they approach stress. Neugarten (1964) argued that people proceed from an active to a passive mastery over their environment. There is some increase in **interiority;** that is, there is a greater preoccupation with the inner self. Those beginning middle age believe that taking risks and exploring new avenues are worthwhile and will pay off. Sixty-year-olds see the environment as more complex and are wary of taking risks (Katchadourian, 1987). As an individual develops from 40 to 60, he or she changes from actively confronting the environment and its challenges to being more accepting of the way things are. Women in their 50s show decreased dependence on others and less self-criticism; they are more confident and decisive and are better able to tolerate ambiguity and analyze problems logically (Helson & Wink, 1992).

Roles also change in middle age. Children are growing up and being launched into the world. Caring for elderly parents increases. Workers in middle age have greater responsibilities. Figure 17.2 shows the results of a study that asked women between 22 and 42 which roles were most involving, defined in terms of interest and expenditure of time. Notice the large increase in parenting responsibilities, peaking in the late 20s, and then the reduction and the increase in commitment to work (Helson & Moane, 1987).

Personality change occurs within a stable foundation in adulthood. Personality traits remain generally stable. A serious person at 30 will continue to be a serious person at 60, and the person who is a optimistic will remain so. Other aspects of personality do change. People become more self-assured, gender stereotypes mean less, coping styles change, generativity increases, and people become

interiority The introspection and preoccupation with one's inner life that occurs during the later stages of middle age and old age.

less critical of themselves. People may also become more cautious and passive.

Some changes are gender related. On negotiating middle adulthood, men become more nurturant and women become more assertive. Women in the empty nest display more of what we might consider stereotypical masculine traits (Cooper & Gutmann, 1987). The man who has spent his whole life living up to a masculine image and achieving at work may find it unnecessary to continue to do so in middle age. The woman who has submerged her more dominant, achievement-oriented, assertive self may find that now that the child-rearing years are over, she can devote more time to a career and can reveal this part of her self (Tamir, 1989).

These changes are presented as age-related changes caused by a combination of role modifications and the biological and social changes that occur during middle age. Another possibility is that some of the apparent differences between young, middle-aged, and elderly people may not be age related but cohort related. Some authorities admit that older people become somewhat less active and experience the gender-related changes just mentioned, but do not believe they undergo any other age-related transformations (Schaie & Willis, 1986). Any additional changes are not the result of age but occur because people are raised in different generations and are taught to act a particular way and to see the world in a certain manner.

The fifties are a time of new optimism, freedom and adventure.

Family Life at Middle Adulthood

Love and work are the areas of greatest concern in adulthood. They are the cause of our greatest satisfaction in life, but they are also the cause of our greatest trials. Middle-aged parents are likely to have teenage children. If parents married in their mid 20s and had their first child a few years later, by the time they are in their 40s, their children are into adolescence. Within the next 10 years, when the parents reach their 50s, their children are being launched into the world. After the last child leaves home, the empty-nest period begins. By the time middle age rolls around, marriages that have survived are about 20 years old. The poor tend to enter and leave these stages before their middle-class cohorts.

Marriage in Middle Adulthood

Marriage in middle adulthood has stood the test of time but still faces many challenges. First, raising teenagers is stressful. Young adult parents have to spend large amounts of time attending to the physical care of their young children. Parents in middle adulthood watch as their children become more independent, and launching their grown children into the adult world becomes their prime concern (Brubaker, 1990). Second, the period of middle age is one of reevaluation, and marriage is one of the areas that is reevaluated. Third, our spouses are likely to remind us that we are aging, and this itself can be a source of stress. Fourth, both spouses are likely to be employed and to some extent may be leading their own lives; new energy may have to be infused into the marriage to revitalize it. Finally, the empty nest can bring many surprises as children no longer dominate their parents' every motivation and action.

The elements that comprise a happy and successful marriage come as no surprise. When middle-aged, middle-class spouses who had indicated they were very happy were interviewed, they reported similar sexual needs and viewed sex as a way of expressing deep emotional commitment. There was evidence of mutual support, and the couples made it clear that they cared very much for each other. Each was very committed to the marriage and expressed a deep desire to work things through. Each person was a fully functioning, mature, independent individual with a solid ego (Fincham & O'Leary, 1983). There is a greater sense of sharing in successful middle-age marriages (Katchadourian, 1987).

Marriages between middle-aged adults differ from what they will become later. Children are a greater source of conflict among 40- to 50-year-olds than among 60- to 70-year-olds (Levenson, Carstensen, & Gottman, 1993). As in early adulthood, men are more satisfied than women; some reduction in marital satisfaction is present at the beginning of middle age, perhaps because of the reevaluation that commonly occurs in this age group (Strong & DeVault, 1995).

In successful marriages positive actions are the rule and are not related to any specific situation; in unhappy marriages negative behaviors are extensive and considered to be deliberate. The ability to take the perspective of one's spouse predicts each spouse's marital adjustment (Long & Andrews, 1990). Spouses who could understand and adopt the point of view of the other were rated superior in marital adjustment. A generous level of perspective taking may be necessary for successful marital interaction.

The position of the couple in the family life cycle is also a factor in marital satisfaction (Spanier, Sauer, & Larzelere, 1979). Marital satisfaction is very high right after marriage and then declines afterward. It increases during the later stages of marriage. Marital satisfaction, particularly for women, is low at the beginning of middle age and rises in later middle age. A steady decline from the beginning of marriage to the time children are of school age occurs for women (Rollins & Feldman, 1970). The decline then levels off, and satisfaction rises rapidly from the empty-nest stage to the retirement stage. For husbands, a slight decline is found from the beginning of the marriage to the time children are of school age, then there is an increase to the empty-nest stage and all through the retirement stage.

The evidence demonstrates that quality of marriage increases as children begin to leave home (White & Edwards, 1990; Rollins, 1989), and marital happiness is quite high during the empty-nest stage (Steinberg & Silverberg, 1987). We can conclude that the earliest and later stages of marriage are the most satisfying (Benin & Nienstedt, 1985). As noted earlier, some theorists doubt the strength of the relationship between marital satisfaction and the life cycle; position on the life cycle is only one of a number of factors related to life satisfaction (Rollins, 1989).

One interesting pattern that arises in middle adulthood is that as men progress through this stage of life, they become more interested in their families and perhaps see their work as somewhat less important. Women, on the other hand, may be just emerging from either not being employed or being able to take only part-time work and may place somewhat more emphasis on work (Katchadourian, 1987). This is especially true if work is seen as helping them fulfill personal missions in life. Marital happiness is highly correlated with general happiness and life satisfaction for men in their 40s, whereas there is a negligible relationship between work satisfaction and life satisfaction for middle-aged males (Tamir, 1982). Relationships with children become more important as well. Men who have very good relationships with their children and spouse find it easier to cope with the challenges that occur during middle age (Julian, McKenry, & Arnold, 1990).

Continuity in marital relationships is the most common pattern. Those who have had positive and rewarding relationships will continue to have them, and those that experience difficulties will continue to experience them (Brubaker, 1990). If the couple is well matched as to personality and aspirations and there are few significant changes in personalities or goals, the relationship is likely to remain satisfying.

Divorce at Mid-Life

Not many couples in middle age divorce, but divorce does occur. Although there is evidence that the divorce rate among middle-aged couples has increased markedly (Price & McKenry, 1989), this may simply mirror the increase in divorce in the general population or the fact that people are getting married later in life. In other words, divorce has increased for marriages of all durations. The divorce rate among middle-aged people is still much lower than that among early adults. Divorce among middle-aged people may seem more prevalent than it is, because when someone who has been married for 20 years gets divorced, it is more noticeable (Tamir, 1989).

> ***True or False?***
> More couples divorce during middle adulthood than during early adulthood.

The reasons for the lower divorce rate are easy to understand. Those who are most likely to get divorced have already done so. Those who are still married in middle age are survivors of sorts; the attrition process has already taken place (White, 1990). Another possibility is that the partners are truly happy with each other. It is difficult to differentiate between age and marital duration. Are people in their 40s more mature and therefore somewhat more understanding of each other's needs, or is it simply that they have been married for many years (White, 1990)? Second, as the marriage continues, each partner has invested more energy and time, and there is a tendency to be reluctant to break up. Third, there is greater cost to breaking up, and there are anticipated rewards from the upcoming empty-nest stage. Many people by middle age can now see a time when they will be more financially secure. Last, there may be some fear of starting over.

Although the evidence is not unanimous, the predictors of divorce, including poor communication, are the same for marriages in early and middle adulthood (White, 1990). Still, there are some reasons that relate specifically to middle age that should be mentioned. For one, some people stay together for the good of the children, and as the children leave home, these people may divorce. Another is the possibility that during the marriage, the people have grown in different directions. When the children leave, there is less of the glue that bound them together, and so they divorce. For still others, an extramarital affair or excessive fear of aging may be the problem.

How does divorce affect middle-aged people? Some argue that middle-aged people are more mature and have greater resources. Others argue that the commitment to a long-term marriage is not so easily discarded and middle-aged people who get divorced may perceive divorce as a failure of their entire adulthood. The partner initiating the divorce views it as a necessary escape, but the other partner often feels betrayed and sad (Golan, 1986). When people aged 20 through 75 who were recently separated were analyzed in terms of morale, physical health, and other factors, people in their 50s were the most maladapted. Adults over 50 reported greater psychological stress than did younger people, a greater disruption in their social lives, and more difficulty going alone to restaurants and theater. They felt more disorganized and out of control, and were unhappier and less optimistic. Divorce, then, appears to have serious consequences in mid-life and people see themselves as having fewer choices.

People divorcing in middle age are faced with many challenges. For men, there is the loss of the stability and the routine that has been put together over many years. At the age of 40 or 50, men are forced to do household chores like cooking and laundry, often for the first time, and may need to get used to apartment living. After so many years as a part of a couple, they may want to find new friends, yet meeting new people is difficult. If they are happy being by themselves, the problems are less severe. However, many men are lonely and bored and have difficulty finding their place. Middle-aged men must come to grips with the question, "Is this all I've got to show for all these years of work and strife?" (Myers, 1989). These men become painfully aware of the aging process. Unless they are very successful in life, they find it difficult to compete with younger men.

For women, the need to learn to socialize is also a major problem. In addition, financial problems may become important. Women's vocational skills may not be current, and women may have difficulty entering or reentering the world of work. Women also face the problem of having to face a coupled world as a mature single. Middle-aged women may find dating even more difficult than their ex-husbands because men tend to date younger women (Katchadourian, 1987).

Remarriage is less likely when divorce occurs at mid-life (Blumstein & Schwartz, 1983). Men are more likely to remarry, especially if they are professionals or well-off financially. Women who are very successful in middle age and who divorce are not as likely to remarry, especially if they had a relatively late first marriage. A successful middle-aged woman may not want to remarry because her professional and business life is very satisfying and she may not want to be encumbered by marriage and household responsibilities.

Parents and Adolescents

People in middle age find themselves parenting teenagers, then acting as a launching center for their children, and finally negotiating the empty-nest period. This is not true for all middle-aged parents as some may have married much later, others earlier (Strong & De Vault, 1995). Parenting adolescents can be a difficult challenge for middle-aged people.

As we saw in earlier chapters, conflict between parents and teens tends to be overemphasized, although some conflict does take place. Both middle-aged people and teenagers are going through a period of evaluation or reevaluation. The middle-aged couple is concerned about aging, about the disparity between dreams and reality, about keeping meaning in life, and about how to deal with aging parents. These middle-agers' children are dealing with their own identities, hopes for the future, and concerns about adulthood while trying to get along with their parents. Parents may be overburdened by the problems of both generations—their adolescent children on one side and their elderly parents on the other.

The tasks of parenting adolescents involve the need to give up control gradually, and a shift in parent-child relationships to allow the adolescent to move into the increased freedom and responsibility of adulthood. It requires refocusing on one's marriage as well (Carter & McGoldrick, 1989). Parents cannot retain complete authority and adolescents may say things that may upset parents. Some parents try to control every aspect of their children's lives, making conflict inevitable. Parents feel less powerful because their influence is less than it was in the past (Carter & McGoldrick, 1989). Flexible boundaries are necessary but this does not mean that parents should not influence their children. Rather, a long, gradual, movement towards equality is the rule. The family needs to change from a unit that protects, nurtures, and controls young children to one that is more of a preparation center for the adolescent's entrance into the adult world. Most families handle these challenges well despite some initial difficulties (Preto, 1989). Increased family conflict occurs as adolescents assert autonomy and independence. Conflicts over tidiness, study habits, communication, and lack of responsibility occur. Despite these growing pains, adolescents and parental bonds generally remain strong (Strong & DeVault, 1995).

Little research has been done on the effects adolescents have on their parents. We do know, however, that middle-aged parents generally feel good about their children (Troll, 1989). A very modest relationship exists between parental well-being and adolescent development (Silverberg & Steinberg, 1990). In other words, just having teenage children does not seem to have that much of an effect on a parent's feelings of well-being. This is especially true when the parents, especially the mother, is employed. However, there is one major exception to this, and it concerns daughters' relationships with their mothers. Mothers report more intense mid-life concerns if their daughters are more physically advanced. There is a negative relationship between pubertal maturation and mothers' mental health, which transcends maternal employment. Perhaps there is more mother-daughter conflict because the daughter's development requires the mother to reevaluate her own stage of life. It may be that mothers' well-being is somewhat lower here, which causes conflict, or perhaps mothers are just concerned with their daughters' dating behavior, and supervision becomes more difficult. When sons date, they are often seen as bringing increased freedom to the parents; daughters are more monitored when they date. Mothers with a high work role are more likely than those with a low work role to report mid-life identity concerns when their daughters date, and some authorities believe that a daughter's adolescence is the most stressful period in a mother's life (Field & Widmayer, 1982). Perhaps these mothers have less time to monitor their daughters and are thus more concerned. The rapidly changing relationship affects the mother because she may find it difficult to allow her children more freedom.

How do parents see this period? The majority of middle-aged parents who had experienced all family stages mentioned the prepubertal and adolescent years as least enjoyable (Genevie & Margolies, 1987). Mothers felt less loved and less appreciated and found the rebelliousness difficult to handle. They interpreted what we might consider typical adolescent behavior such as moodiness and reaction to peer pressure as rejection. Most knew it was not, but still this understanding did not make accepting the behavior easier to tolerate. Although parents said they wanted their adolescent children to be their own people, their attitudes were not matched by their expressed feelings. They were aware that their children's values were somewhat different, and only 25% felt very positively about this; 75% felt to varying degrees that their children's opinions and values were hard to accept. It seems most would like their sons and daughters to be their own person as long as that person was someone they wanted their children to be! About 10% of the parents enjoyed these years the most because they had no difficulty accepting their children's independence and most liked and agreed with their children's lifestyle and ideas.

True or False?
Most parents see the period of raising adolescent children as the most satisfying of their parenting careers.

The father with teenage children finds himself no longer as powerful, and his control wanes. He may need some recognition and overt signals that he is making the right decisions, while his teenagers may be rejecting or modifying his decisions as a way to be independent (Bozett, 1985). Consider the father who is proud of his achievements in business and in providing a good home whose son tells him that materialism is "the pits." Consider the father who is proud of his involvement in community activities, only to be told by his daughter that politics is dirty. Conflict reaches its height during early to middle adolescence and then declines. Fathers often have different relationships with their sons and daughters and are more concerned with a son's success than a daughter's (Bozett, 1985). Fathering is very important to a man's life satisfaction, and satisfaction with father's role is highly related to a man's satisfaction at mid-life (McKenry et al., 1987). Men who communicate more effectively with adolescent children experience less stress during mid-life transition (Julian, McKenry, & Arnold, 1990). Parents with outside activities who identify with their work role seem to have fewer problems, while those without any satisfying outside activities have more difficulties (Silverberg & Steinberg, 1990). These other interests buffer the parents against the problems of raising teens.

Parents of adolescents have special concerns. One parent once told me, "When you have small children you have small worries, but when you have big children you have big worries." Parents of teens worry about their children's companions, their future, their sexual activities, their choice of vocation and school, and their values. Parents are concerned that their children not get trapped into an unwanted pregnancy, make a poor choice of spouse, or get involved in a dead-end job. During this period of life, conflict has a different quality to it. Younger children may argue about bedtime, but such arguments pale next to disagreements about curfews, dating, and other adolescent concerns. Parents hope their children will make reasonable career decisions and would like to help, but they must be careful not to be overinvolved or underinvolved. During these years, parenting requires delicacy, a sense of balance, and skill.

The Empty Nest

The empty nest, the time at which all children have left home, is a longer period than ever before. At the turn of the century parents could only expect about 2 years in this period but today it lasts for an average of 13 years (Schulz & Ewen, 1993). This is because of increased longevity and smaller families. A couple with two children born 3 years apart is more likely to experience an extensive empty-nest period.

How does this affect middle-aged parents? Two different scenarios can be anticipated. First, consider the woman who has invested a tremendous amount of energy in raising children. Her children are her career, but when they leave home, her role expires, and with it her self-esteem decreases, resulting in depression. Some evidence for this view is found in a study showing that women who are employed exhibit less depression during the empty-nest period than women who were full-time homemakers (Powell, 1977). Women who are employed tend to adapt to changes more easily and see such changes more positively than those who are not employed in middle age (Adelmann et al., 1989). Employed mothers have followed a dual-career life path and do not find their role reduced as much during the empty-nest stage. In the other scenario, the empty-nest period is a time of renewal, of improved financial status, of spouses becoming reacquainted, and of relief that the task of raising children is over.

Which scenario is closer to the truth? There is little controversy in this area. Although the evidence shows that employed women experience fewer problems than full-time homemakers, the overwhelming majority of studies show that most women in both groups find increased satisfaction during this stage (Neugarten, 1977) and that the most common reaction is relief (Neugarten, 1974). One of the most quoted studies questioned middle-aged women who had given up their jobs to assume a traditional housewife role for 10 years or longer (Rubin, 1979). These women had invested a great amount of time and effort in their children and had made personal sacrifices to stay at home with them. If any group should show symptoms of empty-nest problems, this group should. But they did not. Some experienced moments of sadness and loneliness after the children had gone, but they were definitely not depressed, and again, their most common feeling was relief. Now they could spend time on other pursuits. Renewal of interest in oneself and a feeling of being released are also reported quite often (Glenn, 1975; Harkins, 1978). The period is seen as liberating. The sense of increased freedom and opportunity far outweighs the supposed loss of role (Neugarten & Datan, 1973). Launching of one's children is a major transition but most see it as a positive one. When it is not, it is most commonly linked to dissatisfaction with the marriage (Harris, Ellicott, & Holmes, 1986).

Questions Students Often Ask

I have some difficulty with the idea that parents experience relief when their children leave home. Don't they really miss their children?

Yes, they do miss them, and some feelings of loneliness occur, but most parents are pleased to see their children happy and achieving independently. In addition, the change from a house full of children to the empty nest is usually gradual, with less and less contact taking place within the home. Most parents see and talk to their adult children regularly, so contact is maintained.

Most studies find no negative effects and significant positive effects of children leaving home (Adelmann et al., 1989). The empty nest is anticipated and prepared for, and great disruptions in women's roles do not occur in most cases (Smith & Moen, 1988). Consider also the fact that most women do not hurry back to the labor force when their children leave home but resume their employment (if they have taken time out for child-rearing) while their children are still at home (Moen, 1991). This does not mean that there aren't some bittersweet feelings. Many women do experience a mixture of happiness and sadness, of gain and loss, and women are more likely to experience feelings of loss than men (Troll, 1989). Although women who are employed are perhaps less likely to feel these emotions, both employed and nonemployed women adjust well to the empty nest. On the whole, increased personal freedom and feelings of relief predominate.

Not as much research has been done on the effect of the empty nest on men. The evidence that is available shows the empty-nest stage to be a happy time in men's lives (Fiske & Weiss, 1977). In late middle age men become less work oriented and concentrate more on the family, and this may contribute to the reported increase in marital satisfaction (Lowenthal & Chiriboga, 1972).

True or False?

The empty-nest stage, the time at which all the children have left home, is experienced positively by most adults.

The Not-So-Empty Nest: The Boomerang Generation

The family life cycle is not as smooth as one might think. One out of every four homes has an adult child living in it. The majority of unmarried children do not leave home until they are more than 24 years old (Strong & DeVault, 1995).

Children may not leave home because housing is expensive and they may not have sufficient resources to live on their own. In other cases, it may be more comfortable to continue living at home. One returning 30-year-old student told me that he got along fine with his parents, gives them rent, and finds that it is a good situation for everyone concerned. Others return home following a divorce, sometimes with their children. Almost a third of all divorced men and women return home (Saluter, 1992). The fact that so many adult children are living at home has led some authorities to argue that a term called ***adult children at home*** should be coined for this stage (Aldous, 1990). Most parents did not anticipate this situation, and although some relationships may not be marked by conflict, some parents report serious conflicts over the hours their children keep and responsibility for household chores (Clemens & Axelson, 1985).

Reflections on Adult Children

Parenting does not stop when children leave home. The relationship continues but changes once children are on their own. Most studies show that parents and their adult children feel close and are not estranged from each other. They keep in touch and visit each other frequently. When this is not possible because of distance, they telephone each other on a regular basis (Troll, 1989). As children leave home, some of the petty problems of living together disappear.

Parents help their adult children in a number of ways, such as baby-sitting for their grandchildren. In addition, they give their children emotional and sometimes financial support, such as helping with a down payment on a house. Early adults and their middle-aged parents often report some embarrassment about having a close relationship with each other (Troll, 1989). The conventional wisdom that both generations should be essentially separate leads to some feelings of uneasiness when mutual support is present. After spending much of the adult years involved with the children, the children leave home to make their own way in the world. Parents can now take much pleasure in the accomplishments of their adult children and their adjustment (Seltzer & Ryff, 1994). Parents who believe their children are doing well have more positive views of themselves and their parenting skills. When parents in their 50s were questioned concerning their adult children's accomplishments, parents who considered their children successful, especially in the occupational and educational spheres of life, and well adjusted had high levels of self-acceptance, feelings of environmental mastery, and purpose in life (Ryff et al., 1994). How parents view their children is an important factor in determining their sense of well-being, which is not surprising since parents have invested so much time in their children's upbringing.

Relationships With the Older Generation

The relationship between grown children and their parents is often looked at in terms of formal obligations and financial help. The picture is one of the dutiful child—usually a daughter—taking care of elderly parents in a role reversal. Instead of parents taking care of children, the children now take care of their parents. The older person is seen as dependent (Shanas, 1973). However, the truth is quite different.

The relationship between parents and children in middle age is actually quite good and characterized by mutual support and voluntary activity. Most middle-aged people get along well with their parents, and there is no evidence of wholesale abandonment of parents (Baruch & Barnett, 1983; Troll, 1989). One married woman of 35 was asked whom she liked to be with when she felt down, and said, "It's really embarrassing to say, but it's my mother." Contrary to the popular stereotype, the relationship between adult child and mother is marked by concern and close emotional attachment (Shanas, 1979a). Most parents live close to their children and see them often (Shanas, 1979b). Positive relationships between parents and children are common and a longitudinal study of high-achieving women found that these relationships were related to self-esteem (Welsh & Stewart, 1995). The middle generation's relationships with their parents are quite good, and middle-aged children often show a greater degree of obligation than their parents expect.

True or False?
The relationship between middle-aged people and their parents is marked by strain and obligation.

Older people prefer adult children to provide emotional support and financial management but not income. They expect their middle-aged children to modify family schedules for the sake of their elderly parents, but the majority of each generation believes that adult children should not share households with elderly parents (Brody, Johnsen, & Fulcomer, 1984).

A significant minority of middle-aged people though, do share their homes with their parents. An estimated one in six middle-aged couples will have an aged parent in the household at some time or another (Beck & Beck, 1984). Sharing one's home with an elderly parent is often a last resort and frequently occurs when the parent cannot live independently for financial or medical reasons. But sharing a home has a positive side that is often left unmentioned. The older person has much to give—for example, household and baby-sitting help or sometimes a financial contribution.

The relationship between parent and child changes in middle adulthood. Slowly, parents reduce the amount of support that they give and the relationship takes on more mutuality (Cooney & Uhlenberg, 1992). When middle-aged adults not living with their parents were surveyed, a pattern of reduced support was found in such areas as receiving services, advice, and other forms of support. The most precipitous drop is found at the beginning of middle age both in services and advice. Elderly parents are seen as potential sources of help less and less as the

We sometimes think of the relationship between middle-aged people and older people in terms of obligation. However, there is often a great affinity between the two, and friendship is quite common.

children negotiate middle age. The evidence shows that parental support declines gradually until middle age and substantially during middle age as parents age.

Concern for the family's elderly members is the rule, not the exception. But as parents age, chronic illness may set in, parents require more care, and the situation becomes increasingly difficult. Both generations want their independence, and as long as this is possible, relationships stay quite good. Role reversal and major problems arise when additional daily help is required and when medical needs become more serious, usually late in the middle-adulthood period, during the empty-nest stage. When this occurs, the elderly person requires a great deal of care. For every disabled person in a nursing home, two or more equally disabled people are cared for by their family (Troll, 1989). It is estimated that between 70% and 80% of all help received by elderly people comes from adult children (Chiriboga, 1989). Most of the care is provided by daughters who make numerous sacrifices (Brubaker, 1990).

There is usually one person who emerges as the main provider of services (Brody & Schoonover, 1986); equal sharing occurs only in a small number of families, for example, if there are two daughters who live close to each other (Matthews, 1987). Sons help, but often in a different manner. Daughters provide more of the routine care whereas sons provide assistance in specific situations. Sons may shop, speak to the doctor, and repair things around the home. However, the type of help given by the children depends upon the circumstances of each child and the functional impairment of the elderly individual (Matthews, Werkner, & Delaney, 1989). The greater the functional impairment, the more the care-giver is affected (Tonwsend & Franks, 1995). Although the extent of the cognitive and physical impairments may affect the care-giver, cognitive impairment is more likely to negatively affect the care-giver than functional impairment; cognitive impairment takes a terrible toll on the relationship (Townsend & Franks, 1995). A parent with a significant cognitive impairment may not seem like the same person you knew, and cognitive impairment often progressively worsens with time whereas functional impairment may not.

Often, families come together when the need arises and provide the necessary assistance. One child may be in a better position to give money than the others whereas someone else living closer may be better able to do the shopping. Everyone in the family is affected by the older person's plight. In such care-giving situations, both husbands and wives feel the strain (Kleban et al., 1989). Taking care of the impaired elderly person is stressful. When daughters and daughters-in-law who had the primary responsibility for caring for the elderly person were studied, both stress and rewards were found (Tables 17.1 and 17.2). Notice that being criticized, being unresponsive, or being uncooperative are the most common stressors, while knowing that the loved one is well cared for and the knowledge that one is fulfilling one's obligation as well as just spending more time with the elderly person were perceived rewards (Stephens, Frank, & Townsend, 1994). Isolating the care-giver role and relating it to stress may not be sufficient because role

Table 17.1 **Rank Order of Stressors Identified in the Care-giver Role**

STRESSOR	PERCENTAGE ENDORSING
Care recipient criticized or complained	71.6
Care recipient was unresponsive	67.4
Care recipient was uncooperative or demanding	67.4
Helped care recipient with personal care needs	67.3
Care recipient asked repetitive questions	67.3
Care recipient was agitated	66.4
Managed legal/financial affairs of care recipient	66.4
Care recipient's health declined	66.3
Supervised care recipient	63.1
Did not receive help with care-giving from family or friends	61.1
Had extra expenses due to care-giving	54.7
Care recipient was forgetful	53.6

Note: n = 95.
Source: Stephens, Franks, & Townsend, 1994.

Table 17.2 **Rank Order of Rewards Identified in the Care-giver Role**

REWARD	PERCENTAGE ENDORSING
Knew care recipient was well cared for	100.0
Fulfilled family obligation	93.7
Spent time in the company of care recipient	92.6
Gave care because wanted to not because had to	89.5
Saw care recipient enjoy small things	84.2
Care recipient showed affection or appreciation	81.1
Helped care recipient with personal care	81.0
Care recipient was cooperative or not demanding	77.8
Care recipient's good side came through despite the illness	73.7
Care recipient was calm or content	70.5
Relationship with care recipient became closer	64.2
Care recipient's health improved	47.3

Note: n = 95.
Source: Stephens, Franks, & Townsend, 1994.

stress is cumulative and having stress in other roles in addition to the care-giver role may cause more emotional difficulties.

Questions Students Often Ask

I've seen middle-aged people try to take care of elderly people, and it seems very difficult. I was surprised to find that there were rewards and that it did not always affect them adversely. I don't understand this.

As newspaper articles trumpet the loneliness and often the desertion of elderly people or the troubles of dealing with an elderly infirm individual, it is uncommon to see any statement of the rewards. Role strain can be found in every role—be it parent, spouse, or care-giver. Both stress and rewards are related to well-being. Care-givers do find some aspects of their roles rewarding and this may have some positive influence on their sense of well-being.

Middle-aged people do not suddenly become interested in, and prime care-givers for, their parents when they become very ill. Often this situation develops gradually, and the duties intensify rather than change suddenly. Many elderly people do not go abruptly from being fully independent to needing nursing home assistance. The process is often gradual, so the care-giving involvement with one's parents is also gradual. Elaine Brody (1981, 1990) calls women in this situation "women in the middle," because they are in the middle of everything. They are middle-aged and caught between the traditional role of caring and the newer emphasis on women to be employed and independent. The increase in the number of chronically ill elderly people and the falling birth rate means that there are fewer people to help out. Women especially pick up the responsibility for helping their parents (Welsh & Stewart, 1995).

Although the relationship between middle-aged children and their elderly parents is good, they do not agree on everything. The same pattern as is found in adolescence is seen here. Elderly parents tend to minimize differences between themselves and their middle-aged children and the children tend to exaggerate these differences (Fingerman, 1995). This is understandable because elderly parents want to believe that their children are closer to them in values and attitudes, as a symbol of their own continuity, while middle-aged children are striving to find and maintain their niche in the world. Elderly people tend to see their relationship with their daughters in a more positive light than daughters do. Mothers overestimate daughters' constructive behavior, such as listening to the other person's point of view, and minimize the extent of a daughter's avoidant behavior (not calling or becoming quiet) and destructive behaviors (yelling). Mothers also report using more constructive behaviors than daughters realize and feel better about conflict afterward than do daughters.

Friends Through It All

Friendships become more stable in middle age (Blieszner & Adams, 1993). Many friends in middle age can be described as "old friends" and being close and conveniently located are not as important in middle age as they were in early adulthood (Rybash, Roodin, & Hoyer, 1995). When middle-aged adults who had moved within the past 5 years were asked about their best friend, a majority named someone from their former neighborhood (Hess, 1971). Middle-aged people do not have to live close to one another in order to be considered intimate friends; they often travel long distances to see their old friends. They can do this because they do not have very young children to care for and have more freedom.

As people progress through middle age, they take more time for friends (Blieszner & Adams, 1993). Middle-aged people also try harder to reduce conflicts with friends than younger adults do (Fox et al., 1985).

Social scientists often use the term **social convoy** to describe the network of close relationships that accompany an individual throughout life. The size of this convoy stays about the same with between two and five close friends throughout adulthood (Antonucci, 1990). The actual people may change but the number of close friends remains relatively stable throughout adulthood (Antonucci, 1985). No significant decline in number of friends takes place in middle age, yet some changes take place. (Costa, Zonderman, & McCrae, 1983) Casual friendships become somewhat less common with age (Schulz & Ewen, 1993). Women continue to have somewhat larger convoys and maintain their friendships somewhat longer.

Gender differences in friendship remain. When people ages 18 to 75 were studied, men were less expressive in their friendships than women at every age (Fox, Gibbs, & Auerbach, 1985). Men talked about sports, politics, and business whereas women shared personal feelings and problems.

Friendships continue to have the same meaning in middle age as they had in early adulthood with one additional responsibility: middle-aged people are likely to suffer personal losses as they progress through these years and friends may be an important source of comfort and social support during these crises.

On the Job

One reward of middle adulthood is financial. Middle-aged people earn more and are often found in management positions. Because men rarely interrupt their vocational life voluntarily—for example, to stay home with the children, as many women do—they are likely to be at the top of their earning power. Most middle-aged women are employed, and the middle-aged woman who has been working throughout her adult years is also probably at the top of her earning power. Even if she delayed enter-

social convoy The changing group of significant others who serve as sources of social support for an individual during the course of his or her life.

ing the work force or interrupted her career to raise her children, she will probably reach her earnings peak sometime in late middle adulthood.

We should not forget the difficulties a middle-aged woman might have in reentering the work world in middle age, or even entering it for the first time. Three problems stand out (Hall, 1986). First, the woman's skills may be either outmoded or unpracticed. A former office manager of years ago may not be familiar with the technologically advanced office of the 1990s, or a former health care professional may not know the latest methods of performing a certain procedure. Second, self-concept and self-esteem problems may become evident. Job interviews are not easy for anyone, but they may be particularly difficult for someone who has been out of touch with the business world for several years. Last, support and encouragement from husband and family are needed, and the greater the encouragement, the easier the transition to employment.

Job Satisfaction

Most middle-aged people are satisfied with their jobs (Maas, 1989; Tamir, 1989), and there is a relationship between job satisfaction and age (Warr, 1992). Those who do better than they thought they would are the most satisfied, but even those who achieve a lower level generally evaluate their jobs positively (Clausen, 1981). When asked to rate job satisfaction, older people report that it increased up to late middle age—ages 50 to 59—then decreased thereafter, often during the last 5 years of their working life (Saleh & Otis, 1964). Job satisfaction takes a U-shaped curve with age; after being high at the beginning of employment, it declines during the 20s and 30s and then increases in the 40s (Warr, 1992).

The research on job satisfaction can be interpreted in many ways. People become used to their jobs in middle adulthood and, faced with fewer opportunities to change jobs, simply adapt to them. In a more positive vein, middle-aged workers are more likely than their younger cohorts to have attained a favorable position, received promotions, and to make good salaries. Their position may allow for more self-direction and choice. Middle-aged workers say that autonomy on the job is very important to them (Schaie & Willis, 1996), and the high level of job satisfaction may reflect the increased individual freedom available in higher-level positions. Job satisfaction is related to how challenging the position is as well as to the financial security it offers, and higher-level positions are more likely to be challenging.

Salary is the most important factor affecting job satisfaction among low-income workers, but this is not true among middle-class blue-collar or white-collar workers who already earn good salaries. People who have certain abilities and skills want to use them. The decline in satisfaction during the later years of middle adulthood may stem from an awareness that promotion is no longer likely and that one's dream will not be realized. In fact, promotion rates decline with age—the older one gets, the less likely one is to be promoted. The corporate ladder is similar to a pyramid, with less room at the top than at the bottom. It is relatively easy to get the first few promotions, but in later middle age fewer positions are available. The decline in job satisfaction in late middle age may also reflect the vision of retirement. It is easier to retire from one's job if one focuses on the negative rather than the positive aspects of the job. However, age-related changes in satisfaction should not be overemphasized. Chronological age is probably less important than other job-related variables, such as the type of job, the company one works for, and the challenges the job offers (Chown, 1977).

In middle age, employment as a source of primary personal fulfillment decreases (Tamir, 1982). This finding meshes well with the trend toward emphasizing other aspects of one's life, especially one's family. Some theorists believe that people are not as happy as they seem but are unwilling to express their dissatisfaction. This is especially true if one has invested much time in preparation and if the job is viewed by the world as important and interesting.

There are some interesting gender differences in employment in middle age that were alluded to earlier in the chapter. For women, the middle years often are a time of reentry or primary entry into careers, with gains in self-esteem as they look for new sources of satisfaction. Many women may

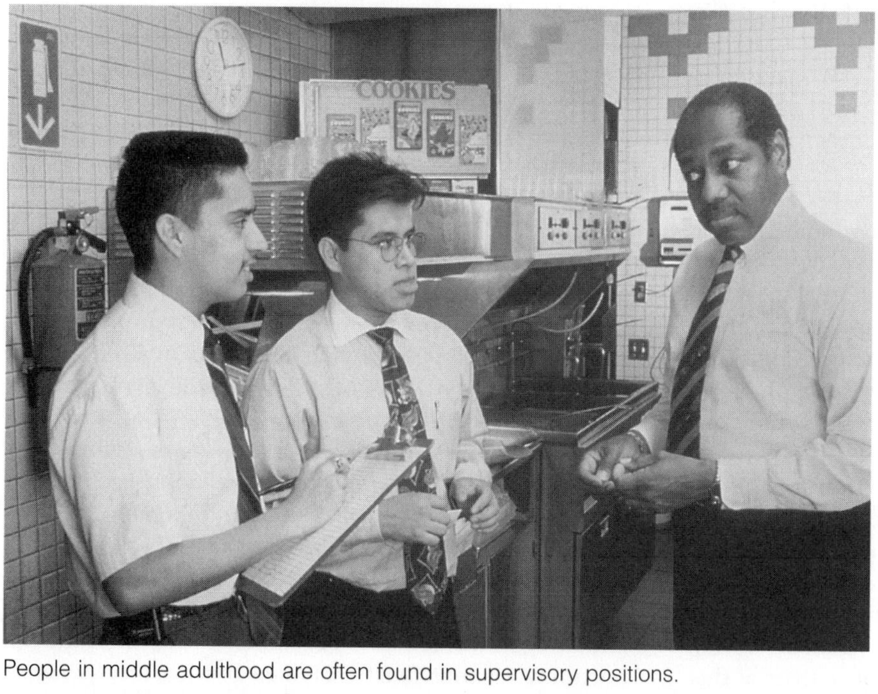

People in middle adulthood are often found in supervisory positions.

Forming Your Own Opinion: Who Would You Hire?

You are an employer seeking to hire a worker for a marketing job that requires some computer skills. The individual will have to be hard-working and a self-starter and to learn new marketing techniques using computer data bases. The two finalists for the position differ greatly in age: one is 28 years old, and the other is 53 years old. Would age enter into your decision?

You are the supervisor on your floor and you have to recommend someone to be promoted to a new position that will require much training. The employee must be able to learn and then teach others these skills. Two finalists for the job appear after an exhaustive evaluation process: one is 25 years old; the other, 48 years old. Would you take age into account when making your decision?

Questions surrounding age and job performance are important, and will become even more important as baby boomers begin to reach the 50-year mark. Even though federal law makes it illegal to discriminate on the basis of age between ages 40 and 70 years, a variety of discriminatory practices exist. Older workers may be laid off, fired, involuntarily retired, not given the promotions they deserve, or even denied a job on the basis of age alone (Pritchard, Maxwell, & Jordan, 1984). Discrimination can take the form of refusing to hire an older worker, not promoting the worker, or giving the older worker a less than glowing recommendation. Older workers perceive that they are discriminated against (Barnes-Farrell, 1993), and 20% of all discrimination cases filed in 1994 involved age (Eisler, 1995).

Much of the discrimination in hiring, promotion, and training is based upon the conventional wisdom that job performance declines with age (Rhodes, 1983; Stagner, 1985). Many people, especially younger less-educated males, believe that older workers do not perform as well on the job as younger workers (Taylor, Crino, & Rubinfeld, 1989). Having younger supervisors increases difficulties in evaluation, often leading to decreases in promotional opportunities (Barnes-Farrell, 1993). Since middle-aged people are slower than younger workers, one would expect some decline in performance. However, middle-aged people are better, more efficient workers because they have more experience. For instance, an experienced salesperson may know which leads are best to follow whereas a younger worker may waste time following all the leads. Others argue that it is a standoff—that the middle-aged worker's experience compensates for any loss of speed.

The available evidence does not reveal any significant age differences in work performance (Avolio, Waldman, & McDaniel, 1990). The only exceptions involve jobs that demand physical strength or speed (Avolio et al., 1990). It may be unfair to make any generalization in this area because there are so many individual differences. Older workers with directly related experience may show performance equal to or even higher than that of younger workers. Older, inexperienced workers in technically complex and rapidly changing work environments may not compare as well (Waldman & Avolio, 1986). Individual differences should be taken into account because two workers of the same age may perform quite differently. Age in itself is not a useful predictor of job competence.

It is difficult to compare older workers to younger workers in productivity because they are not in the same jobs and when they are, their styles may differ. For example, older workers in managerial positions delegate decision-making responsibilities more often and make more use of time management techniques. But what does this mean? Do these managers delegate more because they are confident of their ability and position and see the need to do so, or is it because they are compensating for declines in competence and using others to make up for these deficits? The answer that Rebok and colleagues (1986) found was that both time management and delegation were related to feelings of confidence and experience. Managers who perceived themselves as very competent were more likely to use time management strategies such as keeping a log of tasks and scheduling carefully during times of

have been employed, but they may have limited their hours because of having young children. Now they can show a part of themselves that they could not show before. For men the situation is different. Especially in their 50s, men see diminished rewards from work (Chiriboga, 1989) and do not show as much involvement with work, possibly because they realize that their career options are limited.

The relationship between work satisfaction and life satisfaction is less than it was in earlier ages. In middle age, work satisfaction has little or no bearing on emotional well-being (Tamir, 1989; 1982), and an emotional disengagement from work occurs. Disengagement is also found in blue-collar, nonmanagerial workers (Harlan, 1983). Some workaholics show an increase in job activity at this stage, remaining busy so as not to have to deal with other problems; others are completely absorbed by their work or feel that one great push will get them to the top. However middle-aged people may take a different perspective towards their employment and be more involved in their family and personal lives than they were at a younger age.

Not all middle-aged people are so happy at their jobs. Some may be dissatisfied with their progress, others may not be sure about keeping these positions. Factors that make younger workers satisfied are not the same as those for older workers. Younger workers are more concerned with salary, job security, opportunities for advancement, and relationships with both supervisors and coworkers. Middle-aged workers are more likely to focus on the opportunity for individual challenge and mastery, personal

Forming Your Own Opinion: Who Would You Hire? (continued)

heavy stress. Their delegation of responsibilities was related to their considerable experience in supervision and their knowledge of how to work with people.

The middle-aged unemployed worker may find it very difficult to overcome age-related prejudices. Unemployed middle-aged managers may find that they have to overcome common myths, for instance, that they have reduced capabilities, do not keep up with the world, are a drain on the pension plan, are absent more, cost more in benefits, have something wrong with them, are not as adaptable, or will not be as loyal (Birsner, 1985). Older workers are *not* absent more and do not change jobs as often as younger workers. The increased use of health benefits can be offset by savings in turnover and training, and whether older workers can meet the physical demands of the job depends on the job and the individual's ability (Waldrop, 1991; Kossen, 1983).

Older workers have a number of advantages over their younger colleagues. Their attitudes toward work tend to be stable (Staw & Ross, 1985), and an older worker who has a history of positive work attitudes is less likely to be affected by situational and external influences. A survey of attitudes and values of workers ranging in age from 17 to 65 found that older workers placed greater emphasis on the moral importance of work and took greater pride in craftsmanship whereas younger workers placed greater emphasis on money and the importance of friends (Cherrington, 1983). Some interesting advantages are found among mid-life executives (Tamir, 1989). As noted previously, these workers delegate details to younger people and are able to visualize the bigger picture better than younger workers. Because of their experience, they have enhanced judgment, manage contradiction better, and have a greater desire for challenge. They are more likely to have a sense of company loyalty. Once enrolled in a training program, older workers are more likely than younger ones to complete the training and stay on the job (Morgan, 1987).

One area of great concern for older workers that they can control is skill obsolescence (Smither, 1993). Technology is evolving so quickly that one's job skills can easily become obsolete. People's skills usually become obsolete not because their original jobs have been eliminated but because they have not kept up with new trends (AARP, 1992). It is estimated that half of what you need to know to do a job will be obsolete within 4.5 years; in some fields such as software engineering this figure is 2.2 years (AARP, 1992). This means that a person needs to continue learning throughout life to be competitive and valuable in the work setting.

Middle-aged workers seem to be aware of these new realities. Studies show that middle-aged and older adults understand company needs and are accurate in their assessment of how they contribute to the company and what skills are needed to continue doing so (Fletcher, Hansson, & Bailey, 1992). They often gauge their performance and assess their need to learn new skills more accurately than younger workers.

Americans are aware of the importance of lifelong learning and of keeping current. In one survey, 81% of adult workers said that additional education is important for them to be successful on the job, and 80% had received job-related training in the past 3 years. Just being educated once is not sufficient (Kelly, 1995).

Middle-aged people cannot afford to be complacent. In the fast-changing world of work one can no longer find much safety in seniority. There are no guarantees, but having the skills necessary to compete requires continuous training. This is the responsibility of the middle-aged individual. However, those in the positions of hiring and promoting must also be educated about the unfair and incorrect stereotypes that dog the mature worker. Only if people understand the real nature of the abilities and characteristics that middle-aged and older workers bring to their jobs can a fair environment be created in which people are hired, promoted, and trained based on their true abilities and performance rather than on some caricature or stereotype.

achievement, freedom to be creative, and how their contribution at work relates to the larger whole (Rybash, Roodin, & Hoyer, 1995).

Unemployment

The threat of unemployment for people in middle age is greater than it has been in the past (Sheehy, 1995). Corporations are more likely than ever to sweep away layers of middle management in an effort called *downsizing.* About one-third of all layoffs are of middle management, who are often middle aged (Downs, 1996); this is often done in an effort to restructure the organization (Farber, 1996). Employee morale often declines while the hoped-for economic benefits in productivity may or may not occur (Harper's Magazine, May, 1996).

When middle-aged people do lose their jobs, chances are that they will be unemployed longer than their younger colleagues. Middle-aged workers are faced with fewer options, and older workers are harder hit by economic downturns and unemployment (Brenner, 1985). The effects of long-term unemployment are serious. When workers aged 35 to 60 years who were unemployed were compared with a similar group who had jobs, the unemployed group showed many more symptoms of depression and anxiety (Linn et al. 1985). The changes in self-concept depended on the social support received from family and friends. Those with family support did better, but in general the self-esteem of the unemployed group was lower. Many middle-aged people who have been laid off find that they do not have the

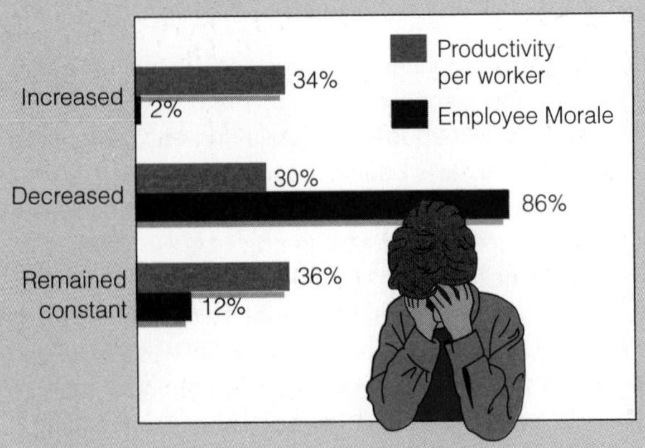

Downsizing has not necessarily resulted in productivity increases but has a negative impact on employee morale.

Datagraphic
The Results of Downsizing (Major firms from 1989–1994)
Source: Data from American Management Association, 1996.

necessary job skills and have to lower their expectations and lifestyles, (Sheehy, 1995). They also experience discrimination in hiring and training programs (see Forming Your Own Opinion: Who Would You Hire? pp. 410–411).

Perhaps some differentiation should be made between people in their 40s and those in their late 50s. Often people in their 40s find unemployment to be an intolerable financial burden because of very strong financial needs. People who are 55 may find themselves retired early, and although they may have some financial difficulty, they may not be as severely burdened with financial responsibilities as people in their 40s (Warr, Jackson, & Banks, 1988). When a number of unemployed men were divided into age groups and tested on a general health questionnaire, the group of people suffering the most were between 40 and 49 years of age, with the 30- to 39-year age group just behind. Those older or younger showed better mental health than these two groups. After 2 years of unemployment, some small improvements in mental health were found, but the middle-aged men showed the least improvement (Warr et al., 1988).

The older worker often has nowhere to go after being laid off. The chances of landing a new job at the same or a more advanced level are slim (Barnes-Farrell, 1993). In a Ford Foundation study of formerly unemployed people who were able to get new jobs, workers under the age of 35 years received far more jobs that paid more than their previous jobs, but after age 40, more of the jobs paid less. After the age of age 55, the chances of finding a higher-paying job were slight (Kossen, 1983). Many adults find that they are trapped: they cannot reach their goals in the job they have, but they have nowhere else to go. This may be one cause of the depression and other psychological problems that sometimes occur during middle age.

Table 17.3 **Some Mid-Life Intergenerational Myths**

1. Mid-life men and women live as far apart from their children and their parents as they can.
2. Mid-life men and women rarely visit or receive visits from their adult children or their parents.
3. Mid-life men and women rarely phone (or get phone calls) or write (or receive letters) from their adult children or their parents.
4. Mid-life men and women do not exchange help with either their adult children or their parents.
5. Mid-life men and women do not feel emotionally close to either their adult children or their parents.
6. Mid-life men and women are distraught when their children grow up and leave their homes.
7. Mid-life men and women are narcissistic, dwelling only on their own needs and wants and unconcerned about those of their adult children or their parents.
8. Mid-life men and women abandon their parents when they get old and sick.
9. Mid-life parents and their adult children are more likely to stay in touch and feel close if they share values and personality.
10. The family is a dying institution.
11. Grandparents lose their grandchildren if their children divorce.
12. Grandparents are avid for close and frequent contact with their grandchildren.
13. Grandparents feel they know how to raise their grandchildren better than their children are doing and are eager to interfere.
14. Extensive extended-family contact is deleterious to mental health.
15. Adults should not live with their relatives other than their young children and spouses.

Source: Troll, 1989.

Remodeling Middle Adulthood

Middle adulthood is a time of facing and answering specific questions. Most people deal quite well with these challenges. This period is both a time of stability and a time of change. Middle-aged people have the experience, financial resources, and maturity to deal with the basic questions of life, enjoy their newfound freedom, and recommit themselves to family, others, and community. This recommitment satisfies Erikson's concept of generativity, of growing as a result of experiencing and giving to others. This chapter has described some of the many myths of middle age that have been exploded by research (see Table 17.3 for these and others). Instead of seeing middle age as a time of stress and struggle, perhaps we should regard it as a time of growth, choice, and opportunity. It may be true that life begins at 40!

Summary

1. Middle-aged people must learn to deal with their own mortality, use their time wisely, recognize their

physical limitations, deal with long-standing health habits, reassess the value of their careers and family relationships, and identify which parts of the self remain unfulfilled.

2. Theorists generally see middle adulthood as a time of reevaluation, reassessment, and commitment. The positive outcome of the psychosocial crisis of middle age, according to Erikson, is attaining a sense of generativity that involves helping the younger generation. The negative outcome is stagnation. Middle-aged people are more likely to show behaviors indicative of caring for the next generation.
3. By middle age, many lifestyle choices have been made. Some people have been able to achieve their dream while others are still working on it. Dream support is more important than achieving the dream for womens' emotional well being.
4. Levinson views middle age as a turbulent time of reassessment and of solving great dilemmas. Although middle age is a time for reevaluation, most psychologists today believe it need not be a time of crisis.
5. People in their 50s see life as more exciting. They see themselves as psychologically in between. They feel younger than they know they are physically. They also believe they have wisdom and take a broader perspective on life.
6. Personality traits remain stable in middle adulthood. However, some age-related and gender-related changes do occur, often in late middle age, and continue through later maturity.
7. Marital satisfaction, especially for women, is low at the beginning of middle age but increases later for both men and women. Dealing with teenage children can create tension, but this aspect is often overemphasized. Adolescents complain that parents are overprotective and interfering.
8. The empty-nest stage is a time of considerable opportunity, and most people look forward to it. The most common reaction is relief, and negative reactions are few.
9. Many unmarried adult children are still living with their families because of economic constraints or because they prefer to do so. Children may also move back to the parental home after getting divorced. The relationship between parents and their adult children is usually positive. Parents' perceptions of their adult children's success is related to their own sense of well-being.
10. The relationship of middle-aged people to their aging parents is generally good and characterized by mutual support. Middle-agers visit their parents often, and both generations desire independence. When their parents cannot care for themselves fully, middle-aged people, especially women, often help out. The care-giver role, like all others, presents both stresses and rewards.
11. Middle-aged people have fewer casual friends but keep the same number of close friends. Physical proximity is not as important because middle-aged people are willing to travel distances to see their friends.
12. Middle-aged people usually express satisfaction with their jobs. Many have attained positions that are challenging and allow for self-direction and expression as well as financial rewards.
13. In middle age, men often turn from investing primarily in their jobs to their own private lives, marriages, and families. Women who may have started full-time employment somewhat later in the life cycle may emphasize their careers more as well as concentrate on fulfilling other aspects of their personal lives.

Multiple-Choice Questions

1. Middle-aged people are said to be in the _____ generation.
   a. sandwich
   b. limelight
   c. forgotten
   d. conservative
2. Which of the following is a task or challenge of middle adulthood?
   a. dealing with one's own mortality.
   b. appreciating physiological change.
   c. reorienting oneself to work and achievement goals.
   d. All of these are tasks and challenges of middle age.
3. The changing time perspective in middle age is best shown by a person's looking at:
   a. the time she has left rather than time since birth.
   b. what is going right in her life rather than what is going wrong.
   c. age in terms of her children's ages rather than her own.
   d. looking forward to holidays rather than dreading them.
4. Which of the following statements about generativity is *correct?*
   a. Generativity involves nurturing the next generation, for example, through one's children.
   b. Generativity may involve creative activities that produce products of enduring worth.
   c. Generativity may involve community work.
   d. All of the above are correct.
5. Women's "dream" in middle age changes in which of the following ways?
   a. a significant decrease in emphasis on work and a reduction in focus on the family.
   b. a significant increase in her focus on work and family.
   c. a significant increase in focus on self-fulfillment.
   d. a radical decrease in focus on work, and stability in emphasis on family.

6. A middle-aged man tells you that he doesn't know how involved with others he should really be at this point in his life. Which of Levinson's polarities does this reflect?
   a. young/old.
   b. family/work.
   c. attachment/separation.
   d. helpfulness/self-fulfillment.
7. Which term does *not* belong in a description of people in their 50s?
   a. freedom.
   b. excitement.
   c. self-confidence.
   d. non-conformity.
8. Jack is measuring such personality traits as activity level, optimism, and sociability longitudinally in a sample of middle-aged people over a 20-year cycle. He should expect:
   a. no particular trend and some characteristics will increase, some will stay the same, and some will decrease.
   b. a pattern of stability.
   c. a pattern of decreased self-assurance and increased pessimism.
   d. a trend towards being more materialistic and less people oriented.
9. You are researching the pattern of interest in work and family for both husbands and wives throughout middle age. If your study agrees with others in the field you should find:
   a. an increase in work interest for men but not women, and stability of interest in family for both husbands and wives.
   b. a decrease in work interest for both husbands and wives, stability of interest in family for women, and an increase in interest in the family for men.
   c. a decline in interest in family for both men and women, and an increase in work interest for both husbands and wives.
   d. an increase in interest for men in their families and an increase in interest in work for women.
10. When people at different ages were studied those who were divorced in their __________ were most greatly affected.
    a. 20s
    b. 30s
    c. 40s
    d. 50s
11. Which of the following statements about middle age parents and their teenage children is *incorrect?*
    a. Relationships usually remain strong.
    b. The period is seen as the most enjoyable parenting period by the majority of parents.
    c. Issues of control are quite important for fathers.
    d. Those parents with outside interests, such as work involvement, tend to be more satisfied.
12. The empty nest is best described as a period of:
    a. yearning and longing.
    b. happiness and opportunities with some longing.
    c. feeling neither happy nor sad, but neutral.
    d. loneliness and bitterness.
13. Which statement concerning the relationship between middle-aged parents and their adult children is *correct?*
    a. Conflict is very common and often serious.
    b. They see or hear from each other often.
    c. How parents view their children's accomplishments is not related to well-being.
    d. All of the above are correct.
14. Mrs. Johnson claims that the relationship between middle-aged children and their parents is marked by little affection, but great amounts of obligation. According to research in the field, Mrs. Johnson is:
    a. correct for both sons and daughters.
    b. incorrect for sons but correct for daughters.
    c. incorrect for daughters but correct for sons.
    d. incorrect for both sons and daughters.
15. Which of the following statements is *correct?*
    a. Parents give their children less advice as the children negotiate middle age.
    b. Older parents generally expect their children to support them financially.
    c. Most elderly people would like to share a home with their adult children.
    d. All of the above are correct.
16. In which situation would the relationship between adult children and their elderly parents be most troublesome?
    a. The elderly parent cannot walk.
    b. The elderly parent needs help in eating.
    c. The elderly parent has difficulty remembering anything.
    d. The elderly parent cannot hear very well.
17. Which statement concerning conflicts between elderly parents and their middle-aged children is *correct?*
    a. Both middle-aged and elderly people exaggerate their differences.
    b. Elderly parents minimize differences whereas middle-aged people exaggerate them.
    c. Middle-aged people minimize the differences whereas elderly people exaggerate them.
    d. Middle-aged and elderly people both minimize the differences.
18. Ed says that middle-aged people are not concerned with how close their friends live to them, make more time for their friends, and the number of friends stays about the same. According to studies in the area, Ed is:
    a. correct.
    b. incorrect about them not being concerned with distance, but correct about everything else.
    c. incorrect about them making more time for their friends, but correct about everything else.
    d. incorrect about the number of friends, but correct about everything else.

19. Most middle-aged people say they are:
    a. neither satisfied nor dissatisfied with their job, but somewhat neutral.
    b. satisfied with their job.
    c. dissatisfied with their job.
    d. satisfied with their salary but dissatisfied with the job duties themselves.
20. Two workers, one 25 years old and the other 45 years old, are laid off from their companies. According to research in the field:
    a. they should be out of work about the same time, and both should find jobs that paid about the same amount of money.
    b. the younger workers will be out of work longer than the middle-aged person but will probably get a job that pays more than the one from which he was laid off.
    c. the middle-aged worker will be out of work longer, and is less likely to find a job that pays as much as the previous one.
    d. the middle-aged worker will be out of work longer, but is more likely to find a job that pays more than the previous one.

Answers to Multiple-Choice Questions

1. a 2. d 3. a 4. d 5. c 6. c 7. d 8. b 9. d
10. d 11. b 12. b 13. b 14. d 15. a 16. c 17. b
18. a 19. b 20. c

Chapter 18

Physical and Cognitive Development in Later Adulthood

Chapter Outline

- Exception or Rule?
- Life Span
- Are People Living Longer? Life Expectancy
- The Health of Older People
- Mental Health
- Predictors of Longevity and Functioning
- Sensory Changes in Later Adulthood
- Cognitive Development in Later Adulthood
- Controversial Issues: The Older Driver
- Intelligence in Later Adulthood
- Memory in Later Adulthood
- The Triple Challenge

Are the Following Statements True or False?

1. After years of gain in life expectancy, recently there has been a gradual reduction in the number of years a person can be expected to live.
2. Although women outlive men in the United States, this is not true in western Europe or in industrialized countries in other parts of the world.
3. The elderly have the highest accident rate of any age group.
4. Most elderly people rate their health positively.
5. The most common emotional problem found in elderly people is depression.
6. The majority of elderly people over 70 years have some form of disorder that causes senility, such as Alzheimer's disease.
7. Most people show some hearing loss by the time they are in their 70s.
8. Elderly people experience pain more intensely than younger adults.
9. Most elderly people show significant declines in most elements of intelligence in their 60s.
10. Elderly people remember the general idea of what they hear or see as well as younger adults.

Answers to True-False Statements 1. False: see p. 419 2. False: see p. 419 3. False: see p. 421 4. True 5. True 6. False: see p. 424 7. True 8. False: see p. 429 9. False: see p. 429 10. True

Exception or Rule?

Dr. Benjamin Spock was over 90 years old when he wrote a book on children. Mother Teresa, at the age of 84, continued to work with sick and poor people in Calcutta, India. Former president of the United States, Jimmy Carter, was 70 when he represented the United States in talks with North Korea and Haiti, and continues to help build housing for poor people. Nelson Mandela, 75, president of South Africa, won the Nobel Peace Prize in 1994 (Schrof, 1994). Golda Meir was 71 years old when she became Prime Minister of Israel. Benjamin Franklin signed the Constitution of the United States when he was 81. These are just a few examples of people who have achieved greatness in their later years.

Do you consider a physically active or intellectually capable elderly person an exception to the rule? The stereotype that many people have of elderly people involves physical and mental decline. People often believe that elderly people are sick all the time and that a steep mental decline is inevitable, that elderly people cannot remember much, and cannot learn or change. As we shall see, each of these is patently untrue.

The issues that surround the physical and intellectual functioning of elderly people are especially relevant because people can expect to live much longer today than ever before. What can people expect from their "golden years?" The answer is: much more than most people think.

Life Span

Even if we eliminated all diseases, people would not live forever. All species seem to be bounded in how long they live. The maximum longevity of the species, sometimes called the **life span,** is the biological limit of life (DiGiovanna, 1994). Each species has its own life span: the Norway rat lives for 4 years, the gray squirrel can live for 15 years, the kangaroo for 20 years, the capuchin monkey for 40, the coyote for 16, the Asiatic elephant for 70, and the hippopotamus for 51 (Sacher, 1977). The maximum number of years that humans live is somewhat over 100, perhaps up to 120 years or so. In 1995 the oldest recorded living human being, Jeanne Calment, turned 120 years old (Newsday, October 16, 1995).

Questions Students Often Ask

What about all those people on commercials claiming to be 150 years old? How can the life span be 150?

I've seen these claims, too, but those people aren't really that old. Occasionally, some elders in a rural mountainous part of a particular country, such as Ecuador or Russia, may claim that people in their village are that old, but scientific investigation proves these claims to be untrue. In one case, people actually showed researchers birth certificates. The only problem was that they actually belonged to their grandparents whom they were named after. One reason these villages seem to have so many elderly people is that many of the younger people have left to find better economic opportunities, leaving a greater percentage of elderly people.

This does not mean that these people have nothing to teach us. Many elderly people in these societies are quite active and do not show the negative effects of aging, especially in their cardiovascular system, perhaps because of their activity level and diet.

Evidence exists that the maximum longevity increased rapidly for human beings until about 100,000 years ago.

life span The biological limit to the length of life of a particular species.

Since then, any increase has been very slight (Hayflick, 1994). This does not mean that a change cannot take place, either through evolution or through intervention to alter genes.

The maximum longevity appears to be determined by between 7 and 20 genes (DiGiovanna, 1994). The position of these genes on the chromosomes has not been identified, but the search for genes involved in the aging process is ongoing; these genes in some way control the biological process of aging.

Some evidence for genetic control comes from animal studies showing that rats, for example, can be bred for longevity. Other evidence for genetic involvement in aging comes from twin studies. When 1000 pairs of twins were followed for years to study their aging processes, identical twins were consistently more likely than fraternal twins to contract certain diseases like cancer and to die closer together than fraternal twins (Hayflick, 1994; Jarvik & Falek, 1962).

The most fascinating evidence in favor of the genetic theory of aging comes from some unique studies performed by Leonard Hayflick (1994; 1977; 1974). Hayflick grew embryonic tissue in the laboratory in a disease-free environment and found that the cells grew and divided perfectly for months. The cells then began to slow down, stopped dividing, and died, after undergoing 50 cell divisions. Cells obtained from young adults multiplied only about 30 times. Some cultures were allowed to divide 30 times and then were frozen. When thawed, the cultures divided only another 20 times or so and then died. As these cells aged, it took more time for them to double. In addition, a definite reduction in metabolic rate was evident. An accumulation of cellular debris and a total degeneration of the cell tissue took place. People do not die because their cells stop regenerating. We all die well before this. What is most important is the potential limit on life and the possibility that the changes in cell biochemistry associated with the aging cell may tell us something about why we age.

One's genes may affect the aging process through changes in the chemical processes within the cell. Changes in these processes, including a loss of efficiency in the cell's operation, might be built in (Watkin, 1983). Another possibility involves genetic control over our immune system. As we age our immune system may weaken, making us more vulnerable to many diseases (Walford, 1983). This theory may well explain why the elderly are more vulnerable to disease, but whether it can explain the aging process itself is still controversial.

Perhaps errors in cellular regeneration are responsible for aging and susceptibility to disease. For the body to survive, cells must reproduce, and the result must be a perfect copy of the parent cell. According to the cellular error theory of aging, as we age, more mistakes occur in the copying process, allowing inaccurate genetic information to be delivered to the next generation of cells. This impairs the functioning of these cells, and aging—perhaps even death—results when the errors are great (Saxon & Etten, 1978).

If we found out why we age, could we increase our life span and live perhaps 200 years? If there are specific genes that control the aging process, it may be possible in the far future to alter these genes so that we age more slowly. However, even if these genes are identified, it is doubtful that scientists will be able to increase the maximum life expectancy of human beings in the near future (Hayflick, 1994).

Are People Living Longer? Life Expectancy

Perhaps we should forget about living 200 years and concentrate on living the full 100 or so years that we appear to be programmed to live. **Life expectancy,** sometimes called *average longevity,* is the average remaining lifetime for a population at any given age (Jackson, 1980). A person's life expectancy from birth cannot exceed the life span, but it can approximate it.

Progress in this area is nothing short of sensational, and people in the United States and in many other countries throughout the world are living longer. Someone born in

life expectancy The average remaining lifetime for a particular population at a given age.

Table 18.1 **Expectation of Life at Selected Ages, by Race and Sex: Death-Registration States, 1900–1902, and United States, 1959–1961, 1969–1971, 1979–1981, and 1994**

LIFE TABLE VALUE, PERIOD, AND AGE	TOTAL	WHITE		ALL OTHER: TOTAL		ALL OTHER: AFRICAN AMERICAN	
		Male	Female	Male	Female	Male	Female
Expectation of life							
At birth							
1994	75.7	73.2	79.6	67.5	75.8	64.9	74.1
1979–1981	73.88	70.82	78.22	65.63	74.00	64.10	72.88
1969–1971	70.75	67.94	75.49	60.98	69.05	60.00	68.32
1959–1961	69.89	67.55	74.19	61.48	66.47	—	—
1900–1902	49.24	48.23	51.08	—	—	32.54	35.04

Source: Data from Department of Health and Human Services, 1991, *Statistical Abstract,* 1996.

1850 in the United States could expect to live for 38.3 years; someone born in the 1951 could expect to live for about 68 years, and an American infant born in 1994 could expect to live for 75.7 years (Statistical Abstract, 1996; see Table 18.1). Some authorities predict that by the beginning of the next century an infant will have a life expectancy of 80. These gains in life expectancy are not continuous; relative stagnation was the rule in the 1960s whereas the 1970s saw significant increases (Metropolitan Life, 1986a).

True or False?
After years of gain in life expectancy, recently there has been a gradual reduction in the number of years a person can be expected to live.

As much as 85% of the increase in average life expectancy is the result of the decline in infant mortality (Go, Brustrom, Lynch, & Aldwin, 1995). Improvements in medical care and nutrition have helped reduce the numbers of children who die in infancy and early childhood. In 1900, 100 of every 1000 infants died during the first year of life; today that number is about 12 per 1000, and this has greatly affected the average life expectancy (Chiras, 1993).

Life expectancy tables also offer figures for average expected life at various ages. For example, a person born in 1994 could expect to live 75.7 years; but if you were 65 years old in 1994, you could expect to live another 17 years or so. It seems that the older you are, the longer you are expected to live! This is true because by the time you have reached 65, you have escaped disease at earlier ages, and statistics tell us that you have a better chance of living even past the average life expectancy. If you are 85 years old, your life expectancy is 6 years.

Some people claim that any future gains in life expectancy will be modest, even if major causes of death, such as heart disease and cancer, are eliminated (Olshansky, Carnes, & Cassel, 1990). Others believe that we can expect rather impressive gains in the future (Cooke, 1990). It remains to be seen which prediction is correct.

Do Women Live Longer Than Men?

At every age, the life expectancy of women is significantly higher than that for men. For example, among newborn white males in 1994, life expectancy increased to 73.2 years whereas the life expectancy for white females rose to 79.6 years (Statistical Abstract, 1996). The same female superiority in life expectancy is found among the nonwhite population as well. This pattern of women outliving men is found in developed countries throughout the world (Metropolitan Life, 1986). This superiority continues throughout life. The gender differential for people over 65 has actually widened since the turn of the century (Turner, 1982).

True or False?
Although women outlive men in the United States, this is not true in western Europe or in industrialized countries in other parts of the world.

We do not know for certain why women outlive men (Hayflick, 1994). Genetic differences may explain some of the pattern (Huyck, 1990). Females have more resistance than males to infectious diseases, presumably because X chromosomes carry genes for producing disease-fighting immunities (Goble & Konopka, 1973). In addition, men's higher metabolic rate may reduce their average longevity (Hayflick, 1994). Infant mortality is also considerably higher for males than for females, a difference that cannot be attributed to variations in socialization; genetic differences, then, may be one key.

Lifestyle differences are also important. The most common causes of male death at older ages are heart disease, cancer, stroke, and cirrhosis of the liver. Although genetic factors may be involved in these diseases, environmental factors as reflected in lifestyle are also important. Men are more likely to die from traffic and hunting accidents. Diet may be still another factor because until re-

Women outlive men in Western societies, although the reasons for this are still under study.

cently, women were much more likely than men to watch their diets.

Males are also much less likely to survive illnesses than females. For example, men are much more likely to succumb to heart attacks, strokes, cancer, various respiratory diseases, accidents, liver disease, and attempted suicide and more likely to be murdered than women (Center for Health Statistics, 1993). Males postpone going to the doctor and do not seem to take care of themselves as well. If the differences in lifestyle and vulnerability to mortality from these causes could be resolved, the gender gap would be substantially reduced or would even disappear. Genetic and lifestyle factors are both involved (Anstey et al., 1993).

Racial Differences in Life Expectancy

Tables of life expectancy are also stratified by race. Throughout life, white males have longer life expectancies than African-American males, and the same relationship holds for females. However, African American females live longer than white males. The gaps are narrowing considerably. Since 1980 longevity gains among African Americans have actually outpaced those of whites.

The racial differences in survival appear to be due mostly to social factors, such as medical care and nutrition. Also, minorities in the United States tend to live in environments where violent crime is more common. If social factors are controlled, African Americans have either lower or equivalent rates on most causes of mortality (Rogers, 1992). The narrowing continues to occur, but does so more slowly. It will take many years for the statistics to show no difference between whites and nonwhites.

Despite the size and rapid growth of the Latino population, little is known about the mortality and health of elderly Latinos because of the absence of national data as well as the wide variations among various Latino populations (Markides & Black, 1996). What data exists shows that Latinos generally are more similar to non-Latino whites than to African Americans, probably because of cultural factors such as diet as well as other factors not well understood. The life expectancy for Asian Americans is at least as high as for white Americans and probably higher, perhaps because of diet and better socioeconomic status. The life expectancy of Native Americans has also been increasing, although it is still lower than that for whites; the improvement is the result of better control of infectious diseases and better acute care.

Social class differences, regardless of race, also exist. Evidence indicates that poor people do not live as long as people in the upper socioeconomic level. Reduced access to health care, greater stress, and greater exposure to crime reduce life expectancy. The lower educational level that often correlates with lower income status may make it more difficult to understand and use some health information. Although certainly genetic factors are involved in aging and life expectancy, it is also clear that lifestyle choices and social factors are important.

The Health of Older People

Old age is often linked with illness and, indeed, elderly people are more likely to be ill than younger people. As we age, chronic diseases become more frequent whereas acute diseases become less so. **Chronic diseases,** such as diabetes, heart disease, and arthritis, are long, lingering illnesses that are usually progressive and irreversible. About 85% of all people over age 65 suffer from at least one chronic disease (Belsky, 1990). **Acute diseases** occur suddenly, run their course, and disappear. The elderly are more likely to suffer from chronic health problems (Metropolitan Life, 1984).

Aging and illness are not the same. Most of the common problems of the elderly do not begin in old age, but are the result of lifestyle choices that begin much earlier, such as poor diet and lack of exercise. This is why a lifespan perspective is so useful. Some of the physical changes of aging may result in health problems. For example, increases in blood pressure and reduced elasticity of the arteries may cause heart and circulatory problems. However, most physical aging can be summed up as a general slowing and is not in itself related to illness.

Heart Disease, Cancer, and Stroke

Heart disease (see p. 373) is the most common cause of death in the elderly, even though the incidence of death from heart disease has been declining for decades (DiGiovanna, 1994). Hypertension, or high blood pressure, rises with advancing years (Hockheimer, 1989).

The second most common cause of death among the elderly is cancer (see p. 375) (Kochanek & Hudson, 1994). The incidence and mortality of most cancers increase with age (Williamson & Schulz, 1995). About two thirds of all cancer deaths occur in the elderly (Manton et al., 1991). The reason for the elderly's special vulnerability to cancer is still unknown.

Stroke, also called cerebrovascular disease, the third leading cause of death among the elderly, results from a disruption in cerebral blood flow and affects more than 550,000 people each year (Lane, 1995). A stroke may result either from a substantial reduction in blood flow to the brain or from bleeding in the brain (Kaufman & Becker, 1991). The reduced blood flow is sometimes caused by a blood clot in the lining of the cerebral artery. Bleeding may be caused by a rupture of blood vessels in the brain, causing brain damage.

Strokes are related to hypertension and arteriosclerosis. They are characterized by periods of unconsciousness and some degree of paralysis. The severity of a stroke depends upon where the blockage in the brain is located

chronic diseases Diseases, such as arthritis, that linger on for an extended period of time.

acute diseases Diseases with a sharp onset and rapid development.

as well as the amount of brain tissue involved. Although all strokes cause some permanent damage, their effects vary greatly. About 30% of all strokes are fatal (Lane, 1995). Some people experience loss of muscular function that may respond to rehabilitation whereas still others become greatly impaired.

Stroke is considered one of the most crippling of all human disabilities (Statistical Bulletin, 1989). Stroke survivors often face years of physical and mental impairment, emotional stress, and great expense. The long-term nature of the disease has led many researchers to look for ways to prevent strokes by identifying people who are at risk. Recently, new medications that prevent blood clots have been discovered which may prevent strokes in people who suffer from a condition in which the heart beats rapidly and irregularly, allowing the blood to pool, causing clots that travel to the brain causing strokes (Lane, 1995). There is hope that vascular surgery and medications now being developed may help to prevent strokes in the future.

Osteoporosis

Osteoporosis, which involves a gradual decrease in bone mass (Figure 18.1), is most commonly found in postmenopausal women. By about 60 years of age, 20% to 25% of women and 5% of men have osteoporosis (Hongladarom, McCorkle, & Woods, 1982).

osteoporosis A disorder, mostly of postmenopausal women, characterized by a loss of bone tissue that causes the bones to become porous and fracture easily.

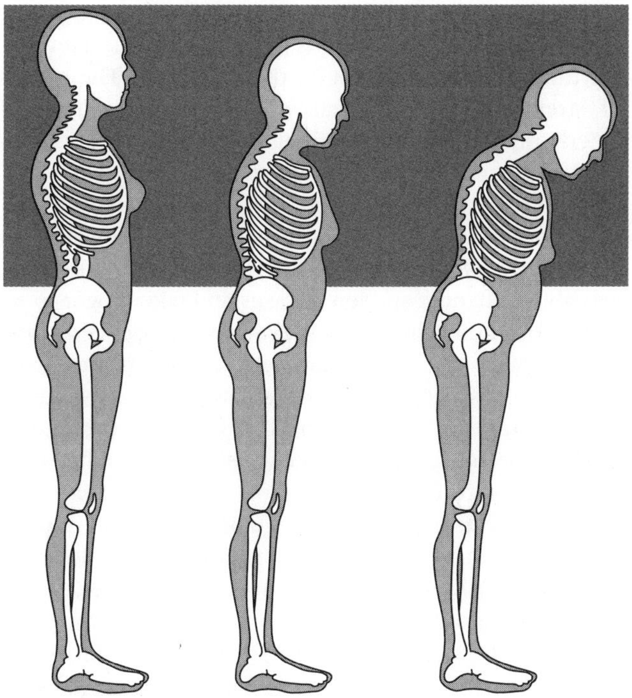

Figure 18.1
Osteoporosis Spinal vertebrae weakened by osteoporosis collapse, causing loss of height (all from the upper part of the body), inward curvature of the lower spine, outward curvature of the upper spine, and protrusion of the abdomen.
Source: Notelovitz & Ware, 1982.

Everyone loses bone mass with age, but the process can be dangerous if it is accelerated. As bones become more brittle and weak, fractures are more likely to occur—one of the most dangerous of these is the hip fracture (Wolinsky & Fitzgerald, 1994). Osteoporosis can also lead to physical deformities, including a stooping posture (Notelovitz & Ware, 1982).

The cause of osteoporosis is thought to be a longstanding calcium deficiency along with the decrease in the ability to absorb the mineral (Hamilton, Whitney, & Sizer, 1991). The calcium need of late middle-aged and elderly people is greater than that of younger people, but older people may not consume enough food containing calcium.

The sex hormones—estrogen and androgen—both work against the process by which bone is broken down. The reduced estrogen production in menopause increases the rate of bone loss. There is no way to restore bone that has been lost, but the rate of loss can be reduced and perhaps prevented through diet, adequate exercise, and sometimes hormone treatment (Anderson, 1987). Hormone therapy consisting of estrogen and progestin is sometimes used (Notelovitz & Ware, 1982).

Accidents

Children have the highest accident rate in the United States; accidents are the leading cause of death among children and adolescents (Statistical Bulletin, 1996). The accident rate among older adults is relatively low compared with other age groups, but when the elderly have an accident, it tends to be more serious (Sterns et al., 1985).

> ***True or False?***
> The elderly have the highest accident rate of any age group.

Degeneration and brittleness of bones, often caused by osteoporosis, frequently result in fractures from falls. Fractures in elderly people take a long time to heal, and the elderly are more likely to suffer from complications. Most falls occur in the home, but outside environmental hazards, such as ice and stairs, also take their toll (Burker et al., 1995); fear of falling is the most common fear in elderly people (Walker & Howland, 1990).

The Health Status of Older People

Considering all this, you would probably be surprised to discover that elderly people are actually fairly healthy! The majority are in good health and rate their own health positively (see Table 18.2) (Ferraro, 1980). Most elderly people are active, and although they suffer from chronic conditions, they deal with them well (Botwinick, 1984). Timothy Salthouse and colleagues (1990) investigated how adults from age 20 through 70 rated their own

Table 18.2 **How the Elderly Rate Their Own Health**
Most elderly perceive their health as good, very good, or excellent.

PERCEIVED HEALTH STATUS	65–74 YEARS	75 YEARS AND OVER
Excellent	15.5%	15.8%
Very good	19.6%	18.6%
Good	32.5%	30.8%
Fair	21.4%	21.3%
Poor	10.6%	13.0%

Source: Data from National Center for Health Statistics, 1986.

health. As one would expect, as people got older, heart and blood pressure problems as well as the use of medications increased. However, there was *no* relationship between age and self-assessed health status. Older adults rate their health better than one might expect if a more objective view based on medical records is taken (Tran, Wright, & Chatters, 1991). Despite their health problems, elderly people are more positive in their evaluation of their overall quality of life than younger adults.

True or False?
Most elderly people rate their health positively.

Questions Students Often Ask

How can elderly people rate their health positively and still suffer from all these chronic disorders?
A number of reasons explain this paradox. First, elderly people compare their health status to others of their own age group. Second, they are not as active as younger people, so a chronic disorder may not limit their sources of enjoyment as much as it would in a younger individual.

This unusual state of affairs exists because the elderly compare their health status with others of the same age instead of with younger people. In addition, people rate their health as negative when it requires some limitation of activity. Because elderly people are usually less active, their symptoms do not limit their activity as much as one would think. This explains why people in their 60s actually define their health as better than the health of younger adults (Cockerman, Sharp, & Wilcox, 1983).

Stress

The life stresses the elderly are most likely to experience, as detailed by the life events scale (see p. 326), include the death of a spouse (the greatest stress on the scale), death of close family members, injury and illness, retirement, change in a family member's health, change in residence, and change in financial status. Stress also arises from everyday hassles. The elderly experience fewer of these daily hassles—for example, they do not have a daily commute. Even if they are employed, they are not likely to be trying to claw their way up through the ranks. They have also finished raising their children. Elderly people deal with daily health-related hassles, such as dressing themselves despite experiencing arthritis pain, but their daily lives can be organized around what they want to do—the daily rushing around of younger years is over.

Older people reported fewer sources of stress than younger individuals (Chiriboga & Cutler, 1980). They also seemed to be less preoccupied with stress. They worry much less about money and social relationships than younger adults (Powers, Wisocki, & Whitbourne, 1992). Not only do they have less stress, but the elderly also appear better able to distance themselves from stress (Chiriboga & Dean, 1978).

Some types of stress are reduced in old age whereas other types are not. For example, elderly people report more health-related stress and less stress relating to family and work (McCrae, 1982). Many of the stresses of old age entail "exit events" such as the death of a loved one and retirement whereas the stresses of youth involve "entrance events" such as starting a family. Elderly people who are poor or trying to live on a fixed income can have significant financial stresses and daily life can be stressful as they try to pay their bills.

Stress is related to physical and psychological problems at every age. It can accelerate the aging process or lead to physical disease by reducing the organism's capacity to respond to it (Eisdorfer & Wilkie, 1977). On the other hand, some people may consider a stressful situation a challenge. As discussed in earlier chapters, the cognitive interpretation of the stress is a vital factor in determining the influence of stress on the individual. The effects of stress on psychological well-being are reduced if elderly people are independent and perceive themselves as in control of events (Roberts, Dunkle, & Haug, 1994).

Although the results of studies are somewhat mixed, older people seem to cope with stress similarly to younger people (McCrae, 1982). However, the elderly are less able to handle sudden stresses and take longer to regain their equilibrium after they have experienced stress (Saxon & Etten, 1978). Others believe that a change from active to passive mastery of stress occurs. Especially when it appears that nothing can be done, the elderly seem to be more likely to accept situations rather than challenge or confront them.

The conclusion concerning elderly people's health runs somewhat counter to conventional wisdom. Although the elderly are more vulnerable to disease, a great deal depends upon the choices they make throughout their lives. In an important study called The MacArthur Field Study of Successful Aging, high-functioning 70- to 79-year-old men and women were compared with medium- and low-functioning subjects over time (Beckman et al., 1993). Both declines and improvements in functioning were found. Health declines were related to lack of economic resources and poorer initial health profiles, including higher body mass index, poorer breathing, high blood pressure, or diabetes. Those who were healthiest remained so. Although some subjects did show declines in performance, a majority maintained or improved their relatively high levels of physical functioning over time. Physical exercise and emotional support from one's social network predicted better physical performance, even when socioeconomic factors and health status were taken into consideration (Seeman et al., 1995). People who practice good health habits continue to practice them and are more resistant to disease. Even in later maturity, people can make decisions that can help them maintain their health and increase their ability to function independently.

Mental Health

Most elderly people are in good mental health (Cohen, 1990). However, mental illness does occur more often in older adults than in younger people. The most important are chronic organic mental disorders, such as depression and Alzheimer's disease.

Depression

The most prevalent emotional problem found in elderly people is depression (Gatz & Hurwicz, 1990). About 3% to 5% of older adults experience major clinical depression and another 12% to 15% suffer from significant depressive symptoms (Thompson, Heller, & Rody, 1994). Certain economic and medical risk factors are related to depression in elderly people (Rabbitt et al., 1995). A relationship exists between pain, functional disability, and depression. As pain increases over time, so does activity restriction, which predicts increases in depression. Although younger people are somewhat more distressed by reduced activity than older people, older people are also affected (Williamson & Schulz, 1995). Generally, daily strains, especially those of coping with physical limitations, are more strongly associated with depression than life events (Roberts et al., 1994). When elderly patients have psychological problems, such as depression, they consult their primary care physicians rather than mental health professionals; therefore, doctors must recognize and treat depression in the elderly (Callahan et al., 1994).

> ***True or False?***
> The most common emotional problem found in elderly people is depression.

The causes of depression in elderly people include isolation and loneliness, bereavement, loss of role, poor health, alcoholism, and changes in brain chemistry (researchers have linked depression to changes in neurotransmitters; Callahan et al., 1994; LaRue, Dessonville, & Jarvik, 1985). Sometimes depression is a side effect of some of the medications elderly people take.

Loss of role is an important environmental factor in depression. Unlike other societies in which the role of elderly people is spelled out clearly and older adults are rewarded for their status and wisdom, the elderly population in the United States is not given a socially important role. Elderly people who live in societies where they have such a role suffer less depression (Altrocchi, 1980).

Social support may help to prevent depression as well as to reduce depressive symptoms. Deficits in social support have a direct effect on level of depression even 1 year after a major stress, and lack of social support increases the likelihood of experiencing stressful daily hassles (Russell & Cutrona, 1991). Social support communicates a regard for personal value and provides encouragement and assistance.

Depression is the most treatable psychiatric disorder of later life (Blazer, 1989), and is often treated successfully if the cause is environmental and not caused by deterioration of the brain (Van der Plaats, 1983). Medication, improved nutrition, increased social support and social interaction, and psychotherapy can be successful.

Suicide Among Older People

The rate of suicide is higher among elderly people than among any other age group (Sorenson, 1991). The rate of suicide by Americans over 65 increased substantially between 1980 and 1992, accounting for almost 20% of all suicides (JAMA, 1996a). From the end of World War II to 1980, the suicide rate among elderly people had shown a significant decrease, probably because of improvements in the economic status of elderly people (McCall, 1991). The reasons for the increase since 1981 are unknown. Technological advances that extend the lives of elderly people but do not add to the quality of their lives and medical treatments that deplete family savings may lead to depression and/or suicide (Tolchin, 1989). This theory is supported by the fact that the increase in the suicide rate is found largely in those aged 75 or over (McCall, 1991). Women are less likely to be suicide victims, perhaps because they seek professional help more often for depression and feelings of hopelessness, which are the most common emotional factors preceding a suicide attempt (Canetto, 1992).

Elderly people commonly do not threaten suicide and give fewer hints of their intentions than younger people. Most elderly suicide victims visit a doctor in the month before committing suicide, but the doctor probably does not recognize the suicide potential (Sorenson, 1991). Among the warning signs of suicide are depression, withdrawal, bereavement, expectation of death, less organization and complexity of behavior, helplessness, physical illness and pain, alcoholism, reaching a decision that one's life has no purpose, and organic deterioration. Loneliness is a prime cause. Elderly people are more likely to be lonely because their friends die, they live alone, suffer depression, and are more reluctant to seek help (Kastenbaum, 1992). However, these are symptoms that are found in many people who do not attempt suicide. Although predicting suicide is difficult in many cases, being aware of the possibility of it is a starting place.

Organic Syndromes

Although depression may be the most common mental health problem, senile **dementia** is the most feared (Gatz, Smyer, & Lawton, 1980). The most serious threats to the mental health of elderly people are chronic brain dysfunctions. About 15% of those over 65 years suffer from some form of dementia—brain tissue deterioration resulting in reduced intellectual ability to the point that social and vocational functioning is impaired (Davison & Neale, 1995). That means that 85% of elderly people do *not* show such dementia—an important and often unpublicized fact. The symptoms of dementia include mental confusion, memory loss, disorientation, cognitive decline, and inappropriate social behavior (Huang, Cartwright, & Hu, 1988). Senile dementia is better thought of as a syndrome—a collection of symptoms—than as one disease. There are some 60 disorders that can cause dementia (Elias, Elias, & Elias, 1990), but the most common is **Alzheimer's disease.**

True or False?
The majority of elderly people over 70 years have some form of disorder that causes senility, such as Alzheimer's disease.

The announcement that Ronald Reagan, former president of the United States, has Alzheimer's disease has focused attention on this disease.

Alzheimer's Disease

Ronald Reagan, former president of the United States, announced in a press statement that he had Alzheimer's disease. His wife, Nancy Reagan, noted in an advertisement that "Alzheimer's disease can change your life. It changed mine" (Newsday, March 23, 1995); Alzheimer's disease affects the entire family.

Alzheimer's disease is the fourth leading cause of death in the United States (Kolata, 1991), although this fact is not always clearly reflected in the statistics. Patients with Alzheimer's often linger in a very weakened state for 15 or more years and finally die from another disorder because of their weakened condition (Heckler, 1985). Pneumonia is the most common cause of death in elderly patients suffering from Alzheimer's disease; in 30% of all such cases, Alzheimer's disease is not even stated as a contributing cause of death (Burns et al., 1990).

Alzheimer's disease is a progressive and irreversible deterioration of brain tissue that is marked by mental disorientation, social withdrawal, and loss of memory (Monti et al., 1995; Anderson, 1987). Alzheimer's patients have difficulty naming objects and show other language problems, such as not being able to describe how a table and a chair are alike (Bayles & Trosset, 1992; Nebes, Boller, & Holland, 1986). The symptoms of memory loss, bizarre behavior, and intellectual deficits result from changes that take place within the brain. Although memory problems are the hallmark of the disorder (Lipinska, Backman, & Herlitz, 1992), it is the behavioral or psychiatric problems that make home care difficult and may cause institutionalization. Personality changes also occur as sufferers become more self-centered, agitated, and suspicious (Rubin et al., 1986). Estimates of the disease's prevalence vary, but about 6% of people aged 65 to 75 have the disorder, about 10% of the population between 75 and 85 have it, and 20% of those over 85 suffer from it (Heckler, 1985). Four million Americans have the disease (Kolata, 1991).

Since Alzheimer's disease was first identified in 1906 much has been learned about it, but its cause remains unknown. Diagnosis is difficult because the symptoms are common to other disorders found in the elderly. The only way to positively diagnose Alzheimer's disease is through examination of brain tissue (Heckler, 1985); of course, this is not practical. When autopsies are performed on victims of Alzheimer's disease, certain irregularities of the brain can be observed. One of these irregularities is the accumulation of abnormal fibers in the neurons, called neurofibrillary tangles. These fibers occur mostly in a part of the brain called the hippocampus, which controls memory and emotion, which might explain the memory and emotional problems. Other observable irregularities in the brain are neuritic plaques (collections of degenerated cell material) and granulovacuolar degeneration, which occurs when the cell becomes filled with cavities (vacuoles) and fluid and other material. The greater the degeneration, the greater the loss of mental function. The most common method of diagnosis is to rule out all other possible reasons for the behavior. The search is on for new ways to diagnose the disease by brain scans and behavioral and psychological measures (Baltes, Kuhl, Gutzmann, & Sowarka, 1995).

New research relates certain linguistic and memory abilities to the early stages of the disease; other studies are searching for early markers that may predict a significant risk of later developing Alzheimer's disease. New

dementia A condition consisting of impaired judgment and a reduction in intellectual ability that interferes with daily functioning and is caused by physical deterioration of brain tissue.

Alzheimer's disease An organic disorder of the elderly involving progressive and irreversible deterioration of brain tissue, causing cognitive and behavioral deficits.

ways of diagnosing and predicting Alzheimer's disease may come from such research. In one study, handwritten biographies of a group of nuns born before 1917 were analyzed. The nuns averaged about 22 years when these statements were written. Two linguistic abilities, idea density and grammatical complexity, were analyzed. Idea density is the average number of ideas expressed in a certain number of words; grammatical complexity refers to the complexity of clauses and sentence structure (see Table 18.3 for an example of the lowest and highest scores on these linguistic variables).

Between 1991 and 1993 the cognitive functioning of these nuns, who were then between 75 and 96 years of age, were analyzed. Low linguistic ability at 22 years was related to poor cognitive functioning and an increased risk of Alzheimer's disease later in life. Low idea density in early life was present in 90% of those with Alzheimer's disease compared with 13% in those without Alzheimer's disease. These findings support a strong relationship between cognitive ability in early life as indicated by linguistic ability and cognitive function and Alzheimer's disease in later life (Snowdon et al., 1996). A weaker association was found for grammatical complexity. The researchers suggest that low linguistic ability in early life may be an early expression of Alzheimer's disease pathology. However, the researchers do not know whether changes in the brain produce low linguistic ability in early life or whether low linguistic ability in early life accelerates the development of neurological problems later in life.

What causes the disease? Some researchers believe that neurotransmitter and neurochemical deficits are the culprits; others point to an excessive accumulation of toxins in the brain, one being aluminum. Abnormally high levels of aluminum have been found in many (but not all) people suffering from the disease. Although we are all exposed to large amounts of aluminum, most healthy people show very little of it in their systems. Why and how people with Alzheimer's retain such quantities of the substance is not yet known (Turkington, 1987).

Some researchers believe that Alzheimer's disease is an autoimmune disorder, (Heckler, 1985) whereas other authorities believe that some cases of Alzheimer's disease have a genetic basis (Kolata, 1991). Some of the genes that might be involved are associated with the brain protein called beta amyloid. In Alzheimer's disease, fragments of the protein form masses outside the dead and dying nerve cells in the brain, and there is evidence for a mutation on chromosome 21 that directs the cells to produce beta amyloid. Other researchers argue that the disease is inherited through genes found on other chromosomes, yet family histories are not present in many cases (Rosenhan & Seligman, 1995).

The course of the disease varies, but it can be described in terms of four phases. In the first phase, the person has less energy and reacts slowly. Throughout the course of the disease, memory impairment becomes progressively more serious (Vitaliano et al., 1986). Linguistic problems such as the inability to find the correct word are common (Bayles & Tomoeda, 1991). These problems emerge early, and an inability to complete sentences, a failure to recognize humor, speaking inappropriately, reading comprehension problems, and a tendency to utter meaningless sentences occur. Depression is seen in between 20% and 30% of these cases (Teri & Wagner, 1991). In the second phase, the patient's speech slows, and the patient has difficulty planning ahead, becomes mentally confused, cannot follow a story, and becomes self-absorbed and in-

Table 18.3 **Examples of the Computation of Idea Density (ID) and Grammatical Complexity (GC)***

SISTER A	SISTER B
I was born in Eau Claire, Wis, on May 24, 1913 and was baptized in St James Church. (ID = 3.9; GC = 0)	The happiest day of my life so far was my First Communion Day which was in June nineteen hundred and twenty when I was but eight years of age, and four years later in the same month I was confirmed by Bishop D. D. McGavick. (ID = 8.6; GC = 7)
Two of the boys are dead. (ID = 3.3; GC = 0)	I visited the capitol in Madison and also the Motherhouse of the Franciscan Sisters of Perpetual Adoration at Duluth which visit increased my love for Notre Dame, because it was and is Notre Dame. (ID = 9.1; GC = 7)
I prefer teaching music to any other profession. (ID = 5.0; GC = 5)	Now I am wandering about in "Dove's Lane" waiting, yet only three more weeks, to follow in the footprints of my Spouse, bound to Him by the Holy Vows of Poverty, Chastity, and Obedience. (ID = 9.1; GC = 7)

*Of the 93 Milwaukee sisters, sisters A and B had the lowest and highest scores on ID and GC. Each of their autobiographies contained 10 sentences, and this table includes their first, fifth, and 10th sentences. Ideas expressed in sister A's first sentence were (1) I was born; (2) born in Eau Claire Wis; (3) born on May 24, 1913; (4) I was baptized; (5) was baptized in church; (6) was baptized in St James Church; and (7) I was born . . . and was baptized. There were 18 words or utterances in that sentence. The ID for that sentence was 3.9 (i.e., 7 ideas divided by 18 words and multiplied by 10 to yield a score of 3.9 ideas per 10 words). Sister A died with neuropathologically confirmed Alzheimer's disease: sister B is alive without cognitive impairment. To ensure anonymity, all dates and proper nouns in each autobiography were changed.
Source: Snowden et al., 1996.

sensitive to the needs of others. In the third phase, the patient loses orientation to time and place and may not be able to identify familiar people. In the fourth and last phase, the patient is apathetic and completely unable to function, even in familiar surroundings, and requires help with everyday living. Sometimes delusions and delirium occur.

Alzheimer's disease affects the whole family (Lieberman & Fisher, 1995; Wright, 1991). The aged spouse or adult children must contend with economic responsibilities and household chores. Communication becomes difficult. Tension increases in the family. The spouse of the afflicted individual loses companionship and may be overwhelmed. The people who care for Alzheimer's patients may experience depression and anxiety disorders (Dura et al., 1990; 1991). Although the chronic stress of care-giving is associated with declines in psychological and immunological function, not all care-givers are equally affected. The severity of the patient's symptoms certainly affects the care-givers. The greater the patient's memory and behavior difficulties, the greater the care-giver's burden and depression (Majerovitz, 1995). The care-giver's abilities are important and those high in adaptability do better. Adaptability is the ability of the family to change power structure, role relationships, and relationship rules in response to new situations (Olson 1991). Such factors as good social contacts, high family cohesiveness, and religious faith seem to moderate stress (Lee & Gottlib, 1994; Uchino, Kiecolt-Glaser & Cacioppo, 1994). Even family members not responsible for the patient's daily care are adversely affected (Lieberman & Fisher, 1995).

Treatment involves administration of drugs to limit symptoms. Research into Alzheimer's disease is expanding rapidly, but it will be some time before we have all the answers.

Predictors of Longevity and Functioning

Only a minority of all elderly people are depressed and suffer from dementia and most do not consider themselves disabled by their physical difficulties. People are living longer and functioning independently in most cases. What factors contribute to longevity and to remaining fully functional in old age?

Longevity studies are correlational and do not indicate cause and effect. In addition, the correlations are not perfect. However, the predictors do present us with some interesting data. Nine factors stand out that slow the rate of aging, delay the development of disease, and correlate with longevity: exercise, not smoking, moderation of alcohol consumption, not being obese, proper diet, avoidance of environmental toxins, use of mature defense mechanisms (such as humor, altruism, mild denial, or suppression), a belief in one's own worth, and avoidance of injury by taking such precautions as wearing seat belts (Fries & Crapo, 1981). Genetic endowment is also a factor, but the extent to which genetics is involved is not known at this time. Notice with the exception of genetic factors, other factors involve lifestyle choices. Two of these factors require further explanation: exercise and nutrition.

Exercise

Elderly people are generally not physically fit. In the areas of strength, endurance, flexibility, and speed, older people do quite poorly (Kozma, Stones, & Hannah, 1991). Many elderly people cannot complete even simple tests of physical strength, and the lack of strength is sometimes blamed for the falls that are so devastating to them (Campbell, Borrie, & Spears, 1989). Vigorous exercise can reduce the signs of aging, and there is a positive correlation between exercise and good health. About 50% of what is called aging results from disuse and degeneration of muscle and bone tissue (O'Brien & Vertinsky, 1991).

Exercise is a low priority on elderly people's list of preferred leisure activities, and elderly people hold a more negative view of physical exercise than any other group (Burrus-Bammel & Bammel, 1985). This is unfortunate, because the benefits of exercise are great.

The immediate benefits of exercise include an improved sense of well-being, a sense of achievement, an improved self-image, more positive mood, and a reduction in stress. Exercise is linked to better sleep patterns as well. Exercise is a social activity and reduces social isolation. Exercise can also reduce depressive symptoms, at least on a short-term basis (McNeil, LeBlanc, & Joyner, 1991). The long-term benefits include better health, resistance to disease, independence, and reduced mortality (Bolla-Wilson & Bleecker, 1989). Exercise helps to develop and maintain an efficient cardiovascular system, lowers blood pressure, controls body fat, and decelerates the deterioration of bone tissue.

Physical exercise also preserves some cognitive functions (Shay & Roth, 1992). Declines in cardiovascular functioning that are related to reductions in cerebral circulation may lead to declines in cognitive functioning, probably because of a reduction in the oxygenation of brain tissues with age (Gur et al., 1987; Warren et al., 1985). These declines can be partially reversed through participation in exercise programs, thereby leading to better cognitive functioning (Hawkins, Kramer, & Capaldi, 1992). People who exercise in adulthood outperform nonexercisers on a variety of cognitive tasks. A 10-week exercise program led to substantial improvements in measures of divided attention (Hawkins et al., 1992), and another short-term program led to a reduction in participants' complaints about their memory (Molloy et al., 1988). A positive correlation exists between exercise and reaction time, and performance on nonverbal reasoning tasks and working memory tasks (Clarkson-Smith & Hartley, 1990). It is clear that active elderly people are likely to show better cognitive functioning.

Most age-related decreases in muscle strength are caused by inactivity (Spirduso & MacRae, 1990), but this is not inevitable. After 8 weeks of strength training, both older and younger adults were able to improve their arm strength by 20% (Moritani & deVries, 1980). After 15 weeks of an exercise program, muscle strength increased greatly and the gains remained over a 1-year period (Pyka, Lindengberger, Charette, & Marcus, 1994).

Elderly people may not exercise because of ageist views about what is appropriate, embarrassment at their body image, or physical pain, such as from arthritis. The elderly should consult a doctor before beginning an exercise program. Since many young and middle-aged adults are currently more physically active, perhaps we shall see more older adults exercising as today's younger adults reach their later years.

Nutrition

Between one third and one half of the health problems experienced by elderly people are related to nutrition (Long & Shannon, 1983). The American Dietetic Association notes that for every dollar spent on nutrition screening and intervention, at least $3.25 in medical costs are saved because well-nourished elderly people become ill less often and recover from illness and injury more quickly (New York Times, July 3, 1995). Disorders such as iron deficiency anemia, vitamin deficiency, and obesity are directly related to nutritional difficulties, and diabetes, hypertension, cardiovascular diseases, and osteoporosis are influenced by nutrition (Long & Shannon, 1983). Some emotional and behavioral problems, such as listlessness and confusion, may be caused by nutritional deficiencies as well, and dehydration among elderly people is a significant health concern (Steffl, 1981).

Nutritional needs change with age; unfortunately, at the present time there are no set recommended daily allowances for elderly people and all people over 50 years are grouped together. This may change in the near future, and recommended daily allowances for people between 50 and 70 years and over 70 are now being considered. A person's need for calories declines with age because physical activity and basal metabolism decrease. People who remain physically active into their senior years maintain muscle mass and have a somewhat higher need for calories. Requirements for certain nutrients such as protein, vitamins C and D, and calcium may increase because of the body's decreased ability to absorb vitamin C and calcium (Brown 1995). The answer is to eat less fat and fewer fried foods, increase consumption of fiber, decrease salt, and take in sufficient fluids.

Elderly people are making dietary changes consistent with recommendations to cut down on fat and eat more fiber (Nutrition Reviews, 1993). When they do not do so, many reasons may be cited. For some, but not the majority, poverty does not allow for balanced meals. For most, however, it is a matter of poor food choices rather than economic difficulties. Older people with time on their hands are apt to snack on high-sugar foods. Certain life changes may cause nutritional problems. Many elderly adults lose interest in food when their spouse and friends die. Men living alone are the most likely group of elderly to be poorly nourished (Davis et al., 1990). Depression also cause a loss of appetite. Eating is a social activity, and many people are not used to eating alone. Another important element is loss of teeth and problems with dentures that make it difficult to eat.

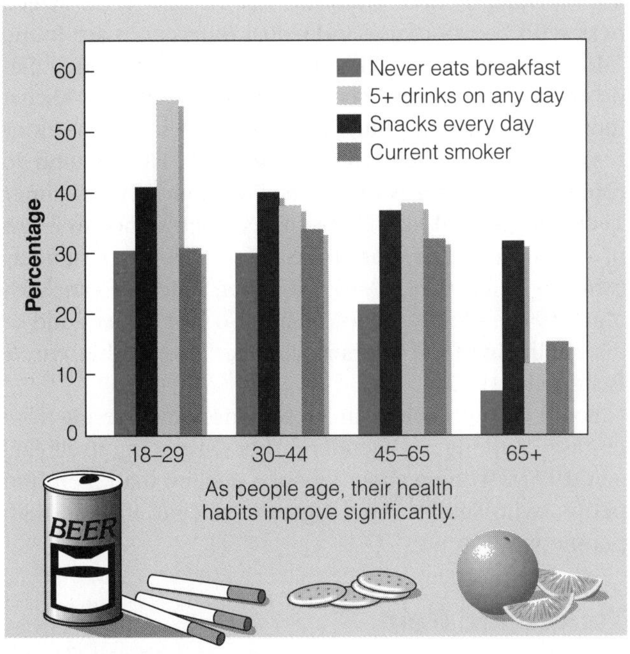

Datagraphic
Health Practices and Age
Source: Data from U.S. Center for Health Statistics, 1993.

Sensory Changes in Later Adulthood

The quality of daily life for older people depends partly on how well their senses operate. In fact, sensory abilities are related to cognitive functioning (Baltes & Lindenberger, 1997). Just as in other areas of aging, some declines occur but these need not adversely affect the functioning of elderly people.

Vision

The editors of the *Miami Herald* conducted a series of focus groups in the late 1980s during which readers made it clear that they "didn't like what they were seeing or rather, what they weren't seeing" (Braus, 1995). In almost every focus group, readers asked the editors to make the type larger. Many elderly people read the *Herald* and, in the future, more newspapers and book publishers will be in the same situation. As we age, the quality of our vision declines both because of normal age-related changes and an increase in eye disease. Simple modifications, such as bigger print, allow elderly people to cope with these changes.

Vision becomes somewhat more limited with advancing age, with most changes simply progressing from middle age. Accommodation, acuity, and adaptation decline with age (Long & Crambert, 1990). Elderly people often complain of difficulty seeing in conditions of glare. They are less sensitive to low-level illumination and find it harder to adapt to the dark (Fozard, 1990). The ability to discriminate objects at a distance also decreases. The speed at which visual processing occurs decreases, so elderly people read somewhat more slowly (Fozard, 1990).

Although these seem like an impressive list, the effects of aging on vision are gradual and can be compensated for by wearing glasses and being careful. However, the elderly are also more likely than younger adults to suffer from eye disease, although most elderly will not experience serious visual impairment. The most common visual problems among the elderly are cataracts and glaucoma. A cataract is a pathological increase in the opacity of the lens (Botwinick, 1984). Cataracts diminish visual acuity and can cause blindness, but the condition can be surgically corrected, and the procedure is now the fifth most frequent major surgery performed in the United States. Glaucoma is really a group of disorders characterized by an increase in pressure in the eyeball and a degeneration of the optic nerve. Unfortunately, the most prevalent type of glaucoma among the elderly does not produce symptoms until damage to the retina has already occurred. It can be detected by a simple test in the doctor's office and treated through medication.

Hearing

From a behavioral and social viewpoint, the decline in the auditory sense may be more important than the decline in the visual sense. Hearing disorders can cause problems in social interaction and make it difficult for elderly people to maintain their interpersonal relationships (Hume & Roberts, 1990). The incidence of hearing impairment rises sharply after age 60, and by the 70s as many as 75% have some hearing problem (Botwinick, 1984). A decline in pure tone sensitivity occurs, especially at higher frequencies (Slawinski, Hartel, & Kline, 1993). Hearing becomes more difficult when elderly people are listening to speech under conditions of background noise (Slawinski et al., 1993), and men experience greater hearing loss at high frequencies (Schaie, 1981). Some authorities claim that women suffer greater hearing loss at low frequencies, whereas others say that it is about equal (Schaie, 1981; Corso, 1977). Because of their greater hearing loss at high frequencies, men are likely to show more problems in speech discrimination than women, especially when the environment is noisy.

True or False?
Most people show some hearing loss by the time they are in their 70s.

The ability to understand speech is vital to ensuring that older people remain independent and fully functional. Unfortunately, elderly people experience a decline in language-processing abilities, especially under demanding conditions (Tun, Wingfield, & Stine, 1991). Understanding speech entails more than just hearing it. The sounds must be processed, which an elderly individual may take somewhat longer to do (Tun, Wingfield, Stine, & Mecsas, 1992). Having a hearing problem only compounds the difficulty because only some of the verbal input is picked up.

Under typical conditions, elderly people compensate for their hearing problems by depending on the context of the words to get the general gist of the speaker's meaning. They become better at inferring meaning from context (Fozard, 1990). When speech is rapid or there are many extraneous noises, elderly people suffer a disproportionately greater decrease in comprehension.

Elderly people may sometimes be helped by hearing aids that amplify sound, but hearing aids do not help everyone. Some changes in the environment are helpful as well, such as rearranging furniture to provide more face-to-face contact and reducing background noise generated by household appliances (Olsho et al., 1985). Finally, speaking slightly louder, at a normal rate but not rapidly, keeping lip movements visible, making certain you have the attention of the elderly person before speaking, and rephrasing rather than merely repeating the message can also help (Hull, 1984).

Taste and Smell

Some evidence indicates that taste preferences change with age. There is an increase in sensitivity to bitter tastes and a decrease in sensitivity to saltiness (Engen, 1977). Older people gradually lose sensitivity to sweetness with age, but large individual differences are found (Moore, Nielsen, & Mistretta, 1982). Taste buds that detect salt and sweet sensations deteriorate somewhat more, whereas taste buds for bitter and sour sensations remain intact longer, which is why the elderly tend to report that things taste bitter or sour (Hockheimer, 1989). In general, the elderly rated high concentrations of salt and sugar as more pleasant than younger subjects (Murphy & Withee, 1986; de Graaf, Polet, & van Staveren, 1994). Elderly people may also not be as good at discriminating food odors as younger adults (Shiffman & Pasternale, 1979).

Some of the decline in these senses may result from disease, smoking, and gender rather than aging itself (Engen, 1977). Women show less of a decline than men, and people who smoke show a greater decline in taste than people who do not.

Touch and Pain

Sensitivity to touch and pain decreases with age (Thornbury & Mistretta, 1981, Walk, 1981). However, significant individual differences are found, and the decreasing sensitivity does not interfere with normal functioning because it is relatively minor.

Older people do not feel pain as intensely as younger people. The time it takes them to become aware of pain increases slightly up to age 60, after which the increase is even more noticeable (Botwinick, 1984). If this is so, why would elderly people feel pain less but seem to complain about it more? First, this reduction in pain sensitivity does not mean that the elderly do not experience pain, only that the pain is relatively less intense than when they were younger. Second, elderly people suffer from chronic pain, such as from arthritis, much more than the young. The experience of chronic pain can be very difficult for elderly people, and there is a relationship between chronic pain and depression (Parmelee, Katz, & Lawton, 1991).

True or False?
Elderly people experience pain more intensely than younger adults.

Reaction Time

Perhaps the most common finding in the aging research concerns the general slowing that occurs with age (Jagacinski, Liao, & Hayyad, 1995; Fozard et al., 1994: Sliwinski et al., 1994). Activities that are a part of daily living, such as dialing a telephone, zipping up a jacket, or using a knife, are all slowed with age (Salthouse, 1994; 1993). Older adults make and execute their decisions more slowly. They react to unpredictable events or disruptions more slowly, even if they are experienced in the area (Carlson, Hasher, Connelly, & Zacks, 1995). This slowing may be the result of physiological changes in the sense organs and the decrease in the speed of neural transmission. All processes slow as people age, including those involved in sensation, perception, and cognitive abilities. The extent to which each of these contributes to the slowness in behavior is debatable. Other causes are the tendency of older adults to react with more caution than younger adults and their desire to be accurate rather than simply fast (Botwinick, 1984).

Although age itself is a reason for slowing, other factors, such as health, affect the degree of slowing (Earles & Salthouse, 1995). Reaction time is related to age, self-related health status, and exercise (Emery, Huppert, & Schein, 1995). In addition, the more complex the task the more the slowing (Fozard et al., 1994). Women also appear to slow more than men.

Predicting a person's speed of performance on the basis of age alone is hazardous, because individual differences are plentiful. Healthy individuals of all ages react faster than people in poorer health, and physically healthy older adults who are physically active have faster reaction times than sedentary middle-aged adults. It is then possible to find physically active, healthy older adults who may be equal or superior to physically inactive, unhealthy younger adults in reaction time (Salthouse, 1985). One interesting finding is that older people who are allowed practice respond well, improving significantly on speed-related tasks (Welford, 1977).

Aging and the Real World

Whatever declines occur with age are relatively minor. Almost all the changes noted here can be compensated for through medical intervention, environmental manipulation, and careful individual planning. For instance, visual and auditory problems can be reduced with eyeglasses and hearing aids. The environment can be manipulated so that the elderly can pay greater attention to what is being said and done. Older people who understand that they react more slowly or do not see well can avoid driving at night and can drive slower but not so slowly as to hinder traffic (see Forming Your Own Opinion: The Elderly Driver, p. 430). The decreases in sensory acuity need not unduly affect the enjoyment of life for most elderly people.

Older people, even those who are not in good physical health, manage to maintain positive psychological functioning and most say they are happy (Heidrich & Ryff, 1993). Physical health certainly affects mental health (Blazer, Hughes, & George, 1987), but having meaningful and valuable roles and strong friendships are also related to psychological well-being. If the individual's social networks are satisfying and the person can perform multiple roles, his or her mental health remains good despite physical problems (Heiderich & Ryff, 1993).

The commonly held belief that aging and illness go hand in hand, are the same, or that aging involves a tremendous and inevitable decline in physical and sensory functioning is false. Although some decline does occur, the health habits of the individual greatly affect the extent of these changes. The same pattern of choice and individuality is true of cognitive development.

Cognitive Development in Later Adulthood

One of the many misconceptions about aging is that it leads to a steep and inevitable mental decline. There are changes in cognitive functioning that occur with aging, but the elderly individual can stay intellectually alert and active. A number of difficulties occur when older people's cognitive abilities are compared to younger adults' abilities. In some studies of intelligence, healthy younger people were inadvertently compared to older people who were not very healthy, thereby confusing aging and health. When healthy older adults are used, the picture changes greatly.

Questions concerning the interpretation of any comparison also arise. Consider the following: The cognitive abilities of elderly people are tested in a number of areas, such as planning, problem solving, and memory, and differences are found between them and groups of younger adults. How would you interpret these differ-

Have you ever seen an elderly person driving very slowly while clinging to the steering wheel? Has the thought that elderly people should be required to take a driving test each year ever entered your mind? If the answer to these questions is yes, some of the changes in the sensory and neurological system described in this chapter probably have fortified your opinion. A number of visual and auditory declines occur, some of which affect driving. Declines in visual acuity and accommodation and problems with glare and dark adaptation affect driving ability. The reduction in speed of all cognitive processes make it less likely that the elderly can quickly process information and make split-second decisions. An elderly driver going 60 miles an hour who says he did not see the sign until the last minute and could not react quickly enough is probably telling the truth. Studies of elderly drivers have linked certain visual decrements—among which are slowing of information processing, impaired ability to divide attention, and impaired ability to ignore distractions—as being related to driving problems and accidents; cognitive impairments are also related to accidents (Owsley et al., 1991).

But are the elderly worse drivers? If we look at the number of accidents in which elderly drivers are involved, it does not appear that they are poorer drivers. Older drivers have fewer accidents and fatalities than their numbers would indicate. For example, in 1995 only 7.7% of all accidents involved drivers over age 65, whereas 13.9% of all the drivers in the United States were over 65 (National Safety Council, 1995). Elderly drivers were involved in 11.1% of the fatal accidents; these statistics seem to indicate that there is no "older driver problem." However, the elderly driver does not drive as many miles as the younger adult. When statistics are adjusted for this fact, drivers over the age of 60 years and below the age of 25 years are involved in more accidents than other age groups (National Research Council, 1995).

The accident record of older drivers is nearly as bad as the record of young drivers (Malfetti & Winter, 1991). Older drivers are more likely to be involved in accidents involving improper lane changes, improper turning, failing to yield right of way, and ignoring traffic signals. Drivers under the age of 25 years are involved in far more accidents involving excessive speed, fatigue, or driving on the wrong side of the road. Many accidents involving elderly people are the result of an inability to process information quickly or to notice signs while traveling fast (Salthouse, 1982). Elderly people have more difficulty driving under dimly-lit conditions, and show poorer visual search strategies as well (Kline et al., 1992). In addition, some of the medications that elderly people take may reduce their effectiveness as drivers.

Older drivers are not oblivious to their own physical changes. They compensate by driving more cautiously and more slowly, driving less, using less demanding roads, and not driving at night (Sterns, Barrett, & Alexander, 1985). Most studies show that older drivers can do well on driving-related tasks when the pace of making decisions on the road is similar to the speed at which they process information. It is when faster-paced decision making is required that they do not do as well (Sterns et al., 1985). Older drivers who know that they must slow down, however, may still cause problems if they creep along on interstates, impeding traffic and sometimes encouraging other drivers to take risks, such as passing under dangerous conditions (Malfetti & Winter, 1991). Some elderly drivers claim that even when they drive at the speed limit they are tailgated by those who want to exceed the limit. When they slow down because it is raining, they are bothered by drivers who do not want to take the more dangerous conditions into account.

It would be wrong to conclude that most elderly drivers constitute a safety hazard on the road, just as it is incorrect to argue that all young drivers are safety hazards. I have heard calls for the elderly to give up their licenses after age 70, but this ignores the wide range of individual differences among elderly people. Stereotyping elderly people is just as objectionable as stereotyping any other age group. Most elderly drivers do not believe they drive unsafely, and they think they are better than younger drivers (Malfetti & Winter, 1991). The suggestion that all drivers over 65 years of age should be given an annual mandatory road test will not work. If we want to curb the most dangerous drivers, all young drivers would have to be tested annually as well, and this would not be politically realistic.

Some steps could be taken to reduce the "older driver problem." First, older drivers could be forced to take yearly visual tests. Periodic physical examinations to find such conditions as cataracts or Alzheimer's disease are possible. A home-based exercise program could improve an older driver's range of body movements, allowing for better hand-eye coordination and more efficient driving skills (Malfetti & Winter, 1991). Driver improvement courses for those over 50 years are given under the auspices of the American Automobile Association, the American Association of Retired Persons, and the National Safety Council; an individual can be encouraged to take these courses by receiving a reduction in car insurance premiums.

Currently in most states an older person may either keep the license and all privileges or lose it altogether if he or she is an unsafe driver. A graded license, sometimes called a *restricted* or *limited license,* could be used as a third alternative, allowing a driver to operate in some areas and times and not others. For instance, a driver may not be able to drive in dense, urban traffic but may be capable of driving around his or her suburban or rural area. An individual may not be able to drive at night. A person with poor peripheral vision may be required to use a special mirror to compensate for the problem.

As our elderly population increases, there will be more older people on the road. To the elderly population, driving means freedom and independence. Public transportation is not always available, and to get to and from the grocery store or the doctor's office may require a car. Elderly drivers should be checked for physical and sensory problems and encouraged to take refresher courses—but an entire age group should not be labeled unsafe.

ences? Age differences in a variety of areas are easy to document, but their interpretation is very difficult.

The Competency-Performance Argument

If you show a group of pictures to subjects ranging in age from 20 to 90 years and tell them their task is to ask questions until they can guess the picture you are thinking of—a task similar to the game of 20 questions—you'll find that the elderly subjects need to ask more questions than young or middle-aged adults do. In addition, young adults are more likely to ask more general questions, like "Is it made of wood?" or "Is it bigger than a breadbox?" whereas older adults use more specific questions that do not eliminate as many items (Denney & Denney, 1982). We could conclude that older adults do not play the game as well and are not as competent as younger adults. But research has found that after simple training, elderly adults can ask the same types of questions younger people do—that is, that elderly people have the ability to use more efficient methods but, for whatever reason, simply do not (Denney, Jones, & Krigel, 1979). It is therefore difficult to come to any definite conclusions about competence based merely on performance.

Differences Versus Deficits

If you present groups of subjects with 50 pictures of everyday objects to sort, you'll find differences between how elderly subjects and younger subjects classify the items. Older subjects will place a frying pan with the stove because a stove is where a frying pan is used, but younger subjects are more likely to create categories, such as "utensils" and "appliances" (Cicirelli, 1976). Someone who considers abstract grouping to be superior would see lack of abstract grouping as a deficit, such a lack would not be seen as a deficit by someone who believes that this type of sorting is reasonable for elderly people. Some researchers believe that we have been too quick to label differences as deficits just because we think that the way young adults reason is optimal (Labouvie-Vief, 1982).

Ecological Validity

What if the elderly do not perform as well on skills that relate to success in school, such as many of those tested on intelligence tests? Such measurements may have great meaning for younger people but much less meaning for older people. This presents us with a problem of **ecological validity**—whether the tasks being tested are those that the average elderly person usually faces in the environment. It is not easy to find problems that both the elderly and the young deal with in their daily lives. Even when such problems are found, differences may reflect varying experience, not ability level. The fact that most elderly people function well in their daily lives and cope well with familiar challenges makes it difficult to interpret deficits found in artificial tasks performed in a laboratory.

ecological validity The question of whether the tasks tested in a special environment, such as the laboratory, are relevant to those in real life.

If intelligence is looked at in terms of successful adaption to one's environment, an individual may see a change from an academic type of intelligence to one of working and dealing with everyday problems (Berg & Sternberg, 1992). Most adults of every age, 77% in one survey, believe that intellectual abilities such as reasoning, problem solving, using one's past experiences, understanding others, and general knowledge improved with age. Most people also believe that some abilities, such as memory, decline with age (Berg & Sternberg, 1992). The overwhelming majority of people believe that people of any age can become more intelligent if they read more, obtain more education, and have interpersonal relationships with stimulating people. They may become less intelligent if they are very ill, lack mental stimulation, or do not have any interest in learning new material.

Intelligence in Later Life

The Wechsler Adult Intelligence Scale (WAIS) allows a researcher to break down intelligence into different parts. The WAIS contains 11 subtests (Table 18.4) that can be grouped into two categories—verbal and performance (Wechsler, 1981). When older people are tested for verbal intelligence, common developmental patterns are found. Vocabulary either remains stable or increases up to about age 70. Information shows no age-related pattern at all in adulthood. Comprehension shows no difference until age 50 or 60, after which it may decline somewhat. Similarities show a slight reduction with increased age (Salthouse, 1982). The phrase that would best describe older people's scores on these tests is "relative stability." The data on the arithmetic test show relative stability with age through age 50, after which some decrease is found. However, studies with other arithmetic tests yield mixed results, apparently depending greatly on the type of arithmetic problem presented. The evidence for digit span shows that poorer performance accompanies age.

True or False?
Most elderly people show significant declines in most elements of intelligence in their 60s.

The pattern of achievement on the performance subtests is quite different. Scores on tests of block design and picture arrangement show decreases starting early in adulthood and continuing throughout later maturity (Salthouse, 1982). Many of the verbal tests in the WAIS represent crystallized intelligence whereas the performance tests measure fluid intelligence. Generally, fluid intelligence decreases with age, showing a steeper decline after age 50, and crystallized intelligence improves even into old age up to around age 70 (Horn & Donaldson, 1980).

Table 18.4 **The Weschler Adult Intelligence Scale—Revised Edition (WAIS-R)**
The WAIS-R comprises 11 subtests. Six subtests constitute the Verbal Scale and 5 the Performance Scale. These subtests are listed and briefly described below. They are numbered in the order of their administration, in which verbal and performance tests are alternated.

VERBAL SCALE	PERFORMANCE SCALE
1. *Information:* 29 questions covering a wide variety of information that adults have presumably had an opportunity to acquire in our culture. An effort was made to avoid specialized or academic knowledge. It might be added that questions of general information have been used for a long time in informal psychiatric examinations to establish the individual's intellectual level and reality orientation.	2. *Picture Completion:* 20 cards, each containing a picture from which some part is missing. Examinee must tell what is missing from each picture.
3. *Digit Span:* Orally presented lists of three to nine digits are to be orally reproduced. In the second part, the examinee must reproduce lists of two to eight digits backwards.	4. *Picture Arrangement:* Each of the 10 items consists of a set of cards containing pictures to be rearranged in the proper sequence so as to tell a story.
5. *Vocabulary:* 35 words of increasing difficulty are presented both orally and visually. The examinee is asked what each word means.	6. *Block Design:* This subtest uses a set of nine cards containing designs in red and white and a set of identical one-inch blocks whose sides are painted red, white, and red-and-white. The examinee is shown one design at a time, which he must reproduce by choosing and assembling the proper blocks.
7. *Arithmetic:* 14 problems similar to those encountered in elementary school arithmetic. Each problem is orally presented and is to be solved without the use of paper and pencil.	8. *Object Assembly:* In each of the four parts of this subtest, cutouts are to be assembled to make a flat picture of a familiar object.
9. *Comprehension:* 16 items, in each of which the examinee explains what should be done under certain circumstances, why certain practices are followed, the meaning of proverbs, etc. Designed to measure practical judgment and common sense, this test is similar to the Stanford-Binet Comprehension items; but its specific content was chosen so as to be more consonant with the interests and activities of adults.	10. *Digit Symbol:* This is a version of the familiar code-substitution test which has often been included in nonlanguage intelligence scales. The key contains nine symbols paired with the nine digits. With this key before him, the examinee has 1½ minutes to fill in as many symbols as he can under the numbers on the answer sheet.
11. *Similarities:* 14 items requiring the examinee to say in what way two things are alike.	

Source: Anastasi, 1988.

These patterns of relative stability in verbal performance and continuous decline in nonverbal performance are known as the **classic pattern of aging** (Belsky, 1990; Botwinick, 1984). Longitudinal studies of intelligence show that performance intelligence declines with age but that intelligence scores on many tests of verbal learning remain relatively stable (Shay & Roth, 1992). For example, in the Seattle Longitudinal Study, discussed in Chapter 16, only word fluency (which has a significant speed component) showed any meaningful decline in the 50s (Schaie, 1994). The declines that were found were quite limited until the 80s. Even at age 81, fewer than half of all observed individuals showed significant decrements over a 7-year period. Compared with age 25, at age 88 almost no decline in verbal ability was found, but inductive reasoning and verbal memory declined somewhat, and spatial orientation, numerical ability, and perceptual speed declined significantly. Much of these declines are attributed to slowing of speed. When the consequences of this slowing with age are removed, declines are much less significant.

Both cross-sectional studies, in which people of various ages are tested at about the same time, and longitudinal studies, in which the same people are tested periodically over a period of years, show declines in general intelligence, but they differ as to when the decline begins and the extent of the decline. Cross-sectional studies show a greater decline in intelligence and that the decline begins earlier than longitudinal studies (Belsky, 1990).

classic pattern of aging The pattern of relative stability on verbal measures and decline in performance on nonverbal tests, commonly found when testing elderly people.

When studies of intelligence are performed on a number of people, often individual differences are forgotten. This is unfortunate because it leaves the impression that the pattern is true for all subjects, which is not the case. Despite the evidence for some general decline in old age, individual differences are striking. Figure 18.2 shows that the proportion of subjects with stable levels of functioning on some specific abilities for 7-year periods ranges from 60% to 85% in the Seattle Longitudinal Study (Schaie, 1990). Thus, although there is definite evidence for decline in old age it is important to specify the skill measured and account for individual differences (Hultsch et al., 1992).

Factors Affecting Intelligence

The evidence shows some decline in cognitive functioning with advancing age but also much individual variability. The factors that affect the relationship between aging and intelligence can be categorized into age-graded

Elderly people who keep intellectually active can maintain the function of their mental abilities at a high level.

influences, history-graded influences, and nonnormative influences (Arbuckle et al., 1992; Willis & Baltes, 1980).

Age-Graded Influences Biological and environmental factors that are highly correlated with chronological age are referred to as **age-graded influences.** For example, the slowing of behavior with age is one of the most common findings. Many intelligence tests contain timed subtests, and elderly people are adversely affected by the time limitations on such tests (Schaie, 1990). When time limits are removed, elderly people do better but still not as well as younger people. Still, such timed tests may accentuate the differences between older and younger samples, making the deficit seem greater than it really is.

History-Graded Influences Events that are correlated with historical change are referred to as **history-graded influences.** For example, wars, revolutions, depressions, epidemics, social movements, and technological changes affect each generation differently. When-

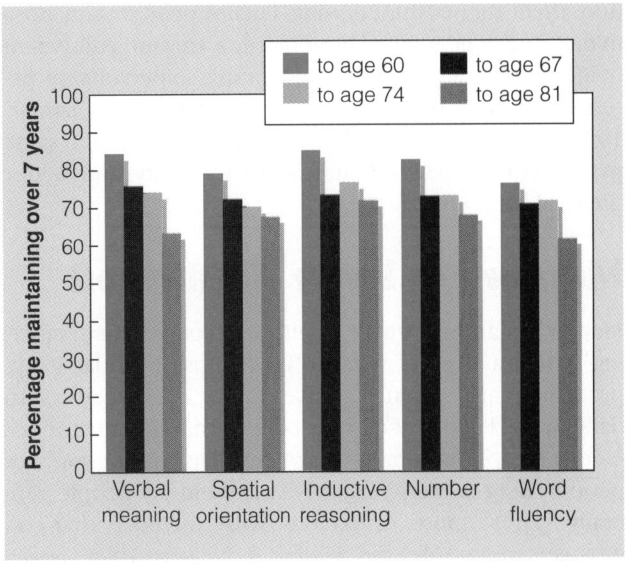

Figure 18.2
Proportion of individuals who maintain stable levels of performance over 7 years on five primary mental abilities.
Source: Schaie, 1990.

ever one is comparing elderly people with young adults, historical periods must be taken into account.

History-graded influences affect intelligence largely through generational differences in education. One reason older people do not do as well as younger people on intelligence tests is that they lack education. Generally speaking, each generation is better educated than the previous one, so comparing people born in 1900, who are now in their 90s, with those born in 1960, who are in their 30s, puts the older generation at a disadvantage (Labouvie-Vief, 1985). Future generations of elderly will be better educated than today's elderly. When educational differences are minimized, so are performance differences on intelligence tests.

Nonnormative Influences Events that relate to one's individual life pattern are known as **nonnormative influences,** which can affect intelligence by narrowing or broadening one's experiences. Travel, adult education, medical problems, divorce, or periods of unemployment are examples of such influences. Individual differences in maintaining intellectual functioning are predicted by the early favorable life experiences, greater education, economic status, active engagement in social and intellectual activities, and a flexible personality style (Schaie, 1994; Schaie, 1983).

Each person's unique life experiences affect cognitive functioning. The more a skill is used, the less it declines over the life span (Denney, 1982) so it is generally inaccurate to predict an individual's cognitive functioning solely on the basis of age. Health also plays a part because a relationship exists between poor health status and a decline in mental abilities. In addition, exercise and nutri-

age-graded influences Biological and environmental factors that are related to chronological age and may affect intelligence. For example, the increase in reaction time is generally age-related.

history-graded influences Events, such as wars, depressions, revolutions, and social movements, that are related to historical change and may affect the measurement of intelligence. For instance, the educational experiences of different generations differ.

nonnormative influences Events, such as medical problems or divorce, that affect a particular individual's life and may affect intelligence and development.

tion affect mental functioning. Finally, people with positive attitudes generally show more optimism, enjoyment of life, and better cognitive functioning, so personality factors also enter the picture (La Rue, Swan, & Carmelli, 1995). If this sounds familiar, it should; these are the same psychological factors that lead to longevity and better physical functioning.

Memory in Later Adulthood

Memory is an important cognitive resource. Remembering where a store is, what to buy, whose birthday is approaching, and when to make dinner are necessary to daily living. People of all ages believe that the memory of elderly people is somewhat worse than that of younger people (Berg & Sternberg, 1992), and elderly people generally report more difficulties with memory than do younger adults (McEvoy, Holley, & Nelson, 1995; Yesavage et al., 1990). When elderly people make the same mistakes as younger people, people of various ages rate them as more serious (Erber, 1989). Memory lapses in older people are often attributed to lack of ability whereas in the young they are attributed to lack of effort (Parr & Siegert, 1993; Erber & Rothberg, 1990).

Sensory, Short-Term, and Working Memory

When a stimulus is presented, it is first registered in sensory memory. Age differences in sensory memory are small or nonexistent (Poon, 1985). Information is transferred from sensory memory to short-term memory. Short-term memory involves holding things in memory for a brief time while working memory involves holding something in memory while carrying out some other operation (Swanson, 1994). The time period for short-term memory is described variously as anywhere between 15 seconds (Bransford, 1979) and 30 seconds (Best, 1986). Short-term memory has a limited capacity (Hultsch et al., 1992). Some evidence indicates a slight reduction in short-term memory with age. For example, when subjects are presented with a list of digits and asked to repeat them immediately in order, the memory span or average number of digits that can be reproduced without error after one presentation declines from seven to six sometime in the late 50s and then remains at that level (Winfield & Byrnes, 1981). So short-term memory is not really much of a problem.

Evidence suggests that some decline in working memory occurs with age (Salthouse & Babcock, 1991; Campbell & Charness, 1990). The most important change in working memory is a reduction in speed of executing various simple operations (Salthouse & Babcock, 1991). When some process must be performed on material in working memory, significant age-related differences arise in favor of younger people. For example, if we demand that subjects recall the digits in reverse order, the elderly perform much more poorly than younger subjects (Botwinick & Storandt, 1974). Under simple conditions, slight short-term memory deficits are found but they become more prominent if elderly people must reorganize or manipulate the material or require some division of attention (Hultsch & Dixon, 1990).

Long-Term Memory

The memory of older people is generally better than what most people think. Any declines depend greatly upon the task and type of memory tested. For example, older adults remember the general points and gist of what they hear and see as well as younger adults, but often show some deficit in remembering the details (Verhaeghen & Marcoen, 1993; Hashtroudi, Johnson, & Chrosniak, 1990). In a study of eyewitness testimony to a videotaped crime, elderly people were just as accurate as younger adults but not as complete in their stories (List, 1986). However, not all studies show this, and one study found no differences in recall of main points or details with age (Adams-Price, 1992). Although age is the most important variable in many studies of memory, individual differences are very important (West, Crook, & Barron, 1992).

True or False?
Elderly people remember the general idea of what they hear or see as well as younger adults.

Questions Students Often Ask

Why do elderly people have difficulty remembering what happened yesterday but seem to remember what happened 50 years ago?

This is a question that has been much debated by psychologists. Not everyone agrees with the premise. For one thing, just because the elderly person seems to remember the past does not mean that their memory is accurate. We tend to pay attention to the memory lapses of elderly people in the present, but have no way of checking the possibility that the person may not be telling us what really happened in the past.

If elderly people truly remember what happened in the past and not yesterday, the problem may be one of poor encoding. Elderly people may not be paying attention to what is happening around them. It may also reflect some possible neurological difficulty.

Older people are also not as good at remembering the source of a particular piece of information. The average deficit is relatively modest and having expertise in a given area reduces the difference somewhat (Brown, Jones & Davis, 1995). The source memory of older adults can be improved if they are encouraged to focus on the details of a situation and are reminded to pay attention to the source (Multhaup, 1995).

Encoding, Storage, and Retrieval

If we compare the performance of elderly people and younger subjects a few days after learning a list, we will find that the younger people remember more of the list.

The difficulty may be caused by problems either at the encoding stage or at the retrieval stage (or perhaps both), but not in storage (Birren et al., 1983; Labouvie-Vief & Schell, 1982). Some studies try to separate encoding and retrieval, but it is becoming more obvious that they interact—that encoding affects retrieval. Older people have more difficulty organizing material for memory, therefore showing some problems in the encoding stage (Witte, Freund, & Sebby, 1990). Elderly people use less effective memory strategies. Studies show that when older people are shown how to organize material for easier encoding, they significantly improve their performance on memory tests (Floyd & Scogin, 1997; Hultsch, 1969).

Older people also take longer to encode information. If older people are allowed sufficient time to respond to a test but are rushed in their initial acquisition of the material, they still perform more poorly than younger people (Botwinick, 1973). Older people benefit much more than younger people when the rate of presentation is slowed down or when they are allowed to go at their own pace (Poon, 1985). When the elderly have time to encode and are taught how to use efficient strategies, the differences between older and younger adults are minimized (Smith, 1980).

Retrieval is another possible source of difficulty with long-term memory. Recall is a more active and more difficult retrieval process than recognition. The elderly show more problems in recall. Further evidence for retrieval deficits comes from studies showing that if the elderly are given longer to respond, they perform better on memory tests. In this case the material is encoded and stored, but there is some delay in retrieval (Labouvie-Vief & Schell, 1982).

Explaining the Changes in Memory and Intelligence

At present it is not clear why the changes in intelligence and memory occur (Spencer & Raz, 1994). One problem is that not all processes of memory and components of intelligence show the same patterns. Those that involve speed, novelty, and complexity are more likely to show deficits whereas those that are practiced often or involve familiar materials show little or even no difference (Craik & Dirkx, 1992; Crossley & Hiscock, 1992). In addition, aging is a highly individualized process and large individual differences are found (Hockheimer, 1989).

A number of mechanisms have been suggested to explain the changes that occur with age (Light, 1991). One possibility is the age-related loss of neurons in the brain. Between the ages of 20 and 80, about 17% of neurons in the prefrontal cortex are lost. Changes in the cell itself may lead to a loss of speed in neural transmission or to the loss of certain neurotransmitters called catecholamines in the prefrontal cortex (Parkin & Walter, 1992). Others believe that the generalized slowing with age occurs throughout the information-processing system, and that something is lost at each stage of processing (Cerella, 1990; Myerson et al., 1990). Significant genetic influences also underlie differences in retention and memory processes (Finkel, Pedersen, & McGue, 1995; Finkel & McGue, 1993).

Although physiological explanations may be one factor in these findings, psychological and educational factors may also be important. For example, as people age they turn inward and become more reflective. They tend to interpret information even more in terms of thoughts and feelings rather than objectively. They become more easily distracted. When older adults are told to focus on the content of a story specifically, their memory improves and the difference between older and younger adults is reduced (Hashtroudi, Johnson, Vnek, & Ferguson, 1994). It is also possible that elderly people are more likely to try to be accurate rather than fast, and that they hesitate in order to increase their chances of being accurate.

Practical Consequences of Cognitive Research

The practical importance of these findings is clear. In order for older people to learn and remember something, they must be given more time to encode and retrieve, the material must be carefully organized, their attention must be undivided, and their anxiety level must be lowered. People who work with elderly people can be more effective if they are aware of the circumstances under which elderly people are less likely to show these deficits.

Although some processing changes, such as the need for more time to learn something and the inability to recall details troubles elderly people, in everyday life familiar material is so overlearned that any pronounced deficit here is viewed by many as a sign of depression or organic damage (Schaie, 1981). The evidence on ecologically valid tasks shows that the deficits decrease as the familiarity of the material is increased. The extent of memory problems depends on many individual factors, including education, intellectual ability, and one's knowledge base (Hultsch, Hertzog, & Dixon, 1990). Factors that seem to lead to less decline in memory are better health, higher education, being intellectually active, and being more satisfied with one's social support (Arbuckle et al., 1992). Elderly adults can improve their memory if taught memory strategies. When elderly people were shown how information processing changed with age and were taught to use mnemonic devices their memory significantly improved (Verhaeghen, Marcoen, & Goossens, 1992).

Problem Solving

Everyone is faced with hundreds of problems each day. Such important practical decisions as what foods to eat, which medications to take, how to get from place to place and how to use the telephone are vital to living an independent existence (Diehl, Willis, & Schaie, 1995). The data show some interesting differences in how younger adults and the elderly approach and solve problems.

Cautiousness "Look before you leap." This saying best describes what might go through the minds of older people confronted with a task. Young adults make more

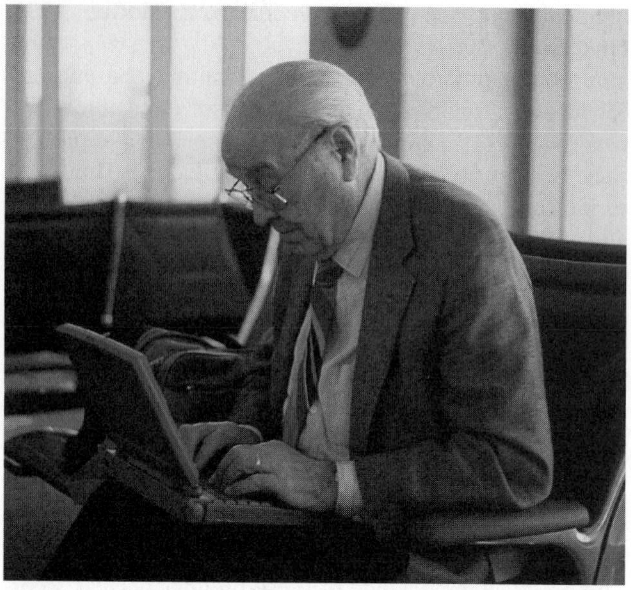

Elderly workers are often very careful and accurate, although they may lack the speed of younger workers.

errors of commission; older adults are more likely to make errors of omission (Botwinick, 1967). Elderly people are less likely to guess, and they tend to leave questions unanswered when they are not certain of the answers; younger people are more likely to venture a guess even if it is wrong (Heyn, Barry, & Pollack, 1978). Older people value accuracy over speed (Smith & Brewer, 1995; Botwinick, 1984) and do not like to take risks (Labouvie-Vief, 1985). This is carried over into daily life, as the elderly are less likely to drive in poor weather, invest their money in something new, or experiment with a new food. This behavior may be functional, as the elderly may recognize that their sensory and motor mechanisms are less efficient, that their money cannot easily be replaced, and that the consequences of mistakes in life are greater for them; cautiousness can be a rational response to the aging process (Okun, 1976).

Flexibility and Rigidity Older adults are more rigid in solving problems. In a variety of studies, older adults show a reluctance to change from one strategy to another when the task calls for it (Salthouse, 1982). They appear to be less flexible, but this may be because they feel safer doing things in the accustomed ways.

Abstract and Concrete Problems Everyone does better when problems are meaningful and concrete than when they are irrelevant and abstract. This is partly explained by differences in interest and motivation. When tasks are meaningful and concrete, motivation is likely to be higher. When older adults are tested on concrete problems, they perform significantly better than they do on abstract problems, although they still do not do as well as younger adults (Labouvie-Vief, 1985).

Forming Hypotheses and Concepts Older people take longer to form concepts and hypotheses (West, Odom, & Aschkenasy, 1978). When adult subjects were tested on their ability to interpret the meaning of such proverbs as "large oaks from little acorns grow" and how objects drawn on three cards were alike, older individuals had more difficulty producing abstract interpretation and had more difficulty abstracting similar characteristics (Alpert, Wolfe, & Lafleche, 1990); the difficulty was most significant after age 70. There seems to be an age-related drop in ability that is not related to memory or intelligence level. The authors suggest that older people show less cognitive flexibility; that is, they are more rigid in analyzing problems. Elderly people also show deficits in using the best strategy—defined as the most appropriate and efficient—to solve a problem (Salthouse, 1982).

Seeking Information Older people seek out much less information when faced with a decision, such as which medical treatment would be best. They do not attend to details as much as younger people do (Sinnott, 1989), and use their experience more, putting less energy in the decision-making process (Streufert, Pogash, Piasecki, & Post, 1990). Older adults require less information to arrive at decisions but often make decisions similar to the ones that younger people make. When women between the ages of 18 and 88 were given scenarios concerning women with breast cancer having to make decisions about what treatment is best, older women sought less information but the outcome of their decisions were similar to those of younger women. Older women also made these decisions more quickly than younger women. A second study of women of various ages who had actually made these decisions confirmed these findings. Older women sought less information and did so less systematically but the outcomes were similar (Meyer, Russo, & Talbot, 1995).

Elderly people can also be helped to improve their problem-solving skills. When young, middle-aged, and older adults were taught a way of squaring numbers mentally, each group improved greatly, although the older groups did not reach the same level of performance as the young group (Campbell & Charness, 1990).

What do the elderly themselves think of their problem-solving skills? In one study, 76% believed that such skills had increased with age, about 20% reported no change, and only 4% reported some decline. When presented with facts from laboratory experiments showing the opposite, the majority simply stated that they were referring to different problems. Everyday challenges were different (Denney & Palmer, 1981). Most elderly people have a positive view of how they solve their everyday problems.

Lifelong Learning

You are a nurse who must tell an elderly man when to take his medications.

You are a music teacher trying to teach an elderly student to play the guitar.

You are a social worker trying to help an elderly women take care of her ailing husband.

You are an investment adviser discussing investment options with an elderly couple.

In any of these situations, and dozens more, it is important for the professional to understand how sensory, memory, and problem-solving changes can affect interpersonal communication and learning. Learning is a lifelong activity, and many elderly people are involved in formal and informal learning activities. We can optimize the elderly adult's ability to learn by manipulating the environment in the following ways:

Alter the Physical Environment The elderly are especially sensitive to environmental factors. Large print, comfortable rooms, and a reasonable level of sound are essential. In addition, it helps to minimize extraneous noise that can interfere with concentration. Because elderly people do poorly if their attention is divided or if they have to attend to two tasks simultaneously, focusing their attention on one item at a time improves their performance.

Change the Pace Older adults need more time to learn material and more time to respond. Giving older people this additional time improves their performance. Any new procedures should be explained more slowly, and the elderly should be given more practice in performing the new skill.

Do More Than Merely Ask "Do You Have Any Questions?" After explaining to an elderly patient his medication responsibilities one nurse was surprised when her patient mixed up the medications and landed in the hospital. Some type of communication in which the elderly person tells you what has to happen is necessary.

Reduce Anxiety Everyone does better when anxiety is reduced and praise is plentiful, but the elderly seem especially sensitive to these conditions. The elderly also need more social support and encouragement.

Use Two Sense Modalities When at all possible, older people learn better when they can both see and hear the information. This can be accomplished through audiovisual presentations and a combination of reading, lecture, and recitation.

Make the Material Relevant The more meaningful the material, the better the learning and the recall. It is best to use examples that are relevant to the daily lives of older people because this helps them encode information more efficiently.

Teach Memory and Learning Strategies Because encoding can be a problem, elderly people sometimes need help in organizing information. The use of mnemonic devices and other memory-training techniques can be helpful. As we have seen, memory, reasoning, and problem solving can be improved through practice and education.

Compensate for Problems Because many elderly people know that their memory is not as good as it once was, they compensate by using other devices more frequently, such as making notes.

Single Out the Important Points The elderly learner often has difficulty singling out the important details from the less crucial details. When faced with information overload, mistakes are common. This can be reduced through training in such skills as understanding the main points and through very specific instructions about what is and is not vital to learn.

Practice Although everyone requires practice, elderly people seem to benefit from it even more. Since studies show that elderly people improve greatly when they have time to practice, rehearsal should be built into the learning process.

Questions Students Often Ask

What about the saying, "You can't teach an old dog new tricks?"

The saying is actually wrong. No one claims that teaching an 80-year-old is as quick and easy as teaching a 10-year-old. However, the evidence is overwhelming that older people can learn. However, they are rarely given the opportunity to learn, and often the material is presented in a way that places them at a disadvantage. For example, the material may be presented too fast.

Compensate for Any Sensory Deficits Hearing and visual problems can certainly interfere with learning and communication. Making certain that these deficits are compensated for can help to improve the situation.

One last point is vital to success in dealing with elderly people. Many people dealing with elderly people use patronizing speech patterns. They may speak not only more slowly, which can be defended, but also more simplistically and may use such expressions as "poor dear" and "good girl" as well as short commands (Ryan, Bourhis, & Knops, 1991). When adults aged 18 to 82 read passages of a conversation between a nurse and a nursing home patient, using either patronizing speech or a more neutral variant, respondents evaluated the nurse in the patronizing situation as less respectful and less nurturant and the recipient as more frustrated. The nurse was also rated as less competent and kind. Therefore, style of communication is an important variable in effectively interacting with elderly people.

Wisdom

One of the few cognitive advantages that older people are afforded by society is an increase in what is called wisdom. Most people see wisdom as a characteristic of older people (Labouvie-Vief, 1990). Psychological research into wisdom is quite recent (Simonton, 1990).

Jacqui Smith and Paul Baltes (1990) define wisdom as expert knowledge in the fundamental pragmatics of life, such as life planning, management, and life review. Their specific criteria for wisdom include (a) rich factual knowledge about life matters, (b) extensive procedural knowledge about ways of dealing with life problems, (c) life span contextualism—knowledge about the multiple contexts of life and their relationships over the life span, (d) relativism—knowledge about the differences in values and priorities, and (e) uncertainty—knowledge about the relative unpredictability of life and ways to manage it. These criteria may seem familiar because some of them, such as relativism and uncertainty, are mentioned prominently in postformal operational reasoning studies (Arlin, 1990).

In a study by Smith and Baltes (1990), young, middle-aged, and elderly adults were presented with specific problems. After some practice in mastering the skill of thinking aloud, subjects were asked to analyze and solve the problems. Using a criterion reflecting the definition, responses were rated as to their "wise" content. Only 5% of the responses were rated as wise, and these responses were found in all groups to about the same degree. Some older adults were among the top performers, but some middle-aged and younger adults also scored high. In other words, age itself was found to be a poor predictor of wisdom. However, the fact that older people were equally represented shows a difference from the studies of cognition that often show declines.

Another study found that wisdom did not involve expertise in a particular area (Baltes et al., 1995). A group of adults picked for their wisdom solved complicated life problems similarly to an expert group of clinical psychologists and significantly outperformed a group of younger and older adults. Wisdom is not merely professional expertise.

Wisdom, then, can be found in some people at all age levels—including elderly people. This conclusion fits well with what older people actually believe, for older people are far less likely to link wisdom with old age than are younger people. As Dean Keith Simonton (1990) notes, this in itself may be a sign of wisdom.

Living Young

Physical and cognitive changes that occur with age are more complicated than the simplistic and incorrect stereotype of inevitable steep decline. Slowing occurs with age, but the extent of any decrease in abilities is based upon lifestyle choices. Studies show that we can minimize any declines through various intervention strategies. Some strategies, such as teaching memory and problem-solving skills, are cognitive; others may involve nutrition and medical care because the relationship between health and cognitive functioning is strong (Coleman, 1983).

Individual differences are very important and age alone is not a particularly good predictor of intelligence. Statistical averages are not especially useful in predicting individual performance, and intelligent people tend to show fewer deficits upon aging (Salthouse, 1982). Experience compensates for some losses and is a factor that should not be taken lightly.

A change has begun to appear in the literature on aging. The inevitability of age-related declines in functional ability has been challenged by a growing awareness that some people do not seem to be as adversely affected by the aging process as others. Although a relationship certain exists between age and risk of disability, these problems are not inevitable or even uniform across groups (Seeman et al., 1994). This has focused increased interest on the factors associated with maintaining functional abilities in old age. The same factors appear consistently in our studies, including life choices in the areas of activity, health practices, social activity and support, and cognitive activity.

The Triple Challenge

With more and more people living longer and evidence on aging countering stereotypes a number of changes will have to occur. First, people's attitudes towards elderly people need to change. Too often, we have focused on the declines. We may benefit by turning some of our attention towards those people who show none or very little decline in old age. If we do so, we may discover strategies that might be used to forestall or at least reduce whatever declines in physical and cognitive functioning might occur.

Second, the improvement in life expectancy during this century has been truly sensational, but along with longer life has come the expectation that some of one's later years will be spent in disability (Guralnik et al., 1991). We must focus more energy on reducing and preventing disability, both mental and physical, and reducing the cognitive deficits that may result from chronic disability. With life expectancy increasing and medical costs associated with chronic conditions escalating, we must do more to promote health in elderly people. For instance, we know that smoking cessation is healthy for the younger adult, but it is also beneficial for the elderly. There is evidence that changes in behavior, including weight reduction or control, moderate alcohol consumption, and avoidance of excess dietary fat and cholesterol, are as beneficial for elderly people as they are for younger people (Lowik et al., 1991). Exercise and physical fitness are also as beneficial to the older individual as they are to the younger adult. If we are to truly improve the life of elderly people, we must improve both the quantity and the quality of their lives, not only in this generation but also in the generations to come.

Summary

1. *Maximum longevity* or *life span* is the maximum life expected of a species; *life expectancy* or *average longevity* is the number of years remaining to a group at a particular age within a society. The human life span has not changed for thousands of years, and is thought to be controlled by several genes.
2. *Life expectancy,* also called *average longevity* has increased dramatically in western countries since the turn of the century. The life expectancy for females is greater than that for males. The reasons may be genetic and/or environmental. Although whites have a longer life expectancy than African Americans, this gap is narrowing.
3. Aging and illness are not the same. In general, with aging comes a slowing of body processes. Elderly people are more likely than younger people to suffer from chronic diseases, and heart disease, cancer, and cerebrovascular disease (stroke) are the three most common causes of death for elderly people.
4. Although the accident rate is lower among elderly people than among some younger groups, elderly people are more likely to suffer death or disability from accidents. Falls are relatively common and often result in fractures, one cause of which is the condition of bone loss in elderly people known as osteoporosis. Most elderly people rate their health positively.
5. Elderly people are less likely to experience daily hassles or stress caused by entrance events, such as starting a family, but they are more likely to suffer from health-related stresses and stresses arising from exit events, such as loss of a loved one. The elderly take a longer time to return to equilibrium after experiencing stress. If elderly people view themselves as independent and in control of their lives, the negative effect of stress is reduced.
6. Most elderly people show good mental health, but mental illness is more prevalent among the aged than among younger people. Depression is the most common problem, and the suicide rate among the elderly has actually increased since 1980. A number of organic disorders are major causes of mental illness. The most prominent of these is Alzheimer's disease, which involves a progressive deterioration of brain tissue resulting in cognitive impairments in memory and judgment and disorganized behavior. The cause of this disease is not known.
7. Factors relating to longevity and functional ability include genetic factors, good health habits, avoidance of drug use, exercise and nutrition, and the use of mature coping mechanisms. Elderly people can benefit greatly from exercise and proper diet. A positive attitude towards life and one's health is also important.
8. Some decline in the functioning of the senses occurs with advancing age, but much of the decline can be compensated for by elderly people. The most important difference is an increase in reaction time caused by changes in the nervous system.
9. Verbal intelligence remains rather stable well into old age before it declines somewhat. Nonverbal skills show a decline in young adulthood that continues throughout life. When intelligence is examined in terms of crystallized and fluid intelligence, the same pattern is seen. Crystallized intelligence is much more stable than fluid intelligence.
10. Research from both cross-sectional and longitudinal studies shows a decrease in intelligence in old age. Usually cross-sectional studies show these deficits occurring earlier and being more severe than longitudinal studies show.
11. Influences on intelligence can be grouped into three categories. Age-graded influences are biological and environmental factors that correlate with age, such as a decline in speed. History-graded influences are events that correlate with historical change, such as a revolution or educational practices. Nonnormative influences are events that relate to our own unique life pattern, including divorce, travel, and unemployment.
12. Complaints about memory are common in elderly people. Short-term memory shows some decline but working memory is affected much more, especially under demanding situations. Older people are as good as younger people in remembering the main ideas. Some decline in source memory is found. A variety of studies show declines in long-term memory that may be caused by problems in encoding and/or retrieval.
13. The elderly are more cautious and rigid in confronting and solving problems. They perform better on realistic, concrete problems than on abstract ones. They take longer to form concepts and hypotheses and use less efficient problem-solving strategies. The elderly can be taught to solve problems more efficiently.
14. The elderly believe they are better at solving daily, practical problems now than they were in the past. They seek out less information when they have to make a decision, but the decisions they make do not differ appreciably from those made by younger people in the same situation. The importance of experience in problem solving should not be minimized.
15. Wisdom is one of the few cognitive advantages society affords to older people. Studies show that wisdom is found in the same percentage of people at all ages. The elderly are less likely to link wisdom with old age than are younger people.
16. Learning continues throughout life. Studies show that the elderly learn best in surroundings that meet their sensory needs, when the pace of instruction is slower, when anxiety is reduced, and when the material is meaningful. The elderly frequently require

help in organizing material, and they benefit when important points are emphasized. Although these practices may help people of all age groups, they benefit the elderly even more.

Multiple-Choice Questions

1. The term *life span* refers to:
   a. the average amount of time people in a particular society live.
   b. the maximum amount of life any species attains.
   c. the span of years that the average individual who has survived infancy lives.
   d. the maximum amount of years during which an individual is capable of functioning independently.
2. Most of the gains in life expectancy are caused by:
   a. reductions in deaths caused by violent crime.
   b. reductions in death during middle age.
   c. reductions in infant mortality rates.
   d. improvements in medical treatment for elementary school children.
3. Which of the following statements is *true?*
   a. Women in Western countries live longer than men.
   b. African American women live longer than white American men.
   c. Infant mortality is higher for males than for females.
   d. All of the above are correct.
4. Diseases such as cancer, heart disease, and diabetes are called:
   a. lethal diseases.
   b. chronic diseases.
   c. acute diseases.
   d. innate diseases.
5. Which statement concerning the health status of elderly people is *correct?*
   a. Most elderly people rate their health as poor or fair.
   b. Elderly people do not like to talk about their health, therefore no research exists in this area.
   c. No objective evidence exists showing that elderly people are in worse health than younger people.
   d. Elderly people rate their health and lifestyle optimistically.
6. The three most common cause of death for people above the age of 65 years in order of incidence are:
   a. cancer, heart disease, AIDS.
   b. heart disease, cancer, stroke.
   c. cancer, stroke, accidents.
   d. heart disease, cancer, accidents.
7. The accident rate for adults is:
   a. about the same as for adolescents.
   b. considerably lower than for children and adolescents.
   c. a little higher than for children and adolescents.
   d. a great deal higher for children and about the same as for adolescents.
8. Jane argues that elderly people are less affected by daily hassles than are younger people. Ahmed says that elderly people worry less about relationships and stress than younger people. Cora says that elderly people are better able to distance themselves from stress, and Dirk claims that elderly people experience far fewer stressful life events than young adults. All of these people are correct *except:*
   a. Jane.
   b. Ahmed.
   c. Cora.
   d. Dirk.
9. The most common psychological problem found in the elderly is:
   a. fear of aging.
   b. separation anxiety.
   c. depression.
   d. paranoia.
10. Which statement concerning suicide and the elderly is *correct?*
    a. The suicide rate is higher for the elderly than for younger age groups.
    b. Elderly women have higher suicide rates than elderly men.
    c. Most elderly people write extensive notes before attempting suicide.
    d. Anger, rather than depression or loneliness, is the prime emotional state that precedes suicide in elderly people.
11. Alzheimer's disease:
    a. is the fourth leading cause of death among the elderly.
    b. causes no physical changes in the brain that are observable during autopsies.
    c. leads to cancer in the majority of sufferers.
    d. is described by all of the above.
12. To the elderly, exercise:
    a. is low on their priority of activities.
    b. does not lead to as many benefits as it does for younger people.
    c. means competing with younger adults, something they do not want to do.
    d. is described by all of the above.
13. The most common group of elderly people to be malnourished are:
    a. women living alone.
    b. men living alone.
    c. men who are married and living with their spouses.
    d. women who are married and living with their spouses.
14. The decline in which sense can be the most important in reducing social interaction?
    a. touch.
    b. vision.

c. hearing.
d. balance.

15. The most common finding in the research on aging is a/an:
    a. reduction in measures of mental health beginning in the 60s.
    b. increase in feelings of being at peace with oneself.
    c. reduction in speed of response with age.
    d. increase in wisdom and a decrease in intelligence measured by standardized intelligence tests.
16. Joanne claims that giving an intelligence test to an elderly person doesn't make much sense because it does not test any skills the elderly person needs in daily life. Such an argument demonstrates the principle of:
    a. competence and performance.
    b. means-ends analysis.
    c. ecological validity.
    d. primary versus secondary functioning.
17. If an individual tells you to expect the classic pattern of aging when giving intelligence tests to aging individuals, you would find:
    a. significant decreases in fluid and crystallized intelligence beginning in middle adulthood.
    b. an increase in fluid intelligence and a decrease in crystallized intelligence beginning in the decade of the 60s.
    c. relative stability in verbal skills and a decline in nonverbal skills.
    d. increasing verbal skills through age 85 and then a plateau, with relative stability in nonverbal skills.
18. Ellen, aged 12, Jon, aged 25, and Keith, aged 60, forget items at the supermarket. Most people would judge:
    a. the memory mistakes as just as serious for all of these people.
    b. Ellen's memory mistake most serious for it shows psychopathology.
    c. Jon's memory mistake most serious since at this age few if any memory mistakes should be made.
    d. Keith's memory mistake the most serious.
19. Which statement concerning the memory ability of elderly people is *correct?*
    a. Elderly people do not remember the source of information as readily as younger people.
    b. Elderly people remember the general theme of what they read or hear as well as younger people.
    c. Elderly people can use mnemonic devices to improve their memory.
    d. All of the above are correct.
20. Which of the following statements concerning elderly people's problem-solving strategies is *false?*
    a. Elderly people are more interested in accuracy than speed.
    b. Older people are less likely to change strategies when solving a problem.
    c. Older people do better on practical than abstract problems.
    d. Elderly people seek out more information when trying to solve problems than younger people.

Answers to Multiple-Choice Questions

1. b 2. c 3. d 4. b 5. d 6. b 7. b 8. d 9. c
10. a 11. a 12. a 13. b 14. c 15. c 16. c 17. c
18. d 19. d 20. d

Chapter 19

Social and Personality Development in Later Adulthood

Chapter Outline

The New Breed
Portrait of a Population
The Economic Status of Older People
Housing
Nursing Homes
New Perspectives: Stereotypes About Older People
Personality in Later Adulthood
Religion in Later Adulthood
Developmental Tasks of Older People
Interpersonal Relationships in Later Adulthood
Cross-Cultural Studies of Aging
The Minority Elderly
Retirement
Work and Leisure in Later Adulthood
Successful Aging
A New Look at Aging

Are the Following Statements True or False?

1. Elderly people comprise more than 10% of the population today, and will increase to more than 20% by the year 2040.
2. Elderly people are more likely to live in poverty than people of any other age group.
3. Most elderly people would move from their homes if they had the financial resources to do so.
4. Most people in nursing homes do not have much need for the special services provided.
5. Most elderly couples express great satisfaction with their marriages.
6. Most elderly people have frequent contact with their middle-aged children.
7. Many people who abuse their elderly relatives are actually financially dependent upon them.
8. Children raised by their grandparents do not show any more behavioral or health problems than those children raised by single parents.
9. Eighteen months after retirement, most people are happier and more satisfied with their lives than they were a month after retirement.
10. The most common leisure-time activity for elderly people is watching television.

Answers to True-False Statements 1. True 2. False: see p. 445 3. False: see p. 445 4. False: see p. 448 5. True 6. True 7. True 8. True 9. False: see p. 460 10. True

The New Breed

Rebecca and Bill Stone live in a retirement community in Boca Raton, Florida. Every morning Bill works out in the gym and swims in the pool while Rebecca attends aerobics class and does household chores. The Stone's afternoons are spent visiting friends, participating in one of many planned daily activities, or going to town. The Stones spend their evenings attending special shows, socializing, or just watching television.

Rebecca had looked forward to retiring from her job as a cashier for the New York State Motor Vehicles Bureau, but Bill, who owned a fashionable women's clothing store, was not so sure about retirement. He had always spent long hours at work and considered business a challenge. How would he do without his work? Twice a year or so, the Stones fly north to see their family, spending a few months at a time in a small apartment. They have a positive view of themselves and their lifestyle.

The media tend to concentrate on the plight of the elderly living in poverty. We read almost daily about those who live from hand to mouth or who cannot afford to live in dignity and comfort. The stories about the elderly who become impoverished providing nursing care for their beloved spouses move us emotionally, and the newspapers are filled with reports of elderly people living in fear in squalid surroundings with no one to care for them. To what extent is this the real picture of the social and personal functioning of the elderly? Are Rebecca and Bill Stone simply an exception to the depressing picture of the elderly, or are they a new and growing breed?

Portrait of a Population

The elderly are a growing segment of our population. In 1900, people over 65 years of age made up only 4% of the population. Today they comprise somewhat more than 12%. By the year 2040, older people will total approximately 23% of the U.S. population (Cantor, 1991; Kranczer, 1994; Schneider & Guralnik, 1990). The same population growth is taking place in developing nations, and by 2025, more than two thirds of the world's elderly will be in developing countries (Myers, 1990).

> ***True or False?***
> Elderly people comprise more than 10% of the population today, and will increase to more than 20% by the year 2040.

The age structure of a population is the result of fertility, mortality, and migration, all of which have affected the number of aging people in the United States. Because the fertility rate has declined, the percentage of elderly in the country has risen. The mortality rate also has declined, allowing more people to live to older ages. Migration is not a factor in the growth of the elderly in the overall U.S. population, but it is important at the city or regional level, with some states, such as Florida, having many more elderly than other states (Grigsby, 1991). The elderly population today is predominantly female. In 1900 the ratio of elderly males to females was 102 : 100, probably because many women died in childbirth. Today it is 69 : 100 (Statistical Abstract, 1996).

This increase in the numbers of elderly in the population has implications for social and medical services. The number of people receiving Social Security has increased and will continue to do so. As the baby-boom generation born after World War II enters old age, social and medical services will be strained. Because older people experience more chronic disorders, more long-term health care facilities and specialized housing will be needed in the future. Elderly people also comprise a potent eco-

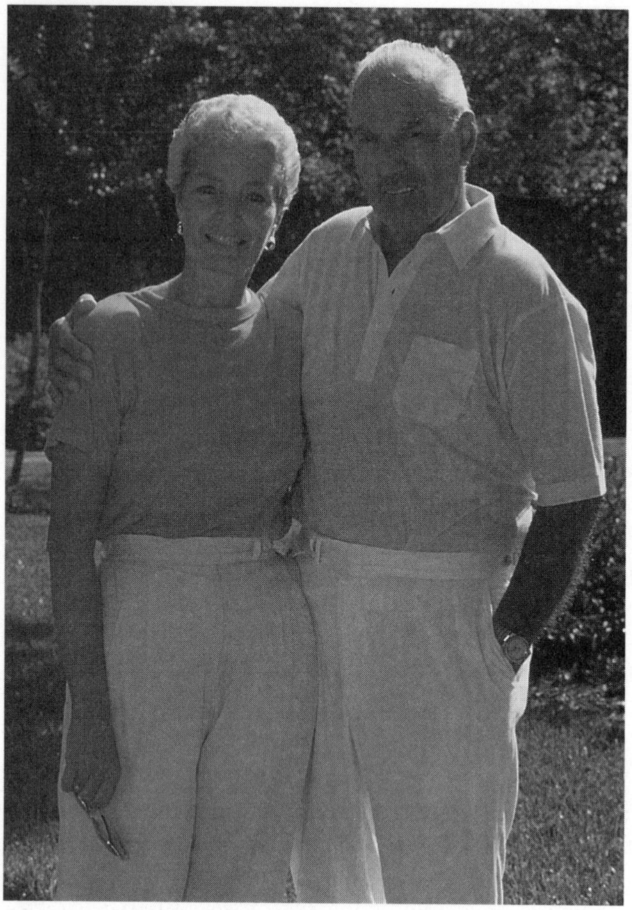

Most elderly people are not poor, although the media seems to concentrate on the plight of the elderly poor.

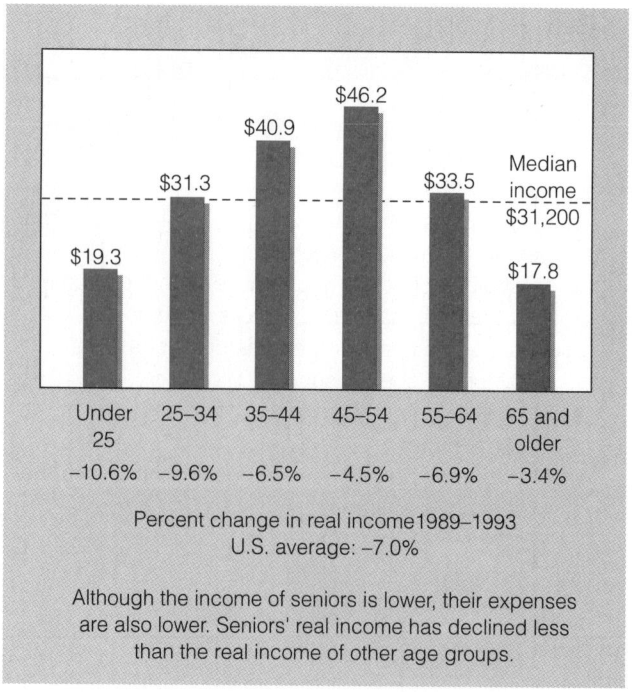

Figure 19.1
Household Income by Age Median household income in thousands by age of householder, 1993, and percent change in 1993 dollars, 1989–1993.
Source: Francese, 1995; American Demographics' calculations from Census Bureau surveys.

nomic force in the country, one that is far larger than the younger generations, and companies will be scrambling for a larger share of this growing consumer market (Wolfe, 1994; Kahn, 1986).

The Economic Status of Older People

Is the average elderly person poor, trying desperately to manage on an insufficient income, or comfortably part of the middle class? Income figures are readily available, but they can be interpreted in many ways. Traditionally, the elderly have been poor; and economic trends, such as inflation, were thought to reduce the elderly's buying power. Indeed, elderly households earn less than half that of households headed by 35- to 44-year-olds (Francese, 1995; see Figure 19.1). Many elderly go through periods of pressing financial concerns (Holden, Burkhauser, & Myers, 1986). The results of studies in the United States and in Japan show that financial problems erode feelings of control and self-worth and lead to depression (Krause, Jay, & Liang, 1991). The media tend to concentrate on the elderly poor and the public believes that most elderly people are poor (see New Perspectives: Stereotypes About Older People, p. 446), but this is not the case.

Most elderly are not poor and the economic status of the elderly has improved greatly in the last 20 years compared with other groups (Dodge, 1995). The percentage of older people living in poverty is about half what it was in 1969, with about 12% living in poverty today (Lichter & Eggebeen, 1994). The average elderly person has an income level twice the level of poverty.

These gains have not been uniform across all groups. Elderly African Americans and Latinos are two to three times more likely to be poor than their non-Latino, white counterparts (Public Health Reports, 1994). Unmarried and widowed women are most likely to live in poverty (Bound et al., 1991).

Many women over 65 are widowed and because these women have not spent many years in the labor force, they may not have many Social Security and other retirement benefits of their own. Women generally earn less than men and many women drop out of the labor force for a period of time to raise their children. Some authorities argue that changes in the law need to be made so as not to penalize women for performing the unpaid but vital work of raising children (Iams & Sandell, 1994).

As a group, the elderly are better off today than they were years ago. However, many still live at or near the poverty level. Age itself is not a particularly good predictor of need. As a group, children are more likely to live in poverty than older people.

True or False?
Elderly people are more likely to live in poverty than people of any other age group.

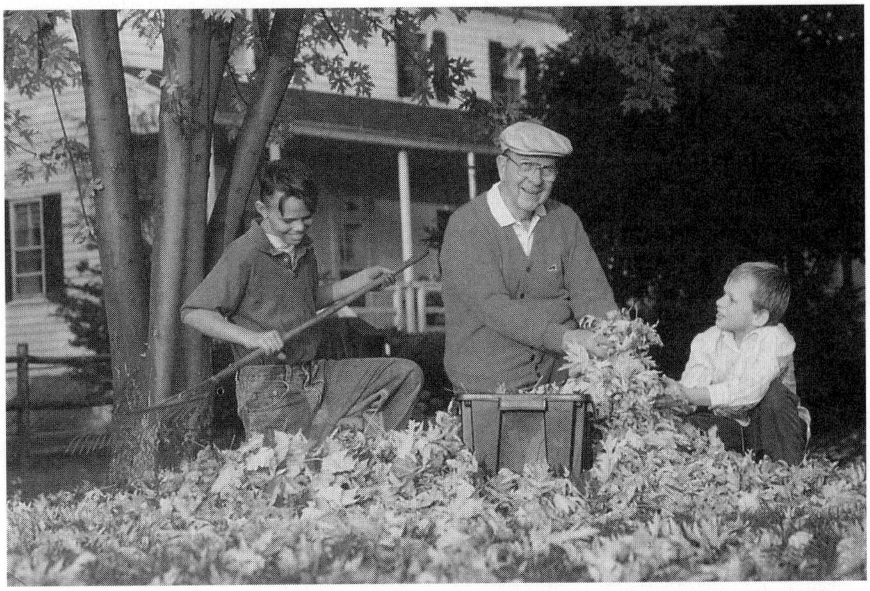

Most elderly people own their homes and want to continue living in them as they age.

The improving status of elderly people is the result of many factors. The elderly pay very little income tax and have smaller households. Their expenses may not be as great in some areas, such as food. In addition, the Social Security payment that most elderly receive is linked to inflation, and as inflation increases, so do Social Security payments. The Social Security program is credited with sharply reducing poverty among the elderly (Cloud, 1995). Most of the sources of income for the elderly rise with increasing prices, and inflation may not have the crippling effect on the elderly that has been traditionally assumed (Clark & Sumner, 1985). Finally, especially since 1970 the elderly depend more on public and private pensions and much less on their own savings, and in the future even more people will have pensions (Woods, 1994).

Housing

About 75% of all eldery people own their own home (Neugarten, 1989), and the overwhelming majority are mortgage free (Kendig, 1990; Neugarten & Neugarten, 1989). About 20% of the elderly live in hotels or public housing projects, or rent apartments, and 5% are institutionalized in nursing homes.

Most elderly people want to stay in their homes (The Economist, 1993). This phenomenon is called **aging in place** (Golant & LaGreca, 1994), and is becoming even more pronounced. However, upkeep can become expensive and older people living alone have the worst housing problems (Stevens-Long & Commons, 1992). Still, most elderly people rate their housing as satisfactory even when it appears less than adequate to an objective viewer. Perhaps this is because they do not think that they have a suitable alternative and see no purpose in complaining.

True or False?
Most elderly people would move from their homes if they had the financial resources to do so.

In many cases, the value of these homes has increased and the house may be the person's largest asset. Elderly homeowners may sometimes elect to move to a retirement community, often made up of condominiums, or to a smaller home of their own. Moving means making new friends and breaking old ties. Rebecca and Bill Stone were able to maintain a small apartment in their old community; most elderly cannot.

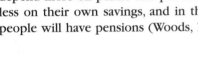

aging in place The phenomenon in which elderly people tend to live their postretirement years in the same place in which they raised their family.

There has been a well-publicized migration of relatively affluent elderly to the Sun-Belt regions of the United States. Such moves, called *amenity moves,* are made for reasons of personal freedom and leisure. Retirement communities in such areas offer those in good health access to leisure activities and other people of their age, and an environment conducive to interpersonal relationships (Hendricks & Cutler, 1990). Some people need help from their families and move closer to them (Longino et al., 1991). However, most elderly people stay in their present home or at least in the same community. Most elderly do not live in cities but in the suburbs and this proportion of the elderly population is growing (Reitzes, Mutran, & Pope, 1991).

Older adults are proud of their independent existence and their ability to take care of themselves and their homes. When they need help, they prefer to have a relative or a paid helper come to their home. A full 80% who need help receive such help in their own home, most often from family members (Moen, Robison, & Fields, 1994). They fear and do not want to enter a nursing home but generally prefer this alternative to living with their children (McAuley & Blieszner, 1985).

Nursing Homes

Even though only 5% of the elderly live in nursing homes, 43% of all the people who turned 65 years in the past year can expect to live in one some time in their lifetime (Montgomery & Kowloski, 1994; Hubbard et al., 1992). The percentage of the elderly living in nursing homes in-

New Perspectives: Stereotypes About Older People

Older people are easily angered and irritable.
Older people are often bored, lonely, and unhappy.
Older people are poor.
Older people cannot adapt to change.
Most older people live in institutions.
Older people are senile.
Older people cannot work as effectively as younger people.

According to a study by the American Association of Retired Persons about two thirds of all people sampled believe that older people are poor, frequently bored, easily irritated, and lonely (AARP, 1994). More than half all adults think elderly people have more work-related accidents and cannot adapt to change. Research shows these beliefs are not based upon fact. Most elderly people are not poor, actually have fewer work-related accidents, most do not live in institutions, and they are certainly not senile. The poll of AARP members also found that the elderly people surveyed did not see themselves as often angry or bored. Three quarters of the AARP members sampled were healthy enough to carry out normal daily routines, most live independent lives and remain socially active. They also stated that they do learn and adapt to change. Other studies find that the public generally believes that elderly people are frequently abandoned by their families and retirement has many adverse effects. These are also not true (Atchley, 1994).

Some perceptions by younger people sampled in the AARP study were considered valid by older people. These included a decrease in physical strength, slower reaction time, some decline in sensory abilities, and a need for more time to learn new things (AARP, 1994). The perceptions of elderly people in this study are substantiated by research, but many of the beliefs held by younger people are not.

Studies generally show that there are two stereotypes about the elderly: one negative and severely limiting, the other positive and essentially an idealization of aging (Lubomudrov, 1987). Traditionally, studies of how people see the elderly show that the elderly are not considered physically active or appealing or very capable but have many good personality traits, along with some negative ones. When college students were asked to generate all the positive and negative terms associated with the elderly, different stereotypes emerged (Schmidt & Boland, 1986). Negative physical stereotypes were common, including the idea that older people were frail. Two types of social stereotypes were found, one positive, the other negative. The students used terms that were often in conflict with one another: for example, *sedentary* and *active, poor* and *wealthy.* The students used many positive terms, such as *tough, happy, alert, generous,* and *courageous,* and many negative ones, including *dependent on family, fragile,* and *poor.*

Other studies find the same pattern of positive and negative stereotypes. The elderly are generally seen as inactive, unhappy, irritable, isolated, depressed, slow, and not intellectually alert (Kite, Deaux, & Miele, 1991; Runback & Carr, 1984). The elderly are also seen as enjoying hobbies, being family oriented, generous to others, and friendly as well as having health problems. They are seen as critical and hard of hearing but also as likable, intelligent, and experienced (Kite & Johnson, 1988).

College students do not always believe that negative stereotypes are more typical of the elderly than positive ones, with the exception of the oldest of the elderly (Hummert, 1990). Attitudes toward the elderly are certainly more negative than for younger people, but smaller differences are found when studies use personality traits rather than measures of competence (Kite & Johnson, 1988). These stereotypes of the elderly are more potent than are gender stereotypes for determining attitudes (Kite, Deaux, & Miele, 1991).

creases with age and the number of elderly in nursing homes is increasing (Montgomery & Kosloski, 1994; Braus, 1994a).

Nursing homes have a tremendous image problem. The elderly view nursing homes in terms of loss of independence and rejection, and as a prelude to death. The public's conception of nursing homes is generally poor, mainly because of the negative publicity the industry has received in the recent past. Horror stories concerning mistreatment and bad conditions capture the public's attention. Stories of abuse and maltreatment are relatively common. When nursing home aides and nurses were interviewed, about one third had seen at least one incident of abuse in the past year and 10% revealed that they had committed at least one act of physical abuse. Psychological abuse was more widespread, with most saying they had seen one incident of yelling, insulting, or swearing and a little less than half admitting to doing so on at least one occasion (Pillemer & Moore, 1989). These statistics can obscure the fact that a great deal of sympathetic care goes on as well, despite enormous physical and psychological demands on the staff (Foner, 1994).

Questions Students Often Ask

My grandmother says she would rather die than go into a nursing home. Are they really that bad?

Some are and some aren't. Many elderly people view nursing homes as places to go to die. They read about the awful conditions in some of them and do not want to consider nursing homes as alternatives. This is understandable because only the most severe cases are

New Perspectives: Stereotypes About Older People (continued)

How do elderly people themselves feel about aging? Do they believe the stereotypes? The answers to these questions depend to a great extent on their education, financial status, marital status (married elderly people are happier and less lonely), and other variables. Most elderly people living in the community have a positive outlook on this stage and an understanding of the problems and limitations involved in aging (Keller et al., 1989). Older people in a Florida retirement community saw the elderly as active, competent, and optimistic (Kahana, Kahana, & McLenigan, 1982). Many cite a feeling of serenity and self-acceptance and see old age as a time of doing things they have always wanted to do (AARP, 1994; Arnett, 1995). Most elderly people hold positive self-images and feel that life is better than anticipated. Less than 20%—about the same proportion as young people—report loneliness as a serious problem (Neugarten, 1989).

Elderly people do not subscribe to all the stereotypes; they know that most older people are not poor or senile. However, a minority do share some of the stereotypes of younger people, but are much less extreme in these beliefs. Most importantly, they see themselves as exceptions to the rule. For example, in one poll, only 35% of the young adults believed the elderly were very good at getting things done, while 38% of the people over 65 believed that their cohorts (others over 65) could accomplish tasks well. However, 55% believed they themselves were good at getting things done. Elderly people who are either educated or affluent are not as likely as those who are uneducated or poor to hold stereotypes of their cohorts (Hellebrandt, 1980). Older people have a tendency to feel younger than their age (Barnes-Farrell & Piotrowski, 1989). Many older people do not think of themselves as old, and this may cause them to reject the stereotypes referred to in the research (Hayslip & Panek, 1993).

How do these stereotypes affect the elderly? Comedian George Burns, who died at the age of 100 in 1996, noted that older people can convince themselves to act according to the stereotype and think of themselves as passive and unproductive. People practice getting old. "They start to walk slower and they hold on to things. They start practicing when they're 70, and when they're 75 they're a hit. They've made it. They are now old" (Butler, 1985, p. 72).

One place people always point to for perpetuation of stereotypes is television. The portrayal of elderly people on weekly programs, especially dramatic series, has improved and intergenerational cooperation is shown often (Atchley, 1994). However, news reports and documentaries often emphasize the limitations and problems of aging, especially the vulnerability of the aging population. Reports on nursing homes and poverty, although necessary, leave the impression that most elderly live in poverty and in nursing homes. Elderly people claim that the media often show sensational stories that stereotype the elderly as cheap or trivialize them in stories of 100-year-old grandmothers who sky dive (Arnett, 1995).

It is unfortunate that people believe so many of the myths and stereotypes about elderly people because these may affect how elderly people are treated. For example, believing that elderly people cannot make decisions and are often times confused may lead to the paternalistic assumption that elderly people always need help and are incapable of accomplishing anything independently. These beliefs also limit the opportunities available for elderly people in the job market and in training. They make it more difficult for a growing proportion of our society to take their rightful place in society and to continue to use their considerable talents and abilities.

found in these homes and some news programs emphasize the negative features of these facilities.

The simple fact of the matter is that nursing homes are one alternative for people who need extensive help with eating, dressing, or bathing. Although some deserve their poor reputation, others do a decent job. It is difficult to change the opinions of elderly people who see a nursing home as a last stop before dying. This is especially true if they have to break up their homes to enter an institution, knowing that they can never again be independent.

A recent poll showed that Americans are more frightened by the idea of placing their parent in a nursing home than by the thought of a parent dying suddenly (Braus, 1994a)! It is often with a great deal of guilt and anguish that both the elderly and their children find themselves in a position where they have no other alternative. The typical patient is female, white, widowed, and age 79, and most patients come from another institution, such as a hospital, rather than from their own homes. The typical patient has multiple physical problems and is confused, angry, and depressed. More than half show psychological difficulties, many times resulting from dementia (Sakauye & Camp, 1992). Substantial percentages of people in nursing homes require assistance in dressing, eating, elimination, and bathing (see Table 19.1); many have visual and auditory problems as well (Horowitz, 1994). With such needs, professional full-time care is often necessary, but there are negative consequences to institutionalization—for example, low morale, negative self-image, feelings of personal insignificance, anxiety,

Table 19.1 **The Status of the Elderly in Nursing Homes**
More than half the elderly in nursing homes require assistance in bathing, dressing, and performing other normal daily chores.

DEPENDENCY STATUS	TOTAL	AGE: 65–74 YEARS	AGE: 75–84 YEARS	AGE: 85 YEARS AND OVER	SEX: MALE	SEX: FEMALE
Type of Dependency			**Percentage**			
Requires assistance in bathing	91.2	84.8	90.3	94.1	86.9	92.6
Requires assistance in dressing	77.7	70.2	75.9	81.9	71.5	79.7
Requires assistance in using toilet	63.3	56.6	60.3	68.2	56.2	65.7
Requires assistance in transferring	62.7	52.1	59.7	69.0	55.3	65.2
Lack of continence—difficulty with bowel and/or bladder control	54.5	42.9	55.0	58.1	51.9	55.3
Requires assistance in eating	40.4	33.4	39.1	44.0	34.8	42.3

Source: Data from National Center for Health Statistics, 1987.

depression, and premature death (Tobin & Lieberman, 1981). In addition, many nursing homes do not offer many activities, and boredom is a great problem.

True or False?
Most people in nursing homes do not have much need for the special services provided.

The picture may not be as bad as it first seems and some argue that nursing homes are frequently blamed for conditions they did not cause. Many of the problems associated with nursing homes, such as isolation and depression, existed prior to institutionalization but increase in severity when the older person is placed in the home (Tobin & Lieberman, 1981). Institutionalization may not cause these problems, but it may make them worse.

These symptoms need not be inevitable (Moos & Lemke, 1985). Homes with better staff/patient ratios, better medical recordkeeping procedures, and superior nutrition programs are associated with improvement in patient functioning (Linn, Giurel, & Linn, 1977). An institution that provides a more stimulating environment with activities, encourages interpersonal relationships, provides a healthy nutritional program, and has a good staff is likely to produce beneficial results (Voelkl, Fries, & Galecki, 1995). When a group of institutionalized elderly and community residents with the same level of illness and disability were compared, the nursing home residents had a higher subjective rating of health, which is an important determinant of morale (Myles, 1978). Another positive finding is that family interaction improves after admission to an institution, as intergenerational stress is reduced (Montgomery, 1982).

Institutions frequently rob the elderly of any feelings of responsibility and control. In a series of studies people in nursing homes were divided into two groups, each of which received potted plants. Subjects in the experimental group were given responsibility for the day-to-day care of the plant, while subjects in the control group had someone else taking care of the plant for them. Experimental group subjects participated in many more daily social activities and nursing home projects, and demonstrated better health over the next year and a half; many more of the control group died than the experimental group (Rodin & Langer, 1977; Langer & Rodin, 1976). In a rather creative program, seniors without cognitive impairment in nursing homes were taught to use an on-line computer service with diverse features including electronic mail, encyclopedias, bulletin boards, and games. Subjective evaluations from the participants showed that they were quite satisfied and the staff were amazed at how quickly the residents learned to use the system. This reduced the isolation of these elderly people, increased mental stimulation, improved self-esteem, and increased scores on an index measuring their ability to perform daily maintenance skills (McConatha, McConatha, & Dermigny, 1994).

Alternatives to Nursing Homes

Although the nursing home population will certainly increase in the next century, alternatives to nursing homes are now being sought because of their substantial cost and the public's negative perception of them. Nursing home use is the largest out-of-pocket health care cost for older people, and government programs pay for about half of all nursing home costs (Montgomery & Kosloski, 1994).

Most elderly people who live alone require few if any services to keep their independence, but many do need some assistance with daily or weekly chores. Two thirds of such assistance is provided without charge by family or friends (Braus, 1994b). Women devote about twice the time to helping their elderly parents as men. Women also spend somewhat more time on such indirect chores as paying bills and shopping, but here the gap between men and women is smaller (Braus, 1994b). Home care aides and registered nurses may be hired to help as well.

***Table 19.2* Home and Community Living Options**
Following are the types of care available in Oregon's home- and community-living options.

In-home services
- Meal preparation
- Shopping and transportation
- Home health services
- Assistance with medication
- Housekeeping and laundry
- Money management
- Assistance with medical equipment
- Help with dressing and personal hygiene

Licensed adult foster care
- Homelike environment with a family
- Flexible rules and routines
- Safe, supervised place to live
- Medication management
- Nursing care
- Help with dressing and personal hygiene

Licensed assisted-living facilities
- Room and board in private apartment
- 24-hour supervision and protection
- Organized activities
- Intermittent nursing services
- Medication management
- Help with dressing and personal hygiene
- Behavior management (for such things as wandering or confusion)
- Licensed nurse available

Licensed residential care
- Room and board
- 24-hour supervision and protection
- Medication management
- Organized activities
- Assistance with dressing and bathing

Source: Concannon, 1995.

It is to everyone's benefit to help elderly people stay in the community and most elderly prefer to stay at home as long as possible (Montgomery & Kosloski, 1994). Many alternatives have been suggested and some states, such as Oregon, have inaugurated successful programs to increase the number of options open to the elderly in need of special care while at the same time saving money (Concannon, 1995). Table 19.2 shows some of the services specifically matched to the specific individual's needs. Oregon's program is such a success that Oregon is the only state with fewer elderly people in nursing homes in 1995 than in 1985!

Personality in Later Adulthood

Just as was the case in middle adulthood, the overwhelming majority of modern studies find that personality characteristics remain rather stable in adulthood and through old age (Costa & McCrae, 1992; Kogan, 1990; Costa et al., 1986). Generally, the individual who is bitter at 35 is bitter at 75 and the individual who is talkative at 40 is talkative at 80! Certain personality traits may express themselves in different ways at different ages. If people were active in their younger years, they are likely to remain active in older adulthood if their health is good, but not in the same way. We might expect a young adult to play basketball whereas an older adult might walk. Normal life stresses, such as retirement and bereavement, do not have significant effects on personality over the long term, but catastrophic stressors, such as stroke, may affect personality (Costa & McCrae, 1992).

Older people are more likely to show an increase in interiority—a preoccupation with the inner life (Neugarten, 1968a). Older people are likely to be more introspective (Atchley, 1990; Schulz, 1985) and to participate in life review (Butler, 1963), which is the process of looking back and evaluating life (described in Chapter 20). Such a process may be important in putting one's life into perspective. Other changes include a tendency to be more cautious, slower, and more practical, which are reasonable adaptations to the challenges of aging; older people also show more self-acceptance.

Religion in Later Adulthood

The increase in introspection and interiority are attempts to place one's life into perspective and to come to grips with one's own mortality. Older people are faced with many terminal events, such as the death of loved ones and physical incapacity. Religion may help people to understand and deal with these events. In addition, religious involvement may be a source of social contact with the community and the religious institution a place to interact with other people. Religion allows people to extract meaning from their life experiences and helps individuals cope with various stressors (Levin, Taylor, & Chatters, 1994).

Older people are more likely than younger people to believe that religion is very important in their lives (Ward, 1984). In addition, certain personal activities such as reading the Bible, listening to religious programs on radio and television, and personal prayer increase in old age. Older people generally show fairly high levels of religiosity, attend religious services at least a few times per month, and pray on a regular basis (Levin et al., 1994). Older women display higher levels of religiosity than older men, and older African Americans display higher degrees of religious involvement than whites (Levin et al., 1994). There is little evidence that older people turn radically to religion as they age, but religion certainly plays a part in the lives of many elderly people.

Developmental Tasks of Older People

People negotiating old age must cope with diminished physical skills, chronic illness, loss of friends and family members, and recognition of their own mortality. According to Erikson (1963), the psychosocial crisis of old age is **ego integrity** versus **despair**. The older person reviews his or her life and accomplishments. If the sum total of life's achievements in all spheres is positive, a sense of satisfaction emerges and ego integrity is achieved. But if the life of the elderly person is full of failures and missed opportunities, a sense of despair emerges, which exhibits itself in bitterness and frustration. Peck (1968) noted that the elderly have to meet three challenges. Older people must value leisure time and make meaningful use of it; they must come to terms with their own mortality and transcend their fear of death; and they must live a satisfying life, including having good interpersonal relations, despite chronic illness.

Interpersonal Relationships in Later Adulthood

Satisfying interpersonal relationships are important at every age and there is reason to believe that intimate or close relationships are even more important to older people. As people age, they narrow their social contacts, the number of people they interact with in a friendly manner is reduced (Carstenson, 1992).

Marriage in the Golden Years

After a decline in marital satisfaction lasting until late middle age, marriages become increasingly satisfying (Carstensen, Gottman, & Levenson, 1995; Ward, 1993). Elderly people express significantly more satisfaction with marriage than at earlier times (Mathis & Tanner, 1991). The increase begins in the empty-nest stage and continues into later maturity.

> ***True or False?***
> Most elderly couples express great satisfaction with their marriages.

Some changes do take place in the marriage. More sharing occurs, and more activities are performed together (Keating & Cole, 1980). When married couples ages 40–50 and 60–70 were compared, older couples showed reduced potential for conflict and greater potential for engaging in pleasurable activities, such as dancing or travel, with each other (Levenson, Carstensen, & Gottman, 1993). Middle-aged couples disagreed more than older couples about money, religion, recreation, and children. Older couples derived more enjoyment from talking about children or grandchildren, taking vacations, and doing things together. More emphasis is placed on relating to each other in an honest, expressive manner (Ward, 1993). Middle-aged couples display higher levels of anger, belligerence, and whining than older couples, and older couples express more affection (Carstensen, Gottman, & Levenson, 1995). In addition, older couples resolve conflict with less negative emotion (Vaillant & Vaillant, 1993).

Gender roles are often blurred in older marriages (Ward, 1984). Older males do not need to live up to a male stereotype that no longer has much meaning to them. Older women may be still working when their husbands retire or taking care of older, physically ill husbands. For whatever reason, older women find themselves with more power.

> ***Questions Students Often Ask***
> I see my grandmother now rules the house. Is this unusual?
> *No, it isn't. In old age, women often gain power. After retirement, men's work role is gone. They exist largely in the home, an area that traditionally and especially for this cohort belongs to the wife. She is also probably younger and more likely to be in better health.*

These changes should not be interpreted to mean that a truly egalitarian marriage emerges and that housework and other responsibilities are shared equally. Middle-aged and older couples exhibit substantial continuity in the division of household labor established earlier in marriage (Dorfman, 1992). Immediately after retirement, more sharing of the household duties is evident, but gradually it reverts to a more stereotyped pattern (Szinovacz & Harpster, 1994). The increase in sharing is not even as great as the couple themselves expect (Vinick & Ekerdt, 1992). Elderly wives report doing many more household tasks and a great inequity exists in performing household chores (Ward, 1993).

When the husband does a chore it has both practical and symbolic value. It symbolizes love and support and therefore her perception of his help makes a difference. Wives who continue to be employed after their husbands retire often report lower levels of marital satisfaction than do wives in marriages in which both spouses retire at the same time or the husband retires first (Lee & Shehan, 1989). If the husband retires first, the wife may be somewhat annoyed if the division of labor does not improve and may resent this inequity. Wives who perceive that their husbands help out at home are more satisfied with their husband's support and less likely to report that their husbands make too many demands on them. These perceptions are associated with wives' reports of greater marital quality and less depression. The division of household chores clearly affects wives' feelings of being supported, which is related to marital happiness (Pina & Bengtson, 1995).

There is an old saying that when a man retires, his wife receives half the income and twice the husband. After retirement, husbands are around the house more and see their wives doing chores. Husbands may become more

ego integrity The positive outcome of Erikson's last psychosocial stage, in which an older person experiences a sense of satisfaction with life.

despair The negative outcome of Erikson's last psychosocial stage, in which an older person experiences a sense of bitterness over lost opportunities.

critical. Housewives who were asked about their reaction to the early years of their husband's retirement said that they were happy that the time available to do things together had increased substantially and that companionship was more plentiful. Some noted that husbands helped with more of the housework, and many stated that their husbands were happier. The most negative aspects were financial problems, husbands with not enough to do, and too much togetherness (Hill & Dorfman, 1982). When asked what advice they would give to other wives, most women stated that wives should try to keep their husbands busy, continue their own preretirement activities, do more with their husbands, and maintain their privacy.

Retirement itself does not have an effect on marital satisfaction, but being satisfied with one's retirement may. If an individual is unhappy in retirement, depression may result and depressive symptoms predict lower marital satisfaction. Satisfaction with retirement is related to having a sense of purpose from one's activities, being able to structure one's time satisfactorily, and the nature of one's interpersonal contacts (Higginbottom, Barling, & Kelloway, 1993). If retired individuals are satisfied, they are less likely to be depressed and more likely to find their marriages satisfying.

Sex and Older People

If people have difficulty seeing their parents in sexual terms, imagine how difficult it is to view their grandparents as sexual beings. When undergraduates were questioned about the degree to which they approved of sexuality in the elderly, there was overwhelming approval of the elderly (over 70 years) having unmarried intercourse, living together, and having sex in nursing homes (Pratt & Schmall, 1989). However, as the closeness of the relationship of the elderly to them increased, the acceptance of sexual activity for the elderly decreased. Many elderly people believe that sex is the province of the young (McCammon, Knox, & Schacht, 1993). This is unfortunate because sexual activity can remain a satisfying part of life throughout old age. Other cultures do not shackle their elderly with such stereotypes. In one survey, 70% of the societies researched expected continued sexual activity, especially for males (Winn & Newton, 1982).

A national survey of marital sex found that the incidence and frequency of marital sex changes drastically over the life span. The percentage of couples who have marital sex gradually declines until about age 50 when the declines become sharper. However, 27% of those 75 and older say that they have engaged in sexual activity in the past month. Touching and caressing without intercourse was the most common sexual activity.

Frequency and quality are not the same, and in one study of elderly people, 75% of those who were still sexually active believed that their lovemaking had improved with age (Starr & Weiner, 1982). For older men, quality of performance was more important to self-esteem than frequency (Stimson, Wase, & Stimson, 1981). Many older couples actually report that their relationships are more romantic now and as sexually satisfying as they were at a younger age (Dychtwald & Flower, 1989).

A significant number of elderly people do not continue to engage in sex. For women, lack of a partner is the most significant problem. Women are much more likely than men to live a portion of old age without a spouse because men die at an earlier age than women. For women living with a spouse, continued sexual activity depends on the male (Ward, 1984). Continued sexual activity in the elderly male is related to the man's sexual practices at the earlier stages of life. Those who were high in sexual interest and activity in early adulthood continue to be sexually active later in life (Pfeiffer & Davis, 1972).

Widowhood

On the Life Events Stress Scale devised by Holmes and Rahe (see p. 326), the death of a spouse is the most stressful situation, achieving a 100-point score. When one becomes a widow or widower, life changes considerably. Years ago, widows were incorporated into the extended family and considered a family responsibility, but times have changed. Today women are more independent, have full inheritance rights, and are more likely to have outside social activities than in the past. On the other hand, widows are also more isolated from family and often suffer financial problems (Lopata, 1979).

Much more is written about widows than about widowers. Three out of four women can expect to become widowed whereas only if a man lives to be 85 does he have an even chance of losing his wife (Barrow, 1986). Older men are far more likely than older women to be married because of the greater longevity of women, the tendency of men to marry younger women, and because widowed men are much more likely to remarry. The probability of widowhood increases with age (Cantor, 1991).

When a spouse dies, the sense of personal loss is extreme. Normally the bereavement period, of which depression is a part, lasts for about 1 year, but for a sizable minority, depression continues longer than that. Widows often must deal with new and strange situations. For instance, the husband may have always taken care of the car or the finances, and suddenly the widow must learn about car maintenance and investments. Stories of widows being tricked by irresponsible and even criminal "advisers" are frequently true. Some widows are left in poverty, and unwise investments strip many others of their financial resources.

The more the widow has identified with the wifely homemaker role, the more she will be affected by the loss of her spouse. Most widows continue to live alone, and half find loneliness to be a great problem (Lopata, 1973). Widows are also apt to curtail their social activities, often because they do not feel accepted and are uncomfortable in couple-oriented situations.

Most widows eventually regain their equilibrium and create a new life, yet one in five claims never to have recovered from the loss (Lopata, 1973). The process of coping with widowhood involves initial recognition of the loss, followed by a temporary disengagement and a period of limbo. Finally, a new life structure is built (Barrow, 1986). The deceased spouse is often idealized (Gentry & Shulman, 1988), and most women say they do not remarry because they cannot find anyone as nice as their first husband, not because of a scarcity of available men. Many widows prefer to remain single. Remarried individuals may find that problems of loneliness, money management, and home maintenance are reduced but that remarriage can produce other stresses and problems (Gentry & Shulman, 1988).

Questions Students Often Ask

My grandmother was fine until my grandfather died, and now she does nothing and is always depressed. What can we do to help her?

Imagine being married for many years and having had your whole life revolve around coupled activities. Perhaps for a year or so, you devoted all your time to your ailing spouse who then dies. One lonely widow suffering from malnutrition did not eat because she was so used to making food for her husband and eating with him. It was no fun eating alone. Another rather depressed widow told me that you can't play Scrabble alone.

Although it cannot be rushed, it is important for widows and widowers to find someone to talk to, perhaps in a bereavement group of others who have suffered similar losses. At the same time, the family must make sure that the elderly individual continues to eat well. There are many groups available and many widows do reenter the community. However, some are so depressed that they do not, and medical help is required and should be actively sought.

Some women find help in self-help groups in which widows get together to discuss their feelings and problems, and give each other companionship. These programs are useful for the full range of widows, not only for those who seem to be at high risk for isolation and continuing depression (Corr, Nabe, & Corr, 1994).

Some authorities believe that the widower has an even more difficult job adjusting to the loss (Bernardo, 1968). The incidence of low morale, mental disorders, and suicide and death is higher for widowers than for widows (Stroebe & Stroebe, 1983). The widower must learn how to do many tasks he may never have performed before, such as cooking or doing the laundry. A widower is more likely to find a mate than a widow is, simply because there are more older women than older men.

Relationships With Children

Most elderly people are pleased with their relationship with their middle-aged children. The large majority of elderly people report active family ties. Most see or talk with their children often and help their children out when they can (Neugarten & Neugarten, 1989). Families in later life are frequently in contact, show affection to each other, and communicate openly (Motenko & Greenberg, 1995).

True or False?

Most elderly people have frequent contact with their middle-aged children.

It is popular to mourn the death of the extended family and to extol its virtues. It is claimed that in the past, three-generation families living together and constantly helping one another were common, but with the advent of industrialization and urbanization, the extended family became almost extinct and this special closeness was lost. This belief is generally untrue. The extended family was never common in the United States. Even in our earliest days of colonization in the 17th century, the extended family was rare, if for no other reason than that grandparents were not as likely to be alive (Ward, 1984). At no point in American history did the percentage of extended families living in the same house exceed 10% (Aizenberg & Treas, 1985). In addition, the overwhelming majority of older people did not then and do not now want to live with their adult children (Bengtson & DeTerre, 1980). Our society values independence, and older people show a great desire to live independently without interfering much in their children's lives.

The elderly have a very strong desire to live independently whenever possible (Wahl, 1991). When they need help, older people expect and receive a great deal of assistance from their children, especially during crises. However, the help is reciprocal, and older people emphasize their contributions to the welfare of their adult children. Many elderly assist their children financially and provide personal services (Aldous, 1987), such as helping to take care of the grandchildren. They are much more likely to assist children who are single or divorced or children they believe need help.

Relationships between elderly parents and their adult children are marked by warmth, but the best relationships occur when neither interferes with the other. This sort of *distant intimacy* is the cultural norm, in which the independence of each is respected (Stevens-Long & Commons, 1992). However, when elderly parents become depressed or very sick, the relationship can become strained. Relationships with the frail elderly change because the elderly cannot visit their children and often cannot see their grandchildren. Illness demoralizes older people and alienates family members as the burden of responsibilities grows (Aizenberg & Treas, 1985).

When elderly people become seriously ill and need considerable care, the quality of their relationships with their middle-aged children declines (Richards, Bengtson, & Miller, 1989). Adult children provide a great deal of care for their elderly parents (Himes, 1992), but the situation is complicated as their children age. One in ten elderly people has a child who is at least 65 years old, and these adult children may not be in good health themselves (Aizenberg & Treas, 1985). It is not easy for elderly people to ask their children for help and to maintain their self-esteem in these circumstances (Motenko & Greenberg, 1995). Being able to provide for the needs of elderly people allows the younger generation to feel that they are giving back something to those who have done so much for them; however, older people must continue to be as autonomous as possible and to exercise choice whenever possible.

Elder Abuse

The frustrations of taking care of the frail elderly sometimes erupt into abuse. It is estimated that between 1% and 10% of the elderly population is abused (Pillemer & Suitor, 1988), and the rates of abuse of older men and women are similar (Pillemer & Finkelhor, 1988). Most states have passed mandatory laws for reporting elder abuse and provide for protective service programs when elder abuse is identified (Johnson, 1995; Wolf & Pillemer, 1994). The abuse of the elderly can take many forms, including physical or psychological abuse, nutritional or medical neglect, and financial exploitation.

All definitions of elder abuse include physical violence and most contain some mention of psychological abuse or maltreatment, usually defined as the intention of causing emotional pain or injury, including such behaviors as verbal aggression in the form of threats and insults, humiliation, or threats of abandonment or institutionalization. Many definitions include exploitation, including theft of pension checks or financial coercion. Neglect involves failure to meet the needs of the individual, such as failing to fulfill caretaking responsibility or withholding food or medication. It is problematic to determine who is responsible for the elderly person and whether the neglect is intentional or unintentional (Lachs & Pillemer, 1995). Although the public is very concerned about physical abuse of the elderly, most elderly people and care-givers surveyed suggest that neglect is the primary form of elder abuse (Johnson, 1995). Care-givers are more likely to identify legal agencies as neglectful, whereas elderly people claim family as more neglectful. The victims of elder abuse are likely to be frail, cognitively and physically impaired, and to view themselves as helpless (Myers & Shelton, 1987). Frailty is a predisposing factor and it interacts with the characteristics of the care-giver. Three care-giver characteristics emerge as the most important: substance abuse or psychiatric problems, excessive dependence on the elderly person for financial assistance or housing, and a history of violence or antisocial behavior in other contexts (Lachs & Pillemer, 1995). Table 19.3 presents the possible risk factors for abuse or neglect of the elderly.

Studies of elder abuse yield some surprises. It is certainly true that the care of the elderly may become so frustrating that the care-giver's anger may result in abuse of the elderly. However, studies find that most abusers are actually dependent upon the elderly person for financial support or housing (Pillemer, 1985). The abuser is frequently a very dependent spouse or child (Pillemer, 1986), perhaps one who is trying to compensate for his or her lack of power. In addition, abusers are more likely to be under stress and to use alcohol or other drugs; sometimes they are getting back at their parents for past grievances.

True or False?
Many people who abuse their elderly relatives are actually financially dependent upon them.

Elder abuse was formally recognized only in the 1970s (Johnson, 1995). It has only recently become the focus

Table 19.3 **Risk Factors for Abuse of the Elderly**

RISK FACTOR	MECHANISM
Poor health and functional impairment in the elderly person	Disability reduces the elderly person's ability to seek help and defend himself or herself.
Cognitive impairment in the elderly person	Aggression toward the care giver and disruptive behavior resulting from dementia may precipitate abuse. Higher rates of abuse have been found among patients with dementia.
Substance abuse or mental illness on the part of the abuser	Abusers are likely to abuse alcohol or drugs and to have serious mental illness, which in turn leads to abusive behavior.
Dependence of the abuser on the victim	Abusers are very likely to depend on the victim financially, for housing, and in other areas. Abuse results from attempts by a relative (especially an adult child) to obtain resources from the elderly person.
Shared living arrangement	Abuse is much less likely among elderly people living alone. A shared living situation provides greater opportunities for tension and conflict, which generally precede incidents of abuse.
External factors causing stress	Stressful life events and continuing financial strain decrease the family's resistance and increase the likelihood of abuse.
Social isolation	Elderly people with fewer social contacts are more likely to be victims. Isolation reduces the likelihood that abuse will be detected and stopped. In addition, social support can buffer the effects of stress.
History of violence	Particularly among spouses, a history of violence in the relationship may predict abuse in later life.

Source: Lachs & Pillemer, 1995.

of public interest and more research must be done if we are to understand it and devise effective interventions for this serious problem.

Grandparenting

Some 70% of the middle-aged and elderly population can expect to become grandparents (Smith, 1995). A grandparent today is much more likely to be in good physical health than grandparents from years ago (Aizenberg & Treas, 1985). Most studies find that the contacts grandparents have with grandchildren are relatively frequent and satisfying (Smith, 1995). Grandparents are likely to have considerable contact with their grandchildren if they live close by (Hodgson, 1992).

Grandparents engage in many activities with their grandchildren, some social, such as playing with them and taking trips together; some spiritual, such as taking them to religious services; some educational, such as teaching them skills or games; and some that involve guidance, such as discussing problems and giving advice (Cherlin & Furstenberg, 1986; Smith, 1995). Children may be directly influenced by their grandparents through their frequent contacts with them. They may also be affected indirectly because grandparents give advice to parents about discipline and punishment (Tomlin & Passman, 1991).

The overwhelming majority of grandparents take a positive view of their new role as grandparents, but one third do not feel quite comfortable with it (Johnson, 1983; Neugarten & Weinstein, 1964). Some feel they are too young to be grandparents or find it difficult to play the role of grandparent (Timberlake & Chipungu, 1992). Those who first become grandparents in their 70s may be disappointed because they may feel too old to engage in the types of activities they want with their young grandchildren (Burton & Bengtson, 1985).

Young grandchildren look forward to their grandparents' indulgence. As grandchildren age and create lives of their own, the relationship becomes less satisfying. Parents influence how involved their children will be with their grandparents. If the children's parents are not close to their own parents, it is unlikely that the children will be close to the grandparents (King & Elder, 1995; Matthews & Sprey, 1985).

Culture also has a significant influence on the kind of roles grandparents play in the lives of their grandchildren. For example, much is written about the importance of the grandmother in African American homes. Historically, grandmothers are important figures who provide support and cultural continuity in families and act as supplementary or surrogate parents (Smith, 1995). When African American and white grandmothers were sampled in a rural area, some differences in perceived parenting attitudes, behaviors, and involvement were found. African American grandmothers gave more help to and received more help from grandchildren than white grandmothers. African American grandfathers both expected to have more association with, and actually had more contacts with their grandchildren than white grandfathers (Kivett, 1993). They saw their role as grandparents as more central to their lives than white grandfathers did (Kivett, 1991), and they reported feeling closer to their grandchildren. There were many similarities as well; all grandparents reported that the grandparent role was more affectionate than instrumental and high levels of closeness were found for both African Americans and whites (Kivett, 1993).

Grandparents Raising Grandchildren

About 5% of all American children live with their grandparents. An increase has occurred across all ethnic groups, but has been particularly significant in the African American community where about 12% of all children live with their grandparents (Brooks-Gunn & Chase-Lansdale, 1995). In some inner cities, the proportions are substantially higher (Gross, 1992). About half these grandparents provide child care and over half a million are raising their grandchildren without help (U.S. News and World Report, September 18, 1995).

The growth of single-parent families, lack of affordable housing, teenage pregnancy, and drug addiction are factors that sometimes cause grandparents to take in their children and grandchildren (Burton, 1992). During such emergencies grandparents take on the clear role of surrogate parent or at least of helper (Smith, 1995). Grandparents may reduce the impact of family disruption caused by drug abuse, divorce, or single parenthood (Solomon & Marx, 1995). Grandmothers are also the primary care-givers for children under the age of 5 whose mothers work (Presser, 1989).

The roles taken by grandparents depend on the situation. Certainly a grandmother is likely to be more involved with the child of a 16-year-old single adolescent parent than with a 30-year-old daughter who is getting a divorce and has her own apartment. Grandparents may be actively involved in any or every area of parenting or simply act as baby-sitters on a regular basis. Young adolescent parents are very likely to live with their parents. Most are not married and whatever assistance the father can provide is usually not enough to allow the mother to live independently (Brooks-Gunn & Furstenberg, 1989).

When grandmothers and low-income adolescent mothers with toddlers were interviewed, four different models appeared (Apfel & Seitz, 1991). In the *parental replacement model,* which was 20% of the sample, the mother of the adolescent assumes the complete responsibility for raising the child. It may occur through mutual agreement, such as when the mother is away at college or in the military. It may also occur if the daughter lives with the family but assumes little responsibility for her child, maintaining the lifestyle of her peers. Sometimes the mother is incompetent or negligent or simply abandons the child. The *parental supplement model* involves the child care being shared between grandmother and daughter. Sometimes, siblings and other family members may also help out. The organization varies depending upon the task to be completed and the time in which it must be done; slightly more than 50% adopted this role. The young mother may live with her family or apart.

In the *supported primary parent model,* which was 20% of the sample, the young mother is responsible for the care of the child but receives support through regular communication or visitation, financial help, and baby-sitting and aid with household tasks. About half lived independently but close by, while the other half resided with the grandparents. The fourth model, the *parent apprentice model,* used by 10% of the sample, involved the grandmother acting as a mentor to her daughter. The grandmother acts as a source of knowledge and a model, quickly giving control to the daughter.

There are potential benefits for both the mother and the child from extensive grandparent involvement, and also some potential drawbacks. Grandmothers may be very effective role models for their daughters as far as parenting is concerned. This is especially true for a young adolescent mother with no experience. Regular and sustained contact can result in a secure attachment forming between the grandchild and grandparent and the greater the involvement, the greater the attachment (Tomlin & Passman, 1989). Such an attachment does not injure the parent-child relationship. However, being a grandparent does not ensure excellent parenting skills. Grandparents may also be poor models or mixed models. Unfortunately, punitive and harsh patterns of parenting are somewhat more likely to be modeled than positive styles (Patterson, 1986). Mothers and maternal grandmothers deal with children somewhat differently. When compared in a laboratory setting, grandmothers were more rewarding and less punishing (Blackwilder & Passman, 1986). The greater the responsibility for caring for the child, the more likely it was that the grandmothers used a more disciplinary style.

In any situation in which grandparent help is required, both their emotional and tangible support may be crucial. For example, right after a divorce, a daughter may require some time to recover; an adolescent parent may require some years to graduate, learn job skills, and become independent. When grandparents help to raise the child, a young mother or a divorced mother may be allowed to finish school and receive appropriate job training (Brooks-Gunn & Chase-Lansdale, 1991). However, the adolescent who found her mother's help and advice so welcome when she was young may resent it now that she is somewhat older. Living together can be stressful for both the mother and the grandparent. The single 18-year-old mother may be balancing her need for autonomy and her need for help caring for her child. The grandmother must balance her need to work and continue her other roles and relationships with the reality of helping to parent her grandchildren (Brooks-Gunn & Chase-Landsdale, 1995). In many of these homes, poverty also adds to the stress.

Some additional concerns involve the effects of beginning all over again to raise or help raise one's grandchildren. Less family support is available today in both the African American and white communities (Johnson & Barer, 1990). Extended families may be living farther from each other and potential helpers may have other obligations. Grandparents may feel ambivalent about their new role; they may enjoy their grandchildren but may resent the resulting loss of freedom.

Generally, children living with a grandparent do well when compared with those living with a single mother (Solomon & Marx, 1995). The grandmother typically carries almost the whole burden and may be poor as well. When grandfathers are present and involved, children are more obedient, healthier, and benefit from the presence of a warm, accepting male role model. Studies show that children raised by their grandparents are not at a disadvantage when measurements of health or behavior are compared with those for children raised in single-parent families. These children are less likely to show behavior problems in school than children raised by single parents and show about the same number of behavior problems as those raised in nuclear families. Children in nuclear families are more academically successful as they repeat fewer grades and are better students. However, children raised by their grandparents are equal in achievement to those raised in single-parent families. The health of these children is about equal to those in intact families and somewhat superior to those raised in single-parent families. The only area of concern is academics and it is possible that these problems are caused by excessive absences that may have begun prior to a divorce (Larson, 1990/1991).

True or False?
Children raised by their grandparents do not show any more behavioral or health problems than those children raised by single parents.

One very special area of concern today is grandparents who become substitute parents for a daughter with a drug problem who just gave birth. The drug problem adds greatly to the normal stress of substitute parenting. Grandmothers, especially African American grandmothers, are often stereotyped as powerful matriarchs with tremendous almost inexhaustible strength, wisdom, and patience. This view is too simplistic. Their twin duties to their daughters and grandchildren, especially if the daughter is addicted to drugs, may leave them economically, physically, and emotionally drained (Burton, 1992). Grandparents in this role identify three different types of stressors—contextual, familial, and individual. The greatest contextual problems involve the danger within the neighborhood, especially the drug trafficking. The timing of the drug trade in the community impacts their daily organization, determining when it is safe to shop or to allow children to play outdoors. The familial stressors include financial problems and the need to continue their previous role of spouse and mother to other children. Sometimes the grandmother has to care for more than one grandchild. Individual sources of stress may involve not having much time for themselves. These grandparents are loving and committed, receive gratification from what they are doing but may be overwhelmed.

These grandparents admit that such stresses sometimes lead to problems such as physical illness, alcoholism, increased smoking, or depression and anxiety (Burton, 1992). Grandparents require special services from churches as well as governmental agencies. More than three quarters need economic assistance but do not receive any from their children or social services agencies. Many need respite services so they can go out. Legal counseling, especially concerning guardianship, parenting programs to help reduce isolation, and job counseling are also needed. When interviewed, most refused to dwell on their health problems because they wanted to protect their grandchildren who they feared would be placed in foster care (Minkler, Roe, & Price, 1992). They were glad they could be there for their grandchildren and noted that the new care-giver role was worth the costs. This is in keeping with the traditional and idealized role of strong grandmothers. However, it is not a desired role for many grandmothers who clearly need greater support services.

Great-Grandparenting

A relatively new status is great-grandparenthood as four-generation families become more common. Great-grandparenting differs from grandparenting in at least two ways. First, great-grandparents are much older. Second, instead of there being only one generation between grandparent and child, there are now two so the relationship is mediated by both parents and grandparents (Robertson, 1975). Grandparents visit their grandchildren, but because of their age and lack of transportation, great-grandparents must wait for visits from their great-grandchildren, who have grandparents to visit as well.

Little research exists on the subject of great-grandparenting. When great-grandmothers were interviewed, they showed a preference for younger great-grandchildren (Wentowski, 1985). One great-grandmother said, "Young children don't think about age the same way grownups do. They love you anyway. Even if you are old, they don't notice. If they did notice, they would say so" (Wentowski, 1985, p. 593). Also, whereas younger grandparents have the energy to play and deal with grandchildren, great-grandparents often feel that youngsters are more wearing.

Great-grandparents realize that they cannot do as much for their great-grandchildren, and they recognize their limitations. They tend to be less involved than they are with their grandchildren. Great-grandparents experience pleasure from and a degree of ambivalence with their role. Having great-grandchildren is also an undeniable sign of aging. Great-grandparents are emotionally remote from the younger generation and admit to being closer to their grandchildren. Relationships with their children are most important, then with their grandchildren, and finally with their great-grandchildren.

Siblings

A person's longest-lasting relationship is most likely to be with siblings (Bengtson, Rosenthal, & Burton, 1990). Contact is fairly frequent, especially by telephone, although the figures differ widely. Most report feeling close to at least one sibling, a long-term feeling beginning in childhood and adolescence (Dunn, 1983). Sibling rivalry decreases after adolescence but contact may be less frequent because of distance, marriage, and the pressures of raising children. In some cases, the relationship between siblings becomes closer in old age, once other family responsibilities decrease (Manney, 1975). Most elderly people say they would like to see their siblings more often than the typical two or three times a year (Goode, 1994).

Women have more sibling contact than men, and people who have children have less contact with siblings than people without children (Bengtson et al., 1990). Earlier relationship patterns tend to be maintained; that is, those who are close in childhood and adolescence tend to remain friends in adulthood (Hayslip & Panek, 1993). Both men and women tend to name sisters and middle-born siblings as their closest sibling (Cicirelli, 1980). Gender also affects sibling closeness. Sister-sister relationships are the closest, followed by brother-sister, and then finally brother-brother relationships (Barrow, 1986). Sisters play an interesting role in middle and older families, acting as sources of reassurance and emotional security. Elderly men with sisters report greater feelings of happiness and less worry and less depression about their life circumstances (Goode, 1994).

Siblings' memories may be similar; they are of the same generation, and as they age, they can form part of a social network that will support each other in times of grief and crisis. Sibling relationships are especially important to the married elderly who have no children and to the widowed, the divorced, and the never-married (Watson, 1982). The death of a sibling is a tremendous shock and one that deeply affects the elderly. The youngest member of the family is especially hard hit because he or she may experience the loss of a number of older siblings with age.

Friendships

Friends do not replace family in times of crisis but the social network of elderly people is one predictor of good adjustment, being satisfied with life, and having a positive self-concept (Busse & Maddox, 1985; Jones & Vaughn, 1990). Social support is related to well-being and feelings of efficacy and social competence (Sarason, Sarason, & Pierce, 1989). The concept of the social convoy (see p. 408) is useful here (Antonucci, 1990; Kahn & Antonucci, 1980). Friends provide a buffer against stress and help maintain high morale in old age (Burrus-Bammel &

Bammel, 1985). Many leisure activities, such as playing cards, require social interaction. Proximity to friends becomes very important in old age because poor health and lack of transportation make it difficult to travel long distances. The social convoy helps an individual cope with life's changes and its shocks, such as the death of a loved one, retirement, or poor health. The nature of the social convoy changes over the life span; children and young adults may depend on their parents whereas older people may depend on siblings and friends. People with a well-structured, well-defined convoy system can better deal with life's stresses.

Although the actual number of friends people have usually decreases in old age, the importance of friends increases (Ebersole & Hess, 1981). One trend that occurs in social relationships in the elderly is a greater selectivity in such relationships (Carstensen, 1987). This selectivity allows people to conserve physical energy and regulate their experiences better. Interacting with familiar peers is more predictable and minimizes the chances for negative experiences. The change to being more selective is gradual and based upon the preferences of the older person (Fredrickson & Carstensen, 1990). Younger people are often interested in potential relationships because they see prospects for the future, but most elderly people are more concerned with immediate rewards and interactions. Most elderly people say that they feel no need to make new friends but would like to interact more with the friends they already have (Atchley, 1977).

Women tend to have more friends and to have more frequent contact with their friends (George, 1990), and women receive more social support from their friends than do men (Depner & Ingersoll-Dayton, 1988). Women are also more likely to have more intimate friends with whom they can share personal secrets and problems whereas men are more likely to have friends who share recreational pursuits. Older men usually stress the importance of similarities in interest; understanding and support are more important for women (Lowenthal, Thurnher, & Chiriboga, 1975). These differences hold up across cultures and subcultures and are true for whites, African Americans, French, Italians, Israelis, and Japanese (Antonucci, 1990).

Cross-Cultural Studies of Aging

Most Americans believe that the position of elderly people in Eastern societies is much better than it is in Western societies. A number of researchers have recently taken an interest in Japanese society because it combines an Eastern heritage with a Western technological base. Some interesting facts emerge. For example, most large Japanese firms retire their workers at the young age of 55 or 57, even though traditional Japanese society defines old age as over 60 (Maeda, 1978). Traditionally, a ceremony marks the person's 61st birthday in which a red vest is presented to the person, signifying the beginning of a second childhood. The person is now permitted to become dependent again, usually on adult sons, and is no longer obligated to work for a living, although most elderly people continue to work for money or satisfaction.

Early retirement causes a number of problems, for often the last child is still attending college, with all the costs this entails. In addition, pension benefits are rather low, and retired people are forced to take jobs with much lower pay and prestige than the jobs from which they were forced to retire. Most Japanese would rather stay on the job.

In Japan, as the last child leaves home, it is not unusual for the older couple to move in with their children, with the eldest son taking responsibility for them. Older people are expected to be dependent on their children. A popular Japanese proverb is "When old, obey your children." Most Japanese elderly and middle-aged people believe it is natural for the generations to live together. This is in sharp contrast to feelings of the elderly in Western cultures, where independent living is a badge of honor (Havighurst, 1978).

Most studies confirm that by and large the elderly are more respected and better treated in less industrialized societies than in industrialized countries (Lehr, 1983). As the proportion of elderly people increases, it is possible that their prestige will decrease. However, if the elderly can perform some valuable function, their status is high (Lehr, 1983). In a rural African culture called the Gesuii, elderly people often become healers or spiritual leaders who can perform certain ceremonies that increase their power (LeVine, 1978). In some societies the elderly control valuable information and are respected for this (Maxwell & Silverman, 1970). For example, in the Bakongo culture in Zaire, the elderly have technical information about fishing that is not available to others (Missinne, 1980); in other cultures the elderly control land or cattle or have political power (Fry, 1985).

Questions Students Often Ask

I think it is terrible that elderly people are not as honored in our society as they are in other cultures. I think the jokes about elderly people are in poor taste. Why is their position so low?

A number of reasons for the low status of elderly people have been advanced. We live in a very fast-changing society where new skills are needed for every new generation. We tend to see the elderly as not having these new skills. We have generalized this to mean that the elderly do not have anything of value to share. We do not seek out their opinions or appreciate their wisdom. In addition, as a youth-oriented society we see beauty and desirable traits in terms of youth and shy away from aging. In some societies, special roles are available for the elderly; our society does not ascribe a special and important role to them. For these and many other reasons, we do not venerate elderly people.

Treatment of elderly people differs according to culture. In many East Asian cultures, older people are more likely to be living with their children or grandchildren.

When industrialization occurs, the status of elderly people decreases quickly (Rosenmayr, 1985). The elderly no longer have essential skills, and as their children leave the traditional village or lifestyle for industry, they lose their control and power. Industrialization has come to be linked with loss of the extended family and an increase in the nuclear family and with a subsequent decrease in power and status for the elderly. There is some indication that in the later stages of industrialization, the status of elderly people improves again (Palmore & Manton, 1974), though not everyone believes that this occurs.

Sometimes the attitude toward the aged is very positive but the actual treatment of them is less so. Studies in a number of cultures—including the Ibo in Nigeria and various areas of Hong Kong and Taiwan—show that behavior does not always match attitudes (Fry, 1985).

Three important points stand out. First, each society gives older people certain duties and rights. Second, while looking at aging, we must consider both the attitudes and practices of a given society toward older people. Third, where older people are seen as serving a useful purpose, they tend to have a higher status. This purpose may involve transmission of culture, special knowledge, control of production, or wisdom. As we look at such areas as changes in personality, family and work relationships, and the entire area of retirement, the cultural context of these changes should be kept in mind.

The Minority Elderly

Recently a great deal of interest has arisen regarding the elderly who are members of minority groups (Cantor, 1991). The poverty rate for African Americans and Latinos is much higher than for white Americans, although some improvement has occurred. Even so, the poverty rate for elderly members of minority groups is still somewhat lower than the overall poverty rates for their respective groups generally.

To understand the older members of a minority, we must take a life-span perspective. Elderly people who are members of minority groups are more likely to have experienced single parenthood, childhood disease, poor diet and medical care, a poor neighborhood, poverty, violence, periods of unemployment, alcohol, other drug problems, and divorce (Jackson, Antonucci, & Gibson, 1990). This may affect the elderly person's health status, opportunities for recreation, and self-esteem later in life (Chatters, 1988).

Members of minority groups have a tendency to retire at earlier ages, and their death rates are higher until age 80 years or so. Some significant progress has been made, however, such as the reduction in hypertension among African Americans. Heart disease, although still more prevalent among elderly members of minority groups, has declined.

Elderly people belonging to minority groups show some interesting sociological differences. Elderly minority group members are more likely to live in multigenerational homes and less likely to be well educated. They are also more likely to be involved in their religious institutions, and religion plays a somewhat greater role in their social and spiritual life than it does for nonminority group elderly. Minority elderly are also more likely to live in larger families, have more frequent family contact, and to be taking care of the younger generations.

Retirement

Retirement is a relatively new concept. In the early years of this century, no one planned to retire. People worked until they were too ill to continue working or until they died. Most people over 65 today are no longer in the labor force (Morgenbagen, 1994). Now that people live longer, a new viewpoint has emerged: voluntary retirement. Early retirement—retirement before age

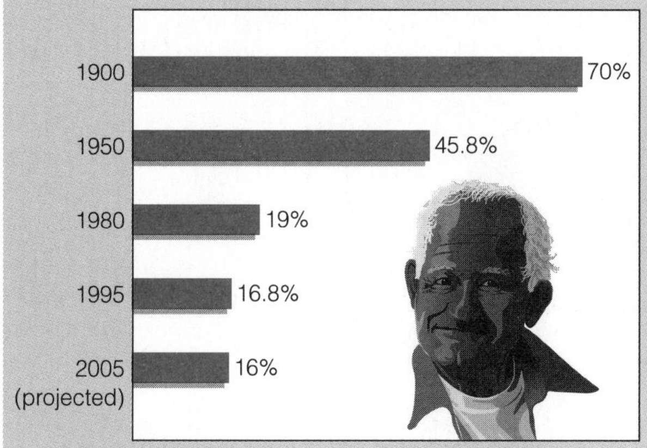

The percentage of men over 65 in the labor force has declined significantly—to a little more than 16%. Today, 8.8% of all women over 65 are in the labor force.

Datagraphic
A Shrinking Portion of the Workforce: Employed Elderly Men
Source: Data from Donovan, 1984; Gendell & Siegel, 1992; Statistical Abstract, 1996.

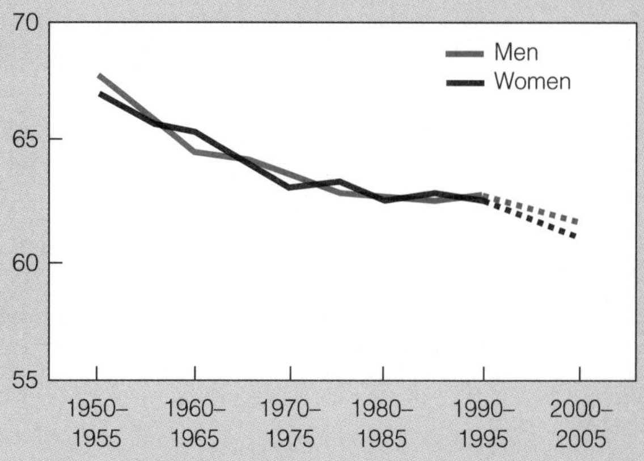

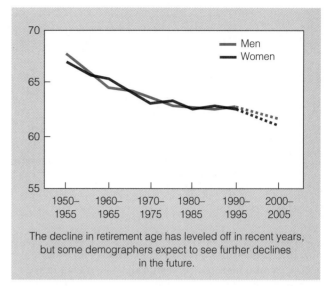

The decline in retirement age has leveled off in recent years, but some demographers expect to see further declines in the future.

Figure 19.2
Lower Expectations Median age of retirement by sex, for 5-year periods, 1950–1990, and projections to 2005.
Source: Morgenbagen, 1994; data from Bureau of Labor Statistics, Monthly Labor Review, July 1992.

65—has become very popular. Many firms and some government agencies give bonuses to people who retire early so that they can replace these workers with younger, less expensive employees. Most people retire before age 65 and take Social Security benefits at 62 or 63. The median age of retirement for both men and women in the United States is 63 (Morgenbagen, 1994). As Figure 19.2 shows, the age of retirement has declined for several decades, although it has now leveled off. Some authorities believe that it will continue to decline again relatively soon (Morgenbagen, 1994).

Questions Students Often Ask

I think older workers should be forced to retire. We won't have any jobs if everyone works into old age. Why shouldn't they be required to make room for others?

Relatively few elderly people continue working so this is really not an important issue at this point. Many companies do, indeed, offer retirement incentives for economic reasons; they can hire younger workers at lower pay to take the place of more senior, more highly paid workers. However, forced retirement assumes that older workers cannot succeed at the job, which is a very dubious assumption. It is also based upon the idea that older people do not need to work. Many still do. Last, an old saying states that you should be careful about what you wish for because you may get it. Someday you will be older and may find your perspective on the subject very different. Federal law prohibits age discrimination and, except for some public safety jobs such as airline pilot, forced retirement is illegal.

Phases of Retirement

Retirement is an exciting time. No longer do you have to get up at 6 in the morning or fight traffic on the way to work. Everything seems perfect—there is no other way to live. Does this feeling continue?

Preretirement and retirement occur in a series of phases (see Figure 19.3) (Atchley, 1977). The first retirement phase, called the **honeymoon phase** is a time of joy and excitement. People are very busy doing all the things they could not do when working full time. This phase may last for months or years. Not everyone goes through a honeymoon period; attitudes and financial resources may prevent some people from enjoying their immediate retirement activities.

After the honeymoon phase is over, many people experience a letdown or even become depressed. Poor planning may show itself in this **disenchantment phase,** as the original choices may have been unrealistic. One retired man told me he intended to spend 6 hours a day at the beach and would make other plans only after he was "thoroughly rested." Another was certain that fishing and camping would suffice, and for a time, both did; but after a year or so, disenchantment set in. When men who had been retired for 13 to 18 months were compared with new retirees, those retired for more than a year were less satisfied and less optimistic about the future than the new retirees (Ekerdt et al., 1985).

honeymoon phase The first phase after retirement, a time of joy and excitement.

disenchantment phase The letdown and sometimes the depression that follow the honeymoon phase, often experienced by people whose retirement planning may have been unrealistic.

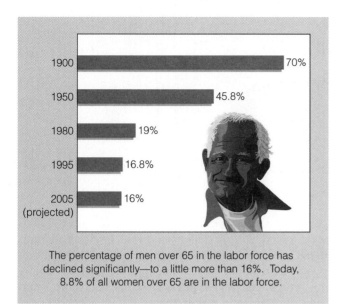

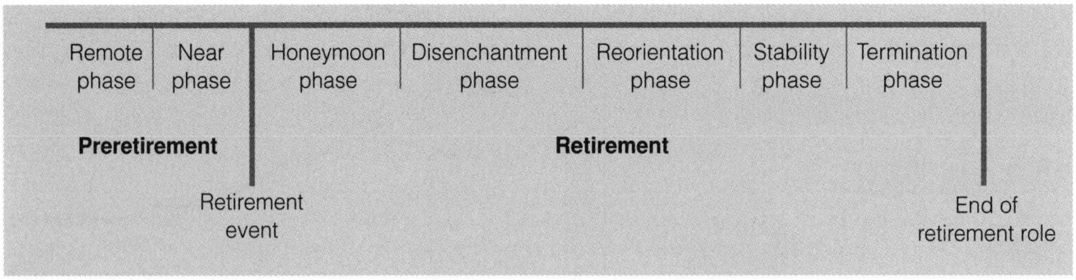

Figure 19.3
Atchley's Phases of Preretirement and Retirement Robert Atchley suggests that people negotiate preretirement and retirement itself in a series of phases.
Source: Atchley, 1977.

True or False?
Eighteen months after retirement, most people are happier and more satisfied with their lives than they were a month after retirement.

The letdown often requires a reevaluation, which leads to the **reorientation phase** as retirees begin to take stock of their lives and develop realistic alternatives. People may become involved in senior citizen clubs (which they might have shunned earlier) and begin to make realistic plans. This leads directly into the **stability phase,** during which these realistic plans come to fruition. Now life is pleasant, satisfying, and predictable.

Finally, there is the **termination phase,** in which people either return to work or have their more active retirement role disrupted by illness or disability. People may pass directly from the honeymoon to the stability phase, while others may never attain stability in retirement.

The Consequences of Retirement

People who retire do not show any sharp decline in health and may even show some improvement, perhaps because of reduced stress (Ekerdt, Bosse, & LoCastro, 1983). We all hear stories about people who retire and suddenly die from a heart attack. Actually, this is the exception to the rule as there is no relationship between retirement and cardiac arrest in retired people (Siscovick et al., 1990).

Most retired people are satisfied with their lives. Most people cope well with retirement and report high levels of satisfaction (Neugarten & Neugarten, 1989). Satisfaction with retirement is related to good health, adequate income, and substituting new activities for old ones (Botwinick, 1984). Poorly adapted people have inadequate financial resources, poor health, and few friends or family. They also lack clear-cut goals and often feel they were forced to retire (Fillenbaum et al, 1985). In addition, those who are forced to retire are more likely to show poorer adjustment to retirement, more illnesses following retirement, poorer physical status, and more symptoms of depression (Swan, Dame, & Carmelli, 1991).

Some experts in the field differentiate retirement from the transition to retirement. The decision to retire may cause some stress because it is a transition. However, retirement itself does not seem to cause much stress. Raymond Bosse and co-workers (1991) compared employed men to retired men. Among those who had retired in the past year, respondents and their spouses rated retirement

reorientation phase The retirement phase following the disenchantment phase, during which realistic plans are put into effect.

stability phase The retirement phase following the reorientation phase, during which realistic plans are put into effect.

termination phase The last phase of retirement, during which people either return to work or find their stable lifestyle disrupted and sometimes ended by illness or disability.

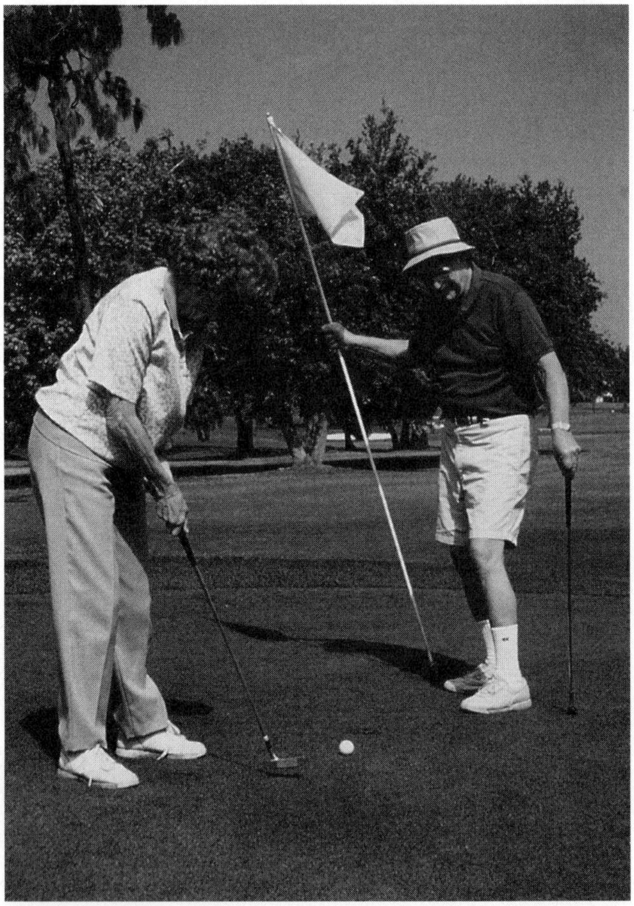

Retirement often marks the change from a work-oriented to a leisure-oriented lifestyle.

as least stressful from a list of 31 possible stressful events. Only 30% found retirement stressful at all, and retirement hassles were less frequently reported than work hassles. When the retirees were asked about problems during the past year, more than two thirds reported no retirement-related problems. Those who reported problems considered boredom and financial problems the greatest. The predictors of problems were poor health and problems with finances. Personality variables did not predict retirement stress (see Table 19.4).

Questions Students Often Ask

My parents are facing the possibility of retirement soon. How can they best prepare?

Preparation for retirement is necessary and this includes financial preparation. Satisfaction in retirement requires the ability to live the kind of lifestyle that one wants. There are other areas for consideration, such as planning meaningful and enjoyable activities. Another consideration is where to live. Although most people stay in their communities, some elderly relocate, sometimes without adequate investigation. It is often better to rent first in the prospective area and to read the local newspaper. The AARP and other organizations can suggest other planning activities.

Although most people adjust well to retirement, about one third have some difficulty in the transition (Floyd et al., 1992; Fletcher & Hansson, 1991). Retirement is a milestone and a transition, and some adjustment is perhaps required. Those who adjust better have planned more realistically and are able to fill their time with meaningful leisure activities. People who find all their satisfaction in work are likely to have difficulty adjusting to retirement (Atchley, 1990). People also have more difficulty coping with retirement if it disrupts long-term friendships and support and if making friends is not easy. To adjust successfully, people who retire must develop new interests or rediscover old talents and most manage to do this (Fletcher & Hansson, 1991).

Women and Retirement

Most studies of retirees involve only men. When studying women who retire, the cohort effect is likely to be formidable. Most of today's elderly female retirees entered the work force late, they interrupted their careers to raise their children for many years, and many of these older women hold positions that do not pay well.

Single women seem to be affected by the same factors as single or married men. Their retirement decision is affected by health, monetary matters, and a positive attitude toward retirement and leisure. However, married women are generally affected by their husband's work. More and more, retirement is a couple phenomenon with husbands and wives retiring at about the same time (Szinovacz & Harpster, 1994).

The key to retirement planning is saving early, and this applies even more to women because they live longer in retirement and earn less. Yet, fewer women than men start preparing for retirement early in adulthood and fewer women say that they are saving for retirement (CQ Researcher, 1993). Twice as many women as men claim that they are uninformed about retirement planning, and married women know less than married men about their own retirement savings and are less likely to manage their accounts.

Studies on women and retirement show mixed results. Some studies show that women generally have a more difficult time than men in retirement (Szinovacz, 1982).

Table 19.4 **Retirement-Related and Work-Related Hassles Experienced by Retirees and Workers During the Past 3 Months**

RETIREES			WORKERS		
Retirement Problems	**Number**	**Percentage**	**Work Problems**	**Number**	**Percentage**
No problems	466	68.9	No problems	295	35.1
Boredom	42	6.2	Organizational	167	19.9
Financial	41	6.1	Interpersonal	110	13.1
Tasks	22	3.3	Retirement planning	79	9.4
Too busy	20	3.0	New job or task	45	5.4
Planning	18	2.7	Financial	44	5.2
Adaptation	16	2.4	Dislike	42	5.0
Health	15	2.2	Work loss	30	3.6
Loneliness	9	1.3	Health	22	2.6
Marital	8	1.2	Multiple	4	0.5
Legal	8	1.2	Environmental	2	0.2
Job seeking	6	0.8			
Multiple	5	0.7			
	676	100.0		840	100.0

Source: Bossé et al., 1991.

Women have fewer financial resources (Rogers, 1985). They are more likely than men to miss the people at work and the positive feeling of achievement that sometimes comes with employment (Streib & Schneider, 1971). Other studies find that retirement has less effect on women's self-esteem and satisfaction than on men's (Palmore et al., 1979), and that retired women were more likely than men to be happy if money was adequate (Jaslow, 1976).

Certain groups of women adjust better to retirement than others. Never-married women adjust better to retirement than widowed, divorced, or separated women (Keith, 1985). Because never-married women are more likely to have participated longer in the labor market, this difference may simply mirror their better financial position.

Work and Leisure in Later Adulthood

Not all elderly people want to retire, and those who do retire sometimes return to work, taking full-time or part-time jobs (Quinn & Burkhauser, 1990).

Working Through Old Age

People may choose to continue to work for many reasons. Lack of financial resources may force someone to work past the time the individual would have liked to retire (Pampel, 1985). Some people continue to work even when they are financially capable of retiring. Such people are most often in good health, have a psychological commitment to work, and find retirement distasteful (Parnes & Sommers, 1994). Being married to someone who is still working is also a factor and feelings of usefulness and value are certainly important (Ruchlin & Morris, 1991). The relationship of work to well-being in later life depends mostly on whether people work because they want to or because they have to. Those who continue to work because they want to report higher levels of physical and psychological well-being than do those who work because they have to (Herzog, House, & Morgan, 1991). After retirement, only about 9% actually return to full-time work, and the majority do not want to return to work at all (Myers, 1991). Some retired people may be forced by circumstances to take part-time positions to supplement their income or may even want to work in order to keep busy.

Among those who do not retire, job satisfaction is rather high and there is a trend toward increasing satisfaction with age (Warr, 1992). More than 80% of employed people age 70 and older say they are very satisfied with their work. The cohort effect needs to be considered, however, because each generation has recently been less satisfied with work than its predecessor. This cohort of elderly may have more positive feelings toward work than the next generation of elderly.

The elderly seeking work or trying to stay in their present job face serious barriers of discrimination. Discrimination against the elderly in hiring, training, and even keeping jobs is extensive (Stagner, 1985). This discrimination against the aged, referred to as **ageism,** is based on faulty premises. Some believe that the elderly are absent more often, are less productive, and do not have the skills required for the job. Each of these is either untrue or a half-truth. Absenteeism actually declines with age (Martocchio, 1989; Coberly & Newquist, 1984). The elderly also have a better safety record than younger workers. The lowest accident rates are found in the 70-to-74 age group (Barrow, 1986; National Safety Council, 1995). The elderly are very reliable and punctual. In addition, their performance on the job tends to be quite good (Foner & Schwab, 1981).

Some elderly may not have the necessary skills for the jobs they apply for, but discrimination in training often does not allow the older worker a chance to learn new skills. Again, because trained younger workers tend to leave jobs quickly while older workers tend to stay, this is a shortsighted policy.

Recently, a study of two American corporations (Days Inn of America and the Travelers Corporation of Hartford) and a large British retail chain (B & Q) showed that older workers are quite productive. The studies measured such variables as how quickly reservation agents worked and workers' success rates, absentee rates, and turnover rates. Analysts found that at Days Inn, the older workers talked a minute or so longer with callers but had a higher success rate in making reservations and stayed on the job longer. The B & Q company found that older workers were more familiar with housewares and construction products. To prove their capabilities, the company staffed a store with only workers over 50, and the store was 18% more profitable, the turnover rate 6 times lower, and absenteeism 39% less than in other stores. In addition, such studies find that older workers can be retrained in new technologies (Teltsch, 1991).

Leisure

When older people are asked what the best thing about being over 65 is, they often say having more leisure time (National Council on the Aging, 1975). A strong relationship exists between the number of hours spent on leisure activities and the degree of life satisfaction (Parnes & Less, 1985). The late adult's world is focused upon leisure activities (Hendricks & Cutler, 1990). Many middle-aged children do not understand that these activities are very important and sometimes become confused or even angry if their elderly parents say that they cannot visit on a particular day because they have a weekly card game or bowling league. What they fail to understand is that just as work is the activity that serves as the focus of the lives of younger people, leisure activities are the central focus of the lives of the elderly. Many elderly see these activities as commitments. For example, one elderly grandparent who played bridge flatly told her daughter

ageism Discrimination on the basis of age.

that her Tuesday game was a responsibility, as they did not have a game without her.

A number of factors influence participation in leisure activities. First, some people are so work oriented that they find it almost impossible to deal with increased leisure. Second, people in poor health cannot always participate in their desired leisure activities. A person may love to play golf but not be physically able to do so. There is more of an opportunity for active leisure among the elderly today because more are in good health for a longer time (Hendricks & Cutler, 1990). Mobility is also a prime concern. Many older adults depend on others for transportation, and some have difficulty walking or climbing stairs. The elderly person who likes to bowl but cannot get to the bowling alley cannot participate in this activity. In addition, lack of companionship is often a major problem (Burrus-Bammel & Bammel, 1985). If you enjoy playing poker, bridge, or gin rummy, you need a group. Finally, financial constraints can be a problem: you may have always wanted to travel, but find you cannot afford to.

Health and financial stability predict leisure pursuits. Health affects not only activity level but also preferences for the type of activity. The lower the overall health rating, the more passive the elderly person (Cutler & Hendricks, 1990). Having enough money allows for more varied activities and more choice.

The most common finding of studies looking into time use in old age is stability in the types of leisure activities, but an increase in the amount of time devoted to them. Most elderly people don't start many new activities, but they spend more time on the leisure activities that they enjoyed earlier in life (Cutler & Hendricks, 1990).

Some of the elderly's increased time goes into housework. Older men almost double their household work, and older women spend about one third more time doing housework (Robinson, 1991). The increase is greatest in the areas of yard work and gardening, but there is also an increase in cooking and cleaning. Mealtimes are also more leisurely and take longer. The elderly spend much more time watching television, which takes up about 50% of their free time (see Table 19.5). The amount of time spent reading and playing cards and other games increases as well. The elderly spend more time walking, writing letters, and attending religious services than do younger people (Robinson, 1991). Travel is also an important leisure activity for elderly people in good health.

As people age, they devote more time to less active pursuits, such as television viewing. Declining health, the loss of friends, and limited mobility may be the reasons why this is so. This is unfortunate, because people who are more involved with other people through such pursuits as bridge, photography competitions, civic projects, and square dancing are more satisfied with life (Gordon & Gaitz, 1983). For those who move to retirement communities, a high degree of participation in activities is related to increased life satisfaction (Gordon & Gaitz, 1983).

Table 19.5 **Time on Their Hands**
Elderly Americans spend almost half of their free time watching television (average time spent in selected activities for the population aged 65 and older, in minutes per day, by sex, 1985).

	TOTAL	MEN	WOMEN
Paid Work			
Working	50	63	42
Commuting to work	5	7	4
Family Care			
Cooking	54	24	74
Cleaning dishes	17	8	23
Housecleaning	34	18	44
Laundry	13	4	18
Yard work	16	28	8
Repairs	9	19	2
Plant/pet care	13	17	10
Other household	20	24	17
Child care and transport	7	3	9
Shopping	24	19	26
Services	9	10	8
Travel, shopping	19	20	19
Personal Care			
Hygiene	55	52	57
Eating out	17	16	17
Eating meals at home	79	85	76
Sleeping	478	470	479
Napping	34	34	34
Travel, personal	10	13	9
Free Time			
Classes/homework	3	3	2
Organizations	6	4	7
Religion	15	13	16
Going to movies, events	2	2	2
Visiting	33	34	33
Other social	4	5	3
Travel, social	12	12	11
Sports, outdoor	20	26	16
Hobbies, crafts	21	12	26
Games, computers	14	17	12
Travel, recreation	4	6	3
Watching TV	199	213	190
Listening to radio, records	7	10	5
Reading	51	56	47
Conversation	24	20	26
Resting, relaxing	15	17	13
Activity not ascertained	29	34	26

Source: Robinson, 1991.

True or False?
The most common leisure-time activity for elderly people is watching television.

Volunteering

In the past 25 years, the proportion of elderly people who volunteer in their communities has increased; about 40% of all elderly people do some volunteer work (Chambre,

1993). More than half devote 10 hours a week or more to community service (Crooke, 1989). When the increased probability of poor health and mobility is taken into account, this percentage is impressive. Elderly volunteers are found in a wide variety of areas, including child care facilities, the Red Cross and other health-promoting organizations, and schools. Many offer their considerable skills in business to new small business owners, sometimes through the government-sponsored Service Corps of Retired Executives (SCORE). The Foster Grandparent program enrolls volunteers to help children, some of whom have disabilities or have been abused or neglected. The largest program, called the Retired Senior Volunteer Program (RSVP), places volunteers into many positions ranging from working with infants to providing tax assistance.

People who volunteer their time extensively have more purpose in life and are less bored (Weinstein, Xie, & Cleanthous, 1995). Volunteering satisfies the need to give to others, increases life satisfaction, and can even be an opportunity to meet others. Many worthwhile community programs depend upon elderly volunteers for their existence and volunteering is a satisfying activity for many elderly people.

Successful Aging

Is the key to successful aging changing the nature of relationships and reducing the ties that bind elderly people to society or trying to keep up the same level of activity that one had in middle age? According to the **disengagement theory,** it is both normal and inevitable that people and society "disengage" from each other (Cumming & Henry, 1961). As individuals negotiate old age, they reduce the ties that bind them to others, becoming more isolated, less socially active, more introspective, and more passive. After an initial period of depression and anxiety, the person accepts disengagement and establishes tranquility. Some of the changes we have seen in old age—including the change from active to passive mastery, the increase in introspection, the reduction of activity, and narrowing of interests—fit this model. Successful aging in the context of this theory would be the progressive disengagement and acceptance of one's position, which should eventually lead to higher morale (Atchley, 1996).

Criticisms of this approach are many, and most research either is mixed or runs contrary to its predictions. For many, what may seem like disengagement—such as the decrease in community involvement and a reduction in interpersonal contacts—may actually be caused by poor health and travel difficulties (Kleiber & Kelly, 1985). Lack of opportunity may also lead to an unwilling disengagement, as when older people do not live near other elderly people (Carp, 1968). In addition, many lives simply do not fit this pattern. One major study of 80-year-olds did not find a general trend toward disengagement (Granick & Patterson, 1971). Also, morale does not seem to increase with disengagement (Tallmer & Kutner, 1970). Last, many studies find some positive relationship between activity, social involvement, and life satisfaction (Markides & Martin, 1979). Many elderly are not satisfied with their "disengagement" because they place great importance on social interaction.

The **activity theory** emphasizes the importance of social activity in promoting life satisfaction and sees the maintenance of the activities and attitudes of middle age to be most important in successful adjustment to aging (Havighurst, 1961; Havighurst & Albrecht, 1953). If a role is lost, such as through widowhood or retirement, some substitute must be found.

This approach is too simplistic because the link between social activity and life satisfaction is moderately positive, but not as strong as would be required to base a case for successful aging on this variable. In addition, activity level can decline without affecting morale (Maddox, 1970). Some research also shows that loss of role is not related to a decrease in life satisfaction (Lemon, Bengtson, & Peterson, 1972). Although many older people remain active, activity may not be the key to everyone's happiness.

Three Keys: Health, Choice, and Personality

Neither the disengagement theory nor the activity theory is entirely successful in predicting successful aging (George, 1990). It may be that both theories have something to offer, but to understand aging we must look at other factors that influence one's adaptation to life. Three such factors have been identified. The first, which has been discussed in both this and the previous chapter, is health. The health status of an elderly person certainly affects and limits lifestyle and adaptation to change.

The second factor is choice. People who choose to reduce some of their bonds, for whatever reason, are likely to show high morale with disengagement (Neugarten, Havighurst, & Tobin, 1968). People who retire because they want to, and not because they are forced to, are happier. Choice is related to control. People who maintain some degree of personal control over their own life decisions are more likely to be happy in old age.

Personality is the third factor. People who are flexible, mature, open to new stimuli, and function well in the cognitive domain show high levels of life satisfaction. Neugarten and colleagues (1968; 1961) called this type of personality an *integrated personality.* Those who try to hold onto middle age as long as possible, those who show high dependency needs or apathy, as well as those who show deteriorating thought processes show less satisfaction with life.

disengagement theory The theory relating successful aging to the reduction in the bonds that tie the elderly person to society.

activity theory The theory relating successful aging to the maintenance of activity throughout later maturity.

A New Look at Aging

It is common to dwell on the problems of old age—inadequate income and housing, poor health, and general decline. These problems are real. Providing adequate care for the very old who may need constant monitoring is a challenge that must be faced. On the other hand, if we merely focus on the problems of aging, we overlook the possibilities for great satisfaction in later life. Because of increases in longevity and better health, many of today's elderly are living active, involved, satisfying lives.

We tend to think of choice as being central to the lives of young and middle-aged adults and to see older adults as having most decisions forced on them or made by someone else. This is not true. Most elderly are independent and have a number of choices concerning their engagement or disengagement, activity or lack of activity. As is true of young and middle-aged adults, the elderly make their choices on the basis of their needs and circumstances. By emphasizing the possibilities for personal choice and satisfaction, we are not neglecting the real problems of aging. We are merely realistically echoing sentiments that are present in the elderly community today.

Summary

1. The proportion of elderly people in the United States stands at more than 10% today, and will increase substantially during the first half of the next century. The elderly population is predominantly female. Although the elderly are better off financially today than years ago, some still live below or near the poverty level.
2. Only 5% of the elderly live in nursing homes. Institutionalization takes place when no other alternatives are open. Most elderly nursing home patients have serious chronic disorders and need help eating and dressing. Depression and other psychological symptoms are common, but if the nursing home is excellent, these symptoms may not appear. Many new housing options are now available for the elderly who need various degrees of support.
3. Most personality characteristics are rather stable throughout adulthood. Older people do tend to be more cautious, slower, more introspective, and more practical than younger people.
4. Marital satisfaction among the elderly is quite high. More sharing takes place in old age, and more activities are performed together. Gender-role distinctions blur somewhat. Sexuality can be a source of satisfaction, but many elderly cease to be sexually active.
5. Women are much more likely than men to become widowed. Most widows and widowers eventually build a new life.
6. The extended family—where three generations live together—was never common in America. Most elderly people want to live independent lives. Older people are frequently visited by and visit their adult children and receive help from them in times of crisis. However, older people also help their children. Their relationship with their children is good, although it may become more strained if the elderly become very ill and require more attention and care.
7. Some elderly people are abused by their spouses or their children. Although sometimes the abuser is a frustrated care-giver, many times the abuse is perpetrated by a person who actually depends on the elderly person for housing or money.
8. Most grandparents have frequent contact with their grandchildren and enjoy the role. Today, more grandparents are involved in raising their grandchildren than in previous generations because of the increase in single and teenage parents. Many do an excellent job under trying circumstances. Great-grandparents are less involved with their great-grandchildren than they are with their grandchildren.
9. Siblings are also important to older people, and closeness may increase with age. Most elderly adults have at least one very close friend who acts as a confidant. Women are more likely to have close friends than men.
10. The retired individual may pass from the satisfaction of the initial honeymoon stage to disenchantment. This is frequently followed by a reorientation phase, when a more realistic lifestyle is built. In the stability phase, life becomes satisfying and predictable. The last phase, called termination, occurs when the retiree either returns to work or cannot continue normal activities because of illness or disability.
11. Most elderly who continue to work show high job satisfaction. Discrimination on the basis of age, called ageism, seriously hampers older workers. Older workers are more safety conscious than younger workers and are absent fewer days. Their performance on the job is good.
12. Each culture has its own roles and responsibilities for older people. In tribal or preindustrial societies, the status of the elderly is somewhat higher than it is in industrialized societies.
13. In the future a greater proportion of the elderly will be members of minority groups. They are more likely to live in poverty. Minority elderly people tend to be more religious and family oriented.
14. The most common leisure activity for elderly people is watching television. When the elderly retire, they are likely to spend more time doing chores and to take meals more leisurely. They are more likely to spend an increasing amount of time on activities they enjoyed earlier in their lives than to start new interests. Many find meaning in volunteering.
15. The disengagement theory states that successful aging involves progressively loosening the bonds that bind the individual to society. The activity theory states that people who stay active and maintain middle-aged attitudes are more likely to be satisfied

in old age. Neither theory, by itself, is totally accepted. Three important variables involved in successful aging are health, choice, and personality.

Multiple-Choice Questions

1. The proportion of elderly people in the population of the United States is expected to:
   a. stay about the same for the next 50 years.
   b. almost double between now and the year 2040.
   c. almost triple by the year 2030.
   d. decline slowly and modestly in the next 50 years.
2. Which statement concerning the economic situation of elderly people in the United States is *correct?*
   a. Elderly people are about twice as likely to be poor as they were 25 years ago.
   b. Elderly people are more likely to be living in poverty than children.
   c. Elderly people have about the same rate of poverty as they had 25 years ago.
   d. Elderly people are less likely to live in poverty than 25 years ago.
3. If the Smiths are like the average elderly couple, they are most likely to live in:
   a. an apartment.
   b. an adult leisure community.
   c. their own home.
   d. a nursing home or other assisted-living facility.
4. If the Smiths are like the average elderly couple, they want to:
   a. move from the area where they have lived to the Sun Belt.
   b. stay where they are.
   c. move to another apartment or home about 100 miles from their present residence.
   d. move nearer to their adult children.
5. Most people in nursing homes:
   a. do not have much wrong with them but do not have anyone to help them with such chores as shopping.
   b. need a variety of important services and are incapable of living independently.
   c. are placed in such homes because families do not want to visit or deal with them.
   d. are there because they want to live in a place where other elderly people congregate.
6. Which of the following best describes personality traits in *later* adulthood?
   a. rapid change
   b. stability
   c. regression
   d. moderate change
7. Erik Erikson argued that the positive outcome of the stage of later maturity is gaining a sense of:
   a. ego integrity.
   b. ego satisfaction.
   c. self-tolerance.
   d. interpersonal fulfillment.
8. Which of the following best describes elderly people's satisfaction with their marriages?
   a. unsatisfied
   b. highly satisfied
   c. neutral
   d. mixed, in that half are satisfied and half dissatisfied
9. Which of the following statements about sexuality in later life is *correct?*
   a. Most cultures expect elderly people to continue their sexual expression.
   b. The frequency of sex within marriage continues to decline in old age.
   c. Most elderly people who are sexually active believe their lovemaking has improved with age.
   d. All of the following are correct.
10. Most elderly people with children:
    a. do not see or hear from their children often.
    b. have frequent contact with their children.
    c. do not believe their children have much interest in them.
    d. perceive their children to be interested more in what the elderly can give the children than in having a "friendly" relationship.
11. David says that elder abuse is a relatively new concept. Jean claims that much of the abuse is perpetrated by people who are dependent on the elderly person. Elaine claims that the elderly believe that physical abuse is more common than neglect, and Margarita adds that abused elderly people are likely to be frail and cognitively and physically impaired. Each of these people is correct *except:*
    a. David.
    b. Jean.
    c. Elaine.
    d. Margarita.
12. The model of grandparent help in which child care duties are shared between the child's mother and grandmother is called:
    a. surrogate parent model.
    b. parental supplement model.
    c. primary parent model.
    d. parent apprentice model.
13. Most elderly people:
    a. would like more contact with their siblings.
    b. have relatively frequent contact with siblings.
    c. find that their sibling rivalry has decreased.
    d. would agree with all of the above.
14. A phrase that describes the changing nature of friends in older adulthood is:
    a. more active.
    b. less involved.
    c. more selective.
    d. increasingly open.
15. In the third phase of retirement, or the ______ phase, people begin to make more reasonable and practical plans.

a. honeymoon
b. disenchantment
c. reorientation
d. stability

16. In a study of the adjustment of retired people, the most common complaint was:
a. marital hassles.
b. boredom.
c. lack of friends.
d. worry about impending death.

17. Which group of women would be expected to adjust best to retirement?
a. never-married women
b. separated women
c. divorced women
d. widows

18. Among those elderly people who continue to work, satisfaction is:
a. high.
b. low.
c. medium.
d. very low.

19. If you know that a couple has just retired, it is probable that they will:
a. find completely new leisure activities.
b. spend more time in the activities they enjoyed before they retired.
c. spend less time in leisure activities with the exception of travel.
d. complain about not having enough leisure time.

20. The theory of aging that argues that older people reduce the ties that bind them to others in society is called:
a. disactivity theory.
b. reduction theory.
c. interagency theory.
d. disengagement theory.

Answers to Multiple-Choice Questions
1. b 2. d 3. c 4. b 5. b 6. b 7. a 8. b 9. d
10. b 11. c 12. b 13. d 14. c 15. c 16. b 17. a
18. a 19. b 20. d

Chapter 20

Death, Dying, and Coping With Loss

Chapter Outline

Are the Following Statements True or False?

1. Because most people die in old age in our society, children are neither exposed to death very much nor think about it much.
2. By the age of 6 or so, children have a mature understanding of the meaning of death.
3. Middle-aged people show more fear of death than elderly people.
4. Most elderly people who die were in good health a year before they died.
5. The tendency of older people to dwell on the past is a definite sign of organic deterioration.
6. Every dying patient goes through a particular series of stages that ends with acceptance.
7. Most people die in their own homes.
8. Hospices offer terminally ill patients high-tech services in a home-like setting.
9. If a person does not grieve openly and intensely after the death of a loved one, the result is most frequently mental illness.
10. Grieving for a child is the most intense form of grief.

Answers to True-False Statements 1. False: see p. 470 2. False: see p. 470 3. True 4. True 5. False: see p. 473 6. False: see p. 475 7. False: see p. 476 8. False: see p. 477 9. False: see p. 484 10. True

Your First Experience With Death

Do you remember your first experience with death? Was it the death of a favorite pet or of an older relative? In our society, death is very much the province of the elderly. In 1900, only 25% of those who died were over the age of 65 (Albert & Steffl, 1984); today the figure stands at about 77%. The death rate for elderly people is much higher than for younger people (Singh et al., 1995) (see Table 20.1).

For many years death and dying were not discussed. Many people did not even want to use the word, and euphemisms such as "passing away" or "gone" were used. Many people do not want to think about planning for their own death or plan for their funeral. Many do not provide for the needs of their children by making wills or discussing their wishes with those most involved.

This situation is changing. As medical treatment allows people to live longer, issues related to death and dying have come to the forefront. Medical treatment may allow a person to stay alive but in a state of permanent unconsciousness for many years. Two spectacular cases brought this situation to the public's attention. In the Karen Ann Quinlan case, decided in 1974, the Supreme Court declared that people had the right to refuse life-sustaining treatment (McCord, 1992). Ms. Quinlan was kept alive on life support systems in a coma that the doctors considered to be irreversible. When asked that the machines be disconnected, the hospital refused. This led to a court battle ending in the decision to give the individual or the surrogate the right to refuse treatment. That right, sometimes called *the right to pull the plug,* is now relatively well established. In Missouri, the parents of Nancy Cruzan went to court to gain the right to instruct the hospital in which their daughter lay in an irreversible coma to disconnect the feeding tube and allow their daughter to die (Smolowe, 1990). The court decided that although competent patients have the right to refuse life-sustaining treatments, in the absence of a specific statement from the patient the states do not have to give family members the right to do so (Neuhaus, 1994). In this case, a witness came forward and stated that the patient had made such a statement.

Table 20.1 **Estimated Death Rates by Age**

AGE	1994
All ages	876.9
Under 1 year	811.1
1–4 years	44.5
5–14 years	22.7
15–24 years	99.6
25–34 years	141.0
35–44 years	239.5
45–54 years	452.3
55–64 years	1139.0
65–74 years	2590.9
75–84 years	5909.7
85 years and over	15,312.6

Note: Rates per 100,000 population in specified group.
Source: Singh, 1995.

Understanding Death Across the Life Span

Most people would like to believe that children are sheltered from information about death (Moore, 1989). According to this thinking, death is and should be a stranger to children (Ward, 1984). Unlike years ago, children today are not likely to experience the death of parents and siblings. Still, children are exposed to death early and often (Moore, 1989). Every child sees death on television—much of it violent. Every child has experienced the death of a plant or other living thing. Many children's games, nursery rhymes, and fairy tales deal with death (Achte et al., 1990).

Some theorists believe that these stories allow children to work through their fears and anxieties about death in a healthy manner (Bettelheim, 1977). Although children may not be able to put it into words or understand its full significance, death is real to young children. Parents are reluctant to allow their children to participate in studies on death and do not talk to their children about death. However, 83% of 6- and 7-year-olds in one study said that they think about death (Lazar & Torney-Purta, 1991).

> ***True or False?***
> Because most people die in old age in our society, children are neither exposed to death very much nor think about it much.

Perhaps the most widely quoted study on children's understanding of death was conducted by Maria Nagy (1948) in Budapest, Hungary on children ranging in age from 3 to 10. A clear developmental progression was found.

Stage 1: Ages 3 to 5 Children between the ages of 3 and 5 do not view death as universal, inevitable, or irreversible. Rather, they believe that the dead are just a little less alive and that the dead can return to life. Even after seeming to accept the fact that grandma has died, they may ask when grandma will visit next. To young children, death may be akin to a separation or a trip in that it is transitory and reversible. When the child finally acknowledges that grandma is not going to visit any more, he or she may ask such questions as "Who is going to bring me candy?" This may infuriate the grieving parent, who would like grandma to be remembered for other reasons. Yet at this age, children often think instrumentally; they mean no disrespect.

> ***True or False?***
> By the age of 6 or so, children have a mature understanding of the meaning of death.

Young children often equate sleep with death, which can cause some problems at bedtime (Kastenbaum, 1977). Preschoolers are also very curious about death. They are interested in details and may want to know why it occurs. Preschoolers often believe that death is caused by some misbehavior on the part of the deceased, such as "eating a dirty bug" (Koocher, 1973). Children are frequently very interested in the concrete aspects of death and often think that dead people are alive but under different conditions (Stambrook & Parker, 1987).

Stage 2: Ages 5 or 6 to 9 Children slowly learn that death is indeed final, although they may not completely accept it until the end of this stage. Despite the advancement in understanding, children still think that death can be avoided by being clever. This reflects the child's real experiences. Children understand that people can be killed crossing the street, but they know that this will not happen if one is careful (Kastenbaum, 1977). Kastenbaum describes the child's understanding of death at this stage as "finality with an escape hatch" (1977, p. 119). Children often link death with frightening events in the outside world (Leming & Dickinson, 1994).

Stage 3: Ages 9 or 10 and Older Children now understand that death is universal and inevitable. Death is understood as the termination of life, and every living thing is acknowledged as having an end point in time.

Nagy's conclusions that children proceed through an orderly, sequential stage-related progression in understanding death has been generally supported by other research (Childers & Wimmer, 1971). However, the situation is not as simple as it seems. The idea that children gain an understanding of death in an invariant stage-like progression does not fit the facts. Studies differ on when children fully understand the central concepts underlying death. Some studies show that fewer than half of all fourth graders understand irreversibility; other studies show that many younger children understand this. Some studies show that young children understand that dead people cannot eat or speak but do not understand that they cannot feel cold or smell flowers, and many children do not understand that they cannot dream (Kane, 1979).

People often overestimate their children's understanding of death. The global concept of death contains a number of subconcepts, such as irreversibility, cessation, causality, inevitability and universality. The last concept to develop is causality, the child's ability to understand the objective causes of death, but studies disagree on the order in which the others are developed (Lazar & Torney-Purta, 1991). Studying and understanding death as a global concept is difficult because these subconcepts develop differently (Lazar & Torney-Purta, 1991).

Other factors such as cognitive level, intelligence, and prior experiences with death may be important in children's understanding of death (Corr et al., 1994). Children must have sufficient verbal ability, understand the concept of time, appreciate causality, differentiate the self from others, and differentiate between objects and living creatures to fully understand death (Orbach et al., 1994/1995). A child's performance on various Piagetian tests relates to understanding of death (Koocher, 1973). The experience of anxiety impairs cognitive performance and children may find the death of people close to them somewhat harder to understand that the death of a bird in the wild. Some personal experience with death hastens the process of understanding. We might expect that children exposed to war, as in Lebanon, Israel, and Vietnam, would develop a more sophisticated understanding of death at an earlier age. Children who frequently come into contact with personal death at an earlier age because of violence and accidents are more advanced in their understanding of death (Kastenbaum & Costa, 1977).

Some studies indicate that terminally ill children understand death at earlier ages than the developmental progression just described would indicate (Bluebond-Langner, 1977). Everyone admits that terminally ill children understand the changes in their own condition from how their parents, doctors, and nurses respond. Their time perspective changes, and they talk very little about the future and much more about the present.

Three important points stand out in the developmental progression of children's understanding of death. First, such understanding progresses in an orderly manner, although variation in understanding the subconcepts of death must be considered. Second, understanding death is associated with changes in intelligence, cognitive development, and age (Orbach et al., 1994/1995). Third, from a very early age children are exposed to death and are curious about it, even if they cannot understand the entire concept or put their thoughts into words.

Helping Children Deal With Death

When Will Lee, who played Mr. Hooper, the shopkeeper, on the children's television show *Sesame Street,* died in December 1982, the program's writers were in a quandary. How should they explain his absence to the millions of preschoolers who watch the program every day?

It would have been dishonest to tell viewers that Mr. Hooper had moved to Florida, so the writers decided to deal with the difficult concept of death. They did not do this by explaining the causes of death or the process of aging. Instead, the resident 5-year-old on the show, Big Bird, was forthrightly told that Mr. Hooper had died. Like most preschoolers, Big Bird did not understand the irreversibility of death and asked when his friend Mr. Hooper was coming back.

Later, as the reality sunk in, Big Bird's attention centered on his own loss. "Who will make me birdseed milkshakes and tell me stories?" he asked. Told that his friend David would do that, Big Bird remained unhappy, knowing it would never be the same. He drew a picture of Mr. Hooper and hung it over his nest. But Big Bird's mood brightened as a new baby was presented on the show, demonstrating the continuity of life ("Death of a Character Is *Sesame Street* Topic," *New York Times,* August 31, 1983.).

Eventually all parents must explain death to their children and decide whether the child should attend the funeral of someone they know who has died. Although death is a difficult subject to discuss with one's children, the following guidelines may help.

1. *Be honest.* Parents should not tell children that the dead individual has gone on a trip. It should not be intimated that the deceased will return or is alive in some way. Although young children may not understand the finality of death, the important thing is that the communication be honest.
2. *Do not confuse death with any other state.* Have you ever heard parents tell their children that the dead are only sleeping? This is dishonest and may cause major problems at bedtime.
3. *Be a good listener and observer.* Parents are sometimes more interested in explaining death to the child than in observing and listening to the child. By observing and listening, you can gain a better understanding of what the child does and does not understand.
4. *Do not explain everything at one sitting.* Some parents try to explain everything to the child when grandma dies. However, the topic may come up at different times, and explaining a little at a time is reasonable.
5. *Explain death in simple terms and do not sermonize.* Sometimes parents get so involved in the subject that they drone on and on. Instead, ask the child to repeat to you in his or her own words what you just explained.
6. *Do not use euphemisms, but use terms children can understand.* Using simple words and phrases like "dead," "stopped working," and "wore out," that establish the fact that the body has ceased to function is reasonable. Sometimes using a euphemism can be troublesome. When a child was told that "grandfather can breathe easier now," an asthmatic child wanted to join grandfather because he himself wanted the chance to breathe easier, too (Dickinson, 1992).
7. *It is O.K. to express emotion.* Children should be told that some people cry when someone dies and it is O.K. to do so if the child feels like it. It is also fine not to do so if the child does not feel like crying. Tell the child that not everyone cries.
8. *Remember the developmental progression.* Many parents expect a child to grieve the same way they do, but because young children do not understand death in an adult manner, this is impossible.
9. *Allow children to talk about fear.* Children are both very curious about death and fearful of it. Children may need to express their feelings and talk about their experiences.
10. *Use natural events to discuss death.* Too often, the first time a parent has spoken with a child about death is when someone close to the family has died. Parents can use a chance occurrence such as the death of a pet or finding a dead bird on the lawn as a starting point in discussing death with their children (Corr et al., 1994).
11. *When discussing the dead individual, talk about good times with the person and what the person meant to everyone.* Looking at a picture or taking out the scrapbook is a reasonable activity (Corr et al., 1994).
12. *Prepare the child for funerals.* How early should children be allowed to attend funerals? A definite age cannot be given. Some children are more mature than others. Hardt (1979) suggests that children age 7 and above may go but should never be forced to. Other people may argue in favor of different ages. The child should always be told what to expect at the funeral.

Adolescents, Young Adults, and Death

Adolescents are likely to have more experience with death than many people think (Balk, 1995). In studies of college students, more than 30% reported the death of a close friend or family member within the past year (Balk, 1991; 1990). Adolescents are likely to experience the death of distant elderly relatives such as grandparents, again reinforcing the relationship between aging and death. Adolescents will also probably come into contact with sudden death, most commonly from motor vehicle accidents, suicide, and homicide. The unfairness of death—its randomness—is what may impress them.

Adolescents romanticize death somewhat. In one study, high school students were given a group of metaphors that describe death and asked to rank the metaphors in terms of how appropriate they were for describing death. Overall, high school students saw death as the "last adventure," "the end of a song," and a "misty abyss." Males were a bit less romantic than females (Farley, 1979). Death is a significant theme in rock music aimed at teenagers. One study of the top 40 songs from 1955 through 1991 found that songs about death comprise a disproportionately popular subset, that males were more likely to die, and that grieving is greatly restricted (Plopper & Ness, 1993).

Young adults do not seem to think much about death. After all, marriage, having children, and beginning an occupation are entrance events, and the future seems somewhat predictable. There is less romanticizing about death, and most young adults tend to avoid thinking about it (Gesser, Wong, & Reker, 1987/1988). When they do think about death it is often in response to events such as wars, accidents, or natural disasters (Lowenthal, Thurnhur, & Chiriboga, 1975). Early adulthood is a time of greater stability than adolescence and anxiety about one's own death is less prominent (Corr, Nabe, & Corr, 1994).

Questions Students Often Ask

We just had our first child last month, and my parents told us to make a will. I don't know why we should since we're so young and neither of us even want to think about death.

They're right; it is very important for young families to have a will. Who would take care of your child if both of you were killed in an accident? Without clear instructions, you and your spouse's family may fight over custody, and someone you may not have wished to raise your child may end up doing so. It is important for you to discuss this issue with the people you wish to raise your child in case of this emergency, and to receive their acceptance of this responsibility. Competent legal advice should always be sought when making out a will because state laws differ.

Middle Age and Death

Most theorists of adulthood see middle age as the time many people are first forced to come to grips with death. Younger people see death in terms of a specific occurrence, such as an accident or something that happens to much older people. The middle-aged person does not have that luxury. Experiences with the death of one's parents or the heart attack that takes the life of a friend force thoughts concerning one's own mortality into consciousness. The death of one's parents is the most common form of bereavement in developed societies and most often occurs when the children are in middle age (Douglas, 1991; Scharlach & Fuller-Thomson, 1994).

The dread of death is more common in middle age than in the elderly (Cohen, 1990). Middle-aged people show a fear of dying before one's time (Stricherz & Cunnington, 1982). This is in keeping with the changing time perspective of middle age when people begin to think about the time they have left rather than time since birth. After the age of 55 or so, an increase in belief about the afterlife and heaven occurs (Spilka, Hood, & Gorsuch, 1985).

True or False?
Middle-aged people show more fear of death than elderly people.

Older People Talk About Death

Older people are more likely to think and talk about death but less likely to show a fear or dread of death (Cohen, 1990). When death anxiety was measured in groups of young adults (aged 18–26), middle-aged people (aged 35–50), and the elderly (aged 60 and older), death anxiety was highest in the middle group and lowest in the elderly (Gesser, Wong, & Reker, 1988). Thinking and talking about death are not the same as experiencing tremendous anxiety about it (de Vries, Bluck & Birren, 1993). The elderly frequently talk about death, which is understandable. First, they are more likely to have friends and relatives who are dying or have died recently. Second, they are aware of the finite time they have left, and talking about death may allow them to come to terms with it.

Older adults show less fear or anxiety than younger adults because older people may recognize the limits of life, and those who are beset by health and economic problems see their more active roles as behind them (Campanelli, 1996). They see many of their tasks in life as completed (Leming & Dickinson, 1994). When older people were asked whether they wanted to live to be 100 years old, many answered no, and none said yes without qualifying the answer (Marshall, 1980). Older people anticipated a life span of 65 to 75 years, and many seemed to have outlived their own expectations. Religion also may be a factor explaining why the elderly are less fearful of death because they are somewhat more religious, which may provide them with comfort. Elderly people are more likely to believe in an afterlife (Kastenbaum, 1992). It is faith, spirituality, and strong feelings that life is meaningful rather than the actual practice of religion or ritual that are related to lower death anxiety (Bivens et al., 1994/1995; Rasmussen & Johnson, 1994). In addition, people are socialized to understand that death and aging are related. By the time people reach old age, they have suffered through the deaths of many other people (Kalish, 1985) and have been forced by circumstances to admit their own mortality. Furthermore, although elderly people understand that their future is limited, most do not expect to die soon. A National Institute of Aging study of people over 65 who had since died found that health did not deteriorate until fairly near the end in most cases. Over 50% were in good or excellent health a year before they died; 10% were even in good health the day before they died; only about one-third knew that death was approaching (McCarthy, 1991).

True or False?
Most elderly people who die were in good health a year before they died.

Although the elderly show less death anxiety, they do not welcome death nor are they fearless of death. Indeed, anxiety about dying may be lower in older people than in middle-aged people, but anxiety about the process of dying itself is greater (Belsky, 1987). Older adults fear the circumstances of death (de Vries, Bluck, & Birren, 1993). Many fear the loss of control, the unknown, and losing those who are close to them and still alive. They fear a long, painful illness (Leming & Dickinson, 1994). Some may fear dying itself, suffering pain, or being dependent on others rather than being dead (Belsky, 1987). The relationship between age and fear of death is not a simple matter. When adults are interviewed, some people in each age group show high, moderate, and low fear of death (McCrae et al., 1976).

Older people are a heterogeneous group. Those who are in poor physical and emotional health, those in institutions, those who have unrealized dreams or who have not been satisfied with their lives, report a greater fear of death (Ross, Braga, & Braga, 1975). Although as a group the aged fear death less, to say that they do not fear death is patently false.

Cultural beliefs are especially important in an individual's attitude toward death and dying. For example, the attitudes of East Indian and English older people towards death differ. Research shows that the elderly in both cultures accept death and face it with confidence. However, the East Indian belief in reincarnation provides a somewhat larger context against which to view life and death. The English sample showed a wider range of beliefs about death and the hereafter (Thomas, 1994).

The Life Review

The finding that people's evaluation of their past affects their attitude toward death fits well with Erikson's concept of ego integrity as well as with some of the changes in attitude and outlook discussed in Chapters 18 and 19. The increase in interiority and evaluation of one's life—called **life review** (Butler, 1974, 1975)—is part of the process of accepting death.

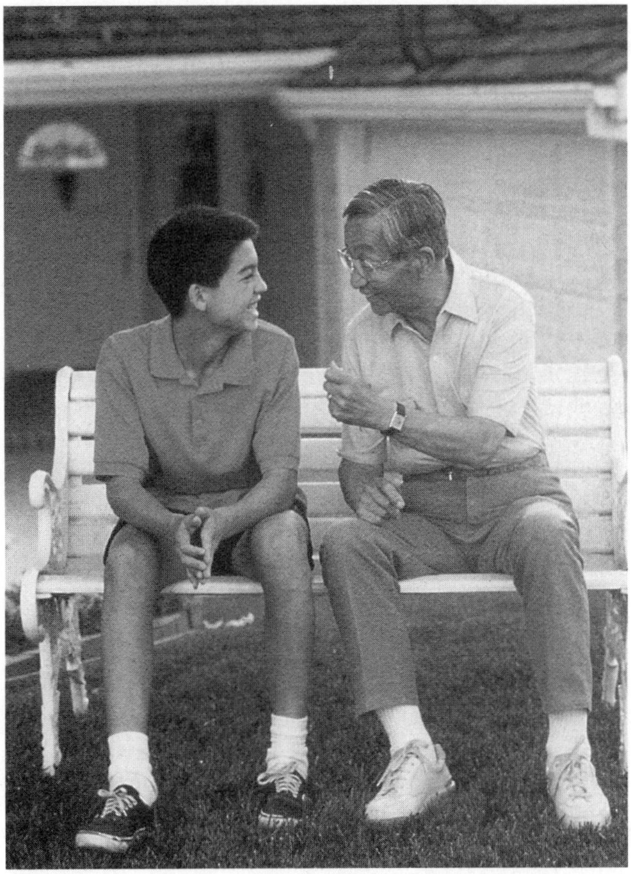

Elderly people often talk about the past as they try to find meaning in their lives. During this time, younger people can learn about family history.

The elderly frequently talk about and dwell on the past. They are deeply involved with their past opportunities, relationships, and mistakes. Too often these reminiscences have been undervalued or even regarded as symptoms of senility. Such a life review fills a need because it permits the elderly to make their peace with life and to accept death. It strengthens their sense of integrity and allows them to integrate their life experiences and find meaning in their lives (Zins, 1987). During these reviews the elderly put their life decisions into perspective and work out conflicts and mistakes. The preoccupation may be mild and show itself as nostalgia or regret, or in its most severe form, it may take the form of anxiety and depression (Botwinick, 1984).

True or False?
The tendency of older people to dwell on the past is a definite sign of organic deterioration.

life review The process, usually found in older people, of reviewing and evaluating one's past.

Such reviews can take place anytime in life. In some African tribes young adults make their own funeral arrangements, including some statement of their accomplishments and social value (Fry, 1985). They are encouraged to do this at other times in their lives as well. In the United States, such a life review often occurs during late middle age, as men begin to think about retirement and as women evaluate their lives after their children leave home. However, the nature of the review in old age is more global. The reminiscences that make up the life review represent living history, and it is unfortunate that we have not taken more of an interest in them. Such reflections can serve as a valuable source of family history. Some families have taped stories about life years ago and preserved them for generations to come. The life review is a natural and functional attempt to place one's life in order and work through conflicts. Its value to the older person and to the family itself is just beginning to be appreciated.

On Dying

Until recently there was little research on how people deal with the knowledge of their own impending death. There was a reluctance to investigate this area at all, and the idea that dying patients wanted an opportunity to discuss their condition openly rather than hiding it was radical in itself. It was the great pioneering studies of Elisabeth Kübler-Ross that opened up new vistas in understanding death.

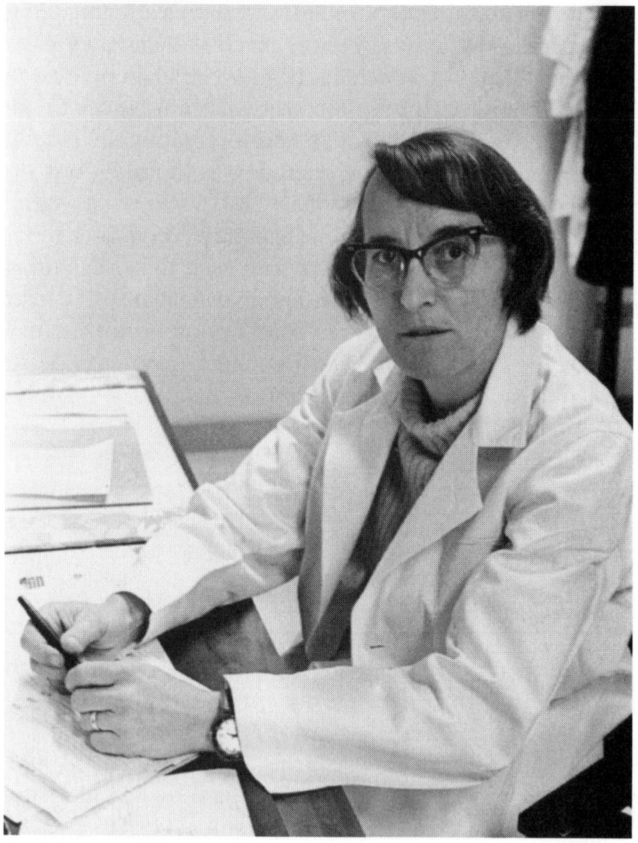

We owe a great debt of gratitude to Elisabeth Kübler-Ross for her pathfinding research on how fatally ill people deal with death. She is shown here around the time of publication of her book *On Death and Dying.*

From Denial to Acceptance

After interviewing many dying patients, Kübler-Ross (1969, 1972) suggested that people come to accept their own death by going through five specific stages.

Stage 1: Denial "No, Not Me. It Can't Be True." The first reaction to being told one is dying is denial. This is a time of disbelief when the person may prefer to believe that a mistake was made, such as the results of a medical test being incorrect (Leming & Dickinson, 1994). Some people become isolated and talk about their own death very objectively, as if it were happening to someone else. This is the time when families come to visit but do not know what to say. They are uncomfortable and become distant. They may avoid the subject or simply engage in hours of small talk.

Stage 2: Anger "Why Me?" Denial often gives way to anger. "Why am I dying while others live?" This is a very difficult stage for the dying patient, the family, and health care professionals who must deal with the patients who displace their anger onto everyone and everything. Such patients may criticize the nurse for coming into the room and shaking the pillow when they want to nap, or criticize the nurse for not shaking the pillow for them. They may be critical because the family is always too early or too late. Such anger is understandable because family members and nurses can come and go as they please, while the patient is left with pain and a death sentence. Dying patients need to express this anger (Kübler-Ross, 1972).

Stage 3: Bargaining "Yes, me, but please let me live long enough to attend my son's wedding." After the anger has abated, the dying patient may begin to bargain with God or the doctors. Some of the bargains with God are kept secret. Most are meant to postpone the inevitable, but Kübler-Ross found that few bargains are kept. One patient in extreme pain who was taught self-hypnosis to allow her to attend her son's wedding for a few hours returned from the wedding and told Kübler-Ross, "Now, don't forget I have another son." Kübler-Ross suggests that the clergy may play a significant role here, for some bargaining with God may reflect guilt, as when a person would like to live long enough to make amends for a past misdeed. The dying patient may need to work through these feelings.

Stage 4: Depression "Yes, me." Depression is the most common response to dying (Hinton, 1972). Patients at this stage may be grieving for loss of independence, loss of a body part, or loss of relationships with others. The depression may be one way of withdrawing into themselves to prepare for the loss of everything they have loved.

Stage 5: Acceptance In this last stage, the patient has accepted his or her fate. Feelings of envy for the healthy living and feelings of anger have been expressed. Losses have been mourned. Acceptance is not a happy stage. By this time, the patient may be very weak and have little emotion left. The patient has now found peace and acceptance, and interest in the outside world is reduced. He or she is not talkative and prefers short visits. Being able to sit in silence with another person is greatly appreciated. Although it is difficult, most elderly who are dying come to terms with their fate and accept their condition.

Evaluation of Kübler-Ross's Work

We owe a great debt to Elisabeth Kübler-Ross for her sensitive treatment of dying patients. The attention she drew to the needs of dying patients has greatly affected the way health care professionals view and treat dying patients. Kübler-Ross showed that death was not a state but a process in which emotional changes occur (Rinaldi & Kearl, 1990). Her efforts led to other studies showing that personal interactions between doctors and people with terminal illness decrease as doctors have less contact with these patients (Rinaldi & Kearl, 1990). Doctors do not receive much training on how to deal with dying patients, and hospitals sometimes consider death a failure by doctors.

Many people have enthusiastically accepted Kübler-Ross's stage theory, but little evidence exists that this sequence is either universal or invariable (Burnell, 1993). Patients can and do switch back and forth—for example, from bargaining to denial and back again. Many do not proceed through these stages in any particular order, and others never enter some of them (Shneidman, 1977). Some dying people may experience two emotions indicative of different stages of dying at the same time, such as showing depression and anger simultaneously (Leming & Dickinson, 1994). In addition, although acceptance is a frequent response, so are apathy and apprehension (Weisman & Kastenbaum, 1968). The data from a number of studies simply do not support rigid stages or schedules for either terminal illness or mourning (Feifel, 1990).

True or False?
Every dying patient goes through a particular series of stages that ends with acceptance.

Other criticisms have focused on Kübler-Ross' methodology or argued that other factors, such as the nature of the illness, may affect the patient's emotional response to it. For instance, a person with a serious heart condition who could die tomorrow or next month or next year may react differently from someone with advanced pancreatic cancer who is told that he has 2 months to live. Kübler-Ross's theory gives little attention to the particular illness, mode of treatment, ethnicity, or lifestyle. Some experts, such as Robert Kastenbaum (1982), argue that each person's death is unique and that personality, age, and the entire context must be taken into consideration. Still others point to the danger in wholesale acceptance of this progression. The dying patient may be pressured to leave one stage and graduate to the next, and acceptance may be demanded before the patient is ready (Burnell, 1993; Kastenbaum, 1978). Kübler-Ross did recognize that individual differences occurred, that not all people go through these stages, and that the stages are not as formal as first thought (Kübler-Ross, 1985). However, her cautions were lost in the excitement of finally having a useful guide for understanding the experiences of dying people.

Choices for Dying Patients

Patients want to know about their medical condition so that they can control what they can. Concern about being in control of events increases with age (Thorson & Powell, 1988). Control is certainly reduced in the dying, who must cope with feelings of helplessness. Among the elderly, control and autonomy are highly correlated with better psychological and physical functioning whereas loss of control has an adverse effect on many areas of functioning (Schulz, 1978). The greater the opportunity and time for people to prepare for death and the more they feel in control, the less anxiety they experience (Schulz, 1978). It is important that dying people be told of available treatment options and be allowed maximum control over various areas of their lives. Patients have the right to know their condition, to choose or decline treatment, to choose or reject attempts to prolong their lives (Rinaldi & Kearl, 1990).

Questions Students Often Ask

Should dying patients be told that they are dying?

At one time, there was some doubt about this, but not today. The answer is yes. Almost all doctors now believe that people should be honestly told about their condition, their prognosis, and the treatment options available. However, this must be done in a sensitive manner because hope is part of the dying process. An individual has the right to say that he thinks he can beat the disease. Telling the patient is only fair, since an individual may have financial and personal affairs to set in order. In addition, most people will guess their condition after a while, and trying to conceal it puts a heavy strain on everyone.

Part of the desire for control is to be able to settle financial and interpersonal affairs. People are sometimes afraid of being a burden to others or of leaving loved family members inadequately cared for (Carey, 1975). It is important to deal with these practical issues, because this allows the patient time to deal with his or her own inner feelings about death.

Personal control means control over treatment decisions and one's everyday decisions such as what to wear and what to watch on television. The concern for personal control has increased greatly over the past 30 years. Traditionally, people were cared for by family in their home and made comfortable. Then, with the development of technology people died in the hospital and more medical machinery was used. The patient lost much control, including privacy and the right to make decisions concerning treatment (Rinaldi & Kearl, 1990). Today, the care for the dying is shifting back into compassionate care, together with alleviating pain (DePaola, Neimeyer, & Ross, 1994).

Appropriate Death

Medical care has advanced to the point that the final drama of life takes longer and longer to be played out. Life can now be prolonged through the use of technology, and new medicines hold out hope for extending life for an additional period of time. Today, many people who would not have survived just 20 years ago are alive. This tendency to prolong life is seen as a blessing by some, but others have pointed out that the patient often lives with extreme pain and that the burdens on the dying person and his or her family are tremendous. A role reversal may occur, and children may have to provide the care necessary for the dying patient's daily existence. Bitterness may mix with pain, creating stress in relationships with loved ones. Some have focused on what is called an **appropriate death**—a death that fulfills the expectations of the individual, shows adequate concern for the needs and desires of the patient, and gives the patient control over his or her destiny (Weisman, 1972). An appropriate death is what one might choose for oneself (Stephen, 1991/1992). People differ in their understanding of this term and every society has its own concept of the proper way to die. People in the United States and many western societies use phrases such as "death with dignity" and "appropriate death." In our society, a death from natural causes, with the dying patient surrounded by family and friends, suffering little or no pain, with a minimum of technological interference, and with the dying person having sufficient time and ability to place his or her affairs in order is considered the ideal (Marshall & Levy, 1990). In this regard, we will look at two issues typifying issues involved in control: the right to choose where one dies and issues relating to euthanasia.

The Place of Death

Although most fatally ill people want to die at home, relatively few will do so (Marshall & Levy, 1990). In the early 1900s only between 10% and 20% of all people died outside their homes; today over 80% die in institutions (Guillemin, 1992; Rinaldi & Kearl, 1990). On the average, two people die each month in a nursing home (Ingram & Barry, 1977), and this contributes to the depressing atmosphere in some nursing homes as well as to the difficulty nursing homes have keeping adequate staff. If some elderly see nursing homes merely as places where they stay while waiting to die, their view is reinforced by these mortality figures. Although only 5% of the elderly are presently in nursing homes, about 25% of all elderly deaths occur in such homes. More patients are now being cared for at home because of changes in the length of hospital stay permitted for Medicare patients (Guillemin, 1992).

appropriate death A death that fulfills the needs and expectations of the patient and gives the individual some control over his or her destiny.

True or False?
Most people die in their own homes.

Perhaps we should not look at death in the patient's own home as the ideal for everyone. There may be no one living at home who can take care of the patient and the symptoms and suffering of the terminally ill patient can be severe. Yet, hospitals do not seem especially capable of caring for terminally ill people either.

Dying in a Hospital

Hospitals are not prepared to serve the needs of the dying person, including their need to feel valued, to talk, to be listened to with understanding, to preserve personal identity, to maintain self-respect, to come to terms with the inevitability of death, to give and receive love, and to be free from pain (Dowling, 1995; Ebersole & Hess, 1981). The average general hospital does not—and perhaps cannot—meet these needs. For example, visiting rules make no sense for the dying patient, who may want to see family members at other times. The terminally ill person may need to have a loved one nearby to hold hands or cry with at a time other than during visiting hours. The family also may find visiting hours inconvenient. The patient may need more time and understanding than busy doctors and nurses can provide.

Hospitals are ineffective when it comes to reducing or eliminating pain for the terminally ill patient (Council on Scientific Affairs, AMA, 1996; Lo, 1995). The basic rule of many hospitals is to wait until the patient complains or needs a painkiller; hospitals do not try to prevent the onset of pain. The basic worry is that the patient will become habituated to the painkiller, but such a worry is not reasonable when working with terminally ill people. Furthermore, the hospital philosophy is strongly weighted toward the patient's getting better, which is as it should be, but the disease is treated rather than the person. All hospital medical procedures are directed toward the ultimate aim of defeating the disease. Such an orientation is incorrect for the terminally ill patient, who requires services directed not only at the disease but at the person and his or her family (Cassell, 1974). Finally, death in hospitals is often seen as the failure of medical technology. Extensive and heroic efforts are used to keep patients alive, requiring all types of medical machinery, but this may not be the desire of the patient or the family. The conclusion that many general hospitals cannot offer the dying the services they need is inescapable.

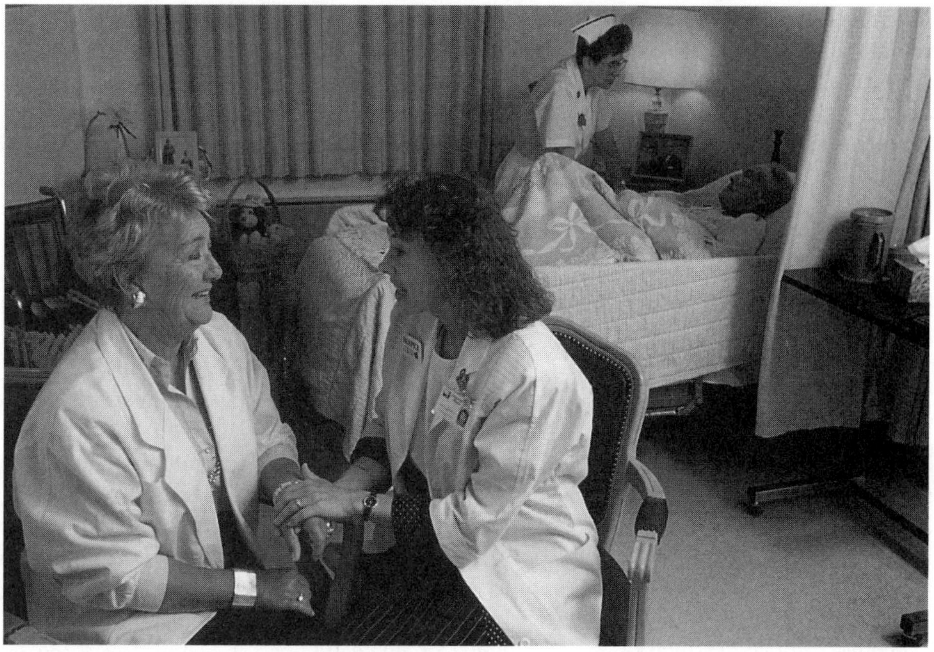

The hospice is a short-term facility where terminally ill people live out their remaining time in a brighter atmosphere. Pain is managed, but no high-tech medical services are offered.

The Hospice Movement

Most patients do not expect miracles. They need care and sensitive handling of their emotional needs. They need to have some input into their treatment and other major decisions regarding their situation. When they have such input, they show less depression and project blame onto others less often, and their loved ones suffer fewer feelings of guilt and inadequacy (Feifel, 1990).

The **hospice** is specifically designed for the care of terminally ill patients (Rinaldi & Kearl, 1990); the majority of hospice patients have cancer (Kastenbaum, 1994). Hospices do not offer high-tech medical services or advanced medication for the treatment of diseases such as cancer or AIDS. Rather, the hospice offers a concern for the patient and family and extensive pain control (Beresford, 1993). The patient's family and friends are intimately involved (Mesler, 1994/1995). The hospice emphasizes care, not cure (Rinaldi & Kearl, 1990), and terminally ill people retain as much control as possible. Rather than wait for a patient to request a painkiller, the medical staff administers doses of special painkillers to prevent the onset of pain. The staff is encouraged to form relationships with the patients, and the clergy plays a significant role in helping patients come to grips with their fate. Death is not considered failure, and the nursing staff and volunteers who work at the hospice are sensitive to the needs of patients and their families. Time is willingly spent with these people, the atmosphere is more cheerful, and families may visit at any time. Children are welcome, and hospices have nursery services available as well. The clergy is also involved providing ministry.

True or False?
Hospices offer terminally ill patients high-tech services in a home-like setting.

The hospice is a developing institution and its founder, Dame Cicely Saunders, argued that all hospices should be involved in research (Kastenbaum, 1994). Some hospices are experimenting with visits from artists, letters from school children, and the presence of plants and even pets (Conley, 1992).

Hospices are not extended-care facilities but rather short-term facilities that cater to the special needs of the terminally ill (Campanelli, 1996). They offer a middle ground between two undesirable approaches, high-technology medicine on one hand and euthanasia on the other. Death in a hospice is neither hastened (precluding euthanasia) nor postponed (precluding high-tech medicine) (Campbell, Hare, & Matthews, 1995). Hospices offer compassionate care, symptom control, and pain management (Beresford, 1993). People who work in hospices see their institutions as distinctly different from and as alternatives to hospitals. When social workers were asked how death in a hospice differs from death in a typical hospital, patient control was seen as the most significant difference (Rinaldi & Kearl, 1990).

The model for most hospices today is St. Christopher's in London, England. The first hospice in the United States was opened in New Haven, Connecticut in 1974. Today, there are more than 1800 hospices in the United States (Beresford, 1993). Although some hospices are institutions like St. Christopher's, many are not. The hospice movement is also a philosophy. Some hospices provide home-care service for dying patients and their families, others function as houses where the terminally ill and their loved ones can go for counseling (Barrow, 1986). At any given time the staff of St. Christopher's is caring for at least twice as many people at home as in their hospice facility itself (Kastenbaum, 1994).

Hospices provide an alternative to death in the hospital, one that is recognized by the public and its elected officials. A hospice benefit is included among Medicare benefits (Marshall & Levy, 1990). However, the hospice

hospice A center specifically designed for short-term care of the terminally ill. Hospices offer pain control and an atmosphere of understanding and concern, but no high-tech medical services.

does not solve the problem of long-term care for the terminally ill who are unable live at home. It remains an option for those who want to live their lives out in an accepting, caring setting without machines or experimental drugs.

Do People Have a Right to Die?

Should an elderly woman with failing mental powers have the right to refuse an operation for cancer that might cure her?

Should a hospital allow a severely burned man to leave, even though the man will probably die from infection within 48 hours if he does so?

Should a hospital refuse to disconnect life-support systems from a victim of a drug overdose who suffers from irreversible and extensive brain damage when taking the person off the respirator would mean immediate death?

Should a former athlete, now weighing 80 pounds after an 8-year struggle with AIDS, who is losing his sight and memory and is terrified of AIDS dementia be given the option of physician-assisted suicide (Quill, Cassel, & Meier, 1992)?

These are just a few of the dilemmas institutions and families face in the area of **euthanasia**—the act of putting a person to death painlessly. Euthanasia can involve acts of omission or commission. For instance, a doctor may not make the maximum effort to revive a patient who is terminal and comatose—an act of omission. An act of commission would involve taking someone off a respirator, even though doing so will probably speed the person's death. Because the gap between commission and omission is tenuous at best, euthanasia has been conceptualized in terms of four categories (Koza, 1977).

Voluntary and Direct Euthanasia The death is voluntary and carried out by the patient. Suicide falls into this category, as does refusal to take medication.

Voluntary but Indirect Euthanasia The patient gives to the doctor, family, or any other person the right to discontinue life-prolonging medical treatment if he or she becomes comatose or dysfunctional.

Involuntary and Direct Euthanasia This is an active form of euthanasia in which something is done to hasten death, such as giving a person a lethal injection to end life. It is involuntary because the person is not able to give consent and is close to what most people mean by the term *mercy killing.*

Involuntary and Indirect Euthanasia In this case, treatment is stopped, and the patient is allowed to die a natural death. In some circumstances, a doctor may not do everything possible to save a terminally ill person; this is sometimes called *passive euthanasia.*

euthanasia A general term defining an act of putting a person to death painlessly. Euthanasia may involve passive acts—such as not giving exceptional treatment—or may be active—as when a terminally ill person in great pain is given something that causes death.

Ethical Considerations of Euthanasia

The practice of euthanasia raises serious ethical questions. For example, under what circumstances can we allow others to make conscious decisions to end their own lives? Consider the case of a severely burned person whose chances of survival are slim. Some physicians will tell the victim, "We cannot predict the future. We can only say that to our knowledge, no one in the past of your age and with your size burn has ever survived this injury either with or without maximum treatment." The burn victim, who at this early point may not be in great pain, is then allowed to make his or her own decision. If the patient wants to receive maximum care, everything possible is done. If not, the patient is allowed visitors, and only ordinary medical care is administered. In this case, the individual makes the decision. But what if the patient is in extreme pain or not mentally healthy? Should such a person be allowed to choose?

Proponents of euthanasia note that medical science has developed to the point where people can be artificially kept alive to suffer lingering deaths but that such medical treatment is not effective if its aim is to cure. Euthanasia is a compassionate answer that recognizes the anguish of suffering and the right of the individual to make a choice based on the best information available. Advocates argue that doctors should not be obligated to continue heroic medical measures to keep someone alive. These arguments are much easier to make if the dying patient is conscious, rational, and capable of making his or her own decision. When this is not the case and other people must decide, the moral and ethical problems multiply. For example, how do we know that a family is acting in the best interests of the dying person?

Opponents of euthanasia note that medicine is not an exact science and that there have been cases of people who have been diagnosed as terminally ill who have gone into remission. In addition, most advocates of euthanasia differentiate between heroic, extraordinary measures and normal, regular care. However, what was considered heroic years ago might be considered normal today. Opponents also argue that last-minute medical developments might save some patients, although the odds are against this. Opponents fear that any reduction in the prohibition against taking life or not doing everything possible to prolong life might lead to serious social collapse. For example, what would stop someone from terminating the life of people with disabilities or who are senile. What would stop someone from ending the life of a terminally ill person because one or more functioning organs is needed for a transplant? Finally, most dying patients are depressed and in pain. Under such conditions, can we really consider any decision they make truly voluntary?

New Attitudes Toward the Dying

Most people today would agree that dying people who are competent should have the right to refuse treatment and that this refusal should be honored. Furthermore, most believe that if the individual cannot make such a decision, family members should be allowed to do so. Americans overwhelmingly support the right of patients to make their own decisions about receiving life-sustaining medical care (Colasanto, 1991). Perhaps this reflects the respondents' desire to have these options available for themselves under such circumstances. Most would want life-sustaining treatment withdrawn if they suffered a terminal illness with great pain and total dependency.

A great many Americans also believe that it is not always appropriate for doctors to do everything they can to save a patient. In a nationwide poll, 80% believed that there are sometimes circumstances when a patient should be allowed to die, and only 15% thought that medical personnel should always do everything possible to save a patient (Colasanto, 1991). People who are very religious and the elderly themselves are slightly more likely to argue that a person's life should always be saved. However, even here a clear majority now believes that at least in some cases no life-sustaining treatment should be given. Most people also agree with living wills and the use of a durable power of attorney to choose one's health care proxy (discussed later in this chapter), although only a small percentage have discussed these issues with anyone. To a considerable degree, however, people's attitudes depend upon the specific situations that are used in the poll (Holloway et al., 1994/1995). When elderly people were given a number of scenarios concerning terminal illness and life with severe mental and physical limitations, slightly more than half wanted to continue living even under conditions that involved immobility and dependency. About 10% favored a decision to end their lives, and about a third wanted family members to make the important decision for them (Cicirelli, 1997). One reason this study found lower percentages of elderly people wanting to end their lives is that people were asked specifically what *they* would do rather than their general attitudes towards euthanasia. Many older people want options available but far fewer believe that they would use these options.

The public has certainly embraced the idea that people who are dying should have some control over their treatment. However, the public is more divided when the patient is an infant or a young child rather than an adult or an elderly person. In fact, about half flatly reject the idea that parents can refuse life-sustaining treatment for severely disabled infants. Religious people are less likely than nonreligious people to agree with withholding treatment.

One area, though, in which the public has not really come to a decision concerns more active forms of euthanasia, including physician-assisted suicide (see Controversial Issues: Physician-Assisted Suicide on pp. 480–481). The public is divided on whether people with an incurable disease should be allowed to end their lives, but there is more tolerance of such a position than in the past (Ward, 1980, 1984). Acceptance of passive euthanasia is always greater than of more active forms of euthanasia.

The Dutch Experience

The western nation most associated with active forms of euthanasia is Holland (The Netherlands). In 1973, a Dutch judge refused to punish a doctor convicted of killing her ailing mother by lethal injection. The judge ruled that the physician had stayed within certain informal policy barriers against patient abuse (Smith, 1994). In 1993, the Dutch legislature agreed to legalize euthanasia under certain conditions that have prevailed for years (The Economist, 1994). Only patients who are experiencing unbearable pain, and repeatedly and voluntarily request death are supposed to be euthanized (Smith, 1994). In practice, however, Dutch physicians sometimes ignore these rules, and some patients who are not terminally ill but are in pain are euthanized. Euthanasia of infants with severe birth defects may also be occurring. A Dutch association for disabled people gives its members a card indicating that they do not want to be euthanized if they are ill. Although only 150 cases of euthanasia are reported annually to government officials, unofficial estimates range from 2000 to 6000 and as high as 25,000 physician-aided deaths per year (Markson, 1992; McCord, 1992). Are they all voluntary? Some evidence indicates that euthanasia of severely disabled children and incompetent individuals may take place and not be officially reported (Council on Scientific Affairs, AMA, 1996). Most requests for euthanasia come from people in their mid-60s, which is somewhat surprising. Perhaps the clustering of suicidal desire among patients in their 60s can be explained by the end of one's work life and a resultant crisis in self-esteem, and the fact that their roles are changing. Those who were refused euthanasia or change their minds rarely desired to die later even if their health and independence declined. Some dissenters from the Dutch experience ask whether this is not a cry of despair and a panic response (Conley, 1992).

Advocates of active euthanasia say that the Dutch system demonstrates that a system of euthanasia can work with appropriate safeguards whereas others claim that the safeguards are not effective. Doctors face prosecution if they fail to follow strict guidelines that require that the patient be in unbearable suffering, show a lasting desire to die, make the decision freely, and that the patient have a clear understanding of the condition. Some evidence does exist in an official report that some euthanasia is taking place without formal patient requests (The Remmelink Report, 1990).

One of the great problems in all discussions of euthanasia is pain. Almost everyone agrees that pain management in hospitals can be greatly improved and there is little reason why most people with terminal illness should suffer pain (Smith, 1994). Up to 60% of cancer patients do not receive adequate pain medication. In addition, hospitals do a poor job of treating depression, which is a common symptom in dying patients (Smith, 1994).

Controversial Issues: Physician-Assisted Suicide

No scenario is as controversial as that of physician-assisted suicide. The debate became more heated in 1990 when Dr. Jack Kevorkian assisted an Alzheimer's patient, Janet Adkins, to commit suicide by building a machine that allowed the woman to end her life by delivering a deadly poison to herself (Borger, 1990). Dr. Kevorkian has been involved in many assisted suicides and some of these were patients who were in great pain, but who were not terminally ill (Gibbs, 1991). His actions have caused a storm of legal and moral debate on the issue of physician-assisted suicide. In another case reported in the prestigious New England Journal of Medicine, Dr. Timothy Quill told the story of Diane, a leukemia patient for whom he prescribed barbiturates knowing that she wanted to die (Quill, 1991). Legally, a doctor may prescribe medication that might kill the patient as long as the medication has a legitimate purpose (The Economist, 1994). Dr. Quill openly declared his role in this death and a grand jury refused to indict him. Dr. Kevorkian has been in legal difficulties for some time but has not yet been convicted of any crime.

Physician-assisted suicide differs from other forms of active euthanasia for it is the patient who makes the ultimate decision and carries it out. Quill argues that the risk of abuse in many forms of euthanasia is too great, since the doctor is given too much power and is forced to perform some final act (Quill, Cassel, & Meier, 1992). The balance of power, Quill feels, is more equal in physician-assisted suicide.

The arguments in favor of this practice are somewhat similar to those used to support more active forms of euthanasia, but with some interesting additions. First, medicine has progressed to the point that it can keep alive people who are in failing health and may be suffering. Physician-assisted suicide is seen as a humane response to this condition. Second, advocates argue that people have the right to make decisions about their treatment and about the timing, circumstances, and place of their death (Stephany, 1994). Society is extending more rights to the dying patient, and it should extend the ultimate right: the right to be allowed to die when one wants. Third, unlike other forms of euthanasia, physician-assisted euthanasia does not require someone else to perform the last act. The doctor facilitates the patient's desire, which is clearly, consistently and voluntarily made. Fourth, although people opposed to physician-assisted suicide often say that pain is controllable, Quill argues that no empirical evidence exists to show that all physical suffering can be relieved (Quill et al., 1992). Fifth, most people accept a number of forms of passive euthanasia but balk at more active forms. Kevorkian asks whether it is humane to withdraw life support services and allow an individual to suffer or starve to death. Finally, it is estimated that 80% of the American health care budget is spent on patients who are in the last months of life, often to provide extraordinary treatment for people with incurable diseases (Burnell, 1993; The Economist, 1993). Often, families cannot afford this cost and society must pick up the bill, leaving less for others. The legalization of physician-assisted suicide would allow vital resources to be spent elsewhere.

Advocates note that adequate safeguards are not only possible but are and should be required by law. Quill would require that the patient freely, clearly, and repeatedly ask to die, the patient's judgment not be distorted, the physician be certain that the patient's suffering is not the product of inadequate care, and that the patient must have a condition that is incurable and involves unrelenting suffering (though not necessarily immediately fatal). The suicide is also carried out solely in the context of a meaningful doctor/patient relationship and the doctor must consult with another experienced physician to ensure that the request is voluntary and the medical situation as dire as reported. Finally, each step must be well documented. Although Quill strongly recommends informing the family of the decision, this is not a requirement (Quill et al., 1993).

Kevorkian's position goes beyond personal autonomy and self-determination, arguing that the physician should present the patient with a series of options, including death, if faced with an incurable disease. Kevorkian argues that dying people should donate their organs to save others or agree to experimentation that would take place under anesthesia from which they would not awaken (Kevorkian, 1991). Even some supporters of euthanasia are somewhat dismayed by Kevorkian's practices and ideas (Conley, 1992). Quill's action took place within the context of a long doctor-patient relationship whereas Kevorkian hardly knows those whom he helps to commit suicide.

The arguments against physician-assisted suicide are impressive. Doctors take a vow to heal, a vow that since ancient time has prohibited doctors from assisting directly in a patient's death (Beauchamp & Veatch, 1996). Involving doctors purposefully in suicides goes against this commitment to life. The decision to allow or not to allow such an action would rest totally on the physician's shoulders, excluding the clergy and other family members (Markson, 1992). Second, an acceptance of physician-assisted suicide may compromise the doctor-patient relationship (Pelligrino, 1996). It may affect how vigorously a doctor treats the patient, or the doctor may subtly influence the patient to choose suicide (Pelligrino, 1996).

Third, physician-assisted suicide is seen as exploiting the most vulnerable—the elderly and the poor—and where it is tolerated it reduces the value of life (Barry, 1992). Some argue that it is a thinly veiled way to eliminate those who are seen as burdensome to society (Conley, 1992). Fourth, it is open to abuse. For example, greedy family members or others could manipulate the patient into thinking that this is best (Barry, 1992). Fifth, people opposed to physician-assisted suicide argue that prescribing lethal medications requires doctors to become actively involved in the suicide and the doctor cannot avoid responsibility just because the final act of throwing a switch or taking the medication is performed by the patient (McCord, 1992). Opponents argue

Controversial Issues: Physician-Assisted Suicide (continued)

that much pain is controllable and doubt that many people need to remain in pain (Barry, 1992). Opponents also argue that suicide is an act of desperation if an individual is suffering and is *not* a rational act (Barry, 1992). While their lives are being prolonged many dying patients live in a technological world of machines and may feel frightened and isolated. Doctors tend to avoid personal involvement with their dying patients (Seravalli & Fashing, 1992). Depression and mental disorders may not be easy to identify in the patient, and a dying person may not be rational enough to consider any alternatives (Capron, 1994).

Finally, there is the "slippery slope" argument. If physician-assisted suicide is accepted, will the right to die become the duty to die for those who are old, sick, dependent, or who see themselves a burden to society (Fenigsen, 1989). The poor and dependent elderly population may feel pressured to agree to euthanasia because their families cannot pay for more medical care (Smith, 1994). Some believe that this is already happening in the Netherlands. For example, a doctor assisted in the suicide of a severely depressed woman who had no other ailment and the Dutch Supreme Court ruled out prosecution (The Economist, 1994). If such a right is conceded to the elderly ill where will it stop? People with disabilities argue that it will inevitably be extended and society will see some people as expendable.

A slight majority of Americans favor physician-assisted suicide under very specific circumstances (Markson, 1992), such as the patient being in tremendous pain with no hope of recovery (The Economist, 1994). However, public support often changes when the public is asked to vote on legalization (Neuhaus, 1994). Measures to allow physician-assisted suicide have failed in many countries and at least in two states. In some countries physician-assisted suicide has been legalized with safeguards against abuse, such as in the Northern Territories of Australia in 1995 (Ryan & Kaye, 1996).

The Supreme Court of the United States in 1997 declared that there is no constitutional right to physician-assisted suicide, allowing laws against it to stand, but left open the question of a state's right to allow such a practice (Maier, 1997).

In November 1994, Oregon voters passed by a close vote a law called the Death With Dignity Act that allows doctors to prescribe fatal doses of drugs for terminally ill people, thereby legalizing physician-assisted suicide (Campbell, Hare, & Matthews, 1995; Capron, 1995) (see the end of this feature for its main points). The measure is silent on who is to administer the lethal medication. The assumption is that the patient self-administers the medication, but this may not be the case. In December 1994 a federal judge issued an injunction preventing the law from being put into effect for an indefinite period of time (Beauchamp & Veatch, 1996). It will be voted on again.

How much control should a patient have? Does giving the patient more control mean giving the patient total control? Even Kevorkian acknowledges that physician-assisted suicide is an option only for rational patients. For example, Janet Adkins, who was Kevorkian's first case of assisted suicide, had Alzheimer's disease and had lost her memory but was considered rational by Kevorkian. Some ask how someone who has lost her memory can be considered rational (Conley, 1992). "Slippery-slope" arguments are difficult to defend or refute because by their very nature they require a prediction of the future, which is impossible (Beauchamp & Veatch, 1996). Some argue that the Netherlands has indeed slipped into involuntary euthanasia, especially in nursing homes (Fenigsen, 1989), whereas others argue that the Netherlands has not exactly collapsed as a moral society because of this practice (McCord, 1992). However, it is difficult to tell if safeguards can be totally secure or whether they will all erode with time.

The issues surrounding physician-assisted suicide and other forms of euthanasia are complex and difficult. They need to be debated and clarified, for the public will eventually have to make up its mind about how much control and autonomy it wishes to give to patients, and when society's interests differ and perhaps supersede the wishes of the individual.

The Death with Dignity Act

1. The patient must be at least 18, terminally ill (having less than 6 months to live), and an Oregon resident.
2. The patient must voluntarily make an oral request to the attending medical/osteopathic physician for a prescription for medication to end his or her life. A 15-day waiting period then begins.
3. The attending physician ensures the patient understands the diagnosis and prognosis. The patient is informed of all options, including pain control, hospice care, and comfort care, as well as the risks and expected result of taking the medication.
4. The attending physician (a) determines whether the patient is capable of making health care decisions and is acting voluntarily; (b) encourages the patient to notify his or her next of kin; (c) informs the patient that he or she can withdraw the request for medication at any time and in any manner; and (d) refers the patient to a consulting physician who is asked to confirm the attending physician's diagnosis and prognosis.
5. The consulting physician also decides whether the patient is capable of making the decision and is acting voluntarily. If either or both physicians believe the patient is suffering from a psychiatric illness or depression that causes impaired judgment, the patient will be referred for counseling.
6. Once the preceding steps have been satisfied, the patient voluntarily signs a written request witnessed by two people. At least one witness cannot be a relative or an heir of the patient.
7. The patient then makes a second oral request to the attending physician for medication to end his or her life.
8. The attending physician again informs the patient that he or she can withdraw the request for medication at any time and in any manner.
9. No sooner than 15 days after the first oral request and 48 hours after the written request, the patient may receive a prescription for medicine to end his or her life. The attending physician again verifies at this time that the patient is making an informed decision.

Attitudes toward dying in our society are changing rapidly. Because they are so difficult to define, catchy phrases such as "death with dignity," "the right to die," and "heroic efforts" do not solve problems. It is clear that people want control over the process of dying whenever possible and want their wishes respected. It is also clear that the public wants to give people more control over the process through advance directives that inform the doctor of the patient's wishes. In some areas, such as passive euthanasia, there is considerable agreement and general guidelines exist; there is much less agreement about active euthanasia. However, guidelines will always be general and controversial, and although they will be of some help, each case will eventually have to be decided on its own merits.

Living Wills

Various alternatives are available for people who would like their treatment decisions known in advance. Some people have signed a **living will**—a document that states their treatment wishes in such circumstances. For example, they may not want technologically advanced treatment for such conditions as irreversible brain damage (Marshall & Levy, 1990). A living will may also direct medical care when an individual is not terminally ill but is severely incapacitated (Neuhaus, 1994). It may direct a doctor to withdraw particular types of medical attention or refrain from withdrawing life support if the patient is in an incurable comatose state (Conley, 1992). Living wills are legal in every state (Cicirelli, 1997). As of December 1991, federal law requires health care facilities to inform patients about their right to prepare advance directives (Markson, 1992). Living wills have been accepted by most religions and medical organizations as valid. In a survey of physicians, 78% favored withdrawing life support from hopelessly ill or irreversibly comatose patients if they or their families request it (Brody, 1989).

Living wills sometimes create their own problems, especially with details. Although general wishes can easily be construed from living wills, it is impossible to foresee every treatment decision. Often, living wills are too vague and leave the patient's intent in question (Hoffman, 1994). For instance, in one New York case a court allowed a hospital to insert a tube into a dying patient unable to eat or drink despite the objections of the patient's daughter, who claimed that this was contrary to the wishes the patient expressed while competent. The court ruled that the statements were not specific enough to cover this eventuality (Fox, 1991). In addition, these wills may not reach the medical personnel at the appropriate time.

The Medical Durable Power of Attorney and Health Care Proxies

To counter these problems, an individual may appoint someone else to make medical decisions if the individual is incapacitated. A health care proxy may be appointed in the text of a living will or a separate document giving an agent a **durable power of attorney for health care or medical treatment** (Burnell, 1993; Fox, 1991). Since state laws differ regarding advanced directives, an individual should seek competent legal help in drawing up these documents. Unlike a living will, which requires specific choices to be enumerated for possible events in the future, an agent has the right to make the decision for the incapacitated individual. One does not have to anticipate all future medical conditions and possible alternatives. It is important for the individual named in the proxy to understand fully the wishes of the dying individual so that the proxy can order or refuse treatment.

A study found that physicians and spouses were *not* generally accurate in predicting a person's wishes about being resuscitated. In one study, physicians were asked about their patients' preferences under a number of scenarios, such as having a stroke that left them paralyzed and dependent. Spouses were also questioned about what their husbands or wives would prefer (Uhlmann et al., 1988). Although more than three-quarters of the physicians and spouses thought they knew the patients' preferences, their accuracy was no greater than what would be expected due to chance alone. Physicians underestimated patients' preferences for resuscitation whereas spouses overestimated them in most cases. So communication with the individual named in the proxy before the emergency is of utmost importance. Some people advocate changing the law to give the next of kin an automatic proxy that would allow this individual to make decisions for the incapacitated relative even if no advance directives have been signed (Neuhaus, 1994).

Doctors and Patients' Wishes

Do doctors who are told of a patient's wishes honor them? The answer appears to be "no" (Gilbert, 1995). In a study that has sparked much debate, researchers found that 31% of all terminally ill patients said they did not want cardiopulmonary resuscitation, but 80% of the doctors either misunderstood or ignored the patients' wishes. Almost half of all the patients who wanted to avoid cardiopulmonary resuscitation by having their doctors write "do not resuscitate" orders did not get them written. When the patient's orders were complied with, it often took quite a number of days before their doctors did so. Better communication did not seem to solve the problem. In a second phase of the study, nurses met daily with each patient and the patient's family to discuss the patient's wishes for treatment, then relayed the information to the doctors and hospital staff. Still, no improvement was found in compliance with patient's "do not resuscitate" requests. Many doctors simply chose to ignore this information (The SUPPORT Principal Investigators, 1995).

living will A document stating that under certain conditions an individual does not wish all available technology or life-saving treatment used.

durable power of attorney for health care or medical treatment A document that may be used to appoint another person as an agent to make treatment decisions if an individual is no longer capable of making those decisions.

The fault may lie with medical education, which does not train doctors to discuss dying with their patients. One AMA survey found that only 26% of residency programs offered instruction on death and dying issues; only 5 medical schools currently have a separate course on such issues and 117 medical schools include some information as part of other courses (Council on Scientific Affairs, AMA, 1996). Only if families or the patient are very insistent are their wishes followed.

Hospital culture is geared to high-tech treatments; the ethic that if we have all these machines available we should be using them is pervasive. Although the study did not deal with living wills the authors believe their findings call into question the value of living wills. Although advance directives are accepted as valid by most people, a considerable gap exists between acceptance of them and their implementation (Westman, Lewandowski & Procter, 1993). It is necessary to change the hospital culture and educate doctors on issues relating to death and dying as well as on improving pain control.

Bereavement, Grief, and Mourning

The death of a spouse, a parent, a sibling, a friend, or a child can leave a void, a feeling of emptiness in our lives. The task of recovery is difficult and fraught with mental and sometimes physical pain. **Bereavement** involves the status of having lost someone, of having been deprived of someone (Corr et al., 1994). **Grief** is the state of distress that occurs after the death. **Mourning** includes the cultural behaviors that follow such a loss (Kastenbaum & Costa, 1977). Bereavement and grief affect the physical, emotional, and intellectual aspects of life. Physical reactions accompany grief, especially right after the death of a loved one. Emotional reactions such as depression, anger, and sometimes guilt, may occur. The intellectual aspects involve coming to grips with the loss (Zins, 1987). In addition, there are social and religious/philosophical manifestations of grief. Problems with personal relationships may occur as do changes in the way an individual looks at God and other religious aspects of life (Corr et al., 1994).

How do people deal with the death of someone they love? The most important work in this area was performed by Erich Lindemann (1944), who observed and interviewed a number of people who had just experienced loss. He found that the reaction to the losses followed a common progression. At first, somatic distress occurred in waves, lasting from 20 minutes to 1 hour and including a tightness in the throat, choking or shortness of breath, need to sigh, an empty feeling in the abdomen, muscular weakness, and tension and mental anguish. Just the mention of the deceased's name can bring on these symptoms.

bereavement The status of having lost someone.

grief The state of distress occurring after someone's death.

mourning The cultural and societal behaviors that follow someone's death.

The grieving person is often preoccupied with the deceased and shows some desire for emotional distance from others. Sometimes, feelings of guilt are present, as those who survive blame themselves for supposed negligence and exaggerated minor injustices to the deceased. For example, after her husband died, one young woman felt guilty because they had quarreled the day before. Some grieving people express hostility to others. Some are restless, cannot attend to anything, and appear aimless and disorganized.

The most intense period of grief lasts 4 to 6 weeks, but depression and grief can last several months, and mourning can last a year or longer (Strong & DeVault, 1989). It is very common for people to reminisce about the deceased loved one, and these memories, often discussed with others, involve shared experiences (Rosenblatt & Elde, 1990). Reminiscence is often part of the ritual of mourning. It occurs most often right after death, and is an important part of grieving. Lindemann's work has been verified by other research and is now well accepted (Vargas, Loya, & Hodde-Vargas, 1989).

Reactions to grief lessen in intensity with time. Table 20.2 shows the initial and lasting grief reactions of a group of middle-aged adults who had experienced the death of a parent 1 to 5 years earlier (Scharlach, 1991). The most frequent behavioral reactions to a parent's death include difficulties with sleeping, working, keeping up with everyday activities, and getting along with certain people. There were no significant differences between initial reactions to the deaths of mothers and fathers. The residual reactions are interesting. A quarter or more of the respondents years later still became upset when thinking about the parent who died, found the memory painful, still cried when thinking about the parent, could not avoid thinking about the parent, and felt the death was unfair. They missed the parent very much.

Most models posit an initial phase of shock and denial, followed by a stage of awareness in which the emotional and behavioral reactions defined by Lindemann occur. Then comes a prolonged intermediate phase, in which the individual resumes daily activities and gradually thinks less about the deceased but still experiences feelings of sadness. A recovery phase then occurs, when there is a more positive attitude toward life and some pride in recovering from the loss (Parkes, 1987; 1972).

The stage concept of adaptation should not be overstated. Not all people who suffer a loss experience deep grief, show great outward expressions of grief, or move through the stages of recovery; nor does apparent lack of grief necessarily predict later problems (Wortman & Silver, 1988). There are many reasons why people may not grieve openly and intensely, including a lack of attachment, relief after someone has watched a loved one suffer, and having grieved before the actual death (Hansson, Stroebe, & Stroebe, 1988). If the relationship was not a strong or meaningful one, intense grief would not be expected (Stroebe, Van den Bout, & Schut, 1994). In addition, some cultures and subcultures encourage different degrees of outward emotional expression than others. There is no universal way to react. The absence of grief does not necessarily indicate pathology (Wortman & Silver, 1988), but in a small minority of cases it may (Stroebe et al., 1994). Although the stages previously described are commonly found, each individual takes his or her own time to grieve and these averages should not be considered rigid (Stroebe, Van den Bout, & Schut, 1994). People need to work through their grief at their own pace and in their own way. Some will grieve openly, some not. Last, there is no complete ending to grief (Wortman & Silver, 1988); it may reemerge at different times and at different situations.

Table 20.2 **Initial and Residual Grief Reactions to the Death of a Parent***

ITEM	MOTHER (*N* = 136)	FATHER (*N* = 119)
Initial Reaction		
Found it hard to get along with certain people	26.5%	31.9%
Found it hard to work well	32.3	26.0
Lost interest in family, friends, and outside activities	16.2	13.5
Felt the need to do things that the deceased had wanted to do	17.7	20.2
Was unusually irritable	23.5	22.6
Couldn't keep up with normal activities	32.4	24.3
Was angry that the person left me	31.6	22.7
Found it hard to sleep	38.2	29.4
Residual Grief		
Still cry when I think about the person	21.4	25.2
Still get upset when I think about the person	30.8	32.0
Cannot accept this person's death	8.1	12.6
Sometimes very much miss the person	79.4	73.1
Painful to recall memories of the person	36.8	24.4
Preoccupied with thoughts about the person	22.1	21.0
Hide my tears when I think about the person	17.7	14.3
No one will ever take this person's place in my life	82.4	82.4
Can't avoid thinking about the person	49.3	41.2
Feel it's unfair that this person died	28.7	30.3
Things and people around me still remind me of the person	64.7	60.5
Unable to accept this person's death	8.1	10.1
At times still feel the need to cry for the person	57.3	50.4

*Percentage of respondents indicating "completely true" or "mostly true."
Source: Scharlach, 1991.

True or False?

If a person does not grieve openly and intensely after the death of a loved one, the result is most frequently mental illness.

Questions Students Often Ask

My friend lost her mother 5 years ago and still occasionally seems to be sad and upset about it. When should grief end?

Grief doesn't end. Even years after the death of a parent or a close friend, sadness may well up inside an individual. This may occur at a family gathering or when some other happy occasion occurs and one thinks about those who are not present.

Factors That Affect the Grieving Process

One obvious factor affecting the grieving process is the centrality of one's relationship with the individual. We grieve more for a parent than for a great-uncle whom we rarely saw. We also grieve more when we think the death could have been prevented. For example, the parents of a young girl killed in a tragic automobile accident by a drunk driver had left the house a few minutes late that day. The girl's mother believed that if she had been on time, the accident would not have happened. It is the person's belief about preventability that matters, not the facts themselves. Table 20.3 shows how the two factors of centrality and preventability interact to affect the grief process.

The effectiveness with which the person is able to work through the complex emotions that accompany the death of a loved one is another factor that affects the duration and intensity of grieving (Burnside, 1981). The suddenness of the death is still another factor. If the family knows that the end is coming, they can prepare for it. **Anticipatory grief** involves doing some of the work of grieving before the death of the loved one. The person anticipating the death of a relative has time to adjust to it and to visit and share some last moments with the dying person. The family can also make their peace with the dying individual and know they are forgiven for past indiscretions. Recovery from grief is more rapid when the death is anticipated and less so when the death is sudden or unexpected (Campanelli, 1996; Kalish, 1981). Grief is also greater when the relationship is marked by ambivalence or dependence rather than by autonomy (Bowlby, 1980; Scharlach, 1991).

Social support is also important. If the grieving family is given a great deal of support, postdeath adjustment is better. Support given during the bereavement pe-

anticipatory grief The grieving that occurs prior to the expected death of a loved one.

riod reduces stress and helps the individual to adjust (Diamond, Lund, & Caserta, 1987). However, support during the care-giving stage is often considered very special by those experiencing a loss (Bass et al., 1990). Such social support includes shopping for the caregiver, cooking meals, helping with child care, cleaning the house, doing laundry, driving the care-giver, running errands, assisting at work if possible, making phone calls and writing letters, and visiting. Social support, such as kind words, being a good and active listener, and doing things for the bereaved, can help the individual recover. However, if this support consists of unwanted advice or encouragement to recover too quickly, it may not help at all. People often find it difficult to talk to someone who has just suffered a loss. Grieving people may become somewhat annoyed with platitudes. It may be important to admit that you don't know what to say and to offer specific ways of assisting, such as taking care of the children for a few days or making phone calls for the bereaved individual (Osterweis, Solomon, & Green, 1984).

One's cultural and religious beliefs are also important factors in the grieving process. Funerals and formal mourning rituals often help survivors accept the death of the loved one and express their grief in an acceptable manner. Customs and traditions vary, but they all encourage acceptance of the basic fact of the individual's death.

Finally, the grieving process is also affected by the age of the person who has died and the place in the life cycle a family finds itself (De Vries, Lana, & Falck, 1994). For example, parents who lose infants or young children often grieve not only for the infant or child but also for the person that the child might have been (Callahan, Brasted, & Granados, 1983). Parents grieving for a young child may often experience guilt, perhaps because they believe they could have prevented the fatal accident or illness. Evidence indicates that grief over a child who has died is the most intense grief and lasts the longest (Sanders, 1988).

True or False?
Grieving for a child is the most intense form of grief.

Table 20.3 **The Interaction of Preventability and the Centrality of the Relationship to the Experience of Grief**

	DEATH PERCEIVED AS PREVENTABLE	DEATH PERCEIVED AS UNPREVENTABLE
Central relationship	Intense and prolonged	Intense and brief
Peripheral relationship	Mild and prolonged	Mild and brief

Source: Bugen, 1977.

Questions Students Often Ask

When I go to a funeral or make a condolence call, I'm afraid of saying the wrong thing. What should I avoid?
It is often difficult to know what to say at a funeral. Just saying that you are sorry and volunteering to do something, such as picking up the children, is helpful. Visiting the individual after the funeral and during the mourning period is also appreciated. Allow the individual to express grief without holding back. Take your cue from what he or she wants to talk about. There are also things that ought not to be said because they are not helpful. For example, avoid saying that you know how they feel.

The Death of a Child

Although people may not want to think about it, they fully expect their parents to die before them. It is part of the normative life cycle that the older generation dies before the younger generation (De Vries et al., 1994). A child is not supposed to die; the event is unexpected and statistically unusual.

Support from others is an important factor in recovering from the death of a loved one. Helping during the care-giving stage is especially appreciated.

Yet some children do not survive their youth. Some die because of accidents, homicides, or suicides; others die from diseases such as cancer. About 39,000 children die each year during their first year of life, most commonly from congenital problems, sudden infant death syndrome, prematurity, and respiratory distress (most often connected with prematurity) (National Center for Health Statistics, 1993). After the first year and throughout childhood and adolescence, accidents are the leading cause of death; AIDS has also become a significant cause of death in children as well. In the rest of the world children also die from war-related tragedies and from starvation.

The death of a child is the most profound loss that anyone can experience and parental grief is intense and longlasting (Romanoff, 1993; Cook & Oltjenbruns, 1989). Longitudinal studies show that grief actually intensifies in the third year after the death and significant depression continues as far into the future as the seventh year (De Vries, et al., 1994), far greater than for any other loss. It may also have a lasting effect on the parents, who may be overprotective of a subsequent child. Parents whose children have died often experience considerable anger (Kübler-Ross & Goleman, 1976). Children carry many of the hopes and dreams of their parents and when the child dies part of the parent dies. In addition, the loss of the parenting role, if it is an only child, can be devastating. Some parents also have feelings of guilt, which even if irrational, may be difficult to work through. Some parents lose hope for the future as well (Schwab, 1992). The untimeliness of the child's death leaves parents unsure of everything. Surviving one's parents is normal, but we do not expect to survive our children. As Catherine Sanders (1988) notes, parents are unequipped to deal with the death of a child.

Although both parents mourn a great deal, mothers show greater levels of guilt and anger, even years later, and often feel that they are the only ones mourning the child's death (Fish, 1986). Fathers and mothers mourn somewhat differently. Mothers express their feelings more openly than fathers, causing the mother not to believe that the father is grieving as much as she is. Fathers take on the responsibility of notifying relatives, arranging the funeral, helping others manage their grief, and making certain that other family members are working through their feelings. Feeling responsible for everyone else may cause the father to postpone working through his own grief until his wife has recovered (De Vries et al., 1994). Fathers also have far fewer emotional supports.

Perhaps this is why the divorce and separation rate among grieving parents is greater than that among the rest of the population (Sanders, 1988). Spouses may find it hard to share their feelings, and the loss of physical and emotional resources makes grief resolution difficult. In addition, caring for an ill child may have been the focus of the family, so much so that other aspects of the marriage may have been put on hold. Parents may feel especially guilty if the death was the result of an accident or some other chance occurrence (Corr, Nabe, & Corr, 1994). They may also feel guilty about not having been perfect parents. Also, people are less tolerant of their spouses and more irritable (Schwab, 1992). Parents may be helped by participating in bereavement groups composed of people who have also suffered the death of a child. They may also do something positive, such as starting a fund or a memorial in their child's memory.

The death of a sibling can change the lives of the other children in the family. A very young child who may not understand the death of a brother or sister will be affected by the stress and disruption around them. Parents are also likely to become overprotective of their other children (Kalish, 1985). On the other hand, parents may not have much energy left (Adams & Deveau, 1987). Often, the dying child may have received all the attention, causing siblings to feel confused, rejected, and unable to express their feelings (Bluebond-Langner, 1989). Siblings also fear normal physical illness and show more death anxiety.

Recovery From Loss

The process of grieving is a trying one. A casual look at the symptoms most frequently reported by widows during the first month after bereavement (see Figure 20.1) is sufficient to show why the grieving process often weakens the person who has just suffered a loss. The incidence of physical and mental disorders, as well as death itself, increases for those most affected by the loss (LaRue, Dessonville, & Jarvik, 1985; Sanders, 1988). For these reasons working through one's grief is vital, but people do so in different ways.

Most people do eventually recover from their loss. For some, bereavement counseling, perhaps from clergy, is helpful. Others use self-help groups to meet with people who have suffered similar losses. Relatively few people in mourning require professional psychological counseling, but it is available for those who do. However, it is important to understand the normality of grieving and not to expect people who lose someone close to them to recover immediately.

Personal Choices

This book emphasizes the concept of personal choice. As people mature, the number of choices they make increases, and the nature of these choices changes. Although we cannot control everything in our lives, we do have some control over the paths our lives take and the way we cope with life's challenges. Although death is inevitable, people have many choices about how, when, and in what manner they will die. These choices represent the last choices in a long list of choices and alternatives available to people at different times in their lives. The choices we make concerning our own death and how we handle the loss of loved ones express our personal needs and values as much as any other choices made at any other time in life.

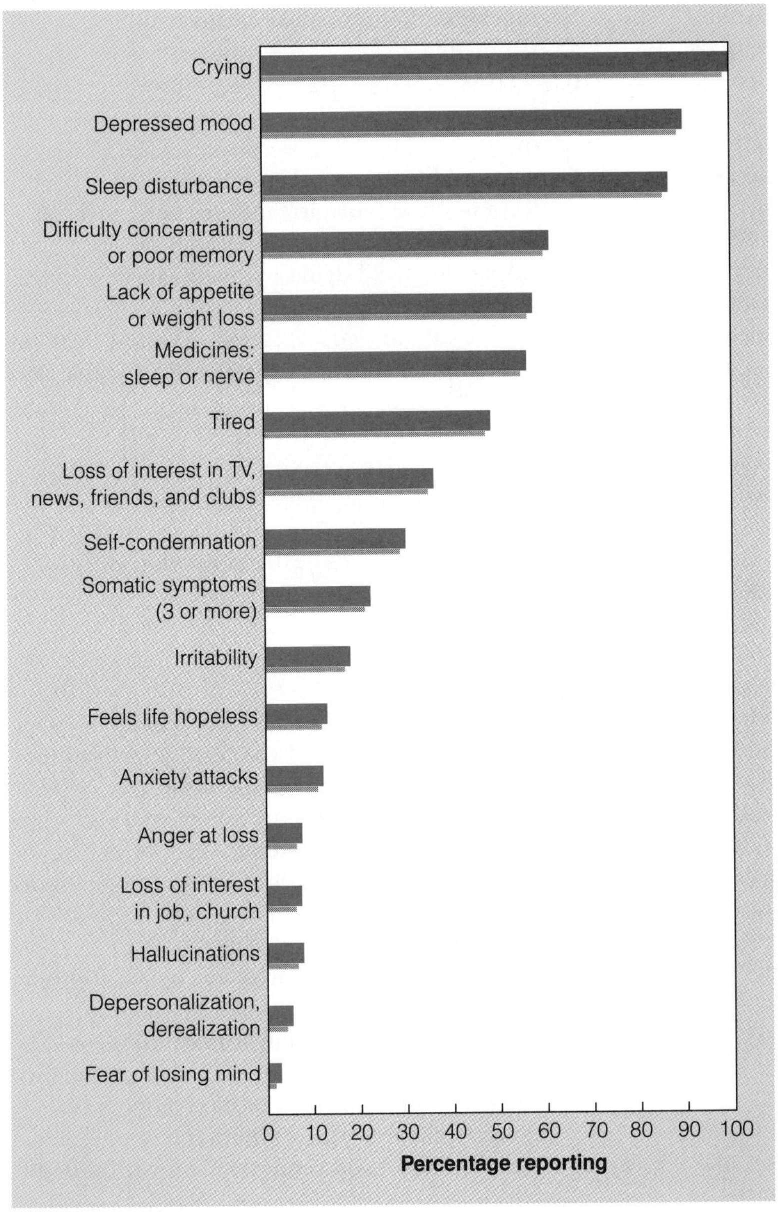

Figure 20.1
Symptoms of Bereavement as Reported by New Widows The process of grieving is an emotionally trying one that often weakens the person who has suffered a loss.
Source: Clayton et al., 1971.

Summary

1. There is currently more interest in the areas of death and dying than at any time in recent past, partly because of the moral issues surrounding death raised by improvements in medical technology as well as by society's increased awareness of the importance of the dying experience.
2. Children understand death through a progression of three stages. In the first stage (3 to 5 years), death is seen as reversible and transitory, and the dead are merely less alive. From ages 5 to 9 death is known to be irreversible but can be avoided. By about the age of 9 or 10, children understand that death is universal and irreversible, although some children within this age group still have not developed a completely adultlike understanding of death. The child's cognitive level and personal experience with death may influence his or her understanding of the concept.
3. Adolescents are more likely than children to come into contact with death, and often romanticize it. Early adults seldom think about death but in middle adulthood people are forced to come to grips with death. Older people do not experience as much death anxiety as people in middle age, but elderly people think and talk about death more often than younger people do.
4. Older people negotiate a life review process that allows them to put their lives into perspective. Their stories and reminiscences can be a source of living history.
5. After conducting many interviews, Elisabeth Kübler-Ross described the process by which dying people come to accept their fate. She described five stages, denial, anger, bargaining, depression, and acceptance. The approach has been criticized because the stages are neither universal nor invariable. Dying people can go through a certain stage more than once, sometimes experience two emotions at the same time, and sometimes do not negotiate all the stages. The nature of the illness and the person's beliefs and background may affect how the dying person copes with death.
6. Family members and medical staff should understand the needs of the dying patient. The patient should be treated as a distinct individual and allowed to participate as much as possible in choices concerning treatment and daily activities.
7. Although most elderly people would prefer to die at home, most will die in hospitals or nursing homes. The average hospital is not well equipped to serve the emotional needs of the dying patient. Another alternative is the hospice, a short-term facility specializing in pain reduction as well as in serving the emotional needs of the patient. The hospice does not offer highly technical medical care for treating disease.
8. Euthanasia is the process of putting a person to death painlessly. It can be passive or indirect, in which an individual is allowed to die, or active and direct, in which death is hastened. It can be voluntary, in which the patient either performs the act or asks someone

to do something that hastens the death, or involuntary, in which the family or doctor makes the decision. Physician-assisted suicide is a controversial issue today. The Netherlands has already legalized some active forms of euthanasia. Many important ethical questions surround the entire practice of euthanasia.

9. Most states allow for living wills in which an individual makes his or her wishes known in advance of a medical emergency. Durable power of attorney for health care decisions is a document that appoints an agent to make such medical decisions for a patient if the person is not capable of making them.
10. The most common symptoms of bereavement are somatic distress, preoccupation with the deceased, guilt and hostility, and disorganized, restless behavior. Most models posit an initial phase of shock and denial, followed by a stage of awareness, in which many emotional and behavioral reactions occur. This is followed by a prolonged intermediate phase in which the individual resumes regular activities and slowly becomes less obsessed with the deceased but still has feelings of great sadness. Then a recovery phase occurs, when a more positive attitude toward life develops and the person may show some pride in having recovered from the loss.
11. The intensity and duration of mourning depend on the centrality of the bereaved person's relationship with the deceased, whether the bereaved believes the death was preventable, the ability of the grieving person to work through the grief, whether the death was expected or unexpected, and the person's cultural and religious beliefs.

Multiple-Choice Questions

1. In the case of ____________, the Supreme Court stated that people had the right to refuse life-sustaining treatments under certain circumstances.
   a. Stephen Wolfe
   b. Jennifer Stevenson
   c. Karen Quinlan
   d. Jonna Dherland
2. Which statement concerning children and death is *correct?*
   a. Most parents want to shelter their children from death experiences.
   b. Children's fairy tales and nursery rhymes often have themes of death.
   c. Parents are very reluctant to allow their children to take part in studies dealing with children's understanding of death.
   d. All of the above are correct.
3. Gene is 3 years old. He probably sees death as:
   a. irreversible.
   b. irrevocable.
   c. universal.
   d. none of the above.
4. Young children often equate death with:
   a. bad people.
   b. sleep.
   c. injury.
   d. toys.
5. Eight-year-old Greg probably believes that:
   a. death is irreversible, irrevocable, and universal.
   b. dead people are just a little less alive.
   c. people can avoid dying by being clever.
   d. all of the above are correct.
6. Children at about age ____________ now first understand that death is irreversible, irrevocable, and universal.
   a. 5
   b. 7
   c. 10
   d. 15
7. The last subconcept of death to develop is:
   a. universality.
   b. reversibility.
   c. cessation of functions.
   d. causation.
8. A 9-year-old child is dying. We can expect:
   a. the child to understand the finality of death better than other children of the same age.
   b. the child to understand the nature of the changes in his/her medical condition.
   c. the child to talk little about the future and more about the present.
   d. all of the above from this child.
9. Which of the following would *not* be an appropriate guideline for explaining death to children?
   a. Do not explain everything at one sitting.
   b. Use an analogy that children will understand, such as that the deceased is breathing more easily.
   c. It is acceptable to show emotion.
   d. Talk about the good times you had with the individual.
10. Which term best describes the attitude of adolescents towards death?
    a. terror.
    b. romanticism.
    c. annoyance.
    d. denial.
11. People in the ____________ years are most likely to show a fear or dread of death.
    a. early adulthood
    b. middle adulthood
    c. late adulthood
    d. adolescent
12. Compared with early and middle adults, elderly people talk about death ____________, but fear it ____________.
    a. more, less
    b. less, more
    c. less, less
    d. more, more

13. Jennifer argues that most elderly people know that their lives are coming to an end in a very short time, such as a week or a month. According to research, Jennifer is:
    a. correct for people over 65.
    b. correct, but only for people over 75.
    c. incorrect, for most people are in good health the day before they die and death is unexpected.
    d. incorrect, for most are in good health a year before they die and less than half know that death is approaching.
14. Doris' grandmother is talking about her childhood and her feelings towards her sister and how she made up with her after not speaking for a considerable amount of time. This is called:
    a. ego processing.
    b. equilibration.
    c. ego transcendence.
    d. life review.
15. According to Kübler-Ross, when people are told that they have a terminal illness, their first reaction is:
    a. anger.
    b. jealousy.
    c. denial.
    d. resignation.
16. Which of the following is a valid criticism of Kübler-Ross' stage theory?
    a. The stages are neither invariable nor universal.
    b. The stages do not take the nature of the illness into account.
    c. Some dying patients show two emotions indicative of different stages of dying at the same time.
    d. All of the above are valid criticisms.
17. Which of the following statements concerning the place of death is *correct?*
    a. Most people want to die in their homes.
    b. Most people die in hospitals or other institutions.
    c. In the early part of this century, only between 10% and 20% of all people died in hospitals.
    d. All of the above are correct.
18. In voluntary and indirect euthanasia the patient:
    a. gives the doctor the right to end medical treatment if the patient is comatose and has no hope of recovery.
    b. takes his or her own life with the help of a physician who prescribes medication.
    c. is subjected to something that hastens death.
    d. does not tell the doctor of any decision to stop treatment but the doctor does so because death is inevitable and the patient is in considerable pain.
19. Your aunt leaves a document stating that she does not wish to be placed on life support if she is comatose with no hope of recovery. This document is called a:
    a. durable power of attorney.
    b. last will.
    c. living will.
    d. dying declaration.
20. The most intense and long-lasting grief follows the death of a:
    a. parent.
    b. child.
    c. friend.
    d. sibling.

Answers to Multiple-Choice Questions

1. c 2. d 3. d 4. b 5. c 6. c 7. d 8. d 9. b
10. b 11. b 12. a 13. d 14. d 15. c 16. d 17. d
18. a 19. c 20. b

Glossary

accommodation The process by which one's existing structures are altered to fit new information.

acculturation The process by which contact between cultures affects the cultural patterns of one or both groups.

activity theory The theory relating successful aging to the maintenance of activity throughout later maturity.

acute diseases Diseases with a sharp onset and rapid development.

adolescence The psychological experience of the child from puberty to adulthood.

adolescent egocentrism The adolescent failure to differentiate between what one is thinking and what others are considering.

age-graded influences Biological and environmental factors that are related to chronological age and may affect intelligence. For example, the increase in reaction time is generally age-related.

ageism Discrimination on the basis of age.

aging in place The phenomenon in which elderly people tend to live their postretirement years in the same place in which they raised their family.

AIDS (acquired immune deficiency syndrome) A fatal disorder affecting the immunological system, leading to inability to fight off disease.

altruism A type of prosocial behavior that involves actions that help people, that are internally motivated, and for which no reward is expected.

Alzheimer's disease An organic disorder of the elderly involving progressive and irreversible deterioration of brain tissue, causing cognitive and behavioral deficits.

amniocentesis A procedure in which fluid is taken from a pregnant woman's uterus to check fetal cells for genetic and chromosomal abnormalities.

androgens A group of male hormones, including testosterone.

animism The preschooler's tendency to ascribe the attributes of living things to inanimate objects.

anorexia nervosa A condition of self-imposed starvation found most often among adolescent females.

anoxia A condition in which the infant does not receive a sufficient supply of oxygen.

anticipatory grief The grieving that occurs prior to the expected death of a loved one.

anxious attachment A general classification of insecure attachment shown in the strange situation consisting of avoidant behavior, ambivalent attachment behavior, or disorganized/disoriented attachment behavior.

anxious/ambivalent attachment A type of attachment behavior shown during the strange situation in which the child both seeks close contact and yet resists it during the mother's reentrance after a brief separation.

anxious/avoidant attachment A type of attachment behavior shown in the strange situation in which the child avoids reestablishing contact with the mother as she reenters the room after a brief separation.

anxious/disorganized-disoriented A type of attachment behavior shown during the strange situation, in which the child shows a variety of behaviors, such as fear of the care-giver, or contradictory behaviors, such as approaching while not looking at the care-giver during the mother's reentrance after a brief separation.

Apgar Scoring System A relatively simple system that gives a gross measure of infant survivability.

appropriate death A death that fulfills the needs and expectations of the patient and gives the individual some control over his or her destiny.

arteriosclerosis A condition in which the arteries lose their elasticity as they harden.

artificialism The belief that natural phenomena are caused by human beings.

assimilation The process by which information is altered to fit into one's already existing structures.

associative play A type of play seen in preschoolers in which they are actively involved with one another but cannot sustain these interactions.

atherosclerosis A condition in which the inner walls of the artery become thick and irregular because of a buildup of plaque.

attachment An emotional tie binding people together over space and time.

attachment behavior Actions by a child that result in the child's gaining proximity to care-givers.

attention deficit/hyperactivity disorder (ADHD) A condition used to describe children who are impulsive, overly active, easily distracted, and inattentive.

attention span The time period during which an individual can focus psychological resources on a particular stimulus or task.

authoritarian parenting A style of parenting in which parents rigidly control their children's behavior by establishing rules while discouraging questioning.

authoritative parenting A style of parenting in which parents establish limits but allow open communication and some freedom for children to make their own decisions in certain areas.

autonomy The positive outcome of the second stage of Erikson's psychosocial stage, an understanding that the child is someone on his or her own.

babbling Verbal production of vowel and consonant sounds strung together and often repeated.

Babinski reflex The reflex in which stroking the soles of a baby's feet results in the baby's toes fanning out.

baby boom generation The generation born between 1946 and 1964, now entering or negotiating middle age. It is the largest generation in the history of the United States.

Bayley Scales of Infant Development A test of intelligence administered to infants between 2 months and 2½ years of age.

behaviorist A psychologist who explains behavior in terms of the processes of learning, such as classical and operant conditioning, and emphasizes the importance of the environment in determining behavior.

bereavement The status of having lost someone.

blastocyst The stage of development in which the organism consists of layers of cells around a central cavity forming a hollow sphere.

Brazelton Neonatal Behavior Scale An involved system for evaluating an infant's reflexes and sensory and behavioral abilities.

Broca's area An area in the brain responsible for producing speech.

bulimia An eating disorder marked by episodic binge eating and purging.

carrier A person who possesses a particular gene or group of genes for a trait, who does not show the trait but can pass it on to his or her offspring.

case study A method of research in which one person's progress is followed for an extended period.

centering The tendency to attend to only one dimension at a time.

cephalocaudal principle The growth principle stating that growth proceeds from the head downward to the trunk and feet.

Cesarean section The birth procedure by which the fetus is surgically delivered through the abdominal wall and uterus.

child abuse A general term used to denote an injury intentionally perpetrated on a child.

child neglect A term used to describe a situation in which the care and supervision of a child is insufficient or improper.

choice reaction time The time required to make one of a number of choices, depending on the stimulus presented.

chorionic villus sampling A diagnostic procedure in which cells are obtained from the chorion (an early structure that later becomes the lining of the placenta) during the 8th to 12th week of pregnancy and checked for genetic abnormalities.

chromosomal abnormalities Conditions caused by too many, too few, or incomplete chromosomes.

chromosomes Rod-shaped structures that carry the genes.

chronic diseases Diseases, such as arthritis, that linger on for an extended period.

classic pattern of aging The pattern of relative stability on verbal measures and decline in performance on nonverbal tests, commonly found when testing elderly people.

classical conditioning A learning process in which a neutral stimulus is paired with a stimulus that elicits a response until the originally neutral stimulus elicits that response.

classification The process of placing objects into different classes.

climacteric A term used to describe all the physical changes bringing someone from a state of fertility to one of infertility.

cohabitation The state of living together without being married.

cohort effect The effect of living in a particular generation or historical period, particularly important to consider when comparing generations.

commitment In psychosocial theory, making a decision concerning some question involved in identity formation and following a plan of action reflecting this decision.

communication The process of sharing information.

compensatory education The use of educational strategies in an attempt to reduce or eliminate some perceived difference between groups of children.

concordance rate A measure of the frequency with which both members of a pair of twins show the same particular trait.

concrete operational stage Piaget's third stage of cognitive development, lasting roughly from 7 through 11 years of age, in which children develop the ability to perform logical operations, such as conservation.

conditioned response The learned response to the conditioned stimulus.

conditioned stimulus The stimulus that the organism has learned to associate with the unconditioned stimulus.

conscience Part of the superego that causes the individual to experience guilt when transgressing.

conscious Freudian term for thoughts or memories of which a person is immediately aware.

conservation The principle that quantities remain the same despite changes in their appearance.

contact comfort The need for physical touching and fondling.

control group The group in an experiment that does not receive any treatment and acts as a comparison group against which the experimental treatment is evaluated.

conventional morality Kohlberg's second level of moral reasoning, in which conformity to the expectations of others and of society in general serves as the basis for moral decision making.

cooing Verbal production of single-syllable sounds, such as "oo."

cooperative play A type of play seen in the later part of the preschool period and continuing into middle childhood, marked by group play, specific roles, and active cooperation for sustained periods.

correlation A term denoting a relationship between two variables.

crisis In psychosocial theory a time in which a person actively faces and questions aspects of his or her own identity.

critical period The period during which a particular event has its greatest impact.

crossing over The process occurring during meiosis in which genetic material on one chromosome is exchanged with material from the other.

cross-sectional study A research design in which subjects of different ages are studied to obtain information about changes in some variable.

crowning The point in labor at which the baby's head appears.

crystallized intelligence Learned knowledge and skills.

cystic fibrosis A severe genetic disease marked by digestive and respiratory problems.

deciduous teeth The scientific term for baby teeth.

deductive reasoning Reasoning that begins with a general rule and is then applied to specific cases.

defense mechanism A behavior that serves to relieve or reduce feelings of anxiety or emotional conflict.

deferred imitation The ability to observe an act and imitate it at a later time.

delivery of the placenta The third and last stage of birth, in which the placenta is delivered.

dementia A condition consisting of impaired judgment and a reduction in intellectual ability that interferes with daily functioning and is caused by physical deterioration of brain tissue.

dependent variables The factors in a study that will be measured by the researcher.

despair The negative outcome of Erikson's last psychosocial stage, in which an older person experiences a sense of bitterness about lost opportunities.

dialectical thinking Thinking that shows the appreciation of constant change in life and shows the capability of accepting contradiction in the real world.

dilation The first stage of labor, in which the uterus contracts and the cervix flattens and dilates to allow the fetus to pass.

discrimination The process by which a person learns to differentiate among stimuli.

disenchantment phase The letdown and sometimes the depression that follow the honeymoon phase, often experienced by people whose retirement planning may have been unrealistic.

disengagement theory The theory relating successful aging to the reduction in the bonds that tie the elderly person to society.

dizygotic (fraternal) twins Twins who develop from two fertilized eggs and are no more genetically similar than any other sibling pair.

dominant traits Traits that require the presence of only one gene.

Down syndrome A disorder caused by the presence of an extra chromosome, leading to a distinct physical appearance and mental retardation of varying degree.

dream A vision of what a person would like his or her life to be like in the future.

durable power of attorney for health care or medical treatment A document that may be used to appoint another person as an agent to make treatment decisions if an individual is no longer capable of making those decisions.

ecological theory A broad theory that attempts to describe the many environments in which people exist and the relationships between people and these environments.

ecological validity The question of whether the tasks tested in a special environment, such as the laboratory, are relevant to those in real life.

ego In Freudian theory, the part of the mind that mediates between the real world and the desires of the id.

ego ideal The individual's positive and desirable standards of behavior.

ego integrity The positive outcome of Erikson's last psychosocial stage, in which an older person experiences a sense of satisfaction with life.

egocentrism A thought process in which young children believe everyone is experiencing the environment in the same way they are. Children who are egocentric have difficulty understanding someone else's point of view.

Electra complex The female equivalent to the Oedipus complex in which the female experiences sexual feelings toward her father and wishes to do away with her mother.

embryonic stage The stage of prenatal development, from about 2 weeks to about 8 weeks, when bone cells begin to replace cartilage.

emotional or psychological abuse Psychological damage perpetrated on the child by parental actions that often involve rejecting, isolating, terrorizing, ignoring, or corrupting.

empathy An emotional response resulting from understanding another person's state or condition.

empty nest The state of the family after the last child leaves home.

environmentality The proportion of the variation between people in a given population on a particular characteristic that is caused by environmental factors.

epigenetic principle The preset developmental plan in Erikson's theory, consisting of two elements: that personality develops according to maturationally determined steps and that each society is structured to encourage challenges that arise during these stages.

equilibration In Piagetian theory, the process by which children seek a balance between what they know and what they are experiencing.

estrogens A group of female hormones, including estradiol.

euthanasia A general term defining an act of putting a person to death painlessly. Euthanasia may involve passive acts—such as not giving exceptional treatment—or may be active—such as when a terminally ill person in great pain is given something that causes death.

exosystem Settings in which the individual is not actively involved, at least at the present time, but that affect the individual.

experiment A research strategy using controls that allows the researcher to discover cause-and-effect relationships.

expressive children Children who use words involved in social interactions, such as "stop" and "bye."

expulsion The second stage of birth, involving the actual delivery of the fetus.

extinction The weakening and disappearance of a learned response.

fear of strangers A common phenomenon beginning in the second half of the first year, consisting of a fear response to new people.

fetal alcohol effect An umbrella term used to describe damage to a child caused by the mother's imbibing alcohol during pregnancy; somewhat less pronounced than fetal alcohol syndrome.

fetal alcohol syndrome A number of characteristics—including retardation, facial abnormalities, growth defects, and poor coordination—caused by maternal alcohol consumption.

fetal stage The stage of prenatal development that begins at about 8 weeks and continues until birth.

fine tuning theory A theory noting that parents tune their language to a child's linguistic ability.

fluid intelligence The basic capacity for learning and problem solving. It is independent of education and experience.

fontanels The soft spots on the top of a baby's head.

formal operations stage The last Piagetian stage of cognitive development, in which a person develops the ability to deal with abstractions in a scientific manner.

full inclusion A movement that would provide all special services for children with disabilities in the regular classroom.

functional invariants Processes that characterize all organisms and operate throughout the life span.

gametes The scientific term for the sex cells.

gender consistency (constancy) Children's knowledge that they will remain boys or girls regardless of how they act, dress, or groom.

gender differences The differences between males and females that have been established through scientific investigation.

gender identity One's awareness of being a male or female.

gender roles Behaviors expected of people in a given society on the basis of whether an individual is male or female.

gender schema theory A theory of gender role acquisition, in which, after developing gender identity the child acquires a body of knowledge about the behaviors of each gender, which helps the child organize and interpret information and helps guide behavior.

gender stability Children's knowledge that they were of a particular gender when younger and will remain so throughout life.

gene The basic unit of heredity.

generational forgetting The phenomenon in which the older generation knows more about a particular area than the newer generation.

generativity The positive outcome of Erikson's psychosocial crisis of middle age, which involves giving of oneself and one's talents to others.

genotype The genetic configuration of the individual.

germinal stage The earliest stage of prenatal development, lasting from conception to about 2 weeks.

grammar A general term that refers to the total linguistic knowledge of phonology, morphology, syntax, and semantics.

grasping reflex A reflex in which a stroke on the palm causes the infant to make a fist.

grief The state of distress occurring after someone's death.

guilt The negative outcome of the psychosocial crisis of the preschool period, resulting in a sense that the child's acts and desires are bad.

habituation The process by which organisms spend less and less time attending to familiar stimuli.

health maintenance organizations (HMOs) Medical organizations that have an organized system for providing health care to members within a geographic area and that offer an agreed-upon set of basic and supplemental health and treatment services.

heart attack (myocardial infarction) The death of a part of the heart muscle because of interruption of the blood supply.

heritability The proportion of the measured differences between people in a given population on a particular characteristic due to genetic factors.

history-graded influences Events, such as wars, depressions, revolutions, and social movements, that are related to historical change and may affect the measurement of intelligence. For instance, the educational experiences of different generations differ.

holophrase One word used to stand for an entire thought.

HOME scale A scale that provides a measure of the quality and quantity of the emotional and cognitive elements in the home.

honeymoon phase The first phase after retirement, a time of joy and excitement.

horizontal decalage The unevenness of development in which a child may be able to solve one type of problem but not others, even though a common principle underlies them all.

hospice A center specifically designed for short-term care of the terminally ill. Hospices offer pain control and an atmosphere of understanding and concern, but no high-tech medical services.

hospitalism A condition found in children from substandard institutions, marked by emotional disturbances, failure to gain weight, and retardation.

Huntington's disease A dominant and fatal genetic disorder affecting the central nervous system.

hypertension High blood pressure.

id In Freudian theory, the portion of the mind that serves as the depository for wishes and desires.

identification The process by which children take on the characteristics of another person, often a parent.

identity The sense of knowing who you are.

identity achievement An identity status in which a person has developed a solid personal identity.

identity diffusion An identity status resulting in confusion, aimlessness, and a sense of emptiness.

identity foreclosure An identity status marked by a premature identity decision.

identity moratorium An identity status in which a person actively searches for an identity.

imaginary audience A term used to describe adolescents' belief that they are the focus of attention and being evaluated by everyone.

implantation The process by which the fertilized egg burrows into the lining of the mother's uterus and obtains nourishment from her system.

imprinting An irreversible, rigid behavior pattern of attachment.

independent variables The factors in a study that will be manipulated by the researcher.

inductive reasoning Reasoning that proceeds from specific cases to the formation of a general rule.

industry The positive outcome of the psychosocial crisis in the middle years of childhood, involving a feeling of self-confidence and pride in one's achievements.

inferiority The negative outcome of the psychosocial crisis in the middle years of childhood, involving the child's belief that his or her work and achievements are below par.

information processing theory An approach to understanding cognition that delves deeply into the way information is taken in, processed, and then acted upon.

initiative The positive outcome of the psychosocial crisis of the preschool period, involving development of a respect for one's own wishes and desires.

intelligence The ability to profit from experience; a cluster of abilities, such as reasoning and memory; the ability to solve problems or fashion a product valued in one's society.

intelligence quotient (IQ) A method of computing intelligence by dividing the mental age by the chronological age and multiplying by 100.

interiority The introspection and preoccupation with one's inner life that occurs during the later stages of middle age and old age.

intimacy The positive outcome of Erikson's psychosocial crisis of young adulthood involving development of close interpersonal relations, most often typified by marriage.

isolation The negative outcome of Erikson's psychosocial crisis of young adulthood, resulting in a lack of commitment to others.

labor A term used to describe the general process of expelling the fetus from the mother's womb.

Lamaze method A method of prepared childbirth that requires active participation by both parents.

language The use of symbols to represent meaning in some medium.

language-acquisition device An assumed biological device used in the acquisition of language.

lanugo The fine hair that covers a newborn infant.

latchkey or self-care children Elementary school children who must care for themselves after school hours. (Junior high school students are sometimes included in the definition.)

latency stage The psychosexual phase, occurring during middle childhood, in which sexuality is hidden.

learning Relatively permanent changes in behavior resulting from interaction with the environment.

learning disabilities A group of disorders marked by significant difficulties in acquiring and using listening, speaking, reading, writing, reasoning, or math skills.

life expectancy The average remaining lifetime for a particular population at a given age.

life review The process, usually found in older people, of reviewing and evaluating one's past.

life span The biological limit to the length of life of a particular species.

life-span developmental psychology The study of human development that is concerned with describing, explaining, and at times modifying the changes that occur over the entire life span.

living will A document stating that under certain conditions an individual does not wish all available technology or life-saving treatment used.

longitudinal study A research design in which the same subjects are followed over an extended period of time to note developmental changes in some variable.

love-oriented discipline A type of discipline relying on the use of reasoning or love.

macrosystem The ideology or belief system inherent in social institutions, including ethnic, cultural, and religious influences, as well as the economic and political systems that exist.

mass to specific principle A principle of muscular development stating that control of the mass or large muscles precedes control of the fine muscles.

maturation A term used to describe changes that result from the unfolding of an individual's genetic plan. These changes are relatively immune to environmental influence.

meiosis The process by which sex cells divide to form two cells, each containing 23 chromosomes.

menopause The cessation of a woman's menstrual cycle.

mental age The age at which an individual is functioning.

mental retardation A condition marked by subaverage intellectual functioning and adjustment difficulties that occurs before a person is 18 years of age.

mesosystem The interrelationships among two or more settings in which the person actively participates.

metamemory A person's knowledge of his or her own memory process.

microsystem The immediate interactions between the individual and the environment.

mid-life crisis A perceived state of physical and psychological distress that results when a person's internal resources and external social support systems are overwhelmed by developmental tasks that require new adaptive resources. (*Note:* Both *mid-life crisis* and *mid-life transition* are used interchangeably to refer to the period of questioning that may occur at the beginning of middle age. There is a general agreement that questioning does occur, but whether the term *crisis* should be applied is controversial.)

mistrust The negative outcome of Erikson's first psychosocial stage, an attitude of suspiciousness.

monozygotic (identical) twins Twins who develop from one fertilized egg and have an identical genetic structure.

moral realism The Piagetian stage of moral reasoning, during which rules are viewed as sacred and justice is whatever the authority figure says.

moral reasoning An approach to the study of moral development, stressing the importance of the child's ideas and reasoning about justice and right and wrong.

moral relativism The Piagetian stage of moral reasoning in which children weigh the intentions of others before judging their actions as right or wrong.

Moro reflex A reflex elicited by a sudden loud noise or momentary change in position, causing arching of the back, extension of the arms and legs, and finally their contraction into a hugging position.

morpheme The smallest unit of meaning in a language.

morphology The study of the patterns of word formation in a particular language.

motherese (parentese) The use of simple repetitive sentences with young children.

mourning The cultural and societal behaviors that follow someone's death.

multicultural education A multidisciplinary approach to education aimed at teaching students about the cultural heritage of various groups and the many contributions each group makes to society.

multifactorial inheritance Traits influenced both by genes and by the environment.

nativist explanation An explanation of language development based on biological or innate factors.

naturalistic observation A method of research in which the researcher observes organisms in their natural habitat.

neonate The scientific term for the baby in the first month of life.

nonnormative influences Events, such as medical problems or divorce, that affect a particular individual's life and may affect intelligence and development.

norms Rules that regulate behavior in particular situations.

object permanence The understanding that an object exists even when it is out of one's visual field.

Oedipus complex The conflict in Freudian theory in which a boy experiences sexual feelings toward his mother and wishes to rid himself of his father.

onlooker play A type of play in which the child watches others play and shows some interest but is unable to join in.

operant conditioning The learning process in which behavior is governed by its consequences.

operation An internalized action that is part of the child's cognitive structure.

osteoporosis A disorder, mostly of postmenopausal women, characterized by a loss of bone tissue that causes the bones to become porous and fracture easily.

overextension A type of error in which children apply a term more broadly than it should be.

overregularization (overgeneralization) A type of error in which children overuse the basic rules of the language. For instance, once they learn to use plural nouns, they may say "mans" instead of "men."

parallel play A type of play, common in 2-year-olds, in which children play in the presence of other children but not with them.

permissive parenting A style of parenting marked by open communication and a lack of parental demand for good behavior.

personal fable The adolescent's belief that their experiences are unique and original.

phallic stage Freud's third psychosexual stage, occurring during early childhood, in which the sexual energy is located in the genital area.

phenotype The observable characteristics of the organism.

phenylketonuria (PKU) A recessive genetic disorder marked by the inability to digest a particular amino acid and leading to mental retardation if not treated.

phonology The study of the sounds of language, the rules for combining the sounds to make words, and the stress and intonation patterns of the language.

play An activity dominated by the child and performed with a positive feeling.

polygenic (multigenic) inheritance Characteristics influenced by more than one pair of genes.

postconventional morality Kohlberg's third level of moral reasoning, in which moral decisions are made on the basis of individual values that have been internalized.

postformal operational reasoning An expression used to describe any qualitatively different reasoning style that goes beyond formal operational reasoning and develops during adulthood.

power-assertive discipline A type of discipline relying on the use of power, such as physical punishment or forceful commands.

pragmatics The study of how people use language in various contexts.

preconscious Freudian term for thoughts or memories that, although not immediately conscious, can easily become conscious.

preconventional morality Kohlberg's first level of moral reasoning, in which satisfaction of one's own needs, and rewards and punishment, serve as the basis for moral decision making.

premature infants Infants weighing less than 5½ pounds or born less than 37 weeks after conception.

preoperational stage Piaget's second stage of cognitive development, marked by the appearance of language and symbolic function and the child's inability to understand logical concepts, such as conservation.

presbycusis The decline in the ability to hear high-pitched sounds.

pretend play (dramatic play) A type of play in which children take on the roles of others.

preterm infants Infants born before 37 weeks of gestation.

primary circular reactions Actions that are repeated over and over again by infants and are centered on the body.

primary process The process by which the id seeks to gratify its desires.

primary sex characteristics Body changes directly associated with sexual reproduction.

Project Head Start A federally funded compensatory education program aimed at reducing or eliminating the differences in educational achievement between poor and middle-class youngsters.

prosocial behaviors Actions that are intended to help or benefit another individual or group.

prototype The most typical instance of a category.

proximodistal principle The growth principle stating that development occurs from the inside out—that the internal organs develop faster than the extremities.

psychosomatic or psychophysiological disorders Physical disorders, such as ulcers and colitis, that are contributed to or caused by emotional factors, including reactions to stress.

puberty Physiological changes involved in sexual maturation, as well as other body changes that occur during the teen years.

punishment The process by which some aversive consequence is administered to reduce the probability that misbehavior will recur.

qualitative changes Changes in process, function, structure, or organization.

quantitative changes Changes that can be considered solely in terms of increases or decreases, such as changes in height or weight.

readiness The point in development at which a child has the necessary skills to master a new challenge.

realistic or companionate love Love that is characteristic of people in a long-term relationship involving steady concern and caring.

recall A way of testing retention in which the subject must produce the correct response given very limited cues.

recessive traits Traits that require the presence of two genes.

reciprocal interaction The process by which an organism constantly affects and is affected by the environment.

recognition A way of testing retention in which the subject is required to choose the correct answer from a group of choices.

referential children Children whose early language is used to name objects, such as "dog" or "bed."

reflex A relatively simple automatic reaction to a particular stimulus.

reinforcer An event that increases the likelihood that the behavior that preceded it will recur.

rejecting-neglecting parenting A parenting style in which parents are not involved in their children's lives, being neither demanding nor responsive.

relativistic thinking Thinking that involves the appreciation that knowledge depends on the subjective experiences and perspective of the individual.

reorientation phase The retirement phase following the disenchantment phase, during which realistic plans are put into effect.

retinopathy of prematurity A condition of blindness resulting from an oversupply of oxygen most often administered to premature infants.

reversibility Beginning at the end of an operation and working one's way back to the start.

Rh factor An antibody often but not always found in human beings.

rite of passage A ceremony or ritual that marks an individual's transition from one status to another.

role A set of behaviors, attitudes, obligations and privileges expected of an individual who occupies a status.

role conflict A state in which the performance of one role makes it difficult to meet the requirements of another role.

role confusion In psychosocial theory, the negative outcome of adolescence, which involves a failure to develop a personal identity and feelings of aimlessness.

role overload A state in which the responsibilities required in a particular role are more than the energy and time available to perform the duties.

romantic love Love that is basically erotic in nature and involves a strong need for the physical presence of the other and for physical contact.

rooting reflex The reflex in young infants in which a stroke on a cheek causes the infant to turn in the direction of the stimulus.

rough-and-tumble play Physical play, such as play fighting, chasing, and wrestling.

rubella A disease responsible for many cases of birth defects.

schema (Piagetian theory) A method of dealing with the environment that can be generalized to many situations.

schema (information processing) An organized body of knowledge that functions as a framework describing objects and relationships that generally occur.

schizophrenia A severe mental disorder marked by hallucinations, delusions, and emotional disturbances.

script A structure that describes an appropriate sequence of events in a particular context.

secondary circular reactions Repetitive actions that are intended to create some environmental reaction.

secondary process or **reality principle** The process by which the ego satisfies the organism's needs in a socially appropriate manner.

secondary sex characteristics Physical changes that distinguish males from females but are not associated with sexual reproduction.

secular trend The trend toward earlier maturation today, compared with past generations.

secure attachment A type of attachment behavior in which the infant in the strange situation uses the mother as a secure base of operations.

selective attention The ability to concentrate on one stimulus and ignore extraneous stimuli.

self-concept The picture people have of themselves.

self-efficacy People's beliefs about what they can and cannot do.

self-esteem The value people place on various aspects of their self.

semantic feature theory A theory of semantic and concept acquisition arguing that people develop concepts in terms of a concept's basic features.

semantics The study of the meaning of words.

sensorimotor stage The first stage in Piaget's theory of cognitive development, in which the child discovers the world using the senses and motor activity.

separation anxiety Fear of being separated from care-givers, beginning at 8 or 9 months and peaking at between 12 and 16 months.

sequential design The use of at least two cross-sectional or longitudinal studies in one research study.

seriation The process of placing objects in size order.

sex chromosomes The 23rd pair of chromosomes, which determines the gender of an organism.

sex typing The process by which an individual acquires the attitudes, values, and behaviors viewed as appropriate for one gender or another in a particular culture.

sex-linked traits Traits inherited through genes found on the sex chromosomes.

sexual abuse Forced, tricked, or coerced sexual behavior between a younger person and an older person.

shame or doubt The negative outcome of Erikson's second psychosocial stage, in which the child has a sense of shame or doubt about being a separate individual.

sickle cell anemia An inherited defect in the structure of red blood cells, found mostly in African Americans and Latinos.

similarity theory of mate selection The theory of mate selection emphasizing that people attract and marry on the basis of underlying similarities in a variety of areas.

simple reaction time The time required to make a response after detecting a stimulus.

small-for-date infants Infants born below the weight expected for their gestational age.

social clock The internalized sense of timing that tells people whether they are progressing too fast or too slow in terms of social events.

social cognition The relationship between cognition and knowledge about and behavior regarding social situations and relationships.

social convoy The changing group of significant others who serve as sources of social support for an individual during the course of his or her life.

social learning theory The theoretical view emphasizing the process by which people learn through observing others and imitating their behaviors.

social referencing The phenomenon in which a person uses information received from others to appraise events and regulate behavior.

solitary play Independent play in which the child plays by himself or herself.

sonogram A "picture" taken of the fetus through the use of ultrasonic soundwaves.

stability phase The retirement phase following the reorientation phase, during which realistic plans are put into effect.

stagnation The negative outcome of Erikson's psychosocial crisis of middle age, in which one becomes completely absorbed in oneself.

stimulus deprivation The absence of adequate environmental stimulation.

stimulus generalization The tendency of an organism that has learned to associate a certain behavior with a particular stimulus to show this behavior when confronted with similar stimuli.

stimulus-value-role theory The theory of mate selection that sees the selection of a marital partner as a three-stage progression involving initial attraction, value comparisons, and analyses of role compatibility.

strange situation An experimental procedure used to measure attachment behaviors.

stress An unpleasant state in which people perceive the demands of an event as taxing or exceeding their ability to satisfy or alter those demands.

sucking reflex A reflex found in young infants, in which an infant automatically sucks when something is placed in the mouth.

superego In Freudian theory, the part of the mind that includes a set of principles, violation of which leads to feelings of guilt.

survey A method of study in which data are collected through written questionnaires or oral interviews from a number of people.

synchrony The coordination between infant and care-giver, in which each can respond to the subtle verbal and nonverbal cues of the other.

syntax The rules for combining words to make sentences.

Tay-Sachs disease A fatal genetic disease found most often in Jews who can trace their ancestry back to Eastern Europe.

telegraphic speech Sentences in which only the basic words necessary to communicate meaning are used, with helping words such as "a" or "to" left out.

temperament A group of characteristics reflecting an individual's way of responding to the environment and thought to be genetic.

teratogen Any agent that causes birth defects.

termination phase The last phase of retirement, during which people either return to work or find their stable lifestyle disrupted and sometimes ended by illness or disability.

tertiary circular reactions Repetitive actions with some variations each time.

Theory of Multiple Intelligences A conception of intelligence advanced by Howard Gardner, who argues that there are seven different types of intelligence.

time-buying behavior Buying timesaving goods and shopping more efficiently.

time-lag study A study that compares data presently gathered to data gathered at an earlier time, before the study was contemplated.

transductive reasoning Preoperational reasoning in which young children reason from particular to particular.

transition A period, late in labor, in which contractions become more difficult.

transitive inferences Statements of comparison, such as, "If X is taller than Y and Y is taller than Z, then X is taller than Z."

trust The positive outcome of Erik Erikson's first psychosocial stage, a feeling that one lives among friends.

unconditioned response The response to the unconditioned stimulus.

unconditioned stimulus The stimulus that elicits the response prior to conditioning.

unconscious Freudian term for memories that lie beyond one's normal awareness.

underextension The use of a word in a more narrow context than is proper.

unoccupied behavior A type of play in which children sit and look at others or perform simple movements that are not goal related.

vernix caseosa A thick liquid that protects the skin of the fetus.

visual cliff A device used to measure depth perception in infants.

walking (stepping) reflex A reflex in which, if the baby is held upright and the soles of the feet are placed on a hard surface while the baby is tipped slightly forward, the infant makes a stepping movement.

Wernicke's area An area in the brain responsible for comprehension of language.

zygote A fertilized egg.

References

AARP. (1992). How to stay employable: A guide for midlife and older worker. Washington, DC: American Association of Retired Persons.

Abernathy, T. J., Massad, L., & Romano-Dweyer, L. (1995). The relationship between smoking and self-esteem. *Adolescence, 30,* 899–907.

Abramovitch, R., Corter, C., Pepler, D. J., & Stanhope, L. (1986). Sibling and peer interaction: A final follow-up and a comparison. *Child Development, 57,* 217–229.

Abromowitz, A. J., & O'Leary, G. (1991). Behavioral interventions for the classroom: Implications for students with ADHD. *School Psychology Review, 20,* 220–234.

Achte, K., Fagerstrom, R., Pentikainen, J. & Farberow, N. L. (1990). Themes of death and violence in lullabies of different countries. *Omega, 20,* 193–204.

Ackerman-Ross, S., & Khanna, P. (1989). The relationship of high quality day care to middle-class 3-year-olds' language performance. *Early Childhood Research Quarterly, 4,* 97–116.

Adams, D. W., & Deveau, E. J. (1986). When a brother or sister is dying of cancer: The vulnerability of the adolescent sibling. *Death Studies, 11,* 279–295.

Adams, J. M. (1996, March 26). A symbolic celebration. *Newsday,* p. A17.

Adams, M. J. (1990). *Learning to read: Thinking and learning about print.* Cambridge, MA: MIT Press.

Adams P. F., & Benson, V. (1990). Current estimates from the National Health Interview Survey, 1989. *Vital and Health Statistics Series 10,* No. 176 (DHHS Pub. No. Phs 90–1504). Hyattsville, MD: National Center for Health Statistics.

Adams, P. F., & Hardy, A. M. (1991, April 1). AIDS knowledge and attitudes for July–September 1990. *Advance data from vital and health statistics of the National Center for Health Statistics.* Washington, DC: U.S. Department of Health and Human Services (DHHS Publication No. PHS 91–1250).

Adams, P. R., & Adams, G. R. (1984). Mount Saint Helen's ashfall: Evidence for a disaster stress reaction. *American Psychologist, 39,* 252–260.

Adams, R. J. (1987). An evaluation of color preference in early infancy. *Infant Behavior and Development, 10,* 143–150.

Adams, R. J. (1989). Newborns' discrimination among mid- and long-wavelength stimuli. *Journal of Experimental Child Psychology, 47,* 130–141.

Adams, R. J. (1995). Further exploration of human neonatal chromatic-achromatic discrimination. *Journal of Experimental Child Psychology, 60,* 344–360.

Adams-Price, C. (1992). Eyewitness memory and aging: Predictors of accuracy in recall and person recognition. *Psychology and Aging, 7,* 602–608.

Adelmann, P. K., Antonucci, T. C., Crohan, S. E., & Coleman, L. M. (1989). Empty nest, cohort, and employment in the well-being of midlife women. *Sex Roles, 20,* 173–189.

Adelson, J. (1996, January). Up with feelings. *Commentary, 101,* 59–61.

Adler, L. L. (1982). Cross-cultural research and theory. In B. B. Wolman (Ed.), *Handbook of developmental psychology* (pp. 76–88). Englewood Cliffs, NJ: Prentice Hall.

Adler, N., & Matthews, K. (1994). Health psychology: Why do some people get sick and some stay well? *Annual Review of psychology, 45,* 229–259.

Adler, N. E., Boyce, T., Chesney, M. A., Cohen, S., Folkman, S., Kahn, R. L., & Syme, S. L. (1994). Socioeconomic status and health: The challenge of the gradient. *American Psychologist, 49,* 15–24.

Adler, T. (1991, July). Women's expectations are menopause villains. *APA Monitor.* Washington, DC: American Psychological Association.

Adler, T. (1991). Seeing double? Controversial twins study is widely reported, debated. *APA Monitor, 22,* 1+.

Affleck, G., Tennen, H., Urrows, S., & Higgins, P. (1994). Personal and contextual features of daily stress reactivity: Individual differences in relations of undesirable daily events with mood disturbance and chronic pain intensity. *Journal of Personality and Social Psychology, 66,* 329–340.

Ainslie, R. C. (1985). *The psychology of twinship.* Lincoln, NE: University of Nebraska Press.

Ainsworth, M. D. S. (1967). *Infancy in Uganda: Infant care and growth of attachment.* Baltimore: Johns Hopkins University Press.

Ainsworth, M. D. S. (1974). The development of infant-mother attachment. In B. Caldwell and H. Riciutti (Eds.), *Review of child development* (Vol. 3). Chicago: University of Chicago Press.

Ainsworth, M. D. S. (1979). Infant-mother attachment. *American Psychologist, 34,* 932–938.

Ainsworth, M. D. S., Blehar, M. C., Waters, E., & Wall, S. (1978). *Patterns of attachment.* Hillsdale, NJ: Erlbaum.

Ainsworth, M. D. S., & Wittig, B. A. (1969). Attachment and the exploratory behavior of one-year-olds in a strange situation. In B. M. Foss (Ed.), *Determinants of infant behavior* (Vol. 4, pp. 113–136). London: Methuen.

Aizenberg, R., & Treas, J. (1985). The family in later life. In J. E. Birren & K. W. Schaie (Eds.), *Handbook of the psychology of aging* (2nd ed.) (pp. 169–190). New York: Van Nostrand Reinhold.

Akhtar, N., Carpenter, M., & Tomasello, M. (1996). The role of discourse novelty in early word learning. *Child Development, 67,* 635–645.

Akiyama, M. M. (1985). Denials in young children from a cross-linguistic perspective. *Child Development, 56,* 95–102.

The Alan Guttmacher Institute (1989). *Risk and responsibility: Teaching Sex educa-*

tion in America's schools today. New York.

Albert, M. S., & Heaton, R. K. (1988). Intelligence testing. In M. S. Albert & M. B. Moss (Eds.), *Geriatric neuropsychology* (pp. 13–33). New York: Guilford Press.

Albert, M. S., Wolfe, J., & Lafleche, G. (1990). Differences in abstraction ability with age. *Psychology and Aging, 5,* 94–100.

Albert, M. V. L., & Steffl, B. M. (1984). Loss, grief, and death in old age. In B. M. Steffl (Ed.). *Handbook of Gerontological Nursing*. New York: Van Nostrand Reinhold. 73–87.

Aldous, J. (1987). New views on the family life of the elderly and near-elderly. *Journal of Marriage and the Family, 49,* 227–234.

Aldous, J. (1990). Perspectives on family change. *Journal of Marriage and the Family, 52,* 571–583.

Aleser, K. H., Brix, K. A., Fine, L. J., Kallenbach, L. R., & Wolfe, R. A. (1989). Occupational mercury exposure and male reproductive health. *American Journal of Industrial Medicine, 15,* 517–529.

Alessandri, S. M., & Wozniak, R. H. (1989). Perception of the family environment and intrafamilial agreement in belief concerning the adolescent. *Journal of Early Adolescence, 9,* 67–81.

Alexander, C. S., Youth, Y. J., Ensminger, M., Johnson, K. E., Smith, B., & Dolan, L. J. (1990). A measure of risk taking for young adolescents: Reliability and validity assessments. *Journal of Youth and Adolescence, 19,* 559–569.

Alexander, G. M., & Hines, M. (1994). Gender labels and play styles: Their relative contribution to children's selection of playmates. *Child Development, 65,* 869–879.

Alexander, J. M., & Schwanenflugel, P. J. (1994). Strategy regulation: The role of intelligence, metacognitive attributions, and knowledge base. *Developmental Psychology, 30,* 709–723.

Alexander, K. L., Entwisle, D. R., & Dauber, S. L. (1993). First-grade classroom behavior: Its short- and long-term consequences for school performance. *Child Development, 64,* 801–814.

Allen, J. G. (1993). *Complying with the ADA*. New York: Wiley.

Allen, K. R., & Demo, D. H. (1995). The families of lesbians and gay men: A new frontier in family research. *Journal of Marriage and the Family, 57,* 111–127.

Allen-Hagen, B., Sickmund, M., & Snyder, H. N. (1994). *Juveniles and violence: Juvenile offending and victimization.* Washington, DC: U.S. Department of Justice.

Allgood-Merten, B., & Lewinsohn, P. (1990). Research cited in *Education Week,* June 6, 1990, p. 9.

Allison, P. D., & Furstenberg, F. F.; Jr., (1989). How marital dissolution affects children: Variations by age and sex. *Developmental Psychology, 25,* 540–550.

Allport, G. W. (1954). The nature of prejudice. Reading, MA: Addison-Wesley.

Alperstein, G., Rappaport, C., & Flanigan, J. M. (1988). Health problems of homeless children in New York City. *American Journal of Public Health, 78,* 1232–1233.

Alsaker, F. D., & Olweus, D. (1992). Stability of global self-evaluations in early adolescence: A cohort longitudinal study. *Journal of Research on Adolescence, 2,* 123–145.

Altman, D. (1986). *AIDS in the mind of America.* Garden City, NY: Anchor/Doubleday.

Alton, E. (1996, Feb. 1). Gene therapy. *The New England Journal of Medicine, 334,* p. 332.

Altrocchi, J. (1980). *Abnormal psychology.* New York: Harcourt Brace Jovanovich.

Alwin, D. F., Converse, P. E., & Martin, S. S. (1985). Living arrangements and social integration. *Journal of Marriage and the Family, 47,* 319–334.

Amato, P. R., & Partridge, S. (1987). Women and divorce with dependent children: Maternal, personal, family, and social wellbeing. *Family Relations, 36,* 316–320.

Ambry, M. K. (1992, April) Childless chances. *American Demographics, 14,* p. 55.

American Association of Retired Persons (AARP) (1994). *Images of Aging.* Washington, DC: AARP.

American Association of University Women (1992). *How schools shortchange girls.* Washington, DC: AAUW Educational Foundation.

American Association on Mental Retardation (1992). *Mental retardation: Definition, classification, and systems of supports.* (9th ed.). Washington, DC: Author.

American College Health Association (1986). *Acquaintance rape: Is dating dangerous?* Rockville, MD: American College Health Association.

American Enterprise Institute (1994 January/February) The twenty somethings. *The American Enterprise,* 88–98.

American Medical Association's Council on Scientific Affairs. (1992, June 17). Violence against women: Relevance for medical practitioners. *Journal of the American Medical Association,* p. 3185.

American Psychiatric Association (1994). *Diagnostic and statistical manual of mental disorders* (4th ed.) (DSM IV) Washington, DC: Author.

Ames, R. (1957). Physical maturing among boys as related to adult social behavior: A longitudinal study. *California Journal of Educational Research, 8,* 69–75.

Anand, K. J. S., & Hickey, P. R. (1987). Pain and its effects in the human neonate and fetus. *New England Journal of Medicine, 317,* 1321–1329.

Anderson, D. R., & Levin, S. R. (1976). Young children's attention to Sesame Street. *Child Development, 47,* 806–811.

Anderson, E. A., & Koblinsky, S. A. (1995). Homeless policy: The need to speak to families. *Family Relations, 44,* 13–18.

Anderson, G. L., Sedmak, D. D., & Lairmore, M. D. (1994). Placenta as barrier. In P. A. Pizzo & C. M. Wilfert (Eds.), *Pediatric AIDS: The Challenge of HIV infection in infants, children, and adolescents* (2nd ed., pp. 159–160) Baltimore: Williams & Wilkins.

Anderson, K. (1987). *Symptoms after 40.* New York: Arbor House.

Anderson, K. E., Lytton, H., & Romney, D. M. (1986). Mothers' interactions with normal and conduct-disordered boys: Who affects whom? *Developmental Psychology, 22,* 604–609.

Andersson, B. E. (1989). Effects of public day-care: A longitudinal study. *Child Development, 60,* 857–866.

Andersson, B. E. (1992). Effects of daycare on cognitive and socioemotional competence of thirteen-year-old Swedish schoolchildren. *Developmental Psychology, 63,* 20–36.

Andersson, T. & Magnusson, D. (1990). Biological maturation in adolescence and the development of drinking habits and alcohol abuse among young males: A prospective longitudinal study. *Journal of Youth and Adolescence, 19,* 33–42.

Andrews, B., & Brewin, C. R. (1990). Attributions of blame for marital violence: A study of antecedents and consequences. *Journal of Marriage and the Family, 52,* 757–767.

Angell, M. (1990). New ways to get pregnant. *New England Journal of Medicine, 323,* 1200–1202.

Angell, M. (1993, July 22). Caring for women's health—What is the problem? *New England Journal of Medicine,* 271–272.

Angier, N. (1990a, September 21). Team cures cells in cystic fibrosis by gene insertion. *New York Times,* p. 1+.

Angier, T. (1990b, December 14). Gene-treated girl is raising hopes. *New York Times,* p. A24.

Anglin, J. M. (1977). *Word, object, and conceptual development.* New York: Norton.

Anisfield, M. (1991). Neonatal imitation. *Developmental Review, 11,* 60–97.

Annis, L. F. (1978). *The child before birth.* Ithaca, NY: Cornell University Press.

Anstey, K., Stankov, L., & Lord, S. (1993). Primary aging, secondary aging, and intelligence. *Psychology and Aging, 8,* 562–570.

Antell, S. E., Caron, A. J., & Myers, R. S. (1985). Perception of relational invariants by newborns. *Developmental Psychology, 21,* 942–948.

Antonarakis, S. E. (1991, March 28). Parental origin of the extra chromosome in Trisomy 21 as indicated by analysis of DNA polymorphisms: Down syndrome collaborative group. *New England Journal of Medicine, 324,* 872–876.

Antonucci, T. C. (1985). Personal characteristics, social support, and social behavior. In R. Binstock & E. Shanas (Eds.), *Handbook of aging and the social sciences.* pp. 94–128). New York: Van Nostrand.

Antonucci, T. C. (1990). Social supports and social relationships. In R. H. Binstock & K. K. George (Eds.), *Handbook of Aging and the Social Sciences* (3rd ed.). New York: Academic Press.

Apfel, N. H. & Seitz, V. (1991). Four models of adolescent mother-grandmother relationships in black-inner-city families. *Family Relations, 40,* 421–431.

Apgar, V. (1953). A proposal for a new method of evaluation of the newborn infant. *Current Researches in Anesthesia and Analgesia, 32,* 260–267.

Apgar, V., & Beck, J. (1974). *Is my baby all right?* New York: Pocket Books.

Apgar, V., Holaday, D. A., James, L. S., Weisbrot, I. M., & Berien, C. (1958). Evaluation of the newborn infant: Second report. *Journal of the American Psychological Association, 168,* 1985–1988.

Appel, L. F., Cooper, R. G., McCarrell, N., et al. (1972). The development of the distinction between perceiving and memorizing. *Child Development, 43,* 1365–1381.

Appelbaum, M. I., & McCall, R. B. (1983). Design and analysis in developmental psychology. In P. H. Mussen (Ed.), *Handbook of child psychology* (4th ed.) (Vol. 1, pp. 415–477). New York: Wiley.

Applebome, P. (1996, March 27). Education summit calls for tough standards to be set by states and local school districts. *New York Times,* p. B9.

Arbuckle, T. Y., Gold, D. P., Andres, D., Schwartzman, A., & Chaikelson, J. (1992). The role of psychosocial context, age, and intelligence in memory performance of older men. *Psychology and Aging, 7,* 25–36.

Archer, S. L. (1982). The lower boundaries of identity development. *Child Development, 53,* 1555–1556.

Ard, B. N. (1990). *The sexual realm in long-term marriages: A longitudinal study following marital partners over twenty years.* San Francisco: Mellen Research University Press.

Are older Americans making better food choices to meet diet and health recommendations? *Nutrition Reviews, 1993, 51,* 20–23.

Arenberg, D., & Robertson-Tchabo, E. A. (1977). Learning and aging. In J. E. Birren & K. W. Schaie (Eds.), *Handbook of the psychology of aging* (pp. 421–450). New York: Van Nostrand Reinhold.

Arlin, P. K. (1990). Wisdom: The art of problem finding. In R. J. Sternberg (Ed.), *Wisdom: Its nature, origins, and development.* (pp. 230–244). Cambridge: Cambridge University Press.

Armon-Lotem, S. (1995). Locating parameters: Evidence from early word-order. In E. V. Clark (Ed.), *The child language research forum.* Center for the study of language and information. Leland Stanford Junior University, pp. 71–81.

Arnett, E. C. (1995, March 26). Society must wise up, maligned seniors say. *The Sentinel,* p. 16C.

Arnett, J. (1992). Reckless behavior in adolescence: A developmental perspective. *Developmental Review, 12,* 339–373.

Arnett, J., & Balle-Jensen, L. (1993). Cultural bases of risk behavior: Danish adolescents. *Child Development, 64,* 1842–1855.

Arnetz, B. B., Wasserman, J., Petrini, B., Brenner, S. O., Levi, L., Eneroth, P., Salovaara, H., Helm, R., Salovaara, L., Theoret, T., & Petterson, I. L. (1987). Immune function in unemployed women. *Psychosomatic Medicine, 49,* 3–12.

Arnold, D. S., Lonigan, C. J., Whitehurst, G. J., & Epstein, J. N. (1994). Accelerating language development through picture book reading: Replication and extension to a videotape training format. *Journal of Educational Psychology, 86,* 235–243.

Aro, H., & Taipale, V. (1987). The impact of timing of puberty on psychosomatic symptoms among fourteen- to sixteen-year-old Finnish girls. *Child Development, 58,* 261–268.

Artman, L., & Cahan, S. (1993). Schooling and the development of transitive inference. *Developmental Psychology, 19,* 753–759.

Arvey, R. D., Bouchard, T. J., Segal, N. L., & Abraham, L. M. (1989). Job satisfaction: Environmental and genetic components. *Journal of Applied Psychology, 74,* 187–192.

Asendorpf, J. B., Warkentin, V., & Baudonniere (1996). Self-awareness and other-awareness II: Mirror self-recognition, social contingency awareness, and synchronic imitation. *Developmental Psychology, 32,* 313–321.

Aslin, R. N. (1987). Visual and auditory development in infancy. In J. Osofsky (Ed.). *Handbook of infant development* (2d ed.) (pp. 5–98). New York: Wiley.

Aslin, R. N., & Dumais, S. T. (1980). Binocular vision in infants: A review and a theoretical framework. In L. Lipsitt & H. Reese (Eds.), *Advances in child development and behavior.* New York: Academic Press.

Aslin, R. N., Pisoni, D. B., & Jusczyk, P. W. (1983). Auditory development and speech perception in infancy. In P. H. Mussen (Ed.), *Handbook of child development* (4th ed.) (Vol. 2, pp. 573–689). New York: Wiley.

At 120, she becomes world's oldest. (October 16, 1995). *Newsday,* p. A8.

Atchley, R. C. (1977). *The social forces in later life* (2d ed.). Belmont, CA: Wadsworth.

Atchley, R. C. (1990). *Social forces and aging* (6th ed.). Belmont, CA: Wadsworth.

Atchley, R. C. (1996). *Social forces and aging* (7th ed.). Belmont, CA: Wadsworth.

Athanasion, R., & Yushioka, G. A. (1973). The special character of friendship formation. *Environment and Behavior, 5,* 143–165.

Atkinson, A. M. (1987). Fathers' participation and evaluation of family day care. *Family Relations, 36,* 146–151.

Atkinson, M. P., & Blackwelder, S. P. (1993). Fathering in the 20th century. *Journal of Marriage and the Family, 55,* 975–986.

Atwater, E. (1996). *Adolescence* (4th ed.). Englewood Cliffs, NJ: Prentice Hall.

Au, T. K., Sidle, A. L., & Rollins, K. B. (1993). Developing an intuitive understanding of conservation and contamination: Invisible particles as a plausible mechanism. *Developmental Psychology, 19,* 186–199.

Ault, R. (1977). *Children's cognitive devel-*

opment. New York: Oxford University Press.

Austin, A. B., & Draper, D. C. (1981). Peer relationships of the academically gifted: A review. *Gifted Child Quarterly, 25,* 129–133.

Austrom, D., & Hanel, K. (1985). Psychological issues of single life in Canada: An exploratory study. *International Journal of Women's Studies, 8,* 12–23.

Avis, J., & Harris, P. (1991). Belief-desire reasoning among Baka children: Evidence for a universal conception of mind. *Child Development, 62,* 460–467.

Avis, N. E., Kaufert, P. A., Lock, M., McKinlay, S. M., & Voss, K. (1993). The evolution of menopausal symptoms. In H. Burger (Ed.), *Baillere's clinical endocrinology and metabolism, 7,* pp. 17–32. London, England: Baillere Tindall.

Avolio, B. J. & Waldman, D. A. (1994). Variations in cognitive, perceptual, and psychomotor abilities across the working life span: Examining the effects of race, sex, experience, education, and occupational type. *Psychology and Aging, 9,* 430–442.

Avolio, B. J., Waldman, D. A., & McDaniel, M. A. (1990). Age and work performance in nonmanagerial jobs: the effects of experience and occupational type. *Academy of Management Journal, 33,* 407–422.

Axinn, W., & Thornton, A. (1992). The relationship between cohabitation and divorce: Selectivity or causal influence? *Demography, 29,* 357–374.

Azar, B. (1994, December). Psychology weighs in on Bell Curve debate. *APA Monitor, 25,* 1, 22.

Azar, B. (1995, May). Several genetic traits linked to alcoholism. *APA Monitor, 26,* 21–22.

Azar, B. (1996, December). Research seeks to soothe infant pain. *APA Monitor,* p. 21.

Bachman, J. G., Johnston, L. D., & O'Malley, P. M. (1993). *Monitoring the future: Questionnaire responses from the nation's high school seniors, 1992.* Ann Arbor, MI: Institute for Social Research, University of Michigan.

Backley, J. V., Warren, S. A., & Bird, G. W. (1988). Determinants of body image in women at midlife. *Psychological Reports, 62,* 9–10.

Bagley, C. A., Copeland, E. J. (1994). African and African American graduate students' racial identity and personal problem-solving strategies. *Journal of Counseling & Development, 73,* 157–173.

Bagnato, S. J., Neisworth, J. T., & Munson, S. M. (1993). Sensible strategies for assessment in early intervention. In D. M. Bryant & M. A. Graham (Eds.), *Implementing Early Intervention* (pp. 148–157) New York: The Guilford Press.

Bahrick, H. P., Bahrick, P. O., & Wittlinger, R. P. (1975). Fifty years of memory for names and faces: A cross-sectional approach. *Journal of Experimental Psychology: General, 104,* 54–75.

Bailey, J. M., Bobrow, D., Wolfe, M., & Mikach, S. (1995). Sexual orientation of adult sons of gay fathers. *Developmental Psychology, 31,* 124–129.

Bailey, J. M., & Pillard, R. C. (1991). A genetic study of male sexual orientation. *Archives of General Psychiatry, 48,* 1089–1096.

Bailey, W. T. (1994). A longitudinal study of fathers' involvement with young children: Infancy to age 5 years. *The Journal of Genetic Psychology, 155,* 331–339.

Baillargeon, R. (1987). Object permanence in 3-1/2- and 4-1/2-month infants. *Developmental Psychology, 23,* 655–665.

Baillargeon, R., & Graber, M. (1988). Evidence of location memory in 8-month-old infants in a nonsearch AB task. *Developmental Psychology, 24,* 502–512.

Baillargeon, R., Spelke, E. S., & Wasserman, S. (1985). Object permanence in Five-month-old infants. *Cognition, 20,* 191–208.

Baird, L. L. (1990). A 24-year longitudinal study of the development of religious ideas. *Psychological Reports, 66,* 479–482.

Baird, P. A., & Sadovnick, A. D. (1987). Life expectancy in Down syndrome. *Journal of Pediatrics, 849,* 110.

Baker, K. A., & de Kanter, A. A. (1981). *Effectiveness of bilingual education: A review of the literature.* Washington, DC: U.S. Department of Education, Office of Planning, Budget, and Evaluation.

Balk, D. (1990). Death and adolescent bereavement. *Journal of Adolescent Research, 6,* 41–58.

Balk, D. E. (1990). The many faces of bereavement on the college campus. In D. E. Balk, (1995). *Adolescent development.* Pacific Grove, CA: Brooks/Cole.

Balk, D. E. (1995). *Adolescent Development.* Pacific Grove, CA: Brooks/Cole.

Ball, S., & Bogatz, G. (1970). *The first year of "Sesame Street:" An evaluation.* Princeton: Educational Testing Service.

Baltes, M. M., Kulh, K. P., Gutzmann, H., & Sowarka, D. (1995). Potential of cognitive plasticity as a diagnostic instrument: A cross-validation and extension. *Psychology and Aging, 19,* 167–172.

Baltes, P. B. (1987). Theoretical propositions of life-span developmental psychology: On the dynamics between growth and decline. *Developmental Psychology, 23,* 611–626.

Baltes, P. B. & Lindenberger, U. (1997). Emergence of a powerful connection between sensory and cognitive functions across the adult life span: A new window to the study of cognitive aging? *Psychology and Aging, 12,* 12–21.

Baltes, P. B., Reese, H. W., & Lipsitt, L. P. (1980). Life-span developmental psychology. *Annual Review of Psychology, 31,* 65–111.

Bandura, A. (1977). *Social learning theory.* Englewood Cliffs, NJ: Prentice Hall.

Bandura, A. (1982). Self-efficacy mechanism in human agency. *American Psychologist, 37,* 122–147.

Bandura, A. (1982). The psychology of chance encounters and life paths. *American Psychologist, 3,* 747–755.

Bandura, A. (1986). *Social foundations of thought and action: A social cognitive theory.* Englewood Cliffs, NJ: Prentice Hall.

Bandura, A., Barbaranelli, C., Caprara, G. V., & Pastorelli, C. (1996). Multifaceted impact of self-efficacy beliefs on academic functioning. *Child Development, 67,* 1206–1222.

Bandura, A., Ross, D., & Ross, S. A. (1961). Transmission of aggression through imitation of aggressive models. *Journal of Abnormal and Social Psychology, 63,* 575–582.

Banks, M. S., & Salapatek, P. (1983). Infant visual perception. In P. H. Mussen (Ed.), *Handbook of child development* (4th ed.) (Vol. 2, pp. 435–573). New York: Wiley.

Banner, L. (1992). *In full flower: Aging women, power and sexuality.* New York: Knopf.

Baranowski, M. D., Schilmoeller, G. L., & Higgins, B. S. (1990). Parenting attitudes of adolescent and older mothers. *Adolescence, 25,* 781–789.

Barglow, P., Vaughn, B. E., & Molitor, N. (1987). Effects of maternal absence due to employment on the quality of infant mother attachment in low-risk sample. *Child Development, 58,* 945–955.

Barkley, R. A. (1990). *Attention deficit hyperactivity disorder.* New York: Guilford.

Barkley, R. A., Karlsson, J., Strzelecki, E., & Murphy, J. V. (1984). Effects of age and Ritalin dosage on the mother-child interactions of hyperactive children.

Journal of Consulting and Clinical Psychology, 52, 750–758.

Barnard, K. E., & Martell, L. K. (1995). Mothering. In M. H. Bornstein (Ed.), *Handbook of Parenting* (Vol. 3., pp. 3–27) Mahwah, NJ: Erlbaum.

Barnes, H. L., & Olson, D. H. (1985). Parent-adolescent communication and the circumplex model. *Child Development, 56,* 438–447.

Barnes, K. E. (1971). Preschool play norms: A replication. *Developmental Psychology, 5,* 99–103.

Barnes-Farrell, J. L. (1993). Contextual variables that enhance/inhibit career development opportunities for older adults: The case of supervisor-subordinate age disparity. In E. Demick & P. M. Miller (Eds.), *Development in the workplace* (pp. 141–155). Hillsdale, NJ: Erlbaum.

Barnes-Farrell, J. L., & Piotrowski, M. J. (1989). Workers' perceptions of discrepancies between chronological age and personal age: You're only as old as you feel. *Psychology and Aging, 4,* 376–377.

Barnett, R. C. (1994). Home-to-work spillover revisited: A study of full-time employed women in dual-earner couples. *Journal of Marriage and the Family, 56,* 647–656.

Barnett, S. (1993, May 19). Does Head Start fade out? *Education Week,* p. 40.

Barnett, W. S., (1995). Long-term effects of early childhood programs on cognitive and school outcomes. *The Future of Children, 5,* 25–51.

Barney, J. & Koford, J. (1987, October). Schools and single parents. *The Education Digest.* (pp. 40–43).

Barrera, M., Jr., Chassin, L., & Rogosch, F. (1993). Effects of social support and conflict on adolescent children of alcoholic and nonalcoholic fathers. *Journal of Personality and Social Psychology, 64,* 602–612.

Barrera, M. E., & Maurer, D. (1981). Recognition of mother's photographed face by the three-month-old infant. *Child Development, 52,* 714–716.

Barret, R. L., & Robinson, B. E. (1981). Teen-age fathers: A profile. *Personnel and Guidance Journal, 60,* 226–228.

Barrett, M., Harris, M., & Chasin, J. (1991). Early lexical development and maternal speech: A comparison of children's initial and subsequent uses of words. *Journal of Child Language, 18,* 21–40.

Barringer, F. (1990, September 2). What America did after the war: A tale told by the Census. *New York Times,* pp. 1, 5.

Barron, J. (1987, November 8). Sex education programs that work in public schools. *New York Times,* Section 12, pp. 16–19.

Barron, J. (1989, November 5). Silent majority. *New York Times Educational Supplement,* p. 27.

Barrow, G. M., & Smith, P. A. (1983). *Aging, the individual, and society* (2d ed.). St. Paul, MN: West.

Barry, R. (1992 July/August). The paradoxes of "rational" death. *Reason, 29,* 25–28.

Bartera, R. L. (1990). The effects of workplace health promotion on absenteeism and employment costs in a large industrial population. *American Journal of Public Health, 80,* 1101–1104.

Barth, J. M., & Parke, R. D. (1993). Parent-child relationship influences on children's transition to school *Merrill-Palmer Quarterly, 39,* 173–195.

Barton, S. (1994). Chaos, self-organization, and psychology. *American Psychologist, 49,* 5–14.

Baruch, G., & Barnett, R. (1983). Adult daughters' relationships with their mothers. *Journal of Marriage and the Family, 45,* 601–606.

Baruch, G. K. & Barnett, R. C. (1986). Determinants of fathers' participation in family work and children's sex role attitudes. *Child Development, 57,* 1210–1223.

Bass, D. M., Noelker, L. S., Townsend, A. L., & Deimling, G. T. (1990). Losing an aged relative: Perceptual differences between spouses and adult children. *Omega, 21,* 21–40.

Basseches, M. (1980). A framework for the empirical study of the development of dialectical thinking. *Human Development, 23,* 400–421.

Basseches, M. A. (1984a). Dialectical thinking as a metasystematic form of cognitive organization. In M. L. Commons, F. A. Richards, & C. Armon (Eds.)., *Beyond formal operations* (pp. 216–239) New York: Praeger.

Basseches, M. A. (1984b). *Dialectical thinking and adult development.* Norwood, NJ: Ablex.

Bassuk, E., & Rosenberg, L. (1988). Why does family homelessness occur? A case-control study. *American Journal of Public Health, 78,* 783–787.

Bassuk, E., & Rubin, L. (1987). Homeless children: A neglected population. *American Journal of Orthopsychiatry, 57,* 279–286.

Bassuk, E., Rubin, L. & Lauriat, A. (1986). Characteristics of sheltered homeless families. *American Journal of Public Health, 76,* 1097–1100.

Bates, J. E., Marvinney, D., Kelly, T., Dodge, K. A., Bennett, D. S., & Pettit, G. S. (1994). Child-care history and kindergarten adjustment. *Developmental Psychology, 30,* 690–700.

Bauer, G. (1987, March). Teaching morality in the classroom. *Education Digest,* pp. 2–5.

Bauer, P. J., & Thal, D. J. (1990). Scripts or scraps: Reconsidering the development of sequential understanding. *Journal of Experimental Psychology, 50,* 287–304.

Baum, W. B., Bernacki, E. J., & Sai, S. P. (1986). A preliminary investigation: Effect of a corporate fitness program on absenteeism and health care cost. *Journal of Occupational Medicine, 28,* 18–22.

Baumrind, D. (1967). Child care practices anteceding three patterns of preschool behavior. *Genetic Psychology Monographs, 75,* 43–88.

Baumrind, D. (1971). Current patterns of parental authority. *Developmental Psychology Monograph, 4,* No. 1, Pt 2.

Baumrind, D. (1972). An exploratory study of socialization effects on black children: Some black-white comparisons. *Child Development, 43,* 261–267.

Baumrind, D. (1978). Parental disciplinary patterns and social competence in children. *Youth and Society, 9,* 239–276.

Baumrind, D. (1980). New directions in socialization research. *American Psychologist, 35,* 639–652.

Baumrind, D. (1985). Research using intentional deception: Ethical issues revisited. *American Psychologist, 40,* 165–175.

Baumrind, D. (1989). Rearing competent children. In W. Damon (Ed.). *Child Development Today And Tomorrow* pp. 349–379. San Francisco: Jossey-Bass.

Baumrind, D. (1993). The average expectable environment is not good enough: A response to Scarr. *Child Development, 64,* 1299–1318.

Baumrind, D. (1994). The social context of child maltreatment. *Family Relations, 43,* 360–368.

Baxter, S. (1995, March). Arizona's constitutional babel. *Freedom Review* 45–47.

Baydar, N., & Brooks-Gunn, J. (1991). Effects of maternal employment and child-care arrangements on preschoolers' cognitive and behavioral outcomes: Evidence from the Children of the National Longitudinal Survey of Youth. *Developmental Psychology, 27,* 932–945.

Bayles, K. A., & Tomoeda, C. K. (1991). Caregiver report of prevalence and appearance order of linguistic symptoms in Alzheimer's patients. *Gerontologist, 31,* 210–215.

Bayles, K. A. & Trosset, M. W. (1992). Confrontation naming in Alzheimer's patients: Relation to disease severity. *Psychology and Aging, 7,* 197–203.

Bayley, N. (1969). *The Bayley scales of infant development.* New York: Psychological Corp.

Bayley, N. (1970). Development of mental abilities. In P. H. Mussen (Ed.), *Carmichael's manual of child psychology.* New York: Wiley.

Beal, C. R. (1985). Development of knowledge about the use of cues to aid prospective retrieval. *Child Development, 56,* 287–304.

Beauchamp, T. L., & Veatch, R. M. (1996). *Ethical issues in death and dying,* Englewood Cliffs, NJ: Prentice Hall.

Beck, S. H., & Beck, R. W. (1984). The formation of extended households during middle age. *Journal of Marriage and the Family, 46,* 277–286.

Becker, J. (1988). The success of parents' indirect techniques for teaching their preschoolers pragmatic skills. *First Language, 8,* 173–182.

Becker, J. V., Barham, J., Eron, L. D. & Chen, S. A. (1994). The present status and future directions for psychological research on youth violence. In L. D. Eron, J. H. Gentry, & P. Schlegel (Eds.), *Reason to hope: A psychosocial perspective on violence and youth.* (pp. 435–447) Washington, DC: American Psychological Association.

Becker, W. C. (1964). Consequences of different kinds of parental discipline. In M. L. Hoffman & H. W. Hoffman (Eds.), *Review of child development research* (Vol. 1). New York: Russell Sage Foundation.

Beckman, L. F., Seeman, T. E., Albert M., et al. (1993). High, usual and impaired functioning in community-dwelling older men and women: Findings from the MacArthur Foundation Research Network on Successful Aging. *Journal of Clinical Epidemiology, 46,* 1129–1140.

Bee, H. (1978). *Social issues in developmental psychology* (2d ed.). New York: Harper & Row.

Beilin, H. (1992). Piaget's enduring contribution to developmental psychology. *Developmental Psychology, 28,* 191–205.

Bell, A., et al. (1981). *Sexual preference: Its development in men and women.* Bloomington, IN: Indiana University Press.

Bell, A. P., Weinberg, M. S. & Hammersmith, S. K. (1981). *Sexual preference: Its development in men and women.* Bloomington, IN: Indiana University Press.

Bell, D. M., et al. (1989). Illness associated with child day care: A study of incidence and cost. *American Journal of Public Health, 79,* 479–484.

Bell, R. Q. (1968). A reinterpretation of the direction of effects in socialization. *Psychological Review, 75,* 81–95.

Bell, R. Q. (1979). Parent, child, and reciprocal influences. *American Psychologist, 34,* 821–827.

Bell, S. M., & Ainsworth, M. D. (1972). Infant crying and maternal responsiveness. *Child Development, 43,* 1171–1190.

Bellamy, C. (1996). *The state of the world's children, 1996.* Oxford: Oxford University Press.

Belsky, J. (1984). Determinants of parenting: A process model. *Child Development, 55,* 83–96.

Belsky, J. (1988). *Here today: Making the most of life after fifty.* Baltimore: Johns Hopkins University Press.

Belsky, J. (1988). The "effects" of infant day care reconsidered. *Early Childhood Research Quarterly, 3,* 235–273.

Belsky, J., & Braungart, J. M. (1991). Are insecure-avoidant infants with extensive day-care experience less stressed by and more independent in the Strange Situation. *Child Development, 62,* 567–571.

Belsky, J., & Eggebeen, D. (1991). Early and extensive maternal employment and young children's socioemotional development: Children of the National Longitudinal Survey of Youth. *Journal of Marriage and the Family, 53,* 1083–1110.

Belsky, J., & Most, R. K. (1982). Infant exploration and play. In J. Belsky (Ed.), *In the beginning: Readings on infancy* (pp. 109–121). New York: Columbia University Press.

Belsky, J., & Rovine, M. (1987). Temperament and attachment security in the strange situation: An empirical rapprochement. *Child Development, 58,* 787–795.

Belsky, J. & Steinberg, L. D. (1978). The effects of day care: A critical review. *Child Development, 49,* 929–949.

Belsky, J., & Steinberg, L. D. (1979). What does research teach us about day care? *Children Today, 8,* 21–26.

Belsky, J. K. (1987). *The psychology of aging* (2d ed.). Pacific Grove, CA: Brooks/Cole.

Belsky, J. K. (1990) *The psychology of aging* (2nd ed.). Pacific Grove, CA: Brooks/Cole.

Belsky, J., Steinberg, L., & Draper, P. (1991). Childhood experience, interpersonal development, and reproductive strategy: An evolutionary theory of socialization. *Child Development, 62,* 647–670.

Belsky, J., Woodworth, S., & Crnic, K. (1996). Trouble in the second year: Three questions about family interaction. *Child Development, 67,* 556–578.

Bem, S. L. (1981). Gender schema theory: A cognitive account of sex typing. *Psychological Review, 88,* 354–364.

Benenson, J. F. (1993). Greater preference among females than males for dyadic interaction in early childhood. *Child Development, 64,* 544–555.

Bengtson, V., Rosenthal, C., & Burton, L. (1990). Families and aging: Diversity and heterogeneity. In R. H. Binstock & L. K. George (Eds.), *Handbook of aging and the social sciences* (3rd ed.). (pp. 263–280). New York: Academic Press.

Bengtson, V. L., & DeTerre, E. (1980). Aging and family relations. *Marriage and Family Review, 3,* 51–76.

Benin, M., & Agostinelli, J. (1988). Husbands' and wives' satisfaction with the division of labor. *Journal of Marriage and the Family, 47,* 975–984.

Benin, M. H., & Nienstedt, B. C. (1985). Happiness in single- and dual-earner families: The effects of marital happiness, job satisfaction, and life cycle. *Journal of Marriage and the Family, 47,* 975–984.

Benoit, D., & Parker, K. (1994). Stability and transmission of attachment across three generations. *Child Development, 65,* 1444–1456.

Benson, J. B., Cherny, S. S., Haith, M. M., & Fulker, D. W. (1993). Rapid assessment of infant predictors of adult IQ: Midtwin-midparent analyses. *Developmental Psychology, 29,* 434–447.

Benson, P., Donahue, M., & Erickson, J. (1989). Adolescence and religion: Review of the literature from 1970–1986. *Research in the Social Scientific Study of Religion, 1,* 153–181.

Benson, P. L. (1993). *The troubled journey: A portrait of 6th–12th grade youth.* Minneapolis, MN: Search Institute.

Berardo, F. M. (1990). Trends and directions in family research in the 1980s. *Journal of Marriage and the Family, 52,* 809–817.

Berenbaum, S. A., & Snyder, E. (1995). Early hormonal influences on childhood sex-typed activity and playmate preferences: implications for the development of sexual orientation. *Developmental Psychology, 31,* 31–42.

Berenson, G., Frank, G., Hunter, S., Srinivasan, S., Voors, A., & Webber, L. (1982). Cardiovascular risk factors in children: Should they concern the pediatrician. *American Journal of Diseases of Children, 136,* 855–862.

Beresford, L. (1993). *The hospice book.* Boston: Little, Brown.

Berg, C. A., & Sternberg, R. J. (1992). Adults' conceptions of intelligence across the adult life span. *Psychology and Aging, 7,* 221–231.

Berg, F., (1992 July/August). Harmful weight loss practices are widespread among adolescents. *HWJ Obesity & Health, 6,* 69–72.

Berg, W. K., Adkinson, C. D., & Strock, B. D. (1973). Duration and frequency of periods of alertness in the newborn. *Developmental Psychology, 9,* 434.

Berg, W. K., & Berg, K. M. (1979). Psychophysiological development in infancy: State, sensory functioning, and attention. In J. Osofsky (Ed.), *Handbook of infant development* (pp. 283–344). New York: Wiley.

Berger, B. G., & Owen, D. R. (1983). Mood alteration with swimming; Swimmers really do "feel better." *Psychosomatic Medicine, 45,* 425–433.

Berger, C. S., Sorensen, L., Gendler, B., & Fitzsimmons, J. (1990). Cocaine and pregnancy: A challenge for health care providers. *Health and Social Work, 15,* 310–316.

Berger, E. P. (1995). *Parents as partners in education* (4th ed.). Englewood Cliffs, NJ: Prentice Hall.

Berger, R. M. (1990). Men together: Understanding the gay couple. *Journal of Homosexuality, 19,* 31–49.

Berko, E.G. (1992). The Americans with Disabilities Act of 1990. Albany, NY: Advocate for the Disabled.

Berkowitz, G. S., Skovron, M. L., Lapinski, R. H., & Berkowitz, R. L. (1990). Delayed childbearing and the outcome of pregnancy. *New England Journal of Medicine, 322,* 659–663.

Berman, C. (1987). The cold facts about remarriage: Money, prenuptial agreements and wills. In J. Belovitch (Ed.), *Making remarriage work* (pp. 15–17). Lexington, MA: Heath.

Berman, S. L., Kurtines, W. M., Silverman, W. K., & Serafini, L. T. (1996). The impact of exposure to crime and violence on urban youth. *American Journal of Orthopsychiatry, 66,* 329–333.

Bernard, H. S. (1981). Identity formation during late adolescence: A review of some empirical findings. *Adolescence, 16,* 349–356.

Bernardo, F. M. (1968). Widowhood status in the United States: Perspectives on a neglected aspect of the family cycle. *Family Coordinator, 17,* 191–203.

Berndt, T. (1979). Developmental changes in conformity to peers and parents. *Developmental Psychology, 15,* 608–617.

Berndt, T. J. (1981). Relations between social cognition, nonsocial cognition, and social behavior: The case of friendship. In J. H. Flavell & L. Ross (Eds.), *Social cognitive development.* Cambridge: Cambridge University Press.

Berndt, T. J. (1989). Friendships in childhood and adolescence. In W. Damon (Ed.), *Child development: Today and tomorrow* (pp. 332–349). San Francisco: Jossey-Bass.

Berndt, T. J., & Hoyle, S. G. (1985). Stability and change in childhood and adolescent friendship. *Developmental Psychology, 21,* 1007–1015.

Berndt, T. J., & Keefe, K. (1995). Friends' influence on adolescents' adjustment to school. *Child Development, 66,* 1312–1329.

Berndt, T. J., Ping, C. C., Sing, L., Kit-Tai, H., & Lew, W. J. F., (1993). Perceptions of parenting in mainland China, Taiwan, and Hong Kong: Sex differences and societal differences. *Developmental Psychology, 29,* 156–164.

Bernhardt, B., & Rauch, J. B. (1993). Genetic family histories: An aid to social work assessment. *Families in Society, 74,* 195–205.

Bernstein, M. E., & Morrison, M. E. (1992). Are we ready for PL 99–457? *AAD, 137,* 7–15.

Berrueta-Clement, J. R., Schweinhart, L., J., Barnett, W. S., Epstein, A. S., & Weikart, D. P. (1985). *Changed lives: The effects of the Perry Preschool Program on youths through age 19.* Ypsilanti, MI: High/Scope.

Bertenthal, B. I., & Campos, J. J. (1987). Commentary—New directions in the study of early experience. *Child Development, 58,* 560–568.

Besharov, D. J. (1989, Fall). Children of crack. *Public Welfare,* pp. 6–11.

Best, J. B. (1986). *Cognitive psychology.* St. Paul, MN: West.

Bettelheim, B. (1977). *The uses of enchantment: The meaning and importance of fairy tales.* New York: Vintage Books.

Beyth-Marom, R., Austin, L., Fischoff, B., Palmgren, C., & Jacobs-Quadrel, M. (1993). Perceived consequences of risky behaviors: Adults and adolescents. *Developmental Psychology, 29,* 549–563.

Bhatt, R. S. & Rovee-Collier, C. (1994). Perception and 24-hour retention of feature relations in infancy. *Developmental Psychology, 30,* 142–150.

Bhatt, R. S., & Rovee-Collier, C. (1996). Infants' forgetting of correlated attributes and object recognition. *Child Development,* 172–187.

Bhavnagri, N. & Parke, R. D. (1991). Parents as direct facilitators of children's peer relationships: Effects of age of child and sex of parent. *Journal of Social and Personal Relationships, 8,* 423–440.

Bielski, V. (1996, May). Daycare, just down the hall. *Parenting,* pp. 44, 46.

Bierman, K. L., & Furman, W. (1984). The effects of social skills training and peer involvement on the social adjustment of preadolescents. *Child Development, 55,* 151–162.

Bigler, R. S., & Liben, L. S. (1990). The role of attitudes and interventions in gender-schematic processing. *Child Development, 61,* 144–1452.

Bigner, J. J. (1994). *Parent-child relations: An introduction to parenting.* New York: Macmillan.

Bilchik, S. (1995). *Delinquency prevention works.* Washington, DC: Office of Juvenile Justice and Delinquency Prevention, U.S. Justice Department.

Biller, H. B. (1982). Fatherhood: Implications for child and adult development. In B. B. Wolman (Ed.), *Handbook of developmental psychology* (pp. 702–720). Englewood Cliffs, NJ: Prentice Hall.

Bingaman, J., Frank, R. G., & Billy, C. L. (1993). Combining a global health budget with a market-driven delivery system: Can it be done? *American Psychologist, 48,* 270–276.

Birch, H. G. (1971, March). Functional effects of fetal malnutrition. *Hospital Practice,* pp. 134–148.

Birch, L. L. (1979). Preschool children's food preferences and consumption patterns. *Journal of Nutrition Education, 11,* 189–192.

Birch, L. L. (1986). Children's food preferences: Developmental patterns and environmental influences. In G. Whitehurst & R. Vasta (Eds.), *Annals of Child Development,* (Vol.4). Greenwich, CT: JAI Press.

Birch, L. L. (1987). The acquisition of food acceptance patterns in children. In R. A. Boakes, D. A. Popplewell, & M. J. Burton (Eds.), *Eating habits: Food, physiology and learned behaviour.* New York: Wiley.

Birch, L. L., & Fisher, J. A. (1996). The role of experience in the development of children's eating behavior. In E. D. Capaldi (Ed.), (pp. 113–145) Washington, DC: American Psychological Association.

Birch, L. L., Johnson, S. L., Andresen, G., Petersen, J. C. & Schulte, M. C. (1991). The variability of young children's energy intake. *New England Journal of Medicine, 324,* 232–235.

Birch, L. L., Johnson, S. L., Jones, M. B. & Peters, J. C. (1993). Effects of a non-energy fat substitute on children's energy and macronutrient intake. *American Journal of Clinical Nutrition, 58,* 326–333.

Biringen, Z., Emde, R. N., Campos, J. J., & Appelbaum, M. I. (1995). Affective reorganization in the infant, the mother, and the dyad: The role of upright locomotion and its timing. *Child Development, 66,* 499–514.

Birren, J. E. (Ed.), (1964). *Relations of development and aging.* Springfield, IL: Thomas.

Birren, J. E., Kinney, D. K., Schaie, K. W., & Woodruff, D. S. (1981). *Developmental psychology: A life-span approach.* Boston: Houghton Mifflin.

Birren, J. E., & Fisher, L. M. (1992). Aging and slowing of behavior: Consequences for cognition and survival. In T. B. Sonderegger (Ed.), *Psychology and aging: Nebraska symposium on motivation,* (pp. 1–39). Lincoln, NE: University of Nebraska Press.

Birren, J. E., & Renner, V. J. (1983). Health, behaviour, and aging. In J. E. Birren et al. (Eds.), *Aging: A challenge to science and society,* (Vol. 3, pp. 9–35). New York: Oxford University Press.

Birsner, E. P. (1985). *Job hunting for the 40+ executive.* New York: Facts on File Publications.

Bisanz, J., Morrison, F. J., & Dunn, M. (1995). Effects of age and schooling on the acquisition of elementary quantitative skills. *Developmental Psychology, 31,* 221–236.

Bischof, L. J. (1976). *Adult Psychology* (2nd ed.). New York: Harper & Row.

Bivens, A. J., Neimeyer, R. A., Kirchberg, T. M., & Moore, M. K. (1994/1995). Death concern and religious beliefs among gays and bisexuals of variable proximity to AIDS. *Omega, 30,* 105–120.

Bjorklund, D. F. (1995). *Children's thinking: Developmental function and individual differences.* Pacific Grove, CA: Brooks/Cole.

Black, J. K., & Puckett, M. B. (1996). *The young child: Development from prebirth through age eight.* Englewood Cliffs, NJ: Merrill.

Blackwilder, D. E., Passman, R. H. (1986). Grandmothers' and mothers' disciplining in three-generational families: The role of social responsibility in rewarding and punishing grandchildren. *Journal of Personality and Social Psychology, 50,* 80–86.

Blair, S. N., Kohl, H. W., Paffenbarger, R. S., Clark, D. G., Cooper, K. H., & Gibbons, L. W. (1989). Physical fitness and all-cause mortality: A prospective study of healthy men and women. *JAMA, 262,* 2395–2401.

Blair, S. N., Piserchia, P. V., Wilbur, C. S., & Crowder, J. H. (1986). A public health intervention model for worksite health promotion. *JAMA, 255,* 921–926.

Blakemore, J. E. O. (1981). Age and sex differences in interaction with a human infant. *Child Development, 52,* 386–388.

Blane, D. (1995). Editorial: Social determinants of health, socioeconomic status, social class, and ethnicity. *American Journal of Public Health, 85,* 903–904.

Blank, M. (1982). Intelligence testing. In C. B. Kopp & J. B. Krakow (Eds.), *The child: Development in a social context* (pp. 708–715). Reading, MA: Addison-Wesley.

Blasi, A. (1980). Bridging moral cognition and moral action: A critical review of the literature. *Psychological Bulletin, 88,* 1–45.

Blazer, D. (1989). Depression in the elderly. *New England Journal of Medicine, 320,* 164–166.

Blazer, D. G., Hughes, D. C., & George, L. K. (1987). The epidemiology of depression in an elderly community population. *The Gerontologist, 27,* 281–287.

Blehar, M. C. (1974). Anxious attachment and defensive reactions associated with day care. *Child Development, 45,* 683–692.

Blendon, R. J., Marttila, J., Benson, J. M., Shelter, M. C., Connoly, F. J., & Kiley, T. (1994). The beliefs and values shaping today's health reform debate. *Health Affairs, 13,* 274–284.

Blewitt, P. (1994). Understanding categorical hierarchies: The earliest levels of skill. *Child Development, 65,* 1279–1298.

Blieszner, R., & Adams, R. G., (1992). *Adult friendship.* Newbury Park, CA: Sage.

Block, J., Block, J. H., & Keyes, S. (1988). Longitudinally foretelling drug usage in adolescence: Early childhood personality and environmental precursors. *Child Development, 59,* 336–355.

Block, J., & Robins, R. W. (1993). A longitudinal study of consistency and change in self-esteem from early adolescence to early adulthood. *Child Development, 64,* 909–923.

Block, J. H. (1976). Assessing sex differences: Issues, problems, and pitfalls. *Merrill-Palmer Quarterly, 22,* 283–308.

Block, J. H. (1979). Socialization influences on personality development in males and females. *American Psychological Association's Master Lecture Series.* Washington, DC: American Psychological Association.

Block, J. H. (1983). Differential premises arising from differential socialization of the sexes: Some conjectures. *Child Development, 54,* 1335–1354.

Block, J. H., Block, J., & Gjerde, P. F. (1986). The personality of children prior to divorce: A prospective study. *Child Development, 57,* 827–840.

Bloom, L. M., (1975). Language development. In F. D. Horowitz (Ed.), *Review of child development research* (Vol. 4). Chicago: University of Chicago Press.

Bluebond-Langner, M. (1977). The meanings of death to children. In H. Feifel (Ed.). *New Meanings of Death.* New York: McGraw-Hill.

Bluebond-Langner, M. (1989). Worlds of dying children and their well siblings. *Death Studies, 13,* 1–16.

Blumberg, M. L., & Lester, D. (1991). High school and college students' attitudes towards rape. *Adolescence, 26,* 727–720.

Blumenthal, J. A., Emery, C. F., Cox, D. R., Walsh, M. A., Kuhn, C. M., Williams, R. B., & Williams, R. S. (1988). Exercise training in healthy type A middle aged men: Effects on behavioral and cardiovascular response. *Psychosomatic Medicine, 50,* 418–433.

Blumenthal, J. A., & McCubbin, J. A. (1987). Physical exercise as stress management. In A. Baim & J. Singer (Eds.), *The handbook of psychology and health* (pp. 303–331). New York: Erlbaum.

Blumstein, P., & Schwartz, P. (1983). *American couples.* New York: Morrow.

Blyth, D. Simmons, R., & Zakin, D. (1985). Satisfaction with body image for early adolescent females: The impact of pubertal timing within different school environments. *Journal of Youth and Adolescence, 14,* 227–236.

Boeck, S., & Lynn, G. (1995, December 27). Why teens choose to use. *USA Today,* p. 1A.

Bogatz, G., & Ball, S. (1971). *The second year of "Sesame Street:" A continuing evaluation.* Princeton: Educational Testing Service.

Bohannon, J. N., MacWhinney, B., & Snow, C. (1990). No negative evidence revisited: Beyond learnability—or who has to prove what to whom. *Developmental Psychology, 26,* 221–227.

Bohannon, J. N., & Marquis, A. L. (1977). Children's control of adult speech. *Child Development, 48,* 1002–1008.

Bohannon, J. N. & Stanowicz, L. (1988). The issue of negative evidence: Adult responses to children's language errors. *Developmental Psychology, 24,* 684–689.

Bohannon, J. N., Padgett, R. J., Nelson, K. E., & Mark, M. (1996). Useful evidence on negative evidence. *Developmental Psychology, 32,* 551–555.

Bohman, M. (1978). Some genetic aspects of alcoholism and criminality: A population of adoptees. *Archives of General Psychiatry, 335,* 269–276.

Boland, J. P., & Follingstead, D. R. (1987). The relationship between communication and marital satisfaction: A review. *Journal of Sex and Marital Therapy, 13,* 286–313.

Bolger, N., DeLongis, A., Kessler, R., & Schilling, E. (1989). Effects of daily stress on negative mood. *Journal of Personality and Social Psychology, 57,* 808–818.

Bolla-Wilson, K., & Bleeker, M. L. (1989). Absence of depression in elderly adults. *Journal of Gerontology, 44,* 53–55.

Booth, A., & Johnson, D. R. (1988). Premarital cohabitation and marital success. *Journal of Family Issues, 9,* 255–272.

Borger, G. (1990, December 17). The shadows lurking behind Dr. Death. *U.S. News and World Report,* p. 31.

Borland, R., Chapman, S., Owen, N., & Hill, D. (1990). Effects of workplace smoking bans on cigarette consumption. *American Journal of Public Health, 80,* 178–180.

Bornstein, M. H. (1991) Approaches to parenting in culture. In M. H. Bornstein (Ed.), *Cultural approaches to parenting* (pp. 3–19). Hillsdale, NJ: Erlbaum.

Bornstein, M. H. (1995). Parenting infants. In M. H. Bornstein (Ed.), *Handbook of parenting,* (pp. 3–41) Mahwah, NJ: Erlbaum.

Bornstein, M. H., Matis-Lemonda, C. S., Pecheux, M. G., & Rahn, C. W. (1991). Mother and infant activity and interaction in France and the United States. A comparative study. *International Journal of Behavioral Development, 14,* 21–43.

Bornstein, M. H., & Sigman, M. D. (1986). Continuity in mental development from infancy. *Child Development, 57,* 251–274.

Bornstein, M. H., Tal, J., Rahn, C., Gaperin, C. Z., Pecheux, M. G., Lamour, M., Today, S., Azuma, H., Ogino, M., & Tamis-LeMonde, C. S. (1992). Functional analysis of the contents of maternal speech to infants of 5 and 13 months in four cultures: Argentina, France, Japan, and the United States. *Developmental Psychology, 28,* 593–603.

Bosse, R., Aldwin, C. M., Levenson, M. R., & Workman-Daniels, K. (1991). How stressful is retirement? Findings from the normative aging study. *Journal of Gerontology, 46,* 9–14.

Botwinick, J. (1967). *Cognitive processes in maturity and old age.* New York: Springer.

Botwinick, J. (1973). *Aging and behavior: A comprehensive integration of research findings.* New York: Springer.

Botwinick, J. (1977). Intellectual abilities. In J. E. Birren & K. W. Schaie (Eds.), *Handbook of the psychology of aging* (pp. 580–605). New York: Van Nostrand Reinhold.

Botwinick, J. (1984). *Aging and behavior* (3rd ed.). New York: Springer.

Botwinick, J., & Storandt, M. (1974). *Memory, related functions, and age.* Springfield, IL: Thomas.

Botwinick, J., & Thompson, L. W. (1968). Age differences in reaction time: An artifact? *Gerontologist, 8,* 25–28.

Bouchard, T. J. (1984). Twins reared together and apart: What they tell us about human diversity. In S. W. Fox (Ed.). *Individuality and Determinism.* New York: Plenum.

Bouchard, T. J., Lykken, D. T., McGue, M., Segal, N. L., & Tellgen, A. (1990). Sources of human psychological differences: The Minnesota study of twins reared apart. *Science, 250,* 223–228.

Bound, J., Duncan, G. J., Laren, D. S., & Oleinick, L. (1991). Poverty dynamics in widowhood. *Journal of Gerontology, 46,* S115–124.

Bowerman, M. (1981). Language development. In H. C. Triandis & A. Heron (Eds.), *Handbook of cross-cultural psychology* (Vol. 4, pp. 93–187). Boston: Allyn and Bacon.

Bowlby, J. (1969). *Attachment and loss.* New York: Basic Books.

Bowlby, J. (1969). *Attachment.* New York: Basic Books.

Bowlby, J. (1980). Attachment and loss, Vol. 3. *Sadness and Depression.* New York: Basic Books.

Bowlby, J. (1982). Attachment and loss: Retrospect and prospect. *American Journal of Orthopsychiatry, 52,* 664–678.

Boyatzis, C. J., Matillo, G. M., & Nesbitt, K. M. (1995). Effects of "The Mighty Morphin Power Rangers" on children's aggression with peers. *Child Study Journal, 22,* 45–55.

Boyer, P. J., Dillon, M., Navaie, M., Deveikis, A., Keller, M., O'Rourke, S., & Bryson, Y. J. (1994, June 22/29). Factors predictive of maternal-fetal transmission of HIV-1: Preliminary analysis of zidovudine given during pregnancy and/or delivery. *JAMA, 271,* 1925–1935.

Boyle, M. A. & Whitney, E. N. (1989). *Personal Nutrition.* St. Paul, MN: West Pub. Co.

Bozett, F. W. (1985). Male development and fathering throughout the life cycle. *American Behavioral Scientist, 29,* 41–54.

Bracey, G. W. (1996). 75 years of elementary education. *Principal, 75,* 17–21.

Brackbill, Y. (1979). Obstetrical medication and infant behavior. In J. D. Osofsky (Ed.), *Handbook of infant development* (pp. 76–125). New York: Wiley.

Brackbill, Y. (1982). Lasting effects of obstetrical medication on children. In J. Belsky (Ed.), *In the beginning* (pp. 50–55). New York: Columbia University Press.

Bradley, A. (1991, May 15). Newly diverse suburbs facing city-style woes. *Education Week,* pp. 1, 15+.

Bradley, R. H. (1989). HOME measurement of maternal responsiveness. In M. H. Bornstein (Ed.), *Maternal responsiveness: Characteristics and consequences* (pp. 63–75). San Francisco: Jossey-Bass.

Bradley, R. H. (1993, November) Children's HOME environments, health, behavior and intervention effects: A review of the HOME. *Genetic Social and General Psychology Monographs, 119,* 439–491.

Bradley, R. H. (1995). Environment and parenting. In M. H. Bornstein (Ed.), Vol. 2, pp. 235–261. Mahwah, NJ: Erlbaum.

Bradley, R. H. & Caldwell, B. M. (1980). The relation of home environment, cognitive competence and IQ among males and females. *Child Development, 51,* 1140–1148.

Bradley, R. H., Mundfrom, D. J., Whiteside, L., Casey, P. H., & Barrett, K. (1994). A factor analytic study of the infant-toddler and early childhood versions of the HOME Inventory administered to white, Black and Hispanic American parents of children born preterm. *Child Development, 65,* 880–888.

Bradsher, K. (1995, October 27). Widest gap in incomes? Research points to U.S. *The New York Times,* p. D2.

Brainerd, C. J. (1978). *Piaget's theory of intelligence.* Englewood Cliffs, NJ: Prentice Hall.

Brainerd, C. J. & Reyna, V. F. (1995). Learning rate, learning opportunities, and the development of forgetting. *Developmental Psychology, 31,* 251–262.

Brand, E., Clingempeel, W. E., & Bowen-Woodward, K. (1988). Family relationships and children's psychological adjustment in stepmother and stepfather families: Findings and conclusions from the Philadelphia Stepfamily Research Project. In E. M. Heatherington & J. D. Arasteh (Eds.), *Impact of divorce, single parenting and stepparenting on children* (pp. 299–324). Hillsdale, NJ: Erlbaum.

Bransford, J. D. (1979). *Human cognition: Learning, understanding, and remembering.* Belmont, CA: Wadsworth.

Braus, P. (1994a, March). Nursing Homes: The hard facts. *American Demographics, 16,* 46–47.

Braus, P. (1994b, March). When mom needs help. *American Demographics, 16,* 38–46.

Braus, P. (1995, June). Vision in an aging America. *American Demographics,* 35–39.

Bray, J. H. (1988). Children's development during early remarriage. In E. M. Hetherington & J. D. Arasteh (Eds.), *Impact of divorce, single parenting and stepparenting on children* (pp. 279–298). Hillsdale, NJ: Erlbaum.

Brayfield, A. (1992). Employment resources and housework in Canada. *Journal of Marriage and the Family, 54,* 19–30.

Brayfield, A. (1995). Juggling jobs and kids: The impact of employment schedules and fathers' caring for children. *Journal of Marriage and the Family, 57,* 321–332.

Brazelton, T. B. (1990). Saving the bathwater. *Child Development, 61,* 1661–1671.

Brazelton, T. B. (1992). *Touchpoints.* Reading, MA: Addison-Wesley.

Brazelton, T. B., Koslowski, B., & Main, H. (1974). The origins of reciprocity: The early infant-mother interaction. In M. Lewis & L. A. Rosenblum (Eds.), *The effect of the infant on its caretaker* (pp. 49–76). New York: Wiley.

Breast cancer tied to adopted home (1995, August 3). *Newsday,* p. A19.

Brehm, S. S., & Kassin, S. M., (1996). *Social psychology* (3rd ed.). Boston: Houghton Mifflin.

Bremner, J. G. (1988). *Infancy.* New York: Basil Blackwell.

Brenneman, K., & Gelman, R. (1993). Reasoning about object identities in the appearance-reality situation. Cited in C. Rice et al., When 3-year-olds pass the appearance-reality test, *Developmental Psychology, 33,* 54–61.

Brenner, M. H. (1985). Economic change and the suicide rate: A population model including loss, separation, illness, and alcohol consumption. In M. R. Zales (Ed.), *Stress in health and disease* (pp. 160–185). New York: Brunner/Mazel.

Breslau, N., & Peterson, E. L. (1996). Smoking cessation in young adults: age of initiation of cigarette smoking and other suspected influences. *American Journal of Public Health, 86,* 214–236.

Brickey, M., & Campbell, K. (1981). Fast food employment for moderately and mildly mentally retarded adults. *Mental Retardation, 19,* 113–116.

Bridges, L. J., Connell, J. P., & Belsky, J. (1988). Similarities and differences in infant-mother and infant-father interaction in the strange situation: A component process analysis. *Developmental Psychology, 24,* 92–101.

Brierly, J. (1976). *The growing brain.* Windsor, England: NFER.

Brim, O. G., & Kagan, J. (1980). Constancy and change: A view of the issues. In O. G. Brim & J. Kagan (Eds.), *Constancy and change in human development* (pp. 1–26). Cambridge, MA: Harvard University Press.

Bringuier, J. C. (1980). *Conversations with Jean Piaget.* Chicago: University of Chicago Press.

Brink, S. (1995, May 15). Smart moves. *U.S. News and World Report,* pp. 76–84.

Broberg, A. G., Wessels, H., Lamb, M. E., & Hwang, C. P. (1997). Effects of day care on the development of cognitive abilities in 8-year-olds: A longitudinal study. *Developmental Psychology, 33,* 62–69.

Brody, E. M. (1981). Women in the middle and family help to older people. *Gerontologist, 25,* 19–29.

Brody, E. M. (1990). *Women in the middle: Their parent-care years.* New York: Springer.

Brody, E. M., Johnsen, P. T., & Fulcomer, M. C. (1984). What should adult children do for elderly parents? Opinions and preferences of three generations of women. *Journal of Gerontology, 39,* 736–746.

Brody, E. M., & Schoonover, C. B. (1986). Patterns of parent-care when adult daughters work and when they do not. *Gerontologist, 26,* 372–381.

Brody, G. H., & Forehand, R. (1988). Multiple determinants of parenting: Research findings and implications of the divorce process. In E. M. Hetherington & J. D. Arasteh (Eds.). *Impact of Divorce, single parenting, and stepparenting on children* (pp. 117–135). Hillsdale, NJ: Erlbaum.

Brody, G. H., Stoneman, Z., & Burke, M. (1987). Family system and individual child correlates of sibling behavior. *American Journal of Orthopsychiatry, 57,* 561–569.

Brody, J. E. (1989, July 13). Personal health. *New York Times,* p. B5.

Brody, J. E. (1989, September 21). The living will. *New York Times,* p. B20.

Brody, L. R. (1981). Visual short-term recall memory in infancy. *Child Development, 52,* 242–250.

Bromley, D. B. (1974). *The psychology of human aging* (2nd ed.). Baltimore: Penguin.

Bronfenbrenner, U. (1979). *The ecology of human development.* Cambridge, MA: Harvard University Press.

Bronfenbrenner, U. (1986). Ecology of the family as a context for human development: Research perspectives. *Developmental Psychology, 22,* 723–743.

Bronfenbrenner, U., & Ceci, S. J. (1994). Nature-nurture reconceptualized in developmental perspective: A bioecological model. *Psychological Review, 101,* 568–586.

Bronfenbrenner, U., & Crouter, A. C. (1983). The evolution of environmental models in developmental research. In P. H. Mussen (Ed.), *Handbook of Child Development* (4th ed., pp. 357–415). New York: Wiley.

Bronson, G. (1968). The development of fear. *Child Development, 39,* 409–432.

Bronson, G. W., (1994). Infants' transitions toward adult-like scanning. *Child Development, 65,* 1243–1261.

Bronstein, P., Stoll, M. F., Caluson, J. A., Abrams, C. L., & Briones, M. (1994). Fathering after separation or divorce: Factors predicting children's adjustment. *Family Relations, 43,* 460–473.

Brook, J. S., Nomura, C., & Cohen, P. (1989). Prenatal, perinatal, and early childhood risk factors and drug involvement in adolescence. *Genetic, Social, and General Psychology Monographs, 115,* 221–241.

Brook, J. S., Whiteman, M., Brook, D. W., & Gordon, A. S. (1981). Paternal determinants of male adolescent marijuana use. *Developmental Psychology, 17,* 841–847.

Brooks-Gunn, J., & Chase-Lansdale, P. L. (1991). Children having children: Effects on the family system, *Pediatric Annals, 20,* 467–481.

Brooks-Gunn, J., & Chase-Landsdale, P. L. (1995). Adolescent Parenthood. In M. H. Bornstein (Ed.), Handbook of Parenting. Vol. 3, (pp. 113–151) Mahway, NJ: Erlbaum.

Brooks-Gunn, J., & Furstenberg, F. F. (1989). Adolescent sexual behavior. *American Psychologist, 44,* 249–157.

Brooks-Gunn, J., Guo, G., & Furstenberg, F. F. Jr. (1993). Who drops out of and who continues beyond high school? A twenty-year follow-up of black urban youth. *Journal of Research on Adolescence, 3,* 271–294.

Brooks-Gunn, J., & Klebanov, P. K. (1996). Ethnic differences in children's intelligence test scores: Rule of economic deprivation, home environment, and maternal characteristics. *Child Development, 67,* 396–408.

Brooks-Gunn, J., Klebanov, P. K., & Duncan, G. J. (1996). Ethnic differences in children's intelligence test scores: Role of economic deprivation, home environment, and maternal characteristics. *Child Development, 67,* 396–409.

Brooks-Gunn, J., & Ruble, D. N. (1982). The development of menstrual-related beliefs and behavior during adolescence. *Child Development, 53,* 1567–1577.

Brooks-Gunn, J., & Warren, M. P. (1985). The effects of delayed menarche in different contexts: Dance and non-dance students. *Journal of Youth and Adolescence, 14,* 285–299.

Brooks-Gunn, J., & Warren, M. P. (1988). Mother-daughter differences in menarcheal age in adolescent dancers and nondancers. *Annals of Human Biology, 15,* 35–43.

Broussard, E. R. (1995). Infant attachment in a sample of adolescent mothers. *Child Psychiatry and Human Development, 25,* 211–219.

Browder, S. (1988, June). Is living together such a good idea? *New Woman,* pp. 120, 122, 124.

Brown, A. L., Bransford, J. D., Ferrara, R. A., & Campione, J. C. (1983). Learning, remembering, and understanding. In J. H. Flavell & E. M. Markman (Eds.), *Handbook of Child Psychology* (4th ed.) (pp. 77–167). New York: Wiley.

Brown, A. L., & Smiley, S. S. (1977). Rating the importance of structural units of prose passages: A problem of metacognitive development. *Child Development, 48,* 1–8.

Brown, A. S., Jones, E. M., & Davis, T. L. (1995). Age differences in conversational source monitoring. *Psychology and Aging, 10,* 111–122.

Brown, B. B., Clasen, D. R., & Eicher, S. A. (1986). Perceptions of peer pressure, peer conformity, dispositions, and self-reported behavior among adolescents. *Developmental Psychology, 22,* 521–530.

Brown, C. (11 October 1993). The vanished Native Americans. *The Nation, 257,* 384–389.

Brown, F. G. (1983). *Principles of educational and psychological testing.* New York: Holt, Rinehart and Winston.

Brown, J. E. (1995). *Nutrition Now.* St. Paul, MN: West.

Brown, L. (1995). *Statement by White House drug czar Lee P. Brown on the 1995 Monitoring the Future survey,* Washington, DC: Office of National Drug Control Policy.

Brown, R. (1973). Development of the first language in the human species. *American Psychologist, 28,* 97–106.

Brubaker, T. H. (1990). Families in later life: A burgeoning research area. *Journal of Marriage and the Family, 52,* 959–981.

Bruch, H. (1978). *The golden cage: The enigma of anorexia nervosa.* Cambridge, MA: Harvard University Press.

Bruch, H. (1986). Anorexia nervosa: The therapeutic task. In K. D. Brownell & J. P. Forey (Eds.), *Handbook of eating disorders: Physiology, psychology, and treatment of obesity, anorexia, and bulimia.* New York: Basic Books.

Bruner, J. (1978a, September). Learning the mother tongue. *Human Nature,* pp. 11–19.

Bruner, J. (1978b). Learning how to do things with words. In J. S. Bruner & A. Garton (Eds.), *Human growth and development: Wolfson College lectures* (pp. 62–85). Oxford: Clarendon Press.

Bruskin, Goldring Research, Parental Discipline. *Education Week,* May 19, 1993. p. 3.

Brynie, F. H. (1995). *Genetics & human health.* Brookfield, CN: The Millbrook Press.

Bucher, H. C., & Ragland, D. R. (1995). Socioeconomic indicators and mortality from coronary heart disease and cancer: A 22-year follow-up of middle-aged men. *American Journal of Public Health, 85,* 1231–1236.

Buckley, W. F. (1995, October 9). Se habla Ingles. *National Review, p. 70–72.*

Buhrmester, D., & Furman, W. (1987). The development of companionship and intimacy. *Child Development, 58,* 1101–1114.

Buis, J. M., & Thompson, D. N. (1989). Imaginary audience and personal fable: A brief review. *Adolescence, 24,* 773–781.

Bullock, M. (1985). Animism in childhood thinking: A new look at an old question. *Developmental Psychology, 21,* 217–226.

Bullock, M., & Lutkenhaus, P. (1988). The development of volitional behavior in the toddler years. *Child Development, 59,* 664–675.

Bumpass, L., & Sweet, J. (1989). National estimates of cohabitation: Cohort levels and union stability. Cited in D. Knox & C. Schacht, *Choices in relationships* (3rd ed.). St. Paul, MN: West.

Bumpass, L. L., & Sweet, J. A. (1989). National estimates of cohabitation. *Demography, 26,* 615–625.

Bumpass, L., Sweet, J., & Martin, T. C. (1990/ August). Changing patterns of remarriage. *Journal of Marriage and the Family, 52,* 747–756.

Bunce, D. J., Warr, P. B., & Cochrane, T. (1993). Blocks in choice responding as a function of age and physical fitness. *Psychology and Aging, 8,* 26–33.

Burcham, B., & Carlson, L. (1995, March). Attention deficit hyperactivity disorder. *The Education Digest,* 42–44.

Burchinal, M., Lee, M., & Ramey, C. (1989). Type of day-care and preschool intellectual development in disadvantaged children. *Child Development, 60,* 128–138.

Burchinal, M. R., Ramey, S. L., Reid, M. K., & Jaccard, J. (1995). Early child care experiences and their association with family and child characteristics during middle childhood. *Early Childhood Research Quarterly, 10,* 33–61.

Burke, J. R. (1990, July 13). "Super" son, 5, aids mother by dialing 911. *Newsday,* pp. 20, 26.

Burker, E. J., Wong, H., Sloane, P. D., Mattingly, D., Preisser, J., & Mitchell, C. M. (1995). Predictors of fear of falling in dizzy and nondizzy elderly. *Psychology and Aging, 10,* 104–110.

Burlton-Bennet, J. A., & Robinson, V. M. J. (1987). A single subject evaluation of the K-P diet for hyperkinesis. *Journal of Learning Disabilities, 20,* 331–335.

Burnell, G. M., (1993). *Final choices: To live or die in an age of medical technology.* New York: Plenum.

Burns, A., Jacoby, R. Luthert, P., & Levy, R. (1990). Cause of death in Alzheimer's disease. *Age and Aging, 19,* 341–344.

Burns, A., & Scott, C. (1994). *Mother-Headed Families and Why they Have Increased.* Hillsdale, NJ: Erlbaum.

Burns, K., Chethik, L., Burns, W., & Clark,

R. (1991). Dyadic disturbances in cocaine-abusing mothers and their infants. *Journal of Clinical Psychology, 47,* 316–319.

Burns, R. B. (1979). *The self-concept: Theory, measurement, development, and behaviour.* New York: Longman.

Burnside, I. M. (1981). Mental health and the aged. In I. M. Burnside (Ed.), *Nursing and the aged* (2nd ed.) (pp. 70–85). New York: McGraw-Hill.

Burros, M. (1996, Jan. 3). In an about-face, U.S. says alcohol has health benefits. *New York Times,* pp. A1, C2.

Burrus-Bammel, L. L., & Bammel, G. (1985). Leisure and recreation. In J. E. Birren & K. W. Schaie (Eds.), *Handbook of the psychology of aging* (2d ed.) (pp. 848–864). New York: Van Nostrand Reinhold.

Burton, L. M. (1992). Black grandparents rearing grandchildren of drug-addicted parents: Stressors, outcomes, and social service needs. *The Gerontologist, 32,* 744–751.

Burton, L. M., & Bengstrom, V. L. (1985). Black grandmothers: Issues of timing and continuity of roles. In V. L. Bengston & J. F. Robinson (Eds.), *Grandparenthood* (pp. 61–77). Beverly Hills, CA: Sage.

Burton, L. M. & Dilworth-Anderson, P. (1991). The intergenerational family roles of aged Black Americans. *Marriage and Family Review, 16,* 311–330.

Burton, R. V. (1963). Generality of honesty reconsidered. *Psychological Review, 70,* 481–499.

Bushnell, I. W. R., Sai, F., & Mullin, J. T. (1989). Neonatal recognition of the mother's face. *British Journal of Developmental Psychology, 7,* 3–15.

Buss, A. H., & Plomin, R. (1984). Temperament: Early developing personality traits. Hillsdale, NJ: Erlbaum.

Busse, E. W., & Maddox, G. L. (1985). *The Duke longitudinal studies of normal aging: 1955–1980.* New York: Springer.

Butler, D. L. (1995). Promoting strategic learning by postsecondary students with learning disabilities. *Journal of Learning Disabilities, 28,* 170–190.

Butler, R. N. (1963). The life review: An interpretation of reminiscence in the aged. *Psychiatry, 26,* 65–76.

Butler, R. N. (1975). *Why Survive? Being Old in America.* New York: Harper and Row.

Butler, R. N. (1985). Ageism. In H. Cox (Ed.), *Aging.* Guilford, CT: Dushkin.

Butterfield, E. C., & Siperstein, G. N. (1972). Influence of contingent auditory stimulation upon non-nutritional suckle. In J. F. Bosma (Ed.), *Third symposium on oral sensation and perception: The mouth of the infant.* Springfield, IL: Thomas.

Bybee, J., Glock, M., & Zigler, E. (1990). Differences across gender, grade level, and academic track in the content of the ideal self-image. *Sex Roles, 22,* 349–359.

Byrnes, J. P. (1988). Formal operations; A systematic reformulation. *Developmental Review, 8,* 66–87.

CQ Researcher, (May 13, 1994). Women's health initiative: Is it too ambitious? 4, 400.

CQ Researcher, (1993, June 18). The U.N.'s global immunization triumph. 3, p. 546.

CQ Researcher, (1993, November 5). How women fare in retirement. 3, 978.

Cahan, S., & Cohen, N. (1989). Age versus schooling effects on intelligence development. *Child Development, 60,* 1239–1249.

Cairns, E., & Dawes, A. (1996). Children: Ethnic and political violence—A commentary. *Child Development, 67,* 129–140.

Cairns, R. B. (1979). *Social development: The origins and plasticity of interchanges.* San Francisco: Freeman.

Cairns, R. B. (1983). The emergence of developmental psychology. In P. H. Mussen (Ed.), *Handbook of child development* (4th ed.) (Vol. 1, pp. 41–103). New York: Wiley.

Cairns, R. B., Cairns, B. D., Neckerman, H. J., Gest, S. D., & Gariepy, J. L. (1988). Social networks and aggressive behavior: Peer support or peer rejection? *Developmental Psychology, 24,* 815–823.

Caldwell, B. M. (1989). All-day kindergarten—assumptions, precautions, and overgeneralizations. *Early Childhood Research Quarterly, 4,* 261–267.

Caldwell, M. A., & Peplau, L. A. (1982). Sex differences in same-sex relationships. *Sex Roles, 8,* 721.

Calkins, S., & Fox, N. (1992). The relations among infant temperament, security of attachment, and behavioral inhibition at twenty-four months. *Child Development, 63,* 1456–1472.

Calkins, S. D., & Fox, N. A. (1994). Individual differences in the biological aspects of temperament. In J. E. Bates & T. D. Wachs (Eds.), *Temperament: Individual differences at the interface of biology and behavior.* (pp. 199–219) Washington, DC: American Psychological Association.

Calkins, S. D., Fox, N. A., & Marshall, T. R. (1996). Behavioral and physiological antecedents of inhibited and uninhibited behavior. *Child Development, 67,* 523–540.

Call, V., Sprecher, S., & Schwartz, P. (1995). The incidence and frequency of marital sex in a national sample. *Journal of Marriage and the Family, 57,* 639–652.

Callahan, C. M., Hendrie, H. C., Dittus, R. S., Brater, D. C., Hui, S. L., & Tierney, W. M., (1994). Depression in later life: The use of clinical characteristics to focus screening efforts. *Journal of Gerontology: Medical Sciences, 49,* M9–M14.

Callahan, E. J., Brasted, W. S., & Granados, J. L. (1983). Fetal loss and sudden infant death: grieving and adjustment for families. In E. J. Callahan and K. A. McCluskey (Eds.) *Life-Span Developmental Psychology: Nonnormative Events* pp. 145–166. New York: Academic Press.

Campanelli, L. C. (1996). Working with the dying older patient. In C. B. Lewis (Ed.), *Aging: The health care challenge* (3rd ed., pp. 392–402). Philadelphia: F. A. Davis.

Campbell, A. J., Borrie, M. J., & Spears, C. F. (1989). Risk factors for falls in a community-based prospective study of people 70 years and older. *Journal of Gerontology, 44,* 112–117.

Campbell, C. S., Hare, J., & Matthews, P. (1995, May/June). Conflict of conscience: Hospice and assisted suicide. *Hastings Center Report.*

Campbell, J. I. D., & Charness, N. (1990). Age-related declines in working-memory skills: Evidence from a complex calculation task. *Developmental Psychology, 26,* 879–889.

Campbell, L. P., & Flake, A. E. (1985). Latchkey children—What is the answer? *The Clearing House, 58,* 381–383.

Campos, J., Langer, A., & Krowtiz, A. (1970). Cardiac responses on the visual cliff in pre-locomotor human infants. *Science, 170,* 196–197.

Campos, J. J., Kermoian, R., & Zumbahlen, M. B. (1992). Socioemotional transformations in the family system following infant crawling onset. In N. Eisenberg & R. A. Fabes (Eds.), Emotion and its regulation in early development. *New directions for child development.* San Francisco: Jossey-Bass.

Camras, L. A. (1992). Expressive development and basic emotions. *Cognition and Emotion, 6,* 269–283.

Camras, L. A., & Sachs, V. B. (1991). Social referencing and caregiver expressive behavior in a day care setting. *Infant Behavior and Development, 14,* 27–36.

Camras, L., Oster, L. A., Campos, J. J., Miyake, K., & Bradshaw, D. (1992). Japanese and American infants' response to arm restraint. *Developmental Psychology, 28,* 578–583.

Canetto, S. S. (1992). Gender and suicide in the elderly. *Suicide and Life-Threatening Behavior, 22,* 80–97.

Cantor, M. H. (1991). Family and community: Changing roles in an aging society. *Gerontologist, 31,* 337–346.

Capaldi, D. M., Crosby, L., & Stoolmiller, M. (1996). Predicting the timing of first sexual intercourse for at-risk adolescent males. *Child Development, 67,* 344–359.

Capell, E. J. Vugia, D. J., Mordaunt, V. L., Marelich, W. D., Ascher, M. S., Trachtenberg, A. I., Cunningham, G. C., Arnon, S. S., & Kizer, K. W. (1992). Distribution of HIV Type 1 infection in childbearing women in California. *Journal of Public Health, 82,* 254–256.

Capron, A. M. (1994, July/August). Easing the passing. *Hastings Center Report, 33,* 25–26.

Capron, A. M. (1995, January/February). Sledding in Oregon. *Hastings Center Report,* 34–35.

Carbo, M., & Cole, R. W. (1995, January). Nurture love of reading and test scores. *Instructional Leader, 8,* 1–3, 12.

Carey, R. G. (1975). Living until death: A program of service and research for the terminally ill. In E. Kübler-Ross (Ed.), *Death: The final stages of growth,* (pp. 75–86). Englewood Cliffs, NJ: Prentice Hall.

Carey, S. (1978). The child as word learner. In M. Halle, G. A. Miller and U. Bresnan (Eds.), *Linguistic theory and psychological reality.* Cambridge, MA: MIT Press.

Carlo, G., Koller, S. H., Eisenberg, N., Da Silva, M. S., & Frohlich, C. B., (1996). A cross-national study on the relations among prosocial moral reasoning, gender role orientations, and prosocial behaviors. *Developmental Psychology, 32,* 231–240.

Carlson, M. C., Hasher, L., Connelly, S. L., & Zacks, R. T. (1995). Aging, distraction, and the benefits of predictable location. *Psychology and Aging, 10,* 427–437.

Carlson, V., Cicchetti, D., Barnett, D., & Baunwald, K. (1989). Disorganized/disoriented attachment relationships in maltreated infants. *Developmental Psychology, 25,* 525–531.

Carmody, D. (1988, September 21). Head Start gets credit for rise in scores. *New York Times,* p. B9.

Carnegie Council on Adolescent Development (1990). *Turning Points.* New York: Carnegie Council.

Carnegie Council on Adolescent Development (1994). *A Matter of time: Risk and opportunity in the out-of-school hours.* New York: The Carnegie Corporation of New York.

Carnegie Council on Adolescent Development (1995). *Great transitions: Preparing adolescents for the new century.* Washington, DC: Author.

Carnegie Foundation for the Advancement of Teaching (1991). *Reading to learn: A mandate for the nation.* New York: Author.

Carp, F. M. (1968). Some components of disengagement. *Journal of Gerontology, 23,* 383–386.

Carpendale, J. I. M., & Krebs, D. L. (1995). Variations in level of moral judgment as a function of type of dilemma and moral choice. *Journal of Personality, 63,* 289–313.

Carr, J. (1994). Annotation: Long term outcome for people with Down Syndrome. *Journal of Child Psychology, Psychiatry and Allied Disciplines, 35,* 425–439.

Carroll, D. W. (1994). *Psychology of language.* Pacific Grove, CA: Brooks/Cole.

Carroll, J. L., & Rest, J. R. (1982). Moral development. In B. B. Wolman (Ed.), *Handbook of developmental psychology* (pp. 434–452). Englewood Cliffs, NJ: Prentice Hall.

Carruth, B., & Goldberg, D. (1990). Nutritional issues of adolescents. *Journal of Early Adolescence, 10,* 122–140.

Carson, E. (1995). Heh, heh, work is cool. *Reason, 27,* 18.

Carstensen, L. L. (1987). Age-related changes in social activity. In L. L. Carstensen & B. A. Edelstein (Eds.), *Handbook of clinical gerontology.* (pp. 222–237). New York: Pergamon Press.

Carstensen, L. L. (1992). Social and emotional patterns in adulthood: Support for socioemotional selectivity theory. *Psychology and Aging, 7,* 331–338.

Carstensen, L. L., Gottman, J. M., & Levenson, R. W. (1995). Emotional behavior in long-term marriage. *Psychology and Aging, 10,* 140–149.

Carstensen, L. L., & Turk-Charles, S. (1994). The salience of emotion across the adult life span. *Psychology and Aging, 9,* 259–265.

Carter, B., & McGoldrick, M. (1989). Introduction in *The changing family life cycle* (2nd ed., pp. 3–29). Boston: Allyn & Bacon.

Carter, D. B., & Levy, G. D. (1988). Cognitive aspects of children's early sex-role development: The influence of gender schemas on preschoolers' memories and preferences for sex-typed toys and activities. *Child Development, 59,* 782–793.

Carter, D. B., & Patterson, C. J. (1982). Sex roles as social conventions: The development of children's conceptions of sex-role stereotypes. *Developmental Psychology, 18,* 812–825.

Carver, V. C., Kittleson, M. J., & Lacey, E. P. (1990). Adolescent pregnancy: A reason to examine gender knowledge in sexual knowledge, attitudes and behavior. *Health Values, 14,* 24–29.

Casiro, O. (1994, March). When pregnant women drink. *NEA Today,* p. 17.

Casper, L. M., (1990). Does family interaction prevent adolescent pregnancy? *Family Planning Perspectives, 22,* 109–114.

Caspi, A., & Bem, D. J. (1990). Personality continuity across the life span. In L. A. Pervin (Ed.), *Handbook of personality: Theory and research* (pp. 549–576).

Caspi, A., Elder, G. H., & Bem, D. J. (1987). Moving against the world: Life-course patterns of explosive children. *Developmental Psychology, 23,* 308–313.

Caspi, A., Henry, B., McGeen, R. O., Moffitt, T. E., & Silva, P. A. (1995). Temperamental origins of child and adolescent behavior problems: From age three to age fifteen. *Child Development, 66,* 55–69.

Caspi, A., & Moffitt, T. (1991). Individual differences and personal transitions: The sample case of girls at puberty. *Journal of Personality and Social Psychology, 61,* 157–168.

Caspi, A., & Silva, P. A. (1995). Temperamental qualities at age three predict personality traits in young adulthood: Longitudinal evidence from a birth cohort. *Child Development, 66,* 486–498.

Cassell, E. J. (1974). Dying in a technological society. In L. A. Bugen and D. S. Davenport (1981). A closer look at the "healthy" grieving process. *Personnel and Guidance Journal, 59,* 332–335.

Cassidy, J. (1988). Child-mother attachment and the self in six-year olds. *Child Development, 59,* 121–134.

Cassidy, J. (1994). Emotion regulation: influences of attachment relationships. In N. Fox (Ed.). The development of emotion regulation (pp. 228–249). *Monographs of the Society for Research in Child Development, 59* (2–3, Serial No. 240).

Cassidy, L., & Hurrell, R. M. (1995). The influence of victim's attire on adolescents' judgments of date rape. *Adolescence, 30,* 319-324.

Catalano, R. F. & Hawkins, J. D. (1995). *Risk focused prevention. Using the social development strategy.* Seattle, WA:

Developmental Research and Programs, Inc.

Cataldo, C. B., & Whitney, E. N. (1986). *Nutrition and diet therapy: Principles and practices*. St. Paul, MN: West.

Catania, J. A., Binson, D., Dolcini, M., Stall, R., Choi, K. H., Pollack, L. M., Hudes, E. S., Canchola, J., Phillips, K., Moskowitz, J. T., & Coates, T. J. (1995). Risk factors for HIV and other sexually transmitted diseases and prevention practices among U.S. heterosexual adults: Changes from 1990 to 1992. *American Journal of Public Health, 85,* 1492–1499.

Catron, T. F., & Masters, J. C. (1993). Mothers' and children's conceptualizations of corporal punishment. *Child Development, 64,* 1815–1828.

Cattell, R. B. (1963). Theory of fluid and crystallized intelligence: A critical experiment. *Journal of Educational Psychology, 54,* 1–22.

Caughy, M. O., DePietro, J. A., & Strobino, D. M. (1994). Day-care participation as a protective factor in the cognitive development of low-income children. *Child Development, 65,* 457–471.

Cauley, K. & Tyler, B. (1989). The relationship of self-concept to prosocial behavior in children. *Early Childhood Research Quarterly, 4,* 51–61.

Cavalli-Sforza, L. L. (1991). Genes, people and languages. *Scientific American, 265,* 104–111.

Cavanaugh, J. C. 1993. *Adult development and aging* (2nd ed.). Pacific Grove, CA: Brooks/Cole.

Cazden, C. B. (1981). Language development and the preschool environment. In C. B. Cazden (Ed.), *Language in early childhood education*. Washington, DC: National Association for the Education of Young Children.

Celermajer, D. S., Adams, M. R., Clarkson, P., Robinson, J., McCredie, R., Donald, A., & Deansfield, J. E. (1996, January 18). Passive smoking and impaired endothelium-dependent arterial dilation in healthy young adults. *The New England Journal of Medicine, 334,* 150–154.

Census paints a new picture of family life. (1994, August 30). *New York Times,* p. A17.

Center on Addiction and Substance Abuse (1995, August 2). A matter of opinion. *Education Week,* p. 4.

Centers for Disease Control (1991b). Premarital sexual experiences among adolescent women—US, 1970–1988 *MMWR, 39,* 929–932.

Centers for Disease Control (1992) Selected behaviors that increase risk for HIV infection among high school students—United States, 1990. *Morbidity and Mortality Weekly Report, 41,* 237–240.

Centers for Disease Control (1993) *HIV/AIDS Surveillance Report.* Atlanta, GA: Centers for Disease Control and Prevention.

Centers for Disease Control and Prevention. (1992, June 1–6). Proceedings of the 26th National Immunization Conference (p. 20) Author.

Centers for Disease Control and Prevention Ad Hoc Working Group for the Development of Standards for Pediatric Immunization Practices. (1993, April 14) Standards for pediatric immunization practices. *Journal of the American Medical Association,* 1818–1821.

Centers for Disease Control (CDC) (1991a). Dieting and purging behavior in black and white high school students: *JAPA, 92,* 306–312.

Cerella, J. (1990). Aging and information-processing. In J. E. Birren & K. W. Schaie (Eds.), *Handbook of the psychology of aging* (3rd ed., pp. 201–221). San Diego, CA: Academic Press.

Cernoch, J. M., & Porter, R. H. (1985). Recognition of axillary odors by infants. *Child Development, 56,* 1593–1598.

Chambre, S. M. (1993). Volunteerism by elders: Past trends and future prospects. *The Gerontologist, 33,* 221–228.

Chandler, M., & Boyes, M. (1982). Social-cognitive development. In B. B. Wolman (Ed.), *Handbook of developmental psychology* (pp. 387–400). Englewood Cliffs, NJ: Prentice Hall.

Chao, R. K. (1994). Beyond parental control and authoritarian parenting style: Understanding Chinese parenting through the cultural notion of training. *Child Development, 65,* 1111–1119.

Chase-Lansdale, P. L., Cherlin, A. J., & Kiernan, K. E. (1995). The long-term effects of parental divorce on the mental health of young adults: A developmental perspective. *Child Development, 66,* 1614–1634.

Chasnoff, I. J. (1987). Perinatal effects of cocaine. *Contemporary Ob/Gyn, 26,* (March of Dimes reprint) entire issue.

Chasnoff, I. J., Burns, W. J., Schnoll, S. H., & Burns, K. (1985). Cocaine use in pregnancy. *New England Journal of Medicine, 313,* 666–669.

Chasnoff, I. J., Griffith, D. R., Freier, C., & Murray, J. (1992). Cocaine/polydrug use in pregnancy: Two-year follow-up. *Pediatrics, 89,* 284–289.

Chassin, L., Pillow, D. R., Curran, P. L., Molina, B. S., & Barrera, M. (1993). Relation of parental alcoholism to early adolescent substance use: A test of three mediating mechanisms. *Journal of Abnormal Psychology, 102,* 3–19.

Chatters, L. M. (1988). Subjective well-being evaluations among older black Americans. *Psychology and Aging, 3,* 184–190.

Chavkin, W., Kristal, A., Seabron, C. & Guiogli, P. E. (1987). Reproductive experience of women living in hotels for the homeless in New York City. *New York State Journal of Medicine, 87,* 10–13.

Chen, K., & Kandel, D. B. (1995). The natural history of drug use from adolescence to the mid-thirties in a general population sample. *American Journal of Public Health, 85,* 41–47.

Cherlin, A. J., & Furstenberg, F. F. (1986). *The new American grandparent: A place in the family, a life apart.* New York: Basic Books.

Cherrington, D. J. (1983). The work ethic: Working values and values that work. Cited in R. Albanese & D. D. Van Fleet, *Organizational behavior: A managerial viewpoint.* Chicago: Dryden.

Chervenak, F. A., Isaacson, G., & Mahoney, M. J. (1986). Advances in the diagnosis of fetal defects. *New England Journal of Medicine, 315,* 305–307.

Chess, S. & Thomas, A. (1981). Infant bonding: Mystique and reality. *American Journal of Orthopsychiatry, 52,* 213–222.

Chew, P. (1976). *The inner world of the middle-aged man.* New York: Macmillan.

Chi, M. T. H., & Glaser, R. (1985). Problem solving ability. In R. J. Sternberg (Ed.), *Human abilities: An information processing approach* (pp. 227–251). New York: Freeman.

Chilamkurti, C., & Milner, J. S. (1993). Perceptions and evaluations of child transgressions and disciplinary techniques in high-and low-risk mothers and their children. *Child Development, 64,* 1801–1814.

Children's Defense Fund. (1992, January). *Children's defense fund, Medicaid and childhood immunizations: A national study.* p. 7–8.

Chilman, C. S. (1983). *Adolescent sexuality in a changing American society* (2nd ed.). New York: Wiley.

Chipuer, H. M., Plomin, R., Pedersen, N. L., McClearn, G. E., & Nesselroade, J. R., (1993). Genetic influence on family environment: The role of personality. *Developmental Psychology, 29,* 110–119.

Chira, S. (1996, April 21). Study says babies in child care keep secure bonds to mothers. *The New York Times,* pp. A1, A31.

Chiras, D. C. (1993). *Biology: The web of life.* St. Paul, MN: West.

Chiriboga, D., & Cutler, L. (1980). Stress and adaptation: Life span perspectives. In L. W. Poon (Ed.), *Aging in the 1980s: Psychological issues* (pp. 347–362). Washington, DC: American Psychological Association.

Chiriboga, D. A. (1989). Mental health at the midpoint: Crisis, challenge, or relief? In S. Hunter & M. Sundel (Eds.), *Midlife myths: Issues, findings, and practical implications* (pp. 116–145). Newbury Park, CA: Sage.

Chiriboga, D. A., & Dean, H. (1978). Dimensions of stress: Perspectives from a longitudinal study. *Journal of Psychosomatic Research, 22,* 47–55.

Chiu, L. H. (1987). Child-rearing attitudes of Chinese, Chinese-American, and Anglo-American mothers. *International Journal of Psychology, 2,* 409–419.

Choi, K. H., Catania, J. A., & Dolcini, M. M. (1994). Extramarital sex and HIV risk behavior among U.S. adults: Results from the National AIDS behavioral survey. *American Journal of Public Health, 84,* 2003–2007.

Chomitz, V. R., Cheung, L. W. Y., & Lieberman, E. (1995, Spring). The role of lifestyle in preventing low birth weight. *The Future of Children, 5,* 121–138.

Chomsky, N. (1959). A review of B. F. Skinner's *Verbal behavior language, 35,* 26–58.

Chomsky, N. (1965). *Aspects of the theory of syntax.* Cambridge, MA: M.I.T. Press.

Chomsky, N. (1972). *Language and mind* (enl. ed.). New York: Harcourt Brace Jovanovich.

Chown, S. M. (1977). Personality and aging. In J. E. Birren & K. W. Schaie, (Eds.), *Handbook of the psychology of aging* (pp. 672–692). New York: Van Nostrand.

Christopoulos, C., Cohn, D. A., Shaw, D. S., Joyce, S., Sullivan-Hanson, J., Draft, S. P., & Emery, R. (1987). Children of abused women: Adjustment at time of shelter residence. *Journal of Marriage and the Family, 49,* 611–619.

Cicero, T. J. (1994). Effects of paternal exposure to alcohol on offspring development. *Family Planning Perspectives, 18,* 37–41.

Cicirelli, V. G. (1976). Categorization behaviors in aging subjects. *Journal of Gerontology, 31,* 676–680.

Cicirelli, V. G. (1980a). Sibling relationships in adulthood. In L. W. Poon (Ed.), *Aging in the 1980s* (pp. 455–463). Washington, DC: American Psychological Association.

Cicirelli, V. G. (1997). Relationship of psychosocial and background variables to older adults' end-of-life decisions. *Psychology and Aging, 12,* 72–83.

Clark, C. A., Worthington, E. L., Jr. & Danser, D. B., (1988). The transmission of religious beliefs and practices from parents to first born early adolescent sons. *Journal of Marriage and the Family, 50,* 463–472.

Clark, C. S. (1992, August 14). Work family and stress. *CQ Researcher,* 15–26.

Clark, C. S. (1993, Jaunary 15). Child sexual abuse. *CQ Researcher, 3,* 38–44.

Clark, E. (1974). Some aspects of the conceptual basis for first language acquisition. In R. Schiefelbusch & L. Lloyd (Eds.), *Language perspectives—Acquisition, retardation and intervention.* Baltimore: University Park Press.

Clark, E. V. (1978). Strategies for communicating. *Child Development, 49,* 953–959.

Clark, R. L., & Sumner, D. A. (1985). Inflation and the real income of the elderly: Recent evidence and expectations for the future. *Gerontologist, 25,* 146–152.

Clark, S. L., & DeVore, G. R. (1989). Prenatal diagnosis for couples who would not consider abortion. *Obstetrics and Gynecology, 73,* 1035–1037.

Clarke, A. M., & Clarke, A. D. S. (Eds.). (1976). *Early experience: Myth and evidence.* New York: Free Press.

Clarke-Stewart, A. (1982, September). The Day-care child. *Parents,* 65–72.

Clarke-Stewart, K. A. (1988). The "effects" of infant day care reconsidered, *American Psychologist, 3,* 293–319.

Clarke-Setwart, K. A. (1989). Infant day care: Maligned or malignant? *American Psychologist, 44,* 266–274.

Clarke-Stewart, K. A., Alhusen, V. D., & Clements, D. C. (1995). Nonparental caregiving. In M. H. Bornstein (Ed.), *Handbook of parenting* (Vol. 3, pp. 161–176). Mahwah, NJ: Erlbaum.

Clarke-Stewart, K. A., & Fein, G. G. (1983). Early childhood programs. In M. M. Haith & J. J. Campos (Eds.), *Handbook of child psychology* (Vol. 2, pp. 917–1001). New York: Wiley.

Clarkson-Smith, L., & Hartley, A. A. (1990). Structural equation models of relationships between exercise and cognitive abilities. *Psychology and Aging, 5,* 437–446.

Clausen, J. A. (1981). Men's occupational careers in middle years. In D. H. Eichorn, J. A. Clausen, N. Haan, M. P. Honzik, & P. H. Mussen (Eds.), *Present and past in middle life* (pp. 321–351). New York: Academic Press.

Clemens, A., & Axelson, L. (1985). The not-so-empty nest: The return of the fledgling adult. *Family Relations, 34,* 259–264.

Clingempeel, W. G., & Segal, S. (1986). Stepparent-stepchild relationships and the psychological adjustment of children in stepmother and stepfather families. *Child Development, 57,* 474–484.

Cloninger, C. R. (1987). Neurogenetic adaptive mechanisms in alcoholism. *Science, 236,* 410–416.

Cloud, D. S. (1995, March 18). Social security funds not immune forever. *Congressional Quarterly Weekly Report, 53,* 838–839.

Coberly, S., & Newquist, D. (1984, February-March). Hiring older workers: Employment concerns. *Aging,* pp. 18–21.

Cockerman, W. C., Sharp, K., & Wilcox, J. A. (1983). Aging and perceived health status. *Journal of Gerontology, 38,* 349–355.

Cogan, R. (1980). Effects of childbirth preparation. *Clinical Obstetrics and Gynecology, 23,* 1–14.

Cohen, E. N., Brown, B. W., Wu, M. L., Whitcher, C. E., Brodsky, J., et al. (1980). Occupational disease in dentistry and chronic exposure to trace anesthetic gases. *Journal of American Dental Association, 101,* 21–31.

Cohen, G. D. (1990). Psychopathology and mental health. In J. E. Birren & J. W. Schaie (Eds.), *Handbook of the psychology of aging* (3rd ed.). (pp. 359–368). New York: Academic Press.

Cohen, L., & Campos, J. (1974). Father, mother, and stranger as elicitors of attachment behavior in infancy. *Developmental Psychology, 10,* 146–154.

Cohen, L. B. (1979). Our developing knowledge of infant perception and cognition. *American Psychologist, 34,* 894–899.

Cohen, L. B., DeLoache, J. S., & Strauss, M. S. (1979). Infant visual perception. In J. Osofsky (Ed.), *Handbook of infant development* (pp. 393–439). New York: Wiley.

Cohen, M. (1982, January). Effective schools: Accumulating research findings. *American Education,* pp. 13–16.

Cohen, R., Duncan, M., & Cohen, S. L. (1994). Classroom peer relations of children participating in a pull-out enrichment program. *Gifted Child Quarterly, 38,* 33–37.

Cohen, S., Lichtenstein, E., Prochaska, J. O. et al., (1989). Evidence from 10 prospective studies of persons who attempt to quit smoking by themselves: debunking myths about self-quitting. *American Psychologist, 44,* 1355–1365.

Cohen, S., Tyrrell, D., & Smith, A. (1991). Psychological stress and susceptibility to the common cold. *The New England Journal of Medicine, 325,* 606–612.

Cohen, S., & Williamson, G. (1991). Stress and infectious disease. *Psychological Bulletin, 109,* 5–24.

Cohn, J. F., & Tronick, E. Z. (1988). Mother-infant face-to-face interaction: Influence is bidirectional and unrelated to periodic cycles in either partner's behavior. *Developmental Psychology, 24,* 386–393.

Coie, J. D., Dodge, K. A., & Christopoulus, K. (1991). Cited in T. J. Dishion, G. R. Patterson, M. Stoolmiller, & M. L. Skinner. Family, school, and behavioral antecedents to early adolescent involvement with antisocial peers. *Developmental Psychology, 27,* 172–280.

Colasanto, D. (1991, May). What Americans think. *USA Today,* p. 62.

Colby, A., Kohlberg, L., Gibbs, J., & Lieberman, M. (1980). A longitudinal study of moral judgment. Unpublished manuscript, Harvard University.

Cole, D. A. (1991). Preliminary support for a competency-based model of depression in children. *Journal of Abnormal Psychology, 100,* 181–190.

Cole, M. (1992). Culture in development. In M. H. Bornstein & M.E. Lamb (Eds.), *Developmental psychology: An advanced textbook* (3rd ed., pp. 731–789). Hillsdale, NJ: Erlbaum.

Coleman, E. (1981). Counseling adolescent males. *American Personnel and Guidance Journal, 60,* 215–219.

Coleman, J. C. (1978). Current contradictions in adolescent theory. *Journal of Youth and Adolescence, 7,* 1–11.

Coleman, M., & Ganong, L. (1991). Remarriage and stepfamily research in the 1980s: Increased interest in an old form. In A. Booth (Ed.). *Contemporary families: Looking forward, looking back.* Minneapolis, MN: National Council on Family Relations.

Coleman, M., Ganong, L. H., & Ellis, P. (1985). Family structure and dating behavior of adolescents. *Adolescence,* 537–543.

Coleman, P. G. (1983). Cognitive functioning and health. In J. E. Birren et al. (Eds.), *Aging: A challenge to science and society* (Vol. 3, pp. 57–67). New York: Oxford University Press.

Colin, V. L. (1996) *Human attachment.* New York: McGraw Hill.

Collins, W. A., Harris, M. L., & Sussman, A. (1995). Parenting during middle childhood. In M. H. Bornstein (Ed.), *Handbook of Parenting* (Vol. 1., pp. 65–91). Mahwah, NJ: Erlbaum.

Collins, W. A., & Russell, G. (1991). Mother-child and father-child relationships in middle childhood and adolescence: A developmental analysis. *Developmental Review, 11,* 99–136.

Colombo, J., & Horowitz, F. D. (1987). Behavioral state as a lead variable in neonatal research. *Merrill-Palmer Quarterly, 33,* 234–437.

Colt, G. H. (1983, September-October). Suicide. *Harvard Magazine,* pp. 46–53, 63–66.

Coltrane, S. (1996). *Family man.* New York: Oxford.

Comer, J. P. (1985). Empowering black children's educational environments. In H. P. McAdoo & J. L. McAdoo (Eds.), *Black children* (pp. 123–139). Beverly Hills, Sage.

Comer, R. J. (1995). *Abnormal psychology* (2nd ed.). New York: Freeman.

Committee on Diet and Health and Singh, V. N., & Gaby, S. K. (1989). Premalignant lesions: Role of antioxidant vitamins and beta-carotene in risk reduction and prevention of malignant transformation. *American Journal of Clinical Nutrition,* 1991, 53, 386S–390S.

Committee on Nutrition: (1992). The use of whole cow's milk in infancy. *Pediatrics, 89,* 1105–1109.

Comstock, G., & Paik, H. (1991). *Television and the American child.* San Diego, CA: Academic Press.

Comstock, G. A., & Paik, H (1994). The effects of television violence on antisocial behavior: A meta-analysis. *Communication Research, 21,* 516–546.

Concannon, K. W. (1995, Spring). Home and community care in Oregon. *Public Welfare, 53,* 10–17.

Condon, W. S., & Sander, L. W. (1974). Synchrony demonstrated between movements of the neonate and adult speech. *Child Development, 65,* 456–462.

Condry, J. (1989). *The psychology of television.* Hillsdale, NJ: Erlbaum.

Condry, J., Bence, P., & Scheibe, C. (1988). Nonprogram content of children's television. *Journal of Broadcasting and Electronic Media, 32,* 255–269.

Conger, J. J., & Petersen, A. C. (1984). *Adolescence and youth* (3rd ed.). New York: Harper & Row.

Conley, J. J. (1984). Longitudinal consistency of adult personality: Self-reported psychological characteristics across 45 years. *Journal of Personality and Social Psychology, 47,* 1325–1333.

Conley, J. J. (1992, July/August). Masks of autonomy. *Reason, 29,* 11–15.

Connolly, J., & Doyle, A. B. (1984). relations of social fantasy play to competence in preschoolers. *Developmental Psychology, 20,* 797–806.

Cook, A. S., & Oltjenbruns, K. A. (1989). *Dying and grieving: Lifespan and family perspectives,* New York: Holt, Rinehart & Winston.

Cook, P. S., Petersen, R. C., & Moore, D. T. (1990). Alcohol, tobacco, and other drugs may harm the unborn. Rockville, MD: DHHS.

Cooke, R. (1990, November 2). Study puts cap on human lifespan. *Newsday,* p. 4.

Cooke, R. (1991, September 3). Getting cancer cells to grow up, behave. *Newsday,* p. 59.

Cooke, R. A. (1982). The ethics and regulation of research involving children. In B. B. Wolman (Ed.), *Handbook of developmental psychology* (pp. 149–175). Englewood Cliffs, NJ: Prentice Hall.

Cooney, T. M., & Uhlenberg, P. (1992). Support from parents over the life course: The adult child's perspective. *Social Forces, 71,* 63–84.

Cooper, C. R., Grotevant, H. D., & Condon, S. M. (1982). Methodological challenges of selectivity in family interaction: Assessing temporal patterns of individuation. *Journal of Marriage and the Family, 44,* 749–754.

Cooper, K. L., & Gutmann, D. L. (1987). Gender identity and ego mastery in middle age pre- and post-empty nest women. *Gerontologist, 27,* 347–352.

Cooper, M. H. (1992, July 31). Infant mortality. *CQ Researcher, 2,* 643–663.

Cooper, M. H. (1995, June 9). Combating infectious disease, *CQ Researcher, 5,* 489–469.

Cooperman, A. (1996, Feb. 12), Bert and Ernie go to Moscow. *U.S. News and World Report,* pp. 4–5.

Coopersmith, S. (1967). *The antecedents of self-esteem.* San Francisco: Freeman.

Corbin, C. B. (1980b). The physical fitness of children: A discussion and point of view. In C. B. Corbin (Ed.), *A textbook of motor development* (pp. 100–107). Dubuque, IA: Brown.

Corcoran, M., Duncan, G. J., & Hill, M. S. (1984). The economic fortunes of women and children: Lessons from the panel study of income dynamics. *Signs, 10,* 232–248.

Cordier, S., Deplan, F., Mandereau, L., & Hermon, D. (1991). Paternal exposure to mercury and spontaneous abortions. *British Journal of Industrial Medicine, 48,* 375–381.

Corey, L., & Spear, P. G. (1986). Infections with herpes simplex viruses. *New England Journal of Medicine, 314,* 749–754.

Cornelius, S. W. (1984). Classic pattern of intellectual aging: Test familiarity, difficulty, and performance. *Journal of Gerontology, 39,* 201–206.

Cornelius, S. W., & Caspi, A. (1987). Everyday problem solving in adulthood and old age. *Psychology and Aging, 2,* 144–153.

Corr, C. A., Nabe, C. M., & Corr, D. M. (1994). *Death and dying life and living.* Pacific Grove, CA: Brooks/Cole.

Corso, J. F. (1971). Sensory processes and age effects in normal adults. *Journal of Gerontology, 26,* 90–105.

Corso, J. F. (1977). Auditory perception and communication. In J. E. Birren & K. W. Schaie (Eds.), *Handbook of the psychology of aging* (pp. 535–553). New York: Van Nostrand Reinhold.

Corso, J. F. (1981). *Aging sensory systems and perception.* New York: Praeger.

Corter, C. M., & Fleming, A. S. (1995). Psychobiology of maternal behavior in human beings. In M. H. Bornstein (Ed.), *Handbook of parenting* (Vol. 2., pp. 87–116). Mahwah, NJ: Erlbaum.

Costa, P. T., & McCrae, R. R. (1986). Cross-sectional studies of personality in a national sample I: Development and validation of survey measures. *Psychology and Aging, 1,* 140–143.

Costa, P. T. & McCrae, R. R. (1992). Trait Psychology comes of age. In T. B. Sonderegger (Ed.), *Nebraska Symposium on Motivation, 1991: Psychology and Aging,* pp. 169–205. Lincoln, NE: University of Nebraska Press.

Costa, P. T. Jr., & McCrae, R. R. (1988). Personality in adulthood: A six-year longitudinal study of self-reports and spouse ratings on the NEO personality inventory. *Journal of Personality and Social Psychology, 54,* 853–863.

Costa, P. T., Jr., McCrae, R. R., Zonderman, A. B., Barbano, H. C., Lebowitz, B., & Larson, D. M. (1986). Cross-sectional studies of personality in a national sample. Part 2: Stability in neuroticism, extroversion and openness. *Psychology and Aging, 1,* 144–149.

Costa, P. T., Jr., Zonderman, A. B., & McCrae, R. R. (1983). Longitudinal course of social support in the Baltimore Longitudinal Study of Aging cited in R. Schulz & R. B. Ewen: *Adult development and aging* (2nd ed.). New York: Macmillan.

Cotton, D., Currier, J. S., & Wofsy, C. (1994). Information for caretakers of children about women infected with HIV. In P. A. Pizzo & C. M. Wilfert (Eds.), *Pediatric AIDS: The Challenge of HIV infection in infants, children, and adolescents* (2nd ed., pp. 83–97) Baltimore: Williams & Wilkins.

Coulton, C. J., Korbin, J. E., Su, M., & Chow, J. (1995). Community level factors and child maltreatment rates. *Child Development, 66,* 1262–1276.

Council on Scientific Affairs, American Medical Association (1996, February 14). Good care of the dying patient. *JAMA, 275,* 474–478.

Coutinho, R. A. (1995). Annotation: Needle exchange programs—do they work? *American Journal of Public Health, 85,* 1490–1491.

Cowan, C. P., & Cowan, P. A. (1992). *When partners become parents.* New York: Basic Books.

Cox, F. D. (1990). *Human intimacy: Marriage, the family and its meaning.* St. Paul, MN: West.

Craik, F. I. M. & Dirkx, E. (1992). Age-related differences in three tests of visual imagery. *Psychology and Aging, 7,* 661–665.

Craik, F. I. M. & Jennings, J. M. (1992). Human memory. In F. I. M. Craik and T. A. Salthouse (Ed.), *Handbook of Aging and Cognition.* Hillsdale, NJ: Erlbaum.

Crain, W. (1992). *Theories of development* (3rd ed.). Englewood Cliffs, NJ: Prentice Hall.

Cratty, B. J. (1970). *Perceptual and motor development in infants and children.* New York: Macmillan.

Cratty, B. J. (1979). Perceptual and motor development in infants and children. (2nd ed.). New York: MacMillan.

Cratty, B. J. (1986). *Perceptual and motor development in infants and children* (3rd ed.). Englewood Cliffs, NJ: Prentice Hall.

Crawford, J. (1987, March 25). Bilingual education works, study finds. *Education Week,* p. 16.

Creedy, K. B. (1994, November/December). What makes your child tick? *Adoptive Families,* pp. 8–13.

Crichton, M. (1990) *Jurassic Park.* New York: Ballantine.

Crick, N. R., & Dodge, K. A. (1996). Social information-processing mechanisms in reactive and proactive aggression. *Child Development, 67,* 993–1002.

Crispell, D. (1995, July). Dual-earner diversity. *American Demographics,* 32–37, 55.

Crockenberg, S., & McCluskey, K. (1986). Change in maternal behavior during the baby's first year of life. *Child Development, 57,* 746–754.

Crook, T. H. & West R. (1990). Name recall performance across the adult lifespan. *British Journal of Psychology, 81,* 335–349.

Crooke, L. (1989, April/May). Volunteer workers: Our greatest asset. *Modern Maturity, 32,* 10–11.

Cross, H. J., & Allen, J. G. (1970). Ego identity status, adjustment, and academic achievement. *Journal of Consulting and Clinical Psychology, 34,* 288.

Cross, W. E., Jr. (1971). The Negro-to-Black conversion experience: Toward a psychology of Black liberation. *Black World, 20,* 13–27.

Cross, W. E., Jr. (1978). The Cross and Thomas models of psychological nigresence. *Journal of Black Psychology, 5,* 13–19.

Cross, W. E., Jr. (1989). Nigrescence: A nondiaphanous phenomenon. *The Counseling Psychologist, 17,* 273–276.

Crossley, M., & Hiscock, M. (1992). Age-related differences in concurrent-task performance of normal adults: Evidence for a decline in processing resources. *Psychology and Aging, 7,* 499–507.

Crouter, A. C., MacDermid, S. M., McHale, S. M., & Perry-Jenkins, M. (1990). Parental monitoring and perceptions of children's school performance and conduct in dual- and single-earner families. *Developmental Psychology, 26,* 649–657.

Crouter, A. C., Perry-Jenkins, M., Huston, T. L. & McHale, S. M. (1987). Processes underlying father involvement in dual-earner and single-earner families. *Developmental Psychology, 23,* 431–440.

Crystal, D. S., Chuansheng, C., Fuligni, A. J., & Stevenson, H. W. (1994). Psychological maladjustment and academic achievement: A cross-cultural study of Japanese, Chinese, and American high school students. *Child Development, 65,* 738–753.

Cullinan, D., & Epstein, M. H. (1982). Behavior disorders. In N. G. Haring (Ed.), *Exceptional children and youth* (3rd ed.) (pp. 207–239). Columbus, OH: Merrill.

Culp, R. E., Culp, A. M., Osofsky, J. D., & Osofsky, H. (1991). Adolescent and older mothers' interaction with their six-month-old infants. *Journal of Adolescence, 14,* 195–200, p. 29.

Cumming, E., & Henry, W. (1961). *Growing old.* New York: Basic Books.

Cummings, M. R. (1995). *Human heredity: Principles and issues.* St. Paul, MN: West.

Cummins, J. (1989) A theoretical framework for bilingual special education. *Exceptional Children, 56,* 111–119.

Curfman, G. D., Gregory, T. S., & Paffenbarger, R. S. (1985). Physical activity and primary prevention of cardiovascular disease. *Cardiology Clinics, 3,* 203–222.

Curry, K., & Rosensteel, L. (1995). National vaccination week: Marketing vaccinations to Hispanics. In Newark, DE, *Public Health Reports, 110,* p. 202.

Curtis, S. (1977). *Genie: A psychological study of a modern-day wild child.* New York: Academic Press.

Cutler, B. (1990, November), Where does the free time go? *American Demographics,* pp. 36–39.

Cutler, S. J., & Hendricks, J. (1990). Leisure and time use across the life course. In R. H. Binstock & L. K. George (Eds.), *Handbook of aging and the social sciences* (3rd ed.) (pp. 169–185). New York: Academic Press.

Cytrynbaum, S., Blum, L., Patrick, R., Stein, J., Wadner, D., & Wilk, C. (1980). Midlife development: A personality and social systems perspective. In L. W. Poon (Ed.), *Aging in the 1980s* (pp. 463–475). Washington, DC: American Psychological Association.

Daly, K. (1993). Reshaping fatherhood: Finding the models. *Journal of Family Issues, 14,* 510–530.

Damon, W. (1983). *Social and personality development,* New York: Norton.

Damon, W., & Hart, D. (1982). The development of self-understanding from infancy through adolescence. *Child Development, 53,* 841–864.

Damon, W., & Hart, D. (1988). *Self-understanding in childhood and adolescence.* Cambridge: Cambridge University Press.

Dan, A. J., & Bernhard, L. A. (1989). Menopause and other health issues for midlife women. In S. Hunter & M. Sundel (Eds.), *Midlife myths* (pp. 51–67). Newbury Park, CA: Sage.

Danielson, K., & Cytrynbaum, S. (1980). Midlife development for blue-collar working men. In Cytrynbaum S. et al. Midlife development: A personality and social systems perspective. In L. W. Poon (Ed.), *Aging in the 1980s* (pp. 463–475). Washington, DC: American Psychological Association.

Dannemiller, J. L. & Stephens, B. R. (1988). A critical test of infant pattern preference models. *Child Development, 59,* 210–217.

Danner, F. W., & Day, M. C. (1977). Eliciting formal operations. *Child Development, 48.* 1600–1606.

Darling, N. & Steinberg, L. (1993). Parenting style as context: An integrative model. *Psychological Bulletin, 113,* 487–496.

Darling-Hammond, L. (1994, September). Will 21st century schools really be different? *The Education Digest,* pp. 4–8.

Daschle, T. A., Cohen, R. J., & Rice, C. L. (1993). Health-Care Reform: Singer-Payer models. *American Psychologist, 48,* 265–269.

Dasen, P., & Heron, A. (1981). Cross-cultural tests of Piaget's theory. In H. C. Triandis & A. Heron (Eds.), *Handbook of cross-cultural psychology* (Vol. 4, pp. 295–343). Boston: Allyn and Bacon.

D'Augelli, A. R. (1992). Lesbian and gay male undergraduates' experiences of harassment and fear on campus. *Journal of Interpersonal Violence, 7,* 383–395.

Davidson, R. J., & Fox, N. A. (1989). Frontal brain asymmetry predicts infants' response to maternal separation. *Journal of Abnormal Psychology, 98,* 127–131.

Davis, C. M. (1928). Self-selection of diet by newly weaned infants. *American Journal of Diseases of Children, 36,* 651–679.

Davis C. M. (1939). Results of the self-selection of diets by young children. *Canadian Medical Association Journal, 95,* 759–764.

Davis, D. T., Bustamante, A., Brown, C. P., Wolde-Tsadik, G., Savage, E. W., Cheng, X, & Howland, L. (1994, July). The urban church and cancer control: A source of social influence in minority communities. *Public Health Reports, 109,* 500–507.

Davis, G. A. (1983). *Educational psychology: Theory and practice.* Reading, MA: Addison-Wesley.

Davis, G. A., & Rimm, S. B. (1994). *Education of the gifted and talented* (3rd ed.). Needham, MA: Allyn & Bacon.

Davis, M. A. et al. (1995). Living arrangements and dietary quality of older U.S. adults. *Journal of the American Dietetic Association, 90,* 1667–1672.

Davis, P. W. (1994). The changing meanings of spanking. In J. Best (Ed.). *Troubling children: Studies of children and social problems* (pp. 133–153). New York: Aldine de Gruyter.

Davis, P. W. (1996). Threats of corporal punishment as verbal aggression: A naturalistic study. *Child Abuse & Neglect, 20,* 289–304.

Davis, R. A. (1989). Teenage pregnancy: A theoretical analysis of a social problem. *Adolescence, 24,* 19–27.

Davison, G. C., & Neale, J. M. (1995). *Abnormal psychology* (6th ed.). New York: Wiley.

Deak, G. O., & Bauer, P. J. (1996). The dynamics of preschoolers' categorization choices. *Child Development, 67,* 740–767.

Dean, A. L., Malik, M. M., Richards, W., & Stringer, S. A. (1986). Effects of parental maltreatment on children's conceptions of interpersonal relationships. *Developmental Psychology, 22,* 617–626.

DeAngelis, T. (1993, July). Science meets practice on PKU findings. *The APA Monitor,* 16–17.

DeAngelis, T. (1994, December). Perceptions influence student drinking. *APA Monitor,* p. 35.

DeAngelis, T. (1995). New threat associated with child abuse. *APA Monitor, 26,* pp. 1, 38.

Death of a character is "Sesame Street" topic, (1983, August 31). *New York Times,* p. D3.

Death toll from smoking is worsening. (1991, February 1). *New York Times,* p. A14.

Deautsch, F. M., Zalenski, C. M., & Clark, M. E. (1986). Is there a double standard of aging? *Journal of Applied Social Psychology, 16,* 771–785.

DeBlassie, A. M., & DeBlassie, R. R., (1996). Education of Hispanic youth: A cultural lag. *Adolescence, 31,* 205–215.

DeBruyne, L. K., & Rolfes, S. R. (1989). *Life cycle nutrition: Conception through adolescence.* St. Paul, MN: West.

DeCasper, A. J., & Fifer, W. P. (1980). Of human bonding: Newborns prefer their mothers' voices. *Science, 208,* 1174–1176.

DeCasper, A. J., & Spence, M. J. (1986). Prenatal maternal speech influences newborns' perception of speech sounds. *Infant Behavior and Development, 9,* 133–150.

Deely, K. (1996, May). Who's doing what? *Parenting,* p. 44.

De Gaston, J. F., Weed, S., & Jensen, L. (1996). Understanding gender differences in adolescent sexuality. *Adolescence, 31,* 217–231.

de Graaf, C., Polet, P., & van Staveren, W. A. (1994). Sensory perception and pleasantness of food flavors in elderly subjects. *Journal of Gerontology: Psychological Sciences, 49,* P93–P99.

De La Pena (1993, August 13). Should the United States adopt English as its "official" language: Yes. *CQ Researcher,* p. 713.

Delaney, C. H. (1995). Rites of passage in adolescence. *Adolescence, 30,* 891–898.

Delgado-Gaitan, C. & Trueba, H. T. (1985). Ethnographic study of participant structures in task completion: Reinterpretation of "handicaps" in Mexican children. *Learning Disability Quarterly, 8,* 67–75.

Delisle, J. R. (1992). *Guiding the social and emotional development of gifted children.* New York: Longman.

DeLoache, J. S. (1987). Rapid change in the symbolic functioning of very young children. *Science, 238,* 1556–1557.

DeLoache, J. S. (1991). Symbolic functioning in very young children: Understanding of pictures and models. *Child Development, 62,* 736–753.

DeLoache, J. S. & Todd, C. M. (1988). Young children's use of spatial categorization as a mnemonic strategy. *Journal of Experimental Child Psychology, 46,* 1–20.

DeLoache, J. S., Cassidy, D. J., & Brown, A. L. (1985). Precursors of mnemonic strategies in very young children's memory. *Child Development, 56,* 125–137.

DeLoache, J. S., Kolstad, V., & Anderson, K. N. (1991). Physical similarity and young children's understanding of scale models. *Child Development, 62,* 111–126.

DeLongis, A., Folkman, S., & Lazarus, R. S. (1988). The impact of daily stress on health and mood: Psychological and social resources as mediators. *Journal of Personality and Social Psychology, 54,* 486–495.

de Lorimier, S., Doyle, A. B., & Tessier, O. (1995). Social coordination during pretend play: Comparisons with nonpretend play and effects on expressive content. *Merrill-Palmer Quarterly, 41,* 497–516.

DeMaris, A., & Leslie, G. R. (1984, February). Cohabitation with the future spouse: Its influence upon marital satisfaction and communication. *Journal of Marriage and the Family, 46,* 77–84.

DeMaris, A., & Rao, K. V. (1992). Premarital cohabitation and subsequent marital stability in the United States: A reassessment. *Journal of Marriage and the Family, 54,* 178–190.

Demo, D. H., & Acock, A. C. (1993). Family diversity and the division of domestic labor: How much have things really changed? *Family Relations, 42,* 323–331.

Dempster, F. N. (1992). The rise and fall of the inhibitory mechanism: Toward a unified theory of cognitive development and aging. *Developmental Review, 12,* 45–75.

Demuth, K. (1995). Current approaches to phonological development: An introduction. In (E. V. Clark, Ed.). *The child language research forum.* (pp. 3–7). Center for the Study of Language and Information. Leland Stanford Junior University.

Denney, N., & Denney, D. (1982). The relationship between classification and questioning strategies among adults. *Journal of Gerontology, 37,* 190–196.

Denney, N., Jones, F., & Krigel, S. (1979). Modifying the questioning strategies of young children and elderly adults with strategy-modeling techniques. *Human Development, 22,* 23–36.

Denney, N., & Palmer, A. (1981). Adult age differences on traditional and practical problem-solving measures. *Journal of Gerontology, 36,* 323–328.

Denney, N. W. (1982). Aging and cognitive changes. In B. B. Wolman (Ed.), *Handbook of developmental psychology* (pp. 807–827). Englewood Cliffs, NJ: Prentice Hall.

Dennis, W. (1973). *Children of the creche.* New York: Appleton-Century-Crofts.

Dennis, W., & Dennis, M. G. (1940). Cradles and cradling customs of the Pueblo Indians. *American Anthrolopogist, 42,* 107–115.

Dennis, W., & Najarian, P. (1957). Infant development under environmental handicap. *Psychological Monographs, 71,* 1–13.

Denzin, N. K. (1992 July/August). The suicide machine. *Reason, 29,* 7–10.

DeOreo, K., & Keough, J. (1980). Performance of fundamental motor tasks. In C. B. Corbin (Ed.), *A textbook of motor development* (2nd ed.) (pp. 76–91). Dubuque, IA: Brown.

DePaola, S. J., Neimeyer, R. A., & Ross, S. K. (1994). Death concern and attitudes toward the elderly in nursing home personnel as a function of training. *Omega, 29,* 231–248.

Depner, C. E., & Ingersoll-Dayton, B. (1988). Supportive relationships in later life. *Psychology and Aging, 3,* 348–357.

Depue, R. A., & Monroe, S. M. (1986). Conceptualization and measurement of human disorder in life stress research: The problem of chronic disturbance. *Psychological Bulletin, 99,* 36–51.

Desai, S., Chase-Lansdale, P. L., & Michael, R. T. (1989). Mother or market? Effects of maternal employment on the intellectual ability of 4-year-old children. *Demography, 26,* 545–561.

Desiderato, L. L., & Crawford, H. J. (1995). Risky sexual behavior in college students: Relationships between number of sexual partners, disclosure of previous risky behavior, and alcohol use. *Journal of Youth and Adolescence, 24,* 55–68.

Deutsch, F. M., Lussier, J. B., & Servic, L. J. (1993). Husbands at home: Predictors of paternal participation in childcare and housework. *Journal of Personality and Social Psychology, 65,* 1154-1166.

deVilliers, J. G., & deVilliers, P. A. (1978). *Language acquisition.* Cambridge, MA: Harvard University Press.

Devlin, A. S., Brown, E. H., Beebe, J., & Parulis, E. (1992). Parent education for divorced fathers. *Family Relations, 41,* 290–296.

De Vries, B., Bluck, S., & Birren, J. E. (1993). The understanding of death and dying in a life-span perspective. *The Gerontologist, 33,* 366–372.

De Vries, B., Lana, R. D., & Falck, V. T. (1994). Parental bereavement over the life course: A theoretical intersection and empirical review. *Omega, 29,* 47–69.

Diamond, A., Cruttenden, L., & Neiderman, D. (1994). AB with multiple wells: 1. Why are multiple wells sometimes easier than two wells? 2. Memory or memory + inhibition? *Developmental Psychology, 30,* 192–205.

Diamond, J. M., Kataria, S., & Messer, S. C. (1989). Latchkey children: A pilot study investigating behavior and academic achievement. *Child and Youth Care Quarterly, 18,* 131–140.

Diamond, M., Lund, D., & Caserta, M. S. (1987). The role of social support in the first two years of bereavement in an elderly sample. *Gerontologist, 27,* 599–604.

Diamond, N. (1982). Cognitive theory. In B. B. Wolman (Ed.), *Handbook of developmental psychology* (pp. 3–23). Englewood Cliffs, NJ: Prentice Hall.

Diaz, R. M. (1985). Bilingual cognitive development: Addressing three gaps in current research. *Child Development, 56,* 1376–1388.

DiCaprio, N. S. (1983). *Personality theories: A guide to human nature* (2nd ed.). New York: Holt, Rinehart and Winston.

Dickinson, G. E. (1992). First childhood death experiences. *Omega, 25,* 169–182.

Dickover, R. E., Garratty, E. M., Herman,

S. A., Sim, M. S., Plaeger, S., Boyer, P. J., Keller, M., Deveikis, A., Stiehm, E. R., & Bryson, Y. J. (1996, February 28). Identification of levels of maternal HIV-1 RNA associated with risk of perinatal transmission. *Journal of the American Medical Association, 275,* 599–605.

Diehl, M., Willis, S. L., & Schaie, K. W. (1995). Everyday problem solving in older adults: Observational assessment and cognitive correlates. *Psychology and Aging, 10,* 478–491.

Diekelmann, N. (1977). *Primary health care of the well adult.* New York: McGraw-Hill.

DiGiovanna, A. G. (1994). *Human aging: Biological perspectives.* New York: McGraw Hill.

Dignan, M. B., Michielutte, R., Jones-Lighty, D., & Bahnson, J. (1994 July/August). Factors influencing the return rate in a direct mail campaign to inform minority women about prevention of cervical cancer. *Public Health Reports, 109,* 507–512.

DiLalla, L. F., Thompson, L. A., Plomin, R., Phillips, K., Fagan, J. F., Haith, M. M., Cyphers, L. H., & Fulker, D. W. (1990). Infant predictors of preschool and adult IQ: A study of twins and their parents. *Developmental Psychology, 26,* 759–770.

Dillon, P. A., Emery, R. E. (1996). Divorce mediation and resolution of child custody disputes: Long-term effects. *American Journal of Orthopsychiatry, 66,* 131–140.

Dion, K. K. (1973). Young children's stereotyping of facial attractiveness. *Developmental Psychology, 9,* 183–188.

Dirks, J., & Neisser, U. (1977). Memory for objects in real scenes: The development of recognition and recall. *Journal of Experimental Child Psychology, 23,* 315–328.

Dishion, T. J. (1990). The family ecology of boys' peer relations in middle childhood. *Child Development, 61,* 874–892.

Dishion, T. J., Andrews, D. W., & Crosby, L. (1995). Antisocial boys and their friends in early adolescence: Relationship characteristics, quality, and interactional process. *Child Development, 66,* 139–151.

Dishion, T. J., Patterson, G. R., Stoolmiller, M., & Skinner, M. L. (1991). Family, school, and behavioral antecedents to early adolescent involvement with antisocial peers. *Developmental Psychology, 27,* 172–280.

DiVaney, S., Hughey, A. W., & Osborne, W. L. (1994). Comparative effects of exercise reduction and relaxation training on mood states and type A scores in habitual aerobic exercisers. *Perceptual and Motor Skills, 79,* 1635–1644.

Dix, T., Reinhold, D., & Zambarano, R. (1990). Mothers' judgments in moments of anger. *Merrill-Palmer Quarterly, 36,* 465–486.

Dix, T., Ruble, D. N., & Zambarano, R. J. (1989). Mother's implicit theories of discipline: Child effects, parental effects and the attribution process. *Child Development, 60,* 1373–1392.

Dobbs, A. R., & Rule, B. G. (1989). Adult age differences in working memory. *Psychology and Aging, 4,* 500–503.

Dobkin, P. L., Tremblay, R. E., Masse, L. C., & Vitaro, F. (1995). Individual and peer characteristics in predicting boys' early onset of substance abuse: A seven-year longitudinal study. *Child Development, 66,* 1198–1214.

Dodge, H. D. (1995). Movements out of poverty among elderly widows. *Journal of Gerontology, 50B,* S240–S249.

Dodge, K. A., Coie, J. D., Pettit, G. S., & Price, J. M. (1990). Peer status and aggression in boys' groups: Developmental and contextual analyses. *Child Development, 61,* 1289–1310.

Dodge, K. A., & Frame, C. L. (1982). Social cognitive biases and deficits in aggressive boys. *Child Development, 53,* 620–635.

Doering, C. H. (1980). The endocrine system. In O. G. Brim & J. Kagan (Eds.), *Constancy and change in human development* (pp. 229–272). Cambridge, MA: Harvard University Press.

Doherty, W. J. & Needle, P. H. (1991). Psychological adjustment and substance use among adolescents before and after a parental divorce. *Child Development, 62,* 328–337.

Dolcini, M. M., Cohn, L. D., Adler, N. E., Millstein, S. G., Irwin, C. E., Kegeles, S. M., & Stone, G. C. (1989). Adolescent egocentrism and feelings of invulnerability: Are they related? *Journal of Early Adolescence, 9,* 409–418.

Donahue, M. J., & Benson, P. L. (1995). Religion and the well-being of adolescents. *Journal of Social Issues, 51,* 145–160.

Donegan, C. (1996, January 19). Debate over bilingualism. *CQ Researcher,* 49–70.

Donnerstein, E., Slaby, R. G., & Eron, L. D. (1994). The mass media and youth aggression in L. D. Eron, J. H. Gentry, & P. Schlegel (Eds.). *Reason to hope: A psychosocial perspective on violence & youth,* pp. 219–251, Washington, DC: APA.

Donohue, R. P., Abbott, R. D., Reed, D. M., & Yano, K. (1988). Physical activity and coronary heart disease in middle-aged and elderly men: The Honolulu Heart Program. *American Journal of Public Health, 78,* 683–685.

Donovan, J. M. (1975). Identity status and interpersonal style. *Journal of Youth and Adolescence, 4,* 37–55.

Dorfman, L. (1992). Couples in retirement: Division of household labor. In M. Szinovacz, D. Ekerdt, & B. Vinick (Eds.). *Families and retirement,* pp. 159–173 Newbury Park, CA: Sage.

Dornbusch, S., Ritter, P., Liederman, P., Roberts, D., & Fraleigh, M. (1987). The relation of parenting style to adolescent school performance. *Child Development, 58,* 1244–1257.

Dornbusch, S. M., Carlsmith, J. M., Bushwall, S. J., Ritter, P. L., Leiderman, H., Hastof, A. H., & Gross, R. T. (1985). Single parents, extended households and the control of adolescence. *Child Development, 56,* 326–341.

Dorr, A., & Rabin, B. E. (1995). Parents, children, and television. In M. H. Bornstein (Ed.), *Handbook of Parenting* (Vol. 4, pp. 323–353). Mahwah, NJ: Erlbaum.

Dougherty, T. M., & Haith, M. M. (1997). Infant expectations and reaction time as predictors of childhood speed of processing and IQ. *Developmental Psychology, 23,* 146–156.

Douglas, J. D. (1991). Patterns of change following parent death in midlife adults. *Omega, 22,* 123–137.

Dowling, K. (1995, December 11, 1995). A hospital isn't the best place to die. *Newsday,* p. A28.

Downs, A. (1996, July/August). The Wages of Downsizing. *Mother Jones, 21,* 6–12.

Downs, W. R., Miller, B. A., Testa, M., & Panek, D. (1992). Long-term effects of parent-to-child violence for women. *Journal of Interpersonal Violence, 7,* 365–382.

Doyle, J. A., & Paludi, M. A. (1991). *Sex and gender: The human experience* (2nd ed.). Dubuque, IA: Brown.

Drabman, R. S., & Thomas, M. H. (1975). Does TV violence breed indifference? *Journal of Communication, 25,* 86–89.

Drebing, C., & Gooden, W. (1991). The impact of the dreams on mental health functioning in the male midlife transition. *International Journal of Aging and Human Development, 32,* 277–287.

Drebing, C. E., De Kemp, H., Gooden, W. E., Malony, H. N., & Drebing, S. M. (1995). The dream in midlife women: Its impact on mental health. *40,* 73–87.

Dreyer, P. H. (1982). Sexuality during adolescence. In B. B. Wolman (Ed.), *Handbook of Developmental Psychology* (pp. 559–602). Englewood Cliffs, NJ: Prentice Hall.

Drummond, R. J., & Ryan, C. W. (1995). *Career counseling: A developmental approach*. Englewood Cliffs, NJ: Prentice Hall.

Duberman, L. (1973). Step-kin relationships. *Journal of Marriage and the Family, 35,* 283–292.

Dubow, E. F., & Luster, T. (1990). Adjustment of children born to teenage mothers: The contribution of risk and protective factors. *Journal of Marriage and the Family, 52,* 393–404.

Duke, M. P. (1994). Chaos theory and psychology: Seven propositions. *Genetic, Social, and General Psychology Monographs, 120,* 267–286.

Dullea, A. (1989, October 12). Opening the world to a generation. *New York Times,* pp. C1, C6.

Duncan, G. J., Brooks-Gunn, J., & Klebanov, P. K. (1994). Economic deprivation and early childhood development. *Child Development 65,* 296–318.

Duncan, P., Ritter, P., Dornbusch, S., Gross, R., & Carlsmith, M. J. (1985). The effects of pubertal timing on body image, social behavior, and deviance. *Journal of Youth and Adolescence, 14,* 227–236.

Dunham, P. J., Dunham, F., & Curwin, A. (1993). Joint-attentional states and lexical acquisition at 18 months. *Developmental Psychology, 29,* 827–831.

Dunn, J. (1983). Sibling relationships in early childhood. *Child Development, 54,* 787–812.

Dunn, J. & Kendrick, C. (1982). *Siblings: Love, envy and understanding*. Cambridge, MA: Harvard University Press.

Dunn, J., & McGuire, S. (1992). Sibling and peer relationships in childhood. *Journal of Child Psychology and Psychiatry, 33,* 67–105.

Dunn, J. & Shatz, M. (1989). Becoming a conversationalist despite (or because of) having an older sibling. *Child Development, 60,* 399–410.

DuPaul, G. J., & Barkley, R. A. (1993). Behavioral contributions to pharmacotherapy: The utility of behavioral methodology in medical treatment of children with attention deficit hyperactivity disorder. *Behavior Therapy, 24,* 47–64.

Dura, J. R., Stukenberg, K. W., & Kiecolt Glaser, J. K. (1990). Chronic stress and depressive disorders in older adults. *Journal of Abnormal Psychology, 99,* 284–290.

Dura, J. R., Stukenberg, K. W., & Kiecolt Glaser, J. K. (1991). Anxiety and depressive disorders in adult children caring for demented parents. *Psychology and Aging, 6,* 467–473.

Duran, R. P. (1989). Assessment and instruction of at-risk Hispanic students. *Exceptional Children, 56,* 154–159.

Durkin, K. (1995). *Developmental social psychology*. Cambridge, MA: Blackwell.

Durrett, M. E., O'Bryant, S., & Pennebaker, J. W. (1975). Child-rearing reports of white, Black, and Mexican-American families. *Developmental Psychology, 11,* 871.

Dusek, J. B. (1996). *Adolescent development & behavior* (3rd ed.). Englewood Cliffs, NJ: Prentice Hall.

Dustman, R. E., Ruhling, R. O., Russell, E. M., Shearer, D. E., Bonekat, H. W., Shigeoka, J. W., Wood, J. S., & Bradford, D. C. (1984). Aerobic exercise training and improved neuropsychological function of older individuals. *Neurobiology of Aging, 5,* 355–42.

Duvall, E. & Miller, B. (1985). *Marriage and family development* (6th ed.). New York: Harper & Row.

Dworetzsky, J. P. (1984). *Introduction to child development* (2nd ed.). St. Paul, MN: West.

Dychtwald, K. & Flower, J. (1989) *Age wave*. Los Angeles: Tarcher.

Eagly, A. H. (1978). Sex differences in influenceability. *Psychological Bulletin, 85,* 86–116.

Earles, J. L., & Salthouse, T. A. (1995). Interrelations of age, health, and speed. *Journal of Gerontology: Psychological Sciences, 50B,* P33–P41.

Easterlin, R. A. (1996). Economic and social implications of demographic patterns. In R. H. Binstock & L. K. George (Eds.), *Handbook of Aging and The Social Sciences* (4th ed., pp. 73–93). San Diego, CA: Academic Press.

Eastern Paralyzed Veterans Association (1992). *Understanding the Americans with Disabilities Act*. New York: Author.

Eaton, W. O., & Ennis, L. R. (1986). Sex differences in human motor activity level. *Psychological Bulletin, 100,* 19–28.

Eaton, W. O., & Ritchot, K. F. M., (1995). Physical maturation and information-processing speed in middle childhood. *Developmental Psychology, 31,* 967–972.

Ebersole, P., & Hess, P. (1981). *Toward healthy aging: Human needs and nursing response*. St. Louis, MO: Mosby.

Eccles, J., Wigfield, A., Harold, R. D., & Blumenfield, P. (1993). Age and gender differences in children's self- and task perceptions during elementary school. *Child Development, 64,* 830–847.

Eccles, J. S., Midgley, C., Wigfield, A., Buchanan, C. M., Reuman, D., Flanagan, C., & MacIver, D. (1993). Development during adolescence: The impact of stage-environment fit on young adolescents' experience in schools and families. *American Psychologist, 48,* 90–101.

Echols, L. D., West, R. F., Stonovich, K. E., & Zehr, K. S. (1996). Using children's literacy activities to predict growth in verbal cognitive skills: A longitudinal investigation. *Journal of Educational Psychology, 88,* 296–304.

Eckerman, C. O., & Didow, S. M. (1996). Nonverbal imitation and toddlers' mastery of verbal means of achieving coordinated action. *Developmental Psychology, 32,* 141–152.

The Economist (1993a, December 4) In never-never land. *The Economist, 329,* p. 30.

The Economist (1993b, November 13) Death's dissident. *The Economist, 329,* p. 34.

The Economist (1994a, October 1) How poor are the poor? *The Economist, 323,* p. 106.

The Economist (1994b, September 14). The cease upon midnight. *The Economist, 332,* 21–24.

The Economist (1995a, July 1). Painful jabs, *The Economist, 336,* 20–22.

The Economist (1995b, March 4). Extra dry. *The Economist, 334,* p. 80.

Edelman, M. W. (1985). The sea is so wide and my boat is so small: Problems facing black children today. In H. P. McAdoo & J. L. McAdoo (Eds.), *Black children* (pp. 72–85). Beverly Hills, CA: Sage.

Eder, R. A. (1989). The emergent personalogist: The structure and content of 3-1/2, 5-1/2, and 7-1/2-year-olds' concepts of themselves and other persons. *Child Development, 60,* 1218–1229.

Edmonds, P. (1994, November 14). Children get poorer; Nation gets Richer. *USA Today,* p. 1A, 2A.

Edmonds, P. (1995, November 29). They're lost in the system and out on their own. *USA Today,* p. 6A.

Edmondson, B. (1993, January). Harvest time, *American Demographics,* 2.

Education poll: Many fear schools lack teaching tools (1996, May 14). *USA Today* p. 2A.

Education Week. (1993, May). Focusing on education, p. 3.

Education Week. (1993, November 3). Hispanic dropouts, p. 3.

Edwards, C. P. (1995). Parenting toddlers.

In M. H. Bornstein (Ed.), *Handbook of parenting* (Vol. 1, pp. 41–63). Mahwah, NJ: Erlbaum.

Egeland, B., & Hiester, M. (1995). The long-term consequences of infant daycare and mother-infant attachment. *Child Development, 66,* 474–485.

Egeland, B., Jacobovitz, D., & Sroufe, L. A. (1988). Breaking the cycle of abuse. *Child Development, 59,* 1080–1089.

Ehrenhaft, P. M., Wagner, J. L., & Herdman, R. C. (1989). Changing prognosis for very low birth weight infants. *Obstetrics and Gynecology, 74,* 528–535.

Eidelberg, L. (Ed.). (1968). *Encyclopedia of Psychoanalysis.* New York: Free Press.

Eimas, P. D., Sigueland, E. R., Jusczyk, P., & Vigorito, J. (1971). Speech perception in infants. *Science, 171,* 303–306.

Eisdorfer, C., & Wilkie, F. (1977). Stress, disease, aging, and behavior. In J. E. Birren & K. W. Schaie (Eds.), *Handbook of the Psychology of Aging* (pp. 251–276). New York: Van Nostrand Reinhold.

Eisele, J., Hertsgaard, D., & Light, H. K. (1986). Factors related to eating disorders in young adolescent girls. *Adolescence, 21,* 283–290.

Eisen, L. M., Field, T. M., Bandstra, E. S., Roberts, J. P., Morrow, C., Larson, S. K., & Steele, B. M. (1991). Perinatal cocaine effects on neonatal stress behavior and performance on Brazelton scale. *Pediatrics, 88,* 477–479.

Eisenberg, N. (1989). The development of prosocial and aggressive behavior. In M. H. Bornstein & M. E. Lamb (Eds.), *Social, emotional and personality development* (pp. 461–486). Hillsdale, NJ: Erlbaum.

Eisenberg, N., & Fabes, R. A. (1994). Mothers' reactions to children's negative emotions: Relations to children's temperament and anger behavior. *Merrill-Palmer Quarterly, 40,* 138–156.

Eisenberg, N., Fabes, R. A., Karbon, M., Murphy, B. C., Wosinski, M., Polazzi, L., Carlo, G., & Juhnke, C. (1996). The relations of children's dispositional prosocial behavior to emotionality, regulation, and social functioning. *Child Development, 67,* 974–992.

Eisenberg, N., Fabes, R. A., Murphy, B., Karbon, M., Smith, M., & Maszk, P. (1996). The relations of children's dispositional empathy-related responding to their emotionality, regulation, and social functioning. *Developmental Psychology, 32,* 195–209.

Eisenberg, N., & Mussen, P. H. (1989). *The roots of prosocial behavior in children.* New York: Cambridge University Press.

Eisenberg, N. & Mussen, P. H. (1989). *The roots of prosocial behavior in children.* New York: Cambridge University Press.

Eisenberg, N., Shell, R., Lennon, R., Bellover, R., & Mathy, R. M. (1987). Prosocial development in middle childhood: A longitudinal study, *Developmental Psychology, 23,* 712–718.

Eisenberg, N., Wolchik, S. A., Hernandez, R., & Pasternack, J. F. (1985). Parental socialization of young children's play: A short term longitudinal study. *Child Development, 56,* 1506–1513.

Eisenberg, R. B. (1970). The organization of auditory behavior. *Journal of Speech and Hearing Research, 13,* 461–464.

Eiser, C., Eiser, J. R., & Jones, B. A. (1990). Scene schemata and scripts in children's understanding of hospital. *Child Care, Health and Development, 16,* 303–317.

Eisler, P,. (1995, August 15). Complaints now sit for at least a year. *USA Today,* A1, A2, A10.

Ekerdt, D. J., Bosse, R., & Levkoff, S. (1985). An empirical test for phases of retirement: Findings from the normative aging study. *Journal of Gerontology, 40,* 95–101.

Ekerdt, D. J., Bosse, R., & LoCastro, J. S. (1983). Claims that retirement improves health. *Journal of Gerontology, 38,* 231–236.

Elardo, R., Bradley, R., & Caldwell, B. M. (1975). The relation of infants' home environments to mental test performance from six to thirty-six months: A longitudinal analysis. *Child Development, 46,* 71–76.

Elardo, R., Bradley, R., & Caldwell, B. M. (1977). A longitudinal study of the relation of infants' home environments to language development at age three. *Child Development, 48,* 595–603.

Elder, G. H., Modell, J., & Parke, R. D. (Eds.). (1993). *Children in time and place.* Cambridge, England: Cambridge University Press.

Elder, G. H., Jr. & Caspi, A. (1988). Economic stress: Developmental perspectives. *Journal of Social Issues, 44,* 25–45.

Elias, M. (1996, April 15). Black, white student scores stay steady. *USA Today,* p. D1.

Elias, M. F., Elias, J. W., & Elias, P. K. (1990). Biological and health influences on behavior. In J. E. Birren & K. W. Schaie (Eds.), *Handbook of the psychology of aging* (3rd ed.) (pp. 80–103). New York: Academic Press.

Elkind, D. (1967). Egocentrism in adolescence. *Child Development, 38,* 1025–1034.

Elkind, D. (1985). Egocentrism redux. *Developmental Review, 5,* 218–226.

Elkind, D. (1987). *Miseducation.* New York: Knopf.

Elkind, D., & Bowen, R. (1979). Imaginary audience behavior in children and adolescence. *Developmental Psychology, 15,* 38–44.

Ellison, C. G. (1991). Religious involvement and subjective well-being. *Journal of Health and Social Behavior, 32,* 80–99.

Elsayed, M., Ismail, A. H., & Young, R. J. (1980). Intellectual differences of adult men related to age and physical fitness before and after an exercise program. *Journal of Gerontology, 35,* 383–387.

Elsen, H. (1995). Linguistic team-work—The interaction of linguistic modules in first language acquisition. In E. V. Clark (Ed.). *The child language research forum.* Center for the study of language and information. Leland Stanford Junior University, pp. 123–137.

Elster, A. B., & Panzarine, S. (1983). Teenage fathers: Stresses during gestation and early parenthood. *Clinical Pediatrics, 22,* 700–703.

Emde, R. N. (1992). Individual meeting and increasing complexity: Contributions of Sigmund Freud and Rene Spitz to developmental psychology. *Developmental Psychology, 28,* 347–360.

Emde, R. N., Izard, C., Huebner, R., Sorce, J. F., & Klinnert, M. (1985). Adult judgments of infant emotions: Replication studies within and across laboratories. *Infant Behavior and Development, 8,* 79–88.

Emery, C. F., Huppert, F. A., & Schein, R. L. (1995). Relationships among age, exercise, health, and cognitive function in a British sample. *The Gerontologist, 35,* 378–385.

Emery, R. E. (1982). Interparental conflict and the children of discord and divorce. *Psychological Bulletin, 92,* 310–330.

Emery, R. E., Matthews, S. G., & Kitzmann, K. M. (1994). Child custody mediation and litigation: Parents' satisfaction and functioning one year after settlement. *Journal of Consulting and Clinical Psychology, 62,* 124–129.

Engen, T. (1977). Taste and smell. In J. E. Birren & K. W. Schaie (Eds.), *Handbook of the psychology of aging* (pp. 554–562). New York: Van Nostrand Reinhold.

Engen, T., Lipsitt, L. P., & Peck, M. B. (1973). Ability of newborn infants to discriminate sapid substances. *Developmental Psychology, 10,* 741–744.

Entwisle, D. R. (1995). The role of schools in sustaining early childhood program benefits. *The Future of Children, 5,* 133–145.

Entwisle, D. R. & Alexander, K. L. (1987). Long-term effects of cesarean delivery on parents' beliefs and children's schooling. *Developmental Psychology, 23,* 676–682.

Entwisle, D. R., & Baker, D. P. (1983). Gender and young children's expectations for performance in arithmetic. *Developmental Psychology, 19,* 100–209.

Epstein, L. H., (1987). Behavioral treatment of childhood obesity. *Psychological Bulletin, 101,* 331–342.

Erber, J. T. (1989). Young and older adults' appraisal of memory failure in young and older adult target persons. *Journal of Gerontology, 44,* 170–175.

Erber, J. T. & Rothberg, S. T. (1991). Here's looking at you. The relative effect of age and attractiveness on judgements about memory failure. *Journal of Gerontology: Psychological Sciences, 46,* 116–123.

Ericksen, K. P., & Trocki, K. F. (1994). Sex, alcohol and sexually transmitted diseases: A national survey. *Family Planning Perspectives, 26,* 257–263.

Erickson, M. F., Sroufe, L. A., & Egeland, B. (1985). The relationship between quality of attachment and behavior problems in preschool in a high-risk sample. In I. Bretherton & E. Waters (Eds.), Growing points of attachment theory and research. *Monographs of the Society for Research in Child Development, 50* (1–2, Serial No. 209), pp. 147–167.

Erikson, E. (1958). *Young man Luther: A study in psychoanalysis and history.* New York: Norton.

Erikson, E. (1959). The problem of ego identity. In *Identity and the life cycle.* New York: Norton.

Erikson, E. (1963a). *Youth and society.* New York: Norton.

Erikson, E. H. (1963b). *Childhood and society* (Rev. ed.). New York: Norton.

Erikson, E. (1968). *Identity: Youth and crisis.* New York: Norton.

Erikson, E. (1969). *Gandhi's truth.* New York: Norton.

Erikson, E. (1975) *Life history and the historical moment.* New York: Norton.

Eron, L. D. (1982). Parent-child interaction, television violence, and aggression of children. *American Psychologist, 37,* 197–212.

Eron, L. D., Huesmann, L. R., Brice, P., Fischer, P., & Mermelstein, R. (1983). Age trends in the development of aggression, sex typing, and related television habits. *Developmental Psychology, 19,* 71–78.

Eron, L. D., Walder, L. O., & Lefkowitz, M. M. (1971). *Learning of aggression in children.* Boston: Little, Brown.

Escobedo, L. G., & Peddicord, J. P. (1996). Smoking prevalence in US birth cohorts: The influence of gender and education. *American Journal of Public Health, 86,* 231–236.

Eskenazi, B., Prehn, A. W., & Christianson, R. E. (1995). Passive and active maternal smoking as measured by serum cotinine: The effect on birthweight. *American Journal of Public Health, 85,* 395–398.

Etaugh, C. (1980). Effects of nonmaternal care on children: Research evidence and popular views. *American Psychologist, 35,* 309–319.

Etaugh, C., & Hughes, V. (1975). Teachers' evaluations of sex-typed behaviors in children: The role of teacher sex and school setting. *Developmental Psychology, 11,* 394–395.

Fabes, R. A., Eisenberg, N., Karbon, M., Troyer, D., & Switzer, G. (1994). The relations of children's emotion regulation to their vicarious emotional responses and comforting behavior. *Child Development, 65,* 1678–1693.

Fabes, R. A., Eisenberg, N., Smith, M. C. & Murphy, B. C. (1996). Getting angry at peers: Associations with liking of the provocateur. *Child Development, 67,* 942–956.

Face up to sex education (1993, June 8). *USA Today.* p. 12A.

Fagan, J. F. (1973). Infants' delayed recognition memory and forgetting. *Journal of Experimental Child Psychology, 16,* 424–450.

Fagot, B. I. (1978). The influence of sex of child on parental reactions to toddler children. *Child Development, 49,* 459–465.

Fagot, B. I. (1995). Parenting boys and girls. In M. H. Bornstein (Ed.). *Handbook of parenting* (Vol. 1., pp. 163–183). Mahwah, NJ: Erlbaum.

Fagot, B. I., Hagan, R., Leinbach, M. D., & Kronsberg, S. (1985). Differential reactions to assertive and communicative acts of toddler boys and girls. *Child Development, 56,* 1499–1505.

Fagot, B. I., & Kavanagh, K. (1993). Parenting during the second year: Influences of age, sex of child, and attachment classification. *Child Development, 63,* 258–271.

Fagot, B. J. (1977). Influence of teacher behavior in the preschool. *Developmental Psychology, 9,* 198–206.

Fagot, B. J. (1997). Attachment, parenting, and peer interactions of toddler children. *Developmental Psychology, 33,* 489–499.

Fagot, B. K., & Hagan, R. (1991). Observations of parent reactions to sex-stereotyped behaviors: Age and sex effects. *Child Development, 62,* 617–628.

Fahy, T. A., & Eisler, I. (1993). Impulsivity and eating disorders. *British Journal of Psychiatry, 162,* 193–197.

Fairburn, C. G., Jones, R., Pevel, R. C., Carr, S. J., Solomon, R. A., O'Connor, M. E., Burton, J., & Hope, R. A. (1991). Three psychological treatments for bulimia nervosa. *Archives of General Psychiatry, 48,* 463–469.

Falbo, T., & Polit, D. (1986). Quantitative review of the only child literature: Research evidence and theory development. *Psychological Bulletin, 100,* 176–189.

Falbo, T. & Poston, D. L., Jr. (1993). The academic, personality, and physical outcomes of only children in China. *Child Development, 64,* 18–35.

Falk, P. J. (1989). Lesbian mothers. *American Psychologist, 44,* 941–947.

Fantz, R. L. (1961, May). The origin of form perception. *Scientific American,* pp. 16–21.

Fantz, R. L., & Miranda, S. B. (1975). Newborn infant's attention to form of contour. *Child Development, 46,* 224–228.

Farber, H. (1996, October 26). Corporate downsizing *Economist, 341,* 79–81.

Farberow, N. L. (1985). Youth suicide: A summary. In M. L. Peck, N. L. Farberow, & R. E. Litman (Eds.), *Youth suicide* (pp. 191–205). New York: Springer.

Farguhar, J. W., Fortmann, S. P., Flora, J. A., Taylor, C. B., Haskell, W. L., Williams, P. T., Maccoby, N., & Wood, P. D. (1990). Effects of communitywide education on cardiovascular disease and risk factors. *JAMA, 264,* 359–365.

Farley, F. H. (1979). The hypostatization of death in adolescence. *Adolescence, 14,* 341–351.

Farmer, H. S. (1978). Career counseling implications for the lower social class and women. *Personnel and Guidance Journal, 56,* 467–472.

Farrar, M. J., & Goodman, G. S. (1992). Developmental changes in event memory. *Child Development, 63,* 173–187.

Farver, J. A. M., & Branstetter, W. H. (1994). Preschoolers' responses to their peers' distress. *Developmental Psychology, 30,* 334–341.

Fay, R., Turner, C., Klassen, A., & Gagnon, J. (1989, January 20). Prevalence and patterns of same-gender sexual contact among men. *Science, 243,* 338–348.

Featherman, D. L. (1980). Schooling and occupational careers: Constancy and change in worldly success. In O. G. Brim & J. Kagan (Eds.), *Constancy and change in human development* (pp. 675–739). Cambridge, MA: Harvard University Press.

Federal Register (1977). Education of handicapped children, U. S. Office of Education. *Federal Register, 42,* 65082–65085.

Feifel, H. (1990). Psychology and death: Meaningful rediscovery. *American Psychologist, 45,* 537–544.

Fein, R. A. (1978). Research on fathering: Social policy and an emergent perspective. *Journal of Social Issues, 34,* 122–135.

Feingold, B. F. (1975). Hyperkinesis and learning disabilities linked to artificial food flavors and colors. *American Journal of Nursing, 75,* 797–803.

Feldhusen, J. F. (1991). Saturday and summer programs. In N. Colangelo & G. A. Davis (Eds.), *Handbook of gifted education* (pp. 197–209). Needham Heights, MA: Allyn & Bacon.

Feldhusen, J. F., Proctor, T. B., & Black, K. N. (1986). Guidelines for grade advancement of precocious children. *Roeper Review, 9,* 25–27.

Feldman, J. F., Brody, N., & Miller, S. A. (1980). Sex differences in non-elicited neonatal behaviors. *Merrill-Palmer Quarterly, 26,* 63–73.

Feldman, M. W., & Lewontin, R. C. (1975). The heritability hang-up. *Science, 190,* 1163–1168.

Feldman, S. S., & Gehring, T. M. (1988). Changing perceptions of family cohesion and power across adolescence. *Child Development, 59,* 1034–1045.

Feldman, S. S., & Quatman, T. (1988). Factors influencing age expectations for adolescent autonomy: A study of early adolescents and parents. *Journal of Early Adolescence, 8,* 325–343.

Feltey, K., Ainslie, J. J., & Geib, I. (1991). Sexual coercion attitudes among high school students. *Youth and Society, 23,* 229–250.

Felton, J. (Ed.) (1991). *Prevention's giant book .of health facts.* Emmaus, PA: Rodale Press.

Fenigsen, R. (1989, January/February). A case against Dutch euthanasia. *Hastings Center Report Special Supplement,* pp. 22–30.

Ferguson, T. J., & Rule, B. G. (1982). Influence of inferential set, outcome intent, and outcome severity on children's moral judgments. *Developmental Psychology, 18,* 843–851.

Fernald, A. (1985). Four-month-old infants prefer to listen to motherese. *Infant Behavior and Development, 8,* 181–195.

Fernald, A., & Kuhl, P. (1987). Acoustic determinants of infant preference for motherese speech. *Infant Behavior and Development, 10,* 279–293.

Fernald, A., & Morikawa, H. (1993). Common themes and cultural variations in Japanese and American mothers' speech to infants. *Child Development, 64,* 637–657.

Fernald, A. & Simon, T. (1984). Expanded intonation contours in mothers' speech to newborns. *Developmental Psychology, 20,* 104–113.

Ferraro, K. F. (1980). Self-ratings of health among the old and old-old. *Journal of Health and Social Behavior, 21,* 377–383.

Field, T. (1986). Interventions for premature infants. *Journal of Pediatrics, 109,* 183–190.

Field, T. (1991). Quality infant day care and grade school behavior and performance. *Child Development, 62,* 863–870.

Field, T. (1995). Psychologically depressed parents. In M. H. Bornstein (Ed.). *Handbook of parenting* (Vol.4, pp. 85–101). Mahwah, NJ: Erlbaum.

Field, T., Masi, W., Goldstein, S., Perry, S., & Parl, S. (1988). Infant day care facilitates preschool social behavior. *Early Childhood Research Quarterly, 3,* 341–361.

Field, T., Masi, W., Goldstein, S., Perry, S., & Pearl, S. (1988). Infant day care facilitates preschool social behavior. *Early Childhood Research Quarterly, 3,* 341–359.

Field, T. M. (1980). Early development of infants born to teenage mothers. In K. Scott, T. Field, & E. Robertson (Eds.), *Teenage parents and their offspring.* New York: Grune and Stratton.

Field, T. M., & Widmayer, S. M. (1982). Marriage and the family. In B. B. Wolman (Ed.), *Handbook of the psychology of aging* (pp. 681–697). Englewood Cliffs, NJ: Prentice Hall.

Fields, G. (1994, May 20–22). 1.6 Million kids home alone. *USA Today,* p. 1A.

Fifer, W. P. & Moon, C. (1984). Discrimination and preference for voices in newborns. Cited in C. Rovee-Collier learning and memory in infancy in J. D. Osofsky (Ed.) *Handbook of Infant Development* (p. 122). New York: Wiley.

Fillenbaum, G., et al. (1985). Determinants and consequences of retirement. *Journal of Gerontology, 40,* 85–94.

Fincham, F., & O'Leary, K. D. (1983). Causal inferences for spouse behavior in maritally distressed and nondistressed couples. *Journal of Clinical and Social Psychology, 1,* 42–57.

Findlay, S. (1985, November 7). Active dads see rewards and snags. *USA Today,* p. 3D.

Fine, M. A. (1989). A social science perspective on stepfamily law: Suggestions for legal reform. *Family Relations, 38,* 53–58.

Fingerman, K. L. (1995). Aging mothers' and their adult daughters' perceptions of conflict behaviors. *Psychology and Aging, 10,* 639–649.

Finkel, D., & McGue, M. (1993). The origins of individual differences in memory among the elderly: A behavior genetic analysis. *Psychology and Aging, 8,* 527–537.

Finkel, D., Pedersen, N., & McGue, M. (1995). Genetic influences on memory performance in adulthood: Comparison of Minnesota and Swedish twin data. *Psychology and Aging, 10,* 437–466.

Finkelhor, D., & Baron, L. (1986). High risk children. In D. Finkelhor (Ed.), *A sourcebook on child sexual abuse.* (pp. 60–88). Beverly Hills, CA: Sage.

Finkelson, L., & Oswalt, R. (1995). College data rape: incidence and reporting. *Psychological Reports, 77,* 526.

Finn, C. E. (1995, January). For whom it tolls. *Commentary, 99,* 76–81.

Finster, M., Pedersen, H., & Morishima, H. O. (1984). Principles of fetal exposure to drugs used in obstetric anesthesia. In B. Krauer, F. Krauer, F. E. Hytten, & E. del Pozo (Eds.), *Drugs and pregnancy,* (pp. 95–101) New York: Academic Press.

Firestone, W. A. (1994). The content and context of sexuality education: An exploratory study in one study. *Family Planning Perspectives, 26,* 125–131.

Fischer, K. W. (1980). A theory of cognitive development: The control and construction of hierarchies of skills. *Psychological Review, 87,* 477–531.

Fischer, K. W. (1987). Commentary-relations between brain and cognitive development. *Child Development, 58,* 623–633.

Fischer, K. W., & Silvern, L. (1985). Stages and individual differences in cognitive development. In M. R. Rosenzweig & L. W. Porter, *Annual Review of Psychology, 36,* 613–649.

Fish, W. C. (1986). Differences of grief intensity in bereaved parents. In T. A.

Rando (Ed.), *Parental loss of a child* (pp. 415–428). Champaign, IL: Research Press.

Fisher, C. B., & Lerner, R. M. (1994). Foundations of applied developmental psychology. In C. B. Fisher & R. M. Lerner (Eds.), *Applied Developmental Psychology,* New York: McGraw Hill, 3–23.

Fisher, C. B., & Tryon, W. W. (1988). Ethical issues in the research and practice of applied developmental psychology. *Journal of Applied Developmental Psychology, 9,* 27–39.

Fisher, J. A. & Birch, L. L. (1995). Fat preferences and fat consumption of 3- to-5-year-old children are related to parental adiposity. *Journal of the American Dietetic Association, 95,* 759–764.

Fisher, W. A., Fisher, J. D., & Rye, B. J. (1995). Understanding and promoting AIDS—Peventive behavior: Insights from the theory of reasoned action. *Health Psychology, 14,* 255–264.

Fiske, M., & Weiss, L. (1977). Intimacy and crises in adulthood. In N. K. Schlossberg & A. D. Entine, *Counseling adults* (pp. 19–34). Pacific Grove, CA: Brooks/Cole.

Fitch, S. A., & Adams, G. R. (1983). Ego identity and intimacy: Replication and extension. *Developmental Psychology, 19,* 839–845.

Fivush, R., Kuebli, J., & Clubb, P. A. (1992). The structure of events and event representations. A developmental analysis. *Child Development, 63,* 188–201.

Flaks, D. K., Ficher, I., Masterpasqua, F., & Joseph, G. (1995). Lesbians choosing motherhood: A comparative study of lesbian and heterosexual parents and their children. *Developmental Psychology, 31,* 105–115.

Flavell, J. H. (1985). *Cognitive development* (2nd ed.). Englewood Cliffs, NJ: Prentice Hall.

Flavell, J. H (1986). The development of children's knowledge about the apperance-reality distinction. *American Psychologist, 41,* 418–426.

Flavell, J. H. (1992). Cognitive development: Past, present and future. *Developmental Psychology, 28,* 998–1006.

Flavell, J. H., Beach, D. H., & Clinsky, J. M. (1966). Spontaneous verbal rehearsal in memory tasks as a function of age. *Child Development, 37,* 283–299.

Flavell, J. H., Flavell, E. R., & Green, F. L. (1983). Development of the appearance-reality distinction. *Cognitive Development, 15,* 95–120.

Flavell, J. H., Flavell, E. R., Green, F. L., & Wilcox, S. A. (1981). The development of three spatial perspective-taking rules. *Child Development, 52,* 356–358.

Flavell, J. H., Friedrichs, A. G., & Hoyt, J. D. (1970). Developmental changes in memorization processes. *Cognitive Psychology, 1,* 324–340.

Flavell, J. H., Miller, P. H., & Miller, S. A. (1993). *Cognitive development* (3rd ed.). Englewood Cliffs, NJ: Prentice Hall.

Flavell, J. H., Mumme, D. L., Green, F. L., & Flavell, E. R. (1992). Young children's understanding of different types of beliefs. *Child Development, 63,* 960–978.

Flavell, J. H., & Wellman, H. M. (1977). Metamemory. In R. V. Kail & J. W. Hagen (Eds.), *Perspectives on the development of memory and cognition.* Hillsdale, NJ: Erlbaum.

Flavell, J. H., & Wohlwill, J. F. (1969). Formal and functional aspects of cognitive development. In D. Elkind & J. H. Flavell (Eds.), *Studies in cognitive development* (pp. 67–120). New York: Oxford University Press.

Flax, E. (1987, June 24). Koop warns of an explosion of AIDS among teenagers. *Education Week 3.*

Fleck, K. M. (1995, November). Easing into elementary school. *The Education Digest, 74,* 25–27.

Fletcher, A. C., Darling, N. E., Steinberg, L., & Dornbusch, S. M., (1995). The company they keep: Relation of adolescents' adjustment and behavior to their friends' perceptions of authoritative parenting in the social network. *Developmental Psychology, 31,* 300–310.

Fletcher, W. L., & Hansson, R. L. (1991). Assessing the social components of retirement anxiety. *Psychology and Aging, 6,* 76–85.

Flowers, B. J., & Eisen, M. (1994). Cardiac change scale: A brief, self-report research measure. *Current Psychology, 13,* 185–193.

Floyd, F. J., Haynes, S. N., Doll, E. R., Winemiller, D., Lemsky, C., Burgy, T. M., Werle, M., & Heilman, N. (1992). Assessing retirement satisfaction and perceptions of retirement experiences. *Psychology and Aging, 7,* 609–621.

Floyd, M. & Scogin, F. (1997). Effects of memory training on the subjective memory functioning and mental health of older adults: A meta-analysis. *Psychology and Aging, 12,* 150–161.

Floyd, R. L., Rimer, B. K. Giovino, G. A., Mullen, P. D., & Sullivan, S. E. (1993). A review of smoking in pregnancy: Effects on pregnancy outcomes and cessation efforts. *Annual Review of Public Health, 14,* 379–411.

Flum, H. (1994). Styles of identity formation in early and middle adolescence. *Genetic, Social, and General Psychology Monographs, 120,* 435–467.

Flynn, C. P. (1990). Relationship violence by women: Issues and implications. *Family Relations, 39,* 194–198.

Fogel, A., Nwokah, E., & Karns, J. (1993) Parent-infant games as dynamic social systems. In K. MacDonald (Ed.), *Parent-child play.* Albany, NY: SUNY Press.

Fomon, S. J. (1993). *Nutrition of normal infants.* St. Louis, MO: Mosby.

Fonagy, P., Steele, H., & Steele, M. (1991). Maternal representations of attachment during pregnancy predict the organization of infant-mother attachment at one year of age. *Child Development, 62,* 891–905.

Foner, A., & Schwab, K. (1981). *Aging and retirement.* Pacific Grove, CA: Brooks/Cole.

Foner, N. (1994). Nursing home aides: Saints or monsters. *The Gerontologist, 34,* 245–250.

Fonteyn, V. J., & Isada, N. B. (1988). Non-genetic implications of childbearing after age thirty-five. *Obstetrical and Gynecological Survey, 43,* 709–719.

Footlick, J. K. (1990). What happened to the family? *Newsweek,* pp. 14–18.

Forbes, D. (1987). Saying no to Ron and Nancy: School-based drug abuse prevention Program in the 1980s. *Journal of Education, 169,* 80–90.

Ford, D. Y., & Harris, J. J. III. (1996). Perceptions and attitudes of black students toward school, achievement, and other educational variables. *Child Development, 67,* 1141–1152.

Ford, K. & Labbok, M. (1990). Who is breastfeeding? *American Journal of Clinical Nutrition, 52,* 451–456.

Ford, M. E. (1979). The construct validity of egocentrism. *Psychological Bulletin, 86,* 1169–1188.

Forgatch, M. S., Patterson, G. R., & Skinner, M. L. (1988). A mediational model for the effect of divorce on antisocial behavior in boys. In E. M. Hetherington & J. D. Arasteh (Eds.), *Impact of divorce, single parenting, and stepparenting on children* (pp. 135–155). Hillsdale, NJ: Erlbaum.

Forness, S. R., & Kavale, K. A. (1988). Psychopharmacological treatment: A note on classroom effects. *Journal of Learning Disabilities, 21,* 144–147.

Foscarinis, M. (1991). The politics of homelessness: A call to action. *American Psychologist, 46,* 1232–1238.

Fowler, B. A. (1989). The relationship of body image perception and weight status to recent change in weight status of the adolescent female. *Adolescence, 24,* 557–567.

Fowler, M. (1991, September). *Attention deficit disorder.* Washington, DC: National Information Center for Children and Youth with Disabilities.

Fox, M. (1991, January 18). *New York Law Journal,* pp. 1, 4.

Fox, M., Gibbs, M., & Auerbach, D. (1985). Age and gender dimensions of friendship. *Psychology and Women Quarterly, 9,* 489–501.

Fox, N. A., Kimmerly, N. L., & Schafer, W. D. (1991). Attachment to mother/attachment to father: A meta-analysis. *Child Development, 62,* 210–225.

Fox, V. (1985). *Introduction to criminology* (2nd ed.). Englewood Cliffs, NJ: Prentice Hall.

Fozard, J. L. (1990). Vision and hearing in aging. In J. E. Birren & K. W. Schaie (Eds.), *Handbook of the psychology of aging* (3rd ed.) (pp. 150–171). New York: Academic Press.

Fozard, J. L., Vercruyssen, M., Reynolds, S. L., Hancock, P. A., & Quilter, R. E. (1994). Age differences and changes in reaction time: The Baltimore Longitudinal Study of aging. *Journal of Gerontology, 49,* pp. 179–189.

Francese, P. (1993, October). The trend evolution. *American Demographics,* p. 2.

Francis, H. (1975). *Language in childhood: Form and function in language development.* New York: St. Martin's Press.

Francis, P. L., Self, P. A., & Horowitz, F. D. (1987). The behavioral assessment of the neonate: An overview. In J. D. Osofsky (Ed.), *Handbook of infant development,* (pp. 723–780). New York: Wiley.

Frank, R. G. (1993). Health-care reform: An introduction. *American Psychologist, 48,* 258–260.

Frank, R. G., Sullivan, M. J., & DeLeon, P. H. (1994). Health care reform in the states. *American Psychologist, 49,* 855–867.

Frank, R. G., & VandenBos, G. R. (1994). Health care reform: The 1993–1994 evolution. *American Psychologist, 49,* 851–854.

Frank, S. J., Jacobson, S., & Tuer, M. (1990). Psychological predictors of young adults' drinking behaviors. *Journal of Personality and Social Psychology, 59,* 770–780.

Frankel, A. J. (1994). Family day care in the United States. *Families in Society: The Journal of Contemporary Human Services, 75,* 550–560.

Frankel, K. A. & Bates, J. E. (1990). Mother-toddler problem solving: Antecedents in attachment, home behavior, and temperament. *Child Development, 61,* 810–820.

Franklin, D. L., Smith, S. E., & McMiller, E. P. (1995). Correlates of marital status among African American mothers in Chicago neighborhoods of concentrated poverty. *Journal of Marriage and the Family, 57,* 141–153.

Franklin, M. E. (1992). Culturally sensitive instructional practices for African-American learners. *Exceptional Children, 59,* 115–123.

Fraser, A. M., Brockert, J. E., & Ward, R. H. (1995). Association of young maternal age with adverse reproductive outcomes. *New England Journal of Medicine, 332,* 113–117.

Frede, E. C. (1995). The role of program quality in producing early childhood program benefits. *The Future of Children, 5,* 115–133.

Fredrickson, B. L., & Carstensen, L. L. (1990). Choosing social partners: How old age and anticipated endings make people more selective. *Psychology and Aging, 5,* 335–347.

Freedman, S. G. (1986, December 2). New focus placed on young unwed fathers. *New York Times,* p. 1.

Freiberg, P. (1996, September). Latchkey kids not always trouble-prone. *APA Monitor,* p. 48.

Freidrich, L. K., & Stein, A. H. (1975). Prosocial television and young children: the effects of verbal labeling and role playing on learning and behavior. *Child Development, 46,* 27–38.

French, S. A., Perry, C. L., Leon, G. R., & Fulkerson, J. A. (1995). Dieting behaviors and weight change history in female adolescents. *Health Psychology, 14,* 548–555.

Fresco, R. (1995, March 13). Gaps widen for minorities in college. *Newsday,* p. A6.

Freud, S. (1900). The interpretation of dreams. In J. J. Strachey (Ed.), *The standard edition of the complete psychological works of Sigmund Freud* Vol. 4. London: Hogarth Press.

Freud, S. (1923). *The ego and the id.* New York: Norton.

Freud, S. (1925, 1953). *Three essays on the theory of sexuality.* London: Hogarth.

Freud, S. (1933). *New Introductory lectures on psychoanalysis.* New York: Norton.

Freud, S. (1933/1961). *New introductory lectures on psychoanalysis.* New York: Norton.

Freud, S. (1935). *A General introduction to psychoanalysis.* New York: Doubleday.

Freud, S. (1949). *An outline of psychoanalysis.* New York: Norton (originally published 1940).

Freud, S. A. (1953). *General introduction to psychoanalysis.* New York: Doubleday (originally published 1935).

Freud, S. (1957). The interpretation of dreams. In J. Strachey (Ed.), *The standard edition of the complete psychological works of Sigmund Freud,* Vol. 4. London: Hogarth (originally published 1900).

Freud, S. (1961). *New introductory lectures on psychoanalysis.* New York: Norton (originally published 1933).

Freud, S. (1962). *The ego and the id.* New York: Norton (originally published 1923).

Frey, K. S., & Ruble, D. N. (1992). Gender constancy and the "cost" of sex-typed behavior: A test of conflict hypothesis. *Developmental Psychology, 28,* 714–721.

Friedman, S., & Carpenter, G. C. (1971). Visual response decrement as a function of age of human newborn. *Child Development, 42,* 1967–1973.

Friedrich, L. K., & Stein, A. H. (1975). Prosocial television and young children. The effects of verbal labeling and role playing on learning and behavior. *Child Development, 46,* 27–38.

Friedrich, W. N., & Boriskin, J. A. (1976). The role of the child in abuse: A review of the literature. *American Journal of Orthopsychiatry, 46,* 580–591.

Friend, T. (1994, November 1). Genes may cause manic depression. *USA Today,* p. 1D.

Friend, T. (1994, October 11). DNA test to spot cancer early. *USA Today,* p. D1.

Friend, T. (1996, May 24-27). Teen smoking rate highest since 1970s. *USA Today,* p. A1.

Fries, J. A., & Crapo, L. M. (1981). *Vitality and aging: Implications of the rectangular curve.* San Francisco: Freeman.

Froming, W. J., Allen, L., & Jensen, R. (1985). Altruism, role-taking, and self-awareness: The acquisition of norms governing altruistic behavior. *Child Development, 56,* 1223–1228.

Frost, J. J., & Forrest, J. D. (1995). Understanding the impact of effective teenage pregnancy prevention programs. *Family Planning Perspectives, 27,* 188–195.

Fry, C. L. (1985). Culture, behavior, and aging in the comparative perspective. In J. E. Birren & K. W. Schaie (Eds.), *Handbook of the psychology of aging* (2nd ed.) (pp. 216–245). New York: Van Nostrand Reinhold.

Fuligni, A. J., & Eccles, J. S. (1993). Perceived parent-child relationships and early adolescents' orientation toward peers. *Developmental Psychology, 29,* 622–632.

Fuligni, A. J. & Stevenson, H. W. (1995). Time use and mathematics achievement among American, Chinese, and Japanese high school students. *Child Development, 66,* 830–842.

Fulkerson, K. F., Furr, S., & Brown, D. (1983). Expectations and achievement among third-, sixth-, and ninth-grade black and white males and females. *Developmental Psychology, 19,* 231–236.

Furman, L. N., & Walden, T. A. (1990). Effect of script knowledge on preschool children's communicative interactions. *Developmental Psychology, 26,* 227–233.

Furman, W. (1996). Parenting siblings. In M. H. Bornstein (Ed.), *Handbook of parenting* Vol. 1, pp. 143–162. Mahway, NJ: Erlbaum.

Furman, W. & Bierman, K. L. (1983). Developmental changes in young children's conception of friendship. *Child Development, 54,* 549–556.

Furman, W., & Buhrmester, D. (1992). Age and sex differences in perceptions of networks of personal relationships. *Child Development, 63,* 103–115.

Furstenberg, F., Jr. (1976). The social consequences of teenage parenthood. *Family Planning Perspectives. 8,* 148–164.

Furstenberg, F. F. (1981). Implicating the family: Teenage parenthood and kinship involvements. In T. Ooms (Ed.), *Teenage pregnancy in a family context: Implications for policy* (pp. 131–165). Philadelphia: Temple University Press.

Furstenberg, F. F. (1982). Conjugal succession: Reentering marriage and divorce. In P. B. Baltes & O. G. Brim, *Life-span development and behavior* (Vol. 4, pp. 107–146). New York: Academic Press.

Furstenberg, F. F. (1987). The new extended family: The experience of parents and children after remarriage. In K. Pasley & M. Ihinger-Talman, (Eds.), *Remarriage and stepparenting* (pp. 42–61). New York: Guilford Press.

Furstenberg, F. F., Brooks-Gunn, J., & Chase-Lansdale, L. (1989). Teenaged pregnancy and childbearing. *American Psychologist, 44,* 313–320.

Furstenberg, F. F., & Spanier, G. (1987). *Recycling the family: Remarriage after divorce* (Rev. ed.). Beverly Hills, CA: Sage.

Futterman, D., & Hein, K. (1994). Medical management of adolescents with HIV infection. In P. A. Pizzo & C. M. Wilfert (Eds.). *Pediatric AIDS: The challenge of HIV infection in infants, children, and adolescents* (2nd ed., pp. 757–772) Baltimore: Williams & Wilkins.

Gable, D. (1994, May 10). Reality-based violence hits harder. *USA Today,* p. 3D.

Gadberry, S. (1980). Effects of restricting first graders' TV-viewing on leisure time use, IQ change, and cognitive style. *Journal of Applied Developmental Psychology, 1,* 45–57.

Gadow, K. D. (1983). Effects of stimulant drugs on academic hyperactive and learning disabled children. *Journal of Learning Disabilities, 16,* 290–299.

Galambos, N. L., Almeida, D. M., & Petersen, A. C. (1990). Masculinity, femininity, and sex role attitudes in early adolescence: Exploring gender intensification. *Child Development, 61,* 1905–1914.

Galef, B. G., Jr. (1991). A contrarian view of the wisdom of the body as it relates to dietary self-selection. *Psychology Review, 98,* 759–764.

Galinsky, A. S., & Judd, B. B. (1994). Working memory and bias in reasoning across the life-span. *Psychology and Aging, 9,* 356–371.

Gallimore, R., Weiss, L., & Finney, R. (1974). Cultural differences in delay of gratification: A problem of behavior classification. *Journal of Personality and Social Psychology, 30,* 72–80.

Gallup, G. H. Jr., & Castelli, J. (1989). *The people's religion: American faith in the 90s.* New York: Macmillan.

Galotti, K. M. (1989). Gender differences in self-reported moral reasoning: A review and new evidence. *Journal of Youth and Adolescence, 18,* 475–487.

Ganong, L., & Coleman, M. (1994). *Remarried family relationships,* Newbury Park, CA: Sage Publications.

Garbarino, J. (1982). Sociocultural risk: Dangers to competence. In C. B. Kopp & J. B. Krakow (Eds.), *The child: Development in a social context,* (pp. 630–686). Reading, MA: Addison-Wesley.

Garbarino, J., Guttman, E., & Seeley, J. (1986). *The psychologically battered child: Strategies for identification, assessment, and intervention.* San Francisco: Jossey-Bass.

Garbarino, J., & Kostelny, K. (1996). The effects of political violence on Palestinian children's behavior problems: A risk accumulation model. *Child Development, 67,* 33–46.

Garcia, J., & Pugh, S. L. (1992, November). Multicultural education in teacher preparation programs. *Phi Delta Kappan,* 214–219.

Garcia Coll, C. T., Meyer, E. C., & Brillon, L. (1995). Ethnic and minority parenting. In M. H. Bornstein (Ed.), *Handbook of parenting* (Vol. 2., pp. 189–209). Mahwah, NJ: Erlbaum.

Garcia-Coll, C., Hoffman, J., & Oh., W. (1987). The social ecology of early parenting of Caucasian adolescent mothers. *Child Development, 58,* 955–964.

Garcia-Coll, C., Kagan, J., & Reznick, J. S. (1984). Behavioral inhibition in young children. *Child Development, 55,* 1005–1019.

Gardner, H. (1983). *Frames of mind.* New York: Basic Books.

Gardner, H. (1987). Beyond the IQ: Education and human development. *Harvard Educational Review, 57,* 187–193.

Gardner, H. (1993). *Multiple intelligences: The theory in practice.* New York: Basic Books.

Gargiulo, J., Attie, I., Brooks-Gunn, J., & Warren, M. P. (1987). Girls' dating behavior as a function of social context and maturation. *Developmental Psychology, 23,* 730–737.

Garland, A. F., & Zigler, E. (1993). Adolescent suicide prevention: Current research and social policy implications. *American Psychologist, 48,* 169–182.

Garn, S. M. (1980). Continuities and change in maturational timing. In O. G. Brim, Jr. & J. Kagan (Eds.), *Constancy and change in human development* (pp. 113–162). Cambridge, MA: Harvard University Press.

Garner, D. M., Fairburn, C. G., & Davis, R. (1987). Cognitive behavioral treatment for bulimia nervosa: A critical appraisal. *Behavioral Medicine, 11,* 398–431.

Garnica, O. K. (1977). Some prosodic and paralinguistic features of speech directed to young children. In C. E. Snow & C. A. Ferguson (Eds.), *Talking to children: Language input and acquisition.* Cambridge: Cambridge University Press.

Garrity, T. F., Kotchen, J. M., McKean, H. E., Gurley, D., & McFadden, M. (1990). The association between type A behavior and changes in coronary risk factors among young adults. *American Journal of Public Health, 80,* 1354–1357.

Gasner, D. & McCleary, E. H. (1982). *The American Medical Association's book of heart care.* New York: Random House.

Gates, H. L. (1994, November 7). Don't blame Darwin. *New Republic, 211,* 10–13.

Gatz, M., & Hurwicz, M. L. (1990). Are old

people more depressed? Cross-sectional data on center for epidemiological studies depression scale factors. *Psychology and Aging, 5,* 284–290.

Gatz, M., Smyer, M. A., & Lawton, M. P. (1980). The mental health system and the older adult. In L. W. Poon (Ed.), *Aging in the 1980s* (pp. 5–19). Washington, DC: American Psychological Association.

Gavin, L. A., & Furman, W. (1989). Age differences in adolescents' perceptions of their peer groups. *Developmental Psychology, 25,* 827–834.

Gaylord-Ross, R. J., Forte, J., Storey, K., Gaylord-Ross, C., & Jameson, D. (1987). Community-referenced instruction in technological work settings. *Exceptional Children, 54,* 112–120.

Ge, X., Lorenz, F. O., Conger, R. D., Elder, G. H., Jr., & Simons, R. L. (1994). Trajectories of stressful life events and depressive symptoms during adolescence. *Developmental Psychology, 30,* 467–483.

Gebhardt, D. L., & Crump, C. E. (1990). Employee fitness and wellness programs in the workplace. *American Psychologist, 45,* 262–272.

Gecas, V., & Seff, M. (1990). Families and adolescents: A review of the 1980s. *Journal of Marriage and the Family, 52,* 467–483.

Gelles, R., & Harrop, J. W. (1989). Violence, battering, and psychological distress among women. *Journal of Interpersonal Violence, 4,* 400–420.

Gelles, R. J. (1978). Violence toward children in the United States. *American Journal of Orthopsychiatry, 48,* 580–592.

Gelles, R. J. (1980). Violence in the family: A review of research in the family. *Journal of Marriage and the Family, 42,* 873–885.

Gelles R. J. (1987). *Family violence.* Newbury Park, CA: Sage.

Gelles, R. J. (1989). Child abuse and violence in single parent families: Parent absence and economic deprivation. *American Journal of Orthopsychiatry, 59,* 492–501.

Gelles, R. J. (1994). Research and advocacy: Can one wear two hats? *Family Process, 33,* 93–96.

Gelles, R. J., & Conte, J. R. (1990). Domestic violence and sexual abuse of children: A review of research in the eighties. *Journal of Marriage and the Family, 52,* 1045–1058.

Gelman, D., Foote, D., Barrett, T., & Talbot, M. (1992, February 24) Born or bred? *Newsweek,* 46–53.

Gelman, R. (1969). Conservation acquisition: A problem of learning to attend to relevant attributes. *Journal of Experimental Child Psychology, 7,* 167–187.

Gelman, R., & Baillargeon, R. A. (1983). A review of some Piagetian concepts. In P. H. Mussen (Ed.), *Handbook of child psychology* (4th ed.) (Vol. 3, pp. 167–231). New York: Wiley.

Gelman, R., Spelke, E., & Meck, E. (1983). What preschoolers know about animate and inanimate objects. In D. Rogers & J. Sloboda (Eds.). *The Acquisition of Symbolic Skills* (pp. 232–252). New York: Plenum.

Genevie, L., & Margolies, E. (1987). *The motherhood report: How women feel about being mothers.* New York: Macmillan.

Gentry, M., & Shulman, A. D. (1988). Remarriage as a coping response for widowhood. *Psychology and Aging, 3,* 191–196.

George, L. K. (1990). Social structure, social processes, and social-psychological states. In R. H. Binstock & L. K. George (Eds.), *Handbook of aging and the social sciences* (3rd ed.) (pp. 186–200). New York: Academic Press.

George, L. K. (1996). Social factors and illness. In R. H. Binstock & L. K. George (Eds.), *Handbook of Aging and the Social Sciences* (4th ed., pp. 229–248). San Diego: Academic Press.

Gerber, P. J., Ginsberg, R., & Reiff, H. B. (1992). Identifying alterable patterns in employment success for highly successful adults with learning disabilities. *Journal of Learning Disabilities, 25,* 475–487.

Gerber, P. J., Schneider, C. A., Paradise, L. V., Reiff, H. B., Ginsberg, R. J., & Popp, P. A. (1990). Persisting problems of adults with learning disabilities: Self-reported comparisons from their school-age and adult years. *Journal of Learning Disabilities, 23,* 569–573.

Gerbner, G., & Gross, L. (1980). The violent face of television and its lessons. In E. L. Palmer & A. Dorr (Eds.), *Children and the faces of television: Teaching, violence, selling* (pp. 149–162). New York: Academic Press.

Gerstein, R., & Woodward, J. (1994). The language-minority student and special education: Issues, trends and paradoxes. *Exceptional Children, 61,* 310–322.

Gesser, G., Wong, P. T., & Reker, G. T. (1987/1988). Death attitudes across the life-span: The development and validation of the death attitude profile (DAP) *Omega, 18,* 113–118.

Gesser, G., Wong, P. T. P., & Reker, G. T. (1988). Death attitudes across the life-span: The development and validation of the death attitude profile. *Omega, 2,* 113–128.

Gewirtzman, R., & Fodor, I. (1987). The homeless child at school: From welfare hotel to classroom. *Child Welfare, 66,* 237–245.

Giambra, L. M., Arenberg, D., Zonderman, A. B., Kawas, C. & Costa, P. T., Jr. (1995). Adult life span changes in immediate visual memory and verbal intelligence. *Psychology and Aging, 10,* 123–129.

Gibbs, J. T., & Huang, L. N. (1989). A conceptual framework for assessing and treating minority youth. In Children of color: Psychological interventions with minority youth (pp. 1–30). San Francisco: Jossey-Bass.

Gibbs, N. (1989, April 24). How America has run out of time. *Time,* pp. 58–62+.

Gibbs, N. (1991, November 4). Dr. Death strikes again. *Time,* p. 78.

Gibson, C. (1993, November). The four baby booms. *American Demographics,* 36–40.

Gibson, E. J., & Walk, R. D. (1960, April). The "visual cliff." *Scientific American.* pp. 64–71.

Gifted and Talented Children's Act of 1978: PL95–562, Section 902.

Gil, D. G. (1970). *Violence against children: Physical child abuse in the United States.* Cambridge, MA: Harvard University Press.

Gilbert, S. (1995, November 22). Study finds doctors refuse patients' requests on death. *The New York Times,* pp. A1, C7.

Giles-Sims, J., & Crosbie-Burnett, M. (1989). Stepfamily research: Implications for policy, clinical interventions, and further research. *Family Relations, 38,* 19–23.

Gilligan, C. (1982). *In a different voice.* Cambridge, MA: Harvard University Press.

Gilligan, C. (1988). Exit-voice dilemmas in adolescent development. In C. Gilligan, J. V. Ward, J. M. Taylor, & B. Bardige (Eds.), *Mapping the moral domain.* Cambridge, MA: Harvard University Press.

Gilligan, C., Brown, L. M., & Rogers, A. G. (1990). Psyche embedded: A place for body, relationships, and culture in personality theory. In A. I. Rabin, R. A. Zuker, R. A. Emmons, & S. Frank (Eds.). *Studying persons and lives.* New York: Springer.

Gilligan, C., Murphy, J. M., & Tappan, M. B. (1990). Moral development beyond adolescence. In C. N. Alexander & E. J. Langer (Eds.), *Higher stages of human development* (pp. 208–229). New York: Oxford University Press.

Ginott, H. G. (1969). *Between parent and teenager.* New York: Macmillan.

Ginsburg, G. S., & Bronstein, P. (1993). Family factors related to children's intrinsic/extrinsic motivational orientation and academic performance. *Child Development, 64,* 1461–1474.

Glaser, R., Rice, J., Sheridan, J., Fertel, R., Stout, J., Speicher, C. E., Pinsky, D., Kotur, M., Post, A., Beck, M., & Kiecolt-Glaser, J. K. (1987). Stress-related immune suppression: Health implications. *Brain, Behavior and Immunity, 1,* 7–20.

Glazer, S. (1994, May 13). Women's health issues. *CQ Researcher, 4,* 409–429.

Gleason, J. B. (1985). *The development of language.* Columbus, OH: Merrill.

Glenn, N. D. (1975). Psychological well-being in the post-parental stage: Some evidence from national surveys. *Journal of Marriage and the Family, 32,* 105–110.

Glenn, N. D. (1980). Values, attitudes, and beliefs. In O. G. Brim & J. Kagan (Eds.), *Constancy and change in human development* (pp. 596–641). Cambridge, MA: Harvard University Press.

Glenn, N. D. (1990). Quantitative research on marital quality in the 1980s: A critical review. *Journal of Marriage and the Family, 52,* 818–831.

Glenn, N. D., & Weaver, C. N. (1985). Cohort, and reported job satisfaction in the United States. In Z. S. Blau (Ed.). *Current perspectives on aging and the life cycle* (Vol. 1, pp. 89–111). Greenwich, CT: Jai Press.

Glick, P. C. (1984). How American families are changing. *American Demographics, 6,* 20–25.

Go, C. G., Brustrom, J. E., Lynch, M. F., & Aldwin, C. M. (1995). Ethnic trends in survival curves and mortality. *The Gerontologist, 35,* 318–326.

Goble, F. C., & Konopka, E. A. (1973). Sex as a factor in infectious disease. *Transactions of the New York Academy of Science, 35,* 325.

Goertzel, V., & Goertzel, M. G. (1962). *Cradles of eminence.* Boston: Little, Brown.

Golambos, N. L., & Maggs, J. L. (1991). Out-of-school care of young adolescents and self-reported behavior. *Developmental Psychology, 27,* 644–655.

Golan, N. (1986). *The perilous bridge: Helping clients through midlife transitons.* New York: Free Press.

Golant, S. M., & LaGreca, A. J. (1994). Housing quality of U.S. elderly households: Does aging in place matter? *The Gerontologist, 34,* 803–813.

Goldenberg, R. L., Tamura, T., Neggers, Y., Cooper, R. L., Johnston, K. E., DuBard, M. B., & Hauth, J. C. (1995). The effect of zinc supplementation on pregnancy outcome. *JAMA, 274,* 463–468.

Goldfield, B. A. (1990). Pointing, naming, and talk about objects: Referential behaviour in children and mothers. *First Language, 10,* 231–242.

Goldfield, B. A., & Reznick, J. S. (1989). Early lexical acquisition: Rate, content, and the vocabulary spurt. *Journal of Child Language, 17,* 171–183.

Goldman, G., Pineault, R., Potvin, L., Blais, R., & Bilodueau, H. (1993). Factors influencing the practice of vaginal birth after cesarean section. *American Journal of Public Health, 83,* 1104–1131.

Goldsmith, H. H. & Alansky, J. A. (1987). Maternal and infant temperamental predictors of attachment: A meta-analytic review. *Journal of Consulting and Clinical Psychology, 55,* 805–816.

Goldsmith, H. H. et al. (1987). What is temperament? Four approaches. *Child Development, 58,* 505–530.

Goleman, D. (1985, April 16). Marriage: Research reveals ingredients of happiness. *New York Times,* pp. C1, C4.

Goleman, D. (1989, June 6). New research overturns a milestone of infancy. *New York Times,* p. C1+.

Goleman, D. (1995). *Emotional intelligence: Why it can matter more than IQ.* New York: Bantam.

Goleman, D. G. (1986a, October 21). Child development theory stresses small moments. *New York Times,* pp. C1, C3.

Golombok, S., & Tasker, F. (1996). Do parents influence the sexual orientation of their children? Findings from a longitudinal study of lesbian families. *Developmental Psychology, 32,* 3–12.

Gomby, D. S., Larner, M. B., Stevenson, C. S., Lewit, E. M., & Behrman, R. E. (1995). Long-term outcomes of early childhood programs: Analysis and recommendations. *The Future of Children, 5,* 6–25.

Gong, V. (1985). Signs and symptoms of AIDS. In V. Gong (Ed.), *Understanding AIDS* (pp. 36–40). New Brunswick, NJ: Rutgers University Press.

Gonzalez-Mena, J. (1986). Toddlers: What to expect. *Young Children, 42,* 85–90.

Good, T. L., Sikes, J. N., & Brophy, J. E. (1973). Effects of teacher sex and student sex in classroom interaction. *Journal of Educational Psychology, 65,* 74–87.

Goode, E. E. (1994, January 11). The secret world of siblings. *U.S. News and World Report,* 45–50.

Goodluck, H. (1986). Language acquisition and linguistic theory. In P. Fletcher & M. Garman (Eds.), *Language acquisition* (2nd ed.) (pp. 49–69). London: Cambridge University Press.

Goodstadt, M. S. (1987, February). School-based drug education: What is wrong? *Education Digest,* pp. 44–47.

Goossens, F. A. & Ijzendoorn, M. H. (1990). Quality of infants' attachments to professional caregivers: Relation to infant-parent attachment and day-care characteristics. *Child Development, 61,* 832–837.

Gopnik, A., & Astington, J. W. (1988). Children's understanding of representational change and its relation to the understanding of false belief and the appearance-reality distinction. *Child Development, 59,* 26–37.

Gopnick, A., & Meltzoff, A. (1987). The development of categorization in the second year and its relation to other cognitive and linguistic developments. *Child Development, 58,* 1523–1531.

Gordis, E., Tabakoff, B., Goldman, D., & Berg, K. (1990). Finding the gene(s) for alcoholism. *Journal of the American Medical Association, 263,* 2094–2095.

Gordon, C., & Gaitz, C. M. (1983). Leisure activities late in the life span. In J. E. Birren et al. (Eds.), *Aging: A challenge to science and society* (Vol. 3, pp. 169–186). New York: Oxford University Press.

Gordon, P. (1990). Learnability and feedback. *Developmental Psychology, 26,* 217–221.

Gorsuch, R. L. (1988). Psychology of religion. *Annual Review of Psychology, 39,* 201–221.

Gorsuch, R. L. (1995). Religious aspects of substance abuse and recovery. *Journal of Social Issues, 51,* 65–83.

Gottesman, I. L, & Shields, J. (1982). *Schizophrenia: The epigenetic puzzle.* Cambridge, UK: Cambridge University Press.

Gottfried, A. E., Bathurst, K. & Gottfried, A. W. (1994). Role of maternal and dual-earner employment status in children's development: A longitudinal study from infancy through early adolescence. In A. E. Gottfried & A. W. Gottfried (Eds.). *Redefining families: Implications for children's development* (pp. 55–97). New York: Plenum.

Gottfried, A. E., Gottfried, A. W., &

Bathurst, K. (1988). Maternal employment, family environment, and children's development: Infancy through the school years. In A. E. Gottfried & A. W. Gottfried (Eds.), *Maternal employment and children's development: Longitudinal research* (pp. 11–58). New York: Plenum.

Gottfried, A. E., Gottfried, A. W., & Bathurst, K. (1995). Maternal and dual-earner employment status and parenting. In M. H. Bornstein (Ed.), *Handbook of Parenting* (Vol. 2, pp. 139–160).

Gottlieb, G., (1991). Experiential canalization of behavioral development: Theory. *Developmental Psychology, 27,* 4–14.

Gould, R. L. (1975, February). Adult life stages: Growth toward self-tolerance. *Psychology Today,* pp. 74–78.

Gould, R. L. (1978). *Transformations: Growth and change in adult life.* New York: Simon & Schuster.

Graber, J. A., Brooks-Gunn, J., Paikoff, R. L., & Warren, M. P. (1994). Prediction of eating problems: An 8-year study of adolescent girls. *Developmental Psychology, 30,* 823–834.

Graham, J. (1994, January 28). TV executives lash out at violence study. *USA Today,* p. 1D.

Graham, J. W., Marks, G., & Hansen, W. B. (1991). Social influence processes affecting adolescent substance use. *Journal of Applied Psychology, 76,* 291–298.

Granick, S., & Patterson, R. D. (1971). *Human aging, 2: Age 11–up, follow-up biomedical and behavioral study.* Publ. No. (HSM) 71–9037. Rockville, MD: Public Health Service.

Grant, C. L., & Fodor, I. G. (1986). Adolescent attitudes toward body image and anorexic behavior. *Adolescence, 21,* 269–281.

Grant, J. P. (1988). *The state of the world's children,* 1988. New York: Published for UNICEF by Oxford University Press.

Grant, L., Simpson, L. A., Rong, X. L., & Peters-Golden, H. (1990). Gender, parenthood, and work hours of physicians. *Journal of Marriage and the Family, 52,* 39–49.

Gratch, G. (1979). The development of thought and language in infancy. In J. Osofsky (Ed.), *Handbook of infant development* (pp. 439–461). New York: Wiley.

Gray, E., & Coolsen, P. (1987, July/August). How do kids really feel about being home alone? *Children Today,* pp. 30–32.

Greaney, V. (1980). Factors related to amount and type of leisure time reading. *Reading Research Quarterly, 15,* 337–357.

Green, A. H., Gaines, R. W., & Sandgrund, A. (1974). Child abuse: Pathological syndrome of family reaction. *American Journal of Psychiatry, 131,* 882–886.

Green, R. (1978). Sexual identity of 37 children raised by homosexual or transsexual parents. *American Journal of Psychiatry, 135,* 692–697.

Green, R. (1982). The best interests of the child with lesbian mother. *Bulletin of the American Academy of Psychiatry and the Law, 10,* 7–15.

Green, R. (1987). *The "sissy boy" syndrome and the development of homosexuality.* New Haven, CT: Yale University Press.

Greenberg, J. S., Bruess, C. E., Mullen, K. D., & Sands, D. W. (1989). *Sexuality: Insights and issues.* Dubuque, IA: Brown.

Greenberger, E., & O'Neil, R. (1993). Spouse, parent, worker: Role commitments and role-related experiences in the construction of adults' well being. *Developmental Psychology, 29,* 181–197.

Greenberger, E., O'Neil, R. O., & Nagel, S. K. (1994). Linking workplace and homeplace: Relations between the nature of adults' work and their parenting behaviors. *Developmental Psychology, 20,* 990–1004.

Greendlinger, V., & Byrne, D (1987). Coercive sexual fantasies of college men as predictors of self-reported likelihood of rape and overt sexual aggression. *The Journal of Sex Research, 23,* 1–11.

Greene, S. (1994). Reactivity in infants: A cross-national comparison. *Developmental Psychology, 30,* 342–345.

Greenough, W. T., Black, J. E., & Wallace, C. S. (1987). Experience and brain development. *Child Development, 58,* 539–560.

Greenstein, T. H. (1995). Gender ideology, marital disruption, and the employment of married women. *Journal of Marriage and the Family, 57,* 31–42.

Griffen, J. (1977). A cross-cultural investigation of behavioral changes at menopause. *Social Science Journal, 14,* 49–55.

Griffith, D. R., (1992, September). Prenatal exposure to cocaine and other drugs: Developmental and educational prognoses. *Phi Delta Kappan,* 30–34.

Griffiths, M. D. (1991). Amusement machine playing in childhood and adolescents: A comparative analysis of video games and machines. *Adolescence, 14,* 53–73.

Griffiths, P. (1986). Early Vocabulary. In P. Fletcher & M. Garman (Eds.). *Language acquisition* (2nd ed.) (pp. 279–307). London: Cambridge University Press.

Grigsby, J. S. (1991). Paths for future population aging. *Gerontologist, 31,* 195–203.

Grossman, K. E., & Grossman K. (1990). The wider concept of attachment in cross-cultural research. *Human Development, 33,* 31–47.

Grotevant, H. D. (1987). Toward a process model of identity formation. *Journal of Adolescent Research, 2,* 203–222.

Grotevant, H. D., & Cooper, C. R. (1985). Patterns of interaction in family relationships and the development of identity exploration in adolescence. *Child Development, 56,* 415–428.

Grotevant, H. D., & Cooper, C. R. (1986). Individuation in family relationships. *Human Development, 29,* 82–100.

Grundy, S. M. (1986). Cholesterol and coronary heart disease: A new era. *JAMA, 256,* 2352–2355.

Grusec, J. E., Dix, T., & Mills, R. (1982). The effects of type, severity and victim of children's transgressions on maternal discipline. *Canadian Journal of Behavioural Science, 14,* 276–289.

Grusec, J. E., & Goodnow, J. J. (1994a). Impact of parental discipline methods on the child's internalization of values: A reconceptualization of current points of view. *Developmental Psychology, 30,* 4–19.

Grusec, J. E. & Goodnow, J. J. (1994b). Summing up and looking to the future. *Developmental Psychology, 30,* 29–31.

Grych, J. H., & Fincham, F. D. (1993). Children's appraisals of marital conflict: Initial investigations of the cognitive-contextual framework. *Child Development, 64,* 215–230.

Guelzow, M. G., Bird, G. W., & Koball, E. H. (1991). An exploratory path analysis of the stress process for dual-career men and women. *Journal of Marriage and the Family, 53,* 151–164.

Guendelman, S., & Abrams, B. (1995). Dietary intake among Mexican-American women: Generational differences and a comparison with white non-Hispanic women. *American Journal of Public Health, 85,* 20–25.

Guerra, N. G., & Slaby, R. (1990). Cognitive mediators of aggression in adolescent offenders: 2. Intervention. *Developmental Psychology, 26,* 269–277.

Guillemin, J. (1992 July/August). Planning to die. *Reason, 29,* 29–33.

Gunnar, M. R., Porter, F. L., Wolf, C. M., Rigatuso, J., & Larson, M. C. (1995). Neonatal stress reactivity: Predictions to later emotional temperament. *Child Development, 66,* 1–14.

Gur, R. C., Gur, R. E., Obrist, W., Skolnick, B., & Reivitch, M. (1987). Age and regional cerebral blood flow at rest and during cognitive activity. *Archives of General Psychiatry, 44,* 617–621.

Guralnik, J. M., LaCroix, A. Z., Branch, L. G., Kasl, S. V., & Wallace, R. B. (1991). Morbidity and disability in older persons in the years prior to death. *American Journal of Public Health, 81,* 443–447.

Gurney, P. (1987). Self-esteem enhancement in children: A review of research findings. *Educational Research, 29,* 130–135.

Gustafson, G. E., & Harris, K. L. (1990). Women's responses to young infants' cries. *Developmental Psychology, 26,* 144–152.

Guttman, D. (1987). *Reclaimed powers: Towards a new psychology of men and women in later life.* New York: Basic Books.

Haager, , D., & Vaughn, S. (1995). Parent, teacher, peer, and self-reports of the social competence of students with learning disabilities. *Journal of Learning Disabilities, 28,* 205–215, 231.

Haan, N., Millsap, R., & Hartka, E. (1986). As time goes by: Change and stability in personality over fifty years. *Psychology and Aging, 1,* 220–232.

Hack, M., Klein, N. K., & Taylor, H. G. (1995) Long-term developmental outcomes of low birth weight infants. *The Future of Children: Low Birthweight* (pp. 176–197). Los Altos, CA: The David and Lucile Packard Foundation.

Hadeed, A., & Siegel, S. R. (1989). Maternal cocaine use during pregnancy: Effect on the newborn infant. *Pediatrics, 84,* 205–210.

Haeuser, A. A. (1990). Can we stop physical punishment of children? *Holistic education review, 3,* 53–56.

Haffner, D. W. (1992). *1992 report card on the states: Sexual rights in America.* SIECUS Report 20, 1–7.

Haft, W. L., & Slade, A. (1989). Affect attunement and maternal attachment: A pilot study. *Infant Mental Health Journal, 10,* 157–172.

Hagekull, B., & Bohlin, G. (1995). Day care quality, family and child characteristics and socioemotional development. *Early Childhood Research Quarterly, 10,* 505–526.

Haith, M. M. (1980). *Rules babies look by: The organization of newborn visual activity.* Hillsdale, NJ: Erlbaum.

Haith, M. M. (1990). Progress in the understanding of sensory and perceptual processes in early infancy. *Merrill-Palmer Quarterly, 36,* 1–26.

Haith, M. M., Hazan, C., & Goodman, G. S. (1988). Expectation and anticipation of dynamic visual events by 3 5-month-old babies. *Child Development, 59,* 467–479.

Hajek, P., West, R., & Wilson, J. (1995). Regular smokers, lifetime very light smokers, and reduced smokers: Comparison of psychosocial and smoking characteristics in women. *Health Psychology, 14,* 195–201.

Hall, D. R. & Zhao, J. Z. (1995). Cohabitation and divorce in Canada: Testing the selectivity hypothesis. *Journal of Marriage and the Family, 57,* 421–427.

Hall, M. (1994, November 2). Violence up in 38 of schools. *USA TODAY,* p. 1A.

Hall, R. H. *Dimensions of Work.* (1986) Beverly Hills, CA: Sage.

Halpern, D. F. (1986). *Sex differences in cognitive abilities.* Hillsdale, NJ: Erlbaum.

Halpern, S. (1989). Infertility: Playing the odds. *Ms,* pp. 147–151, 154–156.

Hamachek, D. E. (1988). Evaluating self-concept and ego development within Erikson's psychosocial framework: A formulation. *Journal of Counseling and Developing, 66,* 354–360.

Hamburg, D. A. (1994). *Today's children: Creating a future for a generation in crisis.* New York: Times Books.

Hamill, P. V. V. (1977). *NCHS growth curves for children.* Vital and Health Statistics, Series 11, Data from the National Health Survey, No. 165. (DWEH No. 78–1650). Washington, DC: U.S. Government Printing Office.

Hamilton, E. M. N., & Whitney, E. N. (1982). *Nutrition: Concepts and controversies* (2nd ed.). St. Paul, MN: West.

Hamilton, E. M. N., Whitney, E. N., & Sizer, F. S. (1985). *Nutrition: Concepts and controversies* (3rd ed.). St. Paul, MN: West.

Hamilton, E. M. N., Whitney, E. N., & Sizer, F. S. (1991). *Nutrition: Concepts and controversies* (5th ed.). St. Paul, MN: West.

Hamond, N. R., & Fivush, R. (1991). Memories of Mickey Mouse: Young children recount their trip to Disneyworld. *Cognitive Development, 6,* 443–448.

Hansen, B. (1995, August 15). Bias in the workplace: More claims, more backlog. *USA Today,* p. 10A.

Hansen, J., & Bowey, J. A. (1994). Phonological analysis skills, verbal working memory, and reading ability in second-grade children. *Child Development, 65,* 938–950.

Hansson, R. O., Stroebe, M. S., & Stroebe, W. (1988). In conclusion: Current themes in bereavement and widowhood research. *Journal of Social Issues, 44,* 207–216.

Haponski, W. C., & McCabe, A. L. (1982). Back to school: The college guide for adults. Princeton: Peterson's Guides.

Hardt, D. V. (1979). *Death: The Final Frontier.* Englewood Cliffs, New Jersey: Prentice Hall.

Hardy, J., & Duggan, A. (1988). Teenage fathers and the fathers of infants of urban, teenage mothers. *American Journal of Public Health, 78,* 919–922.

Hardy, J. B., Welcher, D. W., Mellits, E. D., & Kagan, J. (1976). Pitfalls in the measurement of intelligence: Are standardized tests valid for measuring the intellectual potential of urban children? *Journal of Psychology, 94,* 43–51.

Harkins, E. B. (1978). Effects of empty nest transition on self-report of psychological and physical well-being. *Journal of Marriage and the Family, 40,* 549–558.

Harlan, S. L. (1983). Opportunity and anomie: Attitudes toward job advancement in a manufacturing firm. Cited in L. M. Tamir, Modern myths about men at midlife: An assessment. In S. Hunter & M. Sundel (Eds.). *Midlife myths: Issues, findings, and practical implications* (pp. 157–181). Newbury Pack, CA: Sage.

Harlap, S., & Shiono, P. (1980, July 26). Alcohol and incidence of spontaneous abortions in the first and second trimester. *Lancet,* pp. 173–176.

Harlow, H. F., & Harlow, M. K. (1962). Social deprivation in monkeys. *Scientific American, 207,* 136–146.

Harper, J. A. (1995). Preventive preschool programming that works. *Phi Delta Kappan, 69,* 81–82.

Harper's Magazine. (1996, May). A roundtable discussion. *29,* 35–45.

Harris G., Thomas, A., & Booth, D. (1990). Development of salt taste in infancy. *Developmental Psychology, 26,* 534–539.

Harris, J. C. (1995). *Developmental neuropsychiatry* Vol. 1. New York: Oxford University Press.

Harris, M. B., & Turner, P. H. (1985/1986). Gay and lesbian parents. *Journal of Homosexuality, 12,* 101–113.

Harris, P. L. (1989). Object permanence in infancy. In A. Slater & G. Bremner (Eds.), *Infant Development.* Hillsdale, NJ: Erlbaum.

Harris, R. L., Ellicott, A. M., & Holmes, D. S. (1986). The timing of psychosocial transitions and changes in women's lives: An examination of women aged 45 to 60. *Journal of personality and Social Psychology, 51,* 409–416.

Harrison, A .O. Wilson, M. N., Pine, C. J., Chan, S. Q., & Buriel, R. (1990). Family ecologies of ethnic minority children. *Child Development, 61,* 347–362.

Harrison, M. (1994, May 13). Should women's health be a separate medical specialty? No! *CQ Researcher, 4,* 425.

Harrison, N. S. (1979). *Understanding behavioral research.* Belmont, CA: Wadsworth.

Harrison, R. J., & Bennett, C. E., (1995). Racial and ethnic diversity. In R. Farley *State of the Union: America in the 1990s* (2nd ed. Vol. 2, pp. 141–211). New York: Russell Sage.

Harry, B. (1992). Restructuring the participation of African-American parents in special education. *Exceptional Children, 59,* 123–132.

Hart, B. (1991). Input frequency and children's first words. *First Language, 11,* 289–300.

Hart, B., & Riley, T. R. (1992). American parenting of language-learning children: Persisting differences in family-child interactions observed in natural home environments. *Developmental Psychology, 28,* 1096–1105.

Hart, C. H., Ladd, G. W., & Burleson, B. R. (1990). Children's expectations of the outcomes of social strategies: Relations with sociometric status and maternal disciplinary styles. *Child Development, 61,* 127–138.

Harter, S. (1983). Developmental perspective on the self-system. In P. H. Mussen (Ed.), *Handbook of child psychology* (4th ed.) (Vol. 4, pp. 275–387). New York: Wiley.

Hartshorne, H., & May, M. A. (1928). *Studies in the nature of character* (Vol. 1). New York: Macmillan.

Hartup, W. W. (1970). Peer interaction and social organization. In P. H. Mussen (Ed.), *Carmichael's manual of child development* (3rd ed.). New York: Wiley.

Hartup, W. W. (1983). Peer relations. In P. H. Mussen (Ed.), *Handbook of child psychology: Socialization, personality, and social development,* (4th ed.) (Vol. 4, pp. 103–197). New York: Wiley.

Hartup, W. W. (1996). The company they keep: friendships and their developmental significance. *Child Development, 67,* 1–13.

Harvey, S. M., & Spigner, C. (1995). Factors associated with sexual behavior among adolescents: A multivariate analysis. *Adolescence, 30,* 253–264.

Harwood, R. L. (1992). The influence of culturally derived values on Anglo and Puerto Rican mothers' perceptions of attachment behavior. *Child Development, 63,* 822–839.

Hashtroudi, S., Johnson, M. K., Vnek, N., & Ferguson, S. A. (1994). Aging and the effects of affective and factual focus on source monitoring and recall. *Psychology and Aging, 9,* 160–170.

Hatcher, P. J., Hulme, C., & Ellis, A. W. (1994). Ameliorating early reading failure by integrating the teaching of reading and phonological skills: The phonological linkage hypothesis. *Child Development, 65,* 41–57.

Hauser-Cram, P. (1996). Mastery motivation in toddlers with developmental disabilities. *Child Development, 67,* 236–248.

Hausman, B., & Hammen, C. (1993). Parenting in homeless families: the double crisis. *American Journal of Orthopsychiatry, 63,* 358–368.

Havighurst, R. J. (1961). Successful aging. *Gerontologist, 1,* 8–13.

Harvighurst, R. J. (1978). Aging in western societies. In D. Hobman (Ed.). *The social challenge of aging* (pp. 15–45). New York: St. Martin's Press.

Havighurst, R. J., & Albrecht, R. (1953). *Older people.* New York: Longmans, Green.

Hawkins, H. L., Kramer, A. F., & Capaldi, D. (1992). Aging, exercise, and attention. *Psychology and Aging, 7,* 643–653.

Hawkins, J. D., Catalano, R. F., & Brewer, D. D. (1995). Preventing serious violent and chronic juvenile offending: effective strategies from conception to age six. In *Guide for implementing the comprehensive strategy for serious, violent, and chronic juvenile offenders.* Washington, DC: Office of Juvenile Justice and Delinquency Prevention, U.S. Department of Justice.

Hayes, M. P., Stinnett, N., & DeFrain, J. (1981). Learning about marriage from the divorced. *Journal of Divorce, 4,* 23–29.

Hayes, R. (1986). Men's decisions to enter or avoid nontraditional occupations. *Career Development Quarterly, 34,* 89–101.

Hayflick, L. (1974). The strategy of senescence. *Journal of Gerontology, 14,* 37–43.

Hayflick, L. (1977). The cellular basis for biological aging. In C. E. Finch & L. Hayflick (Eds.), *Handbook of the psychology of aging* (pp. 159–179). New York: Van Nostrand.

Hayflick, L. (1994). *How and why we age.* New York: Ballantine.

Hayne, H. (1990). The effect of multiple reminders on long-term retention in human infants. *Developmental Psychology, 23,* 453–477.

Hayne, H., & Rovee-Collier, C. (1995). The organization of reactivated memory in infancy. *Child Development, 66,* 893–906.

Hays, R., (1992). AIDS and gays: Look for a second wave. *Med Asp Human Sexuality, 26,* 61.

Hayslip, B., & Panek, P. E. (1993). *Adult Development & Aging* (2nd ed.). New York: Harper Collins.

Hazzard, W. R. (1995, December 27). Cardinal features of successful preventive gerontology. *JAMA, 274,* 1964–1965.

Headden, S. (1996, September 25). Tongue-tied in the schools. *U.S. News and World Report,* pp. 44–46.

Healey, J. (1995). Proposed electroic "V-chip" complicates the view. *Congressional Quarterly Weekly Report, 53,* 1994–1997.

Heath, D. T. (1994). The impact of delayed fatherhood on the father-child relationship. *Journal of Genetic Psychology, 155,* 511–531.

Heckler, M. M. (1985). The fight against Alzheimer's disease. *American Psychologist, 40,* 1240–1245.

Heckman, J. J. (1995, March). Cracked bell. *Reason, 26,* 49–56.

Hedlund, B., & Ebersole, P. (1983). A test of Levinson's mid-life reevaluation. *Journal of Genetic Psychology, 143,* 189–192.

Hegde, M. N. (1995). *Introduction to communication disorders* (2nd ed.) Austin, TX: Pro-Ed.

Heidrich, S. M., & Ryff, C. D. (1993). Physical and Mental health in Later Life: The self-system as mediator. *Psychology and Aging, 8,* 327–338.

Hein, K. (1993). "Getting real" about HIV in adolescents. *American Journal of Public Health, 83,* 492–494.

Heinicke, C. M. (1979). Development from two and one-half to four years. In J. D. Noshpitz (Ed.), *Basic handbook of child psychiatry.* (Vol. 1, pp. 167–178). New York: Basic Books.

Heinicke, C. M. (1995). Determinants of the transition to parenting in M. H. Bornstein (Ed.). *Handbook of Parenting* (Vol. 3, pp. 277–305). Mahwah, NJ: Erlbaum.

Heinrich, R., Corbine, J., & Thomas, K. (1990). Counseling Native Americans. *Journal of Counseling and Development, 69,* 128–132.

Heinrichs, C., Munson, P. J., Counts, D. R., Cutler, G. B., & Baron, J. (1995, April 21). Patterns of human growth. *Science, 268,* 443–444.

Hellebrandt, F. (1980). Aging among the advantaged: A new look at the stereotype of the elderly. *Gerontologist, 20,* 404–414.

Heller, K., Sher, K. J., & Benson, C. S. (1982). Problems associated with risk of over-prediction in studies of offspring of alcoholics: Implications for prevention. *Clinical Psychology Review, 2,* 183–200.

Hellmich, N. (1994, October 4). Nip weight gain in the body for better health. *USA Today,* p. 1D.

Hellmich, N., & Peterson, K. S. (1996, April 24). More parents putting kids in formal day care. *USA Today,* pp. 1, 2D.

Helms, J. E. (1992). Why is there no study of cultural equivalence in standardized cognitive testing. *American Psychologist, 47,* 1083–1102.

Helson, R., & Moane, G. (1987). Personality change in women from college to midlife. *Journal of Personality and Social Psychology, 53,* 176–186.

Helson, R., & Wink, P. (1992). Personality change in women from the early 40s to the early 50s. *Psychology and Aging, 7,* 46–55.

Hendricks, J., & Cutler, S. J. (1990). Leisure and the structure of our life world. *Aging and Society, 10,* 85–94.

Henggeler, S. W., Rodick, J. D., Borduin, C. M., Hanson, C. L., Watson, S. M., & Urey, J. R. (1986). Multisystemic treatment of juvenile offenders: Effects on adolescent behavior and family interaction. *Developmental Psychology, 22,* 132–141.

Hennessy, K. D., Robideau, G. J., Cicchetti, D., & Cummings, E. M. (1994). Responses of physically abused and nonabused children to different forms of interadult anger. *Child Development, 65,* 815–828.

Henry, T. (1994, January 6). Violence in schools grows more severe. *USA Today,* p. D1.

Henry, T. (1996, Feb. 22). Principals urge broad changes in high schools. *USA Today,* p. 1D.

Henry, T. (1996, March 13). Fear of crime change kids daily routine. *USA Today,* p. 1D.

Herbert, T. B., Silver, R. C., & Ellard, J. H. (1991). Coping with an abusive relationship: 1. How and why do women stay? *Journal of Marriage and the Family, 53,* 311–325.

Herbert, W. with Daniel, M. (1996, June 3). The moral child. *U.S. News and World Reports,* 52–59.

Hernandez, D. J. (1995). Changing demographics: Past and future demands for early childhood programs. *The Future of Children, 5,* 156–161.

Hernandez, H. (1989). *Multicultural education: A teacher's guide to content and process.* New York: Merrill.

Hero, 5, Can do it but can't say it. (1986, August 7). *Los Angeles Times,* p. 2.

Heron, A., & Kroeger, E. (1981). Introduction to developmental psychology. In H. C. Triandis & A. Heron (Eds.), *Handbook of cross-cultural psychology* (Vol. 4, pp. 1–17). Boston: Allyn and Bacon.

Herrenkohl, E. C. Herrenkohl, R. C., & Egolf, B. (1994). Resilient early school age children from maltreating homes: Outcome in late adolescence. *American Journal of Orthopsychiatry, 64,* 301–309.

Herrnstein, R. J., & Murray, C. (1994). *The bell curve: Intelligence and class structure in american life.* New York: Free Press.

Hershey, M. (1988, February). Gifted child education. *The Clearing House,* 280–282.

Hertsgaard, L., Gunnar, M., Erickson, M. F., & Nachmias, M. (1995). Adrenocordical responses to the strange situation in infants with disorganized/disoriented attachment relationships. *Child Development, 66,* 1100–1106.

Hertzler, A. A., & Frary, R. B. (1989). Food behavior of college students. *Adolescence, 24,* 349–355.

Hertzog, C. (1989). Influences of cognitive slowing on age differences in intelligence. *Developmental Psychology, 25,* 636–651.

Herzog, A. R., House, J. S., & Morgan, J. N. (1991). Relation of work and retirement to health and well-being in older age. *Psychology and Aging, 6,* 202–211.

Herzog, D. B., Keller, M. B., Sacks, N. R., Yeh, C. J., & Levori, P. W. (1992). Psychiatric comorbidity in treatment-seeking anorexics and bulimics. *Journal of the American Academy of Child and Adolescent Psychiatry, 31,* 810–818.

Hess, B. (1971). Amicability cited. In J. M. Rybash, P. A. Roodin, & W. J. Hoyer. *Adult development and aging* (3rd ed.). Dubuque, IA: Brown & Benchmark.

Hess, R., & Shipman, V. (1972). Parents as teachers: How lower and middle class mothers teach. In C. S. Lavatelli & F. Stendler (Eds.), *Readings in child behavior and development* (3rd ed., pp. 436–446). New York: Harcourt Brace Jovanovich.

Hess, R. D., & Camara, K. A. (1979). Post-divorce family relationships as mediating variables in the consequences of divorce for children. *Journal of Social Issues, 35,* 4.

Hess, R. D., Hiroshi, A., & Kashiwagi, K., et al. (1986). Family influences on school readiness and achievement in Japan and the United States: An overview of a longitudinal study. In H. Stevenson, H. Azuma, & K. Makuta (Eds.), *Child development and education in Japan* (pp. 147–166). New York: Freeman.

Hetherington, E. M. (1972). Effects of father absence on personality: Development in adolescent daughters. *Developmental Psychology, 7,* 313–321.

Hetherington, E. M. (1979). Divorce: A child's perspective. *American Psychologist, 34,* 851–858.

Hetherington, E. M. (1993). An overview of the virginal Longitudinal study of divorce and remarriage: A focus on early adolescence. *Journal of Family Psychology, 7,* 39–56.

Hetherington, E. M., Cox, M., & Cox, R. (1976). Divorced fathers. *Family Coordinator, 25,* 417–428.

Hetherington, E. M., Cox, M., & Cox, R. (1978). The development of children in mother headed families. In H. Hoffman & D. Reiss (Eds.), *The American family: Dying and developing.* New York: Plenum.

Hetherington, E. M., Hagan, M. S., & Anderson, E. R. (1989). Marital transitions: A child's perspective. *American Psychologist, 44,* 303–313.

Hetherington, E. M., Stanley-Hagan, M., & Anderson, E. R. (1989). Marital transitions. *American Psychologist, 44,* 303–312.

Hetherington, E. M., & Stanley-Hagan, M. M. (1995). Parenting in divorced and remarried families. In M. H. Bornstein (Ed.). *Handbook of parenting* (Vol. 3., pp. 233–254). Mahwah, NJ: Erlbaum.

Heyn, J. E., Barry, J. R., & Pollack, R. H. (1978). Problem solving as a function of age, sex, and role appropriateness of the problem context. *Experimental Aging Research, 5,* 505–519.

Hickson, L., Blackman, L. S., & Reis, E. M. (1995). *Mental retardation: Foundations of educational programming.* Boston, MA: Allyn & Bacon.

Higginbottom, S. F., Barling, J., & Kelloway, E. K. (1993). Linking retirement experiences and marital satisfaction: A mediational model. *Psychology and Aging, 8,* 508–516.

Higgins, B. S. (1990). Couple infertility: From the perspective of the close-relationship model. *Family Relations, 39,* 81–86.

High/Scope Educational Research Foundation. (1993). *Significant benefits: The High/Scope Perry Preschool study through age 27.* Ypsilanti, MI: High/Scope Educational Research Foundation.

High-tech toddler. (1990, April 25). *New York Times,* p. 28.

Hill, E. A., & Dorfman, L. T. (1982). Reaction of housewives to the retirement of their husbands. *Family Relations, 31,* 195–200.

Hill, J. P. (1987). Research on adolescents and their families: Past and prospect. In C. E. Irwin (Ed.), *Adolescent social behavior and health* (pp. 15–32). San Francisco: Jossey-Bass.

Hilliard, A. G. (1980). Cultural diversity and special education. *Exceptional Children, 46,* 584–588.

Himes, C. L. (1992). Future caregivers: Projected family structures of older persons. *Journal of Gerontology, 47,* S17–26.

Hinshaw, S. P., & Erhardt, D. (1993). Behavioral treatment in V. B. Van Hasselt & M. Hersen (Eds.). *Handbook of behavior therapy and pharmacotherapy for children: A comparative analysis.* Boston: Allyn & Bacon.

Hinton, J. (1972). *Dying.* Baltimore: Penguin.

Hobart, C. (1993). Interest in marriage among Canadian students at the end of the eighties. *Journal of Comparative Family Studies, 24,* 45–61.

Hochschild, A. (1989). *The second shift,* New York: Viking.

Hock, E. (1980). Working and nonworking mothers and their infants: A comparative study of maternal caregiving characteristics and infant social behavior. *Merrill-Palmer Quarterly, 26,* 79–101.

Hock, E., & DeMeis, D. (1990). Depression in mothers of infants; the role of maternal employment. *Developmental Psychology, 26,* 285–291.

Hock, E., DeMeis, D., & McBride, S. (1988). Maternal separation anxiety: Its role in the balance of employment and motherhood in mothers of infants. In A. E. Gottfried & A. W. Gottfried (Eds.), *Maternal employment and children's development: Longitudinal research* (pp. 191–229). New York: Plenum.

Hockheimer, E. F. (1989). *Health promotion of the elderly in the community.* Philadelphia: W.B. Saunders.

Hodapp, R. M., & Mueller, E. (1982). Early social development. In B. B. Wolman (Ed.), *Handbook of developmental psychology,* 284–298. Englewood Cliffs, NJ: Prentice Hall.

Hodgkinson, S., Sherrington, R., Gurling, H., Marchbanks, R., Reeders, S., Mallet, J., McInnis, M., Petursson, H., & Brynjolfsson, J. (1987). Molecular genetic evidence for heterogeneity in manic depression. *Nature, 325,* 805–806.

Hodgson, L. G. (1992). Adult grandchildren and their grandparents: The enduring bond. *International Journal of Aging and Human Development, 34,* 209–225.

Hofer, M. A. (1988). On the nature and function of prenatal behavior. In W. P. Smotherman & C. R. Robinson (Eds.), *Behavior of the fetus* (pp. 3–19). Caldwell, NJ: Telford Press.

Hoff-Ginsberg, E. (1986). Function and structure in maternal speech: Their relation to the child's development of syntax. *Developmental Psychology, 22,* 155–163.

Hoff-Ginsberg, E. (1990). Maternal speech and the child's development of syntax: A further look. *Journal of Child Language, 17,* 85–99.

Hoffman, L. W. (1982, April). Social change and its effects on parents and children: Limitations to knowledge. In P. W. Berman & E. R. Ramey (Eds.), *Women: A developmental perspective.* NIH Pub. No. 82-2298. Washington, DC: U.S. Department of Health and Human Services, Public Health Services.

Hoffman, L. W. (1989). Effects of maternal employment in the two-parent family. *American Psychologist, 44,* 283–292.

Hoffman, M. K. (1994). Use of advance directives: A social work perspective on the myth versus the reality. *Death Studies, 18,* 229–241.

Hoffman, M. L. (1979). Development of moral thought, feeling, and behavior. *American Psychologist, 34,* 958–967.

Hoffman, M. L. (1988). Moral development. In M. H. Bornstein & M. E. Lamb (Eds.) *Personality, emotional and personality development* (2nd ed.) (pp. 497–541.) Hillsdale, NJ: Erlbaum.

Hoffman, M. L. (1994). Discipline and internalization. *Developmental Psychology, 30,* 26–28.

Hogan, D. P., & Lichter, D. T. (1995). Children and youth: Living arrangements and welfare. In R. Farley (Ed.), *State of the Union: America in the 1990s* (Vol. 2, pp. 93–139). New York: Russell Sage Foundation.

Hoge, D. R., & Bender, I. E. (1974). Factors influencing value change among college graduates in adult life. *Journal of Personality and Social Psychology, 29,* 572–585.

Hogue, A., & Steinberg, L. (1995). Homophily of internalized distress in adolescent peer groups. *Developmental Psychology, 31,* 897–906.

Holden, C. (1987). The genetics of personality. *Science, 237,* 598–601.

Holden, C., Burkhauser, R., & Myers, D. (1986). Income transitions at older stages in life: The dynamics of poverty. *Gerontologist, 26,* 292–297.

Holden, G. W. (1995). Parental attitudes toward childrearing. In M. H. Bornstein (Ed.), *Handbook of parenting* (Vol. 3, pp. 359–392.

Holden, G. W., Coleman, S. M., & Schmidt, K. L. (1995). Why 3-year-old children get spanked: Parent and child determinants as reported by college educated mothers. *Merrill-Palmer Quarterly,*

Holden, G. W., & Ritchie, K. L. (1991). Linking extreme marital discord, child rearing, and child behavior problems: Evidence from battered women. *Child Development, 62,* 311–327.

Hollander, D. (1996). Nonmarital childbearing in the United States: A governmental report. *Family Planning Perspectives,* 28–32, 41.

Holloway, H. D., et al. (1994–1995). Measuring attitudes toward euthanasia. *Omega, 30,* 53–65.

Holmes, D. S. (1976a). Debriefing after psychological experiments, I: Effectiveness of post-deception dehoaxing. *American Psychologist, 31,* 858–868.

Holmes, D. S. (1976b). Debriefing after psychological experiments, II: Effectiveness of post-experimental desensitization. *American Psychologist, 31,* 868–876.

Holmes, S. A. (1991, May 25). Conference on black males finds many problems but no consensus. *New York Times,* p. 11.

Holmes, T. H., & Rahe, R. H. (1967). The social readjustment rating scale. *Journal of Psychosomatic Research, 11,* 213–218.

Holstein, C. B. (1976). Irreversible, stepwise sequence in the development of moral judgement: A longitudinal study of males and females. *Child Development, 47,* 51–61.

Holt, J. (1964). *How children fail.* New York: Pitman.

Holtzen, D. W., & Agresti, A. A. (1990). Parental responses to gay and lesbian children. *Journal of Social and Clinical Psychology, 9,* 390–399.

Holtzman, N. A., Kronmal, R. A., Van Doorninck, W., Azen, C., & Koch, R. (1986). Effect of age at loss of dietary control on intellectual performance and behavior of children with phenylketonuria. *New England Journal of Medicine, 314,* 593–597.

Homosexual families and the law. (1989, July 17). *Newsweek,* p. 48.

Hongladarom, G., McCorkle, R., & Woods, N. F. (1982). *The complete book of women's health.* Englewood Cliffs, NJ: Prentice Hall.

Honig, A. S. (1988). The art of talking to a baby. *Baby, 3,* 12–14, 16–17.

Honig, A. S. (1995). Choosing child care for young children. In M. H. Bornstein (Ed.), *Handbook of Parenting* (Vol. 4, pp. 411–435). Mahwah, NJ: Erlbaum.

Honzik, M. P. (1984). Life-span psychology. *Annual Review of Psychology, 35,* 309–333.

Hooker, K. & Kaus, C. R. (1994). Health-related possible selves in young and middle adulthood. *Psychology and Aging, 9,* 126–133.

Hopkins, B., & Westra, T. (1990). Motor development, maternal expectations, and the role of handling. *Infant Behavior and Development, 13,* 117–122.

Hopkins, J., Marcus, M., & Campbell, S. R. (1984). Postpartum depression: A critical review. *Psychological Bulletin, 95,* 498–515.

Horbar, J. D., & Lucey, J. F. (1995, Spring). Evaluation of neonatal intensive care technologies. *The Future of Children, 5,* 139–161.

Horn, J. L. & Cattell, R. B. (1966). Age Differences in Primary Mental Ability Factors. *Journal of Gerontology, 21,* 210–222.

Horn, J. L., & Donaldson, G. (1980). Cognitive development in adulthood. In O. G. Brim & J. Kagan (Eds.), *Constancy and change in human development* (pp. 445–530). Cambridge, MA: Harvard University Press.

Horn, J. M. (1983). The Texas adoption project: Adopted children and their intellectual resemblance to biological and adoptive parents. *Child Development, 54,* 268–275.

Horn, J. M. (1985). Bias? Indeed! *Child Development, 56,* 779–781.

Horney, K. (1939). *New ways in psychoanalysis.* New York: Norton.

Horney, K. (1967). *Feminine psychology.* New York: Norton.

Hornik, R., & Gunnar, M. R. (1988). A descriptive analysis of infant social referencing. *Child Development, 59,* 626–635.

Horowitz, A. (1994). Vision impairment and functional disability among nursing home residents. *The Gerontologist, 34,* 316–323.

Horowitz, T. R. (1992). "Dropout—Mertonian or reproduction scheme? *Adolescence, 27,* 451–459.

Hotelling, K., & Forrest, L. (1985, November). Gilligan's theory of sex-role development: A perspective for counseling. *Journal of Counseling and Development, 64,* 183–186.

House, I. S., et al., (1990). Age, socioeconomic status, and health. *Milbank Quarterly, 68,* 383–411.

House, J. S., Landis, K. R., & Umberson, D. (1988). Social relationships and health. *Science, 241,* 540–545.

Householder, J., Hatcher, R., Burns, W., & Chasnoff, I. (1982). Infants born to narcotic-addicted mothers. *Psychological Bulletin, 2,* 453–468.

Houseknecht, S. (1987). Voluntary childlessness. In M. B. Sussman & S. K. Steinmetz (Eds.), *Handbook of Marriage and the Family* (pp. 369–392). New York: Plenum Pub.

Hovell, M. F., Schumaker, J. B., & Sherman, J. A. (1978). A comparison of parents' models and expansions in promoting children's acquisition of adjectives. *Journal of Experimental Child Psychology, 25,* 41–57.

Howard, M. (1985). Postponing sexual involvement among adolescents: An alternative approach to prevention of sexually transmitted diseases. *Journal of Adolescent Health Care, 6,* 271–277.

Howard, V. F., Williams, B. F., Port, P. D., & Lepper, C. (1997). *Very young children with special needs.* Upper Saddle River, NJ: Merrill.

Howe, M. L. (1991). Misleading children's story recall: Forgetting and reminiscence of the facts. *Developmental Psychology, 27,* 746–762.

Howe, M. L. (1995). Interference effects in young children's long-term retention. *Developmental Psychology, 31,* 579–596.

Howe, M. L., Courage, M. L., & Bryant-Brown, L. (1993). Reinstating preschoolers' memories. *Developmental Psychology, 29,* 854–869.

Howe, N., & Ross, H. S. (1990). Socialization, perspective-taking, and the sibling relationship. *Developmental Psychology, 26,* 160–165.

Howell, J. C. (1994). Gangs. Fact Sheet #12. Washington, DC: U.S. Department of Justice, Office of Juvenile Justice and Delinquency Prevention.

Howes, C. (1988). Peer interaction of young children. *Monographs of the Society for Research in Child Development, 53* (1, Serial No. 217).

Howes, C. (1990). Can the age of entry into child care and the quality of child care predict adjustment in kindergarten. *Developmental Psychology, 26,* 292–304.

Howes, C., & Hamilton, C. E. (1992a). Children's relationships with caregivers: Mothers and child care teachers. *Child Development, 63,* 859–866.

Howes, C., & Hamilton, C. E. (1992b). Children's relationships with child care teachers and concordance with parental attachments. *Child Development, 63,* 867–878.

Howes, C., Phillips, D. A., & Whitebook, M. (1992). Thresholds of quality: Implications for the social development of children in center-based child care. *Developmental Psychology, 63,* 449–460.

Howes, C., & Smith, E. W. (1995). Relations among child care quality, teacher behavior, children's play activities, emotional security, and cognitive activity in child care. *Early Childhood Research Quarterly, 10,* 381–404.

Howes, M. B. (1990). *The psychology of human cognition.* New York: Pergamon Press.

Huang, L., Cartwright, W. S., & Hu, T. (1988). The economic cost of senile dementia in the United States, 1985. *Public Health Reports, 103,* 3–7.

Huang, L. H. (1989). Southeast Asian refugee children and adolescents. In J. T. Gibbs & L. H. Huang (Eds.). *Children of color* (pp. 278–321). San Francisco: Jossey-Bass.

Hubbs-Tait, L., & Garmon, L. C. (1995). The relationship of moral reasoning and AIDS knowledge to risky sexual behavior. *Adolescence, 30,* 549–564.

Hudley, C., & Graham, S. (1993). An attributional intervention to reduce peer-directed aggression among African-American boys. *Child Development, 64,* 124–138.

Hudson, J. A. (1990). Constructive processing in children's event memory. *Developmental Psychology, 26,* 180–187.

Hudson, J. A., Shapiro, L. R., & Sosa, B. B. (1995). Planning in the real world: Preschool children's scripts and plans for familiar events. *Child Development, 66,* 984–998.

Hudson, L., & Gray, W. (1986). Formal operations, the imaginary audience, and the personal fable. *Adolescence, 21,* 751–765.

Huerta-Franco, R., de Leon, J. D., & Malacara, J. M., (1996). Knowledge and attitudes toward sexuality in adolescents and their association with the family and other factors. *Adolescence, 31,* 179–191.

Huesmann, L. R., Eron, L. D., & Lefkowitz, M. M. (1984). Stability of aggression over time and generations. *Developmental Psychology, 20,* 1120–1134.

Huesmann, L. R., Lagerspetz, K. & Eron, L. D. (1984). Intervening variables in TV violence—Aggression relation: Evidence from two countries. *Developmental Psychology, 20,* 746–776.

Hughes, D., Galinsky, E., & Morris, A. (1992). The effects of job characteristics on marital quality: specifying linking mechanisms. *Journal of Marriage and the Family, 54,* 31–42.

Hughes, P. H., Coletti, S. D., Neri, R. L., Urmann, C. F., Stahl, S., Sicilian, D. M., & Anthony, J. C. (1995). Retaining cocaine-abusing women in a therapeutic community: The effect of a child live-in program. *American Journal of Public Health, 85,* 1149–1152.

Hull, R. H. (1984). Talking to the hearing-impaired older person. In J. Botwinick, *Aging and Behavior* (3rd ed.). New York: Springer.

Hulley, S. B., Sherwin, R., Nestle, M., & Lee, P. R. (1991). Epidemiology as a guide to clinical decisions #2 diet and coronary heart disease. *Western Journal of Medicine, 135,* 25–33.

Hultsch, D. F. (1969). Adult age differences in the organization of free recall. *Developmental Psychology, 1,* 673–678.

Hultsch, D. F., & Dixon, R. A. (1990). Learning and memory in aging. In J. E. Birren & K. W. Schaie (Eds.), *Handbook of the psychology of aging* (3rd ed.) (pp. 258–274). New York: Academic Press.

Hultsch, D. F., Hertzog, C., & Dixon, R. A. (1990). Ability correlates of memory performance in adulthood and aging. *Psychology and Aging, 5,* 356–368.

Hultsch, D. F., Hertzog, C., Small, B. J., McDonald-Miszczak, L., & Dixon, R. A. (1992). Short-term longitudinal change in cognitive performance in later life. *Psychology and Aging, 7,* 571–584.

Humble, C., Croft, J., Gerber, A., Casper, M., Hames, C. G., & Tyroler, H. A. (1990). Passive smoking and 20-year cardiovascular disease mortality among nonsmoking wives, Evans County, Georgia. *American Journal of Public Health, 80,* 599–601.

Hume, J. E., & Roberts, L. (1990). Speech-recognition difficulties of the hearing-impaired elderly: The contribution of audibility. *Journal of Speech and Hearing Research, 33,* 726–735.

Hummert, M. L. (1990). Multiple stereotypes of elderly and young adults: A comparison of structure and evaluations. *Psychology and Aging, 5,* 182–193.

Humphreys, A. P., & Smith, P. K. (1987). Rough and tumble friendship and dominance in school children: Evidence for continuity and change with age in middle childhood. *Child Development, 58,* 201–212.

Hunt, J. McV. (1961). *Intelligence and experience.* New York: Ronald.

Hunt, J. R., Kristal, A. R., White, E., Lynch, J. C., & Fries, E. (1995). Physician recommendations for dietary change: Their prevalence and impact in a population-based sample. *American Journal of Public Health, 85,* 722–726.

Hunt, M. (1974). *Sexual behavior in the 1970s.* Chicago: Playboy Press.

Hunter, F. T. (1984). Socializing procedures in parent-child and friendship relations during adolescence. *Developmental Psychology, 20,* 1092–1100.

Hunter, F. T. (1985). Adolescents' perception of discussions with parents and friends. *Developmental Psychology, 21,* 443–450.

Hunter, F. T., & Youniss, J. (1982). Changes in functions of three relations during adolescence. *Developmental Psychology, 18,* 806–812.

Hura, S. L., & Echols, C. H. (1996). The role of stress and articulatory difficult in children's early production. *Developmental Psychology, 21,* 165–176.

Huston, A. C. (1983). Sex-typing. In E. H. Hetherington (Ed.), *Handbook of child psychology* (4th ed.) (Vol. 4, pp. 387–469). New York: Wiley.

Huston, A. C. (1991). Children in poverty: Developmental and policy issues (pp. 1–23). In A. C. Huston (Ed.). *Children in poverty* New York: Cambridge University Press.

Huston, A. C., McLoyd, V. C. & Coll, C. G. (1994). Children and poverty: Issues in contemporary research. *Child Development, 65,* 275–283.

Hutt, S. J., & Hutt, C. R. (1973). *Early human development.* London: Oxford University Press.

Huyck, M. H. (1990). Gender differences in aging. In J. E. Birren & K. W. Schaie (Eds.), *Handbook of the psychology of aging.* (pp. 124–132). New York: Academic Press.

Hyde, J. S. (1985). *Half the human experience: The psychology of women* (3rd ed.). Lexington, MA: Heath.

Hymel, S., Rubin, K. H., Rowden, L., & LeMare, L. (1990). Children's peer relationships: Longitudinal prediction of internalizing and externalizing problems from middle to late childhood. *Child Development, 61,* 2004–2022.

Hymes, J. L. (1987). Public school for four-year-olds. *Young Children, 62,* 51–52.

Iaffaldano, M. T., & Muchinsky, P. M. (1985). Job satisfaction and job performance: A meta-analysis. *Psychological Bulletin, 97,* 251–273.

Iams, H. M., & Sandell, S. H. (1994). Changing Social Security benefits to reflect child-care years: A policy proposal whose time has come. *Social Security Bulletin, 57,* 10–25.

Ihinger-Tallman, M., & Pasley, K. (1987). *Remarriage.* Beverly Hills, CA: Sage.

Illingworth, R. S. (1974). *The development of the infant and young child: Normal and abnormal.* Edinburgh: Livingstone.

Ingram, D., & Barry, J. (1977). National statistics on deaths in nursing homes: interpretations and implications. *The Gerontologist, 17,* 303–308.

Inhelder, B., & Piaget, J. (1958). *The growth of logical thinking.* New York: Basic Books.

International Food Information Council (1992). *Kids make the nutritional grade.* Washington, DC: Author.

Intons-Peterson, M. J., & Reddel, M. (1984). What do people ask about a neonate? *Developmental Psychology, 20,* 358–360.

Isabella, R. (1993). Origins of attachment: Maternal interactive behavior across the first year. *Child Development, 64,* 605–621.

Isabella, R. A., & Belsky, J. (1991). Interactional synchrony and the origins of infant-mother attachment: A replication study. *Child Development, 62,* 373–384.

Isabella, R. A., Belsky, J., & von Eye, A. (1989). The origins of infant-mother attachment: An examination of interactional synchrony during the infant's first year. *Developmental Psychology, 25,* 12–21.

Isenberg, J., & Quisenberry, N. L. (1988, February). Play: A necessity for all children. *Childhood Education,* pp. 138–145.

Izard, C. E. (1994). Innate and universal facial expressions: Evidence from developmental and cross-cultural research. *Psychological Bulletin, 115,* 288–299.

Izard, C. E., Fantauzzo, C. A., Castle, J. M., Haynes, O. M., Rayias, M. F., & Putnam, P. H. (1995). The ontogeny and significance of infants' facial expressions in the first 9 months of life. *Developmental Psychology, 31,* 997–1013.

Izard, C. E., Haynes, O. M., Chisholm, G., & Baak, K. (1991). Emotional determinants of infant-mother attachment. *Child Development, 62,* 906–017.

Izard, C. E., Huebner, R., Risser, D., McGinnes, G., & Dougherty, L. (1980). The young infant's ability to produce discrete emotion expressions. *Developmental Psychology, 16,* 132–140.

Izard, C. E., & Malatesta, C. Z. (1987). Perspectives on emotional development 1: Differential emotions theory of early emotional development. In J. D. Osofsky (Ed.), *Handbook of infant development,* (pp. 494–555). New York: Wiley.

Jack, B. W., & Culpepper, L. (1990). Preconception care. *Journal of the American Medical Society, 264,* 1147–1149.

Jackson, J. F. (1993). Human behavioral genetics, Scarr's theory, and her views on interventions: A critical review and commentary on their implications for African-American children. *Child Development, 64,* 1318–1333.

Jackson, J. J. (1980). *Minorities and aging.* Belmont, CA: Wadsworth.

Jackson, J. S., Antonucci, T. C., & Gibson, R. C. (1990). Cultural, racial, and ethnic minority influences on aging. In J. E. Birren & K. W. Schaie (Eds.), *Handbook of the psychology of aging* (pp. 103–123). New York: Academic Press.

Jacobson, A. L. (1978, July). Infant day care: Toward a more human environment. *Young Children,* 151–158.

Jacobson, J. L., & Jacobson, S. W. (1996, September 12). Intellectual impairment in children exposed to polychlorinated biphenyls in utero. *New England Journal of Medicine, 335,* 783–789.

Jacobson, J. L., Jacobson, S. W., Fein, G., Schwartz, P. M., & Dowler, J. K. (1984). Prenatal exposure to an environmental toxin: A test of the multiple effects model. *Developmental Psychology, 20,* 523–533.

Jacobson, J. L., Jacobson, S. W., Padgett, R. J., Brumitt, G. A., & Billings, R. L. (1992). Effects of prenatal PCB exposure on cognitive processing efficiency and sustained attention. *Developmental Psychology, 28,* 297–306.

Jagacinski, R. J., Liao, M. J., & Hayyad, E. A. (1995). Generalized slowing in sinusoidal tracking by older adults. *Psychology and Aging, 10,* 8–20.

Jahoda, G. (1983). European "lag" in the development of an economic concept: A study in Zimbabwe. *British Journal of Developmental Psychology, 1,* 113–120.

JAMA. (1996, February 21). Suicide among older persons–United States, 1980–1992. 275, 509.

Janerich, D. T., et al. (1990). Lung cancer and exposure to tobacco smoke in the household. *New England Journal of Medicine, 323,* 632–636.

Jarvik, L. F., & Falek, A. (1962). Comparative data on cancer in aging twins. *Cancer, 15,* 1009–1018.

Jaslow, P. (1976). Employment, retirement, and morale among older women. *Journal of Gerontology, 31,* 212–218.

Jemmott, J. B., & Locke, S. E. (1984). Psychosocial factors, immunologic mediation, and human susceptibility to infectious diseases. *Psychological Bulletin, 95,* 78–108.

Jemmott, J. B., & Magloire, K. (1988). Academic stress, social support, and secretary immunoglobulin A. *Journal of Personality and Social Psychology, 55,* 803–810.

Jencks, C. (1972). *Inequality: A reassessment of the effects of family and schooling in America.* New York: Basic Books.

Jepson, C., Kessler, L. G., Portnoy, B., & Gibbs, T. (1991). Black-white differences in cancer retention knowledge and behavior. *American Journal of Public Health, 81,* 501–503.

Jessor, R., Van Den Bos, J., Vanderryn, J., Costa, F. M., & Turbin, M. S. (1995). Protective factors in adolescent problem behavior: Moderator effects and developmental change. *Developmental Psychology, 31,* 923–933.

Joffe, L. S., & Vaughn, B. E. (1982). Infant-mother attachment: Theory, assessment and implications for development. In B. B. Wolman (Ed.), *Handbook of developmental psychology* (pp. 190–204). Englewood Cliffs, NJ: Prentice Hall.

Johansen, A. S., Leibowitz, A., & Waite, L. J. (1988). Child care and children's illness. *American Journal of Public Health, 78,* 1175–1177.

John, O. P., Caspi, A., Robins, R. W., Moffitt, T. E., & Stouthamer-Loeber, M. (1994). The "little five": Exploring the nomological network of the five-factor model of personality in adolescent boys. *Child Development, 65,* 160–178.

Johnson, C. C., Myers, L., Webber, L. S., Hunter, S. M., Srinivasan, S. R., & Berenson, G. S. (1995). Alcohol consumption among adolescents and young adults: The Bogalusa Heart Study, 1981 to 1001. *American Journal of Public Health, 85,* 979–982.

Johnson, C. L. (1983). A cultural analysis of the grandmother. *Research on Aging, 5,* 547–567.

Johnson, C. M. (1995). Verb errors in the early acquisition of Mexican and Castilian Spanish. In E. V. Clark (Ed.), *The child language research forum.* Center for the study of language and information. Leland Stanford Junior University.

Johnson, I. M. (1995). Family members' perceptions of and attitudes toward elder abuse. *Families in Society: The Journal of Contemporary Human Services, 76,* 220–229.

Johnson, J. A. (1981). The etiology of hyperactivity. *Exceptional Children, 47,* 348–354.

Johnson, J. E., & Yawkey, T. D. (1988). Play and integration. In T. D. Yawkey, & J. E. Johnson (Eds.), *Integrative processes and socialization* (pp. 97–119). Hillsdale, NJ: Erlbaum.

Johnson K. (1994, May 13). Should women's health be a separate medical specialty? Yes! *CQ Researcher, 4,* 425.

Johnson, M. P. (1995). Patriarchal terrorism and common couple violence: Two forms of violence against women. *Journal of Marriage and the Family, 57,* 283–294.

Johnson, R. R., Cooper, H. I. & Chance, J. (1982). The relation of children's television viewing to school achievement and I.Q. *Journal of Educational Research, 76,* 294–297.

Johnson, S. L., & Birch, L. L. (1994). Parents' and children's adiposity and eating style. *Pediatrics, 94,* 653–661.

Johnson, S. P., & Aslin, R. N. (1995). Perception of object unity in 2-month-old infants. *Developmental Psychology, 31,* 739–745.

Johnson, S. P., & Nanez, J. E., Sr. (1995). Young infants' perception of object unity in two-dimensional displays. *Infant behavior and Development, 18,* 133–143.

Johnston, L., Bachman, J. & O'Malley, P. (1995). *Monitoring the future: The national high school seniors survey.* Ann Arbor, MI: University of Michigan Survey Research Center.

Johnston, L. D., O'Malley, P. M., Bachman, J. G. (1993). *National survey results on drug use from the monitoring of the future study, 1975–1992,* Washington, DC: U.S. Department of Health and Human Services, Public Health Service; 1993: NIH Pub. 93-3598.

Jones, D. C., & Vaughan, K. (1990). Close friendships among senior adults. *Psychology and Aging, 5,* 451–457.

Jones, E., & Gallois, C. (1989). Spouses' impressions of roles for communication in public and private marital conflicts.

Journal of Marriage and the Family, 51, 957–967.

Jones, J. M., Levine, I. S., & Rosenberg, A. A. (1991). Homelessness research, services, and social policy. *American Psychologist, 46,* 1109–1111.

Jones, K. L., Smith, D. W., Streissguth, A. P., & Myrianthopoulus, N. (1974). Outcomes in offspring of chronic alcoholic women. *Lancet, 1,* 1076–1078.

Jones, M. C. (1957). The later careers of boys who are early and late maturers. *Child Development, 28,* 113–128.

Jones, M. C. (1965). Psychological correlates of somatic development. *Child Development, 36,* 899–911.

Jones, M. C., & Bayley, N. (1950). Physical maturing among boys as related to behavior. *Journal of Educational Psychology, 41,* 129–148.

Jones, R. T., McDonald, D. W., Fiore, M. F., Arrington, T., & Randall, J. (1990). A primary preventive approach to children's drug refusal behavior: The impact of rehearsal plus. *Journal of Pediatric Psychology, 15,* 211–223.

Joseph, J. G., Adib, S. M., Koopman, J. S., & Ostrow, D. G. (1990). Behavioral change in longitudinal studies: Adoption of condom use by homosexual/bisexual men. *American Journal of Public Health, 80,* 1513–1514.

Jost, K. (1993). Childhood immunizations. *CQ Researcher, 23,* 531–551.

Julian, T. W., McKenry, P. C., & Arnold, K. (1990). Psychosocial predictors of stress associated with the male midlife transition. *Sex Roles, 22,* 707–722.

Junge, M. E., & Dretzke, B. J. (1995). Mathematical self-efficacy gender differences in gifted/talented adolescents. *Gifted Child Quarterly, 39,* 22–28.

Juntune, J. Myth: (1982). The gifted constitutes a single homogeneous group! *Gifted Child Quarterly, 26,* 9–10.

Jusczyk, P. W. (1995). Infants' detection of the sound patterns of words in fluent speech. *Cognitive Psychology, 29,* 1–23.

Jusczyk, P. W., Cutler, A., & Redanz, N. J. (1993). Infants' preference for the predominant stress patterns of English words. *Child Development, 64,* 675–687.

Justice, E. (1985). Categorization as a preferred memory strategy: Developmental changes during elementary school. *Developmental Psychology, 21,* 1105–1110.

Kagan, J. (1979). Overview: Perspectives on human infancy. In J. Osofsky (Ed.), *Handbook of infant development* (pp. 1–29) New York: Wiley.

Kagan, J. (1984). *The nature of the child,* New York: Basic Books.

Kagan, J. (1992). Yesterday's premises, tomorrow's promises. *Developmental Psychology, 28,* 990–998.

Kagan, J. Reznick, J. S., & Snidman, N. (1987). Physiology and psychology of behavioral inhibition. *Child Development, 59,* 1459–1473.

Kahana, B., Kahana, E., & McLenigan, P. (1982). Cited in B. Kahana, Social behavior and aging. In B. B. Wolman (Ed.), *Handbook of developmental psychology* (pp. 871–889). Englewood Cliffs, NJ: Prentice Hall.

Kahn, A. S. (Ed.). (1984). *Social psychology.* Dubuque, IA: Brown.

Kahn, D. (1986, March 3). A fresh young market seen in affluent over-50s. *Newsday,* Pt. 3, p. 9.

Kahn, R., & Antonucci, T. (1980). Convoys over the life course: Attachment roles and social support. In P. B. Baltes & O. G. Brim, Jr. (Eds.), *Life-span development and behavior* (Vol. 3, pp. 254–286). New York: Academic Press.

Kail, R. (1990). *The development of memory in children* (3rd ed.). New York: W. H. Freeman.

Kail, R., & Hagen, J. W. (1982). Memory in childhood. In B. B. Wolman (Ed.), *Handbook of developmental psychology* (pp. 350–367). Englewood Cliffs, NJ: Prentice Hall.

Kaitz, M., Meschlach-Sarfaty, O., Auerbach, J., & Eidelman,A. (1988). A reexamination of newborns' ability to imitate facial expressions. *Developmental Psychology, 24,* 3–8.

Kalat, J. W. (1981). *Biological psychology.* Belmont, CA: Wadsworth.

Kaler, S. R., & Kopp, C. (1990). Compliance and comprehension in very young toddlers. *Child Development, 61,* 1997–2003.

Kalish, R. (1981). *Death, Grief, and Caring Relationships.* Pacific Grove, CA: Brooks/Cole.

Kalish, R. A. (1985). *Death, grief, and caring relationships* (2nd ed.). Pacific Grove, CA: Brooks/Cole.

Kamii, C., & Radin, N. (1967). Class differences in the socialization practices of Negro mothers. In R. Staples (Ed.), *The Black family: Essays and studies.* Belmont, CA: Wadsworth.

Kamisar, Y. (1993, May/June). Are laws against assisted suicide unconstitutional? *Hastings Center Report, 23,* 32–41.

Kandel, D., & Lesser, G. S. (1969). Parent-adolescent relationships and adolescent independence in the United States and Denmark. *Journal of Marriage and the Family, 31,* 348–358.

Kandel, D. B., Wu, P., & Davies, M. (1994). Maternal smoking during pregnancy and smoking by adolescent daughters. *American Journal of Public Health, 84,* 1407–1413.

Kanner, A. D., Coyne, J. C., Schaefer, C., & Lazarus, R. S. (1981). Comparison of two modes of stress measurement: Daily hassles and uplifts versus major life events. *Journal of Behavioral Medicine, 4,* 1–39.

Kaplan, P. S. (1977, March 13). It's the I.Q. tests that flunk. *New York Times,* p. 26.

Kaplan, P. S. (1986). *A Child's Odyssey.* St. Paul, MN: West.

Kaplan, P. S. (1990). *Educational psychology for tomororow's teacher.* St. Paul, MN: West.

Kaplan, P. S. (1996). *Pathways for Exceptional Children.* St. Paul, MN: West.

Karen, R. (1990, February). Becoming attached. *The Atlantic Monthly,* pp. 35–50, 63–70.

Karp, D. A. (1988). A decade of reminders: Changing age consciousness between fifty and sixty years old. *Gerontologist, 28,* 727–738.

Karpatkin, R. H., & Shearer, G. E. (1995). A short-term consumer agenda for health care reform. *American Journal of Public health, 85,* 1352–1355.

Kasarda, J. D. (1995). Industrial restructuring and the changing location of jobs. In R. Farley (Ed.), *State of the union: America in the 1990s* (Vol. 1, pp. 215–269). New York: Russell Sage.

Kastenbaum, R. (1977). *Death, Society, and Human Experience.* St. Louis, MO: Mosby.

Kastenbaum, R. (1978, May/June). Death, dying and bereavement in old age. *Aged Care and Services Review.*

Kastenbaum, R. (1982). New frontiers in American death system. *Death Education, 6,* 155–166.

Kastenbaum, R. (1992). Death, suicide and the older adult. *Suicide and life-threatening behavior, 22,* 1–14.

Kastenbaum, R., & Costa, P. (1977). Psychological perspectives on death. *Annual Review of Psychology, 28,* 225–249.

Katchadourian, H. (1977). *The biology of adolescence.* San Francisco: Freeman.

Katchadourian, H. (1987). *Fifty: Midlife in perspective.* New York: Freeman.

Katz, L. G. (1980, August). Should you be your child's parents? *Parents,* pp. 88–90.

Katz, P. A., & Ksansnak, K. R. (1994). Developmental aspects of gender role flexibility and traditionality in middle childhood and adolescence. *Developmental Psychology, 30,* 272–282.

Katz, P. A., & Walsh, P. V. (1991). Modification of children's gender-stereotyped behavior. *Child Development, 62,* 338–351.

Katzel, L. I., Bleecker, E. R., Colman, E. G., Rogus, E. M., Sorkin, J. D., & Goldberg, A. P. (1995, December 27). Effects of weight loss vs aerobic exercise training on risk factors to coronary disease in healthy, obese, middle-aged, and older men. *JAMA, 274,* 1915–1921.

Kaufman, J., & Zigler, E. (1987). Do abused children become abusive parents. *American Journal of Orthopsychiatry, 57,* 186–192.

Kaufman, S. R., & Becker, G. (1991). Content and boundaries of medicine in long-term care: Physicians talk about stroke. *Gerontologist, 31,* 238–245.

Kavanaugh, R. E. (1972). *Facing death.* Los Angeles: Nash.

Kazdin, A. E. (1994). Interventions for aggressive and antisocial children. In L. D. Eron, U. H. Gentry, & P. Schlegel (Eds.), *Reason to hope: A psychosocial perspective on violence and youth,* (pp. 341–383) Washington, DC: American Psychological Association.

Keating, N. C., & Cole, P. (1980). What do I do with him 24 hours a day? Changes in the housewife role after retirement. *Gerontologist, 20,* 804–809.

Kegan, R. (1982). *The evolving self: Problem and process in human development.* Cambridge, MA: Harvard University Press.

Keil, F. C. (1989). *Concepts, word meanings, and cognitive development.* Cambridge, MA: MIT Press.

Keil, J. E., Sutherland, S. E., Knapp, R. G., & Tyroler, H. A. (1992). Does equal socioeconomic status in black and white mean equal risk of mortality? *American Journal of Public Health, 82,* 1133–1139.

Keith, P. M. (1985). Work, retirement, and well-being among unmarried men and women. *Gerontologist, 25,* 410–416.

Keller, A., Ford, L. M., & Meacham, J. A. (1978). Dimensions of self-concept in preschool children. *Developmental Psychology, 14,* 483–489.

Keller, L. M., Bouchard, T. J., Arvey, R. D., Segal, N. L., & Dawis, R. V. (1992). Work values: Genetic and environmental influences. *Journal of Applied Psychology, 77,* 79–88.

Keller, M. Leventhal, E., & Larson, B. (1989). Aging: The lived experience. *International Journal of Aging and Human Development, 29,* 67–82.

Kelley, M. L., Grace, N., & Elliott, S. N. (1990). Acceptability of positive and punitive discipline methods: Comparisons among abusive, potentially abusive, and nonabusive parents. *Child Abuse & Neglect, 14,* 219–226.

Kelley, M. L., Power, T. G., & Wimbush, D. D. (1992). Determinants of disciplinary practices in low-income black mothers. *Child Development, 63,* 573–582.

Kelley, M. L., Sanchez-Huckles, J., & Walker, R. R. (1993). Correlates of disciplinary practices in working-to-middle-class African-American mothers. *Merrill-Palmer Quarterly, 39,* 252–264.

Kelley, M. L., & Tseng, H. (1992). Cultural differences in child rearing: A comparison of immigrant Chinese and Caucasian American mothers. *Journal of Cross-Cultural Psychology, 23,* 444–455.

Kellogg, R. (1970). *Analyzing children's art.* Palo Alto, CA: Mayfield.

Kelly, D. (1995, September 13). Adults say lifelong learning critical to job success. *USA Today,* p. 7D.

Kelly, J. A., Lawrence, J. S., Diaz, Y. E., Stevenson, L. Y., Hauth, A. C., Brasfield, R. T., & Andrew, M. E. (1991). HIV risk behavior reduction following intervention with key opinion leaders of population: An experimental analysis. *American Journal of Public Health, 81,* 168–171.

Kelly, J. B. (1982). Divorce: The adult perspective. In B. B. Wolman (Ed.), *Handbook of developmental psychology* (pp. 734–750). Englewood Cliffs, NJ: Prentice Hall.

Kelly, J. B., & Wallerstein, J. S. (1976). The effects of parental divorce: Experiences of the child in early latency. *American Journal of Orthopsychiatry, 46,* 20–33.

Kendig, H. L. (1990). Comparative perspectives on housing, aging, and social structure. In R. H. Binstock & L. K. George (Eds.), *Handbook of aging and the social sciences* (3rd ed.) (pp. 288–303). New York: Academic Press.

Kendler, K. S., MacLean, C., Neale, M., Kessler, R., Heath, A., & Eaves, L. (1991). The genetic epidemiology of bulimia nervosa. *American Journal of Psychiatry, 148,* 1627–1637.

Kerig, P. K., Cowan, P. A., & Cowan, C. P. (1993). Marital quality and gender difference in parent-child interaction. *Developmental Psychology, 29,* 931–939.

Kermis, M. D. (1984). *The psychology of human aging.* Boston: Allyn and Bacon.

Kern, D. L., McPhee, L., Fisher, J., Johnson, S., & Birch, L. L. (1993). The postingestive consequences of fat condition preferences for flavors associated with high dietary fat. *Physiology & Behavior, 54,* 71–76.

Kerr, B. (1991). Educating gifted girls. In N. Colangelo & G. A. Davis (Eds.), *Handbook of gifted education* (pp. 402–416). Needham Heights, MA: Allyn & Bacon.

Kerrey, B., & Hofschire, P. J. (1993). Hidden problems in current health-care financing and potential changes. *American Psychologist, 48,* 261–264.

Kershner, R., (1996). Adolescent attitudes about rape. *Adolescence, 31,* 29–33.

Kevorkian, J. (1991). *Prescription: medicide—The goodness of planned death.* Buffalo, NY: Prometheus Books.

Kidwell, J. S., Dunham, R. M., Bachno, R. A., Pastorino, E., & Portes, P. R. (1995). Adolescent identity exploration: A test of Erikson's theory of transitional crisis. *Adolescence, 30,* 785–793.

Kiekolt-Glaser, J. K. & Glaser, R. (1992). Psychoneuroimmunology: Can psychological interventions modulate immunity? *Journal of Consulting and Clinical Psychology, 60l,* 569–575.

Kiecolt-Glaser, J. K., Fisher, L. D., Ogrocki, P., Stout, J. C., Speicher, C. E., & Glaser, R. (1987). Marital quality, marital disruption and immune function. *Psychosomatic Medicine, 49,* 13–34.

Kiecolt-Glaser, J. K., Kennedy, S., Malkoff, S., Fisher, L., Spreicher, C. E., & Glass, R. (1988). Marital discord and immunity in males. *Psychosomatic Medicine, 50,* 213–229.

Kimball, M. (1989). A new perspective on women's math achievement. *Psychological Bulletin, 105,* 198–214.

Kimble, G. A. (1993). Evolution of the nature-nurture issue in the history of psychology. In R. Plomin & G. E. McClearn (Eds.), *Nature, Nurture, & Psychology* (pp. 3–27). Washington, DC: American Psychological Association.

King, V., & Elder, G. H. (1995). American children view their grandparents: Linked lives across three rural generations. *Journal of Marriage and the Family, 57,* 165–178.

Kirby, D., et al. (1994). School-based programs to reduce sexual risk behaviors: A review of effectiveness. *Public Health Reports, 109,* 339–360.

Kite, M. E., Deaux, K., & Miele, M. (1991). Stereotypes of young and old: Does age outweigh gender? *Psychology and Aging, 6,* 19–27.

Kite, M. E., & Johnson, B. T. (1988). Attitudes towards older and younger adults: A meta-analysis. *Psychology and Aging, 3,* 233–244.

Kitson, G. C., & Morgan, L. A. (1990). The multiple consequences of divorce: A decade review. *Journal of Marriage and the Family, 52,* 913–924.

Kivett, V. R. (1991). Centrality of the grandfather role among older rural black and white men. *Journal of Gerontology: Social Sciences, 46,* D250–258.

Kivett, V. R. (1993). Racial comparisons of the grandmother role: implications for strengthening the family support system of older black women. *Family Relations,* 165–172.

Klass, D. (1987). Marriage and divorce among bereaved parents in a self-help group. *Omega, 17,* 237–249.

Klaus, M. H., & Kennel, J. H. (1976). *Maternal-infant bonding.* St. Louis, MO: Mosby.

Kleban, M. H., Brody, E., & Shoonover, C. B., & Hoffman, C. (1989). Family help to the elderly: Perceptions of sons-in-law regarding parent care. *Journal of Marriage and the Family, 51,* 303–312.

Kleiber, D. A., & Kelly, J. R. (1985). Cited in L. L. Burrus-Bammel, & G. Bammel, Leisure and recreation. In J. E. Birren & K. W. Schaie (Eds.), *Handbook of the psychology of Aging* (2nd ed., pp. 848–863). New York: Van Nostrand Reinhold.

Klepinger, D. H., Lundberg, S., & Plotnick, R. D. (1995). Adolescent fertility and the educational attainment of young women. *Family Planning Perspectives, 27,* 23–28.

Klesges, R. C., Shelton, M. L., & Klesges, L. M. (1993). Effects of television on metabolic rate: Potential implications for childhood obesity. *Pediatrics, 91,* 281–286.

Klesges, R. E., et al. (1991). Parental influence on food selection in young children and its relationships to childhood obesity. *American Journal of Clinical Nutrition, 53,* 859–864.

Klimoski, R., & Palmer, S. N. (1995). The ADA and the hiring process in organizations. In S. M. Bruyere & J. O'Keeffe (Eds.), *Implications of the Americans with Disabilities Act for psychology* (pp. 37–85). New York: American Psychological Association and Springer.

Kline, D. W., Kline, T. J. B., Fozard, J. L., Kosnik, W., Schieber, F., & Sekuler, R. (1992). Vision, aging, and driving: The problems of older drivers. *Journal of Gerontology: Psychological Sciences, 47,* pp. 27–34.

Kline, D. W., & Scialfa, C. T. (1996). Visual and auditory aging. In J. E. Birren & K. W. Schaie (Eds.), *Handbook of the psychology of aging* (4th ed). San Diego, CA: Academic Press.

Kline, P. (1972). *Fact and fantasy in Freudian theory.* London: Methuen.

Knothe, H., & Dette, G. A. (1985). Antibiotics and pregnancy: Toxicity and teratogenicity. *Infection, 49,* 13.

Knowles, M., & Boucher, R. (1996, February 1). Gene therapy. *The New England Journal of Medicine, 334,* p. 333.

Knox, D. (1985). *Choices in relationships.* St. Paul, MN: West.

Knox, D., & Schacht, C. (1991). *Choices in relationships* (3rd ed.). St. Paul, MN: West.

Koch, M. (1994, Fall). Opening up technology to both genders. *Technos, 3,* 14–19.

Kochanek, K. D., & Hudson, B. L., Advance report of final mortality statistics, 1992. Washington, DC: U.S. Department of Health and Human Services.

Kochanska, G. (1994). Beyond cognition: Expanding the search for the early roots of internalization and conscience. *Developmental Psychology, 30,* 20–22.

Kochanska, G. (1995). Children's temperament, mothers' discipline, and security of attachment: Multiple pathways to emerging internalization. *Child Development, 66,* 597–615.

Kochanska, G., & Aksan, N. (1995). Mother-child mutually positive affect, the quality of child compliance to requests and prohibitions, and maternal control as correlates of early internalization. *Child Development, 66,* 236–254.

Kochanska, G., Aksan, N., & Koenig, A. L. (1995). A longitudinal study of the roots of preschoolers' conscience: Committed compliance and emerging internalization. *Child Development, 66,* 1752–1769.

Koff, E., & Rierdan, J. (1995). Preparing girls for menstruation: Recommendations from adolescent girls. *Adolescence, 30,* 795–811.

Kogan, N. (1990). Personality and aging. In J. E. Birren & K. W. Schaie (Eds.), *Handbook of the psychology of aging* (pp. 330–343). New York: Academic Press.

Kohlberg, L. (1969). Stage and sequence: The cognitive-developmental approach to socialization. In D. A. Goslin (Ed.), *Handbook of socialization theory and research.* Chicago: Rand-McNally.

Kolberg, L. (1976). Moral stages and moralization: The cognitive-developmental approach. In T. Lickona (Ed.), *Moral development and behavior.* New York: Holt, Rinehart and Winston.

Kolberg, L. (1987a). The development of moral judgment and moral action. In L. Kohlberg (Ed.). *Child psychology and childhood education: A cognitive-developmental view* (pp. 259–329). New York: Longman.

Kohlberg, L., & Kramer, R. (1969). Continuities and discontinuities in childhood and adult moral development. *Human Development, 12,* 83–120.

Kohn, R. R. (1977). Heart and cardiovascular system. In C. Finch & L. Hayflick (Eds.), *Handbook of the physiology of aging* (pp. 281–317). New York: Van Nostrand.

Kolata, G. (1989, December 5). Understanding Down syndrome: A chromosome holds the key. *New York Times,* p. C3.

Kolata, G. (1991, February 26). Alzheimer's researchers close in on causes. *New York Times,* pp. C1, C7.

Komarovsky, M. (1985). *Women in college.* New York: Basic Books.

Kontos, S. (1994). The ecology of family day care. *Early Childhood Research Quarterly, 9,* 87–110.

Koocher, G. (1973). Childhood, death, and cognitive development. *Development Psychology, 9,* 369–375.

Kopp, C. (1992). Emotional distress and control in young children. *New Directions for Child Development, 55,* 41–56.

Kopp, C. B., & Kaler, S. R. (1989). Risk in infancy. *American Psychologist, 44,* 224–231.

Kopp, C. B., & Parmelee, A. H. (1979). Prenatal and perinatal influences on infant behavior. In J. D. Osofsky (Ed.), *Handbook of infant development* (pp. 29–75). New York: Wiley.

Korner, A. F., (1973). Sex differences in newborns with special reference to differences in the organization of oral behavior. *Journal of Child Psychology and Psychiatry, 14,* 17–29.

Koslowski, B. (1980). Quantitative and qualitative changes in the development of seriation. *Merrill-Palmer Quarterly, 26,* 391–405.

Koss, M., et al. (1987, April). The scope of rape: Incidence and prevalence of sexual aggression and victimization in a national sample of higher education students. *Journal of Consulting and Clinical Psychology, 55,* 162–170.

Kossen, S. (1983). *The human side of or-*

ganizations (3rd ed.). New York: Harper & Row.

Koup, R. A., & Wilson, C. B. (1994). Clinical immunology of HIV-infected children. In P. A. Pizzo & C. M. Wilfert (Eds.), *Pediatric AIDS: The challenge of HIV infection in infants, children, and adolescents* (2nd ed., pp. 129–159). Baltimore: Williams & Wilkins.

Koza, P. E. (1977). Euthanasia: Some legal considerations. In L. A. Bugen (Ed.), *Death and dying* (pp. 311–323), Dubuque, IA: Brown.

Kozma, A., Stones, M. J., & Hannah, T. E. (1991). Age, activity, and physical performance: An evaluation of performance models. *Psychology and Aging, 6,* 43–49.

Kramer, D. (1983). Post-formal operations? A need for further conceptualization. *Human Development, 16,* 91–105.

Kramer, D. A., Kahlbaugh, P. E., & Goldston, R. B. (1992). A measure of paradigm beliefs about the social world. *Journal of Gerontology: Psychological Aspects, 47,* 180–189.

Kramer, L. (1996). What's real in children's fantasy play? Fantasy play across the transition to becoming a sibling. *Journal of Child Psychology and Psychiatry, 37,* 329–337.

Kramer, L. R. (1986). Career awareness and personal development: A naturalistic study of gifted adolescent girls' concerns. *Adolescence, 21,* 123–131.

Kramer, R. A., Allen, L, & Gergen, P. J. (1995). Health and social characteristics and children's cognitive functioning: Results from a national cohort. *American Journal of Public Health, 85,* 312–318.

Kranczer, S. (1994, October-December). Outlook for U.S. population growth. *Statistical Bulletin,* 19–26.

Krantz, D. S., Grunberg, N. E., & Baum, A. (1985). Health psychology. *Annual Review of Psychology, 36,* 349–385.

Krappman, L. (1989). Family relationships and peer relationships in middle childhood: an exploratory study of the associations between children's integration into the social network of peers and family development. In K. Kreppner & R. M. Lerner (Eds.), *Family systems and life-span development* (pp. 93–104). Hillsdale, NJ: Erlbaum.

Kraus, M. A., & Redman, E. S. (1986). Postpartum depression: An interactional view. *Journal of Marriage and the Family, 12,* 63–74.

Krause, N., Jay, G., & Liang, J. (1991). Financial strain and psychological well-being among the American and Japanese elderly. *Psychology and Aging, 6,* 170–181.

Krausz, M. (1982). Policies of organizational choice at different vocational life stages. *Vocational Guidance Quarterly, 31,* 60–68.

Krauthammer, C. (1990, August 6). The tribalization of America. *Washington Post,* p. A11.

Krebs-Smith, S. M., Cook, A., Subar, A. F., Cleveland, L. & Friday, J. (1995). US adults' fruit and vegetable intakes, 1989–1991: A revised baseline for the Healthy People 2000 objective. *American Journal of Public Health, 85,* 1623–1629.

Kreppner, K., & Lerner, R. M. (1989). Family systems and life-span development: Issues and perspectives. In K. Kreppner & R. M. Lerner (Eds.), *Family systems and life-span development* (pp. 1–15). Hillsdale, NJ: Erlbaum.

Kreutzer, M. A., & Charlesworth, W. R. (1973). Infants' reactions to different expressions of emotion. In C. A. Nelson, The recognition of facial expressions in the first two years of life: Mechanisms of development. *Child Development, 58,* 889–909.

Krogman, W. M. (1980). *Child growth.* Ann Arbor: University of Michigan Press.

Kroninger, S. (1995, September 25). That's entertaining. *Forbes,* p. 31.

Kruesi, M. J. & Rapoport, J. L. (1986). Diet and human behavior: How much do they affect each other? *Annual Reviews of Nutrition, 6,* 113–130.

Kruger, A. (1994). The midlife transition, crisis or chimera? *Psychological Reports, 75,* 1299–1305.

Ku, L. C., Sonenstein, F. L., & Pleck, J. H. (1993). Factors affecting first intercourse among young men. *Public Health Reports, 108,* 680–694.

Kübler-Ross, E. (1969). *On death and dying.* New York: Macmillan.

Kübler-Ross, E. (1972, February). On death and dying. *Journal of the American Medical Association.*

Kübler-Ross, E. (1985). *AIDS, the ultimate challenge.* New York: Macmillan.

Kübler-Ross, E. & Goleman, D. (1976). The child will always be there: Real love doesn't die. *Psychology Today, 10,* 48–52.

Kubiszyn, T., & Borich, C. (1987). *Educational testing and measurement* (2nd ed.). Glenview, IL: Scott, Foresman.

Kuhn, D., Ho, V., & Adams, C. (1979). Formal reasoning among pre and late adolescents. *Child Development, 50,* 1149–1152.

Kuhn, D., Pennington, N., & Leadbeater, B. (1983). Adult thinking in developmental perspective. In P. B. Baltes & O. G. Brim (Eds.), *Life-span development and behavior* (Vol. 5, pp. 158–193). New York: Academic Press.

Kupersmidt, J. B., Griesler, P. C., DeRosier, M. E., Patterson, C. J., & Davis, P. W. (1995). Childhood aggression and peer relations in the context of family and neighborhood factors. *Child Development, 66,* 360–375.

Kurdek, L. (1991). Predictors of increases in marital distress in newlywed couples: A 3-year prospective longitudinal study. *Developmental Psychology, 27,* 627–636.

Kurdek, L. A. (1981). An integrative perspective on children's divorce adjustment. *American Psychologist, 36,* 856–866.

Kurdek, L. A. (1993b). The allocation of household labor in gay, lesbian, and heterosexual married couples. *Journal of Social Issues, 49,* 127–139.

Kurdek, L. A. (1994). Areas of conflict for gay, lesbian, and heterosexual couples: What couples argue about influences relationship satisfaction. *Journal of Marriage and the Family, 56,* 923–934.

Kurdek, L. A. (1995). Predicting change in marital satisfaction from husbands' and wives' conflict resolution styles. *Journal of Marriage and the Family, 57,* 153–164.

Kurdek, L. A., & Fine, M. A. (1994). Family acceptance and family control as predictors of adjustment in young adolescents: Linear, curvilinear, or interactive. *Child Development, 64,* 1137–1146.

Kurdek, L. A., Fine, M. A., & Sinclair, R. J. (1995). School adjustment in sixth graders: Parenting transitions, family climate, and per norm effects. *Child Development, 66,* 430–445.

Kurz, D. (1991). Corporal punishment and adult use of violence: A critique of "discipline and deviance." *Social Problems, 38,* 155–166.

Kurzweil, S. R. (1988). Recognition of mother from multisensory interactions in early infancy. *Infant Behavior and Development, 11,* 235–243.

Laboratory of Comparative Human Cognition, Culture, and Cognitive Development. (1983). In P. H. Mussen (Ed.), *Handbook of child development* (4th ed.) (Vol. 1, pp. 295–357). New York: Wiley.

Labouvie-Vief, G. (1980). Beyond formal operations: Uses and limits of pure logic in life-span development. *Human Development, 23,* 141–161.

Labouvie-Vief, G. (1982). Growth and aging in life-span perspective. *Human Development, 25,* 65–78.

Labouvie-Vief, G. (1984). Logic and self-regulation from youth to maturity: A model. In M. L. Commons, F. A. Richards, & C. Armon (Eds.), *Beyond formal operations* (pp. 158–181). New York: Praeger.

Labouvie-Vief, G. (1985). Intelligence and cognition. In J. E. Birren & K. W. Schaie (Eds.), *Handbook of the psychology of aging* (2nd ed., pp. 500–531). New York: Van Nostrand Reinhold.

Labouvie-Vief, G. (1990). Wisdom as integrated thought: Historical and developmental perspectives. In R. J. Sternberg (Ed.), *Wisdom: Its Nature, Origins, and Development* (pp. 52–87). Cambridge: Cambridge University Press.

Labouvie-Vief, G., & Schell, D. A. (1982). Learning and memory in later life. In B. B. Wolman (Ed.), *Handbook of developmental psychology* (pp. 828–847). Englewood Cliffs, NJ: Prentice Hall.

Lachs, M. S., & Pillemer, K. (1995, February 16). Abuse and neglect of elderly persons. *The New England Journal of Medicine, 332,* 437–443.

Lackey, C., & Williams, K. R. (1995). Social bonding and the cessation of partner violence across generations. *Journal of Marriage and the Family, 57,* 295–305.

Ladd, G. W., & Le Sieur, K. D. (1995). Parents and children's peer relationships. In M. H. Bornstein (Ed.), *Handbook of parenting* (Vol. 4, pp. 377–411). Mahwah, NJ: Erlbaum.

Ladd, G. W., & Price, J. M. (1993). Play styles of peer-accepted and peer-rejected children on the playground. In C. H. Hart (Ed.), *Children on playgrounds: Research perspectives and applications* (pp. 130–161). Albany, NY: SUNY Press.

Ladner, J. (1987). Black teenage pregnancy: A challenge for educators. *Journal of Negro Education, 56,* 53–63.

LaFromboise, T. D., & Low, K. G. (1989). American Indian children and adolescents. In *Children of color: Psychological interventions with minority youth* (pp. 114–148). San Francisco: Jossey-Bass.

Laks, D. R., Beckwith, L., & Cohen, S. E. (1990). Mothers' use of personal pronouns when talking with toddlers. *Journal of Genetic Psychology, 151,* 25–32.

Lamaze, F. (1970). *Painless childbirth.* Chicago: Regnery.

Lamb, M. E. (1988). Social and emotional development in infancy. In M. H. Bornstein & M. E. Lamb (Eds.), *Social, emotional and personality development* (pp. 359–411). Hillsdale, NJ: Erlbaum.

Lamb, M. E., Frodi, M., Hwang, C. P., & Frodi, A. M. (1983). Effects of paternal involvement on infant preferences for mothers and fathers. *Child Development, 54,* 450–458.

Lamborn, S., Mounts, N., Steinberg, L., & Dornbusch, S., (1991). Patterns of competence and adjustment among adolescents from authoritative, authoritarian, indulgent and neglectful homes. *Child Development, 62,* 1049–1065.

Lampl, M., Cameron, N., Veldhuis, J. D., & Jonson, M. L. (1995, April 21). Response. *Science, 268,* 445–447.

Lampl, M., Veldhuis, J. D., & Johnson, M. L. (1992). Saltation and status: A model of human growth. *Science, 258,* 801–803.

Lancashare, J. (1995). National center for health statistics data line. *Public Health Reports, 110,* 105–106.

Landau-Stanton, J., & Clements, C. D., (1993). *AIDS health and mental health: A primary sourcebook.* New York: Brunner/Mazel.

Lando, H. A., Pechacek, T. F., Pirie, P. L., Murray, D. M., Mittelmark, M. B., Lichtenstein, E., Nothwehr, F., & Gray, C., (1995). Changes in adult cigarette smoking in the Minnesota Heart Health Program. *American Journal of Public Health, 85,* 201–208.

Lane, E. (1995, April 11). Teen surveys vs. parental consent. *Newsday,* p. B29.

Lane, E. (1995, September 8) Drug's use urged as stroke curb. *Newsday,* p. A19.

Lane, K. E., & Gwartney-Gibbs, P. A. (1985). Violence in the context of dating and sex. *Journal of Family Issues, 6,* 45–49.

Langer, E. J., & Rodin, J. (1976). The effects of choice and enhanced personal responsibility for the aged: A field experiment in an institutional setting. *Journal of Personality and Social Psychology, 34,* 191–198.

Langhinrichsen-Rolhling, J. & Smutzler, N. (1994) Positivity in marriage: The role of discord and physical aggression against women. *Journal of Marriage and the Family, 56,* 69–80.

Langlois, J. H., & Downs, A. C. (1980). Mothers, fathers, and peers as socialization agents of sex-typed play behavior in young children. *Child Development, 51,* 1237–1247.

Lapsley, D. K., Milstead, M., & Quintana, S. M. (1986). Adolescent egocentrism and formal operations: Tests of a theoretical assumption. *Developmental Psychology, 22,* 800–807.

Larroque, B., Karminski, M., Dehaene, P., Subtil, D., Delfosse, M. J., & Querleu, D. (1995). Moderate prenatal alcohol exposure and psychomotor development at preschool age. *American Journal of Public Health, 85,* 1654–1661.

Larsen, J. M., & Robinson, C. C. (1989). Later effects of preschool on low-risk children. *Early Childhood Research Quarterly, 4,* 133–144.

Larson, D. (1990/1991). Unplanned parenthood. *Modern Maturity,* 32–36.

Larson, J. (1992, June). Understanding stepfamilies. *American Demographics,* 36–42.

Larson, R., & Ham, M. (1993). Stress and "storm and stress" in early adolescence: The relationship of negative events with dysphoric affect. *Developmental Psychology, 29,* 130–140.

LaRue, A., Dessonville, C., & Jarvik, L. F. (1985). Aging and mental disorders. In J. E. Birren & K. W. Schaie (Eds.), *Handbook of the psychology of aging* (2nd ed.) (pp. 664–703). New York: Van Nostrand Reinhold.

La Rue, A., Swan, G. E., & Carmelli, D. (1995). Cognition and depression in a cohort of aging men: Results from the western collaborative group study. *Psychology and Aging, 10,* 30–34.

Laughlin, H. P. (1970). *The ego and its defenses.* New York: Appleton-Century-Crofts.

Laumann, E. O., Gagnon, J. H., Michael, R. T., & Michaels, S. (1994). *The social organization of sexuality: sexual practices in the United States.* Chicago: University of Chicago Press.

Lauresen, B., & Hartup, W. W. (1989). The dynamics of preschool children's conflicts. *Merrill-Palmer Quarterly, 35,* 281–297.

Lawrence, R. (1989). *Breastfeeding guide for the medical profession.* St. Louis, MO: Mosby.

Lawrence, R. (1991). Breast-feeding trends: A cause for action. *Pediatrics, 88,* 867–868.

Lawton, M. (1991, April 10). More than a third of teens surveyed say they have contemplated suicide. *Education Week,* p. 5.

Lawton, M. (1994, November 9). Violence-prevention curricula: What works best? *Education Week, 14,* pp. 1, 10.

Lawton, M. (1995b, November 8) Students post dismal results on history test. *Education Week,* pp. 1, 12.

Lawton, M. (1995c, October 25). Students fall short in NAEP geography test. *Education Week,* pp. 1, 23.

Lawton, M. (1996a, February 28). Teenagers have little trouble buying cigarettes, study finds. *Education Week,* p. 7.

Lazar, A., & Torney-Purta, J. (1991). The development of the subconcepts of death in young children: A short-term longitudinal study. *Child Development, 62,* 1321–1333.

Lazar, I., & Darlington, R. (1982). Lasting effects of early education: A report from the consortium for longitudinal studies. *Monographs of the Society for Research in Child Development, 47* (2–3, Serial No. 195).

Lazarus, R. S. (1993). From psychological stress to the emotions.: A history of changing outlooks. *Annual Review of Psychology, 44,* 1–21.

Lazarus, R. S., & Folkman, S. (1984). *Stress, appraisal, and coping.* New York: Springer.

Leahy, T. H., & Harris, R. J. (1997). *Learning and cognition* (4th ed.). Englewood Cliffs, NJ: Prentice Hall.

Learner, R. M. (1991). Changing Organism-context relations as the basis process of development. *Developmental Psychology, 27,* 27–33.

Lee, C. M., & Gotlib, I. H. (1993). Mental illness and the family. In L. L'Abate (Ed.), *Handbook of Developmental Family Psychology and Psychopathology,* (pp. 243–264). New York: Wiley.

Lee, G., & Shehan, C. (1989). Retirement and marital satisfaction. *Journal of Gerontology, 44,* S226–230.

Lee, I., Chung-Cheng, H., & Pafenbarger, R. S. (1995). Exercise intensity and longevity in men. *JAMA, 273,* 1179–1184.

Leepson, M. (1992, November 6) Physical fitness: Has the fitness boom of the 1970s and 1980s run out of steam. *CQ Researcher,* 955–1015.

Lehr, U. (1983). Stereotypes of aging and age norms. In J. E. Birren et al. (Eds.), *Aging: A challenge to science and society* (Vol. 3, pp. 101–112). New York: Oxford University Press.

Leland, N. L., & Barth, R. P. (1992). Gender differences in knowledge, intentions, and behaviors concerning pregnancy and sexually transmitted disease prevention among adolescents. *Journal of Adolescent Health, 13,* 589–599.

Leland, N. L., Petersen, D. J., Braddock, M., & Alexander, G. R. (1995). Variations in pregnancy outcomes by race among 10–14-year-old mothers in the United States. *Public Health Reports, 110,* 53–58.

Leming, M. R., & Dickinson, G. E. (1994). *Understanding dying, death, and bereavement* (3rd ed.). Orlando, FL: Harcourt.

Lemme, B. H. (1995). *Development in adulthood.* Boston: Allyn & Bacon.

Lemon, B. W., Bengtson, V. L., & Peterson, J. A. (1972). An explanation of the activity theory of aging: Activity types and life satisfaction among in-movers to a retirement community. *Journal of Gerontology, 27,* 511–523.

Lemp, G. et al. (1994). Seroprevalence of HIV and risk behaviors among young homosexual and bisexual men. *JAMA, 272,* 449–454.

Lenfant, C. (1987). Advancements in meeting the 1990 hypertension objectives, *JAMA, 257,* 2709–2718.

Lenneberg, E. H. (1967). *Biological foundations of language.* New York: Wiley.

Leon, G. R., & Dinklage, D. (1989). Obesity and anorexia nervosa. In T. H. Ollendick and M. Hersen (Eds.), *Handbook of Child Psychopathology* (2nd ed., pp. 247–264). New York: Plenum.

Lerner, J. V., & Abrams, L. A. (1994). Developmental correlates of maternal employment influences on children. In C. B. Fisher & R. M. Lerner (Eds.), *Applied developmental psychology* (pp. 174–192). New York: McGraw-Hill.

Lerner, R. M. Karson, M., Meisels, M., & Knapp, J. R. (1975). Actual and perceived attitudes of late adolescents and their parents: The phenomenon of the generation gap. *Journal of Genetic Psychology, 126,* 195–207.

Leshner, A. I. (1995). *Statement of Alan I. Leshner, Director, National Institute on Drug Abuse, National Institute of Health,* Washington, DC: U.S. Department of Health & Human Services.

Lester, B. M., & Dreher, M. (1989). Effects of marijuana use during pregnancy on newborn cry. *Child Development, 60,* 765–771.

Lester, B. M., Heidelise, A., & Brazelton, T. B. (1982). Regional obstetric anesthesia and newborn behavior: A reanalysis toward synergistic effects. *Child Development, 53,* 687–692.

Levant, R. E., & Doyle, G. F. (1983). An evaluation of a parent education program for fathers of school-aged children. *Family Relations, 32,* 29–37.

LeVay, S. (1991). A difference in hypothalamic structure between heterosexual and homosexual men. *Science, 253,* 1034–1037.

Levenson, R. W., Carstensen, L. L., & Gottman, J. M. (1993). Long-term marriage: Age, gender and satisfaction. *Psychology and Aging, 8,* 301–313.

Levin, J. S., Taylor, R. J., & Chatters, L. M., (1994). Race and gender differences in religiosity among older adults: Findings from four national surveys. *Journal of Gerontology: Social Sciences, 49,* S137–S145.

Levin, W. C. (1988). Age stereotyping: College student evaluations. *Research on Aging, 10,* 134–148.

Levine, K., & Mueller, E. (1988). In T. D. Yawkey & J. E. Johnson (Eds.), *Integrative processes and socialization: Early to middle childhood* (pp. 207–225). Hillsdale, NJ: Erlbaum.

LeVine, R. (1985). Adulthood and aging in cross-cultural perspective. Cited in J. E. Birren & K. W. Schaie (Eds.), *Handbook of the psychology of aging* (2nd ed. pp. 216–245). New York: Van Nostrand Reinhold.

Levinson, D. (1986). A conception of adult development. *American Psychologist, 41,* 3–13.

Levinson, D. (1990). A theory of life structure development in adulthood. In C. N. Alexander & E. J. Langer (Eds.), *Higher states of human development* (pp. 35–54). New York: Oxford University Press.

Levinson, D. J. (1978). *The seasons of a man's life.* New York: Knopf.

Levinson, D. J. (1980). Toward a conception of the adult life course. In N. J. Smelser & E. H. Erikson (Eds.), *Themes of work and love in adulthood* (pp. 265–291). Cambridge, MA: Harvard University Press.

Levinson, D. J. (1996). *The seasons of a woman's life.* New York: Knopf.

Leviton, A. (1995). Editorial: Reform without change? Look beyond the curriculum. *American Journal of Public Health, 85,* 907–908.

Levitt, M. J., Guacci-Franco, N., & Levitt, J. L. (1994). Social support and achievement in childhood and early adolescence: A multicultural study. *Journal of Applied Developmental Psychology, 15,* 207–222.

Levy, C. W. (1994, February). The bad news about Barney. *Parents,* 191–192.

Levy, F. (1995). Incomes and income inequality. In R. Farley (Ed.), *State of the Union: America in the 1990s* (pp. 1–59). New York: Russell Sage.

Levy, G. D., & Carter, D. B. (1989). Gender schema, gender constancy, and gender-role knowledge: The roles of cognitive factors in preschoolers' gender-role stereotype attributions. *Developmental Psychology, 25,* 444–450.

Levy, J. M., Jesspo, D. J., Rimmerman, A., & Levy, P. H. (1992). Attitudes of Fortune 500 corporate executives toward the employability of persons with severe disabilities: A national study. *Mental Retardation, 30,* 67–75.

Levy-Shiff, R. (1994). Individual and contextual correlates of marital change across transition to parenthood. *Developmental Psychology, 30,* 591–601.

Lewis, M. (1987). Social development in infancy and early childhood. In J. Osofsky (Ed.), *Handbook of infant development* (2nd ed., pp. 419–493). New York: Wiley.

Lewis, M., Alessandri, S. M., & Sullivan, M. W. (1990). Violation of expectancy, loss of control, and anger expressions in young infants. *Developmental Psychology, 26,* 745–751.

Lewis, M., Alessandri, S. M., & Sullivan, M. W. (1992). Differences in shame and pride as a function of children's gender and task difficulty. *Child Development, 63,* 630–638.

Lewis, M., & Brooks-Gunn, J. (1979). *Social cognition and the acquisition of self.* New York: Plenum.

Lewis, M., & Feiring, C. (1989). Infant, mother, and mother-infant interaction behavior and subsequent attachment. *Child Development, 60,* 831–838.

Lewis, M., & Rosenblum, L. A. (Eds.), (1975). *Friendship and peer relations.* New York: Wiley.

Lewis, M., Stanger, C., & Sullivan, M. W. (1989). Deception in 3-year-olds. *Developmental Psychology, 25,* 439–443.

Lewis, M., Sullivan, M. W., Stanger, C., & Weiss, M. (1989). Self development and self-conscious emotion. *Child Development, 60,* 146–156.

Lewis, R. G., & Ho, M. K. (1979). Social work with Native Americans. *Social Work, 20,* 379–392.

Lewit, E. M., & Baker, L. S. (1995). Health insurance coverage. *The Future of Children: Long-term outcomes of early childhood programs, 5,* 192–204.

Lewkowicz, D. J. (1996). Infants' response to the audible and visible properties of the human face 1. Role of lexical-syntactic content, temporal synchrony, gender, and manner of speech. *Developmental Psychology, 32,* 347–366.

Lezotte, L. W. (1982, November). Characteristics of effective schools and programs for realizing them. *Education Digest,* pp. 27–29.

Liben, L. S., & Signorella, M. L. (1993). Gender-schematic processing in children: The role of initial interpretations of stimuli. *Developmental Psychology, 29,* 141–149.

Lichter, D. T., & Eggebeen, D. J. (1994). The effect of parental employment on child poverty. *Journal of Marriage and the Family, 56,* 633–646.

Lieberman, A. F. (1993). *The emotional life of the toddler.* New York: MacMillan.

Lieberman, E. & Ryan, K. J. (1989, Dec. 28). Birth-day choices. *The New England Journal of Medicine, 321,* 1824–1825.

Lieberman, E., Gremy, I., Lang, J. M., & Cohen, A. P. (1995). Low birthweight at term and the timing of fetal exposure to maternal smoking. *American Journal of Public Health, 84,* 1127–1131.

Lieberman, M. A., & Fisher, L. (1995). The impact of chronic illness on the health and well-being of family members. *The Gerontologist, 35,* 94–102.

Liebert, R. M., & Sprafkin, J. (1988). *The early window: Effects of television on children and youth* (3rd ed.). New York: Pergamon Press.

Light, D., Keller, S., & Calhoun, C. (1989). *Sociology* (5th ed.). New York: Knopf.

Light, D., Keller, S., & Calhoun, C. (1994). *Sociology* (7th ed.). New York: Knopf.

Light, L. L. (1991). Memory and aging: Four hypotheses in search of data. *Annual Review of Psychology, 42,* 333–376.

Light, P. C. (1988). *Baby boomers.* New York: Norton.

Lillard, A. S. (1993). Pretend play skills and the child's theory of mind. *Child Development, 64,* 348–371.

Lin, C. C., & Fu, V. R. (1990). A comparison of child-rearing practices among Chinese, immigrant Chinese, and Caucasian-American parents. *Child Development, 61,* 429–433.

Lin, K. M., Poland, R. E., & Lesser, I. M. (1986). Ethnicity and psychopharmacology. *Culture, Medicine and Psychiatry, 10,* 151–165.

Lindbaum, M. L., Sallmen, M., Antila, A., Taskinen, H., Hemminski, K., (1991). Paternal occupational lead exposure and spontaneous abortion. *Scandinavian Journal of Work Environment Health, 81,* 1029–1033.

Lindberg, L. D. (1996). Women's decisions about breastfeeding and maternal employment. *Journal of Marriage and The Family, 58,* 239–252.

Lindberg, M. (1980). The role of knowledge structures in the ontogeny of learning. *Journal of Experimental Child Psychology, 30,* 401–410.

Lindemann, E. (1944). Symptomatology and management of acute grief. In L. A. Bugen (Ed.) (1979). *Death and Dying.* Dubuque, IA: Brown, 7–17.

Lindenberger, U., Kliegl, R., & Baltes, P. B. (1992). Professional expertise does not eliminate age differences in imagery-based memory performance during adulthood. *Psychology and Aging, 7,* 585–593.

Link, B., Phelan, J., Bresnahan, M., Stueve, A., Moore, R., & Susser, E. (1995). Lifetime and five-year prevalence of homelessness in the United States: New evidence on an old debate. *American Journal of Orthopsychiatry, 65,* 347–354.

Linn, M. W., Giurel, L., & Linn, B. S. (1977). Patient outcome as a measure of quality of nursing home care. *American Journal of Public Health, 67,* 337–344.

Linn, M. W., Sandifer, R., & Stein, S. (1985). Effects of unemployment on mental and physical health. *American Journal of Public Health, 75,* 502–506.

Lipinska, B., Backman, L., & Herlitz, A. (1992). When Greta Garbo is easier to remember than Stefan Edberg: Influences of prior knowledge of recognition memory in Alzheimer's disease. *Psychology and Aging, 7,* 214–220.

Lipsitt, L. P. (1990). Learning and memory in infants. *Merrill-Palmer Quarterly, 36,* 53–66.

Lipsitt, L. P., & Kaye, H. (1964). Conditioned sucking in the newborn. *Psychonomic Science, 1,* 29–30.

Lipsitt, L. P., & Levy, N. (1959). Electrotactual threshold in the neonate. *Child Development, 30,* 547–554.

List, J. A. (1986). Age and schematic differences in the reliability of eyewitness testimony. *Developmental Psychology, 22,* 50–58.

Little, R. E., & Sing, C. F. (1987). Father's drinking and infant birth weight: Report of an association. *Teratology, 36,* 59–65.

Lo, B. (1995, November 22/29). Improving care near the end of life: Why is it so hard? *Journal of the American Medical Association, 274,* 1634–1636.

Lobel, T. E., & Menashri, J. (1993). Relations of conceptions of gender-role transgressions and gender constancy to gender-typed toy preferences. *Developmental Psychology, 29,* 150–155.

Lockhart, A. S. (1980). Motor learning and motor development during infancy and childhood. In C. B. Corbin (Ed.), *A textbook of motor development* (2nd ed., pp. 246–253). Dubuque, IA: Brown.

Loeber, R., & Stouthamer-Loeber, M. (1986). Family factors as correlates and predictors of juvenile conduct problems and delinquency. In M. Tonry & N. Morris (Eds.), *Crime and justice: An annual review of research* (Vol. 7). Chicago: University of Chicago Press.

Loehlin, J. C. (1992). *Genes and environment in personality development.* Newbury Park, CA: Sage.

Loehlin, J. C., Horn, J. M., & Willerman, L. (1989). Modeling IQ change: Evidence from the Texas Adoption Project. *Child Development, 60,* 993–1005.

Lombard, D. N., Lombard, T. N., & Winett, R. A. (1995). Walking to meet health guidelines: The effect of prompting frequency and prompt structure. *Health Psychology, 14,* 164–170.

Lombroso, P. J., Pauls, D. L., & Leckman, J. F. (1994). Genetic mechanisms in childhood psychiatric disorders. *Journal of the Academy of Child Adolescent Psychiatry, 33,* 921–938.

Londerville, S., & Main, M. (1981). Security, compliance, and maternal training methods in the second year of life. *Developmental Psychology, 17,* 289–299.

London, K. A. (1991, January 4). Cohabitation, marriage, marital dissolution, and remarriage: United States, 1988. Data from the National Survey of Family Growth. Washington, DC: U.S. Department of Health and Human Services.

Long, E. C. J., & Andrews, D. W. (1990). Perspective taking as a predictor of marital adjustment. *Journal of Personality and Social Psychology, 59,* 126–131.

Long, G. M., & Crambert, R. F. (1990). The nature and basis of age-related changes in dynamic visual acuity. *Psychology and Aging, 5,* 138–143.

Long, P. J., & Shannon, B. (1983). *Nutrition: An inquiry into the issues.* Englewood Cliffs, NJ: Prentice Hall.

Longino, C. F., Jackson, D. J., Zimmerman, R. S., & Bradsher, J. E. (1991). The second move: Health and geographic mobility. *Journal of Gerontology, 46,* S218–224.

Longino, C. F., Jr. (1994 August). Myths of an aging America. *American Demographics, 16,* 36–44.

Longstreth, L. E. (1981). Revisiting Skeel's final study: A critique. *Developmental Psychology, 17,* 620–625.

Loomis, L. S., & Landale, N. S. (1994). Nonmarital cohabitation and childbearing among black and white American women. *Journal of Marriage and the Family, 56,* 949–962.

Lopata, H. Z. (1973). *Widowhood in an American city.* Cambridge, MA: Schenkman.

Lopata, H. Z. (1979). *Women as widows: Support systems.* New York: Elsevier.

Lorenz, K. (1937). The companion in the bird's world. *AUK, 54,* 245–273.

Lorion, R. P., & Saltzman, W. (1993). Children's exposure to community violence: Following a path from concern to research to action. *Psychiatry, 56,* 55–65.

Lovett, M. W., Borden, S. L., DeLuca, T., Lacerenza, L., Benson, N. J., & Brackstone, D. (1994). Treating the core deficits of developmental dyslexia: Evidence of transfer of learning after phonologically- and strategy-based reading training programs. *Developmental Psychology, 30,* 805–822.

Lowenthal, M., Thurnher, M., & Chiriboga, D. (1975). *Four stages of life.* San Francisco: Jossey-Bass.

Lowenthal, M. F., & Chiriboga, D. (1972). Transition to the empty nest. *Archives of General Psychiatry, 26,* 8–14.

Lowik, M. R. H., Wedel, M., Kok, F. J., Odink, J., Westenbrink, S., & Meulmeester, J. F. (1991). Nutrition and serum cholesterol levels among elderly men and women (Dutch Nutrition Surveillance System). *Journal of Gerontology, 46,* 23–28.

Lowrey, G. (1978). *Growth and Development of Children* (7th ed.). Chicago: Year Book Medical Publishers.

Lubomudrov, S. (1987). Congressional perceptions of the elderly: The use of stereotypes in the legislative process. *Journal of Gerontology, 27,* 77–81.

Lucas, A., Morley, R., Cole, T. J., Lister, G., & Leeson-Payne, (1992). Breast milk and subsequent intelligence quotient in children born preterm. *Lancet, 339,* 261–264.

Luster, T., & McAdoo, H. P. (1994). Factors related to the achievement and adjustment of young African American children. *Child Development, 65,* 1080–1094.

Lyon, T. D., & Flavell, J. H. (1993). Young children's understanding of forgetting over time. *Child Development, 64,* 789–800.

Lyons, N. P. (1990). Listening to voices we have not heard. In C. Gilligan, N. P. Lyons, T. J. Hammer (Eds.), *Making connections.* Cambridge, MA: Harvard University Press.

Lyons-Ruth, K., Alpern, L., & Repacholi, B. (1993). Disorganized infant attachment classification and maternal psychosocial problems as predictors of hostile-aggressive behavior in the preschool classroom. *Child Development, 64,* 572–585.

Lytton, H. & Romney, D. M. (1991). Parents' differential socialization of boys and girls: A meta-analysis. *Psychological Bulletin, 109,* 267–296.

Lytton, H., Watts, D., & Dunn, B. E. (1988). Continuity and change in child characteristics and maternal practices between ages 2 and 9: An analysis of interview responses. *Child Study Journal, 18,* 1–15.

Maas, H. S. (1989). Social responsibility in middle age: Prospective and preconditions. In S. Hunter & M. Sundel (Eds.). *Midlife myths: Issues, findings, and practical implications* (pp. 253–272). Newbury Park, CA: Sage.

Maccoby, E., & Martin, J. (1983). Socialization in the context of the family: Parent-child interaction. In E. M. Hetherington & P. H. Mussen (Eds.), *Handbook of Child Psychology:* (Vol. 4, pp. 1–101). New York: Wiley.

Maccoby, E. E. (1980). *Social development: Psychological growth and the parent-child relationship.* New York: Harcourt Brace Jovanovich.

Maccoby, E. E. (1990). Gender and relationships: A developmental account. *American Psychologist, 45,* 513–521.

Maccoby, E. E., Buchanan, C. M., Mnookin, R. H., & Dornbush, S. M. (1993). Post-divorce roles of mothers and fathers in the lives of their children. *Journal of Family Psychology, 7,* 24–38.

Maccoby, E. E., & Jacklin, C. N. (1974). *The psychology of sex differences.* Stanford, CA: Stanford University Press.

Maccoby, E. E., & Jacklin, C. (1980). Sex differences in aggression: A rejoinder and reprise. *Child Development, 51,* 964–980.

Maccoby, E. E., & Martin, J. A. (1983). Socialization in the context of the family: Parent-child interaction. In P. H. Mussen (Ed.), *Handbook of child development* (4th ed.) (Vol. 4, pp. 1–103). New York: Wiley.

MacDormand, M. F., & Rosenberg, H. M. (1993). Trends in infant mortality by cause of death and other characteristics. *Vital Health Statistics, 1993:* DHHS Publication PHS 93–1857.

MacFarlane, A. (1981). Olfaction in the development of social preferences in the human neonate. Cited in T. B. Brazelton, *On becoming a family: The growth of attachment.* New York: Delacorte.

MacKinnon, D. (1978). *In search of human effectiveness.* Buffalo: Creative Education Foundation.

MacMillan, H. L., MacMillan, J. H., Offord, D. R., Griffith, L., & MacMillan, A. (1994a). Primary prevention of child abuse and neglect: A critical review. Part 1. *Journal of Child Psychology and Psychiatry and Allied Disciplines, 35,* 835–856.

MacMillan, H. L., MacMillan, J. H., Offord, D. R., Griffth, L., & MacMillan, A. (1994b). Primary prevention of child sexual abuse: A critical review. Part II. *Journal of Child Psychology and Psychiatry and Allied Disciplines, 35,* 857–876.

Madden, M., (1996, June 18). Kids take parents' lead to read and succeed. *USA Today,* p. 1D.

Maddox, G. (1970). Fact and artifact: Evidence bearing on disengagement theory. In E. Palmore (Ed.), *Normal aging*. Durham, NC: Duke University Press.

Madrid, A. (1993, August 13). Should the United States adopt English as its "official" language? No. *CQ Researcher*, p. 713.

Maeda, D. (1978). Aging in Eastern society. In D. Hobman (Ed.), *The social challenge of aging* (pp. 45–73). New York: St. Martin's Press.

Maeroff, G. I. (1996, March 6). Apathy and anonymity: Combating the twin scourges of modern post-adolescence. *Education Week*, pp. 46, 60.

Maglio, C. J., & Robinson, S. E. (1994). The effects of death education on death anxiety: A meta-analysis. *Omega, 29*, 319–335.

Mahler, K. (1996). Delay in first sex is seen among British teenagers in sex education program. *Family Planning Perspectives, 28*, 83–84.

Maier, T. (1997, June 27). Back to states: Supreme Court sees no right to M.D.-aided suicide. *Newsday*, 2-3, 4, 40.

Main, M., & Cassidy, J. (1988). Categories of response to reunion with the parent at age 6: Predictable from infant attachment classifications and stable over a one-month period. *Developmental Psychology, 24*, 415–427.

Main, M., Kaplan, N., & Cassidy, J. (1985). Security in infancy, childhood and adulthood: A move to the level of representation. In I. Bretherton & E. Waters (Eds.), Growing points in attachment theory and research. *Monographs of the Society for Research in Child Development, 50*, 66–104.

Main, M., & Soloman, J. (1990). Procedures for identifying infants as disorganized/disoriented during the Ainsworth strange situation. In M. Greenberg, D. Cicchetti, & M. Cummings (Eds.), *Attachment in the preschool years: Theory, research, and intervention* (pp. 121–160). Chicago: University of Chicago Press.

Main, M., & Weston, D. R. (1981). The quality of the toddler's relationship to mother and to father: Related to conflict behavior and readiness to establish new relationships. *Child Development, 52*, 932–940.

Majerovitz, S. D. (1995). Role of family adaptability in the psychological adjustment of spouse caregivers to patents with dementia. *Psychology and Aging, 10*, 447–457.

Makin, J. W., & Porter, R. H. (1989). Attractiveness of lactating females' breast odors to neonates. *Child Development, 60*, 803–811.

Making money by making babies. (1992, June 10). *New York Times*, p. A22.

Malatesta, C. Z., Culver, C., Tesman, J. R., & Shepard, B. (1989). The development of emotion expression during the first two years of life. *Monographs of the Society for Research in Child Development, 54* (1–2, Serial No. 219).

Malatesta, C. Z., Grigoryev, P., Lamb, C., Albin, M., & Culver, C. (1986). Emotion socialization and expressive development in preterm and full-term infants. *Child Development, 57*, 316–330.

Malatesta, C. Z., & Haviland, J. M. (1982). Learning display rules: The socialization of emotion expression in infancy. *Child Development, 53*, 991–1003.

Malfetti, J. L., & Winter, D. J. (1991). Concerned about an older driver?: A guide for families and friends. Washington, DC: AAA Foundation for Traffic Safety.

Malinowski, C. I., & Smith, C. P. (1985). Moral reasoning and moral conduct: An investigation prompted by Kohlberg's theory. *Journal of Personality and Social Psychology, 49*, 1016–1027.

Malnutrition hits many elderly. (July 3, 1995). *New York Times*, p. 28.

Mandel, D. R. (1995). Chaos theory, sensitive dependence, and the logistic equation. *American Psychologist, 50*, 106–107.

Mandel, D. R., Jusczyk, P. W., & Pisoni, D. B. (1995). Infants' recognition of the sound patterns of their own names. *Psychological Science, 6*, 314–317.

Mandler, J., & Johnson, N. (1977). Remembrance of things passed: Story structure and recall. *Cognitive Development, 9*, 111–151.

Mandler, J. M. (1990). A new perspective on cognitive development in infancy. *American Scientist, 78*, 236–243.

Manney, J. D. (1975). *Aging*, Washington, DC: Department of Health, Education, and Welfare.

Manning, A. (1994, October 21). Trouble follows armed students. *USA Today*, p. 1D.

Manning, M. L., & Allen, M. G. (1987). Social development in early adolescence, *Childhood Education, 18*, 172–176.

Manson, J. E., Colditz, G. A., Stampfer, M. J. H., et al. (1990). A prospective study of obesity and risk of coronary heart diseases in women. *New England Journal of Medicine, 322*, 882–990.

Manton, K. G., Wrigley, J. M., Cohen, H. J., & Woodbury, M. A. (1991). Cancer mortality, aging, and patterns of comorbidity in the United States: 1968 to 1986. *Journal of Gerontology, 46*, 225–233.

Many overestimate breast cancer risk. (1995, May 17). *Newsday*, p. A16.

Maples, M. F. (1981). Dual career marriages: Elements for potential success. *Personnel and Guidance Journal, 60*, 19–25.

March of Dimes (1983). *Be good to your baby before it is born*. White Plains, NY: March of Dimes.

March of Dimes (1986b). *PKU*. Public health information series.

March of Dimes (1989). *VDT Facts*. Public Health Education Information Sheet.

March of Dimes (1990). Personal communication.

Marcia, J. (1967). Ego identity status: Relationship to change in self-esteem, "general maladjustment," and authoritarianism. *Journal of Personality, 35*, 118–133.

Marcia, J. (1980). Identity in adolescence. In J. Adelson (Ed.), *Handbook of adolescent psychology*, New York: Wiley.

Marcus, G. F., Pinker, S., Ullman, M., Hollander, M., Rosen, T. J., & Xu, F. (1992). Overregularization in language acquisition. *Monographs of the Society for Research in Child Development, 57*, No. 228.

Marczely, B. (1993). The Americans with Disabilities Act: Confronting the shortcomings of section 504 in public education. *West's Education Law Reporter, 78*, 199–207.

Mare, R. D. (1995). Changes in educational attainment and School Enrollment. In R. Farley (Ed.), *State of the Union: America in the 1990s* (pp. 155–115). New York: Russell Sage Foundation.

Marean, G. C., Werner, L. A., & Kuhl, P. K. (1992). Vowel categorization by very young infants. *Developmental Psychology, 28*, 396–405.

Mariner, W. K. (1995). AIDS phobia: Public health warnings, and lawsuits: deterring harm or rewarding ignorance? *American Journal of Public Health, 85*, 1562–1568.

Markides, K. S., & Black, S. A. (1996). Race, ethnicity, and aging: The impact of inequality. In R. H. Binstock & L. K. George (Eds.), *Handbook of Aging and the Social Sciences* (4th ed., pp. 153–170). San Diego, CA: Academic Press.

Markides, K. S., & Martin, H. W. (1979). A causal model of life satisfaction among the elderly. *Journal of Gerontology, 34*, 36–93.

Markson, E. W. (1992, July/August). Moral dilemmas. *Society, 29*, 4–6.

Marsh, G. R., & Thompson, L. W. (1977).

Psychophysiology of aging. In J. E. Birren & K. W. Schaie (Eds.), *Handbook of the psychology of aging* (pp. 219–241). New York: Van Nostrand.

Marshall, J. (1983). Reducing the effects of work oriented values on the lives of male American workers. *Vocational and Guidance Journal, 32,* 109–115.

Marshall, J. R. (1995). Editorial: Improving Americans' diet—Setting public policy with limited knowledge. *American Journal of Public Health, 85,* 1609–1611.

Marshall, S. P., & Smith, J. D. (1987). Sex differences in learning mathematics. A longitudinal study with item and error analysis. *Journal of Education Psychology, 79,* 372–381.

Marshall, V. (1980). *Last Chapters: A Sociology of Aging and Dying.* Pacific Grove, CA: Brooks/Cole.

Marshall, V. W. (1995). The next half-century of aging research—and thoughts for the past. *The Journal of Gerontology, 50B,* s131–133.

Marshall, V. W., & Levy, J. A. (1990). Aging and dying. In R. H. Binstock & L. K. George (Eds.), *Handbook of aging and the social sciences* (3rd ed., pp. 245–260). New York: Academic Press.

Marsiglio, W. (1993). Attitudes toward homosexual activity and gays as friends: A national survey of heterosexual 15- to 19-year-old males. *Journal of sex research, 30,* 12–17.

Martin, B. (1975). Parent-child relationships. In F. D. Horowitz (Ed.), *Review of child development research* (Vol. 4, pp. 463–540). Chicago: University of Chicago Press.

Martin, C. L., Eisenbud, L., & Rose, H. (1995). Children's gender-based reasoning about toys. *Child Development, 66,* 1453–1471.

Martin, C. L., & Halverson, C. F. (1981). A schematic processing model of sex-typing and stereotyping in children. *Child Development, 52,* 1119–1132.

Martin, H. A. (1978). Child-oriented approach to prevention of abuse. In A. W. Franklin (Ed.), *Child abuse* (pp. 9–20). London: Churchill-Livingston.

Martin, S. (1995, October). Practitioners may misunderstand black families. *Monitor,* p. 36.

Martin, T. C., & Bumpass, L. L. (1989). Recent trends in marital disruption. *Demography, 26,* 37–52.

Martinez, F. D., Wright, A. L., Taussig, L. M., & the Group Health Medical Associates (1994). The Effect of paternal smoking on the birthweight of newborns whose mothers did not smoke. *American Journal of Public Health, 84,* 1489–1491.

Martinez, P. & Richters, J. E. (1993). The NIMH community violence project II. Children's distress symptoms associated with violence exposure. *Psychiatry, 56,* 22–35.

Martocchio, J. J. (1989). Age-related differences in employee absenteeism: A meta-analysis. *Psychology and Aging, 4,* 409–414.

Masheter, C. (1991). Postdivorce relationships between ex-spouses: The roles of attachment and interpersonal conflict. *Journal of Marriage and the Family, 53,* 103–110.

Mason, J. O. (1993). The dimensions of an epidemic of violence. *Public Health Reports, 108,* 1–4.

Mason, S. E., & Smith, A. D. (1977). Imagery in the aged. *Experimental Aging Research, 3,* 17–32.

Masters, H. H., Johnson, V. E., & Kolondy, R. C. (1991). *Human sexuality.* Boston: Little, Brown.

Masters, W., & Johnson, V. E. (1966). *Human sexual response.* Boston: Little, Brown.

Masters, W. H., Johnson, V. E., & Kolodny, R. C. (1988). *Masters and Johnson on sex and human loving.* Glenview, IL: Scott, Foresman.

Matas, L., Arend, R., & Sroufe, L. A. (1978). Continuity of adaptation in the second year: The relationship between quality of attachment and later competence. *Child Development, 49,* 547–556.

Mates, B. F., & Strommen, L. (1995, December). Why Ernie can't read. . . . Who reads on *Sesame Street? The Reading Teacher, 49,* 300–306.

Matis, R., & Cohn, J. F. (1993). Are Max-specified infant facial expressions during face-to-face interaction consistent with differential emotions theory? *Developmental Psychology, 29,* 524–531.

Matis, R., Cohn, J. F., & Ross, S. (1989). A comparison of two systems that code infant affective expression. *Developmental Psychology, 25,* 483–489.

Matthews, K. A. (1992). Myths and realities of the menopause. *Psychosomatic Medicine, 54,* 1–9.

Matthews, K. A., Wing, R. R., Kuller, L. H., Meilahn, E. N., Kelsey, S. F., Costello, E. J., Caggiula, A. W. (1990). Influences of natural menopause on psychological characteristics and symptoms of middle-aged healthy women. *Journal of Consulting and Clinical Psychology, 58,* 345–351.

Matthews, S. H. (1987). Provision of care to old parents: Division of responsibility among adult children. *Research on Aging, 9,* 455–460.

Matthews, S. H., & Sprey, J. (1985). Adolescents' relationships with grandparents: An empirical contribution to conceptual clarification. *Journal of Gerontology, 40,* 621–626.

Matthews, S. H., Werkner, J. E., & Delaney, P. J. (1989). Relative contributions of help by employed and nonemployed sisters to their elderly parents. *Journal of Gerontology, 44,* S36–44.

Mattox, W. R., Jr. (1996, August 8). Too pooped to parent. *USA Today,* p. 14A.

Mauldon, J., & Luker, K. (1996). The effects of contraceptive education on method use at first intercourse. *Family Planning Perspectives, 28,* 19–24, 41.

Maurer, D., & Salapatek, P. (1976). Developmental changes in the scanning of faces by young infants. *Child Development, 47,* 523–527.

Maxwell, R. J., & Silverman, P. (1970). Information and esteem. *Aging and Human Development, 1,* 127–146.

Mayaux, M. J., Burgard, M., Telas, J. P., Cottalorda, J., Keivine, A., Simon, F. et al. (1996, February 28). Neonatal characteristics in rapidly progressive perinatally acquired HIV-1 Disease. *Journal of the American Medical Association, 275,* 506–610.

Mayer, J. E., & Ligman, J. D. (1989). Personality characteristics of adolescent marijuana users. *Adolescence, 24,* 965–975.

Mayes, L. C. (1995). Substance abuse and parenting. In M. H. Bornstein (Ed.), *Handbook of parenting.* Vol. 4, Mahway, NJ: Erlbaum, 101–125.

Mayes, L. C., Granger, R. H., Bornstein, M. H., & Zuckerman, B. (1992). The problem of prenatal cocaine exposure: A rush to judgment. *JAMA, 267,* 406–408.

Maynard, R., & Rangarajan, A. (1994). Contraceptive use and repeat pregnancies among welfare-dependent teenage mothers. *Family Planning Perspectives, 26,* 198–205.

McAdams, D. P., & de St. Aubin, E. (1992). A theory of generativity and its assessment through self-report, behavioral acts, and narrative themes in autobiography. *Journal of Personality and Social Psychology, 62,* 1003–1015.

McAdams, D. P., de St. Aubin, E., & Logan, R. L. (1993). Generativity among Young, Midlife, and Older Adults. *Psychology and Aging, 8,* 221–230.

McAdoo, H. P. (1991). Family values and outcomes for children. *Journal of Negro Education, 60,* 361–365.

McAuley, W., & Blieszner, R. (1985). Selection of long-term care arrangements. *Gerontologist, 25,* 188–193.

McBride, B. A., & Darragh, J. (1995). Interpreting data on father involvement: implications for parenting programs for men. *Families in Society, 78,* 490–497.

McBride, B. A., & McBride, R. J. (1993). Parent education and support programs for fathers: Research guiding practice. *Childhood Education, 70,* 4–9.

McBride, B. A., & Mills, G. (1993). A comparison of mother and father involvement with their preschool age children. *Early Childhood Research Quarterly, 8,* 457-477.

McBride-Chang, C. (1995). What is phonological awareness? *Journal of Educational Psychology, 87,* 179–192.

McBroom, P. (1980). *Behavioral genetics.* National Institute of Mental Health Science Monograph. Washington, DC: Department of Health, Education, and Welfare.

McCabe, A. E. & Siegel, L. S. (1987). The stability of training effects in young children's class inclusion reasoning. *Merrill-Palmer Quarterly, 33,* 187–194.

McCall, P. L. (1991). Adolescent and elderly white male suicide trends: Evidence of changing well-being? *Journal of Gerontology, 46,* 43–51.

McCall, R. B. (1979). The development of intellectual functioning in infancy and the prediction of later I.Q. In J. Osofsky (Ed.), *Handbook of infant development* (pp. 707–742). New York: Wiley.

McCall, R. B. (1981). Nature-nurture and the two realms of development: A proposed integration with respect to mental development. *Child Development, 52,* 1–12.

McCall, R. B. (1987). Developmental function, individual differences, and the plasticity of intelligence. In J. J. Gallagher & C. T. Ramey (Eds.), *The malleability of children* (pp. 15–25). Baltimore: Paul Brookes.

McCall, R. B., Hogarty, P. S., & Hurlburt, N. (1972). Transitions in infant sensorimotor development and the prediction of childhood I.Q. *American Psychologist, 27,* 728–748.

McCammon, S., Knox, D., & Schacht, C. (1993). *Choices in Sexuality.* St. Paul, MN: West.

McCarthy, A. (1991, September). The country of the old. *Commonweal, 118,* 505–506.

McCarthy, A. (1994 June 3). Generations aren't seamless. *Commonweal, 121,* 9–11.

McCarthy, K. (1993, July). Research on women's health doesn't show whole picture. *APA Monitor,* 14–15.

McCauley, K. (1992). Preventing child abuse through the schools. *Children Today, 21,* 8–11. Washington, DC: Administration for Children and Families, Department of Health & Human Services.

McClanahan, S., & Booth, K. (1991). Mother-only families: Problems, prospects, and politics. In A. Booth (Ed.), *Contemporary families: Looking forward, looking back.* Minneapolis, MN: National Council on Family Relations.

McClearn, G. E. (1993). Behavioral genetics: The last century and the next. In R. Plomin & G. E. McClearn (Eds.), *Nature, nurture, & psychology* (pp. 27–55). Washington, DC: American Psychological Association.

McConatha, D., McConatha, J. T., & Dermigny, R. (1994). The use of interactive computer services to enhance the quality of life for long-term care residents. *The Gerontologist, 34,* 553–556.

McCord, J. (1991). Questioning the value of punishment. *Social Problems, 38,* 167–179.

McCord, W. (1992, July/August). Dignity, choice, and care. *Reason,* 20–24.

McCrae, R. R. (1982). Age differences in the use of coping mechanisms. *Journal of Gerontology, 37,* 454–460.

McCrae, R. R., Bartone, P. T., & Costa, P. T. (1976). Age, personality, and self-reported health. *International Journal of Aging and Human Development, 6,* 49–58.

McCrae, R. R. & Costa, P. T., Jr. (1990). *Personality in adulthood.* New York: Guilford Press.

McCrone, W. P. (1994). A two-year report card on Title 1 of the Americans with Disabilities Act: Implications for Rehabilitation counseling with deaf people. *Journal of Rehabilitation of the Deaf, 28,* 1–20.

McCubbin, H. I., et al. (1988). *Family types and strengths: A life cycle and ecological approach.* Edina, MN: Bellwether.

McEnroe, J. (1991, February). Split-shift parenting. *American Demographics,* pp. 50–52.

McEvoy, C. A., Holley, P. E., & Nelson, D. L. (1995). Age effects in cued recall: Sources from implicit and explicit memory. *Psychology and Aging, 10,* 314–325.

McGinnis, J. M., & Lee, P. R. (1995, April 12). Healthy People 2000 at mid decade. *JAMA, 273,* 1123–1229.

McGraw, M. B. (1940). Neural maturation as exemplified in achievement of bladder control. *Journal of Pediatrics, 16,* 580–589.

McGue, M. (1993). From proteins to cognitions: The behavioral genetics of alcoholism. In R. Plomin & G. E. McClearn (Eds.), *Nature, nurture, & psychology* (pp. 245–269). Washington, DC: American Psychological Association.

McGue, M., Bacon, S., & Lykken, D. T. (1993). Personality stability and change in early adulthood: A behavioral genetic analysis. *Developmental Psychology, 29,* 96–110.

McGue, M., Bouchard, T. J., Iacono, W. G., & Lykken, D. T. (1993). Behavioral genetics of cognitive ability: A life-span perspective. In R. Plomin & G. E. McClearn (Eds.), *Nature, nurture, & psychology* (pp. 59–76). Washington, DC: American Psychological Association.

McGuinness, D. (1976). Sex differences in the organization of perception and cognition. In B. Lloyd & J. Archer (Eds.), *Exploring sex differences* (pp. 123–157). London: Academic Press.

McGuinness, D. (1979). How schools discriminate against boys. In S. Hochman & P. S. Kaplan (Eds.), *Readings in psychology: A soft approach* (Rev. ed.) (pp. 74–79). Lexington, MA: Ginn.

McGuire, S., Neiderhiser, J. M., Reiss, D., Hetherington, E. M., & Plomin, R. (1994). Genetic and environmental influences on perceptions of self-worth and competence in adolescence: A study of twins, full siblings and step-siblings. *Child Development, 65,* 785–799.

McHale, S. M., & Crouter, A. C. (1992). You can't always get what you want: Incongruence between sex-role attitudes and family work roles and its implications for marriage. *Journal of Marriage and the Family, 54,* 537–547.

McHale, S. M., & Huston, T. L. (1984). Men and women as parents: Sex role orientations, employment, and parental roles with infants. *Child Development, 55,* 1349–1361.

McIlroy, J. H. (1984). Midlife in the 1980s: Philosophy, economy, and psychology. *Personnel and Guidance Journal, 62,* 623–628.

McKenry, P., Arnold, K., Julian, T., & Kuo, J. (1987). Interpersonal influences on the well-being of men at mid-life. *Family Relations, 21,* 225–233.

McKenry, P. C., Julian, T. W., & Gavazzi, S. M. (1995). Toward a biopsychosocial model of domestic violence. *Journal of Marriage and the Family, 57,* 307–320.

McKinlay, S. M., Brambilla, D. J., & Posner, J. G. (1992). The normal menopause transition. *Journal of Human Biology, 4,* 37–46.

McKinlay, S. M., Brambilla, D. J., Avis, N. E., & McKinlay, J. B. (1991). Women's experience of menopause. *Current Obstetrics and Gynecology, 1,* 3–7.

McKinlay, S. M., & Jeffreys, M. (1974). The menopausal syndrome. *British Journal of Preventive and Social Medicine, 28,* 108.

McKinlay, S. M., McKinlay, S. M., & Brambilla, D. (1987). The relative contribution of endocrine changes and social circumstances to depression in mid-aged women. *Journal of Health and Social behavior, 28,* 345–363.

McKusick, V. A. (1989, April 6). Mapping and sequencing the human genome. *New England Journal of Medicine,* pp. 910–915.

McLanahan, S. & Booth, K. (1989). Mother-only families: Problems, prospects, and politics. *Journal of Marriage and the Family, 51,* 557–580.

McLaughlin, B. (1977). Second-language learning in children. *Psychological Bulletin, 84,* 438–459.

McLaughlin, B. (1978). *Second-language acquisition in childhood.* Hillsdale, NJ: Erlbaum.

McLaughlin, B. (1983). Child compliance to parental control techniques. *Developmental Psychology, 19,* 667–674.

McLoyd, V. C. & & Wilson, L. (1991). The strain of living poor: Parenting, social support, and child mental health. (pp. 105–136) In A. C. Huston (Ed.), *Children in poverty.* New York: Cambridge University Press.

McNally, S., Eisenberg, N., & Harris, J. D. (1991). Consistency and change in maternal child-rearing practices and values: A longitudinal study. *Child Development, 62,* 190–198.

McNeil, J. K., LeBlanc, E. M., & Joyner, M. (1991). The effect of exercise on depressive symptoms in the moderately depressed elderly. *Psychology and Aging, 6,* 487–488.

McNeill, D. (1970). The development of language. In P. H. Mussen (Ed.), *Carmichael's manual of child psychology* (3rd ed.). New York: Wiley.

Meeus, W., & Dekovic, M. (1995). Identity development, parental, and peer support in adolescence: Results of a national Dutch study. *Adolescence, 30,* 931–944.

Mehler, J., Jusczyk, P. W., Lambertz, G., Halsted, L., Bertoncini, J., & Amiel-Tison, C. (1988). A precursor of language acquisition in young infants. *Cognition, 29,* 143–178.

Meier, R. P., & Newport, E. L. (1990). Out of the hands of babes: On a possible sign advantage in language acquisition. *Language, 66,* 1–23.

Meilman, P. W. (1979). Cross-sectional age changes in ego identity status during adolescence. *Developmental Psychology, 15,* 230–231.

Meltzoff, A. (1988). Infant imitation and memory: Nine-month-olds in immediate and deferred tests. *Child Development, 59,* 217–226.

Meltzoff, A. N. (1977). Imitation of facial and manual gestures by human neonates. *Science, 198,* 75–78.

Meltzoff, A. N. (1988). Infant imitation and memory: Nine-month-olds in immediate and deferred tests. *Child Development, 59,* 217–226.

Meltzoff, A. N., & Moore, M. K. (1989). Imitation in newborn infants: Exploring the range of gestures imitated and the underlying mechanisms. *Developmental Psychology, 25,* 954–963.

Melzack, R. (1984). The myth of painless childbirth. *Pain, 19,* 321.

Mendelson, B. K., & White, D. R. (1985). Development of self-body-esteem in overweight youngsters. *Developmental Psychology, 21,* 90–97.

Mendelson, J. H. & Mello, N. K. (1985). *Alcohol: Use and abuse in America.* Boston: Little Brown.

Menyuk, P. (1977). *Language and maturation.* Cambridge, MA: M.I.T. Press.

Meredith, G., & Schewe, C. (1994, December). The power of cohorts. *American Demographics,* 22–31.

Mervis, C. B., & Bertrand, J. (1994). Acquisition of the novel name-nameless category (N3C) principle. *Child Development, 65,* 1646–1662.

Mesler, M. A. (1994/1995). The philosophy and practice of patient control in hospice: The dynamics of autonomy versus paternalism. *Omega, 30,* 173–189.

Metcalf, D. R. (1979). Organizers of the psyche and EEG development: Birth through adolescence. In R. L. Noshpitz (Ed.), *Basic handbook of child psychiatry* (Vol. 1, pp. 63–72). New York: Basic Books.

Metcoff, J., Coistiloe, P., Crosby, W. M., Sandstread, H. H., & Milne, D. (1989). Smoking in pregnancy: Relation of birth weight to maternal plasma carotene and cholesterol levels. *Obstetrics and Gynecology, 302,* 302–308.

Metropolitan Life Insurance Co. (1984, April–June). Projections of population growth at the older ages. *Statistical Bulletin,* pp. 8–10.

Metropolitan Life Insurance Co. (1986a, January–March). Variations in mortality from cancer. *Statistical Bulletin,* pp. 22–27.

Metropolitan Life Insurance Co. (1986b, January–March). Recent international changes in longevity. *Statistical Bulletin,* pp. 16–21.

Meyer, B. J. F., Russo, C., & Talbot, A. (1995). Discourse comprehension and problem solving: Decisions about the treatment of breast cancer by women across the life span. *Psychology and Aging, 10,* 84–103.

Meyer, D. R., & Garasky, S. (1993). Custodial fathers: Myths, realities, and child support policy. *Journal of Marriage and the Family, 55,* 73–89.

Meyer, J. & Sobieszek (1972). Effect of a child's sex on adult interpretations of its behavior. *Developmental Psychology, 6,* 42–48.

Meyer-Bahlburg, H. F. L., Ehrhardt, A. A., Rosen, L. R., Gruen, R. S., Verdiano, N. P., Vann, F. H., & Neuwalder, H. F. (1995). Prenatal estrogens and the development of homosexual orientation. *Developmental Psychology, 31,* 12–21.

Michael, R., Gagnon, J., Laumann, E., & Kolata, G. (1994). *Sex in America: The definitive story.* Boston: Little, Brown.

Michelsson, K., Rinne, A., & Paajanen, S. (1990). Crying, feeding and sleeping patterns in 1- to 12-month-old infants. *Child, Health and Development, 16,* 99–111.

Milburn, N., & D'Ercole, A. (1991). Homeless women, children, and families. *American Psychologist, 46,* 1159–1160.

Milewski, A. E. (1976). Infants' discrimination of internal and external pattern elements. *Journal of Experimental Child Psychology, 22,* 229–246.

Miller, B. C. & Sollie, D. L. (1980). Normal stresses during the transition to parenting. *Family Relations, 29,* 459–465.

Miller, D. C. (1964). Industry and the worker. In H. Borow (Ed.), *Man in a world at work.* Boston: Houghton Mifflin.

Miller, D. J., Ryan, E. B., Short, E. J., Ries, P. G., McGuire, M. D., & Culler, M. P. (1977). Relationships between early habituation and later cognitive performance in infancy. *Child Development, 48,* 658–661.

Miller, F. T. (1980). Measurement and monitoring of stress in communities. In L. W. Poon (Ed.), *Aging in the 1980s* (pp. 383–391). Washington, DC: American Psychological Association.

Miller, L. (1995, February 8). Child-care study finds mediocre level of services. *Education Week,* pp. 1, 11.

Miller, L. (1995, July 12) Children and Families. *Education Week,* p. 9.

Miller, L. (1995, November 8). Inadequate laws put children in day care at risk, CDF says. *Education Week,* p. 16.

Miller, P. H. (1989). *Theories of developmental psychology.* New York: Freeman.

Miller, P. H. (1993). *Theories of developmental psychology* (3rd ed.). New York: Freeman.

Miller, P. H., & Harris, Y. R. (1988). Preschoolers' strategies of attention on a same-different task. *Developmental Psychology, 24,* 628–634.

Miller, P. M., Danaher, D. L., & Forbes, D. (1986). Sex-related strategies for coping with interpersonal conflict in children aged five and seven. *Developmental Psychology, 22,* 543–548.

Miller, S., & Cunningham, B. (1992). A guided look experience program for minority students. *Journal of College Student Development, 33,* 373–374.

Mills, J. L., Braubard, B. I., Harley, E. E., Rhoads, G. G., & Berendes, H. W. (1984). Maternal alcohol consumption and birth weight: How much drinking during pregnancy is safe? *Journal of the American Medical Association, 252,* 1875–1879.

Mills, R. S. L., & Rubin, K. H. (1990). Parental beliefs about problematic social behaviors in early childhood. *Child Development, 61,* 138–152.

Millstein, S. G. (1989). Adolescent health: Challenges for behavioral scientists. *American Psychologist, 44,* 837–843.

Milner, J. S., & Chilamkurti, C. (1991). Physical child abuse perpetrator characteristics: A review of the literature. *Journal of Interpersonal Violence, 6,* 345–366.

Milsum, J. H. (1984). Health, stress, and illness: A systems approach. New York: Praeger.

Milunsky, A. (1989). *Choices not chances.* Boston: Little, Brown.

Minard, J., Coleman, D., Williams, G., & Ingledyne, E. (1968). Cumulative REM of three- to five-day-olds: Effect of normal external noise and maturation. *Psychophysiology, 5,* 232.

Minkler, M., Roe, K. M., & Price, M. (1992). The physical and emotional health of grandmothers raising grandchildren in the crack cocaine epidemic. *The Gerontologist, 32,* 752–761.

Minkoff, H. L., & Duerr, A. (1994). Obstetric issues—relevance to women and children. In P. A. Pizzo & C. M. Wilfert (Eds.), *Pediatric AIDS: The Challenge of HIV infection in infants, children, and adolescents* (2nd ed., pp. 809–828). Baltimore: Williams & Wilkins.

Minuchin, P. P., & Shapiro, E. K. (1983). The school as a context for social development. In E. M. Hetherington (Ed.), *Handbook of child psychology: Socialization, personality, and social development* (4th ed.), (Vol. 4, pp. 197–275). New York: Wiley.

Mirsky, A. F., & Duncan, C. C. (1986). Etiology and expression of schizophrenia: Neurobiological and psychosocial factors. *Annual Review of Psychology, 37,* 291–321.

Mischel, W. (1970). Sex-typing and socialization. In P. H. Mussen (Ed.), *Carmichael's manual of child psychology* (3rd ed.). New York: Wiley.

Missinne, L. E. (1980). Aging in Bakongo culture. *International Journal of Aging and Human Development, 11,* 283–295.

Mitchell, S. (1994, September). How boomers save. *American Demographics,* 22–27.

Mitchell, V. & Helson, R. (1990). Women's prime of life. Is it the 50s? *Psychology of Women Quarterly, 14,* 451–470.

Miyake, K., Chen, S., & Campos, J. (1985). Infants' temperament, mothers' mode of interaction and attachment in Japan: An interim report. In I. Bretherton & E. Waters (Eds.), Growing points of attachment theory and research. *Monographs of the Society for Research in Child Development, 50* (1–2 Serial No. 109), 276–297.

Moen, P. (1991). Transitions in mid-life: Women's work and family roles in the 1970s. *Journal of Marriage and the Family, 53,* 135–150.

Moen, P., Robison, J., & Fields, V. (1994). Women's work and caregiving roles: A life course approach. *Journal of Gerontology: Social Sciences, 49,* S176–S186.

Moerk, E. L. (1989). The LAD was a lady and the tasks were ill-defined. *Developmental Review, 9,* 21–57.

Mofenson, L. M., & Wolinsky, S. M. (1994). Current insights regarding vertical transmission. In P. A. Pizzo & C. M. Wilfert (Eds.), *Pediatric AIDS: The Challenge of HIV infection in infants, children, and adolescents* (2nd ed., pp. 179–203). Baltimore: Williams & Wilkins.

Moffitt, T. E. (1990). Juvenile delinquency and attention deficit disorder: Boys' developmental trajectories from age 13 to age 15. *Child Development, 61,* 893–910.

Moffitt, T. E., Caspi, A., Belsky, J., & Silva, P. A. (1992). Childhood experience and the onset of menarche: A test of a sociobiological model. *Child Development, 63,* 47–58.

Mohar, C. J. (1988). Applying the concept of temperament to child care. *Child and Youth Care Quarterly, 17,* 221–238.

Molfese, D. L., Molfese, V. J., & Carroll, P. L. (1982). Early language development. In B. B. Wolman (Ed.), *Handbook of developmental psychology* (pp. 301–323). Englewood Cliffs, NJ: Prentice Hall.

Molloy, D. W., Beerschoten, D. A., Borrie, M. J., Crilly, R. G., & Cape, R. D. T. (1988). Acute effects of exercise on neuropsychological function in elderly subjects. *Journal of the American Geriatrics Society, 36,* 29–33.

Molnar, J. M., Rath, W. R., & Klein, T. P. (1990). Constantly compromised: The impact of homelessness on children. *Journal of Social Issues, 46,* 109–124.

Monaco, N. M. & Gaier, N. M. (1987). Developmental level and children's responses to the explosion of the space shuttle *Challenger. Early Childhood Research Quarterly, 2,* 83–95.

Money, J. (1987). Sin, sickness, or status? Homosexual gender identity and psychoneuroendocrinology. *American Psychologist, 42,* 384–399.

Money, J., & Ehrhardt, A. (1972). *Man and woman, boy and girl.* Baltimore: Johns Hopkins University Press.

Monroe, S. M., Thase, M., & Simons, A. (1992). Social factors and psychobiology of depression: Relations between life stress and rapid eye movement sleep latency. *Journal of Abnormal Psychology, 101,* 528–537.

Montepare, J. M., & Lachman, M. E. (1989). "You're only as old as you feel": Self-perceptions of age, fear of aging, and life satisfaction from adolescence to old age. *Psychology and Aging, 4,* 73–78.

Montgomery, R. (1982). Impact of institutional care policies on family integration. *The Gerontologist, 22,* 54–58.

Monti, L. A., Gabrieli, J. D. E., Wilson, R. S., & Reminger, S. L. (1995). Intact text specific implicit memory in patients with Alzheimer's Disease. *Psychology and Aging, 9,* 64–71.

Moon, S. M., & Dillon, D. R. (1995). Multiple exceptionalities: A case study. *Journal for the Education of the Gifted, 18,* 111–130.

Moore, C. M. (1989). Teaching about loss

and death to junior high school students. *Family Relations, 38,* 3–7.
Moore, K. L., & Persaud, T. V. N. (1993). *Before we are born* (4th ed.). Philadelphia: W. B. Saunders.
Moore, L. M., Nielsen, C. R., & Mistretta, C. M. (1982). Sucrose taste thresholds: Age related differences. *Journal of Gerontology, 37,* 64–69.
Moorehouse, M. J. (1991). Linking maternal employment patterns to mother-child activities and children's school competence. *Developmental Psychology, 27,* 295–303.
Moos, R. H., & Lemke, S. (1985). Specialized living environments for older people. In J. E. Birren & K. W. Schaie (Eds.), *Handbook of the psychology of aging* (2nd ed., pp. 864–891). New York: Van Nostrand Reinhold.
Morbidity and Mortality Report (1995). Update AIDS-United States, *Centers for Disease Control 44,* 64–67.
Morelli, G. A., Rogoff, B., Oppenheim, D., & Goldsmith, D. (1992). Cultural variation in infants' sleeping arrangements: Questions of independence. *Developmental Psychology, 28,* 604–613.
Morgan, J. (1987). *Getting a job after 50.* New York: Wiley.
Morgan, J. L. (1996). Finding relations between input and outcome in language acquisition. *Developmental Psychology, 32,* 556–559.
Morgan, J. L., Bonamo, K. M., & Travis, L. L. (1995). Negative evidence on negative evidence. *Developmental Psychology, 31,* 180–197.
Morgenbagen, P. (1994, June). Rethinking retirement. *American Demographics,* 28–33.
Moritani, T., & deVries, H. A. (1980). Potential for gross muscle hypertrophy in older men. *Journal of Gerontology, 35,* 265–265.
Morrell, P., & Norton, W. T. (1980). Myelin. *Scientific American, 242,* 88–119.
Morris, J. N., Everitt, M. G., Pollard, R., et al. (1980). Vigorous exercise in leisure-time: Protection against coronary heart-disease. *Lancet, 2,* 1207.
Morrison, D. M. (1985). Adolescent contraceptive behavior: A review. *Psychological Bulletin, 98,* 538–568.
Morrison, G. S. (1991). *Early childhood education today* (5th ed.). Columbus, OH: Merrill.
Morrow, D., Leirer, V., Altieri, P., & Fitzsimons, C. (1994). When expertise reduces age differences in performance. *Psychology and Aging, 9,* 134–148.
Morrow, R. D. (1987, November). Cultural differences—Be Aware! *Academic Therapy, 23,* 143–149.
Morse, C. K. (1993). Does variability increase with age?: An archival study of cognitive measures. *Psychology and Aging, 8,* 156–165.
Motenko, A. K. & Greenberg, S. (1995). Reframing dependence in old age: A positive transition for families. *Social Work, 40,* 382–390.
Muir, D., & Field, J. (1979). Newborn infants orient to sounds. *Child Development, 50,* 431–436.
Muir, M. A. (1991). *The environmental contexts of AIDS.* New York: Praeger.
Mujica, M. (1996a, January 29). U.S. English, Inc. *National Review.* pp. 46–48.
Mujica, M. (1996b, January 19). Should English be the official language of the United States. *CQ Researcher,* p. 65.
Mullahy, P. (1948). *Oedipus: Myth and complex.* New York: Grove.
Multhaup, K. S. (1995). Aging, source, and decision criteria: When false fame errors do and do not occur. *Psychology and Aging, 10,* 492–497.
Munley, P. H. (1975). Erik Erikson's theory of psychosocial development and career development. *Journal of Counseling Psychology, 22,* 314–319.
Munley, P. H. (1977). Erikson's theory of psychosocial development and career development. *Journal of Vocational Behavior, 10,* 261–269.
Murphy, C., & Withee, J. (1986). Age-related differences in the pleasantness of chemosensory stimuli. *Psychology and Aging, 4,* 312–318.
Murphy, J. M., & Gilligan, C. (1980). Moral development in late adolescence and adulthood: A critique and reconstruction of Kohlberg's theory. *Human Development, 23,* 77–104.
Murray, B. (1995a, November). Gender gap in math scores is closing. *APA Monitor,* p. 43.
Murray B. (1995b, November) Programs go beyond "just saying no" *APA Monitor,* p. 41.
Murray, B. (1995c, November). Key skill for teen parents: Having realistic expectations. *APA Monitor,* p. 51.
Murray, S. F., Dolby, R. M., Nation, R. L., & Thomas, D. B. (1981). Effects of epidural anesthesia on newborns and their mothers. *Child Development, 52,* 71–82.
Murstein, B. I. (1976). *Who will marry whom? Theories and research in marital choice.* New York: Springer.
Murstein, B. I. (1982). Marital choice. In B. B. Wolman (Ed.), *Handbook of developmental psychology,* 652–667. Englewood Cliffs, NJ: Prentice Hall.
Murstein, B. I. (1987). A clarification and extension of the SVR theory of dyadic pairing. *Journal of Marriage and the Family, 49,* 929–933.
Muscat, J. E., Axelrad, C., Ray, K., Weston, R., Landers, C., Vaccaro, D., Orlandi, M. A., & Haley, N. J. (1994, January/February). Cholesterol screening in a community health promotion program: Epidemiologic results from a biracial population. *Public Health Reports, 109,* 93–99.
Mussen, P. H., & Eisenberg-Berg, N. (1977). *Roots of caring, sharing, and helping.* San Francisco: Freeman.
Mussen, P. H., & Jones, M. C. (1957). Some conceptions, motivations, and interpersonal attitudes of late- and early-maturing boys. *Child Development, 28,* 242–256.
Muuss, R. E. (1982). *Theories of adolescence* (4th ed.). New York: Random House.
Muuss, R. E. (1985). Adolescent eating disorder: Anorexia nervosa. *Adolescence, 20,* 525–536.
Muuss, R. E. (1986). Adolescent eating disorder: Bulimia. *Adolescence, 21,* 257–267.
Muuss, R. E. (1988). Carol Gilligan's theory of sex differences in the development of moral reasoning during adolescence. *Adolescence, 23,* 235–243.
Myers, B. J., Jarvis, P. A., & Creasey, G. L. (1987). Infants' behavior with their mothers and grandmothers. *Infant Behavior and Development, 10,* 245–259.
Myers, D. A. (1991). Work after cessation of career job. *Journal of Gerontology, 46,* S93–102.
Myers, G. C. (1990). Demography of aging. In R. H. Binstock & L. K. George (Eds.), *Handbook of aging and the social sciences* (3rd ed.) (pp. 19–41). New York: Academic Press.
Myers, J. E., & Shelton, B. (1987). Abuse and older persons: Issues and implications for counselors. *Journal of Counseling and Development, 65,* 376–380.
Myers, M. F. (1989). *Men and divorce.* New York: Guilford Press.
Myerson, J., Hale, S., Wagstaff, D., Poon, L. W., & Smith, G. A. (1990). The information loss model: A mathematical theory of age-related cognitive slowing. *Psychological Review, 97,* 475–487.
Myles, J. F. (1978). Institutionalization and sick role identification among the elderly. *American Sociological Review, 43,* 508–521.
Nachmias, M., Gunnar, M., Mangelsdorf, S., Parritz, R. H., & Buss, K. (1996). Behavioral inhibition and stress reactivity:

The moderating role of attachment security. *Child Development, 67,* 508–522.

Nadel, M. V. (1993). *Needle exchange programs: Research suggests promise as an AIDS prevention strategy.* Report GAO/HRD 93-60. Washington, DC: United States General Accounting Office: 1993.

Naeye, R. L. & Peters, E. C. (1984). Mental development of children whose mothers smoked during pregnancy. *Obstetrics & Gynecology, 64,* 601–607.

Nagel, K. L., & Jones, K. H. (1992). Sociological factors in the development of eating disorders. *Adolescence, 27,* 107–113.

Nagy, M. (1948). The child's theories concerning death. *Journal of Genetic Psychology, 73,* 3–27.

Nakonezny, P. A., Shull, R. D., & Rodgers, J. L. (1995). The effect of no-fault divorce law on the divorce rate across the 50 states and its relation to income, education, and religiosity. *Journal of Marriage and the Family, 57,* 477–488.

Nall, S. W. (1982). Bridging the gap: Preschool to kindergarten. *Childhood Education, 59,* 107–110.

Nancy Reagan Fights Back (1995, March 23). *Newsday,* p. A19.

Napoli, M. (1982). *Health facts: A critical evaluation of the major problems, treatments, and alternatives facing medical consumers.* Westock, NY: Overlook.

NARIC (National Rehabilitation Information Center). (1993, August 15). *The Americans with Disabilities Act* (ADA) A NARIC Resource Guide.

Nathanielsz, P. W. (1995, Spring). The role of basic science in preventing low birth weight. *The Future of Children, 5,* 57–70.

National Alliance to End Homelessness. (1991). *What you can do to help the homeless.* New York: Simon & Schuster.

National Center for Health Statistics (1993). Advance report of final mortality statistics, *Monthly and Vital Statistics Report, 41,* (7) Hyattsville, MD: United States Department of Health and Human Services, Public Health Service, CDC.

National Center for Health Statistics (1995). *Health, United States, 1994.* Hyattsville, MD: Public Health Service.

National Center for Nutrition and Dietetics, International Food Information Council, (1991). *Kids at the table: Who's placing the orders?* Chicago: American Dietetic Association.

National Center on Excellence in Education (1981). *A nation at risk.* Washington, DC: U.S. Department of Education.

National commission on excellence in education (1981). *A Nation At Risk,* Washington, DC: U.S. Department of Education.

National Committee to Prevent Child Abuse (1996). *Current trends in child abuse reporting and fatalities: The results of the 1995 annual fifty state survey.* Chicago: NCPCA.

National Council on the Aging. (1975). *The myth and reality of aging in America.* Washington, DC: National Council on the Aging.

National Institute on Aging (1986). The menopause of life. Washington, DC: U.S. Department of Health and Human Services.

National Safety Council (1995). *Accident facts,* Itasca, IL: Author.

National Vaccine Advisory Committee: The measles epidemic: The problems, barriers and recommendations. (1991, September 18). *JAMA, 266,* 1547–1552.

Nazarro, J. N. (Ed.). (1981). *Culturally diverse exceptional children.* Reston, VA: Council for Exceptional Children.

Nebes, R. D., Boller, F., & Holland, D. (1986). Use of semantic context by patients with Alzheimer's disease. *Psychology and Aging, 1,* 261–269.

Neiger, B. L., & Hopkins, R. W. (1988). Adolescent suicide: Character traits of high-risk teenagers. *Adolescence, 23,* 469–475.

Neimark, E. D. (1975). Intellectual development during adolescence. In F. D. Horowitz (Ed.), *Review of child development research,* (Vol. 4). Chicago: University of Chicago Press.

Nelson, C. A. (1987). The recognition of facial expressions in the first two years of life: Mechanisms of development, *Child Development, 58,* 889–910.

Nelson, C. A., & Horowitz, F. D. (1983). The perception of facial expressions and stimulus motion by two- and five-month-old infants using holographic stimuli. *Child Development, 54,* 868–878.

Nelson, D. E., Giovino, G. A., Shopland, D. R., Mowery, P. D., Mills, S. L., & Eriksen, M. P. (1995). Trends in cigarette smoking among U.S. adolescents, 1974 through 1991. *American Journal of Public Health, 85,* 34–40.

Nelson, F. L. (1987). Evaluation of a youth suicide school program. *Adolescence, 22,* 813–825.

Nelson, K. (1973). Structure and strategy in learning to talk. *Monograph of the Society for Research in Child Development, 38* (1–2, Serial No. 149).

Nelson, K. (1978). How children represent knowledge of their world in and out of language: A preliminary report. In R. S. Siegler (Ed.), *Children's thinking: What develops.* Hillsdale, NJ: Erlbaum.

Nelson, K. & Gruendel, J. (1981). Generalized event representations: Basic building blocks of cognitive development. In M. E. Lamb & A. L. Brown (Eds.), *Advances in developmental psychology.* (Vol. 1). Hillsdale, NJ: Erlbaum.

Nelson, K., Rescorla, L., Gruendel, J., & Benedict, H. (1978). Early lexicons: What do they mean? *Child Development, 49,* 960–968.

Neugarten, B. L. (1964). *Personality in middle and later life.* New York: Atherton.

Neugartern, B. L. (1968). The awareness of middle age. In B. L. Neugarten (Ed.), *Middle age and aging* (pp. 93–98). Chicago: University of Chicago Press.

Neugarten, B. L. (1968a). Adult personality: Toward a psychology of the life cycle. In B. L. Neugarten (Ed.), *Middle age and aging.* Chicago: University of Chicago Press.

Neugarten, B. L. (1970). Dynamics of transition of middle age to old age. *Journal of Geriatric Psychiatry, 4,* 71–87.

Neugarten, B. L. (1976). Adaptation and the life cycle. *Journal of Geriatric Psychiatry, 4,* 71–87.

Neugarten, B. L. (1977). Personality and aging. In J. E. Birren & K. W. Schaie (Eds.), *Handbook of the psychology of aging* (pp. 626–644). New York: Van Nostrand Reinhold.

Neugarten, B. L., & Datan, N. (1973). Sociological perspectives on the life cycle. In P. B. Baltes & K. W. Schaie (Eds.), *Life-span developmental psychology.* New York: Academic Press.

Neugarten, B. L., Havighurst, R. J., & Tobin, S. S. (1961). The measurement of life satisfaction. *Journal of Gerontology, 16,* 134–143.

Neugarten, B. L., Havighurst, R. J., & Tobin, S. S. (1968). Personality and patterns of aging. In B. L. Neugarten (Ed.), *Middle age and aging.* Chicago: University of Chicago Press.

Neugarten, B. L., & Moore, J. W. (1968). The changing age-status system. In B. L. Neugarten (Ed.), *Middle age and aging.* Chicago: University of Chicago Press.

Neugarten, B. L., & Neugarten, D. A. (1989). Policy issues in an aging society. In M. Storandt & G. R. VandenBos (Eds.), *The adult years: Continuity and change* (pp. 143–167). Washington, DC: American Psychological Association.

Neugarten, B. L., & Weinstein, K. (1964). The changing American grandparent. *Journal of Marriage and the Family, 26,* 199–204.

Neugarten, B. L., Wood, V., Kraines, R. J., & Loomis, B. (1963). Women's attitudes toward the menopause. *Vita Humana, 6,* 140–151.

Neuhaus, R. J. (1994, April 4). Live and let die. *National Review, 46,* 40.

Neuman, S. B. (1982). Television viewing and leisure reading: A qualitative analysis. *Journal of Educational Research, 75,* 299–304.

Neuspiel, D. R., & Hamel, S. C. (1991). Cocaine and infant behavior. *Developmental and Behavioral Pediatrics, 12,* 55–64.

New face of America. (1991, March 12). *Newsday,* p. 10.

New York State Council on Alcoholism (1986). *Alcohol Abuse.* New York State Division of Alcohol and Alcohol Abuse.

New York State Department of Health (1979). DES: *The wonder drug women should wonder about.* New York: Author.

Newell, G. K., Hammig, C. L., Jurich, A. P., & Johnson, D. E. (1990). Self-concept as a factor in the quality of diets of adolescent girls. *Adolescence, 25,* 117–127.

Newman, B. M. (1982). Mid-life development. In B. B. Wolman (Ed.), *Handbook of developmental psychology* (pp. 617–634). Englewood Cliffs, NJ: Prentice Hall.

Newman, B. M. (1989). The changing nature of the parent-adolescent relationship from early to late adolescence. *Adolescence, 96,* 915–923.

Newman, B. S., & Muzzonigro, P. G. (1993) The effects of traditional family values on the coming out process of gay male adolescents. *Adolescence, 28,* 213–226.

Newman, B., Selby, J. V., Quesenberry, C. P., King, M. C., Friedman, G. D., & Fabsizt, R. R. (1990). Nongenetic influences of obesity on other cardiovascular disease risk factors: An analysis of identical twins. *American Journal of Public Health, 80,* 675–677.

Newmann, J. P. (1989). Aging and depression. *Psychology and Aging, 4,* 150–165.

NICHD. (1996). Infant child care and attachment security: Results of the NICHD study of early child care. Washington, DC: Symposium, International Conference on Infant Studies, Providence, RI.

NIDA Capsules. (1995). *Facts about teenagers and drug abuse.* Washington, DC: National Institute on Drug Abuse.

Nigg, J. T., & Goldsmith, H. H. (1994). Genetics of personality disorders: Perspectives from personality and psychopathology research. *Psychological Bulletin, 115,* 346–380.

Niknian, M., Lefebvre, R. C., & Carleton, R. A. (1991). Are people more health conscious? A longitudinal study of one community. *American Journal of Public Health, 81,* 203–205.

Ninio, A., & Rinott, N. (1988). Fathers' involvement in the care of their infants and their attributions of cognitive competence to infants. *Child Development, 59,* 652–664.

Nisbett, R. (1994, October 31). Blue genes. *New Republic, 211,* 15–16.

Nogata, D. K. (1989). Japanese American children and adolescence. In J. T. Gibbs & L. N. Huang (Eds.). *Children of color* (pp. 67–114). San Francisco: Jossey-Bass.

Nolen-Hoeksema, S., Girgus, J. S., & Seligman, M. E. P. (1992). Predictors and consequences of childhood depressive symptoms: A 5-year longitudinal study. *Journal of Abnormal Psychology, 101,* 405–422.

Noller, P., & Fitzpatrick, M. A. (1990). Marital communication in the eighties. *Journal of Marriage and the Family, 52,* 832–843.

Notelovitz, M., & Ware, M. (1982). *Stand tall: The informed woman's guide to preventing osteoporosis.* Gainesville, FL: Triad.

Nunnally, J. C. (1982). The study of change: Measurement, research strategies, and methods of analysis. In B. B. Wolman (Ed.), *Handbook of developmental psychology* (pp. 133–149). Englewood Cliffs, NJ: Prentice Hall.

Nye, R. D. (1975). *Three views of man.* Pacific Grove, CA: Brooks/Cole.

Nyhan, W. L. (1986). Neonatal screening for inherited disease. *New England Journal of Medicine, 313,* 43–44.

Nyiti, R. M. (1982). The validity of "cultural differences explanations" for cross-cultural variation in the rate of Piagetian cognitive development. In D. A. Wagner & H. W. Stevenson (Eds.), *Cultural perspectives on child development* (pp. 146–166). San Francisco: Freeman.

Obarzanek, E., et al., (1994). Energy intake and physical activity in relation to indexes of body fat: The National Heart, Lung, and Blood Institute Growth and Height Study. *American Journal of Clinical Nutrition, 60,* 15–22.

O'Brien, M., & Huston, A. C. (1985a). Development of sex-typed play behaviors in toddlers. *Developmental Psychology, 21,* 866–871.

O'Brien, M., & Huston, A. C. (1985b). Activity level and sex stereotyped toy choice in toddler boys and girls. *Journal of Genetic Psychology,* 527–534.

O'Brien, S. F., & Bierman, K. L. (1988). Conceptions and perceived influence of peer groups: Interviews with preadolescent and adolescents. *Child Development, 59,* 1360–1365.

O'Brien, S. J., & Vertinsky, P. A. (1991). Unfit survivors: Exercise as a resource for aging women. *Gerontologist, 31,* 347–357.

O'Campo, P. O., Gielen, A. C., Faden, R. R., Xiaonan, X., Kass, N., & Wang, M. C. (1995). Violence by male partners against women during the childbearing years: A contextual analysis. *American Journal of Public Health, 85,* 1092–1097.

Ochs, E. (1988). *Culture and language development: Language acquisition and language socialization in a Samoan village.* New York: Cambridge University Press.

Ockene, J. K., Kuller, L. W., Svendsen, K. H., & Meilahn, E. (1990). The relationship of smoking cessation to coronary heart disease and lung cancer in the multiple risk factor intervention trial (MRFIT). *American Journal of Public Health, 80,* 954–958.

O'Connor, R. E., Jenkins, J. R., & Slocum, T. A. (1995). Transfer among phonological tasks in kindergarten: Essential instructional content. *Journal of Educational Psychology, 87,* 202–217.

O'Connor, T. G., Hetherington, E. M., Reiss, D., & Plomin, R. (1995). A twin-sibling study of observed parent-adolescent interactions. *Child Development, 66,* 812–829.

Office of National Drug Control Policy (1996). *President Clinton's accomplishments in the fight against drugs in defense of our children and our families.* Washington, DC: Author.

Ogbu, J. U. (1978). *Minority education and caste. New York: Academic Press.*

Ogbu, J. U. (1981). Origins of human competence: A cultural-ecological perspective. *Child Development, 52,* 413–429.

Ogbu, J. U. (1992). Understanding cultural diversity and learning. *Educational Reseacher, 21,* 5–14.

O'Hare, W. P., & Frey, W. H. (1992, September) Booming, suburban and black. *American Demographics,* 30–38.

Okun, M. A. (1976). Adult age and cautiousness in decision: A review of the literature. *Human Development, 19,* 220–233.

O'Leary, A. (1990). Stress, emotion, and human immune function. *Psychological Bulletin, 108,* 363–382.

Olim, E. G., Hess, R. D., & Shipman, V. C. (1967). Role of mothers' language styles in mediating their preschool children's development. *School Review, 78,* 414–424.

Olsen, D., & Zigler, E. (1989). An assessment of the all-day kindergarten movement. *Early Childhood Research Quarterly, 4,* 167–187.

Olshan, A. F., & Faustman, E. M. (1993). Male-mediated developmental toxicity. *Annual Review of Public Health, 14,* 159–181.

Olshansky, S. J., Carnes, B., & Cassel, C. (1990, November). In search of Methuselah: Estimating the upper limits to longevity. *Science, 250,* 634–640.

Olsho, L. W., Harkins, S. W., & Lenhardt, M. I. (1985). Aging and the auditory system. In J. E. Birren & K. W. Schaie (Eds.), *Handbook of the psychology of aging* (pp. 332–378). New York: Van Nostrand Reinhold.

Olson, D. H. (1991). Family types and response to stress. *Journal of Marriage and the Family, 53,* 786–798.

Olvera-Ezzell, N., Power, T. G., Cousins, J. H., Guerra, A. M., & Trujillo, M. (1994). The development of health knowledge in low-income Mexican-American children. *Child Development, 65,* 416–427.

Olweus, D. (1977). Aggression and peer acceptance in adolescent boys: Two short-term longitudinal studies of ratings. *Child Development, 48,* 1301–1313.

Olweus, D. (1979). Stability and aggressive reaction patterns in males: A review. *Psychological Bulletin, 86,* 852–875.

Olweus, D. (1982). Development of stable aggressive reaction patterns in males. In R. Blanchard & C. Blanchard, *Advances in the study of aggression* (Vol. 1). New York: Academic Press.

Onorato, I. M., Gwinn, M., & Dondero, T. J. (1994). Applications of data from the CDC family of surveys. *Public Health Reports, 109,* 204–212.

Oppel, W. C., Harper, P. A., & Rider, R. V. (1968). The age of attaining bladder control. *Pediatrics, 42,* 614–626.

Orbach, I., Weiner, M., Har-Even, D., & Eshel, Y. (1994/1995). Children's perception of death and interpersonal closeness to the dead person. *Omega, 30,* 1–12.

Orenberg, C. L. (1981). *DES: The complete story.* New York: St. Martin's Press.

Orlofsky, J. L., Marcia, J. E., & Lessor, I. M. (1973). Ego identity status and the intimacy versus isolation crisis of young adulthood. *Journal of Personality and Social Psychology, 27,* 211–219.

Ornish, D. (1990). The life style heart trial. *Lancet, 242,* 133–147.

Ortho Diagnostic Systems. (1981). *What every Rh negative woman should know about RhoGAM.* Raritan, NJ: Ortho Diagnostic Systems.

Oser, F. K. (1990). Kohlberg's educational legacy. In D. Schrader (Ed.), *The legacy of Lawrence Kohlberg* (pp. 81–89). San Francisco: Jossey-Bass.

Oshima-Takane, Y., Goodz, E., & Derevensky, J. L. (1996). Birth order effects on early language development: Do secondborn children learn from overheard speech? *Child Development, 67,* 621–634.

Oshman, H., & Manosevitz, M. (1974). The impact of the identity crisis on the adjustment of late adolescent males. *Journal of Youth and Adolescence, 3,* 207–217.

Oshman, H. P., & Manosevitz, M. (1976). Father absence: Effects of stepfathers upon psychosocial development in males. *Developmental Psychology, 12,* 477–480.

Oskamp, S. (1984). *Applied social psychology.* Englewood Cliffs, NJ: Prentice Hall.

Osofsky, J. D., & Connors, K. (1979). Mother-infant interaction: An integrative view of a complex system. In J. Osofsky (Ed.), *Handbook of infant development* (pp. 519–549). New York: Wiley.

Osofsky, J. D., Wewers, S., Hann, D. M., & Fick, A. C. (1993). Chronic community violence: What is happening to our children? *Psychiatry, 56,* 36–45.

Ossip-Klein, D. J., Doyne, E. J., Bowman, E. D., Osborn, K. M., McDougall-Wilson, I. B., & Neimeyer, R. A. (1989). Effects of running or weight lifting on self-concept in clinically depressed women. *Journal of Counseling and Clinical Psychology, 57,* 158–161.

Oster, H., Hegley, D., & Nagel, L. (1992). Adult judgments and fine-grained analysis of infant facial expressions: Testing the validity of a priori coding formulas. *Developmental Psychology, 28,* 1115–1131.

Osterweis, M., Solomon, F., & Green, M. (1984). *Bereavement: Reactions, consequences, and care.* Washington, DC: National Academy Press.

Ostroff, C. (1992). The relationship between satisfaction, attitudes, and performance: An organizational level analysis. *Journal of Applied Psychology, 77,* 963–974.

Owens, R. E. (1988). *Language development.* Columbus, OH: Merrill.

Owens, R. E. (1992) *Language development: An introduction* (3rd ed.). New York: Macmillan.

Owens, R. E. (1994). Development of communication, language and speech. In G. H. Shames, E. H. Wiig, & W. A. Second (Eds.), *Human communication disorders* (4th ed., pp. 36–82). New York: Macmillan.

Owsley, C., Ball, K., Sloane, M. E., Roenker, D. L., & Bruni, J. R. (1991). Visual/cognitive correlates of vehicle accidents in older drivers. *Psychology and Aging, 6,* 403–415.

Oxtoby, M. J. (1994). Vertically acquired HIV infection in the United States. In P. A. Pizzo & C. M. Wilfert (Eds.), *Pediatric AIDS: The challenge of HIV infection in infants, children, and adolescents* (2nd ed., pp. 3–21). Baltimore: Williams and Wilkins.

Oyemade, U. J. (1985). The rationale for Head Start as a vehicle for the upward mobility of minority families: A minority perspective. *American Journal of Orthopsychiatry, 55,* 591–602.

Paar, W. V., & Siegert, R. (1993). Adults' conceptions of everyday memory failures in others: Factors that mediate the effects of target age. *Psychology and Aging, 8,* 599–605.

Paden, S. L., & Buehler, C. (1995). Coping with the dual-income lifestyle. *Journal of Marriage and the Family, 57,* 101–110.

Padilla, A. M., & Baird, T. L. (1991). Mexican-American adolescent sexuality and sexual knowledge: An exploratory study. *Hispanic journal of Behavioral Sciences, 13,* 95–104.

Padilla, A. M., Lindholm, K. J., Chen, A., Duran, R., Hakuta, K., Lambert, W., & Tucker, G. R. (1991). The English-only movement: Myths, reality, and implications for psychology. *American Psychologist, 46,* 120–131.

Paffenbarger, R. S., Hyde, R. T., Wing, A. L., Lee, I. Jung, D. L., & Kampert, J. B. (1993). The association of changes in physical-activity level and other lifestyle characteristics with mortality among men. *New England Journal of Medicine, 328,* 538–545.

Paffenbarger, R. S., Jr., Wing, A. L., Hyde, R. T., et al. (1978). Chronic disease in former college students: Physical activ-

ity as an index of heart attack risk in college alumni. *American Journal of Epidemiology, 108,* 151.
Painter, K. (1996, February 21). Heavy marijuana use may impair learning. *USA Today,* p. 1D.
Palkovitz, R. (1985). Father's birth attendance, early contact, and extended contact with their newborns: A critical review. *Child Development, 56,* 392–407.
Pallone, N. J. (1992, July/August). Costs and benefits of medicine. *Reason, 29,* 34–36.
Palmore, E., Cleveland, W. P., Nowlin, J. G., Ramm, D., & Siegler, I. C. (1979). Stress and adaptation in later life. *Journal of Gerontology, 34,* 841–851.
Palmore, E., & Manton, K. (1974). Modernization and the status of the aged: International correlations. *Journal of Gerontology, 29,* 205–210.
Paloutzian, R. F., & Kirkpatrick, L. A. (1995). Introduction: The scope of religious influences on personal and societal well-being. *Journal of Social Issues, 51,* 1–11.
Pampel, F. C. (1985). Determinants of labor force participation rates of aged males in developed and developing nations, 1965–1975. In Z. S. Blau (Ed.), *Current perspectives on aging and the life cycle* (Vol. 1, pp. 243–275). Greenwich, CT: Jai.
Paneth, N. S. (1995, Spring). The problem of low birth weight. *The future of children, 5,* 19–34.
Parcel, G. S., Simons-Morton, B. G., O'Hara, N. M., Baranowski, T., Kolbe, L. J., & Bee, D. E. (1987). School promotion of healthful diet and exercise behavior: An integration of organizational change and social learning theory interventions. *Journal of School Health, 57,* 150–156.
Parham, T. A. (1989). Cycles of psychological nigrescence. *The Counseling Psychologist, 17,* 187–226.
Paris, S. G., & Lindauer, B. K. (1982). The development of cognitive skills during childhood. In B. B. Wolman (Ed.), *Handbook of developmental psychology* (pp. 333–350). Englewood Cliffs, NJ: Prentice Hall.
Parish, T. S. (1982). Locus of control as a function of father loss and the presence of stepfather. *Journal of Genetic Psychology, 140,* 321–322.
Parish, T. S. (1990). Evaluations of family by youth: Do they vary as a function of family structure, gender, and birth order. *Adolescence, 25,* 353–356.
Park, K. A., Lay, K. L., & Ramsay, L. (1993). Individual differences and developmental changes in preschoolers' friendships. *Developmental Psychology, 29,* 264–270.
Parke, K. A., & Waters, E. (1989). Security of attachment and preschool friendships. *Child Development, 60,* 1076–1082.
Parke, R. D. (1979). Perspectives on father-infant interaction. In J. Osofsky (Ed.), *Handbook of infant development* (pp. 549–591). New York: Wiley.
Parke, R. D. (1981). *Fathers.* Cambridge, MA: Harvard University Press.
Parke, R. D. (1995). Fathers and families. Mothering. In M. H. Bornstein (Ed.), *Handbook of parenting* (Vol. 3, pp. 27–65). Mahwah, NJ: Erlbaum.
Parke, R. D., & Collmer, C. W. (1975). Child abuse: An interdisciplinary analysis. In E. M. Hetherington (Ed.), *Review of child development research* (Vol. 5). Chicago: University of Chicago Press.
Parke, R. D., & Slaby, R. G. (1983). The development of aggression. In E. M. Hetherington (Ed.), *Handbook of child psychology: Socialization, personality, and social development* (4th ed., Vol. 4, pp. 547–643). New York: Wiley.
Parke, R. D., Ornstein, P. A., Reiser, J. J., & Zahn-Waxler, C. (1994). Reflections on a century of developmental development (pp. 547–549). Washington, DC: American Psychological Association.
Parker, J. G., & Gottman, J. M. (1989). Social and emotional development in a relational context: Friendship interaction from early childhood to adolescence. In T. J. Berndt & G. W. Ladd (Eds.), *Peer relationships in child development* (pp. 95–133). New York: Wiley.
Parkes, C. M. (1972). *Bereavement.* New York: International Universities Press.
Parkes, C. M. (1987). Models of bereavement care. *Death Studies, 11,* 257–261.
Parkin, A. J., & Walter, B. M. (1992). Recollective experience, normal aging, and frontal dysfunction. *Psychology and Aging, 7,* 290–298.
Parmelee, A. H., & Sigman, M. D. (1983). Perinatal brain development and behavior. In P. H. Mussen (Ed.), *Handbook of child development* (3rd ed., Vol. 2, pp. 95–157). New York: Wiley.
Parmelee, P. A., Katz, I. R., & Lawton, M. P. (1991). The relation of pain to depression among institutionalized aged. *Journal of Gerontology, 46,* 15–21.
Parnes, H., & Less, L. (1985). Variation in selected forms of leisure activity among elderly males. In Z. S. Blau (Ed.), *Current perspectives on aging and the life cycle* (Vol. 1, pp. 223–243). Greenwich, CT: Jai.
Parnes, H. S., & Sommers, D. G. (1994). Shunning retirement: Work experience of men in their seventies and early eighties. *Journal of Gerontology: Social Sciences, 49,* S117–S124.
Parten, M. (1932). Social participation among preschool children. *Journal of Abnormal and Social Psychology, 27,* 243–269.
Patterson, B. H., Block, G., Rosenberger, W. F., Rosenberger, W. F., Pee, D., & Kahle, L. L. (1990). Fruit and vegetables in the American diet: Data from the NHANES 2 survey. *American Journal of Public Health, 80,* 1443–1449.
Patterson, C. J. (1992). Children of lesbian and gay parents. *Child Development, 63,* 1025–1042.
Patterson, C. J. (1995). Families of the lesbian baby boom: Parents' division of labor and children's adjustment. *Developmental Psychology, 31,* 115–1254.
Patterson, C. J., Kupersmidt, J. B., & Griesler, P. C. (1990). Children's perceptions of self and of relationships with others as a function of sociometric status. *Child Development, 61,* 1335–1350.
Patterson, G. R. (1986). Performance models for antisocial boys. *American Psychologist, 41,* 432–444.
Patterson, G. R., DeBaryshe, B. D., & Ramsey, E. (1989). A developmental perspective on antisocial behavior. *American Psychologist, 44,* 329–335.
Paul, J. (1993). Childhood cross-gender behavior and adult homosexuality: The resurgence of biological models of sexuality. *Journal of Homosexuality, 24,* 41–54.
Paulsen, K., & Johnson, M. (1983). Sex role attitudes and mathematical ability in 4th-, 8th-, and 11th-grade students from a high socioeconomic area. *Developmental Psychology, 19,* 210–214.
Paxton, S. J., Wertheim, E. H., Gibbons, K., Szmukler, G. I., Hillier, L., & Petrovich, J. L. (1991). Body image satisfaction, dieting beliefs, and weight loss behaviors in adolescent girls and boys. *Journal of Youth and Adolescence, 20,* 361–379.
Pearson, D. A., & Lane, D. M. (1991). Auditory attention switching: A developmental study. *Journal of Experimental Child Psychology, 51,* 320–334.
Peck, R. C. (1968). Psychological developments in the second half of life. In B. L. Neugarten (Ed.), *Middle age and aging.* Chicago: University of Chicago Press.
Peckham, C., & Gibb, D. (1995). Mother-to-child transmission of the human immunodeficiency virus. *New England Journal of Medicine, 333,* 298–302.
Pederson, D. R., & Moran, G. (1996). Ex-

pressions of the attachment relationship outside of the strange situation. *Child Development, 67,* 915–927.

Pedlow, R., Sanson, A., Prior, M., & Oberklaid, F. (1993). Stability of maternally reported temperament from infancy to 8 years. *Developmental Psychology, 29,* 998–1007.

Pellegrini, A. D. (1987). Rough-and-tumble play: Developmental and educational significance. *Educational Psychologist, 22,* 23–43.

Pellegrini, A. D. (1988). Elementary-school children's rough-and-tumble play and social competence. *Developmental Psychology, 24,* 802–807.

Pellegrini, A. D. (1995). A longitudinal study of boys' rough-and-tumble play and dominance during early adolescence. *Journal of Applied Developmental Psychology, 16,* 77–93.

Pellegrini, A. D., & Perlmutter, J. C. (1989). Classroom contextual effects on children's play. *Developmental Psychology, 25,* 289–297.

Pelletier, K. R. (1977). Mind as healer, mind as slayer. *Psychology Today,* p. 35.

Pelletier, K. R. (1988). Database: Research and evaluation of results. *American Journal of Health Promotion, 2,* 52–57.

Pelligrino, E. D. (1996). Distortion of the healing relationship. In T. L. Beauchamp & R. M. Veatch (Eds.), *Ethical issues in death and dying* (pp. 161–165). Englewood Cliffs, NJ: Prentice Hall.

Pendarvis, E. D., Howley, A. A., & Howley, C. B. (1990). *The abilities of gifted children.* Englewood Cliffs, NJ: Prentice Hall.

Peplau, L. (1981). What homosexuals want. *Psychology Today, 15,* 28–38.

Peplau, L., & Gordon, S. (1982). The intimate relationships of lesbians and gay men. In E. Allgeier & N. McCormick (Eds.), *Gender roles and sexual behavior.* Mountain View, CA: Mayfield.

Pepper, E. C. (1976). Teaching the American Indian child in mainstream settings. In R. L. Jones (Ed.), *Mainstreaming and the Minority Child.* Reston, VA: Council for Exceptional Children.

Perl, D. P. (1991, February 17). No proof for diet switch-cancer risk. *New York Times,* p. A12.

Perlmutter, M., & Myers, N. A. (1979). Recognition memory development in two-to-four-year-olds. *Developmental Psychology, 15,* 73–83.

Perry, D. G. (1994). Comments on Grusec and Goodnow (1994) Model of the role of discipline in moral internalization. *Developmental Psychology, 30,* 23–25.

Perry, D. G., Perry, L. C., & Rasmussen, P. (1986). Cognitive social learning mediators of aggression. *Child Development, 57,* 700–711.

Perry, W. B. (1968). *Forms of intellectual and ethical development in the college years: A scheme.* New York: Holt, Rinehart and Winston.

Perry, W. B. (1981). Cognitive and ethical growth: The making of meaning. In A. Chickering (Ed.), *The modern American college* (pp. 76–117). San Francisco: Jossey-Bass.

Perry-Jenkins, M., & Folk, K. (1994). Class, couples, and conflict: Effects of the division of labor on assessments of marriage in dual-earner marriages. *Journal of Marriage and the Family, 56,* 226–228.

Personick, V. A. (1990). Industry output and employment: A slower trend for the nineties. In *Outlook 2000.* Washington, DC: Bureau of Labor Statistics, Bulletin 2352, pp. 24–40.

Peskin, H. (1967). Pubertal onset and ego functioning. *Journal of Abnormal Psychology, 72,* 1–15.

Peskin, H. (1973). Influences of the development schedule on learning and ego functioning. *Journal of Youth and Adolescence, 2,* 273–290.

Pestrak, V. A., & Martin, D. (1985). Cognitive development and aspects of adolescent sexuality. *Adolescence, 20,* 981–987.

Peters, A. M. (1986). Early syntax. In P. Fletcher & M. Garman (Eds.), *Language acquisition* (2nd ed., pp. 307–326). London: Cambridge University Press.

Peters, D. L. (1977). Early childhood education: An overview and evaluation. In H. L. Hom & P. A. Robinson (Eds.), *Psychological processes in early education* (pp. 1–23). New York: Academic Press.

Peterson, B. E., & Klohnen, E. C. (1995). Realization of generativity in two samples of women at midlife. *Psychology and Aging, 10,* 20–29.

Peterson, C., Seligman, M. E. P., & Vaillant, G. E. (1988). Pessimistic explanatory style is a risk factor for physical illness: A thirty-five year longitudinal study. *Journal of Personality and Social Psychology, 55,* 23–27.

Peterson, J. L., & Nord, C. W. (1990). The regular receipt of child support: A multistep process. *Journal of Marriage and the Family, 52,* 539–551.

Peterson, K. L., & Roscoe, B. (1991). Imaginary audience behavior in older adolescent females. *Adolescence, 26,* 195–200.

Peterson, L. (1983). Influence of age, task competence, and responsibility focus on children's altruism. *Developmental Psychology, 19,* 141–148.

Peterson, L. (1990). PhoneFriend: A developmental description of needs expressed by child callers to a community telephone support system for children. *Journal of Applied Developmental Psychology, 11,* 105–122.

Petitpas, A. (1978). Identity foreclosure: A unique challenge. *American Personnel and Guidance Journal, 56,* 558–562.

Petti, M. (1987). Educational implications of the nonverbal WISC-R. *Academic Therapy, 23,* 177–181.

Petty, M. (1988). Educational implications of the verbal WISC-R. *Academic Therapy, 23,* 279–286.

Pettit, G. S., & Bates, J. E. (1989). Family interaction patterns and children's behavior problems from infancy to 4 years. *Developmental Psychology, 25,* 413–421.

Pfeiffer, E., & Davis, G. C. (1972). Determinants of sexual behavior in middle and old age. *Journal of the American Geriatric Society, 20,* 151–158.

Pfeiffer, E., Verwoerdt, A., & Davis, G. C. (1974). Sexual behavior in midlife. In E. Palmore (Ed.), *Normal aging 2: Reports from the Duke longitudinal studies, 1970–1973.* Durham, NC: Duke University Press.

Pfost, K. S., Stevens, M. J., & Matejcak, A. J. (1990). A counselor's primer on postpartum depression. *Journal of Counseling and Development, 69,* 149–151.

Phelps, K. E., & Woolley, J. D. (1994). The form and function of young children's magical beliefs. *Developmental Psychology, 30,* 385–394.

Phillips, D., McCartney, K., & Scarr, S. (1987). Child-care quality and children's social development. *Developmental Psychology, 23,* 537–543.

Phillips, D. A., Voran, M., Kisker, E., Howes, C., & Whitebook, M. (1994). Child care for children in poverty: Opportunity or inequity. *Child Development, 65,* 472–492.

Phillips, J. L. (1975). *The origins of intellect: Piaget's theory* (2nd ed.). San Francisco: Freeman.

Phillips, S., & Lobar, S. L. (1990). Literature summary of some Navajo child health beliefs and rearing practices within a transcultural nursing framework. *Journal of Transcultural Nursing, 1,* 13–20.

Phillips, S. C. (1994, April 8). Reproductive ethics. *CQ Magazine, 4,* 289–310.
Phillips, S. C. (1995, April 14). Dieting and health. *CQ Researcher, 5,* 321–343.
Phinney, J. S., (1989). Stages of ethnic identity development in minority group adolescents. *Journal of Early Adolescence, 9,* 34–49.
Phinney, J. S., Chavira, V., & Williamson, L. (1992). Acculturation attitudes and self-esteem among high-school and college students. *Youth and Society, 23,* 299–312.
Phinney, J. S., & Tarver, S. (1988). Ethnic identity seach and commitment in black and white eighth graders. *Journal of Early Adolescence, 8,* 265–277.
Piaget, J. (1928). *Judgment and reasoning in the young child.* New York: Harcourt, Brace, and World.
Piaget, J. (1930). *The child's conception of physical causality.* London: Kegan Paul, Trench, & Trubner.
Piaget, J. (1952). *The child's conception of number.* New York: Humanities Press.
Piaget, J. (1952a). *The origins of intelligence in children.* New York: Norton.
Piaget, J. (1954). *The construction of reality in the child.* New York: Basic Books (originally published 1937).
Piaget, J. (1962). *Play, dreams, and imitation in childhood.* New York: Norton.
Piaget, J. (1962). The stages of intellectual development of the child, *Bulletin of the Meninger Clinic, 26,* 120–128.
Pieaget, J. (1967). *Six psychological studies.* New York: Vintage.
Piaget, J. (1968). *On the development of memory and identity.* Worcester, MA: Clark University Press.
Piaget, J. (1969). *The child's conception of the world.* Totowa, NJ: Littlefield & Adams.
Piaget, J. (1970). Piaget's theory. *The child's conception of time.* London: Routledge and Kegan Paul, (originally published 1926).
Piaget, J. (1972). Intellectual evolution from adolescence to adulthood. *Human Development, 15,* 1–12.
Piaget, J. (1974). Piaget's theory. *Understanding causality.* New York: Norton.
Piaget, J., & Inhelder, B. (1969). *The psychology of the child.* New York: Basic Books.
Piaget, J. & Inhelder, B. (1974). *The child's construction of quantities: Conservation and atomism.* London: Routledge and Kegan Paul.
Pickens, J. (1994). Perception of auditory-visual distance relations by 5-month-old infants. *Developmental Psychology, 30,* 537–544.
Pierce, C. (1994). Importance of classroom climate for at-risk learners. *Journal of Educational Research, 88,* 37–43.
Pierce, J. P. (1989). International comparisons of trends in cigarette smoking prevalence. *American Journal of Public Health, 79,* 152–257.
Pierce, J. P., Fiore, M. C., Novotny, T. E. Hatziodreu, E. J., & Davis, R. M. (1989). Trends in cigarette smoking in the United States: Projections to the year 2000. *JAMA, 261,* 61–65.
Pillemer, K. (1986). The dangers of dependency: New findings on domestic violence against the elderly. *Social Problems, 33,* 147–156.
Pillemer, K., & Finkelhor, D. (1988). The prevalence of elder abuse: A random sample survey. *Gerontologist, 28,* 51–57.
Pillemer, K., & Moore, D. (1989). Abuse of patients in nursing homes: Findings from a survey of staff. *The Gerontologist, 29,* 314–320.
Pillemer, K., & Suitor, J. J. (1988). Elder abuse. In V. B. Van Hasselt, R. L. Morrison, A. S. Bellack, & M. Hersen (Eds.), *Handbook of family violence* (pp. 247–270). New York: Plenum.
Pillitteri, A. (1992). *Maternal and child health nursing: Care of the childbearing and childrearing family.* Philadelphia: Lippincott.
Pina, D. L., & Bengtson, V. L. (1993). The division of household labor and wives' happiness: Ideology, employment, and perceptions of support. *Journal of Marriage and the Family, 55,* 901—912.
Pina, D. L., & Bergtson, V. L. (1995). Division of household labor and the well-being of retirement-aged wives. *The Gerontologist, 35,* 308–317.
Pina, P. (1995, September 13). More teenagers using marijuana. *USA Today,* p. 7D.
Pine, J. M. (1995). Variation in vocabulary development as a function of birth order. *Child Development, 66,* 272–281.
Pleck, J. H. (1985). *Working wives/working husbands.* Beverly Hills, CA: Sage.
Plepys, C., & Klein, R. (1995, September). Health status indicators: Differentials by race and hispanic origin. *U.S. Department of Health and Human Services,* DHHS Pub. No. (PHS), pp. 95–1237.
Plomin, R., & Daniels, D. (1987). Why are children in the same family so different from each other. *The Behavioral and Brain Sciences, 10,* 1–16.
Plomin, R., & DeFries, J. C. (1980). Genetics and intelligence: Recent data. *Intelligence, 4,* 15–24.
Plomin, R., DeFries, J. C., & Loehlin, J. C. (1977). Genotype-environment interaction and correlation in the analysis of human behavior. *Psychological Bulletin, 84,* 309–322.
Plomin, R., DeFries, J. C. & McClearn, G. E. (1990). *Behavioral genetics: A primer* (2nd ed.). New York: Freeman.
Plomin, R., Emde, R. N., Braungart, J. M., Campos, J., Corley, R., Fuler, D. W., Kagan, J., Reznick, J. S., Robinson, J., Zahn-Waxler, C., & DeFries, J. C. (1993). Genetic change and continuity from fourteen to twenty months: The MacArthur Longitudinal Twin Study. *Child Development, 64,* 1354–1377.
Plopper, B., & Ness, E. M. (1993). Death as portrayed to adolescents through top-40 rock songs. *Adolescence, 28,* 793–807.
Plumert, J. M., (1995). Relations between children's overestimation of their physical abilities and accident proneness. *Developmental Psychology, 31,* 866–876.
Pocs, O., & Godow, A. (1976). Can students view parents as sexual beings? *Family Coordinator, 26,* 31–36.
Poirier, L. A. (1987). Stages in carcinogenesis: Alteration by diet. *American Journal of Clinical Nutrition, 45,* 185–191.
Polit, D. F., & Falbo, T. (1987). Only children and personality development: A quantitative review. *Journal of Marriage and the Family, 49,* 309–325.
Polivy, J., & Thomsen, L. (1988). Dieting and other eating disorders. In E. A. Blechman & K. D. Brownell (Eds.), *Handbook of behavioral medicine for women.* New York: Pergamon.
Pollock, R. (1994). Shots in the dark. *Reason, 26,* 51–54.
Pomerleau, A., Bolduck, D., Malcuit, G., & Cossette, L. (1990). Pink or blue: Environmental gender stereotypes in the first two years of life. *Sex Roles, 22,* 359–367.
Poon, L. W. (1985). Differences in human memory with aging: Nature, causes, and clinical implications. In J. E. Birren & K. W. Schaie (Eds.), *Handbook of the psychology of aging* (2nd ed., pp. 427–463). New York: Van Nostrand Reinhold.
Popkin, B. M., Sieg-Riz, A. M., & Haines, P. S. (1996, September 5). A comparison of dietary trends among racial and socioeconomic groups in the United States. *The New England Journal of Medicine, 335,* 716–720.
Porter, R. H., Bologh, R. D., & Makin, J. W.

(1988). Olfactory influences on mother-infant interactions. In C. Rovee-Collier & L. P. Lipsitt (Eds.), *Advances in infancy research* (Vol. 5, pp. 39–69). Norwood, NJ: Ablex.

Porter, R. P. (1990, May 17). Tongue-tied by bilingual education. *Newsday, 36.*

Portes, P. R., Haas, R., & Brown, J. H., (1991). Predicting children's adjustment to divorce. *Journal of Divorce, 15,* 87–103.

Portes, P. R., Howell, S. C., Brown, J. H., Eichenberger, S., & Mas, C. A. (1992). Family functions and children's postdivorce adjustment. *American Journal of Orthopsychiatry, 62,* 613–617.

Portner, J. (1995, April 19). Two studies link high-quality day care and child development. *Education Week,* p. 6.

Portner, J. (1996, February 28). Some students report feeling safer at school. *Education Week,* p. 7.

Potts, R., Doppler, M., & Hernandez, M. (1994). Effects of television content on physical risk-taking in children. *Journal of Experimental Child Psychology, 58,* 321–331.

Potts, R., & Henderson, J. (1991). The dangerous world of television: A content analysis of physical injuries in children's television programming. *Children's Environment, 8,* 7–14.

Powell, B. (1977). The empty nest, employment, and psychiatric symptoms in college-educated women. *Psychology of Women Quarterly, 2,* 253–265.

Powell, K. E., Thompson, P. D., Casperson, C. J., & Kendrich, J. S. (1987). Physical activity and incidence of coronary heart disease. *Annual Review of Public Health, 8,* 253–287.

Power, T. (1985). Mother- and father-infant play: A developmental analysis. *Child Development, 56,* 1514–1525.

Power, T. G., & Chapieski, M. L. (1986). Childrearing and impulse control in toddlers: A naturalistic investigation. *Developmental Psychology, 22,* 271–275.

Powers, C. B., Wisocki, P. A., & Whitbourne, S. K. (1992). Age differences and correlates of worrying in young and elderly adults. *Gerontologist, 32,* 82–88.

Powlishta, K. K. (1995). Intergroup processes in childhood: Social categorization and sex role development. *Developmental Psychology, 31,* 781–788.

Prager, K., Turczyn, K., & Smith, S. S. (1993, November/December). NCHS Annual summary shows drop in life expectancy. *Public Health Reports, 108,* 789–793.

Prager, K., Turczyn, K., Lancashire, J., & Smith, S. (1994, September). National health overview shows one in five without health insurance coverage. *Public Health Reports, 109,* 713–715.

Pratt, C. C., & Schmall, V. L. (1989). College students' attitudes toward elderly sexual behavior: Implications for family life education. *Family Relations, 38,* 137–141.

Presser, H. B. (1989). Some economic complexities of child care provided by grandmothers. *Journal of Marriage and the Family, 51,* 581–591.

Preto, N. G. (1989). Transformation of the family system in adolescence. In B. Carter & M. McGoldrick (Eds.), *The changing family life cycle* (pp. 265–285). Boston: Allyn & Bacon.

Price, H. B. (1992, November). Multiculturalism: Myths and realities. *Phi Delta Kappan,* 208–213.

Price, R. H., Cowen, E. L., Lorion, R. P., & Ramos-McKay, J. (1989). The search for effective prevention programs: What we learned along the way. *American Journal of Orthopsychiatry, 59,* 49–58.

Price, S. J., & McKenry, P. C. (1989). Current trends and issues in divorce: An agenda for family scientists in the 1990's. *Family Science Review, 2,* 219–236.

Princeton Religious Research Center. (1980). *Religion in America, 1979–1980.* (Princeton, NJ: Princeton University Press).

Pritchard, R. D., Maxwell, S. E., & Jordan, W. C. (1984). Interpreting relationships between age and promotion in age-discrimination cases. *Journal of Applied Psychology, 69,* 199–206.

Pritchard, R. E., & Potter, G. C. (1990). *Fitness, Inc.: A guide to corporate health and wellness programs.* Homewood, IL: Dow Jones-Irwin.

The Progressive (1994, March). Technology and choice. *The Progressive, 58,* 10.

Prohaska, T. R., Leventhal, E. A., Leventhal, H., & Keller, M. L. (1985). Health practices and illness cognition in young middle aged and elderly adults. *Journal of Gerontology, 40,* 569–578.

Psychological Corporation (1993). *The Bayley scales of infant development,* (2nd ed.). San Antonio, Texas: Author.

Psychology Today. (1993, May/June). Chaos comes to psychology. *Psychology Today, 26,* 21.

Public Health Reports. (1993a, July/August). PHS funds five minority health research centers. *Public Health Reports, 108,* 523.

Public Health Reports. (1993b, March/April). More Indians smoke, PHS study shows. *Public Health Reports, 108,* 262.

Public Health Reports. (1993c, July/August). Evaluation of telephoned computer-generated reminders to improve immunization coverage at inner-city clinics. *Public Health Reports, 108,* 426–430.

Public Health Reports, (1993d, July/August). WHO acts to prevent vaccine crises in former USSR. *Public Health Reports, 108,* 525.

Public Health Reports. (1994a, January/February). NIAAA report says U.S. drinking problem ebbs. *Public Health Reports, 109,* 145.

Public Health Reports (1994b, September/October). WHO scientific group formulates new research agenda on menopause. *Public Health Reports, 109,* 715.

Public Health Reports (1994c, November). Research committee views aging populations's effect on future policies. *Public Health Reports, 109,* 830–832.

Public Health Service. (1991). *Healthy people 2000: National health promotion and disease prevention objectives.* Washington, DC: U.S. Department of Health and Human Services. Pub. No. 91–50212.

Pulaski, M. A. S. (1980). *Understanding Piaget: An introduction to children's cognitive development* (rev. ed.). New York: Harper & Row.

Punamaki, R. L. (1996). Can ideological commitment protect children's psychosocial well-being in situations of political violence? *Child Development, 67,* 55–70.

Pyka, G., Lindenberger, E., Charette, S., & Marcus, R. (1994). Muscle strength and fiber adaptations to a year-old resistance training program in elderly men and women. *Journal of Gerontology: Medical Sciences, 49,* M22–M27.

Quadrel, M. J., Fischoff, B., & Davis, W. (1993). Adolescent (in)vulnerability. *American Psychologist, 48,* 102–116.

Quarrel, O. W. Q., Tykler, A., Upadhyaya, M., Meredith, A. L., Youngman, S., & Harper, P. S. (1987). Exclusion testing for Huntington's disease in pregnancy with a closely linked DNA marker. *Lancet, 1,* 1281.

Quill, T. E. (1991). Death and dignity: A case of individualized decision making. *New England Journal of Medicine, 324,* 691–694.

Quill, T. E. (1993). *Death and dignity: Making choices and taking charge.* New York: Norton.

Quill, T. E., Cassel, C. K., & Meier, D. E. (1992). Care of the hopelessly ill: Proposed clinical criteria for physician-assisted suicide. *New England Journal of Medicine, 327,* 1380–1384.

Quilligan, E. J. (1995). Obstetrics and gynecology. *JAMA, 273,* 1700–1701.

Quinn, J. F., & Burkhauser, R. V. (1990). Work and retirement. In R. H. Binstock & L. K. George (Eds.), *Handbook of aging and the social sciences* (3rd ed., pp. 308–323). New York: Academic Press.

Rabbitt, P., Donlan, C., Watson, P., McInnes, L., & Bent, N. (1995). Unique and interactive effects of depression, age, socioeconomic advantage, and gender on cognitive performance of normal health older people. *Psychology and Aging, 10,* 307—314.

Rabkin, J., Fremien, R., & Wilson, C. (1994). *Good doctors good patients: Partners in HIV treatment.* New York: NCM Pub.

Rader, N., Spiro, D. J., & Firestone, P. B. (1979). Performance on a stage 4 object-permanence task with standard and non-standard covers. *Child Development, 50,* 905–910.

Radin, N. (1994). Primary caregiving fathers in intact families. In A. E. Gottfriend & A. W. Gottfried (Eds.), *Redefining families: implications or children's development* (pp. 11–54). New York: Plenum.

Rafferty, Y., & Shinn, M. (1991). The impact of homelessness on children. *American Psychologist, 46,* 1170–1179.

Ragone, H. (1994). *Surrogate motherhood: conception in the heart.* Boulder, CO: Westview Press.

Ragozin, A. S., Basham, R. B., Crnic, K. A., Greenberg, M. T., & Robinson, N. M. (1982). Effects of maternal age on parenting role. *Developmental Psychology, 18,* 627–635.

Ramey, C. T., Farran, D. C., & Campbell, F. A. (1979). Predicting I.Q. from mother-infant interaction. *Child Development, 50,* 804–814.

Ramirez, J. D. (1992). Executive summary. *Bilingual Research Journal, 16,* 1–62.

Ramsey, P. G., (1995). Changing social dynamics in early childhood classrooms. *Child Development, 66,* 764–773.

Randal, J. E. (1988, December 6). Risks of cesarean sections. *Newsday,* p. 11.

Raschke, H. (1987). Divorce. In M. Sussman & S. Sussman (Eds.), *Handbook of marriage and the family.* New York: Plenum.

Rasmussen, C. H., & Johnson, M. E. (1994). Spirituality and religiosity: Relative relationships to death anxiety. *Omega, 29,* 313–318.

Raths, L. E., Harmin, M., & Simon, S. B. (1966). *Values and teaching.* Columbus, OH: Charles E. Merrill.

Raz, I. S., & Bryant, P. (1990). Social background, phonological awareness and children's reading. *British Journal of Developmental Psychology, 8,* 209–225.

Razel, M. (1988). Call for a follow-up study of experiments on long-term deprivation of human infants. *Perceptual and Motor Skills, 67,* 147–158.

Rebok, G., Offerman, L. R., Wirtz, G., & Montaglione, C. J. (1986). Work and intellectual aging: The psychological concomitants of social-organizational conditions. *Educational Gerontology, 12,* 359–374.

Rech, J., & Stevens, D. J. (1996). Variables related to mathematics achievement among black students. *The Journal of Educational Research, 89,* 346–350.

Reed, R. (1988). Education and achievement of young black males. In J. T. Gibbs (Ed.), *Young, black, and male in America: An endangered species.* Dover, MA: Auburn House.

Reedy, M. N., Birren, J. E., & Schaie, K. W. (1982). Age and sex differences in satisfying love relationships across the life-span. *Human Development, 24,* 52–66.

Rees, N. (1994). *The catchphrase handbook.* London: Sterling.

Reese, H. W., & Lipsitt, L. P. (1973). *Experimental Child Psychology.* New York: Academic Press.

Reinemer, M. (1995). Work happy. *American Demographics,* 26–31, 45.

Reiss, D. (1993). Genes and the environment: Siblings and synthesis. In R. Plomin & G. E. McClearn (Eds.). *Nature, nurture, & psychology* (pp. 417–433). Washington, DC: American Psychological Association.

Reissland, N. (1988). Neonatal imitation in the first hour of life: Observations in rural Nepal. *Developmental Psychology, 24,* 464–470.

Reitzes, D. C., Mutran, E., & Pope, H. (1991). Location and well-being among retired men. *Journal of Gerontology, 46,* S195–203.

The Remmelink Report (1990). Medical practice with regard to euthanasia and related medical decisions in the Netherlands. In T. L. Beauchamp & R. M. Veatch (Eds.), *Ethical issues in death and dying* (1996, pp. 181–185). Upper Sadle River, NJ: Prentice Hall.

Rende, R. D., Slomkowski, C. L., Stocker, C., Fulker, D. W., & Plomin, R. (1990). Genetic and environmental influences on maternal and sibling interaction in middle childhood: A sibling adoption study. *Developmental Psychology, 28,* 484–491.

Repetti, R. L. (1989). Effects of daily workload on subsequent behavior during marital interaction: The roles of social withdrawal and spouse support. *Journal of Personality and Social Psychology, 57,* 651–659.

Repp, A. C., Nieminen, G. S., Olinger, E., & Brusca, R. (1988). Direct observation: Factors affecting the accuracy of observers. *Exceptional Children, 55,* 29–36.

Rescorla, L., Parker, R., & Stolley, P. (1991). Ability, achievement, and adjustment in homeless children. *American Journal of Orthopsychiatry, 6,* 210–220.

Rest, J. R. (1983). Morality. In P. H. Mussen (Ed.), *Handbook of child psychology: Cognitive development* (4th ed., Vol. 3, pp. 556–630). New York: Wiley.

Restak, R. M. (1988). *The mind.* New York: Bantam.

Revelle, W. (1995). Personality processes. *Annual Review of Psychology, 46,* 295–328.

Rexcoat, C., & Shehan, C. (1987). The family life cycle and spouses' time in housework. *Journal of Marriage and the Family, 49,* 737–750.

Reynolds, M. C., & Birch, J. W. (1988). *Adaptive mainstreaming* (3rd ed.). New York: Longman.

Reznick, J. S., & Goldfield, B. A. (1992). Rapid change in lexical development in comprehension and production. *Developmental Psychology, 28,* 406–413.

Rheingold, H., & Cook, K. (1975). The contents of boys' and girls' rooms as an index of parents' behavior. *Child Development, 46,* 459–463.

Rheingold, H. L., & Eckerman, C. O. (1973). Fear of the stranger: A critical examination. In H. W. Reese (Ed.), *Advances in child development and behavior* (Vol. 8). New York: Academic Press.

Rhodes, S. R. (1983). Age-related differences in work attitudes and behavior: A review and conceptual analysis. *Psychological Bulletin, 93,* 328–367.

Ricciuti, H. (1974). Fear and development of social attachments in the first year of life. In M. Lewis & L. A. Rosenblum (Eds.), *The origins of human behavior: Fear.* New York: Wiley.

Ricciuti, H. N. (1980). Adverse environmental and nutritional influences on mental development: A perspective. Paper presented at American Dietetic Association Meeting, Atlanta.

Rice, C., Koinis, D., Sullivan, K., Tager-Flusberg, H., & Winner, E. (1997). When 3-year-olds pass the appearance-reality test. *Developmental Psychology, 33,* 54–62.

Rice, F. P. (1989). *Human sexuality.* Dubuque, IA: Brown.

Rice, M. L. (1989). Children's language acquisition. *American Psychologist, 44,* 149–157.

Rice, M. L., Burh, J. C., & Nemeth, M. (1990). Fast mapping word-learning abilities of language-delayed preschoolers. *Journal of Speech and Hearing Disorders, 55,* 33–42.

Rice, M. L., Huston, A. C., Truglio, R., & Wright, J. (1990). Words from *Sesame Street:* Learning vocabulary while viewing. *Developmental Psychology, 26,* 421–429.

Rice, M. L., & Woodsmall, L. (1988). Lessons from television: Children's word learning when viewing. *Child Development, 59,* 420–429.

Rich, M. (1991, May 1). Y.W.C.A. Official discusses the need for anti-rape education. *Education Week,* pp. 6, 7.

Richards, L. N., Bengtson, V. L., & Miller, R. B. (1989). The "generation in the middle": Perceptions of changes in adults' intergenerational relationships. In K. Kreppner & R. M. Lerner (Eds.), *Family systems and life-span development.* Hillsdale, NJ: Erlbaum.

Richards, M. H., Boxer, A. M., Petersen, A. C., & Albrecht, R. (1990). Relation of weight to body image in pubertal girls and boys from two communities. *Developmental Psychology, 26,* 313–321.

Richmond, J. (1990). Low-birth-weight infants: Can we enhance their development? *Journal of the American Medical Association, 263,* 3069–3070.

Richmond-Abbott, M. (1983). *Masculine and feminine.* Reading, MA: Addison-Wesley.

Rickert, E. S. (1981). Media mirrors of the gifted: E. Susanne Richert's review of the film *Simon. Gifted Child Quarterly, 25,* 3–4.

Rickman, M. D., & Davidson, R. J. (1994). Personality and behavior in parents of temperamentally inhibited and uninhibited children. *Developmental Psychology, 30,* 346–354.

Rimm, E. B., Ascherio, A., Giovannucci, E., Spiegelman, D., Stampfer, M. J., & Willett, W. C. (1996, February 14). Vegetable, fruit, and cereal fiber intake and risk of coronary heart disease among men. *JAMA, 275,* 447–451.

Rinaldi, A., & Kearl, M. C. (1990). The hospice farewell: Ideological perspectives of its professional practitioners. *Omega, 21,* 283–300.

Rindfuss, R. R., & Vanden Heuvel, A. (1990). Cohabitation: A precursor to marriage or an alternative to being single? *Population and Developmental Review 16,* 703–726.

Rist, M. C. (1990, January). "Crack babies" in school. *American School Board Journal,* pp. 19–24.

Ritchie, K. (1995, April). Marketing to Generation X. *American Demographics,* 34–39.

Rivers, C., & Barnett, C. (1996, August 8). Families faring just fine, thanks. *USA Today,* p. 14A.

Roberge, J. R., & Flexer, B. K. (1979). Further examination of formal operational reasoning abilities. *Child Development, 50,* 478–484.

Roberts, B. L., Dunkle, R., & Haug, M. (1994). Physical, psychological, and social resources as moderators of the relationship of stress to mental health of the very old. *Journal of Gerontology: Social Sciences, 49,* S35–S43.

Roberts, L., & Krokoff, L. J. (1990). A time-series analysis of withdrawal, hostility, and displeasure in satisfied and dissatisfied marriages. *Journal of Marriage and the Family, 52,* 95–105.

Roberts, P., & Newton, P. M. (1987). Levinsonian studies of women's adult development. *Psychology and Aging, 2,* 154–164.

Roberts, W., & Strayer, J. (1996). Empathy, emotional expressiveness, and prosocial behavior. *Child Development, 67,* 449–470.

Robertson, J. F. (1975). Interaction in three-generation families, parents as mediators: Towards a theoretical perspective. *International Journal of Aging and Human Development, 6,* 103–110.

Robertson, M. J. (1991). Homeless women with children. *American Psychologist, 46,* 1198–1204.

Robinson, J. L., Kagan, J., Reznick, J. S., & Corley, R. (1992). The heritability of inhibited and uninhibited behavior: A twin study. *Developmental Psychology, 28,* 1030–1038.

Robinson, J. P. (1990, February). The time squeeze. *American Demographics,* pp. 30–33.

Robinson, J. P. (1991, May). Quitting time. *American Demographics,* pp. 34–37.

Roche, A. F., & Davila, G. H. (1972). Late adolescent growth in stature. *Pediatrics, 50,* 874–880.

Roche, J. P. (1986). Premarital sex: Attitudes and behavior by dating stage. *Adolescence, 81,* 107–121.

Roche, J. P., & Ramsey, T. W. (1993.) Premarital sexuality: A five-year follow-up study of attitudes and behavior by dating stage. *Adolescence, 28,* 67–80.

Rodin, J., & Langer, E. J. (1977). Long-term effects of a control-relevant intervention with the institutionalized aged. *Journal of Personality and Social Psychology, 35,* 897–902.

Rodman, H., Pratto, D. J., & Nelson, R. S. (1985). Child care arrangements and children's functioning: A comparison of self-care and adult-care children. *Developmental Psychology, 21,* 413–418.

Rodriguez, C., & Moore, N. B. (1995). Perceptions of pregnant/parenting teens: Reframing issues for an integrated approach to pregnancy problems. *Adolescence, 30,* 685–706.

Roffwarg, H. P., Muzio, J. N., & Dement, W. C. (1966). Ontogenic development of the human sleep-dream cycle. *Science, 152,* 604–619.

Rog, D. J., Holupka, C. S., McCombs-Thornton, K. L. (1995a). Implementation of the homeless families program: 1. Service models and preliminary outcomes. *American Journal of Orthopsychiatry, 65,* 502–513.

Rog, D. J., McCombs-Thornton, K. L., Gilbert-Mongelli, A. M., Brito, C., & Holupka, C. S. (1995b). Implementation of the homeless family program: 2. Characteristics, strengths, and needs of participant families. *American Journal of Orthopsychiatry, 65,* 514–527.

Rogers, G. T. (1985). Nonmarried women approaching retirement: Who are they and when do they retire? In Z. S. Blau (Ed.), *Current perspectives on aging and the life cycle* (pp. 169–193). Greenwich, CT: Jai.

Rogers, L. (1976). Male hormones and behaviour. In B. B. Lloyd & J. Archer (Eds.), *Exploring sex differences* (pp. 185–213). London: Academic Press.

Rogers, M. F., Shocehetman, G., & Hoff, R. (1994). Advances in diagnosis of HIV-1 infection. In P. A. Pizzo & C. M. Wilfert (Eds.), *Pediatric AIDS: The challenge of HIV infection in infants, children, and adolescents* (2nd ed., pp. 219–240). Baltimore: Williams & Wilkins.

Rogers, R. G. (1992). Living and dying in the USA: Sociodemographic determinants of death among African-Americans and whites. *Demography, 29,* 287–303.

Roggman, L. A., Langlois, J. H., Hubbs-Tait, L., & Rieser-Danner, L. A. (1994). Infant day-care, attachment, and the "file drawer problem." *Child Development, 65,* 1429–1443.

Rogler, L. H., Cortes, D. E., & Malgady, R. G. (1991). Acculturation and mental health status among Hispanics. *American Psychologist, 46,* 585–597.

Rogoff, B. (1981). Schooling and the development of cognitive skills. In H. C. Triandis & A. Heron, *Handbook of cross-cultural psychology* (Vol. 4: *Developmental psychology,* pp. 233–295). Boston: Allyn and Bacon.

Rogoff, B., Mistry, J., Goncu, A., & Mosier, C. (1993). Guided participation in cultural activity by toddlers and caregivers. *Monographs of the Society for Research in Child Development, 58,* (8 Serial No. 236).

Rogoff, B., & Morelli, G. (1989). Culture and American children: Section introduction. *American Psychologist, 44,* 341–343.

Rogoff, B., Newcombe, N., & Kagan, J. (1974). Planfulness and recognition memory. *Child Development, 45,* 972–977.

Rolfes, S. R., & DeBruyne, L. K. (1989). *Life span nutrition: Conception through life.* St. Paul, MN: West.

Rolfes, S. R., & DeBruyne, L. K. (1990). *Life span nutrition.* St. Paul, MN: West.

Rollins, B., & Feldman, H. (1970). Marital satisfaction over the life span. *Journal of Marriage and the Family, 32,* 20–28.

Rollins, B. C. (1989). Marital quality at midlife. In S. Hunter & M. Sundel (Eds.), *Midlife myths: Issues, findings, and practical implications* (pp. 184–195). Newbury Park, CA: Sage.

Romanoff, B. D. (1993). When a child dies: special considerations for providing mental health counseling for bereaved parents. *Journal of Mental Health Counseling, 15,* 384–393.

Rooks, J. P., Weatherby, N. L., Eunice, K. M., Stapleton, S., Rosen, D., & Rosenfield, A. (1989). Outcomes of care in birth centers. *New England Journal of Medicine, 321,* 1804–1810.

Roper Organization, Inc. (1991). *AIDS: Public attitudes and education needs.* New York.

Rose, R. J. (1995). Genes and human behavior. *Annual review of psychology, 46,* 615–654.

Rose, S. A. (1981). Developmental changes in infants' retention of visual stimuli. *Child Development, 52,* 227–233.

Rose, S. A., & Wallace, I. F. (1985a). Visual recognition memory: A predictor of later cognitive functioning. *Child Development, 56,* 853–861.

Rosen, K. S., & Rothbaum, F. (1993). Quality of parental caregiving and security of attachment. *Developmental Psychology, 29,* 358–367.

Rosen, R., & Rosen, L. R. (1981). *Human sexuality.* New York: Knopf.

Rosen, W. D., Adamson, L. B., & Bakeman, R. (1992). An experimental investigation of infant social referencing: Mothers' messages and gender differences. *Developmental Psychology, 28,* 1172–1178.

Rosenberg, S., & Farrell, M. (1981). *Men at midlife.* Boston: Auburn House.

Rosenberg, S. D., & Farrell, M. P. (1976). Identity and crisis in middle-age men. *International Journal of Aging and Human Development, 7,* 153–170.

Rosenberg, Z. F., & Fauci, A. S. (1994). Immunopathology and pathogenesis of HIV infection. In P. A. Pizzo & C. M. Wilfert (Eds.), *Pediatric AIDS: The challenge of HIV infection in infants, children, and adolescents* (2nd ed., pp. 115–128). Baltimore: Williams & Wilkins.

Rosenblatt, P., & Elde, C. (1990). Shared reminiscence about a deceased parent: Implications for grief education and grief counseling. *Family Relations, 39,* 206–210.

Rosenhan, D. L., & Seligman, M. E. P. (1995). *Abnormal psychology* (3rd ed.). New York: Norton.

Rosenmayr, L. (1985). Changing values and positions of aging in Western culture. In J. E. Birren & K. W. Schaie (Eds.), *Handbook of the psychology of aging* (2nd ed., pp. 190–216). New York: Van Nostrand Reinhold.

Rosenstein, D. & Oster, H. (1988). Differential facial responses to four basic tastes. *Child Development, 59,* 1555–1569.

Rosenthal, E. (1992, May 26). Cost of high-tech fertility: too many tiny babies. *New York Times: Science Times,* pp. C1, C10.

Rosentsweig, J. (1980). Motor development through life. In C. B. Corbin (Ed.), *A textbook of motor development* (2nd ed., pp. 283–290). Dubuque, IA: Brown.

Rosenzweig, M. R., Bennett, E. L., & Diamond, M. C. (1972, February). Brain changes in response to experience. *Scientific American,* 22–29.

Ross, H. S. (1996). Negotiating principles of entitlement in sibling property disputes. *Developmental Psychology, 32,* 90–101.

Ross, H. S., & Lollis, S. P. (1989). A social relations analysis of toddler peer relationships. *Child Development, 60,* 1082–1091.

Ross, K., Braga, J., & Braga, L. Z. (1975). Omega. In E. Kübler-Ross (Ed.), *Death: The final stage of growth* (pp. 164–166). Englewood Cliffs, New Jersey: Prentice Hall.

Rothenberg, K. H., & Paskey, S. J. (1995). The risk of domestic violence and women with HIV infection: Implications for partner notification, public policy, and the law. *American Journal of Public Health, 85,* 1569–1575.

Rothman, R. (1990, June 13). Students spend little time reading or writing in school, NAEP finds. *Education Week,* 1, 9.

Rothman, R. (1991, March 13). Psychologist's cross-national studies in math show U.S.'s long road to "first in the world." *Education Week,* 6–7.

Rothstein, L. E. (1995). *Special education law* (2nd ed.). White Plains, NY: Longman.

Rowe, D. C., & Waldman, I. D. (1993). The question "how?" reconsidered. In R. Plomin & G. E. McClearn (Eds.), *Nature, nurture, & psychology,* Washington, DC: American Psychological Association, pp. 355–375.

Rowlison, R. T., & Felner, R. D. (1988). Major life events, hassles, and adaptation in adolescence: Confounding in the conceptualization and measurement of life stress and adjustment revisited. *Journal of Personality and Social Psychology, 55,* 432–444.

Rozin, P. (1996). Sociocultural influences on human food selection. In E. D. Capaldi (Ed.), *Why we eat what we eat.* Washington, DC: American Psychological Association, pp. 233–267.

Rubin, A. M. (1995, July 21). Using pop culture to fight teen violence. *The Chronicle of Higher Education,* p. A5.

Rubin, E. H., Morris. J. C., Storandt, M., & Berg, I. (1986). Behavioral changes in patients with mild senile demential of the Alzheimer's type. *Psychiatric Research, 21,* 55–62.

Rubin, J., Provenzano, F., & Luria, Z. (1974). The eye of the beholder: Parents' views of sex of newborns. *American Journal of Orthopsychiatry, 43,* 720–731.

Rubin, K. H., Fein, G. G., & Vandenberg, B. (1983). Play. In P. H. Mussen (Ed.), *Handbook of child psychology* (4th ed., Vol. 4, pp. 693–775). New York: Wiley.

Rubin, K. H., & Howe, N. (1986). Social play and perspective taking. In G. Fein & M. Rivkin (Eds.), *The young child at play: Reviews of research* (Vol 4. pp. 113–125). Washington, DC: National Association for the Education of Young Children.

Rubin, L. (1979). *Women of a certain age.* New York: Harper & Row.

Rubin, R. (1996, February 5). The war on cancer. *U.S. News and World Report,* 54–61.

Rubin, R. A., & Balow, B. (1979). Measures of infant development and socioeconomic status as predictors of later intelligence and school achievement. *Developmental Psychology, 15,* 225–227.

Rubin, Z. (1980). *Children's friendships.*

Cambridge, MA: Harvard University Press.
Rubinson, L., & De Rubertis, L. (1991). Trends in sexual attitudes and behaviors of a college population over a 15 year period. *Journal of Sex Education and Therapy, 17,* 32–42.
Ruble, D. N. (1988). Sex role development. In M. H. Bornstein & M. E. Lamb (Eds.), *Social, emotional and personality development* (2nd ed., pp. 411–451). Hillsdale, NJ: Erlbaum.
Ruble, D. N., & Brooks-Gunn, J. (1982). The experience of menarche. *Child Development, 53,* 1557–1566.
Rubonis, A. V., & Bickman, L. (1991). Psychological impairment in the wake of disaster: The disaster-psychopathology relationship. *Psychological Bulletin, 109,* 384–399.
Ruchlin, H. S., & Morris, J. N. (1991). Impact of work on the quality of life of community-residing young elderly. *American Journal of Public Health, 81,* 498–500.
Ruddy, M. G., & Bornstein, M. H. (1982). Cognitive correlates of infant attention and maternal stimulation over the first year of life. *Child Development, 53,* 183–188.
Rueter, M. A., & Conger, R. D. (1995). Antecedents of parent-adolescent disagreements. *Journal of Marriage and the Family, 57,* 435–448.
Ruff, H. A., & Lawson, K. R. (1990). Development of sustained, focused attention in young children during free play. *Developmental Psychology, 26,* 85–93.
Ruittenbeck, H. M. (1964). *The individual and the crowd: A study of identity in America.* New York: New American Library.
Runback, R. B., & Carr, T. S. (1984). Schema guided information search in stereotyping of the elderly. *Journal of Applied Social Psychology, 14,* 57–68.
Ruopp, R., Travers, J., Glantz, F., & Coelen, C. (1983). *Children at the center* (Final report of the National Day Care Study). Cited in E. Zigler & S. Muenchow. Infant day care and infant-care leaves: A policy vacuum. *American Psychologist, 38,* 91–95.
Rush, D. (1992). Folate supplements and neural tube defects. *Nutrition Reviews, 50,* 25–26.
Russell, C. (1993, October). The master trend. *American Demographics,* 28–37.
Russell, C. (1995a, November). Glass ceilings can break. *American Demographics,* 8.
Russell, C. (1995b, December). The baby boom turns 50. *American Demographics,* 23–33.
Russell, C., & Mitchell, S. (1995, April). Talking about whose generation? *American Demographics,* 32–33.
Russell, D. W., & Cutrona, C. E. (1991). Social support, stress, and depressive symptoms among the elderly: Test of a process model. *Psychology and Aging, 6,* 190–201.
Rutter, M. (1979). Maternal deprivation, 1972–1978: New findings, new concepts, new approaches. *Child Development, 50,* 283–305.
Rutter, M. (1981). Social-emotional consequences of day care for preschool children. *American Journal of Orthopsychiatry, 51,* 4–29.
Rutter, M. (1983). School effects on pupil progress: Research findings and policy implications. *Child Development, 54,* 1–29.
Rutter, M. (1995). Maternal deprivation. In M. H. Bornstein (Ed.), *Handbook of parenting* (Vol. 4, pp. 3–33). Mahwah, NJ: Erlbaum.
Rutter, M., & Rutter, M. (1993). *Developing minds.* New York: Basic Books.
Ryan, A. S., Rush, D., Krieger, F. W., & Lewandowski, G. E. (1991b). Recent declines in breast-feeding in the United States, 1984–1989. *Pediatrics,* 719–726.
Ryan, C. J., & Kaye, M. (1996, February 1). Euthanasia in Australia—The Northern Territory Rights of the Terminally Ill Act. *The New England Journal of Medicine, 334,* 326–328.
Ryan, E. B., Bourhis, R. Y., & Knops, U. (1991). Evaluative perceptions of patronizing speech addressed to elders. *Psychology and Aging, 6,* 442–450.
Ryan, E. J. (1994, February). Will multiculturalism undercut student individuality? *Education Digest,* 26–28.
Ryan, K. (1981). *Questions and answers on moral education.* Bloomington, IN: Phi Delta Kappa Educational Foundation.
Ryan, K., & Greer, P. (1990, January). Putting moral education back in schools. *Education Digest,* 31–34.
Ryan, R. M., & Lynch, J. H. (1989). Emotional autonomy versus detachment: Revising the vicissitudes of adolescence and young adulthood. *Child Development, 60,* 340–356.
Rybash, J. M., Roodin, P. A., & Hoyer, W. J. (1995). *Adult development and aging* (3rd ed.). Dubuque, IA: Brown & Benchmark.
Rychlak, J. F. (1985). Eclecticism in psychological theorizing: Good and bad. *Journal of Counseling and Development, 63,* 351–354.
Ryff, C. D., Lee, Y. H., Essex, M. J., & Schmutte, P. S. (1994). My children and me: Midlife evaluations of grown children and of self. *Psychology and Aging, 9,* 195–205.
Sacher, G. A. (1977). Life table modification and life prolongation. In C. E. Finch & L. Hayflick, *Handbook of the biology of aging* (pp. 582–638). New York: Van Nostrand.
Sadker, M., & Sadker, D. (1985). Sexism in the schoolroom in the '80s. *Psychology Today, 19,* 54–57.
Sadker, M., & Sadker, D. (1994). *Failing at fairness: How America's schools cheat girls.* New York: Macmillan.
Sagi, A., van Izendoorn, M. H., Scharf, M., Koren-Karie, N., Joels, T., & Mayseless, O., (1994). Stability and discriminant validity of the adult attachment interview: A psychometric study in young Israeli adults. *Developmental Psychology, 30,* 771–777.
Sakauye, K. M., & Camp, C. J. (1992). Introducing psychiatric care into nursing homes. *The Gerontologist, 32,* 849–852.
Saleh, S. D., & Otis, J. L. (1964). Age and level of job satisfaction. *Personnel Psychology, 17,* 425–430.
Salend, S. J., & Taylor, L. (1993). Working with families: A cross-cultural perspective. *Remedial and Special Education, 14,* 25–32, 39.
Salkind, N. J. (1981). *Theories of human development.* New York: Van Nostrand.
Salt, R. (1991). Child support in context: Comments on Rettig, Christensen, and Dahl. *Family Relations, 40,* 175–178.
Salthouse, T. A. (1982). *Adult cognition: An experimental psychology of human aging.* New York: Springer-Verlag.
Salthouse, T. A. (1985). Speed of behavior and its implications for cognition. In J. E. Birren & K. W. Schaie (Eds.), *Handbook of the psychology of aging* (2nd ed., pp. 400–427). New York: Van Nostrand Reinhold.
Salthouse, T. A. (1989). Age-related changes in basic cognitive processes. In P. T. Costa et al., *The adult years: Continuity and Change* (pp. 5–41). Washington, DC: American Psychological Association.
Salthouse, T. A. (1993). Speed mediation of adult age differences in cognition. *Psychology and Aging, 29,* 722–738.
Salthouse, T. A. (1994). The nature of the influence of speed on adult age differences in cognition. *Developmental Psychology, 30,* 240–259.
Salthouse, T. A., & Babcock, R. L. (1991). Decomposing adult age differences in

working memory. *Developmental Psychology, 27,* 763–777.

Salthouse, T. A., & Kail, R. (1983). Memory development throughout the life span. In P. B. Baltes & O. G. Brim (Eds.), *Life-span development and behavior* (Vol. 5, pp. 90–118). New York: Academic Press.

Salthouse, T. A., Kausler, D. H., & Saults, J. S. (1990). Age, self-assessed health status, and cognition. *Journal of Gerontology, 45,* 156–160.

Saltz, E., & Johnson, J. (1974). Training for thematic-fantasy play in culturally disadvantaged children. *Journal of Educational Psychology, 66,* 523–630.

Saluter, A. (1992). Marital status and living arrangements. *Bureau of the Census Current Population Reports Population Characteristics Series.* (p. 20, No. 468) Washington, DC: U.S. Government Printing Office.

Salzinger, S., Feldman, R. S., Hammer, M., & Rosario, M. (1993). The effects of physical abuse on children's social relationships. *Child Development, 64,* 169–187.

Sameroff, A. J., & Cavanagh, P. J. (1979). Learning in infancy: A developmental perspective. In J. Osofsky (Ed.), *Handbook of infant development* (pp. 344–393). New York: Wiley.

Sameroff, A. J., & Chandler, M. J. (1975). Reproductive risk and the continuum of caretaker causality. In F. D. Horowitz (Ed.), *Review of child development research* (Vol. 4). Chicago: University of Chicago Press.

Sampson, P. D., Bookstein, F. L., Barr, H. M., & Streissguth, A. P. (1994). Prenatal alcohol exposure, birthweight, and measures of child size from birth to age 14 years. *American Journal of Public Health, 84,* 1421–1428.

Sandberg, E. C. (1989). Only an attitude away: The potential for reproductive surrogacy. *American Journal of Obstetrics and Gynecology, 160,* 1441–1446.

Sande, M. A. (1986). Transmission of AIDS: The case against casual contagion. *New England Journal of Medicine, 314,* 380–382.

Sanders, C. M. (1988). Risk factors in bereavement outcome. *Journal of Social Issues, 44,* 97–111.

Sanders-Phillips, K., Strauss, M. E., & Gutberlet, R. L. (1988). The effect of obstetric medication on newborn infant feeding behavior. *Infant Behavior and Development, 11,* 251–263.

Sandler, I. N., Tein, J. Y., & West, S. G. (1994). Coping, stress, and the psychological symptoms of children of divorce: A cross-sectional and longitudinal study. *Child Development, 65,* 1744–1763.

Sands, L. P., Terry, H., & Meredith, W. (1989). Change and stability in adult intellectual functioning assessee by Wechsler item responses. *Psychology and Aging, 4,* 79–87.

Sansavini, A., Bertoncini, J., & Giovanelli, G. (1997). Newborns discriminate the rhythm of multisyllabic stressed words. *Developmental Psychology, 23,* 3–12.

Santrock, J. W. (1972). Relation of type and onset of father absence to cognitive development. *Child Development, 43,* 455–469.

Sarafino, E. P. (1994). *Health psychology.* New York: Wiley.

Sarafino, E. P. (1996). *Principles of behavior Change.* New York: Wiley.

Sarason, I., Johnson, J., & Siegel, J. (1978). Assessing impact of life changes: Development of the life experiences survey. *Journal of Clinical and Consulting Psychology, 46,* 932–946.

Sarason, I. G., Sarason, B. R., & Pierce, G. R. (1989). *Social support: An interactional view.* New York: Wiley.

Satcher, D. (1995, June 9). Is the new vaccines for children program improving immunization rates in the United States. Yes. *CQ Researcher, 5,* 505.

Sattler, J. M. (1974). *Assessment of children's intelligence* (Rev. ed.). Philadelphia: Saunders.

Saunders, S. E., & Carroll, J. (1988). The use of whole cow's milk in infancy. *Journal of the American Dietetic Association, 88,* 213–215.

Sautter, R. C. (1992, November). Crack: Healing the children. *Phi Delta Kappan,* (Kappan Special Report) K1–K12.

Savin-Williams, R. C. (1988). Theoretical perspectives accounting for adolescent homosexuality. *Journal of Adolescent Health Care, 9,* 95–105.

Savin-Williams, R. C., & Small, S. A. (1986). The timing of puberty and its relationship to adolescent and parent perceptions of family interactions. *Developmental Psychology, 22,* 342–348.

Savitz, D. A., Schwingle, P. J., Keels, M. A. (1991). Influence of paternal age, smoking, and alcohol consumption on congenital anomalies. *Teratology, 44,* 429–440.

Sax, L. J., Astin, A. W., Korn, W. S., Mahoney, K. M. (1995). *The American freshman: National norms for 1995.* Los Angeles: Higher Education Research Institute, UCLA.

Saxon, S. V., & Etten, M. J. (1978). *Physical change and aging.* New York: Tiresias.

Sayler, M. E., & Brookshire, W. K. (1993). Social, emotional, and behavioral adjustment of accelerated students, students in gifted classes, and regular students in eighth grade. *Gifted Child Quarterly, 37,* 150–154.

Scales, P. (1981). Sex education and the prevention of teenage pregnancy: An overview of policies and programs in the United States. In T. Ooms (Ed.), *Teenage pregnancy in family context: Implications for policy* (pp. 213–254). Philadelphia: Temple University Press.

Scarr, S. (1981). Testing for children: Assessment and the many determinants of intellectual competence. *American Psychologist, 36,* 1159–1167.

Scarr, S., (1992). Developmental theories for the 1990s: Development and individual differences. *Child Development, 63,* 1–20.

Scarr, S. (1993). Biological and cultural diversity: The legacy of Darwin for development. *Child Development, 64,* 1333–1354.

Scarr, S., Eisenberg, M., & Deater-Deckard, K. (1994). Measurement of quality in child care centers. *Early Childhood Research Quarterly, 9,* 131–151.

Scarr, S., & McCartney, K. (1983). How people make their own environments: A theory of genotype-environment effects. *Child Development, 54,* 424–436.

Scarr-Salapatek, S. (1975). Genetics and the development of intelligence. In E. M. Hetherington, S. Scarr-Salapatek, & G. M. Siegel (Eds.), *Review of child development research* (Vol. 4, pp. 1–58). Chicago: University of Chicago Press.

Schachter, F. F. (1981). Toddlers with employed mothers. *Child Development, 52,* 958–964.

Schachter, J. (1989). Why we need a program for the control of chylamydia trachomatis. *New England Journal of Medicine, 320,* 802–803.

Schaeffer, R. T., & Lamm, R. P. (1995). *Sociology* (5th ed.). New York: McGraw-Hill.

Schaffer, H. R. (1996). *Social development.* Oxford: Blackwell.

Schaffer, K. F. (1981). *Sex roles and human behavior.* Cambridge, MA: Winthrop.

Schaffer, R. (1977). *Mothering.* Cambridge, MA: Harvard University Press.

Schaie, K. W. (1981). Psychological changes from midlife to early old age: Implications for the maintenance of mental health. *American Journal of Orthopsychiatry, 51,* 199–219.

Schaie, K. W. (1983) The Seattle Longitudinal Study: A 21-year exploration of psychometric intelligence in adulthood. In K. W. Schaie (Ed.), *Longitudinal studies of adult cognitive development,* (pp. 64–135). New York: Guilford Press.

Schaie, K. W. (1989). Perceptual speed in adulthood: Cross-section and longitudinal studies. *Psychology and Aging, 4,* 443–453.

Schaie, K. W. (1990). Intellectual development in adulthood. In J. E. Birren & K. W. Schaie (Eds.), *Handbook of the psychology of aging* (3rd ed., pp. 291–309). New York: Academic Press.

Schaie, K. W. (1994). The course of adult intellectual development. *American Psychologist, 49,* 304–313.

Schaie, K. W., & Geitwitz, J. (1982). *Adult development and aging*. Boston: Little, Brown.

Schaie, K. W., & Hertzog, C. (1982). Longitudinal methods. In B. B. Wolman (Ed.), *Handbook of developmental psychology* (pp. 91–116). Englewood Cliffs, NJ: Prentice Hall.

Schaie, K. W., & Hertzog, C. (1983). Fourteen-year cohort-sequential analyses of adult intellectual development. *Developmental Psychology, 19,* 531–544.

Schaie, K. W., & Parham, I. A. (1977). Cohort-sequential analyses of adult intellectual development. *Developmental Psychology, 13,* 649–653.

Schaie, K. W., Plomin, R., Willis, S. L., Gruber-Baldini, A., & Dutta, R. (1992). Natural cohorts: Family similarity in adult cognition. In T.B. Sonderegger (Ed.). *Psychology and aging: Nebraska Symposium on Motivation, 1991* (pp. 205–243). Lincoln, NE: University of Nebraska Press.

Schaie, K. W., & Willis, S. L. (1986). *Adult development and aging* (2nd ed.). Boston: Little, Brown.

Schaie, K. W., & Willis, S. L. (1993). Age difference patterns of psychometric intelligence in adulthood: Generalizability within and across ability domains. *Psychology and Aging, 8,* 44–55.

Schaie, K. W., & Willis, S. L. (1996). *Adult development and aging* (4th ed.). New York: Harper Collins.

Scharlach, A. E. (1991). Factors associated with filial grief following the death of an elderly parent. *American Journal of Orthopsychiatry, 61,* 307–313.

Scharlach, A. E., & Fuller-Thomson, E. (1994). Coping strategies following the death of an elderly parent. *Journal of Gerontological Social Work, 21,* 85–102.

Schechtman, K. B., Barzilai, B., Rost, K., & Fisher, E. B. (1991). Measuring physical activity with a single question. *American Journal of Public Health, 81,* 771–773.

Scherling, D. (1994). Prenatal cocaine exposure and childhood psychopathology. *American Journal of Orthopsychiatry, 64,* 9–19.

Schiedel, D. G., & Marcia, J. E. (1985). Ego identity, intimacy, sex role orientation and gender. *Developmental Psychology, 21,* 149–160.

Schiever, S. W., & Maker, C. J. (1991). Enrichment and acceleration: An overview and new directions. In N. Colangelo & G. David (Ed.), *Handbook of gifted education* (pp. 99–111). Needham Heights, MA: Allyn & Bacon.

Schiffman, S., & Pasternale, M. (1979). Decreased discrimination of food odors in the elderly. *Journal of Gerontology, 34,* 73–79.

Schilmoeller, G. L., Baranowski, M. D., & Higgins, B. S. (1991). Long-term support and personal adjustment of adolescent and older mothers. *Adolescence, 26,* 787–797.

Schlessinger, A. M., (1994, January 7). Does multicultural education contribute to racial tensions? *CQ Researcher, 4,* 17–18.

Schlicker, S. A., Borra, S. T., & Regan, C. (1994). The weight and fitness status of United States children. *Nutrition Reviews, 52,* 11–17.

Schlossberg, N. K. (1984). Exploring the adult years. In A. M. Rogers & C. J. Scheirer (Eds.), *The G. Stanley Hall lecture series* (Vol. 4, pp. 101–155). Washington, DC: American Psychological Association.

Schmeck, H. M. (1995, October 3). Study of chimps strongly backs salt's link to high blood pressure. *The New York Times,* p. C3.

Schmidt, D. F., & Boland, S. M. (1986). Structure of perceptions of older adults: Evidence for multiple stereotypes. *Psychology and Aging, 1,* 255–260.

Schmidt, P. (1994, September). Idea of "gender gap" under attack. *Education Week,* 1, 16.

Schmidt, P. (1995, March 1). Gap between white, black dropout rates has virtually closed. *Education Week,* 6.

Schmitt, M. H. (1979, July). Superiority of breast-feeding: Fact or fancy. *American Journal of Nursing,* 1488–1493.

Schmitt, N., Gogate, J., Rothert, M. Rovner, D., Holmes, M., Talarcyzk, G., Given, B., & Kroll, J. (1991). Capturing and clustering women's judgment policies: The case of hormonal therapy for menopause. *Journal of Gerontology: Psychological Sciences, 46,* S92–101.

Schnaiberg, L. (1996a, January 17). Educating Rafael. *Education Week,* 18–26.

Schnaiberg, L. (1996b, August 7). Hispanic immigrants trail other groups, study says. *Education Week, 16,* 12.

Schneider, J. (1993, July/August 16). Vanguard centers selected for women's health research studies. *CQ Researcher, 108,* 520–522.

Schneider, W., & Pressley, M. (1989). *Memory development between 2 and 20*. New York: Springer-Verlag.

Schneider-Rosen, K., & Wenz-Gross, M. (1990). Patterns of compliance from eighteen to thirty months of age. *Child Development, 61,* 104–112.

Schofield, J. W. (1981). Complementary and conflicting identities: Images and interaction in an interracial school. In S. R. Asher & J. M. Gottman (Eds.), *The development of children's friendships* (pp. 53–91). Cambridge: Cambridge University Press.

Schucker, B., Bailey, K., Heimbach, J. T., et al. (1987). Change in public perspective on cholesterol and heart disease: Results from two national surveys. *JAMA, 258,* 3527–3531.

Schuckit, M. (1986). Genetic and clinical implications of alcoholism and affective disorder. *American Journal of Psychiatry, 143,* 140–153.

Schuckit, M. (1987). Biological vulnerability to alcoholism. *Journal of Consulting and Clinical Psychology, 55,* 301–309.

Schultz, D. A. (1984). *Human sexuality*. Englewood Cliffs, NJ: Prentice Hall.

Schultz, D. P. (1978). *Psychology and industry today* (2nd ed.). New York: Macmillan.

Schultz, E. A., & Levenda, R. H. (1987). *Cultural anthropology*. St. Paul MN: West.

Schulz, R. (1985). Emotion and affect. In J. E. Birren & K. W. Schaie (Eds.), *Handbook of the psychology of aging* (2nd ed., pp. 531–544). New York: Van Nostrand Reinhold.

Schulz, R., & Ewen, R. B. (1993). *Adult development and aging* (2nd ed.). New York: Macmillan.

Schwab, R. (1992). Effects of a child's death on the marital relationship: A preliminary study. *Death Studies, 16,* 141–154.

Schwartz, P., & Jackson, D. (1989, February). How to have a model marriage. *New Woman,* 66–74.

Schweinghart, L. J., & Weikert, D. P. (1981). Effects of the Perry Preschool Program on youth through age 15. *Journal of the Division of Early Childhood, 4,* 29–39.

Scott, C. S., Shifman, L., Or, L., Owen, R. G., & Fawcett, N. (1988). Hispanic and black American adolescents' beliefs relating to sexuality and contraception. *Adolescence, 23,* 667–688.

Scott, M. E. (1988, Spring). Learning strategies can help. *Teaching Exceptional Children,* 30–34.

Sears, R. R., Maccoby, E. E., & Levin, H. (1957). *Patterns of child rearing.* New York: Harper & Row.

Sears, R. R., Roe, L., & Alpert, R. (1965). *Identification and child rearing.* Stanford, CA: Stanford University Press.

Seeman, T. E., Berkman, L. F., Charpentier, P. A., Blazer, D. G., Albert, M. S., & Tinettio, M. E. (1995). Behavioral and psychosocial predictors of physical performance: MacArthur studies of successful aging. *Journal of Gerontology: Medical Sciences, 50,* M177–M183.

Seeman, T. E., Charpentier, P. A., Berkman, L. F., Tinetti, M. E., Guarlnik, J. M., Albvert, M., Blazer, D., & Rowe, J. W. (1994). Predicting changes in physical performance in a high-functioning elderly cohort: MacArthur studies of successful aging. *Journal of Gerontology: Medical Sciences, 49,* M97–M108.

Segalowitz, N. S. (1981). Issues in the cross-cultural study of bilingual development. In H. C. Triandis & A. Heron (Eds.), *Handbook of cross-cultural psychology* (Vol. 4, pp. 55–93). Boston: Allyn and Bacon.

Seifer, R., Sameroff, A. J., Barrett, L. C., & Krafchuk, E. (1994). Infant temperament measured by multiple observations and mother report. *Child Development, 65,* 1478–1490.

Seifer, R., Schiller, M., Sameroff, A., Resnick, S., & Riordan, K. (1996). Attachment, maternal sensitivity, and infant temperament during the first year of life. *Developmental Psychology, 32,* 12–25.

Seitz, V., & Apfel, N. H. (1994). Effects of a school for pregnant students on the incidence of low-birthweight deliveries. *Child Development, 65,* 409–414.

Seligman, D., & Sullum, M. D. (1995, November 11). Books in brief: Emotional intelligence. *National Review, 47,* 69–71.

Seligmann, J. (1990, Winter/Spring). Variation on a theme. *Newsweek* (Special ed., The 21st Century Family), 38–46.

Selkoe, D. J. (1991, November). Amyloid protein and Alzheimer's disease. *Scientific American,* 68–78.

Sellers, D. E., McGraw, S. A., & McKinlay, J. B. (1994). Does the promotion and distribution of condoms increase teen sexual activity? Evidence from an HIV prevention program for Latino youth. *American Journal of Public Health, 84,* 1952–1959.

Sells, C. W., & Blum, R. M. (1996). Morbidity and mortality among US adolescents: An overview of data and trends. *American Journal of Public Health, 86,* 513–519.

Seltzer, J. A. (1991). Relationships between fathers and children who live apart: The father's role after separation. *Journal of Marriage and the Family, 53,* 79–101.

Seltzer, M. M., & Ryff, C. D. (1994). Parenting across the life span: The normative and nonnormative cases. In D. L. Featherman, R. M. Lerner, & M. Perlmutter (Eds.), *Life-span development and behavior* (Vol. 12, pp. 1–40). Hillsdale, NJ.: Erlbaum.

Seravalli, E. (1992, July/August). Medical art and immortality. *Reason, 29,* 37–38.

Serbin, L. A., Powlishta, K. K., & Gulko, J. (1993). The development of sex typing in middle childhood. *Monographs of the Society for Research in Child Development, 58,* (2, Serial No. 232).

Serdula, M. K., Collins, M. E., Williamson, D. F., Anda, R. F., Pamuk, E. R., & Byers, T. E. (1993). Weight control practices of U.S. adolescents and adults. *Annals of Internal Medicine, 119,* 667–671.

Serdula, M. K., Williamson, D. F., Anda, R. F., Levy, A., Heaton, A., & Byers, T. (1994). Weight control practices in adults: Results of a multistate telephone survey. *American Journal of Public Health, 84,* 1821–1824.

Sexias, J. S., & Youcha, G. (1985). *Children of alcoholism.* New York: Crown.

Shakoor, B. H., & Chalmer, D. (1991). Covictimization of African-American children who witness violence: Effects on cognitive, emotional and behavioral development. *JAMA, 83,* 233–238.

Shalala, D. E. (1993, April). Giving pediatric immunizations the priority they deserve. *JAMA,* 1845.

Shanan, J. (1983). Transitional phases of human development in transient society. In J. E. Birren et al. (Eds.), *Aging: A challenge to science and society* (pp. 112–125). New York: Oxford University Press.

Shanas, E. (1973). Family-kin networks and aging: A cross-cultural perspective. *Journal of Marriage and the Family, 35,* 505–511.

Schanas, E. (1979a). Social myth as hypothesis: The case of the family relations of old people. *The Gerontologist, 19,* 3–20.

Shanas, E. (1979b). The family as a social support system in old age. *Gerontologist, 19,* 169–174.

Shantz, C. U. (1983). Social cognition. In P. H. Mussen (Ed.), *Handbook of child psychology: Cognitive development* (4th ed., Vol. 4, pp. 495–556). New York: Wiley.

Shatz, M. (1983). Communication. In P. H. Mussen (Ed.), *Handbook of child psychology* (4th ed., pp. 841–891). New York: Wiley.

Shaver, J. P., & Strong, W. (1976). *Facing value decisions: Rationale-building for teachers.* Belmont, CA: Wadsworth.

Shay, K. A., & Roth, D. L. (1992). Association between aerobic fitness and visuospatial performance in healthy older adults. *Psychology and Aging, 7,* 15–24.

Shedler, J., & Block, J. (1990). Adolescent drug use and psychological health: A longitudinal inquiry. *American Psychologist, 45,* 612–630.

Sheehy, G. (1991). *Silent passage.* New York: Random House.

Sheehy, G. (1995). *New passages.* New York: Knopf.

Shinn, M., Knickman, J. R., & Weitzman, B. C. (1991). Social relationships and vulnerability to becoming homeless among poor families. *American Psychologist, 46,* 1180–1187.

Shiono, P. H., & Behrman, R. E. (1995, Spring). Low birth weight: Analysis and recommendations. *The Future of Children, 5,* 4–18.

Shirley, M. M. (1931). *The first two years: A study of twenty-five babies* (Vol. 1: *Postural and locomotor development*). Minneapolis, MN: University of Minnesota Press.

Shirley, M. M. (1933). *The first two years: A study of twenty-five babies* (Vol. 2: *Intellectual development.* Minneapolis, MN: University of Minnesota Press.

Siegel, J., & Shaughnesy, M. F. (1995). There's a first time for everything: Understanding adolescence. *Adolescence, 30,* 217–222.

Siegel, L. J., & Senna, J. J. (1991). *Juvenile delinquency* (4th ed.). St. Paul, MN: West.

Siegel, O. (1982). Personality development in adolescence. In B. B. Wolman (Ed.), *Handbook of developmental psychology* (pp. 537–549). Englewood Cliffs, NJ: Prentice Hall.

Siegel, P. Z., Brackbill, R. M., & Heath, R., (1995). The epidemiology of walking for exercise: Implication. *American Journal of Public Health, 85,* 706–711.

Siegel, P. Z., Deeb, L. C., Wolfe, W. E., Wilcox, D., & Maks, J. S. (1993). Stroke mortality and its socioeconomiic, racial, and behavioral correlates in Florida. *Public Health Reports, 108,* 454–459.

Siegler, R. S. (1991). *Children's thinking* (2nd ed.). Englewood Cliffs, NJ: Prentice Hall.

Sigman, M., Neumann, C., Carter, E., Cattle, D. C., D'Souza, S. D., & Bwibo, N. (1988). Home interactions and the development of Embu toddlers in Kenya. *Child Development, 59,* 1251–1261.

Signorella, M. L., & Liben, L. S. (1984). Recall and reconstruction of gender-related pictures: Effects of attitude, task difficulty, and age. *Child Development, 55,* 393–405.

Silver, L. B. (1987). The "magic cure": A review of the current controversial approaches for treating learning disabilities. *Journal of Learning Disabilities, 20,* 498–504.

Silver, L. B. (1990). Attention deficit hyperactivity disorder: Is it a learning disability or a related disorder? *Journal of Learning Disabilities, 23,* 394–397.

Silverberg, S. B., & Steinberg, L. (1990). Psychological well-being of parents with early adolescent children. *Developmental Psychology, 216,* 658–666.

Silverman, E.H. (1995). *Speech, language, and hearing disorders.* Needham, MA: Allyn & Bacon.

Silverman, W. K., La Greca, A. M., & Waserstein, S. (1995). What do children worry about? Worries and their relation to anxiety. *Child Development, 66,* 671–686.

Simkin, P., Whalley, J., & Keppler, A. (1984). *Pregnancy, childbirth, and the newborn.* Deephaven, MN: Meadowbrook Books.

Simmons, R. G., Blyth, D. A., Van Cleave, E. F., & Bush, D. M. (1979). Entry into early adolescence: The impact of school structure, puberty, and early dating on self-esteem. *American Sociological Review, 38,* 553–568.

Simoes, E. J., Byers, T., Coates, R. J., Serdula, M. K., Mokdad, A. H., & Heath, G. W. (1995). The association between leisure-time physical activity and dietary fat in American adults. *American Journal of Public Health, 85,* 240–244.

Simons, M., Whitbeck, L. B., Conger, R. D., & Chyi-in, W. (1991). Intergenerational transmission of harsh parenting. *Developmental Psychology, 27,* 159–172.

Simons, R. G., & Blyth, D. A. (1987). *Moving into adolescence: The impact of pubertal change and school context.* Hawthorne, NY: Aldine & deGruyter.

Simons, R. L., Johnson, C., Beaman, J., & Conger, R. D. (1993). Explaining women's double jeopardy: Factors that mediate the association between harsh treatment as a child and violence by a husband. *Journal of Marriage and the Family, 55,* 713–723.

Simonton, D. K. (1990). Creativity and wisdom in aging. In J. E. Birren & K. W. Schaie (Eds.), *Handbook of the psychology of aging* (3rd ed., pp. 320–329). New York: Academic Press.

Singer, D. G., & Singer, J. L. (1976). Family television viewing habits and the spontaneous play of preschool children. *American Journal of Orthopsychiatry, 46,* 496–502.

Singer, J. L., & Singer, D. G. (1983). Psychologists look at television: Cognitive, developmental, personality, and social policy implications. *American Psychologist, 38,* 826–835.

Singer, S., & Hilgard, H. R. (1978). *The biology of people.* San Francisco: Freeman.

Singh, G. K., Matthews, T. J., Clarke, S. C., Yannicos, T., & Smith, B. L. (1995, October 23). *Annual summary of births, marriages, divorces, and deaths: United States, 1994.* Washington, DC: U.S. Department of Health and Human Services.

Singh, G. K., & Yu, S. M. (1995). Infant mortality in the United States: Trends, differentials, and projections, 1950 through 2010. *American Journal of Public Health, 85,* 957–964.

Sinnott, J. D. (1981). The theory of relativity. *Human Development, 24,* 293–311.

Sinnott, J. D. (1984). Postformal reasoning: The relativistic stage. In M. L. Commons, F. A. Richards, & C. Armon (Eds.), *Beyond formal operations* (pp. 298–326). New York: Praeger.

Sinnott, J. D. (1989). A model for solution of ill-structured problems: Implications for everyday and abstract problem solving. In J. D. Sinnott (Ed.), *Everyday problem solving: Theory and applications* (pp. 72–99). New York: Praeger.

Siscovick, D. S., Strogatz, D. S., Weiss, N. S., & Rennert, G. (1990). Retirement and primary cardiac arrest in males. *American Journal of Public Health, 80,* 207–208.

Sizer, F. S., & Whitney, E. N. (1988). *Life choices: Health concepts and strategies.* St. Paul, MN: West.

Skarin, K. (1977). Cognitive and contextual determinants of stranger fear in six- and eleven-month-old infants. *Child Development, 48,* 537–544.

Skeels, H. M. (1966). Adult status of children with contrasting early life experiences: A follow-up study: *Monographs of the Society for Research in Child Development, 31*(3).

Skinner, B. F. (1957). *Verbal behavior.* New York: Appleton-Century-Croft.

Slaby, R. G., & Frey, K. S. (1975). Development of gender constancy and selective attention to same-sex models. *Child Development, 46,* 849–856.

Slater, A., Johnson, S. P., Kellman, P. J., & Spelke, E. S. (1994). The role of three-dimensional depth cues in infants' perception of partly occluded objects. *Early Development and Parenting, 3,* 187–191.

Slaughter-Defoe, D., Nakagawa, K., Takanishi, R., & Johnson, D. J. (1990). Toward cultural/ecological perspectives on schooling and achievement in African- and Asian-American children. *Child Development, 61,* 363–383.

Slawinski, E. B., Hartel, D. M., & Kline, D. W. (1993). Self-reported hearing problems in daily life throughout adulthood. *Psychology and Aging, 8,* 552–561.

Sleeter, C. E., (1993, March). Multicultural education: Five views. *Education Digest,* 53–57.

Sliwinski, M., Buschke, H., Kuslansky, G., Senior, G., & Scarisbrick, D. (1994). Proportional slowing and addition speed in old and young adults. *Psychology and Aging, 9,* 72–80.

Slobin, D. I. (1972, July). Children and language: They learn the same way all around the world. *Psychology Today,* p. 18.

Slobin, D. I. (1973). Cognitive prerequisites for the development of grammar. In C. A. Ferguson & D. I. Slovin (Eds.), *Studies of child language development.* New York: Holt, Rinehart and Winston.

Slonim, M. B. (1991). *Children, culture and ethnicity.* New York: Garland Publishing Co.

Slonim-Nevo, V., Auslander, W. F., Ozawa, M. N., & Jung, K. G. (1996). The long-term impact of AIDS-preventive interventions for delinquent and abused adolescents. *Adolescence, 31,* 409–421.

Small, M. Y. (1990). *Cognitive development.* San Diego, CA: Harcourt Brace Jovanovich.

Smart, D. E., Beaumont, P. J., & George, G. C. (1976). Some personality characteristics of patients with anorexia nervosa. *British Journal of Psychiatry, 128,* 57–60.

Smetana, J. G. (1986). Preschool children's conceptions of sex-role transgressions. *Child Development, 57,* 862–871.

Smetana, J. G. (1989). Adolescents' and parents' reasoning about actual family conflict. *Child Development, 60,* 1052–1067.

Smith, A. D. (1980). Age differences in encoding, storage, and retrieval. In L. W. Poon, J. L. Fozard, L. S. Cermak, D. Arenberg, & L. W. Thompson (Eds.), *New directions in memory and aging.* Hillsdale, NJ: Erlbaum.

Smith, C., & Lloyd, B. (1978). Maternal behavior and perceived sex of infant: Revisited. *Child Development, 49,* 1263–1265.

Smith, C. R. (1991). *Learning disabilities* (2nd ed.). Boston: Allyn & Bacon.

Smith, E. (1991). Ethnic identity development: Toward the development of a theory within the context of majority/minority status. *Journal of Counseling & Development, 70,* 181–188.

Smith, G. A., & Brewer, N. (1995). Slowness and age: Speed-accuracy mechanisms. *Psychology and Aging, 10,* 238–247.

Smith, J., & Baltes, P. B. (1990). Wisdom-related knowledge: Age/cohort differences in response to life-planning problems. *Developmental Psychology, 26,* 494–505.

Smith, K. R., & Moen, P. (1988). Passage through midlife: Women's changing family roles and economic well-being. *Sociological Quarterly, 29,* 503–524.

Smith, P. B., & Pederson, D. R. (1988). Maternal sensitivity and patterns of infant-mother attachment. *Child Development, 59,* 1097–1102.

Smith, P. K. (1978). A longitudinal study of social participation in pre-school children: Solitary and parallel play reexamined. *Developmental Psychology, 14,* 517–523.

Smith, P. K. (1995). Grandparenthood. In M. H. Bornstein (Ed.), *Handbook of Parenting* (Vol. 3, pp. 89–113). Mahwah, NJ: Erlbaum.

Smith, R. E., & Smoll, F. L. (1990). Self-esteem and children's reactions to youth sport coaching behaviors: A field study of self-enhancement. *Developmental Psychology, 26,* 987–993.

Smith, T. E. C. (1987). *Introduction to education.* St. Paul, MN: West.

Smith, W. J. (1994, October 10). *National Review, 46,* 60–64.

Smither, R. D. (1994). *The psychology of work and human performance* (2nd ed.). New York: HarperCollins.

Smolowe, J. (1990, December 24). *Time,* p. 64.

Snow, M. E., Jacklin, C. N., & Maccoby, E. E. (1983). Sex-of-child differences in father-child interaction at one year of age. *Child Development, 54,* 227–232.

Snowdon, D. A., Kemper, S. J., Mortimer, J. A., Greiner, L. H., Wekstein, D. R., & Markesbery, W. R. (1996, February 21). Linguistic ability in early life and cognitive function and Alzheimer's disease in later life. *JAMA, 275,* 528–532.

Snyder, H. N. (1994). *Are juveniles driving the violent crime trends?* Washington, DC: U.S. Department of Justice, Office of Juvenile Justice and Delinquency Prevention, May 1994, Fact Sheet #16.

Snyderman, M., & Rothman, S. (1987). Survey of expert opinion on intelligence and aptitude testing. *American Psychologist, 42,* 137–144.

Sobesky, W. E. (1983). The effects of situational factors on moral judgments. *Child Development, 54,* 575–584.

Sokolov, J. L. (1993). A local contingency analysis of the fine-tuning hypothesis. *Developmental Psychology, 29,* 1008–1023.

Solnit, A. J., Call, J. D., & Feinstein, C. B. (1979). Psychosexual development: Five to ten years. In J. D. Noshpitz (Ed.), *Basic handbook of child psychiatry* (pp. 184–190). New York: Basic Books.

Solomon, J. C., & Marx, J. (1995). "To grandmother's house we go": Health and school adjustment of children raised solely by grandparents. *The Gerontologist, 35,* 386–394.

Somers, M. D. (1993). A comparison of voluntarily childfree adults and parents. *Journal of Marriage and the Family, 55,* 643–650.

Somerville, S. C., Wellman, H. M., & Cultice, J. C. (1983). Young children's deliberate reminding. *Journal of Genetic Psychology, 143,* 87–96.

Sommer, B. B. (1978). *Puberty and adolescence.* New York: Oxford University Press.

Sommerfeld, M. (1995, May 10). New generation of activists channels their idealism. *Education Week,* 1, 10.

Sommers, C. H. (1994, October 26). The spouse abuse myth. *USA Today,* 13A.

Sontag, S. (1972). The double standard of aging. *Saturday Review, 50,* 29–38.

Sontag, S. (1977). The double standard of aging. In J. H. Williams (Ed.), *Psychology of women: Selected readings* (pp. 462–478). New York: Norton.

Sorce, J. F., Emde, R. N., Campos, J., & Klinnert, M. D. (1985). Maternal emotional signaling: Its effect on the visual cliff behavior of one-year olds. *Developmental Psychology, 21,* 195–200.

Sorenson, S. (1991). Suicide among the elderly: Issues facing public health. *American Journal of Public Health, 81,* 1109–1110.

Spafkin, J., Gadow, K. D., & Abelman, R. (1992). *Television and the exceptional child: A forgotten audience.* Hillsdale, NJ: Erlbaum.

Spaide, D. (1995). *Teaching your kids to care.* New York: Citadel.

Spangler, G., & Grossmann, K. E. (1995). Biobehavioral organization in securely and insecurely attached infants. *Child Development, 64,* 1439–1450.

Spanier, G. B., Sauer, W., & Larzelere, R. (1979). An empirical evaluation of the family life cycle. *Journal of Marriage and the Family, 41,* 27–38.

Speicher, B. (1994). Family patterns of moral judgment during adolescence and early adulthood. *Developmental Psychology, 30,* 624–632.

Spence, A. P. (1989). *Biology of human aging.* Englewood Cliffs, NJ: Prentice Hall.

Spencer, M. B., & Markstrom-Adams, C. (1990). Identity processes among racial and ethnic minority children in America. *Child Development, 61,* 290–311.

Spencer, W. D., & Raz, N. (1994). Memory for facts, source, and context: Can frontal lobe dysfunction explain age-related differences? *Psychology and Aging, 9,* 149–159.

Sperling, H. S., et al. (1996, November 28). Maternal viral load, zidovudine treatment, and the risk of transmission of human immunodeficiency virus type 1 from mother to infant. *The New England Journal of Medicine, 335,* 1621–1629.

Spilka, B., Hood, R. W., & Gorsuch, R. L. (1985). *The psychology of religion: An empirical approach.* Englewood Cliffs, NJ: Prentice Hall.

Spirduso, W. W., & MacRae, P. G. (1990). Motor performance and aging. In J. E. Birren & K. W. Schaie (Eds.), *Handbook of the psychology of aging* (3rd ed., pp. 183–200). New York: Academic Press.

Spitz, R. (1945). Hospitalism: An inquiry into the genesis of psychiatric conditions in early childhood. *Psychoanalytic Study of the Child, 1,* 53–71.

Spitz, R. (1965). *The first year of life: A psychoanalytic study of normal and deviant development of object relations.* New York: International Universities Press.

Sprafkin, J. N., Liebert, R. M., & Poulos, R. W. (1975). Effects of a prosocial televised example on children's helping. *Journal of Experimental Child Psychology, 20,* 119–126.

Sprafkin, J., Watkins, L. T., & Gadow, K. D. (1990). Efficacy of television literacy curriculum for emotionally disturbed and learning disabled children. *Journal of Applied Developmental Psychology, 11,* 225–244.

Sprigle, J. E., & Schaefer, L. (1985). Longitudinal evaluation of the effects of two compensatory preschool programs on fourth- through sixth-grade students. *Developmental Psychology, 21,* 702–709.

Sprintall, N. A., & Collins, W. A. (1984). *Adolescent psychology: A developmental view.* New York: Random House.

Spurlock, J., & Lawrence, L. E. (1979). The black child. In J. D. Noshpitz (Ed.), *Basic handbook of child psychiatry* (Vol. 1, pp. 248–256). New York: Basic Books.

SRCD (Society for Research in Child Development) (1991). *U.S. children and their families: Current conditions and recent trends, 1989.* Washington, DC: SRCD.

Sroufe, L. A. (1985). Attachment classification from the perspective of infant-caregiver relationships and infant temperament. *Child Development, 56,* 1–14.

Sroufe, L. A., Carlson, E., & Shulman, S. (1993). Individuals in relationships: Development from infancy through adolescence. In D. C. Funder, R. D. Parke, C. Tomlinson-Keasey, & Widaman K. (Eds.), *Studying lives through time* (pp. 315–343). Washington, DC: American Psychological Association.

Sroufe, L. A., & Wunsch, J. (1972). The development of laughter in the first year of life. *Child Development, 43,* 1326–1344.

St. George-Hyslip, P. H., et al. (1987). The genetic defect causing familial Alzheimer's disease maps on chromosome 21. *Science, 235,* 885–886.

St. George-Hyslow, P., Haines, J., et al. (1992). Genetic evidence for a novel familial Alzheimer's disease locus on chromosome 14. *Nature Genetics, 2,* 330–334.

Stagner, R. (1985). Aging in industry. In J. E. Birren & K. W. Schaie (Eds.), *Handbook of the psychology of aging* (2nd ed., pp. 789–818). New York: Van Nostrand Reinhold.

Stagno, S., & Whiteley, R. J. (1985). Herpes simplex virus and varicella-zoster virus infections. *New England Journal of Medicine, 313,* 1327–1329.

Stainback, S., & Stainback, W. (1991). Schools as inclusive communities in S. Stainback & W. Stainback (Eds.), *Controversial issues confronting special education* (pp. 27–44). Needham Heights, MA: Allyn and Bacon.

Stainback, W., & Stainback, S. (1984). A rationale for the merger of special and regular education. *Exceptional Children, 51,* 102–111.

Stambrook, M., & Parker, K. C. H. (1987). The development of the concept of death in childhood: A review of the literature. *Merrill-Palmer Quarterly, 33,* 133–137.

Stanford, L. D., & Hynd, G. W. (1994). Congruence of behavioral symptomatology in children with ADD/H, ADD.WO, and learning disabilities. *Journal of Learning Disabilities, 27,* 243–253.

Stark, E. (1986, May). Friends through it all. *Psychology Today,* 54–60.

Starr, B. D., & Weiner, M. B. (1982). The Starr-Weiner report on sex and sexuality in the mature years. New York: McGraw-Hill.

Statistical Abstract of the United States, 1996. Washington, DC: U.S. Department of Commerce.

Statistical Bulletin (1989, April/June). Hypertension in the United States: 1960 to 1980 and 1987 estimates. *Statistical Bulletin,* 13–15.

Statistical Bulletin (1993, October-December). Selected health behaviors and perceptions among U.S. adults in 1990. *Statistical Bulletin,* 2–9.

Staton, A. Q., & Oseroff, Varnell, D. (1990). Becoming a middle school student. In A. Q. Staton. *Communication and student socialization* (pp. 72–99). Norwood, NJ: Ablex.

Staw, B. M., & Ross, J. (1985). Stability in the midst of change: A dispositional approach to job attributes. *Journal of Applied Psychology, 70,* 469–480.

Steele, H., Steele, M., & Fonagy, P. (1996). Associations among attachment classifications of mothers, fathers, and their infants. *Child Development, 67,* 541–555.

Steffl, B. M. (1981). Assessment of safety factors. In I. M. Burnside (Ed.), *Nursing and the aged.* New York: McGraw-Hill.

Stein, J. A., Newcomb, M. D., & Bentler, P. M. (1993). Differential effects of parent and grandparent drug use on behavior problems of male and female children. *Developmental Psychology, 29,* 31–43.

Stein, Z. A. (1995). Editorial: More on women and the prevention of HIV infection. *American Journal of Public Health, 85,* 1485–1487.

Steinberg, L. (1986). Latchkey children and susceptibility to peer pressure: An ecological analysis. *Developmental Psychology, 24,* 295–296.

Steinberg, L. (1987). Single parents, stepparents, and the susceptibility of adolescents to antisocial peer presssure. *Child Devleopment, 58,* 269–275.

Steinberg, L. (1988). Reciprocal relation between parent-child distance and pubertal maturation. *Developmental Psychology, 24,* 122–128.

Steinberg, L. (1989). *Adolescence* (2nd ed.). New York: McGraw-Hill.

Steinberg, L., Brown, B., & Dornbusch, S. (1996). *Beyond the classroom: Why school reform has failied and what parents need to do.* New York: Simon & Schuster.

Steinberg, L., Elmen, J. D., & Mounts, N. S. (1989). Authoritative parenting, psychosocial maturity, and academic success among adolescents. *Child Development, 60,* 1424–1436.

Steinberg, L., & Levine, A. (1991). *You and your adolescent: A parents' guide for ages 10 to 20.* New York: Harper Perennial.

Steinberg, L., & Silverberg, S. (1987). Marital satisfaction in middle stages of family life cycle. *Journal of Marriage and the Family, 49,* 751–760.

Steinberg, L., & Silverberg, S. B. (1986). The vicissitudes of autonomy in early adolescence. *Child Development, 57,* 841–851.

Steinberg, L. D., Catalano, R., & Dooley, D. (1981). Economic antecedents of child abuse. *Child Development, 52,* 975–985.

Stephen, D. L. (1991–1992). A discussion of Avery Weisman's notion of appropriate death. *Omega, 24,* 301–308.

Stephens, M. A. P., Franks. M. M., & Townsend, A. L. (1994). Stress and rewards in women's multiple roles: The case of women in the middle. *Psychology and Aging, 9,* 34–52.

Stephens, R. C., Feucht, T. E., & Roman, S. W. (1991). Effects of an intervention program on AIDS-related drug and needle behavior among intravenous drug users. *American Journal of Public Health, 81,* 568–571.

Stephenson, A. L., Henry, C. S., & Robinson, L. C. (1996). Family characteristics and adolescence substance abuse. *Adolescence, 31,* 59–77.

Stern, D. N., Spieker, S., & MacKain, K. (1982). Intonation contours as signals in maternal speech to prelinguistic infants. *Developmental Psychology, 18,* 727–736.

Stern, M., & Karraker, K. H. (1989). Sex stereotyping of infants: A review of gender labeling studies. *Sex Roles, 20,* 501–522.

Sternberg, R. (1986). A triangular theory of love. *Psychological Review, 93,* 119–135.

Sternberg, R., & Grajek, S. (1984). The nature of love. *Journal of Personality and Social Psychology, 47,* 312–327.

Sternberg, R. J. (1985). General intellectual ability. In R. J. Sternberg (Ed.), *Human abilities: An information processing approach* (pp. 5–31). New York: Freeman.

Sterns, H. L., Barrett, G. V., & Alexander, R. A. (1985). Accidents and the aging individual. In J. E. Birren & K. W. Schaie (Eds.), *Handbook of the psychology of aging* (2nd ed., pp. 703–725). New York: Van Nostrand Reinhold.

Stets, J. E. (1990). Verbal and physical aggression in marriage. *Journal of Marriage and the Family, 52,* 501–514.

Stets, J. E., & Straus, M. A. (1989). The marriage as a hitting license: A comparison of assaults in dating, cohabiting, and married couples. (pp. 33–52). New York: Greenwood Press.

Stevens-Long, J. (1984). *Adult life* (2nd ed.). Palo Alto, CA: Mayfield.

Stevens-Long, J. (1990). Adult development: Theories past and future. In R. A. Nermiroff & C. B. Colarusso (Eds.), *New Dimensions in Adult Development* (pp. 125–165). New York: Basic Books.

Stevens-Long, J., & Commons, M. L. (1992). *Adult life: Developmental processes* Mountain View, CA: Mayfield Publishing Co.

Stevenson, H. W. (1991). The development of prosocial behavior in large-scale collective societies: China and Japan. In R. A. Hinde & J. Groebel (Eds.), *Cooperation and prosocial behaviour.* Cambridge: Cambridge University Press.

Stevenson, H. W., Chen, C., & Lee, S. Y. (1993). Mathematics achievement of Chinese, Japanese & American children: Ten years later. *Science, 259,* 53–58.

Stevenson, J., & Fredman, G. (1990). The social environmental correlates of reading ability. *Journal of Child Psychology and Psychiatry, 31,* 681–698.

Stevenson, R. E. (1973). *The fetus and newly born infant: Influences of the prenatal environment.* St. Louis: Mosby.

Stewart, M. J. (1980). Fundamental locomotor skills. In C. J. Corbin (Ed.), *A textbook of motor development* (pp. 44–52). Dubuque, IA: Brown.

Stifter, C. A., Coulehan, C. M., & Fish, M. (1993). Linking employment to attachment: The mediating effects of maternal separation anxiety and interactive behavior. *Child Development, 64,* 1451–1460.

Stigler, J. W., Lee, S. Y., & Stevenson, H. W. (1987). Mathematics classrooms in Japan, Taiwan, and the United States. *Child Development, 58,* 1272–1286.

Stimson, A., Wase, J., & Stimson, J. (1981). Sexuality and self-esteem among the aged. *Research on Aging, 3,* 228–239.

Stine, G. J. (1993). *AIDS: Biological, medical, social and legal issues.* Englewood Cliffs, NJ: Prentice Hall.

Stine, G. J. (1996). *Acquired immune deficiency syndrome* (2nd ed.). Englewood Cliffs, NJ: Prentice Hall.

Stines, J. A. (1983). A daycare checklist and personal communication.

Stipek, D., Feiler, R., Daniels, D., & Milburn, S. (1995). Effects of different instructional approaches on young children's achievement and motivation. *Child Development, 66,* 209–223.

Stipek, D., & Recchia, S., & McClintic, S. (1992). Self-evaluation in young children. *Monographs of the Society for Research in Child Development, 57,* No. 1 (Serial no. 226).

Stipek, D. J., Gralinski, H., & Kopp, C. B. (1990). Self-concept development in the toddler years. *Developmental Psychology, 26,* 972–977.

Stone, E. (1989, September). Quoted in *Reader's Digest,* 34.

Stoneman, Z., & Brody, G. H. (1993). Sibling temperaments, conflict, warmth, and role asymmetry. *Child Development, 64,* 1786–1800.

Storfer, M. D. (1990). *Intelligence and giftedness.* San Francisco: Jossey-Bass.

Strand, F. L. (1983). *Physiology* (2nd ed.). New York: Macmillan.

Strassberg, Z. (1995). Social information processing in compliance situations by mothers of behavior-problem boys. *Child Development, 66,* 176–189.

Straus, M. A. (1991a). Discipline and deviance: Physical punishment of children and violence and other crime in adulthood. *Social Problems, 38,* 133–152.

Straus, M. A. (1991b). New theory and old canards about family violence research. *Social Problems, 38,* 180–197.

Straus, M., Gelles, R., & Steinmetz, S. (1980). *Behind closed doors: Violence in the American family.* New York: Anchor.

Streib, G., & Schneider, C. (1971). *Retirement in American society.* Ithaca, NY: Cornell University Press.

Streissguth, A. P., Martin, D. C., Barr, H. M., Sandman, B. M., Kirchner, G. L., & Darby, B. L. (1984). Intrauterine alcohol and nicotine exposure: Attention and reaction time in four-year-old children. *Developmental Psychology, 20,* 533–542.

Streri, A., & Pecheux, M. G. (1986). Tactual habituation and discrimination of form in infancy: A comparison with vision. *Child Development, 57,* 100–104.

Streufert, S., Pogash, R., Piasecki, M., & Post, G. M. (1990). Age and management team performance. *Psychology and Aging, 5,* 551–559.

Stricherz, M., & Cunnington, L. (1982). Death concerns of students, employed persons, and retired persons. *Omega, 12,* 373–379.

Strickland, B. R. (1988). Menopause. In E. A. Blechman & K. D. Brownell (Eds.), *Handbook of behavioral medicine for women* (pp. 41–47). New York: Pergaman.

Stroebe, M. S., & Stroebe, W. (1983). Who suffers more? Sex differences in health risks of the widowed. *Psychological Bulletin, 93,* 279–301.

Stroebe, M., Van den Bout, J., & Schut, H. (1994). Myths and misconceptions about bereavement: The opening of a debate. *Omega, 29,* 187–203.

Strong, B., & DeVault, C. (1990). *The marriage and family experience* (4th ed.). St. Paul, MN: West.

Strong, B., & DeVault, C. (1995). *The marriage and family experience* (6th ed). St. Paul, MN: West.

Strouse, J. S., Buerkel-Rothfuss, N., & Long, E. C. (1995). Gender and family as moderators of the relationship between music video exposure and adolescent sexual permissiveness. *Adolescence, 30,* 505–522.

Strube, M. J., & Barbour, L. S. (1983). The decision to leave an abusive relationship: Economic dependence and psychological commitment. *Journal of Marriage and the Family, 45,* 785–794.

Stuckey, M. F., McGhee, P. E., & Bell, N. J. (1982). Parent-child interaction: The influence of maternal employment. *Developmental Psychology, 18,* 635–644.

Study: Less violence on TV. (1996, October 16). *Newsday,* A10.

Stunkard, A. J., et al. (1986). An adoption study of human obesity. *New England Journal of Medicine, 314,* 193–197.

Sue, D., Sue, D. W., & Sue, S. (1990). *Understanding abnormal behavior* (3rd ed.). Boston: Houghton Mifflin.

Suitor, J. J. (1991). Marital quality and satisfaction with the division of household labor across the family life cycle. *Journal of Marriage and the Family, 53,* 221–230.

Sullivan, K., & Winner, K. (1993). Three-year-olds' understanding of mental states: The influence of trickery. *Journal of Experimental Child Psychology, 56,* 135–148.

Sullivan, M. W., Lewis, M., & Alessandri, S. M., (1992). Cross-age stability in emotional expression: During learning and extinction. *Developmental Psychology 28,* 58–63.

Sullivan, S. A., & Birch, L. L. (1990). Pass the sugar, pass the salt: Experience dictates preference. *Developmental Psychology, 26,* 536–552.

Super, C. M., (1976). Environmental effects on motor development: The case of "African infant precocity." *Developmental Medicine and Child Neurology, 18,* 561–567.

Super, D. (1953). A theory of vocational development. *American Psychologist, 8,* 185–190.

The SUPPORT Principal Investigators (1995, November 22/29). A controlled trial to improve care for seriously ill hospitalized patients. *Journal of the American Medical Association, 274,* 1591–1598.

Surra, C. (1990). Research and theory on mate selection and premarital relationships in the 1980s. *Journal of Marriage and the Family, 52,* 844–865.

Surra, C., Arizzi, P., & Asmussen, L. I. (1988). The association between reasons for commitment and the development of and outcome of marital relationships. *Journal of Social and Personal Relationships, 5,* 47–63.

Swain, I. U., Zelazo, P. R., & Clifton, R. K. (1993). Newborn infants' memory for speech sounds retained over 24 hours. *Developmental Psychology, 29,* 312–323.

Swain, R. C., Oetting, E. R., Edwards, R. W., & Beauvais, F. (1989). Links from emotional distress to adolescent drug use: A path model. *Journal of Consulting and Clinical Psychology, 57,* 227–231.

Swan, G. E., Dame, A., & Carmelli, D. (1991). Involuntary retirement, type A behavior, and current functioning in elderly men: 27-year follow-up of the Western Collaborative Group study. *Psychology and Aging, 6,* 384–391.

Swanson, H. L. (1994). Short-term memory and working memory: Do both contribute to our understanding of academic achievement in children and adults with learning disabilities? *Journal of Learning Disabilities, 27,* 34–50.

Swanson, J. M., Cantwell, D., Lerner, M., McBurnett, K., & Hanna, G. (1991). Effects of stimulant medication on learning in children with ADHD. *Journal of Learning Disabilities, 24,* 219–230.

Swiatek, M. A., & Benbow, C. P. (1991). Ten-year longitudinal follow-up of ability-matched accelerated and unaccelerated gifted students. *Journal of Educational Psychology, 83,* 528–538.

Symons, D. K., & Moran, G. (1987). The behavioral dynamics of mutual responsiveness in early face-to-face mother-infant interactions. *Child Development, 58,* 1488–1496.

Sytkowski, P. A., Kannel, W. B., & D'Agostino, R. B. (1990). Changes in risk factors and the decline in mortality from cardiovascular disease. *New England Journal of Medicine, 322,* 1635–1641.

Szinovacz, M. (1982). Introduction: Research on women's retirement. In M. Szinovacz (Ed.), *Women's retirement.* Beverly Hills, CA: Sage.

Szinovacz, M., & Harpster, P. (1994). Couples' employment/retirement status and the division of household tasks. *Journal of Gerontology: Social Sciences, 49,* S125–S136.

Tait, M., Padgett, M. Y., & Baldwin, T. T. (1988). Job and life satisfaction: A reevaluation of the strength of the relationship and gender effects as a function of the date of the study. *Journal of Applied Psychology, 74,* 502–507.

Tallmer, M., & Kutner, B. (1970). Disengagement and morale. *Gerontologist, 10,* 317–320.

Tamir, L. M. (1989). Modern myths about men at midlife: An assessment. In S. Hunter & M. Sundel (Eds.), *Midlife myths: Issues, findings, and practical implications* (pp. 157–181). Newbury Park, CA: Sage.

Tamir, L. W. (1982). *Men in their forties: The transition to middle age.* New York: Springer.

Tanner, J. M. (1964). The adolescent growth-spurt and developmental age. In G. A. Harrison, J. S. Werner, J. M. Tannert, & N. A. Barnicot (Eds.), *Human biology: An introduction to human evolution, variation, and growth* (pp. 321–339). Oxford: Carendon Press.

Tanner, J. M. (1970). Physical growth. In P. H. Mussen (Ed.), *Carmichael's manual of child development* (3rd ed., pp. 77–155). New York: Wiley.

Tanner, J. M. (1990). *Fetus into man.* Cambridge, MA: Harvard University Press.

Taras, H. L., Sallis, J. F., Patterson, T. L., Nader, P. R., & Nelson, J. A. (1989). Television's influence on children's diet and physical activity. *Developmental and Behavioral Pediatrics, 10,* 176–180.

Taskinen, H., Antitila, A., Lindbohm, M. L., Sallmen, M., Hemminki, K. (1989). Spontaneous abortions and congenital malformations among the wives of men occupationally exposed to organic solvents. *Scandinavian Journal of Work Environment: Health, 15,* 345–352.

Taylor, G. S., Crino, M. D., & Rubinfeld, S. (1989). Coworker attributes as potential correlates to the perceptions of older workers' job performance: An exploratory study. *Journal of Business and Psychology, 3,* 449–458.

Teachman, J., & Polonko, K. (1990). Cohabitation and marital stability in the United States. *Social Forces, 69,* 207–220.

Teale, W. H. (1986). Home background and young children's literacy development. In W.H. Teale & E. Sutzby (Eds.), *Emergent literacy: Writing and reading* (pp. 173–206). Norwood, NJ: Ablex.

Teare, J. F., Garrett, C. R., Coughlin, D. D., Shanahan, D. L., & Daly, D.L. (1995). American's children in crisis: Adolescents' requests for support from a national telephone hotline. *Journal of Applied Developmental Psychology, 16,* 21–33.

Tellegen, A., Lykken, D. T., & Bouchard, T. (1988). Personality similarity in twins reared apart and together. *Journal of Personality and Social Psychology, 54,* 1032–1039.

Teltsch, K. (1991, May 21). New study of older workers finds they can become good investments. *New York Times,* A16.

Teri, L., & Wagner, A. W. (1991). Assessment of depression in Alzheimer's patients: Concordance among informants. *Psychology and Aging, 6,* 280–285.

Terman, L. M. (1925). *Mental and physical traits of 1,000 gifted children: Genetic studies of genius* (Vol. 1). Stanford, CA: Stanford University Press.

Termine, N. T., & Izard, C. E. (1988). Infants' responses to their mothers' expressions of joy and sadness. *Developmental Psychology, 24,* 223–230.

Terwilliger, J. S., & Titus, J. C. (1995). Gender differences in attitudes and attitude changes among mathematicallly talented youth. *Gifted Child Quarterly, 39,* 29–35.

Tessor, A. (1993). The importance of heritability in psychological research: The case of attitudes. *Psychological Review, 100,* 129–142.

Thelen, E. (1986). Treadmill-elicited stepping in seven-month-old infants. *Child Development, 57,* 1498–1506.

Thelen, E., & Fisher, D. M. (1982). Newborn stepping: An explanation for a "disappearing" reflex. *Developmental Psychology, 18,* 760–775.

Thomas, A., Chess, S., & Birch, H. G. (1970, August). The origins of personality. *Scientific American,* 102–109.

Thomas, D. G., & Lykins, M. S. (1995). Event-related potential measures of 24-hour Retention in 5-month old infants. *Developmental Psychology, 31,* 946–958.

Thomas, H. (1995). Modeling class inclusion strategies. *Developmental Psychology, 31,* 170–179.

Thomas, L. E. (1994). Reflections on death by spiritually mature elders. *Omega, 29,* 177–185.

Thomas, R. M. (1979). *Comparing theories of child development.* Belmont, CA: Wadsworth.

Thompson, F. E., Jr. (1995, June 9). Is the new vaccines for children program improving immunization rates in the United States. No., 5, 505.

Thompson, L., & Walker, A. (1989). Gender in families: Women and men in marriage, work, and parenthood. *Journal of Marriage and the Family, 51,* 845–857.

Thompson, M. G, Heller, K., & Rody, C. A. (1994). Recruitment challenges in studying late-life depression: Do community samples adequately represent depressed older adults? *Psychology and Aging, 9,* 121–125.

Thompson, R. A. (1988). The effects of infant day care through the prism of attachment theory: A critical appraisal. *Early Childhood Research Quarterly, 3,* 273–283.

Thompson, R. A. (1990). Vulnerability in research: A developmental perspective on research risk. *Child Development, 61,* 1–17.

Thornburg, H. D., & Glider, P. (1984). Dimensions of early adolescent social perceptions and preferences. *Journal of Early Adolescence, 4,* 387–406.

Thornbury, J., & Mistretta, C. M. (1981). Tactile sensitivity as a function of age. *Journal of Gerontology, 36,* 34–39.

Thornton, A. (1990). The courtship process and adolescent sexuality. *Journal of Family Research, 11,* 239–273.

Thornton, A., Axinn, W. G., & Hill, D. H. (1992). Reciprocal effects of religiosity, cohabitation, and marriage. *Journal of Marriage and the Family, 98,* 628–651.

Thorson, J. A., & Powell, F. C. (1988). Elements of anxiety and meanings of death. *Journal of Clinical Psychology, 44,* 691–701.

Thun, M. J., Day-Lally, C. A., Calle, E. E., Flanders, W. D., & Heath, C. W. (1995, September). Excess mortality among cigarette smokers: Changes in a 20-Year interval. *American Journal of Public Health, 85,* 1223–1230.

Timberlake, E. M., & Chipungu, S. S. (1992). Grandmotherhood: Contemporary meaning among African-American middle-class grandmothers. *Social Work, 37,* 216–221.

Timiras, P. S. (1972). *Developmental physiology and aging.* New York: Macmillan.

Timiras, P. S., & Meisami, E. (1972). Changes in gonadal function. In P. S. Timiras (Ed.), *Developmental physiology and aging* (pp. 527–542). New York: Macmillan.

Tisak, M. S. (1986). Children's conceptions of parental authority. *Child Development, 57,* 166–176.

Tobin, S., & Lieberman, M. (1981). Last home for the aged. Cited in P. Ebersole & P. Hess. *Toward healthy aging: Human needs and nursing response.* St. Louis, MO: Mosby.

Tobler, N. S. (1986). Meta-analysis of 143 adolescent drug prevention programs: Quantitative outcome results of program participants compared to a control or comparison group. *Journal of Drug Issues, 16,* 537–568.

Toch, T., Bennefield, R. M., & Bernstein, A. (1996, April 1). The case for tough standards. *U.S. News and World Report,* 52–56.

Tolchin, M. (1989, July 19). When long life is too much: Suicide rises among elderly. *New York Times,* 1.

Toledo-Dreves, V., Zabin, L. S., & Emerson, M. R. (1995). Durations of adolescent sexual relationships before and after conception. *Journal of Adolescent Health, 17,* 163–172.

Tomasello, M., & Barton, M. (1994). Learning words in nonostensive contexts. *Developmental Psychology, 30,* 639–650.

Tomasello, M., & Ferrar, J. (1984). Cognitive bases of lexical development: Object permanence and relational words. *Journal of Child Language, 13,* 495–505.

Tomasello, M., & Kruger, A. (1992). Acquiring verbs in ostensive and nonostensive contexts. *Journal of Child Language, 19,* 311–333.

Tomasello, M., & Mannle, S. (1985). Pragmatics of sibling speech to one-year-olds. *Child Development, 56,* 911–917.

Tomlin, A. M., & Passman, R. H. (1989). Grandmothers' responsibility in raising two-year-olds facilitates their grandchildren's adaptive behavior: A preliminary intrafamilial investigation of mothers' and maternal grandmothers' effects. *Psychology and Aging, 4,* 119–121.

Tomlin, A. M., & Passman, R. H. (1991). Grandmothers' advice about disciplining grandchildren: Is it accepted by mothers, and does its rejection influence grandmothers' subsequent guidance? *Psychology and Aging, 6,* 182–189.

Tomporowski, P. D., & Ellis, N. R. (1986). Effects of exercise on cognitive processes: A review. *Psychological Bulletin, 99,* 338–346.

Torgersen, A. M. (1989). Genetic and environmental influences on temperamental development: Longitudinal study of twins from infancy to adolescence. In S. Doxiadis (Ed.), *Early influences shaping the individual* (pp. 269–283). New York: Plenum.

Tosteson, A. N., Weinstein, M. C., Williams, L. W., & Goldman, L. (1990). Long-term impact of smoking cessation on the incidence of coronary heart disease. *American Journal of Public Health, 80,* 1481–1486.

Tower, R. B., Singer, D. G., Singer, J. J., & Biggs, A. (1979). Differential effects of television programming on preschoolers' cognition, imagination, and social play. *American Journal of Orthopsychiatry, 49,* 265–281.

Tower, R. L. (1987). *How schools can help combat student drug and alcohol abuse.* Washington, DC: NEA Professional Library.

Townsend, A. L., & Franks, M. M. (1995). Binding ties: Closeness and conflict in adult children's caregiving relationships. *Psychology and Aging, 10,* 343–351.

Townsend, B., & O'Neil, K. (1990, August). Women get mad. *American Demographics,* pp. 26–32.

Tran, T. V., Wright, R., Jr., & Chatters, L. (1991). Health stress, psychological resources, and subjective well-being among older blacks. *Psychology and Aging, 6,* 100–108.

Treffinger, D. J. (1982). Demythologizing gifted education: An editorial essay. *Gifted Child Quarterly, 26,* 3–8.

Trehub, S. (1973). Infants' sensitivity to vowel and tonal contrasts. *Developmental Psychology, 9,* 81–96.

Trickett, P. K., & Kuczynski, L. (1986). Children's misbehavior and parental discipline in abusive and non-abusive families. *Developmental Psychology, 22,* 115–123.

Trickett, P. K., & McBride-Chang, C. (1995).

The development impact of different forms of child abuse and neglect. *Developmental Review, 15,* 311–337.

Troll, L. E. (1985). *Early and middle adulthood* (2nd ed.). Pacific Grove, CA: Brooks/Cole.

Troll, L. E. (1989). Myths of midlife intergenerational relationships. In S. Hunter & M. Sundel (Eds.), *Midlife myths: Issues, findings, and practical implications* (pp. 210–233). Newbury Park, CA: Sage.

Tubman, J. G., Windle, M., & Windle, R. C. (1996). The onset and cross-temporal patterning of sexual intercourse in middle adolescence: Prospective relations with behavioral and emotional problems. *Child Development, 67,* 327–343.

Tucker, T., & Bing, E. (1975). *Prepared childbirth.* New Canaan, CT: Tobey.

Tulkin, S., & Kagan, J. (1972). Mother-child interaction in the first year of life. *Child Development, 43,* 31–41.

Tun, P. A., Wingfield, A., & Stine, A. L. (1991). Speech-processing capacity in young and older adults: A dual-task study. *Psychology and Aging, 6,* 3–9.

Tun, P. A., Wingfield, A., Stine, E. A. L., & Mecsas, C. (1992). Rapid speech processing and divided attention: Processing rate versus processing resources as an explanation of age effects. *Psychology and Aging, 7,* 546–550.

Turiel, E. (1990). Moral judgment, action, and development. In D. Schrader (Ed.), *The legacy of Lawrence Kohlberg,* (pp. 31–51). San Francisco: Jossey-Bass.

Tur-Kaspa, H., & Bryan, T. (1995). Teachers' ratings of the social competence and school adjustment of students with LD in elementary and junior high school. *Journal of Learning Disabilities, 28,* 44–52.

Turkheimer, E., & Gottesman, I. (1991). Individual differences and the canalization of human behavior. *Developmental Psychology, 27,* 18–23.

Turkington, C. (1987, January). Alzheimer's and aluminum. *APA Monitor,* 13.

Turner, B. F. (1982). Sex-related differences in aging. In B. B. Wolman (Ed.), *Handbook of developmental psychology* (pp. 912–936). Englewood Cliffs, NJ: Prentice Hall.

Turner, P. J., & Gervai, J. (1995). A multidimensional study of gender typing in preschool children and their parents: Personality, attitudes, preferences, behavior, and cultural differences. *Developmental Psychology, 31,* 759–772.

Tuttle, E. B., Becker, L. A., & Sousa, J. A. (1988). *Characteristics and identification of gifted and talented students.* Washington, DC: NEA Publications.

Twomey, J. G., Jr., & Fletcher, J. C. (1994). Ethical issues surrounding care of HIV-infected children. In P. A. Pizzo & C. M. Wilfert (Eds.), *Pediatric AIDS: The Challenge of HIV infection in infants, children, and adolescents* (2nd ed., pp. 713–724). Baltimore: Williams & Wilkins.

Uchino, B. N., Kiecolt-Glaser, J. K., & Cacioppo, J. T. (1994). Construals of preillness relationship quality predict cardiovascular response in family caregivers of Alzheimer's disease victims. *Psychology and Aging, 9,* 113–120.

Uhlmann, R. F., Pearlman, R. A., & Cain, K. C. (1988). Physicians and spouses' predictions of elderly patients' resuscitation preferences. *Journal of Gerontology, 43,* M115–121.

Underwood, R. A. (1996, January 19). Should English be the official language of the United States. *CQ Researcher,* 47.

UNICEF (1993). The state of the world's children, 1993. New York: Author.

UNICEF (1996). The state of the world's children. New York: Oxford.

Urberg, K. A., Segirmencioglu, S. M., Tolson, J. M., & Halliday-Scher, K. (1995). The structure of adolescent peer networks. *Developmental Psychology, 31,* 540–548.

U.S. Bureau of the Census, (1994). *Current population Reports,* P20-477. Washington, DC: Author.

U.S. Congress, Office of Technology Assessment (1992). *Adolescent Health: Volume II—Effectiveness of Selected Prevention and Treatment Services.* Washington, DC: U.S. Government Printing Office.

U.S. Department of Education (1993a) *Fifteenth annual report to Congress on the implementation of the Education of the Handicapped Act.* Washington, DC: Author.

U.S. Department of Education (1993b). *National excellence: A case for developing America's talent.* Washington, DC: Author.

U.S. Department of Education (1994). *To assure the free appropriate public education of all children with disabilities: Sixteenth annual report to congress on the implementation of the individuals with disabilities act.* Washington, DC: U.S. Department of Education.

U.S. Department of Education (1995a). *The Educational progress of black students.* Washington, DC: Author.

U.S. Department of Education (1995b). *The educational progress of Hispanic students.* Washington, DC: Author.

U.S. Department of Education (1995c). *The educational progress of women.* Washington, DC: Author.

U.S. Department of Health and Human Services (1988). The health consequences of smoking: Nicotine addiction: A report of the Surgeon General. Rockville, MD: U.S. Department of Health and Human Services (Pub. PHSA 88-8406). Office on Smoking and Health.

U.S. Department of Health and Human Services (1989a). *The surgeon general's report on nutrition and health.* Rocklin, CA: Prima Publishing and Communications.

U. S. Department of Health and Human Services (1989b). *Promoting health/preventing disease: Year 2000 objectives for the nation.* Washington, DC: Author.

U.S. Department of Health and Human Services (1991a). *Promoting health/ preventing disease: objectives for the nation.* Washington, DC: U.S. Government Printing Office.

U.S. Department of Health and Human Services (1991b). *Health: United States, 1990:* Pub. No. PHS 91-12312. Washington, DC: U.S. Government Printing Office.

U.S. Department of Health and Human Services (1993). *Eighth special report to the U.S. Congress on alcohol and health,* NIH Pub. No. 94–3699.

U. S. Department of Health and Human Services (1995a). *Health: United States, 1994.* Hyattsville, MD: Author. DHHS Pub. No. (PHS) 95-1232.

U.S. Department of Health and Human Services (1995b). *HHS NEWS: Annual survey shows increases in tobacco and drug use by youth.* Washington, DC: Author.

U.S. Department of Health and Human Services (1996). *Trends in the well-being of America's children and youth.* Washington, DC: Author.

U.S. Department of Labor (1993, December). *Work and family: turning thirty—job mobility and labor market attachment.* Washington, DC: U.S. Department of Labor, Report 862.

U.S. Department of Labor (1994). Bulletin 2307. Washington, DC: Author.

Use of alcohol linked to rise in fetal illness. (1995, April 7). *New York Times,* A27.

Uzgiris, I. C. (1973). Patterns of cognitive development in infancy. *Merrill-Palmer Quarterly, 19,* 181–204.

Vaillant, C. O., & Vaillant, G. E. (1993). Is the U-curve of marital satisfaction an illusion? A 40-year study of marriage. *Journal of Marriage and the Family, 55,* 230–239.

Vaillant, G. E. (1977). *Adaptation to life.* Boston: Little, Brown.

van den Bloom, D. C. (1994). The influence of temperament and mothering on attachment and exploration: An experimental manipulation of sensitive responsiveness among lower-class mothers and irritable infants. *Child Development, 65,* 1457–1478.

van den Boom, D. C., & Hoeksma, J. B. (1994). The effect of infant irritability on mother-infant interaction: A growth-curve analysis. *Developmental Psychology, 30,* 581–590.

Van der Plaats, M. (1983). Health. In J. E. Birren, et al. (Eds.), *Aging: A challenge to science and society* (Vol. 3, pp. 397–398). New York: Oxford University Press.

Van Evra, J. (1990). *Television and child development.* Hillsdale, NJ: Erlbaum.

van Ijzendoorn, M. H., Goldberg, S., Kroonenberg, P. M., & Frenkel, O. J. (1992). The relative effects of maternal and child problems on the quality of attachment: A meta-analysis of attachment in clinical samples. *Child Development, 63,* 840–858.

Van Itallie, T. B. (1990). The perils of obesity in middle-aged women. *New England Journal of Medicine, 322,* 928–929.

Vandell, D. L., & Bailey, M. D. (1992). Conflicts between siblings. In C. U. Shatz & W. W. Hartup (Eds.), *Conflict in child and adolescent development* (pp. 242–269). Cambridge, MA: Cambridge University Press.

Vandell, D. L., & Corasaniti, M. A. (1988). The relation between third graders' after-school care and social, academic, and emotional functioning. *Child Development, 59,* 868–876.

Vandell, D. L., Henderson, V. K., & Wilson, K. S. (1988). A longitudinal study of children with day-care experiences of varying quality. *Child Development, 59,* 1286–1293.

Vandenberg, B. (1978). Play and development from an ethological perspective. *American Psychologist, 33,* 724–739.

Vandenberg, S. G., & Kuse, A. R. (1979). Spatial ability: A critical review of the sex-linked major-gene hypothesis. In M. Whittig & A. Petersen (Eds.), *Determinants of sex related differences in cognitive functioning.* New York: Academic Press.

Vargas, L. A., Loya, F., & Hodde-Vargas, J. (1989). Exploring the multidimensional aspects of grief reactions. *American Journal of Psychiatry, 146,* 1484–1488.

Vaughn, B. E., Deane, K. E., & Waters, E. (1985). The impact of out-of-home care on child-mother attachment quality: Another look at some enduring questions. In I. Bretherton & E. Waters (Eds.), Growing points of attachment theory and research. *Monographs of the Society for Research in Child Development, 50* (1–2, Serial No. 209, pp. 110–136).

Vaughn, B. E., Goldberg, S., Atkinson, L, Marcovitch, S., MacGregor, D., & Seifer, R. (1994). Quality of toddler-mother attachment in children with Down syndrome: Limits to interpretation of strange situation behavior. *Child Development, 65,* 95–108.

Vaughn, B. E., Stevenson-Hinde, J., Waters, E., Kotsaftis, A., Lefever, G. B., Shoudice, A., Trudel, M., & Belsky, J. (1992). Attachment security and temperament in infancy and early childhood: Some conceptual clarifications. *Developmental Psychology, 28,* 463–471.

Vaughn, S. (1985). Why teach social skills to learning disabled students? *Journal of Learning Disabilities, 18,* 588–591.

Vega, W. A. (1990). Hispanic families in the 1980s: A decade of research. *Journal of Marriage and the Family, 52,* 1015–1024.

Vergason, G. A. (1990). *Dictionary of special education and rehabilitation* (3rd ed.). Denver, CO: Love Pub. Co.

Verhaeghen, P., & Marcoen, A. (1993). Memory aging as a general phenomenon: Episodic recall of older adults is a function of episodic recall of young adults. *Psychology and Aging, 8,* 380–388.

Verhaeghen, P., Marcoen, A., & Goossens, L. (1992). Improving memory performance in the aged through mnemonic training: A meta-analytic study. *Psychology and Aging, 7,* 242–251.

Vermund, S. H. (1995). Editorial: Casual sex and HIV transmission. *American Journal of Public Health, 85,* 1488–1489,

Vernon, P. E. (1976). Environment and intelligence. In V. P. Varma & P. Williams (Eds.), *Piaget, psychology, and education* (pp. 31–42). Itasca, IL: Peacock.

Vespo, J. E., Pedersen, J., & Hay, D. F. (1995). Young children's conflicts with peers and siblings: Gender effects. *Child Study Journal, 25,* 189–212.

Viadero, C. (1987, January 28). Panel to develop model suicide-prevention program for schools. *Education Week,* 5.

Viadero, D. (1989, May 3). 7 of 10 Handicapped graduates found "productive". *Education Week,* 6.

Viadero, D. (5 May, 1993). Special education update. *Education Week,* 10.

Viadero, D. (1994, April 20). Fade-out in Head Start Gains linked to later schooling. *Education Week,* 9.

Viadero, D. (1995a, July 12). Counter Intelligence. *Education Week,* 35–36.

Viadero, D. (1995b, January 11). RAND documents academic gains since 1970. *Education Week,* 9.

Viadero, D. (1996a, February 24). Teen culture seen impeding school reform. *Education Week,* 1, 10.

Viadero, D. (1996b, January 10). Study finds variation in math, science tests in 7 nations. *Education Week,* 13.

Vihman, M. M., Kay, E., de Boysson-Barides, B., Durand, C., & Sundberg, U. (1994). External sources of individual differences? A cross-linguistic analysis of the phonetics of mothers' speech to 1-year-old children. *Developmental Psychology, 30,* 651–662.

Vitaliano, P. P., Russo, J., Breen, A. R., Vitiello, M. J., & Prinz, P. N. (1986). Functional decline in the early stages of Alzheimer's disease. *Psychology and Aging, 1,* 41–47.

Vitz, P. C. (1990). The use of stories in moral development: New psychological reasons for an old education method. *American Psychologist, 45,* 709–720.

Voeller, B. (1980). Society and the gay movement. In J. Marmor (Ed.), *Homosexual behavior.* New York: Basic Books.

Voget, F. X. (1985). Bulimia. *Adolescence, 20,* 46–50.

Volling, B. L., & Feagans, L. V. (1995). Infant day care and children's social competence. *Infant Behavior and Development, 18,* 177–188.

Vorhees, C. V., & Mullnow, E. (1987). Behavioral teratogenesis: Long-term influences on behavior from early exposure to environmental agents. In J. Osofsky (Ed.), *Handbook of infant development* (2nd ed., pp. 913–971). New York: John Wiley.

Wachs, T. D., Uzgiris, I. C., & Hunt, J. M. (1971). Cognitive development in infants of different age levels and from different environmental backgrounds: An explanatory investigation. *Merrill-Palmer Quarterly, 17,* 283–317.

Waddington, C. H. (1957). *The strategy of genes.* Winchester, MA: Allen & Unwin.

Wagner, R. K., Torgesen, J. K., & Rashotte, C. A. (1994). Development of reading-related phonological processing abilities: New evidence of bidirectional causality from a latent variable longitudinal study. *Developmental Psychology, 30,* 73–87.

Wagner, T. (1996, October 9). Creating community consensus on core values. *Education Week,* 36, 38.

Wahl, H. W. (1991). Dependence in the elderly from an interactional point of view: Verbal and observational data. *Psychology and Aging, 6,* 238–246.

Wainryb, C. (1993). The application of moral judgments to other cultures: Relativism and universality. *Child Development, 64,* 924–933.

Walden, E. L., & Thompson, S. A. (1981). A review of some alternative approaches to drug management of hyperactivity in children. *Journal of Learning Disabilities, 4,* 213–217.

Walden, T. A., & Ogan, T. A. (1988). The development of social referencing. *Child Development, 59,* 1230–1241.

Waldman, D. A., & Avolio, B. J. (1986). A meta-analysis of age differences in job performance. *Journal of Applied Psychology, 71,* 33–38.

Waldrop, J. (1991, January). The baby boom turns 45. *American Demographics,* 22–27.

Walford, R. L. (1983). *Maximum life span.* New York: Norton.

Walk, R. D. (1981). *Perceptual development.* Pacific Grove, CA: Brooks/Cole.

Walker, D., Greenwood, C., Hart, B., & Carta, J. (1994). Prediction of school outcomes based on early language production and socioeconomic factors. *Child Development, 65,* 606–621.

Walker, E., & Emory, E. (1985). Commentary: Interpretive bias and behavioral genetic research. *Child Development, 56,* 775–779.

Walker, J. E., & Howland, J. (1990). Falls and fear of falling among elderly persons living in the community: Occupational therapy interventions. *American Journal of Occupational Therapy, 15,* 119–122.

Walker, J. H., Kozma, E. J., & Green, R. P. (1989). *American education: Foundations and policy.* St. Paul, MN: West.

Walker, L. J. (1984). Sex differences in the development of moral reasoning: A critical review. *Child Development, 55,* 677–691.

Walker, L. J. (1988). The development of moral reasoning. *Annals of Child Development, 5,* 33–78.

Walker, L. J. (1989). A longitudinal study of moral reasoning. *Child Development, 60,* 157–166.

Walker, L. J., & Taylor, J. H. (1991b). Family interactions and the development of moral reasoning. *Child Development, 62,* 264–283.

Wall, S. M., Pickert, S. M., & Bigson, W. B. (1989). Fantasy play in 5- and 6-year-old children. *Journal of Psychology, 123,* 245–256.

Wallace, I., Wallechinsky, D., Wallace, A., & Wallace, S. (1981) *The book of lists: 2.* New York: Bantam.

Wallerstein, J. S. (1983). Children of divorce: The psychological tasks of the child. *American Journal of Orthopsychiatry, 53,* 230–243.

Wallerstein, J. S. (1986). Women after divorce: Preliminary report from a ten-year follow-up. *American Journal of Orthopsychiatry, 56,* 65–77.

Wallerstein, J. S. (1987). Children of divorce: Report of a ten-year follow-up of early latency-age children. *American Journal of Orthopsychiatry, 57,* 199–211.

Wallerstein, J. S., Corbin, S. B., & Lewis, J. M. (1988). Children of divorce: A 10-year study. In E. M. Hetherington & J. D. Arasteh (Eds.), *Impact of divorce, single parenting, and stepparenting on children* (pp. 197–215). Hillsdale, NJ: Erlbaum.

Wallerstein, J. S., & Kelly, J. (1980). Effects of divorce on the visiting father-child relationship. *American Journal of Psychiatry, 137,* 1534–1539.

Walsh, D. J. (1989). Changes in kindergarten: Why here? Why now? *Early Childhood Research Quarterly, 4,* 377–393.

Walsh, M. (1996, December 6). "Sesame Street" incorporates theories on cognition. *Education Week,* 3.

Wan, C., Fan, C., Lin, G., & Jing, Q. (1994). Comparison of personality traits of only and sibling children in Beijing. *Journal of Genetic Psychology, 155,* 377–389.

Ward, M. J., & Carlson, E. A. (1995). Associations among adult attachment representations, maternal sensitivity, and infant-mother attachment in a sample of adolescent mothers. *Child Development, 66,* 69–79.

Ward, R. A. (1980). Age and acceptance of euthanasia. *Journal of Gerontology, 35,* 421–431.

Ward, R. A. (1984). *The aging experience: An introduction to social gerontology* (2nd ed.). New York: Harper & Row.

Ward, R. A. (1993). Marital happiness and household equity in later life. *Journal of Marriage and the Family, 55,* 427–438.

Ward, S. K., Chapman, K., Cohn, E., White, S., & Williams, K. (1991). Acquaintance rape and the college social scene. *Family Relations, 40,* 65–71.

Warfield-Coppock, N. (1992). The rites of passage movement: A resurgence of African-centered practices for socializing American youth. *Journal of Negro Education, 61,* 471–481.

Wark, G. R., & Krebs, D. L. (1996). Gender and dilemma differences in real-life moral judgment. *Developmental Psychology, 32,* 220–230.

Warner, K. E., Wickizer, T. M., Wolfe, R. A., Schildroth, J. E., & Samuelson, M. H. (1988). Economic implications of workplace health promotion programs: Review of the literature. *Journal of Occupational Medicine, 30,* 106–112.

Warr, P. (1992). Age and occupational well-being. *Psychology and Aging, 7,* 37–45.

Warr, P., Jackson, P., & Banks, M. (1988). Unemployment and mental health: Some British studies. *Journal of Social Issues, 44,* 47–68.

Warren, L., Butler, R. M., Katholi, C., & Halsey, J. (1985). Age differences in cerebral blood flow during mental activation measurements with and without monetary incentive. *Journal of Gerontology, 40,* 53–59.

Warren, M. P., Brooks-Gunn, J., Fox, R., Lancelot, C., Newman, D., & Hamilton, W. G. (1991). Lack of bone accretion and amenorrhea in young dancers: Evidence for a relative osteopenia in weight bearing bones. *Journal of Clinical Endocrinology and Metabolism, 72,* 847–853.

Warren, M. P., Brooks-Gunn, J., Hamilton, L. H., Hamilton, W. G., & Warren, L. F. (1986). Scoliosis and fractures in young ballet dancers: Relationships to delayed menarcheal age and secondary amenorrhea. *New England Journal of Medicine, 314,* 1348–1353.

Wasserman, G. A., Rauh, V. A., Brunelli, S. A., Garcia-Castro, M., & Necos, B. (1990). Psychosocial attributes and life experiences of disadvantaged minority mothers: Age and ethnic variations. *Child Development, 61,* 566–580.

Waterman, A. S. (1982). Identity development from adolescence to adulthood: An extension of theory and a review of the literature. *Developmental Psychology, 18,* 341–359.

Waterman, A. S., & Waterman, C. K. (1971). A longitudinal study of changes in ego identity status during the freshman year at college. *Developmental Psychology, 5,* 167–173.

Waters, E. (1978). The reliability and stability of individual differences in infant-mother attachment. *Child Development, 49,* 483–494.

Waters, E., & Deane, K. E. (1982). Theories, models, recent data, and some tasks for comparative developmental analysis. In L. Hoffman, R. Gandelman, & R. Schiffman (Eds.), *Parenting: Its causes and consequences* (pp. 19–54). Hillsdale, NJ: Erlbaum.

Waters, E., Wippman, J., & Sroufe, L. A. (1979). Attachment, positive affect, and competence in the peer group: Two studies in construct validation. *Child Development, 50,* 821–829.

Watkin, D. M. (1983). *Handbook of nutrition, health, and aging.* Park Ridge, NJ: Noyes.

Watkins, B. A., Huston-Stein, A., & Wright, J. C. (1980). Effects of planned television programming. In E. L. Palmer & A. Dorr (Eds.), *Children and the faces of television: Teaching, violence, selling* (pp. 49–71). New York: Academic Press.

Watkins, H. D., & Bradbard, M. R. (1984, Fall). The social development of young children in day care: What practitioners should know. *Child Care Quarterly,* pp. 169–187.

Watson, R. E., & DeMeo, P. W. (1987, April). Premarital cohabitation vs. traditional courtship and subsequent marital adjustment: A replication and follow-up. *Family Relations,* pp. 193–197.

Watson, W. H. (1982). *Aging and social behavior.* Belmont, CA: Wadsworth.

Wattleton, F. (1987). American teens: Sexually active, sexually illiterate. *Journal of School Health, 57,* 379–380.

Wauchope, B., & Straus, M. A. (1990). Physical punishment and physical abuse of American children: Incidence rates by age, gender, and occupational class. In M. S. Straus & R. J. Gelles (Eds.), *Physical violence in the American family* (pp. 133–148). New York: Doubleday/Anchor. New Brunswick, N.J.

Weatherley, D. (1964). Self-perceived rate of physical maturation and personality in late adolescence. *Child Development, 35,* 1197–1210.

Webster, R. L., Steinhardt, M. H., & Senter, M. G. (1972). Changes in infants' vocalizations as a function of differential acoustic stimulation. *Developmental Psychology, 7,* 39–43.

Wechsler, D. (1981). *WAIS-R manual.* New York: Psychological Corp.

Wechsler, D. (1991). *Manual for the Wechsler Intelligence Scale for children, III.* San Antonio, TX: Psychological Corp.

Weg, R. B. (1989). Sensuality/sexuality of the middle years. In S. Hunter & M. Sundel (Eds.), *Midlife myths* (pp. 31–51). Newbury Park: CA: Sage.

Weiffenbach, J. M., Cowart, B. J., & Baum, B. J. (1986). Taste insensitivity and aging. *Journal of Gerontology, 41,* 460–468.

Weikart, D. B. (1988). Quality in early childhood education. In C. Warger (Ed.), *A resource guide to public school early childhood programs* (pp. 63–72). Alexandria, VA: Association for Supervision and Curriculum Development.

Weiner, J. P. (1994). Forecasting the effects of health reform on U.S. physician workforce requirement: Evidence from HMO staffing patterns. *Journal of the American Medical Association, 272,* 222–230.

Weinraub, M., & Gringlas, M. B. (1995). Single parenthood. In M. H. Bornstein (Ed.), *Handbook of parenting* (Vol. 3, pp. 65–87). Mahwah, NJ: Erlbaum.

Weinstein, L., Xie, X., & Cleanthous, C. C. (1995). Purpose in life, boredom, and volunteerism in a goup of retirees. *Psychological Reports, 76,* 482.

Weis, D. L., & Felton, J. (1987). Marital exclusivity and the potential for future marital conflict. *Social Work, 32,* 45–49.

Weisenfeld, A. R., & Klorman, R. C. (1978). The mother's psychological reactions to contrasting affective expressions by her own and unfamiliar infants. *Developmental Psychology, 14,* 294–304.

Weisman, A. A. (1972). *On Dying and denying: A psychiatric study of terminality.* New York: Behavioral Publications.

Weisman, A. D., & Kastenbaum, R. (1968). *The psychological autopsy: A study of the terminal phase of life.* Community Mental Health Journal Monograph. New York: Behavioral Publications.

Weiss, C. D., & Lillywhite, H. S. (1976). *Communication disorders: A handbook for prevention and early intervention.* St. Louis, MO: Mosby.

Weiss, G. (1990). Hyperactivity in childhood. *New England Journal of Medicine, 323,* 1413–1414.

Weiss, L., & Lowenthal, M. (1975). Life-course perspectives on friendship. In M. Lowenthal, M. Thurnher, & D. Chiriboga (Eds.), *Four stages of life.* San Francisco, CA: Jossey-Bass.

Weitzman, L. J. (1985). *The divorce revolution: The unexpected consequences for women and children in America.* New York: Free Press.

Welch-Ross, M. K., & Schmidt, C. R. (1996). Gender-schema development and children's constructive story memory: Evidence for a developmental model. *Child Development, 67,* 820–835.

Welford, A. T. (1977). Motor performance. In J. E. Birren & K. W. Schaie (Eds.), *Handbook of the psychology of aging* (pp. 450–497). New York: Van Nostrand Reinhold.

Wellman, H. M., Cross, D., & Bartsch, K. (1987). Infant search and object permanence: A meta-analysis of the A-not-B error. Washington, DC: *Monographs of the Society for Research in Child Development, 51* (3), (Serial No. 214).

Wells, K. (1987). Scientific issues in the conduct of case studies. *Journal of Child Psychology and Psychiatry and Allied Disciplines, 28,* 783–790.

Wells, L. E., & Rankin, J. H. (1991). Families and delinquency: A meta-analysis of the impact of broken homes. *Social Problems, 38,* 71–93.

Welsh, W .M., & Stewart, A. J. (1995). Relationships between women and their parents: Implications for midlife well-being. *Psychology and Aging, 10,* 181–190.

Wenar, C. (1994). *Developmental psychopathology* (3rd ed.). New York: McGraw-Hill.

Wentowski, G. J. (1985). Older women's perceptions of great-grandmotherhood: A research note. *Gerontologist, 25,* 593–596.

Wertheimer, M. (1961). Psycho-motor coordination of auditory-visual space at birth. *Science, 134,* 1962.

West, J., Hausken, E. G., & Chandler, K. (1992). *Home activities of 3- to 8-year-olds: Statistics in brief.* Washington, DC: National Center for Education Statistics (ERIC Document Reproduction Service No. ED341 513).

West, P. (1994, October 12). Report links increased enrollments in math, science to reforms of 80s. *Education Week,* 11.

West, R. L., Crook, T. H., & Barron, K. L. (1992). Everyday memory performance across the life span: Effects of age and noncognitive individual differences. *Psychology and Aging, 7,* 72–82.

West, R. L., Odom, R. D., & Aschkenasy,

J. R. (1978). Perceptual sensitivity and conceptual coordination in children and younger and older adults. *Human Development, 21,* 334–345.

Westinghouse Learning Corporation (1969, June). *The impact of Head Start: An evaluation of effects of Head Start on children's cognitive and affective development.* Executive Summary. Ohio University, Report to the Office of Economic Opportunity. Washington, DC: Clearinghouse for Federal Scientific and Technical Information, (EDO93497).

Weyant, J. M. (1986). *Applied social psychology.* New York: Oxford University Press.

Whalen, H., Henker, B., Buhurmester, D., Hinshaw, S. P., Huber, A., & Laski, K. (1989). Does stimulant medication improve the peer status of hyperactive children? *Journal of Consulting and Clinical Psychology, 57,* 545–549.

Wheeler, D. L. (1995, July 14). Few successes in gene therapy. *The Chronicle of Higher Education,* A8, A12.

Whitall, J., & Getchell, N. (1995). From walking to running: Applying a dynamical systems approach to the development of locomotor skills. *Child Development, 66,* 1541–1553.

Whitbourne, S. K., & Weinstock, C. S. (1979). *Adult development: The differentiation of experience.* New York: Holt, Rinehart and Winston.

Whitbourne, S. K., Zuschlag, M. K., Eliot, L. B., & Waterman, A. S. (1992). Psychosocial development in adulthood: A 22-year sequential study. *Journal of Personality and Social Psychology, 63,* 260–271.

White, B. (1993). *The first three years of life.* New York: Simon & Schuster.

White, B. L. (1971). *Human infants: Experience and psychological development.* Englewood Cliffs, NJ: Prentice Hall.

White, K. R. (1982). The relation between socioeconomic status and academic achievement. *Psychological Bulletin, 91,* 461–481.

White, L., & Edwards, J. N. (1990). Emptying the nest and parental well-being: An analysis of national panel data. *American Sociological Review, 55,* 235–242.

White, L. K. (1990). Determinants of divorce: A review of research in the eighties. *Journal of Marriage and the Family, 52,* 904–912.

White, S. D., & DeBlassie, R. (1992). Adolescent sexual behavior. *Adolescence, 27,* 183–191.

White, S. H. (1994). G. Stanley Hall: From philosophy to developmental psychology. In R. D. Parke, P. A. Ornstein, J. J. Rieser, & C. Zahn-Waxler (Eds.), *A century of developmental psychology* (pp. 204–225). Washington, DC: APA.

Whitehead, B. M., Cain, K. C., & Graves, G. (1994, March). Put computers into elementary classrooms—not labs. *The American School Board Journal, 181,* 48–49.

Whitehurst, G. J. (1982). Language development. In B. B. Wolman (Ed.), *Handbook of developmental psychology* (pp. 367–384). Englewood Cliffs, NJ: Prentice Hall.

Whitehurst, G. J., Arnold, D. S., Epstein, J. N., Angell, A. L., Smith, M., & Fischel, J. E. (1994). A picture book reading intervention in day care and home for children from low-income families. *Developmental Psychology, 30,* 679–689.

Whitehurst, G. J., Epstein, J. N., Angell, A. L., Payne, A. C., Crone, D. A., & Fischel, J. E. (1994). Outcomes of an emergent literacy intervention in head start. *Journal of Educational Psychology, 86,* 542–555.

Whitehurst, G. J., Falco, F. L., Lonigan, C. J., Fischel, J. E., DeBaryshe, B. D., Valdez-Menchaca, M. C., & Caulfield, M. (1988). Accelerating language development through picture book reading. *Developmental Psychology, 24,* 552–560.

Whitehurst, G. J., & Valdez-Menchaca, M. C. (1988). What is the role of reinforcement in early language acquisition? *Child Development, 59,* 430–441.

Whitehurst, G. J., & Vasta, R. (1977). *Child behavior.* Boston: Houghton Mifflin.

Whiteman, F. L., Diamond, M., & Martin, J. (1993). Homosexual orientation in twins: A report on 61 pairs and three triplet sets. *Archives of Sexual Behavior, 22,* 187–206.

Whiting, B. B., & Edwards, C. P. (1988). *Children of different worlds: The formation of social behavior.* Cambridge, MA: Harvard University Press.

Whitley, B. E., Jr., (1993). Reliability and aspects of the construct validity of Sternberg's triangular love scale. *Journal of Social and Personal Relationships, 10,* 475–480.

Whitman, B., Accordo, P., Boyert, M., & Kendagor, R. (1990). Homelessness and cognitive performance in children: A possible link. *Social Work, 35,* 516–519.

Whitney, E. N., Cataldo, C. B., & Rolfes, S. R. (1994). *Understanding normal and clinical nutrition* (4th ed.). St. Paul, MN: West.

Whitney, E. N. W., & Hamilton, E. M. N. (1984). *Understanding nutrition* (3rd ed.). St. Paul, MN: West.

Whitney, E. N., & Rolfes, S. R. (1996). *Understanding nutrition* (7th ed.). St. Paul, MN: West.

Why heart disease is harder on blacks (1996, March 28). *Newsday,* A50.

Wicks-Nelson, R., & Israel, A. C. (1997). *Behavior disorders of childhood* (3rd ed.). Englewood Cliffs, NJ: Prentice Hall.

Wierson, M., Forehand, R., Fauber, R., & McCombs, A. (1989). Buffering young male adolescents against negative parental divorce influences: The role of good parent-adolescent relations. *Child Study Journal, 19,* 101–115.

Wiesel, T. N., & Hubel, D. H. (1965). Extent of recovery from the effects of visual deprivation in kittens. *Journal of Neurophysiology, 28,* 1060–1072.

Willemsen, E. (1979). *Understanding infancy.* San Francisco: Freeman.

Willert, M., & Kamii, C. (1985). Reading in kindergarten: Direct vs. indirect teaching. *Young Children, 40,* 3–9.

Williams, D. R. (1990). Socioeconomic differences in health: A review and redirection. *Social Psychology Quarterly, 53,* 81–99.

Williams, D. R., Lavizzo-Mourey, R., & Warren, R. C. (1994). The concept of race and health status in America. *Public Health Reports, 109,* 26–43.

Williams, G. M. (1991). Causes and prevention of cancer. *Statistical Bulletin,* April/June, 6–10.

Williams, H. B. (1979). Some aspects of childrearing practices in three minority subcultures in the United States. *Journal of Negro Education, 48,* 408–418.

Williams, J. H. (1977). *Psychology of women: Behavior in a biosocial context.* New York: Norton.

Williams, J. W., & Stith, M. (1980). *Middle childhood: Behavior and development* (2nd ed.). New York: Macmillan.

Williamson, G. M., & Schulz, R. (1995). Activity restriction mediates the association between pain and depressed affect: A study of younger and older adult cancer patients. *Psychology and Aging, 10,* 369–379.

Willig, A. E. (1985). A meta-analysis of selected studies on the effectiveness of bilingual education. *Review of Educational Research, 55,* 269–317.

Willis, S. (1989). Adult intelligence. In S. Hunter & M. Sundel (Eds.), *Midlife myths* (pp. 97–113). Newbury Park, CA: Sage.

Willis, S. L., & Baltes, P. B. (1980). Intelligence in adulthood and aging: Contemporary issues. In L. W. Poon (Ed.), *Aging in the 1980s: Psychological issues* (pp. 260–273). Washington, DC: American Psychological Association.

Wilson, B. J., & Gottman, J. M., (1995). Marital interaction and parenting. In M. H. Bornstein (Ed.), *Handbook of parenting* (Vol. 4, pp. 33–56). Mahwah, NJ: Erlbaum.

Wilson, G. T., & Fairburn, C. G. (1993). Cognitive treatments for eating disorders. *Journal of Consulting and Clinical Psychology, 61,* 261–269.

Wilson, J. Q., & Herrnstein, R. J. (1985). *Crime and human nature.* New York: Simon & Schuster.

Wilson, R. S. (1983). The Louisville Twin Study: Developmental synchronies in behavior. *Child Development, 54,* 298–316.

Wilson, S. M., & Medora, N. P. (1990). Gender comparisons of college students' attitudes toward sexual behavior. *Adolescence, 25,* 615–627.

Wimmer, H. (1979). Processing of script deviations by young children. *Discourse Processes, 2,* 301–310.

Wimmer, H. (1980). Children's understanding of stories: Assimilation by a general schema for actions or coordination of temporal relations? In F. Wilkening, J. Becker, & T. Trabasso (Eds.), *Information integration by children.* Hillsdale, NJ: Erlbaum.

Winch, R. (1958). *Mate selection: A study of complementary needs.* New York: Harper & Row.

Wineberg, H. (1990). Childbearing after remarriage. *Journal of Marriage and the Family, 52,* 31–38.

Wineberg, H. (1994). Marital reconciliation in the United States: Which couples are successful. *Journal of Marriage and the Family, 56,* 80–8.

Winfield, A., & Byrnes, D. L. (1981). *The psychology of human memory.* New York: Academic Press.

Wing, L. A. (1995). Play is not the work of the child: Young children's perceptions of work and play. *Early Childhood Research Quarterly, 10,* 223–247.

Winick, M. (1976). *Malnutrition and brain damage.* New York: Oxford University Press.

Winkler, K. J. (1990, November). Proponents of "multicultural" humanities research call for a critical look at its achievements. *Chronicle of Higher Education, 28,* A5.

Winn, R. L., & Newton, N. (1982). Sexuality in aging: A study of 106 cultures. *Archives of Sexual Behavior, 11,* 283–299.

Winter, S. W. (1994/1995). Diversity: A program for all children. *Childhood Education, 70,* 91–95.

Wisdom, C. S. (1989). Does violence beget violence? A critical examination of the literature. *Psychological Bulletin, 106,* 3–28.

Wise, S., & Grossman, F. K. (1980). Adolescent mothers and their infants: Psychological factors in early attachment and interaction. *American Journal of Orthopsychiatry, 50,* 454–468.

Wittrock, M. C. (1986). Students' thought processes. In M. C. Wittrock (Ed.), *Handbook of research on teaching* (3rd ed., pp. 247–315). New York: MacMillan.

Wodarski, J. S. (1990). Adolescent substance use: Practical implications. *Adolescence, 25,* 667–687.

Wolf, R. (1995, October 6). A positive turn for the poor. *USA Today,* 6A.

Wolf, R. (1996). *Marriages and families in a diverse society.* New York: Harper Collins.

Wolf, R. S., & Pillemer, K. (1994). What's new in elder abuse programming? Four bright ideas. *The Gerontologist, 34,* 126–129.

Wolfson, J. C. (1996, January 15). Women with cystic fibrosis defy the odds by having babies. *Newsday,* B17–B18.

Wolinsky, F. D., & Fitzgerald, J. F. (1994). The risk of hip fracture among noninstitutionalized older adults. *Journal of Gerontology: Social Sciences, 49,* S165–175.

Wood, D. (1995, June). Vaccination levels in Los Angeles public health centers: The contribution of missed opportunities. *American Journal of Public Health, 85,* 850–854.

Wood, W., Wong, F., & Chachere, G. J. (1991). Effects of media violence on viewers' aggression in unconstrained social interaction. *Psychological Bulletin, 78,* 371–383.

Woodard, C. (1992, January 15). Magic nudges Bush: Tells president to get more involved in AIDS fight. *Newsday,* 5.

Woodruff, C. W. (1978). The science of infant nutrition and the art of infant feeding. *Journal of the American Medical Association, 240,* 657–661.

Woods, J. R. (1994). Pension coverage among the baby boomers: Initial findings from a 1993 survey. *Social Security Bulletin, 57,* 12–26.

Woodward, A. L., Markman, E. M., & Fitzsimmons, C. M. (1994). Rapid word learning in 13- and 18-month-olds. *Developmental Psychology, 30,* 553–566.

Woody-Ramsey, J., & Miller, P. H. (1988). The facilitation of selective attention in pre-schoolers. *Child Development, 59,* 1504–1514.

Woolley, J. D., & Wellman, H. M. (1990). Young children's understanding of realities, nonrealities, and appearances. *Child Development, 61,* 946–961.

World Press Review (1994, December). Measles Shots. *World Press Review,* 41, 45.

Worobey, J., & Blajda, V. M. (1989). Temperament ratings at 2 weeks, 2 months and 1 year: Differential stability of activity and emotionality. *Developmental Psychology, 25,* 257–264.

Woronov, T. (1994, December). Myths bout the magic of technology in schools. *The Education Digest,* 12–15.

Worsnop, R. L. (1991). Teenage suicide. *CQ Researcher, 1:* 371–391.

Wortman, C. B., & Silver, R. C. (1988). Coping with irrevocable loss. In G. R. VandenBos & B. K. Bryant (Eds.), *Cataclysms, crises, and catastrophes* (pp. 185–235). Washington, DC: American Psychological Association.

Wright, J. C., Huston, A. C., Ross, R. P., Calvert, S. L., Rolandelli, D., Weeks, L. A., Raeisse, P., & Potts, R. (1984). Pace and continuity of television programs: Effects on children's attention and comprehension. *Developmental Psychology, 20,* 653–667.

Wright, K. N., & Wright, K. E. (1995). *Family life, delinquency, and crime: A Policymaker's guide.* Washington, DC: Office of Juveile Justice and Delinquency Prevention, Department of Justice.

Wright, L. K. (1991). The impact of Alzheimer's disease on the marital relationship. *Gerontologist, 31,* 224–237.

Wright, R. (1994, October 24). Technology and choice. *New Republic, 211,* 6–7.

Wright, R. (1995, January 2). Dumb bell. *New Republic, 212,* 6–7.

Wrightman, M. J. (1991). Criteria for placement decisions with cocaine-exposed infants. *Child Welfare,* 653–663.

Wurtele, S. K., & Miller-Perrin, C. L. (1987a). Sexual abuse prevention: Are school programs harmful? *Journal of School Health, 57,* 228–231.

Wurtele, S. K., & Miller-Perrin, C. L. (1987b). Harmful effects of school-based sexual abuse prevention programs? Reassure the parents. In C. C. Tower (Ed.), *How schools can help combat child abuse and neglect* (2nd ed., pp. 146–154). Washington, DC: NEA Library.

Wyrobek, A. J. (1993). Methods and concepts in detecting abnormal reproductive outcomes of paternal origin. *Reproductive Toxicology, 7,* 3–16.

Yang, B., Ollendick, T. H., Dong, Q., Xia, Y., & Lin, L. (1995). Only children and children with siblings in the People's Republic of China: Levels of fear, anxiety, and depression. *Child Development, 66,* 1301–1311.

Yang-Lewis, P. (1995, February). A collaborative regional model for obstetrical care in New York state. *American Journal of Public Health, 85,* 264–266.

Yankelovich, D. (1982, April). New rules in American life: Searching for self-fulfillment in a world turned upside down. *Psychology Today,* 35–41, 91.

Yarrow, M. R., Scott, P., de Leeuw, I. D. & Heinig, C. (1962). Child rearing in families of working and non-working mothers. In H. Bee (Ed.), *Social issues in developmental psychology* (2nd ed., pp. 112–129) New York: Harper and Row, 1978.

Yatsko, C., & Larsen, J. D. (1990). Relationship between sex-role and moral decision-making. *Psychological Reports, 66,* 59–64.

Yesavage, J. A., Sheikh, J. I., Friedman, L., & Tanke, E. (1990). Learning mnemonics: Roles of aging and subtle cognitive impairment. *Psychology and Aging, 5,* 133–137.

Yoon, Y. H., & Waite, L. J. (1994). Converging employment patterns of black, white, and Hispanic women: Return to work after first birth. *Journal of Marriage and the Family, 56,* 209–217.

Yoshikawa, H. (1995). Long-term effects of early childhood programs on social outcomes and delinquency. *The Future of Children, 5,* 51–76.

Youngblood, S. A., Mobley, W. H., & Meglino, B. M. (1983). A longitudinal analysis of the turnover process. *Journal of Applied Psychology, 68,* 507–516.

Zabin, L. S., Sedivy, V., & Emerson, M. R. (1994). Subsequent risk of childbearing among adolescents with a negative pregnancy test. *Family Planning Perspectives, 26,* 212–217.

Zahr, L. (1996). Effects of war on the behavior of Lebanese preschool children: Influence of home environment and family functioning. *American Journal of Orthopsychiatry, 66,* 401–408.

Zelazo, N. A., Zelazo, P. R., Cohen, K. M., & Zelazo, P. D. (1993). Specificity of practice effects on elementary neuromotor patterns. *Developmental Psychology, 29,* 686–691.

Zelazo, P. R., Zelazo, N. A., & Kolb, S. (1972). "Walking" in the newborn. *Science, 176,* 314–315.

Zeskind, P. S., Sale, J., Maio, L. W., & Weiseman, J. R. (1985). Adult perceptions of pain and hunger cries: A synchrony of arousal. *Child Development, 56,* 549–554.

Zigler, E., & Berman, W. (1983). Discerning the future of early childhood intervention. *American Psychologist, 38,* 894–907.

Zigler, E., & Muenchow, S. (1992). *Head Start: The inside story of America's most successful educational experiment.* New York: Basic Books.

Zigler, E., Taussig, C., & Black, K. (1992). Early childhood intervention: A promising preventative for juvenile delinquency. *American Psychologist, 47,* 997–1006.

Zill, N. (1996, January/February). Parental schooling and children's health. *Public Health Reports, 111,* 34–44.

Zill, N., Collins, M., West, J., & Germino-Hauken, E. (1995). *Approaching kindergarten: A look at preschoolers in the United States.* Washington, DC: U.S. Department of Education, National Center for Educational Statistics.

Zill, N., & Robinson, J. (1995, April). The Generation X difference. *American Demographics,* 24–33.

Zins, S. (1987). *Aging in America.* Albany, NY: Delmar.

Zinsser, C. (1981, October). The preschool pressure cooker. *Working Mother,* 61–64.

Zivian, M. T., & Darjes, M. T. (1983). Free recall by in-school and out-of-school adults: Performance and metamemory. *Developmental Psychology, 19,* 513–520.

Zmiles, H., & Lee, V. E. (1991). Adolescent family structure and educational progress. *Developmental Psychology, 27,* 314–320.

Zuckerman, B., et al. (1989). Effects of maternal marijuana and cocaine use on fetal growth. *New England Journal of Medicine, 320,* 762–768.

Zuckerman, B., & Frank, D. A. (1992). "Crack kids": Not broken. *Pediatrics, 89,* 337–339.

Author Index

Subject Index

Credits

This page constitutes an extension of the copyright page. We have made every effort to trace the ownership of all copyrighted material and to secure permission from copyright holders. In the event of any question arising as to the use of any material, we will be pleased to make the necessary corrections in future printings. Thanks are due to the following authors, publishers, and agents for permission to use the material indicated.

Chapter 1: 7: Figure 1.1 from "The Power of Cohorts," by G. Meredith and C. Schewe, *American Demographics,* December, 1994, pp. 26–27. Copyright © 1994 *American Demographics* Magazine. Reprinted with permission. **9:** Figure 1.2 from "Cross-Sectional Studies of Personality in a National Sample 2—Stability in Neuroticism, Extraversion, Openness," by Paul T. Costa et al., *Psychology and Aging,* June 1986, p. 148. Copyright © 1986 American Psychological Association. Reprinted by permission of the author.

Chapter 2: 40: Table 2.2 from "The Prime of Our Lives," by A. Rosenfeld and E. Stark, May 1987, *Psychology Today, 66,* pp. 68–72. Reprinted with permission from Psychology Today Magazine. Copyright © 1987 (Sussex Publishers, Inc.).

Chapter 3: 58: Table 3.1 adapted from "The Origin of Personality," by Alexander Thomas, Stella Chess, and Herbert G. Birch, August 1970, *Scientific American,* pp. 106–107. Illustration by A. D. Iselin. Copyright © May 1961 by Scientific American, Inc. All rights reserved. Reprinted by permission.

Chapter 4: 73: Figure 4.1 from Moore, K. L., and Persaud, T. V. N., *Before We Are Born,* 4th, Philadelphia, W. B. Saunders, Co., 1993. Reprinted by permission.

Chapter 5: 93: Figure 5.1 adapted from "The Origin of Form Perception," by Robert L. Fantz, May 1961, *Scientific American,* p. 72. Illustration by Alex Semenoick. Copyright © 1961 by Scientific American, Inc. All rights reserved. Reprinted by permission. **98:** Table 5.1 from *Introduction to Child Development,* Second Edition, by J. P. Dworetzky. Copyright © 1984 West Publishing Company, 1996 Brooks/Cole Publishing Company. **101:** Figure 5.4 from *The First Two Years: A Study of Twenty-Five Babies,* Vol. *2: Intellectual Development,* by M. M. Shirley. Copyright © 1933 University of Minnesota Press. Reprinted by permission. **113:** Figure 5.6 from "Object Permanence in 3 1/2- and 4 1/2-Month-Old Infants," by R. Baillargeon, *Developmental Psychology, 23,* p. 656. Copyright © 1987 American Psychological Association. Reprinted by permission. **116:** Table 5.2 from "HOME Measurement of Maternal Responsiveness," by R. H. Bradley. In M. H. Bornstein (Ed.), *Maternal Responsiveness: Characteristics and Consequences,* pp. 63–75. Copyright 1989 Jossey-Bass. Reprinted by permission.

Chapter 6: 127: Table 6.1 from *From Human Attachment,* by V. L. Colin, p. 36. Copyright © 1996 McGraw Hill. Reprinted by permission of The McGraw-Hill Companies. **138:** Figure 6.2 from "Can the Age of Entry Into Child Care and the Quality of Child Care Predict Adjustment in Kindergarten?" by C. Howes, *Developmental Psychology, 26,* p. 299. Copyright © 1990 American Psychological Association. Reprinted by permission.

Chapter 7: 147: Figure 7.1 from *Language Development: An Introduction,* by R. E. Owens, Jr., p. 15. Copyright © 1992 Allyn & Bacon. Reprinted by permission of Allyn & Bacon.

Chapter 8: 170: Figure 8.1 from "Under-5 Mortality Rate Falling," in the *State of the World's Children, 1996,* p. 59, copyright © 1996 UNICEF. Reprinted with permission. **171:** Table 8.2 from "Social Goals: 1995 and 2000," in the *State of the World's Children, 1996,* p. 72, copyright © 1996 UNICEF. Reprinted with permission.

Chapter 9: 201: Table 9.1 adapted from "Beyond Parental Control and Authoritarian Parenting Style: Understanding Chinese Parenting Through the Cultural Notion of Training," by R. K. Chao, *Child Development, 65,* pp. 111–119. Copyright © 1994 Society for Research In Child Development. Reprinted by permission.

Chapter 10: 219: Table 10.1 from *Maternal and Child Health Nursing,* by A. Pillitteri, p. 947. Copyright © 1992 J. B. Lippincott Company. Reprinted by permission. **229:** Figure 10.1 from "7 Ways to Be Bright," *U. S. News and World Report.* Copyright © November 23, 1987, U. S. News and World Report. Reprinted by permission. **236:** Table 10.3 from *Mental Retardation: Definition, Classification, and Systems of Supports,* Ninth Edition. Copyright © 1992 American Association on Mental Retardation (AAMR). Reprinted by permission.

Chapter 12: 278: Table 12.3 from "The Influence of Victim's Attire on Adolescents' Judgments of Date Rape," by L. Cassidy and R. M. Hurrell, Summer 1995, *Adolescence, 30,* pp. 319–324. Copyright © 1995 Libra Publishing. Reprinted by permission. **282:** Table 12.4 reproduced with the permission of The Alan Guttmacher Institute from Jennifer J. Frost and Jacqueline Darroch Forrest, "Understanding the Impact of Effective Teenage Pregnancy Prevention Programs," *Family Planning Perspectives,* Volume *27,* Number 5, September/October 1995.

Chapter 13: 293: Table 13.1 from "Identity Status and Academic Achievement in Female Adolescents," by R. Hummel and L. L. Roselli, 1983, *Adolescence, 18.* Copyright © 1983 Libra Publishing. Reprinted by permission. **298:** Table 13.2 from "Factors Influencing Age Expectations for Adolescent Autonomy: A Study of Early Adolescents and Parents," by S. S. Feldman and T. Quatman, 1988, *Journal of Early Adolescence, 8,* pp. 325 343. Copyright © 1988 by Sage Publications. Reprinted by permission of Sage Publications, Inc.

Chapter 14: 318: Table 14.1 from "Selected Health Behaviors and Perceptions Among U. S. Adults in 1990," Table

1, October-December 1993, *Statistical Bulletin,* p. 5. Copyright © 1990 Metropolitan Life Insurance Company. Reprinted by permission. **326:** Table 14.2 reprinted with permission from "The Social Readjustment Scale," by T. Holmes and R. H. Rahe in *Journal of Psychosomatic Research, 11.* Copyright © 1967 Elsevier Science Inc. **329:** Table 14.3 from *Adult Cognition and Aging,* by J. M. Rybash, W. J. Hoyer, and P. A. Roodin, p. 297. Copyright © 1986 Pergamon Press. Reprinted by permission of the author. **330:** Figure 14.1 reprinted by permission of the publisher from "Cognitive Development in Adulthood," by J. L. Horn and G. Donaldson, in *Constancy and Change in Human Development,* by O. G. Brim and J. Kagan, eds., Cambridge, Mass: Harvard University Press, Copyright © 1980 by the President and Fellows of Harvard University. **331:** Figure 14.2 reprinted by permission of the publisher from "Cognitive Development in Adulthood," by J. L. Horn and G. Donaldson, in *Constancy and Change in Human Development,* by O. G. Brim and J. Kagan, eds., Cambridge, Mass: Harvard University Press, Copyright © 1980 by the President and Fellows of Harvard University.

Chapter 15: 339: Figure 15.1 from *The Seasons of a Man's Life,* by D. J. Levinson et al. Copyright © 1978 by Daniel J. Levinson. Reprinted by permission of Alfred A. Knopf Inc. **344:** Table 15.1 from *Choices in Relationships,* by D. Knox. Copyright © 1985 West Publishing Company. Reprinted by permission of Wadsworth Publishing Company. **347:** Figure 15.2 adapted from "Marital Satisfaction Over the Family Life Cycle," by B. C. Rollins and H. Feldman, 1970, *Journal of Marriage and the Family, 32*(1), pp. 20–28. Copyright © 1970 by the National Council on Family Relations, 3989 Central Ave. NE, Suite 550, Minneapolis, MN 55421. Reprinted by permission. Adaptation from *Adulthood Development and Aging,* by K. W. Schaie and S. L. Willis, HarperCollins, 1996.

Chapter 16: 366: Figure 16.2 from "The Baby Boom Turns 50," by C. Russell, December 1995, *American Demographics,* p. 27. Copyright © 1995 American Demographics Magazine. Reprinted with permission. **369:** Figure 16.3 from "The Incidence and Frequency of Marital Sex in a National Sample," by V. Call, S. Sprecher, and P. Schwartz, 1995, *Journal of Marriage and the Family, 57*(3), pp. 639–652. Copyright © 1995 by the National Council on Family Relations, 3989 Central Ave., NE, Suite 550, Minneapolis, MN 55421. Reprinted by permission. **385:** Figure 16.4 from "The Course of Adult Intellectual Development," by K. W. Schaie, 1994, *American Psychologist, 49,* pp. 304–313. Copyright © 1994 American Psychological Association. Reprinted by permission. **385:** Figure 16.5 from "The Course of Adult Intellectual Development," by K. W. Schaie, 1994, *American Psychologist, 49,* pp. 304–313. Copyright © 1994 American Psychological Association. Reprinted by permission. **389:** Table 16.2 from "Everyday Problem Solving in Adulthood and Old Age," by S. W. Cornelius and A. Caspi, 1987, *Psychology and Aging, 2,* pp. 144–153. Copyright © 1987 American Psychological Association. Reprinted by permission. **390:** Figure 16.6 from "Aging and Cognitive Changes," by N. W. Denney. In Benjamin B. Wolman (Ed.), *Handbook of Developmental Psychology,* p. 819. Copyright © 1982 Prentice-Hall. Reprinted by permission.

Chapter 17: 399: Figure 17.1 from "Women's Prime of Life. Is It in the 50's?" by V. Mitchell and R. Helson, 1990, *Psychology of Women Quarterly 1990, 14,* p. 456, Figure 1. Copyright © Cambridge University Press. Reprinted with permission of Cambridge University Press. **400:** Figure 17.2 from "Personality Change in Women from College to Midlife," by R. Helson and G. Moane, 1987, *Journal of Personality and Social Psychology, 53,* pp. 176–186. Copyright © 1987 American Psychological Association. Reprinted by permission. **407:** Table 17.1 from "Stress and Rewards in Women's Multiple Roles: The Case of Women in the Middle," by M. A. P. Stephens, M. M. Franks, and A. L. Townsend, 1994, *Psychology and Aging, 9,* pp. 34–52. Copyright © 1994 American Psychological Association. Reprinted by permission. **407:** Table 17.2 from "Stress and Rewards in Women's Multiple Roles: The Case of Women in the Middle," by M. A. P. Stephens, M. M. Franks, and A. L. Townsend, 1994, *Psychology and Aging, 9,* pp. 34–52. Copyright © 1994 American Psychological Association. Reprinted by permission. **412:** Table 17.3 from "Myths of Midlife Intergenerational Relationship," by L. E. Troll. In S. Hunter and M. Sundel (Eds.), *Midlife Myths: Issues, Findings, and Practical Implications,* pp. 210–233. Copyright © 1989 by Sage Publications. Reprinted by permission of Sage Publications, Inc.

Chapter 18: 421: Figure 18.1 from *Stand Tall! The Informed Woman's Guide to Preventing Osteoporosis,* by M. Notelovitz and M. Wave, p. 32. Copyright © 1982 Triad Publishing Co. Reprinted by permission. **425:** Table 18.3 from "Linguistic Ability in Early Life and Cognitive Function and Alzheimer's Disease in Later Life," by D. A. Snowdon, S. J. Kemper, J. A. Mortimer, L. H. Greiner, D. R. Wekstein, and W. R. Markesbery, February 21, 1996, *Journal of the American Medical Association, 275,* pp. 528–532. Copyright © 1996 American Medical Association. Reprinted by permission. **432:** Table 18.4 from *Psychological Testing,* Sixth Edition, by A. Anastasi, pp. 250–251. Copyright © 1988 Macmillan. Adapted by permission of Prentice-Hall, Inc. Upper Saddle River, NJ. **433:** Figure 18.2 from "Intellectual Development in Adulthood," by K. W. Schaie. In J. E. Birren and W. K. Schaie (Eds.), *Handbook of the Psychology of Aging,* Third Edition, p. 297. Copyright © 1990 Academic Press. Reprinted by permission.

Chapter 19: 444: Figure 19.1 from "America at Mid-Decade," by P. Francese, February 1995, *American Demographics,* p. 29. Copyright © 1995 American Demographics Magazine. Reprinted with permission. **449:** Table 19.2 from "Home and Community Care in Oregon," by K. W. Concannon, Spring 1995, *Public Welfare,* p. 12. Copyright © 1995 American Public Welfare Association. Reprinted by permission. **453:** Table 19.3 from "Abuse and Neglect of Elderly Persons," by M. S. Lachs and K. Pillemer, 1995, *The New England Journal of Medicine, 332,* pp. 437–443. Copyright © 1995 Massachusetts Medical Society. Reprinted by permission of *The New England Journal of Medicine.* **459:** Figure 19.2 from "Rethinking Retirement," by P. Morgenbagen, June 1994, *American Demographics,* pp. 28–33. Copyright © 1994 American Demographics Magazine. Reprinted with permission. **460:** Figure 19.3 from *The Social Forces in Later Life,* Second Edition, by R. C. Atchley. Copyright © 1977 Wadsworth Publishing Company. Reprinted by permission. **461:** Table 19.4 from "How Stressful is Retirement? Findings from the Normative Aging Study" by R. Bossé, C. M. Aldwin, M. R. Levenson, and K. Workman-Daniels, 1991, *Journal of Gerontology, 46,* pp. 9–14. Copyright © 1991 Gerontological Society of America. Reprinted by permission. **463:** Table 19.5 from "Quitting Time," by J. P. Robinson, May 1991, *American Demographics,* p. 34–37. Copyright © 1991 American Demographics Magazine. Reprinted with permission.

Chapter 20: 484: Table 20.2 from "Factors Associated with Filial Grief Following the Death of an Elderly Parent," by A. E. Scharlach, 1991, *American Journal of Orthopsychiatry, 61,* pp. 307–313. Reprinted, with permission, from the *American Journal of Orthopsychiatry.* Copyright © 1991 by the American Orthopsychiatric Association, Inc. **485:** Table 20.3 from "Human Grief: A Model for Prediction and Intervention," by L. A. Bugen, 1977, *American Journal of Orthopsychiatry, 2,* pp. 196–207. Reprinted, with permission, from the *American Journal of Orthopsychiatry.* Copyright © 1977 by the American Orthopsychiatric Association, Inc. **487:** Figure 20.1 from "The Bereavement of the Widowed," by P. J. Clayton, J. A. Halikes, W. L. Maurice, 1971, *Diseases of the Nervous System, 32,* pp. 597–604. Copyright © 1971 Physicians Postgraduate Press. Reprinted by permission.

Photo Credits

5: Corbis-Bettmann, **8:** AP/Wide World Photos, **3:** ©Bill Bachmann/PhotoEdit, **15:** Jeff Greenberg/PhotoEdit, **37:** Albert Bandura, Stanford University, **39:** Paul Conklin/PhotoEdit, **32:** Bill Anderson/Monkmeyer, **29:** ©Tony Freeman/PhotoEdit, **55:** ©Will and Deni McIntyre/Science Source, Photo Researchers, Inc., **56:** Susan Woog Wagner Photography © 1991 All rights reserved/Photo Researchers, **65:** Richard G. Anderson, **49:** Mary Kate Denny/PhotoEdit, **78:** ©Tom Stewart/The Stock Market, **80:** ©Michael Tweed/*New York Times* Pictures, **82:** ©Russell D. Curtis/Photo Researchers, Inc., **85:** ©Jonathan Nourok/PhotoEdit, **95:** ©PhotoEdit (photo courtesy of Joe Campos & Rosanne Kermoian), **96:** Rosenstein, D. and Oster, H. (1988) *Child Development,* **105:** ©Bill Bachman/Photo Researchers, Inc., **111:** ©Elizabeth Crews, **131:** ©Ursula Markus/Photo Researchers, Inc., **126:** Courtesy of the University of Wisconsin Primate Laboratory, **133:** ©Spencer Grant/Photo Researchers, Inc., **139:** ©Elizabeth Crews, **149:** ©Myrleen Ferguson/PhotoEdit, **152:** ©Myrleen Ferguson/PhotoEdit, **157:** ©Myrleen Ferguson/PhotoEdit, **159:** Kathy Sloane/Photo Researchers, Inc., **166:** AP/Wide World Photos, Inc., **169:** ©Robert Brenner/PhotoEdit, **179:** ©Tom McCarthy/PhotoEdit, **181:** AP/Wide World Photos, **194:** ©1992 Richard G. Anderson, **196:** ©David Young-Wolff/PhotoEdit, **199:** Tony Freeman/Photo Edit, **209:** ©Michelle Bridwell/PhotoEdit, **218:** ©Robert Finken/Photo Researchers, Inc., **223:** ©David Young-Wolff/PhotoEdit, **226:** ©Susan Woog Wagner Photography/Photo Researchers, Inc., **233:** ©Robin L. Sachs/PhotoEdit, **246:** ©Erika Stone/Photo Researchers, Inc., **248:** ©Tony Freeman/PhotoEdit, **250:** ©Paul Barton/The Stock Market, **251:** Elizabeth Crews, **265:** AP/Wide World Photos, **272:** ©Jeff Greenberg/PhotoEdit, **274:** Tony Freeman/Photo Edit, **283:** ©Rhoda Sidney/Photo Edit, **297:** ©David Young Wolff/PhotoEdit, **300:** ©Mary Kate Denny/PhotoEdit, **302:** ©1990 Doug Plummer/Photo Researchers, Inc., **309:** Mary Kate Denny/PhotoEdit, **319:** ©David Young-Wolff/PhotoEdit, **324:** ©Reuters/Corbis-Bettmann, **321:** Merritt Vincent/PhotoEdit, **328:** PhotoEdit, **340:** ©Kathy Sloane/Photo Researchers, Inc., **343:** ©David Young-Wolff/PhotoEdit, **352:** ©Richard Hutchings/PhotoEdit, **357:** ©Michael Newman/PhotoEdit, **366:** Amy Etra/PhotoEdit, **373:** AP/Wide World Photos, **383:** Robert Brenner/PhotoEdit, **388:** Steven Lunetta/PhotoEdit, **395:** Jon Feingersh/The Stock Market, **401:** Henley and Savage/The Stock Market, **406:** ©Merritt Vincent/PhotoEdit, **409:** Michael Newman/PhotoEdit, **419:** Bill Aron/PhotoEdit, **424:** Reuters/Corbis-Bettmann, **433:** Rafael Macia/Photo Researchers, Inc., **436:** Tony Freeman/PhotoEdit, **444:** Bill Bachmann/PhotoEdit, **445:** Bill Bachmann/PhotoEdit, **458:** ©Michael Newman/PhotoEdit, **460:** Myrleen Ferguson/PhotoEdit, **473:** David Young-Wolff/PhotoEdit, **474:** AP/Wide World Photos, **477:** A. Ramey/PhotoEdit, **485:** Amy C. Etra/PhotoEdit.